Immigration & Nationality Law Handbook

2006–07 Edition

AILA Titles of Interest

AILA's Occupational Guidebooks

Immigration Options for Physicians

*Immigration Options for Nurses
& Allied Health Care Professionals*

Immigration Options for Religious Workers

Immigration Options for Academics and Researchers

Immigration Options for Investors and Entrepreneurs

Statutes, Regulations, Agency Materials & Case Law

Immigration & Nationality Act (INA)

Immigration Regulations (CFR)

*Agency Interpretations of Immigration Policy
(Cables, Memos, and Liaison Minutes)*

AILA's Immigration Case Summaries

Core Curriculum

Selected Fundamentals of Immigration Law

*Immigration Law for Paralegals**

*AILA's Guide to Technology and Legal Research for the
Immigration Lawyer*

CD Products & Toolbox Series

AILALink CD-ROM

The AILA Immigration Practice Toolbox

The AILA Litigation Toolbox

Client Brochures (10 Titles)

For Your Clients

Client Brochures (10 Titles)

*U.S. Tax Guides for Foreign Persons and Those Who Pay Them,
3 volumes (H-1Bs, L-1s, J-1s)**

Treatises & Primers

Kurzban's Immigration Law Sourcebook
by Ira J. Kurzban

Professionals: A Matter of Degree
by Martin J. Lawler

AILA's Asylum Primer
by Regina Germain

*Immigration Consequences
of Criminal Activity*
by Mary E. Kramer

Essentials of Removal and Relief
by Joseph A. Vail

Essentials of Immigration Law
by Richard A. Boswell

Other Titles

David Stanton Manual on Labor Certification

*AILA's Global Immigration Guide:
A Country-by-Country Survey*

Immigration & Nationality Law Handbook

The Visa Processing Guide

Ethics in a Brave New World

*Immigration Practice Under NAFTA
and Other Free Trade Agreements*

Government Reprints

BIA Practice Manual

Immigration Judge Benchbook (Print or CD)

Citizenship Laws of the World

EB-5 Manual

Tables of Contents and other information about these publications can be found at
www.ailapubs.com. Orders may be placed at that site or by calling 1-800-982-2839.

*An AILA-distributed title

IMMIGRATION & NATIONALITY LAW HANDBOOK

2006-07 EDITION

SENIOR EDITORS

Gregory P. Adams

Dan H. Berger

Jan H. Brown

Leigh Polk Cole

James P. Eyster II

Carl Falstrom

Ester Greenfield

David W. Leopold

Nancy-Jo Merritt

Steven A. Morley

Allen Orr, Jr.

John L. Pinnix

Rita Kushner Sostrin

William A. Stock

T. Douglas Stump

Elizabeth A. Thompson

EDITOR-IN-CHIEF
Stephanie L. Browning

ASSOCIATE EDITORS
Tatia L. Gordon-Troy

Silvia S. Wang

PRODUCTION ASSISTANT
Elizabeth R. Bartels

AMERICAN IMMIGRATION LAWYERS ASSOCIATION
918 F Street NW, Washington DC 20004 ♦ (202) 216-2400 ♦ *www.aila.org*

Website for Corrections and Updates

Corrections and other updates to AILA publications
can be found online at: *www.aila.org/BookUpdates.*

If you have any corrections or updates to the information in this book, please let us know by
sending a note to the address below, or e-mail us at *books@aila.org*.

This publication is designed to provide accurate and authoritative information in regard to the
subject matter covered. It is distributed with the understanding that the publisher is not
engaged in rendering legal, accounting, or other professional service. If legal advice or other
expert assistance is required, the services of a competent professional should be sought.

*—from a Declaration of Principles jointly adopted by a committee of the American Bar
Association and a committee of publishers*

Printed in the United States of America

ISBN 1-57370-197-1
Stock No. 81-97

TABLE OF CONTENTS

Preface..xi
About the Editors...xiii
Table of Authors...723
Index...729

Practice Management and Ethics

BEST PRACTICES FOR IMMIGRATION LAW OFFICE MANAGEMENT
by Davis C. Bae, Jeffrey W. Goldman, and Dinesh P. Shenoy..1

TECHNOLOGY FOR THE IMMIGRATION PRACTITIONER
by David S. Jones, Randy P. Auerbach, and Cletus M. Weber...11

THE IMPORTANCE OF ADVANCE BUSINESS PLANNING
IN THE INITIAL REPRESENTATION DECISION
by Roxana C. Bacon..23

MANAGING CLIENT EXPECTATIONS
by Edwin R. Rubin and Carl Falstrom...27

INITIAL INTERVIEWS
by Stephen Yale-Loehr...32

MANAGING ETHICAL CONFLICTS IN A BUSINESS PRACTICE
by Kristina K. Rost..38

ETHICAL CONSIDERATIONS FOR IMMIGRATION ATTORNEYS
REGARDING EMPLOYMENT OF PARALEGALS
by Mark A. Mancini..44

WHY "WALK THE LINE"? EFFECTIVE, EFFICIENT,
AND ETHICAL PRACTICES FOR IMMIGRATION PARALEGALS
by Jasmine Chehrazi and Matthew I. Hirsch, with contributions from Alison Walters................67

Removal and Relief

RELIEF FROM REMOVAL: DOES IT CURRENTLY EXIST?
by Vikram K. Badrinath and Barbara Hines 73

WHAT YOU STILL NEED TO KNOW ABOUT §212(C)
by Jodi Goodwin, Ilana E. Greenstein, and Philip Smith...84

FRAUD AND MISREPRESENTATION WAIVERS—PLANNING FOR SUCCESS
by Richard M. Ginsburg...96

Waivers of the §212(a)(9)(c) Permanent Bar—How to Get Them
If You Need Them—and What Is a 'Removal Order' Anyway?
by Philip Hornik 104

Nonimmigrant Waivers for Canadian Citizens
and Instability in the Processing System
by William Z. Reich and Jill A. Apa 108

The Hardship of Proving Hardship
by B. John Ovink 114

Preventative Medicine: Avoiding Removal for
Noncitizen Criminal Defendants Using Pre- and Post-Conviction Relief
by Robert Frank, Linda Kenepaske, and Jay S. Marks 124

Into the Rabbit's Hole: When a Misdemeanor Is a Felony
The Davis/Barrett Hypothetical Federal Felony Analysis of Drug Crimes
by Ilana Etkin Greenstein 137

Remedies of Last Resort: Private Bills and Pardons
by Anna Marie Gallagher 144

Strategies Before the Courts

The Immigration Judge War
by Jonathan D. Montag and Socheat Chea 160

Here We Go Again: Motions to Reopen, Reconsider, and Rescind
Before the Board of Immigration Appeals
by Zachary Nightingale and Avantika Shastri 169

Appealing Words for the BIA and AAO
by Dagmar Butte, Martin J. Lawler, Stanley Mailman, Estelle M. McKee, and Lory D. Rosenberg 184

Habeas Corpus and the REAL ID Act: Some Constitutional Concerns
by Lisa S. Brodyaga 204

Getting Out: Strategies for Challenging Unlawful Detention in Federal Court
by Jeff Joseph, Holly S. Cooper, and David W. Leopold 213

Plyler v. Doe, The Education of Undocumented Children, and the Polity
by Michael A. Olivas 224

Asylum and Other Forms of Protection

Asylum Grab Bag: Sexual Orientation, Gangs, Children, and Presentation of
Background Country Condition Evidence
by Salvador Colon, Hilary A. Han, and Mary E. Kramer 239

BRIEF HISTORY OF LESBIAN, GAY, BISEXUAL, TRANSGENDER, AND HIV
(LGBT/H ASYLUM) LAW
excerpted from *LGBT/HIV Based Asylum Handbook: Winning Asylum, Withholding,*
and CAT Cases Based on Sexual Orientation, Transgender Identity and/or HIV-Positive Status 248

"MAYBE YOU SHOULD," "YES, YOU MUST," "NO, YOU CAN'T": SHIFTING STANDARDS AND
PRACTICES FOR ENSURING DOCUMENT RELIABILITY IN ASYLUM CASES
by Virgil Wiebe 263

NACARA FOR GUATEMALANS, SALVADORANS, AND FORMER SOVIET BLOC NATIONALS
by Mark Silverman and Linton Joaquin 280

THE ABCs OF WORKING WITH IMMIGRANT CHILDREN TO OBTAIN SPECIAL
IMMIGRANT JUVENILE STATUS FOR THOSE ABUSED, NEGLECTED, OR ABANDONED
by Anne Chandler, Judy Flanagan, and Kathleen A. Moccio 300

Family Immigration and Adoption

FAMILY IMMIGRATION ISSUES: LOVE CONQUERS ALL?
by Jan H. Brown 312

YES, SAME-SEX COUPLES CAN GET MARRIED IN FOUR COUNTRIES AND MASSACHUSETTS—
NO, THEY STILL ARE NOT I-130 ELIGIBLE
by Noemi E. Masliah and Lavi S. Soloway 317

STOPPING TIME AND IGNORING THE REALITY OF AGING: THE SIMPLE BEAUTY
OF THE CHILD STATUS PROTECTION ACT
by Royal F. Berg and Ronald H. Ng 323

VIOLENCE AGAINST WOMEN ACT (VAWA) SELF-PETITIONS
by Julie E. Dinnerstein 331

INTERNATIONAL ADOPTION—A BASIC GUIDE TO THE THREE VISA CATEGORIES
by Daniel E. Marcus and Irene A. Steffas, with contributions from Boyd F. Campbell 364

INTERCOUNTRY ADOPTIONS FROM INDIA
by Anil Malhotra and Ranjit Malhotra 375

Strategies for Obtaining LPR Status

"SHOULD I STAY OR SHOULD I GO?"
by Dyann DelVecchio, Cyrus D. Mehta, Shannon M. Underwood, and Paul W. Virtue 387

PRIORITY DATES: MORE IMPORTANT THAN EVER
by Jeffrey A. Devore and Xiomara M. Hernández 399

PULLING THE RABBIT OUT OF THE HAT: USING WESTERN HEMISPHERE
PRIORITY DATES TO MOVE BUSINESS- AND FAMILY-BASED IMMIGRATION
by Kathrin S. Mautino 409

Employment-Based Immigrant Visas

DOL Proposes Drastic Changes to the Labor Certification Program
by Mitchell L. Wexler and Careen B. Shannon..417

Labor Certifications and the Law of Recruitment
by Rómulo E. Guevara 424

Perm Strategies and Ad Hoc Rules for Beneficiaries with
Three-Year Bachelor's Degrees
by Ronald Y. Wada 432

The Revival of Schedule A, Group II: Is "Exceptional" in Vogue?
by Rita Kushner Sostrin 443

National Interest Waiver: Case Study
by Nathan A. Waxman 454

EB-5 Immigrant Investors
by Stephen Yale-Loehr..480

How Much Is Enough? Documenting the Ability to Pay
in Religious Worker Cases
Updated by James D. Eiss and Danielle Rizzo...497

Summary of AAO Decisions on "Religious Visas"
by Rodney M. Barker and Dhara Sharma 501

Employment and Security Compliance

Employment Verification Systems—Where Are We and Where Are We Going?
by Eileen M.G. Scofield, Newton J. Chu, Leigh N. Ganchan, and Austin T. Fragomen, Jr. 508

A Proactive Approach to DOL Audits—Bingo Revisited
by Alan Tafapolsky, Neil S. Dornbaum, Peter T. Shiron, Jr., and Andrew L. Wizner 521

Security Clearances and Technology Licenses
by Mark J. Newman and Michael H. Gladstone...530

Employment-Based Nonimmigrant Visas

B-1 Business Visitors
updated by Teri A. Simmons, Warren R. Leiden, and Lincoln Stone.......................................536

E-1 Nonimmigrant Status
by Henry J. Chang..544

MAKING SENSE OF THE FAM NOTES ON TREATY INVESTOR VISAS
by Paul W. Ferrell 562

CHALLENGES IN REPRESENTING NONIMMIGRANT PROFESSIONALS:
A ROUNDTABLE Q&A WITH PRACTITIONERS
by Janet L. Henner, Eleanor Pelta, and Tarik H. Sultan 571

MAKING DO: AC21 IN A REGULATORY VACUUM
by Naomi Schorr 583

CURRENT STATE OF THE U.S. GUEST WORKER PROGRAM: H-2B AND H-2A STATUS
FOR EMPLOYING ESSENTIAL WORKERS AND PROPOSED IMMIGRATION REFORM
by Jay C. Ruby and Robert D. Kershaw..605

STRATEGIES FOR L-1As
by Kelly M. McCown, Gerard M. Chapman, and Joycelyn L. Fleming 628

OVERCOMING HURDLES WITH L-1B INTRACOMPANY TRANSFEREES
by Sherry L. Neal 643

PRACTICE POINTERS FOR O AND P VISAS
by Kathleen L. Grzegorek, Laya R. Kushner, and Jenifer M. Brown 648

Nonimmigrant Visas for Students, Trainees, and Victims of Crime

WORKSTUDY: EMPLOYMENT OPTIONS FOR STUDENTS WITH F, J, OR M VISAS
by Elizabeth S. Goss, Craig Peterson, and Scott D. Pollock 658

TRAINING AMERICAN STYLE
by Cora D. Tekach, Lori T. Chesser, Scott F. Cooper, and M. Mercedes Badia-Tavas............668

U.S. GOVERNMENT FUNDING IN J-1 WAIVER CASES—THE WORST FORM OF THE DISEASE
by Bruce A. Hake 681

PROTECTING VICTIMS OF CRIME
by Aimee Clark Todd, Sally Kinoshita, Sheila Neville, and Gail Pendleton 692

Entry and Exit Issues

VWP & CBP: PERFECT TOGETHER?
by Susan Borowski Storch..705

THE NEW ADMISSION CONUNDRUM
by David L.P. Garson and Gregg Rodgers 707

Naturalization

ALL IN THE FAMILY: HOW MESSY DIVORCES CAN MAKE A MESS OF NATURALIZATION
by Jonathan S. Greene 717

PREFACE

As you read through this year's *Immigration & Nationality Law Handbook*, you might notice, despite the volume of articles, that some old friends are absent. This year, we decided to forego updating the core curriculum articles; two developments brought us to this choice. First, the panelists on the advanced and master's tracks turned in a sheer bounty of very topical articles—not surprising, given the added complexities over the last year stemming from the REAL ID Act and retrogression in even more immigrant visa categories. In past editions, about 40 articles comprised the advanced portion of the book; this year, there are over 60 articles and they particularly shore up the asylum/protection, administrative appeal/judicial review, and practice management/ethics categories. I urge you to mine this book; I have no doubt that many of these articles will assist AILA members, no matter what your niche.

Beginning practitioners should not feel abandoned. Having more advanced articles in the *Handbook* complements the fundamentals-track sessions, as those sessions themselves will cover the basics. These articles, in turn, will decrease your learning curve as you acquire the tricky cases in your practices by providing handy tips and strategies from the experienced practitioners. However, should you want the comfort of having immigration law basics close by, we offer you in tandem with this book, our new *Essentials of Immigration Law* by Richard A. Boswell. Professor Boswell has written a comprehensive and well-constructed primer on the entire body of immigration law. I would like to personally thank Professor Boswell for his tenacity and diligence preparing his manuscript in time to be part of AILA's 2006–07 Annual Conference offerings.

And, of course, I'd like to thank the authors of the articles within this *Handbook* for their enthusiasm in committing their knowledge, insights, and experience to a book on which immigration law practitioners can rely for another year (or until comprehensive immigration reform is passed). Thanks, too, to the senior editors, who really devoted themselves this year by reviewing so many advanced and sophisticated articles. I would be remiss if I did not express my gratitude to Tatia L. Gordon-Troy, Silvia S. Wang, Elizabeth R. Bartels, Kathy J. Frazier, and Randy P. Auerbach—the rest of the AILA Publications team—who endeavored mightily to bring this *Handbook* and many other books to fruition for this year's Annual Conference.

Stephanie L. Browning
June 2006

ABOUT THE EDITORS

GREGORY P. ADAMS *(senior editor)* is a partner in the Cincinnati office of Dinsmore & Shohl LLP. Mr. Adams has served as chair of the AILA Connecticut and Ohio chapters, has co-authored "Foreign Students and Educational Visitors," a chapter in R. Rapp, *Education Law*, and has authored numerous articles for AILA publications. Mr. Adams has been an editor of AILA's *Immigration & Nationality Law Handbook* since 1993. He is a graduate of Middlebury College, Vermont, and Suffolk University Law School in Boston.

DAN H. BERGER *(senior editor)* is a graduate of Harvard College and Cornell Law School. He won the 1995 AILA Edward L. Dubroff Memorial writing competition for an article on INS policies toward international adoptions and has recently been appointed chair of the AILA Publications Committee. He also has been an outside editor for *Immigration Law and Procedure* since 1993 and is an author/editor of the NAFSA *Adviser's Manual*. He developed his interest in immigration in college, where he studied immigration history and taught English as a Second Language classes for adult refugees. He now specializes in serving academic clients in New England for the firm of Curran & Berger in Northampton, Mass.

JAN H. BROWN *(senior editor)* is a principal in the New York City-based law firm of Jan H. Brown, P.C. Mr. Brown has been practicing in the field of immigration law since 1979. He has lectured on many occasions on the subject and is also a reviewing editor for *Kurzban's Immigration Law Sourcebook* and contributing author to *The Visa Processing Guide*, both published by AILA. Mr. Brown is currently a chair of the Immigration and Nationality Law Committee of the New York State Bar Association International Law and Practice Section and is an Executive Committee officer for AILA's New York Chapter.

STEPHANIE L. BROWNING *(editor-in-chief)* is senior legal editor for AILA, where she is the managing editor for various AILA publications, and a contributing writer for *AILA's Immigration Law Today*. Ms. Browning received a B.A. from the University of Chicago (1996), and a J.D. from the University of Michigan Law School (2002), where she served as editor-in-chief of the *Michigan Journal of International Law*. She clerked for the EOIR at the Detroit Immigration Court during the summer of 2000.

JAMES P. EYSTER *(senior editor)*, an assistant clinical professor at Ave Maria School of Law, has practiced immigration law in Ann Arbor for nine years. Prior to that, he served first as executive director of the Princeton-in-Asia Foundation and then in the same capacity for the University of Michigan's Southeast Asia Business Program, for which he edited the *Journal of Asian Business*. He is a graduate of Princeton University and Fordham Law School, where he served as editor-in-chief of the *Fordham International Law Journal*. Mr. Eyster is listed in *Who's Who in American Law*.

CARL FALSTROM *(senior editor)* is principal of the Law Office of Carl Falstrom in San Francisco. He received his bachelor's degree from the University of Chicago and his law degree from the University of California, Hastings College of the Law. Mr. Falstrom is a former AILA Northern California Chapter chair and has served on the AILA California Service Center Liaison Committee. He also has been appointed adjunct professor of immigration law at University of San Francisco and Golden Gate University Schools of Law.

ESTER GREENFIELD *(senior editor)* is a director at MacDonald, Hoague & Bayless, where her practice is limited to immigration law. She is a past chair of the AILA Washington State Chapter and has taught immigration law and a seminar on VAWA as an adjunct professor at Seattle University. Ms. Greenfield has written and lectured nationally on immigration topics, with an emphasis on labor certification and has served on local and national Department of Labor liaison committees. She was co–editor-in-chief of the Third Edition of AILA's *David Stanton Manual on Labor Certification* (2005), co-editor of *AILA's Department of Labor Directory for Immigration Lawyers* (2002–03 eds.), and has been an editor of the *Immigration & Nationality Law Handbook* for many years. Ms. Greenfield is listed in *The Best Lawyers in America* in immigration law and the *International Who's Who of Business Lawyers* in corporate immigration Law.

Tatia L. Gordon-Troy *(associate editor)* is associate director and managing editor for the American Immigration Lawyers Association's (AILA) Publications Department and has been with AILA for seven years. A 1995 graduate of the University of Baltimore School of Law and member of the Maryland bar, Ms. Gordon-Troy practiced in the areas of employment, family, and administrative law as an associate with the Baltimore firm of Gohn, Hankey & Stichel. In a past life, she was deputy editor for *The Daily Record* in Baltimore and press secretary to U.S. Representative (Md.) Elijah E. Cummings.

Rita Kushner Sostrin *(senior editor)* is senior counsel at Wolfsdorf Immigration Law Group, one of the largest immigration firms in Los Angeles, and the seventh largest in the United States. She is listed in *An International Who's Who of Corporate Immigration Lawyers*, and is a frequent speaker and author on employment-based immigration law topics. Ms. Kushner Sostrin's practice is focused on immigration of academics and international medical graduates, and she represents several major academic institutions, hospitals, and scientific laboratories around the United States. She has been selected to serve as the 2006–07 chair of AILA's California Service Center Liaison Committee.

Nancy-Jo Merritt *(senior editor)*, a director in the Phoenix office of Fennemore Craig, P.C., has more than two decades of practice in the field of immigration law. Her practice is broad-based and includes the representation of domestic and international companies regarding visa and work authorization issues for foreign national employees. She also assists employers with federal compliance issues in the contexts of mergers and acquisitions and government audits. Ms. Merritt has bachelor's (1964) and master's (1974) degrees in English from Arizona State University and a law degree from the same institution (1978).

Steven A. Morley *(senior editor)* is a partner in the Philadelphia-based law firm of Morley, Surin & Griffin, where he concentrates in all facets of immigration law and criminal defense. He has served as an officer and chair of the AILA Philadelphia Chapter and as chair of the Criminal Justice Section of the Philadelphia Bar Association. Mr. Morley is a frequent regional and national lecturer on immigration law. He has successfully argued matters before the Third Circuit Court of Appeals and before the U.S. Supreme Court in the decision of *Mitchell v. United States*, extending the Fifth Amendment right to remain silent to sentencing proceedings. Mr. Morley is an honors graduate of the University of Wisconsin Law School.

Allen Orr, Jr. *(senior editor)* is an associate in the International Practice Group at Baker & McKenzie, specializing in immigration law. Mr. Orr's area of practice includes the representation of businesses and individuals before the U.S. Department of State and the U.S. Department of Homeland Security. He is the associate editor of *AILA's Global Immigration Guide: A Country-by-Country Survey*. Mr. Orr graduated from Howard University School of Law.

John L. Pinnix *(senior editor)* is a past president of AILA (2002–03) and a founding member of AILA's Carolinas Chapter. Mr. Pinnix attained B.A. and M.A. degrees in History at the University of North Carolina at Greensboro, and his J.D. at the Wake Forest University School of Law. He has served as an adjunct professor at North Carolina Central University School of Law and as a senior lecturing fellow at Duke University School of Law. He is a principal in the Raleigh law firm, Allen and Pinnix, P.A., and is a North Carolina board-certified immigration specialist.

Leigh Polk Cole *(senior editor)* is a shareholder and director of Dinse, Knapp & McAndrew, P.C., in Burlington, Vt. Her immigration practice primarily consists of representing U.S. and foreign companies and U.S. educational and health care institutions employing foreign nationals in the United States. She received a B.A. from Cornell University in 1985 in government and international trade policy, and a J.D. from Albany Law School of Union University in 1991, where she served as editor-in-chief of the *Albany Law Review*.

WILLIAM "BILL" STOCK *(senior editor)* is a founding partner of Klasko, Rulon, Stock & Seltzer, LLP. He handles all aspects of immigration law, including assisting companies and individuals in obtaining employment- and family-based visas; resolving citizenship issues and obtaining naturalization; and defending clients in ICE and DOL enforcement proceedings. Mr. Stock, who is an adjunct faculty member at Villanova University School of Law, currently serves as the chair of AILA's Philadelphia Chapter, is a past member of the AILA Board of Governors, and has received the Joseph Minsky Award. In 2003, he was selected for inclusion in *Best Lawyers in America*. He is a member of editorial boards for Matthew Bender and has authored many articles on immigration law topics.

T. DOUGLAS STUMP *(senior editor)* is an attorney with over 23 years of experience in a practice focused on employment-based immigration law, complex deportation, asylum, and family immigration matters. He maintains offices in Oklahoma City and Tulsa. Mr. Stump is serving a second three-year term as one of the 22 elected directors governing AILA. He is the past president of the Texas Chapter and an adjunct professor of immigration law. He serves as chair of AILA's Citizenship and Immigration Services National Security Liaison Committee and is a member of the Customs & Border Protection Committee. Mr. Stump is past chair of the AILA/Administrative Appeals Office Liaison Committee and served as a member of the AILA/USCIS Service Center Operations, Nomination, and Benefits Policy Committees. He is a past chair of the AILA Texas Service Center Liaison Committee. Mr. Stump has been listed in the Bar Register of Preeminent Lawyers since 1996, and is recognized in *Best Lawyers in America* for immigration law.

ELIZABETH A. THOMPSON *(senior editor)* is co-founder of the firm of Myers Thompson, P.A., in Minneapolis. She practices in the area of business-related immigration. Ms. Thompson has served as chair of the AILA Minnesota Dakotas Chapter, co-chair of the NSC Liaison Committee, chair of the Canada-U.S. Free Trade Agreement Committee, and co-chair of the Employment Creation/Investors Immigrant Category Committee. She also has served on the AILA-SSA Liaison Committee. Ms. Thompson has been an editor of this *Handbook* and other publications since 1991, and was an AILA Board of Governors member from 1991 to 1994. She is listed in *Best Lawyers in America*.

SILVIA S. WANG *(associate editor)* is a legal editor for AILA. A member of the Massachusetts bar, Ms. Wang previously served as staff attorney at Greater Boston Legal Services. She received a B.A. in English from Duke University and a J.D. from Boston College Law School.

DAVID WOLFE LEOPOLD *(senior editor)* practices removal defense and business and family immigration law in Cleveland. He is currently AILA's national secretary and served as an elected director on AILA's Board of Governors (2003–05). Mr. Leopold is former chair of the AILA ICE Liaison Committee (2003–04), former chair of the AILA Due Process Committee (2002–03), and former member of the AILA General Counsel Liaison Committee (2004–05). He served as Ohio Chapter chair (2001–03) and is a co-founder of the AILA/AILF Litigation Institute.

ABOUT AILA

The American Immigration Lawyers Association (AILA) is a national bar association of nearly 10,000 attorneys who practice immigration law and/or work as teaching professionals. AILA member attorneys represent tens of thousands of U.S. families who have applied for permanent residence for their spouses, children, and other close relatives for lawful entry and residence in the United States. AILA members also represent thousands of U.S. businesses and industries who sponsor highly skilled foreign workers seeking to enter the United States on a temporary or permanent basis. In addition, AILA members represent foreign students, entertainers, athletes, and asylum-seekers, often on a pro bono basis. Founded in 1946, AILA is a nonpartisan, not-for-profit organization that provides its members with continuing legal education, publications, information, professional services, and expertise through its 35 chapters and over 50 national committees. AILA is an affiliated organization of the American Bar Association and is represented in the ABA House of Delegates.

American Immigration Lawyers Association
918 F Street, NW
Washington, DC 20004
Tel: (202) 216-2400
Fax: (202) 783-7853
www.aila.org

BEST PRACTICES FOR IMMIGRATION LAW OFFICE MANAGEMENT

by Davis C. Bae, Jeffrey W. Goldman, and Dinesh P. Shenoy[*]

The practice of immigration law continues to increase in complexity and competitiveness. It is difficult to run a practice that focuses solely on delivering quality work. It has become necessary to take action to be competitive in terms of pricing, service, and speed. The authors of this article provide key guidelines for running not only a competitive immigration practice but also a quality business. The first five points are general guidelines to consider when running a business and are applicable to firms of all ranges and attorneys of all levels. The second five points are guidelines specific to the practice of immigration law. We hope that when applied together, these guidelines will provide great value and immediate tools of use to the readers of this article.

UNDERSTAND THE BUSINESS YOU ARE IN

Failure to understand the business side of your practice can result in a cycle of frustration and struggle without the opportunity for advancement. In the end, a law firm is just another form of business. Ventures built on great ideas that fail to generate revenue are merely hobbies rather than businesses.

[*] **Davis C. Bae** is the founder and managing attorney of the Bae Law Group. Mr. Bae's practice focuses on comprehensive immigration planning for multinational and fast-growth corporations. Mr. Bae regularly speaks to professional associations and companies on a variety of immigration issues including corporate changes, human resources, legal advocacy, foreign recruitment, and employee retention. Mr. Bae teaches the course "Small & Solo Practice" at the University of Washington Law School.

Jeff Goldman is a partner with Mintz Levin in Boston, with a concentration on employment-based immigration, particularly national interest waiver and extraordinary ability petitions. He is a frequent speaker at AILA and various colleges and universities, and in 2002, was named Pro Bono Attorney of the Year by the nationally recognized PAIR Project in Boston. Mr. Goldman has been a solo practitioner, small firm associate, and large firm partner.

Dinesh Shenoy practices with Ingber & Aronson PA in Minneapolis, with emphasis on employment/family cases as well as immigration consequences of crimes. He has spoken at many AILA conferences and teleconferences, and published articles on the "concurrent filing rule" and H-1B issues. Mr. Shenoy received the 2003 AILA Mentor Award and was a member of the AILA-NSC Liaison Committee (2004–05).

The following is a list of ideas on how to avoid having a potentially great law practice turn into a hobby:

- *Balance Legal Education with Business Education*: When providing assistance to other attorneys with struggling practices, the authors ask the attorney how many hours they spend on CLEs per year. The authors then ask them how many hours they spend on education related to running a business. Almost invariably, the lawyers who struggle spend most of their time on legal CLEs and almost no time on business education. These include understanding issues like cash flow, human resources, tax planning, technology, and benefits administration.

- *Understand Marketing vs. Sales*: Marketing is an outbound message with little control on the inflowing business opportunities. Sales is the process of closing those opportunities. To illustrate this point, a website is an effective marketing tool, but it generally does not result in direct revenue until a sales process is initiated to engage the website viewer. Websites are becoming the yellow pages of the new millennium, as almost all firms have a website that provides basic information about the law firm. One possible method for incorporating a sales aspect into your website marketing campaign is to use tools to track users, getting permission to contact them via the most direct path, and then following through with those leads in the most direct way possible (*e.g.*, phone, e-mail, or in-person visit).

- Review the seasonal aspects of the business in terms of revenues and costs. Many businesses will have sales and temporary hires based upon their seasonal revenue expectations. The immigration business is highly seasonal and careful review of revenue would demonstrate increases in certain types of petitions (H-1B, H-2B, and even marriage-based adjustment of status) depending on the time of year. Effective law office management would include making the correct staffing decisions, initiating marketing campaigns, and even discounting rates depending on the flow of legal revenue.

DEVELOP, REVIEW, AND ADHERE TO YOUR BUSINESS PLAN

Business plans keep individuals and organizations on a consistent plan of advancement. Business plans can be both personal and entity-wide. It is not enough simply to carefully create a thoughtful business plan, however. Regardless of whether you are an entry-level associate, sole practitioner, or a senior partner, attorneys should regularly take the time to stop, evaluate, and improve their business plans. The following are tips on how to develop and utilize business plans properly:

- After you have taken the time to carefully develop your business plan, have others review it. Often a business plan is not successful because the goals are unobtainable or because there are obstacles that the writer of the plan does not have the experience to recognize or is too close to the business to see. Do not hesitate to obtain advice on your business plan from individuals who are outside of your area of practice or outside of the legal field entirely. Amazing insight can be achieved by borrowing the perspective of individuals in other businesses. In the end, a law firm is just another type of business that shares more similarities than differences with other businesses.

- No business plan has value unless you can measure how your business is progressing. To measure your success and failure, the business must have clear metrics to measure progress. Metrics can take numerous forms including gross and net profitability, cases filed, client satisfaction, and goal completion. Carefully analyze which metrics are essential to your business and then track them.

- Create an accountability structure comprised of members within your own organization, an advisory board, or other colleagues who will provide honest feedback and advise you when you diverge from your business plan. To obtain quality support, you may require compensation or trade in services to properly motivate your advisors.

- Conduct a power retreat annually. Retreats are opportunities to sit back and review the business with members of management and staff. Retreats should be special events where the management and staff provide input and gain a sense of investment in the business. Creative exercises are available online and in many management books. One simple but effective exercise that is a regular element of many retreats is the SWOT analysis.

SWOT is an acronym for Strengths, Weaknesses, Opportunity, and Threats. In this exercise, individuals at the retreat list items that fall into those four categories. From here, a discussion can take place to determine how to take advantage of the Strengths and Opportunities that address the Weaknesses and Threats. A sample of a SWOT analysis is at Appendix A.

CREATE A CULTURE AND CORE VALUES FOR YOUR BUSINESS

This is the starting point for all well-run businesses that is too often ignored by law firms. A law firm's culture can be described as the "personality" of a firm. Specifically, the culture is made up of the business's attitudes, values, beliefs, norms, and customs. A business's culture is not necessarily the business's mission and/or core values, but the culture should reflect those ideals. The culture of an organization operates at both conscious and unconscious levels. At its most subconscious level, it involves deeply rooted beliefs, values, and norms held by members of the organization but are often difficult to describe for insiders who have "grown up" in the business culture. Public values, on the other hand, exist at a more conscious level; these are the values people discuss, promote, and try to live by.

- *Core Values*: If you are starting your business, establishing these Core Values early on will make the business simpler to run because a good values set should be easy to comply with. If you are in a mature business and have not clearly defined the business's Core Values, it is a valuable utilization of time and energy to determine what the business's Core Values are. Once these values are clear, it is essential that management and staff consistently strive to achieve these values.

- *Reinforce your Core Values*: Core Values must be consistently maintained throughout an organization. This requires a consistent message and alignment and creation of incentives that are based on the business's Core Values. In one author's firm, annual reviews and awards are based upon employee behavior consistent with the firm/business's Core Values that have long been: innovation, integrity, and inspiration.

- *Be the Chief of Culture!* The owner or head of an organization is its Chief of Culture. By living the culture of your business, the head sets the example for the rest of the organization. Although culture is profoundly shaped by the company's leader and senior managers, it is essential that all members of an organization are consistent with the tone set by management.

ALWAYS LOOK TO CREATE GOOD WILL

Good will is an essential asset of a law firm that never shows up in a balance sheet as a line item but can be evaluated nonetheless. Good will can exist in different forms and with different groups. Below is a summary of good will that attorneys should strive to develop:

- *With Colleagues*: Develop a close set of colleagues/mentors from whom to draw information and experience. Immigration is a business that requires direct knowledge and/or experience with a wide array of immigration issues. Without a clearly established set of colleagues to draw from, too much of our time is spent looking for answers that do not exist in a treatise or regulation. Once you establish good will with colleagues by sharing valuable gained information, they will return the favor. When one of the authors started his own practice, he contacted several prominent solo attorneys and moderated brown bag lunches where they could discuss common but difficult immigration issues. Ten years later, most of this group still communicates about difficult cases and shares valuable information.

- *With Clients*: Good will with clients is established by going beyond the simple processing of a visa or permanent residence. Taking a vested interest in a client, educating them on the law, and exceeding their expectations are ways to develop client good will. Good will with clients is clearly evidenced in their feedback and desire to refer you to others. At some point in their career, almost all attorneys will eventually have a case go wrong. When this happens, good will from previous excellent client service will often buy forgiveness and understanding from even the most demanding client.

- *With Strategic Alliances*: Strategic alliances include referral sources, vendors, and members of your various communities. In addition to creating balance in one's professional and personal life, good will in these areas will frequently bring financial benefit through referrals and boost your reputation as a quality service provider.

- *With Staff*: Good will internally within your organization promotes a sense of integrity and loyalty. Offering quality employee benefits beyond

salary, sincere consideration of staff input, a quality work environment, and a culture of employee appreciation are all ways to develop good will with staff. Downturns in business such as those caused by 9/11, the dot-com crash, and negative changes in the law can make it very compelling for talented individuals to leave immigration law firms. However, high levels of internal good will within an immigration firm can be the motivation for employees to stand by employers during difficult periods.

FOCUS ON EFFICIENCY

Inefficiency is the fat on an organization that keeps it from running smoothly. An inefficient organization requires more revenue to maintain profitability. In that way, a dollar saved is more valuable than a dollar earned. Businesses that focus on efficiency will often avoid issues that become a drag on larger but less efficient businesses, thereby enjoying better net revenues.

- Software and templates are just the first steps toward efficiency. The real key to efficiency is the review of procedures in all elements of your business. This includes the integration of new staff, the acceleration of payment from clients, and the balancing of technology, processes, and staff for maximum efficiency.

- Software solutions can be effective solutions, but they also can be costly tools that provide little benefit. While almost any issue can be resolved by an engineered solution, many of those solutions are prohibitively expensive. Oftentimes, simple combinations of procedure and basic technology can make up for expensive software tools that may be unnecessary.

- Employment handbooks may seem like restrictive guidelines for employees, but well-drafted and balanced employment guidelines will provide a common knowledge base for employees to understand how the business operates. A well-drafted handbook will also resolve many of the issues that could grow into large problems within an organization, as the employees can determine proper procedure prior to problems growing out of hand. Inefficiency in dealing with employee dissatisfaction can be extremely time-consuming and a cancer on a business culture.

- Reviews of financial issues such as cash flow, investment, taxes, and retirement benefits will often result in financial gains that were previously unutilized. By utilizing firm resources more carefully, the firm can invest and develop a deeper war chest of funds should the need arise.

BE A MANAGER AS WELL AS A LAWYER

Many of us were taught in law school to learn to "love the law." The "pure" practice of law can indeed be a love, but practicing law in the real world is more than just analyzing facts, applying the law, and churning out a conclusion. A successful law practice quickly grows beyond a handful of cases that a lawyer can personally manage by reacting to events as they happen. Being a manager is as much a part of an immigration attorney's daily and weekly and monthly job duties as are legal strategizing, marketing, and appearing in court or at interviews. Once you have exceeded the capacity of how many cases, cold calls, referrals, and responses to unexpected new issues (*e.g.*, requests for evidence) that you can deal with individually on a given day, you have reached the point of needing support staff and assistance. Once your practice involves utilizing the efforts of any human being other than yourself to accomplish what you need to for your clients, your role as manager becomes equal in importance to your role as lawyer. In terms of client satisfaction and your own personal satisfaction with your career, perhaps nothing is more important than properly managing your caseload, your staff, and your time. The following practices are recommended for moving from just "practicing law" to "managing a law practice":

- Define staff roles in writing. Many kinds of employment-based and family-based petitions and applications can be successfully delegated to legal assistants to prepare for interim and final review by attorneys for filing. However, delegating has its limits, and staff need to be clearly instructed that giving legal advice, formulating core case strategy, and quoting fees for any potential new case can only be performed by the responsible attorney(s) for that particular client.

- Cross-Train staff so that two or more employees are available at any given time, all of whom are well-trained in particular kinds of cases (*e.g.*, L-1s, asylum cases, adjustment of status procedures). This ensures that the office is adequately covered so that one employee going on vacation or leaving the firm does not disrupt the flow of work. Different employees have different work styles and strengths/weakness that naturally suit them to different kinds of cases; however, over-

specialization of staff can lead to significant disruption whenever an employee leaves the firm.

- Require consistency by staff in file maintenance. Each case file should speak for itself, meaning if an employee assigned to the case is unavailable at any given time, the remaining office staff should be able to quickly and easily familiarize themselves with the client's particular facts and current situation. This is vital in an area of law where urgent questions such as travel and visa problems, job changes, and/or new facts arise randomly and suddenly. Establishing and enforcing office-wide consistent practices for how client information and communications are recorded in the physical case files as well as a case management software system such as Immigration Tracker or INS Zoom is strongly recommended.

CREATE SYSTEMS FOR REGULAR, SYSTEMATIC FILE REVIEW

Nothing is as great as getting a phone call from a potential client who says they were referred by a past satisfied client (particularly one whom you remember fondly). On the other hand, nothing is as scary as getting two or three or more such calls, plus several e-mails, plus maybe a new case from an existing corporate client, plus an unexpected RFE, etc. Being able to meet your duty to zealously represent all your clients properly requires maintaining files according to a systematic format *and* planning for regularly reviewing those case files. The following methods are suggested for achieving a regular, systematic review:

- Use two different systems to create a redundant safety net for tracking the progress of your cases to make sure that due dates and deadlines are not falling through the cracks. One suggested way is to use a combination of a case management software system like Immigration Tracker or INS Zoom (or similar products) that have a "tickler" feature, backed up by physically annotating files for when you next want to see or discuss the file (*e.g.*, three months after I-130/485/765/131 are filed, or six months in advance of when H-1B status expires, or four days after you have assigned an L-1 to an associate). Your file room should be combed once a week so that these "come-up" dates are effective in getting your files back to your office well in advance of when you need to act on them or delegate tasks on them.

- Effectively using a case management software package can eliminate the need to physically obtain each file from the file room. One author has a system where Immigration Tracker notifies two different people of each "tickle" or "reminder" that has been entered in to the system. Clear notes and accurate dates are tracked right in the software package, so it is not necessary to actually have the physical file in front of you to e-mail a client a timely reminder about an H-1B extension that must be filed in six months.

- Track priority dates each month. In family-based and employment-based practice, it is critical not to miss precious weeks or months when a visa number has become available or will soon become available. The attached template at Appendix B suggests an easy method for creating a simple 3-ring binder that enables you to quickly check all your cases against the Visa Bulletin when it is released each month.

- Perform monthly total case review. At least once a month, use your case management software to print off a complete list of all open/in preparation or filed/pending cases for which you are responsible. Most programs allow relevant information to be easily captured in one entry for quick review (*e.g.*, what kind of case it is, relevant expiration dates such as I-94, EAD, and what dates you filed various petitions/applications on).

- Send news flash updates to your client e-mail list on a mostly regular basis. Particularly in the case of employment-based immigration practice, it is important to regularly update corporate clients of upcoming milestones (such as April 1 when new H-1B visa numbers become available for filing toward the following fiscal year's cap). While there is something to be said for not bombarding clients with so many "flash" e-mails that they grow weary of seeing your name in their Inbox, short, periodic e-mails that are targeted to clients' interests are largely appreciated and welcomed by corporate clients. Not only is this a recommended strategy for building and keeping clients loyal through periodically reminding them of your existence, but it ensures that you are giving your clients the information needed to do their own hiring planning. One of the authors bills his corporate clients through flat-fee arrangements tied to each individual alien's case. The approval and closing of each particular case file does not mean the attorney-client relationship between the company and the law firm is severed. To the con-

trary, the clients expect this attorney to keep them informed of major immigration news that the company needs to factor into its larger planning even if it is not tied to an immediate new case. As an example, if a company is planning for a round of hiring in the spring, hoping to hire new foreign workers during the summer, the H-1B cap might well be exhausted by that time. The company may depend on your foresight to help protect their interests.

START AND END ATTORNEY-CLIENT RELATIONSHIPS IN WRITING

With the number of reports of attorney discipline actions seemingly on the increase, it is more important than ever to clearly delineate who has and who has not become a client and who no longer is one for which you are responsible for tracking and advising.

- For phone and e-mail contacts with potential clients, if the potential client does not agree to do an initial consultation or hire you according to your usual terms, then make clear that you are not their attorney simply because you have had a conversation with them about a potential case. Immigration is a very deadline-driven practice, and it is very important to be clear whose deadlines you are *not* responsible for tracking.

- After an initial consultation with a potential client, always send a written follow-up making clear what the potential client must do to become a client (*e.g.*, sign a contract with your firm and/or pay an initial retainer). Once hired, sending an engagement letter is critical to make clear what work you will and will *not* be doing, what the total fee is, and when it is due.

- When the immigration objective is achieved at the end of a case, make sure to send a close-out letter that leaves the client not only with your well wishes, but also a clear statement the attorney-client relationship has ended.

MANAGE INFORMATION AND DOCUMENTS CONSISTENTLY

One key to successfully managing a large case load and the regular flow of new work is to standardize how you take in client information and how you communicate information out to clients and the immigration agencies.

- *Require all new clients to complete a standard questionnaire.* Each and every foreign national client should complete a comprehensive initial questionnaire that reviews the client's immigration history and asks essential questions affecting the client's admissibility and eligibility for various immigration benefits. Keep your questionnaires current with changes in the law.

- *Establish intraoffice standards for database maintenance.* The many case management software tools available to immigration attorneys require intraoffice agreement on how client information is stored in the database. This is particularly true of company information in an employment-based practice where the same information about the same company is updated yearly and used regularly, such as for multiple I-129 petitions and PERM filings. At any given time, if the attorney and legal assistant assigned to a case are both unavailable, other attorneys/staff in the office should be able to determine quickly what the most recent communication has been with the client and the status of the case, whether in preparation or pending at U.S. Citizenship and Immigration Services (USCIS). This also properly prepares your office for turnover amongst staff with minimal disruption.

- *Use template letters, with necessary customization.* Many AILA members regularly criticize USCIS for using too much "boilerplate" when communicating with them. On the other hand, because there is a great deal of repetition in the kinds of cases the attorneys file, it is vital that the attorneys too make use of template letters as long as each client's particular facts are taken into consideration in the advice given. There is a lot of general immigration advice that attorneys need to repeat over and over to all clients (such as the need for a nonimmigrant visa stamp for future international travel). At the same time, for certain clients, the advice must be tailored or changed entirely from what attorneys might normally advise most clients to do (for example, using or not using the "automatic visa revalidation rule" in 22 CFR §41.112(d), depending on the purpose of a client's trip to Canada or Mexico). Many of the case management software products (and even Microsoft Word itself) offer easy template features for standardizing letters that you use over and over.

REMEMBER THAT THE DEVIL IS IN THE DETAILS

If you are like the authors and are fortunate enough to have smart, capable, and competent support staff, then you may be lucky enough that many of your forms, supporting documentation, and cover letters are prepared by your staff and presented to you in almost-ready-to-file format. It is dangerously alluring to just sign off on a cover letter and the forms without reading them closely, particularly if your support staff are professionals who do not need to be micromanaged. Yet an attorney should never sign off on a case he or she has not personally reviewed. Even if you are solo and do all your own work, this point bears repeating. As lawyers, we take pride in knowing all the substantive laws and having our legal citations in support of our arguments laid out clearly in our briefs or cover letters. But the strongest, most clearly approvable I-129 petition can go awry if you make a simple mistake of forgetting to check a box, or check a box incorrectly (such as forgetting to claim cap exemption when you know the case is cap exempt). The most solid appeal issue can be lost if you send your notice of appeal to the Board of Immigration Appeals' old address. And in a high-pressure, fast-paced law practice environment where support staff are used, there is an inevitable tendency for lawyer and legal assistant to each expect the other to catch small mistakes, when in fact having more than one person responsible for a case can cause mistakes to multiply. Even viewing it from the realistic perspective that time is money (and thus more money is to be made the less time you spend on any given case), the following recommended practices may feel like they take more time in the short term to implement, but in the long term they will inevitably save not only money but time as well (such time not spent trying to fix mistakes suddenly discovered, or time not spent having to apologize to a client.):

- Review forms line by line *twice*; once before forms are sent to a client for signature, and again after signature and before filing the case.

- Double-check the spelling of each alien's name and date of birth against his or her passport, questionnaire, and possibly birth certificate (if it is provided for that kind of case). A misspelling of an alien's name on an immigration document may be a small issue to the attorney, but to the client, a misspelling of a name is a major source of frustration and anxiety about future problems at the time of visa application or immigration inspections, as well as a sign that his or her attorney does not really know who the client is.

- Developing *and using* quality control checklists is an excellent practice, particularly if you establish a "buddy" system of having a different employee other than the responsible attorney (and possibly legal assistant) complete the checklist to look for gross errors such as a filing fee check being written for the wrong amount of fees or to the wrong party, or missing boxes/fields on forms that are likely to cause USCIS to reject the filing. Each year, the *Immigration & Nationality Law Handbook*, published by AILA at the time of the Annual Conference, contains an article on filing procedures with recommended checklists for various types of immigration filings.

Immigration law is simultaneously an exciting and rewarding practice area, yet daunting and fraught with potential pitfalls. Unlike other fields of law involving claims for monetary and other damages, for the most part in immigration law, the outcomes of cases are very much "all or nothing."

A petition is either approved or not approved; there is no half-visa to get for your client. Status expires on a particular day, and the extension of status either was properly filed and accepted or was not, with little room for forgiveness if the deadline is missed. The immigration judge either orders your client removed or grants relief; there is no plea bargaining to a lesser ground of removal. Does this mean that immigration lawyers must always be perfect and never make mistakes? No, but it does mean that immigration lawyers have an obligation to make sure they are managing themselves and their practices properly. The purpose of this article has been to suggest ways to make immigration law practice both manageable and profitable, both personally rewarding and financially rewarding. In the end, proper law office management is part and parcel of meeting our ethical obligations to our clients, because our clients' needs are best served by properly managing ourselves.

APPENDIX A: THE SWOT ANALYSIS

For 15 minutes, please use the colored post-it notes on the table to write a short statement or word on each of the following. If you have difficulty coming up with ideas, review the questions listed below in each category. After completion of the 15-minute period, our answers will be listed and reviewed. We will jointly define the top items under each category and create action items to address each category.

Strengths—Yellow

    1)   What do we do better than anyone else?
    2)   What are you proud of regarding our office?
    3)   What compliments do we regularly get from clients?

Weaknesses—Green

    1)   What is a source of frustration?
    2)   What do other firms do better than us?
    3)   What complaints do we get from clients?

Opportunities—Pink

    1)   What aspects of our business do you get excited about?
    2)   What entrepreneurial opportunities do you see?

Threats—Orange

    1)   What fears do you have for the business?
    2)   Where do you see problems for the business in the future?

Strengths	Weaknesses	Opportunities	Threats
Value	Website	Growing economy	Legal change
Good Will	Consistency	PERM	War
Brand	Need more staff	Branch office	Volatile economy
Staff	Marketing materials	Referral campaign	Financing
Technology			

APPENDIX B: INSTRUCTIONS FOR USING BINDER
TO TRACK MONTHLY VISA BULLETIN DATES

I. The Purpose of This Binder

This binder is designed to systematize and simplify office-wide tracking of any open case in which the client is prevented from filing a 485 (or initiating IV processing overseas through NVC—which will mostly be family cases) because of the unavailability of a visa number on the monthly DOS Visa Bulletin. Since we never know exactly when the Visa Bulletin is going to show an alien's priority date has been reached, the best practice is:

1. Each month when the Bulletin comes out, run it against all such cases, and

2. Be ready to file the clients' 485s by having them either working on drafts or updating us on previously prepared 485s once their particular category's cut-off date has moved up to within 2 months or less of their priority date.

II. How to Use This Binder

1. For each case that has reached this point (either I-130/I-140 is filed and pending or approved, but 485 cannot be filed), the Responsible Attorney should prepare a REMINDER SHEET (attached hereto.)

2. After setting reminders in the database for nonimmigrant status expiration date(s) and other relevant reminders, and before returning the file to the file room with a come-up date maybe 6+ months in the future, the Responsible Attorney should fill out the REMINDER SHEET, *making sure to screen for critical legal issues such as possible earlier retained priority date under 8 CFR § 204.5(e), any cross-chargeability based on country of birth of the spouse/kids if different from the principal alien, and make sure to enter the proper EB or FAM preference category for the principal alien. Please use the date format "01 JAN 98" since that is the format DOS uses on the Bulletin for cut-off dates.*

3. The completed Reminder sheet should go into this 3-ring binder for the next step. The folder is divided in sections of EB-1, EB-2 and EB-3, and Family 1st, 2A, 2B, 3rd & 4th. Sheets should be inserted into the appropriate section, with *oldest* priority date on top.

4. *Each month when the Visa Bulletin comes out,* one person should go through each sheet in the binder, and write down which VB they are looking at (Oct. 2005, Nov. 2005, Dec. 2005, etc.) and write down what cut-off date appears based on the alien's country of birth and preference category. *Please use the date format "01 JAN 98" since that is the format DOS uses on the Bulletin for cut-off dates.*

Whomever does this should make note if the cut-off date has surpassed the alien's priority date or if the cut-off date is approaching within 2 months up to the alien's priority date. If it is, then the case file should immediately be pulled and brought to the attention of the responsible attorney since an I-485 should be able to be filed soon and therefore should be readied for filing.

REMINDER SHEET
FOR CHECKING VISA BULLETIN

This case has reached the point where the principal alien could file an I-485 *but for* unavailability of an immigrant visa number, (*i.e.*, alien has an approved I-140 *or* a pending I-140 in a preference category where we know that upon approval of that 140 the alien is still facing a wait for a visa number, meaning no concurrent 485 filing can be done right now).

The responsible attorney should check this month's Visa Bulletin against the alien's country of chargeability and priority date and preference category below.

ALIEN: (enter First Name, LAST NAME and file number)

COUNTRY: (enter Country of Birth *after* checking for any cross-chargeability)

CATEGORY: (enter EB-1, EB-2 or EB-3, or FAM 1, 2A, 2B, 3 or 4)

PRIORITY DATE: (enter date of I-130 filing, I-140 filing if no Labor Cert, or Labor Cert filing)

I-485 FILED YET?   (Y/N) (If Yes, I-485 has been filed and now priority date reached, call 1-800)

In the chart below, note down which Visa Bulletin you examined, and write down the cut-off date that this month's Bulletin is showing. If the cut-off date is approaching within 2 month or less of the Priority Date shown above, or especially if the cut-off date has moved past the Priority Date shown above, pull this file and bring it to the attention of the responsible attorney ASAP.

Which Visa Bulletin are you looking at?	What "cut-off" date is shown for this country/category?		Which Visa Bulletin are you looking at?	What "cut-off" date is shown for this country/category?

TECHNOLOGY FOR THE IMMIGRATION PRACTITIONER

by David S. Jones, Randy P. Auerbach, and Cletus M. Weber [*]

INTRODUCTION

Success in using technology to improve your immigration law practice is not universal. Small, inexpensive steps sometimes yield fantastic results and large, expensive steps sometimes lead to dead ends (and vice versa, of course). This article focuses on a few bread-and-butter issues of technology for immigration lawyers: case management/forms and online research. It also provides a few tips on other helpful technologies. Additional background and a broader range of technology concepts and choices can be found in *AILA's Guide to Technology and Legal Research for the Immigration Practitioner, Third Edition.*

---

[*] **David Jones** is a partner in the Memphis office of Siskind Susser. He specializes in a wide variety of immigration areas including employment, asylum, J waivers, and extraordinary ability petitions. Mr. Jones oversees the firm's technical innovations and is a contributor to the TechNotes column in *Immigration Law Today*. Mr. Jones graduated from the University of Florida Fredric G. Levin College of Law in 1999, with a focus on international and immigration issues. He has a B.A. magna cum laude in Foreign Languages from the University of Memphis.

Randy Auerbach has been AILA's Director of Publications since 1999. He is a 27-year veteran of the legal-publishing industry, having served as managing editor for BNA Books and *Family Law Reporter*, and the Supreme Court editor for *U.S. Law Week*. A member of the Maryland and D.C. bars, Mr. Auerbach received his J.D. from the University of Baltimore and his B.A. from the University of Rochester.

Cletus Weber is a partner at Peng & Weber in Seattle, where he practices primarily business immigration with an emphasis on national interest waivers, EB-1 petitions, and J-1 waivers. Mr. Weber is Chair of AILA's Washington State Chapter and a contributor to a number of AILA publications including *AILA's Guide to Technology and Legal Research for the Immigration Lawyer, Third Edition*. He earned his B.B.A. at the College of William and Mary and his J.D. from George Washington University, where from 1988 to 1989 he served as Managing Editor of the *George Washington Law Review*.

SOFTWARE FOR THE IMMIGRATION PRACTITIONER

Research

Most of you probably have a large collection of statutes, regulations and treatises, and today almost any immigration issue can be researched online. There are a few products out there, however, that bring all of these together. They provide a one-stop on-line or desktop application to read treatises, review statutes, search cases or study background materials. The three major providers of research materials are AILA*Link*, LexisNexis, and Westlaw, which we will discuss below.

AILALink *(www.ailapubs.org/ailalink.html)*

AILA*Link* is an immigration law library that resides on your local computer or network. Besides an extensive array of primary source information such as statutes and regulations, BIA decisions, and agency memoranda and Liaison minutes, the electronic library includes nearly every new AILA book that is published, including *Kurzban's Sourcebook, The Stanton Manual on Labor Certification*, and the various Occupational Guidebooks. (AILA's Toolbox publications, which are packaged with their own CDs, are the most notable exceptions to the included books.)

All the data is searchable through a robust Folio search engine; searches can query selected sources or the entire library. AILA*Link* also includes a forms component, described *infra*.

LexisNexis

LexisNexis offers both an online research engine covering all areas of the law and a desktop application specifically for immigration research. The online product allows you to search cases and statutes and provides access to a variety of sources, including treatises, the Foreign Affairs Manual, Operating Instructions, Officer Manuals and the Federal Register. The desktop application, LexisNexis CD—Immigration Law Library, provides all primary sources, analysis, practice aids, and administrative decisions. The application also contains the Bender treatise, *Immigration Law and Procedure*, and Bender's Immigration Regulations Service.

Westlaw

Westlaw also offers both an online research engine and desktop application. The online product provides access to federal cases, administrative decisions, statutes, regulations, analytical resources, *Interpreter Releases*, *Immigration Briefings*, and appellate briefs. Treatises such as Fragomen and Bell's *Immigration Procedures Handbook*, *H-1B Handbook*, and *Labor Certification Handbook* also are available. The desktop application, IRIS (Immigration Research Information Service) provides access to primary source materials, including annotated statutes, federal regulations and agency guidance. The CD also provides analysis of immigration topics and access to the *Asylum Case Law Sourcebook*, *Interpreter Releases*, and *Immigration Briefings*.

Case Management and Forms

Immigration case management software products have now been with us for more than 10 years. Today's products are light-years ahead of the early versions and are improving on almost a daily basis. Today there are a variety of immigration tools which simplify and improve the way you prepare your cases and manage your client's needs. Before buying any product, however, you should keep a number of factors in mind.

While it is helpful to have a variety of products available, the immigration bar is still relatively small and it seems unlikely that a large number of different case management products can be supported over the long run. There are probably fewer general case management products serving the entire legal community. It is important to look at the financial viability of the company producing the software, the size of the customer base, and the number of years the company and its key people have been in this field. The consequences of the company's closure could be disastrous.

Closely review features to ensure that the product fits your practice's needs. Some products are geared more for the individual practitioner while others are designed for larger firms. You also should look to see if it is well designed for the types of cases you generally process. Some products may focus on business matters and not work well for family and litigation matters. Clearly define your goals in using the software. Many systems offer a variety of features such as e-mail integration billing, calendaring status tracking, etc. Decide which features are important to you and which features you believe your staff will use. If you just need something to complete forms, it would be a mistake to invest in an extensive case management system.

Another important issue in looking at the company is the level and type of training and support offered. Training and support can be as basic as FAQs on a website or as involved as sending someone to your office. The costs associated with the support also may vary. It may seem that you have saved a lot of money on the software you have chosen, only to make up the difference later paying for support. You also should look at the staff's availability in updating forms, answering questions, and resolving problems. Even the most expensive and extravagant software will be of no use to you if the forms are out of date, your staff cannot use it or if there is no one to help you fix it when there is a crash.

Perhaps the most important question to consider is the type of platform you will use and what will be involved in deploying it. Some products are web-based and host your data. Others are systems that reside on your own computers. Still others may be some sort of hybrid. Two major factors to consider here are the location of your data and the technological investment you will have to make in order to be able to use the product.

If you have a small practice, you may find it advantageous to use a Web-based system where the data is housed by the software company. It will save you money on the technology needed to operate the software and the IT staff needed to maintain it. If your data will be hosted remotely, however, you need to carefully review how the company secures your data from both hackers and disaster. You also should consider what would be involved if you had to reclaim your data from the company. Yet another consideration is the reliability of the Internet connections required to use the product and access your data.

Larger practices with good technological infrastructures and savvy IT staff on the other hand may prefer to house the data at their office, whether they choose a Web-based or desktop product. Such products often allow greater flexibility in customization and control. Doing so, however, requires a close look at your practice. You should be certain you are aware of the additional costs you may accrue if new equipment needs to be purchased or if you have to add IT support staff to manage it. You also still must ensure that you have the capability to protect your data.

Below we provide a quick summary of a number of products that are available and specifically designed for immigration law firms:

EILA, Esq. and EIMMIGRATION from Cerenade (www.cerenade.com)

Cerenade offers a desktop application, EILA, Esq. and a Web-based application, EIMMIGRATION. EILA, Esq. (Electronic Immigration Lawyer Assistant) is available in small office and large enterprise versions. The small office version utilizes the Microsoft Access database and the enterprise version utilizes SQL Server. EILA, Esq. organizes data in client case files that store all information and forms relevant to a particular client. Once data is entered in one form, the data is "shared" with other forms to avoid repetition of entry. Other features include automatic reduction of font size to fit information into form fields, forms e-mail integration, text search, mail merge and over 15 different reports.

EIMMIGRATION is the Web-based version, which can run across the Internet or your office's intranet and is available in three versions, Enterprise, Pay Per Use and Per Month. The Enterprise version allows you to host the data on your own server, utilizing your own SQL database, while Cerenade will host your data with the Pay Per Use and Per Month versions. Being a Web-based ASP application, EIMMIGRATION runs entirely on the host server, eliminating the need for client software. The Web-based version offers the ability to e-mail intake questionnaires to clients, which can be imported to the database. Clients also can access their data remotely using a secure login. Additional features include a contact manger, case manager, reminders, forms manager, and report generation.

EmpPet Professional / EmpPet Enterprise from Compaque Business Software (www.emppet.com)

Both of Compaque Business Software's solutions, EmpPet Enterprise and EmpPet Professional, are desktop applications, which means the data will always be stored in-house. EmpPet Professional is an H-1B/H-4 preparation software providing step by step instructions and guidance for H-1B petitions. The software validates entered information to avoid human mistakes, and maintains all the addresses needed to file a petition. It also provides sample letters, templates, LCA tracking, and automated reminders.

EmpPet Enterprise uses its "NAVIGATOR" and the Microsoft Access database to organize client data. Six windows provide information on companies, clients, contacts, activities, and forms. The "NAVIGATOR" organizes data in a hierarchical structure, where individuals, projects, forms, etc. can be organized under one company or linked to related companies and projects. EmpPet Enterprise comes with built-in wizards to generate forms. Like EmpPet Professional, these wizards can take you step by step to create the petitions. Additional features include Web enabled Case Tracking, more than 20 standard reports, additional customizable reports, auto reminders, database backup, restore and repair, templates, LCA and activity tracking, search features and a calendar. EmpPet Enterprise is available in attorney and corporate versions.

Immigration Law Interactive Drafting System (IDS) from Bender (www.bender.com)

IDS provides over 140 forms from the variety of government agencies needed to complete an immigration case, including Social Security and the Internal Revenue Service. The system also allows you to generate 13 different types of reports and logs, create ticklers and sort cases by petitioner, file number or attorney. A "Personal Organizer" allows you to organize frequently used form and files. IDS also provides government instructions, links to websites and access to O*NET, Occupational Employment Statistics, and the Dictionary of Occupation Titles.

Immigrant Pro and Immigration Forms Gold (www.immigrantsoftware.com)

Immigrant Professional is a forms processor, case tracking, and management tool known to most immigration practitioners. In addition to basic forms completion, it provides a calendaring module and a report builder.

Forms Gold is a step up from Immigrant Professional and comes with the MSSQL Desktop Engine. It can also run on and be upgraded to the full version of SQL. Forms Gold allows association of beneficiaries, petitioners, and forms. It includes reports and automatic tracking of important dates with reminders.

Case Management Gold, as the name suggests, is the case management upgrade to the forms programs. Case Management Gold allows you to track every task and notifies the user when tasks need to be completed. Both Forms Gold and Case Management Gold integrate with a Web component, Immigrant Online.

Immigrant Online allows clients to input and edit their own data. It also permits your staff to access client data and case status remotely. Immigrant Software is currently preparing to release new versions of Case Management Gold and Immigrant Online.

ImmigrationTracker
(www.immigrationtracker.com)

ImmigrationTracker's latest version, Tracker7 Office, uses a smart client interface, allowing you to use a desktop application to access data across the internet. Anywhere you have an Internet connection you have access to all features of the application and your client data. Tracker provides online access to foreign nationals and HR for case tracking and the completion of case questionnaires.

Process Detail Screens give your staff all of the critical information needed for your cases and interface with e-filing and online tracking for USCIS, DOS, DOL, and SEVIS. Tracker also provides a document management system with document and e-mail generators. Additional features include a calendar with automated reminders, synchronization with Outlook and PDAs, a contact manager, and reports wizard (including staff productivity reports). Tracker also integrates with other applications such as Juris, QuickBooks, and Outlook.

For those who do not want to host their own data, ImmigrationTracker provides an online edition where they will host and secure the data. This edition retains the functionality of the office version. Finally, ImmigrationTracker has also released a global version, which provides legal guides for various countries, including a directory of experts in each country. The global version includes country-specific processes with multi-language forms and questionnaires.

Immigration Works (www.immigrationworks.com)

Immigration Works is a comprehensive immigration case management system, which provides access to all case management features and functions from a Web-based platform. It features a "self-service" module allowing clients, petitioners and beneficiaries to check case status and verify information directly. Users have the option of running the software from the Immigration Works website or in-house if they have their own server. Different billing structures apply based on which option you choose. Immigration Works also provides reminder dates for visa expiration, court appearances and other important dates, migration of such dates to Outlook, reports, an integrated billing module, and free 24x7 telephone and e-mail support.

INSZoom (www.inszoom.com)

INSZoom is an Internet immigration application, where users logon using a secure ID and password.

It comes in three packages: U.S. Immigration Management System (usIMS); Global Immigration Management System (globalIMS); and Corporate Immigration Management System (corporateIMS). All versions include more than 600 immigration forms, which support e-filing and status tracking, immigration knowledge-base templates, management and expiration reports, and priority date and processing time calculators.

Additional features include e-mail alerts and reminders for case steps and expirations (including I-9 reminders), Web-portals for foreign nationals and HR, a contacts manager, and integrated billing. In addition this product suite integrates with various third-party applications including Outlook, QuickBooks, Juris, various shipping company software, SAP, PeopleSoft and Oracle. INSZoom also backs up your database every hour at three distinct geographical locations in the United States.

The Global Immigration Management System adds the Global Partner Module to the standard U.S. Immigration Management System product. This module allows a law firm to manage outbound immigration work and currently supports over 45 countries. The Corporate Immigration Management System includes the Global Partner Module and is designed to cater to the specific needs of a corporation.

LawLogix (www.lawlogix.com)

LawLogix is a multi-language Web-based forms and case management system. It can be accessed by staff, foreign nationals, or HR to complete online client questionnaires, check status, view receipts, and securely upload documents. The system allows you to customize various items such as process names, questionnaires, checklists, activities and reports. Features include reminders, automated communications with templates and mail merge, customizable work flow process, customizable reports generator, integrated billing, and integration with Outlook and other systems. Data can be exported to third party programs such as QuickBooks, Oracle, SAP, Juris, and TimeMatters.

LawLogix also has created a Global Outbound Immigration Module and a new secure messaging (SSL-encrypted SureMessage™), which allows safe communication between the user and clients and automatically associates communication with the client's file. LawLogix uses redundant and uninterruptible power supplies, biometric hand-scan entry and cluster servers (a network of servers that share the workload) to ensure your data is secure and always accessible. If you need to retrieve all of your data from LawLogix or wish to back it up yourself, the system provides FTP access to a full copy of the data file, including forms and documents.

VisaManager
(www.windstar-tech.com/public/prodvisa.html)

VisaManager is a case management system geared towards academic institutions. Its forms component is limited to I-20 A/B, I-20 M/N, I-765, DS-2019 and I-539, although an optional module can be added to complete H applications. The system keeps detailed records for each student and scholar (such as visa status, employment, academic program and more) and stores lists of standard information needed to complete the forms. E-mail alerts and reports allow staff to monitor important events and changes and to comply with SEVIS requirements.

FORMS ONLY

AILALink *(www.ailapubs.org/ailalink.html)*

The AILA*Link* immigration library described above also includes a component allowing users to fill out and save immigration forms, utilizing an included product called Adobe Approval. It does not currently include the ability to populate multiple forms with common data.

AILA has recently announced, however, that it expects AILA*Link* to have such database capabilities in an upgrade expected to debut in the last quarter of 2006.

ILW *(www.ilw.com)*

Although ILW is primarily a website dedicated to providing articles on immigration, it provides additional features such as INS forms, instructions, and form filling.

ImmForms Plus from West Group
(www.westgroup.com)

After West Group stopped bundling Immigrant Pro with its Law Desk research software, it developed a similar product called ImmForms Plus. ImmForms Plus provides access to more than 150 immigration forms that can be filled out, edited, saved, or printed and includes line-by-line instructions and procedural guidance. The forms can be accessed by number, title, or subject and are saved in PDF format. ImmForms Plus also provides customized reports to help track cases. Access to the Occupational Outlook Handbook, the U.S. Bureau of Labor Statistics' Occupational Employment Statistics, Dictionary of Occupational Titles, and O*NET™ OnLine is included in the product.

LEI Immigration Software *(www.linely.com)*

LEI version 5.0 is available both as a download or CD-ROM. It provides more than 50 immigration forms in Adobe format. The forms come with government instructions and LEI tips to assist you in their completion. LEI also provides its Attorney Notes Series eGuidebooks, which provide step by step guidance on completing petitions.

Immigration Law Systems (ILS) *(www.ilssys.com)*

ILSForms divides the forms into employment, family and "other" categories. Data is stored for automatic form completion and forms are organized under the individual client. ILSForms also provides an alien information screen and the ability to sort by attorney, employer or family member. Additional features include multiple font choices and size adjustability, spell-check, help files, and backup tools.

NEW AND OLD TECHNOLOGIES THAT CAN HELP YOUR PRACTICE

At whatever level of sophistication, your case management and forms technologies will be the core of your technology efforts. Software for billing, trust accounting, and timekeeping will also play a central role in your office. Following are a few technologies you might consider beyond these basics. Some, such as scanning, can be of benefit to most offices. Others, such as voice recognition, produce mixed-bag results. Some swear by it; others swear at it.

Scanning Hardware and Software

Studies of office efficiency frequently point out that large amounts of time are spent looking for things, especially files and specific documents within files. One approach that can be very helpful in reducing this problem—especially for primary documents, such as approval notices, RFEs, denials, etc.—is scanning the documents into an electronic format. Some advantages of electronic documents: (1) they can be found and reviewed by many people simultaneously; (2) they can be quickly and easily emailed to multiple people instantaneously; and (3) they can be quickly be printed out by anyone who needs a hard copy.

The most common electronic format is portable document format (PDF), which was developed by Adobe (*www.adobe.com*). Please note that the free

Adobe "Reader" does not provide scanning capabilities. You need to buy the full Adobe Acrobat or PDF-creation software from other vendors (such as Nitro PDF Professional, *www.nitroPDF.com*) to support scanning.

The scanning hardware options are myriad, ranging from small portable scanners that you can carry with your laptop to large, in-office high-speed digital photocopiers that can switch between printing to paper and printing to PDF.

Computer-Telephony Integration

Computer-telephony integration is a fancy name for solutions that allow your computer to control your telephone and vice versa. This is not commonly used in immigration law offices, but it can be very helpful.

For example, one approach used by one of the authors is a system developed by Rose Technologies (*www.rosetechnologies.com*). When someone calls, the software instantaneously checks the caller ID information and "pops up" not only the caller's name and number, but the caller's entire Outlook contact information. This allows any person answering the call to immediately see who is calling and quickly determine what their relationship is to other persons, such as clients, foreign nationals, etc. With customization, it could also be made to pop up a client's records from your case management software.

Voice Recognition

Most people think faster than they talk, and they talk faster than they type. One way to speed things up by a considerable amount is to use voice recognition software to "type" as you talk. Voice recognition is very easy to get up and running, but it takes much patience and persistence to use *efficiently*. The software has certainly become easier to use over the last 10 years, and specialized dictionaries for legal terminology (including legal citations) help to lessen the learning curve, but it remains a love-it-or-hate-it solution. Those with the persistence to get past the gravel can find a goldmine of efficiency. The market leader in voice recognition software is Dragon Naturally Speaking, now owned by Nuance (*www.nuance.com*).

Websites

Most lawyers think of websites as tools for bringing in clients, but websites can also be extremely helpful in making staff more efficient and in better serving clients' needs. Although *how* to develop a website is beyond the scope of this article, it is important to keep in mind that the process is continually becoming easier over time. Below are a few of the many ways websites can help your practice.

Client Input

Instead of sending paper or electronic checklists to the client for filling out, only to have your staff retype everything into your case management/forms program, websites can be set up to allow your clients to input their own information directly online without requiring any of your staff time.

Client Reporting

Answering clients' status-update calls takes up expensive attorney and staff time. If you or your staff do not provide prompt enough responses, then the calls result in lower client satisfaction. E-mailing your clients as processing steps are completed can help, but frequently clients delete their mail or in the case of HR managers, have so many cases they are working on that it is difficult for them to dig through their inbox for status updates. Setting up a secure, password-protected area on your website can allow clients to instantaneously access all of their records, without the need to call you and your staff.

Please note: you do *not* need to have an "online" case management/forms program to do this. You can also use *in-house* case management/forms programs and "push" the data out to your website.

Other Useful Technologies

Depending on your practice, one or more of the following technologies might serve your practice well.

Voice Over Internet Protocol (VOIP)

In the old days, most telephone calls traveled over telephone lines, but now you can use the Internet. Why do you care? It can be much cheaper and more flexible. Vonage (*www.vonage.com*) is a market leader, Skype (*www.skype.com*) is another widely used solution, and many others can be found through an online search for "VOIP."

Conference Calling

It is easy to conference with a person or two if you have multiple phone lines at your office, but what if you have 20 or 30 or more people you need to talk with all at the same time? Use third-party conference calling. These outside providers charge—usually by the minute—to allow many people to call into the same number at the same time.

There are options. You can use "open" mode (everyone can hear each other), "presentation" mode (like an AILA teleconference where you can hear only the designated speakers), or "Q&A" mode, (everybody "lines up" to ask questions of the moderator one-by-one). The discussion leader can also switch among these modes during the course of the call.

Here is an example of how one of the authors (and many other immigration lawyers) used conference calling. When the September 2005 *Visa Bulletin* announced the serious retrogression of employment-based numbers for nationals of China and India and elsewhere, there was an immediate need to answer numerous questions about what this meant not only to the clients whose cases had already been filed, but also to those whose cases had a chance to be filed before the visa numbers retrogressed on October 1, 2005.

The difficulty was that even the most efficient system for "status updates" could not answer everyone's questions. On top of that, the emergent circumstances made it even more critical that all attorneys and staff use their time to get as many cases as possible filed before the deadline. A blast email to all those affected could certainly help, and it did, but the questions were so important to each client that there was no way to write an email that answered all the questions about all scenarios.

A conference call proved to be the perfect tool for rapid information dissemination and Q&A. Once everyone understood the general issues and the firm's approach to handling them—and everyone had a chance to ask their questions—the clients understood what they needed to do and what the firm would do to make the best of the short notice. There were almost zero "status update" calls from these clients during the ensuing two-week period, allowing everyone to spend their valuable time working on cases.

You can try large-group conference calling for free at *www.freeconferencecalls.com*. You still have to pay long-distance charges, though.

Working From Home

Virtually everyone works at home from time to time, and the typical approach is to take home the paper file along with an electronic copy of the documents to be worked on. Invariably, an important document or file is left at the office. The same "missing document" problem occurs on business trips.

One solution to this problem is to use a "remote desktop" application. A well-established stand-alone application is Symantec pcAnywhere™ 12.0 (*www.symantec.com*). In recent years, Web-based systems, such GoToMyPC (*www.gotomypc.com*), have entered the market. The advantage of Web-based remote access is that you can obtain access from any computer with access to the Internet without having to reconfigure anything.

These solutions may require some technological knowledge to set them up, but once configured, they can be very helpful in allowing you to access your office computer from somewhere else.

ONLINE RESEARCH FOR THE IMMIGRATION LAWYER

While general search engines such as Google will guide you to sources of legal information on the Internet, we have listed in an appendix to this article a number of sites to take much of the guesswork out of searching for immigration-related information and resources. While the actual URLs of the sites are of course provided, the greater value of the list is the compilation itself—letting you know that these sites (and organizations) exist and are out there to help your research efforts.

CONCLUSION

Technology is certainly not a panacea for immigration practitioners, but when properly aligned with your firm's underlying financial, marketing, and client-service goals, technology can provide substantial long-term benefits. The highest rewards from technological advancement typically come to those practitioners who resist the impulse to possess the latest techno-toys on the one hand and overcome the fear of discarding familiar but inefficient technologies on the other. Careful planning—if it does not reach the level of organizational paralysis—is also essential.

Appendix—Online Resources[*]

Statutes & Codes

Bills & Public Laws (Library of Congress "Thomas" site): *http://thomas.loc.gov*

Cornell University's Legal Information Institute: *www.law.cornell.edu*

Government Printing Office (GPO): *www.gpoaccess.gov/index.html*

o GPO's e-CFR (beta): *www.gpoaccess.gov/ecfr*

o GPO's Public & Private Laws: *www.gpoaccess.gov/plaws/index.html*

House Internet Law Library: *http://uscode.house.gov/search/criteria.shtml*

Federal Courts

U.S. Supreme Court

www.supremecourtus.gov

o LII (Cornell) Supreme Court collection: *http://supct.law.cornell.edu/supct/index.html*

o FindLaw.com's Supreme Court page: *www.findlaw.com/casecode/supreme.html*

U.S. Courts of Appeal & District Courts

uscourts.gov/links.html

(See also Cornell's Legal Information Institute (*www.law.cornell.edu/federal/opinions.html*) for links to alternative sites for circuit court decisions, as well as links to other courts.

Other Judicial Information

Administrative Office of the U.S. Courts: *www.uscourts.gov*

Federal Civil Trials Database: *http://teddy.law.cornell.edu:8090/questtr2.htm*

Federal Courts Finder: *www.law.emory.edu/FEDCTS/*

Federal Judicial Center: *www.fjc.gov*

Federal Rules of Civil Procedure: *www.law.cornell.edu/rules/frcp/*

Federal Rules of Evidence: *www.law.cornell.edu/rules/fre/overview.html*

---

[*] Adopted and abridged, with permission, from AILA*Link* CD-ROM and *AILA's Guide to Technology and Legal Research for the Immigration Practitioner, Third Edition.*

The list excludes, for the most part, the subscription and other fee-based information services, such as Lexis and Westlaw. While the URLs below were checked at the time this article went to press, they may, as is wont in the ethereal world of the Internet, change or otherwise become invalid over the course of time.

Institute for Court Management: *www.ncsconline.org/D_Icm/icmindex.html*

U.S. Sentencing Commission: *www.ussc.gov*

Administrative Courts

Administrative Appeals Office (AAO)

o Decisions issued after 7/31/00: *http://uscis.gov/graphics/lawsregs/admindec3/index.htm*

o Decisions issued prior to 7/31/00: *http://uscis.gov/graphics/lawsregs/admindec/index.htm*

Office of the Chief Administrative Hearing Officer (OCAHO)

o Home Page (including link to all decisions by volume): *www.usdoj.gov/eoir/OcahoMain/ocahosibpage.htm*

o Alphabetical index: *www.usdoj.gov/eoir/efoia/ocaho/ocmnind.htm*

BIA / AG precedent decisions

o On EOIR Web Site: *www.usdoj.gov/eoir/vll/intdec/lib_indecitnet.html*

Selected Federal Agency Sites

Central Intelligence Agency (CIA)

Freedom of Information Act: *www.usdoj.gov/foia/*

World Factbook: *www.odci.gov/cia/publications/factbook/*

Department of Commerce

Bureau of the Census—NAICS: *www.census.gov/epcd/www/naics.html*

Bureau of Economic Analysis: *www.bea.gov*

Economic Development Administration: *www.doc.gov/eda*

FedWorld Information Network: *www.fedworld.gov*

STAT–USA: *www.stat-usa.gov*

Department of Health & Human Services (HHS)

Office of Refugee Resettlement: *www.acf.dhhs.gov/programs/orr/*

Poverty Guidelines: *http://aspe.hhs.gov/poverty/index.shtml*

Department of Homeland Security (DHS)

DHS Home Page: *www.dhs.gov/dhspublic/*

U.S. Citizenship & Immigration Services (USCIS): *http://uscis.gov/graphics/index.htm*

o USCIS Asylum Home Page: *http://uscis.gov/graphics/services/asylum/index.htm*

o USCIS's "Other Government Sites" Page: *http://uscis.gov/graphics/othergov/index.htm*

o Forms on the USCIS Web site: *http://uscis.gov/graphics/formsfee/forms/index.htm*

o Service Center Case Status Search:
  https://egov.immigration.gov/cris/jsps/index.jsp

Bureau of Customs & Border Protection (CBP):
  www.cbp.gov

Bureau of Immigration & Customs Enforcement (ICE):
  www.ice.gov/graphics/index.htm

Directorate of Border & Transportation Security (BTS):
  www.dhs.gov/dhspublic/theme_home4.jsp

Department of Justice (DOJ)

DOJ Home Page: *www.usdoj.gov*

Executive Office for Immigration Review (EOIR):
  www.usdoj.gov/eoir

o Operating Policies & Procedures Memoranda
  (OPPMs):
  www.usdoj.gov/eoir/efoia/ocij/OPPMLG2.htm

o Immigration Virtual Law Library:
  www.usdoj.gov/eoir/vll/libindex.html

o Forms on the EOIR Web site:
  www.usdoj.gov/eoir/formspage.htm

o Freedom of Information Act (FOIA):
  www.usdoj.gov/eoir/efoia/foiainfo.htm

o Office of the Attorney General (OAG):
  www.usdoj.gov/ag/index.html

o Office of Special Counsel for Immigration Related
  Unfair Employment Practices (OSC):
  www.usdoj.gov/crt/osc/

o Office of the Chief Immigration Judge:
  www.usdoj.gov/eoir/efoia/ocij/locop.htm

Office of Special Counsel for Unfair Immigration-Related
  Employment Practices (Civil Rights Division):
  www.usdoj.gov/crt/osc

Department of Labor (DOL)

DOL Home Page: *www.dol.gov*

Bureau of Labor Statistics: *http://stats.bls.gov*

DOL Law Library—Immigration Collection:
  www.oalj.dol.gov/libina.htm

Dictionary of Occupational Titles (DOT):
  www.oalj.dol.gov/libdot.htm

Employment & Training Administration: *www.doleta.gov*

Employment Standards Administration: *www.dol.gov/esa*

FLC Data Center: *www.flcdatacenter.com*

Occupational Employment Statistics: *www.bls.gov/oes*

Occupational Outlook Handbook: *www.bls.gov/oco*

Office of Administrative Law Judges: *www.oalj.dol.gov*

o BALCA En Banc Decisions: *www.oalj.dol.gov/*

Standard Occupational Classification (SOC) System:
  http://stats.bls.gov/soc/

Department of State (DOS)

DOS Home Page: *www.state.gov*

Bureau of Consular Affairs: *http://travel.state.gov*

Bureau of Democracy, Human Rights, & Labor:
  www.state.gov/g/drl

Bureau of Educational & Cultural Affairs:
  http://exchanges.state.gov

Exchange Visitor (J Visa) Program:
  http://exchanges.state.gov/education/jexchanges

Foreign Affairs Manual:
  http://foia.state.gov/REGS/Search.asp

International Information Programs:
  http://usinfo.state.gov

J Visa Waiver Status:
  *http://travel.state.gov/visa/tempvisitors_info_waivers
  .html*

Official Forms: *www.state.gov/m/a/dir/c4455.htm*

U.S. Consulates, Embassies, & Missions:
  http://usembassy.state.gov

UnitedStatesVisas.gov: *www.unitedstatesvisas.gov*

Visa Appointment Reservation System: *www.nvars.com*

Visa Bulletin:
  *http://travel.state.gov/visa/frvi/bulletin/bulletin_1360
  .html*

Visa Reciprocity Tables:
  www.travel.state.gov/visa/reciprocity/index.htm

Social Security Administration (SSA)

Social Security Administration Home Page: *www.ssa.gov*

Immigration Issues: *www.ssa.gov/immigration*

White House

White House: *www.whitehouse.gov*

Executive Orders: *www.whitehouse.gov/news/orders*

Council of Economic Advisers: *www.whitehouse.gov/cea/*

Presidential Documents, Weekly:
  www.gpoaccess.gov/wcomp/index.html

Statements of Administration Policy:
  www.whitehouse.gov/omb/legislative/sap/

Federal Legislative Research

Legislative Research Sites

Legi-Slate: *www.legislate.com*

Thomas (Library of Congress): *http://thomas.loc.gov*

U.S. Congress via GPO Access:
  www.gpoaccess.gov/multidb.html

Congress—House

House of Representatives: *www.house.gov*

House Internet Law Library: *http://uscode.house.gov*

Members of the House:
  www.house.gov/house/MemberWWW.html

Committee on the Judiciary: *www.house.gov/judiciary/*

Miscellaneous House Publications:
  www.gpoaccess.gov/congress/index.html

Congress—Senate

Senate: *www.senate.gov*

Members of the Senate:
  *www.senate.gov/general/contact_information/senator
  s_cfm.cfm*

Senate Committees:
 *www.senate.gov/pagelayout/committees/d_three_sect
 ions_with_teasers/committees_home.htm*
Committee on the Judiciary: *www.judiciary.senate.gov*
Subcommittee on Immigration:
 *http://judiciary.senate.gov/subcommittees/immigratio
 n109.cfm*
Congressional Bills: *www.gpoaccess.gov/bills/index.html*
 www.law.cornell.edu:80/statutes.html
History of Bills: *www.gpoaccess.gov/hob/index.html*
Congressional Committee Reports:
 o *www.gpoaccess.gov/serialset/creports/index.html*
 o *http://thomas.loc.gov/cp105/cp105query.html*
Congressional Record: *http://thomas.loc.gov*
 www.law.cornell.edu:80/statutes.html
Congressional Record Index:
 www.gpoaccess.gov/cri/index.html
Miscellaneous Senate Publications:
 www.gpoaccess.gov/congress/index.html
Public Laws: *www.gpoaccess.gov/plaws/index.html*
U.S. Code: *www.gpoaccess.gov/uscode/index.html*

International Sites & Resources

Foreign Consulates & Embassies

Embassies: *www.embassy.org*
Foreign Consulates:
 www.infoplease.com/ipa/a0004582.html

United Nations System

United Nations: *www.un.org*
International Court of Justice: *www.icj-cij.org*
International Law: *www.un.org/law*
United Nations Educational, Scientific & Cultural Or-
 ganization (UNESCO): *www.unesco.org*
U.N. Children's Fund (UNICEF): *www.unicef.org*
U.N. Development Programme (UNDP): *www.undp.org*
U.N. Environmental Programme (UNEP): *www.unep.org*
U.N. High Commission for Refugees (UNHCR):
 www.unhcr.org

Immigration Policy & Research Sites

Research—Immigration & Migration Policy Sites

Alexis de Tocqueville Institution: *www.adti.net/*
Americans for Better Borders (U.S. Chamber of Com-
 merce): *www.uschamber.org/coalitions/abb/default*
Association of Farmworker Opportunity Programs:
 www.afop.org
Center for Immigration Studies (CIS) [Restrictionists]:
 www.cis.org
Center for Migration Studies of New York:
 www.cmsny.org
Center for World Indigenous Studies: *www.cwis.org*
European Research Centre on Migration & Ethnic Rela-
 tions: *www.ercomer.org*

Expedited Removal Study—University of California's
 Hastings College of the Law:
 http://w3.uchastings.edu/ers/
Forced Migration Projects: *www.forcedmigration.org/*
Migration Policy Group (MPG): *www.migpolgroup.com*
National Clearinghouse on Guestworker Legislation:
 www.crlaf.org/gworkers.htm
National Conference of State Legislatures:
 www.ncsl.org/programs/immig/
Refugee Studies Centre: *www.rsc.ox.ac.uk/*
U.S.-Mexico Border Health Association:
 www.usmbha.org
University of California Migration Dialogue:
 http://migration.ucdavis.edu
Urban Institute—Population Studies Center:
 www.urban.org/center/lhp/index.cfm
World Organization Against Torture: *www.omct.org*

Groups—Immigrant, Migrant, & Refugee Rights

American Immigration Law Foundation: *www.ailf.org*
Americans for Legal Reform: *www.halt.org*
ACLU Immigrant Rights:
 *www.aclu.org/ImmigrantsRights/ImmigrantsRightsM
 ain.cfm*
Battered Immigrant Women's Rights Project:
 http://endabuse.org/programs/immigrant/
Chinese Professionals & Entrepreneurs Association:
 www.chinasite.com/Organizations/Chinaorg.html
Cuban American National Council, Inc.: *www.cnc.org*
European Council on Refugees & Exiles (ECRE):
 www.ecre.org
European Research Centre on Migration & Ethnic Rela-
 tions: *www.ercomer.org*
Immigrants Support Network: *www.isn.org*
Intercultural Mutual Assistance Association:
 www.imaa.net
International Center for Migration, Ethnicity & Citizen-
 ship (ICMEC): *www.newschool.edu/icmec/*
International Organization for Migration: *www.iom.int*
International Rescue Committee: *www.theirc.org/*
Iranian Refugees' Alliance, Inc.: *www.irainc.org*
Lesbian and Gay Immigration Rights Task Force:
 www.lgirtf.org
Massachusetts Immigrant Health Access Coalition:
 http://hcfa.org/
MiCasa–SuCasa: *www.ilw.com/micasa/home.htm*
NAFSA: Association of International Educators:
 www.nafsa.org
National Center for Farmworker Health, Inc.:
 www.ncfh.org
National Immigration Forum: *www.immigrationforum.org*
National Immigration Project of the National Lawyer's
 Guild: *www.NationalImmigrationProject.org*
National Network for Immigrant & Refugee Rights:
 www.nnirr.org
New America Alliance: *www.naaonline.org*

New York Association for New Americans:
www.nyana.org

New York State Defenders Ass'n Criminal Defense Immigration Project:
www.nysda.org/NYSDA_Resources/nysda_resources.html#ImmigrationProject

Refugees International: *www.refintl.org*

Sweatshop Watch: *www.sweatshopwatch.org*

United Nations High Commissioner for Refugees (UNHCR): *www.unhcr.gov*

United States Committee for Refugees: *www.refugees.org*

National Network for Immigrant & Refugee Rights:
www.nnirr.org/immigration/immigration_map.html

Women's Commission for Refugee Women & Children:
www.womenscommission.org/

Groups—Civil Rights, Equal Justice, & Related

Alliance for Justice: *www.afj.org*

American Civil Liberties Union: *www.aclu.org*

American Friends Service Committee (AFSC):
www.afsc.org

Amnesty International: *www.amnesty.org*

Center for Human Rights & Constitutional Law Foundation: *www.centerforhumanrights.org*

Citizens' Commission on Civil Rights: *www.cccr.org*

Citizens for Independent Courts: *www.faircourts.org*

Coalition for International Justice:
www.cij.org/index.cfm?fuseaction=homepage

Equal Justice Network: *www.equaljustice.org*

Equal Rights Advocates: *www.equalrights.org*

Freedom House: *www.freedomhouse.org*

Institute for Civil Justice—RAND:
www.rand.org/centers/icj

Institute for Justice: *www.instituteforjustice.org*

Leadership Council on Civil Rights: *www.civilrights.org*

League of United Latin American Citizens:
www.lulac.org

National Association for the Advancement of Colored People (NAACP): *www.naacp.org*

National Equal Justice Library:
http://nejl.wcl.american.edu

National Health Law Program, Inc.: *www.healthlaw.org*

National Urban League: *www.nul.org*

Open Society Institute: *www.soros.org/*

The Sentencing Project: *www.sentencingproject.org*

Trial Lawyers for Public Justice: *www.tlpj.org*

Asylum, Human Rights, & Refugee Sites & Resources

Asylum & Country Condition Reports

Center for International & European Law on Immigration & Asylum: *http://migration.uni-konstanz.de/content/index.php?lang=en*

Fieldings's Danger Finder:
www.comebackalive.com/df/index.htm

INCORE, Conflict Data Service:
www.incore.ulst.ac.uk/cds/countries

United Nations High Commission for Refugees:
www.unhcr.gov

World Bank: *www.worldbank.org*

World Factbook (CIA):
www.odci.gov/cia/publications/factbook/

Human Rights Sites & Resources

Human Rights Search Engine: *www.hurisearch.org/*

African Human Rights Resource Center:
http://www1.umn.edu/humanrts/africa/

Amnesty International: *www.amnesty.org*

Asylumlaw.org: *www.asylumlaw.org*

Center for Human Rights & Constitutional Law Foundation: *www.centerforhumanrights.org*

Center for Victims of Torture (CVT): *www.cvt.org*

Center for World Indigenous Studies (CWIS)—Fourth World Documentation Project: *www.cwis.org*

Child Rights Information Network: *www.crin.org*

Cultural Survival: *www.cs.org*

Derechos Human Rights: *www.derechos.org/human-rights*

Detained Torture Survivor Legal Support Network:
www.lirs.org/What/programs/torturesurvivor.htm

DIANA—International Human Rights Database:
www.law.uc.edu/Diana

European Research Centre on Migration & Ethnic Relations: *www.ercomer.org*

European Court of Human Rights: *www.echr.coe.int*

Human Rights Interactive Network:
www.Webcom.com/hrin/welcome.html

Human Rights Internet: *www.hri.ca*

Human Rights U.S.A.: *www.hrusa.org*

Human Rights Watch: *www.hrw.org*

Human Rights Web Site: *www.hrWeb.org*

Inter-American Commission on Human Rights (OAS):
www.cidh.oas.org

Inter-American Court of Human Rights (OAS):
www.corteidh.or.cr/index_ing.html

International Centre for Human Rights & Democratic Development: *www.ichrdd.ca*

International Gay & Lesbian Human Rights Commission:
www.iglhrc.org

International Red Cross: *www.icrc.org*

Kresge Law Library, International Human Rights:
www.nd.edu/~lawlib/

Lawyers Committee for Human Rights: *www.lchr.org*

Minnesota Advocates for Human Rights:
www.mnadvocates.org

OneWorld Online:
www.oneworld.net/article/frontpage/10/3

Partners in Human Rights Education:
http://www1.umn.edu/humanrts/education/pihre

Peace Brigades International: *www.igc.apc.org/pbi*

Physicians for Human Rights: *www.phrusa.org*

Project Disappeared: *www.desaparecidos.org*

ReliefWeb: *www.reliefWeb.int*
http://wwwnotes.reliefWeb.int

Survival International: *www.survival-international.org*

Survivors of Torture, International: *www.notorture.org/*

United Nations High Commissioner for Refugees (UNHCR): *www.unhcr.gov*

U.S. Dept. of State Human Rights Reports: *www.state.gov/g/drl/hr/*

Universal Declaration of Human Rights: *www.unhchr.ch/udhr/index.htm*

Witness Program: *www.witness.org*

Women's Human Rights Resources: *www.law-lib.utoronto.ca/diana*

Labor Certifications, Prevailing Wages, & Occupational Data

Government & Regulatory Information

America's Labor Market Information System: *www.almisdb.org/*

Interstate Conference of Employment Security Agencies (ICESA): *www.icesa.org*

LCA Processing Times: *http://ows.doleta.gov/foreign/times.asp*

LMINet: *www.lmi-net.org*

O*NET: *www.onetcenter.org*
www.doleta.gov/programs/onet/

PERM: *www.plc.doleta.gov/*

Standard Occupational Classification System: *www.bls.gov/soc/*

Wages and Trends—Occupation Search: *www.acinet.org/acinet/occ_sea1.htm*

Independent Wage & Occupational Surveys

Abbot, Langer & Associates: *www.abbott-langer.com*

Bay Area Compensation Association: *www.baca-online.org*

College & University Personnel Association: *www.cupa.org*

DataMasters (Computer Industry): *www.datamasters.com/*

Economic Research Institute: *www.erieri.com/*

HomeFair.Com International Salary Calculator: *http://www2.homefair.com/calc/salcalc.html*

JobSmart: *http://jobsmart.org/tools/salary/sal-prof.htm*

KForce Professional Staffing—Experience on Demand: *www.experienceondemand.com*

SalariesReview.com: *www.salariesreview.com*

WageWeb, Salary Survey Data Online: *www.wageWeb.com*

Watson Wyatt Worldwise: *www.watsonwyatt.com*

Ethnic & Cultural Organizations

American-Arab Anti-Discrimination Committee: *www.adc.org*

Asian Community Online Network (ACON): *www.acon.org*

Association of Asian Pacific Community Health Organizations: *www.aapcho.org*

Conference on Asian Pacific American Leadership: *www.capal.org/*

Intercultural Mutual Assistance Association: *www.imaa.net*

Japanese American Citizens League: *www.jacl.org*

League of United Latin American Citizens: *www.lulac.org*

National Asian Pacific American Legal Consortium: *www.napalc.org*

National Council of Churches of Christ in U.S.A.: *www.ncccusa.org*

National Council of La Raza: *www.nclr.org*

National Italian American Foundation: *www.niaf.org*

National Korean American Service & Education Consortium (NAKASEC): *www.nakasec.org*

New York Association for New Americans: *www.nyana.org*

Organization of Chinese Americans: *www.ocanatl.org*

Simon Wiesenthal Center: *www.wiesenthal.com*

Legal Services

California Rural Legal Assistance Foundation: *www.crlaf.org*

Catholic Charities Immigration & Refugee Services: *www.catholiccharitiesla.org/immigration.html*

Catholic Legal Immigration Network (CLINIC): *www.cliniclegal.org/*

Christian Legal Society: *www.clsnet.org/*

Hebrew Immigrant Aid Society: *www.hias.org*

Immigration Counseling Service: *www.immigrationcounseling.org*

Legal Aid Society (District of Columbia): *www.legalaiddc.org*

Legal Aid Foundation of L.A., Immigration Unit: *www.lafla.org/clientservices/immigration/index.asp*

Maryland Services Corporation: *www.mlsc.org*

Mexican American Legal Defense & Educational Fund (MALDEF): *www.maldef.org*

Washington Legal Foundation: *www.wlf.org*

THE IMPORTANCE OF ADVANCE BUSINESS PLANNING IN THE INITIAL REPRESENTATION DECISION

by Roxana C. Bacon[*]

Any discussion of legal and ethical issues that an attorney should consider when deciding whether to represent a client must begin with the attorney understanding and implementing both professional and personal goals. Many attorneys comply with (or at least consider) the Rules of Professional Conduct and all applicable statutes in connection with initial representation. However, too often, because attorneys do no advance business planning, they are unable to intelligently analyze whether a particular client offer the right opportunity for their business and themselves.

Asking yourself a few fundamental questions, and recording and referring to the answers, is the best way to draw up a business plan that works for you. It is also the best way to ensure that you do not accept representation of a client that is outside your competence, interest, or economic model. Take an hour or so and write the answers to these fundamental inquiries:

1. *What do I want my practice to look like?*: What type of clients do I want, what areas of immigration law do I want to emphasize, how much work do I want to manage, what should be the size and composition of my staff, and what are my annual growth goals?

2. *What are my personal and professional strengths and primary interests?*: What do I do best in my practice? What are my major attributes as a lawyer? What clients have I most enjoyed working for during the last year, and why? What clients have given me the most positive feedback on my work during the last year, and why?

3. *What are my personal goals?*: What are my financial needs and expectations annually? What balance between work and non-work do I need? What have I built into my schedule for exercise? What big events (marriage, children, care of elder parents, little league coaching, and so forth) am I expecting this year that will take time from my practice?

4. *What is my business plan to reach my practice and personal goals this year?*: The business plan and written budget should be reviewed monthly to ensure you are in compliance, to identify where and why you are not, and to make corrections accordingly. If you have never done a business or personal goals plan before, hire someone to help you, whether it is a business consultant, your CPA, or even a colleague who has a good track record in this sort of analysis.

Having a business/personal framework allows you to be proactive, not reactive, about your life and career. It also guarantees that your practice will be more enjoyable, more profitable, and less stressful. For the investment of a few hours of your time and perhaps a few hundred dollars in consulting fees, you can develop a business plan that helps you direct your energies toward your own definition of success.

Once you have identified what you want out of your practice, decisions about which clients to pursue and what cases to accept become clearer. More important, a good business plan that you stick with will help you identify which clients you do not want, however tempting they may be in the short run.

CLIENT SELECTION: YOU DO NOT HAVE TO AND SHOULD NOT REPRESENT EVERYONE WHO CALLS

The most critical issue of initial representation is to determine if a potential client is someone you should and want to represent. A client outside the profile that your business/personal plan has developed is *not* the client you should agree to represent. That client will be:

---

[*] **Roxana Bacon** is a managing director in the firm of Littler Global. She is the first woman to serve as president of the State Bar of Arizona, as General Counsel for both AILA and AILF, representative to the Ninth Circuit Court of Appeals and of the International Women's Forum. Ms. Bacon is the recipient of the State's 100 Outstanding Minority and Women Lawyers, the 2001 Sarah Herring Sorin Award, and the 2003 State Bar Distinguished Service Award. Ms. Bacon is an adjunct professor at the Arizona State University College of Law.

- less profitable, since you will have to learn new areas of the law at a level sufficient to provide good representation;

- more likely to annoy you and your staff with questions that you and your staff do not routinely answer;

- more difficult logistically, as the case will be outside your regular processes, templates, forms software, etc.; and

- riskier in terms of malpractice and ethics liability, since you will be in legal areas that are new to you.

HOW TAKING A CLIENT OUTSIDE YOUR BUSINESS/PROFESSIONAL PLAN CAN AFFECT YOU PROFESSIONALLY AND PERSONALLY: A HYPOTHETICAL

To demonstrate the pivotal role a solid business plan can and should play in the initiation of client representation, this section of the article will walk through a hypothetical that embodies the most typical issues confronting an immigration practitioner with a small firm in connection with initial representation.

Assume that you have practiced law for four years, focusing on immigration law for the last two years. You have identified family-based immigration law as your primary interest, particularly in the Spanish-speaking community, since you are fluent in that language. You are an active member of AILA and also of the family law section of your State Bar, as you want to stay current on everything related to family law and have at least 25 percent of your practice in non–immigration-related family law issues.

You have done a budget for your staff of three (two paralegals and one secretary/receptionist). Your total office expenses for the year are $225,000, and you expect gross income of $350,000 this year. That figure assumes a modest growth in family-based petitions and no growth in the non-immigration family law matters. You invested $25,000 last year to modify your forms and case tracking software to accommodate family-based immigration matters and expect that the improved efficiency will let you enjoy the increase in work without having to add staff or work longer hours.

Personally, you have identified the biggest issues that you think will require significant time this year, and you have been able to estimate when they will occur so that you can lighten your practice during those times—namely, you and your brother, a physi-

cian just starting his practice, are planning your parents' 30th anniversary party in September, three months from now, and that same month your youngest child will start in a cooperative kindergarten that requires that you, too, attend with him three mornings a week, from 9 to 11 a.m.

A small construction company, Ajax, has asked for your help in obtaining 100 skilled construction workers (dry wall and tiling), as soon as possible, but absolutely within the next 60 days, so that Ajax can meet its contract obligations with Big Homes, a huge development company with projects all over the West Coast. Ajax's contract with BH is worth $15 million. Ajax says that it will pay you $1,000 per worker if you can obtain valid work authorization for the 100 critical workers.

THE ANALYSIS

Since this is outside your business plan, ask yourself honestly: can your office handle this work?

- What resources will be required? Be as specific as possible, but cover at least the following factors:

  - Technology: What will you need? Can you modify your software to meet those needs? Do your potential new clients have access to PCs?

  - Attorney time: How much time will you have to commit? What is the time frame in which the work will be required? What else are you committed to in the same time frame?

  - Paralegal time: Can they learn what they need to learn in time? Do they want to do this type of work? What else is on their plates during the same period?

  - Support time and costs: What are the hidden costs, *e.g.*, express mail, translations, copying, recruiting abroad, faxes, fees for advertising, consulate fees, and fees for passports for the beneficiaries?

  - Billing: When will you bill? When will the client pay? If the fee is only due when workers enter the United States, how will you carry the costs? If you cannot obtain the workers but do the work well and timely, will you receive nothing?

  - Other work: What about other work in the office or work expected to come from repeat clients/referral sources? Who will handle that core business?

- What is the cost of the required resources?

- What is the cost of any delays that may occur and how will you handle them?

- Are you competent to handle this work? If not, how will you learn the areas of law you need to know?

- How will your staff learn what they need to learn to work on this matter?

- Taking into account all these factors, what is the *actual* potential profit, if any?

- Evaluating the profit and reviewing the resources and work needed to provide competent representation, are you sure this is work you want to do? Does it fit into your life comfortably? If not, who will be compromised and are they willing to cooperate?

Who is your client?

Before you decide yes or no, you should *always* determine who your client is. Every state in which you are licensed has specific Ethical Rules (ERs) that speak directly to determining who is your client and, if you have multiple clients in the same matter, how and whether you are allowed to represent them. ERs 1.6 and 1.7 are most on point, but read all the ERs carefully to be sure that you are in compliance should you agree to this representation. In this matter, you have at least three potential clients: Ajax (which is a corporation, so you represent the business, not the person who called you, who only speaks for the corporation); the foreign national beneficiaries, as yet unknown and unnamed; and the beneficiaries' dependents, if they are planning on accompanying their spouses.

- Do these possible clients have any real or potential conflicts of interest? In answering this question, note the following:

  - All employers and employees have potential conflicts of interest.

  - At a minimum, you will need to outline those potential conflicts, satisfy yourself that they can be waived under the ERs, and draft the appropriate notice and waiver for *all* clients to sign.

  - What will you communicate to Ajax if any beneficiary is excludable for criminal or other "private" reasons, *e.g.*, health? What permis-

sion should you obtain upfront to share any such communications?

- How will you communicate with the beneficiaries?

  - Will they have access to online communication?

  - If not, what are the delays and costs associated with old technology communication, probably from a foreign country?

  - How will you satisfy yourself that they are fully informed about the conditions and requirements of the job? (You want to avoid any problems with fraud.)

Do you need help to handle the work? If so, what kind and what sources will help?

- The only way to avoid a crisis in a matter like this is to think about what you will need and bring in help *early*.

- *Read* all the applicable statutes, regulations, and treatises (*e.g.*, *Kurzban's Immigration Law Sourcebook* (AILA 10th ed.)).

- Identify and contact local and national colleagues who are expert in the substantive areas of law (*e.g.*, possibly H-2B, E, L, TN, depending upon the development of facts about Ajax, its current and possible affiliations outside the United States, and the country of origin of the potential workers).

- Check AILA and other specialized CLE resources.

- Review all relevant government websites, including DOS sites for whatever consulates you think may be involved.

Should you partner with someone else to handle this client, at least in the first matter?

Partnering with someone else, at least to complete the first matter, may be the most efficient and economic strategy to use. Doing so could allow you to learn the area with less exposure to liability in the first matter and would give you backup expertise in case it should be needed. Consult the ERs before agreeing to any fee-sharing arrangement. Ordinarily, lawyers who share fees must reveal their *exact* relationship to Ajax and beneficiaries, and obtain their approval. Everyone involved needs to have a clear understanding of everything relating to the fees, costs, and billing, and have a written agreement regarding the same with any co-counsel as well as all clients. The entire agreement must be in writing and signed by all involved. In most states, the ERs require a written representation and fee agreement.

Note: Remember that resolving all financial issues with all interested parties before agreeing to representation is the best way to avoid monetary disputes!

Assuming you decide to accept the representation, what do you need to do to formalize the decision?

- Know the law and regulations and agencies involved in the matter so you can communicate the process to the client, with a time frame for each critical step.

- Without knowing the process, you cannot draft an effective client representation letter, so you need to factor in unpaid learning time just to determine if you should take the matter and, if so, what the terms of the representation will be.

- Early on, consider meeting with the client at their worksite so you better understand the client's work, culture, resources, etc.

- Be sure everyone in your office (or with whom you affiliate) has complete information about the client—such as names, titles, and means of contact.

- Meet with any local agencies involved (*e.g.*, for H-2Bs, state DOL agencies) to establish relationships, learn about local processing, etc.

- Draft the representation letter, stating fees, costs, and billing requirements.

  - This is required by most State Bars.

  - It should be complete, covering every topic that could lead to a misunderstanding or incorrect expectations.

  - It should outline communication expectations, such as weekly status reports and online access to files.

  - The language should be clear; "legalese" causes problems.

  - The agreement should include a "cooperation" clause so you can terminate the relationship if client does not cooperate (*e.g.*, provide timely information or documentation).

  - It should explain clearly any potential conflicts and seek waiver of them to comply with dual representation ERs.

  - It must be signed by all parties, each of whom should receive a signed copy. The attorney should keep evidence that he or she gave a copy to all parties.

  - It must be translated if that is necessary for a party to understand it.

  - If others will be assisting in representation, the agreement must identify who, and the related financial arrangements.

  - The letter should cover what happens if representation terminates, especially return of the file, costs for copying files, etc.

  - Any changes to the agreement must be in writing and signed by *all* parties again.

Do not be afraid to say "No!"

Deciding not to represent a client can be the most profitable decision an attorney can make. Only having a detailed business and personal plan will give you the baseline you need to evaluate whether you should accept even a seemingly very profitable matter or whether it will end up being the quicksand that takes you down. If you are spending all your time on matters that you do not like and in which you are not experienced and skilled, you are missing opportunities to do work you do like and in which you are competent!

MANAGING CLIENT EXPECTATIONS
by Edwin R. Rubin and Carl Falstrom[*]

INITIAL AND ONGOING CLIENT REPRESENTATION: DOING IT RIGHT

One of the most difficult decisions an attorney must make is whether to accept or decline a potential fee-paying client. In the practice of immigration law, there will be situations, perhaps frequently, where a decision not to undertake representation of a particular client will be the best course of conduct. It may be because there is simply no available remedy under the current law. It may be because the particular undertaking would be beyond your expertise or take more time than can be devoted to the matter in the time frame required. It may be because you have concerns about the facts. Concern about the facts may relate to whether the necessary facts exist or can be proven. At the conclusion of the initial consultation, the attorney may: (1) advise the client that the attorney will not or cannot take the case with an appropriate explanation; (2) set the terms of the fee agreement and determine if the client finds it acceptable; or (3) advise the client that more time is required to determine the applicable facts or law and set a fee for an extended consultation while making it clear that such an arrangement does not obligate the client or attorney to undertake the matter if the extended consultation results in a unfavorable conclusion.

In applications for benefits, an attorney has a duty to present information that is accurate.[1] For example, in removal proceedings, there will be instances where it is proper to make the government prove its case and the respondent may remain silent. In affirmative applications, this is not the case.

A thorough initial interview and evaluation of the applicable law is an essential first step. "A well-structured initial interview can save the new as well as the seasoned attorney many hours of time and lay the foundation for an effective client-attorney relationship."[2] In immigration practice, this may mean a somewhat extended discussion with the foreign national and potential family- or employment-based petitioner. Immigration practice is complicated by the various ways potential cases reach the practitioner. A U.S. citizen spouse may call, or the call may be from the foreign national spouse. The employer or potential employer may call, or the contact may come from the foreign national. The foreign national may be in the United States or abroad. However, when the potential undertaking reaches you, a full understanding of the determinative facts should be made before agreeing to represent the client and preparing the fee agreement. Dual representation presents its own difficulties.[3]

Even before the initial interview, counsel must determine whether and how much to charge as a consultation fee. This must be communicated clearly to potential clients upfront. Counsel must determine how to obtain the information required to reach an informed decision about representation. You may want written questionnaires completed in some cases, perhaps even before talking to the client. In other cases, it may be far better practice to have the potential client come to your office for a thorough review of the facts. For example, it is probably good practice to not undertake a marriage-based case without interviewing the spouses in the office together. Although exceptions may be made where the potential clients are too far away or the beneficiary is outside the United States, it is still good practice

[*] **Edwin Rubin**, whose practice has been limited to immigration matters for over 33 years, served as AILA's National President (1990–91) and senior editor of and contributing author to *Immigration & Nationality Law Handbook* (AILA 1985–1990). He received AILA's Lowenstein Award in 1993 and AILA's Mentor Award in 2001. He is listed in *Martindale-Hubbell Bar Register of Preeminent Lawyers*, *Best Lawyers in America*, *An International Who's Who of Corporate Immigration Lawyers*, and *Superlawyers*.

Carl Falstrom is principal of the Law Office of Carl Falstrom in San Francisco. He received his bachelor's degree from the University of Chicago and law degree from the University of California, Hastings College of the Law. Mr. Falstrom is a former AILA Northern California Chapter Chair and has served on a number of AILA liaison, program, and other committees.

[1] *See generally Ethics in a Brave New World* (AILA 2004) (hereinafter *Ethics*); Edwin R. Rubin, "Filing Immigration Applications and Petitions: Ethical Responsibilities and Criminal Penalties," *Ethics*, at 76.

[2] *See* Stephen Yale-Loehr, "Initial Interviews," elsewhere in this volume.

[3] See discussions regarding dual representation in *Ethics*, *supra* note 1, and form templates regarding dual representation and initial questionnaires in *AILA's Immigration Practice Toolbox* (2d ed. 2006) (hereinafter *Practice Toolbox*).

to communicate with both spouses at length, if at all possible, before taking the case.

This initial fact gathering is critical for several reasons. It allows an assessment of the facts and whether they support a claim for benefits or relief. It allows the attorney to make a judgment as to the appropriate fee. It allows for a determination whether additional facts may be required before a decision can be made as to whether the client's desired result can be achieved. If, as recommended, the initial interview is done in person or by phone, it will allow counsel to make an assessment of the client. The demeanor of the client, the client's ability to communicate, and the nature of the available documentation can best be ascertained in person. Many lawyers find that a brief initial telephonic discussion is helpful. It permits a very preliminary determination of eligibility and allows the potential client to be advised of the consultation fee and the documents to be brought to the office consultation. Setting an initial in-person consultation also allows for a certain amount of screening, although counsel must be just as cautious advising someone on the phone as someone in the office for a full consultation that the individual is ineligible for any relief. Such advice must always be given with caution and with "disclaimers."

Asking the potential client to schedule an in-person initial consultation may provide immediate feedback that this does not appear to be a desirable client. In a marriage case, the caller indicating that his spouse absolutely cannot come in because of her work schedule may be all the information you need that this is not a case worth taking. At the very least, counsel should heed the red flag and be particularly careful in evaluating the bona fides of the relationship. Similarly, a potential client who balks at your established consultation fee may be one who requires a fee agreement with additional safeguards to assure counsel is paid.

The initial interview should serve another critical purpose. Once the facts are gathered and counsel has made a decision to represent the client, it allows counsel to "set" the client's expectations. If an employer in an H-1B petition wants the employee to start work next Monday, counsel can explain the time frame, the possibility of premium processing, and the state of the current H-1B quota availability, among other relevant factors and processes. If the beneficiary of an immediate relative spouse petition is eligible for conditional permanent residence but has overstayed her visitor's status by over 180 days,

the attorney can advise the beneficiary she will not be able to attend her sister's wedding in Uruguay in four weeks because she is ineligible for advance parole, and, more importantly, if it was mistakenly granted, she will be barred from returning to the United States for three years. Of course, it is not possible to set forth all of the possible information to be communicated to clients. It will depend on the facts and applicable law in each case. At a minimum, counsel should clearly indicate the most likely time frame for completion of the matter, what might happen to extend that time frame (*e.g.*, name checks or Requests for Evidence), the issues affecting a successful outcome (as defined by the client expectations), documents required and when needed, and the fees and costs and when they will be due. Possible conflicts should be discussed and appropriate documents prepared.[4]

The fee should be fully set forth in writing and signed by the client. Written fee agreements are now required in many states, and some states have very specific rules relating to the content of the fee agreement and conflict waivers. The fee agreement should be specific about the amount and timing of professional fees. It should, as specifically as possible, state the nature of the undertaking. A fee agreement stating that it is for a permanent labor certification, preference petition, and application for permanent residence is better than one indicating it is "to obtain permanent residence." A fee agreement indicating that it is to file a labor certification for Ms. Smith as a research chemist for Jones Co., file an Employment-Based Third Preference Petition if the labor certification is approved and apply for adjustment of status, if Ms. Smith remains eligible to do so, is probably a better alternative. The fee agreement should always indicate that counsel has made no guarantee with regard to the outcome of the case or the time frame to completion of the matter undertaken. The fee agreement also should contain a clear description and estimate of filing fees and other costs.

Once counsel is retained, the discussions concerning time frames, documentation needed, permissible activity (*e.g.*, travel, employment, marriage, and divorce) should be reinforced either in writing or in clear verbal communication. Exigencies of practice make writing to the client in order to reinforce everything discussed difficult. At the very

---

[4] *See Practice Toolbox, supra* note 3 and *Ethics, supra* note 1.

least, notes should be made in the client file about those communications, and the most important communications must be sent in writing. For example, if you are filing a family second preference petition for an unmarried son or daughter, it is imperative the petitioner and beneficiary understand the effect of a marriage by beneficiary or naturalization by petitioner. As another example, single clients pursuing permanent residence through employment should be advised that the timing of any marriage to a foreign national could be critical since marriage before permanent residence is granted will probably allow the foreign national spouse to take advantage of the priority date and classification of the principal, while marriage after permanent residence is granted places the spouse in the Family Second Preference backlog.

Immigration practice can be particularly frustrating because of ever-changing time frames, procedures, and at times, the lack of transparency of adjudicative standards. These matters should be discussed with the clients upfront and at the various stages of the case. If you have advised your naturalization applicant at the beginning of the filing and again before the interview that even if everything goes well at the interview and the adjudicator says "Congratulations, you have passed the requirements for naturalization," the naturalization may still be delayed because of the required security clearance, that client will be better prepared for the disappointment. Advising the client at the beginning of normal time frames must always include the caveat that time frames vary considerably. Keeping the client accurately informed of current processing times when the client contacts the attorney or when the attorney has reason to contact the client is equally important.

Experienced practitioners have all heard the statement from a potential client that so and so obtained permanent residence in four weeks, frequently by use of a different attorney. If you know that the time frame for the result is patently impossible, you have a red flag warning that this client may be difficult to satisfy. If, after explaining the normal time frame, the potential client does not seem satisfied with the explanation, it may be that you are better off not accepting the case. You may choose to advise the potential client, as a way of making your point about processing times, that he or she may be better off going to that other attorney.

Another aspect of managing client expectations relates to an early explanation of the steps normal to the case, requirements as to amount and timing of payment of professional fees, filing fees, and other costs, what and when documents will be needed and in what format. It is very disturbing to a client with an approved employment-based petition to be advised for the first time that a birth certificate is now needed for the adjustment of status. If the client does not already have the required documents, even a brief delay to obtain something from abroad may be a cause of dissatisfaction. Well-prepared counsel should not hear the phrase, "why didn't you tell me this before?"

In summary, managing client expectations is an important part of the successful client-attorney relationship. Creating unrealistic expectations or allowing such unrealistic expectations to go uncorrected is certain to sour the relationship. Remember, a satisfied client is your best marketing tool.

EFFECTIVE HAND-HOLDING TECHNIQUES

The Importance of Making an Effort (As Distinguished from Merely Getting a Result)

The key to keeping clients happy after a case has been filed is never to forget that while clients *need* results, what they *want* is effort. Jay Foonberg expresses this best in his outstanding *How to Start and Build a Law Practice* (much of what follows in this article draws from Foonberg's work):

New lawyers think that clients want results more than they want effort. Believe it or not, the reverse is true. Clients need favorable results; they want effort. Don't misinterpret what I am saying. I am not saying that clients don't care whether they win or lose. They care very much. I am saying that whether they come back to you when a matter is over with, or whether they recommend other clients to you or pay your fee willingly, or not at all, is determined more by their opinion of your efforts than their opinion of the results.

Ultimately, it is in your interest to demonstrate in as many ways as possible that you are making a maximum effort on your client's behalf, whatever the result in his or her case turns out to be. Here are some time-honored techniques for making sure that the client is aware of and appreciates your effort:

Return phone calls and respond to e-mails promptly. Even if the voicemail or e-mail is a simple "What's going on with my case?" and the answer is basically "Nothing has changed since the last time you asked," it is best to communicate this response to the client the same day, if at all possible. If the client's communication arrives in the late afternoon, then next morning is fine for a reply. If, for whatever reason, you have difficulty responding to a particular communication within 24 hours, ask someone in your office to respond for you, if only to let the client know that you are temporarily busy but will get back to them as soon as possible. This might seem like a lot of trouble, but studies show that clients get unhappy and sue lawyers not so much because lawyers lose cases, but instead because lawyers do not return phone calls or respond to e-mails. A little extra effort in this regard can ensure against a future lawsuit by helping to keep a client happy.

Copy the client on every communication you have to or from the government. The easiest way to let a client know what is going on with his or her case is to give them copies of both everything you send to the government and everything you receive from the government that is related to the case. This might seem self-evident, but some lawyers may not do this. This task can be accomplished quickly and efficiently by scanning all filings and response receipts and letters and sending to the clients as attachments. This saves money in postage and secretarial time and impresses a tech-savvy client. The client appreciates having an electronic document that he or she can print out, archive on a hard disk, or easily forward to another interested party.

"Fondle the file" on a regular basis. Try not to let more than 60 to 90 days go by between communications to clients. Maintaining a longer communication interval than this can cause the client to wonder if anything is being done on his or her behalf and may lay the groundwork for hurt feelings later on. Set up your tickler system so that if you do not have occasion to write or call your client or if your client has not written or called you during this interval, you will be reminded to take a fresh look at the case and to let the client know that his or her file continues to get your attention. A quick e-mail or voice-mail along the lines of the following gets the point across:

> I know it's been some time since we last spoke, but I just wanted to let you know that I'm still tracking the progress of your filing. Since the Vermont Service Center is processing I-140 petitions like yours that were filed nine months ago and yours was only filed six months ago, I'm not expecting to hear any news about your case for another three months. However, I will continue to monitor the situation and advise you as appro-

priate. Feel free to contact me if there's anything further I can do for you at this time.

Stay current with the law and make sure you've explored every possible option for your client. Regularly fondling the file also gives you the opportunity to ensure you are able to explore the ramifications of new developments in the law on your client's case. That memo about unlawful presence may not have made you think of Ms. Doe's file when it was posted to InfoNet a month ago—but taking a look at Ms. Doe's file now may help you make the connection. Furthermore, leading practitioners and commentators regularly publish articles and give presentations that cover common, intractable problems and strategies for dealing with them. If your client's case is languishing due to a government backlog, reading such an article can help make sure that you have exhausted all possibilities for speeding things up. Note, also, that options that appear to you to be unlikely to succeed can still be worth discussing with your client—after all, it is ultimately your client's decision whether or not to take an economic or other risk with his or her case.

Dealing With High-Maintenance Clients

We all have clients for whom all-too-frequent rather than infrequent communication is the issue. While the ability to maintain successful communications with our clients is among our core competencies as lawyers, some clients make this more difficult than it should be by means of multiple daily phone calls, abuse of support staff, and other unpleasantness.

It may be that most people who "pester" their lawyers with constant phone calls, e-mails, and unannounced office visits do not mean to be bothersome. Their behavior can be explained by a combination of factors that would include, among others, anxiety over their cases and their lives as affected by their cases, unrealistic expectations about the lawyer's role in the problem-solving process, and a belief (perhaps not completely unfounded) that "only the squeaky wheel gets the grease."

The key to dealing with this kind of client is to first try to understand where they are coming from and to meet them halfway in this regard, and then to at least make it economically feasible for you to provide them the extra attention that they demand.

Finally, if all else fails, you may need to formally end the relationship.[5]

Here are some tips for holding clients' hands as their matters unfold:

Empower your clients by educating them about "self-help" options. The vast majority of new USCIS filings now have a 13-digit case number assigned to them. Processing time reports are now updated regularly for USCIS service centers and local offices via USCIS's website. A client with access to the Internet can therefore do his or her own "status check" by entering the relevant case number and reviewing the appropriate processing time report without having to involve the lawyer or the lawyer's support staff. Clients who are not Internet-savvy can call the National Customer Service line to get the same information over the telephone. Similarly, the Department of State now posts waiting times for interview appointments on its website for practically every embassy and consulate in the world. Having access to this kind of information is not always a substitute for talking to the lawyer, but many clients get a sense of satisfaction through feeling they have at least some control over what is happening to them if they have the ability to interface with the government themselves in ways such as these.

Charge difficult clients extra if they take up (or you believe they may take up) too much of your time. This might sound controversial for those among you who are accustomed to billing flat rates for common immigration matters. However, it is entirely appropriate to let a client know that because his or her matter is requiring more of your time than you originally anticipated, due to an unforeseen circumstance—namely, the client's constant phone calls, e-mails, and visits—the client's case will require a higher fee. Of course, if you believe that a client may be high-maintenance just based on your initial meeting with him or her, you can include an unstated "high maintenance" premium in your quoted flat fee. You may find that you can more readily

handle giving a difficult client much attention if you believe you are being paid appropriately for doing so. Your bedside manner in setting fees will obviously be an important factor in successfully exercising this maneuver—the trick is to let the client know that you are happy to give them more than the usual attention, but such service will necessarily come at a price. If the client is unwilling to pay that price, then you still have the final arrow in your quiver . . . .

Fire the client. No matter how important the matter or what kind of fee is involved, some clients are frankly so unpleasant to deal with that the burdens of continuing the relationship will outweigh whatever benefits you might be reaping. In that instance, you are better off without that client. Most, if not all, jurisdictions will generally allow you to end a relationship with a client so long as doing so does not harm the client's interest, and the client has ample opportunity to find new counsel without hurting his or her case. Grounds for immediately ending a client relationship may include rudeness or hostility toward support staff, for example. Other kinds of behavior can merit a warning along the following lines:

> When I agreed to be your lawyer and you agreed to be my client, you promised to cooperate with me so that I could represent you to the best of my abilities *(be sure your fee agreement contains language to this effect if it doesn't already).* Your recent conduct has called your ability to cooperate with me into question. It does not benefit either of us to maintain a relationship within which I cannot provide you with the best legal service of which I am capable. Therefore, if you persist in this kind of behavior, I shall have no choice but to end our relationship, subject to the terms of our agreement.

Life is too short, and there are too many fish in the sea for a lawyer to maintain an unhealthy relationship with any client for any length of time.

---

[5] Elsewhere in this volume, in the complementary article to this one by Roxana Bacon, the importance of setting expectations at the onset of the relationship is discussed.

INITIAL INTERVIEWS

by Stephen Yale-Loehr[*]

INTRODUCTION

By the time an immigration attorney has practiced for six months, he or she has already spent countless hours interviewing clients. However, most attorneys, including those who have practiced law for decades, have little or no training in interviewing techniques. Often the typical interview is unstructured, reactive, largely intuitive, and rather ineffective. A well-structured initial interview can save the new as well as the seasoned attorney many hours of time and lay the foundation for an effective client-attorney relationship.

PURPOSE OF THE INITIAL INTERVIEW

The initial interview is essentially a mutual evaluation of the attorney and the prospective client. At this consultation, potential clients decide whether legal services will be of use to them, whether they want to retain the services of the particular lawyer or firm, and whether the proposed terms and fees are satisfactory. The attorney gathers sufficient information to: (1) determine the goals of the client; (2) identify options for action in the case that correspond to the client's goals; (3) establish the attorney-client relationship and the scope of the representation; (4) determine fees; and (5) set a short- and long-range agenda for the case.[1]

Some preparation can significantly increase the effectiveness of the initial interview. It is often helpful to spend a few minutes discussing the client's situation over the telephone when setting the office appointment. This brief exchange has several benefits. First, it puts the potential client at ease and provides assurance that the attorney cares about the case. Second, it provides the attorney with sufficient information to instruct the potential client to bring necessary documents. For example, when the attorney determines that a client's case may involve criminal issues, the client should bring copies of the criminal dispositions to the initial interview. If the client's case will require documentation such as university degrees or other credentials, it is helpful to have at least some of the documents available at the initial interview.

After the attorney speaks to the potential client on the telephone, he or she may decide to conduct some preparatory research about an obvious issue in the case. Even a limited amount of preparatory research suggests to the potential client that the attorney is knowledgeable and allows the attorney to identify the core facts and issues in the case more quickly.

MANNER AND METHOD OF THE INITIAL INTERVIEW

Establish Rapport

The first step in a successful initial interview is to establish rapport with the client. Rapport is the comfortable and unconstrained mutual trust and confidence that exists between two or more persons.[2] An attorney can develop rapport with a potential client by acknowledging the client's feelings and expectations, regardless of how inappropriate or unhelpful those feelings and expectations may be.[3] The client's expectations will be an important factor in the case

[*] Updated from an article by Mr. Yale-Loehr published at 1 *Immigration & Nationality Law Handbook* 37 (2005–06 ed.). Mr. Yale-Loehr thanks Lindsay Schoonmaker, a research assistant at Miller Mayer, for her assistance in updating this article.

Stephen Yale-Loehr (*syl@millermayer.com*) is co-author of *Immigration Law and Procedure*, the leading immigration law treatise, published by LexisNexis Matthew Bender. He also teaches immigration law and refugee law at Cornell Law School, and is of counsel at Miller Mayer (*www.millermayer.com*) in Ithaca, N.Y. Mr. Yale-Loehr co-writes a bi-monthly column on immigration law for the *New York Law Journal*, and also chairs AILA's Business Visa Committee. He used to be the Co-Editor of *Interpreter Releases* and the Executive Editor of *Immigration Briefings*. He graduated from Cornell Law School in 1981 *cum laude*, where he was Editor-in-Chief of the *Cornell International Law Journal*.

[1] *See* Note, "Recognizing and Dealing with Professional Responsibility Issues Arising in Initial Legal Consultations," 18

Creighton L. Rev. 1461, 1461–62 (1985) (hereinafter "Professional Responsibility Issues in Initial Interviews").

[2] Note, "Cross-Cultural Legal Counseling," 18 *Creighton L. Rev.* 1475, 1480 (1985) (hereinafter "Cross-Cultural Counseling").

[3] Abbott, "The Anatomy of a Client Interview," 42 *Prac. Law.* 61, 65 (Dec. 1996).

continued

in the long term, and identifying those expectations provides both a basis for initial rapport as well as important information for evaluation of the case. Establishing rapport assists the attorney in factually developing the case, increases the effectiveness of the attorney's legal advice, and, on a broader scale, enhances the image of the legal profession.[4]

Clarify the Attorney-Client Relationship

It is important that the attorney communicate the ethical obligations and the limits on the scope of the representation to the potential client.[5]

Confidentiality—First, the attorney is more likely to obtain essential information if he or she advises the client that the information is confidential. An attorney is required to maintain confidentiality from the initial interview, throughout the representation, and after termination of the representation.[6] The client may want the attorney to share information about his or her case with one or more family members or acquaintances. In immigration practice, this issue arises frequently where language barriers exist and the client communicates to the attorney with the assistance of third parties. The attorney must ask the client to identify the third parties to whom the attorney may communicate information about the client's case.[7]

Exception: Future Crimes—Attorney-client communication may not be covered by the confidentiality rule if the client informs the attorney that he or she intends to commit a crime. This situation may force the attorney to consider whether he or she has an ethical obligation to withdraw from representation. As confidentiality rules vary among jurisdictions, attorneys should check the rules of individual states for definitive guidance.

Fraud Issues—In some cases, the attorney may suspect that the client is not telling the truth or is seeking to procure a benefit by fraud. An attorney may develop suspicion based on statements, inconsistencies in the client's story, or nonverbal cues. A suspicion of fraud may also arise where the client appears to block communication between the attorney and the other parties in a multiple-party case, such as the spouse in an adjustment case based on marriage, or the employer in a labor certification case. Attorneys should advise the client of the consequences of fraud, including possible withdrawal of representation. Some attorneys advise their clients in writing of the potential consequences of intentional misrepresentation.

Scope of Representation—When representing clients from other countries, it is important for attorneys to anticipate that a client may hold misperceptions of the role or power of an attorney in the U.S. legal system. For example, potential clients may expect that attorneys are willing and able to commit acts such as exerting undue influence over government officials or immigration judges. At times, a potential client may ask a lawyer to commit illegal acts such as bribery or fraud. Conversely, in some societies attorneys are viewed as part of a repressive legal system rather than as the advocate of the client. It is important that the attorney explain the limits of legal representation to establish trust and to avert the possibility of misunderstandings.

Gather Facts

General Techniques—The substance of the initial interview is the fact-gathering component where the attorney prompts the client to talk while at the same time focusing the interview to elicit the most relevant facts.[8] The attorney should be in control of the interview but also allow the client to "tell his or her story" before establishing all of the essential facts. The technique of empathetic listening is a critical tool for a lawyer.[9] For example, if the attorney feels that a prospective client is digressing, he or she might say, "That might be important for later, but right now we need to address . . . ." In this way, the attorney is able to reassume control of the interview while at the same time indicating to the client that he

---

[4] "Cross-Cultural Counseling," *supra* note 2, at 1481.

[5] *See generally* "Professional Responsibility Issues in Initial Interviews," *supra* note 1.

[6] *See ABA/BNA Lawyer's Manual on Professional Conduct.* For a review of breaches of confidentiality, see J. Foonberg, *How to Get and Keep Good Clients* 236–43 (2d ed. 1990).

[7] 81 Am. Jur. 2d *Witness* §§418–26 (1992).

---

[8] For good articles on client interviews, see, e.g., Loue, "A Guide to Better Client Interviews," 89-7 *Immigration Briefings* 10–13 (July 1989) (hereinafter "Guide to Better Client Interviews"); Collins, "Tips for a Successful Client Interview," 85 *Ill. B.J.* 441 (1997); Howarth, "How to Interview the Client," 9 *Litig.* 25 (1983).

[9] Gellhorn, "Law and Language: An Empirically Based Model for the Opening Moments of Client Interviews," 4 *Clinical L. Rev.* 321 (1998); Kessler, "The Lawyer's Intercultural Communication Problems with Clients from Diverse Cultures," 9 *Nw. J. Int'l L. & Bus.* 64, 73 (1988) (hereinafter "Intercultural Communication Problems"); Barkai, "How to Develop the Skill of Active Listening," 30 *Prac. Law.* 73, 74 (1984).

or she is committed to ensuring the successful outcome of the case.

During the course of establishing rapport with the client, the attorney should observe the demeanor of the client and decide whether to conduct a client-directed or attorney-directed interview.[10] In the client-directed interview, the client tells the entire story and then the attorney follows up with questions. This method is effective with clients who are sophisticated and well-organized, and also with clients who are emotional or very nervous. In the attorney-directed interview, the attorney questions the client. This method may be preferred where the client is reticent or inarticulate.[11] Often, the ideal interview technique is a combination of these two styles, where the client begins to provide information and the attorney steers the direction of the discussion.[12]

Regardless of the technique, attorneys should be careful not to prejudge the legal theory of the case and thereby cut off important lines of factual inquiry. After the client has disclosed sufficient facts to establish a legal theory of the case, the attorney should follow up with further relevant questions.

Immigration-Specific Issues—Under the current immigration system of restrictive laws and strict enforcement, several factors are critical in every immigration case. Practitioners should make every effort to determine any past criminal history of all clients. Under the U.S. immigration law, a number of crimes that may seem minor to clients, such as domestic violence, driving under the influence, or shoplifting, may have significant immigration consequences.[13]

Similarly, due to the bars to admissibility based on past immigration violations, it is important that the attorney determine the presence of any previous immigration history and periods of unauthorized presence in the client's case.

Retain the Information

It is essential that the attorney note all of the client's important information. There are a number of techniques for effective retention of information for a client's file. One is the client intake sheet that the client completes before the interview. Another is note-taking on paper or computer. Many attorneys find it helpful to develop customized standard intake questionnaires or checklists to record basic information and then ask clients to sign the document at the end of the interview.

Barriers to Communication in Initial Interviews

Immigration practitioners often experience barriers to effective client communication that are unique to the practice.

Language—Clearly an interview is more difficult to conduct where the attorney and the client do not speak the same language. There are several ways to overcome the language barrier. One is to ask the potential client to bring a family member or other interpreter to the initial interview. If many of an attorney's clients speak a certain language, he or she may choose to employ someone who speaks that language to interpret in client interviews.[14]

Even if the attorney and the client speak the same language, there still may be communication difficulties. For example, the client may not understand complex concepts inherent in immigration law. The attorney may use words that are unfamiliar to the client due to the client's geographic area of origin, age, or socioeconomic status. Conversely, the client may use terminology that the attorney does not understand. The attorney can reduce the impact of these misunderstandings if he or she is attentive to nonverbal cues that indicate that the client may have misunderstood.[15] For example, a client may appear restless, bored, confused, or lost if he or she is having trouble understanding what the attorney is saying. To help alleviate this feeling of discomfort and facilitate the client's understanding of the case, the attorney might ask, "Does this make sense to you?" periodically to make sure the client understands and to reduce the client's feeling of being confused, intimidated, or threatened.

Cultural Barriers—Immigration practice often pairs attorneys and clients of different cultures. The differences between the two parties may lead to cultural barriers other than language that inhibit effec-

---

[10] Beckmeyer, "That Crucial First Contact: Should You Take the Case?" 6 *Compleat Law.* 16, 17 (Winter 1989).

[11] *Id.*

[12] "Guide to Better Client Interviews," *supra* note 8, at 9.

[13] Kaiser, "A Lawyer's Guide: How to Avoid Pitfalls When Dealing with Alien Clients," 86 *Ky. L.J.* 1183 (1998).

[14] For a good law review article on translations, see McCaffrey, "Don't Get Lost in Translation: Teaching Law Students to Work With Language Interpreters," 6 *Clinical L. Rev.* 347 (2000) (discussing the difficulties of translation and ways to overcome its problems).

[15] "Guide to Better Client Interviews," *supra* note 8, at 3.

tive attorney-client communication. Value conflicts can impede communication where the client or the attorney does not understand the reason that the other adheres to certain value constructs.[16] Stereotyping can occur where the client or attorney applies a rigid preconception based on membership in a racial or nationality group to the other party regardless of individual variation. Bias occurs where one of the parties has a prejudice or tendency toward a particular matter based on personal experience.[17] Not recognizing one's own prejudices is ethnocentrism, *i.e.*, viewing the world only through one's own eyes with one's beliefs, values, and attitudes and not acknowledging that others may not see the world in the same way.[18] In general, the attorney should examine his or her own prejudices and work to minimize their clouding effects.

Trauma—Any legal client may require emotional support at some time, but in some immigration cases, fear and trauma may become a significant factor in the attorney-client relationship. First, many clients involved in removal proceedings and other types of immigration proceedings experience tremendous stress. In some cases, past or present experiences can lead to trauma, a condition where an individual experiences intensely unpleasant feelings associated with crisis experiences.[19]

Trauma may pose a barrier to effective communication, particularly in cases where the client has symptoms of disorders such as post-traumatic stress disorder[20] or concentration camp syndrome,[21] resulting from torture or extended detention. These types of conditions may lead to failing memory, inability to concentrate, intense fear, helplessness, and emotional instability. It is often helpful both for the client's mental health as well as for attorney-client communication to refer such clients to a psychologist or psychiatrist for further evaluation.

An issue of concern when dealing with a person experiencing the results of trauma is that the potential client may see the legal counselor as therapist or emotional confidant. For attorneys, it is vital to recognize the fine line between caring legal advice and therapy.[22] Legal counseling is geared toward the resolution of specific and immediate problems, not long-term therapy.[23] In these types of situations, it is advisable for the attorney to express sympathy for the client's situation but not attempt to deal with complex, emotional issues that require professional assistance. In some cases, the attorney should recommend a mental health professional to help alleviate emotional problems. Many communities have referral lists of professionals and peer support groups that address these types of issues. A referral to a mental health professional for an emotionally troubled client will help to clarify the attorney-client relationship, take some pressure off the attorney, and potentially result in long-term benefits to the client.[24]

Special Barriers: Children, Elderly, and the Mentally Ill—Certain clients, including those who are children,[25] elderly, or mentally ill or disabled, present additional barriers to effective communication. It may be more difficult for the attorney to explain the case to the client. There may be legal issues with respect to the client's ability to give consent. A number of techniques can assist the attorney in overcoming these particular barriers. In certain situations it may be necessary to consider the appointment of a

---

[16] *See* N. Connolly & M. Tayler, "Cross-Cultural Client Contact: Achieving Effective Communication," 24 *AILA's Immigration Law Today* 44 (Mar./Apr. 2005).

[17] B. Lott & D. Maluso, *The Social Psychology of Interpersonal Discrimination* (1995); F. Jandt, *Intercultural Communication: An Introduction* (4th ed. 2003); "Cross-Cultural Counseling," *supra* note 2, at 1478–79.

[18] "Intercultural Communication Problems," *supra* note 9, at 68. *See also* Tremblay, "Interviewing and Counseling Across Cultures: Heuristics and Biases," 9 *Clinical L. Rev.* 373 (2002); Bryant, "The Five Habits: Building Cross-Cultural Competence in Lawyers," 8 *Clinical L. Rev.* 33 (2001).

[19] Note, "Lawyers and Clients: The First Meeting," 49 *Mod. L. Rev.* 351 (1986).

[20] *See* American Psychiatric Ass'n, *Diagnostic and Statistical Manual of Mental Disorders* 463–68 (4th ed. [text rev.] 2000).

[21] A. Strom (ed.), "Psychiatric Aspects," *Norwegian Concentration Camp Survivors* 45–85 (1968).

[22] *See generally* Stern, "How to Respond to a Client Who Wants Comfort as Well As Counsel," 26 *Ariz. Att'y* 36 (Mar. 1990).

[23] *See* "Cross-Cultural Counseling," *supra* note 2, at 1476.

[24] *See* Weiner, "Playing Counselor Without Playing Therapist," 2 *Compleat Law.* 22, 22 (Summer 1985).

[25] *See generally* Perry, "Interviewing, Counseling, and Court Examination of Children: Practical Approaches for Attorneys," 18 *Creighton L. Rev.* 1461, 1461–62 (1985); Smith, "Considerations When Interviewing Children," 12 *Children's Legal Rts. J.* 2 (Summer 1992); Lutheran Immigration and Refugee Service (LIRS), *Working with Refugee and Immigrant Children: Issues of Culture Law and Development* (1998), available from LIRS at *www.lirs.org*; Nugent & Schulman, "Giving Voice to the Vulnerable: On Representing Detained Immigrant and Refugee Children," 78 *Interpreter Releases* 1569 (Oct. 8, 2001).

third party to represent the client's interests, such as a guardian ad litem or a conservator. Attorneys should consult with the rules of the appropriate state to be advised of ethical restrictions governing such appointments.

Evaluate the Case

Review Relevant Facts—After the attorney and the client have had the opportunity to discuss the situation, it is time for the attorney to do a preliminary evaluation of the case. A preliminary evaluation begins with a review of the relevant facts. A review of the facts allows the attorney to double check the accuracy of the facts and elicit any final necessary details.

Explain the Law—Next, the attorney should explain the relevant law to the client. A well-educated and informed client is the attorney's most valuable asset in developing relevant facts and documentation. An understanding of the case will allow the client to be an active participant in the process and to provide informed consent.[26] A client who has a grasp of the legal theory of his or her case will best be able to assist the attorney in identifying important facts in the case and is likely to be a more effective witness. Of course, it is necessary to explain the legal parameters in language and concepts that are comprehensible to the client.[27] It is often helpful to use real-life metaphors or analogies to the client's line of work. The attorney should encourage the client to ask questions.

Identify and Rank Goals—After explaining the law the attorney should establish the preferred goals of the client. In immigration cases, it is critical that the attorney identify what the client really wants from the case. For example, in a removal case, some clients wish to remain in the United States as long as possible with permission to work, regardless of the long-term legal consequences. Other clients may wish to return to the country of origin with minimum expense and legal complications.

In the business immigration context, some clients may wish to work in the United States for only a few years without worrying about future visas or permanent immigration. Other clients may have a high priority to leave open all possible routes to future permanent residence.

In some cases, the initial interview is also the only meeting, and the interview serves as an informational consultation where the parties decide that the client will gain no significant benefit in retaining an attorney. In each case, the final decision must reflect the goals of the client. A letter indicating that the attorney no longer represents the client may be useful to avoid any misunderstanding.

Create Realistic Expectations and Identify Risks—Along with understanding the specific needs of each individual client, the attorney should explain the risks involved in the proposed course of action and create realistic expectations. For example, it is to the attorney's benefit to forewarn the client about possible delays in the labor certification process or the risks associated with failing to disclose material information. In addition, the attorney must avoid making promises that he or she cannot or will not keep.

Choose Strategy Toward the Solution—Based on the analysis of the facts within the legal framework, the assessment of the client's goals, and the discussion of potential risks, the attorney and the client need to determine the best solution to the problem. It is important that the attorney does not make personal or legal decisions for the client. For example, it is not appropriate for the attorney to advise a foreign student to marry his U.S. citizen or permanent resident girlfriend, although the lawyer can advise the client on the legal consequences of the decision.

There is debate in the legal community regarding whether the attorney or the client should be the primary decision-maker. A concept that has gained popularity is "client-centered counseling," which emphasizes client-centered decision-making.[28] While a client-centered approach deprives the attorney of some autonomy and authority, its proponents argue that it significantly increases client participation and satisfaction. In any case, the direction the case ultimately takes must reflect the client's priorities.

Outline the Course of Action—After the attorney and client have made the preliminary assessment and set

---

[26] Andersen, "Informed Consent: Giving Clients the Opportunity to Make Fully Informed Decisions," 24 *Trial* 61, 62 (1988).

[27] *See generally* T. Shaffer, *Legal Interviewing and Counseling in a Nutshell* (4th ed. 2004).

[28] For a general discussion of the theory, see Dinerstein et. al, "Legal Interviewing and Counseling: An Introduction," 10 *Clinical L. Rev.* 281 (2003); Binder, "Lawyers as Counselors: A Client-Centered Approach," 35 *N.Y.L. Sch. L. Rev.* 29 (1990); Dinerstein, "Client-Centered Counseling: Reappraisal and Refinement," 32 *Ariz. L. Rev.* 501 (1990). *See also* Hurder, "Negotiating the Lawyer-Client Relationship: A Search for Equality and Collaboration," 44 *Buffalo L. Rev.* 71 (1996).

the direction for the case, the final step at the initial interview is to identify the responsibilities of the attorney and client to further the case. The attorney will likely need to conduct further analysis and research. In most cases, the attorney should provide the client with a list of documentation and other evidence that the client needs to obtain. The attorney and client should agree on a realistic time frame to which the attorney should adhere.

FEES AND RETAINER AGREEMENT

Whether or not the client articulates it, one of the most important factors to every potential client is the cost of legal services. It benefits both attorney and client to establish a clear understanding of fees for the case at the first interview.[29] Many attorneys choose to use written retainer agreements to provide clarity regarding the scope of the legal services and the fees for those services.[30] However, some clients may be intimidated by the complexity of a retainer agreement, particularly if the client is not proficient in the language of the agreement. In this type of situation, the attorney should review the contents of the document with the client before signature.

Some states require written retainer agreements and regulate the contents. Attorneys should consult with the local bar association regarding specific rules.

---

[29] *See* "Professional Responsibility Issues in Initial Interviews," *supra* note 1, at 1467.

[30] Jackson, "Avoiding Malpractice and Client Complaints: Twelve Golden Rules," 47 *Ala. Lawyer* 269, 271 (1986). For an example of a retainer agreement, see 9A C. Gordon, S. Mailman, & S. Yale-Loehr, *Immigration Law and Procedure* Appendix B Exhibit 18 (rev. ed. 2006).

MANAGING ETHICAL CONFLICTS IN A BUSINESS PRACTICE

*by Kristina K. Rost**

INTRODUCTION

Immigration law today is one of the most complex bodies of law that exists in the United States. Faced with constant changes in this area of law, immigration attorneys are required to not only battle legal complexities but also respond to other unique issues involved in the immigration practice. Other AILA attorneys have analyzed the many conflicting roles immigration attorneys juggle in today's practices, and there are numerous articles written on the ethical conflicts faced on a daily basis.[1] The key to success is to practice defensively and to constantly analyze problematic situations. The focus of this article is to address the conflict a business immigration lawyer often faces in representing an employer corporate client without also being deemed to represent the employee foreign worker or family member.

Immigration attorneys deal with ethical issues every day. We represent employers who are unfamiliar with the stringent requirements of immigration statutes and regulations and who cannot fathom the business-based purpose behind these unfriendly laws. We frequently must address the concerns of foreign employees for whom English is, at best, a second language and who are totally unknowledgeable about our legal and cultural system. The increasingly complex practice of immigration law challenges the immigration lawyer's ability to comply with codes of professional conduct, as well as specific ethical advisory opinions that may apply in any given situation. Compliance with these legal

ethical requirements may even seem to contradict the attorney's personal ethics.

GUIDANCE

INA[2] §240(b)(6), 8 USC §1229(a)(b)(6) authorizes the Attorney General to adopt regulations that:

- Define frivolous behavior subject to sanctions in proceedings before an immigration judge (IJ) or administrative body;

- Specify the circumstances under which an administrative appeal of a decision or ruling will be considered frivolous and summarily dismissed;

- Impose sanctions (which may include suspension and disbarment).

INA §274C(a)(5), 8 USC §1324C(a)(5) prohibits filing or assisting in filing an application or document in support of an application with knowledge or reckless disregard of the fact that the application or documents are in whole or in part false, or do not relate to the person on whose behalf they are being submitted.[3]

8 CFR §§1003.101–1003.108 govern professional conduct for practitioners before the Executive Office for Immigration Review (EOIR), which includes the immigration courts and the Board of Immigration Appeals (BIA).

8 CFR §1292.3 provides for the discipline of attorneys and representatives by the IJ or BIA.

8 CFR §1292.2 governs the admission and removal of accredited representatives to practice before "the Service"[4] and EOIR.

---

* **Kristina Rost** is a partner of Boston-based immigration law firm Maged & Rost, P.C. Ms. Rost is a past co-chair of the New England Chapter Young Lawyers Division and is a member of AILA Ethics and Professionalism Committee. She is a writing contributor and columnist to numerous publications on business and family immigration law matters.

Ed. note: The editor would like to thank Lynn Calder of Allen and Pinnix P.A., for her insights and review of this article.

[1] *See, e.g.*, "Ethical Issues for Immigration Lawyers," *Immigration & Nationality Law Handbook* (AILA 2004–05). For a thorough review of professionalism issues affecting immigration lawyers, see Pinnix, ed., *Ethics in a Brave New World* (AILA 2004), distributed in a complimentary mailing to AILA members.

---

[2] Immigration and Nationality Act of 1952, Pub. L. No. 82-414, 66 Stat. 163 (*codified as amended at* 8 USC §§1101 *et seq.*) (INA).

[3] *See also* ABA Model Rule 3.3 prohibiting attorneys from knowingly providing false information to a tribunal, withholding relevant adverse legal authority, and allowing clients or witnesses to provide false information to a tribunal. Rule 3.3 also addresses attorneys' affirmative responsibilities to inform the tribunal of criminal or fraudulent conduct. ABA Model Rules of Professional Conduct. *See infra* note 5.

[4] U.S. Citizenship and Immigration Services (USCIS) (formerly Immigration and Naturalization Service (INS)).

8 CFR §103.2(a)(3) authorizes representation of an applicant or petitioner by an attorney in the United States, an attorney outside of the United States, or by an accredited representative as defined in 8 CFR §1292.1(a)(4).

Codes of Conduct

- **ABA Model Rules of Professional Conduct, amended 2003**—have been adopted in some form by many U.S. jurisdictions and often are used for guidance even in those jurisdictions that have not adopted them.[5] Further, jurisdictions may or may not adopt the ABA Comments to those Model Rules that are adopted.

- **State Rules**—each state has its own code of professional conduct that may include variations of the Model Rules and ABA Comments, and the state's own interpretations of the Rules. State variations are not only stylistic but often reflect substantive differences in professional requirements. Depending on jurisdiction, evaluation of ethical implications of the exact same conduct may result in totally different conclusions.[6] States' rules are published online at *www.legalethics.com*.

- **Agency Rules**—the BIA *Practice Manual*, for example, includes a section on the discipline of practitioners.

DUAL REPRESENTATION IN BUSINESS IMMIGRATION MATTERS

Ethical problems arise in the business immigration practice because attorneys often are expected to fulfill multiple roles, thereby creating potential conflicts of interest. Key questions to consider are how the attorney-client relationship is created and whether the attorney may or may not represent both the employer and the employee—or whether the attorney wants to engage in dual representation even if allowable. If the attorney has appropriately represented both the employer and employee, further analysis must address whether the attorney thereafter may represent either individually.

Dual Representation (Model Rule 1.7)

Specifically, "Rule 1.7, Conflict of Interest: Current Clients," provides as follows:

(a) Except as provided in paragraph (b), a lawyer shall not represent a client if the representation involves a concurrent conflict of interest. A concurrent conflict of interest exists if:

(1) the representation of one client will be directly adverse to another client; or

(2) there is a significant risk that the representation of one or more clients will be materially limited by the lawyer's responsibilities to another client, a former client or a third person or by a personal interest of the lawyer.

(b) Notwithstanding the existence of a concurrent conflict of interest under paragraph (a), a lawyer may represent a client if:

(1) the lawyer reasonably believes that the lawyer will be able to provide competent and diligent representation to each affected client;

(2) the representation is not prohibited by law;

(3) the representation does not involve the assertion of a claim by one client against another client represented by the lawyer in the same litigation or other proceeding before a tribunal; and

(4) each affected client gives informed consent, confirmed in writing.

Representation of One Party after Termination or Conclusion of Dual Representation (Model Rule 1.9)

"Rule 1.9, Duties to Former Clients," provides as follows:

(a) A lawyer who has formerly represented a client in a matter shall not thereafter represent another person in the same or a substantially related matter in which that person's interests are materially adverse to the interests of the former client unless the former client gives informed consent, confirmed in writing.

(b) A lawyer shall not knowingly represent a person in the same or a substantially related matter

---

[5] The ABA Model Rules of Professional Conduct, including Preamble, Scope, Terminology and Comment, were adopted by the ABA House of Delegates on August 2, 1983, and amended in 1987, 1989, 1990, 1991, 1992, 1993, 1994, 1995, 1997, 1998, 2000, 2002, and 2003. The Model Rules may be found on many websites, including the ABA site: *www.abanet.org/cpr/mrpc/model_rules.html*. The American Legal Ethics Library, published by Cornell Law School at *www.law.cornell.edu/ethics*, includes comparative analysis of state codes of professional responsibility.

[6] This jurisdictional conflict is illustrated in an example given by J. Gavin in his article, "Multi-Jurisdictional Disciplinary Enforcement," *Ethics in a Brave New World* 85 (AILA 2004).

in which a firm with which the lawyer formerly was associated had previously represented a client,

> (1) whose interests are materially adverse to that person; and

> (2) about whom the lawyer has acquired information protected by Rule 1.6 and 1.9(c) that is material to the matter; unless the former client gives informed consent, confirmed in writing.

(c) A lawyer who has formerly represented a client in a matter or whose present or former firm has formerly represented a client in a matter shall not thereafter:

> (1) use information relating to the representation to the disadvantage of the former client except as these Rules would permit or require with respect to a client, or when the information has become generally known; or

> (2) reveal information relating to the representation except as these Rules would permit or require with respect to a client.

Analysis of Dual Representation

Hypothetical: A U.S. corporation (hereafter referred to as "US Inc.") frequently employs foreign national workers. Attorney represents US Inc. in all of its immigration matters involving obtaining legal status for these workers, usually through H-1B petitions or labor certifications, I-140 petitions, and adjustment of status. The terms of Attorney's representation of US Inc. usually are expressly formalized in a written representation agreement for each new employee; US Inc. pays all legal fees and expenses. In representing US Inc. in these immigration matters involving filing documents on behalf of foreign national employees (hereafter referred to as FN), Attorney finds she often also must consult with the FN. For example, in preparing documents such as labor certification applications and I-140 petitions, Attorney and her staff can more efficiently obtain necessary personal information directly from FN rather than through US Inc.'s Human Resources (HR) office. Attorney also prefers that she or her staff advise FN directly regarding his or her immigration-related questions rather than risk miscommunication within HR. Attorney is the legal information resource to FN for the complicated immigration process, providing information about the process or status of documents pending with the government.

Attorney feels this "open door" policy with US Inc.'s foreign employees results in her representing the best interests of US Inc. As US Inc.'s fees represent a large portion of Attorney's income, she is attentive to providing the company with the best legal services possible. Attorney is aware that, occasionally, the FNs may assume that Attorney is their attorney as well, even though the employees have no formal legal relationship or representation agreement with her.

Additional discussion of similar dual representation scenarios may be found in articles written by AILA member and frequent writer on immigration ethics, Bruce Hake, and by Jeffery McLellan.[7]

Formation of the Attorney-Client Relationship

The determination of whether an attorney-client relationship exists and continues generally is governed by state agency or contract law and the state's appropriate rules of professional conduct.[8] Creation of the attorney-client relationship can occur through a formal writing and/or by the conduct of the parties, most notably, whether the advice or assistance of the attorney is both sought and received in matters pertinent to the legal profession.[9]

Practice Pointer: If it is reasonable to conclude that legal advice was given and relied upon by the putative client, an attorney-client relationship may be found.[10] Payment of legal fees or the expectation of payment has no bearing on the issue. This standard will subject many business immigration attorneys to implied, if not formal, attorney-client relationships with the foreign employees of the attorneys' corporate clients. Those immigration attorneys—even in-house corporate counsel—who want to limit their representation to the corporate client face some difficulty in insulating themselves from any inference of attorney-client relationship with the foreign national employee.

---

[7] Br. Hake, "Dual Representation in Immigration Practice," *Ethics in a Brave New World* 28 (AILA 2004); J. McLellan, "Hiring Foreign Nationals as Faculty," *Nat'l Ass'n of College & University Attys* (Mar. 2002).

[8] *E.g.*, *Huddleston v. State*, 259 Ga. 45, 46–47, 376 S.E.2d 683 (1989).

[9] *Id.*

[10] *E.g.*, *Guillebeau v. Jenkins*, 182 Ga. App. 225, 231, 355 S.E.2d 453 (1987) (an attorney-client relationship cannot be created unilaterally in the mind of the client—a reasonable belief is required).

Does the Attorney Really Represent the FN?

There are two views that represent two different approaches to this question. On one hand, the relationship among the attorney, corporate employer, and foreign employee involves a particular set of factors that favor the establishment of an attorney-client relationship between the FN and the attorney. This is true even when the attorney is him- or herself expressly retained as US Inc.'s full-time employee. The primary factor for such logic is the very nature of the legal relationship US Inc. and FN must have with government agencies making immigration decisions.

The other view is that the representation may be effectively limited and presented in such a way that the attorney owes his or her duty of loyalty only to the primary client—US Inc. If limited representation is the goal, Attorney for US Inc. must take affirmative steps to avoid the perception that an attorney-client relationship has been established with the FN. Even then, if challenged, a determination of limited representation may be difficult, if not impossible, to achieve.

Factors Contributing to Formation of an Implied Attorney-Client Relationship With the FN

Many FN employees, especially those educated abroad who have spent a limited amount of time in the United States, are neither prepared for nor accustomed to dealing with complex immigration rules. If a FN is a new hire, he or she has little time to tend to the task of immigration matters and instead relies on the advice of the company's attorney. In these circumstances, the likelihood of establishing an implied attorney-client relationship with FN is quite high. This "client" may be viewed as disabled, as that term is contemplated in the Model Rules of Professional Conduct,[11] thus imposing special responsibilities on the attorney to make sure the "client" understands the nature of the relationship.

The FN who has attended undergraduate or graduate school in the United States may be accustomed to receiving comprehensive immigration information and services free of charge from the des-

ignated school official and/or responsible officer. Reliance by the FN on a university's legal department to provide immigration assistance—employment-based or otherwise—may be transferred to the corporate attorney performing the immigration work for the FN's new employer. This expectation of available legal assistance may lead to an implied attorney-client relationship.

The dependants of FNs may seek (and receive) legal assistance from US Inc.'s attorney, thus demonstrating a reliance upon attorney's legal advice.

Affirmative Steps in Attempting to Avoid and/or Limit Representation of the FN

An attorney-client relationship is premised on the provision of and reliance on legal advice. Clearly, the US Inc. attorney must refrain from giving legal advice to the FN; otherwise, arguably, an attorney-client relationship is established. For reasons stated above, this is a difficult mandate to accomplish.

The Model Rules of Professional Conduct provide guidance for dealing with unrepresented persons (FN and family) on behalf of the attorney's client (US Inc.).[12] Under the Model Rules, it is imperative that US Inc.'s attorney communicate the scope of the representation to the FN, preferably during the initial meeting with the FN, and every time a new petition, application, or extension (*e.g.*, I-129, labor certification, or I-140) is filed by US Inc. on behalf of the FN. A written non-representation letter, addressed to the FN, is essential. Some attorneys have the FN sign these non-representation letters. Points addressed in the non-representation letter should clearly limit the scope of representation and include identification of the attorney's corporate client, the lack of confidentiality of the communications with the attorney, and the recommendation that the FN seek independent counsel.[13] The attorney should

---

[11] "When a client's ability to make adequately considered decisions in connection with the representation is diminished, whether because of minority, mental impairment, or for some other reason, the lawyer shall, as far as reasonably possible, maintain a normal client-lawyer relationship with the client." ABA Model Rules of Professional Conduct Rule 1.14(a) (2003).

[12] "In dealing on behalf of a client with a person who is not represented by counsel, a lawyer shall not state or imply that the lawyer is disinterested. When the lawyer knows or reasonably should know that the unrepresented person misunderstands the lawyer's role in the matter, the lawyer shall make reasonable efforts to correct the misunderstanding. The lawyer shall not give legal advice to an unrepresented person, other than the advice to secure counsel, if the lawyer knows or reasonably should know that the interests of such a person are or have a reasonable possibility of being in conflict with the interests of the client." ABA Model Rules of Professional Conduct Rule 4.3 (2003).

[13] Comment, ABA Model Rule 4.3.

then be vigilant in adhering to the terms of the non-representation letter.

USCIS and Department of Labor (DOL) petitions and/or applications requiring the signature of the employer should be the only matters handled by the attorney. Generally, this means US Inc.'s attorney handles only matters pertaining to Trade NAFTA (TN) (change of status and extensions); H-1B and O nonimmigrant petitions; labor certifications; and immigrant petitions (Form I-140) for FNs. Employer involvement in applications for adjustment of status (Form I-485) and applications for immigrant visas (consular processing) is unnecessary. Thus, the US Inc. attorney need not sign or give advice regarding those applications.

Attorney-client relationships also may be established through implication by the provision of services and/or advice to the dependents of the FN, including the concurrent filing of derivative nonimmigrant and immigrant petitions, *e.g.*, for H-4, L-2, and derivative I-485s. The attorney wishing to avoid dual representation should routinely refer the FN and his or her dependents to others for legal representation concerning filing these types of documents.

Although probably not determinative in limiting representation, attention should nevertheless be paid to careful completion of the G-28 as an additional precaution and to ensure consistency of statements regarding representation. The attorney in an immigration case is required to submit a Notice of Entry of Appearance as Attorney or Representative (Form G-28) signed by the employer/petitioner[14] in order to be recognized as US Inc.'s representative in a matter before USCIS. USCIS does not consider the FN beneficiary a party to a petition; the FN beneficiary therefore has no access to information regarding the petition except through the petitioner or the attorney on the G-28.[15] A properly completed G-28 could serve as additional notice to the FN of the representation of only US Inc. by the attorney and of the specific scope of that representation.[16] For this reason, the attorney should complete the "In re: THE ABOVE CONSENT TO DISCLOSURE IS IN CONNECTION WITH THE FOLLOWING MATTER" section of the G-28 to indicate the precise type of petition being submit-

ted, the represented party submitting the petition, and the benefit requested. Even if an attorney-client relationship is found to exist between the US Inc. attorney and the FN, the attorney could try arguing that the scope of that representation is limited by the scope of the representation on the G-28.

Terminating the "Dual Representation" Relationship

Despite his or her best efforts, the business immigration attorney may encounter the situation wherein dual representation arguably exists and the interests of an FN and US Inc. are no longer compatible and become adverse. The attorney must consult the professional conduct rules of the relevant jurisdiction to determine the actions that must be taken. Under the Model Rules of Professional Conduct,[17] the attorney must assess whether the dual representation under the circumstances will not adversely affect the relationship with each client and then gain the consent of each party after consultation as to the acceptability of that assessment. If one of the parties withholds such consent or if the attorney cannot in good faith reasonably conclude that the adverse effect on the parties can be reconciled, the attorney must terminate representation of one or both parties.[18]

Termination of representation carries its own set of professional responsibilities to protect the legal interests of the affected party.[19] One of these responsibilities is to refer the formerly represented party to independent counsel. If the US Inc. attorney is expressly retained/employed by the company, the representation of the FN, whether it exists or not, would likely be the terminated representation with the FN being referred to another attorney. Whether termination from representation of both parties is necessary depends on the specific facts of the case; the Model Rules suggest this possibility, due to the attorney's knowledge of facts adverse to one or both parties. For US Inc. attorneys, such as the

---

[14] 8 CFR §§292.4(a), 1292.4(a).

[15] 8 CFR §103.2(a)(3).

[16] *See generally* B. Hake, "G-28 Notices of Appearance and the Client-Lawyer Relationship," 72 *Interpreter Releases* 757 (1995).

[17] ABA Model Rules of Professional Conduct Rule 1.7(a) and (b) (2003).

[18] ABA Model Rules of Professional Conduct Rule 1.16(a) (2003).

[19] "Upon termination of representation, a lawyer shall take steps to the extent reasonably practicable to protect a client's interests, such as giving reasonable notice to the client, allowing time for employment of other counsel, surrendering papers and property to which the client is entitled and refunding any advance payment of fee or expense that has not been earned or incurred. The lawyer may retain papers relating to the client to the extent permitted by other law." ABA Model Rules of Professional Conduct Rule 1.16(d) (2003).

attorney described in the earlier hypothetical, this scenario is a potential nightmare as it presents the possibility of losing an important client.

If the attorney is going to represent both the employer and employee, clearly the preferred course is to take as many steps as possible to prevent a dual representation conflict. Reducing the possibility of a dual representation conflict is accomplished by the attorney informing both clients clearly and in writing of the limited scope of the representation of each of them.

Additional ABA Model Rules to Note (Not Exhaustive)

- **Duty of Loyalty (Model Rules 1.3 and 1.7)**—One of the fundamental principles of legal representation. Stems from the essence of the attorney-client relationship and principles of agency.

- **Professional Judgment (Model Rule 2.1)**—In representing a client, a lawyer shall exercise independent professional judgment and render candid advice. In rendering advice, a lawyer may refer not only to law but to other considerations such as moral, economic, social, and political factors that may be relevant to the client's situation.

- **Duty of Confidentiality (Model Rule 1.6)**—Circumstances under which an attorney may reveal information given by client.

- **Prohibition against accepting compensation from one not a client (Model Rule 1.8)**—Circumstances under which attorney may accept compensation for representing a client from one other than the client.

- **Prohibition against advising one not represented who is not a client (Model Rule 4.3)**—Guidance regarding limited advice that may be given to unrepresented person.

- **Prohibition against providing false information (Model Rule 3.3)**—Model Rule 1.0(m) defines "Tribunal" as "a court, an arbitrator in a binding arbitration proceeding or a legislative body, administrative agency, or other body acting in an adjudicative capacity. A legislative body, administrative agency, or other body acts in an adjudicative capacity when a neutral official, after the presentation of evidence or legal argument by a party or parties, will render a binding legal judgment directly affecting a party's interests in a particular matter."

CONCLUSION

The materials presented in this article demonstrate how difficult and challenging the immigration law practice is. It is essential that immigration lawyers practice defensively, thus protecting not only their licenses but also the legal interests of their clients. Potential conflict of interest situations arise in a business immigration practice daily where practitioners are faced with issues such as:

- Foreign national employee informs employer's attorney he or she plans to find a new job as soon as possible and asks how long he or she must wait;

- The employer client tells his or her attorney that the approved labor certification position is only part-time and was never intended to be full-time;

- The foreign employee asks the employer's attorney to negotiate a higher salary as a result of a high prevailing wage determination.

Codes and rules of professional conduct, along with the INA and 8 CFR, must be consulted in determining the proper way to address conflicts.

ETHICAL CONSIDERATIONS FOR IMMIGRATION ATTORNEYS REGARDING EMPLOYMENT OF PARALEGALS

*by Mark A. Mancini**

It is a pleasant fact in an unpleasant field that so much concerning ethics for attorneys in general is a question of common sense rather than an exercise in advanced moral theology. This is certainly the case when discussing the place of the paralegal in the daily operations of an immigration practice. As will appear below, both the ABA Model Rules of Professional Conduct and the relevant statutes and regulations reflect this. They distill, to a remarkable degree, principles most probably learned at grandmother's knee, which should be recalled periodically by every practitioner. This article, therefore, is not meant to be academic in nature or tone, but rather to offer some practical advice (by no means exhaustive) on the question of how an immigration attorney can avoid ethical lapses—which can lead to criminal proceedings—while still making the best use of the talents of legal assistants.

A recent rash of attorney disciplinary actions and criminal fraud convictions has piqued the curiosity of immigration lawyers about this very issue. Conversely, paralegals may legitimately ask whether complying with requests from employing attorneys will result in a goodly chunk of jail time. This article will attempt to address these concerns by examining some critical aspects of the roles of both parties in a typical immigration practice.

OBLIGATIONS OF ATTORNEYS IN THE EMPLOYMENT OF LEGAL ASSISTANTS UNDER THE MODEL RULES

First, the good news for attorneys: the employment of paralegals (or legal assistants—the terms are virtually interchangeable) is governed by Rule 5.3 of the Model Rules, allowing the employment of legal assistants in performing almost any function in a law office. There is, however, one crucial proviso: *all work must be supervised by an attorney, and that attorney must be ultimately responsible for the work.*

This rule means that the attorney who supervises the paralegal must assure that the paralegal who performs the work performs it to the same ethical standards as if the attorney him- or herself were performing it, *i.e.*, the attorney and the paralegal are in an *unified interest* and under the same common obligation. A wise attorney should therefore be certain that he or she (among other things):

- Hires paralegals who are trained in the basics of immigration law, or promptly trains them him- or herself, thereby enhancing the competent representation of the client. The more knowledgeable the paralegal, the less time-consuming supervision[1] is necessary. (See reference to common sense, *supra.*[2]);

- Keeps careful watch over both the daily activities of the paralegal and the paralegal's end work product;

- Assures that no paralegal gives *any sort* of legal advice directly to a client;

- Sounds a violent alarm if he or she discovers that a paralegal has engaged in any conduct that would be unethical if *the attorney, him- or herself, engaged in it.*

Examples of this would include such behaviors as:

– A paralegal who offers to "introduce" any alien to any potential employer;

– A paralegal who offers to "introduce" any alien to any potential spouse (or any potential "mother," "father," "sister," "brother" or "child," for that matter; viz., the Chinese paper father cases of yore);

– A paralegal with *any sort* of financial relationship with *any client* of the attorney, no matter how normal this would be if the paralegal were not employed by the attorney.

---

* **Mark A. Mancini** is a Pennsylvania native who has practiced in immigration and nationality law since admission to the bars in Pennsylvania and the District of Columbia. He received his J.D. from Temple University in 1973.

[1] The literal translation of "supervision" is "oversight," which of course means the opposite. I cannot explain this. Bill Safire, call your office.

[2] Attendance at conferences such as this one is certainly a good place to start.

In situations where a sole practitioner employs only one or two paralegals (typical of the younger members of AILA), these guidelines become more, and not less, important. The time spent in supervision and education of paralegals is a capital expenditure of enormous value.

The practice of immigration law often entails idiopathic problems in the use of paralegals that would not appear in other specialty areas. Since the clients often do not have English as a first language, they are most comfortable discussing their legal problems with an attorney who speaks their language. When a paralegal performs a translation function, and where the attorney does not speak the alien's language, the danger of running afoul of the rule referred to above increases exponentially.[3]

An attorney must be confident that any translation activity by a paralegal conforms to the statutory standard discussed here, or he or she would certainly stand liable under any "failure-to-supervise" standard.

STATUTORY AND REGULATORY STANDARD AFFECTING BOTH ATTORNEYS AND LEGAL ASSISTANTS

The major sources for disciplinary actions against attorneys on ethical grounds are contained in the sections of the INA[4] and the regulations discussed below. These sections also are major sources of problems in the unethical use of paralegals. Since no states currently license or discipline paralegals independently, these standards apply to the legal assistants employed by the attorneys in the same way they apply to the attorneys themselves (see discussion of duty to supervise, *supra*).[5]

Section 274C(a)(5) of the INA looms large in the area of attorney discipline, as well as criminal proceedings against immigration lawyers and paralegals. It provides:

> It is unlawful for any person or entity knowingly . . . (5) to prepare, file, or assist another in preparing or filing, any application for benefits

under this Act, or any document required under this Act, or any document submitted in connection with such application or document, with knowledge or in reckless disregard of the fact that such application or document was falsely made or, in whole or in part, does not relate to the person on whose behalf it was or is being submitted.

Further guidance as to what is meant by to "falsely make" is provided by §274C(f), which reads:

> For purposes of this section, the term "falsely make" means to prepare or provide an application or document, with knowledge or in reckless disregard of the fact that the application or document contains a false, fictitious, or fraudulent statement or material representation, or has no basis in law or fact, or otherwise fails to state a fact which is material to the purpose for which it was submitted.

Please note that the statute provides for criminal penalties for any person or entity, and not just attorneys. For attorneys, a criminal conviction will undoubtedly result in discipline by the Board of Immigration Appeals (BIA) under 8 CFR §§1003.101 *et seq.*; the BIA has stated that it has no authority to discipline non-lawyers.[6] On the other hand, the paralegal can certainly go to jail with his or her employer.

These two sections of the Act should give pause to every practitioner and every paralegal because they formed the basis for disciplinary, civil, and criminal actions against *six attorneys and four paralegals* in the Washington area alone, and that happened only in the last three years.[7]

---

[3] *See, e.g., Mags v. Neal*, 938 S.W.2d 830 (Ark. 1992).

[4] Immigration and Nationality Act of 1952, Pub. L. No. 82-414, 66 Stat. 163 (*codified as amended at* 8 USC §§1101 *et seq.*) (INA).

[5] *See generally* M. Newman and R. Ford, "Utilizing Immigration Paraprofessional: The Ethical Consideration," *Ethics in a Brave New World* (AILA 2004).

[6] BIA P.M. Rule 11.3(d), appended here as Appendix I. Attorneys, however, need not be criminally convicted to be disciplined by the Board. See Rule 11.4, in which conviction of a serious crime is only one of 13 types of conduct that will result in discipline, which also include "assisting the unauthorized practice of law" and "improper solicitation of clients or using runners."

See also Matter of Gadda, Attorney, 23 I&N Dec. 645 (BIA 2003); *Matter of Ramos, Attorney*, 23 I&N Dec. 843 (BIA 2005). The BIA rules parallel Model Rule 3.3, which applies of course to all attorneys' disciplinary proceedings.

[7] *See* List of Suspended and Expelled Practitioners, Office of the General Counsel, EOIR (Mar. 7, 2006), attached as Appendix II. The criminal law counterpart to §274C is at 18 USC 1001 *et seq.*

The particular nexus here is clear: it is most often the paralegal who first "prepares" an immigration application, and as such, constitutes the first line of defense against any potential violation of §274C(a)(5).[8]

There is, of course, a broad spectrum of activity involved in "preparing" an immigration document. There should be no ethical quandary involved in pondering whether or not to commit forgery in applying for a benefit.[9] More consideration must be given, however, to the other activities that go into preparing an immigration document. Avoiding ethical difficulties with this section of the statute should include:

- Legal assurances by the clients (both petitioner and beneficiary) that they are in fact who they say they are, such as birth certificates, licenses, passports, and so forth.

- Familiarity with provisions of the Department of State *Foreign Affairs Manual*. One presenting a document provided by a client purporting to be a divorce decree from a country that does not recognize divorce might be called "reckless disregard."

- Avoidance of multiple or repeated substitutions of immigrant visa petition beneficiaries.[10]

- Running away very fast when the answer to the question "Are you married?" is: "Not in this country"; or, when "Are you divorced?" is answered with "I never talk about that."

As was pointed out at the beginning of this article, the use of common sense reaches far in the field of ethics for immigration practitioners.

OBLIGATIONS OF LEGAL ASSISTANTS IN THEIR EMPLOYMENT BY IMMIGRATION ATTORNEYS

Since the same ethical and positive legal rules apply to both the immigration attorney and the paralegal (*see supra*), a legal assistant should take care to guard against violations. As a practical matter (and moving up the ethical scale from a general admonition not to forge signatures), some pointers for paralegals would include:

- Keep copies of original *drafts* of all forms used, even if never revised or submitted to Department of Homeland Security (DHS), in the handwriting of the client. Subsequent revisions and editing should always be translated to and initialed by the client. This will avoid angry cries of "I told you about my perjury conviction already!" at adjustment interviews. No attorneys or paralegal could be accused of "falsely making" where such a document is kept.

- Keep up-to-date with regulatory changes, especially fee schedules. It would not be an ethical lapse for a paralegal to enclose a filing fee check in an incorrect amount (anyone can fail at addition, although one would imagine the minimum standard of care referred to in the Rules must reach at least to long division), but certainly a charge of neglect would lie when DHS returns the check and the deadline for filing has already passed.

Remember: It is the duty of the immigration attorney to supervise the paralegal, even in clerical matters. Attorneys—check your outgoing mail!

- Be brave. No matter how pressed your employer may be, a paralegal should remind him or her that the Rules would be violated by a paralegal attending *any* interviews with a client at DHS, because it would be impossible per se for an attorney to supervise the legal assistant within any interpretation of Rule 5.3. This would certainly include a fortiori such activity as being sent to the Executive Office for Immigration Review (EOIR) to ask for a continuance viva voce. This also would constitute the unauthorized practice of law in most states.

- Do not file any document with any blank spaces or unanswered questions. The expanded definition of "falsely make" in §274C(f) includes "or otherwise fails to state a fact which is material to the purpose for which it was submitted." Form I-485, for instance, on which the question regard-

---

[8] *See* DOJ Press Release, "Two Lawyers Indicted for Immigration Fraud" (May 12, 2005), U.S. Attorney's Office for the District of Maryland, Northern Division, attached as Appendix III.

[9] *See Matters of Ramos*, at 844, "As with misuse of client funds, the Supreme Court of Florida takes a very dim view of Forgery." The author was unable to locate opinions by the Supreme Courts of any other state that held to the contrary. *See also* Expulsion of Kooritzsky, Appendix II, at p.3

[10] As of the date of writing, it has been proposed to discontinue this practice, due to the overheated secondary market in labor certifications.

ing arrests is left blank could be so interpreted. If there is any doubt as to or whether an action constituted an arrest, it is far better to answer "yes" rather then leave it blank, under the civil law doctrine of *tutior pars*, where the inculpatory can later be made exculpatory at the time of adjudication. I guess there is a little moral theology in this after all.

- Make sure the preparers' blanks are signed by the attorney. See the criminal penalties for failure to attend to this, described in §274C(e)(2), *supra*.

CONCLUSION

An overview of the ethical lapse of immigration practitioners over the last few years reveals a spectrum of behaviors that can get either the lawyer or legal assistant into serious disciplinary, tort, or criminal trouble.

The behaviors (using the common law terms) are, in ascending order of badness:

- "Mere" negligence;
- Reckless disregard;
- Malfeasance;
- Misfeasance;
- Criminality.

The author does not think that any AILA member, or any of employee of a member, needs to be warned about criminal behavior being unethical. It is the lower orders of misbehavior that have to be watched carefully by both the lawyer and paralegal. It has been the experience of the author both in his practice and as a witness in Bar Counsel proceedings that most arise out of charge of "reckless disregard" (of how things are being done in the attorney's office), rather than criminality.

In fact, the BIA has set forth in its practice manual 13 examples of activity that would merit disciplinary action (*see* Appendix I). Only *four* involve criminal activity. Since the BIA by regulation sits on cases of attorney discipline for all immigration practitioners,[11] it would be sensible for attorneys and paralegals to refer regularly to the list in daily practice.

One final note: Misprision of felony is a crime in most states. If a paralegal fails to notify the appropriate authority of an instance where clear criminal behavior is taking place, that paralegal could stand accused of a separate crime. Definitions of conspiracy, accomplicity, or accessoriness also could apply.[12]

Have a nice day.

---

[11] 8 CFR §1003.1(d)(2)(iii).

[12] See press release announcing the indictment of I. Jay Fredman, Attorney and Alpo Canseven, Paralegal, in Appendix III: "the indictment further alleges that to facilitate the *conspiracy* some of the payments from the alien applicants were deposited into bank accounts controlled by companies formed by some of the defendants" (emphasis added).

APPENDIX I: BIA PRACTICE MANUAL, RULE 11

11   Discipline of Practitioners

11.1   Practitioner Discipline Generally

The Board has the authority to impose disciplinary sanctions upon attorneys and accredited representatives who violate rules of professional conduct in practice before the Board, the Immigration Courts, and the Department of Homeland Security (DHS). 8 C.F.R. §§ 1003.1(d)(2)(iii), 1003.1(d)(5), 1003.101-106; 1292.3. See also *Matter of Gadda*, 23 I&N Dec. 645 (BIA 2003).

11.2   Definition of Practitioner

For purposes of this Chapter, the term "practitioner" is defined as an attorney or accredited representative, as defined in 8 C.F.R. § 1001.1(f), (j).

11.3   Jurisdiction

(a) *Practitioners.* — The Board is authorized to discipline any practitioner if the Board finds it to be in the public interest to do so. 8 C.F.R. §§ 1003.101(a), 1292.3(a). Pursuant to regulations, it is in the public interest to discipline any practitioner who has engaged in criminal, unethical, or unprofessional conduct or in frivolous behavior. 8 C.F.R. §§ 1003.101(a), 1003.102, 1292.3(b).

(b) *DHS attorneys.* — The Board's disciplinary authority does not extend to attorneys who represent DHS.

(c) *Immigration Judges.* — The Board's disciplinary authority does not extend to Immigration Judges. The conduct of Immigration Judges falls under the jurisdiction of the Department of Justice's Office of Professional Responsibility. 8 C.F.R. § 1003.109.

(d) *Immigration specialists.* — The Board does not have authority to discipline individuals such as "immigration specialists," "visa consultants," "notarios," "asesorios," and other individuals who engage in the unauthorized practice of law. However, the Board has the authority to discipline practitioners who assist in the unauthorized practice of law. 8 C.F.R. § 1003.102(m). The Board encourages anyone harmed by the unauthorized practice of law to report it to the appropriate law enforcement, consumer protection, and other authorities.

Chapter 11   Board of Immigration Appeals

11.4   Conduct

The following conduct may result in discipline by the Board:

- o   frivolous behavior, as defined in 8 C.F.R. § 1003.102(j) and discussed at 8 C.F.R. § 1003.1(d)(2)(iii)

- o   ineffective assistance of counsel as provided in 8 C.F.R. § 1003.102(k)

- o   misconduct resulting in disbarment from, suspension by, or resignation with an admission of misconduct from a state or federal licensing authority

- o   conviction of a serious crime

- o   a false statement of material fact or law made knowingly or with reckless disregard

- o   false certification of a copy of a document made knowingly or with reckless disregard

- o   assisting the unauthorized practice of law

- o   grossly excessive fees

- o   bribery, coercion, or an attempt at either, with the intention of affecting the outcome of an immigration case

- o   improper solicitation of clients or using "runners"

- o   misrepresenting qualifications or services

- o   repeated failure to appear for scheduled hearings in a timely manner without good cause

- o   courtroom conduct that would constitute contempt of court in a judicial proceeding

See 8 C.F.R. § 1003.102. This list is not exhaustive or exclusive, and other grounds for discipline may be identified by the Board. 8 C.F.R. § 1003.102.

11.5　Complaints

(a) *Who may file.* — Anyone may file a complaint against a practitioner, including aggrieved clients, adjudicators, DHS personnel, and other practitioners. 8 C.F.R. § 1003.104(a)(1).

(b) *What to file.* — Complaints must be submitted *in writing* on the Immigration Practitioner Complaint Form (Form EOIR-44), which can be downloaded from the Internet. See Chapter 12.2(b) (Obtaining forms), Appendix E (Forms). The complaint form provides important information about the complaint process, confidentiality, and the kinds of misconduct that the Board can discipline. Complaints should be specific and as detailed as possible, providing supporting documentation when it is available.

(c) *Where to file.* —

(i) *Misconduct before Board or Immigration Judge.* — Complaints alleging misconduct before the Board or an Immigration Court are filed with the Office of General Counsel of the Executive Office for Immigration Review (EOIR). 8 C.F.R. § 1003.104(a)(1). The completed form and supporting documents should be sent to:

> Office of General Counsel
> Executive Office for Immigration Review
> 5107 Leesburg Pike, Suite 2600
> Falls Church, VA 22041
>
> Attn: Bar Counsel

EOIR's Office of General Counsel decides whether or not to initiate disciplinary proceedings. 8 C.F.R. § 1003.104(b).

(ii) *Misconduct before DHS.* — Complaints involving such conduct before DHS are to be filed with the appropriate DHS Office of the Principle Legal Advisor. 8 C.F.R. §§ 1003.104(a)(2); 1292.3(d).

(d) *When to file.* — Complaints based on ineffective assistance of counsel must be filed within one year of a finding of ineffective assistance of counsel by the Board or the Immigration Court. 8 C.F.R. § 1003.102(k).

11.6   Duty to Report

Any attorney or accredited representative who practices before the Board, the Immigration Courts, or DHS has an affirmative duty to report whenever he or she:

     o   has been found guilty of, or pled guilty or *nolo contendere* to, a serious crime (as defined in 8 C.F.R. § 1003.102(h)), *or*

     o   has been suspended or disbarred, or has resigned with an admission of misconduct

8 C.F.R. §§ 1003.103(c), 1292.3(c)(4). The practitioner must report the misconduct, criminal conviction, or discipline both to the EOIR Office of General Counsel and to the appropriate DHS Office of the Principal Legal Advisor within 30 days of the issuance of the relevant initial order. The duty applies even if an appeal of the conviction or discipline is pending.

11.7   Procedure

The regulations provide the procedures for filing complaints and imposing sanctions for misconduct before the Board and the Immigration Courts. See 8 C.F.R. §§ 1003.101 et seq. The regulations also contain procedures for filing complaints regarding misconduct before DHS. 8 C.F.R. § 1292.3.

(a) *Initiation of Proceedings.* —

(i) *Notice of Intent to Discipline.* — Disciplinary proceedings begin when the EOIR Office of General Counsel files a Notice of Intent to Discipline with the Board and serves a copy on the practitioner. The Notice contains a statement of the charge(s) against the practitioner, a copy of the inquiry report (if any), proposed disciplinary sanctions, the procedure for filing an answer to the Notice or requesting a hearing, and the contact information for the Board. 8 C.F.R. § 1003.105(a).

(ii) *Petition for Immediate Suspension.* — When the Notice of Intent to Discipline concerns an attorney who has either been convicted of a serious crime or is subject to suspension or disbarment by a state or federal licensing authority, the Office of General Counsel petitions for the immediate suspension of that attorney. 8 C.F.R. § 1003.103(a)(1).

Usually filed in conjunction with the Notice of Intent to Discipline, the petition for immediate suspension seeks the practitioner's immediate suspension from practice before the Board and the Immigration Courts. 8 C.F.R. § 1003.103(a)(1). DHS may ask that the practitioner be similarly suspended from practice before DHS.

The regulations direct that, upon the filing of a petition for immediate suspension, the Board will suspend the respondent for as long as disciplinary proceedings are pending. 8 C.F.R. § 1003.103(a)(2). The regulations permit the immediate suspension to be set aside when the Board deems it in the interest of justice to do so. 8 C.F.R. § 1003.103(a)(2). The usual hardships that accompany a suspension from practice (e.g., loss of income, duty to complete pending cases) are generally not sufficient to set aside an immediate suspension order.

(b) *Response.* — The subject of a Notice of Intent to Discipline has 30 days from the date of service to file a written answer to the Notice and to request a hearing. 8 C.F.R. § 1003.105(c)(1). An answer is deemed filed at the time it is *received* by the Board. See Chapter 3.1(b) (Must be "timely"). The answer should be served on both the EOIR Office of General Counsel and the appropriate DHS Office of Principal Legal Advisor. The time in which to file an answer may be extended for good cause shown through the filing of a motion no later than 3 working days *before* the filing deadline. 8 C.F.R. § 1003.105(c)(1). Second extension requests are rarely granted.

(i) *Timely answer.* — If an answer is timely received by the Board, the matter will be referred to an appropriate adjudicator, generally an Immigration Judge, to conduct a disciplinary hearing. 8 C.F.R. § 1003.106. The answer must specifically admit or deny each of the allegations in the Notice of Intent to Discipline. Each allegation not denied is deemed admitted. 8 C.F.R. § 1003.105(c)(2).

If the practitioner wishes to have a hearing, the request for a hearing must be contained in the written answer. Otherwise, the opportunity to request a hearing will be deemed waived. 8 C.F.R. § 1003.105(c)(3).

(ii) *No answer or untimely answer.* — If the Board does not receive a timely answer, the failure to answer is deemed an admission of the allegations in the Notice of Intent to Discipline, and the practitioner is thereafter precluded from requesting a hearing on the matter. 8 C.F.R. § 1003.105(d). The regulations require the Board to enter a default order imposing the discipline recommended by the EOIR Office of General Counsel and the DHS Office of Principal Legal Advisor, absent the presence of special considerations. 8 C.F.R. § 1003.105(d)(2).

A practitioner subject to a default order may move to set aside that order, provided that the motion is filed within 15 days of the date of service of the default order and that his or her failure to answer was due to exceptional circumstances beyond the control of the

Chapter 11   Board of Immigration Appeals

practitioner (e.g., the attorney's serious illness, death of an immediate relative). 8 C.F.R. § 1003.105(d)(2).

(c) *Hearing.* — If a practitioner timely requests a hearing, the record is forwarded to an Immigration Judge or other appropriate adjudicator to conduct a disciplinary proceeding, which is described at 8 C.F.R. § 1003.106. For the most part, disciplinary hearings will be conducted in the same manner as immigration proceedings. 8 C.F.R. § 1003.106. However, the Immigration Judge presiding over the disciplinary proceeding will not be one before whom the practitioner regularly appears. 8 C.F.R. § 1003.106(a)(1)(i).

(d) *Appeals.* — The regulations provide that the Board may entertain an appeal filed by a practitioner wishing to challenge the adjudicator's disciplinary ruling. 8 C.F.R. § 1003.106(c). The appeal must be received by the Board within 30 days of the oral decision or, if no oral decision was rendered, 30 days of the date of mailing of the written decision. The proper form for filing a practitioner discipline appeal is the Notice of Appeal (Form EOIR-45), which can be downloaded from the Internet. See Chapter 12.2(b) (Obtaining forms), Appendix E (Forms). (This form is specific to disciplinary proceedings and is different from the Notices of Appeal in other types of proceedings. See Appendix E (Forms).) The parties must comply with all of the other standard provisions for filing appeals with the Board. 8 C.F.R. § 1003.106(c). See Chapter 4 (Appeals of Immigration Judge Decisions).

(e) *Motions.* — As with most motions in immigration proceedings, motions should be filed with the adjudicator who has jurisdiction over the case.

(i) *Prior to the entry of a default order or a timely request for a hearing.* — In this instance, motions should be filed with the Board.

(ii) *After a timely response has been made.* — In this instance, motions should be filed with the Immigration Judge, unless an appeal to the Board has been taken.

(iii) *If a default order has been entered.* — In this instance, motions should be filed with the Board.

11.8   Sanctions

The Board is authorized to impose a broad range of sanctions, including "expulsion" (permanent suspension) from immigration practice, public or private censure, and other sanctions deemed appropriate by the Board. 8 C.F.R. § 1003.101(a). The Board may even increase the level of disciplinary sanction. *Matter of Gadda,* 23 I&N Dec. 645 (BIA 2003). When a practitioner has been expelled or suspended, that information is made available to the public on the EOIR website, at the Board, and at the Immigration Courts. See Chapter 11.9 (Confidentiality).

11.9 Confidentiality

The regulations discuss confidentiality and public disclosure at the various stages of disciplinary proceedings. See 8 C.F.R. § 1003.108. As a general rule, action taken on a Notice of Intent to Discipline may be disclosed to the public. 8 C.F.R. § 1003.108(c).

11.10 Effect on Cases before the Board

(a) *Duty to advise clients.* — A practitioner who is disciplined is obligated to advise all clients with a case pending before either the Board or an Immigration Court that he or she has been disciplined by the Board.

(b) *Pending cases deemed unrepresented.* — Once a practitioner has been disciplined by the Board and is currently not authorized to practice before the Board and the Immigration Courts, the Board will deem that practitioner's pending cases to be unrepresented. Filings that are submitted after a practitioner has been expelled or suspended will be rejected and returned to the party whenever possible. If the practitioner is later reinstated by the Board, he or she must file a new Notice of Entry of Appearance (Form EOIR-27) in every case, even if he or she previously represented that party. See Chapter 11.12(c) (Cases pending at the time of reinstatement).

(c) *Ineffective assistance of counsel.* — The imposition of discipline on an attorney does not constitute *per se* evidence of ineffective assistance of counsel in any case formerly represented by that attorney.

(d) *Filing deadlines.* — An order of practitioner discipline does not automatically excuse parties from meeting any applicable filing deadlines.

11.11 List of Suspended and Expelled Attorneys

A list of practitioners who have been suspended or expelled from immigration practice appears at www.usdoj.gov/eoir. The list is updated periodically. Copies are also posted at the Board and in the Immigration Courts.

Chapter 11   Board of Immigration Appeals

11.12 Reinstatement

(a) *Expiration of suspension.* — When a period of suspension has run, reinstatement is not automatic. 8 C.F.R. § 1003.107(a). An practitioner who has been suspended from immigration practice and who wishes to be reinstated must:

- file a motion with the Board requesting to be reinstated

- show that he or she can meet the definition of "attorney" set forth in 8 C.F.R. § 1001.1(f) (or § 1001.1(j) if an "accredited representative")

Certain attorneys must meet additional criteria to be reinstated. See subsection (b), below.

(b) *Petition for reinstatement.* — A practitioner who has been expelled or has been suspended for a year or more may seek reinstatement with the Board if he or she:

- petitions after one year or one-half of the term of suspension has expired, whichever is greater

- can meet the regulatory definition in 8 C.F.R. § 1001.1(f) or § 1001.1(j)

- can demonstrate by clear, unequivocal, and convincing evidence that he or she possesses the moral and professional qualifications required to return to immigration practice

- can show that reinstatement will not be detrimental to the administration of justice

8 C.F.R. § 1003.107(b)(1). Failure to meet any one of these criteria will result in the request for reinstatement being denied. Once a request for reinstatement is denied, the attorney may not seek reinstatement for another full year. 8 C.F.R. § 1003.107(b)(2). The Board may, in its discretion, hold a hearing to determine if the attorney meets all the regulatory requirements for reinstatement.

All requests for reinstatement must be served on the EOIR Office of General Counsel and the appropriate DHS Office of Principal Legal Advisor. 8 C.F.R. § 1003.107(b)(1).

(c) *Cases pending at the time of reinstatement.* — Suspension or expulsion by the Board terminates representation. A practitioner reinstated to immigration practice by the Board who wishes to represent cases before the Board or the Immigration Courts must enter a new appearance in each case, *even if* he or she was the attorney of record at the time that discipline was imposed. The practitioner should include proof of reinstatement with each new appearance. See Chapter 2.3(c) (Appearances).

updates: www.usdoj.gov/eoir
119
this page last revised: June 15, 2004

APPENDIX II: EOIR LIST OF SUSPENDED AND EXPELLED PRACTITIONERS

LIST OF SUSPENDED AND EXPELLED PRACTITIONERS   Page 1 of 7

U.S. Department of Justice

Executive Office for Immigration Rev

Bar Counse   *5107 Leesburg Pike, Suite 2600* Office of the General Counsel
                                                  Falls Church, Virginia 22041

March 7, 2006

LIST OF DISCIPLINED PRACTITIONERS

* = denotes practitioner(s) most recently disciplined

For more information about a practitioner's disciplinary history, click on the date highlighted in blue.

For more information about the Executive Office for Immigration Review's Attorney Discipline Program,

click on these links: Rules for Professional Conduct & Professional Conduct for Immigration Practitioners - Factsheet

NAME	CITY/STATE	DATE IMMED. SUSPENSION IMPOSED	FINAL DISCIPLINE IMPOSED	EFFECTIVE DATE OF DISCIPLINE	REINSTATED?
Richard Acevedo	San Antonio, TX	10/8/02	Suspended - 5 years	10/8/02	No
Mohamed Alamgir	District of Columbia	------------	Expelled	7/9/04	No
Stephen J. Alexander	Los Angeles, CA	9/16/05			
Mahmoud Alsafty	Maryland/New York	5/7/04	Suspended - 1 year	3/30/04	No
Grosvenor Anschell	Washington	11/30/00	Suspended - 2 years	11/30/00	No
Derrick G. Arjune	New York	8/11/05			
Chris Asher	District of Columbia/ Maryland	7/30/01	Suspended - 5 years	7/30/01	No
Frank A.K. Awuah	District of Columbia/ Maryland	10/1/01	Indefinite Suspension	10/1/01	No
Hani Alex Azzam	Massachussetts	9/1/05	------------	------------	Yes - 12/14/05
Jordan N. Baker	Virginia	11/16/04	Expelled	12/7/04	No
Michael T. Barrett	Oregon	10/4/01	Indefinite Suspension	10/4/01	No
Sharon Bartu	Washington	6/15/01	Suspended - 6 months	6/15/01	No
Mario Antonio Bautista	San Francisco, CA	12/2/05	Indefinite Suspension	12/2/05	No
Mitchil O. Bechet	New York	12/21/00			
Chaim Howard Berglas	New York	5/11/05	Suspended - 1 year	5/11/05	No

LIST OF SUSPENDED AND EXPELLED PRACTITIONERS

Kathleen L. Bilbe	Louisiana	-----------	Suspended - 5 years	6/2/98	No
Roy L. Bischoff	Utah/Nevada	6/27/05	Expelled	6/27/05	No
Ann Bitterman	Florida	3/18/05	Suspended - 91 days	3/18/05	No
Charles H. Bowser	District of Columbia	9/15/00	Expelled	9/15/00	No
Ira Sylvester Brackens	San Francisco, CA	7/24/03	Suspended - 18 months	7/24/03	No
David L. Brehmer	Minnesota	3/8/01	Indefinite Suspension	3/8/01	No
Marcia Jean Brinkley	Texas/San Diego, CA	2/17/05	Suspended - 5 years	2/17/05	No
Brenda C. Brisbon	Maryland	5/12/05	Indefinite Suspension	5/12/05	No
Deloris A. Brown	District of Columbia	5/7/01	Indefinite Suspension	5/7/01	No
Dennis Detmer Burchard	San Diego, CA	4/8/03	Suspended - 9 months	4/8/03	No
Bruce C. Burge	San Francisco, CA	-----------	Suspended - 6 months	10/23/03	No
David Keith Burgess	San Francisco, CA	11/7/02			
Martha L. Burns	Minnesota	12/7/01	Suspended - 9 months	12/7/01	No
Walter Burrier	Connecticut/ Los Angeles, CA	5/13/05	Suspended - 1 year	5/13/05	No
Joel H. Cavadel	Pennsylvania	-----------	Suspended - 9 months	11/14/05	No
Manlin Chee	North Carolina	3/18/05	Expelled	3/18/05	No
Carroll A. Clark	Arizona	-----------	Suspended - 6 months and 1 day	11/5/04	No
Marsden Coates	Maryland	1/24/05	Expelled	1/24/05	No
Marshall L. Cohen	Florida/Georgia	11/8/05			
Kemakolan Comas	New York	3/1/05			
Antonio Cortez	El Paso, TX	11/4/04	Suspended - 12 months	11/4/04	No
Baird Cuber	New York	6/27/05			
Paul Howard Curtis	Los Angeles, CA	7/16/03	Suspended - 6 months	7/16/03	No
Lester Walter Czapelski	New Jersey	2/18/04			
Marcia Lynn Czapelski	New Jersey	2/18/04			
Edward Daneri	San Antonio, TX	4/30/03	Suspended - 5 years	4/30/03	No
Dan P. Danilov	Washington	9/25/03			
Reginald Egan Darbonne	Florida	12/1/00	Suspended - 5 years	12/1/00	No
Earl S. David	New York	-----------	Suspended - 15 months	7/9/04	No
Howard D. Deutsch	New York	5/30/01			
Drew S. Diehl	Ohio	8/12/05	Suspended - 2 years	8/12/05	No
James C. Dragon	Massachussetts	1/30/03	Indefinite Suspension	10/29/03	No
Grisel S. Echavarria	Wisconsin	3/28/05	Expelled	3/28/05	No
Irving Edelman	New York	-----------	Indefinite Suspension	7/10/96	No
Aloysius O. Ejimakor	Maryland	-----------	Suspended - 9 months	1/8/04	No
Allan M. Elster	Florida	12/1/00	Suspended - 3 years	12/1/00	No
Ronald Fanta	New York	12/2/05			

LIST OF SUSPENDED AND EXPELLED PRACTITIONERS

Irwin Jay Fredman	Maryland/District of Columbia	1/11/06			
Paul Ira Freedman	New York	9/18/01	Expelled	9/18/01	No
Miguel Gadda	San Francisco, CA	10/2/01	Expelled	7/8/03	No
*Virginia Gago	New York	2/2/06	Expelled	2/2/06	No
Edward P. Gallagher	Maryland	3/3/05	Expelled	3/3/05	No
Jorge H. Galvez	Utah	1/30/06			
Maximiliano S. Garcia	Arizona/California	10/7/05			
Ruben John Garcia	San Antonio, TX	6/15/01	Suspended - 5 years	6/15/01	No
William R. Gardner	San Francisco, CA	3/8/01	Suspended - 6 months	10/19/00	No
*Richard F. Garza	Dallas, TX	3/7/06			
Gayle S. Ghitelman	Massachusetts	3/9/04	Suspended for 1 year and 1 day	3/9/04	Yes - 12/2/05
Alexander Goldman	Illinois	11/22/05	Expelled	11/22/05	No
Wendy B. Golenbock	Massachusetts	4/17/02	Suspended - 8 years	4/17/02	No
Jeffrey Gonzalez-Perez	Virginia	8/4/04	Suspended - 2 years	8/4/04	No
Nicholas C. Grapsas	Wisconsin	9/15/00	Suspended - 6 months	9/15/00	No
Charles A. Grutman	New York	6/6/02	Suspended - 7 years	6/6/02	No
Rosalynn D. Guillen	Washington	10/29/01	Suspended - 5 years	10/29/01	No
Cheryl Handy	Illinois	1/24/05	Suspended - 1 year	1/24/05	No
Hanna Z. Hanna	New York	4/30/03	Suspended - 3 years	4/30/03	No
Alfred L. Hansen	Louisiana/San Francisco, CA	1/10/05	Suspended - 2 years	1/10/05	No
*Alan J. Harris	New York	2/21/06			
Michael C. Hyde	Florida	9/9/04	Suspended - 30 days	9/9/04	No
John Hykel	Pennsylvania	3/8/01	Suspended - 2 years	3/8/01	No
Richard Allen James	District of Columbia/ Maryland	6/15/01	Suspended - 5 years	6/15/01	No
Walter T. Johnson, Jr.	North Carolina	3/19/04	Suspended - 1 year	3/19/04	No
Alake Johnson-Ford	District of Columbia	9/15/00	Suspended - 5 years	9/15/00	No
Thomas Christopher Jones	Illinois	10/6/04	Suspended - 30 months	10/06/04	No
Lijyasu Kandekore	Florida	11/30/00	Indefinite Suspension	6/20/01	No
Randhir S. Kang	San Francisco, CA	1/27/06			
Deborah J. Kartje	Chicago, IL/Northern IN	12/4/00	Expelled	12/4/00	No
William P. Kaszynski	Minnesota	3/8/01	Expelled	3/8/01	No
Dalia R. Kejbou	Minnesota	2/16/06			
Morris B. Kemper	San Francisco, CA	5/7/01	Suspended - 1 year	5/7/01	No
Claude Henry Kleefield	New York	12/2/05	Suspended - 3 months	12/2/05	No
Alan Edward Koczela	Virginia	8/10/00			
Samuel G. Kooritzky	Virginia	4/8/03	Expelled	4/8/03	No

LIST OF SUSPENDED AND EXPELLED PRACTITIONERS   Page 4 of 7

Robert L. Koven	Maryland	5/7/01	Indefinite Suspension		No
John J. Kozlowski	San Francisco, CA	10/29/01	Suspended - 90 days	10/29/01	No
Dorothea J. Kraeger	Arizona	6/2/05			
Milton Dan Kramer	San Francisco, CA	8/10/00	Indefinite Suspension	3/1/00	No
Boris A. Krivonos	New York	-----------	Expelled	1/30/03	No
Robert M. Kuhnreich	New York	8/11/05	Expelled	8/11/05	No
Steven Y. Lee	District of Columbia/ Virginia	11/22/04	Expelled	12/7/04	No
Eric Levine	Massachusetts	10/25/05	Suspended - 4 years	10/25/05	No
Clyde E. Lindsay	Massachusetts	2/11/04	Suspended - 1 year	2/11/04	No
J. Thomas Logan	Los Angeles, CA	-----------	Suspended - 60 days	12/1/04	
Javier Lopera	Florida	11/4/04	Expelled	12/7/04	No
Mark E. Maier	Maryland	12/4/00	Indefinite Suspension	12/4/00	No
Denise A. Maniscalco	Virginia	9/1/04	Suspended - 32 months and 3 days	10/19/04	No
Brandon Marinoff	Colorado	1/31/05	Suspended - 12 months	1/31/05	No
Allen C. Marra	New York/ New Jersey	7/18/05	Indefinite Suspension	7/18/05	No
Leroy Allan Martin	Los Angeles, CA	-----------	Suspended - 60 days	6/18/05	Yes - 1/31/06
Jason A. Martinez	Arkansas	9/25/03	Expelled	9/25/03	No
Victor Stephen Martinez	Los Angeles, CA	10/9/02	Suspended - 9 months	10/9/02	No
Timothy P. Mason	Los Angeles, CA	7/20/04			
Timothy L. McCandless	Los Angeles, CA	10/6/04	Suspended - 6 months	10/6/04	No
Mackson P. McDowall	New York	3/8/01	Suspended - 2 years	3/8/01	No
Terrence McGuire	Los Angeles, CA	9/1/05	Suspended - 2 years	9/1/05	no
Armando J. Mendez	San Francisco, CA	7/24/03	Suspended - 90 days	7/24/03	No
John Owen Meyers, III	Los Angeles, CA	10/29/01	Suspended - 20 months	10/29/01	No
Maqsood Mir	Maryland	9/16/05			
Wayne M. Mitchell	Maryland	12/2/05	Expelled	12/2/05	No
Carolyn E. Miyashita	North Carolina/San Francisco, CA	8/10/00	Suspended - 5 years	8/10/00	No
Gaetanella Molinini-Rivera	New York	12/2/05			
	Massachusetts	9/25/03	Suspended - 2 years	9/25/03	No
Joseph A. Morris	Illinois	----------	Public Censure	1/13/05	----------
Robert Paul Muenchrath	Minnesota	9/28/00	Indefinite Suspension	9/28/00	No
Joseph Francis Muto	New York	5/3/02	Suspended - 7 years	1/28/03	No
Toritsefe Nanna	New York	8/4/04	Indefinite Suspension	8/4/04	No
Fuad B. Nasrallah	Michigan/Ohio	1/25/01	Indefinite Suspension	1/25/01	No
*Paul Ngobeni	Connecticut	2/24/06			

LIST OF SUSPENDED AND EXPELLED PRACTITIONERS

Thomas James O'Grady	Florida	4/17/02	Suspended - 5 years	4/17/02	No
Michael Imevbore Ojo	Houston, TX	12/2/05			
*Dennis F. Olsen	Washington	2/21/06			
Justin Jin-Lin Ong	Houston, TX	1/25/01	Expelled	1/25/01	No
Oleg Ordinartsev	Washington	6/27/05	Suspended - 2 years	6/27/05	No
Todd Norman Ostergard	Florida	2/18/04	Suspended - 90 days	2/18/04	No
Douglas D. Osterloh	Washington	11/24/04	Suspended - 5 years	11/24/04	No
Sheri B. Paige	Connecticut	11/4/04	Expelled	11/4/04	No
Maria Lara Peet	Florida	2/16/06			
Alfred Perez, Jr.	Los Angeles, CA	7/20/04	Expelled	7/20/04	No
Linda Irene Perez	San Antonio, TX	3/28/05	Suspended - 2 years	3/28/05	No
Horace Hugo Perez	District of Columbia/Virginia	9/15/03	Suspended - 60 days	9/15/03	No
James S. Phillips, Jr.	Kansas	10/22/04			
Ramon R. Pizzini-Amott	Florida/Puerto Rico	7/24/03	Suspended - 6 months	7/24/03	No
John S. Pomeroy	Massachusetts	7/15/05			
Robert E. Porges	New York	5/6/02	Expelled	5/6/02	No
Jose M. Quinones	Los Angeles, CA	----------	Suspended - 90 days	9/16/05	No
Johnny P. Ragasa	Hawaii	7/10/02	Suspended - 5 years	7/10/02	No
Anthony E. Ramos	District of Columbia/Florida	12/6/04	Expelled	7/25/05 11/15/05	No
Jose Louis Ramos	Los Angeles, CA	7/31/01	Suspended - 42 months	7/31/01	No
Kenneth R. Rastello	Michigan	8/10/00	Suspended - 180 days	8/10/00	No
Maritza Regalado	Florida	2/7/05	Suspended - 5 years	2/7/05	No
James C. Regan	Los Angeles, CA	1/30/06			
Rico C. Reyes	Florida	12/2/05	Indefinite Suspension	12/2/05	No
Antonio Reyes-Vidal	San Antonio, TX	----------	Suspended - 90 days	4/1/06	No
Frank William Ricci	Florida/Indiana	9/28/00	Expelled	9/28/00	No
David J. Rodkin	New York	11/8/05	Suspended - 6 months	8/22/05	No
Wayne Anthony Rodney	Pennsylvania	10/7/02	Suspended - 1 year and 1 day	10/07/02	No
Leon Rountree, Jr.	San Francisco, CA	1/25/01	Expelled	1/25/01	No
Sylvia Anita Ryan	District of Columbia	9/15/00	Suspended - 1 year	9/15/00	No
David S. Sabghir	New York	----------	Suspended - 6 months	9/24/97	No
Antonio Salazar	Washington	11/8/05	Suspended - 60 days	11/8/05	Yes - 1/20/06
Libby D. Salberg	New York	5/30/01	Expelled	5/30/01	No
Patrick P. Salley	Michigan	11/23/04	Expelled	11/23/04	No
Paige Elizabeth Samsky	Georgia	9/15/00	Suspended - 3 years	9/15/00	No
Jesus C. Sandoval	New Mexico	3/28/05	Expelled	3/28/05	No

LIST OF SUSPENDED AND EXPELLED PRACTITIONERS   Page 6 of 7

Alfred G. Santos	Houston, TX	11/4/04	Suspended - 14 months	11/4/04	No
Hiam David Schmerin	Los Angeles, CA	10/12/01	Indefinite Suspension	5/8/02	No
Andrew R. Sebok	Virginia	3/8/01	Suspended - 9 months	3/8/01	No
Louis A. Serio	Rhode Island	8/20/03	Suspended - 5 years	8/20/03	No
Catherine M. Shelton	Dalllas, TX	1/21/04	Suspended - 90 days	1/21/04	No
Joseph E. Sheridan	Los Angeles, CA	9/9/04	Expelled	12/7/04	No
Mitchell L. Singer	New York	2/13/06			
Jeanette Elizabeth Smith	Florida	12/20/04	Suspended - 1 year	12/20/04	No
John Roger Snow	North Carolina	9/18/01	Suspended - 5 years	9/18/01	No
Curtis L. Solomon	District of Columbia	10/23/00	Suspended - 30 days	10/23/00	No
Alex Sonson	Hawaii	2/14/05	Suspended - 90 days	2/14/05	No
Victor Sparrow	District of Columbia	----------	Suspended - 10 years	6/22/94	No
Gary M. Spraker	Indiana	5/7/01	Suspended - 2 years	5/7/01	No
Regina D. Steele	San Diego, CA	8/11/05			
Marshall D. Tandy	Arizona/ Florida	6/8/01	Suspended - 5 years	6/8/01	No
Eric Tarankow	Los Angeles, CA	1/10/05	Suspended - 2 years	1/10/05	No
Raymond B. Thompson	District of Columbia	----------	Indefinite Suspension	1/19/94	No
Barbara W.M. Tomaszweski	Washington	3/1/05	Expelled	3/1/05	No
Hoang N. Tran	Houston, TX	10/22/04	Suspended - 5 years	10/22/04	No
Jose Luis Trujillo			Suspended - 5 years	11/6/02	No
Mac Truong	New York	3/19/04			
David P. Ulin	Massachusetts	5/30/01	Indefinite Suspension	5/30/01	No
Ernesto Valdes	Houston, TX	5/29/03	Suspended - 5 years	5/29/03	No
James R. Valinoti	Los Angeles, CA	7/24/03	Suspended - 3 years	7/24/03	No
William P. Vela	San Francisco, CA	9/1/05	Suspended - 1 year	9/1/05	No
Rafael A. Velasquez	Florida	----------	Expelled	3/1/05	No
George A. Verdin	Los Angeles, CA/Hawaii	12/4/00	Indefinite Suspension	12/4/00	No
Rufino J. Villarreal	Nebraska	4/10/03	Suspended - 5 years	4/10/03	No
Sheldon Irwin Walker	New York	9/15/00	Expelled	9/15/00	
Ida Katherine Warren	Indiana	10/31/00	Indefinite Suspension	10/31/00	
Mark L. Weber	Los Angeles, CA	7/9/04	Suspended - 5 years	7/9/04	No
L. Ari Weitzhandler	Colorado	7/20/04			
Walter Wenko	Los Angeles, CA	3/8/01	Suspended - 5 years	3/8/01	No
Chester Lee Wheless	Dallas, TX	10/12/01	Suspended - 5 years	10/12/01	No
James Eduard White	Oregon	1/11/06	Expelled	1/11/06	No
Paul White *aka* Krishan Kumar	Washington	2/11/05	Suspended - 5 years	2/11/05	No
Robert A. Wilkinson	Georgia	9/18/01	Suspended - 3 years	9/18/01	No

LIST OF SUSPENDED AND EXPELLED PRACTITIONERS

Richard A. Williams	Connecticut	5/29/03			
Arthur G. Williamson	New Jersey	12/12/00	Expelled	12/12/00	No
Gregory S. Wilson	Washington	11/22/05	Expelled	11/22/05	No
Rex Wingerter	Maryland	11/14/05	Expelled	11/14/05	No
Frank D. Winston	San Francisco, CA	8/19/03	Suspended - 5 months	8/19/03	No
William Wright, Jr.	New Jersey	12/7/01	Expelled	12/7/01	No
Valerie L. Yaeger	Michigan	3/8/01	Suspended - 180 days	3/8/01	No
Richard P. Zipser	Michigan	3/16/05	Suspended - 180 days	3/16/05	No

APPENDIX III: U.S. ATTORNEY PRESS RELEASE ON IMMIGRATION FRAUD INDICTMENT

U.S. Department of Justice

United States Attorney
District of Maryland
Northern Division

Allen F. Loucks *United States Attorney* *Vickie E. LeDuc* *Public Information Officer*	*36 South Charles Street* *Fourth Floor* *Baltimore. Maryland 21201*	*410-209-4800* *TTY/TDD:410-962-4462* *410-209-4885* *FAX 410-962-3091* *Vickie.LeDuc@usdoj.gov*

MAY 12, 2005
FOR IMMEDIATE RELEASE

FOR FURTHER INFORMATION CONTACT:
VICKIE E. LEDUC, AUSA
(410) 209-4885

TWO LAWYERS INDICTED FOR IMMIGRATION FRAUD

BALTIMORE, Maryland - Allen F. Loucks, United States Attorney for the District of Maryland, announces today the unsealing of a 149-count indictment returned by a federal grand jury on April 26, 2005 charging two law firms and four individuals associated with those firms with conspiracy to commit immigration fraud in Maryland, Washington, D.C.,and Virginia during a four-year period from April 2001 until the present.

The law firms are the Law Offices of I. Jay Fredman, P.C., at 2120 L Street, NW, Suite 210, Washington, D.C., and Sergei Danilov and Associates, LLC. at 900 19th Street, NW, Suite 201, Washington, D.C. The individuals charged in the indictment include two attorneys, Irwin Jay Fredman, 72, of Bethesda, Maryland, and Sergei Danilov. 44, of McLean, Virginia, and two legal assistants, Elnur Veliev, 21, of Silver Spring, Maryland, and Alp Canseven, 30, of Washington, D.C. Except for Alp Canseven, all were arrested this morning. Veliev and Danilov have their initial appearances at 3:00 this afternoon in federal court in Baltimore.

The indictment alleges that the defendants profited from the use of fraudulent practices to thwart immigration laws in order to obtain work visas for alien clients who were charged legal fees as high as $22,000. Under the auspices of the Law Offices of I. Jay Fredman, P.C., and Sergei Danilov and Associates, LLC, the defendants prepared and filed on behalf of alien clients fraudulent labor certification applications with the Department of Labor (DOL) and fraudulent petitions for alien work visas, commonly referred to as "green cards," with the U.S. Citizenship and Immigration Services (USCIS). One of the fraudulent aspects of these applications and petitions was that the defendants listed Maryland businesses, including an employment agency, a pizza restaurant and a construction company, as the official sponsors for the alien applicants when, in fact, the owners of the businesses never agreed to sponsor them. Some of the documents filed by the defendants contained the forged signatures of the business owners and/or listed false work experience for the alien applicants.

The indictment further alleges that to facilitate the conspiracy some of the payments from the alien applicants were deposited into bank accounts controlled by companies formed by some of the defendants. One such company, formed by Alp Canseven and Sergei Danilov and Associates, LLC, is WCIS, LLC, d/b/a the Washington Center for International Solutions, at 900 19th Street, NW, Suite 201, Washington, D.C. Another company formed by Alp Canseven is USCMFS, Inc., at 5501 Baltimore National Pike, Baltimore, Maryland.

Both Sergei Danilov, a Russian national, and Elnur Veliev, an Azerbaijan national, have immigrant status in the U.S. as lawful permanent residents and are deportable if convicted of the allegations. Both Irwin Jay Fredman and Alp Canseven are U.S. citizens.

The defendants face a maximum of 10 years of imprisonment and a $250,000 fine as to each count of conviction.

United States Attorney Allen F. Loucks stated that "No one is above the law, especially those who are entrusted to enforce our laws. Our justice system depends on the integrity of lawyers and professionals to do their jobs ethically and fairly. This indictment ensures that unscrupulous attorneys who exploit the immigration laws in this post 9-11 era and sponsor aliens illegally will be prosecuted to the fullest extent of the law."

Gordon S. Heddell, Inspector General, United States Department of Labor, stated: "Abuse of the foreign labor certification program by unscrupulous law firms victimizes businesses that have a legitimate need for foreign labor. Attorneys who knowingly violate the law for their own profit will be held accountable for their fraudulent acts. My office is committed to maintaining the integrity and lawful use of the Foreign Labor Certification program."

"Today's arrests are the latest enforcement actions in ICE's ongoing effort to restore integrity to the U.S. immigration system," said Special Agent-in-Charge Cynthia O'Connell, who leads ICE investigation in Baltimore. "Through this initiative, we're aggressively targeting criminals responsible for the production of fraudulent documents and exploitation of the immigration system."

An indictment is not a finding of guilt. An individual or company charged by indictment is presumed innocent unless and until proven guilty at some later criminal proceeding.

The criminal charges in this indictment are the result of a joint investigation by the Department of Labor's Office of Inspector General and the United States Immigration and Customs Enforcement, Department of Homeland Security. The case is being prosecuted by Assistant U.S. Attorneys Martin J. Clarke and Joyce K. McDonald.

WHY "WALK THE LINE"?
EFFECTIVE, EFFICIENT, AND ETHICAL PRACTICES FOR IMMIGRATION PARALEGALS

by Jasmine Chehrazi and Matthew I. Hirsch, with contributions from Alison Walters[*]

In law firms of all types, paralegals play a prominent role in client relations, case preparation, and file administration.[1] In few areas of the law is this truer than in immigration.

Paralegals in immigration law firms often find themselves walking the line between activities that are permissible for paralegals and those for which a supervising attorney is responsible.[2] Setting a definitive line is very difficult but can be accomplished through the use of systems to define the scope of paralegals' duties, attributes to consider when hiring paralegals, how to make the best use of a paralegal's talents, and the ways paralegals, supervising attorneys, and clients can communicate.

This article offers suggestions on how paralegals can avoid crossing the line between permissible and impermissible practices,[3] not through a review of laws governing unauthorized practice[4] but through the study of better practices.

WHY NOT CROSS THE LINE?

It is often easier for a paralegal to reply directly and immediately to a client's question, offer analysis and strategy, make recommendations, and advise clients than to act as an intermediary between the client and the supervising attorney. Moreover, an experienced paralegal is often amply qualified to offer sound advice. Such action, however, simply is illegal.[5] All states have laws that prohibit the unauthorized practice of law and restrict paralegals and

---

[*] **Jasmine Chehrazi** has over 10 years of experience assisting with immigration cases at Maggio & Kattar, P.C. She is co-author of "Visa Arts for Visual Artists" and "Waivers for Foreign Medical Graduates in a Nutshell." Her previous American Immigration Lawyers Association (AILA) presentations include "A Paralegal's Role in the Preparation of Nonimmigrant Business Visas," "Successful Strategies for J Waivers," and "How to Obtain and Prepare Declarations in Support of Various Immigration Petitions and Waivers." Ms. Chehrazi attended Georgetown University for her bachelor's studies and also attended the Corcoran College of Art, George Mason University, and the University of the District of Columbia.

Matthew I. Hirsch is a solo practitioner in suburban Philadelphia. A former trial attorney for INS, Mr. Hirsch now specializes in employment- and family-based immigration. He is a past chair of AILA's Philadelphia Chapter and has served on numerous local and national committees. Mr. Hirsch was co-editor of AILA's 2006 Midyear Conference Handbook and associate editor of AILA's *Stanton Manual on Labor Certification*. His articles and updates have been published in *AILA's Immigration Law Today, The Visa Processing Guide and Consular Posts Handbook*, and various AILA conference handbooks. Since 1993, Mr. Hirsch has been adjunct professor of immigration law at Widener University School of Law.

Alison Walters is a senior paralegal at the Law Offices of Carl Shusterman in Los Angeles. She has over 10 years of experience in almost every aspect of business- and family-based immigration law and is a regular contributor to the online Shusterman Immigration Update and other publications. She holds a B.Sc. degree in international relations and linguistics studies (Russian, Swedish) and a diploma in management from the University of Surrey in the United Kingdom.

[1] J. Broderick, *An Emerging Model: Legal Assistant as Colleague*, in Leveraging with Legal Assistants: How to Maximize Team Performance, Improve Quality, and Boost Your Bottom Line (Arthur G. Greene, ed., 1996).

[2] American Bar Association (ABA) Model Rules of Professional Conduct, Rule 5.3.

[3] The unauthorized practice of law may be reported to the Office of Immigration Assistance Attorney General Hotline at (888) 587-0557. Illegal or unethical attorney practices may be reported to the ABA at *www.abanet.org/cpr/regulation/scpd/disciplinary.html*. The *ABA/NBA Lawyers Manual on Professional Conduct*, available at *www.abanet.org*, states, "A lawyer is subject to discipline if he or she assists a nonpayer in engaging in the unauthorized practice of law. For purposes of this prohibition, non-lawyers include not only those without legal training, but also disbarred, suspended, or out-of state lawyers not licensed in the jurisdiction."

[4] M. Lieberman, "Unauthorized Practice of Law by a Paralegal: What It Is and How to Avoid It," DCBA Briefs Online (2002) March 27, 2006, *available at www.dcba.org/brief/mayissue/2002/art40502.htm*.

[5] M. Newman & R. Ford, "Utilizing Immigration Paraprofessionals: The Ethical Considerations," in *Ethics in a Brave New World*, 15–27 (J. Pinnix, ed., 2004).

other support staff from acting too independently. Violations can subject a supervising attorney to disciplinary sanctions and malpractice claims and a paralegal to charges of unauthorized practice of law.

It can also be costly and inefficient for paralegals to counsel clients, work on cases without adequate supervision, and otherwise engage in activities that are within the province of attorneys. For instance, a paralegal in preparing a petition or preparing for a hearing might be unsure of exactly what documents and information are required. In such cases, a paralegal who is not well supervised might waste valuable time and money by pursuing case strategies, research, or evidence that is superfluous, inappropriate or even harmful.

Similarly, though an attorney may *trust* that a paralegal, especially one with years of experience, will be vigilant about maintaining client confidentiality,[6] but even a good paralegal may accidentally and innocently breach that confidence, thereby creating problems for the attorney-client relationship and exposing the attorney to ethical sanctions.

In order to prevent this, lawyers and law firms should have systems that help prevent unintended intrusions into the attorney's realm while also promoting effective and efficient paralegal practices.

Establishing Systems for Keeping Paralegals Effective, Efficient, and Ethical

Each immigration case should begin with a retainer agreement describing the legal services to be provided and the fees for those services. The agreement informs clients, attorneys, and paralegals of their respective roles and responsibilities. The document can include standard information about attorney-client relationships,[7] confidentiality,[8] dual representation,[9] and the nature of nonattorney assistance on the case[10] (that paralegals work under the supervision of an attorney and are therefore bound by the ethical and legal responsibilities arising from the attorney-client relationship).[11] A copy reminds the paralegal of his or her limits and role within a particular case.

An employee manual or office policy that reviews these same issues should be required reading. Moreover, paralegals should be asked to sign or initial a document confirming that they have read and understand the manual. There should be opportunities for questions and a review of scenarios with supervising attorneys where such issues arise. The policy should incorporate procedures that help the paralegal understand how these issues can be raised and to whom concerns may be brought, and also provide channels for confidential inquiries about attorney behavior and ethics and the limits of a paralegal's role. Similarly, an attorney joining a law firm should have resources available that provide a common understanding of the role of the paralegal at the firm.[12]

The Paralegal and the Evidence

A paralegal can be highly effective at the outset of a case. A well-trained paralegal can even lead the client interview and be responsible for putting together a complete record of relevant facts, such as current and former immigration status, education, work experience, family relationships, police incidents, and other factors germane to the analysis of immigration cases. To ensure that the paralegal does this properly, attorneys should have standard checklists for client interviews with several pages calling for general information as well as questions geared for particular case types.[13]

Written instructions from the attorney on the checklist ensure appropriate supervision. For instance, a checklist for an H-1B case might identify such common tasks as obtaining a copy of the beneficiary's degree and any necessary translations; it might remind the paralegal to copy in the supervising attorney on correspondence and to document any substantive communications from the client.

---

[6] R. Anteau & N. Wolff, "Keeping Secrets Secret: Safeguarding Client Confidentiality in Your Law Office," *ABA General Practice, Solo & Small Firm Division Magazine*, September 2000, *www.abanet.org/genpractice/magazine/sept2000/sep2000anteau.html* (accessed Mar. 27, 2006).

[7] H. Vyas, "Ethical Issues for Immigration Lawyers," *Ethics in a Brave New World*, 4–14 (J. Pinnix, ed., 2004).

[8] Anteau & Wolff, *supra* note 6.

[9] B. Hake, "Dual Representation in Immigration Practice," *Ethics in a Brave New World* 28–35 (J. Pinnix, ed., 2004).

[10] Newman & Ford, *supra* note 5.

---

[11] National Association of Legal Assistants, "Model Standards and Guidelines for Utilization of Legal Assistants-Paralegals," *NALA Model Standards* 2005, available at *www.nala.org/98model.htm*, (accessed March 27, 2006).

[12] *Id.* Among other limitations, paralegals cannot establish attorney-client relationships, set legal fees, give legal opinions or advice, or represent a client before a court.

[13] For sample checklists and other helpful law office documents, see *AILA's Immigration Practice Toolbox*, Second Ed. (2006) with CD-ROM, available at *www.ailapubs.org*.

A Paralegal's Role in Spotting Legal Issues

Connected to his or her role in the collection of evidence, the paralegal detects issues that require research, legal advice, or other attorney intervention. To be effective in this role, the paralegal must sufficiently understand the law, and be able to locate and use statutes, regulations, and Web and other resources, such as AILA InfoNet. The supervising attorney and law firm must be clear that the paralegal must be familiar with the laws and regulations and keep informed of current developments.

This aspect of a paralegal's work does not encroach on the role of the attorney; rather, it equips the paralegal with an understanding of the law for more ready identification of issues that require the attorney's intervention.

The Paralegal's Role in Completing Forms

A common responsibility for immigration paralegals is to complete immigration forms. Though some may think of this as merely routine, anyone who has made an error on forms understands their critical importance. Some attorneys and paralegals will have clients sign a form in blank or allow a client to sign a form without fully explaining the contents and significance of the form. These practices are unacceptable practices and unethical; they can lead to future problems. Even if it is time-consuming to explain all parts of forms to clients, many mistakes, misunderstandings, and legal violations can be avoided if paralegals and attorneys take this step.

The Paralegal's Role in Providing Client Copies

Paralegals often transmit a copy of a draft final petition, or other filing to the client. The supervising attorney must ensure that this important task is done. To preserve confidentiality, prevent lost documents, and respect client preferences, the standard checklists should indicate to whom copies should be sent.

The Paralegal's Role as Messenger

Paralegals from communicate legal advice from the supervising attorney to a client. As a messenger, the paralegal should be clear that the legal advice is from the attorney, *not* his or her own advice. Ideally, such communications should be in writing for record-keeping purposes.

Paralegals and attorneys can work together to identify the most effective and ethical ways for attorneys to communicate the necessary legal advice. For example, if a paralegal drafts a memo, e-mail, or letter to a client that communicates advice or guid-

ance, the document should first be reviewed by the supervising attorney for any necessary revision, and then should go out over the attorney's name.

Templates for documents, such as task, document, and information checklists; memoranda to the file; or letters confirming client communications can be helpful tools for paralegals. AILA's *Immigration Practice Toolbox* is an excellent resource for attorneys and firms seeking to improve their office templates. The use of case management software also is helpful for maintaining records, communicating with clients, and helping paralegals walk the line between the legitimate paralegal role and encroaching on the attorney's prerogative.

Hiring Paralegals: Skills to Look for

When hiring a paralegal, a number of factors must be considered: individual strengths, communication skills, the ability to handle deadlines and pressure, organization, compatibility with others, prioritization, and of course personal character, integrity, and honesty. Some can be taught; others are part of a person's character and can be difficult to judge or test. At the heart of the hiring decision is the question of whether and in what way a paralegal is going to contribute to the strength of a law firm.

Handling Diverse Strengths

Paralegals come from a wide variety of ethnic, linguistic, socioeconomic, and educational backgrounds and, thus bring different skills, talents, and attributes to a law firm. Recognizing his or her strengths is a key to optimizing a paralegal's effectiveness.

For example, paralegals who were raised in another culture have a specific knowledge and respect for the ways of that culture. This helps them understand complex interaction with others from that culture. Paralegals who can communicate with clients in their native languages facilitate an open dialogue.

Candidates hold paralegal certificates, associate's degrees, or bachelor's degrees in a variety of academic areas. A paralegal coming from an administrative or secretarial background might possess highly developed organizational skills. Recognizing the qualities, strengths, and talents that spring from such diversity is important for hiring decisions.

Handling Communication

Paralegals generally need strong communication skills and should be comfortable with person-to-person contact. Paralegals must be able to build relationships of trust so that clients will communicate legally relevant information without feeling any distrust, anxiety, or shame. Here, an awareness of cultural issues that affect the nature and extent of communication can be helpful. For example, avoidance of eye contact is a sign of respect in some cultures; in others, it can be construed as reflecting insecurity or dishonesty.

Handling Clients

Supervising attorneys often rely on paralegals for routine communications with clients. This can lead to communication overload when anxious and frustrated clients engage in persistent patterns of frequent calls, e-mails, and unscheduled drop-ins.

In dealing with persistent and annoying client communications, a paralegal should realize that "clients are the purpose of our work, and not interruptions of it." Paralegals must understand what is at stake for clients. Anticipating the concerns of clients and addressing them with periodic updates, returning telephone calls and e-mails, and being proactive in contacting clients helps prevent persistent or inappropriate demands for information.

Handling Workload

A paralegal must know when he or she is overwhelmed or can take on more work. Some idea of workload can be gleaned from a review of case management summaries, revenues generated, client and coworker feedback, the quality of the paralegal's work, and how well records are kept. Just as paralegals should indicate when their workload is too great, they should indicate when they do not understand something, whether it is an attorney's comments or instructions, a client's answer, or some other communication.

Handling Problem Cases

Communication is extremely helpful to the ethical resolution of problem cases, whether the problems resulted from actions or inaction by the paralegal, the attorney, the government, the client, or some combination of these. At fault or not, a paralegal who senses that there is a problem must immediately alert the supervising attorney. This can be systemically accomplished using a simple internal-use form stating the date, description, and timing of the problem and suggestions for the problem's resolution, initialed by the person submitting the form. Copies of the form can be placed in the client's file and circulated as needed.

Handling Client Stress

Even when sympathetic to a client's plight, a paralegal cannot act as a client's therapist or confessor. The paralegal should not be the scapegoat or punching bag for a client who is frustrated and who wants to "vent" or blame the paralegal. Instead, a paralegal must be well equipped to defuse such situations and to manage pressure. A paralegal must remain sensitive to a client's circumstances so that he or she can fairly manage the client's expectations.

The paralegal and the supervising attorney must never inflate a client's expectations. An example of setting client expectations is a paralegal informing a client that he or she will call the client in a set amount of days to inform the client of the case status. This gives the client a date to look forward to and may encourage the client to refrain from making premature inquiries.

Handling Priorities and Multitasking

Contrary to popular belief, multitasking is inefficient.[14] An immigrant of sorts himself, the Syrian-born Publilius Syrus of Rome said, "To do two things at once is to do neither."[15] When a paralegal has an overlong "to do" list, it is difficult to know which task to do first. When every case and every task is important, the paralegal must determine the order in which to execute the tasks by effectively communicating with his or her supervising attorney, by employing common sense assessments, and by understanding the "process flow"[16] in various immigration procedures.

---

[14] "Multitasking and Task Switching," *NALA Model Standards*, University of Michigan Brain, Cognition and Action Laboratory, available at *www.umich.edu/~bcalab/multitasking.html*; P. Anderson, "Study: Multitasking Is Counterproductive," CNN.com/Career (Aug. 5 2001), available at *http://archives.cnn.com/2001/CAREER/trends/08/05/multitasking.focus/index.html*, accessed March 27, 1006.

[15] "Publilius Syrus." *Wikiquote., available at http://en. wikiquote.org/wiki/Publilius_Syrus (accessed* Mar. 27, 2006).

[16] Process flow refers to the standard steps that must be taken in a particular type of immigration case and the order in which the steps are generally taken, which are usually determined by immigration law and procedure, firm procedures, government processing times, and similar factors. An understanding of process flow helps paralegals gain perspective about where a specific case stands in the case type's typical process flow. Paralegals can help attorneys strategize how to make processes for different case types flow most efficiently. For instance, they can draw up charts, diagrams, and other explanatory models to identify current process

continued

Immigration case management software is a highly useful tool for organizing tasks. Some programs allow the user to assign a value or due date to a task to designate its priority. Regardless of the software selected, implementation can be a long and challenging process that requires both attorneys and paralegals to participate.

Training Paralegals and Keeping Them Effective

Internal Training

Throwing paralegals into the pool and seeing who can swim is not the best training practice. A training program for inexperienced paralegals should review U.S. immigration policy and law, and introduce governing regulations, manuals, and common research materials. Paralegal training will also usually include having the new paralegal "shadow" a more seasoned paralegal and gain hands-on experience by helping with tasks under close supervision and instruction.

Whether the paralegal is a new hire or a staff member being trained to assist in new ways, larger immigration law firms can coordinate the paralegal's training with several different staff members, with each training the paralegal in a different area of specialization. Whatever the firm size or the paralegal's experience, there should be one-on-one training with at least daily opportunities for the paralegal to present questions in an organized fashion.

External Training

Besides internal training, there are numerous organizations that offer educational programs and resources for training paralegals. Although such programs add cost to the training process, they are usually an excellent investment in a new paralegal.

Many state bar associations offer seminars on the fundamentals of U.S. immigration law. Although they may be often intended for attorneys from other fields with an interest in immigration law, they are often appropriate for paralegals who want to know more about immigration law and procedure.

Every year, AILA conducts conferences that cover immigration law fundamentals and also periodically offers seminars for immigration paralegals. AILA offers topic-specific conferences hosted by local chapters, an annual conference, Web conferences, and teleconferences.

Continuous and Regular Training

Continuous training is essential because immigration laws constantly change. The following suggestions can help maintain paralegal skills at high level and help attorneys who work with them:

- Updates on procedural changes should be forwarded to all staff, centrally printed, and organized by topic and date for easy firm-wide access.

- Paralegals should periodically conduct research, perhaps using AILA's InfoNet and reviewing statute and regulations, featured articles in *Interpreter Releases*, U.S. Citizenship and Immigration Services (USCIS) memos, etc.

- Attorneys should periodically hold staff meetings to review immigration procedure questions.

- Attorneys can ensure that appropriate opportunities for external professional development for paralegals, recognizing the value these add firm-wide; paralegals can debrief other staff members and take detailed notes for firm-wide distribution.

Retention: Keeping the Job Interesting

Goals and Reviews

It is important to have plans that encourage retention, measure success, and ensure adherence to ethical standards. Paralegals should work with their supervising attorneys to identify short- and long-term goals, perhaps quarterly and annual goals, and should be regularly reviewed by supervising attorneys. Firms may consider the use of self-evaluation and firm evaluation questionnaires as part of a paralegal's performance review to facilitate open discussions of job-related issues.

The Big Picture

Attorneys should step back to consider the big picture by analyzing ethical practices, process flow, the use of case management software, the design and use of systems for improving productivity, diversifying assignments, cross-training, and other ideas to keep a paralegal interested in the job. Paralegals should be part of the process of analyzing the big-picture issues. Who better to help search for, propose, and implement new and better ways of accomplishing tasks and projects and resolving problems than paralegals themselves?

Even a paralegal's simple suggestion that an attorney estimate how long it will take to review the

flow and analyze how to streamline processes and eliminate unnecessary steps.

paralegal's work product can do wonders for the firm's big picture, because the paralegal can more efficiently prioritize work, estimate case preparation time, update clients, and avoid stress and delays.

Looking at the big picture may also allow paralegals to consider how they may become involved in new tasks and cases. In complicated situations requiring legal advice, more experienced paralegals can draft correspondence, which can then be finalized, signed, and transmitted by supervising attorneys. Attorneys may consider offering paralegals conceptual revisions, rather than word-for-word corrections, so that paralegals can offer their own solutions for attorney consideration. Paralegals can be helpful in client receptions and other business development activities. Paralegal support also should be taken into account; a paralegal's ability to rely on other support staff, even if only occasionally when the workload is particularly large, can go a long way toward relieving and retaining the paralegal. Part of the big picture approach in mid-sized and large firms may be to analyze flexibility to shift work between paralegals in the interest of fairness and efficiency.

What It's Worth: Compensation

Paralegal compensation varies significantly depending on years of experience; there is a wealth of information on the Internet about standard paralegal pay.[17] Aside from standard compensation, paralegals also may benefit from bonuses, tuition reimbursement, attendance at immigration courses, and standard transportation benefits.

Most paralegal positions are not exempt from the overtime protection requirement of the Fair Labor Standards Act (FLSA) and, thus, qualify for overtime pay for all hours worked over 40 in a workweek.[18] However, at present, in addition to a salary of at least $23,660 per year or $455 per week,[19] a professional position may be exempt from FLSA overtime protection if the position meets the following DOL-prescribed criteria:

- The employee's primary duty must be the performance of work requiring advanced knowledge;

- The advanced knowledge must be in a field of science or learning; and

- The advanced knowledge must be customarily acquired by a prolonged course of specialized intellectual instruction.[20]

Regardless of the specifics of their compensation, paralegals should not be rewarded for excessive independence, since that might encourage paralegals to avoid the necessary supervision.

CONCLUSION

Drawing the line between ethical and unethical paralegal practices is beyond challenging. Thankfully, what is known of this line can be reinforced through systems that safeguard the ethical partnership between attorneys and paralegals. These systems hinge upon understanding the scope of paralegal duties, the strengths and limitations of each paralegal, fair paralegal compensation, and issues essential to paralegal hiring, training, and development. Through this understanding, the practice of immigration law as a whole can be made more efficient, effective, and, ethical.

---

[17] For example, the National Federation of Paralegal Association offers a Paralegal Compensation and Benefits Report available at *www.nfpa.org*.

[18] "Exempt/Non-Exempt," *WSPA Paralegal Compensation* (Feb. 21, 2006), *www.wspaonline.com/exempt.htm* (*accessed* Mar. 27, 2006).

[19] "DOL's Fair Pay Overtime Initiative," *Fair Pay*. U.S. Department of Labor Employment Standards Administration Wage and Hour Division, at *www.dol.gov/esa/regs/compliance/whd/fairpay/* (*accessed* Mar. 27, 2006).

---

[20] Fact Sheet #17D: Exemption for Professional Employees Under the Fair Labor Standards Act (FLSA), Fair Pay Fact Sheet by Exemption, available at *www.dol.gov/esa/regs/compliance/whd/fairpay/fs17d_professional.htm*. Other DOL FairPay Fact Sheets describe further potential grounds for FLSA exemption.

RELIEF FROM REMOVAL: DOES IT CURRENTLY EXIST?

by Vikram K. Badrinath and Barbara Hines[*]

INTRODUCTION

Practitioners who represent noncitizens in removal and deportation proceedings before the immigration courts and Board of Immigration Appeals (BIA) may begin the first battle against the underlying charges of inadmissibility or deportability. Such a battle may focus on issues such as the divisibility of statutes, lack of evidence against a noncitizen, or a particular provision of federal immigration law. However, once the government has met its burden of demonstrating an alien's inadmissibility or deportability, the weighty question of relief from removal first emerges. Nevertheless, a skilled practitioner should always begin his or her initial case analysis with an overview of the government's ability to demonstrate deportability as well as all potential applications for relief. For example, an application for adjustment of status may require first having an approved immigrant visa petition—a process that may take several months to adjudicate before U.S. Citizenship and Immigration Services (USCIS). Such an application may also entail the completion of a medical examination, obtaining misplaced tax return information for affidavit of support requirements, certified birth certificates, and other documentation not easily obtainable. These needs are often further complicated when a noncitizen is detained by U.S. Immigration and Customs Enforcement (ICE) in a remote location thousands of miles away from his or her home, family, or employment. Understanding the intricacies and subtleties of various relief applications, as well as the mechanics of relief, therefore, is often the foundation upon which a winning removal or deportation case is built. This article aims to inform practitioners of the various subtleties of the most common relief applications, potential pitfalls, and approaches toward obtaining a successful grant.

BACKGROUND

Historically, lawful permanent residents (LPRs) could seek a variety of applications for relief before an immigration judge, such as adjustment of status, waivers of deportability, suspension of deportation, and voluntary departure. Such applications often entail navigating a complex labyrinth consisting of regulations, immigration law, circuit court decisions, and the like. Under current law, an LPR may seek relief from removal in the form of cancellation of removal, former INA §212(c) relief, adjustment of status, or asylum/withholding of removal.

SECTION 212(c) RELIEF

Section 212(c) relief was enacted in 1952[1] to replace the Seventh Proviso to §3 of the Immigration and Nationality Act of 1917.[2] Under the 1917 provisions, a noncitizen otherwise inadmissible under certain provisions of the predecessor to INA §212(a), but returning after a temporary absence to an unrelinquished domicile of seven consecutive years could be admitted in the discretion of the Attorney General under such conditions he might prescribe. This relief was not yet limited to "aliens lawfully admitted for permanent residence." In 1952, however, Congress limited a noncitizen's eligibility for §212(c) relief by requiring that only a noncitizen who was lawfully admitted for permanent residence and had maintained a lawful domicile of seven years could apply.

Under former §212(c) relief, an LPR who was deportable or excludable from the United States could seek a discretionary waiver to avoid deportation or exclusion. Such a waiver required the LPR to demonstrate, inter alia, that the favorable factors present in a particular case outweighed the negative factors of record, and that the noncitizen merited relief as a matter of discretion. Although §212(c) relief was a waiver listed in the grounds of inadmissibility, an LPR seeking

[*] **Vikram Badrinath** has practiced immigration law for more than 10 years. He is a certified specialist in immigration and nationality law by the State Bar of California, Board of Legal Specialization. He has litigated cases before the U.S. court of appeals and U.S. district courts, as well as the immigration courts and BIA. Mr. Badrinath has received an award from the U.S. Department of Justice for his pro bono work before the BIA.

Barbara Hines has practiced in the field since 1975 and is board-certified in immigration and nationality law by the Texas Board of Legal Specialization. She received AILA's Jack Wasserman Award for Excellence in Litigation (1992) and the AILA Texas Chapter Litigation Award (1993).

---

[1] Act of June 27, 1952; 66 Stat. 163; 8 USC §1182(c).

[2] Act of February 5, 1917; 39 Stat. 878, ch. 29, §3.

to waive a ground of deportability could apply[3] for such a waiver provided that he or she could demonstrate that the underlying ground of deportability (rather than the offense itself) had a "comparable" ground of inadmissibility.[4] In this regard, underlying grounds of deportability such as "entry without inspection," firearms convictions, and failure to register changes of address were not grounds of deportability with a corresponding ground of inadmissibility, and hence could not be waived under §212(c).[5] Recently, the BIA has "backtracked" on the previously understood application of §212(c) relief, to preclude its use by individuals charged with being deportable from the United States under INA §101(a)(43)(A) (sexual abuse of a minor) classification,[6] as well as under INA §101(a)(43)(F) (crime of violence) classification.[7] As of the writing of this article, these cases are currently under additional litigation, and it remains to be seen

whether the BIA's holdings will withstand judicial scrutiny. Because the BIA appears to be "chipping" away at the continued scope and applicability of §212(c) relief, practitioners will have to remain on guard and provide justification to immigration judges in individual cases that there is a "comparable" ground of inadmissibility for the underlying ground of deportability.[8] To the extent that it can be argued that a particular ground of deportation could not conceivably have such an analogue among the grounds of inadmissibility, it may be possible to argue for the continued availability of §212(c) in particular cases.[9]

In 1996, Congress passed the Antiterrorism and Effective Death Penalty Act (AEDPA),[10] which effectively removed §212(c) for noncitizens deportable for certain enumerated reasons,[11] such as an "aggravated felony" conviction, controlled substances violations, firearms offenses, sabotage or espionage offenses, or two crimes involving moral turpitude for which both offenses are covered by former §241(a)(2)(A)(i).[12] Subsequently, approximately five months later, Congress passed the Illegal Immigration Reform and Immigrant Responsibility

[3] See, e.g., Francis v. INS, 532 F.2d 268 (2d Cir. 1976) (holding that Immigration and Naturalization Service's (INS's) narrow implementation of §212(c) relief violated the Equal Protection Clause because it irrationally granted relief to those permanent residents in exclusion proceedings who fortuitously departed the United States and sought to return, but not to those permanent residents who had never departed); Matter of Silva, 16 I&N Dec. 26 (BIA 1976) (holding that the Second Circuit's approach in Francis should be applied on a uniform, national level); see also Tapia-Acuna v. INS, 640 F.2d 223, 225 (9th Cir. 1981) (same).

[4] Matter of Hernandez-Casillas, 201 I&N Dec. 262 (A.G. 1991); see also Matter of Montenego, 20 I&N Dec. 603 (BIA 1992); Matter of Meza, 20 I&N Dec. 257 (BIA 1991).

[5] Matter of Wadud, 19 I&N Dec. 182 (BIA 1984) (noting that §212(c) is not available for certain grounds such as entry without inspection (EWI) charge and document fraud because no corresponding ground of excludability); Leal-Rodriguez v. INS, 990 F.2d 939 (7th Cir. 1993); Matter of Montenegro, 20 I&N Dec. at 605 (holding that §212(c) is not available for firearms charge because no corresponding ground of excludability); see also Matter of Esposito, 21 I&N Dec. 1 (BIA 1995); Matter of Jimenez, 21 I&N Dec. 567 (BIA 1996) (no §212(c) waiver for document fraud); but see Bedoya-Valencia v. INS, 6 F.3d 891, 894–95 (2d Cir. 1993) (concluding that §212(c) relief was available for EWI charge despite fact that no corresponding ground exists).

[6] Matter of Blake, 23 I&N Dec. 722 (BIA 2005) (holding that a noncitizen removable on the basis of sexual abuse of a minor is ineligible for a §212(c) waiver because the charged ground of removal has no statutory counterpart in the grounds of inadmissibility).

[7] Matter of Brieva, 23 I&N Dec. 766 (BIA 2005) (holding that a noncitizen removable on the basis of a crime of violence is ineligible for a §212(c) waiver because the charged ground of removal has no statutory counterpart in the grounds of inadmissibility).

[8] See, e.g., Matter of Wadud, 19 I&N at 183–84; Komarenko v. INS, 35 F.3d 432 (9th Cir. 1994) (holding that alien was not denied equal protection when eligibility for §212(c) relief was denied on grounds that firearms deportation charge and moral turpitude exclusion ground were not substantially identical).

[9] See, e.g., Bedoya-Valencia v. INS, 6 F.3d at 894–95 (placing great emphasis on the fact that entry without inspection was "a ground of deportation that could not conceivably have such an analogue" in the exclusion grounds). Arguably, with the passage of IIRAIRA, "entry without inspection" now has a comparable ground of inadmissibility under §212(a)(6)(A)(i) of the Act, and, thus, §212(c) should be available to waive its applicability. See Illegal Immigration Reform and Immigrant Responsibility Act of 1996, Division C of the Omnibus Appropriations Act of 1996 (H.R. 3610), Pub. L. No. 104-208, 110 Stat. 3009 (IIRAIRA).

[10] Pub. L. No. 104-132, 110 Stat. 1214.

[11] See §440(d) of AEDPA (Antiterrorism and Effective Death Penalty Act of 1996, Pub. L. No. 104-132, 110 Stat. 1214).

[12] AEDPA also altered the ground of deportability at §241(a)(2)(A)(i) (1996). See §435(a) of AEDPA; see Matter of Fortiz, 21 I&N Dec. 1199 (BIA 1998) (holding that a noncitizen deportable under INA §241(a)(2)(A)(ii), as an alien convicted of two or more crimes involving moral turpitude, and whose proceedings were initiated prior to AEDPA, was not ineligible for a §212(c) waiver unless more than one conviction resulted in a sentence or confinement of one year or longer pursuant to the former version of §241(a)(2)(A)(i)(II), prior to its amendment by AEDPA).

Act (IIRAIRA),[13] which was a substantial overhaul of the nation's immigration laws, changing not only the traditional regimes of deportation and exclusion, but also repealing altogether §212(c) relief, as it was previously understood.[14] With the passage of IIRAIRA, Congress officially removed §212(c) and replaced it with cancellation of removal.[15]

Nevertheless, after some five years of litigation, the Supreme Court invalidated former Immigration and Naturalization Service's (INS) retroactive interpretation of §440(d) of AEDPA eliminating §212(c), and held that noncitizens who were eligible for §212(c) relief at the time of their plea, remain eligible for such relief despite Congress's repeal of that provision, and regardless as to whether the individual was in deportation or removal proceedings.[16] Previously, the circuit courts of appeals had reached various conclusions regarding the continued availability of §212(c) relief depending upon such themes, inter alia, as reliance, the timing of the service of an order to show cause, and whether a detainer had been lodged against a particular noncitizen.[17] Although §212(c) relief was repealed with the earlier passage of IIRAIRA,[18] Congress substituted it with an entirely new form of relief called cancellation of removal, pursuant to newly enacted INA §240A(a).[19] Although §212(c) has been replaced, it still exists and is a viable form of relief for many noncitizens facing removal proceedings now and in the foreseeable future. In this regard, under St. Cyr,[20] noncitizens who entered a plea of guilty prior to the passage of AEDPA may be eligible for a waiver under §212(c) while in removal proceedings. Regrettably, courts have been reluctant to extend §212(c) waiver for noncitizens convicted before the passage of AEDPA, but after

trial, instead of the formal acceptance of a plea.[21] However, at least one circuit court has recognized that §212(c) relief still exists for individuals who were found guilty after trial, rather than by plea.[22] Hence, although the Supreme Court in St. Cyr did not specifically require a noncitizen to demonstrate reliance upon the availability of §212(c) relief, it remains possible to obtain §212(c) relief if a noncitizen can demonstrate actual, specific reliance upon the availability of §212(c) relief even in the case where the conviction was obtained after trial.

In addition, at least one circuit court of appeal has concluded that §212(c) relief remains for a noncitizen so long as an equal protection violation can be demonstrated.[23] In Cordes,[24] the Ninth Circuit found that the disparate treatment between Cordes and LPRs who are entitled to §212(c) relief under St. Cyr lacked a rational basis. Cordes was convicted on May 30, 1996, between the passage of AEDPA and IIRAIRA. Later, she became deportable as an "aggravated felon," but was not deportable at the time of the passage of AEDPA. As such, had Cordes committed a more serious crime that rendered her deportable from the United States, she would have been eligible for §212(c) relief, even though the offense had been later reclassified as an "aggravated felony" under §321 of IIRAIRA. The court found that this was an irrational distinction and permitted Cordes to seek §212(c) relief based on the equal protection violation between noncitizens who became "aggravated felons" retroactively and had committed deportable offenses at the time of their plea, and noncitizens who became "aggravated felons" retroactively and had not committed deportable offenses at the time of their plea.

Finally, once a noncitizen is deemed eligible for §212(c) relief, he or she is required to further demonstrate that: (1) he or she possesses at least seven years of an unrelinquished lawful domicile;[25] and (2)

---

[13] IIRAIRA, *supra* note 9.

[14] *See, e.g., Matter of Collado,* 21 I&N Dec. 1061 (BIA 1998), *Matter of Punu,* 22 I&N Dec. 224 (BIA 1998), *Matter of Lettman,* 22 I&N Dec. 365 (BIA 1998).

[15] *See* §304(a)(3) of IIRAIRA (adding §240A(a)).

[16] *See INS v. St. Cyr,* 533 U.S. 289 (2001) (holding that §212(c) relief remains for noncitizens who, at the time of their plea, were eligible for §212(c) relief); *see also* 8 CFR §1003.44(a) (2003).

[17] *See, e.g., Magana-Pizano v. INS,* 200 F.3d 603, 611 (9th Cir. 1999); *Wallace v. Reno,* 194 F.3d 275, 285 (1st Cir. 1999), *Alanis-Bustamante v. INS,* 201 F.3d 1303, 1305 (11th Cir. 2000).

[18] *See* IIRAIRA §304(b) (removing §212(c)).

[19] *See* IIRAIRA §304(a)(3) (adding §240A(a)).

[20] *St. Cyr,* 533 U.S. 289.

[21] *Armendariz-Montoya v. Sonchik,* 291 F.3d 1116 (9th Cir. 2002); *Lara-Ruiz v. INS,* 241 F.3d 934, 945 (7th Cir. 2001); *Chambers v. Reno,* 307 F.3d 284 (4th Cir. 2002); *Dias v. INS,* 311 F.3d 456, 458 (1st Cir. 2002); *Swaby v. Ashcroft,* 357 F.3d 156 (2d Cir. 2003).

[22] *Ponnapula v. Ashcroft,* 373 F.3d 480 (3d Cir. 2004).

[23] *Cordes v. Gonzales,* 2005 WL 2060851, *5 (9th Cir., Aug. 24, 2005).

[24] *Id.*

[25] *Matter of Anwo,* 16 I&N Dec. 293 (BIA 1977) (holding that "lawful unrelinquished domicile" refers to domicile subsequent to LPR status), *aff'd Anwo v. INS,* 607 F.2d 435 (D.C. Cir. 1975) (*Matter of Hinojosa,* 17 I&N Dec. 34 (BIA *continued*

the social and humane factors[26] present outweigh the negative factors and the noncitizen's undesirability of being an LPR. Although the scope and extent of §212(c) has been unclear, the continued availability of §212(c) relief is an evolving and fluid process. In this regard, practitioners may continue to build on the foundations laid in cases such as *St. Cyr, Ponnapula*,[27] and *Cordes*, and seek out this form of relief where noncitizens have *specifically* relied upon such relief, where an equal protection violation exists, or fundamental fairness and due process was violated at some point in the process to remove a noncitizen from the United States.[28] Finally, practitioners may wish to explore filing an affirmative application for §212(c) relief with a district director *before* the commencement of formal removal proceedings.[29] Such an approach may yield more successful results, avoid detention, years of litigation, and thorny legal issues before the courts.

CANCELLATION OF REMOVAL RELIEF

While the number of noncitizens who are eligible for §212(c) relief will diminish with time, a new form of relief has been enacted to take its place. With the repeal of §212(c) relief, Congress enacted §240A(a), known as "Cancellation of Removal for Certain Permanent Residents." This new form of relief, although seemingly codified and strict, is open to interpretation. As such, novel issues as to its scope and applicability are continually arising. Since its advent, the BIA and the circuit courts of appeals have begun the process to interpret its subtleties.

Like its predecessor under §212(c), cancellation of removal is a form of discretionary relief that permits an immigration judge to "cancel" the removal of an LPR. If an application for cancellation of removal is granted, the LPR maintains his or her residence status, and the

grounds of either inadmissibility under INA §212 or deportability under INA §237 are waived except for terrorism and the persecution of others.[30] Unlike the former §212(c) waiver inadmissibility, there is no requirement of a "comparable ground of inadmissibility" in order to qualify for §240A(a) relief.[31] In addition, unlike former §212(c) relief, an LPR may only file for cancellation of removal after jurisdiction vests with an immigration judge after the commencement of removal proceedings, and when a Notice to Appear (Form I-862) is officially filed.[32]

The three basic statutory requirements to qualify for cancellation of removal are: (1) lawful admission for permanent residence for at least five years; (2) continuous residence in the United States for at least seven years after having been admitted in any status; and (3) absence of an "aggravated felony" conviction.[33] Although not specifically listed in the statute, the BIA has noted that a noncitizen must also demonstrate that he or she warrants a favorable exercise of discretion, and that the previous concepts and general standards governing the merits of a §212(c) application apply equally to applications for relief under INA §240A(a).[34]

In order to apply for cancellation of removal, an applicant must be a permanent resident for at least five years at the time of the application for cancellation of removal. Recently, the BIA has reiterated its well-established position and held that an application for relief is a "continuing" application.[35] Hence, a

---

1979) (noting that the seven years of lawful domicile may continue to accrue while a noncitizen is outside of the United States).

[26] *Matter of Marin*, 16 I&N Dec. 581 (BIA 1978) (noting factors to be considered in assessing whether to grant a waiver under §212(c) of the Act).

[27] *Ponnapula*, 373 F.3d 480.

[28] *See, e.g., United States v. Leon-Paz*, 340 F.3d 1003 (9th Cir. 2003) (holding that a deportation proceeding was fundamentally unfair and was subject to collateral attack where a noncitizen had been misadvised by an immigration judge).

[29] *See* 8 CFR §1212.3(b) (noting that an application may file an affirmative application for §212(c) at any time prior to departure from the United States).

[30] INA §§240A(c)(4) and (5). There are other grounds of ineligibility, but they apply primarily to non–permanent resident cancellation.

[31] *See, e.g., Matter of Blake*, 23 I&N Dec. 722 (BIA 2005).

[32] *See* 8 CFR §1240.20(b); *see generally Matter of G–N–C–*, 22 I&N Dec. 281 (BIA 1998) (noting that once a notice to appear is filed, exclusive jurisdiction vests with an immigration judge over motions and applications for relief).

[33] INA §240A(a).

[34] *Matter of C–V–T–*, 22 I&N Dec. 7 (BIA 1998) (noting that an immigration judge should consider equities such as length of residency (especially if begun at an early age), family ties, employment, rehabilitation, property ties, community service); *see also Matter of Marin*, 16 I&N Dec. 581, 584–85 (BIA 1978).

[35] *Matter of Ortega-Cabrera*, 23 I&N Dec. 793 (BIA 2005) (holding that because an application for cancellation of removal under INA §240A(b)(1) (2000) is a continuing one for purposes of evaluating a noncitizen's moral character, the period during which good moral character must be established ends with the entry of a final administrative decision by the immigration judge or the BIA).

noncitizen should be able to argue that the five-year requirement of lawful permanent status continues to accrue until the time the application is determined or considered by an immigration judge or the BIA. While a noncitizen's satisfaction of the seven-year requirement is subject to the "stop-time" rule,[36] a noncitizen may continue to accrue five years of lawful permanent resident status until such time his or her application is finally considered. As with its predecessor under §212(c), LPR status that was obtained through fraud or deceit is not considered a "lawful" admission, and, thus, cannot be used toward fulfilling the five-year residency requirement.[37] Ordinarily, a noncitizen's accrual toward the five-year residency requirement begins as of the date the noncitizen is admitted for LPR status.[38] However, in certain cases, a noncitizen may accrue time prior to his or her date of adjustment, such as noncitizens who adjust under the Cuban Refugee Adjustment Act of 1966.[39] In such cases, noncitizens receive 30 months of retroactive residency, or the date of the noncitizen's last arrival in the United States, whichever is later.[40]

Although more applicants for cancellation of removal relief under INA §240(a) may easily meet the five-year permanent residency requirement, many noncitizens may find difficulty in demonstrating that they fulfill the seven-year continuous residency requirement. At the outset, it is important to note that the statutory language of continuous residency under §240A(a)(2) differs from that of former §212(c) relief. Under §212(c), there were conflicting administrative and judicial opinions regarding when residence began and if unlawful residence or temporary residence could be counted.[41] In contrast, however, the cancellation of removal statute only requires continuous residence "after having been admitted in any status." Hence, if a person is lawfully admitted in any status, he or she be-

gins to accrue continuous residence for cancellation purposes, regardless of whether he or she subsequently falls out of status at a later date. In *Matter of Blancas*,[42] the BIA held that a noncitizen who had been admitted to the United States with a border crossing card, who remained in the United States after the expiration of his authorized stay and subsequently adjusted status to that of an LPR, began to accrue continuous residence for cancellation purposes effective as of the date of his original admission with a border crossing card. The BIA reached this conclusion based on the plain language of the statute that requires only a lawful admission, and not the maintenance of status after admission.[43] Under the *Blancas* rule, all of the following individuals would be considered to be eligible for cancellation of removal under INA §240A(a): (1) a noncitizen admitted on a B-2 tourist visa for one year, followed by two years of being out-of-status, followed by LPR status for five years; (2) a noncitizen admitted on an F-1 student visa, followed by permanent resident status for five years; and (3) a noncitizen admitted for temporary resident status for two years followed by five years of permanent resident status. As the statute requires "continuous residence," issues of abandonment of residency may arise in cancellation cases that may affect both the underlying determination of LPR status and continuous residence for cancellation purposes. However, "continuous residence" in other statutory contexts does not require actual physical presence during the entire required period of residence.[44] In addition, practitioners may wish to argue that a minor can use the residence of his or her parents to establish continuous residency (*i.e.*, imputed residency) for cancellation purposes. This issue has arisen in situations in which the cancellation applicant does not have the seven years of continuous residence at the time of application. Because the statute requires seven years of residence "after having been admitted in any status," two indexed and unpublished BIA decisions have both held that a minor who enters the United States without being inspected cannot count his parents' residence because the statute requires a legal admission before residence may begin to accrue.[45]

---

[36] *See* INA §240A(d)(1); *see also* 8 CFR §1240.20(a) (2003).

[37] *Matter of Koloamatangi*, 23 I&N Dec. 548 (BIA 2003). However, it is possible that any underlying fraud could be cured by an INA §237(a)(1)(H) waiver. In such instance, an applicant could apply for cancellation of removal to waive additional grounds of removability. *See* discussion, *infra*, regarding multiple waivers.

[38] Under INA §216, conditional LPRs accrue time retroactively as to the original adjustment date, provided that the condition is removed.

[39] Pub. L. No. 89-732.

[40] *See Matter of Rivera-Rioseco*, 19 I&N Dec. 833 (BIA 1988).

[41] *See, e.g., Pritchard-Ciriza v. INS*, 978 F.2d 219 (5th Cir. 1992).

---

[42] 23 I&N Dec. 458 (BIA 2002).

[43] INA §240A(a)(2) ("has resided in the United States continuously for 7 years after having been admitted in any status. . . .").

[44] *Compare* INA §240A(a)(2) *with* §§240A(b)(1)(A) and 240A(d)(2).

[45] *Matter of Rivera-Becerra* (BIA 1999) (available at 2003 WL 23270115); *Matter of Davila-Hernandez* (BIA 2004)

continued

Recently, the U.S. Court of Appeals for the Ninth Circuit concluded that a parent's admission for permanent residence is imputed to the parent's unemancipated minor children residing with the parent for purposes of establishing continuous residency for cancellation of removal purposes.[46] In *Cuevas*, the noncitizen had unlawfully entered the United States in 1985, at the age of one with his parents. His mother later obtained LPR status in 1990, when Cuevas was seven years old. Cuevas, however, did not obtain LPR status until 1997. In 2002, Cuevas committed an offense that rendered him deportable and, pursuant to the "stop-time" rule under §240A(d)(1), was unable to demonstrate seven years of continuous residence necessary to apply for cancellation of removal under INA §240A(a) since he was not lawfully admitted until 1997. Nevertheless, the Ninth Circuit concluded that Cuevas had sufficient continuous residence for cancellation purposes. In so holding, the Ninth Circuit noted the "high priority [given] to the relation between lawful permanent resident parents and their children," followed its prior holding in *Lepe-Guitron v. INS*,[47] and concluded that its earlier decision also imputed a parent's "admission" to the United States to that of the minor child. Accordingly, practitioners may be able to extend the *Cuevas-Gaspar* rule in other areas of the United States that recognized the doctrine of "imputed" actions from parents to minor children. Finally, it should be noted that a noncitizen LPR who has served 24 months in the Armed Forces and has been honorably discharged is not required to establish continuous residence, provided that he or she enlisted or was inducted while in the United States.[48]

In attempting to demonstrate fulfillment of the seven-year continuous residence requirement[49] in the United States after having been admitted in any status, some noncitizens will encounter difficulty due to two "stop-time" rules.[50] Previously, under INA §212(c), it was unclear as to when the seven-year unrelinquished domicile requirement was spe-

cifically tolled. In most contexts, it was thought to be tolled when an order of deportation or exclusion had become administratively final.[51] However, with passage of IIRAIRA, the statute now makes clear that a noncitizen can no longer continue to accrue time for cancellation of removal purposes after: (1) the service of a Notice to Appear (Form I-862); or (2) the commission of an offense referred to in §§212(a)(2) or 237(a)(2), 237(a)(4) that renders the noncitizen inadmissible under §212(a)(2).

Hence, the mere *service* of the Notice to Appear is sufficient to "stop" a noncitizen's accrual of time necessary for cancellation of removal.[52] It is important to emphasize that it is not the issuance (which could be at an earlier time), nor the filing of the Notice to Appear (which could be later), that will trigger the "stop-time" rule. Because a noncitizen's residence may be cut-off, it is important to review the Notice to Appear to ensure it has been properly served and it is not procedurally deficient. In this regard, a Notice to Appear that has not been properly served may serve as a basis to challenge the application of the "stop-time" rule. Moreover, challenging a Notice to Appear on procedural grounds and obtaining a successful termination may permit the noncitizen client to continue accrual of the required time for cancellation purposes. In this regard, the Notice to Appear that ends continuous residence must also be the one that forms the basis of the current removal hearing.[53] Moreover, it must be a Notice to Appear with a clearly sustainable charge.[54]

Finally, it should be noted that although the statute makes reference to a "notice to appear [served] under §239(a)," the "stop-time" rule has been held to encompass Orders to Show Cause (Form I-221),[55] used previously for noncitizens placed into deporta-

---

(available at 2004 WL 2943458), distinguishing *Lepe-Guitron v. INS*, 16 F.3d 1021 (9th Cir. 1993).

[46] *See Cuevas-Gaspar v. Gonzales*, 430 F.3d 1013 (9th Cir. 2005).

[47] 16 F.3d 1022–24 (9th Cir. 1993).

[48] INA §240A(d)(3).

[49] *See Matter of Bautista-Gomez*, 23 I&N Dec. 893 (BIA 2006) (holding that a noncitizen seeking to reopen proceedings must demonstrate prima facie eligibility under "stop-time" rules pursuant to §240A(d)(1)).

[50] INA §240A(d)(1).

[51] *See, e.g., Jaramillo v. INS*, 1 F.3d 1149 (11th Cir. 1993) (en banc).

[52] INA §240A(d)(1).

[53] *Matter of Cisneros-Gonzales*, 23 I&N Dec. 668 (BIA 2004).

[54] *Matter of Moreno-Chavarin*, 24 *Immigr. Rptr.* B1-138 (BIA 2002) (available in LEXIS Board of Immigration Appeals (BIA) & AAU Non-Precedent Decisions database).

[55] *Matter of Mendoza-Sandino*, 22 I&N Dec. 1236 (BIA 2001) (holding that a noncitizen may not accrue the requisite seven years of continuous physical presence for suspension of deportation after the service of the Order to Show Cause and Notice of Hearing (Form I-221), as service of the Order to Show Cause ends continuous physical presence under §240A(d)(1)); *see also Matter of Nolasco*, 22 I&N Dec. 632 (BIA 1999) (service of NTA ends time for §244(a)(1) relief).

tion proceedings. A special exemption exists for certain Nicaraguans, Salvadorans, Guatemalans, and former Soviet Block country nationals.[56]

Most noncitizens facing removal proceedings for a qualifying offense may encounter difficulty in establishing eligibility for cancellation of removal under INA §240A(a) due to the second "stop-time" rule. Specifically, the statute states, in pertinent part, that a noncitizen's time is stopped when he or she has "committed an offense referred to in §212(a)(2) that renders the alien inadmissible to the United States under §212(a)(2) or removable from the United States under §237(a)(2) or 237(a)(4), whichever is earliest."[57] Importantly, the BIA has concluded that only offenses under §212(a)(2) implicate the "stop-time" rule. The BIA has held that a firearms offense, a deportable offense under §237(a)(2)(C) is not one "referred to" under §212(a)(2), and hence, does not stop the accrual of residence for cancellation purposes.[58] Moreover, the BIA has held the statute requires an offense that renders the LPR "inadmissible," and hence, an offense that meets the "petty offense" exception at §212(a)(2)(A)(ii) does not trigger the "stop-time" rule.[59] Therefore, if a practitioner can demonstrate that a particular offense does not render a noncitizen inadmissible under §212(a)(2), continuous residence for cancellation purposes under INA §240A(a) will continue. In addition, the BIA has interpreted the provision to refer to only the "commission" of the offense, rather than the conviction of an offense.[60] In *Perez*,[61] the BIA held that the "stop-rule" rule encompasses offenses committed *before* passage of IIRAIRA. At least two federal courts have disagreed.[62] Practitioners may argue that because there is

no clear congressional directive that the "stop time" rule be applied to offenses pre-dating its enactment, the principles of retroactivity, as clarified in *INS v. St. Cyr*,[63] counsel against applying the "stop-time" rule to such offenses.[64]

Finally, in order to statutorily qualify for cancellation of removal under INA §240A(a), a noncitizen must demonstrate that he or she has not been convicted of an "aggravated felony" under INA §101(a)(43). This, perhaps, is one of the most problematic parts of the cancellation provision, as it will automatically eliminate an LPR's eligibility for relief under the statute. Hence, where possible, it is critical to challenge the government's classification of an offense as an "aggravated felony." The scope of this article, however, does not address the intricacies and complexities of the "aggravated felony" definition.[65]

Assuming an applicant can meet the above statutory requirements for cancellation, he or she must establish that he or she merits a favorable exercise of discretion. Currently, insofar as the BIA has increased the use of the "affirmance without opinion"[66] procedure, and whereas the circuit courts of appeals have no jurisdiction to review discretionary determinations, presentation of a winning case before the immigration court is paramount. A carefully prepared application with extensive supporting documentation is essential. In addition, practitioners must allow adequate time in every case for trial preparation, both in terms of the documentation and testimonial evidence to be presented. The client's testimony may, in this regard, ultimately break or make the case. Family members, employers, pastors,

---

[56] *See* IIRAIRA §309(c)(5), as amended by the Nicaraguan Adjustment and Central American Relief Act (enacted as Title II of the District of Columbia Appropriations Act for fiscal year 1998, Pub. L. No. 105-100, 111 Stat. 2160 (Nov. 19, 1997) (NACARA)).

[57] INA §240A(d)(1).

[58] *Matter of Campos-Torres*, 22 I&N Dec. 1289 (BIA 2000).

[59] *Matter of Deanda-Romo*, 23 I&N Dec. 597 (BIA 2003).

[60] *Matter of Perez*, 22 I&N Dec. 689 (BIA 1999) (concluding that a retroactivity analysis is unnecessary where Congress's intent was express in the temporal reach of IIRAIRA's removal provisions). Note that retroactivity discussion in *Perez* was made in the absence of the Supreme Court's clarified *Landgraf* analysis in *INS v. St. Cyr*, and is, therefore, no longer persuasive authority on this issue.

[61] *Matter of Perez*, 22 I&N Dec. 689 (BIA 1999).

[62] *Henry v. Ashcroft*, 175 F. Supp. 2d 688 (S.D.N.Y. 2001); *see also Gonzales-Garcia v. Gonzales*, No. 04-60385 (5th continued

Cir., Nov. 15, 2005) (holding that the application of the "stop-time" rule to a pre-enactment offense would be impermissibly retroactive, and that the alien could apply for §212(c) relief).

[63] 533 U.S. 239 (2001); *see also Martin v. Hadix*, 527 U.S. 343 (1999) (discussing retroactivity principles and analysis).

[64] *See* IIRAIRA §304.

[65] For a comprehensive review and analysis of definition of aggravated felony, see D. Kesselbrenner & L. Rosenberg, *Immigration Law & Crimes*; A. Gallagher, "Immigration Consequences of Criminal Convictions: A Primer on What Crimes Can Get Your Client into Trouble," *Immigration & Nationality Law Handbook* 859 (AILA 2005–06 ed.); and M. Kramer, *Immigration Consequences of Criminal Activity: A Guide to Representing Foreign-Born Defendants* (AILA 2005).

[66] *See* 8 CFR §1003.1(a)(7).

and members of the community can provide important testimony and shed light on the subtleties of the client's character and the social and humane aspects of the case. In addition, expert witnesses can evaluate a client's rehabilitation, remorse, danger to the community, and equities.

In order to demonstrate the client merits a favorable exercise of discretion, it is necessary to conclusively show that the positive factors outweigh the negative factors present. As noted previously, an immigration judge must weigh a variety of factors in assessing whether a particular applicant should be granted relief; the general standards employed in assessing a waiver under former INA §212(c) are applicable in the cancellation of removal context.[67]

Unlike its predecessor under former INA §212(c), the BIA has held there is no requirement that a noncitizen demonstrate "unusual and outstanding equities" to overcome serious criminal charges.[68] Moreover, in light of the fact that the "unusual and outstanding" equity test evolved in the context of noncitizens convicted of "aggravated felony" offenses, and inasmuch as "aggravated felons" are rendered statutorily ineligible to apply for cancellation of removal relief under INA §240A(a), this requirement may no longer be necessary. In assessing an application for relief, however, all factors must be considered based on the totality of the evidence. Hence, a criminal conviction is a "serious adverse factor" that is analyzed based upon its recency and severity.[69] Unlike the consideration of a criminal conviction to establish deportability in which the court may *not* go behind the record of conviction, the court may consider the circumstances of the offense in the exercise of discretion. Thus, practitioners should review the indictment, the police report, the pre-sentencing report, and any other documents relating to the crime and prepare the client for questioning by the government or the court.

Lastly, an LPR may obtain a grant of cancellation of removal under INA §240A(a) only once.[70] Accordingly, before "using" the one-and-only cancella-

tion of removal relief, a noncitizen facing removal proceedings should aggressively defend the matter on any available procedural or substantive issues such as challenges to the charged grounds of deportability, defects in the Notice to Appear, divisibility of the statute, Department of Homeland Security's (DHS) inability to meet its burden of proof, and so forth. Or, the noncitizen may want to consider pursuing other available forms of relief such as adjustment of status. Additionally, the statutory prohibition against receiving a cancellation of removal waiver on the basis of a past grant of INA §212(c) or INA §244(a)(1) (suspension of deportation) is unclear and remains to be litigated. Several arguments exists for the practitioner, ranging from impermissible retroactivity to an interpretation of the phrase "previously been" granted relief (*i.e.*, the phrase "previously" does not mean during the current hearing or simultaneous hearing). These issues remain to be explored in the context of future litigation.

ADVANCED WAIVERS—§212(h)/§212(i)

Although many legal strategies remain in pursuing and obtaining cancellation of removal or §212(c) relief, ultimately a practitioner may conclude that a noncitizen cannot meet the stringent requirements of the "stop-time" rule or residence requirements. Hence, practitioners also should explore the possibility of other waivers, either separately or in conjunction with adjustment of status.[71]

Pursuant to INA §212(h), a noncitizen otherwise inadmissible under certain sections of INA §212(a) may seek a discretionary waiver of inadmissibility. This type of waiver is ordinarily combined with another application for admission, such as adjustment of status. Under §212(h), the Attorney General may waive the crimes of moral turpitude, multiple crimes with an aggregate five-year sentence, simple possession of marijuana offenses of less than 30 grams, and prostitution or other commercialized vice.[72] In actuality, the §212(h) waiver consists of two sepa-

---

[67] *Matter of Marin*, 16 I&N Dec. 581 (BIA 1978); *Matter of C–V–T–*, 22 I&N Dec. 7 (BIA 1998).

[68] *Matter of Sotelo-Sotelo*, 23 I&N Dec. 201 (BIA 2001); *cf. Matter of Edwards*, 20 I&N Dec. 191 (BIA 1990).

[69] *See, e.g., Marin*, 16 I&N Dec. 581; *Matter of Buscemi*, 19 I&N Dec. 628 (BIA 1988).

[70] INA §240A(c)(6).

[71] *See Matter of Azurin*, 23 I&N Dec. 695 (BIA 2005) (holding that a noncitizen who, prior to the 1996 amendments made to former §212(c), pleaded guilty to an offense that rendered him inadmissible for a crime involving moral turpitude, as well as removable based on his conviction for an aggravated felony and a firearms offense, may seek a waiver of his inadmissibility under §212(c) in conjunction with an application for adjustment of status, despite regulatory changes relating to the availability of §212(c) relief.)

[72] INA §212(h).

rate, distinct waiver provisions. First, under §212(h)(1)(A), a waiver is available if the noncitizen is inadmissible under INA §212(a)(2)(D), relating to prostitution offenses, or if the activities for which the alien is inadmissible occurred more than 15 years before the date of the noncitizen's application for admission or adjustment of status.[73] In addition, the noncitizen must demonstrate additional requirements, such that: (1) the noncitizen has been rehabilitated; and (2) the admission of the noncitizen would not be contrary to the welfare, safety, or security of the United States.

Alternatively, INA §212(h)(1)(B) provides the availability of a waiver in the case of an immigrant (*i.e.*, an adjustment of status application or admission of an "arriving alien") who is the spouse, parent, son, or daughter of a U.S. citizen or an LPR, if it can be established that the denial of admission would result in "extreme hardship" to the qualifying family member.[74] The BIA has interpreted "extreme hardship" narrowly and consistent with its prior interpretations in the context of relief under former §244(a) (suspension of deportation).[75] The consideration of such a waiver requires a balancing of the favorable and unfavorable factors present in a noncitizen's situation, such as: (1) length of residency (especially at an early age); (2) family ties in the United States; (3) history of employment; (4) property or other assets; (5) rehabilitation and remorse; (6) military service, volunteer work, or community service; and (7) the nature, recency, and severity of the criminal record, among others. Although the §212(h) waiver is discretionary in nature, the BIA must properly balance and consider all applicable factors.[76]

Subsequent to the passage of IIRAIRA, the availability of a waiver under §212(h) has been further limited. In this regard, no waiver may be afforded to an LPR if since the date of admission, the LPR has been convicted of an aggravated felony[77] or

has not *lawfully resided* continuously in the United States for at least seven years as of the date of initiation of proceedings to remove the alien.[78] Although an LPR convicted of an aggravated felony may not seek a §212(h) waiver, an LPR convicted on non–aggravated grounds may seek a §212(h) waiver, provided that he or she could prove seven years of *lawful continuous residence*. (The statute does not require seven years of admission as an LPR.) Hence, applicants admitted as a nonimmigrant or had temporary resident status, or other periods of lawful status, may argue that such periods of time should be counted toward the seven-year requirement.[79] In unpublished decisions, the BIA has held that a conviction for an "aggravated felony" at *any time* after admission also bars the use of a §212(h) waiver. Although the statute specifically refers to "such admission" (referring to and modifying the preceding phrase "as an alien lawfully admitted for permanent residence"), the BIA has interpreted this in a restrictive form. Additional litigation, therefore, is necessary to clarify this aspect of the statute. It is also important to note that noncitizens convicted of "aggravated felony" offenses who have not been admitted for lawful permanent residency, may obtain waivers under §212(h)(1)(B).[80] Most courts that have considered the issue have rejected equal protection arguments regarding the availability of §212(h) waivers of nonresident "aggravated felons" and LPR "aggravated felons."[81]

Practitioners also should note that the applicant must demonstrate seven years of *lawful continuous residence* in the United States prior to the initiation of proceedings. The initiation of proceedings has

---

[73] *Matter of Alarcon*, 20 I&N Dec. 557 (BIA 1992).

[74] *See Matter of Ngai*, 19 I&N Dec. 245 (BIA 1984); *Shooshtary v. INS*, 39 F.3d 1049 (9th Cir. 1994).

[75] *See, e.g., Matter of Mendez-Moralez*, 21 I&N Dec. 296 (BIA 1996) (noting that the factors enunciated in *Matter of Marin* in assessing an application for relief under INA §212(c) are the same for consideration of a §212(h)(1)(B) waiver).

[76] *Hassan v. INS*, 927 F.2d 465 (9th Cir. 1991).

[77] *Matter of Yeung*, 21 I&N Dec. 610 (BIA 1996); *Matter of Ayala*, 22 I&N Dec. 398 (BIA 1998) (noting that an LPR who was found to have been inadmissible or excludable at
continued

the time of entry, but convicted of an "aggravated felony" cannot now claim eligibility for a §212(h) waiver).

[78] *See* §348 of IIRAIRA. The provision became effective "on the date of enactment of [IIRAIRA] and shall apply in the case of any alien who is in exclusion or deportation proceedings as of such date unless a final administrative order in such proceedings has been entered as of such date"; *see also Matter of Pineda*, 21 I&N Dec. 1017 (BIA 1997) (holding that a noncitizen seeking to reopen proceedings to apply for §212(h) relief is subject to IIRAIRA's new limitations).

[79] *See, e.g., Matter of Blancas*, 23 I&N Dec. 458 (BIA 2002).

[80] *Matter of Michel*, 21 I&N Dec. 1101 (BIA 1998).

[81] *Moore v. Ashcroft*, 251 F.3d 919 (11th Cir. 2001); *Taniguchi v. Schultz*, 303 F.3d 950 (9th Cir. 2002); *De Leon-Reynoso v. Ashcroft*, 293 F.3d 633 (3d Cir. 2002); *Jankowski-Burczyk v. INS*, 291 F.3d 172 (2d Cir. 2002); *Lara-Ruiz v. INS*, 241 F.3d 934 (7th Cir. 2001); *Lukowski v. INS*, 279 F.3d 644 (8th Cir. 2002).

been held to constitute the filing of the charging document with the immigration court, rather than service of the Notice to Appear.[82] Hence, practitioners may be able to demonstrate additional periods of residency from the issuance of the charging document, to its actual filing with the immigration court, in order to establish eligibility for the §212(h) waiver. This difference is unlike the cancellation of removal "stop-time" rule discussed earlier, which stops the accumulation of continuous residence after *service* of the charging document. Importantly, there is no "stop-time" rule for the accrual of lawful continuous residence for §212(h) purposes based upon the commission of a qualifying inadmissible offense. Finally, it is important to note that §212(h) waivers are available in conjunction with an application for adjustment of status[83] or on a stand-alone basis for a noncitizen seeking admission to the United States, such as a returning LPR detained at a port of entry.[84]

In 2002, the Attorney General decided a case that laid the groundwork toward revising the standards upon which §212(h) relief is assessed.[85] In *Matter of Jean*, the Attorney General—in a case involving the beating and shaking death of an infant—held that a refugee seeking a waiver under INA §209(c) needed to demonstrate that

> extraordinary circumstances, such as those involving national security or foreign policy considerations, or cases in which an alien clearly demonstrates that the denial of adjustment of status would result in exceptional and extremely unusual hardship. . . .

This new, heightened standard would apply in offenses or crimes that are particularly "violent or dangerous." Moreover, the Attorney General noted that "depending on the gravity of the [noncitizen's] underlying criminal offense, such a showing might still be insufficient."[86]

Subsequently, the Attorney General codified the *Jean* rule into a regulation[87] affecting the scope of

INA §212(h)(2), rather than waivers under §209(c). Pursuant to newly codified 8 CFR §1212.7(d) (2003), noncitizens convicted of "violent or dangerous" offenses must now demonstrate "extraordinary circumstances." This has been further defined as either the existence of: (1) important national security or foreign policy considerations; or (2) exceptional and extremely unusual hardship to a qualifying family member should the application be denied. It is important to note that the regulation refers specifically to "violent criminal acts," rather than "crimes of violence." Although the regulation does not specifically define what constitutes "violent criminal acts," practitioners should argue that only extreme offenses—such as outlined in *Matter of Jean*—would require the heightened standard, such as the shaking and beating death of an infant. Lesser offenses—practitioners should argue—are not covered within the scope of the *Jean* rule. Moreover, the use of the term "dangerous" suggests a degree of violence that is higher than that of a "crime of violence" defined under 18 USC §16. Practitioners should emphasize the actual offense the Attorney General considered in *Jean* and use its graphic nature to illustrate the types of offenses that will necessarily trigger the heightened regulatory standard. In challenging the application of the regulation, practitioners should argue that: (1) the regulation is not retroactive to offenses, acts, or convictions, occurring before its enactment;[88] or (2) the Attorney General's regulation is ultra vires to the statute (*i.e.*, although the §212(h) waiver is discretionary in nature, the Attorney General may not impose new standards substantially and materially affecting the operation of the statute).[89]

In addition to the §212(h) waiver, the INA also affords a discretionary waiver for noncitizens who, through fraud or willful misrepresentation of a material fact, seek to procure, have sought to procure or have procured visas, other documentation, or admission into the United States.[90] This waiver, under INA §212(i), currently waives inadmissibility under INA §212(a)(6)(C)(i) for simple misrepresentations

---

[82] *Matter of Sanchez*, 20 I&N Dec. 223, 225 (BIA 1990); 8 CFR §1003.14(a); *see also Cortez-Felipe v. INS*, 245 F.3d 1054 (9th Cir. 2001).

[83] Note that in the Eleventh Circuit, an application for adjustment of status is not required. *Yeung v. INS*, 72 F.3d 843 (11th Cir. 1996).

[84] *See* Kramer, *supra* note 65, ch. 7.

[85] *Matter of Jean*, 23 &N Dec. 373 (A.G. 2002).

[86] *Id*.

[87] 67 Fed. Reg. 78675 (Dec. 26, 2002).

[88] Dec. 26, 2002; *see, e.g., INS v. St. Cyr*, 533 U.S. 289 (2001).

[89] *See, e.g., Morales-Izquierdo v. Ashcroft*, 388 F.3d 1299 (9th Cir. 2004) (holding that only an immigration judge may order removal against a noncitizen, and legacy INS/ICE's use of the reinstatement procedure under §241(a)(5) with immigration judge involvement was *ultra vires* to the statute).

[90] *See* INA §212(i).

or misuse of documents. Regrettably, Congress has not yet expanded the scope of the §212(i) waiver to include false claims to U.S. citizenship under §212(a)(6)(C)(ii)(I).[91] There is no waiver for this ground of inadmissibility *except* if the noncitizen reasonably believed that he or she was a U.S. citizen, both parents are (or were) U.S. citizens, and the noncitizen permanently resided in the United States prior to attaining the age of 16 years.

As with a waiver under §212(h), a noncitizen seeking a waiver under §212(i) must demonstrate that he or she is an immigrant seeking admission (*i.e.*, either in the case of adjustment of status or an LPR returning resident, "arriving alien"), if "extreme hardship" can be demonstrated to a qualifying family member if the noncitizen is the spouse, son, or daughter of a U.S. citizen. Unlike waivers under §212(h), however, a waiver under §212(i) is not permitted for an immigrant who is the *parent* of a U.S. citizen. Hence, parents who have children who are U.S. citizens and are immediately eligible to immigrate to the United States, but enter with fraudulent documents, or through misrepresentation, are permanently inadmissible and ineligible for a waiver under INA §212(i).[92] Prior to the passage of IIRAIRA, a §212(i) waiver was available if the noncitizen was a parent of a U.S. citizen or if the fraud occurred more than 10 years prior to the application for admission. In assessing whether to grant a waiver under §212(i), the immigration judge must again perform a balancing test and consider: (1) the presence of family ties in and outside the United States; (2) country conditions in the country of relocation; (3) financial impact of departure upon the qualifying family members; and (4) medical or other health considerations (including the availability of treatment or prescription medication).[93] Other considerations, such as length of residence in the United States and cultural relocation factors including language, employment, and culture, are useful in assessing whether to grant a §212(i) waiver. A central purpose of the §212(i) waiver is to reunite families, and hence, it is usually more liberally granted than

§212(h) waivers.[94] It should also be noted that the immigration judge may balance against favorable factors the actual fraud committed requiring the waiver in the first instance.[95] Finally, practitioners should be proactive in demonstrating their client's eligibility—both on a statutory and discretionary basis—insofar as Congress has specifically limited the ability of federal courts to review the Attorney General's decisions regarding these waivers.[96]

CONCLUSION

Although cancellation of removal has replaced former §212(c), the continued availability of §212(c) relief in removal proceedings is likely to be a major recourse to avoiding deportation and removal for noncitizens charged with criminal offenses. Despite having been severely limited in recent years, the use of the §212(c) waiver is important for those convicted of aggravated felony offenses, as well as those who are unable to demonstrate seven years of continuous residence in the United States before the commission of a qualifying "stop-time" offense or the service of the charging document to qualify for cancellation of removal. In addition, practitioners may expand and evolve cancellation of removal relief when confronted with novel and unique fact sets. Once statutory eligibility has been established, a practitioner should supplement the factual record with documentary and testimonial evidence that shed the best light on the noncitizen, his or her family, his or her life in the United States, his or her rehabilitation and remorse, and the social and humane factors present.

Finally, in other situations where a noncitizen may not be eligible for cancellation of removal or §212(c) relief, alternative applications for relief such as adjustment of status in conjunction with an appropriate waiver pursuant to §§212(h) or 212(i) may be sought. Despite the restrictions Congress has placed in the law over the past several years, practitioners still possess a variety of tools in order to keep a noncitizen charged with deportability inside the United States.

---

[91] *See* §344(a) of IIRAIRA, effective for "representations made on or after the date of enactment of [IIRAIRA]."

[92] *See, e.g., Okpa v. INS*, 266 F.3d 212, 318–19 (4th Cir. 2001); *Cervantes-Gonzales v. INS*, 244 F.3d 1001, 1005–06 (9th Cir. 2001).

[93] *Matter of Cervantes*, 22 I&N Dec. 560 (BIA 1999), *aff'd*, *Cervantes-Gonzales v. INS*, 244 F.3d 1001 (9th Cir. 2001).

[94] *See, e.g., Matter of Lopez-Monzon*, 17 I&N Dec. 280 (Comm. 1989); *Delmundo v. INS*, 43 F.3d 436 (9th Cir. 1994).

[95] *Matter of Cervantes*, 22 I&N Dec. at 569.

[96] *See* INA §242(a)(2)(B)(i).

WHAT YOU *STILL* NEED TO KNOW ABOUT §212(c)

by Jodi Goodwin, Ilana E. Greenstein, and Philip Smith[*]

BREAKING DOWN THE BASICS

Until 1997, §212(c) of the Immigration and Nationality Act of 1952 (INA)[1] contained a waiver of deportability or inadmissibility for long-time lawful permanent residents (LPRs). Despite the fact that §212(c) no longer exists, the waiver is still a potential form of relief for noncitizens. This article outlines the basics of what every practitioner should know about a waiver of inadmissibility pursuant to (the old) INA §212(c).

We begin with an overview of §212(c) and its historical counterparts. We move on to the repeal of §212(c) in 1996–1997, and the degree to which the waiver survived thereafter. And we conclude with discussions of some of the issues currently surrounding §212(c) relief: the reclassification of the underlying offense, the doctrine of the comparable ground, and the possibility of combining a §212(c) application with another application when §212(c) standing alone is not enough.

The Statute—INA §212(c) and Its History

The Constitution of the United States grants to Congress plenary power over immigrants, naturalization, and immigration laws.[2] Traditionally, immigration laws have included waivers of deportability or inadmissibility for LPRs. The Seventh Proviso of Section 3 of the 1917 Immigration Act, (the predecessor to §212(c)), was intended "as a 'humane' provision 'to permit the readmission to the United States . . . of aliens who have lived here for a long time and whose exclusion after a temporary absence would result in peculiar or unusual hardship."[3] The Seventh Proviso read: "(A)liens returning after a temporary absence to an unrelinquished United States domicile of seven consecutive years may be admitted in the discretion of the Attorney General, and under such conditions as he may prescribe."

Section 212(c) was modeled after the Seventh Proviso and enacted as part of the INA.[4] It read:

> Aliens lawfully admitted for permanent residence who temporarily proceeded abroad voluntarily and not under an order of deportation, and who are returning to a lawful unrelinquished domicile of seven consecutive years, may be admitted in the discretion of the Attorney General without regard to the provisions of paragraph (1) through (25) and paragraphs (30) and (31) of subsection (a). Nothing contained in this subsection shall limit the authority of the Attorney General to exercise the discretion vested in him under section 211(b).

---

[*] **Jodi Goodwin** is in private practice in Harlingen, Tex., concentrating solely in the area of immigration and nationality law. A graduate of St. Mary's University, she serves as chair of the AILA Texas chapter. Ms. Goodwin frequently speaks on the issues of employer compliance with immigration laws, immigration and family law, and various aspects of the immigration consequences of criminal convictions.

Ilana Greenstein practices immigration law at Kaplan, O'Sullivan and Friedman in Boston. She practices all aspects of immigration law, with a focus on appellate litigation. Ms. Greenstein holds a J.D. from Northeastern University School of Law, and a B.A. in Spanish and International Studies from Macalester College. She served on the board of directors of the Massachusetts Chapter of the National Lawyers Guild from 1996–2002, and on the steering committee of the Boston Bar Association's Individual Rights & Responsibilities section in 2000.

Philip Smith, a founding partner of Hecht & Smith LLP in Portland, Ore., is a member of the Tennessee and Oregon bars and is admitted to the U.S. District Court of Oregon, the Court of Appeals for the Ninth Circuit, and the U.S. Supreme Court. Mr. Smith is currently the AILA chapter chair for Oregon. Prior to life as a lawyer, Mr. Smith served as a Peace Corps volunteer in Sri Lanka.

[1] Immigration and Nationality Act of 1952 (INA), Pub. L. No. 82-414, 66 Stat. 163 (codified as amended at 8 USC §§1101–1524).

[2] *U.S. Const.*, art. I, §8, cl. 4.

[3] *Matter of Hernández Casillas*, 20 I&N Dec. 262, (BIA 1990), at note 3. *See also In re Hector Ponce de Leon-Ruiz*, 21 I&N Dec. 154 (BIA 1996).

[4] Adjudication of a §212(c) application involves a balancing test; in *Matter of Marín*, 16 I&N Dec. 581, (BIA 1988), the BIA listed factors for consideration in balancing hardship, equities, and negative characteristics presented in §212(c) applications. Positive factors include family ties within the United States and residence of long duration, hardship to the respondent and respondent's family members, history of employment, existence of property or business ties, value or service to the community, genuine rehabilitation in cases of a criminal record and evidence of good moral character. Negative factors include the nature and underlying circumstances of the ground of deportation, length and seriousness of criminal record, and additional violations of the immigration laws.

Section 511(a) of the Immigration Act of 1990 (IMMACT 90)[5] provided for a waiver of excludability for LPRs returning to lawful unrelinquished domiciles of at least seven years, but amended INA §212(c), disqualifying from relief any alien "who has been convicted of one or more aggravated felonies and has served for such felony or felonies a term of imprisonment of at least 5 years." By its use of such specific language, Congress clearly intended to exclude noncitizens who had served more than five years' incarceration as a result of convictions for aggravated felonies. Thus, after IMMACT90, a discretionary waiver remained available to those noncitizens who had been LPRs for at least seven years on the date that the application was adjudicated on the merits, providing that they had not served more than five years incarceration for an aggravated felony (or in the aggregate, for more than one aggravated felony).

Everything changed in 1996. First, §440(d) of the Antiterrorism and Effective Death Penalty Act of 1996 (AEDPA)[6] removed §212(c) relief for "any alien who is deportable by reason of having committed any aggravated felony, any controlled substance offense, certain firearms offenses, and multiple crimes of moral turpitude."[7] Then, the Illegal Immigration Reform and Immigrant Responsibility Act of 1996, (IIRAIRA)[8] repealed §212(c) relief completely.

The effect of AEDPA and IIRAIRA was disastrous for many long-time LPRs who had been placed into immigration court proceedings after being convicted of a criminal offense. The government took the position (and the EOIR agreed) that AEDPA and IIRAIRA applied retroactively, rendering any noncitizen convicted of any aggravated felony, controlled substance offense, or crime involving moral turpitude automatically deportable and ineligible for any form of relief, notwithstanding the date of the conviction.[9] Scores of long-time LPRs, some of whose convictions were decades old and whose crimes were not classified as aggravated felonies on the date of commission, were deported as aggravated felons.[10]

The issues of AEDPA's temporal scope and the permissibility of IIRAIRA's retroactive provisions were first argued before immigration judges (IJ), then raised repeatedly at the Board of Immigration Appeals (Board).[11] In *Matter of Soriano*,[12] the Board held that AEDPA §440(d) did not apply to aliens who had applied for §212(c) relief before AEDPA was enacted, but did apply to all other aliens covered in the provision, including those whose proceedings were commenced or whose criminal conduct occurred before AEDPA was enacted. On February 21, 1997, the Attorney General (AG) concluded that AEDPA §440(d) applied to all aliens who had committed one of the specified offenses and who had not been granted §212(c) relief at the time of AEDPA's enactment.

The AG's interpretation of the §440(d)'s amendments spawned litigation in every circuit court of appeals except the D.C. Circuit.[13] Many noncitizens filed petitions for writs of habeas corpus.[14] The former Immigration and Naturalization Service (INS) argued that the federal courts had no jurisdiction pursuant to INA §242(g).

The Fifth Circuit found that AEDPA §440(d)'s bar on discretionary relief applies to convictions that predated AEDPA and that its distinction between excludable and deportable aliens passes constitutional muster. The Fifth Circuit concluded: "AEDPA §440(d) has no retroactive effect when it is triggered by pre-AEDPA convictions . . . ."[15] The Third and Tenth Circuits agreed.[16]

---

[5] Pub. L. No. 101-649, 104 Stat. 4978, 5052 (Nov. 29, 1990).

[6] Pub. L. No. 104-132, 110 Stat. 1214.

[7] INA §§241(a)(2)(A)(iii), (B), (C), (D), and 241(a)(2)(A)(ii); 304(b).

[8] Illegal Immigration Reform and Immigrant Responsibility Act of 1996, Division C of the Omnibus Appropriations Act of 1996 (H.R. 3610), Pub. L. No. 104-208, 110 Stat. 3009.

[9] *Matter of Davis*, 20 I&N Dec. 536 (BIA 1992).

[10] *In re Fuentes Campos*, 21 I&N Dec. 905 (BIA 1997).

[11] *Matter of Fortiz*, 21 I&N Dec. 1199 (BIA 1998); *Matter of Truong*, 22 I&N Dec. 1090 (BIA 1999).

[12] 21 I&N Dec. 516 (BIA 1996, AG 1997) (superseded by regulation).

[13] *See Goncalves v. Reno*, 114 F.3d 110 (1st Cir. 1998); *Henderson v. INS*, 157 F.3d 106 (2d Cir. 1998); *Sandoval v. Reno*, 166 F.3d 225 (3d Cir. 1999); *Tasios v. Reno*, 204 F.3d 544 (4th Cir. 2000); *Requeña-Rodríguez v. Pasquarell*, 190 F.3d 299 (5th Cir. 1999); *Pak v. Reno*, 196 F.3d 666 (6th Cir. 1999); *LaGuerre v. Reno*, 164 F.3d 1035 (7th Cir. 1998); *Shah v. Reno*, 184 F.3d 719 (8th Cir. 1999); *Magaña Pizano v. INS*, 200 F.3d 603 (9th Cir. 1999); *Jurado Gutierrez v. Greene*, 190 F.3d 1135, (10th Cir. 1999); *Mayers v. INS*, 175 F.3d 1289 (11th Cir. 1999).

[14] *Magaña Pizano v. INS*, 200 F.3d 603.

[15] *Requena-Rodriguez v. Pasquarell*, 190 F.3d 299, 300 (5th Cir. 1999).

[16] *DeSousa v. Reno*, 190 F.3d 175 (3d Cir. 1999); *Gutierrez v. Greene*, 190 F.3d 1135 (10th Cir. 1999).

DESPITE REPEAL, AVAILABILITY OF §212(c) FOR CERTAIN PRE-AEDPA AND PRE-IIRAIRA CONVICTIONS CONTINUES

INS v. St. Cyr

In 2000, the litigation surrounding the retroactive repeal of §212(c) reached the Supreme Court, and in 2001, the Court issued its landmark decision in *INS v. St. Cyr*.[17] *St. Cyr* held simply that §212(c) relief remained available to permanent residents who had pleaded guilty to offenses that rendered them deportable, excludable, or removable and who would have been eligible for §212(c) at the time they pleaded.

Enrico St. Cyr, a citizen of Haiti who became an LPR of the United States in 1986, pleaded guilty to a drug trafficking offense in March 1996, and applied for a waiver in removal proceedings.[18] The IJ found that no relief was available as a result of AEDPA §440(d), which renders any person who has been convicted of an offense relating to a controlled substance ineligible for any form of relief. St. Cyr appealed the IJ's finding. The Board upheld the IJ and dismissed the appeal.

St. Cyr subsequently filed a petition for a writ of habeas corpus in the Court of Appeals for the Second Circuit, which held that AEDPA §440(d) is not applicable in the case of an alien in removal proceedings who entered a guilty plea before April 24, 1996.[19] The Office of the Solicitor General filed a petition for certiorari in *St. Cyr* on November 13, 2000.

The Supreme Court held in *St. Cyr* that Congress did not direct with requisite clarity that AEDPA §440(d) be applied retroactively. Further, the Court held that denying §212(c) relief to persons who pleaded guilty in criminal court while relying on its availability in immigration court is manifestly unfair. In sum, the Court ruled, it would be contrary to considerations of fair notice, reasonable reliance, and settled expectations to hold that IIRAIRA removes §212(c) relief for convictions that occurred prior to its enactment.

The absence of a clearly expressed statement of congressional intent also pervades our review of the merits of St. Cyr's claim. Two important legal consequences ensued from respondent's entry of a guilty plea in March 1996: (1) He became subject to deportation, and (2) he became eligible for a discretionary waiver of that deportation under the prevailing interpretation of §212(c). The issue that remains to be resolved is whether IIRAIRA 304(b) eliminated the respondent's eligibility for a waiver.[20]

The Court considered the government's argument that Congress unambiguously communicated its intent that the provisions of IIRAIRA's Title IIIA apply to all removals initiated after the effective date of the statute, regardless of when the convictions occurred. The majority on the Court, however, agreed that the Second Circuit properly relied on its decision in *Landgraf*.[21] Enunciating a refined and venerable precept—that the legal consequences of any action should be evaluated under the law as it existed on the date of its commission—the Court repeated, then explained, the basis for the presumption against retroactivity:

Retroactive statutes raise special concerns.[22] The Legislature's unmatched powers allow it to sweep away settled expectations suddenly and without individualized consideration. Its responsivity to political pressures poses a risk that it may be tempted to use retroactive legislation as a means of retribution against unpopular groups or individuals.

Accordingly, congressional enactments will not be construed to have retroactive effect unless their language requires that result.[23]

The Court found that the language of AEDPA and IIRAIRA did not require retroactive effect. "We find nothing in IIRIRA unmistakably indicating that Congress considered the question whether to apply its repeal of §212(c) retroactively to such aliens."[24] The rationale for the decision was fundamental fairness, and the Court concentrated on the second prong of the *Landgraf* analysis, whether depriving removable aliens of consideration for §212(c) relief produces an impermissible retroactive effect for aliens who were convicted pursuant to a plea agreement at a time when the plea would not have rendered them ineligible for §212(c) relief.[25] The authority of Congress to

---

[17] *INS v. St. Cyr*, 533 U.S. 289 (2001).

[18] *St. Cyr v. INS*, 229 F.3d 406, 408 (2d. Cir. 2000).

[19] *Id.* at 418.

---

[20] *St. Cyr*, 533 U.S. at 314–15.

[21] *Landgraf v. USI Film Products*, 511 U.S. 244 (1994)

[22] *Id.* at 266.

[23] *Bowen v. Georgetown Univ. Hospital*, 488 U.S. 204, 208 (1988).

[24] *St. Cyr*, 533 U.S. at 326.

[25] *St. Cyr*, 533 U.S. 289.

impose retroactive effects must be measured against available rights under existing laws, the Court noted. Taking into account equitable standards of reasonable notice and firm expectations in light of changes in the law, the majority found that applying AEDPA and IIRAIRA to persons who pleaded guilty in reliance on the availability of §212(c) relief as a consequence of a guilty plea occurring before its enactment created an impermissible retroactive effect.[26] And, accordingly, the Court stated:

> We therefore hold that §212(c) relief remains available for aliens, like respondent, whose convictions were obtained through plea agreements and who, notwithstanding those convictions, would have been eligible for §212(c) relief at the time of their plea under the law then in effect.[27]

The Regulation—8 CFR §212.3

On August 13, 2002, the AG issued a proposed rule entitled "§212(c) relief for aliens with certain criminal convictions before April 1, 1997." The AG's guidelines to that rule provide, in relevant part:

> Under this rule, aliens whose pleas were made before April 24th 1996, regardless of when they were entered by the court, will be eligible to apply for §212(c) relief without regard to the amendments made by AEDPA. Thus, an LPR who has not served an aggregate term of at least five years for aggravated felonies may apply for §212(c) relief, if otherwise eligible, with respect to any criminal convictions arising from a plea made before April 24th 1996.[28]

On September 24, 2004, the AG's proposed rule was adopted as a final rule without substantial change.[29]

Thus, the §212(c) regulations now state, in relevant part:

> Certain LPRs who pleaded guilty or *nolo contendere* to crimes before April 1, 1997 may seek section 212(c) relief from being deported or removed from the United States on account of those pleas. Under this rule, eligible LPRs currently in immigration proceedings may file a request to apply for 212(c) relief as in effect on the

date of their plea, regardless of the date the plea was entered by the court. This rule is applicable only to certain eligible aliens who were convicted pursuant to plea agreements made prior to April 1, 1997.[30]

The amendments made by the AG's rule were codified and are now found at 8 CFR §212.3. Those regulations make clear that an application for relief under §212(c) may be made to a USCIS district director or to an IJ.[31] Given the jurisdiction of a district director, applications for the waiver may be made affirmatively (that is, while not in removal proceedings) and may be filed prior to a departure from or arrival to the United States.[32] Although there is no appeal from a decision of a district director denying an application for a waiver, the application may be renewed before an IJ in removal proceedings.[33]

Conviction after Trial versus a Plea

St. Cyr and its resulting regulations left open the question of whether a permanent resident who had been convicted after trial, rather than after pleading guilty to a removable offense, retained the right to apply for §212(c) relief. In *Chambers v. Reno*,[34] the Fourth Circuit considered the "very narrow question" of whether the provisions of IIRAIRA have a retroactive effect on an LPR who pleaded not guilty and was convicted at trial. Chambers was convicted prior to enactment of AEDPA and IIRAIRA. The Fourth Circuit commented on the *St. Cyr* retroactivity analysis and remarked, "In view of these observations by the Court about retroactivity, we have acknowledged that an alien's failure to demonstrate reliance on pre IIRAIRA law might not foreclose a claim that post IIRAIRA version of the INA operates retroactively."[35] It concluded, however, that *St. Cyr* did not extend §212(c) availability to those LRPs who had been convicted *after trial* of aggravated felonies prior to IIRAIRA's enactment.

The Second Circuit followed suit. In *Rankine v. Reno*,[36] the circuit noted, as had the Fourth Circuit in *Chambers*, that the petitioners were ineligible for §212(c) because they could not demonstrate reliance

---

[26] *Id.* at 324.

[27] *Id.* at 326.

[28] 67 Fed. Reg. 52629.

[29] 69 Fed. Reg. 57826 (Sept. 24, 1996).

[30] 69 Fed. Reg. 57826.

[31] 8 CFR §212.3(a).

[32] 8 CFR §212.3(b).

[33] 8 CFR §212.3(c).

[34] *Chambers v. Reno*, 307 F.3d 284 (4th Cir.2002).

[35] *Id.* at 294–95.

[36] *Rankine v. Reno*, 319 F.3d 19 (2d. Cir. 2003).

on the availability of §212(c) in exchange for a guilty plea, as per *St Cyr*. The LPRs in *Chambers* and *Rankine* were removable as aggravated felons immediately upon conviction, because they had relinquished their rights to direct appeal.

In *Ponnapula v. United States Attorney General*,[37] the Third Circuit interpreted *St. Cyr's* holding to include LPRs whose convictions were the result of a jury verdict. Ponnapula was an LPR who turned down the prosecutor's offer of a plea bargain to a misdemeanor and was convicted at trial of grand larceny in the first degree. That offense is a felony, which rendered him removable. When removal proceedings commenced on October 4, 2000, he applied for §212(c) relief. The IJ found the respondent ineligible for relief, as the facts surrounding his conviction did not fit within the parameters of *St. Cyr v. INS*.[38] The respondent appealed, and the Board upheld the IJ's decision, noting that *St. Cyr* applied to those individuals who pleaded guilty, but not to those who had gone to trial.

The respondent sought declaratory relief in the U.S. district court, where INS argued that because he "sought acquittal from the outset," he could not demonstrate that he relied on the availability of relief according to the state of the immigration laws in exchange for a guilty plea. The government argued that such "reliance" was a requirement for *St. Cyr* eligibility.

Ponnapula distinguished his claim from that presented in *St. Cyr*, arguing that he may have received a longer period of incarceration as result of his refusal to enter into a plea agreement, but that he knew he would be eligible for §212(c) in any event. Unlike St. Cyr who relied on the plea agreement to ensure §212(c) eligibility, Ponnapula relied on counsel's considered estimation that he would not serve more than five years incarceration. Ponnapula reasoned that whether or not he pleaded guilty to a misdemeanor, even if he lost at trial and was convicted of a felony, he would remain eligible for relief.[39]

The Third Circuit looked beyond *St. Cyr* and emphasized the necessity of carefully assessing the Supreme Court's perspective on the permissible scope of retroactivity conveyed through a series of decisions, beginning with *Landgraf*.[40] It noted that "[t]he Supreme Court has never required actual reliance or evidence thereof in the *Landgraf* line of cases, and has in fact assiduously eschewed an actual reliance requirement."[41] Rather than making *quid pro quo* its primary consideration, the Third Circuit focused on the reasoning behind *St. Cyr*: "Thus the Supreme Court has avoided an 'actual reliance' formulation in favor of a 'reasonable reliance' formulation in its retroactivity analysis."[42] "[W]e think the Supreme Court regarded *St. Cyr* as a clear and straightforward result flowing from *Landgraf*."[43]

For the Third Circuit, the relevant inquiry for §212(c) eligibility is not the *quid pro quo* exchange of a guilty plea for certain eligibility for discretionary relief. The Third Circuit framed the issue: "What aliens, if any, who went to trial and were convicted did so in reasonable reliance on the availability of §212(c)?"[44] The Third Circuit cited *St. Cyr*, noting the Supreme Court's "recognition that the availability of discretionary relief plays a central role in many aliens' decisions regarding whether to accept a plea agreement."[45] "The reasonable reliance question turns on the nature of the statutory right and the availability of some choice affecting that right, not on the particular choice actually made."[46]

RECLASSIFICATION OF THE UNDERLYING OFFENSE

In *St. Cyr*, the Supreme Court began its analysis by recognizing two important legal consequences of St. Cyr's March 1996 guilty plea: (1) he became subject to deportation, and (2) he became eligible for a §212(c) waiver.[47] The Court quickly noted that the first consequence was unchanged by the 1996 repeal of §212(c) and then proceeded to focus exclusively

---

[37] *Ponnapula v. United States Attorney General*, 373 F.3d. 480 (3d Cir. 2004).

[38] 229 F.3d 406, 483 (2d. Cir. 2000).

[39] *Ponnapula*, 373 F.3d. at 484.

[40] *See also Hughes Aircraft Co. v. United States ex. Rel. Schumer*, 520 U.S. 939, (1997); *Martin v. Hadix*, 527 U.S. 343 (1999).

[41] *Ponnapula*, 373 F.3d. at 491.

[42] *Id.* at 492.

[43] *Id.*

[44] *Id.* at 494.

[45] *Id.* at 596 (citing *INS v. St. Cyr*, 533 U.S. 289, 322–23 (2001)).

[46] *Id.* at 20.

[47] *St. Cyr*, 533 U.S. at 314–15.

on whether IIRAIRA eliminated St. Cyr's eligibility for a §212(c) waiver.[48]

Applying its *Landgraf* two-step retroactivity analysis, the Court held that "212(c) relief remains available for aliens, like respondent, whose convictions were obtained through plea agreements and who, notwithstanding those convictions, would have been eligible for §212(c) relief at the time of their plea under the law then in effect."[49] Thus, St. Cyr, who pleaded guilty to a drug trafficking offense in March 1996, remained eligible for a §212(c) waiver even though he was placed in removal proceedings after the repeal of §212(c) and his conviction constituted an aggravated felony under INA §101(a)(43)(B).

But what if, on the day that St. Cyr pleaded guilty, he was not deportable? If he were not deportable, would he have relied on the availability of §212(c) relief at the time of entering his guilty plea? If his crime were later reclassified as an aggravated felony, would he still be eligible under *St. Cyr* for a §212(c) waiver? What effect, if any, does the reclassification of a conviction from a nondeportable offense to an aggravated felony have on a permanent resident's eligibility to apply for a §212(c) waiver?

Since *St. Cyr*, the Ninth Circuit has taken the lead in addressing these questions. First, in *U.S. v. Velasco-Medina*,[50] the circuit drew a line between guilty pleas entered before the effective date of AEDPA §440(d) (April 24, 1996), and guilty pleas entered after that date. Velasco-Medina pleaded guilty in June 1996 to second-degree burglary and received a one-year sentence for the offense. In finding him ineligible for §212(c) relief, the Ninth Circuit gave two reasons for concluding that the repeal of §212(c) was not impermissibly retroactive as applied to Velasco-Medina.[51] First, the court reasoned that because his plea did not render him deportable at the time, Velasco-Medina was not eligible for §212(c) relief, and he therefore did not possess "vested rights acquired under existing laws."[52] Second, the court emphasized the fact that only six weeks prior to his guilty plea, AEDPA had eliminated §212(c) relief for anyone convicted of an aggravated felony. Therefore, the court concluded,

Velasco-Medina had been given fair notice that §212(c) relief would not be available if his offense were later reclassified as an aggravated felony, and any expectation that he may have had of the future availability of §212(c) relief was neither reasonable nor settled.

Authors' note: It is questionable whether the first prong of the court's analysis is entirely correct. Arguably, a permanent resident who has pleaded guilty to an excludable, but not deportable, offense could still acquire vested rights under existing law because, if that permanent resident were to travel outside the United States, he would have needed and would have been eligible for a §212(c) waiver to return to the United States.

In contrast, the Ninth Circuit found, in *U.S. v. Leon-Paz*,[53] that a permanent resident remains eligible for a §212(c) waiver if he pleaded guilty to an offense that was a nondeportable offense prior to passage of AEDPA but was subsequently reclassified as an aggravated felony by IIRAIRA. There, the court explained that Leon-Paz had double protection against deportation at the time that he entered his guilty plea in 1995. First, he was not deportable for the offense, first-degree burglary with a four-year sentence. And second, if his offense were re-classified as an aggravated felony, he would still be eligible for §212(c) relief. The court distinguished *Velasco-Medina*, finding that AEDPA had provided Velasco-Medina with fair notice of the possible unavailability of §212(c), notice that was not provided to Leon-Paz.

Having drawn a bright line between guilty pleas for nondeportable offenses entered before and after April 24, 1996, the Ninth Circuit recently added a whole new wrinkle, one that may ultimately erase the bright line and restore §212(c) eligibility for post-AEDPA guilty pleas.

In *Cordes v. Gonzales*,[54] the Ninth Circuit considered the situation of Patricia Ann Cordes, a woman from Scotland who had been a lawful permanent resident since 1972. On May 30, 1996, Cordes entered a guilty plea to dissuading a witness from testifying under threat of force and received a two-year sentence. At the time, the plea did not render Cordes deportable; however, IIRAIRA reclassified the offense as an aggravated felony, which under AEDPA precluded Cordes from eligibility for

---

[48] *Id.* at 315.

[49] *Id.* at 326.

[50] *U.S. v. Velasco-Medina*, 305 F.3d 839, 843 (9th Cir. 2002).

[51] *Id.* at 849–50.

[52] *Id.* at 849.

[53] *U.S. v. Leon-Paz*, 340 F.3d 1003, 1005 (9th Cir. 2003).

[54] *Cordes v. Gonzales*, 421 F.3d 889, 896 (9th Cir. 2005).

§212(c) relief. The court held that under *Velasco-Medina*, IIRAIRA's repeal of §212(c) was not impermissibly retroactive as applied to a post-April 24, 1996, guilty plea and did not violate Cordes's right to due process.

At this point in the opinion, it was not looking good for Cordes. But looking to the long history of §212(c) and equal protection jurisprudence, the court held that the principle of equal protection was violated if §212(c) relief was afforded to permanent residents who retroactively became aggravated felons but had committed deportable offenses at the time of their conviction, yet not granted to permanent residents who retroactively became aggravated felons but had not committed deportable offenses at the time of their convictions. The court reasoned that Cordes was similarly situated to those permanent residents who remain eligible for §212(c) relief under *St. Cyr* and that the disparate treatment between Cordes and permanent residents entitled to §212(c) relief lacks a rational basis.[55]

In essence, the circuit court found it irrational to interpret the law to allow permanent residents who had committed more serious crimes to apply for §212(c) relief, but to deny the same opportunity to similarly situated permanent residents who had committed less serious offenses. As a result, even though Cordes pleaded guilty to a nondeportable offense post-AEDPA that was subsequently reclassified as an aggravated felony by IIRAIRA, she was still eligible to apply for a §212(c) waiver. The court's holding effectively modifies the provision of the new regulations that purport to limit §212(c) eligibility to plea agreements for aggravated felonies that were made prior to April 24, 1996.[56]

COMPARABLE GROUND OF INADMISSIBILITY (EXCLUDABILITY) REQUIREMENT

Section 212(c) grants the AG the discretion to admit permanent residents who have temporarily traveled abroad and are seeking readmission, even if they are otherwise excludable or inadmissible. To take that point literally, §212(c) appears to only benefit LPRs in exclusion proceedings or in removal proceedings when they are subject to grounds of inadmissibility. From its very inception, however,

the Board has interpreted §212(c) as being available in some situations to aliens subject to grounds of deportability, as well as to those subject to excludability/inadmissibility.

History of the "Doctrine of the Comparable Ground": The Seventh Proviso

Section 212(c) had its origins in the Seventh Proviso to Section 3 of the Immigration Act of 1917;[57] indeed, as noted above, the language of §212(c) as we know it is nearly identical to its nearly century-old ancestor. In the 1940s, the Board extended the Seventh Proviso's reach, first to noncitizens in deportation proceedings who had departed and returned to the United States after the ground of deportation arose,[58] and then to noncitizens in deportation proceedings, regardless of whether they had departed the country.[59]

Enter the INA

With the passage of the INA in 1952, the Seventh Proviso was replaced by §212(c). And three years later, the Board relied on its previous decisions interpreting the Seventh Proviso to extend §212(c)'s reach to waive grounds of deportability and excludability for an alien who had departed the country after committing an offense that rendered him or her inadmissible, had re-entered, and was thereafter placed into deportation proceedings and charged with being inadmissible. The Board reasoned that if INS permitted an LPR to enter the country and then placed him or her into deportation proceedings, he or she should not be placed in a worse position than he or she would have been had he or she been excluded at the time he or she attempted to enter.[60]

That interpretation, however, produced inequities in its own right. While one LPR who became deportable and then departed the country became eligible for a waiver upon re-entry, another one who was deportable for the same reason but who never departed, did not. Finding this distinction "not rationally related to any legitimate purpose of the statute," the Second Circuit, in *Francis v. INS*,[61] struck it down as violating the Due

---

[55] *Id.* at 897.

[56] *See* 8 CFR §1212.3(f)(4)(i).

[57] 39 Stat. 874.

[58] *Matter of L*, 1 I&N Dec. 1 (1940).

[59] *Matter of A*, 2 I&N Dec. 459 (BIA 1946).

[60] *Matter of G–A*, 7 I&N Dec. 274 (BIA 1956); *see also Matter of S–*, 6 I&N Dec. 392 (BIA 1954, A.G. 1955).

[61] *Francis v. INS*, 532 F.2d 268, 272 (2d Cir. 1976).

Process Clause. In *Matter of Silva*,[62] the Board adopted the *Francis* court's reasoning and held that §212(c) relief was available to deportable aliens regardless of whether they had left the United States after committing the act that rendered them deportable.

Because the rationale for extending §212(c) relief to deportable aliens was to equalize the treatment of noncitizens who were deportable versus excludable on equivalent grounds, the Board extended §212(c) relief only to those aliens whose deportability was based on a ground for which a comparable ground of excludability existed.[63] And thus was born the "doctrine of the comparable ground."

From *Francis* to *Jimenez*—
A Slowly Tightening Noose

In *Silva*, the Board applied the *Francis* rule nationwide, and most of the nation's circuit courts followed.[64] In 1990, the Board departed briefly from the general consensus to hold in *Matter of Hernandez-Casillas (Hernandez-Casillas I)* that §212(c) was available to all permanent residents facing deportation unless the ground of deportability was specifically excluded by §212(c).[65] The momentary liberality was soon curtailed, however, when the AG reversed the Board (and the Fifth Circuit upheld the AG's reversal).[66] The AG ruled that the relevant question in such a case was whether the ground of deportability to which the applicant was subject was comparable to a ground of excludability in §212.[67] This became known as the "*Hernandez-Casillas II* rule."

The question in *Hernandez-Casillas* was whether §212(c) relief should be available to waive the entry

without inspection of the ground of deportability. Because an entry without inspection rendered a noncitizen deportable but not excludable, the AG concluded that no comparable ground of excludability existed for that particular ground of deportability. As such, it held that §212(c) relief was not available to waive that ground.[68]

Thereafter, the Board and the nation's circuit courts followed the *Hernandez-Casillas II* rule to hold that such grounds as entry without inspection[69] and firearms violations[70] were not waivable under §212(c) because they have no comparable ground in §212.

With IMMACT90, a new question arose: Could one who was deportable for having committed an aggravated felony waive that ground of deportability under §212(c), given that the commission of an aggravated felony renders one deportable but not inadmissible?

The Board addressed that question for the first time in 1990. In *Matter of Meza*,[71] the Board considered whether an applicant who was removable as an aggravated felon for having committed a crime involving "illicit trafficking in a controlled substance" could waive that conviction under §212(c) despite the fact that §212 does not render one who has been convicted of an aggravated felony inadmissible.

The Board held that,

[a] waiver under 212(c) is not unavailable to an alien convicted of an aggravated felony simply because there is no ground of exclusion which recites the words, 'convicted of an aggravated felony,' as in section 241(a)(4)(B) of the Act.[72]

Instead, the Board looked to the specific category of aggravated felony charged—in that case, §101(a)(43), which referred to "any illicit trafficking in a controlled substance." It noted that former

---

[62] *Matter of Silva*, 16 I&N Dec. 26, 30 (BIA 1976).

[63] *Matter of Wahud*, 19 I&N Dec. 182, 184 (BIA 1984); *Matter of Granados*, 16 I&N Dec. 726, 728 (BIA 1979).

[64] *De Gonzalez v. INS*, 996 F.2d 804, 806 (6th Cir. 1993); *Leal Rodriguez v. INS*, 990 F.2d 939, 949 (7th Cir. 1993); *Variamparambil v. INS*, 831 F.2d 1362, 1364, n.1 (7th Cir. 1987); *Butros v. INS*, 990 F.2d 1142, 1143 (9th Cir. 1993) (en banc); *Casalena v. INS*, 984 F.2d 105, 106 (4th Cir. 1993); *Ghassan v. INS*, 972 F.2d 631, 633, n.2 (5th Cir. 1992); *Campos v. INS*, 961 F.2d 309, 313 (1st Cir. 1992); *Lozada v. INS*, 857 F.2d 10, 11, n. 1 (1st Cir. 1988); *Vissian v. INS*, 548 F.2d 325, 328, n.3 (10th Cir. 1977).

[65] *Matter of Hernandez-Casillas*, 20 I&N Dec. 262, 268 (BIA 1990).

[66] *Id.* at 280–93, *aff'd mem.*, 983 F.2d 231 (5th Cir. 1993) (*Hernandez-Casillas II*).

[67] *Id.* at 280.

[68] *Id.* at 291–92.

[69] *Leal-Rodriguez v. INS*, 990 F.2d 939 (7th Cir. 1993); *Farquharson v. Ashcroft*, 246 F.3d 1317 (11th Cir. 2001).

[70] *Gjonaj v. INS*, 47 F.3d 824, 827 (6th Cir. 1995); *Rodriguez-Padron v. INS*, 13 F.3d 1455, 1460–61 (11th Cir. 1994); *Chow v. INS*, 12 F.3d 34, 38 (5th Cir. 1993); *Rodriguez v. INS*, 9 F.3d 408, 412 (5th Cir. 1993); *Campos v. INS*, 961 F.2d 309, 316–17 (1st Cir. 1992); *Cabasug v. INS*, 847 F.2d 1321, 1327 (9th Cir. 1988); *Matter of Montenegro*, 20 I&N Dec. 602, 605 (BIA 1992).

[71] *Matter of Meza*, 20 I&N Dec. 257 (BIA 1991).

[72] *Matter of Meza*, 20 I&N Dec. 257, 259 (BIA 1991).

§212(a)(23)(A) provided that convictions for a "violation of, or conspiracy to violate, any law or regulation . . . relating to a controlled substance," rendering the subject inadmissible. And it concluded that,

> [a]s the respondent's conviction for a drug-related aggravated felony clearly could also form the basis for excludability under section 212(a)(23), he is not precluded from establishing eligibility for section 212(c) relief based on his conviction for an aggravated felony.[73]

In *Matter of Montenegro*[74] and *Matter of Esposito*,[75] however, the Board limited *Meza* to its facts. In both of those cases, the Board held that a different aggravated felony—a firearms offense that rendered the respondents deportable under former §241(a)(2)(C)—did not have a comparable ground within §212. Although the offenses for which the respondents in those cases had been convicted were crimes involving moral turpitude, as well as firearms offenses, and although the commission of one or more crimes involving moral turpitude did render an applicant excludable, the Board held that the firearms and moral turpitude provisions were not analogous for the purpose of finding one to be comparable to the other. Each case distinguished *Meza*, and limited it to its facts.[76]

The last of the IMMACT90 aggravated-felony cases was *Matter of Jimenez*.[77] In that case, the Board held that a noncitizen who had been found deportable for a conviction under 18 USC §1546(a) (relating to fraud and misuse of visas, permits, or other entry documents) was not eligible for §212(c) relief because §212(c)(6)(C)(i) (relating to fraud, willful misrepresentation of a material fact in procuring a visa, entry into the United States, or other immigration benefit) was not sufficiently comparable to the ground upon which he was deportable. The Board recognized that there was some "overlap" between the two provisions, but concluded that §1546(a) "encompasses more serious document fraud and misuse offenses not contemplated by the

'willful misrepresentation' language of §212(a)(6)(C)(i)."[78]

The *Jimenez* Board declined to adopt an approach that asks whether the noncitizen's offense or conduct is subsumed under the terms of one of the exclusion grounds. It concluded, instead, that, "[t]he essential analysis is to determine whether the deportation ground under which the alien has been adjudged deportable has a statutory counterpart among the exclusion grounds waivable by §212(c)."[79]

IIRAIRA and *Blake*: Is Anything Comparable?

Soon after *Jimenez* came down, AEDPA and IIRAIRA took effect, generating a whirlwind of litigation over the very existence of §212(c). It was not until 2005 that the Board again took up the issue of the comparable ground, this time in the context of the "new" §212(c), governed by *St. Cyr* and the regulations promulgated in its wake.[80]

In *Matter of Blake*,[81] the Board addressed the availability of §212(c) relief to aggravated felons in the post-IIRAIRA, post–*St. Cyr* context. In that case, the respondent had been found removable under §237(a)(2)(A)(iii), as an alien convicted of sexual abuse of a minor (an aggravated felony under §101(a)(43)(A)). The IJ held that, although §212 did not specifically include convictions for sexual assault of a minor as a ground of inadmissibility, since almost all offenses involving the sexual abuse of a minor would by necessity also constitute crimes involving moral turpitude, the ground of deportability at §237(a)(2)(A)(iii) was sufficiently comparable to §212(a)(2)(A)(i)(I) to render the respondent eligible to apply for a §212(c) waiver.[82]

The Board disagreed. It relied on the newly published *St. Cyr* regulations to explicitly withdraw from any "comments" in *Montenegro* and *Esposito* that "may have suggested a more relaxed approach to the analysis of comparable grounds in cases involving aggravated felony grounds of removal."[83]

---

[73] *Id.*

[74] 20 I&N Dec. 603 (BIA 1992).

[75] 21 I&N Dec. 1 (BIA 1995).

[76] 20 I&N Dec. at 605; 21 I&N Dec. at 9–10.

[77] 21 I&N Dec. 567, 573 (BIA 1996), *aff'd, Jimenez-Santillano v. INS*, 120 F.3d 270 (10th Cir. 1997).

[78] *Matter of Jimenez*, 21 I&N Dec. 567, 573 (BIA 1996).

[79] *Id.* at 574.

[80] Executive Office for Immigration Review; Section 212(c) Relief for Aliens With Certain Criminal Convictions Before April 1, 1997, 69 Fed. Reg. 57826, 57835 (Sept. 28, 2004) (codified at 8 CFR §1212.3(f)(5) (eff. Oct. 28, 2004).

[81] 23 I&N Dec. 722 (BIA 2005).

[82] *Matter of Blake*, 23 I&N Dec. 722, 723 (BIA 2005).

[83] *Id.* at 728.

And it held that the question of whether a deportation or removal ground has a "statutory counterpart" (a term that the regulations and the Board use interchangeably with "comparable ground") in a ground of inadmissibility or excludability "turns on whether Congress has employed similar language to describe substantially equivalent categories of offenses."[84] Although considerable "overlap" existed between those offenses involving sexual abuse of a minor and crimes involving moral turpitude, the Board held that the former is not a "statutory counterpart" of the latter.[85]

The *Blake* Board hastened to assure its readers that the offenses need not be "a perfect match" to be statutory counterparts "so long as the ground of inadmissibility addresses essentially the same category of offenses under which the removal charge is based."[86] Still, it did not offer any clearer rule for determining what *is* a comparable ground than it had had in *Meza, Montenegro, Esposito,* or *Jimenez.*

Indeed, the only case, in the authors' opinion, to set forth a clear rule of law determining what constitutes a comparable ground (or "statutory counterpart") is *Hernandez-Casillas I*; it is also, of course, the only case that has been explicitly overruled. Having rejected *Hernandez-Casillas I*, the AG has since chosen to employ the approach of "we don't know what a comparable ground is, but we know one when we see it and this isn't it."

The only precedential decision to interpret *Blake* and the comparable ground rule in the post-IIRAIRA, post–*St. Cyr* context is *Matter of Brieva-Perez.*[87] In that case, the Board again addressed the comparability of an aggravated felony under §101(a)(43) (this time, a crime of violence under §101(a)(43)(F)) to the crime of moral turpitude ground at §212(a)(2)(A)(i)(I). The Board noted that the particular offense that rendered the noncitizen removable in that case (unauthorized use of a motor vehicle) was not generally considered to be a crime of moral turpitude. It did not, however, rely on that fact explicitly to hold the grounds incomparable. Instead, it looked to the language of the two categories of offenses, and held that the

distinctly different terminology used to describe the two categories of offenses and the significant variance in the types of offenses covered by these two provisions lead us to conclude that they are not 'statutory counterparts' for the purposes of section 212(c) eligibility.[88]

Montenegro, Esposito, and *Jimenez* generated relatively little controversy in the immigration community. *Blake* and *Brieva-Perez,* however, have sparked an uproar, with immigration practitioners wondering whether anything is comparable in this day and age. The problem, of course, is not that *Blake* and its progeny laid forth some new, highly restrictive rule of law—on its face, *Blake* simply reaffirms that *Montenegro, Esposito,* and *Jimenez* survived IIRAIRA and the *St. Cyr* regulations; the problem is that IIRAIRA increased exponentially the number of enumerated offenses that constitute aggravated felonies, while leaving the list of inadmissible offenses small and general.

The largest class of crimes that render one deportable are aggravated felonies. The largest class of crimes that render one inadmissible are crimes involving moral turpitude. Congress chose to enumerate an exhaustive list of 21 specific offenses that constitute aggravated felonies;[89] it chose not to define "crimes involving moral turpitude." In that sense, it is almost impossible to identify a crime that is both a removable offense and has a counterpart in the §212 that closely tracks its terms. The only offenses that are clearly waivable under §212(c) in this new landscape are drug crimes, which may be removable offenses under the aggravated felony provision[90] and under INA §§237(a)(B)(i) or (ii) (relating to controlled substance violations and abusers) and for which the statute also provides two specific grounds of inadmissibility.[91]

Where Do We Go from Here?

The result of the 1996 amendments to the INA is that the rule that evolved in the pre-IIRAIRA context, in which there was much more parity between the grounds of deportability and of excludability, has radically transformed the reality our clients face. From a world in which practically the only offenses not waivable under §212(c) were firearms offenses and entry

---

[84] *Id.*

[85] *Id.*

[86] *Id.* at 729.

[87] 23 I&N Dec. 766 (BIA 2005).

[88] *Id.* at 772–73.

[89] INA §§101(a)(43)(A)–(U).

[90] INA §101(a)(43)(B).

[91] INA §§212(a)(2), 212(c)(i).

without inspection, we arrive in one in which almost nothing except a drug offense *is* waivable.

What to do? We should litigate, litigate, litigate. It appears that IIRAIRA and *Blake* have brought us full circle, back to *Francis* and the pre-*Francis* case law. The comparable ground doctrine as interpreted by *Blake* has again created a situation in which wildly divergent fates attach to aliens who have committed identical offenses merely by dint of the fact that one chose to travel in and out of the United States after committing the offense and another chose not to. It is time to start from *Matter of G*[92] and go forward again.

TWISTS AND TURNS ALONG THE WAY

Combining §212(c) with Other Forms of Relief

Section 212(c) Plus Adjustment of Status

When a permanent resident has a conviction or convictions that constitute two separate grounds of deportability, one of which has a corresponding ground of inadmissibility and the other does not, it is possible to combine a §212(c) waiver with another form of relief. For example, a permanent resident could apply to adjust status to overcome the aggravated felony ground of deportability and concurrently apply for a §212(c) waiver to overcome the crime involving moral turpitude ground of inadmissibility.

This was precisely the situation in *Matter of Azurin*.[93] Azurin was convicted in March 1990 of shooting at an occupied motor vehicle. On the basis of this one conviction, Azurin was charged in 1998 with removability as an aggravated felon and for a conviction on a firearms charge.[94] Azurin sought to adjust status (or, more accurately, "re-adjust") on the basis of his marriage to a U.S. citizen.

The Board, citing *Matter of Rainford*,[95] explained that Azurin was not precluded from adjusting status by the aggravated felony or firearms ground of deportability. Where there is no corresponding ground of inadmissibility, §212(c) relief is not needed in order to adjust status.[96] However, because Azurin's offense also constituted a crime involving

moral turpitude, a §212(c) waiver was required in order to waive the INA §212(a)(2)(i)(I) ground of inadmissibility. In reaffirming *Matter of Gabryelsky*,[97] and finding that Azurin was eligible to apply concurrently for adjustment of status and a §212(c) waiver, the Board expressly rejected an interpretation of the recently promulgated §212(c) regulations that could have been read to preclude concurrently filed applications.[98]

Practice Pointer: Filing concurrent applications for adjustment of status and a §212(c) waiver is one strategy for avoiding the *Matter of Blake* conundrum discussed earlier.

Section 212(c) Plus Cancellation of Removal

Is it possible to apply simultaneously for a §212(c) waiver and a §240A cancellation of removal?

If a permanent resident has been convicted of both a pre–April 24, 1996, aggravated felony and a post-IIRAIRA conviction for a deportable offense, can he or she combine the §212(c) waiver with the §240A cancellation of removal to obtain relief from deportation? A number of creative attorneys have tried the strategy of simultaneously applying for both. So far, this strategy has not worked.[99]

There seems to be two major obstacles to prevailing under this theory. First, under INA §240A(c)(6), a permanent resident is not eligible for cancellation of removal if he or she has been granted relief under section §212(c). Second, under INA §240A(a)(3), a permanent resident is not eligible for cancellation of removal if he or she has been convicted of an aggravated felony. Taken together, it is difficult to structure a compelling argument that, from a temporal perspective, the §212(c) waiver does not precede the grant of cancellation, so as to avoid the §240A(c)(6) prohibition against prior relief and, at the same time, the §212(c) waiver waives the aggravated felony conviction so that the §240A(a)(3) bar to relief for those with aggravated felony convictions does not apply.

---

[92] 9 I&N Dec. 159 (BIA 1960).

[93] *Matter of Azurin*, 23 I&N Dec. 695 (BIA 2005).

[94] INA §§237(a)(2)(A)(iii) and 237(a)(2)(C).

[95] 20 I&N Dec. 598 (BIA 1992).

[96] *Id.*

[97] 20 I&N Dec. 750 (BIA 1993).

[98] 8 CFR §1212.3(f)(5).

[99] *See Rodriguez-Munoz v. Gonzales*, 419 F.3d 245 (3d. Cir. 2005); *Comas v. McDonough*, Civil Action No.: 04-10691, 2005 U.S. LEXIS 4448 (D. Mass. 2005).

Affirmative Applications for
LPRs Who Need to Travel

More often, long-time LPRs are being detained at the airport because of some long-ago criminal conviction. This is the ultimate nightmare scenario facing many permanent residents returning from travel abroad. Often, the permanent resident knows of the risk but needs to travel for emergency reasons, such as to visit an aging parent or dying relative.

A rather simple point that is often overlooked is that a permanent resident who is eligible to apply for a §212(c) waiver does not have to wait until he or she has been arrested at the airport, detained, and placed in removal proceedings before applying for relief. Affirmative §212(c) applications are expressly authorized by regulation.[100]

If a §212(c) eligible permanent resident must travel, it may prove easier and less stressful to prepare and file the §212(c) application directly with the USCIS district director's office prior to traveling, rather than waiting and hoping that the nightmare does not occur.

CONCLUSION

Despite having been deleted from the statute 10 years ago, §212(c) remains alive and well, and very relevant in the post–IIRAIRA world. For that significant (though admittedly dwindling) class of people to whom §212(c) remains available, it can mean all the difference in the world.

---

[100] 8 CFR §212.3(b).

FRAUD AND MISREPRESENTATION WAIVERS—PLANNING FOR SUCCESS

by Richard M. Ginsburg[*]

INTRODUCTION

This article discusses the representation of clients who are alleged to be inadmissible under the fraud and willful misrepresentation grounds of INA §212(a)(6)(C)(i), which applies to applications for both immigrant and nonimmigrant visas. The first section discusses avoiding or challenging a finding of fraud or misrepresentation and applies to both types of applications. The following sections discuss determining eligibility and applying for a waiver of inadmissibility for applicants for immigrant visas under INA §212(i). Waivers for nonimmigrant visa applications under INA §212(d)(3) are not discussed. The article is intended as a practical guide to avoiding a finding of inadmissibility and applying for a waiver of inadmissibility.

Fraud and misrepresentation are far too common and yet not always easy for the practitioner to detect. The ultimate consequence can be visa denial and a lifetime bar to immigration.[1] Thus, avoiding this ground of inadmissibility is of great importance to clients, and cases must be carefully prepared and skillfully presented. While there are rules governing findings of fraud or misrepresentation, overcoming the ground takes the practitioner into imprecise areas such as arguing extreme hardship and circumstances meriting the favorable exercise of discretion. This gives practitioners the opportunity to be creative and appeal to the humanity of the adjudicator.

It is necessary to become thoroughly familiar with the case, analyze the legal ground of inadmissibility, and prepare the waiver application package.

CHALLENGE THE FRAUD

When the client faces inadmissibility based on fraud or willful misrepresentation and may need to apply for a discretionary waiver, the first task is to challenge the grounds. The practitioner must understand the legal basis for such a finding, thoroughly document the facts, and apply the law to argue that the client is not inadmissible based on, for example, statutory language, regulations, case law, and agency policy statements.

Read the Statute

Review the statutory basis of inadmissibility:

Misrepresentation.

In general. "Any alien who, by fraud or willfully misrepresenting a material fact, seeks to procure (or has sought to procure or has procured) a visa, other documentation, or admission into the United States or other benefit provided under this Act is inadmissible.

INA §212(a)(6)(C)(i).

Get the Facts

Exhaustively familiarize yourself with the facts. Clients, and their family members, often intentionally or unknowingly deny that untruthful statements were made to U.S. government officials. This is the starting point. Get the facts. Obtain a detailed chronology directly from the client, using a qualified interpreter if necessary. Review events for fraud or misrepresentation—including signed applications, visa interviews at a consulate, applications for admission at a port of entry, preflight inspection or deferred inspection, applications for extensions or changes of nonimmigrant status, applications for adjustment of status, etc. Review all related documents.

---

[*] **Dick Ginsburg** is a sole practitioner in Hillsboro, Ore., and limits his practice to immigration law. He has been an AILA member since 1975, was a founding member of the Oregon AILA Chapter, and served as its chairperson and treasurer. He has chaired AILA national committees and worked on legislative and regulatory issues. He has written and spoken on immigration topics at state, regional, and national levels including AILA national conferences and continuing legal educations sessions. He received his B.A. from Western Reserve University and his J.D. from The National Law Center at George Washington University.

[1] *See Matter of Shirdel*, 19 I&N Dec. 33, 35 (BIA 1984) and *Matter of Y–G–*, 20 I&N Dec. 794 (BIA 1994) where the Board of Immigration Appeals (BIA) held that facts relating to fraud or misrepresentation are to be closely scrutinized since such a finding may perpetually bar an alien from admission.

Apply the Law

With the facts still fresh, parse the statute. The *Foreign Affairs Manual*[2] (FAM) is an essential tool in applying the statutory ground of inadmissibility to the facts. It gives the Visa Office's thinking on a wide variety of common fact patterns and can be cited as authority.

INA §212(a)(6)(C)(i) Piece by Piece

Any alien who—

This is the client, not a traveling companion or a person speaking on the client's behalf (as long as the client was not aware at the time of the misrepresentation of another).

... by fraud—

"Fraud" is defined in the accepted legal sense and "consists of a false representation of a material fact made with knowledge of its falsity and with intent to deceive the other party. The representation must be believed and acted upon by the party deceived to his disadvantage."[3]

The FAM, citing *Matter of G–G–* (which it refers to as *Matter of G*), defines fraud as requiring a false representation with knowledge of its falsity, with the intent to deceive a consular or immigration officer and with the representation having been believed and acted upon by the officer. It observes that "most cases of ineligibility under this section will involve 'material misrepresentations' rather than 'fraud' since actual proof of an alien's intent to deceive may be hard to come by."[4]

... or willfully misrepresenting a material fact—

This complex phrase requires careful dissection. *Black's Law Dictionary* defines "willful" as "[p]roceeding from a conscious motion of the will; voluntary."[5]

Misrepresentation is an assertion or manifestation not in accordance with the facts. It requires that the alien make an affirmative act and can be made in an oral interview, in written applications, or by submitting evidence containing false information.[6]

The FAM defines a "willful misrepresentation" as "simply a false misrepresentation, willfully made, concerning a fact which is relevant to the alien's visa entitlement." It must be made with knowledge of its falsity. Neither intent to deceive nor belief in and action by the officer upon the misrepresentation are necessary. The standard is lower than what Congress intended for a finding of fraud because it is not necessary to show that the person to whom the misrepresentation was made was motivated to action.[7]

... a material fact—

The Supreme Court held that the test of materiality is whether it can be shown by clear, unequivocal, and convincing evidence to have been capable of affecting the decision, and that the question is one of law, not fact.[8] The FAM states that materiality results not from the lie, but must be "measured pragmatically in the context of the individual case as to whether the misrepresentation was of direct and objective significance to the proper resolution of the alien's application for a visa." A misrepresentation is material[9] if either: (1) the alien is excludable on the true facts or (2) the misrepresentation tends to shut off a line of inquiry which is relevant to the alien's eligibility and which might well have resulted in a proper determination that he or she be excluded.[10]

Under (1), materiality may not result if INA §212 grants relief from ineligibility automatically by operation of law, *i.e.* misrepresenting a crime of moral turpitude covered by the "petty offense" exception to INA §212(a)(2)(A)(i)(I). If the relief requires an evaluation or judgment, the misrepresentation is material.[11]

Under (2), the FAM uses the "rule of probability." If the misrepresentation tended to cut off a line of inquiry and was reasonably expected to foreclose information from the consular officer, it was material. It

---

[2] 22 CFR §40.63, 9 FAM 40.63.

[3] *Matter of G–G–*, 7 I&N 161 (BIA 1956).

[4] 9 FAM 40.63 N.3.

[5] *Black's Law Dictionary*, Revised Fourth Ed., 1968.

[6] 9 FAM 40.63 N.4.1.

[7] 9 FAM 40.63 N.3 (citing *Matter of G–G–*, 7 I&N 161, which required actual intent to deceive to gain a benefit, *Matter of S– and B–C–*, 9 I&N 436, 448–49 (A.G. 1961), which eliminated the actual intent requirement; and *Matter of Kai Hing Hui*, 15 I&N 288 (1975), which affirmed that actual intent is not required).

[8] *Kungys v. U.S.*, 485 U.S. 759 (1988), a denaturalization case under INA §340.

[9] Relying on *Matter of S– and B–C–*, 9 I&N, at 447.

[10] 9 FAM 40.63 N.6.1 and 6.2.

[11] 9 FAM 40.63 N.6.2-1.

does not have to succeed in the foreclosing investigation to be deemed material; it only must reasonably have had the capacity to do so. If visa eligibility is determined based on known circumstances, subsequent discovery of a misrepresentation would not be material if it did not tend to mislead the consular officer, *i.e.*, if an alien is denied as an intending immigrant before a relevant misrepresentation is discovered, the false statement is not material because it had no objective significance to the finding that the alien was not a nonimmigrant. If the truth is otherwise available to the officer, the misrepresentation does not tend to cut off a line of inquiry since the line of inquiry was readily available. However, if the true facts of the misrepresentation disclose an independent ground of ineligibility, the misrepresentation is material under (1).[12]

The FAM provides the following instances of facts considered to be material:

- Residence and identity only if the alien is excludable on the true facts or the misrepresentation tends to cut off a relevant line of inquiry that might have led to a finding of ineligibility;

- A previous visa application or registration for immigration, while not in itself material, can raise questions about nonimmigrant intent. Because this might tend to cut off the line of inquiry into nonimmigrant intent, the misrepresentation is normally considered material, but other factors, including events intervening between the registration and the nonimmigrant visa application, can render the prior registration immaterial unless it also concealed an independent ground of ineligibility;

- A misrepresentation concerning a previous nonimmigrant visa application made as part of an immigrant visa applicant is not of itself considered material;

- A nonimmigrant visa applicant's misrepresentation of only a previous nonimmigrant visa refusal is not material on the assumption that the refusal was based on the facts at the time and eligibility must be decided in light of the current situation. If the misrepresentation conceals only the fact of a prior refusal and not facts not otherwise known or available to the second officer and therefore

did not tend to cut off a line of inquiry, it is not material.[13]

To be material, the misrepresentation must have cut off a relevant line of inquiry that might have resulted in a determination of inadmissibility. The information foreclosed must be significant to visa eligibility. Balanced against all the other information of record, it must be controlling or crucial to a final decision on visa eligibility. The consular officer must be able to state categorically that, if the true state of affairs had been known, no visa would have been issued.[14]

The facts must lead to a proper finding of ineligibility. If they support a finding that the alien is eligible for a visa, the misrepresented fact is not material. A misrepresentation intended to establish an advantageous immigrant visa status is not material if the alien was entitled to another equally advantageous status. Once a misrepresentation is established, the applicant has the burden of establishing that the facts support eligibility or that, had the consular officer known the truth, a visa could not properly have been refused. The consular officer is to be receptive to any further evidence the alien may provide to ensure that a proper finding has been made.[15] The Ninth Circuit Court of Appeals held that in an application for an immigrant visa, failure to disclose an arrest was not material because the charges were dismissed.[16] The Second Circuit, citing *Kungys v. U.S.*,[17] held in an I-751 petition to remove the conditional basis of residence, that a misrepresentation of residence was material and the applicant must be given the opportunity to rebut a presumption of removability.[18]

The FAM provides guidance on when a fraud or a material willful misrepresentation has occurred.

- Silence is golden—"Silence or the failure to volunteer information does not in itself constitute a misrepresentation."[19]

---

[12] 9 FAM 40.63 N.6.3-1.

[13] 9 FAM 40.63 N.6.3-3.

[14] 9 FAM 40.63 N.6.3-4.

[15] 9 FAM 40.63 N.6.3-5.

[16] *Forbes v. INS*, 48 F.3d 439 (9th Cir. 1995).

[17] *Kungys v. U.S.*, 485 U.S. 759 (1988).

[18] *Monter v. Gonzales*, 430 F.3d 546, 548 n. 1 (2nd Cir. 2005), *published on* AILA InfoNet at Doc. No. 06010960 (*posted* Jan. 9, 2006).

[19] 9 FAM 40.63 N.4.2. *See also Matter of D–L– & A–M–*, 20 I&N Dec. 409 (BIA 1991) (applicants who surrendered false

continued

- Agency—If the alien is aware of the misrepresentation of an agent, such as a travel agent or an attorney, the misrepresentation is willful. A misrepresentation at a port of entry by an aider or abettor is attributable to the alien if the alien was aware of the misrepresentation.[20]

- Alien's own application—The misrepresentation must have been made by the alien with respect to the alien's own visa application.[21]

- Before U.S. official—generally, a consular officer or a DHS officer.[22]

- Timely retraction—serves to purge a misrepresentation if it is made at the first opportunity. If the applicant is being interviewed, the retraction must be made during the interview. The applicant must be warned of the penalty imposed by INA §212(a)(6)(C)(i) at the outset of every initial interview.[23]

- 30/60-day rule—Used to determine if misrepresentation occurred where the alien's activities in the United States vary from the purpose of the visa stated in the application or to the consular officer. This could be a failure to maintain nonimmigrant status or applying for adjustment of status to permanent residence. Such actions do not necessarily prove a misrepresentation at the time of application or entry. "The existence of a misrepresentation must therefore be clearly and factually established by direct or circumstantial evidence sufficient to meet the 'reason to believe' standard. [This] requires that a probability exists, supported by evidence which goes beyond mere suspicion."[24]

- If occurring within 30 days, the officer may presume a misrepresentation in seeking a visa or entry.[25] If it is after 30 days but within 60 days, no presumption of misrepresentation arises. If the facts lead to a reasonable belief of a misrepresentation, the alien must be given the opportunity to present countervailing evidence. If it is not persuasive, an advisory opinion must be sought.[26] If it is after 60 days, the conduct does not constitute a basis to apply INA §212(a)(6)(C)(i) ineligibility.[27] There must be evidence of the misrepresentation. If there is reliance on the 30/60-day guidelines, the Visa Office must concur. The alien has the burden of rebutting the presumption and must be given the evidence and the opportunity to overcome it.[28]

... a visa, other documentation, or admission into the United States or other benefit provided under this Act—

This specifies that the fraud or misrepresentation must be in connection with an application for any INA benefit. Carefully gather and analyze the facts to avoid future misrepresentations about past representations. It is usually advisable to disclose past history and argue that the representation was not fraud or willful misrepresentation of a material fact. Where it is concluded that there is a basis for not disclosing, prepare a memo to file with the justification.

WAIVER ELIGIBILITY

If you conclude your client is (or may be found to be) inadmissible, the next question is whether a waiver available and your client is eligible? A waiver for inadmissibility is provided for in INA §212(a)(6)(C)(iii):

(iii) Waiver authorized—For provision authorizing waiver of clause (i), see subsection (i)

INA §212(i) provides:

(i) Admission of immigrant excludable for fraud or willful misrepresentation of material fact.—

(1) The Attorney General may, in the discretion of the Attorney General, waive the application of clause (i) of subsection (a)(6)(C) in the case of an immigrant who is the spouse, son, or daughter of a United States citizen or of an alien lawfully admitted for permanent residence, if it is established to the satisfaction of the Attorney General that the refusal of admission to the United States of such immigrant alien would result in extreme hardship to the citizen or lawfully resident spouse or parent of such an alien or, in the case of an

---

documents at the port of entry and applied for asylum did not commit fraud or misrepresentation)

[20] 9 FAM 40.63 N.4.5.

[21] 9 FAM 40.63 N.4.4.

[22] 9 FAM 40.63 N.4.3. *See also Matter of Y–G–*, 20 I&N Dec. 794 (BIA 1994).

[23] 9 FAM 40.63 N.4.6.

[24] 9 FAM 40.63 N.4.7-1.

[25] 9 FAM 40.63 N.4.7-2.

[26] 9 FAM 40.63 N.4.7-3.

[27] 9 FAM 40.63 N.4.7-4.

[28] 9 FAM 40.63 N.4.8.

alien granted classification under clause (iii) or (iv) of section 204(a)(1)(A) or clause (ii) or (iii) of section 204(a)(1)(B), the alien demonstrates extreme hardship to the alien or the alien's United States citizen, lawful permanent resident, or qualified alien parent or child.

(2) No court shall have jurisdiction to review a decision or action of the Attorney General regarding a waiver under paragraph (1).

To be eligible for this discretionary waiver, your client must be the spouse or child of a U.S. citizen or lawful permanent resident (the qualifying relative) and it must be established that denying admission would result in extreme hardship to the qualifying relative. Also eligible is an alien or a child of the alien who qualifies to immigrate under the VAWA provisions of the INA as having been battered or the subject of extreme cruelty perpetrated by the alien's spouse or intended spouse. These waiver applications must establish extreme hardship to the alien or the alien's U.S. citizen or lawful permanent resident or VAWA-qualified alien parent or child.

PREPARING THE WAIVER APPLICATION

Waiver applications are major undertakings not to be taken lightly by the client or the practitioner. The client has much at stake and there is a high burden to establish extreme hardship and circumstances deserving favorable exercise of discretion. The application should be prepared just as if the case was before an immigration judge. The applicant has the burden of persuasion, using documentation and testimony (if the waiver is part of an application for adjustment of status or to the immigration court). The client must realize what it takes to win and what will be expected in terms of effort and cost. Also, the client must understand the need to be completely truthful with the practitioner and the government.

A §212(i) waiver is filed on Form I-601. The proper fee must be submitted. The waiver is adjudicated by U.S. Citizenship and Immigration Services (USCIS) and will be filed in one of three venues: consular processing, adjustment of status, or removal proceedings. Be prepared by knowing the means of filing in each venue.

Consular Processing

The I-601 is filed with USCIS after a finding by a consular officer of inadmissibility pursuant to INA §212(a)(6)(C)(i). Typically, the I-601 is physically delivered to the consular officer at the time of the denial or within a specified period thereafter for transmission to the USCIS office with jurisdiction. Arguments challenging the determination of inadmissibility are made to the consular officer. Once there has been a finding of inadmissibility, the I-601 is filed. There is no further argument of inadmissibility to USCIS.

The I-601 must be prepared with the awareness that there will be no live contact with the adjudicator. There will be no interviews or testimony. Everything must be in writing. Once the application is submitted, the practitioner's role is effectively finished (unless there is need and opportunity to supplement the application). There is no further opportunity to advocate.

The challenge is to make the adjudicator's job easy. The application must be accompanied by a cover letter that will keep the adjudicator's attention. The letter organizes the presentation of the waiver case and guides the adjudicator to a favorable decision. The application package must be organized, making it easy to find supporting documentation. Since there is no opportunity for live statements or testimony, affidavits should be presented. Participate in the preparation of all affidavits to make sure they are probative and accurate—but they should not sound as though they were written by a lawyer.

Adjustment of Status

In an adjustment interview, the practitioner is present and can advocate. Nonetheless, a cover letter is advisable. Interviews are time-restricted and there is more than the waiver to consider. The district adjudication officer can be expected to review the case beforehand and often will not adjudicate the waiver at the time of the interview. The practitioner's cover letter therefore gives the officer the first impression of the case and is a guide to consideration of the case. Again, it is the opportunity to make the officer's job of making the right decision easy. While the petitioner and beneficiary can make live statements to the officer during the interview, sworn statements from them are still useful because of time limitations and the fact that most officers take few notes. Other witnesses are usually not interviewed so they should also submit sworn statements. To reiterate, carefully supervise preparation of all affidavits.

Removal Hearings

This venue offers an opportunity for live testimony by the petitioner, the beneficiary, and witnesses. However, clients and witnesses often do not testify well in court. The level of scrutiny will be higher because testimony, including that of the expert witness, is subject to cross-examination, and there is an opposing party. Prepare as for any trial.

Documenting the Waiver Application

The waiver application is far more than the I-601 and a few supporting documents. It is story-telling, painting a picture of the client and the client's family. Communicate to the adjudicator what it is that grabs one, what sets the case from other cases. The client's story and hardship must stand out and tip the balance in favor of the second chance provided by a grant of the waiver. The adjudicator must listen to the story with an open mind. Adjudicators will not be satisfied with perfunctory statements of predictable hardship. Develop a theory of the hardship and build on it.

Submit the I-601 with a cover letter that will quickly educate the adjudicator about the hardship asserted and lay out why the client deserves to have the waiver granted. The goal is to make this an easy choice for the adjudicator. The letter should organize the case and make it easy to follow. Use a numbered exhibit list with references from the letter.

In preparing the case, map out how to:

- Introduce the client in the most favorable light.

- Deal early, quickly, and honestly with the negative factors and distance them from the adjudicatory process. The basis for the ground of inadmissibility will be considered.[29]

- Define and establish each hardship element, including: the qualifying relative's family ties in the United States and lack of family ties in the alien's country; conditions in that country; financial impact of departure from the United States; significant medical and psychological health considerations; length of residence of the qualifying relative and the alien in the United States; possibility of other means of adjustment of status; contributions to and position of the qualifying relative and the alien to the United States and the local community; alien's immigration history; and alien's moral character.[30]

- Argue that the hardship is extreme by distinguishing and personalizing it.

- Establish that a balancing of the "alien's undesirability as a permanent resident with the social and human considerations present" provides a basis for a finding that "a grant of relief is in the best interests of this country."[31] Extreme hardship is a favorable discretionary factor.[32]

- The cover letter should document the client's statutorily eligibility for the waiver, state the facts, and present each topics from the case map.

- Suggested sources for case preparation are:

  – *AILA's Essentials of Removal and Relief* by Joseph A. Vail, American Immigration Lawyers Association, *also* found on the AILA*Link* CD-ROM;

  – *Matter of Cervantes-Gonzalez*, 22 I&N Dec. 560 (BIA 1999), for a discussion of hardship factors and the weight to be given to them;

  – "Hardship Standards," by Bruce A. Hake, *Bender's Immigration Bulletin*, January 2002;

  – *Separate Opinion*, "Where Have All the Waivers Gone? An Examination of Extremely and Exceptionally Unusual Discretionary Standards," by Lory Diana Rosenberg, *Bender's Immigration Bulletin*, February 2003; and

  – *Separate Opinion*, "Another Chance: Forensic Psychological Assessment of Recidivism and Dangerous Immigration Adjudication," by Lory Diana Rosenberg and F. Barton Evans, III, *Bender's Immigration Bulletin*, May 2003.

The following are practice tips for preparing and presenting the waiver case:

- *Engage the adjudicator*—The adjudicator may be predisposed to deny but must be objective. He or she is typically looking for a hook on which to hang the denial. Seek to avoid the hook. Hold the adjudicator's attention. If the case grabbed you enough to take it, make it grab the adjudicator. Answer the question, "Why is this waiver case different from all other waiver cases?" Convince the adjudicator to feel obliged to read on and deliberate before deciding. Be intellectually honest.

---

[29] *Matter of Tijam*, 22 I&N Dec. 408 (BIA 1998).

[30] *Matter of Cervantes-Gonzales*, 22 I&N Dec. 560 (BIA, 1999), *Matter of Anderson*, 16 I&N 596 (BIA 1978), *Matter of L–O–G–*, Int. Dec. 3281 (BIA 1996), and *Matter of O–J–O–*, Int. Dec. 3280 (BIA 1996) and *Matter of Tijam*, 22 I&N Dec. 408.

[31] *Matter of Tijam*, 22 I&N Dec. 408.

[32] *Matter of Mendez-Moralez*, 21 I&N Dec. 296 (BIA 1996).

- *Minimize the ground of inadmissibility*—Show the fraud or misrepresentation to be an isolated event that is out of character for the client. Discuss what motivated the client and why such behavior is not likely to recur. Show that on balance, it is an insufficient basis to impose the hardship of denying the visa while acknowledging that the law was violated.

- *Tell the story and do not rely on the obvious*—Nothing is obvious. The obvious makes your clients just like everyone else. Personalize the case and do not let the adjudicator deny it because the hardship to client's family is the same hardship that anyone would suffer and therefore is not extreme.

- *Thoroughly present the facts*—It is a slippery slope to denial once your story loses credibility. Preparation must include detailed client interviews and a review of all relevant documents for positive and negative factors. An adjudicator who wants to deny will scrutinize the record for justification. You must do the same to confront the negatives and argue the positives. This includes criminal records, police reports, pre-sentence reports, probation reports, etc. Leave no stone unturned. If your clients will be interviewed or testify, they must be totally candid and credible. They must be prepped to state the good and the bad—and to tell the truth.

- *Avoid undocumented statements of fact*—The practitioner's job is to discuss and argue the evidence in the record and not to make the record by undocumented statements of facts. The adjudicator's attention will be quickly lost and the hook on which to hang the denial is at hand. You do not want a denial that says: "Counsel asserts that Mrs. Jones might not find sufficient work . . . in Mexico." "The attorney states that she will be forced to find a job… Additionally, he states that she will not be able to stay at home in order to take care of her child who suffers from Down's Syndrome… No evidence has been provided to substantiate that if she finds a job she will not be able to take care of herself and her children."

- *Avoid undocumented assertions*—A story built on thin air or conclusory statements will not convince. Document, document, document! Cite authority. Show the adjudicator you are serious and that the case merits careful consideration. Lay a strong foundation for appeal. If the case succeeds in gaining the adjudicator's attention and sympa-

thy, it will provide a justification for the decision to be defended to a supervisor.

- *Use a psychological evaluation*—A qualified psychological evaluation is expensive, especially one involving testing, which is important to make the report more objective. Yet every separation or move by spouse or children abroad has a psychological impact. A psychologist is an objective expert who will see things that the practitioner and client will not see and will state them in a professional manner. There will be nothing in the record to contest the opinion.

- Send the client and the qualifying relative to the psychologist only after you have a thorough command of the facts. Summarize the case; explain how the report will be used, what questions are to be answered, and what should not appear in the report. Make sure this discussion is off the record, meaning it will not be in the report. Discuss the case with the psychologist after the evaluation. Get a draft of the report. Make sure the facts as you understand them are the same as those the client stated to the expert. The psychologist should not explain the immigration history. This is not his or her area of expertise.

- *Avoid advocacy by the expert*—An expert witness is often sympathetic and will want to be a team member. However, if the expert is not objective, the report or testimony will not be effective. The expert cannot be an advocate—that's the lawyer's job. The expert should not state legal conclusions and should not use the legal term "extreme hardship."

- *Make it clear that hardship to the children is hardship to the spouse*—By statute, the waiver may only consider hardship to the spouse or parent. However, hardship to children is hardship to the parents. Show that the effects of hardship to the children result in hardship on the soon-to-be-single-parent spouse. Document the spouse's situation before the beneficiary appeared on the scene and use an expert and other evidence to predict the consequences of the spouse raising the children alone.

- *Describe the hardship to the qualifying relative of living abroad*—The adjudicator will consider this. Bring out facts such as roots the spouse and children have in the community, with family, etc. Help the adjudicator imagine herself or himself in the qualifying relative's shoes. Use reports of economic conditions and living standards in the foreign country. See if the State Department travel advisories make the place look dangerous. The expert can then report on how this would impact the qualifying relative.

- *Expect that the adjudicator may find that the hardship was self-imposed*—Creating family relationships is not a deliberate, calculated, or rational act. It consists of emotional milestones in one's life. Make the adjudicator see him- or herself in the same dilemma. Use the expert.

- *Avoid unpersuasive evidence*—Making the case look desperate weakens it by losing the adjudicator's attention and providing a hook for denial. Unsworn statements from parties will be given less weight. Handwritten letters should be accompanied by an affidavit from the witness that acknowledges authorship, states that it is the truth to the best of the witness's knowledge, belief, and recollection, and provides the witness's address and telephone number. Statements should evidence familiarity with the facts, especially negative ones. Declarations should not be

pro forma and should have more than gratuitous motivation. Avoid friends and family whom you might expect to say good things—except for mothers-in-law, who are always concerned about the well-being of their children. Conclusory documents are minimally probative if the reason for the conclusion is not stated.

- *Remember the totality of the circumstances*—Beyond serious health conditions, no one positive factor can be expected to carry the day. The argument that convinces is based on the totality of the circumstances.

CONCLUSION

Fraud or willful misrepresentation can have disastrous immigration consequences. A successful waiver is far from a given. Clients must understand what they face and be prepared to undertake the effort and cost of a well-prepared defense to the ground of inadmissibility and prosecution of the waiver application.

WAIVERS OF THE §212(a)(9)(C) PERMANENT BAR
HOW TO GET THEM IF YOU NEED THEM—
AND WHAT IS A 'REMOVAL ORDER' ANYWAY?

*by Philip Hornik**

THE STATUTE

The Immigration and Nationality Act's (INA) §212(a)(9)(C) was created by IIRAIRA.[1] It provides as follows:

Aliens unlawfully present after previous immigration violations.

(i) In general. Any alien who—

(I) has been unlawfully present in the United States for an aggregate period of more than 1 year, or

(II) has been ordered removed under section 235(b)(1) [8 USC §1225(b)(1)], section 240 [8 USC §1229a], or any other provision of law, and who enters or attempts to reenter the United States without being admitted is inadmissible.

(ii) Exception. Clause (I) shall not apply to an alien seeking admission more than 10 years after the date of the alien's last departure from the United States if, prior to the alien's reembarkation at a place outside the United States or attempt to be readmitted from a foreign contiguous territory, the Attorney General has consented to the alien's reapplying for admission. The Attorney General in the Attorney General's discretion may waive the provisions of section 212(a)(9)(C)(i) in the case of an alien to whom the Attorney General has granted classification under clause (iii), (iv), or (v) of section 204(a)(1)(A), or classification under clause (ii), (iii), or (iv) of section 204(a)(1)(B), in any case in which there is a connection between—

(1) the alien's having been battered or subjected to extreme cruelty; and

(2) the alien's—

(A) removal;

(B) departure from the United States;

(C) reentry or reentries into the United States; or

(D) attempted reentry into the United States.

Except for those aliens who are within the narrow group of exceptions set forth in INA §212(a)(9)(C)(ii), it is not even possible to request a waiver of §212(a)(9)(C)(i)(I) inadmissibility until the alien has remained outside the United States for 10 years.

WHAT IS A REMOVAL ORDER?

The answer to this question may be more or less than meets the eye, depending on whose eye it is. There is no definition of the word "removed" in the INA.

There are a number of procedures by which U.S. immigration officials are authorized to send an alien from the United States to another country. These include:

- an immigration judge's Order of Removal, Deportation, or Exclusion after a hearing[2];

- an Order of Expedited Removal;[3]

- an Order of Expedited Removal of an alien convicted of an aggravated felony;[4]

- reinstatement of a removal order;[5] and

- judicial removal.[6]

But what about those aliens who leave the United States pursuant to an order of voluntary departure[7] at

---

* **Philip Hornik** is an attorney in private practice in Portland, Ore. His practice has emphasized immigration law since 1997. Since 1980, he has had a solo law practice handling all aspects of immigration law. He has been the update editor of the National Immigration Project's *Immigration Law and Defense* (a Thomson*West publication) since 1991. Mr. Hornik has been a frequent speaker at AILA National and Northwest immigration conferences.

[1] The Illegal Immigration Reform and Immigrant Responsibility Act of 1996, Division C of Omnibus Appropriations Act of 1996 (HR 3610), Pub. L. No. 104-208, 110 Stat. 3009.

[2] INA §240 or former INA §242.

[3] INA §235(b).

[4] INA §238(b).

[5] INA §241(a)(5).

[6] INA §238(c).

[7] INA §240B.

their own expense? Moreover, regarding individuals who apply for immigrant visas at the U.S. consulate in Cd. Juarez, Mexico—what about those aliens who enter the United States illegally, are arrested by immigration officials, and are promptly returned to Mexico without becoming the subject of a removal or expedited removal proceeding?[8] Before IIRAIRA was enacted, this practice was known as "voluntary departure at government expense under safeguards." It is now known as "voluntary removal."

Voluntary departure is a form of relief from removal or deportation. It offers an alien an alternative to the entry of an order of deportation or removal. An alien who is ordered removed or deported becomes inadmissible for a period ranging from five years to life, depending on the statutory ground underlying the order.[9]

The clear distinction between voluntary departure and a removal order was noted by the Ninth Circuit in *Gallo-Alvarez v. Ashcroft*.[10] In this case, an alien was granted 60 days of voluntary departure at his 1993 deportation hearing, but failed to leave within that time. He departed later and then re-entered illegally and was apprehended by U.S. immigration authorities, who again sought to expel him from the United States without affording him a removal hearing. He challenged[11] the government's efforts to reinstate his 1993 deportation order.

The court stated:

 Of course, §1231 does not apply to all aliens who voluntarily depart under the threat of deportation; it applies only to aliens who, like Gallo, actually received the benefit of formal deportation proceedings prior to their predicate deportation. See 8 USC §1254(e) (repealed 1996). In other words, 1231 does not apply to aliens who received voluntary departure under old INA

§242(b). Under that provision, codified at 8 U.S.C. §1252(b) (repealed 1996), an alien could receive voluntary departure by conceding deportability and waiving the right to formal deportation proceedings. This second form of voluntary departure is a 'rough immigration equivalent to a guilty plea.' *Contreras-Aragon v. INS*, 852 F.2d 1088, 1094 (9th Cir.1988) (internal quotation omitted). Aliens who depart voluntarily under this provision are not leaving 'under an order of removal,' and thus are not subject to reinstatement under 8 U.S.C. §1231(a)(5).[12]

Notwithstanding this analysis, in 2003, U.S. consulate and Department of Homeland Security (DHS) personnel in Cd. Juarez began interpreting INA §212(a)(9)(C)(i)(II) to mean that any expulsion from the United States constitutes a removal under "any other provision of law." Thus, in the consulate's opinion, an alien who has entered the United States without inspection and is then summarily returned to Mexico via "voluntary removal" has been "ordered removed." According to this interpretation, an alien who later enters without inspection after receiving a voluntary removal order becomes inadmissible and ineligible to seek a waiver of inadmissibility until the alien has remained outside the United States for 10 years.[13]

The Visa Office later consulted DHS's general counsel on this issue. They have rethought their interpretation of INA §212(a)(9)(C)(i)(II):

According to the informal opinion of DHS, a 'voluntary removal' (which would normally occur when an alien who entered without inspection agreed to a removal without being issued a removal order at a Port of Entry or by an Immigration Judge) would not be considered an order of removal, and therefore would not meet the criteria in 212(a)(9)(C)(i)(II) for an ineligibility determination under this section.[14]

An informal DHS opinion is better than no opinion at all. Pursuant to INA §103(a), which was created by the Homeland Security Act of 2002,[15] it is

---

[8] It is likely that expedited removal proceedings will be used with increasing frequency to expel those who have been apprehended in the United States near the U.S./Mexico border. The Department of Homeland Security (DHS) has announced that it will be applying expedited removal to those aliens "who have spent 14 days or less in the U.S. and are apprehended within 100 miles of the border with Canada or Mexico or arrive by sea and are apprehended within 100 miles of a coastal border area." *See* DHS's Jan. 30, 2006 Press Release, *published on* AILA InfoNet at Doc. No. 06013018 (*posted* Jan. 30, 2006).

[9] *See* INA §§212(a)(9)(A)(i) and (ii).

[10] 266 F.3d 1123 (9th Cir. 2001).

[11] Pursuant to INA §241(a)(5).

[12] 266 F.3d at 1129.

[13] *See* AILA-State Department Visa Office Liaison Meeting Minutes, Item No. 16 (Mar. 4, 2004), *published on* AILA InfoNet at Doc. No. 04042164 (*posted* Apr. 21, 2004).

[14] *See* AILA-State Department Visa Office Liaison Meeting Minutes, Item No. 40 (Oct. 20, 2005), *published on* AILA InfoNet at Doc. No. 05112874 (*posted* Nov. 28, 2005.)

[15] Homeland Security Act of 2002, Pub. L. No. 107-296, 116 Stat. 2135 (Nov. 25, 2002).

now DHS rather than the State Department that governs visa policy. Hopefully, DHS will issue regulations on this matter soon.

WHO IS SUBJECT TO §212(a)(9)(C)(i)?

Does INA §245(i) trump §212(a)(9)(C)(i)? Decisions in the Ninth and Tenth Circuits say "yes" as to (C)(i)(I); the Fifth Circuit's response is less promising, and the Supreme Court has been asked to weigh in as to (a)(9)(C)(i)(II).

Many aliens who are immediate relatives of U.S. citizens have returned to the United States illegally after being ordered deported or removed by an immigration judge or after accruing more than one year of unlawful presence in the United States. Many of them who were present in the United States on December 20, 2001, are the beneficiaries of immigrant visa petitions or alien labor certification applications filed before May 1, 2001.

DHS, relying on legacy Immigration and Naturalization Service guidance memoranda, has taken the position that such aliens are not eligible to apply for adjustment of status, on the theory that they are inadmissible pursuant to INA §212(a)(9)(C). DHS argues that those who are inadmissible under §212(a)(9)(C)(i)(I) are ineligible to even request a waiver of inadmissibility until they have left the United States, triggering the 10-year bar. Those who are inadmissible under (C)(i)(II) can only obtain a waiver of inadmissibility if they obtain approval of an I-212 application for permission to reapply for admission—and they can only file an I-212 while they are outside the United States.

Fortunately, the Ninth and Tenth Circuits have rejected the DHS position.

In *Perez-Gonzalez v. Ashcroft*,[16] the Ninth Circuit held that an alien who has been removed and has reentered the United States illegally is nonetheless eligible to apply for adjustment of status pursuant to INA §245(i) as amended by the LIFE Act.[17] Essen-

tially, the court concluded that §245(i) waives §212(a)(9)(C)(ii) inadmissibility.

The court rejected as unpersuasive the contrary interpretation in a 1997 INS guidance memorandum of §245(i)'s impact on §212(a)(9)(C)(i)(II).[18] Instead, the court looked to the purpose of the LIFE Act's amendments to INA §245(i) as indicated in the Joint Memorandum, Statement of Senator Kennedy,[19] as well as the absence of anything in the LIFE Act's legislative history that "suggests that aliens who have been previously deported or removed are barred from adjustment of status."[20]

Similarly, in *Padilla-Caldera v. Gonzales*,[21] the Tenth Circuit gave little weight to the 1997 guidance memorandum interpreting §212(a)(C)(i)'s effect on §245(i) adjustment applicants. The court said that "most convincingly, there is evidence in the timing of the passage of the LIFE Act that Congress did not intend that its effect would be blocked by 8 USC §1182(a)(9)(C)(i)."[22]

However, in *Fernandez-Vargas v. Ashcroft*,[23] a different Tenth Circuit panel found "no inherent tension between the allowance of adjustment of status to aliens admitted without inspection under INA §245(i) and the bar to any relief to previously removed aliens who illegally re-enter the United States under INA §241(a)(5)."[24] Fernandez-Vargas, like Perez-Gonzales, re-entered the United States illegally after being deported and applied for adjustment of status pursuant to INA §245(i). He attempted to obtain a waiver of inadmissibility under INA §212(a)(9)(C)(i)(II) by filing an I-212. But, unlike the Ninth Circuit in *Perez-Gonzalez*, the court in *Fernandez-Vargas* rejected the argument that filing the I-212 could cure his inadmissibility.

The Fifth Circuit, in *Mortera-Cruz v. Gonzalez*,[25] rejected the *Padilla-Calderas* analysis and held that the court of appeals should defer to BIA's conclusion that §245(i) does not implicitly waive Mortera-

---

[16] 379 F.3d 783 (9th Cir. 2004), *motion to reconsider denied*, 403 F.3d 1116 (9th Cir. 2005).

[17] Legal Immigration Family Equity Act (LIFE), Pub. L. No. 106-553, 114 Stat. 2762, Title XI of HR 5548 (Dec. 21, 2000), H. Rep. No. 106-1005 at 185; 2000 H.R. 4942 and LIFE Act Amendments, Pub. L. No. 106-554, 114 Stat. 2763, Title XV, Division B, of H.R. 5666 (Dec. 21, 2000), H. Rep. Conf. 106-1033; 146 Cong. Rec. S11850-02 (daily ed. Dec. 15, 2000–Senator's Joint Memorandum).

[18] 379 F.3d at 793.

[19] 146 Cong. Rec. S11850-52 (daily ed. Dec. 2000).

[20] 379 F.3d at 793.

[21] 426 F.3d 1294 (10th Cir. 2005).

[22] *Id.* at 1299.

[23] 394 F.3d 881 (10th Cir. 2005), *cert. granted, sub nom.*, *Fernandez-Vargas v. Gonzales*, 126 S. Ct. 544 (Oct. 31, 2005).

[24] 394 F.3d at 885.

[25] 409 F.3d 246 (5th Cir. 2005).

Cruz's §212(a)(9)(C)(i)(I) inadmissibility. However, the *Mortera-Cruz* holding is narrow, *i.e.*, that the Board, in an unpublished nonprecedent decision, did not act arbitrarily in finding that Mortera-Cruz was ineligible for adjustment of status, notwithstanding INA §245(i).[26]

Most recently, in *Acosta v. Gonzales*,[27] the Ninth Circuit relied on its reasoning in *Perez-Gonzalez*, and concluded that INA §245(i) is "an ameliorative rule designed to forestall harsh results."[28] The court interpreted this statute in "an ameliorative fashion."[29] The court noted that

> [w]ith respect to Acosta's case, there is also nothing to suggest that aliens who reenter the country after accruing more than one year of unlawful presence are ineligible for penalty-fee adjustment of status.[30]

Therefore, the court concluded that "an alien inadmissible for accruing more than one year of unlawful status is eligible for penalty-free adjustment of status."[31]

CONCLUSION

A certain catcher for a noted American League baseball team once opined that "it ain't over til it's over."[32] It is expected that the government will seek further review of the *Acosta* decision. The Supreme Court's resolution of the *Fernandez-Vargas* case may well resolve the extent to which INA §245(i) and an I-212 waiver application can cure inadmissibility for aliens present after previous immigration violations.

As has been said in other forums, for further details, "watch this space."

---

[26] *Id*. at 256.

[27] 2006 WL 408206, 439 F.3d 550 (9th Cir. 2006).

[28] *Id*. (citing *Akhtar v. Burzynski*, 384 F.3d 1193 at 1201 (9th Cir. 2004)).

[29] 2006 WL 408206*4.

[30] 2006 WL 408206*2.

---

[31] 2006 WL 408206*3.

[32] Yogi Berra.

NONIMMIGRANT WAIVERS FOR CANADIAN CITIZENS AND INSTABILITY IN THE PROCESSING SYSTEM

by William Z. Reich and Jill A. Apa[*]

INTRODUCTION

Because we are immigration lawyers practicing near the Northern Border, Canadian citizens make up a majority of our client base. Due to the proximity of the United States and Canada and the traditionally friendly relationship between the countries, Canadians often are subject to a unique collection of U.S. immigration laws. One way Canadians are set apart from all other foreign nationals is how the U.S. government processes an application for a nonimmigrant waiver (NIV).

This article provides a comprehensive description of the general waiver process as it relates to Canadian citizens, as well as an illustration of the instability that has unfortunately plagued the system since the terror attacks of September 11, 2001, the dismemberment of INS, and the subsequent creation of the Department of Homeland Security (DHS).

---

[*] **William Reich** is senior partner of the immigration law firm, Serotte, Reich & Wilson, LLP, based in Buffalo. He is a graduate of Queens College, CUNY, and the State University of New York at Buffalo School of Law. He co-authored two chapters for Gordon, Mailman & Yale-Loehr, *Immigration Law and Procedure*, on the "North American Free Trade Agreement, and Inspection and Entry; Procedure at the Border; Remedies; Penalties and Sanctions." He is also co-editor-in-chief of AILA's *Immigration Procedure Under NAFTA and Other Free Trade Agreements*, Third Ed. (2006). A frequent lecturer and panelist at seminars and AILA conferences, Mr. Reich maintains an extensive practice in NAFTA business applications and border-problem cases.

Jill Apa is an associate attorney in the Buffalo firm of Serotte, Reich & Wilson, LLP. A graduate of the University of New Hampshire and Ohio Northern University Pettit College of Law, Ms. Apa previously served as a staff attorney at the Third District Court of Appeals for the State of Ohio. Ms. Apa's immigration practice includes employment, family, and border issues. Additionally, Ms. Apa has authored various professional articles, including the immigration chapter in *Homeland Security Deskbook* (Matthew Bender), as well as two chapters discussing nonimmigrants and foreign-born fiancé(e)s, which are set for publication in the *2006 Immigration Law and Procedure Desk Edition* (Matthew Bender). Ms. Apa also served as associate editor of AILA's *Immigration Procedure Under NAFTA and Other Free Trade Agreements*, Third Ed. (2006).

TRIAGE OF A CANADIAN NIV WAIVER CASE

Step 1: The Preliminaries— Ask the Questions and Identify the Issues

The Immigration and Nationality Act (INA)[1] sets forth a myriad of grounds of inadmissibility at §212(a). The most common grounds of inadmissibility encountered in everyday practice are those relating to criminal convictions, prior orders of removal—including those for fraud/misrepresentation, which then becomes a separate and distinct ground in and of itself—and health-related issues. In an initial interview with a client, an attorney should make every effort to ask direct questions that, if answered truthfully, would elicit information leading to the belief that a ground of inadmissibility may be implicated.

Step 2: Hunt Down the Docs

The next step is to ask the client for all relevant documentation. Without the proper documentation, a lawyer may be tempted to presume a ground of inadmissibility exists without engaging in a comprehensive analysis of the specific facts of the case. The background, history, and details of the perceived ground of inadmissibility must be thoroughly dissected before making a final determination that a waiver is necessary.

If there has been a criminal conviction, the client should provide certified copies of the trial court records, including the final judgment and sentencing order. If the client no longer has possession of these records, which is often the case, ask if he or she can locate them through the attorney that represented him or her during the criminal proceedings. If there was no attorney or the case occurred so long ago that the attorney no longer practices and/or has destroyed all of the records, you may have to deal with the court directly. In the alternative, if the conviction occurred in Canada, you may want to inquire as to whether the client can obtain at least the basic information about

---

[1] Immigration and Nationality Act of 1952, Pub. L. No. 82-414, 66 Stat. 163 (codified as amended at 8 USC §§1101 *et seq.*) (INA).

the case, *i.e.,* date of incident, charged offense, and disposition through a search conducted by the Royal Canadian Mounted Police (RCMP). In some cases, tracking down the records is no easy task, but again, presuming a ground of inadmissibility does nothing to help the client in the long run. In addition to the court records, obtain a copy of the criminal statute under which the client was convicted. That way, you have the particular language of the law at your fingertips.

In situations involving a prior order of removal, the client should produce the final order from the immigration judge or Board of Immigration Appeals (BIA). If the removal took place under an expedited removal order authorized under INA §235(b)(1), the client should provide all paperwork generated at the port of entry, including the I-867 Q&A, which sets forth the official statement that the client provided to the immigration officers after being placed under oath. Surprisingly, clients frequently fail to foresee the importance of this documentation and they toss or otherwise destroy the information. At present, there is virtually no other way to obtain prior immigration records aside from having to file a Freedom of Information Act (FOIA) request. While FOIA requests once took only weeks to generate, it is not uncommon for clients to wait more than a year for the government to produce these essential records in this post-9/11 era—another symptom of the problems that have arisen since the creation of DHS.

In the case of a health-related ground of inadmissibility, the client should provide medical records, a list of current medications, and any evidence to show participation in a rehabilitation program. Under INA §212(a)(1)(A)(i), an individual is inadmissible for a health-related issue if he or she has "a communicable disease of public health significance," which includes the HIV virus. Additionally, a person who currently has or has had a physical or mental disorder that has caused certain behavior that has posed or may pose a threat to the property, safety, or welfare of the foreign national or other individuals is inadmissible. Lastly, an individual who is determined to be a "drug abuser or addict" is inadmissible to the United States.

Step 3: Analyze That!

Once the applicable documentation has been obtained, the attorney must carefully review the facts and circumstances in light of the particular rules surrounding the potential ground of inadmissibility. While this can get tedious, it may reveal that your client is subject to an exception to the general rules

of inadmissibility. The following are descriptions of scenarios that allow the client to circumvent the waiver requirement:

Convictions Don't Always Equal Inadmissibility

In the case of a past criminal conviction (for a crime involving moral turpitude—CIMT), be sure to notice your client's age at the time of the offense. If he or she was under the age of 18, this could mean that the conviction is exempt from the law regarding inadmissibility[2] or it may even mean that the U.S. government will not recognize the conviction for purposes of immigration.

Additionally, the INA contains a "petty offense exception" which, if applicable, will not render the client inadmissible. This exception obviates the need for a waiver if the client has only one conviction and the "maximum penalty possible for the crime of which the alien was convicted . . . did not exceed imprisonment for one year and, if the alien was convicted of such crime, the alien was not sentenced to a term of imprisonment in excess of 6 months (regardless of the extent to which the sentence was ultimately executed)."[3]

Furthermore, do not assume that all offenses involve moral turpitude that would implicate inadmissibility. Certain offenses may, at first glance, appear to be a CIMT but, upon further inspection, are considered by the government to be merely "regulatory" in nature. Although not formally defined in the INA, "moral turpitude" is frequently described as an act that is "inherently base or vile." Obviously, violent offenses committed against other persons, such as rape or manslaughter, involve moral turpitude. Additionally, it is not difficult to find the element of moral turpitude in serious crimes against property such as arson.

The lines become much more blurred, however, with unusual or uncommon offenses. The *Foreign Affairs Manual* (FAM) specifies that crimes against property or governmental authorities, such as customs violations, generally do not involve moral turpitude unless fraud is an element of the offense. This is why your analysis must focus on the relevant statute as well as the court documents.

---

[2] INA §212(a)(2)(A)(ii)(I)

[3] INA §212(a)(2)(A)(ii)(II).

Is the Order of Removal Vulnerable to Attack?

If the client appears to be inadmissible for a prior order of removal, particularly with a prior expedited removal order issued at the port of entry, be sure to carefully examine the documents generated as a result of the incident. Expedited removal orders, which are authorized under INA §235(b)(1), can only be issued for charges of inadmissibility under INA §212(a)(6) (fraud/material misrepresentation) or 212(a)(7) (lack of proper documentation).

Remember that since the implementation of DHS and the break-up of Immigration and Naturalization Service (INS), three separate agencies are now charged with handling various immigration matters. U.S. Customs and Border Protection (CBP), which is part of this massive trio, is the agency that conducts the immigration inspections when foreign nationals present themselves for admission. The current make-up of the CBP includes officers with INS backgrounds as well as officers who, prior to the creation of DHS, specialized in customs issues only. This lack of experience among many CBP officers sometimes leads to an erroneously issued expedited removal order, especially as it relates to a charge involving fraud or a material misrepresentation.

For these reasons, be sure to compare the client's statement to the officers against the facts presented to you in your subsequent interview. During your interview, it may become obvious that, although the client may have told an untruth during the inspections process, the statement does not rise to the level of fraud and cannot be considered "material" to the ultimate question of admission. Many CBP officers don't understand the issue of materiality and have not yet grasped the concept that a misstatement may not always lead to inadmissibility, particularly if the individual is admissible on the true facts.

The expedited removal laws do not allow for further review of the order by a court or different agency. Thus, if you encounter an expedited removal order that cannot be supported by the facts, your only recourse is to contact the issuing port and argue for reversal or amendment of the order. This is by no means an easy task, and the port officials often do not immediately accept or understand what you are trying to do. Keep in mind, however, that although there is nothing in the law that requires a review of the order, there also is nothing that prohibits the ports from taking a second look and correcting whatever mistakes were made.

Not All Health-Related Issues Signal an Admissibility Death-Knell

Based on the general parameters outlined in INA §212(a)(1)(A), a medical issue may, on the surface, appear to cause an issue of admissibility. However, in certain cases, part of an attorney's due diligence may be to ask the client to undergo a comprehensive medical exam by a designated panel physician who can then make a professional determination as to whether the individual actually comes within the reach of the statute.

For example, the mere existence of a serious physical or mental disorder does not, in and of itself, automatically lead to inadmissibility. Rather, the disorder must have led to certain harmful behavior, which includes the foreign national causing injury to him- or herself or another, threatening the health or safety of him- or herself or another, or causing property damage.[4]

Furthermore, an issue with drug abuse does not, by itself, render the individual inadmissible for a health-related reason. Note that the language of INA §212(a)(1)(A)(iv) provides that inadmissibility is only implicated if the individual *is* determined to be an abuser or addict. The use of the verb *is* clearly requires a present tense determination. This is confirmed by the FAM, which allows for a finding that the individual is in remission from drug use or abuse.[5] A finding of remission occurs if the panel physician determines that a certain period of time—two to three years depending on the particular drug involved—has elapsed since the last incident of use.[6] If the physician records a finding of remission, the foreign national is not considered inadmissible on the health-related ground.

NO WAY OUT—THE CLIENT NEEDS A WAIVER

If, after all of the analyses and assessments of the case, you determine that the client needs a waiver, various laws and processes will apply. Following is a description of the law and the processes and pitfalls that can arise:

---

[4] 9 FAM 40.11 N.8.

[5] *Id.* at N.9.4.

[6] *Id.* at N.9.5.

The NIV Waiver Process for Visa-Exempt Canadian Citizens

Waivers for Criminal/Immigration Law Violations

Pursuant to 22 CFR §41.2, Canadian citizens who wish to enter the United States in nonimmigrant status are generally exempt from having to obtain a visa from a U.S. consulate. (The limited exceptions to this rule for the E-1/E-2 and K-1 classifications are discussed in detail below.) Under INA §212(d)(3)(A)(ii) (formerly INA §212(d)(3)(B)) and 8 CFR §§212.4(b), 1212.4(b), inadmissible Canadian citizens must file an I-192 waiver form along with supporting documentation at a port of entry or pre-flight inspection at a CBP office. The application must be filed in person so that the applicant can be fingerprinted for the FBI background checks.

The situs of adjudication depends on where the application is filed. Various CBP offices have been engaged in a lengthy and nasty turf war that has caused much anguish among applicants and their attorneys. Once filed, certain ports transfer the application directly to the Admissibility Review Office (ARO), which is a part of CBP and headquartered in Minneapolis.[7] Upon its inception, attorneys understood that the ARO was meant to serve as a unified adjudications office for all I-192 waiver applications. This has turned out not to be the case since certain other ports continue to transfer I-192 applications to regional CBP offices for final adjudication. For example, an I-192 filed at the Peace Bridge port of entry in Buffalo is transferred to the CBP office in Champlain, Vt. At this point, it remains to be seen whether this issue will ever be completely resolved. Therefore, it is in everyone's best interest to contact the port where the application will be filed to obtain this important information at the outset. Even then, be prepared for the possibility of unanticipated transfers and difficulty following up on processing of the application.

Adjudication Rules

Adjudication of an I-192 application to waive immigration or criminal law violations is discretionary and based on a balancing test that involves three separate factors. The leading case regarding these applications is *Matter of Hranka*[8] wherein the BIA articulated the following factors for consideration:

1. risk of harm to society if the applicant is admitted;

2. seriousness of the applicant's immigration or criminal law violations; and

3. nature of the applicant's reasons for wishing to enter the United States.

While *Hranka* is the major authority on nonimmigrant waiver applications filed under INA §212(d)(3)(A)(ii), certain steadfast rules and policies surrounding these three factors have developed in recent years.

First, assessment of the risk of harm seems to be tied directly to a demonstration of rehabilitation. Rehabilitation can be shown through a variety of documents, including letters from influential members of the foreign national's community, reports from probation officers, evidence of charitable contributions, and service to the community. Unless the conviction or immigration violation is relatively old (more than five years), this type of evidence can be key to a favorable determination.

Second, although *Hranka* does not require that the applicant show a compelling reason to come to the United States, important personal or business motives carry more weight than the desire to simply enjoy a U.S. vacation. The dream of visiting Disney World is less compelling than the wish to spend a holiday with aging lawful permanent resident parents who can no longer travel due to health risks.

Third, many clients seek the advice of counsel immediately following a criminal conviction or immigration violation with the idea that the inability to travel to the United States will only last a few months. These clients need to be reminded over and over again that the U.S. government does not usually grant waiver applications that were filed shortly after the problem causing the inadmissibility has occurred. If this were the case, the laws would have virtually no impact. The more serious the situation, the longer the applicant should wait before filing the I-192. As a rule of thumb, a minor drug conviction or fraud/material misrepresentation at the border may require at least a two-year wait. That way, the initial sting of the violation has lessened and the applicant can take advantage of the opportunity to show sufficient rehabilitation.

---

[7] This office attempted to obtain certain statistical information from the ARO to include in this article. However, we were unable to convince the ARO officials to provide the information for publication.

[8] *Matter of Hranka*, Int. Dec. 2544 (BIA 1978).

Finally, processing times vary depending on where the adjudication is set to take place. However, the days of having an I-192 adjudicated within three to four months are long gone. An increase in mandatory background and security checks, coupled with the post-9/11 agency-wide opinion that waivers are not high priority, translates into lengthy processing times. Clients must be advised that it is not uncommon to wait up to 12 months before the agency issues a notice of decision. This obviously places a major strain on the case if CBP eventually grants a waiver with a validity period of only one year. This means that the client is essentially forced to file an application for renewal almost immediately after receipt of the decision.

Interplay between I-192 and I-212 Waiver Applications—Possible Changes to Come

Traditionally, the filing of an I-192 application has been the means of waiving all grounds of inadmissibility for a visa-exempt Canadian, save and except for certain security-related issues considered absolutely "unwaivable" under the statute. No separate I-212, "Application for Permission to Reapply for Admission Into the United States After Deportation or Removal," was required to overcome inadmissibility caused by a prior deportation or removal order.

However, CBP is currently reviewing whether an I-212 also must be filed when the individual is inadmissible for a previous removal order as well as a criminal/immigration violation and/or health-related matter. This disturbing obligation for the I-192/I-212 combination has already started to emerge in certain regions in the western United States.

If uniformly implemented, this change in procedure will undoubtedly wreak havoc on the nonimmigrant waiver program. This is especially true since, at present, the regulations require that an I-192 be adjudicated by CBP, while an I-212 application is decided by the U.S. Citizenship and Immigration Services (USCIS). Processing times, confusion, and overall frustration will likely increase ten-fold.

Waivers for Health-Related Grounds of Inadmissibility for Visa-Exempt Canadians

Prior to the terror attacks of 9/11 and the creation of DHS, INS had the authority to decide I-192 waivers for health-related grounds of inadmissibility right at the port of entry. The background checks, fingerprints, and other *Hranka* evidence necessary for the criminal/immigration waivers is generally not required for a health-related I-192. Rather, these waivers are based more on concrete medical evidence and, if applicable, evidence regarding the applicant's desire to seek treatment in the United States.

Currently, however, another jurisdictional war is raging over the authority to adjudicate these waivers at the ports. While certain ports continue to accept and adjudicate these I-192 applications, other ports are convinced that they must be transferred to the ARO along with all the other nonimmigrant waiver applications. There has been no official guidance to resolve this split in opinion. Therefore, even if a client is granted an I-192 medical waiver at one port, another port is not bound by that action, so admission may still be denied. We have been advised that this issue is being reviewed by CBP officials, but as of the time of publication, there has been no final determination.

NIV Waivers for Canadians Who Need a Visa

While the majority of Canadian citizens who are seeking to enter the United States as nonimmigrants do not require visas, persons seeking E-1/E-2 treaty trader or investor status, as well as K-1 fiancé(e)s, must obtain visas before applying for admission. Requests for waivers that are part of a visa application are dictated by INA §212(d)(3)(A)(i). As set forth below, there are significant differences in processing when the waiver application is filed in conjunction with an application for a visa.

E-Visa Applicants

A Canadian E-visa applicant must file all appropriate forms and evidence to support the nonimmigrant visa classification at the U.S. Consulate in Toronto. The consul may accept the application, but, upon discovery of the particular ground of inadmissibility, deny the visa. At that point, the applicant must also submit a request for a waiver. Unlike the I-192 application, the submission to the consular officer does not require any specific form or RCMP fingerprint reports. However, the applicant should still submit documentation regarding the ground of inadmissibility, *i.e.,* certified criminal records, as well as evidence to satisfy the *Hranka* criteria.

Upon submission of the waiver request, the consul will review the file and decide whether to recommend approval to DHS. If DHS approves the waiver, the consul is then authorized to issue the E-visa, which will contain a notation of the waiver on its face. Although processing times for I-192 applications are at an all-time high, DHS seems to issue decisions on the §212(d)(3)(A)(i) waiver requests more expeditiously, in about 60 days.

It should be noted, however, that in this type of case the waiver is tied exclusively to the visa. Therefore, if the E-visa status fails because the supporting business has failed, the applicant cannot enter the United States in a visa-exempt posture without an approved I-192 application.

K-1 Visa Applicants

A Canadian seeking K-1 fiancé(e) status to enter the United States and marry a U.S. citizen within 90 days of the admission, must first file an I-129F petition with the regional USCIS service center having jurisdiction over the petitioner's place of residence. The I-129F simply provides the agency with proper identification of the parties, as well as evidence of the required personal meeting within the past two years and confirmation that the U.S. citizen and foreign national are free and able to marry each other.[9] Once the I-129F is approved, the case is then transferred to the U.S. Consulate in Montreal for purposes of the visa application.

A K-1 visa is widely recognized as a "hybrid." While it is technically classified as a nonimmigrant visa,[10] the K-1 applicant must engage in an application process that is almost identical to that of an individual seeking an immigrant visa (Green Card). The nonimmigrant waiver provisions, therefore, technically apply to a K-1 visa application. However, since the very purpose of the K-1 visa is to allow a foreign-born fiancé(e) to enter the United States, marry a U.S. citizen, and then file for adjustment of status to lawful permanent residency, the consular officers will not issue the visa unless the applicant is eligible for an immigrant waiver under INA §§212(g), (h), or (i); 212(a)(9)(B)(v); 212(d)(11) or (12).[11] The necessary application form corresponds to the type of waiver sought.

Similar to the E-visa situation, the consular officer will review the file and make a determination regarding recommendation for approval. If the consular officials recommend approval, the waiver application will be transferred to the appropriate DHS office for a final determination. The situs of the adjudication is unfortunately unstable at this time. While immigrant waiver applications submitted in Montreal were once adjudicated by the Buffalo INS District Office, they are now being transferred to different locations.

For instance, an I-601 application to waive the prior accrual of unlawful presence under INA §212(a)(9)(B)(v) is now forwarded to the Vermont Service Center. As with any other waiver application, processing times depend on the place of adjudication. If the waiver is ultimately approved, the consul can issue the K-1 visa and the applicant will have a clear path to adjustment.

CONCLUSION

Obtaining a waiver for a client who is a Canadian citizen is no longer a predictable and transparent process. Since 9/11 and the creation of DHS, the nonimmigrant waiver program has undergone a multitude of twists and turns that have led to prolonged processing times and mounting frustration among applicants and attorneys. Due to the continuing battles over jurisdiction among the CBP and USCIS, as well as the designation of waivers as low priority, there is unfortunately no end in sight to this turmoil. This is all the more reason for immigration lawyers to take the time to make a thorough assessment of whether a waiver is even necessary. If a waiver is undoubtedly necessary, the client must be fully aware of the uncertainties that are involved with nonimmigrant waiver applications filed by Canadian citizen applicants.

---

[9] INA §214(d).

[10] 8 CFR §§212.1, 1212.1.

[11] 9 FAM 41.81 N.9.

THE HARDSHIP OF PROVING HARDSHIP

by B. John Ovink[*]

INTRODUCTION

The requirement that an undocumented person prove some kind of hardship in order to be granted relief from removal appears at various places in the Immigration and Nationality Act (INA). Unfortunately, neither the INA nor the regulations yield a workable definition of "hardship," let alone a description of the various adjectives that state the degree of hardship required. This article discusses the requirements, standards, and analyses, as formulated by the Attorney General and the courts that are relevant to proving hardship. It further provides a practical guide for compiling the best possible hardship case.

The Violence Against Women Act now provides that abused spouses and children who face removal are eligible to apply for relief due to "extreme" hardship. Because the preparation for an INA §240(c) cancellation is so complex and so different from preparing other hardship cases, the author has omitted discussion of the Violence Against Women Act in this article.

THE STATUTES

A definition of "hardship" is notably absent from the INA. Yet numerous sections of the act require proof of hardship. For instance, "extreme" hardship is required for relief under INA §§212(a)(9), 212(h) and (i); when applying for a T or U visa; for INA §216(c)(4) waivers; and under the Nicaraguan Adjustment and Central American Relief Act (NACARA) (where hardship is "presumed"). A waiver of the two-year J-1 foreign stay requirement demands "exceptional" hardship. Section 240 has three separate definitions of hardship, ranging from "exceptional" and "extremely unusual" hardship to the alien's spouse, parent, or child, to "extreme hardship" to a battered spouse or child, and to no apparent requirement of hardship at all for a lawful permanent resident seeking cancellation (although in practice, courts still require some kind of hardship to be shown in those cases). Similarly, §212(c), as recently restored by the Supreme Court, does not require any hardship, yet the wording of the section seems to indicate that the "discretion of the Attorney General" requires evidence that one deserves the relief.

Since passage of the Illegal Immigration Reform and Immigrant Responsibility Act (IIRAIRA) in 1996,[1] some of the wording has changed, but the adjectives defining hardship have remained similar. Congress's intent in changing some wording is made clear in the legislative history, which states that Congress "deliberately changed the required showing of hardship from 'extreme hardship' to 'exceptional and extremely unusual hardship' to emphasize that the alien must provide evidence of harm . . . substantially beyond that which ordinarily would be expected to result from the alien's deportation."[2]

The regulations accompanying this section of IIRAIRA make no mention of "exceptional and extremely unusual" hardship.[3] Specifically, the regulations hold: "For cases raised under §240A(b)(2) of the Act, extreme hardship shall be determined as set forth in §1240.58 of this part."[4] Section 1240.58 then proceeds to describe, without defining, that an alien is required to show that the "deportation would result in *extreme* hardship to the . . . alien's spouse, parent or child. . . ."[5] A list of 14 categories accompanies this section, most of which seem to have been derived from case law, and will be discussed in the remainder of this article.

[*] **B. John Ovink** is a sole practitioner with offices in Tampa and Dade City. He practices exclusively immigration law, concentrating on defending criminal immigrant's rights to come to the United States or remain here. He is a frequent speaker and conference organizer, and has published several articles on this topic. He is former chair of the AILA's Central Florida Chapter; chair of the Chapter Chair Orientation Committee, co-chair of the Grassroots and Advocacy Committee, and member of the Asylum Committee. See his website at *www.ovink-immigrationlaw.us*.

---

[1] Illegal Immigration Reform and Immigrant Responsibility Act, Division C of the Omnibus Appropriations Act of 1996 (H.R. 3610), Pub. L. No. 104-208, 110 Stat. 3009.

[2] *Matter of Monreal*, 23 I&N Dec. 56 (BIA 2001).

[3] 8 CFR §§1240.20 and 1240.58.

[4] 8 CFR §1240.20(c).

[5] 8 CFR §1240.58(a).

The Courts

The burden is on the alien to demonstrate both statutory eligibility and equities meriting favorable exercise of the discretion vested in the Attorney General.[6] The Supreme Court, in *INS v. Rios-Pineda*,[7] has recognized that if the Attorney General decides relief should be denied as a matter of discretion, the statutory eligibility requirements need not be addressed. Since neither the statutes nor the regulations define the term "hardship," let alone the distinction between "extreme" and "exceptionally and unusual," it has been left to the Board of Immigration Appeals (BIA) (and in a limited way, the courts) to delimit the field.

In *Hernandez-Patino v. INS*,[8] the court wrestled with the concept of extreme hardship:

As this court has declared, '[t]he scope of 'extreme hardship' is not self-explanatory,' *Bueno-Carrillo*, 682 F.2d 143, at 145 (7th Cir. 1982) (citing *INS v. Jong Ha Wang*, 450 U.S. 139, 144 (1981)). The present suspension of the deportation provision is the product of nearly fifty years of 'modern' legislation, before which no authority existed for doing anything but deporting an illegal alien. See *INS v. Chadha*, 462 U.S. 919 (1983). Legislation in 1940 authorized suspension of deportation upon a showing of 'serious economic detriment.' Viewing this standard to be too lenient, framers of the 1952 Act restricted the availability of suspension only to a person whose deportation would, in the opinion of the Attorney General, result in 'exceptional and extremely unusual hardship'. In 1962, the statute was again amended, authorizing suspension upon a showing of 'extreme hardship.' However, unlike the 1952 revision, the present language was substituted sans clarification, without any expressed intention of either restricting or loosening the remedy ... But nowhere do we find concrete support for the proposition that the amendment of 'exceptional and extremely unusual' to merely 'extreme' hardship entails a broadening of the remedy, much less a departure from norms established by the BIA and approved by the courts. These norms require comparisons of like applications for relief. It is through this means the BIA avoids reaching arbitrary results. Besides, it is not clear how, if it is supposed that the petitioner is not required to show 'unique' hardship, the BIA is then precluded from considering relative claims. * * *. The better view may be to accept the fact that congress, in refusing to define 'extreme' hardship fully, avoided the substantive policy decision and has deferred to agency expertise. Given the power to define extreme hardship, the BIA need merely follow established procedures, support conclusions with evidence and articulate reasons for its decision.[9]

In general, the courts have held the BIA to an "abuse of power" standard, which, combined with the tendency to bar review by federal courts, gives the BIA virtually unbridled power to make arbitrary decisions, in spite of what the Supreme Court has remarked:

While agencies are not directly accountable to the people, the Chief Executive is, and it is entirely appropriate for this political branch of the government to make such policy choices—resolving the competing interests which Congress itself either inadvertently did not resolve, or intentionally left to be resolved by the agency charged with the administration of the statute in light of everyday realities.[10]

The Supreme Court has dealt with the question of hardship in such a way as to avoid having to decide upon a definition. In deferring to the Attorney General, the Court in *INS v. Jong Ha Wang* stated:

The crucial question in this case is what constitutes 'extreme hardship.' These words are not self-explanatory, and reasonable men could easily differ as to their construction. But the Act commits their definition in the first instance to the Attorney General and his delegates, and their construction and application of this standard should not be overturned by a reviewing court

---

[6] Even though the regulations and act still delegate the ultimate decision and discretion of granting relief to the Attorney General, it is unclear whether the Attorney General still has this power since the shifting of legacy Immigration and Naturalization Service (INS) to the Department of Homeland Security (DHS).

[7] 105 S. Ct. 2098, 2102 (1985).

[8] 831 F.2d 750 (7th Cir. 1987).

---

[9] *See Hernandez-Cordero v. INS*, 819 F.2d 558 (5th Cir. 1987).

[10] *See Chevron, U.S.A., Inc. v. Natural Resources Defense Counsel, Inc.*, 467 U.S. 837, 865–66 (1984).

simply because it may prefer another interpretation of the statute.[11]

In other words, if the Attorney General does not define extreme hardship, the courts refuse to do it for him. The Court later underscored this deference to the Attorney General: "In *INS v. Wang*, we rejected a relaxed standard for evaluating the 'extreme hardship' requirement as impermissibly shifting discretionary authority from INS to the courts." This deference to the power of the Attorney General in immigration cases is entirely in line with the long string of Supreme Court decisions regarding the assignment of duty between the courts and the executive branch and with the axiom that "it is emphatically the province and duty of the judicial department to say what the law is," does not seem to apply immigration questions. The Court in *Wang* goes on to say that "[t]he Attorney General and his delegates have the authority to construe 'extreme hardship' narrowly should they deem it wise to do so." The Court than refers to the exceptional nature of the suspension remedy: unfairness to those waiting for a quota, if it were made too easy to acquire suspension.

In holding that nieces who were living as part of the family of respondent were not children for purposes of the deportation statute, the Court in *INS v. Hector* stated that the BIA need not consider hardship that alien's deportation might have on a third party other than "a spouse, parent or child." This decision is in line with the narrow interpretation the Court allows the statute and its deference to the Attorney General. At the same time, this decision overruled the liberal view that some courts of appeal had taken in regard to hardship conditions, by extending the definition of "family" to other than blood relatives.

THE BIA DEFINES HARDSHIP: A STUDY OF THREE CASES

The BIA has made an attempt to define hardship in three recent cases: *Matter of Monreal*,[12] *Matter of Andazola-Rivas*,[13] and *Matter of Recinas*.[14] All three cases deal with "exceptional and unusual" hardship, as required under INA §240A(b) for cancellation of

removal. The fact patterns in the three cases are remarkably similar.

Monreal

The respondent is a 34-year-old native and citizen of Mexico who has been living in the United States since his entry in 1980. He has not returned to Mexico since coming to this country as a 14-year-old child. His wife, who was not statutorily eligible for cancellation of removal, voluntarily departed to Mexico shortly before the respondent's hearing on his application for cancellation of removal, and she took their infant U.S. citizen child with her. The couple's two older children have remained with the respondent in the United States. The oldest child is now 12 years old, and the middle child is 8 years old. Both are U.S. citizens.

The respondent has been gainfully employed in this country since his entry as a teenager, and he provides the sole support for his two citizen children in this country, and sends money to his wife in Mexico. He has worked in an uncle's business continuously since 1991. The respondent's parents lawfully immigrated to this country in 1995, and his children sometimes spend time with these grandparents when their father is working. In addition, the respondent has seven siblings who reside lawfully in the United States, as well as a brother in Mexico who also works for the respondent's uncle. The respondent's oldest child testified at the hearing about his life in this country and his desire not to depart for Mexico, which he would do if his father were required to leave the United States.

Andazola

The respondent is a 30-year-old native and citizen of Mexico who entered the United States without inspection in August 1985. She has two U.S. citizen children, ages 11 and 6. The respondent has had the same employment for four years with a company that provides health insurance for her and her family, as well as a 401(k) retirement savings plan. The respondent bought her own house, valued at $69,000, in 1998. She owns two vehicles, with a combined value of about $12,000. According to her testimony, she also has savings of about $7,000.

The respondent testified that she has no relatives in Mexico who could help her with the children, should she be forced to return there. She further stated that her mother takes the children to school and looks after them while she works. All of the respondent's siblings live in this country, without valid immigration status, as do her aunts and uncles.

---

[11] *INS v. Jong Ha Wang*, 450 U.S. 139 (1981).

[12] 23 I&N Dec. 56 (BIA 2001).

[13] 23 I&N Dec. 319 (BIA 2002).

[14] 23 I&N Dec. 467 (BIA 2002).

The respondent's older child testified to her very close relationship with her grandmother. She did not indicate that she is close to any other relatives in this country.

Although the respondent is not married, when asked at the hearing about the father of her children, she replied, "We're okay, we just live together." She indicated that he has "some form of temporary permit" in this country. Asked if he contributes to the household, the respondent said, "He's working construction so sometimes he does have a job, sometimes he doesn't."

The respondent described the children's health as "fine." She stated that she has had problems with asthma, which is under control, but that this condition would prevent her from working in the fields in Mexico. She also does not believe she could get an office job in Mexico, as she has only a sixth grade education. She is concerned that she would not be able to obtain any employment in Mexico that would be comparable to the job she has here.

The respondent also stated that the schools are better in this country than in Mexico, with better facilities and supplies, and access to computers. She is afraid that her children would not be able to get much education in Mexico, especially when they get older and reach the point where she would have to pay for it.

The respondent testified that the main focus of the family's social life is the church they attend every week. She also stated that she helps out twice a month at her younger child's Head Start program.

Recinas

The adult respondent is a 39-year-old native and citizen of Mexico. She is the single mother of four U.S. citizen children, ages 12, 11, 8, and 5, and the two minor respondents, ages 15 and 16, both of whom are natives and citizens of Mexico. Her parents are lawful permanent residents, and her five siblings are U.S. citizens. She is divorced and has no immediate family in Mexico. The respondent and her children have no close relatives remaining in Mexico. Her entire family lives in the United States, including her lawful permanent resident parents and five U.S. citizen siblings. As in *Matter of Andazola*, the respondent's mother serves as her children's caretaker and watches the children while the respondent manages her own motor vehicle inspection business.

The respondent is divorced from the father of her U.S. citizen children. Although the respondent's former husband at one point was paying $146.50 per month in child support, there is no indication that he remains actively involved in their lives. He is currently out of status and was in immigration proceedings in Denver as of the date of the respondent's last hearing.

The respondent has been operating her own business performing vehicle inspections for two years. The business has two employees. She reported having $4,600 in assets, which is apparently the value of an automobile she owns. The respondent testified that after two months in business, her proceeds were $10,000 a month, but she was also repaying her mother and brother money that she and her former husband had borrowed from them. After meeting expenses, her net profits were $400–500 per month.

The respondent's four U.S. citizen children have all spent their entire lives in this country and have never traveled to Mexico. She and her family live five minutes away from her mother, with whom they have a close relationship. According to the respondent, her children, particularly two of her U.S. citizen children, experience difficulty speaking Spanish and do not read or write in that language.

Finally, the respondent has no alternative means of immigrating to the United States in the foreseeable future. There is a significant backlog of visa availability to Mexican nationals with preference classification. Therefore, the respondent has little hope of immigrating through her U.S. citizen siblings, or even her parents, should they naturalize.

Are There Differences?

In *Monreal*, the immigration judge denied cancellation, and the immigrant appealed. The appeal was dismissed. It is a case from Dallas—the Fifth Circuit. The immigrant lost!

In *Andaloza*, the immigration judge granted cancellation, and certified this case to the BIA. The INS appealed as well. The appeal was granted, and the immigrant lost! It is a case from Phoenix—the Ninth Circuit.

In *Recinas*, the immigration judge denied cancellation, and the immigrant appealed. The immigrant won! It is a case from Los Angeles—the Ninth Circuit.

All three decisions were en banc, and it is interesting to note that (with the exception of Lori Rosenberg), the BIA in *Monreal* and *Recinas* were unanimous, whereas *Andaloza* had nine separate and dissenting opinions.

Looking at the BIA members involved is of no great help either, since the same BIA members are involved:

Monreal: Scialabba, Acting Chairman; Dunne, Vice Chairman; Heilman, Schmidt, Holmes, Hurwitz, Villageliu, Filppu, Cole, Guendelsberger, Mathon, Jones, Grant, Moscato, Miller, Brennan, Espenoza, Osuna, and Ohlson, Board Members. Concurring and Dissenting Opinion: Rosenberg, Board Member.

Andaloza: Scialabba, Acting Chairman; Dunne, Vice Chairman; Holmes, Hurwitz, Filppu, Cole, Grant, Miller, Ohlson, Hess, and Pauley, Board Members. Dissenting Opinions: Espenoza, Board Member, Joined by Rosenberg, Board Member; Osuna, Board Member, Joined by Schmidt, Villageliu, Guendelsberger, Rosenberg, Moscato, and Brennan, Board Members.

Recinas: Scialabba, Chairman; Dunne, Vice Chairman; Schmidt, Holmes, Hurwitz, Villageliu, Filppu, Cole, Guendelsberger, Rosenberg, Grant, Moscato, Miller, Brennan, Espenoza, Osuna, Ohlson, Hess, and Pauley, Board Members.

Especially in *Matter of Monreal*, the BIA went all out to define hardship, give us a history lesson in hardship, and ultimately deny relief to the Mexican father in good health who was able to support his small family. The BIA stated that the applicant must demonstrate that his or her spouse, parent, or child would suffer hardship that is substantially beyond that which would ordinarily be expected to result from the alien's deportation, but need not show that such hardship would be "unconscionable." (Thus, introducing a new category).

Andazola's attempt to distinguish her case from *Monreal* consisted of the following facts: she is a single mother and the sole support of her children; she has no relatives in Mexico to help her there. She also contended that women in Mexico face discrimination in employment and that this would make it particularly difficult as a single mother to support her family. She was unsuccessful in distinguishing her case and was deported.

Recinas's attempt to distinguish her case was more successful: After noting that "the hardship standard is not so restrictive that only a handful of applicants, such as those with a serious medical condition, will qualify for relief," the BIA found the following factors relevant: Recinas raised her family

in the United States since 1988, and the four U.S. citizen children do not speak Spanish well and cannot read or write in Spanish; the citizen children are solely dependent on Recinas for their support, unlike the respondent in *Andazola*; and Recinas's ability to work and support her children depends on the assistance her mother has provided in caring for the children, and with no family in Mexico she would have an especially difficult time finding employment and providing a safe home for her children.

As a practitioner, you should follow the facts and events in *Recinas*, and in your closing argument you should point out that, just as in *Recinas*, the facts prove that your client will suffer extreme and unusual hardship. Rest assured that the trial attorney will argue that this case is completely unlike *Recinas*, and much more like *Monreal* and *Andazola* because the facts do not rise to the level of extreme and unusual hardship. Ultimately, however, this author believes that the way you present your case, the impression your client makes on the judge, and the evidence you present in support of your client will determine whether your client becomes *Recinas* or *Monreal*, rather than the actual facts.

Establishing Hardship

What if the facts of your case do not even come close to *Recinas*? When presented with a case requiring hardship (whether in adjustment cases or cancellation cases, or even when preparing a gubernatorial pardon), this author advises clients that they (or their spouse, or kids) need to suffer more and differently from people in the same situation, and that we are going to prepare evidence to prove that they would.

The first thing to do, to set the requirements, is to look at 8 CFR §1240.58, which lists 14 factors that may be considered in evaluating whether deportation would result in extreme hardship. Then explain to your client that you need this information from him or her:

- age, both at the time of entry to the United States and at the time of application for waiver;

- age, number, and immigration status of your spouse and children and their ability to speak the native language and to adjust to life in the country of return;

- health condition of the client, the children, spouse, or parents, and the availability of any

- required medical treatment in the country to which the client would be returned;

- ability to obtain employment in the country to which the client would be returned;

- the length of residence in the United States, both legal and illegal;

- the existence of other family members who are, or will be, legally residing in the United States;

- the financial impact of the client's departure on family;

- the impact of a disruption of educational opportunities for the client, his or her children, and spouse;

- psychological impact of client's deportation;

- current political and economic conditions in the country to which the client would be returned;

- family and other ties to the country to which the client would be returned;

- contributions to and ties to a community in the United States, including the degree of integration into society;

- immigration history, including any authorized stay in the United States;

- availability of other means of adjusting to lawful permanent resident status.

Trial Strategy

While this may be obvious, start your case by finding out who your judge will be, and what his or her peculiarities are, or what he or she thinks is extremely important or adverse. And prepare your client for the hearing so there are no surprises as to your questions, your client's answers, and the tone and attitude of your client during the hearing. Anticipate what the U.S. Immigration and Customs Enforcement (ICE) trial attorney will ask, and prepare your client for such questions.

Issues that will always come up are the conviction, the rehabilitation, and whether your client pays federal income tax. Since you usually have several months between the master calendar hearing and individual hearing, you can take corrective action like filing back taxes (if necessary) and get your client involved with his or her kids (or grandchildren) and in the community.

Once you have discussed the above list of items with your client, set monthly meetings during which you go over the evidence your client is collecting. Call in friends and family to do an affidavit (the author once had a client call in desperation from an Office Depot store, stating that the store didn't have any "affidavits" and what were they!).

Prepare your evidence in a logical way, label and tab evidence, and use a highlighter to emphasize why you are submitting that particular document. If the document is lengthy, prepare a synopsis and "offer of proof" so the judges don't need to read 20 pages. Submit evidence as far in advance as possible, and submit it all at once. Make sure you have original documents with you in court, should the ICE trial attorney require proof of originality.

If you use psychologists, doctors, or lie detector tests, ask the ICE trial attorneys before trial if they are willing to stipulate to written testimony or if they require that the expert appear in court. Unless you know and can trust your ICE trial attorney, get this in writing.

During trial, the author finds that it is usually best to start with the bad parts—the client's crimes and violations—and slowly build up to rehabilitation and involvement in family and neighborhood. By the time you are done, the judge will have "forgotten" the crimes, and will be convinced that your client is an angel who simply made a mistake in his or her life.

If your client had to amend taxes, bring it up and explain why. It is better that you, rather than the ICE trial attorney, bring out the bad parts.

The person whose hardship you need to establish is a required witness. If this is the parent, prepare him or her to say something more than "I love my son and he helps me!" Establish that your client is the only one in a position to help elderly parents (because of his or her particular skills, or proximity of residence); have brothers and sisters testify why they cannot care for the parents if your client is deported.

It is extremely important that you have the spouse and children testify, and that at least the spouse knows exactly every detail about your client's past mistakes. And make sure that they tell the judge that they have forgiven their spouse/parent. If the children are too young to testify, have them make a drawing about their (to be deported) parent. Bring the children into court. Submit a lot of family pictures.

It is good if an employer is willing to come to court, but remember that it is hardship on the family that counts. The author only brings in employers and friends if it is a weak case. Judges know what these people are going to say anyway ("He's a great worker.").

EXCEPTIONAL AND EXTREMELY UNUSUAL HARDSHIP

As may be deduced from the 1952 law, mere economic hardship does not suffice in establishing "exceptional and extremely unusual hardships," as required when applying for cancellation of removal, and the former 10-year suspension. In *Brown v. INS*,[15] petitioner was unable to provide documentary evidence of circumstances, other than economic hardship. The fact that his U.S. citizen spouse refused to leave with him, and that the resulting separation of the family would cause Mrs. Brown and their child to suffer substantial emotional distress, were mere assertions of counsel. Hence, the court looked only at the alleged economic disruption. In doing so, the court held that it was well established that a showing of economic hardship does not constitute "extreme hardship" and thus would not qualify for the even more restrictive standard of "exceptional and unusual." The court quoted from the Senate report, stating that relief "should be available only in the very limited category of cases in which the deportation of the alien would be unconscionable."[16]

Occasionally, an alien may claim relief under both §240(A) (cancellation), and §212(h) as an alien who has never adjusted status and who has not been convicted of an "aggravated felony." Because of the difference in standards of hardship, it is now advisable to seek §212(h) relief, rather than cancellation. This is demonstrated by the following, interesting case, where an alien, who had been sentenced for five years and five months, had established eligibility for both §212(c) (under the pre-1990 amendments) and §244(a)(2) relief (under the post-1990, and pre-1996 amendments). Here, the court discusses the factors determining the different hardship requirements: "Once an alien is deemed eligible for a waiver under §212(c), the Attorney General . . . balances the social and human considerations in the alien's favor against any adverse factors that demonstrate his or her undesirability as a permanent resi-

dent in the United States."[17] Because of his drug conviction, the immigration judge required Cortes, the alien, to show unusual or outstanding countervailing equities. The court considered proof of rehabilitation an important factor, and remanded to re-evaluate the case and consider updated information concerning employment and rehabilitation, in conjunction with family ties, existence of property, value and service to the community, and other evidence attesting to a good character (*i.e.*, affidavits from family, friends, and responsible community representatives). At the same time, the court decided that the demonstrated evidence would not suffice to establish the more stringent requirement of exceptional and extremely unusual hardship as required by (former) §244(a)(2), stating that hardships, common to most deported aliens, like general allegations of economic and emotional hardship, are insufficient. The court explicitly overruled two 1953 cases[18] that had established criteria for "exceptional and extremely unusual hardship" by saying that

> Congress amended §244(a)(1) in 1962 to require an 'extreme hardship.' Section 244(a)(2), which applies to aliens convicted of crimes, demands a heightened showing of 'exceptional and extremely unusual hardship.' The definition of 'exceptional and extremely unusual hardship' now applied only to aliens seeking relief under §244(a)(2), has become more stringent in the forty years since the Board decided *Matter of S.* and *Matter of U.*

The importance of this case is that aliens faced with a removal order and a cancellation claim as their only option should pursue relief under §212(h) if they can. The court has made it clear that the threshold is lower, and that evidence sufficient to establish "extreme hardship" will probably be insufficient to establish "exceptional and extremely unusual hardship."

CONCLUSION AND RECAP

As the foregoing has demonstrated, there are no clear guidelines as to when an alien has successfully established "hardship." It seems that those who have the best chance of establishing hardship are the old, the sick, the homeless, the uneducated, and the unemployed—particularly when they are honest, have

---

[15] 775 F.2d 383 (D.C.C. 1985).

[16] S. Rep. No. 1137, 82d Cong., 2d. Sess. 25 (1952).

[17] *Cortes-Castillo v. INS*, 997 F.2d 1199 (7th. Cir. 1993).

[18] *Matter of S*, 5 I&N Dec. 409 (BIA 1953), and *Matter of U*, 5 I&N Dec. 413 (BIA 1953).

U.S. citizen children who do not speak the foreign language, and who have lived here a long time. In that sense, one might properly speak of granting relief for humanitarian reasons and as a reward for not having been caught by INS for at least seven years. On the other hand, the fact that no definite criteria have been established allows any alien facing deportation charges, who has otherwise satisfied additional requirements, an equal shot at discretionary relief. In general, the better-documented a claim is, the higher the chances of success.

Medical Hardship

- *Rodriguez-Gutierrez v. INS*, 59 F.3d 504, (5th Cir. 1995) (suspension and adjustment of status)

- *Watkins v. INS*, 63 F.3d 844 (9th Cir. 1995) (motion to reopen to seek suspension and adjustment)

- *Matter of Recinas*, 23 I&N Dec. 467 (BIA 2002) (cancellation)

- *Matter of Andazola-Rivas*, 23 I&N Dec. 319 (BIA 2002) (cancellation)

- *Matter of Cervantes-Gonzalez*, 22 I&N Dec. 560 (BIA 1999) (INA §212(i) case)

- *Matter of Pilch*, 21 I&N Dec. 627 (BIA 1996) (suspension of deportation)

- *Matter of O–J–O–*, 21 I&N Dec. 381 (BIA 1996) (suspension of deportation)

- *Matter of Mendez-Moralez*, 21 I&N Dec. 296 (BIA 1996) (INA §212(h) case)

Economic Hardship

- *INS v. Jong Ha Wang*, 450 U.S. 139 (1981) (suspension of deportation)

- *Gebremichael v. INS*, 10 F.3d 28 (1st Cir. 1993) (suspension of deportation)

- *Blanco v. INS*, 68 F.3d 642 (2nd Cir. 1995) (suspension of deportation)

- *Rodriguez-Gutierrez v. INS*, 59 F.3d 504 (5th Cir. 1995) (suspension of deportation)

- *Salameda v. INS*, 70 F.3d 447 (7th Cir. 1995) (suspension of deportation)

- *Tukhowinich v. INS*, 57 F.3d 869 (9th Cir.) (suspension of deportation)

- *Matter of Kao & Lin*, 23 I&N Dec. 45 (BIA 2001) (suspension of deportation)

- *Matter of Cervantes-Gonzalez*, 22 I&N Dec. 560 (BIA 1999) (INA §212(i) waiver)

- *Matter of Mendez-Moralez*, 21 I&N Dec. 296 (BIA 1996) (INA §212(h) waiver)

Emotional Hardship

- *Hector v. INS*, 479 U.S. 85 (1986) (suspension of deportation)

- *Watkins v. INS*, 63 F.3d 844 (9th Cir. 1995) (suspension of deportation and adjustment)

- *Matter of Recinas*, 23 I&N Dec. 467 (BIA 2002) (cancellation case)

- *Matter of Andazola-Rivas*, 23 I&N Dec. 319 (BIA 2002) (cancellation case)

- *Matter of Jean*, 23 I&N Dec. 373 (A.G. 2002) (adjustment through §209(c))

- *Matter of Cervantes-Gonzalez*, 22 I&N Dec. 560 (BIA 1999) (INA §212(i) waiver)

- *Matter of Pilch*, 21 I&N Dec. 627 (BIA 1996) (suspension of deportation)

- *Matter of O–J–O–*, 21 I&N Dec. 381 (BIA 1996) (suspension of deportation)

SAMPLE LETTER

When the author first sits down with a client to discuss the evidence needed, the above 14 categories are broken down into three areas. Generally, clients have no idea what is important for their case, and what is not. And most do not speak legalese. In line with this, this author has prepared the following letter:

Dear Mr./Ms. _____:

You have been asked to submit a request for waiver of deportation (or application for cancellation) from the United States. By submitting the application you ask that the USCIS use its discretion to allow you to remain here. If the waiver is denied, deportation proceedings will be started against you. The reason you need to request a waiver is because you have done something in your life that makes you removable from, or inadmissible to, the United States. Fortunately for you, the law allows you to ask the immigration service to admit you anyway, provided that you can establish something called "hardship."

First, we need to know who you and your family are, and what you have been doing here. Evidence of this can consist of:

- Immigration records of yourself and your family (was your spouse born in the United States, or somewhere else?) What language(s) do they speak? Can your children speak/read/write your native language?

- School records and transcripts for yourself and your family; including awards, participation in extra-curricular events such as sports, band, debate team.

- Employment records, including statements from current and former employers, proof of all federal income taxes, Social Security records, etc. Make sure they are filed correctly, and correct if necessary. (Example: a married couple cannot file "head of household" unless they do not live together for more than six months of a year, which is the exact opposite of what you need to establish in court.)

- In case you are self-employed or own a business, we would need records of incorporation, payroll, corporate taxes, and proof of ownership of the business.

- Curriculum vitae for yourself and your spouse (and of adult children).

Second, you need to provide evidence of good moral character. Primary evidence of this would include:

- A statement from the police that you have not been arrested.

- A certified copy of *all* your arrest records as well as their final disposition, both in the United States and elsewhere. (Include ones not mentioned on the Notice to Appear, and all traffic violations, however minor. The trial attorney of ICE will have a CIA computer printout, which will include *all* arrests, both in the United States and overseas.)

- Proof that you have completed any type of sentence, including probation and rehabilitation that may have been imposed. Proof of rehabilitation (completion of community service, courses, etc.). Proof of early termination of sentence. Proof that you have gone over and beyond what you were supposed to do (and no, it's not too late to start now).

- Any type of post-conviction relief you may have had, or are able to obtain. Check for a timely (before November 29, 1990) Judicial Recommendation Against Deportation (JRAD), or, if there is time, discuss with criminal counsel the possibilities of filing a motion to set aside the judgment and verdict.

- Details about what you did and why, how old you were, and all circumstances surrounding your actions. Evidence of victims who have forgiven you or were witness to what happened would be extremely useful.

Third, you need to prove that you deserve to remain in the United States. The primary persons benefiting from your remaining here would be your immediate family. Even more important than the suffering you would incur, USCIS will look first and foremost to the effects your potential deportation has on your immediate family, therefore, we would need:

- Proof of bona fide marriage, affidavits from your parents in law, statement from your spouse what he/she will do if you are deported.

- Proof of birth of any and all children of the marriage, involvement in your children's lives, school (participation in PTA, for example), financial support for children, both here and born outside the United States).

- School records and transcripts of your spouse and children, including any awards they may have won or earned; the ability of your spouse and children to speak your native language, and their ability to obtain an education in your native country; evidence of your involvement in your children's lives and participation in school, after-school events, and church.

- Information on any other family members who live in the United States, their whereabouts and their relationship to you.

- Employment and education records for your spouse, and the chances he or she may have of finding employment in your native country.

- Statements from friends, employers and/or employees, testifying to the loss they would suffer if you were to be removed from the United States.

- If anyone in your family would suffer from a physical or psychological condition caused by your removal that would not be treatable in the destination country, either for lack of financing or lack of medical facilities, then proof of such suffering would also be evidence.

- The health condition of yourself and any member of your family, and the availability of doctors, hospitals, and treatment (including whether you could afford that) in your native country.

Finally, and probably most important of all, would be evidence of you and your family's contributions to, and ties to, your community in the United States. Prime evidence of this would be voluntary work that you have been involved in, religious activities, pro bono work, and the degree of involvement in your children's school, and sworn statements from neighbors and friends testifying to your involvement.

Preventative Medicine: Avoiding Removal for Noncitizen Criminal Defendants Using Pre- and Post-conviction Relief

by Robert Frank, Linda Kenepaske, and Jay S. Marks[*]

With greater frequency, colleagues in the criminal defense bar call upon immigration attorneys to craft pleas that either avoid the institution of removal proceedings or preserve any possible waivers or relief to removal. While many criminal defense attorneys have come to understand the importance of sentences of less than a year for crimes of violence and/or theft offenses, most simply cannot dedicate the time or effort necessary to master the nuances of immigration-sensitive pleas. Unfortunately, some defense attorneys continue to plead their noncitizen clients to crimes that guarantee removal, at which point our efforts in postconviction relief become critical.

This article provides practical guidance based on real-world cases from attorneys who are frequently called upon by the criminal defense bar to provide advice to criminal defense attorneys and their noncitizen clients.

A SIMPLE CHECKLIST FOR INITIAL EVALUATION

If you are fortunate enough to have defense counsel contact you before his or her client pleads to any charges, the following is a simple checklist to help you evaluate the case.

First, determine whether the accused is indeed a noncitizen. Sometimes the defendant has become a citizen by operation of law without knowing it. If so, your focus shifts to proving citizenship. As we know, however, the Department of Homeland Security (DHS) may disagree with your assessment of your client's citizenship. Depending on the strength of your citizenship case, you may wish to continue the analysis to devise strategies against removability or inadmissibility.

Second, obtain a complete copy of the charging documents. Read the statement of charges of the investigating officer. These will contain facts that U.S. Immigration and Customs Enforcement (ICE) may try to use against your client in the future, especially in domestic violence cases to prove the relationship between the defendant and alleged victim or cases in which the age of the victim may be relevant to prove the ground of removability. Reviewing the charging documents, as well as any plea agreements and/or discovery in the case provides you with an advance look at what ICE will review in the event the defendant is charged with removability/inadmissibilty.

Third, read the text of the statute under which the defendant is charged to determine whether it charges an offense that renders the defendant either removable or inadmissible to the United States. Entire treatises have been written on this step—it is an area of the law that is too large, complex, and unwieldy for the space constraints of this article. Nevertheless, some simple rules are worth mentioning. Start by reviewing Immigration and Nationality Act (INA)[1] §101(a)(43) (aggravated felonies), §212 (grounds of inadmissibility), and §237 (grounds of removability). Determine whether the BIA has spoken to the exact statute under which the noncitizen defendant has been charged. Research whether the Supreme Court and/or the U.S. court of appeals for the relevant circuit have determined whether the statute is a

[*] **Robert Frank** practices immigration law at Frank & York, a firm listed in the Bar Register of Preeminent Lawyers. Past chair of the AILA New Jersey Chapter, he was named to *Best Lawyers in America* and is rated AV by Martindale-Hubbell. He received the Sam Williamson Mentor Award from AILA. Mr. Frank has been a professor at Montclair State University and often lectures for AILA, the Federal Bar Association, and NJICLE. He has served on various AILA national committees, including EOIR liaison.

Linda Kenepaske has been practicing immigration law in New York City for more than 20 years. As a solo practitioner, she handles all types of immigration cases; however, her first love is deportation/removal defense. Ms. Kenepaske is very active in AILA on both the local and national levels, and lectures frequently on immigration topics before bar associations.

Jay Marks, a founder and principal of Marks & Katz, LLC, practices immigration law and civil litigation, with a focus on the immigration consequences of criminal convictions. He's never met a coram nobis petition he didn't like and welcomes inquiries at *jay@markskatz.com*. Marks & Katz, LLC has a resource-rich website at *www.markskatz.com*.

[1] Immigration and Nationality Act of 1952, Pub. L. No. 82-414, 66 Stat. 163 (*codified as amended at* 8 USC §§1101 *et seq.*) (INA).

removable offense for immigration purposes. For example, the Supreme Court recently decided that Florida's drunk driving statute did not have the mens rea necessary to constitute a crime of violence, and thus an aggravated felony, for removal purposes.[2]

In some instances, it may be unclear whether the conduct described in a state or federal statute constitutes a removable offense. Such cases require analysis under a "categorical approach" to determine whether the generic elements of the offense constitute a removable offense.[3] When it is not clear from the statutory definition that the statute constitutes a removable offense, the courts apply a "modified categorical approach," looking beyond the language of the statute to the "record of conviction," a term of art defined at 8 CFR §1003.41. You may also discover that a criminal statute is divisible, *i.e*, it contains offenses that may render the defendant removable while other offenses within the same statute do not.[4] Again, the BIA and the various circuits consult the "record of conviction" to determine the precise part of the statute under which a defendant was convicted. You will be better positioned to win on a Motion to Terminate on a divisible statute if you have recognized the issue before defendant makes any on-the-record proffers, stipulations, or plea colloquies in the criminal proceeding.

Fourth, interview the noncitizen defendant yourself. Find out whether he or she has had any other arrests or convictions in the past. A prior criminal record may render the individual removable or inadmissible despite your efforts, or it may be relevant for the multiple conviction grounds of removability/inadmissibility. If the defendant pleaded guilty pre-IIRAIRA, he or she may still be eligible for §212(c) relief.[5]

Fifth, determine whether a guilty plea or verdict causes the defendant to lose eligibility to any relief from removal, such as cancellation of removal, §212(h), asylum, or naturalization.

With the above analytical framework in mind, the following are cases and/or opinion letters to criminal defense counsel, based on actual cases.

---

[2] *Leocal v. Ashcroft*, 543 U.S. 1, 125 S. Ct. 377, 160 L. Ed. 2d 271 (2004).

[3] *See Taylor v. U.S.*, 495 U.S. 575, 110 S. Ct. 2143, 109 L. Ed. 2d 607 (1990).

[4] *See Matter of Short*, 20 I&N Dec. 136 (BIA 1989).

[5] *INS v. St. Cyr*, 533 U.S. 289, 121 S. Ct. 2271, 150 L.Ed.2d 347 (2001).

CASE 1: DOMESTIC VIOLENCE/ CRIME OF VIOLENCE/CRIME INVOLVING MORAL TURPITUDE

Joe Smith, a 23-year-old native and citizen of the United Kingdom, has lived in the United States since January 5, 1990, when he entered with an immigrant visa. He was born on January 18, 1983 to a single mother. His mother, who later became a lawful permanent resident (LPR), petitioned for him, and she subsequently naturalized on March 15, 2002. Mr. Smith and Judy Jones, a friend (not a girlfriend) had an argument on September 1, 2003, and Mr. Smith became so angry that he screamed at her, hit the wall next to her, and threatened to hit her if she did not stop arguing with him. Ms. Jones became fearful, called the police, and filed a complaint against Mr. Smith.

On September 15, 2003, the Criminal Court of the City of New York issued an Order of Protection against Mr. Smith, ordering him to stay away from Judy Jones, to refrain from any contact with her, including telephone, e-mail, voice mail, and so forth, and to refrain from assaulting, stalking, or harassing her. Mr. Smith did not take the Order of Protection seriously, and he called Ms. Jones on the telephone several times and left voice mail messages each time. He also followed her home from work one day. Ms. Jones reported this to the police, and as a result, Mr. Smith was prosecuted in Criminal Court in the City of New York. He was charged with the crime of Criminal Contempt in the First Degree, subsections (b)(ii), (iii), and (iv), a Class E felony. On March 15, 2004, he pleaded guilty to Criminal Contempt in the Second Degree, a Class A misdemeanor (§215.50 of the New York State Penal Law). He was placed on probation for three years and ordered to attend anger management courses.

At first, Mr. Smith did well on probation; however, after a few months, he got involved in a fight in a bar. He was arrested and charged with Assault in the Second Degree, a Class D felony (§120 of the New York State Penal Law). On January 15, 2005, he pleaded guilty to Assault in the Third Degree, a Class A misdemeanor. He was sentenced to 15 days in jail.

As Mr. Smith was serving his sentence at Riker's Island, the Department of Homeland Security/Immigration and Customs Enforcement (DHS/ICE) Deportation Office paid him a visit. They placed a detainer on him, and when he finished his sentence, DHS/ICE picked him up and took him to a DHS/ICE detention facility pursuant to the detainer.

ICE filed a Notice to Appear against Mr. Smith, alleging that he was removable from the United States under INA §237(a)(2)(E)(ii), in that he was an alien who at any time after entry had been enjoined under a protection order and had been determined to have engaged in conduct in violation of the order that involves protection against credible threats of violence, repeated harassment, or bodily injury to the person for whom the order was issued. ICE also alleged that Mr. Smith was removable under §237(a)(2)(A)(ii), in that he had been convicted at any time after admission of two crimes of moral turpitude, not arising out of a single scheme of criminal misconduct.

Mr. Smith's family has come to you and asked you to secure his release from DHS/ICE custody on bond and represent him before the immigration court.

Analysis

Is Mr. Smith a U.S. Citizen?

The first inquiry I always make in a case such as Mr. Smith's is whether he is a U.S. citizen. If Mr. Smith's mother naturalized when he was under 18 years old and living in the United States pursuant to lawful permanent residence, he would have derived citizenship under INA §320, and he would not need your services. Unfortunately, when his mother naturalized in March 2002, Mr. Smith was already 19 years old, and therefore, ineligible to derive citizenship when his mother naturalized. The statute does not have retroactive applicability, so it looks as if Mr. Smith is out of luck on that point.

Mr. Smith, unfortunately, if he is removable (which will be discussed later), appears to be ineligible for release on bond, as he is mandatorily detainable under INA §236(c)(1)(B)—a person who has been convicted of two crimes involving moral turpitude, and who served time in prison or jail. The mandatory custody provisions under §236(c) were implemented on October 9, 1998, and any noncitizen released from prison on or after that date and is removable under any of the grounds contained in §236(c) is mandatorily detainable. If Mr. Smith had never been in prison as a result of his criminal convictions, he would not be mandatorily detainable and would be eligible for release on a bond. If Mr. Smith is not removable as charged, however, the removal proceedings will be terminated and Mr. Smith will be released from custody.

Since Mr. Smith is not eligible for release from DHS custody on bond, then it becomes even more important to examine very carefully whether he is even removable from the United States.

Is Mr. Smith Removable as Charged?

DHS must prove by "clear, unequivocal and convincing evidence" that Mr. Smith is removable from the United States as charged in the Notice to Appear, filed with the court.[6] As discussed below, DHS cannot meet its burden of proving by "clear, unequivocal and convincing evidence" that he is removable as charged.

The first conviction listed in the Notice to Appear appears to be a violation of §215.50 of the New York Penal Law. In order for that conviction to fall under the grounds of removability listed under §237(a)(2)(E)(ii) of the Act, it would have to be a violation of an injunction "issued for the purpose of preventing violent or threatening acts of *domestic violence* [emphasis added], including temporary or final orders issued by civil or criminal courts." The purpose of the law, added in 1996, is to provide additional protection for victims of domestic violence.

INA §237(a)(2)(E)(i) contains a definition of "crime of domestic violence," which is as follows:

> For purposes of this clause, the term "crime of domestic violence" means any crime of violence (as defined in section 16 of title 18, United States Code) against a person *committed by a current or former spouse of the person, by an individual with whom the person shares a child in common, by an individual who is cohabiting with or has cohabited with the person as a spouse, by an individual similarly situated to a spouse of the person under the domestic or family violence laws of the jurisdiction where the offense occurs, or by any other individual against a person who is protected from the individual's acts under the domestic or family violence or any State, Indian tribal government or unit of the local government laws of the United States.*" (emphasis added)

The New York Criminal Statutes themselves do not contain a definition of "domestic violence." The definition of "domestic violence," however, is contained in the New York Domestic Violence Prevention Act, Social Services §459-a. It is very similar to the definition set forth above. The New York definition of "domestic violence" covers any person over

---

[6] See Woodby v. INS, 385 U.S. 276 (1966).

the age of 16, who is a *victim of an act* (emphasis added), including disorderly conduct, harassment, menacing, reckless endangerment, kidnapping, assault, or attempted assault or murder *by a family or household member* (emphasis added), which includes a *person related by consanguinity or affinity, persons legally married to one another; persons formerly married to one another;* and *persons who have a child together* (emphasis added).

An offense will fall under INA §237(a)(2)(E)(ii) only if it involves "domestic violence." Mr. Smith and Ms. Jones were only friends. They were not married, never cohabited, never had a child, or were not related to one another in any way. Unless DHS can establish that they had a relationship that fell into one of those categories, Ms. Jones does not fall under the definition of a victim of "domestic violence." Therefore, Mr. Smith did not violate an "order of protection" under INA §237(a)(2)(E)(ii) because the protection order issued against him did not fall under the definition of "protection order" as set forth in §237(a)(2)(E)(i) and (ii). As Mr. Smith did not violate an injunction issued for the purpose of preventing violent or threatening acts of *domestic violence*, he cannot be deportable under §237(a)(2)(E).

In addition, there is no evidence that the court determined Mr. Smith "engaged in conduct that violated a portion of that order that involved protection against credible threats of violence, repeated harassment, or bodily injury to the person or persons for whom the protection order was issued," as DHS alleged in the Notice to Appear issued against Mr. Smith. That particular language is not contained anywhere in §215.50, the section of the New York Penal Law under which Mr. Smith was convicted. Section 215.50 contains no mention whatsoever of threats, violence, bodily injury, and so forth, and does not mirror the language contained in INA §237(a)(2)(E)(ii). New York Penal Law §215.51 "Criminal Contempt in the First Degree" contains the specific language regarding the "violator of the order of protection placing the victim in danger of physical injury, or harassing or threatening the victim"; however, Mr. Smith was not convicted under that section of law.

Although Mr. Smith may not be removable under §237(a)(2)(E)(ii), he may still be removable under §237(a)(2)(A)(ii) (conviction of two crimes involving moral turpitude). Again, DHS will not be able to sustain its burden.

In order to meet its burden, DHS must show that Mr. Smith has been convicted of two crimes of moral turpitude, "refer[ring] generally to conduct which is inherently base, vile, or depraved, and contrary to the accepted rules of morality and the duties owed between persons or to society in general." Moral turpitude has been defined as an act that is per se morally reprehensible and intrinsically wrong.[7] In determining whether a crime involves moral turpitude, the statute under which the person was convicted is controlling.[8] Moral turpitude most usually involves "evil intent."[9] An analysis of the intent behind the action is critical to a determination regarding moral turpitude.[10]

Mr. Smith was convicted under §215.50 of the New York Penal Law, Criminal Contempt in the Second Degree, a divisible statute. His conviction record does not reveal under which subsection of §215.50 he was convicted. If the statute under which Mr. Smith was convicted contains some crimes that may and some that may not involve moral turpitude, he will not be removable on moral turpitude grounds unless the record of conviction itself shows that the particular offense involved moral turpitude.[11] All of the elements of the statute relate to contempt of court, and it is not clear that any of the subsections requires "evil intent," or, with the exception of one subsection, any intent at all. Subsection (3) refers to "intentional disobedience or resistance to the lawful process"; however, it does not rise to the level of "evil intent," and it is not clear from the conviction record itself that Mr. Smith pleaded guilty to that section of the statute. For example, if Mr. Smith had been convicted of "insolent behavior committed during the sitting of a court, in its immediate view and presence and directly tending to interrupt its proceedings or to impair the respect due its authority" (Section (1) of New York Penal Law 215.50), his behavior would not involve the "evil intent" or even

---

[7] *See Matter of L–V–C–*, 22 I&N Dec. 594 (BIA 1999); *Matter of Danesh*, 19 I&N Dec. 669 (BIA 1988).

[8] *Matter of Franklin*, 20 I&N Dec. 867, 868 (BIA 1994), aff'd, 72 F.3d 571 (8th Cir. 1995).

[9] *See Matter of Khourn*, 21 I&N Dec. 1041, 1046 (BIA 1997); *Matter of Flores*, 17 I&N Dec. 225 (BIA 1980); *Matter of Abreu-Semino*, 12 I&N Dec. 775, 777 (BIA 1968).

[10] *See Matter of Serna*, 20 I&N Dec. 579 (BIA 1992).

[11] *See Matter of Short*, 20 I&N Dec. 136 (BIA 1989); *Matter of Esfandiary*, 16 I&N Dec. 659 (BIA 1979); *Matter of Garcia*, 11 I&N Dec. 521 (BIA 1966); *Matter of C–*, 5 I&N Dec. 65 (BIA 1953).

intent at all and would not fall under the definition of a crime involving moral turpitude (CMT). Finally, there is BIA precedent holding that contempt of court is not inherently immoral.[12] DHS will not be able to meet its burden in establishing that Mr. Smith's conviction under §215.50 is a CMT.

It can also be argued that Mr. Smith's conviction for Assault in the Third Degree (no subsection specified) is not a CMT. Under the same divisible statute analysis that we did above, it is clear that, for example, if Mr. Smith had been convicted of assault under Subsection (2) of Section 120, he would have exhibited only "reckless behavior causing physical injury to another person." In *Matter of Fualaau*,[13] the BIA found that a criminally "reckless state of mind must be coupled with an offense involving serious bodily injury," before the offense will be considered a CMT. If Mr. Smith had been convicted under Subsection (2) of Section 120, his reckless behavior caused only physical injury, not serious physical injury. In addition, there are numerous cases holding that simple assault is not a CMT.[14] There is, however, a BIA precedent, *Matter of Wojtkow*,[15] in which the BIA found that a conviction for second degree manslaughter under §125.15(1) of the Penal Law of New York is a crime involving moral turpitude, as it involved "reckless behavior."

Even if the immigration judge finds that Mr. Smith's conviction for assault to be a CMT, it would not subject him to removability under §237(a)(2)(A)(ii), as DHS would not be able to prove that his conviction for contempt fell under the definition of a CMT. In addition, if DHS decided to charge Mr. Smith with removability under §237(a)(2)(A)(i), he would not be removable for either conviction, as the conviction for contempt is not a CMT, and his conviction for assault occurred more than five years after he became an LPR.

If Mr. Smith is not removable, then the immigration judge must grant his motion to terminate proceedings, and he should be released from DHS custody. Mr. Smith and his family will be very happy with you.

---

[12] *See Matter of C–*, I&N Dec. 524 (BIA 1962); *Matter of P–* 6 I&N Dec. 400 (BIA 1954).

[13] 21 I&N Dec. 475 (BIA 1996).

[14] *See Matter of E–*, 1 I&N Dec. 505 (BIA 1943); *Matter of Short*, 20 I&N Dec. 136 (BIA 1989).

[15] 18 I&N Dec. 111 (BIA 1981).

CASE 2: SHERMAN ACT/ ANTITRUST/CRIME INVOLVING MORAL TURPITUDE

Facts

Mr. Dervish is a native and citizen of Turkey. He was born in 1963. He came to the United States for the first time on an F-1 visa in 1980 to study at an university. He has remained in the United States since then, with the exception of short trips two or three times a year outside the United States. He married a U.S. citizen (USC) in 1989. He became a permanent resident in 1990 as an immediate relative. He has two children (from his marriage) who are seven and 10 years old, respectively. He owns his own business, selling supplies to school cafeterias.

Mr. Dervish has been referred to you by his criminal attorney. He is facing charges under the Sherman Antitrust Act, 15 USC §1. He and his criminal attorney want to know the immigration consequences if he pleads guilty to this offense. He had entered into an arrangement with some of his competitors to fix the bids for the contract to supply one of the schools. He and his competitors had agreed to let him win the contract by their offering higher bids. Mr. Dervish felt that his bid was reasonable and not inflated. His bid was for approximately $40,000. He provided the supplies as agreed, but he was only paid $20,000, before the school found out about their scheme.

15 USC §1 reads as follows:

Every contract, combination in the form of trust or otherwise, or conspiracy, in restraint of trade or commerce among the several state, or with foreign nations, is declared to be illegal. Every person who shall make any contract or engage in any combination or conspiracy hereby declared to be illegal shall be deemed guilty of a felony, and, on conviction thereof, shall be punished by fine not exceeding $10,000,000 if a corporation, or, if and other person, $350,000, or by imprisonment not exceeding three years, or by both said punishments, in the discretion of the court.

The criminal attorney wants from you an opinion as to the immigration consequences of a conviction under this Act. The U.S. Attorney has supplied the criminal attorney with a sample indictment from a similar case. The indictment accuses the defendant of that case and co-conspirators of engaging in a combination and conspiracy in unreasonable restraint of interstate trade and commerce. The indictment describes the conspiracy as a continuing agreement, understanding, and concert of action to rig bids and allocate contracts for supplying their products. A second count of the indictment accused that defendant of false and fraudulent acts in violation of 18 USC §371, conspiracy to commit offense or defraud the United States.

As will be shown below, close cooperation between the criminal attorney and the immigration attorney is necessary. The immigration attorney needs to understand the elements of the criminal charge and how the prosecution handles similar acts.

Analysis

One question is whether a violation of the Sherman Antitrust Act is a CMT.[16] The term "crime involving moral turpitude" is not defined in the INA.[17] "Moral turpitude is a nebulous concept, which refers generally to conduct that shocks the public conscience."[18] This does not mean that because bid-rigging may shock someone's conscience that it is a CMT. It is generally defined as act of baseness, vileness, or depravity . . . a crime involving grave infringement of the moral sentiment of the community as distinguished from statutory mala prohibita.[19] The Department of State in its *Foreign Affairs Manual* also uses the term mala prohibita.

> It must not merely be *mala prohibita*, but the act itself must be inherently immoral. The doing of the act itself, and not its prohibition by statute, fixes the moral turpitude.[20]

It appears that the Sherman Act is a clear example of mala prohibita. These acts were not considered crimes under common law. They only became crimes by an Act of Congress in response to anti-competitive business activities at the end of the 19th Century. Generally, CMTs are crimes such as rape, theft, and aggravated assault. Some crimes that at times and according to the statute involved were not considered to be CMTs include manslaughter, drug distribution, bigamy, and possession of a sawed off shotgun. A couple of examples worth noting— incest, marriage, and/or sexual relations between uncle and niece were not considered to be CMT, though it would certainly shock someone's con-

science.[21] Structuring financial transactions was not a CMT though the statute was obviously directed to money laundering by drug dealers.[22]

The *Goldeshtein* case is a good example of how the courts dealt with the mala prohibita concept. My research did not find any case involving the Sherman Act, possibly because legacy Immigration and Naturalization Service (INS) (now DHS) has never instituted proceedings based on convictions for violation of that Act.

Additionally, the conviction for *one* CMT that occurs more than *five* years after entry would not make someone deportable.[23] However, the conviction for even one CMT for which a sentence of one year or longer may be imposed would make an alien inadmissible.[24] Thus, one who is not deportable but possibly inadmissible would not be subject to removal proceedings if he or she did not leave the United States. In view of Mr. Dervish's frequent travels, the problem of inadmissibility could be very important to him and should be part of any consideration in advising him prior to any plea.

An additional factor that affects the evaluation of whether this crime is a CMT is a Memorandum of Understanding (MOU) from legacy INS to the Antitrust Division of the Department of Justice (Mar. 15, 1996) that the U.S. Attorney also gave the criminal attorney. The purpose of the MOU was to gain the assistance of aliens in the prosecution of antitrust violations in spite of the deportation consequences they believed to exist.

The MOU concludes that legacy INS considers a violation of 15 USC §1 to be a CMT. This memorandum does not give any basis for its conclusion that a violation of the Sherman Antitrust Act "may subject an alien to exclusion or deportation from the United States." While, in my opinion, I conclude that an immigration judge or a court of appeal would agree that a conviction for this section of the law is not a deportable offense, the client should be informed that it possible ICE might still institute removal proceedings.

The other possible ground of deportability is that of an aggravated felony.[25] Whether the offence is an

---

[16] INA §§237(a)(2)(A)(i), 212(a)(2)(A)(i).

[17] *See* Norton Tooby, *Crimes of Moral Turpitude: The Complete Guide.*

[18] *Matter of Short*, 20 I&N Dec. 136, 139 (BIA 1989).

[19] *Black's Law Dictionary.*

[20] 9 FAM §40.21(a), Note 2.2.

[21] *Matter of B–*, 2 I&N Dec. 617 (BIA 1946).

[22] *Goldeshtein v. INS*, 8 F.3d 645 (9th Cir. 1993).

[23] *See* INA §237(a)(2)(A)(i).

[24] INA §212(a)(2)(A)(i)(I).

[25] INA §101(a)(43).

aggravated felony may have more impact than if it is a CMT, as there does not exist any waivers for aggravated felonies where the conviction is after April 1, 1997.[26] The Sherman Antitrust Act is not one of the multitude of crimes listed there. The closest would be a crime of fraud or deceit where the loss to the victim exceeded $10,000.[27] It appears that a violation of the Sherman Antitrust Act does not necessarily involve fraud or deceit. It is clearly not an element of the crime (see statute above). The essence of the crime is a conspiracy in restraint of trade. An example would be that if all immigration lawyers agreed on a certain fee to charge clients to obtain permanent residence, this could be considered a restraint of trade, but in no way involves fraud or deceit—just as Mr. Dervish might plea to this charge because he conspired with others to set bids for their contracts.

The best example of this difference is the sample indictment provided by the U.S. Attorney, stating in Count Two that defendant issued "false and fraudulent purchase orders." This language is missing from Count One. This Count speaks of "noncompetitive bids." It does not indicate that the acts were fraudulent or deceitful—merely that the conspirators "arranged for such bids to be submitted."

While deceit may be part of a "bid-rigging" scheme, bid-rigging as such is not a necessary element of a violation of Section 1 of Title 15. Thus, a plea to an indictment or information alleging restraint of trade may not necessarily be an admission to a deceitful bid-rigging scheme.

It certainly could be argued that if the offence does not fall under the category of CMT, then it was not meant to be included in the fraud and deceit category of aggravated felony. Generally, crimes that involve fraud or deceit would be CMTs; these crimes would relate to some kind of theft offense. The aggravated felony section is read quite restrictively, while money laundering in violation of §1956 or §1957 of title 18 of the U.S. Code, structuring financial transactions in violation of 31 USC §5322(b) or §5324(a)(3) is neither an aggravated felony nor even a CMT.[28]

Another consideration in this case is the issue of the loss to the victim. If it were concluded that a violation of the Sherman Act involved fraud or deceit, was there a loss of $10,000 or more? There was not such a loss in this case. Assuming Dervish could prove his $40,000 bid was reasonable, since he was paid only half that amount, there was no loss to the victim. All the goods were delivered.

What the stated loss is—if any—to the victim and what is stated in the plea elocution may affect the immigration consequences. There should be a clear written or statement on the record that the loss to the victim was less than $10,000 to avoid a violation of INA §101(a)(43)(M)(i). The plea elocution also should make no reference to any fraudulent or deceitful conduct. It should not be necessary as it is not an element of a violation of the Sherman Act.

While the conclusion is that Mr. Dervish is not removable for a conviction under 15 USC §1, the client and the criminal attorney should be advised that one cannot predict what DHS might do or guarantee an outcome. As there may be a difference of opinion regarding whether this violation is a CMT, the client should be advised of the risks of travel. As noted above, if the conviction is considered by DHS to be a CMT, he may not be deportable but would be considered inadmissible. A trip out of the country could quite likely trigger the charge of inadmissibility. The client should be so advised.

One way to avoid problems after a trip abroad would be for the client to naturalize. The ability to naturalize can be an important consideration. A conviction for this offence—even if not a CMT—could be considered a lack of good moral character, which is necessary for citizenship. Thus, Mr. Dervish may have to wait five years from the commission of the act or five years from release from prison, if he has to serve more than 180 days, before he is eligible for naturalization.[29] He would never be eligible to naturalize if he were now convicted of an aggravated felony.[30] He would also be ineligible to naturalize while on probation.[31]

---

[26] *See* cancellation of removal for certain permanent residents, at INA §§240A(a), §212(h)(2).

[27] INA §101(a)(43)(M)(i).

[28] See discussion of *Goldeshtein*, *supra*.

[29] INA §101(f)(7).

[30] 8 CFR §316.10(b)(1)(ii).

[31] 8 CFR §316.10(c).

CASE 3: WIRE FRAUD/ AGGRAVATED IDENTITY THEFT

Attorney Work Product

Attorney-Client Privileged Communication

August 2, 2005
Mr. Senior Partner Defense Attorney
Mr. Associate Defense Attorney
000 L Street NW
Washington, D.C. 20036

Re: *U.S. v. Smith*, Case No. 04-000 M-01, U.S. District Court for the District of Columbia

Dear Mr. Partner and Mr. Associate:

It was a pleasure meeting with you concerning the above-referenced matter. You requested an opinion as to the immigration consequences of a guilty plea or conviction in the matter of *U.S. v. Smith*, now pending before the U.S. District Court for the District of Columbia. Herewith, I provide you with my opinion.

Summary Conclusion

If Mr. Smith is found guilty or pleads guilty to aggravated identity theft, and is sentenced to at least one year, regardless of how much time may be suspended or actually served, he could face removal from the United States as an aggravated felon.

If he is found guilty, or pleads guilty, to either wire fraud or aggravated identity theft, or both, he could be removable based on multiple convictions for crimes involving moral turpitude (CMT) because of his prior Texas assault conviction. Although simple assault is not a CMT, assault committed against a family member is considered a CMT. If the record of conviction in the Texas assault case identifies a family member as the victim, Mr. Smith could face removal based on a CMT and/or a conviction for a crime of domestic violence.

There is no Board of Immigration Appeals (BIA) case discussing avoiding arrest or detention. Of all the circuit courts, only the Seventh Circuit has decided a case on the immigration consequences of avoiding arrest—explicitly finding that Illinois's aggravated flight statute is a CMT.

Facts

Mr. Smith entered the United States as a lawful permanent resident (LPR) on February 23, 1999, at the age of 16. He is currently 21 years old. He is single and lives with his parents at their home in Texas. He has not left the United States since his admission in 1999. His mother and father, as well as his two sisters, are LPRs, and his brother is a U.S. citizen.

Mr. Smith is currently facing one count of wire fraud in violation of 18 USC §§1343 and 1342, and one count of aggravated identity theft in violation of 18 USC §1028a.

On December 21, 2001, on the advice of counsel, Mr. Smith pleaded no contest to assault and threatening bodily injury in violation of Texas Penal Code §22.01(a)(2) for threatening to injure and/or hurt his mother after a family dispute—a Class C misdemeanor, carrying a maximum penalty of a fine of $500 and no jail time. He was ordered to pay a fine of $100. Mr. Smith informed me during our interview that his defense attorney did not inquire into his immigration status when advising Mr. Smith to plead no contest.

On November 6, 2003, Mr. Smith pleaded guilty to evading arrest in violation of Texas Penal Code §38.04(a), a Class B misdemeanor, carrying a maximum 180-day sentence and fine of $2,000. He received a two-day sentence.

Discussion

Crime Involving Moral Turpitude (CMT)

Generally

Moral turpitude refers generally to conduct that shocks the public conscience as being inherently base, vile, or depraved, and contrary to the accepted rules of morality and the duties owed between persons or to society in general. Moral turpitude has been defined as an act that is per se morally reprehensible and intrinsically wrong, or malum in se, so it is the nature of the act itself and not the statutory prohibition of it that renders a crime one of moral turpitude. Among the tests to determine if a crime involves moral turpitude is whether the act is accompanied by a vicious motive or a corrupt mind.[32]

Analytical Framework

Whether a crime involves moral turpitude depends on the inherent nature of the crime, as defined in the statute concerned, rather than the circumstances surrounding the particular transgression. A crime involves moral turpitude only if all of the conduct it prohibits is turpitudinous. An exception to

---

[32] *Smalley v. Ashcroft*, 354 F.3d 332 (5th Cir. 2005); *Hamdan v. INS*, 98 F.3d 183 (5th Cir.1996).

this general rule is made if the statute is divisible into discrete subsections of acts that are and those that are not CMTs. In this situation, we look at the alien's record of conviction to determine whether he has been convicted of a subsection that qualifies as a CMT.[33]

INA §237(a)(2)(A)(i), 8 USC §1227(a)(2)(A)(i) provides as follows:

Any alien who—

(I) is convicted of a crime involving moral turpitude committed within five years . . . after the date of admission, and

(II) is convicted of a crime for which a sentence of one year or longer may be imposed, is deportable.[34]

Assault Conviction

On December 21, 2001, Mr. Smith pleaded "no contest" to assault under Texas Penal Code §22.01(a)(2), which states: "A person commits the offense [of assault] if the person . . . (2) intentionally or knowingly threatens another with imminent bodily injury, including the person's spouse." It is classified as a Class C misdemeanor and has a maximum penalty of a fine of $500. There is no incarceration for Class C misdemeanors under the Texas Penal Code.

Simple assault is not a CMT.[35] The BIA has held, however, that assault on a family member is a CMT.[36] In this case, I have not yet seen the record of the Texas conviction, and therefore it is unclear whether Immigration and Customs Enforcement (ICE) would be able to prove that the "victim" was a family member. We must therefore examine the conviction documents to determine if there is any proof that Mr. Smith's assault involved a spouse or a family member.[37]

Mr. Smith would not be exposed to removal for this conviction alone because, although it occurred

within five years of his admission to the United States, the maximum penalty is only a fine.

Note: As discussed below in the section entitled "Multiple Criminal Convictions," however, Mr. Smith could still be exposed to the "multiple convictions" ground of removal found at INA §237(a)(2)(A)(ii), 8 USC §1227(a)(2)(A)(ii).

Conviction for Evading Police

On November 6, 2003, Mr. Smith pleaded guilty to evading arrest or detention in violation of Texas Penal Code §38.04(a), which states that a "person commits an offense if he intentionally flees from a person he knows is a police officer attempting lawfully to arrest or detain him."

In *Mei v. Ashcroft*,[38] the only case at either the BIA or among the Circuits to discuss fleeing arrest, the Seventh Circuit found that Illinois's aggravated fleeing statute was a CMT. In that case, the aggravating factor was that Mei was traveling at more than 21 miles per hour over the limit during the flight. The Texas statute in Mr. Smith's case has an intent element, while the Illinois statute had none.

Although there is no BIA precedent directly on point, the Board might indeed find this to be a CMT because of the intent in the statute and the "malum in se" of fleeing a law enforcement officer.

This conviction, by itself, does not render Mr. Smith removable, because, assuming it is a CMT, the maximum sentence is 180 days. As already discussed, to be removable, the maximum sentence must exceed one year. Moreover, it is not an aggravated felony because his sentence was less than one year.[39]

Nevertheless, in combination with either the assault conviction and/or a conviction for wire fraud and/or identity theft, Mr. Smith could face charges of removal based on multiple convictions for crimes involving moral turpitude. *See* section entitled "Multiple Criminal Convictions," below.

Wire Fraud and Aggravated Identity Theft

A guilty plea or a finding of guilt by judge or jury for wire fraud would constitute a conviction for a CMT.[40] Similarly, a conviction for theft, regardless

---

[33] *Matter of Short*, 20 I&N Dec. 136, (BIA 1989) (internal citations omitted); *Matter of Esfandiary*, 16 I&N Dec. 659 (BIA 1979).

[34] INA §237(a)(2)(A)(i), 8 USC §1227(a)(2)(A)(i).

[35] *Matter of Fualaau*, 21 I&N Dec. 475 (BIA 1996).

[36] *Matter of Tran*, 21 I&N Dec. 291, 294 (BIA 1996).

[37] *Matter of Sweetser*, 22 I&N Dec. 709 (BIA 1999); *Matter of Short*, 20 I&N Dec. 136. (See INA §240(c)(3)(B), 8 USC §1229a(c)(3)(B), for list of documents allowed to prove conviction.)

[38] 393 F.3d 737 (7th Cir. 2004).

[39] *See* INA §101(a)(43)(S), 8 USC §1101(a)(43)(S).

[40] *Jordan v. De George*, 341 U.S. 223, 71 S. Ct. 703, 95 L. Ed. 886 (1951).

of the sentenced imposed or the amount stolen, is also a CMT.[41]

In this case, the maximum sentence for wire fraud under 18 USC §1343 is five years. The maximum sentence under 18 USC §1028A for aggravated identity theft is two years.

According to the criminal complaint, however, Mr. Smith did not commit the alleged crimes until October 2004, more than five years after his February 23, 1999, admission to the United States. Consequently, any conviction on either or both of the counts above would not result in deportability on the grounds of INA §237(a)(2)(A)(i), 8 USC §1227(a)(2)(A)(i).

Multiple Criminal Convictions

Unfortunately, the current criminal complaint, coupled with the Texas assault case, may expose Mr. Smith to removal based on multiple CMT convictions. The Immigration Code provides that:

> Any alien who at any time after admission is convicted of two or more crimes involving moral turpitude, not arising out of a single scheme of criminal misconduct, regardless of whether confined therefore and regardless of whether the convictions were in a single trial, is deportable.

INA §237(a)(2)(A)(ii), 8 USC §1227(a)(2)(A)(ii).

Thus, regardless of the length of sentence, or even absence of sentence, the Texas assault case could indeed be considered in conjunction with a conviction for wire fraud and/or aggravated identity theft, to render Mr. Smith removable.

Theft Offense: Aggravated Felony Ground of Removal

If Mr. Smith is found guilty of aggravated identity theft and receives a sentence of one year or more (regardless of the amount of time actually served), he will be subject to removal as an aggravated felon. The Immigration Code defines an aggravated felony as, inter alia, a theft offense for which the term of imprisonment is at least one year.[42] Aggravated identity theft is a theft offense and, if a sentence is imposed of greater than one year, Mr. Smith will, in all likelihood, face removal and have no defenses. Other than challenging the constitutionality of the conviction or arguing that Aggravated Identity Theft is not a theft offense, Mr. Smith will have no defenses to removal if an immigration judge finds him removable as an aggravated felon.

Domestic Violence

An individual who at any time after admission is convicted of a crime of domestic violence is removable.[43] If the record of conviction in Mr. Smith's Texas assault case reveals that a family member was a complaining witness, then he may be exposed to the domestic violence ground of removal. The term "crime of domestic violence" is defined in the statute as "any crime of violence (as defined in section 16 of title 18, United States Code) against a person committed by . . . any other individual against a person who is protected from that individual's acts under the domestic or family violence laws of the United States or any State. . ."[44]

Under §71.003 of the Texas Family Code, the term "family" means, inter alia, individuals related by consanguinity or affinity. Under §82.002 of the Texas Family Code, a family member may file for a protective order in the event of family violence. It appears that Mr. Smith's mother is a family member entitled to protection under the family violence statutes of Texas, and thus her criminal complaint could render Mr. Smith deportable.

To prove its case, however, ICE would have to prove, using the record of conviction, that the complaining witness was Mr. Smith's mother. I have not yet reviewed the records from the Texas proceeding and thus am unable to conclude whether the record of conviction would support a claim of removal on this ground.

Inadmissibility

I strongly advise Mr. Smith not to leave the continental United States until these immigration matters are completely resolved. An individual is inadmissible to the United States if that person has committed a CMT. While the Texas assault case may be a CMT, it falls into the "petty offense exception" for offenses that have a maximum possible sentence of up to one year, and for which the individual received no more than six months. In Mr.

---

[41] *See Dashto v. INS*, 59 F.3d 697, 699 (7th Cir. 1995) *(citing Soetarto v. INS*, 516 F2d. 778, 780 (7th Cir. 1975); *see also Zaitona v. INS*, 9 F.3d 432, 437 (6th Cir. 1993); *Matter of De La Nues*, 18 I&N Dec. 140, 145 (BIA 1981); *Matter of Leyva*, 16 I&N Dec. 118 (BIA 1977); *Matter of T–*, 3 I&N Dec. 404 (BIA 1948).

[42] INA §101(a)(43)(G), 8 USC §1101(a)(43)(G).

[43] INA §237(a)(2)(E), 8 USC §1227(a)(2)(E).

[44] *Id.*

Smith's case, the Texas assault case would not bar Mr. Smith's admission to the United States; however, he may be questioned about it upon his return from foreign travel and should keep a certified copy of the conviction with him when traveling.

The wire fraud and aggravated identity theft counts would indeed bar Mr. Smith's admission to the United States because they are clearly CMTs and do not fall within the "petty offense exception" discussed above.

Crime of Violence

Mr. Smith is not likely to be charged with removability as an aggravated felon for having committed a crime of violence (assault) because the Immigration Code requires a sentence imposed of more than one year. As previously noted, Mr. Smith received a fine only and no sentence to confinement.

Defenses to Removal

Section 212(h)

If Mr. Smith accumulates seven years of physical presence before he is formally charged by ICE with removal, he would be eligible to apply for a waiver of removability under §212(h) of the Immigration Code.

Cancellation of Removal

Mr. Smith may be eligible for cancellation of removal. However, if he pleads guilty to another CMT before his seventh year of physical presence in the United States, he will lose eligibility for this relief.[45]

Alternative Pleas

Criminal Trespass

Criminal trespass does not normally involve moral turpitude unless it is accompanied by the intent to commit a morally turpitudinous crime, *e.g.*, larceny after entering the building.[46] Thus, if Mr. Smith pleaded guilty to simple criminal trespass, assuming there were no mens rea, he would not have been convicted of a CMT. Additionally, if his sentence were less than one year, he would not be at risk for removal for an aggravated felony.

Receipt of Stolen Property

This is not a viable alternative plea for two reasons. First, it is an aggravated felony if the term of imprisonment is at least one year. Second, it is also a CMT regardless of the length of sentence received.[47]

Destruction of Property

Unfortunately, this potential plea is also fraught with risk. First, if it has a mens rea of at least recklessness, it may be a crime of violence and thus an aggravated felony if the term of imprisonment is at least one year. Second, it is also a CMT, regardless of the length of sentence received, if it has the appropriate mens rea.[48]

Petition for Writ of Error Coram Nobis

As we discussed in your office during our meeting, Mr. Smith may file a Petition for Writ of Error Coram Nobis in the Texas assault case based on ineffective assistance of counsel. His defense attorney in that matter failed to advise him of the immigration consequences of a "no contest" plea, and therefore the plea was neither knowing nor voluntary. Convictions vacated due to underlying constitutional defects, such as Sixth Amendment violations, have no immigration consequences. However, convictions vacated solely to avoid immigration consequences remain valid for immigration purposes.[49] I suggest that Mr. Smith consult with an attorney licensed in Texas who is competent to advise him on the possibility of post-conviction relief and coram nobis litigation.

Conclusion

Please provide me with the Texas record of conviction for the assault so that I may review the potential for a CMT/domestic violence ground of removal. I also look forward to discussing possible plea strategies with you. I hope this discussion has been useful, and I look forward to speaking about it in detail.

---

[45] *Matter of Deanda-Romo*, 23 I&N Dec. 597 (BIA 2003).

[46] *Matter of M–*, 2 I&N Dec. 721, 723 (BIA, A.G. 1946).

[47] *Matter of Fortiz-Zelaya*, 21 I&N Dec. 1199 (BIA 1998) (where it was conceded that receipt of stolen property was a CMT); *Matter of Gordon*, 20 I&N Dec. 52 (BIA 1989) (finding receipt of stolen property is crime of moral turpitude).

[48] *Matter of M–*, 3 I&N Dec. 272 (BIA 1948).

[49] *Matter of Pickering*, 23 I&N Dec. 621 (2003).

CASE 4: CONCEALED DANGEROUS WEAPON/FALSE STATEMENT TO A POLICE OFFICER

ATTORNEY WORK PRODUCT

ATTORNEY-CLIENT PRIVILEGED COMMUNICATION

March 24, 2005

Mr. Solo Practitioner
1243 Main Street
Anytown, MD 20744-1038
Your Client: Mr. Smith

Dear Mr. Practitioner:

You requested an additional opinion letter from me concerning the immigration consequences of a possible guilty plea(s) or conviction(s) in the case of Mr. Smith, your client. I had the pleasure of meeting Mr. Smith on January 17 and 31, and March 23, 2005 here in my office. Below is my analysis of Mr. Smith's case in light of your recent plea negotiations.

Summary Conclusion

If Mr. Smith pleaded guilty to a single count of violating Criminal Law Article §4-101(c)(1), possession of a concealed dangerous weapon, and received a sentence of less than 364 days, he could preserve his defense of cancellation of removal (although he remains potentially deportable). Mere possession of a dangerous weapon, without an element of intent, is neither a CMT nor (with a sentence of less than one year) an aggravated felony. The charging document should be amended, however, to excise all reference to a handgun.

If Mr. Smith pleaded guilty to the charge of making a false statement to a police officer, he would also preserve his immigration defense of cancellation of removal. While DHS could assert that his prior second-degree assault conviction (involving his domestic companion) combined with this turpitudinous crime, render him deportable based on more than one conviction for a CMT, neither the assault nor the false statement is an aggravated felony. Mr. Smith would still be eligible to apply for cancellation of removal.

Mr. Smith's traffic violations do not create a basis for removability.

Facts

Mr. Smith first entered the United States on March 3, 1986, as a tourist. On October 3, 1992, he returned to Guatemala with his family to consular process his immigrant visa and returned to the United States as a lawful permanent resident (LPR) on October 17, 1992. His passports demonstrate that he has departed from the United States once since then, in July 1996, for a short vacation in Guatemala. Since his return in August 1996, he has not left the United States. He is in a common law relationship with a U.S. citizen, and together they have a U.S. citizen daughter, age four.

Current Plea Negotiations

It is my understanding that Mr. Smith has the opportunity to plea to the following:

- Possession of a concealed deadly weapon;
- False statement to a police officer;
- Parking in a handicapped space without special registration in violation of Transportation Article §21-1006 (b) (non-jailable, fine only);
- A total sentence of 360 days, with all but 179 suspended.

Discussion of Pleas that Lower the Risk of Deportation—Concealed Dangerous Weapon

Criminal Law §4-101(c)(1), possession of a concealed dangerous weapon, includes no intent element and specifically excludes firearms. It is likely neither a CMT nor an aggravated felony. If Mr. Smith pleaded guilty to a single count of violating Criminal Law Article §4-101(c)(1), and received a sentence of less than 364 days, he could preserve his defense of cancellation of removal (although he remains potentially deportable). To be sure that Mr. Smith is not exposed to an aggravated felony charge of deportation, the charging document should be amended to excise all reference to a handgun. I strongly suggest that an entirely new charging document, with a new case number, free of any reference to facts underlying prior charges, should be issued. Any statement of facts in the new case must be free of references to a firearm of any kind.

False Statement to A Police Officer

Section §9-502 of the Criminal Law Article of the Annotated Code of Maryland, makes it a misdemeanor to "knowingly, and with intent to deceive, make a false statement to a law enforcement officer concerning the person's identity, address, or date of birth." While clearly morally turpitudinous, such conviction would attain more than five years after Mr. Smith's admission to the United States, and the maximum possible sentence under the statute is less than one year. Thus, a conviction under §9-502 would not render Mr. Smith removable for a CMT under INA §237(a)(2)(A)(i).

Unfortunately, if DHS attempts to classify the second degree assault conviction as a CMT (due to the domestic violence element), Mr. Smith could be deportable based on INA §237(a)(2)(ii), committing more than one CMT. Nevertheless, he would not automatically become ineligible for cancellation of removal.

Cancellation of Removal

If not convicted of an aggravated felony, Mr. Smith appears to be eligible for cancellation of removal, a discretionary defense to removal for a lawful permanent resident (LPR) such as Mr. Smith.

Eligibility for cancellation of removal requires that Mr. Smith have been an LPR of the United States for at least five years before the *commission* (not conviction) of his 1999, CDS possession crime. He also must have accumulated seven years' physical presence in the United States after admission in any status before commission of the 1999, possession crime, and not have a conviction for an aggravated felony.

As a threshold matter, we will argue that Mr. Smith has satisfied the five- and seven-year requirements. Mr. Smith entered the United States as a tourist with a B-1/B-2 visa on March 3, 1986, and remained in the United States until a short trip on October 3, 1992 to Guatemala to obtain his green card at the U.S. Consulate there; he returned on October 17, 1992, two weeks later, and entered as an LPR. He committed his CDS (cocaine) possession crime on May 5, 1999, approximately 6.5 years later. We will argue that the short trip to Guatemala was not meaningfully interruptive of his physical presence and that his time in the United State after admission on his B-1/B-2 visa is counted toward the seven-year physical presence requirement. The Board of Immigration Appeals has already said that time spent in the United States once admitted as a temporary resident or a nonimmigrant may be applied toward the seven-year physical presence requirement.[50]

The Government will most likely argue that his trip to Guatemala stopped the accumulation of the seven years' continuous physical presence and that he is not eligible for cancellation of removal. The Government could move to pretermit (preclude the filing of) Mr. Smith's application for cancellation of removal, arguing that Mr. Smith is not eligible for the relief, and thus, the immigration judge should not even entertain the defense.

If we are allowed to file the application for cancellation of removal, approval is discretionary and far from automatic. Mr. Smith's cancellation defense would turn on the immigration judge's weighing of the evidence in favor of granting discretionary relief, such as: (1) the length of time he has been an LPR; (2) his family ties to the United States; (3) the immigration status of his family; (4) employment; (5) community and civic involvement; (6) comments on his character by those who know him; (7) his prospects in his country of origin and country conditions; (8) the nature of the offense; (9) rehabilitation; (10) extenuating circumstances; and (11) health issues.

Sentence

Mr. Smith is facing a total sentence of 360 days, with all but 179 suspended. The total sentence is less than one year, thus precluding the possibility of a conviction for a "crime of violence" aggravated felony. His sentence for 179 days will preserve his ability, at a future date, to apply for citizenship, assuming he is able to defend successfully against removability.

I also do not recommend, and I counsel against, Mr. Smith leaving the United States until all of these immigration matters have been resolved.

Conclusion

It appears that the pleas contemplated, along with a total sentence of 360 days, with all but 179 suspended, would not disturb Mr. Smith's potential eligibility to apply for cancellation of removal, although his prior convictions might cause the immigration judge to deny, in the exercise of discretion, the application.

I hope you have found this discussion useful. Please call me if you have any questions.

---

[50] *In Re Eduardo Blancas-Lara*, 23 I&N Dec. 458 (BIA 2002); *In re Perez*, 22 I&N Dec. 689 (BIA 1999).

INTO THE RABBIT'S HOLE: WHEN A MISDEMEANOR IS A FELONY
THE *DAVIS/BARRETT* HYPOTHETICAL
FEDERAL FELONY ANALYSIS OF DRUG CRIMES

by Ilana Etkin Greenstein[*]

Ten years after IIRAIRA's[1] expansion of the aggravated felony definition, it has become common knowledge within the immigration law community that a conviction for an aggravated felony is the kiss of death to the noncitizen. A conviction for an aggravated felony at any time after admission to the United States renders a noncitizen deportable (removable).[2] Aggravated felons are precluded from applying for asylum,[3] and from withholding of removal if those crimes constituted "particularly serious" ones.[4] They are ineligible for cancellation of removal,[5] and they are subject to mandatory detention throughout the course of their immigration proceedings.[6] The question whether a particular offense constitutes an aggravated felony can mean the difference between the possibility of remaining in the United States and mandatory detention followed by certain deportation and permanent exclusion from the country. As such, the question of whether an offense constitutes an aggravated felony is of critical importance to noncitizens.

Section 101(a)(43) of the Immigration and Nationality Act (INA) consists of a laundry-list of offenses that constitute aggravated felonies. That list includes drug trafficking crimes, which the statute defines as offenses that either involve trafficking or that are punishable under various federal statutes criminalizing controlled substance violations. When a noncitizen has been convicted of a trafficking offense in any court, or of another drug crime in federal court, then the question of whether the offense is an aggravated felony is a relatively easy one. When the individual has been charged in state court of a non-trafficking offense, however, the answer often becomes much less clear. In those cases, the courts look to the federal drug statutes and ask whether the offense in question could have been prosecuted under federal law had the defendant been subject to federal jurisdiction. When the analysis rests on analogy-drawing, though, a question arises: Can an offense that is a misdemeanor under the law of the convicting jurisdiction be classified as an aggravated *felony* for the purpose of the federal immigration laws? What about an offense that is a felony under state law, but which would only be punishable as a misdemeanor if it were prosecuted under federal law?

The Board of Immigration Appeals (BIA) and the nation's circuit courts of appeals have taken a deep dive into Alice's rabbit hole, and have convoluted, circuitous paths to answering those questions. The result is a body of case law with more twists and turns than the average roller coaster and with truly bizarre results. This article attempts to navigate those paths, lead the reader through the lines of analysis, and describe the state of the case law to date. It also offers a few potential arguments against classifying an offense as an aggravated felony by analogy.

---

[*] **Ilana Greenstein** practices immigration law at Kaplan, O'Sullivan and Friedman in Boston (*www.kof-law.com*). She practices all aspects of immigration law, with a focus on appellate litigation. Ms. Greenstein holds a J.D. from Northeastern University School of Law, and a B.A. in Spanish and International Studies from Macalester College. She served on the Board of Directors of the Massachusetts Chapter of the National Lawyers Guild from 1996–2002, and on the steering committee of the Boston Bar Association's Individual Rights & Responsibilities section in 2000, and remains active in the National Lawyers Guild's Massachusetts chapter.

[1] Illegal Immigration Reform and Immigrant Responsibility Act of 1996, Division C of the Omnibus Appropriations Act of 1996 (H.R. 3610), Pub. L. No. 104-208, 110 Stat. 3009 (IIRAIRA).

[2] Immigration and Nationality Act of 1952, Pub. L. No. 82-414, 66 Stat. 163 (*codified as amended at* 8 USC §§1101 *et seq.*), INA §237(a)(2)(A)(iii). The "after admission" language is not a safe haven. *See Matter of Rosas*, 22 I&N Dec. 616 (BIA 1999).

[3] INA §208(b)(2)(A).

[4] *Matter of L–S–*, 22 I&N Dec. 645 (BIA 1999). *See also Matter of Y–L– et al.*, 23 I&N Dec. 270 (BIA 2002).

[5] INA §§240A(a)(3), 240B(a)(1).

[6] INA §236(c). Of course, mandatory detention is authorized for most criminal-based removal proceedings, not just aggravated felonies.

HISTORY OF THE
AGGRAVATED FELONY CONCEPT

The "aggravated felony" concept was introduced into the INA by the Anti-Drug Abuse Act of 1988 (ADAA).[7] ADAA §7342 added §101(a)(43) to the INA, which defined the term "aggravated felony" as it pertains to drug offenses as "any drug trafficking crime as defined in §924(c)(2) of title 18, United States Code...." ADAA also amended 18 USC §924(c)(2), to define a "drug trafficking crime" as "any felony punishable under the Controlled Substances Act, the Controlled Substance Import and Export Act, or the Maritime Drug Law Enforcement Act."

Prior to 1988, §924(c)(2) had defined the term "drug trafficking crime" simply as "any felony violation of federal law involving the distribution, manufacture, or importation of any controlled substance." Thus, prior to 1988, the term "drug trafficking crime" referred exclusively to federal felony drug offenses.[8] ADAA expanded the term to include state offenses.

THE BIA AND THE
DAVIS/BARRETT HYPOTHETICAL
FEDERAL FELONY DOCTRINE

In the wake of the 1988 amendments, the BIA confronted the question of whether state drug convictions could constitute "drug trafficking crimes" under 18 USC §924(c)(2) and, as such, "aggravated felonies" within the meaning of the new INA §101(a)(43). In *Matter of Barrett*, the BIA answered that question, holding that the definition of a drug trafficking crime under §924(c)(2) encompassed state drug convictions which "include[d] all the elements of an offense for which an alien 'could be convicted and punished'" under the applicable federal statute in §924(c)(2).[9] This analysis came to be known as the "hypothetical federal felony" approach. *Barrett* did not address how the classification of an offense as a felony or a misdemeanor would be relevant to its subsequent classification as an aggravated felony; it held simply that one could be deemed to have committed a felony by analogy, and that that analogy could form the basis for an aggravated felony classification.

The Immigration Act of 1990 (IMMACT90),[10] further amended the definition of an aggravated felony. Under the amended definition, a drug offense constitutes an "aggravated felony" if it involves

> any illicit trafficking in a controlled substance (as defined in section 102 of the Controlled Substances Act), including a drug trafficking crime (as defined in section 924(c) of title 18, United States Code).... Such term applies to offenses described in the previous sentence whether in violation of Federal or State law....[11]

The amendments thus added the phrase "any illicit trafficking in a controlled substance" to the definition, and also specified that the definition of an aggravated felony included violations of state, as well as federal, law. As such, the changes effectively codified *Matter of Barrett*.[12] With the exception of a technical amendment in 1994 that changed INA §101(a)(43)'s reference from "§924(c)(2)" to "§924(c)" (thereby including crimes of violence, as well as drug trafficking crimes, in the aggravated felony definition), the definition has not changed since 1990.

After the 1990 amendments, the BIA elaborated on the question of when a state drug offense could constitute a "drug trafficking crime" under the new aggravated felony definition. In *Matter of Davis*,[13] the BIA held that two alternate routes existed within INA §101(a)(43) to determine whether a drug offense constitutes an aggravated felony.

The first route tracked the language of the new phrase "illicit trafficking in a controlled substance." Under that route, an offense is deemed an aggravated felony if: (1) it is classified as a felony under the law of the convicting jurisdiction; and (2) it contains a "trafficking element." The BIA defined "trafficking" as "the unlawful trading or dealing of a controlled substance."[14] Thus,

---

[7] Pub. L. No. 100-690, 102 Stat. 4181 (1988).

[8] *U.S. v. Palacios-Suarez*, 418 F.3d 692, 698 (6th Cir. 2005).

[9] 20 I&N Dec. 171, 174–77 (BIA 1990).

---

[10] Pub. L. No. 101-649, 104 Stat. 4978 (IMMACT90).

[11] IMMACT90 §501.

[12] *See* H.R. Rep. No. 681 pt. 1 at 147 (1990), *reprinted at* USCCAN 6472, 6553 ("Because the Committee concurs with the recent decision of the Board of Immigration Appeals [in *Matter of Barrett*] and wishes to end further litigation on th[e] issue [of whether a state drug trafficking conviction can render an alien an aggravated felon], §1501 of H.R. 5269 specifies that drug trafficking . . . is an aggravated felony whether or not the conviction occurred in state or Federal Court.").

[13] 20 I&N Dec. 536 (BIA 1992).

[14] *Davis*, 20 I&N Dec. at 541.

an offense that is not a felony and/or an offense which lacks a sufficient nexus to the trade or dealing of controlled substances [does not] constitute[] "illicit trafficking [and, as such, is not an aggravated felony]. . . ."[15]

If an offense is not classifiable as a trafficking offense under §924(c)(2)'s first prong (the plain language analysis), the BIA held, then the adjudicator must determine whether the offense is analogous to a federal drug crime.

This second prong is analyzed under the "hypothetical federal felony" analysis initially set forth in *Barrett*. *Davis* clarified *Barrett* to hold that

if the offense is not designated as a felony [under the law of the convicting sovereign] it may nonetheless be a "drug trafficking crime" (and therefore "illicit trafficking" and an "aggravated felony" if it is analogous to an offense punishable under one of the federal acts specified in 18 USC §924(c)(2), and the offense to which it is analogous is a "felony" under federal law.[16]

Thus, under the hypothetical federal felony analysis, the *Davis* BIA interpreted §924(c)(2)

to encompass convictions for state offenses, however characterized by the state, if those offenses would be 'punishable' under one of the three specified federal statutes if federally prosecuted, so long as the hypothetical federal conviction would be a felony under federal law, *i.e.*, would be punishable by a term of imprisonment of over one year.[17]

As such, the determination of whether an offense constitutes an aggravated felony under INA §101(a)(43)(C) involves two questions: (1) whether the offense involves trafficking in a controlled substance; and, if not, (2) whether it is a felony that can be deemed a "trafficking offense" nonetheless because it would be punishable under 18 USC §924(c)(2) if the offender were prosecuted in federal court.

If the offense on its face involves trafficking in a controlled substance, that is the end of the inquiry; the offense constitutes an aggravated felony under INA §101(a)(43)(C)'s first prong. If it does not involve trafficking, then the court must determine

whether the offense is a felony that would be punishable under the Controlled Substances Act, the Controlled Substance Import and Export Act, or the Maritime Drug Law Enforcement Act. If the offense is not a felony, or would not be punishable under one of those federal statutes (that is, if the offense is not sufficiently analogous to a federal drug offense), then it fails under the second prong of the analysis, and is not an aggravated felony.

If the offense does not involve trafficking, but would be punishable under federal law, then the court must determine whether the offense is a felony. If it is a felony, then it is an aggravated felony. If it is not a felony, then it does not fall within INA §101(a)(43)(C)'s scope, and it is not an aggravated felony.

THE RABBIT'S HOLE: WHEN IS A FELONY NOT A FELONY? WHEN IT IS A MISDEMEANOR . . .

It is in this final step of the analysis that the majority of the litigation has focused. Many of the circuit courts of appeals declined to follow the *Davis/Barrett* hypothetical federal felony analysis and, instead, adopted rules of their own, with the majority of the judicial cases arising in the context of the federal Sentencing Guidelines. The U.S. Sentencing Guidelines Manual §2L1.2, Application Note 1 refers to INA §101(a)(43)'s definition of an "aggravated felony" for the purpose of sentencing enhancements for violations of 18 USC §1326. Section 1326 criminalizes unlawful re-entry into the United States for aliens who have previously been deported or removed from the country. Section 2L1.2 of the Sentencing Guidelines requires the judge to impose a 16-point sentencing enhancement for aggravated felons guilty of illegal re-entry.

The First Circuit authored the seminal interpretation of §924(c)(2) in the Sentencing Guidelines context, diverging significantly from the *Davis/Barrett* test. First articulated in *Amaral v. INS*[18] and in *United States v. Forbes*,[19] the most thorough analysis of the alternate position is found in *United States v. Restrepo-Aguilar*.[20]

Restrepo-Aguilar addressed a state felony that would have been punishable under the Controlled

---

[15] *Id.*

[16] *Id.* at 543.

[17] *Gerbier v. Holmes*, 280 F.3d 297, 306 (3d Cir. 2002) (quoting *Steele v. Blackman*, 236 F.3d 130, 135–36 (3d Cir. 2001)).

[18] 977 F.2d 33, 36 n.3 (1st Cir. 1992).

[19] 16 F.3d 1294, 1301 n.10 (1st Cir. 1994).

[20] 74 F.3d 361 (1st Cir. 1996).

Substances Act as a misdemeanor. In that case, the court looked to the plain language of the statute defining a drug trafficking crime as "any felony punishable under the Controlled Substances Act [*et al.*],"[21] to reject the defendant's argument that "punishable under" meant an offense punishable *as a felony under federal law*. It affirmed its prior holding that §924(c)(2)'s definition had two elements: (1) that the offense be a felony; and (2) that it be punishable under the Controlled Substances Act. And it emphasized that they are "two *separate* elements."[22] The offense in question must be a felony, *and* it must be punishable under the federal drug laws.[23]

The circuit courts of appeals almost unanimously adopted *Restrepo-Aguilar*'s approach in the Sentencing Guidelines context.[24] In response to the widespread criticism of its approach, and in deference to the circuit courts, the BIA, in 2002, retreated from the *Davis/Barrett* test, and determined that in the future, it would follow the approach adopted by whichever circuit had jurisdiction over a particular case and, where the circuit had not spoken on the issue, it would defer to the approach that the majority of the courts had adopted—the *Restrepo-Aguilar* approach.[25]

Thereafter, the §924(c)(2) analysis developed along two divergent paths. In the Sentencing Guidelines context, the First Circuit interpreted its prior decision in *Restrepo-Aguilar* as permitting the adjudicator to look both to the law of the convicting jurisdiction and to the analogous federal law and, if one of those two classified the offense in question as a felony, to designate the offense a felony for the purpose of a §924(c)(2) analysis.[26]

The majority of the other circuits have followed a similar tack. In *U.S. v. Wilson*,[27] the Fourth Circuit articulated the majority view when it held that a state felony analogous to a federal misdemeanor did fall within the Controlled Substances Act's definition of a felony as "any Federal or State offense classified by applicable Federal *or State* law as a felony."[28] It noted that "while the CSA would not *punish* Wilson's conduct as a felony, it does *define* it as a felony given the punishment it receives under Virginia law."[29]

The Sixth Circuit, however, required that the offense be classified as a felony under both state and federal law in order for it to constitute an aggravated felony under the Sentencing Guidelines.[30] Similarly, the Ninth Circuit has held that a state felony could not be considered an aggravated felony under §924(c)(2), regardless of its classification under analogous federal law, unless the state conviction carried a potential sentence of a year's imprisonment or more.[31]

In the deportation context, however, the BIA and some of the circuit courts of appeals have interpreted §924(c)(2) much more stringently, in keeping with fundamental tenets of fairness and deference to sovereign states, and in light of the grave impact that deportation has on its subjects, their families, and their communities. In the deportation context, the BIA has interpreted §924(c)(2) as leaving the classification of felonies up to the convicting jurisdictions. A state conviction, therefore, can only be an aggravated felony if the state classifies the offense as a felony.[32]

The Third Circuit has gone even farther, holding that an offense must be classified as a felony under the law of the convicting jurisdiction and *also* must

---

[21] *Restrepo-Aguilar*, 74 F.3d at 364 (quoting 18 USC §924(c)(2)).

[22] *Id.* (emphasis in original)

[23] *Restrepo-Aguilar*, 74 F.3d at 364.

[24] *U.S. v. Pornes-Garcia*, 171 F.3d 142 (2d Cir. 1999); *U.S. v. Hernandez-Avalos*, 251 F.3d 505 (5th Cir. 2001); *U.S. v. Hinojosa-Lopez*, 130 F.3d 691 (5th Cir. 1997); *U.S. v. Briones-Mata*, 116 F.3d 308 (8th Cir. 1997); *U.S. v. Ibarra-Galindo*, 206 F.3d 1337 (9th Cir. 2000); *U.S. v. Garcia-Olmedo*, 112 F.3d 399 (9th Cir. 1997); *U.S. v. Valenzuela-Escalante*, 130 F.3d 944 (10th Cir. 1997); *U.S. v. Cabrera-Sosa*, 81 F.3d 998 (10th Cir. 1996); and *U.S. v. Simon*, 168 F.3d 1271 (11th Cir. 1999).

[25] *Matter of Yanez-Garcia*, 23 I&N Dec. 390 (BIA 2002).

[26] *U.S. v. Brennick*, 337 F.3d 107 (1st Cir. 2003).

[27] 316 F.3d 506 (4th Cir. 2003).

[28] *Id.* at 512 (quoting 21 USC §802(13) (emphasis in original)).

[29] *Id.* at 513. *See also U.S. v. Pornes-Garcia*, 171 F.3d 142; *U.S. v. Sanchez-Villalobos*, 412 F.3d 572 (5th Cir. 2005); *Hernandez-Avalos*, 251 F.3d 505; *Hinojosa-Lopez*, 130 F.3d 691; *Briones-Mata*, 116 F.3d 308; *Valenzuela-Escalante*, 130 F.3d 944; *Cabrera-Sosa*, 81 F.3d 998; and *Simon*, 168 F.3d 1271.

[30] *Palacios-Suarez*, 418 F.3d at 695.

[31] *United States v. Robles-Rodriguez*, 281 F.3d 900 (9th Cir. 2002); *see also Ibarra-Galindo*, 206 F.3d 1337; *Garcia-Olmedo*, 112 F.3d 399.

[32] *Matter of Santos-Lopez*, 23 I&N Dec. 419 (BIA 2002); *Matter of Elgendi*, 23 I&N Dec. 515 (BIA 2002).

be punishable as a felony under an analogous federal statute in order to be deemed a felony within the meaning of §924(c)(2).[33] Out of deference to the BIA and in order to avoid disparate treatment of similarly situated aliens, the Second Circuit reversed its prior decision in *Jenkins v. INS*,[34] in which it had held that a state felony drug offense punishable as a misdemeanor under the Controlled Substances Act constitutes an aggravated felony. The *Jenkins* court adopted the BIA's rule in *Matter of L–G–*,[35] to hold that a state drug conviction could not constitute a "felony" within the meaning of §924(c)(2) unless it were analogous to a federal felony.

In *Pornes-Garcia*,[36] the Second Circuit noted the propriety of having two separate interpretations of the same term, and the same statutory provision, in different (that is, Sentencing Guidelines versus deportation) contexts.[37] The Fifth Circuit has held that it will not interpret Sentencing Guidelines cases differently from deportation cases.[38] The Eighth Circuit has taken a broader view, holding that "for INA purposes, a drug trafficking crime is an offense which would be punishable under 21 USC §§801 et. seq., and which would qualify as a felony under either state or federal law."[39]

In *Cazarez-Gutierrez v. Ashcroft*, the Ninth Circuit adopted the Second and Third Circuits' rule and cited with approval the BIA's decision in *Elgendi*.[40]

Cazarez-Gutierrez did not explicitly address the question of whether a state misdemeanor analogous to a federal felony would constitute an aggravated felony within the meaning of §924(c)(2). Its adoption of *Gerbier*, and its approval of *Elgendi*, however, imply that it too would hold that an offense may only be deemed a "felony" for the purposes of an aggravated felony analysis if it is both punishable as a felony under federal law *and* is classified as a felony by the convicting jurisdiction.

MAKING THE ANALYSIS

Determining whether a drug offense can be classified as an aggravated felony involves a three-step analysis. The first question is: does the offense involve illicit trafficking in a controlled substance? If so, it is an aggravated felony. If the offense does not involve trafficking, the second question becomes: would the offense be punishable under a federal drug statute if the defendant were subject to federal jurisdiction? And, if so, the third question becomes: is the offense a felony?

The BIA has defined those offenses that fall under the first prong of the analysis (that is, those offenses, which, on their face, involve trafficking) as those that: (1) constitute a felony under the law of the convicting sovereign; and (2) involve the "unlawful trading or dealing of any controlled substance."[41] That "trading or dealing" must by necessity involve commerce—that is, distribution for consideration.

> Essential to the concept of "trading or dealing" is activity of a "business or merchant nature," thus excluding simple possession or *transfer without consideration.*[42]

Thus, an offense that does not have a compensation or consideration element cannot be deemed a trafficking offense, even if it does involve distribution of a controlled substance.

The second question—whether a state offense is "punishable under" a federal statute—turns on the elements of the offense as defined in the relevant statutes, not on the facts of the individual's case.

---

[33] *Gerbier*, 80 F.3d 297, 307 (3d Cir. 2002).

[34] 32 F.3d 11 (2d Cir. 1994).

[35] 21 I&N Dec. 89 (BIA 1995).

[36] 171 F.3d 142, 147 (2d Cir. 1999).

[37] *Pornes-Garcia* was decided before the BIA issued its decisions in *Santos-Lopez* and *Elgendi*, decisions which explicitly overruled *L–G–*, 21 I&N Dec. 89. The Second Circuit has not, to the best of the author's knowledge, had the opportunity to revisit its decision in light of those cases. Given that the rule the court adopted in *Pornes* was the BIA's rule at the time, and given that the court's explicit reason for reversing its prior decisions was a desire to keep its doctrine in line with the BIA's, it is quite likely that the Second Circuit would choose to follow *Santos-Lopez* and *Elgendi* to the extent that they are incompatible with *Pornes*.

[38] *Hernandez-Avalos*, 251 F.3d 505, 509–10 (5th Cir. 2001).

[39] *Lopez v. Gonzales*, 417 F.3d 934, 937 (8th Cir. 2005). The Supreme Court has recently granted certiorari in this case to resolve the split in the circuit courts of appeal. The Court has also granted certiorari in a sentencing case raising the same issue. *See Toledo-Flores*, No. 05-7664, 2006 WL 842994 (2006).

[40] 23 I&N Dec. 515. *Cazarez-Gutierrez v. Ashcroft*, 382 F.3d 905, 912 (9th Cir. 2004).

[41] *Matter of Davis*, 20 I&N Dec. 536, 541 (BIA 1992); *Steele v. Blackman*, 236 F.3d 130 (3d Cir. 2001).

[42] *Steele*, 236 F.3d at 135 (emphasis added) (quoting *Davis*, 20 I&N Dec. at 541); *see also Kuhali v. Reno*, 266 F.3d 93 (2d Cir. 2001) (offense must exhibit business or merchant nature in order to constitute trafficking).

Since the basis for the incapacities under the Immigration Act is 'conviction of an aggravated felony,' 8 USC §1229b(a), the Board looks to what the convicting court must necessarily have found to support the conviction and not to other conduct in which the defendant may have engaged in connection with the offense. Thus, where, as here, the Service is relying on a state misdemeanor conviction, the requirements of this second category of aggravated felony convictions are satisfied only by proving a conviction that includes all the elements of a felony offense for which the alien could be convicted and punished under the cited federal laws. Accordingly, the proposed analogy between the state statutes and offenses under the cited federal statutes will be a matter of law.[43]

Determining whether an offense has a trafficking element, and whether it is analogous to a federal offense, are usually relatively straightforward. It is the third prong of the analysis that becomes the most difficult. The vast majority of the published cases on this issue involve state felonies punishable as misdemeanors under federal law, and the majority of those cases address the question in the context of the Sentencing Guidelines, rather than in that of a deportation/removal claim. And the way in which the majority of the cases are written makes it difficult to glean a clear rule of law.

Rather than stating a clear-cut general rule (for example, "in determining whether an offense constitutes a felony for the purposes of classifying it as an aggravated felony, the classification of the convicting jurisdiction shall control" or "the classification of the federal analogue shall control"), the courts have tended to state their holdings in terms of results rather than rules ("We hold that a state drug offense is properly deemed a 'felony' . . . if the offense is classified as a felony under the law of the relevant state, even if the same offense would be punishable only as a misdemeanor under federal law.").[44] As such, a case holding, for example, that a state felony punishable as a federal misdemeanor does constitute an aggravated felony would not preclude an argument that a state misdemeanor punishable as a federal felony is *not* an aggravated felony.

If your case involves a state misdemeanor punishable as a federal felony, consider an argument that the plain language of the statute (defining an aggravated felony as a "*felony* punishable under" one of the enumerated federal drug statutes) precludes a reading that would classify a state misdemeanor offense as a felony simply because it is analogous to an offense theoretically punishable as a felony under federal law.[45]

Also consider a due process argument: It is absolutely critical that when an alien pleads guilty to a criminal offense, he or she be aware of the consequences of his or her plea. As the Third Circuit noted in *Steele*,

> One cannot suffer the disabilities associated with having been convicted of an aggravated felony unless one has been *convicted* of a felony. This, of course, means that there must be a judicial determination beyond a reasonable doubt of every element of a felony or a constitutionally valid plea that encompasses each of those elements. . . .
>
> The fact that this hypothetical [federal felony] approach imposes such grave consequences on factual determinations made, or pleas entered, in misdemeanor proceedings is one of its more troubling aspects. Misdemeanor charges are frequently not addressed by a defendant with the same care and caution as a felony indictment with its more serious, immediate consequences.[46]

---

[43] *Steele*, 236 F.3d at 136 (quoting *Matter of Barrett*, 20 I&N Dec. 171, 174–77 (BIA 1990)).

[44] *Restrepo-Aguilar*, 74 F.3d 361, 365 (1st Cir. 1996).

---

[45] As Judge Straub noted in his dissent to *U.S. v. Pacheco*:

> Common sense and standard English grammar dictate that when an adjective—such as 'aggravated'—modifies a noun—such as 'felony'—the combination of the terms delineates a subset of the noun. One would never suggest, for example, that by adding the adjective 'blue' to the noun 'car,' one could be attempting to define items that are not, in the first instance, cars. In other words, based on the plain meaning of the terms 'aggravated' and 'felony,' we should presume that the specifics that follow in the definition of 'aggravated felony' under INA §101(a)(43) serve to elucidate what makes these particular felonies 'aggravated;' we certainly should not presume that those specifics would include offenses that are not felonies *at all*.

U.S. v. Pacheco, 225 F.3d 148, 157 (2d Cir. 2000) (Straub, J., dissenting); *cf. Benjamin v. Jacobson*, 172 F.3d 144, 173 n.5 (2d Cir. 1999) (Calabresi, J., concurring) ("When Congress, in a definitional section, seems to say that bananas *are* apples, we should ask whether that is really what Congress meant. . . .").

[46] 236 F.3d at 136–37.

Finally, if the law of your circuit is unhelpful, but only addresses the issue in the context of the Sentencing Guidelines (or in the removal context, if your claim involves the Sentencing Guidelines), consider an argument that it is appropriate to address the classification of an offense as an aggravated felony differently depending on whether the claim arises in the context of a Sentencing Guidelines dispute, or an immigration/deportation dispute.[47]

CONCLUSION

The question of whether and in what context a state drug offense may be classified as an aggravated felony has generated a whirlwind of litigation, leaving the circuits widely split. That split, though resulting in a good deal of confusion and frustration among the courts, leaves the door wide open for litigation. And, in a day and age when the classification of an offense as an aggravated felony can mean the difference between hope and despair for our clients, an open door cannot be a bad thing.

---

[47] *Restrepo-Aguilar*, 74 F.3d at 364) (declining to follow the BIA's holding in *Matter of L–G–*, 21 I&N Dec. 89 (BIA 1995), and noting policy reasons for interpreting Sentencing Guidelines cases more harshly than deportation cases); *Pornes-Garcia*, 171 F.3d 142, 147–48 (2d Cir. 1999) ("our interpretation of 'aggravated felony' in the context of § 2L1.2 [of the Sentencing Guidelines] is informed by the commentary accompanying that guideline. . . . Application note 1 to §2L1.2 mandates a broad definition of 'felony;' it provides that 'felony offense' means any federal, state or local offense punishable by imprisonment for a term exceeding one year."); *see also Aguirre v. INS*, 79 F.3d 315, 317 n.1 (2d Cir. 1996); *Cazarez-Gutierrez*, 382 F.3d 905 (9th Cir. 2004); *but see Hernandez-Avalos*, 251 F.3d 505 (5th Cir. 2001).

REMEDIES OF LAST RESORT: PRIVATE BILLS AND PARDONS

by Anna Marie Gallagher[*]

Over the years, thousands of noncitizens with compelling stories have been deported from the United States because their cases did not fall within the four square corners of public immigration laws. Many have lost their immigration status and been removed because of criminal convictions or behavior, while many others have fallen between the cracks of public immigration and asylum laws, which for the most part are meant to keep families together, provide much needed workers for the U.S. labor market, and protect refugees. When the law fails to provide much needed relief for many deserving cases, the only remaining remedies available may be applying for a private bill in the United States Congress or a pardon—either state or federal—for those with criminal issues.

Congress has a long history of passing private laws in order to provide a remedy in cases where the public law cannot do so.[1] From its first session in 1789 until today, the U.S. Congress has enacted over 7,000 private bills.[2] From the 77th session of Congress in 1942 until the 107th session in 2003, 60,601

immigration-related private bills were introduced. Of that amount, 6,798 were enacted.[3] As noted in the seminal work on private bills written by a former congressional staffer, Bernadette Maguire, the harsher the laws on the books at any given time, the greater the need for private immigration relief.[4] An increase in the number of requested private bills has acted to inform Congress of the need for reform. For example, during the years that immigration quotas were enforced—granting status based on national origin—the only recourse for immigration for those persons from countries not covered by the Act was through private legislation. Large numbers of bills have also been filed by family members of persons excluded from the United States for health grounds and criminal behavior. Finally, the high number of requests for private bills in the area of naturalization—to excuse certain expatriating acts during long periods of residence abroad—has also provided notice to Congress of gaps in the laws. The ongoing requests for private relief as a result of gaps in the immigration law above served to notify Congress of a need for change.[5]

In addition to private fixes through specific legislation, many practitioners representing clients with criminal convictions also turn to pardons to avoid deportation. Changes relating to grounds of inadmissibility and removal included in the Antiterrorism and Effective Death Penalty Act[6] and the Illegal Immigration Reform and Immigrant Responsibility Act[7] resulted in thousands of persons with criminal convictions or past activity being subjected to deportation, with many facing permanent expulsion. The need for state and federal pardons after passage of these laws in 1996 became even greater in order to avoid separation of families and deportation of longtime residents from the United States, many for crimes they had committed years before.

This *Briefing* will address both private bills and pardons. In discussing private bills, it will provide some historical background and statistics relating to private legislation since the formation of our country. It will also explain the procedures to be followed in seeking approval of private legislation. In addressing pardons, it will discuss both state and federal pardons, including the legal framework and procedures.

---

[*] This article was originally published in "Remedies of Last Resort: Private Bills and Pardons," 06-02 Immigration Briefings 1 (Feb. 2006), © 2006 Thomson/West 2006, and draws upon material contained in Ms. Gallagher's treatise, Immigration Law Service 2d, published by Thomson West. It is reprinted here with the permission of Thomson/West. For information on Immigration Law Service 2d, visit *http://west.thomson.com/store/product.asp?product_id =15503434*. For further information on Immigration Briefings, visit *http://west.thomson.com/product/15867088/ product.asp*. Both Immigration Law Service 2d and Immigration Briefings articles are also available on Westlaw®.

Anna Marie Gallagher, a North American attorney based in Spain, teaches international refugee and migration law in Europe and is a consultant to the Jesuit Refugee Service, an international non-governmental organization working with refugees and other forced migrants around the world. Ms. Gallagher, a longtime member of AILA, was the Director of the Legal Action Center of the American Immigration Law Foundation (AILF) (1996–2000), a teaching fellow in the Center for Applied Legal Studies at Georgetown University Law Center (2000–2002) and the Pedro Arrupe Chair of Migration and Refugee Law in Deusto University in Bilbao, Spain (2002–2004). She has published in her areas of interest and practice and is the author of Immigration Law Service 2d, Thomson West's immigration law treatise.

PRIVATE BILLS

What Is the Purpose and Legal Authority of a Private Bill?

A private bill is an individual discretionary exception to the general law. The primary purpose of a private law is to correct an injustice which cannot be remedied under existing public laws. The House of Representatives has defined a private bill as follows:

> A private bill is a bill for the relief of one or several specified persons, corporations, institutions, etc., and is distinguished from a public bill which relates to public matters and deals with individuals only by classes.[8]

Common types of private bills include the following:[9]

- *Adoption cases*: Under the immigration laws, a foreign born child can obtain immigrant status if the adoption takes place when the child is 16 years or younger and the child is either an orphan or the child has resided with the adoptive parents for two years.[10] Private bills have been passed for adopted children who do not fit within these requirements, where the children were young and had a long-standing relationship with the adoptive parents.

- *Certain criminal activity*: Depending on the circumstances of the case and the best interests of the community, Congress will consider private bills involving noncitizens with criminal convictions or activity in their past.

- *Waiver of exclusions/inadmissibility*: Many bills have been passed waiving certain grounds of exclusion/inadmissibility, including health-related grounds.

- *Naturalization cases*: These bills involve compelling cases where the beneficiaries do not qualify for naturalization but present special circumstances warranting a grant.

The House of Representatives indicates in its rules that it looks unfavorably upon the following requests for private relief:[11]

- *Doctors*: Applications for private legislation granting permanent residency status to doctors seeking lucrative job offers rather than practices in medically underserved areas.

- *Medical cases*: Applications for private bills seeking residency for persons who enter the United States for medical treatment. There are nonimmigrant visas available for such persons to enter and seek the necessary treatment and return home when finished. In cases involving such requests, Congress will request opinions to determine the availability of treatment in the home country.

- *Deferred action and parole cases*: Congress is reluctant to grant a private bill to persons who have been granted deferred action or who have been paroled indefinitely into the United States.

- *Draft evaders*: There are few precedent cases involving private bills for persons seeking residency to avoid military recruitment.

- *Visa fraud*: Congress is reluctant to grant relief in cases involving visa fraud.

- *Bills tabled in a previous Congress*: Congress believes that since requests for private relief are given careful consideration, repetitious requests negatively affect other private bills and reflects poorly on the private bill process itself.

Congressional authority over immigration matters is not explicitly provided for in the U.S. Constitution but is considered to derive from several clauses. The United States Supreme Court in its decision in *Plyler v. Doe*,[12] noted that the Constitution confers on Congress the power to 'establish an uniform Rule of Naturalization' under Art. I, §8, cl. 4. Therefore, drawing on its powers relating to naturalization, its plenary authority relating to foreign relations and international commerce and on the inherent power of a sovereign to control its borders, Congress has developed a complicated process governing admission and stay in the United States by noncitizens.[13] The constitutional authority for private legislation is found in the First Amendment prohibition against Congressional actions which would impede the right of the people "to petition the Government for redress of grievances"[14] and the power of Congress to pay the debts of the country.[15]

When the public immigration laws do not permit someone to enter or remain in the United States or to obtain some other immigration benefit, such as naturalization, private immigration bills may provide an alternative route for a person whose case merits special attention. Therefore, private bills are intended to be a remedy of last resort after all other remedies are exhausted.[16]

When Congress enacts legislation which does not include procedures to address hardship cases, there is generally an increase in the number of private bills filed. The majority of private immigration-related legislation grants lawful permanent resident status by waiving general law provisions which precludes the concession or maintenance of such status, waiving numerical allocations or waiving definitions of eligible immigrant categories.

Examples of approved private immigration bills include:

- *Persian Gulf evacuees*: This bill provided lawful permanent residency for 54 families unable to obtain legal status in the United States following their evacuation during the Gulf War.[17]

- *Guy Taylor*: This bill granted lawful resident status to a young Canadian man, orphaned when his father died before his birth and his mother died from a drug overdose after his 16th birthday. During his childhood, Mr. Taylor had attended school in California and Vancouver. His grandmother, a U.S. citizen, flew to Canada after his mother's death and took him back to the U.S. Because he was over 16 years old, adoption by his grandparents would not provide him with residence status. Therefore, a private bill was the only remedy available.[18]

- *Wei Jingsheng*: This bill granted permanent residency status to a Chinese pro-democracy activist who was imprisoned in China for 29 years. He entered the United States on a visitor visa in November of 1997. Columbia University filed a petition to obtain an exchange visitor visa for him which was granted but expired in June 2000.[19]

- *Larry Errol Pieterse*: A private bill was enacted to grant permanent residence and relief from deportation to Mr. Pieterse who had entered the United States in 1981 after marrying his first wife, a U.S. citizen. After the marriage began to fall apart in 1983, his wife began to stalk him, slashed the tires of his car, and planted cocaine in his home after discovering he was seeing another woman. Mr. Pieterse, after being assured that he would not face deportation for a misdemeanor conviction, pleaded guilty to avoid paying high attorney fees. Because of changes in the law, he later became deportable. In the interim, he remarried a U.S. citizen and supported her and her four children. The only remedy available to avoid his deportation was a private bill.[20]

Circumstances under which private bills have been successful include the following: serious family medical conditions;[21] to correct unfair denials of diversity visas due to errors by the National Visa Center;[22] whistleblowing regarding Holocaust-era bank records;[23] granting of U.S. citizenship to make beneficiaries eligible for Nazi reparations;[24] death of a U.S. citizen spouse during pendency of conditional permanent resident petition;[25] waiver of naturalization oath for incapacitated, approved applicant;[26] death of sponsor prior to family immigration;[27] permanent residency for a young adult abandoned as a minor;[28] and cases where the adoption proceedings were finalized after the beneficiaries' 16th birthday.[29]

Requests for private bills may be made to either the Senate Subcommittee on Immigration, Border Security and Citizenship or to the House Subcommittee on Immigration, Border Security and Claims. Each subcommittee has its own rules governing procedures for private immigration bills.[30] The House Rules are much more extensive than the Senate Rules. The processing of requests for private immigration legislation in the House is governed by its rules and precedents.[31] The Senate Subcommittee rules do not discuss specific precedents. Therefore, it may provide greater latitude in permitting the equities of a particular case to overcome negative precedent. Regarding practical procedures, what generally happens is that a constituent family member within a certain congressional district or state contacts his or her representative or Senator requesting that they author a private bill to remedy the case in question. The family members and their attorney, if they retain one, gather the relevant information and provide it to the representative or senator who then will decide on whether to author such a bill.

Procedures in the House Subcommittee on Immigration Border Security and Claims

A request for a private immigration bill must be submitted in writing, in letter form, addressed to the Chairman of the Subcommittee on Immigration, Border Security and Claims, by the author of the bill, stating the relevant facts and attaching any supporting documentation.[32] Only the author of the bill can present information relating to the request. The following relevant documentation must be submitted by the author to the Subcommittee in triplicate:[33]

- Date and place of birth of each beneficiary and contact information for each if in the United States;

- Dates of all (legal and illegal) entries and departures from the United States, along with information on the type of visas used for admission, the consulates where the visas were obtained, and, if relevant, the consulate where the beneficiary or beneficiaries will seek a visa if made available;

- Status of all petitions and proceedings with the Department of Homeland Security (DHS) or the legacy Immigration and Naturalization Service (INS), including nonimmigrant and immigrant petitions filed by the beneficiary or beneficiaries or on his/her/their behalf;

- Names, addresses, and telephone numbers of interested parties;

- Names, addresses, dates and places of birth, and immigration or citizenship status of all close relatives;

- Occupations, recent employment records, and salaries of the beneficiary or beneficiaries;

- Copies of all immigration-related letters to and from U.S. agencies;

- Copies of all administrative and judicial decisions involving the beneficiary or beneficiaries' case;

- A signed statement by each beneficiary or his or her guardian stating that he or she desires the relief requested in the private bill;

- An explanation of how failure to obtain the sought-after relief will result in extreme hardship to the beneficiary or each beneficiary's U.S. citizen spouse, child, or parent;

- A signed statement from the author of the bill confirming that the author met personally with the beneficiary or beneficiaries or with members of the family.

The House rules require additional information to be filed in support of private bills relating to adoption, on behalf of doctors or nurses, in support of a bill waiving certain grounds of exclusion relating to criminal activity, and private bill requests concerning beneficiaries who are receiving medical treatment.[34]

Each request for a private bill must include a statement recognizing that the beneficiary or beneficiaries will apply for the requested relief—if the bill is enacted—no later than two years from the date of enactment of the law.[35] As noted above, no private bill will be scheduled for Subcommittee action until all administrative and judicial remedies have been exhausted.[36] Upon motion, the Subcommittee may request a report on the beneficiary or beneficiaries from the Department of Homeland Security or the Department of State.[37] However, such reports will only be requested in cases involving extreme hardship to the beneficiary or beneficiaries or his/her/their U.S. citizen spouse, parent, or child.[38]

Only the author of the private bill is permitted to present testimony to the Subcommittee.[39]

If the Subcommittee makes a decision to favorably report the bill to the Judiciary Committee it is placed on a special calendar called the Private Calendar.[40] Consideration of bills placed on the Private Calendar is held during the first and, at the discretion of the Speaker of the House, the third Tuesday of each month. Private bills are considered "in the House as in the Committee of the Whole" and there is no period of general debate. During the call of the Private Calendar, if two members object to the consideration of any bill, it will be recommitted to the Subcommittee which can re-report it as a paragraph of an omnibus private bill. In practice, committees seldom re-report private measures once recommitted.[41]

Once the President signs the private bill, the Subcommittee then notifies the relevant agency within the Department of Homeland Security—U.S. Citizenship and Immigration Services (USCIS) and U.S. Immigration and Customs Enforcement (ICE); or the Department of State if the beneficiary or beneficiaries are outside the United States to proceed with implementation of the bill.[42]

Procedures in the Senate Subcommittee on Immigration, Border Security and Citizenship

As noted above, the rules of procedure governing request and consideration of private immigration bills in the Senate Subcommittee are much less detailed than those in the House Subcommittee. The rules of procedure in the Senate are generally similar to those in the House with some exceptions. While the House Subcommittee does not require a report from the relevant government agency on a private bill request, the Senate Subcommittee rules require such.[43] Administrative and judicial remedies must be exhausted before requesting consideration of a private bill.[44] As in the House, a request for a private immigration bill must be made by the author to the Subcommittee in written form and must contain the following information:

- The name, age, place of birth, and contact information of the beneficiary;

- The date and place of the beneficiary's last entry into the United States and his or her immigration status at that time;

- The location of the consulate where he or she obtained a visa, if any;

- In the case of a beneficiary who is physically outside the United States, the persons' age, place of birth, address, and the location of the U.S. consulate before which the application for visa is pending, and the address of the relation of the person primarily interested in his or her admission to the United States;

- In the case of a beneficiary seeking expedited naturalization, the date the noncitizen was admitted to the United States for permanent residents, his or her age, place of birth, and address in the United States.[45]

Previously tabled bills shall generally not be reconsidered unless new evidence is introduced showing a material change of facts.[46]

Any supporting material submitted by the author is limited to three or four typewritten pages and should include a detailed statement establishing the equities in the case and why administrative or judicial remedies are unavailable.[47] Supporting information is used for the Senate report and must be typewritten in order to be cut and pasted into the report. Important original documents, therefore, such as birth certificates, should not be submitted; copies are sufficient.[48] After receipt of all material, including reports from the relevant government departments, private bills are scheduled for subcommittee consideration in the chronological order of their introduction.[49]

Effect of Introduction of
Private Bill on Nonimmigrant Status

Under legacy INS Operations Instructions, the introduction of a private bill seeking to adjust the status of a nonimmigrant in the United States to that of a lawful permanent resident is regarded as prima facie evidence of termination of lawful nonimmigrant status, if that status has not already been terminated.[50] Any deportation or removal proceedings which have been commenced will continue forward to final decision.[51] If proceedings have not already been commenced and the beneficiary was in lawful status as a B, C, D or H nonimmigrant when the private bill was introduced, and either the House or the Senate Subcommittee has requested a report on the bill from the relevant government agency, Form I-177 in duplicate will be served on the beneficiary. If the beneficiary fails to depart or to advise DHS within 30 days of receipt of I-177 that he or she no longer wishes to adjust status through private legislation, a Notice to Appear will be issued and removal proceedings commenced.[52]

If the beneficiary was maintaining status as an ambassador, public minister, career diplomatic or consular officer under INA §101(a)(15)(A), as a foreign government representative under INA §101(a)(15)(G), or as a treaty trader under INA §101(a)(15)(E) at the time the bill was introduced, he or she will be considered to have voluntary departure for the period of time that he or she remains in that status. In these cases, Form I-177 will not be issued.[53] If removal proceedings have not already been instituted but the beneficiary's status as a nonimmigrant was terminated at the time of bill's introduction a Notice to Appear will be issued and removal proceedings will be initiated until a final determination.[54]

If the beneficiary was maintaining status under INA §101(a)(15)(E), (F), (I), (J) or (M), Form I-177 will not be issued nor will removal proceedings be commenced. However, any application for extension of stay will be denied unless the beneficiary overcomes the presumption of termination of status raised by the introduction of a private bill on his or her behalf.[55] Voluntary departure will be granted in increments of one year conditioned upon the beneficiary's otherwise maintaining status or upon complying with the terms and conditions of the beneficiary's exchange program if in J status.[56] Other beneficiaries of these classes (E, F, I, J, M) who have already been placed in removal proceedings because of the bill's introduction will be granted extensions of voluntary departure and stays of removal under similar conditions.[57]

Removal proceedings will not be initiated or reactivated in any case involving compelling humanitarian factors.[58]

Stays of Removal During
Private Bill Consideration

During the processing of a request for a private bill, the House Subcommittee generally will not intervene in deportation or removal proceedings nor will it request a stay of deportation or removal for a beneficiary or beneficiaries with one exception.[59] Where the House Subcommittee requests a report from the Department of Homeland Security on a beneficiary or beneficiaries of a private bill, the U.S. Immigration and Customs Enforcement (ICE) division of DHS generally authorizes a stay of proceedings during the preparation and submission of the report and receipt of the final decision on the bill.[60] The Senate Subcommittee Rules advise that the Subcommittee will only request a stay of removal of a beneficiary or beneficiaries to prevent unusual hardship to the beneficiary or beneficiaries themselves or to U.S. citizens. However, no request for a stay can be granted until all of the documentation in support of the private bill is filed with the Subcommittee.[61]

Contact with DHS and Effect of Enactment of a Private Bill

The relevant Operations Instructions refer to an office within legacy INS—the Private Bill Control Unit—in charge of private bill matters. It appears that this unit no longer exists within either the USCIS or the ICE. When Congress wishes to request reports or needs other relevant information relating to private bills, it generally contacts the Congressional Relations Office in either ICE or USCIS. The Congressional Relations Offices in both divisions only speak with Members of Congress or their staff and do not provide information to the public, including potential beneficiaries or their representatives, on private bill proceedings. They identify the relevant offices within each of their divisions to direct inquiries for reports and other questions from Congress.

As mentioned above, once a private bill is signed by the President notice is sent to the relevant DHS office, usually USCIS, for implementation.[62] If the private law directs that deportation or removal proceedings should be terminated, the relevant DHS office must notify the beneficiary of such.[63] When the private bill grants some other benefit of waiver, the relevant DHS office must notify the beneficiary or any other interested party and offer the appropriate assistance.[64] The Department of Homeland Security cannot institute subsequent removal proceedings against a beneficiary of a private law granting residence status or terminating prior proceedings on grounds based solely on the facts contained in the Judiciary Committee's reports on the bill.[65]

PARDONS

A noncitizen is inadmissible to the United States if he or she has committed or, in some cases admits to committing, a crime involving moral turpitude (unless the person was under 18 years of age at the time the crime was committed, he or she committed only one crime the penalty for which was less than one year imprisonment and a sentence of six months or less was imposed, and the crime was committed or the person was released from confinement more than five years before applying for admission) or multiple criminal convictions for which the aggregate sentences to confinement were five years or

more.[66] A noncitizen may be removed from the United States if he or she was inadmissible at the time of entry[67] or upon conviction of the following: (1) a crime involving moral turpitude committed within five years of entry (or 10 years in the case of an offender with certain lawful permanent resident status) and for which a sentence of one year or longer may be imposed; (2) two or more crimes of moral turpitude not arising out of a single scheme; (3) an aggravated felony; (4) a drug offense (other than one involving possession of 30 grams or less of marijuana for one's own use); (5) certain firearms offenses; (6) certain offenses relating to national security; (7) certain immigration offenses; or, (8) a domestic violence offense.[68]

There are some forms of relief available to noncitizens with criminal convictions under certain conditions which include the following: cancellation of removal for certain permanent residents;[69] former INA §212(c) relief;[70] asylum;[71] withholding of removal;[72] relief under the Convention Against Torture (CAT);[73] general nonimmigrant waiver;[74] waiver for certain criminal conduct;[75] the "petty offense" exception;[76] or pursuing citizenship through naturalization or eligibility through acquired citizenship.[77] Unfortunately, most of the available relief does not eliminate grounds of inadmissibility for a great number of crimes. In those cases, practitioners may want to investigate the possibility of obtaining a pardon to save their clients from deportation from the United States.

Pardon and clemency authority is vested in the President of the United States under the U.S. Constitution. Under state constitutions and legislation, governors or their designated representatives also have the power to issue pardons.

Legal Authority and Applicability of Pardons

Noncitizens subject to removal based on convictions for crimes of moral turpitude, aggravated felonies, high speed flight and multiple criminal convictions may avoid removal if granted a "full and unconditional" pardon by the President, the governor of the State, or a constitutionally recognized executive.[78] A pardon will only waive the grounds of removal specifically set forth in INA §237(a)(2)(A)(v) [8 U.S.C.A. §1227(a)(2)(A)(v)] which are: crimes of moral turpitude, multiple criminal convictions, aggravated felony, and high speed flight from a DHS checkpoint.[79] No implicit waivers may be read into the statute.[80] In its decision addressing the issue of the applicability of pardons for immigration purposes, the

Board of Immigration Appeals (BIA or Board) has held that a noncitizen's conviction for domestic violence or child abuse under INA §237(a)(2)(E)(i) [8 USCA §1127(a)(2)(E)(i)] could not be waived by a pardon.[81]

Pardons are limited to specific crimes, including aggravated felonies. The pardon section specifically does not apply to crimes referred to in INA §237(a)(2)(B) or (C) [8 U.S.C.A. §1227(a)(2)(B) or (C)] involving controlled substances and certain firearms offenses and the Board has held that pardons do not defeat removal for controlled substances offenses.[82] However, since pardons are applicable to aggravated felonies—which are defined under INA 101(a)(43) [8 U.S.C.A. §1101(a)(43)] to include firearms[83] and controlled substance offenses[84]—there appears to be an inconsistency in the law. A pardon would eliminate the ground of removal for a controlled substance or firearms offense under the aggravated felon definition but not under a different provision in the INA. Therefore, a noncitizen who receives a full pardon for a drug or illicit firearms trafficking crime would not be removable as an aggravated felon. If charged as removable under another provision of the INA, however, the pardon would not apply.[85] This is precisely what the Board held in *Matter of Suh*, finding that a pardon which served to eliminate a "sexual battery" as grounds for removal as an aggravated felony did not eliminate the domestic violence offense as a ground for the exact same offense.[86]

A pardon eliminates the immigration consequences of a given crime for future entries.[87] Therefore, a noncitizen who has received a pardon is not deportable as inadmissible at the time of admission for the crime or crimes covered in the pardon. Inadmissibility under INA §212(a)(2)(A)(i)(I) [8 USCA §1181(a)(2)(A)(i)(I)] based on the admission to a crime of moral turpitude will not be found if a pardon has been granted for the crime which the noncitizen admits committing.[88]

When Is a Pardon "Full and Unconditional"?

In order for a pardon to be effective to eliminate the above-mentioned grounds of removal, it must be "full and unconditional."[89] In order to be effective for immigration purposes, it must release the person from all legal consequences flowing from the conviction and it must not be dependent upon the fulfilment of any condition.[90] Additionally, the pardon must be executively, as distinguished from legislatively, granted.[91] In *Matter of Nolan*, the Board held

that an automatically issued pardon to a first felony offender under the Constitution of Louisiana was not a "full and conditional pardon" for immigration purposes.[92] As the Board noted in *Matter of Nolan*, at times states have two different categories of pardons: those granted by the governor and those awarded automatically to first offenders by operation of laws upon the completion of sentences imposed. Those which are valid for immigration purposes are those granted by a governor or his or her designate.

Where the pardon does not release the noncitizen from all legal consequences of the conviction, the pardon is not considered "full and unconditional" for immigration purposes. Under federal law and the law of many states, a conviction for a felony has consequences which may continue long after the sentence has been served. These consequences, or disabilities, include the loss of the right to vote, to hold state office, to sit on a jury. Additionally, felons may be restricted in their ability to gain certain employment and professional licenses. Under federal gun control laws and many state laws, felons also may lose their right to own and use firearms. Restoration of these rights can be achieved either automatically after a certain amount of time has passed or through the occurrence of a specific event such as the completion of a sentence, or through a judicial or executive act such as a pardon.

The laws governing which disabilities exist as a result of a felony conviction vary among the states, especially relating to restoration of civil rights and rights to possess firearms. For example, in many states persons convicted of federal felony offenses cannot avail themselves of state procedures to restore their civil rights either because the law only applies to state offenders through a state pardon—which is not available to federal offenders—or because the state procedures are generally unavailable to federal offenders.[93] Because of the wide differences in availability of state remedies to restore rights to federal offenders, aside from firearms privileges the only mechanism in federal law for restoring rights is a presidential pardon. Therefore, federal felons residing in states which provide no restoration remedies for federal crimes must obtain a presidential pardon in order to exercise certain political rights, including the right to vote, to hold state office, and to sit on a jury.

The area of state laws relating to firearms disabilities is complicated. There are federal and state level regulations concerning loss of the right to bear arms upon conviction of certain offenses and restoration of the right. At the state level, in addition to state statutes and regulations, municipal and county rules may also be in place. There is also considerable variation among the states on the definition of the term "firearm privilege."[94]

The controlling case in the federal system relating to the firearms disability is *Beecham v. United States*.[95] In that case, the Supreme Court addressed the issue of whether the firearms disability imposed upon convicted federal felons is removed by the restoration of rights under state law. The Court held that federal felons remain subject to the firearms disability under 18 USCA §922(g)(1) until their rights are restored by federal procedures. Therefore, the disability continues to apply even if the federal felon's civil rights were restored under a state procedure. The only means for a federal felon to regain firearms privileges is through a presidential pardon or through the restoration process as provided under 18 USCA §925(c) through the Bureau of Alcohol, Tobacco and Firearms (ATF). Since October 1992, however, ATF's annual appropriation has prohibited the use of any funds to investigate or act upon applications for relief from federal firearms disabilities.[96] Therefore, as long as this prohibition remains in place ATF cannot process applications for restoration.

Federal Pardon

Legal authority for pardons and implementation. The Constitution of the United States grants the President the authority to "grant Reprieves and Pardons for Offences against the United States."[97] The Office of the Pardon Attorney with a 12-person staff within the U.S. Department of Justice (DOJ) advises and assists the President in carrying out the pardon power.[98] Regulations have been published governing the processing of pardon requests submitted to the Office of the Pardon Attorney.[99]

A presidential pardon serves as an official statement of forgiveness for the commission of a federal crime and serves to restore basic civil rights.[100] A person is not eligible to file a request for a federal pardon until five years after that person is released from confinement for his or her most recent conviction, or, if no condition of confinement was imposed as part of the sentence, the date of conviction.[101] A petition for a pardon cannot be filed by a person who is on probation, parole, or supervised release.

Note: The regulations governing procedures before the Office of the Pardon Attorney do not bind the President. He or she retains the authority under the Constitution to consider a pardon request from a person who may be ineligible to apply under the DOJ regulations or who has not applied at all, and to grant clemency if the President believes it is appropriate.[102]

Statistics relating to pardons and commutation of sentences granted by different administrations from 1900 through 2001 are available on the Office of the Pardon web page. During the administration of George H. Bush (1988–1992), 731 petitions for pardons were filed, and 74 were approved. During the Clinton administration, 2001 petitions were filed, and 396 were granted. President George W. Bush only granted 11 pardons during the first three years of his administration. During that same period, he denied 580 requests.[103] As with private bills, pardons are difficult to obtain but still may be worth the effort in particularly compelling cases.

Pardon request. An applicant for a pardon must file a formal petition, addressed to the President, and submitted to the Office of the Pardon Attorney, Department of Justice, 500 First Street, N.W., Suite 400, Washington, D.C., 20530.[104] An applicant for a pardon can retain the services of an attorney to aid in the petition process. The standard form used to request a pardon asks the following: information on the offense and any other criminal record of the applicant; employment and residence history since the conviction; other biographical information; any substance abuse and medical history; civil and financial information; military record; civil rights and occupational licensing; charitable and community activities; and the reasons for seeking a pardon.[105] The application must be signed and notarized and the applicant is also required to submit three notarized affidavits from character references unrelated to the applicant but who know of the conviction and support the pardon request.[106]

Investigation and processing of the petition by the Office of Pardon Attorney. Upon receipt of the petition, the Office of the Pardon Attorney will do an initial screening to ensure that the applicant is indeed eligible to seek a pardon; specifically, that the crime for which the pardon is sought is a federal offense and that the applicant has complied with the five year waiting period. The Office will also review the form to determine if any necessary information has not been included or whether the applicant's responses require further elaboration. If the applicant is ineligible to apply, he or she will be informed so.

If the Office needs additional information for the petition, the assigned attorney will request such.[107]

As an initial step in the processing of the petition, the Office of the Pardon Attorney will contact the United States Probation Office for the federal district in which the applicant was prosecuted to obtain copies of the presentence report and the judgment of conviction as well as information regarding the applicant's compliance with any order of court supervision, and to determine the Probation Officer's views regarding the pardon request. If information gathered at this stage reveals information which clearly excludes the applicant from further favorable consideration, the Office of the Pardon Attorney will prepare a report to the President for the signature of the Deputy Attorney General recommending that the pardon be denied. On the other hand, if the initial review indicates that the case may have some merit, it is referred to the Federal Bureau of Investigation (FBI) so that a background investigation can be carried out.[108]

In addition to contacting the probation officer for the federal district court where the applicant was prosecuted, the pardon attorney will provide copies of the petition to the United States Attorney involved in the prosecution.[109] The pardon attorney gives considerable weight to the comments and recommendation of the local U.S. Attorney's Office previously in charge of the case.[110] Additionally, the pardon attorney may request the U.S. Attorney to seek the views and recommendations of the sentencing judge.[111] The United States Attorney, under its own standards, can support, oppose or take no position on a pardon request. The pardon attorney generally asks for a response within 30 days from the U.S. Attorney.[112]

State Pardons

Introduction. Every state in the United States has some sort of mechanism for convicted persons to mitigate the collateral consequences of their convictions through restoration of civil rights procedures upon completion of the sentence and/or some other event or through an executive or board pardon. All state constitutions provide for an executive pardon authority. Unfortunately, these mechanisms are often inaccessible or complex and at times not understandable to the very people that are responsible for administering them. Pardon procedures differ from state to state. Some states exercise this authority only through the governor. Other states have independent boards which investigate and decide upon

pardon petitions. The level of involvement of governors in the process varies widely across the country.

According to a study carried out by the Sentencing Project, only nine states administer the pardon power in a regular manner and issue a significant number of pardons each year. These states are: Alabama, Arkansas, Connecticut, Delaware, Georgia, Nebraska, Oklahoma, Pennsylvania, and South Carolina. All receive a substantial number of pardons each year and grant a significant percentage of the applications filed.[113] Of these nine states, all but Georgia and Arkansas administer the process through a public application and hold regular hearings.[114]

States which administer the greatest number of pardons are generally ones in which the pardon power has some degree of protection from the political process, usually through administration by an independent board.[115] Even in states where pardons are routinely granted to eligible applicants, relatively few people apply. The low number of applications may be attributable to the time and expense involved with the procedure, the uncertainty of success, or doubts about the benefits of a pardon.[116] The American Bar Association has issued a resolution with a report calling for federal and state governments to establish standards which provide greater access to fair procedures in both commutation and pardon processes.[117]

A case of mass clemency. The Illegal Immigration Reform and Immigrant Responsibility Act of 1996 (IIRIRA)[118] automatically expanded the number of noncitizens subject to mandatory removal as aggravated felons overnight. Although Congress intended to create a law to deport serious noncitizen offenders from the United States, the law also affected hundreds if not thousands of non-serious offenders, resulting in their removal, loss of their contribution to communities and the labor market, and separation from their families, including many from their U.S. citizen children. One such case reached the attention of the Georgia Board of Pardons and Parole and led to clemency for 138 noncitizens who were affected by the law.

In January 2000, the Atlanta Journal and Constitution published a story about Mary Anne Gehris, a lawful permanent resident living in Georgia.[119] Ms. Gheris, a married mother of two U.S. citizen children, was born in Germany but came to the United States before her second birthday with her adoptive parents. In 1999, she applied for naturalization which ultimately resulted in her facing deportation for a 12 year old misdemeanor conviction for simple battery. She had been sentenced to a suspended 12 month sentence and placed on probation.[120] The Atlanta newspaper continued with extensive reporting on Ms. Gheris' plight and Georgians learned of the hundreds of people who had been deported for minor crimes across the country as a result of the 1996 laws.[121] Fellow Georgians facing deportation included an Ethiopian who had stolen a chicken sandwich, a Nigerian who had stolen a box of donuts, another Nigerian who had stolen a $15 baby outfit, an English teacher threatened with deportation for underage drinking, and a Laotian man convicted of shoplifting a pair of jeans when he was a teenager.[122] Some of these cases involved people like Ms. Gehris, who had been bought to the United States as children, could not speak the language of the country of origin, and had no relatives or friends to whom to return.

In response to the publicity and a concern that justice be done, the Board of Pardons and Parole created an initiative during 2000 to inform the immigrant community in Georgia that it would entertain pardon applications from noncitizens who would otherwise be deported because of their misdemeanor convictions.[123] From January 1, 2000, to June 1, 2001, the Board received 257 applications for pardons to avoid deportation. As of late 2001, there were 139 grants and 98 denials. Several other applications remained pending for final decision or additional documentation.[124] Of the 139 applications granted, 138 involved misdemeanor convictions. One application submitted by a noncitizen convicted of a felony was also approved. That case involved a well respected Korean businessman in his mid-40s, Dong Jin Park, who was a deacon in his church and a 20-year resident of Georgia. His three adolescent daughters had been born in the United States. In 1996, Mr. Park was convicted of aggravated assault upon an employee arising out of a fight after a night of heavy drinking. The Korean community in Georgia, over 50,000 persons strong, organized a successful drive to have Mr. Park pardoned.[125]

The Georgia Board is part of a small group of executives who have granted mass clemency in response to laws which they perceived as overly harsh or unjust. In the early twentieth century, Governor George W. Donaghey of Arkansas pardoned hundreds of convicts because of his opposition to the convict labor system. In the early 1960s, President John F. Kennedy pardoned over a hundred drug offenders serving mandatory minimum sentences.

New Mexico Governor Tony Anaya commuted the sentences of all five persons on death row before he left office in 1986 and Governor Richard Celeste of Ohio commuted the sentences of eight death row inmates at the end of his term in 1991. Governor George Ryan of Illinois commuted the sentence of 167 death row inmates in 2003, citing the flawed processes which led to the sentences. Several states, including Ohio and Florida, have initiated clemency reviews and releases for women prisoners who killed their batterers, but were precluded under the law from presenting a battered women's defense at the time of trial.[126]

Procedures in Particular States with High Immigrant Populations

California. For first offenders, the pardon power rests exclusively in the Governor, who may request an investigation and an advisory opinion from the Board of Parole Hearings (BPH).[127] For repeat offenders, the governor is required to refer pardon applications to BPH though he or she is not bound by their recommendations.[128] A pardon cannot be granted in such cases unless a majority of the judges of the State Supreme Court so recommend, with four justices concurring. The governor is required to report the pardon to the legislature, stating the facts and including reasons for the grant.[129]

BPH consists of 17 commissioners appointed by the governor to staggered three-year terms which can be renewed. BPH Commissioners are full-time employees and can be removed by the governor for misconduct or incompetence or neglect, but only after a full hearing. Of the 17 commissioners, five are assigned exclusively to juvenile offenders. The other 12 are responsible for adult offenders and act as the Governor's Clemency Advisory Board.[130]

Current policy of the governor's office is to accept pardon applications only after 10 years have passed since discharge from parole or probation.[131] Federal offenders and persons convicted under the laws of another state are ineligible for a gubernatorial pardon, and can only regain their civil rights through a pardon or similar action in the jurisdiction of their conviction.

A California state pardon restores civil rights lost and removes occupational bars. However the conviction may still be considered by a state agency in licensing proceedings.[132] The right to possess a firearm is restored upon the granting of a pardon except when the underlying offense involved the use of a dangerous weapon.[133]

There are two procedural routes to applying for a pardon in California. For those residing in the state the process usually begins with an application for a certificate of rehabilitation in the county of residence.[134] Convicted persons residing outside the state, or who are otherwise ineligible for a certificate of rehabilitation (e.g., sex offenders) may apply directly to the governor.[135]

The certificate of rehabilitation is an order confirming a court's finding that a person has been rehabilitated and a recommendation that the person be pardoned, but this order has no independent legal affect.[136] Upon a person's release from prison the warden is required to inform him or her of the right to apply for this certificate.[137] A person may apply to the court after completion of the period of rehabilitation running from release from prison or release on probation, which is five years residence in the state plus four years for serious offenses and two years for less serious offenses. A court may order additional years in the case of concurrent sentences.[138] Sex offenders who are required to register, except for indecent exposure, must wait for a period of 10 years.

Applicants for pardons are eligible for the assistance of all state rehabilitative agencies, including the right to be assisted by a public defender;[139] the public defender is required to appear for court proceedings relating to the pardon.[140] If a court finds that an applicant has demonstrated rehabilitation, the court will issue a certificate and forward it to the governor, or to the Supreme Court in the case of repeat offenders with a recommendation that the person be pardoned.[141]

Upon receipt of the certificate, the governor may request the BPH to carry out additional investigation and in some cases make a recommendation. The views of the court and the district attorney are requested as well.[142] For repeat offenders, the Supreme Court must hold a hearing and at least four justices must concur. The governor then has the option to grant or deny the pardon.[143] Whenever a person is issued a certificate of rehabilitation or pardon, it is recorded in the person's criminal record and reported to the FBI.[144]

As of June 2005, Governor Schwarzenegger had issued three pardons. Under Governor Davis' administration, no pardons were issued. Previous governors have issued pardons in California as follows: Governor Wilson: 13; Governor Deukmejian: 328; Governor Brown: 403; and Governor Reagan: 575.[145]

Florida. The power to grant a pardon and to restore civil rights in Florida resides with the governor.[146] The governor and three members of the cabinet are designated as the Clemency Board. Currently, the Clemency Board is comprised of the governor, the Attorney General, the Financial Officer, and the Agricultural Commissioner. Under the law, the governor may deny a request for a pardon for any reason. He or she must report to the legislature each pardon case at the beginning of each legislative session.[147]

The Office of Executive Clemency, established in 1975, is in charge of the day-to-day business of the Clemency Board and interprets the Rules of Executive Clemency of Florida.[148] Applicants for a pardon are eligible to apply 10 years after completion of their sentences and must have no outstanding financial obligations as a result of the conviction(s).[149] After waiting the necessary time period, an applicant submits a request for pardon to the Clemency Board.[150] An application for a pardon must include a certified copy of the charging instrument for each conviction and a certified copy of the judgment for each conviction. An application may also include character references, letters of support and any other documents which are relevant to the request.[151] Hearings may be held on the application. The state Parole Commission is charged with providing investigative support to the Clemency Board.[152] When an investigation is completed, the examiners from the Parole Commission put their recommendations into confidential files and provide them to the Clemency Board before any hearing. Applicants may wait years for a hearing. They are not required to attend but do have a right to make an oral presentation.[153] Applicants who are denied a pardon may only reapply after a year.[154]

A full pardon unconditionally releases the person from punishment and forgives guilt. It also entitles the applicant to all rights enjoyed prior to the conviction, including the right to possess, own, or use firearms.[155] However, the governor must specifically grant relief from the disability of firearm possession, ownership, or use.[156]

Illinois. Pardon authority in the state of Illinois is vested in the governor.[157] The Prisoner Review Board (PRB) serves as the board of review and recommendation to assist the governor in exercising clemency power.[158] The PRB is authorized to hear and decide upon applications for pardons and it makes confidential recommendations to the governor.[159] As is the case with federal pardons, exercise of the governor's constitutional pardon authority does not depend on the filing of an application.[160]

The PRB is comprised of 15 members, one of whom is designated chair, and all appointed by the governor. Members serve full-time for six year terms.[161] The Board is charged with hearing and deciding on all requests for pardons.[162] Federal offenders or persons with convictions in other jurisdictions are ineligible to apply for or receive Illinois state pardons.

Under the regulations, a notice of the proposed application for pardon is given by the PRB to the relevant court and to the state's attorney of the county where the conviction occurred. The PRB is required to meet and consider pardon petitions at least four times per year and shall, if requested and upon due notice, provide a hearing to each applicant, permitting representation by counsel if desired. After the hearing, it confidentially advises the governor by written report of its recommendations which are reached by a majority vote. All cases are sent to the governor with a recommendation.[163]

The PRB receives between 500 to 600 pardon requests per year, approximately 30% of which involve misdemeanor convictions. Current Governor Rod Blagojevich has granted 53 pardons after two years in office.[164]

New York. The authority to issue pardons in the state of New York is vested with the governor.[165] Similar to procedures in other states, the governor is required to report annually on the number of pardons and his or her reasons for granting such. The Board of Parole is charged with advising the governor on clemency cases when so requested.[166] Absent compelling reasons, a pardon will not be considered if there are administrative remedies available. In New York, pardons are only considered for the following reasons: (1) to set aside a conviction in cases of innocence; (2) to relieve collateral disability; or (3) to prevent deportation or permit reentry.[167] An Executive Clemency Bureau within the Division of Parole is charged with screening candidates for eligibility requirements, gathering materials relating to applications, and responding to letters from applicants and others relating to the application process.[168] In recent years there have been very few pardons granted in New York. It appears that the only one granted by current Governor George Pataki was a posthumous pardon to Lenny Bruce in 2003.[169]

CONCLUSION AND RECOMMENDATIONS

As demonstrated by the statistics relating to private bills, the likelihood of success is rather slim.[170] That does not mean, however, that practitioners should not consider pursuing a private bill in compelling cases. Many practitioners have had cases with fact patterns similar to many included in private bills which were successful. It is important that practitioners develop good relationships with their local representatives and U.S Senators. Practitioners should begin to develop these relationships early on in their practice by staying in touch with their local congressional offices, raising their concerns with them regarding the law generally, and by participating in the American Immigration Lawyers Association (AILA) activities relating to the national Lobby Day. AILA has materials developed precisely for its membership to learn about and become involved in lobbying local and national officials.[171]

Practitioners who represent noncitizens with criminal convictions should carefully investigate the pardon procedures in the relevant state. As noted in this *Briefing*, those states where the procedure is shielded from the political process are more likely to grant pardons than those where the governor is the primary decision maker. Where a state is inclined to grant a pardon to your client, make sure that the terms of the pardon are unconditional so that it qualifies for immigration purposes.

Private bills and pardons take lots of time and energy to prepare, submit and advocate. Practitioners should think of speaking with large firms to seek their pro bono services in compelling cases. Law students are another potential source of support in researching and working on pardons.[172] For example, law students have been active on pardons involving battered women. The Illinois Clemency Project for Battered Women is comprised of lawyers, activists, and law students from the University of Chicago Law School, the University of Illinois Law School, DePaul University School of Law, Chicago-Kent College of Law, and Northeastern Illinois University. Law students and faculty from the universities prepare the pardon petitions assisted by practicing lawyers in the Chicago area. Such a model could be used in designing a similar one to represent noncitizens facing deportation.

Finally, the support of family and local communities for noncitizens facing deportation from the United States is vital. It is worth mentioning again the case of Mr. Dong Jin Park, the Korean businessman in Georgia who—although convicted of a serious felony—was able to obtain a pardon due primarily to the unprecedented political activism of the local Korean community.[173] Any advocacy strategy relating to private bills and pardons must include grassroots participation by family and community as well as the services of highly trained lawyers. With compelling facts, such a strategy can work to win relief for many deserving noncitizens.

REFERENCES

1. For more detailed information on the history of public legislation in the immigration context, see, Bernadette Maguire, Immigration: Public Legislation and Private Bills (University Press of America 1997).

2. Bernadette Maguire, Immigration: Public Legislation and Private Bills (University Press of America 1997), p. 87; CRS Report, Private Immigration Legislation (2005). p. 2, f. 9.

3. See, U.S. Department of Homeland Security, Yearbook of Immigration Statistics, 2003, Table 51, U.S. Government Printing Office: Washington, D.C. 2004, which is reproduced in the Appendix to this article.

4. Bernadette Maguire, Immigration: Public Legislation and Private Bills (University Press of America 1997), p. xv.

5. Bernadette Maguire, Immigration: Public Legislation and Private Bills (University Press of America 1997), pp. 69–71.

6. Pub. L. No. 104-132, 110 Stat. 1214 (Apr. 24, 1996).

7. Pub. L. No. 104-208, 110 Stat. 3009 (Sept. 30, 1996).

8. Hinds' Precedents of the House of Representatives of the United States, Washington D.C., U.S. Government Printing Office, 1907, IV, 247.

9. See Subcommittee on Immigration, Border Security and Claims of the U.S. House of Representatives Committee on the Judiciary, Rules of Procedure and Statement of Policy for Private Immigration Bills, Rule 3, 108th Congress (2003), Statement of Policy (hereinafter "House Subomm. Rules"); Robert Hopper and Juan Osuna, "Remedies of Last Resort: Private Bills and Deferred Action," 97-06 Immigration Briefings (June 1997), at 3.

10. INA § 101(b)(1)(E) [8 USCA §1101(b)(1)(E)]; Matter of Repuyan, 19 I&N Dec. 119 (BIA 1984).

11. House Subcomm. Rules, Statement of Policy.

12. Plyler v. Doe , 457 U.S. 202, 102 S. Ct. 2382, 72 L. Ed. 2d 786 (1982).

13. Plyler v. Doe, 457 U.S. 202, 225, 102 S. Ct. 2382, 72 L. Ed. 2d 786 (1982); Passenger Cases (Smith v. Turner), 48 U.S. 283, 7 How. 283, 12 L. Ed. 702 (1849) (commerce clause); Chy Lung v. Freeman, 92 U.S. 275, 2 Otto 275, 23 L. Ed. 550 (1876) (foreign relations powers); Chinese Exclusion Case (Chae Chan Ping v. United States), 130 U.S. 581, 9 S. Ct. 623, 32 L. Ed. 1068 (1889) (inherent control over borders). See also Anna Marie Gallagher, Immigration Law Service 2d, §1:233 (2005), discussing Congressional authority over immigration matters.

14. U.S. Const., amend. I, cl. 3.

15. U.S. Const., art. I, §8, cl. 1. See also Bernadette Maguire, Immigration: Public Legislation and Private Bills (University Press of America 1997), p. 2, f. 11. Maguire points out that the courts have interpreted the term "debts" to include moral or honorary debts. United States v. Realty Co., 163 U.S. 427, 440, 16 S. Ct. 1120, 41 L. Ed. 215 (1896).

16. Subcommittee on Immigration, Border Security and Claims of the U.S. House of Representatives Committee on the Judiciary, Rules of Procedure and Statement of Policy for Private Immigration Bills, Rule 3, 108th Congress (2003); Subcommittee on Immigration, Border Security and Citizenship of the Senate Committee on the Judiciary, Rules of Procedure for introducing a private bill (immigration), Rule 3 (as reprinted in S. Prt. 108-58, U.S. Senate Committee on the Judiciary, Legislative and Executive Calendar (Final Edition), 108th Cong. (2005) (hereinafter "Senate Subcomm. Rules"). Although the requirement of exhaustion is generally strictly applied, in at least one case the Senate seems to have waived the requirement. The case involved the Chinese pro-democracy activist Wei Jingsheng who had a pending employment based immigration petition and was a visiting university scholar at the time the private bill was enacted. Private Law No. 106-14 (Nov. 22, 2000).

17. Private Law No. 106-8 (Nov. 7, 2000). See also Memorandum, INS Office of the Deputy Commissioner, Guidance for Treatment of Persian Gulf Evacuees (PGEs); supplemental instructions on PGE's Named in Private Bill, H.R. 1860 (September 11, 1997).

18. Private Law No. 106-22 (Jan. 24, 2000).

19. Private Law No. 106-14 (Nov. 22, 2000).

20. Private Law No. 105-644 (July 24, 1998).

21. Private Law No. 104-3 (October 9, 1996); Private Law No. 106-15 (Nov. 22, 2000); Private Law No. 106-20 (Nov. 22, 2000).

22. Private Law No. 106-364 (Oct. 5, 1999); Private Law No. 106-12 (Nov. 9, 2000).

23. Private Law No. 105-1 (July 29, 1997).

24. Private Law No. 105-3 (Nov. 21, 1997); Private Law No. 105-4 (Nov. 21, 1997).

25. Private Law No. 105-7 (Nov. 10, 1998); Private Law No. 105-8 (Nov. 10, 1998); Private Law No. 106-3 (Dec. 3, 1999); Private Law No. 106-23 (Nov. 22, 2000); Private Law No. 107-6 (Dec. 2, 2002).

26. Private Law No. 105-10 (Nov. 10, 1998).

27. Private Law No. 106-16; Private Law No. 106-19 (Nov. 22, 2000).

28. Private Law No. 106-22 (Nov. 22, 2000).

29. Private Law No. 105-5 (Nov. 10, 1998); Private Law No. 106-7 (Oct. 13, 2000); Private Law No. 107-6 (Dec. 2, 2002).

30. Subcommittee on Immigration, Border Security and Claims of the U.S. House of Representatives Committee on the Judiciary, Rules of Procedure and Statement of Policy for Private Immigration Bills, Rule 3, 108th Congress (2003) (hereinafter "House Subcomm. Rules"); Subcommittee on Immigration, Border Security and Citizenship of the Senate Committee on the Judiciary, Rules of Procedure for introduc-

ing a private bill (immigration), Rule 3 (as reprinted in S. Prt. 108-58, U.S. Senate Committee on the Judiciary, Legislative and Executive Calendar (Final Edition), 108th Cong. (2005) (hereinafter "Senate Subcomm. Rules").

31. Deschler's Precedents of the United States House of Representatives; Cannon's Precedents of the House of Representatives of the United State, Washington, D.C., U.S. Government Printing Office, 1935; Hinds' Precedents of the House of Representatives. *See also* Bernadette Maguire, Immigration: Public Legislation and Private Bills (University Press of America 1997), App. D1, Precedents Case Summaries.

32. For information on members of the Subcommittee and their contact information, the House website at *www.house. gov* and click on Committee Offices.

33. House Subcomm. Rules, no. 1(a) through (l).

34. House Subcomm. Rules, no. 1(l).through (o).

35. House Subcomm. Rules, no. 2.

36. House Subcomm. Rules, no. 3.

37. House Subcomm. Rules, no. 5; 9 FAM Appendix I, 500 Guidelines Regarding Private Bills.

38. House Subcomm. Rules, no. 5.

39. House Subcomm. Rules, no. 7.

40. Rules of the House of Representatives of the United States, prepared by Karen L. Haas, Clerk of the House of Representatives, 109th Congress (2006), Rule XV, cl. 5, XIII, cl. 1 (hereinafter "House Rules").

41. CRS 98-628, Private Bills: Procedure in the House, by Richard S. Beth (October 21, 2004), p. 2.

42. *See* OI §107.1(h)(1). For Department of State procedures, see, 9 FAM Appendix I, 500 General Guidelines Regarding Private Bills.

43. Senate Subcomm. Rules, no. 4.

44. Senate Subcomm. Rules, no. 3.

45. Senate Subcomm. Rules, no. 1(a), (b), (c).

46. Senate Subcomm. Rules, no. 6.

47. Senate Subcomm. Rules, Material to Be Submitted by Author.

48. Senate Subcomm. Rules, Material to Be Submitted by Author.

49. Senate Subcomm. Rules, no. 5.

50. OI §107.1(e). Legacy INS Operations Instructions still remain posted on the USCIS website as part of USCIS's Laws, Regulations and Guides. Although dated and infrequently updated, they still represent valid USCIS guidance on immigration and nationality matters.

51. OI §107.1(e).

52. OI §107.1(e). Although the original OI refers to "deportation" and "order to show cause", this author uses the current terminology as reflected in the Immigration and Nationality Act and relevant regulations addressing removal matters.

53. OI §107.1(e).

54. OI §107.1(e).

55. OI §107.1(e).

56. OI §107.1(e).

57. OI §107.1(e).

58. OI §103.1(a)(1)(ii).

59. House Subcomm. Rules, no. 4.

60. (OI 107.1(c); House Subcomm. Rules, no. 3.

61. Senate Subcomm. Rules, no. 2.

62. OI §107.1(h)(2).

63. OI §107.1(h)(2)

64. OI §107.1(h)(2).

65. OI §107.(h)(2).

66. INA §212(a)(2)(A), (B) [8 USCA §1182(a)(2)(A), (B)].

67. INA §237(a)(1)(A) [8 USCA §1227(a)(1)(A)].

68. INA §237(a)(2) [8 USCA §1227(a)(2)].

69. INA § 240A(a) [8 USCA §1229b(a)].

70. 69 Fed. Reg. 57826 (Sept. 28, 2004).

71. INA §209 [8 U.S.C.A. §1158].

72. INA §241(b)(3) [8 USCA §1231(b)(3)].

73. United Nations Convention against Torture and Other Cruel, Inhumane or Degrading Treatment or Punishment (CAT), 39 UN GAOR Supp. No. 51 at 197, U.N. Doc. A/Res/39/708 (1984) implemented through regulations at 8 CFR §§208.16-208.18, 1208.16-1208.18. For analysis of the CAT, see Feroli, "Trends in Decisions Under the Convention Against Torture," 05-05 *Immigration Briefings* 1 (May 2005); Sklar, "New Convention Against Torture Procedures and Standards," 99-07 *Immigration Briefings* 1 (July 1999); Rosati, "The United Nations Convention Against Torture: A Detailed Examination of the Convention as an Alternative for Asylum Seekers," 97-12 *Immigration Briefings* 1 (Dec. 1997); Rosati, "The United Nations Convention Against Torture: A Viable Alternative for Asylum Seekers," 74 *Interpreter Releases* 1773 (Nov. 21, 1997); 184 A.L.R. Fed. 385.

74. INA §212(d)(3) [8 U.S.C.A. §1182(d)(3)].

75. INA §212(h) [8 U.S.C.A. §1182(h)].

76. INA §212(a)(2)(A)(ii)(II) [8 USCA §1182(a)(2)(A)(ii)(II)].

77. INA §301 [8 U.S.C.A. §1401].

78. INA §237(a)(2)(A)(v) [8 USCA §1227(a)(2)(A)(v)].

79. *Matter of Suh*, 23 I&N Dec. 626 (BIA 2003).

80. *Matter of Suh*, 23 I&N Dec. 626 (BIA 2003).

81. *Matter of Suh*, 23 I&N Dec. 626 (BIA 2003).

82. *Matter of Lindner*, 15 I&N 170 (BIA 1975); *Mullen-Cofee v. INS*, 976 F.2d 1375 (11th Cir. 1992).

83. INA §101(a)(43)(C) (illicit trafficking in firearms).

84. INA §101(a)(43)(B) (illicit trafficking in a controlled substance).

85. *Probert v. INS*, 750 F. Supp. 252 (E.D. Mich. 1990) (judicial recommendation against deportation effective to defeat aggravated felony ground of removal), *aff'd on other grounds*, 954 F.2d 1253 (6th Cir. 1992). The no repealed JRAD was linked to pardons under the former statute as both were included in former 8 USCA §1251(a)(2).

86. *Matter of Suh*, 23 I&N Dec. 626 (BIA 2003).

87. *Matter of H–*, 6 I&N Dec. 90 (BIA 1954).

88. *Matter of E–V–*, 5 I&N Dec. 194 (BIA 1953).

89. *Matter of Nolan*, 19 I&N Dec. 539 (BIA 1988).

90. *Matter of Tajer*, 15 I&N Dec. 125 (BIA 1974); *Matter of L–*, 6 I&N Dec. 355 (BIA 1954); *Matter of T–*, 6 I&N Dec. 214 (BIA 1954); *Matter of C–* , 5 I&N 630 (BIA 1954); *Matter of S–*, 5 I&N Dec. 10 (BIA 1953).

91. *Matter of Nolan*, 19 I&N Dec. 539 (BIA 1988), citing *Matter of K–*, 9 I&N Dec. 336 (BIA 1961); *Matter of D–*, 7 I&N Dec. 476 (BIA 1957); *Matter of R–*, 6 I&N Dec. 444 (BIA 1954); *Matter of R–*, 5 I&N Dec. 612 (BIA 1954).

92. *Matter of Nolan*, 19 I&N Dec. 539 (BIA 1988).

93. For a state-by-state summary of disabilities and applications to remove such, see, U.S. Department of Justice, Office of the Pardon Attorney, Civil Disabilities of Convicted Felons: A State-by-State Survey (October 1996). Readers should be cautioned that this publication is dated and the laws in many states are revised frequently. Therefore, the best source is the current state law.

94. *See* U.S. Department of Justice, Office of the Pardon Attorney, Civil Disabilities of Convicted Felons: A State-by-State Survey (October 1996).

95. *Beecham v. United States*, 511 U.S. 368, 114 S.Ct. 1669, 128 L.Ed. 2d 383 (1994).

96. *See* Pub. L. No. 107-67, 115 Stat. 514 (Nov. 12, 2001). See also the ATF website at *http://www.atf.treas.gov under Firearms FAQ.*

97. *U.S. Const.*, art. II, Section 2; 28 USCA §§ 509, 510.

98. For more information on the Office of the Pardon Attorney, visit its website at *http://usdoj.gov/pardon/.*

99. See 28 CFR §§1.1 *et seq.*

100. *See* Testimony of Roger C. Adams, Pardon Attorney, before the Committee on the Judiciary, United States Senate, February 14, 2001.

101. 28 USCA §1.2.

102. *See* Testimony of Roger C. Adams, Pardon Attorney, before the Committee on the Judiciary, United States Senate, February 14, 2001.

103. *See* American Bar Association Justice Kennedy Commission—Report to the House of Delegates, by Stephen Saltzburgh, Chairperson (August 2004), p. 9, f. 17.

104. 28 CFR §1.1. A copy of this formal petition is available on the DOJ website on the Office of Pardon Attorney page at *www.usdoj.gov/pardon/.*

105. *See* Petition for Pardon After Completion of Sentence, available at *www.usdoj.gov/pardon/.*

106. *See* Petition for Pardon After Completion of Sentence.

107. *See* Testimony of Roger C. Adams, Pardon Attorney, before the Committee on the Judiciary, United States Senate, February 14, 2001.

108. *See* Testimony of Roger C. Adams, Pardon Attorney, before the Committee on the Judiciary, United States Senate, February 14, 2001.

109. United States Attorney's Manual— Standards for Consideration of Clemency Petitions, Section 1-2:111: Role of the United States Attorney in Clemency Matters.

110. United States Attorney's Manual—Standards for Consideration of Clemency Petitions, Section 1-2:111: Role of the United States Attorney in Clemency Matters.

111. United States Attorney's Manual—Standards for Consideration of Clemency Petitions, Section 1-2:111: Role of the United States Attorney in Clemency Matters.

112. United States Attorney's Manual—Standards for Consideration of Clemency Petitions, Section 1-2:111: Role of the United States Attorney in Clemency Matters.

113. Margaret Colgate Love, Relief from the Collateral Consequences of a Criminal Conviction: A State-by-State Resource Guide (July 2005), Table 2—Characteristics of Independent Pardon Boards.

114. Margaret Colgate Love, Relief from the Collateral Consequences of a Criminal Conviction: A State-by-State Resource Guide (July 2005), Executive Summary, p. 8.

115. Margaret Colgate Love, Relief from the Collateral Consequences of a Criminal Conviction: A State-by-State Resource Guide (July 2005), Executive Summary, p. 5.

116. Margaret Colgate Love, Relief from the Collateral Consequences of a Criminal Conviction: A State-by-State Resource Guide (July 2005), Executive Summary, p. 9; Chart 4—Characteristics of the 12 Most Active Pardon Authorities.

117. *See* American Bar Association Justice Kennedy Commission—Report to the House of Delegates, by Stephen Saltzburg (August 2004).

118. Pub. L. No. 104-208, 110 Stat. 3009 (Sept. 30, 1996).

119. Mark Bixler, Atlanta Journal and Constitution, Past's Pull: Old Incident Threatens Deportation. Jan. 10, 2000, at 1B; *see also* Anthony Lewis, "This has Got Me in Some Kind of a Whirlwind," *New York Times*, Jan. 8, 2000, at A13.

120. Mark Bixler, "'I pledge allegiance...; She Goes from Deportation List to Citizenship," *Atlanta Journal and Constitution*, February 10, 2001 at 1A.

121. INS estimated that "the number of people deported nationally for petty crimes such as shoplifting is 'in the hundreds." Mark Dixler, "Deportation Threat May Be Near End," *Atlanta Journal and Constitution*, Jan. 11, 2001, at 1B.

122. Mark Bixler, "Global Atlanta: Easing up on Deportation: Every Monday, a Look at Our Changing Communities," *Atlanta Journal and Constitution*, Aug. 28, 2000, at 1B and Milo Ippolito, "State High Court's Ruling May Aid Immigrants; Judges Have Leeway to Avert Deportation," *Atlanta Journal and Constitution*, Jan. 23, 2001 at 1JJ.

123. Regulations governing the procedures for pardon application and consideration are found at Ga. Code Ann. §§42-9-19, 43, 54, 56.

124. *See* Elizabeth Rapaport, The Georgia Immigration Pardons: A Case Study in Mass Clemency, 13 *Federal Sentencing Reporter* No. 3-4 (2000-2001), p. 185.

125. Mark Bixler, "Unified Front: City's Korean Residents Rally to Fight Man's Deportation," *Atlanta Journal and Constitution*, Feb. 17, 2000 at 14A; Mark Bixler, "Forgiven

Felon is Now Free to Stay," *Atlanta Journal and Constitution*, April 25, 2000 at 1A.

126. *See* Elizabeth Rapaport, "The Georgia Immigration Pardons: A Case Study in Mass Clemency," 13 *Federal Sentencing Reporter* No. 3-4 (2000-2001), p. 185. *See also Chicago Tribune*, January 12, 2003; January 15, 2003.

127. Cal. Const. art. V, §8(a); Cal. Penal Code §§4800, 4812-4813. *See also www.bpt.ca.gov.*

128. Cal. Penal Code §4802.

129. Cal. Const. art. V, §8; Cal. Penal Code § 4852.16

130. *See www.cdcr.ca.gov.*

131. *See* "How to Apply for a Pardon," at *www.bpt.ca.gov/ apply_for_pardon.pdf* (revised Sept. 2004).

132. Cal. Penal Code §§4852.15, 4853.

133. Cal. Penal Code §4852.17.

134. Cal. Penal Code §§4852.06, 4852.19.

135. *See* "How to Apply for a Pardon," at *www.bpt.ca.gov/ apply_for_pardon.pdf* (revised Sept. 2004).

136. Cal. Penal Code §4852.13.

137. Cal. Penal Code §4852.21.

138. Cal. Penal Code §4852.13.

139. Cal. Penal Code §4852.04.

140. *Ligda v. Superior Court of Solano County*, 85 Cal. Rptr. 744, 752 (Cal. Ct. App. 1970).

141. Cal. Penal Code §4852.14.

142. Cal. Penal Code §4803.

143. Cal. Penal Code §4852.16.

144. Cal. Penal Code §4852.17.

145. Margaret Colgate Love, "Relief from the Collateral Consequences of a Criminal Conviction: A State-by-State Resource Guide—California" (July 2005), p. CA 3.

146. Fla. Const. art. IV, §8(a); Fla. Stat. 940.01, 940.05.

147. Fla. Const. art. IV, §8(a); Fla. Stat. 940.01.

148. The rules are available at: *www.state.fl.us/fpc/Policies/ ExecClemency/ROEC12092004.pdf.*

149. Rules of Executive Clemency of Florida, R. 9E.

150. Applications are available on the webpage of the Clemency Board at *www.myflorida.com/fpc/Clemency.htm.*

151. Rules of Executive Clemency of Florida, R. 6.

152. Fla. Stat. 947.01-947.27. See also Office of Executive Clemency, Information and Instructions on Applying for Restoration of Civil Rights, available at *https://fpc.state.fl.us/ PDFs/clemency/instructionsonforrcr.pdf.*

153. Margaret Colgate Love, "Relief from the Collateral Consequences of a Criminal Conviction: A State-by-State Resource Guide—Florida" (July 2005), p. FL3; Rules of Executive Clemency of Florida, R. 11.

154. Rules of Executive Clemency of Florida, R. 14.

155. Rules of Executive Clemency of Florida, R. 4A.

156. Rules of Executive Clemency of Florida, R. 5D.

157. Ill. Const. art. V, §12.

158. 730 Ill. Comp. Stat. 5/3-3-1(a)(3).

159. 730 Ill. Comp. Stat. 5/3-3-2(a)(6).

160. 730 Ill. Comp. Stat. 5/3-1-13(e). *See also People ex rel. Madigan v. Snyder*, 804 N.E. 2d 546, 588 (2004) (constitution does not give legislature power to limit governor's power to act in absence of an application).

161. 730 Ill. Comp. Stat. 5/3-3-1(b).

162. 730 Ill. Comp. Stat. 5/3-3-2(a)(6).

163. Guidelines on the application process are available at *www.state.il.us/prb/docs/exclemexg.pdf.*

164. Margaret Colgate Love, "Relief from the Collateral Consequences of a Criminal Conviction: A State-by-State Resource Guide—Illinois" (July 2005), p. IL3.

165. N.Y. Const. art. 4, §4.

166. N.Y. Exec. Law §259-c.

167. *See* New York State Parole Handbook, §9 (2004), available at *http://parole.state.ny.us/INTROparolehandbook. html.*

168. New York State Parole Handbook, § 9 (2004).

169. Margaret Colgate Love, "Relief from the Collateral Consequences of a Criminal Conviction: A State-by-State Resource Guide—New York" (July 2005), p. NY2. For more information relating to collateral consequences of convictions in New York and available resources on the issue, visit the website of the New York State Defenders' Association (NYSDA) Immigrant Defense Project at *www.immigrant defenseproject.org.*

170. Of the 60,601 private bills introduced since 1942, only 6,798 were enacted as law—an 8.91 percent success rate.

171. For more on its activities and support to its membership on advocacy issues, visit the AILA Advocacy Department page on AILA's website at *www.aila.org.*

172. Students have worked with lawyers and activists on seeking pardons for battered women in several clemency projects across the country. *See* the Battered Women's Clemency Project in Michigan at *www.umich.edu/ ~clemency/*; the Illinois Clemency Project for Battered Women at *www-news.uchicago.edu/releases/95/950525. battered.women.shtml.*

173. Mark Bixler, "Unified Front: City's Korean Residents Rally to Fight Man's Deportation," *Atlanta Journal and Constitution*, Feb. 17, 2000 at 14A; Mark Bixler, "Forgiven Felon is Now Free to Stay," *Atlanta Journal and Constitution*, April 25, 2000 at 1A.

THE IMMIGRATION JUDGE WAR

by Jonathan D. Montag and Socheat Chea[*]

INTRODUCTION

For years, practitioners in immigration court have complained about immigration judges. This is not particularly remarkable. Lawyers everywhere complain about judges. But proving the validity of complaints is difficult. As in Aesop's fable "The Boy Who Cried Wolf," why should anyone believe immigration lawyers' complaints about the courts in which they practice when all lawyers complain about the courts in which they practice?

REASONS WHY IMMIGRATION COURT COMPLAINTS GO UNNOTICED

There are substantial obstacles to airing problems with immigration court. Immigration courts are not part of an independent judiciary, but part of the Justice Department.

Although they are called "judges" (formerly called "special inquiry officers"), the role of immigration judges is different from Article III[1] judges. Immigration judges are administrative judicial officers employed by the U.S. Department of Justice. They assume a more active role in the courtroom than the traditional judge who passively lets the parties present their cases. An immigration judge can "interrogate, examine, and cross-examine the alien and witnesses."[2] The federal courts have defended the activist role for immigration judges and at times have encouraged it. *Calderon-Ontiveros v. INS.*[3] Immigration judges are obligated to fully develop the record in those circumstances where applicants appear without counsel.[4] Because of the nature of the system, immigration judges have a duty to be fair and unbiased, but they are able and sometimes commanded to examine and cross-examine, which invites the appearance of, or actual, partisanship that may provoke complaints but little attention. Further, the courts do not deal with citizens but rather with "foreigners," referred to in immigration law by a term of art: "alien." With aliens defined as outsiders, and with the term "alien" associated with words like "sedition" or "predator," there is no wonder that little interest is aroused when foreign nationals have a difficult time in immigration court. The ultimate punishment, after all, is a free trip home, back to "where they came from."

Immigration lawyers, while at times critical of the way immigration judges conduct proceedings, are wary of trying to air their complaints publicly. This is because of concerns about the propriety of publicly complaining about judges and possible repercussions for themselves and their clients.

Finally, since most immigration court cases deal with persons who have violated immigration or criminal laws, sympathy for the applicants is low. Immigration lawyers tend to minimize the wrong of the initial overstay, but the public often does not and will have little sympathy when unjust things happen to the person in immigration court.

One exception to the lack of sympathy for "law breakers" can be seen in cases of asylum-seekers. There tends to be less hostility toward asylum-seekers

---

[*] **Jonathan Montag** practices immigration law at Montag & Nadalin LLP in San Diego. He is a graduate of the University of Pennsylvania and the University of San Diego School of Law. He is a past chapter chair and a member of the National Benefit Center Liaison Committee, the AILA Annual Conference Planning Committee, the AILA National Membership Committee, and the *Immigration Law Today* Editorial Advisory Board. He was named one of *California Lawyer Magazine's* attorneys of the year for 2006.

Socheat Chea has been practicing immigration law in his own firm for over 10 years in Atlanta. A graduate of Boston College Law School, he was the chair of the AILA Atlanta Chapter for 2001–02. He is a passionate advocate on immigration causes and has served as a faculty member for the past five years for the Institute of Continuing Legal Education in Georgia on immigration issues. Mr. Chea received national prominence in 2000 when he defended against the deportation of long-time permanent residents who had minor brushes with the law. He has been speaking at the AILA annual conference since 2001. He would like to extend a special thanks to his law clerk, Karen Hamilton, for her assistance in this article.

[1] *U.S. Const.* art. III, establishing the judicial branch of government.

[2] 8 USC §1252(b) (1996).

[3] 809 F.2d 1050, 1052 (5th Cir. 1986).

[4] *Jacinto v. INS*, 208 F.3d 725, 727 (9th Cir. 2000).

who have incurred "minor" immigration violations. The law certainly is more tolerant.[5]

All these factors diminish media interest in what occurs in immigration court. Without interest, there is no media attention—no sunlight. And, as Justice Louis Brandeis observed, "Sunlight is the best disinfectant." But the media are not the only source of light. The federal courts are able, albeit once to a greater degree, to review the immigration courts, and federal appellate courts have now published decisions that lambaste some recent decisions of the immigration courts.

SUNLIGHT ILLUMINATES IMMIGRATION COURT PROBLEMS

Public pronouncements by the courts of appeal have attracted some media sunlight. The *New York Times* surveyed cases in the Third, Seventh, and Ninth Circuits, where circuit judges were scathing in their criticisms of immigration courts and the Board of Immigration Appeals (BIA).[6]

Liptak's article highlighted *Benslimane v. Gonzales*,[7] where circuit judge Richard Posner pointed out that the Seventh Circuit reversed the BIA in 40 percent of the cases decided on the merits in the year preceding oral argument in *Benslimane*. He noted that the rate was 18 percent in nonimmigration cases where the United States was the appellee. Judge Posner then explained the reason for the disagreement between the courts of appeal and the administrative adjudicators:

> This tension between judicial and administrative adjudicators is not due to judicial hostility to the nation's immigration policies or to a misconception of the proper standard of judicial review of administrative decisions [*i.e.*, it is not the fault of the courts of appeal]. It is due to the fact that the adjudication of these cases at the administrative level has fallen below the minimum standards of legal justice [*i.e.*, it is the fault of the immigration judges and BIA].[8]

Judge Posner's comment about a "misconception of the proper standard of judicial review" is not incidental or accidental. Some appellate court judges have skewered their colleagues for wasting judicial resources on nitpicking by the immigration judges and BIA when there are bigger fish to fry. In *Jahed v. INS*,[9] taking into account the Supreme Court decision[10] in *INS v. Ventura*,[11] Ninth Circuit Judge Alex Kozinski wrote:

> The question in this case is, in the immortal words of Humpty Dumpty, which is to be the master—that's all. When it comes to the granting of asylum, Congress has said the BIA is the master. The statute provides it, the other courts of appeals recognize it and the Supreme Court keeps reminding us of it. But to no avail. Maybe there's something in the water out here, but our court seems bent on denying the BIA the deference a reviewing court owes an administrative agency. Instead, my colleagues prefer to tinker – to do the job of the Immigration Judge and the BIA, rather than their own.[12]

He then continued, still in light of *Ventura*:

> While the Court was careful to limit its ruling to the facts presented, its message to us was clear to anyone with eyes to see: Stop substituting your judgment for that of the BIA; give proper deference to administrative fact finding; and do not adopt rules of law that take away the agency's ability to do its job. In other words, stop fiddling with the agency's decisions just because you don't like the result.[13]

Although Judge Posner says that 40 percent of immigration cases were reversed because of a misconception of the proper standard of judicial review rather than problems with the immigration court and

---

[5] *See Matter of Pula*, the "circumvention of the immigration laws is only one of a number of factors that should be balanced in exercising discretion in asylum cases." 19 I&N Dec. 467 (BIA 1987).

[6] A. Liptak, "Courts Criticize Judges' Handling of Asylum Cases," *New York Times*, A1 (Dec. 26, 2005).

[7] 430 F.3d 828 (7th Cir. 2005).

[8] *Id.* at 829–30.

[9] 356 F.3d 991, 1002 (9th Cir. 2004).

[10] The case stands for the proposition that, generally speaking, a court of appeal must remand a case to the BIA for a decision of a matter that statutes placed primarily in the BIA's hands when the issue was not previously addressed by the BIA. As a result, in the vast majority of reversals by the courts of appeal, rather than granting relief, cases are remanded to the BIA to consider elements overlooked earlier by the immigration court or BIA. This is likely a major source of congestion at the BIA and immigration courts.

[11] 537 U.S. 12 (2002).

[12] *Jahed*, 356 F.3d 991, at 1002.

[13] *Id.* at 1007.

the BIA, there is merit to Judge Kozinksi's concerns. In a great many cases when the courts of appeal apply the correct law and standards, they find that the immigration courts and BIA are not adjudicating cases to meet the minimum standard of justice.

Some of the fact patterns in the cases cited by Judge Posner and the *New York Times* are instructive. In *Benslimane*, the respondent was arrested by U.S. Immigration and Customs Enforcement (ICE) despite having a valid I-130/I-485 filed with U.S. Citizenship and Immigration Services (USCIS). The immigration judge would not continue the case for I-130 adjudication and ordered removal.[14] (There is an issue in the case concerning the attorney filing an I-485, but this is a red herring.) Relying on a prior Seventh Circuit case, *Subhan v. Ashcroft*,[15] and *Matter of Garcia*,[16] a case the BIA now seems to regret as evidenced by the lengths it goes to distinguish it,[17] the court determined that failing to continue the case while awaiting the I-130 adjudication allowed "Benslimane to be ground to bits in the bureaucratic mill against the will of Congress."[18]

It is odd that Judge Posner's ire was raised by this case, calling the BIA's holding "intelligible but not justifiable" and a case decided "below the minimum standards of legal justice," when immigration judges throughout the country routinely act accordingly. For many reasons—among them concerns about cluttered calendars, arguments about circumventing orderly consular procedures, and the court not being beholden to other agencies—immigration judges routinely deny continuances. The only hope in many of these cases is the fact that the wait for a hearing date in court and BIA appeals is getting longer and longer, while USCIS adjudication times are shortening. Thus, an I-130 may be approved before a removal order becomes administratively final. However, pursuant to *Matter of Velarde-Pacheco*,[19] the BIA will not reopen a case after the 90-day reopening period without the agreement of ICE; and

ICE is often unwilling to agree to reopening. So, delays often do not help without the intervention of a court of appeal.

More typical of immigration judicial misconduct, rather than just shoddy judgment, is *Wang v. Attorney General*.[20] The case is a Chinese family-planning asylum case. The family of four included two daughters, the older one handicapped. They came to the United States without inspection after the Chinese government forcibly sterilized the mother. The father became the respondent in a removal proceeding. The immigration judge took exception to the father on three grounds: not paying a fine in China levied against his family for having a second child without permission; not having produced evidence of efforts to have his older daughter's physical condition analyzed in the United States, and trying to obtain a visa by fraud at a consulate in China, then arranging to be smuggled into the United States. The court noted that the immigration judge considered herself "embarrassed" to have the respondent in her court, termed him "obsessed" with having a son, and accused him of "ignoring" his handicapped daughter.[21]

Commenting on the course of proceedings and quoting extensively from the record, the court wrote, "The proceedings before the IJ were conducted in too intimidating and hostile a manner to afford Wang a meaningful opportunity to develop the factual predicates of his claim, yet alone to respond to any legitimate concerns about his claim."[22] The court concluded that the immigration judge "chose to attack Wang's moral character rather than conduct a fair and impartial inquiry into his asylum claims. The tone, the tenor, the disparagement, and the sarcasm of the IJ seem more appropriate to a court television show than a federal court proceeding."[23]

The court noted that it was not only the judge's demeanor that was inappropriate, but also her analysis. "The IJ's opinion in this case was highly improper for both its contemptuous tone and its consideration of personal issues irrelevant to the merits of Wang's asylum application."[24]

---

[14] Inasmuch as the very first case discussed in the article is not an asylum case at all, the headline, "Courts Criticize Judges' Handling of Asylum Cases," is inaccurate.

[15] 383 F.3d 591 (7th Cir. 2004).

[16] 16 I&N Dec. 653 (BIA 1978).

[17] See, for example, *Matter of Arthur*, 20 I&N Dec. 475 (BIA 1992), and *Matter of Velarde-Pacheco*, 23 I&N Dec. 253 (BIA 2002).

[18] *Benslimane*, at 833.

[19] *Velarde-Pacheco*, 23 I&N Dec. 253

[20] 424 F.3d 260 (3rd Cir. 2005).

[21] *Id.* at 265.

[22] *Id.* at 267.

[23] *Id.* at 269.

[24] *Id.* at 270.

Another example of justice gone awry cited by the *New York Times* was *Recinos de Leon v. Gonzales*,[25] wherein a Los Angeles immigration judge denied asylum, reciting an oral decision that the Court of Appeals for the Ninth Circuit characterized thusly:

> [t]he IJ's opinion jumbles together discussions of Recino's credibility, past persecution, future persecution, changed country circumstances, and relocation. As a result, regarding at least five crucial points, we cannot tell what factual or legal determinations, if any, the IJ made. Accordingly, in many instances, we cannot determine what holdings of the IJ we should review.[26]

The BIA affirmed the opinion without opinion, prompting the court of appeals to write, "By streamlining the case, the BIA offered no coherent alternative explanation for the decision not dependent on the IJ's deficient finding of facts. Instead, the BIA rested on the IJ's indecipherable explanation."[27] At the end of the opinion, the court of appeals appended the immigration judge's decision.

The case highlighted two problems: poor adjudication at the immigration judge level and affirmance without opinion, wherein the BIA affirmed a decision[28] that the court of appeals considered "literally incomprehensible," "incoherent,"[29] and "indecipherable."[30]

PRACTICAL REPRESENTATION CONSIDERATIONS

Because nearly all the circuits are to some extent reversing BIA and immigration judges' decisions that have fallen below the minimum standard of justice, practitioners must realize that to properly repre-

sent a client, the attorney must be focused not only on preparing for court but also creating a record that will carry the day when on appeal. In other words, an attorney must make sure there is a good record for the court of appeals to review. The attorney must preserve issues and must not bend to the will of the immigration court in such a way that will prevent relevant issues and facts from making it into the record.

Preserving Issues

As anyone who has appeared in immigration court knows, there is a tension between satisfying the fact finder—the immigration judge—and ensuring the record is complete. In an asylum case, for example, there are often a great many details involving the life of the asylum-seeker that are relevant to the asylum claim. When an immigration judge becomes impatient and seeks to move the case along, details can be skipped. Should the attorney nevertheless insist on asking his client everything he or she intended, he or she risks aggravating the immigration judge and even souring the judge to the case. While an immigration judge should not deport an alien because of the perceived iniquities of the alien's counsel, a "halo effect" can occur. Since the attorney's first goal is to prevail in immigration court, it is natural not to want to aggravate the fact finder.

In this era of detained aliens and lengthy backlogs,[31] another serious concern is that if a case does not finish in the time allotted to it, the respondent can expect a delay of many months until the continuation of the hearing. A prolonged detention may be the price the foreign national pays for his or her

---

[25] 400 F.3d 1185 (9th Cir. 2005).

[26] *Id.* at 1190.

[27] *Id.* at 1193–94.

[28] The summary affirmance regulations, at 8 CFR §1003.1(e)(4), allow a single BIA member to affirm a decision without opinion if the BIA member determines the decision was correct, that any errors in the decision were harmless or nonmaterial, and the case is covered by established precedent. The court of appeals did not chastise the BIA for its summary affirmance, begging the question of how the BIA could determine the elements of appropriateness for summary affirmance when the decision it was affirming made no sense.

[29] *Recinos de Leon v. Gonzales*, 400 F.3d at 1187.

[30] *Id.* at 1190.

---

[31] In the Supreme Court decision regarding mandatory detention, *Demore v. Kim*, 538 U.S. 510, 529 (U.S. 2003), Chief Justice Rehnquist based his conclusion that mandatory detention was not unconstitutional on government-provided statistics that in 85 percent of cases detention lasts an average time of 47 days and a median of 30 days. In the remaining 15 percent of cases, in which the alien appeals the decision of the immigration judge to the BIA, the appeal takes an average of four months, with a median time that is slightly shorter. *Id.* at 529. For the government to suggest these as accurate statistics to the Supreme Court says more about the conjuring power of government statisticians than government concern for proffering the complete truth. In San Diego, detained aliens do not get to their initial master calendars in much less than 30 days, and cannot expect an individual hearing in much less than two months after that, and often a lot more time than that. Should a case need to be continued, the additional wait will be several more months.

need or desire to present all the details of the case by live testimony.

To avoid being coerced into abbreviating the case and skipping vital details, counsel should present everything that the client will say in court through a detailed application, a detailed declaration, and supporting documentation. Thus, if the client does not have the opportunity to testify about an event, that information is nonetheless in the record.

The importance of developing a written record is illustrated by a recent Ninth Circuit case, *Tchoukhrova v. Gonzales*.[32] In the opening of the opinion, the court described how an infant, Evgueni Tchoukhrova, was harmed during childbirth. The court wrote:

> The next morning, because the induced labor had stopped, hospital personnel decided to forcibly extract the child from its mother's body, breaking its neck in the process. Instead of giving the newborn child medical care, they initially threw Evgueni into a container holding abortion and other medical waste, telling his mother that "they didn't see the reason why he needed to live."

At the hearing, the child's mother, the respondent, did not provide all these details regarding childbirth. Had she tried, the immigration judge would have stopped her. But the details were in the written record. In seeking rehearing, the government proffered an argument that because Ms. Tchoukhrova did not say these things in court, it was "*de novo* fact finding" by the court of appeals. In a dissent, the judges did not accept the argument that declarations found in the administrative record were not part of the record.

Stating at Trial What Needs to Be Stated At Trial

Bullying is unfortunately something that can happen in immigration court. A judge can bully an attorney into not calling a witness or not pursuing a line of questioning. It takes a lot of experience, and sometimes luck, to know what an attorney can skip to appease a judge in the hope of winning a case, without dooming the case by creating an inadequate record on appeal.

In *Wang*, the immigration judge pressured the attorney to skip over issues that needed to be in the record for appeal. One issue was that Mr. Wang fled China, leaving behind parents whose pensions were withheld by the Chinese government as punishment for Mr. Wang's violating the country's birth-control policy. The immigration judge considered Mr. Wang's flight a callous move. Mr. Wang's attorney wanted to explain that he could not pay a fine in China that would have ameliorated his parents' plight and had little alternative but to flee China. The excerpts quoted in the case show the admirable tenacity of the attorney, Yee Ling Poon.

When Poon attempted to question Mr. Wang further about the pension, the IJ instructed her to "[g]et off the pension thing," but she then persisted in pursuing the very theme she told counsel to avoid. Her exchange with Poon went as follows:

JUDGE TO MS. POON:

Q. It's ridiculous. Go away from this issue and move on because it's just insane.

A. I am not trying to stick on it. I'm only trying because I was asked for him to explain why he edits [his asylum claim] now.

Q. I don't even know why he put it in. To me it just makes me more convinced that your client is willing to do anything, even to the detriment of his parents, to take care of himself. You and I both know, there is nothing that happened in this case, nothing in the sworn statement that's even going to begin to explain why he chose to come here at the moment that he did, okay.

A. I will ask him.

Q. And you can ask him and I know what he's going to say. He finally had the money together or whatever he needed to pay the smugglers because there's nothing here at all and maybe we'll learn something suddenly today. That there's nothing here about the timing and there's nothing to convince me that he shouldn't have gone ahead and paid that fine first before he came here.

A. Because he had no money when he was in China.

Q. I don't know about that.

A. That's what he said.

Q. Well, that's what, he can say anything he wants.[33]

---

[32] 404 F.3d 1181 (9th Cir. 2005) *reh'g denied*, 430 F.3d 1222 (9th Cir. 2005).

[33] *Wang*, at 263–64.

In addition to the perseverance of counsel, putting objections in the record is extremely important.

When an immigration judge comes into court and tells you that she is not going to grant a case, either directly or by everything she says and does or has indicated by her track record, the attorney has fewer restraints. Concerns about alienating the one person who can grant the case in immigration court evaporate when the attorney knows success cannot be achieved in the immigration court itself. Then, the only objective is to make a record. In fact, the more apoplectic an immigration judge becomes, the more material needs to be created for the appeal. Of course, a lawyer should create the record within the bounds of propriety and with respect for the court. Such duties are discussed below.

THE GONZALES MEMO

As a result of the sunlight provided by the *New York Times* and other articles discussing the failure of immigration judges to dispense sound and legal decisions, Attorney General Alberto Gonzales issued two memoranda on January 9, 2006, to the immigration judges and the BIA, chiding them for "intemperate and even abusive" behavior to litigants and launching a comprehensive investigation and review of the U.S. immigration courts. Some of the shortcomings of the immigration courts and BIA are due to a lack of resources, overwhelming caseloads, judicial misconduct, and lack of review from the BIA since the streamlining rules initiated by Attorney General John Ashcroft.[34]

THE IMMIGRATION ADJUDICATION STRUCTURE

To understand the governing rules or procedures by which a practitioner can pursue judicial misconduct, it is useful to focus on the structure and confines that immigration judges operate in and to examine common situations faced by immigration practitioners.

Before 1983, immigration judges were part of the Immigration and Naturalization Service (INS) and were known as special inquiry officers. Because of the apparent bias and conflict of interest in this structure, they assumed their current title of immigration judges and were transferred to a new Department of Justice agency, the Executive Office for Immigration Review (EOIR). The EOIR also consisted of the BIA, the Chief Immigration Judge, and other officers.[35] Immigration judges are not administrative law judges but are considered a special type of administrative adjudicative officer.[36] While the Attorney General can directly appoint an immigration judge, the filling of a vacant position is generally announced to the public through various offices in the Department of Justice, with the funneling of the candidates to the Office of Chief of Immigration Judges (OCIJ). The OCIJ makes the recommendation to the deputy director and the director of EOIR, who afterward sends the recommendation to the Deputy Attorney General for the final selection. The requirements to become an immigration judge are that an applicant be a U.S. citizen, possess a J.D. or L.L.B., and have a license and authority to practice law in the United States or its territories. The applicant must have a minimum of seven years of legal experience after bar admission.[37]

THE COMPLAINT STRUCTURE

Before investigating the intricacy of handling judicial misconduct, we must consider some basic concepts of removal proceedings. While immigration proceedings are deemed to be civil and not criminal in nature, the courts and the BIA have consistently held that due process must be provided in immigration court proceedings.[38] In essence, the constitutional requirements of due process are met when the administrative hearing is found to be fair. The BIA has ruled that the alien must suffer prejudice in order to show a denial of a fair hearing.[39] Put another way, harmless error will not suffice to establish the denial of due process. When evaluating a

---

[34] *See* S. Legomsky, "Deportation and the War on Independence," 91 *Cornell L. Rev.* 369, 374 (2006) (discussing the empirical effect of streamlining on the BIA).

[35] *See* Board of Immigration Appeals; Immigration Review Function; Editorial Amendments, 48 Fed. Reg. 8056, 8056 (Feb. 25, 1983) (codified at 28 CFR pt. 0); Board of Immigration Appeals; Immigration Review Function; Editorial Amendments, 48 Fed. Reg. 8038, 8039 (Feb. 25, 1983) (codified at 8 CFR pts. 1, 3, & 100).

[36] *See generally* 3 Gordon & Mailman, *Immigration Law and Procedure* §5.1 (rev. ed. 1989).

[37] *See* AILA-EOIR Liaison Agenda Questions 14 (Oct. 17, 2005), *www.aila.org/content/default.aspx?docid=17987*.

[38] *See, inter alia, Farrokhi v. INS*, 900 F.2d 697, (4th Cir. 1990); *Larita-Martinez v. INS*, 220 F.3d 1092 (9th Cir. 2000); *In re Huete*, 20 I&N Dec. 250 (BIA 1991).

[39] *See In re Santos*, 19 I&N Dec. 105 (BIA 1984).

possible claim of judicial misconduct, one must focus on the concept of due process.

Many practitioners and the American Immigration Lawyers Association (AILA) voiced complaints and sought reform of the disciplinary systems because there is no clear standard for evaluating and disciplining immigration judges,[40] unlike the disciplinary system that exists for private attorneys practicing before EOIR, which is quite efficient. (One can find the list of disciplined attorneys on the EOIR's website posted almost in real time.[41]) But the provisions for disciplining private attorneys do not apply to government attorneys. Instead, government attorneys and immigration judges are subject to the Standard of Conduct for Executive Branch Employees.[42] The Office of Professional Responsibility (OPR) of the Department of Justice is responsible for the investigation of allegations of misconduct by immigration judges.[43] Although the Office of the Chief of the Immigration Judge (OCIJ) also accepts complaints of judicial misconduct,[44] it appears the more effective practice would be to submit allegations of misconduct to the OPR.[45] The EOIR stated at an AILA liaison meeting that the OCIJ will make its own preliminary assessment, and if it determines that the charges have substance, only then will it refer the complaint to the OPR.[46] An immigration practitioner's best approach is to file the charges with OPR, since it is separate from the EOIR branch.[47]

COMPLAINT STANDARDS

What is the standard that governs misconduct by immigration judges? Who investigates to determine whether the charge is actionable? In April 2001, the Director of EOIR sent a memorandum to all BIA members, immigration judges, and administrative law judges outlining the adoption of an ethics manual. According to the memo, the manual is essentially an annotated version of the Standard Conduct for Executive Branch Employees.[48] This manual contains four parts: *Ethics Handbook for Immigration Judges, Members of the Board of Immigration Appeals, and the Administration Law Judges*; Standards of Conduct for Executive Branch Employees and the Supplemental Standards of Conduct for Department of Justice Employees; Departmental Memoranda and Orders that bear on ethical considerations EOIR judges may encounter; and the American Bar Association (ABA) Model Code of Judicial Conduct (MCJC). Importantly, the manual only serves as a "useful guide for anyone seeking guidance on particular ethical issues."[49] Nevertheless, the manual does acknowledge the ABA Model Code of Judicial Conduct by stating that "[a]lthough EOIR judges are not required to comply with the Model Code of Judicial Conduct, its canons and commentary represent principles of ethical conduct EOIR Judges should aspire to achieve."[50] Practitioners should also look to the state rules relating to professional responsibility because the immigration judge, if an attorney, will be a member of a state bar. Members of a state bar are subject to those ethical standards as well.

In looking at the specific provisions that might provide guidance to practitioners, Canon 3 of the MCJC may be helpful:

[40] P. MacLean, "Immigration Bench Plagued by Flaws," 27 *Nat'l L.J.* 1 (Feb. 6, 2006) (describing the difficulty in disciplining immigration judges).

[41] *See* Executive Office for Immigration Review, Disciplinary Release (Feb. 2006), *www.usdoj.gov/eoir* (illustrating the website's near constant updates regarding attorneys whom they discipline).

[42] 5 CFR §2365, *et. seq*.

[43] *See* Jurisdiction for Investigation of Allegations of Misconduct by Department of Justice Employees, Att'y Gen. Order No. 1931-94 (Nov. 8, 1994), *www.usdoj.gov/ag/readingroom/agencymisconducta.htm*.

[44] *See* AILA-EOIR Liaison Agenda Questions (Mar. 7, 2002), *published on* AILA InfoNet at Doc. No. 02041871 (*posted* Apr. 18, 2002).

[45] AILA-EOIR Liaison Agenda Questions (Mar. 16, 2005), *published on* AILA InfoNet at Doc. No. 05051268 (*posted* May 12, 2005).

[46] AILA-EOIR Liaison Minutes of March 7, 2002, *published on* AILA InfoNet at Doc. No. 02041871 (*posted* Apr. 18, 2002). Specifically, on question 4, the response from the EOIR states, "A complaint against an Immigration Judge may be filed with the OCIJ, and it may later be referred to OPR. A complaint can also be filed directly with OPR." A copy of this memo also can be found AILA's *Interpretations of Immigration Policy: Cables, Memos, and Liaison Minutes*
continued

for 2002. For more information or to order a copy of this book, see *www.ailapubs.org*.

[47] Dep't of Justice, *Ethics Manual for Members of the Board of Immigration Appeals, Immigration Judges, and Administrative Law Judges Employed by the Executive Office for Immigration Review* 4 (2001), *www.usdoj.gov/eoir/statspub/handbook.pdf* [hereinafter *Manual*].

[48] 5 CFR §2635 (2005).

[49] *Manual, supra* note 47.

[50] *Id.*

A judge shall be patient, dignified and courteous to litigants, jurors, witnesses, lawyers, and others with whom the judge deals in an official capacity, and shall require similar conduct of lawyers, and of staff, court officials and others subject to the judge's direction and control.[51]

It appears that this problem exists with some immigration judges currently on the bench.[52] "Time and time again, we have cautioned immigration judges against making intemperate or humiliating remarks during immigration proceedings. Three times this year we had to admonish immigration judges who failed to treat the asylum applicants in their court with the appropriate respect."[53]

Another provision of Canon 3 of the MCJC is relevant:

A judge shall perform judicial duties without bias or prejudice. A judge shall not, in the performance of judicial duties, by words or conduct manifest bias or prejudice, including but not limited to bias or prejudice based upon race, sex, religion, national origin, disability, age, sexual orientation or socioeconomic status, and shall not permit staff, court officials and other subject to the judge's direction and control to do so.[54]

Several immigration judges have breached this canon by their actions. The *Los Angeles Times* reported on an immigration judge who wrongly deported a U.S. citizen and "had failed to conduct herself as an impartial judge but rather as a prosecutor anxious to pick holes in the petitioner's story."[55] Another immigration judge, now retired, was often a subject of criticism and motions to recuse by the local bar. He became infamous for various remarks, including his joking reference to himself as "Me Tarzan" to a Ugandan asylum-seeker named Jane, a rape victim. In another case, when the attorney suggested that his client take off his shirt to show his scars, the same immigration judge yelled in the courtroom, "I am not going to turn this courtroom into a monkey house."[56]

WHEN AND HOW TO COMPLAIN

The question remains: How should a litigant handle a situation when he or she encounters bias from the immigration judge? Bias may manifest in many ways: remarks off the record or rulings unsubstantiated by law, assumption of a prosecutorial role in the hearing, a ruling that was appealed and reversed and remanded to the same immigration judge for an additional hearing, or adverse credibility findings on shaky grounds. The key analysis is whether the immigration judge deprived the client of a fair hearing and due process.

If the practitioner feels that the immigration judge denied a fair hearing, the practitioner must make a motion to recuse during the hearing. Whether it is a written or oral motion, the practitioner must take steps to perfect the record for appellate review. The *Immigration Judge Benchbook*[57] provides instructions to immigration judges regarding this matter. The *Benchbook* directs the immigration judge never to go off the record to deal with the issue of recusal. A memorandum issued by the Chief Immigration Judge in March 2005 provides further guidance regarding recusal.[58] The memo sets out the specific criteria under which immigration judges must recuse themselves, as well as the objective criteria for situations that fall outside the mandatory requirement. In a recusal situation, practitioners should refer to this memorandum for guidance.

The practitioner should rely on his or her sound professional judgment in deciding whether to take further steps. If the conduct is egregious, perhaps the next step is the formal filing of a complaint with OPR or OCIJ. The complaint should document in detail the alleged judicial misconduct and cite the alleged violations of the Standards of Conduct for Executive Employee, the *Ethics Manual*, or the MCJC. In this situation, the immigration judge has possibly violated the requirement that "employees shall put forth honest effort in the performance of their duties."[59] The alleged conduct may also violate

---

[51] Model Code of Judicial Conduct Canon 3 (1997), available at *www.abanet.org/cpr/mcjc/mcjc_home.html*.

[52] A. Simmons, "Some Immigrants Meet Harsh Face of Justice," *L.A. Times*, Feb. 12, 2006; A. Liptak, *supra note 6*, at A1.

[53] Wang, *supra note 33* (quoted in MacLean, *supra note 7*).

[54] *Supra* note 51.

[55] Simmons, *supra* note 52.

[56] *Id.*

---

[57] *Immigration Judge Benchbook* 214 (Oct. 2001), *www.usdoj.gov/eoir/statspub/benchbook.pdf*.

[58] Michael J. Creppy, Operating Policies and Procedures Memorandum 05-02: EOIR on Procedures for Issuing Recusal Orders in Immigration Proceedings, Mar. 21, 2005, *www.usdoj.gov/eoir/efoia/ocij/oppm05/05-02.pdf*; *published on* AILA InfoNet at Doc. No. 05032369 (*posted* Mar. 23, 2005).

[59] *See* 5 CFR §2365; *Ethics Manual*, *supra* note 47.

several canons of the MCJC.[60] The drawback of these actions is the requirement of specificity in providing the name of the client and case number, which could invite retaliation. If this is a concern, the practitioner may consult the chair of AILA's EOIR committee regarding the possibility of AILA itself filing an informal and anonymous complaint of judicial misconduct to the regional assistant chief immigration judge. Whatever action is selected for dealing with possible judicial misconduct, a practitioner should keep in mind the client's best interest.

Remember, the litmus test is whether the immigration judge denied the client due process under the law, to wit—was the client denied a fair hearing?

CONCLUSION

With increased awareness that there are serious problems with immigration courts, attorneys must be proactive in preserving issues in court to raise at the courts of appeal. And while attorneys have outlets to register complaints against judges who deny their clients due process, doing so requires careful preparation and documentation.

---

[60] *Supra* note 51.

HERE WE GO AGAIN: MOTIONS TO REOPEN, RECONSIDER, AND RESCIND BEFORE THE BOARD OF IMMIGRATION APPEALS

*by Zachary Nightingale and Avantika Shastri**

INTRODUCTION

This article surveys motions to reconsider, reopen, and rescind before the Board of Immigration Appeals (Board).[1] Filing such motions can be a powerful way to get facts or arguments of your client's case considered (or reconsidered) before a deportation or removal order is executed. It may also be the only way to have certain facts considered if your client already has been issued a final order of deportation or removal.

There are different regimes for each kind of motion, some created by regulation and others by case law. Recognizing the different sources of law is important because many rules that apply are not found in the regulations themselves but are instead based on legal interpretation in precedent decisions or by

statute (whether it is the INA[2] or other sources, such as VAWA,[3] NACARA,[4] HRIFA,[5] and other statutes not explicitly incorporated in the INA).

In determining which type of motion to file, and what the rules are, there are several preliminary questions: kind of proceeding, function of the motion, timing of the motion, evidentiary requirements of each motion, and the practical effect of the motion in delaying or preventing removal. Notably, filing motions is not restricted to filing one at a time, or to only one judge or adjudicator at a time. Thus, thoughtful and creative filing of the motions based on the procedural posture of the case can maximize your client's chances of receiving a rehearing.

This article is primarily concerned with motions to reconsider and reopen. It will provide only general updates related to motions to rescind because excellent articles have been published already on that subject.[6] The article concludes with the general and strategic aspects of filing these motions.[7]

---

* **Zachary Nightingale**, a partner at Van Der Hout, Brigagliano & Nightingale, LLP, (*www.vblaw.com*) received his J.D. and M.S. (mathematics) from Stanford and A.B. from U.C. Berkeley. His practice focuses on deportation defense and federal court litigation. Mr. Nightingale is certified as an expert in immigration law by the state bar of California, and was honored with AILA's 2003 Jack Wasserman Memorial Award for excellence in litigation.

Avantika Shastri is an associate attorney at Van Der Hout, Brigagliano & Nightingale, LLP, in San Francisco.

[1] *See* 8 CFR §1003.2. Motions to reopen and reconsider may also be filed before the immigration judge (IJ), *see* 8 CFR §1003.23; and the Administrative Appeals Office, *see* 8 CFR §§103.3, 1103.3. Although this article will primarily address motions before the Board, the suggestions will almost always apply to motions made to the immigration court as well.

There are two other kinds of motions that are related but will not be discussed in depth here. First, if the Board has granted an appeal of an order that is pending or a motion to reopen, you may file a motion to remand to return jurisdiction of a case pending before the Board to the IJ. *See* 8 CFR §1003.2(c)(4); *Matter of Coelho*, 20 I&N Dec. 464 (BIA 1992); *Matter of L–V–K–*, 22 I&N Dec. 976, 980 (BIA 1999); *see also BIA Practice Manual*, Ch. 5.8. Motions to remand have the same substantive requirements as motions to reopen but are not limited in time or number. *See* discussion *infra*. Second, when you wish to reopen proceedings that have been administratively closed or continued indefinitely, the proper motion is a motion to recalendar, not to remand. *See BIA Practice Manual*, Ch. 5.9(h).

[2] Immigration and Nationality Act of 1952, Pub. L. No. 82-414, 66 Stat. 163 (codified as amended at 8 USC §§1101–1524).

[3] Violence Against Women and Department of Justice Reauthorization Act of 2005 (VAWA 2005), Pub. L. No. 109-162, 119 Stat. 2960 (Jan. 5, 2006).

[4] Nicaraguan Adjustment and Central American Relief Act, Pub. L. No. 105-100, 111 Stat. 2160, 2193; amended by Pub. L. No. 105-139, Pub. L. 106-386, and Pub. L. No. 106-554.

[5] Haitian Refugee Immigration Fairness Act of 1998, Pub. L. No.105-277, Division A, §101(h), Title IX, 112 Stat 2681.

[6] *See, e.g.*, AILF Practice Advisory, "Rescinding an In Absentia Order of Removal," (*amended* May 20, 2002), at *www.ailf.org*; B. Jobe, "Strategies for Reopening In Absentia Deportation Proceedings and Mitigating the Effects of the Time and Numerical Limitations on Motions to Reopen," in *11th AILA California Chapters Conference Handbook* 121 (1998); *see also* I. Kurzban, *Kurzban's Immigration Law Sourcebook*, 10th Ed. (2006).

[7] The Board has also provided an excellent practice manual that lays out in a clear and organized fashion many of the procedural rules for motions. *See BIA Practice Manual* (last revised June 15, 2004). A copy can be found online at the Executive Office of Immigration Review's Virtual Law Library website, or for a bound copy, see *www.ailapubs.org*. Sample motions may be found in *AILA's Immigration Litigation Toolbox* (2005), *www.ailapubs.org* for more information.

MOTIONS FOR RECONSIDERATION

A motion to reconsider is a vehicle for requesting reconsideration of a previous legal decision where there are no new facts to be considered.[8] A motion to reconsider is a "request that the Board reexamine its decision in light of additional legal arguments, a change of law, or perhaps an argument or aspect of the case that was overlooked."[9]

A motion to reconsider must be filed with the Board within 30 days of the Board's decision.[10] A party may file only one motion to reconsider any given decision and may not seek reconsideration of a decision denying a previous motion to reconsider.[11]

Motions to reconsider filed before July 31, 1996, do not count toward the one-motion limit.[12] In contrast to motions to reopen, there are no regulatory exceptions to the numerical and time limitations except that the Board may reconsider on its own motion at any time.[13] There may, however, be equity-based exceptions to those limitations.[14]

A motion to reconsider may be made even if the case was dismissed for lack of jurisdiction when the dismissal was due to an untimely appeal. In *Matter of Lopez*,[15] the Board held that it retained jurisdiction over a motion to reconsider its dismissal of an

untimely appeal, to the extent that the motion challenges the finding of untimeliness or requests consideration of the reasons for untimeliness.

The only materials required to support a motion to reconsider are a statement of the party's arguments about the Board's alleged errors and "pertinent authority."[16] It is implicit in subsection (b)(1) that the Board will reconsider the case using the same evidence used in making its prior decision.[17]

In *Matter of Cerna*, the Board held that motions to reopen and motions to reconsider are distinct motions with different requirements.[18] It said:

> A motion to reconsider asserts that at the time of the Board's previous decision an error was made. It questions the Board's decision for alleged errors in appraising the facts and the law. When we reconsider a decision, we are in effect placing ourselves back in time and considering the case as though a decision in the case on the record before us had never been entered. If the respondent was eligible for relief at the time the original decision was entered, then in reconsidering the decision we would treat his status as that which it had been at the time of the initial decision. The very nature of a motion to reconsider is that the original decision was defective in some regard.

In contrast, the Board said,

> A motion to reopen proceedings, however, is a fundamentally different motion. It does not contest the correctness of (or simply request a reevaluation of) the prior decision on the previous factual record. Rather, a motion to reopen proceedings seeks to reopen proceedings so that new evidence can be presented and so that a new decision can be entered, normally after a further evidentiary hearing.

Despite this apparently clear distinction, in practice, the difference is not always readily apparent, especially where a change in law after the final order affects your client's legal rights.[19] There also may be

---

[8] *See* INA §240(c)(5); 8 CFR §1003.2(b).

[9] *Matter of Ramos*, 23 I&N Dec. 336, 338 (BIA 2002), *aff'd*, 979 F.2d 212 (11th Cir. 1992) (unpublished table decision); *Asemota v. Gonzales*, 420 F.3d 32, 34 (1st Cir. 2005); *Kui Rong Ma v. Ashcroft*, 361 F.3d 553, 558 (9th Cir. 2004); *see also BIA Practice Manual*, Ch. 5.7.

[10] INA §240(c)(5)(B); 8 CFR §1003.2(b)(2).

[11] INA §240(c)(5)(A); 8 CFR §1003.2(b)(2).

[12] *See id.* at §1003.2(b)(2).

[13] *See* 8 CFR §1003.2(a); *cf.* 8 CFR §1003.2(c)(3).

[14] *See* discussion, *infra*. In addition, there are other cases in which untimely motions to reconsider may be filed. For example, following a Board decision, your client's prior representative may have missed the 30-day jurisdictional deadline to file a petition for review in the court of appeals and the 30-day motion to reconsider deadline. Even if such failure to file were the result of deficient representation, the circuit courts have not found ineffective assistance of counsel to be a sufficient basis for accepting a late petition for review. However, the ineffective assistance of counsel may be a valid basis to file a late motion to reconsider with the Board. Even if such motion were denied, a petition for review of that denial could then be timely filed to ultimately obtain review in the circuit court.

[15] *Matter of Lopez*, 22 I&N Dec. 16, 17 (BIA 1998), *modifying Matter of Mladineo*, 14 I&N Dec. 591 (BIA 1974).

[16] *See Iturribarria v. INS*, 321 F.3d 889, 895 (9th Cir. 2003).

[17] *Id.*

[18] 20 I&N Dec. 399, 402–03 (BIA 1991). The Board has made the same distinction between motions to reopen and to rescind. *See Matter of M–S–*, 22 I&N Dec. 349 (BIA 1998).

[19] *Compare Matter of G–D–*, 22 I&N Dec. 1132 (BIA 1999) (motion to reconsider based on the argument that a later decision by the Board warranted reconsideration of respondent's case); *Matter of H–A–*, 22 I&N Dec. 728 (BIA 1999) (motion to reconsider based on the argument that a Board

continued

a strategic reason to characterize a motion as either reopening or reconsideration, given that each has separate evidentiary and jurisdictional requirements.

In confusing circumstances, always refer to relevant precedent in the particular jurisdiction. It may be best to file a motion within the jurisdictional time for a reconsideration motion to best preserve your client's legal options. The motion can always be supplemented, and if necessary be characterized as either or even both types of motions. If you face numerical or time bars to jurisdiction, it may still be possible to file based on equitable reasons for untimely filing.[20]

MOTIONS TO REOPEN

A motion to reopen presents new facts, unavailable at the time of the original proceedings, to the Board or the immigration judge (IJ).[21] A motion to reopen must demonstrate a prima facie case for relief and will shall not be granted unless it appears to the Board that the evidence sought to be offered is material and was not available and could not have been discovered or presented at the former hearing.[22] The applicant must submit any applications for relief along with the motion.[23] A motion to reopen does *not* lead to an automatic stay of removal; the applicant must still request a stay from the Board.[24]

There are strict jurisdictional requirements for motions to reopen. Unless subject to one of the specific exceptions, a party may file only one motion to reopen and that motion must be filed no later than 90 days after the administrative decision.[25] A statutory

exception outside the regulations is that motions to reopen to apply for relief as a battered spouse, parent, or child also do not count towards the one-motion limitation.[26]

Among the regulatory exceptions to the time and numerical limitations are the following:

- The party was subject to an *in absentia* order of removal (see discussion, *infra*, on motions to rescind).

- The party is applying or reapplying for asylum based on changed circumstances in the country from which asylum is sought or to which removal was ordered.

- The government joins in the motion to reopen.

- The government files a motion to reopen deportation or exclusion proceedings where it has discovered fraud in the underlying proceedings, or it believes your client has committed a crime that would support termination of asylum.[27]

The Board may also *sua sponte* reopen any case at any time.[28]

Notably, in a motion to reopen the applicant has the burden of making a *prima facie* case for relief. Thus, applicants will want to submit documentation that not only relates to why the evidence or issues were not raised in the prior hearing, and what the new evidence is, but also relates to the underlying merits of the claim, including any discretionary issues beyond the basic requirements for relief.

The evidence submitted with a motion to reopen must make a *prima facie* case that the movant is eligible for the relief requested.[29] The Board has "found that a respondent demonstrates eligibility where the evidence reveals a reasonable likelihood that the statutory requirements for relief have been satisfied."[30] It has "not required a conclusive showing that

---

decision conflicted with the regulations); 8 CFR §1003.44 (requiring special motion to reopen based on eligibility for relief under INA §212(c) after *St. Cyr* decision); AILF Practice Advisory, "Judicial Provisions of the REAL ID Act: Strategies for Dealing with the Expansion of Jurisdiction in the Court of Appeals" (*amended* June 1, 2005) (providing guidance to file a motion to reopen because of newly enacted changes to circuit court jurisdiction in the REAL ID Act); *see also Iturribarria v. INS*, 321 F.3d 889, 894–97 (9th Cir. 2003) (finding that the Board abused its discretion by characterizing the petitioner's motion to reopen based on ineffective assistance of counsel as a motion to reconsider).

[20] *See* discussion, *infra*.

[21] *See* INA §240(c)(6); 8 CFR §1003.2(c).

[22] *See* 8 CFR §1003.2(c)(1).

[23] *Id.*

[24] *See* 8 CFR §1003.2(f); *see also* discussion, *infra*.

[25] *See* INA §240(c)(6)(C)(i); 8 CFR §1003.2(c)(2).

[26] *See* VAWA 2005 §825.

[27] *See* 8 CFR §1003.2(c)(3). *See also* 8 CFR §§1208.24(e), (f) (applying this rule to removal proceedings and to prior grants of withholding of deportation); 8 CFR §1208.17(d)–(f) (motion for new hearing, rather than motion to reopen required to terminate prior grants of deferral of removal under the Convention Against Torture).

[28] *See* 8 CFR §1003.2(a).

[29] *See INS v. Abudu*, 485 U.S. 94 (1988) (also enumerating other reasons why the Board may deny a motion to reopen).

[30] *Matter of S–V–*, 22 I&N Dec. 1306, 1308 (BIA 2000), citing *Matter of L–O–G–*, 21 I&N Dec. 413, 419 (BIA 1996).

eligibility for relief has been established. Rather, [it has] reopened proceedings where the new facts alleged, when coupled with the facts already of record, satisfy us that it would be worthwhile to develop the issues further at a plenary hearing on reopening."[31]

Statutory and Regulatory Bases for Motions to Reopen

Asylum Applications

Pursuant to 8 CFR §1003.2(c)(3), a motion to reopen may be filed to apply or reapply for asylum or for withholding of deportation/removal based on changed circumstances in the country of nationality or the country to which deportation has been ordered.[32] Here the numeric and time limitations on motions to reopen do not apply.[33] The applicant must show that the evidence is material and could not have been presented earlier.[34]

Personal changes in the United States are not a valid basis for arguing changed circumstances under the reopening regulations.[35] However, there may be ways to argue that the changed personal circumstances constitute a new ground for asylum, which could not have been raised earlier. A *sua sponte* motion or a request for a joint motion are both possible but usually difficult. Legal arguments also appear possible in some situations. For example, the statute provides that after an asylum application is denied, another may be filed if one of the conditions in INA §208(a)(2)(D) is met.[36] Those conditions of course cover more than simply changed conditions in the country from which asylum is being sought. Therefore, the regulation that limits motions to reopen to this singular situation appears to be *ultra vires* to the

statute itself.[37] The fact that the regulations define a denied asylum application as one denied by the immigration court or the Board supports this reading.[38]

Moreover, the requirements under the Convention Against Torture (CAT)[39] that the United States not repatriate an applicant to a country where he or she faces torture would appear to require a mechanism for making a CAT claim even after the 90-day reopening period has expired where the basis of the CAT case arises after the deadline. Again, such a situation would appear to be one in which a late motion to reopen should be accepted based on changed circumstances within the United States in order to uphold the CAT treaty obligations.

Relief Under Former INA §212(c)

Pursuant to 8 CFR §1003.2(c)(1), a motion to reopen proceedings for consideration of an application for relief under former INA §212(c) may be granted if the applicant demonstrates that he or she was eligible for such relief before the final order of deportation was entered.[40] The numerical and time limitations that apply to motions to reopen would apply here as well.[41]

Battered Spouses, Parents, and Children

In late 2005, Congress reauthorized the Violence Against Women Act (VAWA) with significant changes[42] that apply to removal, exclusion, and de-

---

[31] *Id.* (citations omitted). *See, e.g., Ordonez v. INS*, 345 F.3d 777, 784–87 (9th Cir. 2003); *Kay v. Ashcroft*, 387 F.3d 664, 675 (7th Cir. 2004); *Shardar v. Ashcroft*, 382 F.3d 318, 325 (3d Cir. 2004).

[32] 8 CFR §1003.2(c)(3)(ii).

[33] 8 CFR §1003.2(c)(3).

[34] *Id. See, e.g., Matter of J–J–*, 21 I&N Dec. 976 (BIA 1997) (no changed circumstances warranting reopening).

[35] *See, e.g., Haddad v. Gonzales*, 437 F.3d 515 (6th Cir. 2006) (stating that divorce was a purely personal change in circumstances that does not constitute changed conditions or circumstances in Jordan); *Guan v. Board of Immigration Appeals*, 345 F.3d 47, 49 (2d Cir. 2003) (finding that the fact that petitioner now had two children did not constitute a changed circumstance).

[36] INA §208(a)(2)(C).

[37] *See also* 8 CFR §1208.4(a)(4) (enumerating examples of changed circumstances for purposes of determining eligibility for asylum).

[38] *See* 8 CFR §§208.4(a)(3), 1208.4(a)(3).

[39] United Nations Convention Against Torture and Other Cruel, Inhuman or Degrading Treatment or Punishment (CAT), opened for signature Feb. 4, 1985, G.A. Res. 39/46 U.N. GAOR Supp. No. 51, at 197, U.N. doc. A/RES/39/708 (1984), reprinted in 23 I.L.M. 1027 (1984), modified in 24 I.L.M. 535 (1985).

[40] 8 CFR §§1003.2(c)(1); *see also* 8 CFR §§212.3, 1212.3.

[41] *Id.* For some time, the regulations permitted a special motion to reopen to apply for relief under INA §212(c), which was not subject to numerical limitations. However, the period for filing such motions has ended. *See* 8 CFR §1003.44 (special motion to reopen rule to seek §212(c) relief for motions to reopen filed on or before April 26, 2005), explained further at AILF Practice Advisory, "St. Cyr Regulations and Strategies for Applicants Who Are Barred from Section 212(c) Relief Under the Regulations" (Oct. 19, 2004), at *www.ailf.org*.

[42] *See* VAWA 2005.

portation proceedings.[43] VAWA 2005 significantly increased the scope of coverage to persons who had not otherwise been able to self-petition or apply for relief in removal or deportation proceedings. Many of these newly eligible people now may be qualified to file a motion to reopen.

VAWA 2005 permits applicants to file one motion to reopen at any time based on domestic violence, *in addition to* one motion to reopen based on other causes.[44] Notably, however, it retains the requirement that the motion to reopen must be filed within one year of entry of the final order of removal unless the time limitation is waived by the Attorney General.[45]

The motion may be made on behalf of battered spouses, children,[46] and now battered *parents* as well.[47] VAWA 2005 allows reopening for the purpose not only of applying for adjustment as a self-petitioner under INA §204(a), special rule cancellation under INA §240A(b)(2), as it did previously, but now also for VAWA suspension of deportation under INA §244(a)(3) (in effect March 31, 1997).[48]

Lastly, VAWA 2005 added a requirement that an applicant must be physically present in the United States when the motion is filed. It also added a mandatory stay for qualified aliens as described in the Personal Responsibility and Work Opportunity Reconciliation Act of 1998,[49] pending final disposition of the motion, including exhaustion of all appeals, if the motion establishes that the alien is qualified.[50]

Bases to Reopen Established by Case Law

Ineffective Assistance of Counsel

An applicant may have been effectively prevented from presenting evidence in the first hearing because of deficient advice from a lawyer or someone purporting to be a lawyer. A claim of ineffective assistance may be used to explain both the error that resulted in a delay in presenting new evidence that in fact existed or was known of earlier in the case, or the error that may have prevented the new information from being timely presented in a motion to reopen. While we will not claim to recount all the ways assistance could take be ineffective, courts have found ineffective assistance and sometimes equity-based remedies in numerous situations.[51]

A claim of ineffective assistance of counsel almost always requires complying with the basic procedural requirements laid out by the Board or an explanation of why they have not been followed. In *Matter of Lozada*,[52] the Board held that ineffective assistance of counsel could constitute grounds for reopening if certain procedural hurdles were met.[53]

Procedural Requirements of Lozada

Lozada sets forth three requirements for supporting a claim of ineffective assistance of counsel:

- an affidavit by the alien setting forth the agreement with counsel on representation;

- evidence that counsel was informed of the allegations and allowed to respond; and

- an indication that a complaint has been lodged with the state bar, or reasons why it was not.

The Board and the circuit courts generally have been fairly strict in requiring that these procedural hurdles be met before reopening any case. However, there are cases where circuit courts have found that an applicant effectively demonstrated ineffective assistance even when he or she did not meet one or more of the strict *Lozada* requirements.

---

[43] *See* VAWA 2005 §825. *See also* Battered Immigrant Women Protection Act of 2000, Div. B (Violence Against Women Act of 2000), Pub. L. No. 106-386, 114 Stat. 1464 (Oct. 28, 2000), §§1501–1513; Violent Crime Control and Law Enforcement Act of 1994, Tit. IV (Violence Against Women Act of 1994), Pub. L. No. 103-322, 108 Stat. 1796 (Sept. 13, 1994), §40703. Certain provisions of VAWA relating to reopening deportation proceedings were contained only in the statute and never promulgated in regulations.

[44] *See* VAWA 2005 §§825(a)(1), (a)(2)(B).

[45] *See id*. §825(a)(2)(E) (the requirement may be waived if the applicant demonstrates extraordinary circumstances or extreme hardship to his or her child).The "extraordinary circumstances" requirement is distinct from the "exceptional circumstances" required to rescind *in absentia* orders. *Compare* INA §240(c)(7)(C)(iv)(III) *with* §240(e)(1).

[46] VAWA 2005 also expanded the ability of persons who were battered as children to self-petition or apply for relief in removal and deportation proceedings. *See* VAWA 2005 §805.

[47] *See id*. VAWA §825(a)(2)(A).

[48] *See id*. VAWA §825(a)(2)(C).

[49] 8 USC §1641(c)(1)(B).

[50] *See* VAWA §825(a)(2)(F).

[51] *See also* discussion, *infra*.

[52] 19 I&N Dec. 637, 639 (BIA), *aff'd*, 857 F.2d 10 (1st Cir. 1988).

[53] *See also Matter of Assaad*, 23 I&N Dec. 553 (BIA 2003); *Matter of Rivera*, 21 I&N Dec. 599 (BIA 1988).

The Ninth Circuit in particular has recognized several times the flexibility of the *Lozada* requirements. For example, in *Lo v. Ashcroft*,[54] it found that *Lozada's* purpose and reasoning had been served even without a state bar complaint against offending counsel, because prior counsel acknowledged a mistake and actively worked with petitioner to rectify the error. Similarly, in *Escobar-Grijalva v. INS*,[55] the same circuit found that the petitioner did not have to show that she had filed complaints against counsel because the record was clear on its face that she had been subject to the assistance had been ineffective. In that case, an exasperated IJ assigned the petitioner counsel even though the counsel had never before met the petitioner and had no knowledge of her case.[56]

Other examples of courts countenancing less than complete compliance with *Lozada* can be found in several other circuits.[57]

Substantive Requirements of Lozada

The substantive requirements of a *Lozada* claim generally involve showing (1) fundamental unfairness, and (2) prejudice.[58] The standard for funda-

mental unfairness is quite easy to meet given that ineffective assistance of counsel is a due process violation of the Fifth Amendment.[59] Similarly, the standard for prejudice many courts use is also quite low; it is only necessary to show that the outcome of the case "*may* have been affected" by the ineffective assistance of counsel.[60]

A motion to reopen based on ineffective assistance of counsel should provide not only evidence showing that the assistance of counsel was ineffective (as *Lozada* requires) but also clear and strong evidence of your client's eligibility for relief. Evidence in support of eligibility for relief is important to show the prejudice your client suffered from previous counsel's inadequacy. This evidence should address all the elements required for the relief applied for, such as evidence of qualifying relatives, hardship, and good moral character. It should also offer any evidence necessary to support a positive exercise of discretion.

Vacating Convictions

Numerous courts have said that the overturning of a conviction upon which deportability was premised is a basis for reopening proceedings.[61]

The Board itself has found that a conviction that was overturned because it was illegally entered in the first place will be recognized as no longer having immigration consequences.[62] However, a conviction

---

[54] 341 F.3d 934, 938 (9th Cir. 2003).

[55] 206 F.3d 1331(9th Cir. 2000).

[56] *See also Castillo-Perez v. INS*, 212 F.3d 518, 526 (9th Cir. 2000) (stating that "[w]hile the requirements of *Lozada* are generally reasonable, they need not be rigidly enforced where their purpose is fully served by other means. . . . Here, the record of the proceedings themselves is more than adequate to serve those functions. Thus, there has been substantial compliance with the rule.").

[57] *See, e.g., Esposito v. INS*, 987 F.2d 108, 111 (2d Cir. 1993) ("Esposito did not file a complaint with any disciplinary authority, but provided a reasonable explanation in his affidavit (a belief that Maracina had already been suspended from the practice of law) for not doing so"); *Figeroa v. U.S. INS*, 886 F.2d 76, 79 (4th Cir. 1989) (overturning the Board's reasoning that the petitioner had failed to inform his prior counsel of the charges against him on the grounds that "The evidence is clear that Tellez's conduct failed to meet even the minimum level of competence expected of an attorney under these circumstances.").

[58] *See, e.g., Hernandez v. Reno*, 238 F.3d 50, 55 (1st Cir. 2001); *Jian Yun Zheng v. U.S. DOJ*, 409 F.3d 43, 46 (2d Cir. 2005); *Zheng v. Gonzales*, 422 F.3d 98 (3d Cir. 2005); *Goonsuwan v. Ashcroft*, 252 F.3d 383, 385 (5th Cir. 2001); *Allabani v. Gonzales*, 402 F.3d 668 (6th Cir. 2005); *Kay v. Ashcroft*, 387 F.3d 664 (7th Cir. 2004); *Obleshchenko v. Ashcroft*, 392 F.3d 970, 972 (8th Cir. 2004); *Maravilla v. Ashcroft*, 381 F.3d 855, 857–58 (9th Cir. 2004); *Michelson v. INS*, 897 F.2d 465, 468 (10th Cir. 1990).

[59] *Id.*

[60] *Id.*

[61] *See, e.g., De Faria v. INS*, 13 F.3d 422, 423 (1st Cir. 1994); *Johnson v. Ashcroft*, 378 F.3d 164, 171 (2d Cir. 2004); *Escobar v. INS*, 935 F.2d 650, 652 (4th Cir. 1991) (noting that INS had asked Board to "reopen and terminate" deportation proceedings after conviction was expunged); *Wiedersperg v. INS*, 896 F.2d 1179, 1182–83 (9th Cir. 1990) (abuse of discretion to deny reopening in this context); *Becerra-Jimenez v. INS*, 829 F.2d 996, 1000–02 (10th Cir. 1987) (because conviction was expunged, court remands for agency consideration of motion to reopen); *Haghi v. Russell*, 744 F. Supp. 249, 251–52 (D. Col. 1990) (vacation of conviction is "new and material evidence" within 8 CFR §3.2).

[62] *See, e.g., Matter of Rodriguez-Ruiz*, 22 I&N Dec. 1378 (BIA 2000). *Compare Matter of Song*, 23 I&N Dec. 173 (BIA 2001) (finding that the modification of a sentence for theft to less than one year meant that the conviction no longer constituted an aggravated felony), *aff'd*, in *Matter of Cota-Vargas*, 23 I&N Dec. 849 (BIA 2005) (holding that a trial court's decision to modify or reduce an alien's criminal sentence *nunc pro tunc* is entitled to full faith and credit by IJs and the Board, and a modified or reduced sentence is recognized as valid for purposes of immigration law without

continued

vacated for other reasons (such as rehabilitation or other equity grounds, or solely to avoid the immigration consequences) will continue to have the same consequences. In *Matter of Pickering*, the Board held that a criminal conviction vacated for reasons solely related to rehabilitation or immigration hardships would continue to operate as a conviction within the meaning of INA §101(a)(48)(A).[63] The Board concluded that "there is a significant distinction between convictions vacated on the basis of a procedural or substantive defect in the underlying proceedings and those vacated because of post-conviction events, such as rehabilitation or immigration hardships."[64]

The circuit courts have applied this same analysis in looking at the specific reason for vacating when considering whether a conviction continue to have immigration consequences.[65] It is therefore likely that the Board and the circuit courts would apply the same rule to motions to reopen based on vacated convictions. The Ninth Circuit, for example, appears to have endorsed that distinction, finding that a "technical" expungement does not carry the same significance as a legal one when there is a motion to reopen a deportation order based on that conviction. For example, in *Hernandez-Almanza v U.S. DOJ*,[66] the court affirmed a Board decision refusing to reopen deportation proceedings for an alien who had his state court conviction vacated because he had returned to the United States illegally and who successfully attacked his state court conviction only after new deportation proceedings had begun against him. The Ninth Circuit distinguished *Hernandez-Almanza* in two later cases, *Estrada-Rosales v. INS*[67]

and *Wiedersperg v. INS*,[68] *inter alia*, the court emphasized that in each of those cases, the vacature of the conviction went to the merits and the conviction was the sole ground for the petitioner's deportation. It therefore found that the motion to reopen should have been granted.

Although we are not aware of any case to have explicitly held so in this context, such motions to reopen should be granted without regard to the time and numerical limitations of the statute and regulations, for due process reasons: it is basically unfair to uphold a deportation or removal order that is based on a criminal conviction that is now invalid. If the removal order was based on an invalid conviction, due process requires that the removal order be invalid as well. Neither statutory nor regulatory requirements could override the constitutional issue.

Marriage During Proceedings

Until recent Board precedent changed the law, if an individual in deportation or removal proceeding were to enter into a marriage that could be the basis for an application for adjustment of status, a motion to reopen could not be filed until the immediate relative visa petition was approved.[69]

MOTIONS TO RESCIND

Motions to rescind are a special kind of motion to reopen that calls for the reopening of a removal order

---

regard to the trial court's reasons for effecting the modification or reduction).

[63] 23 I&N Dec. 621 (BIA 2003).

[64] *Id.* at 624. *See also Matter of Roldan*, 22 I&N Dec. 512 (BIA 1999) (finding that vacation of a conviction pursuant to a state rehabilitative statute did not eliminate the immigration consequences).

[65] *See, e.g., Herrera-Inirio v. INS*, 208 F.3d 299, 306 (1st Cir. 2000); *U.S. v. Campbell*, 167 F.3d 94, 98 (2d Cir. 1999); *Zaitona v. INS*, 9 F.3d 432, 436–37 (6th Cir. 1993); *Beltran-Leon v. INS*, 134 F.3d 1379, 1380–81 (9th Cir. 1998). *But cf. Renteria-Gonzales v. INS*, 310 F.3d 825 (5th Cir. 2002), *reh. en banc den'd*, 322 F.3d 804 (2003) (finding no reason to distinguish between reasons for vacating and upholding original conviction).

[66] 547 F.2d 100 (9th Cir. 1976).

[67] 645 F.2d 819 (9th Cir. 1981).

[68] 896 F.2d 1179 (9th Cir. 1990).

[69] *See Matter of Arthur*, 20 I&N Dec. 475 (BIA 1002); *Matter of H–A–*, 22 I&N Dec. 728 (BIA 1992); *Rezai v. INS*, 62 F.3d 1286, 1289–92 (10th Cir. 1995); *Dielmann v. INS*, 34 F.3d 851 (9th Cir. 1994).

However, in *Matter of Velarde*, the Board modified this position to allow for motions to reopen where (1) the application for adjustment of status and the visa petition are timely filed within 90 days of the final order, (2) the motion is not numerically barred or barred by *Matter of Shaar*, 21 I&N Dec. 541 (BIA 1996), or any other procedural grounds, and (3) the motion presents clear and convincing evidence that the marriage is bona fide. 23 I&N Dec. 253 (BIA 2002); *Matter of Garcia*, 16 I&N Dec. 653, 656 (BIA 1978); *Bull v. INS*, 790 F.2d 869 (11th Cir. 1986); *cf. Krazoun v. Ashcroft*, 350 F.3d 208 (1st Cir. 2003) (upholding Board's denial in discretion because respondent had two previous marriages that Board deemed fraudulent). The Board suggested that a *Velarde* motion would generally be granted if DHS does not oppose the motion or bases its opposition solely on *Matter of Arthur*. *See, e.g., Matter of Garcia*, 16 I&N Dec. at 653 (stating that the Board "shall hereafter generally reopen the deportation proceedings in such cases unless clear ineligibility is apparent in the record.").

on the grounds that it was unlawfully executed. They have their own specific filing deadlines and carry a mandatory stay of removal. The Board has stated that while a motion to reopen permits you to raise new facts or seek new relief in regard to a prior order, motions to rescind eliminate the prior order of removal completely and return the respondent to the status he or she held before removal proceedings began.[70] The Board's regulations for motions to rescind[71] refer to the regulations for motions to rescind before an IJ.[72]

A motion to rescind requires a showing of one of the following: (1) the failure to appear was caused by "exceptional circumstances" as defined in INA §240(e)(1); (2) the movant did not receive notice in accordance with INA §§239(a)(1) or (2); or (3) the alien was in federal or state custody and so failure to appear was through no fault of his or her own.[73]

The jurisdictional rules for motions to rescind are different depending on whether the proceedings are for deportation, exclusion, or removal. None of these motions is subject to the 90-day time limitations for filing a motion to reopen,[74] and motions to rescind in deportation or exclusion proceedings are also not subject to the numerical limitations for motions to reopen.[75]

What Constitutes an Exceptional Circumstance?

The INA defines exceptional circumstances warranting a motion to reopen under INA §240(e).[76] The Board has interpreted what does and does not constitute exceptional circumstances in several cases.[77]

Notably, under VAWA 2005, domestic violence is now recognized as an exceptional circumstance warranting reopening of an *in absentia* order.[78] The statute applies to a failure to appear that occurs before, on, or after the date the act was passed.[79] Thus,

an exceptional circumstance might be "battery or extreme cruelty to the alien or any child or parent of the alien, battery or exceptional cruelty to the alien or any child or parent of the alien, serious illness of the alien, or serious illness or death of the spouse, child, or parent of the alien, but not including less compelling circumstances)." The section specifies that these circumstances must be "beyond the control of the alien."[80] In the Third Circuit, the timely filing of motion to reopen may also constitute an exceptional circumstance.[81]

In such cases, the applicant must provide detailed statements and evidence and show attempts to notify the court in advance or immediately afterwards. It also helps to show prior diligence in attending hearings and eligibility for relief and no reason to miss the hearing.

Strategic Choices

There may be circumstances in which you have a choice between filing a motion to rescind (because your client was issued an *in absentia* removal order) and a motion to reopen (because there was a due process violation or your client has recently become eligible for a form of relief). Which motion is preferable?

Notably, in *Matter of M–S–*, the Board held that a respondent could file a motion to reopen an *in absentia* removal order without filing a motion to rescind.[82] In *M–S–*, the respondent had been ordered deported pursuant to an *in absentia* order. Soon after, the alien married a U.S. citizen and filed a motion to reopen based on a pending and then approved application for adjustment of status. The respondent did not contest her deportability or any other basis for the removal order.

In contesting the motion to reopen, the government argued that the IJ could not adjudicate the respondent's motion to reopen until it had first granted a motion to rescind. The government argued that to allow her reopen her case without meeting the requirements to rescind the removal order would effectively allow her to bypass the penalties for failing to appear for her removal hearing. Thus, it applied the requirements under INA §242B(c)(3) (1994), which required a showing of exceptional circum-

---

[70] *See Matter of M–S–*, 22 I&N Dec. 349 (BIA 1998).

[71] 8 CFR §1003.2(c).

[72] 8 CFR §1003.23(b)(4)(ii).

[73] *See* INA §240(b)(5); 8 CFR §§1003.23(b)(4)(ii), (iii).

[74] *See* 8 CFR §1003.2(c)(3).

[75] *Id.*

[76] For cases initiated before June 13, 1992, the standard for reopening is "reasonable cause," rather than "exceptional circumstances." *See* INA §242(b) (1982); *Matter of Ruiz*, 20 I&N Dec. 91 (BIA 1989).

[77] *See, e.g.*, "Rescinding an In Absentia Order of Removal," *supra* note 6; Jobe, *supra* note 6.

[78] *See* VAWA 2005 §813(a)(1).

[79] *See id.* §813(a)(2).

[80] *Id.*

[81] *See Barrios v. Attorney General*, 399 F.3d 272 (3d Cir. 2005).

[82] 22 I&N Dec. 349 (BIA 1998) (*en banc*).

stances, incarceration, or lack of proper notice to rescind the removal order. The government also argued that she was barred from filing a motion to reopen to apply for adjustment of status under former INA §242B(c)(e) (now §240(b)(7)), which bars persons with *in absentia* orders from eligibility for certain forms of discretionary relief, including adjustment of status.

The Board rejected these arguments. It held that a motion to reopen and a motion to rescind were distinctive and that an *in absentia* order could be reopened pursuant to a motion to reopen without requiring the applicant to rescind the removal order first, if the alien was not contesting the finding of deportability but was instead applying for a form of relief that had not been considered previously. It also held that because the respondent had not been given proper notice of failing to appear, she was not subject to the limitations on discretionary relief under INA §242B(c)(e): The IJ could exercise discretion to consider why she failed to appear at her prior hearing.

Thus, if circumstances allow a client to choose between these two motions, be aware of the following differences in the motions, some of which are noted in *Matter of M–S–*:

(1) A motion to reopen an *in absentia* order cannot be used to challenge the finding of deportability or removability but can only present an application for relief.

(2) An automatic stay follows from filing a motion to rescind but not a motion to reopen;

(3) The standards for showing exceptional circumstances or lack of notice for a motion to rescind may or may not be more difficult than showing lack of notice of consequences for failing to appear, depending on the unique facts.

(4) Eligibility for a given form of relief may depend on whether the client had been properly notified of the consequences of failing to appear, including loss of eligibility for certain forms of relief (as specified in INA §240(b)(7) or the statute in force at that time).

GENERAL STRATEGY AND CONSIDERATIONS

Exceptions to the Strict Jurisdictional Bars

Equitable Tolling of Limitations

Though each motion has specific numerical and time bars, there are several situations in which exceptions to these bars will apply.

Some circuit courts have recognized equity-based exceptions to the strict regulatory and statutory restrictions on motions to reopen.[83] Generally, these have fallen into two categories: cases where the applicant was prevented from timely filing due to not having received correct legal advice; and cases where the basis for the deportation or removal order has been eliminated for very significant reasons.[84]

Motions to Supplement a Pending Motion

The numerical limit to motions to reopen can often be as problematic as the time limit. For example, if one motion to reopen is pending and another issue arises that would also be the subject of a motion to reopen, it is not clear how to style the second filing to properly raise the new issue.

If a motion to reopen is pending, it may be preferable to file a motion to supplement it. In *Wang v. Ashcroft*,[85] the petitioner had received a final order of deportation when he filed a motion to reopen based on his eligibility for suspension of deportation. He then filed a second motion, a motion to remand, based on his eligibility to adjust status based on his wife's employment. The Board denied both motions—the second for being an untimely motion to reopen.

On appeal to the Fifth Circuit, the petitioner did not contest the Board's decision on the first motion but he argued that his second motion should either have been construed as a supplement to the first, which was timely filed, or as a motion to remand, which was not subject to time limitations.

---

[83] *See, e.g., Jobe v. INS*, 238 F.3d 96, 100-01 (1st Cir. 2001); *Iavorski v. INS*, 232 F.3d 124, 129–135 (2d Cir. 2000); *Borges v. Gonzales*, 402 F.3d 398, 406 (3d Cir. 2005); *Scorteanu v. INS*, 339 F.3d 407, 413 (6th Cir. 2003); *Iturribaria v. INS*, 321 F.3d 889, 897 (9th Cir. 2003); *but cf. Mejia-Rodriguez v. Reno*, 178 F.3d 1139 (11th Cir. 1999), *cert. denied*, 531 U.S. 1010 (2000) (upholding 90-day limitation as not raising a constitutional concern).

[84] *See* discussion, *infra*, on ineffective assistance of counsel.

[85] 260 F.3d 448, 452 (5th Cir. 2001).

The court first rejected the argument that the motion constituted a motion to remand because it held that motions to remand could only be filed if the case had been reopened or if an appeal of the IJ's order were pending. Given that the first motion to reopen had been pending when the second motion was filed, the court found that there was no open case to remand.

Second, the court found that the motion did not constitute a supplement to the earlier motion to reopen. Although it found the argument "plausible," it rejected it on the facts, which showed that petitioner never had referred to the second motion as a supplement to the first.[86]

Joint Motions with DHS

If your client is barred on other grounds, it may be possible to file a joint motion before the Board with the cooperation of DHS that bypasses the need to meet any filing requirements.[87]

Requesting Sua Sponte Reopening

The Board may in extraordinary cases exercise its *sua sponte* powers to reopen a case.[88] In *Matter of X–G–W–,*[89] the Board granted an untimely motion to reopen because soon after the case was denied, Congress passed §601(a)(1) of the IIRAIRA,[90] which amended the definition of a "refugee" to include persons who have been subject to coercive population control policies.[91] In finding that this fundamental change in the law warranted untimely reopening, the Board stated:

> This case presents a difficult dilemma for the Board because a marked change in the refugee

law, which was meant to provide relief to individuals suffering persecution on account of coerced population control policies, is running up against a change in the regulations intended to bring finality to immigration decisions and to prevent successive and frivolous motions designed to delay deportation.

> We believe that the change in the asylum law supports reopening in this case for reasons similar to those that allow reopening to apply for asylum based on changes in country conditions in the alien's country of nationality. 8 CFR §3.2(c)(3)(ii). There is no indication that the applicant in this proceeding delayed applying for asylum or purposefully filed dilatory motions, which is what the 1996 motions regulations sought to prevent. Rather, a significant change in the immigration law made relief available to the applicant on the basis of the same asylum application he filed initially, and he has filed his motion promptly following the new developments.[92]

Of course, counsel will have to bring a case warranting reopening to the Board's attention by filing a request to the Board to exercise its *sua sponte* authority to reopen a case. We recommend that the request be made as an additional basis to reopen in any case where an exception to the jurisdictional requirements is being requested.[93]

Review After the Client Has Been Removed[94]

Filing a motion to reopen *after* your client has left the United States can be particularly difficult; generally, such motions are barred under 8 CFR

---

[86] *See also Guzman v. INS*, 318 F.3d 911, 913 (9th Cir. 2003) (holding that it was within the discretion of the Board to treat a motion to remand as something other than a barred second motion to reopen, such as a motion to supplement).

[87] *See* 8 CFR §1003.2(c)(3)(iii). *See also* Memo, Martin, General Counsel, INS, HQ COU 90/16.11-P (Dec. 23, 1997), *reprinted in* 75 No. 7 *Interpreter Releases* 259, 275, 277 (Feb. 23, 1998) (laying out factors that would lead the government to consent to reopening the case); Memo, Cooper, Gen. Counsel, HQCOU 90/16.22.1 (May 17, 2001), *reprinted in* 78 No. 27 *Interpreter Releases* 1166, 1181–84 (July 16, 2001) (same).

[88] *See* 8 CFR §1003.2(a).

[89] 22 I&N Dec. 71 (BIA 1998).

[90] Illegal Immigration Reform and Immigrant Responsibility Act of 1996, Division C of the Omnibus Appropriations Act of 1996 (H.R. 3610), Pub. L. No. 104-208, 110 Stat. 3009–689, 110 Stat. at 3009.

[91] *See* INA §101(a)(42); *Matter of X–G–W–*, 22 I&N Dec. at 72.

[92] *Id.* at 73; *Cf. Matter of G–C–L–*, 23 I&N Dec. 359 (BIA 2002); *Matter of G–D–*, 22 I&N Dec. 1132, 1136 (BIA 1999) (en banc) (finding that the Board's decision in *Matter of O–Z– & I–Z–*, 22 I&N Dec. 23 (BIA 1998), constituted an "incremental" change in the law, which did not warrant reconsideration of the case); *Matter of J–J–*, 21 I&N Dec. 976, 984 (BIA 1997).

[93] The Board has specified that the *sua sponte* authority is not intended to provide an exception allowing reopening in cases otherwise jurisdictionally barred. *Matter of J–J–*, 21 I&N Dec. 976 ("The power to reopen on our own motion is not meant to be used as a general cure for filing defects or to otherwise circumvent the regulations, where enforcing them might result in hardship."). For this reason, counsel will want to explain in the motion why *sua sponte* reopening is particularly warranted.

[94] *See* T. Hasche, "'Reopening' the Executed Removal Order," at Appendix, for hypothetical issues and analysis of review after a client has been removed.

§1003.2(d). If you client has re-entered the United States illegally, the problem is compounded. However, under Ninth Circuit and Board case law, a motion to reopen prior deportation proceedings may be filed after an alien has re-entered the United States after being deported if that deportation was pursuant to an unlawful order. Either a due process violation or gross miscarriage of justice can render the prior deportation order unlawful.[95]

But although this may provide a jurisdictional argument for reopening the case, difficult issues may remain about how to address a later unlawful entry.[96] If your client was a lawful permanent resident before removal, reopening or reconsidering the case may allow you to argue that your client should be restored to the status he or she held before the unlawful order, and that the later entry would have been authorized. However, presence in the United States could subject your client to reinstatement of removal under INA §241(a)(5), expedited removal under INA §235, administrative removal under INA §238(b), or a new removal proceeding under INA §240. Each of these has its own complications but also might be a venue in which to challenge the prior removal (or in which to appeal based on invalidity of the prior removal). These concerns are beyond the scope of this article but should be seriously considered when planning a legal strategy.

Effect on Eligibility for a Stay of Removal

Each motion may have different practical effects on your client's eligibility to have removal stayed while the motion is pending. A motion to rescind or a motion to reopen based on domestic violence may automatically stay deportation and permit your client to litigate the merits of the hearing.[97] A motion to rescind an *in absentia* deportation order will invoke an automatic stay of deportation while the case is pending before the immigration court and the Board. A similar motion to rescind an *in absentia* removal order, however, will invoke an automatic stay only until the IJ adjudicates the motion, but not while an appeal is pending before the Board.[98]

However, general motions to reopen or reconsider will *not* mandate an automatic stay of removal.[99] Instead, file a separate motion for a stay, with supporting documentation, before the Board. In some cases, deportation officers will respect these motions and upon proof of filing informally delay your client's removal. However, if removal is imminent, you may ask the Board to expedite the adjudication of your motion for a stay.[100]

Tolling the Voluntary Departure Period

An additional issue arises if your client has been granted voluntary departure but would also like to file a motion to reopen or reconsider. In *Matter of Shaar*, the Board held that filing a motion to reopen deportation proceedings does not stop the voluntary departure period from running.[101] Under INA §240B(d) (1994), any person who was granted voluntary departure but fails to timely depart faces civil penalties. These penalties include being barred for ten years from being granted cancellation of removal, adjustment of status, change of status, registry, and voluntary departure.

However, sometimes facts or legal arguments arise after voluntary departure has been granted, which may warrant filing a motion to reopen or reconsider. Often the new facts render the noncitizen eligible for a form of relief from which he or she would be barred if there is an overstay of the voluntary departure period. Because the Board rarely adjudicates motions within the brief voluntary departure period, those persons would be faced with a difficult decision under *Shaar*: whether to depart voluntarily in a timely manner (and not be subject to the bar) and thereby abandon the motion to reopen, or to litigate the motion to reopen, only to be barred from the very relief for which he or she would otherwise be eligible.[102]

---

[95] *See, e.g., Matter of Farinas*, 12 I&N Dec. 467 (BIA 1967) (requiring a showing of a gross miscarriage of justice); *Matter of Malone*, 11 I&N Dec. 730 (BIA 1966) (gross miscarriage of justice); *Hernandez-Almanza v. U.S. DOJ*, 547 F.2d 100 (9th Cir. 1976) (gross miscarriage of justice); *Mendez v. INS*, 563 F.2d 956 (9th Cir. 1977) (due process violation); *Estrada-Rosales v. INS*, 645 F.2d 819 (9th Cir. 1981) (due process violation); *Wiedersperg v. INS*, 896 F.2d 1179 (9th Cir. 1990) (due process violation).

[96] *See, e.g., Hernandez-Almanza v. U.S. DOJ*, 547 F.2d 100.

[97] *See* 8 CFR §1003.3(f); VAWA 2005 §825(a)(2)(F).

[98] *Compare* 8 CFR §1003.23(b)(4)(ii) *with* §1003.23(b)(4)(iii)(C).

[99] *See* 1003.3(f).

[100] *See BIA Practice Manual*, Ch. 6.

[101] 21 I&N Dec. 541 (BIA 1996), *aff'd*, 141 F.3d 953 (9th Cir. 1998) (upholding *Shaar* for pre-IIRAIRA cases).

[102] In such cases, persons with final orders of deportation would be in a better position than those granted voluntary departure because overstaying their removal order would not subject them to the same bars to relief under INA §240B(d) (1994). Counsel, therefore, should strongly
continued

Fortunately, some circuits have created exceptions to this *Shaar* problem.[103] Recently, in *Azarte v. Ashcroft*,[104] the Ninth Circuit found that the reasoning of *Shaar* did not apply in post-IIRAIRA cases. The *Azarte* court held that statutory changes to motions to reopen and voluntary departure created potentially conflicting terms, which was not the case when *Shaar* was decided. Thus, the court interpreted IIRAIRA to find that in cases in which the motion to reopen is filed within the voluntary departure period and stay of removal or stay of voluntary departure is requested, the voluntary departure would be tolled while the motion is pending.

Thus, while *Shaar* continues to govern deportation proceedings in circuits other than the Third, it has been modified in the Ninth, Eighth, and Third Circuits for removal cases.[105] In these circuits, it is crucial to file the motion to reopen (with the stay request, if needed) as soon as possible to preserve as much of the voluntary departure period as possible.[106]

New Criminal Issues

In filing motions, the party should state whether any new criminal proceedings have commenced against the client since the last Board action.[107] Thus, in some cases, it may be in your client's interest to postpone filing the motion until any new criminal charges have been dismissed or are otherwise concluded. The government can file a motion to reopen based on new charges for removal.[108]

Government Use of Motions to Reopen

The regulations make clear that the government also may file motions to reopen. Especially, the government may move to reopen, without any limitations, deportation or exclusion cases if it has discov-

ered fraud in the underlying proceedings, or if it believes that your client has committed a crime that would support termination of asylum.[109] The government does *not* have to file a motion to reopen to terminate a deferral of removal that has been granted under the Convention Against Torture.[110]

The government has also used motions to reopen to lodge new charges of deportability. Pursuant to 8 CFR §242.16(d), INS "may at any time during a hearing lodge additional charges of deportability, including factual allegations, against the respondent." This regulation has been held to apply to reopened proceedings.[111]

However, the government is subject to the same substantive requirements for motions to reopen. For example, in *Ramon-Sepulveda v. INS*,[112] the Ninth Circuit rejected the government's efforts to reopen a case on the grounds that it had not reasonably shown why the new evidence it proffered had not been available at the prior proceedings.

CONCLUSION

Often, a post-final order motion will be the only way to preserve your client's right to relief from removal. As is evident, the regulatory framework and case law for motions to reopen, reconsider, and rescind are constantly evolving at the Board and in the circuit courts. Thus, when strategizing in this complicated area, carefully review not only the current regulations and other statutes that might apply but also the administrative and judicial case law.

---

consider not requesting voluntary departure before the immigration court under some circumstances.

[103] *See, e.g., Barrios v. Attorney General*, 399 F.3d 272 (3d Cir. 2005) (overruling *Shaar* in the Third Circuit and finding that the proper filing of a motion to reopen constitutes an exceptional circumstance).

[104] 394 F.3d 1278 (9th Cir. 2005).

[105] *See also Sidikhouya v. Gonzales*, 407 F.3d 950 (8th Cir. 2005) (same, but not requiring a motion for a stay); *Kanivets v. Gonzales*, 424 F.3d 330 (3d Cir. 2005) (same, but not requiring a motion for a stay).

[106] For more information, see the AILF Practice Advisory, "Staying the Voluntary Departure Period When Filing a Motion to Reopen" (*amended* October 21, 2005), at *www.ailf.org*.

[107] *See* 8 CFR §1003.2(e).

[108] *See infra.*

[109] *See* 8 CFR §1003.3(c)(3)(iv); *see also* 8 CFR §§1208.24(e), (f) (applying this rule to removal proceedings and to prior grants of withholding of deportation).

[110] *See* 8 CFR §§208.17(d), 1208.17(d) (requiring only that the government file a motion before the immigration court to schedule a hearing to consider whether the deferral of removal should be reconsidered).

[111] *See, e.g., De Faria v. INS*, 13 F.3d 422, 423 (1st Cir. 1994), citing *Rosenberg v. Fleuti*, 374 U.S. 449, 450 (1963). *Cf. Matter of Guevara*, 20 I&N Dec. 238 (BIA 1991) ("in the instant case, the Service does not seek to advance additional charges of deportability, nor does it seek to advance additional factual allegations. The Service does not wish to modify its case against the respondent at all, but rather requests the opportunity to make a second effort at proving the same allegations and charge which have already been advanced unsuccessfully").

[112] 743 F.2d 1307 (9th Cir. 1984).

APPENDIX—"REOPENING" THE EXECUTED REMOVAL ORDER

by Tilman Hasche[*]

QUESTION

What do you do if your client, who is physically present in the United States, is subject to a final removal[113] order that would be subject to reopening but cannot be reopened because it has been executed by the client's departure from the United States?

FACT SCENARIO 1

Phong is a citizen of Laos. In 1990 Phong travels to the United States to visit his two sons, both of whom are lawful permanent residents, one living in Houston, one in Boston. While visiting Son #1 in Houston, Phong lives in a rooming house with several other Laotians. He applies for asylum, but his claim is denied, and legacy INS commences deportation proceedings against him. Meanwhile, Phong moves to Boston to stay with Son #2, who has just obtained U.S. citizenship. Phong and Son #2 file a one-step immediate relative /adjustment of status package with the local district office of INS. Meanwhile, INS in Houston sends an Order to Show Cause (the predecessor of today's Notice to Appear) by certified mail to Phong's Houston residence. Someone at the house signs the certified mail receipt card for the INS letter, which contains the OSC placing Phong in deportation proceedings. Phong never learns of the pending deportation proceeding, however. As a result, the immigration court in Houston enters an *in absentia* order of deportation against him. Four months after the deportation order is entered, the INS office in Boston, which is unaware of the deportation proceeding in Houston, adjusts Phong's status to that of a lawful permanent resident. In 1995, Phong travels to Canada for a wedding, executing the deportation order. On his return to the United States, he is inspected and readmitted on the basis of his Green Card. In 1999, he files for naturalization, and INS realizes that it granted his adjustment while he was subject to an outstanding, unexecuted deportation order.

FACT SCENARIO 2:

Maria is a citizen of Guatemala. In 1992, an IJ denies her asylum claim and orders her deported. She timely appeals her case to the Board. While her case is on appeal, she marries Yuri, a citizen of Russia. Yuri has an affirmative asylum application pending before legacy INS. In 1994, at his affirmative asylum interview, Yuri asks the asylum officer to "add" Maria to his case as his dependent. To do this, the asylum officer instructs him, Maria will have to dismiss her appeal. Pursuant to the asylum officer's instructions, Maria does just that, setting forth in detail the reasons for the motion. She serves copies of the motion as well as the Board's subsequent order of dismissal on the asylum officer and the INS deportation officer monitoring her file in the local INS district office. By operation of law, the dismissal of Maria's appeal renders the IJ's deportation order against her final. Nevertheless, shortly after her appeal is dismissed, INS approves Yuri's asylum claim and grants Maria derivative asylee status. Two years later, INS grants her INA §209 asylee application to adjust status and issues her a Green Card. In 1999, Maria makes a brief trip back to Guatemala for a family emergency. On her return to the United States, she is inspected and readmitted based on her Green Card. In 2004, she applies to the U.S. Citizenship and Immigration Services (USCIS) for naturalization. She passes all tests at her interview with flying colors. However, USCIS does not know what to do: The record shows she is subject to an executed order of deportation, namely, the IJ's 1992 order.

ANALYSIS

An alien who has been ordered removed remains in removal proceedings until such time as the order has been executed. Pursuant to *Matter of Vizcarra-Delgadillo*,[114] a removal proceeding may be terminated as

---

[*] **Tilman Hasche** is a shareholder with Parker, Bush & Lane, P.C. a seven-attorney law firm in Portland, Ore., with a wide-ranging immigration practice. Mr. Hasche's practice emphasizes family-based immigration, removal defense, and asylum.

[113] For purposes of this discussion the term "removal order" subsumes orders of removal under the post–IIRAIRA INA, as well as orders of deportation and orders of exclusion under the pre–IIRAIRA Act.

[114] 13 I&N Dec. 51 (BIA 1968).

"improvidently begun" even after a final order is entered. This situation may arise, for example, if the original order is entered by mistake, the legal predicate for the order is removed, or dismissal of the proceedings is consistent with a judicious exercise of prosecutorial discretion.

In *Vizcarra-Delgadillo*, for example, the alien had been ordered deported based on his having been convicted, on a plea of guilty, of aiding and abetting the alteration and possession of a false immigration document. After the deportation order was entered, the alien moved to set aside the criminal conviction on the basis that the criminal defense attorney had been ineffective. The district court denied the motion, and the Ninth Circuit affirmed.[115] The alien then filed a petition for writ of certiorari to the Supreme Court. Later, the alien entered into an agreement with the government to dismiss the appeal if the INS district director would join in a motion to terminate the deportation proceedings notwithstanding the outstanding deportation order. Although the district director filed the motion, the IJ[116] denied it. On appeal, the Board reversed and granted the motion, noting that "Even a criminal judgment of conviction affirmed on appeal may be set aside on the prosecutor's motion on the ground that the proceeding violated prosecutive policy. *Petite v. United States*, 361 U.S. 529 (1960). An administrative deportation is not entitled to greater inviolability."[117]

If an order of removal has been entered, the subsequent departure from the United States of the alien executes the order.[118] Under *Matter of Okoh*[119] and *Matter of G– y B–*,[120] once a deportation or removal order has been executed, there is nothing for the immigration court or Board of Immigration Appeals to reopen. When the order is executed, the Executive Office for Immigration Review (EOIR) loses jurisdiction over the case.

So what can Maria and Phong do? Each is subject to removal proceedings because their adjustment of status by INS was not "lawful": INS did not have jurisdiction to grant them the legal benefit they received. One solution might be to file a new one-step I-130 petition/adjustment of status application. This assumes that they have a qualifying U.S. citizen relative, *e.g.*, Phong's Son #2 or Maria's husband Yuri, provided he has obtained citizenship and is still married to Maria.

In some cases, unfortunately, the alien in this situation does not have a white knight who can provide the legal basis for a "readjustment." Then what can the alien do?

Get him- or herself placed in proceedings and move to set aside the earlier removal order on the grounds that not doing so would result in a "gross miscarriage of justice"![121]

Malone concerned a Canadian woman who had been admitted to permanent residence as a child, in 1925. In 1953 she had been deported on a legally unsupported charge of engaging in prostitution. She later reentered and was deported again for reentering after deportation without the Attorney General's consent. Illegally reentering a second time, she was again placed in deportation proceedings. There, she moved to set aside the 1953 deportation order as a "gross miscarriage of justice" and retroactively applied for permission to reenter for each illegal reentry. The IJ granted relief, finding that there had been a "gross miscarriage of justice," and the Service appealed.

The Service, pointing to judicial decisions holding that a collateral attack on a prior deportation proceeding cannot be made unless there was a lack of due process or a jurisdictional issue, contends that neither of

---

[115] *See Vizcarra-Delgadillo v. United States*, 395 F.2d 70 (9th Cir. 1968).

[116] Consistent with the law at that time, the term used in the opinion is "special inquiry officer," which is roughly equivalent to today's "immigration judge."

[117] 13 I&N Dec. at 54.

[118] INA §101(g).

[119] 20 I&N Dec. 864 (BIA 1994).

[120] 6 I&N Dec. 159 (BIA 1954).

[121] *See Matter of Malone*, 11 I&N Dec. 730 (BIA 1966); *Matter of Farinas*, 12 I&N Dec. 467 (BIA 1967); *Matter of Agdinaoay*, 16 I&N Dec. 545 (BIA 1978); *Matter of Roman*, 19 I&N Dec. 855 (BIA 1988); *Ramirez-Juarez v. INS*, 633 F.2d 174 (9th Cir. 1980); *Hernandez-Almanza v. INS*, 547 F.2d 100 (9th Cir. 1976).

these elements is present here. The short answer is that the special inquiry officer relied upon judicial and administrative authority permitting collateral attack where there has been a gross miscarriage of justice.[122]

Dismissing the Service's appeal, the Board affirmed the IJ's vacating of the 1953 deportation order and permitted the alien to apply, with *nunc pro tunc* effect, for permission to reenter for each unlawful reentry since the 1953 deportation order.

Farinas dealt with a Filipino crewman who had been deported in 1950. The deportation order entered against him was based on a reading of the law that was directly counter to Supreme Court authority at the time. Reentering unlawfully in 1966, the alien was again placed in proceedings and moved to set aside the 1950 deportation order and for *nunc pro tunc* permission to reenter. On appeal, the Board granted relief, finding that the misinterpretation of Supreme Court precedent at his 1950 deportation hearing constituted a "gross miscarriage of justice."[123]

CONCLUSION

Within the last year, the author has had two cases similar to these fact patterns. Discussions with supervisory adjudication officers at USCIS suggest that the legal problem presented—the agency's having granted permanent residence when there was an outstanding order of removal, deportation, or exclusion, so that it did not have jurisdiction to enter the order—is not uncommon. The hypotheticals offer a conceptual framework for removing an earlier removal order from an alien's record and thereby ratifying lawful permanent resident status, notwithstanding the fact that the original grant of LPR status was unlawful. By filing an I-212 in conjunction with the motion to set aside the earlier removal order, the alien will not only clean up his record but will also preserve the equities he has accumulated during his years as an alien who was unlawfully granted lawful permanent residence. All's well that ends well.

Of course, the practitioner has to be cognizant of the reinstatement provision of INA §241(a)(5) that would permit DHS to simply remove the client without a new proceeding based on the prior order. However, this caveat should not interfere with pursuing the actions outlined here in the appropriate case.

---

[122] 11 I&N Dec. at 731.

[123] 12 I&N Dec. 472.

APPEALING WORDS FOR THE BIA AND AAO

by Dagmar Butte, Martin J. Lawler, Stanley Mailman, Estelle M. McKee, and Lory D. Rosenberg[*]

INTRODUCTION

The subject is advocacy—representing a client on appeal or on certification before the Board of Immigration Appeals (BIA or Board), the Administrative Appeals Office (AAO) of the U.S. Citizenship and Immigration Services (USCIS), or USCIS service centers. Each of these forums is distinct

---

[*] **Dagmar Butte** is an elected member of AILA's Board of Governors and serves on the AILA General Counsel and Due Process Committees. She practices in all areas of immigration law with Parker, Bush & Lane in Portland, Ore. Ms. Butte has been on the faculty for the AILF Litigation Institute and has spoken at and written for AILA conferences both regionally and nationally since 1998. She also is an adjunct professor at Lewis & Clark Law School where she teaches legal writing as part of substantive international law and moot court courses.

Martin Lawler named in *Best Lawyers in America*, is recognized as an exceptional lawyer by his clients, colleagues, and others. His lectures on immigration law have included such prestigious venues as Harvard University. During his 28 years as an immigration lawyer, Mr. Lawler has authored many books, book chapters, and articles. His two-volume treatise, *Professionals: A Matter of Degree*, is the leading authoritative text on business visas and published by AILA. He is the 1996 recipient of AILA's Jack Wassermann Memorial Award honoring excellence in immigration litigation.

Stanley Mailman is a past president of AILA, and co-author of the Matthew Bender/LEXIS treatise, *Immigration Law and Procedure*. He has written on immigration law for various professional publications including the *New York Law Journal* (since 1976). He is of counsel to the New York firm of Satterlee Stephens Burke & Burke, LLP, of which he was formerly a member.

Estelle McKee is a full-time lecturer at Cornell Law School. She co-teaches the Asylum and Convention Against Torture Appellate Clinic and a first-year legal writing course. Before joining the Cornell faculty, she practiced legal services and death penalty law. She was also a pro se clerk in the Second Circuit for two years.

Lory Rosenberg is of counsel to Paparelli & Partners, LLP, where she handles complex immigration litigation, enforcement, asylum, and removal matters. She is the founder of Immigration Defense & Expert Assistance (IDEA)©, a resource for legal professionals, and she is a featured columnist for *Bender's Immigration Bulletin*. Ms. Rosenberg served as Board member on the Board of Immigration Appeals (1995–2002). She is co-author of *Immigration Law and Crimes*, and a director on the AILA Board of Governors.

from the other in its composition, the kinds of matters it adjudicates, and the format and formality of its procedures.

The main purpose of this article is to describe principles of advocacy that apply when representing clients before the BIA and AAO, and to provide specific techniques that are appropriate for each forum. To a lesser extent it also addresses those issues as they pertain to a USCIS service center. Finally, this article describes certain mistakes to avoid when advocating in each forum. Hopefully, these suggestions will assist both new and experienced counsel as they continue to represent clients before these forums, and provide some guidance for counsel to effectively advocate in each of them.

PRINCIPLES OF ADVOCACY

Generally, winning a case on appeal (or certification) is a matter of making your client's cause as sympathetic as possible, and helping the adjudicator(s) to see its virtues. Regardless of which forum they are in, advocates will usually do well in championing a client's cause if they observe certain common principles of advocacy. Those principles are described here.

- Before you start writing, develop a clear understanding of the path the appellate body must take in order to overturn the adverse decision below. That is, you should have a "theory of the appeal." The brief should illuminate the findings of fact and/or conclusions of law needed for reversal; at the same time, by telling a persuasive and sympathetic story, particularly through the statement of facts, the brief should make the BIA or AAO want to walk down that path. Every fact or comment in the brief should relate to one or both of these goals. Keep to the path throughout the brief, and be sure the path is clear to the adjudicator(s).

- If there is a simple basis on which the BIA or AAO can rule for your client, emphasize it.[1]

---

[1] *See* A. Kozinski, "The Wrong Stuff," 1992 *BYU L. Rev.* 325, 326 (1992) ("Keep in mind that simple arguments are
continued

- Understand which facts and arguments are *dispositive* (that require the adjudicator to overturn the decision) and which are *persuasive* (make the adjudicator want to overturn the decision). If you don't know why a sentence is in your brief, the adjudicator won't know either.

- Write the statement of the facts clearly, as favorably to the client's cause as the record permits, and as briefly as possible without sacrificing clarity and fairness.

- Concede what obviously needs to be conceded—graciously, not grudgingly. It's better to array your client's vulnerability yourself than to leave it to your opponent's attack. Hiding adverse facts only hurts your credibility; instead, put a positive emphasis on them. For example, rather than failing to mention your client's earlier, failed application for permanent residence, perhaps present that fact in the context of a discussion of her long and demonstrated commitment to making a permanent home here. A good statement of facts should go a long way toward kindly predisposing the reader to the client personally and to her case.

- Frame the issues simply, clearly, and as favorably to the client as possible. As we have seen in the national political arena, it is easier to win the argument when you frame the issues your way.[2]

- Write argumentative Point Headings, such as: "Respondent Should Receive Asylum Because All the Credible Evidence Shows She Will Be Persecuted," not "The Credible Evidence or The Respondent Will Be Persecuted."

- Whenever possible, use short, everyday words rather than words that slow the reader down; write in the active, not the passive, voice. A punchy style often works well for brief writers. At the same time, if a sentence is clear and goes down easily, there is nothing wrong with length itself when needed for emphasis and dramatic effect, or to make necessary qualifications. The arts of rhetoric—metaphor and other flourishes—can be effective if used to push a point home, but not to show off verbal dexterity.

- Challenge factual or legal errors but don't personally attack an adjudicator or adversary. First,

there is something unfair in attacking a trial judge or lawyer who has no role in the appeal and cannot defend herself; attack the decision, not the writer. Second, tones of anger and outrage are seldom effective and may invite a backlash. If you describe the prejudicial behavior or persistent error calmly, patiently, and one item at a time, you can make misconduct seem all the more egregious. If the situation cries for outrage, build up to it inevitably rather than embracing it enthusiastically. Indeed, an understanding tone often works well. It can be a helpful tactic, for example, to suggest sympathetically why the judge took the wrong tack, misunderstood the testimony, or failed to give enough credence to newspaper reports of persecution. In short, explain how and why the judge went wrong; give the judge the benefit of the doubt rather than painting him as an ignorant bigot. After all, the government's trial lawyer and the immigration judge are part of the same government family as BIA members, face many of the same frustrations, and are subject to many of the same fears.[3] And they may be next-door neighbors.

- Ordinarily you would put the strongest arguments up front. However, if your case is complex and hard to digest, or controversial and liable to provoke the reader's resistance, it may be better to lead off with points.

STYLE

Whether your submission is an appellate brief or a response to a request for evidence (RFE), its style can have significant impact upon whether the case is ultimately successful. Some lawyers, especially young ones, seem to think that they do not sound sufficiently "lawyerlike" if they eschew words such as "heretofore," "henceforward," "thusly," "hereinabove," and the like. In fact, there is anecdotal evidence that clients think they are being short-changed by their high-priced lawyers if a brief is too simple and easy to follow and does not contain words that sound as if they leapt off the page of an 18th-century novel. However, there are plenty of $40 words in the English language to

---

winning arguments; convoluted arguments are sleeping pills on paper.").

[2] *See* G. Lakoff, *Moral Politics: How Liberals and Conservatives Think* (2nd ed. 2002).

[3] *See* S. Legomsky, "Deportation and the War on Independence," 91 *Cornell L. Rev.* 369, 370 (2006) (arguing among other things how the current national administration has conducted an "all-out war on the very notion of decisional independence in the adjudication of immigration cases").

make a writer sound knowledgeable without resort to antiquated legal terms that add nothing to the substance of the argument.

The key thing to remember is that a written submission in any legal proceeding must, above all, be persuasive. Simple, clear, and direct writing is always more persuasive than dense, complex writing. Sending the adjudicator rushing to the dictionary to see what a word means or evoking images of Jane Austen characters in a Regency drawing room is counter-productive.

The appendix to this article provides some practical guidelines that you can use to produce effective, compelling legal writing.

APPEALS TO THE BIA

In almost every case, the BIA's jurisdiction arises from an appeal or certification of a decision below. That decision, most often by an immigration judge, usually resolves a removal proceeding, but the BIA also reviews a service center's decisions on family-based visa petitions, and sometimes other matters, such as proceedings on fines or penalties.

What sets the BIA apart from the AAO, particularly in reviewing decisions in removal proceedings, is that it resembles an appellate court. For example, the issues for decision are ordinarily limited to the four corners of the record below. The BIA rarely takes oral argument, but when it does, a three-member panel appears in judicial black robes. (Note, however, that most cases are assigned to a single member who is authorized to affirm without opinion, issue a brief order, or refer the appeal to a panel.) What is at stake in a case before the BIA is often graver than the usual matter at issue before the other two forums: whether an individual should be removed from the United States, perhaps after living here most of one's life, or face persecution in the country of deportation. These considerations suggest a solemnity and a formality of presentation usually absent in arguing cases to the AAO or to the USCIS service centers. Each case deserves its own strategy and a tone appropriate to that strategy.[4]

---

[4] The BIA provides guidelines and requirements for counsel in the *BIA Practice Manual* (*Practice Manual*) (2004), at *www.usdoj.gov/eoir/bia/qapracmanual/BIA_Practice_Man _FullVer.pdf*. Also available in a bound copy from AILA Publications at *www.ailapubs.org*. These guidelines are the equivalent of local court rules, and no practitioner should *continued*

BIA Appeal Advocacy

Preparation for an appeal to the BIA starts long before the immigration judge has issued a decision denying relief or ordering removal. From the start, counsel should investigate and verify the charges, examine and explore the individual facts, determine whether the respondent is eligible for any form of relief from removal, and develop a theory of the case that directs his or her presentation of the case before the immigration judge. The specific facts and all related issues, including points to be raised in anticipation of possible appeal, must be brought out and included in the record made in the hearing before the immigration judge.

Theory of the Case

An effective "theory of the case" should be founded on existing BIA precedent opinions, applicable circuit court rulings, and proposed legal interpretations of the governing statutes and regulations that accommodate the particular facts and details of a case. Imagine, for example, this hypothetical case:

A respondent has been living in Los Pasos, Texizona, since he arrived as a visitor from Syria in August 1985 at age 10. He stayed with relatives, got his driver's license in 1993, and graduated from high school in June 1994. He was a bit of a "hot dog" during his youth and was arrested for DUI in April 1994, in December 1994, and again in August 1995.

The first two times, he was convicted and placed on probation. At the time of the third arrest, his driver's license was suspended while the charges were pending, and that led to his January 1996 arrest for operating a vehicle on a suspended license, because he had to get his Colombian girlfriend to the hospital to give birth to their twins. One month later, these last two cases were consolidated, and the respondent was convicted and sentenced to five years, suspended, with ten years probation.

In the 10 years since his kids were born, the respondent has stopped drinking, held a steady job to support his family, married his girlfriend, had another set of twins, began taking the children both to the mosque and to church, and has become a more careful driver. Just as he successfully completed probation, his situation came to

---

attempt to advocate before the BIA without first becoming familiar with them.

the attention of the immigration authorities, and he was apprehended and placed in removal proceedings.

Given these facts and the existing legal authority, the theory of the case might be:

The respondent is eligible to apply for and can satisfy the "extreme and exceptionally unusual hardship" standard for cancellation of removal under INA §240A(b), based on evidence establishing his role as the sole provider for his family, the significance of his parenting, the adverse country conditions in both Syria and Colombia, the oppressive religious climate for Christians in Syria, and other factors that would cause all four children to experience extreme and exceptionally unusual hardship whether they accompany him to Syria, try to go to Colombia, or remain in the United States without him.

The theory should also address obvious counter-arguments:

Although the respondent overstayed the period of his admission as a visitor and has a record of DUIs, a simple DUI is not a crime involving moral turpitude and would not render the respondent inadmissible or deportable under INA §240A(d)(1). The respondent committed the crime of driving on a suspended license and received a five-year sentence for two crimes only after the passage of more than 10 years of continuous physical presence from the time of his original admission.[5] He can also demonstrate good moral character for a 10-year period dating back from his hearing in 2006 to January 1996.[6]

Evidence and Findings of Fact

As a matter of prudent practice, as well as in anticipation of appeal, the record made in the hearing before the immigration judge should include all of the legal issues and evidentiary factors that could have a bearing on the outcome of the case.[7] First, under the 2002 Procedural Reforms to Improve Case Management ("streamlining") regulations,[8] the

Board cannot entertain new evidence on appeal and is precluded from making factual findings.[9] The Board must accept an immigration judge's findings of fact, including credibility findings, as conclusive, unless those findings are clearly erroneous.[10] If the findings are found to be clearly erroneous, the case must be remanded to the immigration judge.

Accordingly, to avoid a piecemeal adjudication or, at best, a remand, counsel should present all of the pertinent evidence that is discoverable and available, and encourage the immigration judge to make factual findings on all of the evidence presented. This can be done by making an oral request on the record or by submitting a motion containing proposed findings of fact. If the immigration judge does not permit a witness to appear, cuts off testimony on a particular subject, or refuses to mark or admit a document as an exhibit, it is prudent to make an offer of proof, on the record, indicating the expected content of the testimony or listing the documents that are offered. The proposed evidence, under cover of a written offer of proof, should be submitted with the request that it be included in the record for purposes of appeal.[11] (This important point of establishing and preserving the record in immigration court is also discussed in the article by J. Montag and S. Chea, "The Immigration Judge War," included in this *Handbook*.)

Exhaustion of Remedies

A respondent must exhaust administrative remedies by raising claims before the immigration judge and appealing them to the BIA. The INA expressly restricts judicial review to cases in which "the alien has exhausted all administrative remedies available to the alien as of right."[12] This statutory jurisdictional requirement is applied strictly. The purpose of the exhaustion requirement is to "ensure that the INS, as the agency responsible for construing and applying the immigration laws and implementing

---

[5] *See Matter of Cisneros-Gonzalez*, 23 I&N Dec. 668 (BIA 2000).

[6] *See Matter of Ortega-Cabrera*, 23 I&N Dec. 793 (BIA 2005).

[7] *See, e.g.*, INA §240(c); 8 CFR §1240.9.

[8] Board of Immigration Appeals: Procedural Reforms to Improve Case Management, 67 Fed. Reg. 54, 878 (Aug. 26, *continued*

2002, eff. Sept. 25, 2002). These regulations are now codified at 8 CFR Parts 1003 and 1280.

[9] *See Matter of S–H–*, 23 I&N Dec. 462, 463–64 (BIA 2002) (acknowledging the loss of the BIA's *de novo* review authority in relation to credibility and other factual findings).

[10] 8 CFR §1003.1(d)(3).

[11] If compliance with local filing rules is not possible or is excusable, an attorney should provide an explanation accompanied by the reasons that the interests of justice favor the documents or affidavits being allowed.

[12] INA §242(d)(1).

regulations, has had a full opportunity to consider a petitioner's claims."[13] For example, in *Abdulrahman v. Ashcroft*,[14] the Third Circuit insisted on exhaustion as to "each claim or ground for relief if he or she is to preserve the right of judicial review of that claim." Similarly, the Sixth Circuit has held that "only claims properly presented to the BIA and considered on their merits can be reviewed by this court in an immigration appeal."[15] Although some courts have acknowledged an exception to exhaustion in the case of constitutional claims that the agency cannot address, jurisdiction does not extend to "due process claims based on correctable procedural errors unless the alien raised them below."[16]

Theory of the Appeal

The "theory of the appeal" often differs from the theory of the case by its focus on BIA jurisdiction and the standard of review that the BIA is authorized to exercise. As an appellate body, and because the regulations prohibit the BIA from engaging in review of an immigration judge's factual findings other than for clear error, the BIA principally is concerned with questions of law and the review of discretionary decisions made by immigration judges, over which it exercises de novo review authority.[17]

To continue the hypothetical given above, suppose that at a May 2006 removal hearing, the immigration judge ruled that the respondent was subject to removal as charged for failing to maintain a lawful status under INA §237(a)(1)(C). The immigration judge then pretermitted the respondent's application for cancellation of removal under INA §240A(b), finding that the respondent's crimes, considered together, prevented him from accruing 10 years of continuous physical presence, rendering him ineligible for cancellation of removal.

Given such a ruling, the theory of the appeal would rest entirely on a legal challenge and be argued this way:

The immigration judge erred as a matter of law in denying the respondent an opportunity to apply for cancellation of removal, by failing to properly apply Board precedent,[18] and by misreading the "stop-time" rule in the statute, because:

(1) a simple DUI conviction is not a crime involving moral turpitude,[19] even if the offense is repeated;

(2) a conviction for driving on a suspended license is not a crime involving moral turpitude, because the statute contains no *mens rea* element, it can be committed by a driver who has no knowledge his license was suspended, and suspension of a license can result from a late registration payment or outstanding tickets, as well as a pending DUI charge;[20] and,

(3) building on the BIA decision in *Matter of Deandra-Romos*,[21] where a first crime involving moral turpitude offense qualifying under the "petty offense" exception of INA §212(a)(2)(A)(ii)(II) did not "stop time" despite being followed by a second conviction, after the accrual of the requisite time,

(a) the respondent should continue to accrue physical presence time and can qualify for cancellation unless he is rendered inadmissible under INA §212(a)(2)(B) as the result of multiple convictions that have an aggregate sentence of more than five years within the qualifying time period; and,

(b) the respondent can establish the requisite period of physical presence *even if* the offense of driving on a suspended license is determined to be a crime involving moral turpitude, where that offense was committed *after* the qualifying time period.

---

[13] *Theodoropoulos v. INS*, 358 F.3d 162, 171 (2d Cir. 2004); *see also Sun v. Ashcroft*, 370 F.3d 932, 940 (9th Cir. 2004) (ruling that exhaustion will "avoid premature interference with the agency's processes"); *Dokic v. INS*, 899 F.2d 530, 532 (6th Cir. 1990) (ruling that exhaustion "allow[s] the BIA to compile a record which is adequate for judicial review").

[14] 330 F. 3d 587, 595 (3d. Cir. 2003).

[15] *Ramani v. Ashcroft*, 378 F.3d 554, 560 (6th Cir. 2004). *But see Zhang v. Ashcroft*, 388 F.3d 713, 721 (9th Cir. 2004) (holding that "Zhang's request [for reversal] was sufficient to put the BIA on notice that he was challenging the IJ's Convention determination, and the agency had an opportunity to pass on this issue"); *Ladha v. INS*, 215 F.3d 889, 903 (9th Cir. 2000) (holding, in turn, that petitioners exhausted claim by raising it in their notice of appeal, even though it was not discussed in the briefs before the BIA).

[16] *Barron v. Ashcroft*, 358 F.3d 674, 678 (9th Cir. 2004) (citing *Agyeman v. INS*, 296 F.3d 871, 877 (9th Cir. 2002)).

[17] 8 CFR §1003.1(d)(3).

[18] The BIA is bound to follow its own precedent. 8 CFR §1003.1(g).

[19] *Matter of Torres-Varela*, 23 I&N Dec. 78 (BIA 2002).

[20] *See Matter of Lopez-Meza*, 22 I&N Dec. 1188 (BIA 1999).

[21] 23 I&N Dec. 597 (BIA 2003).

The five-year sentence for the consolidated crimes was not imposed until the respondent had committed an offense in January 1996, after the respondent had accrued 10 years of physical presence as of August 1995. Accordingly, he was not subject to termination of physical presence under INA §240A(d)(1), despite the fact he had more than two convictions prior to August 1995, and his last conviction was consolidated with an August 1995 DUI. Although *Matter of Deandra-Romos*[22] addressed a different statutory section, the BIA precedent provides persuasive guidance and should be followed. Moreover, because none of the criminal offenses was committed within the past 10 years and there is no statutory bar to good moral character, the immigration judge should have engaged in a discretionary weighing of the respondent's good moral character under INA §101(f).

The theory of the appeal in this example provides the path that counsel wants the BIA to follow in adjudicating the appeal, and that path points directly to remand to permit the respondent to apply for cancellation of removal.

Practical Considerations

Counsel must be prepared to provide the immigration judge and the BIA with the legal authority that supports the respondent's defense to the removal charges and the respondent's claim of eligibility for discretionary relief—not only to prevail in the hearing before the immigration judge or to construct a coherent appellate record but as a way to punctuate the persuasive force of the testimonial and documentary evidence. In many cases, counsel should consider submitting the legal authority as an exhibit during the hearing or addressing it in a trial brief. This approach can only help the immigration judge reach a favorable decision by underscoring the authority that the BIA will undoubtedly refer to in deciding any appeal.

Counsel should bear in mind the volume of appeals that come to the Board, and be aware that each week the attorney-advisor staff and Board members review hundreds of records, address multiple issues, and apply hundreds of administrative and federal precedents. An appeal raising a common issue governed by controlling law may not require a lengthy discussion if accompanied by citations to precedent or regulations that cover each dispositive point. An appeal that raises multiple issues or contains an extremely complicated factual or procedural pattern will benefit from simplification and logical organization. In some cases, including actual quotations from portions of the transcript can be quite helpful if they are brief and precisely illustrate a specific point in the appeal. In other cases, providing a chronology or an annotated list of documents in the record is very useful and can create the "path" that counsel wishes the BIA to follow.

The Notice of Appeal

BIA advocacy begins with preparation of the Notice of Appeal (NOA). The NOA presents an opportunity to avoid both summary dismissal and summary affirmance under the regulations.

The NOA is the respondent-appellant's first contact with the BIA. It initiates the appellate process and offers your first chance to articulate the theory of the appeal, such as the three-point, one-paragraph theory of appeal developed for the hypothetical case above. The NOA should serve as an outline of the substantive bases for challenging the immigration judge's opinion, and an introduction to the topics that will be addressed more fully in the respondent's brief on appeal. Although the NOA is a pre-printed form, the respondent is not limited to the space provided for indicating the reasons for appeal, and may attach additional sheets of paper. To comply with future judicial-exhaustion requirements, it is critical that your NOA assert every claim or issue capable of being raised on appeal to the BIA, to the extent it is possible to do so without the benefit of a transcript, including a transcription of the immigration judge's oral opinion.

In the event that counsel did not represent the respondent before the immigration judge, it is critical to listen to the tape of the hearing. Counsel also must review the administrative record, which in many districts must be obtained through a FOIA request, to ascertain that it is complete and accurate with respect to such matters as whether the hearing was properly conducted, the documents submitted by the respondent were entered into the record, the respondent and witnesses were understood, the tape was properly transcribed, respondent's prior counsel was effective, and the immigration judge's decision accurately reflects the evidence in the record.

Summary Dismissal Factors

Summary dismissal is a form of discretionary regulatory authority used to terminate an appeal to the BIA. The regulations require that the party taking the appeal identify the reasons for the appeal in

---

[22] *Id.*

order to avoid getting a summary dismissal pursuant to 8 CFR §1003.1(d)(2)(i).[23] In addition, an appeal may be dismissed if a party indicates in the NOA that a brief will be filed in support of the appeal but then fails to file a brief.[24]

In *Matter of Valencia*,[25] the BIA outlined the specificity required to avoid summary dismissal, stating that it is "insufficient to merely assert that the immigration judge improperly found that deportability had been established," and that if "eligibility for discretionary relief is at issue, it should be stated whether the error relates to grounds of statutory eligibility or to the exercise of discretion . . . [and] . . . should be clear whether the alleged impropriety in the decision lies with the immigration judge's interpretation of the facts or his application of legal standards."[26] The BIA continued, "Where a question of law is presented, supporting authority should be included, and where the dispute is on the facts, there should be a discussion of the particular details contested."[27] Thus, the NOA must specifically identify the findings of fact, or the conclusions of law, or both, that are being challenged, and differentiate and discuss the inappropriate aspects of the decision.[28]

Summary Affirmance Factors

Summary affirmance is a form of mandatory regulatory authority used to affirm the decision of the immigration judge.[29] Under 8 CFR §1003.1(e)(4)(ii), the streamlining regulations require affirmance using a uniform order containing specific boilerplate language if a single Board member determines that:

- the immigration judge's decision was correct;
- any errors were harmless or nonmaterial; and that

----

[23] *See also Practice Manual*, *supra* note 5, ch. 4.16(b) (failure to specify grounds for appeal).

[24] *See id.* chs. 4.7(e) (decision not to file a brief), 4.16 (summary dismissal).

[25] 19 I&N Dec. 354, 355 (BIA 1986).

[26] *Id.*

[27] *Id.*

[28] Some circuit courts have found these requirements to violate due process in certain circumstances. *See, e.g., Vargas-Garcia v. INS*, 287 F.3d 882, 885 (9th Cir. 2002) (involving a pro se petitioner); *Castillo-Manzanarez v. INS*, 65 F.3d 793, 796 (9th Cir. 1995) (involving a petitioner with language difficulties).

[29] 8 CFR §1003.1(e)(4).

- the issues on appeal are squarely controlled by existing Board or federal court precedent and do not involve the application of precedent to a novel factual situation; or

- the factual and legal issues raised on appeal are not so substantial that the case warrants the issuance of a written opinion.[30]

Draft Language and Checklist

All NOAs should track the regulations and governing standards. To avoid summary dismissal, summary affirmance, or one-member review, counsel might consider adapting and enlarging upon the portions of the following text for an NOA in which it is appropriate:

I. The appeal should not be dismissed summarily under 8 CFR §1003.1(d)(2)(i) because under (d)(2)(i),

(A) the appellant *does* specify the reasons for appeal below; and under

(B) the reason for appeal *does not* involve a finding of fact or conclusion of law that was conceded below, *or,* such concession was unknowing and involuntary because [*state reasons*]; and under

(C) the order *did not* grant the requested relief because [*state reasons*];* * * and under

(E) if so indicated, a timely brief will be filed.

None of the other grounds for summary dismissal apply, and summary dismissal of this appeal is not warranted as a matter of discretion.

II. The appeal should not be affirmed summarily under 8 CFR§1003.1(e)(4) because the immigration judge's decision is not correct because he [*state reasons*], and under (i) there are "errors in the decision [that] are not harmless or nonmaterial" because [*state reasons*]; and under (e)(4)(i)

(A) the issues are [*state issues*], and they are not controlled squarely by existing BIA or federal precedent; and

(B) the factual and legal issues *are* substantial and *do* warrant a written opinion, because [*state reasons*]. *Cf.* 8 CFR §1003.1(e)(4); and

III. Three-member BIA review is warranted under 8 CFR §1003.1(e)(6) because of [*state reasons*], which reflect the need to [*select one or more as applicable*]:

----

[30] 8 CFR §1003.1(e)(4)(i).

(i) settle inconsistencies between the rulings of different immigration judges;

(ii) establish a precedent to clarify ambiguous laws, regulations, or procedures;

(iii) correct a decision by an IJ or the INS that is plainly not in conformity with the law or with applicable precedents;

(iv) resolve a case or controversy of major national import; or

(v) correct a clearly erroneous factual determination by an IJ.

In completing the NOA, counsel should follow five essential practice mandates that can make or break an appeal to the BIA:

- Raise every finding, aspect of the hearing, and legal issue with specificity—to insure review and exhaust administrative remedies.

- Assert that the immigration judge's decision is incorrect, the errors not harmless, the issues not squarely controlled by precedent, and not insubstantial—to avoid one-member review.

- Identify the specific factual or legal bases why the case is novel or complex and requires a consistent ruling—to warrant three-member review.

- Satisfy all requirements for timely filing and service on the opposing party.

- Commit to briefing the appeal, request a one-time extension within the briefing deadline if needed, or notify the BIA if a promised brief will not be filed.

The *BIA Practice Manual* recommends that appellate briefs contain the following sections: a concise statement of facts and procedural history of the case, a statement of issues, the standard of review, a summary of the argument and the argument itself, and a short conclusion stating the precise relief or remedy sought.[31] Following are descriptions of how to use these sections to advocate in your brief:

Statement of Facts

The Statement of Facts has two purposes: to educate the adjudicator about the issues on appeal and to persuade the adjudicator that the facts in this particular case compel only one sound outcome.[32] An advocate must accomplish both of these goals as

succinctly as possible, because the BIA's case load is staggering.[33] The BIA is so concerned with efficiency that its own *Practice Manual*, in two locations, encourages parties to limit their briefs to 25 pages.[34] At the same time, an advocate must persuade the adjudicator to slow down and pay close attention to the advocate's specific appeal. The BIA has narrow subject matter jurisdiction, and each adjudicator has likely seen thousands of appeals similar to yours. Do not let the adjudicator skim the Statement of Facts. Educate the judge by interesting him or her in your client's story, and persuade him or her by causing him or her to believe you. Following are a few techniques to accomplish these goals:

Educate

- *Every fact you refer to elsewhere in your brief must also appear in your statement of facts.* Do not surprise the adjudicator later with a new fact in the Argument. Instead, include that fact in your Statement of Facts so that it is emotionally persuasive before it is legally persuasive. In addition, summarize the relevant portions of the immigration judge's conclusions, reasoning, and findings of fact. Do so fairly, without slanting the decision. Do not make the adjudicator find the opinion and hunt for the portions that you are challenging.

- *Encourage the adjudicator to believe your facts by citing to the record.* Refer the adjudicator to specific pages of the transcripts, exhibits, or opinion so that he or she can verify your facts. Where the record is voluminous, attach significant factual sources to the back of your brief and highlight the relevant passages.[35]

- *Do not misstate or omit relevant facts.* Although you can use the persuasive techniques described below, do not sacrifice the integrity of your brief by using the Statement of Facts to characterize

---

[31] *Practice Manual, supra* note 5, ch. 4.6(c)(iv).

[32] *See id.*

[33] *See* "Attorney General Issues Final Rule Reforming Board of Immigration Appeals Procedures," Press Release, Dep't of Justice (Aug. 23, 2002) (noting that before the streamlining regulations the BIA was processing over 5,000 appeals per month). As of October 2004, the BIA had a backlog of 33,000 cases. S. Mailman & S. Yale-Loehr, "Immigration Appeals Overwhelm Federal Courts," *N.Y.L.J.* 3 (Dec. 27, 2004).

[34] *Practice Manual, supra* note 5, chs. 4.6(b), 3.33(i)(C)(iii). Although such limits are not always possible, counsel should strive to keep the brief concise.

[35] *See id.*, ch. 3.3(e)(iii).

facts or engage in legal argument. Avoid heavy-handed adjectives and adverbs in favor of details and vivid verbs to emphasize facts. For example, instead of "A military officer brutally beat Mr. X with his rifle," try "A military officer shoved the butt of his rifle into Mr. X's face, breaking several of Mr. X's teeth." Also include negative facts, minimizing them by using the techniques outlined below.

Persuade

- *Write your facts only after deciding on your theory of appeal (the path the BIA should take to overturn or affirm the decision).* Your theory of appeal should tie all of your arguments together and focus the adjudicator on the "big idea" of how justice requires a decision for your client.[36] This theory dictates which facts are positive and which facts you must overcome.

- *Organize your Statement of Facts to highlight positive facts and minimize negative facts.* Start with your most positive facts so that the adjudicator can absorb them while he or she is still fresh. Typically, advocates fall back on chronology as the default organizational scheme. Catch the adjudicator's attention by instead starting with a particularly compelling scene, filling in background facts as necessary to acquaint the adjudicator with your case. For example, where persecution is at issue, begin with the scene of the persecution taking place. Alternatively, if your facts are complex, begin your Statement of Facts with a paragraph that provides an overview of your client's story. Do not start out by boring the adjudicator with procedural history unless your case hinges on that.

  After the initial scene or overview paragraph, the facts should then proceed chronologically, by subject matter, or according to some consciously chosen over-arching organizational scheme. Topic headings can also help organize the facts so that they are easier to understand.

  Minimize negative facts by sandwiching them between positive facts, so that you neither begin

nor end with a negative fact. Bury negative facts in subordinate clauses (beginning with "although," "even though," and similar marker words) and juxtapose them with positive facts. For instance, an advocate who argues that the Turkish government acquiesces to torture through the use of unmodified ECT (electroconvulsive therapy without anesthesia) must deal with the negative fact that Turkey has denounced unmodified ECT and created a "state of the art" ECT Center in which to use ECT with anesthesia. Relying on a report by Mental Disability Rights International (MDRI) as the source of both positive and negative facts, an advocate could minimize the negative facts as follows:

  According to MDRI, the use of unmodified ECT is common in Turkish state mental hospitals. (Exh. 3 at 1). Although Turkey announced to the European Union that it would try to stop the use of unmodified ECT, the doctors MDRI interviewed in state mental hospitals did not know that Turkey had made such an announcement. (Exh. 3 at 5). Turkey also assured the European Union that it could administer anesthesia with ECT using its "state of the art" ECT center and neurosurgery department at Bakirkoy State Hospital (Exh. 3 at 4), but doctors there still administer ECT on the patients' ward without anesthesia (Exh. 3 at 6). To date, Turkey has not passed any laws banning or even limiting the use of unmodified ECT. (Exh. 3 at 8).

- *Keep your facts simple and omit all detail outside the focus of your theory.* Reserve your use of detail, including quotes, to emphasize strong and relevant facts. Do not dwell on details that are legally irrelevant, even if they are emotionally compelling. Otherwise, your adjudicator will begin to doubt whether you understand what the legal issues are and whether you really have sufficient facts to support your arguments. For example, if the immigration judge ruled against your client because she believed that doctors did not specifically intend the severe pain and suffering caused by unmodified ECT, then overcoming that point should be the focus of your appeal. Do not dwell on the details establishing how ECT causes broken bones, amnesia, and fear—these facts establish that ECT causes severe pain and suffering, but not the specific intent to inflict it. Instead, use details such as the following quote: "According to the Chief of Bakirkoy's ECT Cen-

---

[36] *See* S. Stark, *Writing to Win* 64 (Broadway Books 1999). Karl Llewellyn states that a brief should concentrate its fire: "Even three points, or two, can prove troublesome as dividers of attention unless a way can be found to make them subpoints of a single simple line of attack…" K. Llewellyn, *The Common Law Tradition: Deciding Appeals* 239 (Wm. Hein & Co. 1960).

ter, 'Patients with major depression feel that they need to be punished. If we use anesthesia the ECT won't be as effective because they won't feel punished.'" You could even start your Statement of Facts with that particular quote. In particular, use quotes from the transcript with due-process claims, such as adjudicator bias. Do not make the adjudicator flip back and forth through the record.

Supplementary Parts of the Submission

The supplementary portions of your brief are the Statement of Issues (also known as the "Questions Presented"), the Index of Authority, and the Table of Contents. Each of these sections represents another opportunity to persuade.

Statement of Issues

The important issues should be phrased as questions that suggest within them the desired result. This is one of the few times that a leading question is the optimum end-product in a legal argument.

Index of Authorities

This section should be clear, should pin-point the location of the authority in the body of the brief, and be organized visually in a way that is easy to read. It should be divided into categories to indicate the different types of authority that you relied on in the body of the submission. This gives the adjudicator an idea of where the argument is headed and where to find any authority that the adjudicator may be particularly concerned about or interested in.

Table of Contents

Here you should reproduce the various section headings verbatim and you should make sure that each heading provides the adjudicator with information about that section and suggests within it the desired result. For example, consider this heading:

THE LEGAL STANDARD FOR ASYLUM

It is much less effective and useful than this point heading:

RESPONDENT QUALIFIES FOR ASYLUM BECAUSE HE HAS SHOWN A CREDIBLE FEAR OF PERSECUTION BASED ON HIS RELIGION

If the headings are clear and communicate the objective of the submission, they will not only aid the adjudicator in parsing the submission but will also help in the writing of the Summary of the Argument.

Together, the point headings and subheadings should provide a roadmap of your arguments. The point headings should generally assert the relief you seek and each independent ground for relief. The subheadings should be more specific: include both the legal conclusion that you want the BIA to adopt and brief reasoning based on the facts of your case. Consider, for example, this subheading:

The current government of Laos will more likely than not torture Respondent Y.

This subheading is more informative and persuasive:

The current government of Laos will more likely than not torture Respondent Y because he and his brother, the vice-president of Amnesty International, continue to publicly protest the actions of the current Laotian government.

Summary of the Argument

The Summary of the Argument is a part of the written submission, irrespective of the forum, that is too often ignored or given short shrift. Given that tribunals are notoriously overburdened, this is the one section—in addition to the facts—that you can rely on the adjudicator to read. Even the most overworked adjudicator has time to carefully read a three-page summary, but may find it more difficult to give equally close scrutiny to the 25 pages that follow.

With this in mind, the summary should be something more than a mere restatement of the various subheadings of the brief. It should be written only after the final submission has been completed and edited. It should be concise and direct. This is the first step in fulfilling the old maxim (to be revisited later in this article): "Tell 'em what you're going to tell 'em, tell 'em, then tell 'em what you told 'em." You should clearly lay out each principal argument, the main authority that will be relied on in support of the argument, the manner in which that authority leads to the requested result, and the result. This is a chance to prime the adjudicator for what is to come and set up the proper frame of mind to ensure that the decision maker is receptive to the arguments that follow.

If the submission is some sort of response or reply brief, the Summary of the Argument should also include refutation of the other side's argument when appropriate. You should be careful that it is in fact a refutation rather than a restatement of the opposing position, and should clearly negate any particularly devastating or effective arguments raised by the other side by pointing to the authority and reasoning that compels the contrary result.

The Argument: Organization

When organizing your Summary of the Argument, keep in mind the goals of educating and persuading the adjudicator in the most efficient way possible. The following are a few techniques to accomplish these goals:

▪ *An appellant's first argument should explain to the BIA screening panel why the appeal requires review by three members and should not be affirmed without opinion by a single member.* This section may be omitted from the brief if it appears in the NOA, as described above. This portion of the argument should specifically address why the appeal meets at least one of the six regulatory requirements for review by the three-member panel and why it does not meet the requirements for affirmance without opinion.[37]

▪ *Raise your strongest arguments first, and only address counter-arguments afterwards.* Present the strongest arguments that support your theory first, so that they stand out and the adjudicator can more easily remember them. The exception to this rule is a threshold argument, such as a jurisdictional argument, or an argument that is especially controversial. Always raise your own arguments before resolving counter-arguments so that you, and not the government, set the terms of the debate.[38] The government's story should never be the focal point of your brief.

▪ *State the premise of each argument at the beginning.* Do not wait until the end of the argument to state the conclusion you want the adjudicator to adopt. Just as a person would not get on a bus without knowing where it is going, your adjudicator will not want to wade through a lot of reasoning without knowing where it leads.

▪ *Organize the law from broad to narrow rules.* Briefly present broad, statutory law before moving to narrower regulatory law and case-defined legal definitions. The adjudicator must understand the foundation of your arguments before you launch into them. For example, provide the statutory definition of asylum before you address the regulatory meaning of "on account of" and the case law defining "particular social group." In addition, always provide law *before* applying it to your specific facts. However, there is no need to dwell on well-known background law—your adjudicator will be an expert in this area.

▪ *Cite mandatory authority first.* Where possible, always cite decisions of the BIA, the Supreme Court, and the court of appeals in the circuit that oversees the immigration court from which you are appealing. Do not move to persuasive authority, such as federal district court cases or federal appellate cases outside your circuit, except when (1) no mandatory authority exists, (2) you are arguing that the BIA should reverse its prior stance (and your federal circuit court has not passed on the issue), or (3) your facts are similar to a helpful persuasive case that applies equivalent law (and even then, also include mandatory authority if it exists). If you must rely on unpublished opinions that are not easily accessible, attach them to your brief.[39]

The Argument: Substance

There are a number of tips that will improve the substance of your written submission and make everything you write clearer and more persuasive:

▪ *Connect the law and facts to the basic premise.* You must connect every legal principle you cite to the facts of your case and compare and contrast the two to reach the desired result. After you have done that with narrow sub-points, you must be sure to connect these narrow sub-points to the broader main premises of your argument.

▪ *Do not argue by assertion.* Many legal writers state a legal rule and then, without analysis, simply state that their client satisfies the rule and should therefore win. This is sometimes called "argument by assertion," and it is never persuasive. You should always analyze why a rule does or does not govern the facts of your case before concluding that your case does or does not satisfy the rule.

▪ *Do not assume the reader knows your issue as well as you do.* This is a common trap for the advocate who knows her case too well. Always make sure you have built a proper foundation for your argument by clearly laying out the legal principles that underlie your ultimate conclusions. Do not skip intermediate steps. For those who remember high school geometry: you have to show all your work and cannot leave out a part of the proof. One good mantra in this context is

---

[37] See text accompanying notes 29–31.

[38] *See* Stark, *supra* note 36, at 126.

[39] *Practice Manual, supra* note 5, ch. 1.4(d)(iii).

to write everything in such a way that a reader who knows nothing about your subject matter could not only understand your argument but would reach the same result that you want the adjudicator to reach. You might even want to try having your spouse or a friend read your (redacted) work to see if it is clear and persuasive. (In the latter case, you should offer an appropriate inducement, reward, or bribe.)

- *Phrase the issues presented in an affirmative manner*. Do not forget that the brief is a piece of advocacy, as opposed to a law review article. Structure your sentences in such a way that they compel the result you want even if, theoretically, there could be other results.

- *Never engage in intellectual or factual dishonesty*. No explanation needed—if you're caught, you're dead!

- *Do not flesh out counter-arguments*. Let the other side do that. At the same time, do not ignore them. Instead, devote your energies to resolving them in your client's favor.

- *Have a unified "theory of the appeal."* Develop a theory that ties all your arguments together. As discussed above, your theory will be based on an understanding of the path the BIA must take in order to overturn the adverse decision below. The theory should govern what themes you want to emphasize and the labels you use. For example, is your client the "alien," the "asylum applicant," the "Respondent," or "Ms. Uzuner"?

- *Preserve claims for higher tribunals*. Although your theory will help to focus and narrow your claims for appeal, do not forget the importance of preserving claims for federal court petitions, whether they be petitions for review or habeas corpus claims. Although federal courts do not require counsel to argue claims before the BIA that would be futile (for example, arguing that a particular immigration statute is unconstitutional), federal courts will also refuse to consider new claims that could have been raised below. Don't leave anything out that could limit the client later.

- *Avoid long quotes, especially block quotes*. Revise the court's language to persuade and to distill the key legal principle from the decision.

If you follow these simple pointers in your substantive presentation, your end result should be a brief that is concise, clear, and effective advocacy—the Holy Grail in legal writing.

Conclusion of the Brief

The remaining portion of your written submission—whether a brief on appeal or a response to an RFE—is the Conclusion. Sadly, the Conclusion is often tacked on at the last minute, and opportunity is lost for one final piece of advocacy. While it is true that the Conclusion should not be too long, it is the last opportunity the writer has to summarize the client's position and remind the adjudicator of what the client wants. It is also one final opportunity to make the best policy statement respecting why the result the client seeks is the appropriate result.

Often, a Conclusion will begin with the following words: "For the aforementioned reasons . . . ." This approach is not helpful. First, if the submission is longer than 10 pages, the adjudicator likely will have no clear memory of what specific reasons were "aforementioned." Second, the phrase is a perfect example of the type of legalese so abhorred by most contemporary adjudicators because it adds nothing to the substance of the argument. Third, it waives that last opportunity to remind the adjudicator in the case of what the client wants and why the adjudicator should feel good about giving that to the client. The Conclusion is the written embodiment of the last part of that adage noted before: "Tell 'em what you're going to tell 'em, tell 'em, and then tell 'em what you told 'em."

A good Conclusion *briefly* restates the major issues and provides the reasoning that leads to the requested result. The structure of the sentence should be something akin to:

> Respondent's request for asylum should be granted, because, pursuant to the holding in _____ [*insert case authority for your Circuit here*], Respondent's credible and unrebutted testimony alone is sufficient to sustain his claim for asylum.

Such a sentence reminds the decision maker of the basic premise presented, the authority underlying the premise, the factors needed to sustain the requested result, and that those factors are present in the case that is the subject of the submission.

If the case lends itself to a policy argument, or is winnable on technical grounds but potentially unappealing to the decision maker—*e.g.*, the law is on the client's side but the client is not likeable—then the conclusion should include a policy argument. For example, in an asylum case, the conclusion could include a sentence that reads something like this:

It is reasonable to sustain an inherently credible asylum claim without additional corroborating evidence because of the difficulty often inherent in obtaining supporting documentation while fleeing from persecution, and because of the very real threat to the life and safety of an asylum seeker who delays escape in an effort to obtain this evidence.

If this policy statement is actually contained in a decision by a tribunal, the decision should be cited. Including this type of policy argument at the end of the submission is a potent reminder that, at least in the Anglo-American legal tradition, cases do not exist in a vacuum and stare decisis considerations may require a result that does not seem inherently palatable when one considers only the facts of the case under consideration. Of course, the converse is also true. Sometimes, a policy argument is necessary to overcome bad precedent and help the decision maker feel comfortable about differentiating your case from other similar cases. The key is to keep the policy argument short, concise, and result-focused.

A final consideration respecting the Conclusion is that the writer must be sure that it clearly states what the client wants the adjudicator to do. State clearly whether the requested result is an affirmance, a remand, a decision on the merits, or some other action. Many Conclusions end without this crucial request and thus look more like a piece of scholarly writing than a piece of advocacy. Remember—every word in the submission is an opportunity to persuade, and these opportunities should be seized wholeheartedly.

APPEALS BEFORE THE ADMINISTRATIVE APPEALS OFFICE (AAO)[40]

The AAO is the appellate body that considers cases under the appellate jurisdiction of the Associate Commissioner, Examinations.[41] That official's jurisdiction is supposed to be lodged at §103.1(f)(2) of the Department of Homeland Security regulations (DHS);[42] however, that regulation no longer con-

tains this information. After the terror attacks of September 11, the authority to administer the immigration laws was vested in the Secretary of Homeland Security, and that authority may be subdelegated to any DHS employee without publication in the *Federal Register*.[43] While the appellate jurisdiction of the Associate Commissioner and his AAO may officially be a secret, it appears from practice and the appeal forms that it still includes a wide variety of appeals from decisions on various types of applications, including nonimmigrant and immigrant visa petitions and citizenship applications.

Briefs in support of AAO appeals tend to be less formal than those submitted to the BIA. However, form should follow function. Complicated factual and legal issues in an immigrant-investor case or a derivative-citizenship case might well warrant a formal brief. But whether written as a brief or as a letter, the same general principles of advocacy apply here as before the BIA. As discussed below, there is often more latitude at the AAO in supplementing the record with material on appeal. But advocates should not assume that their factual representations can substitute for material from the record: such representations are not evidence. It is usually effective to suggest instead that the decision invites a factual answer, which is therefore attached in the form of a further affidavit or other document.

In the past, adjudicators at the AAO were not lawyers, unlike members of the BIA. Today, most AAO adjudicators are lawyers, and are well-trained in the rules they administer. Although some of their decisions seem to contain canned sections from prepared paragraphs, they discuss the facts at length and are amenable to reasoning. Good organization, clear exposition, plain writing, candor in the presentation of the facts and the law, and avoidance of personal attack are appreciated no less in this forum than by members of the BIA, and arguably predispose the AAO in favor of the appeal.

Many appeals in employment-based visa petition cases involve high-tech occupations, some with a highly specialized vocabulary. Practitioners, even within this panel, may differ as to the amount of material, argument and/or evidence that works best on an appeal in a given case. But we agree that neither bulk nor brevity is a substitute for clarity. No matter how technical the occupation, the facts have to be stated so as to be understood. As the AAO points

---

[40] Hope M. Frye, past AILA president and co-author of *The Employers' Immigration Compliance Guide* (Matthew Bender), contributed significantly to this portion of the article.

[41] *See* 8 CFR §103.3(a)(1)(iv). Although USCIS refers to "the Administrative Appeals Office" in its memoranda and other communications, that office is still named "the Administrative Appeals Unit" in this regulation.

[42] *See* 8 CFR §103.3(a)(1)(ii).

[43] *See id.* §2.1.

out almost ad nauseum but properly, the burden is on the petitioner to make out a case.

Burden and Standard of Proof

The petitioner has the burden of proof in visa petition matters.[44] The burden of proof is separate and apart from the standard of proof.

Visa petitions are civil proceedings and thus the standard of proof the petitioner must meet is "preponderance of the evidence."[45] "Preponderance of the evidence" means "probably true" or "more likely than not."[46] This is not conclusive proof and not beyond a reasonable doubt—it is simply a majority. It is 50 percent plus a fraction.

The BIA gave this explanation of "preponderance of the evidence":

> For example, when something has to be proved beyond a reasonable doubt, the proof must demonstrate that something must be almost certainly true. And when something has to be proved by clear and convincing evidence, the proof must demonstrate that it is highly probably true. But, when something is to be established by a preponderance of the evidence it is sufficient that the proof only establish that it is *probably true*.[47]

The AAO in *Matter of Chawathe*,[48] an "adopted decision," reaffirmed that most petitions should be judged by "preponderance of the evidence" standard. (Its choice of *Chawathe* to reaffirm this standard, however, is curious. The issue in this case was whether Chevron Texaco is a U.S. corporation for Section 316(b)[49] purposes. It would seem that own-ership of Chevron Texaco is of such common knowledge that judicial notice could be taken, rendering unnecessary a discussion of how to weigh evidence.)

An AAO decision must be based on "substantial evidence."[50] In other words, the decision must explain the evidence on which it is made. Decisions also must be limited to the relevant facts related to the petition. For example, relying on irrelevant facts, such as the size of the employer, rather than the job duties (for determining specialist/professional positions for an H-1B petition), is unreasonable.[51]

Expert Testimony

An adjudicator has broad latitude to determine who qualifies as an expert.[52] In the past few years, USCIS has increasingly dismissed opinions of experts in H-1B[53] Extraordinary Ability, Outstanding Researcher, and National Interest cases. There are various reasons given. For example, an expert's letter will be disregarded if the writer has worked with the beneficiary, coauthored even one article, or attended the same university.

The USCIS California Service Center sometimes goes even further by only accepting testimony if the expert has never met the beneficiary. Prominent professors and researchers who speak at international conferences tend to meet other prominent experts. Barring a prominent expert's testimony just because he or she sat on a panel with an international expert at a conference or had other professional contact is not a legitimate basis for ignoring testimony.

In the denial of an EB-1 outstanding researcher petition, the California Service Center said:

> The fact that most of the letters were from past acquaintances, employers, and people who knew her from various research groups she worked

---

[44] *Matter of Brantigan*, 11 I&N Dec. 493 (BIA 1966).

[45] *Matter of Martinez*, 21 I&N Dec. 1035 (BIA 1997); *Matter of Patel*, 19 I&N Dec. 774 (BIA 1988); *Matter of Soo Hoo*, 11 I&N Dec. 151 (BIA 1965). There is a higher standard of proof, "clear and convincing," needed to rebut the presumption of a prior fraudulent marriage for certain I-130 petitions. INA §204(a)(2)(A)(ii).

[46] *Matter of E–M–*, 20 I&N Dec. 77 (Comm. 1989) [Emphasis added]; *see also Matter of J–E–*, 23 I&N Dec. 291 (BIA 2002); *Fischl v. Armitage*, 128 F.3d 50, 55 (2d. Cir. 1997); *Modern Federal Jury Instructions* §73.01 (1997).

[47] 20 I&N Dec. at 80.

[48] Adopted Decision 06-0003, File No. A74-254-994 (AAO January 11, 2006), *available at www.uscis.gov/graphics/lawsregs/admindec3/Chawathe011106.pdf* (last visited May 10, 2006). USCIS personnel are directed to follow the reasoning of "adopted decisions" in similar cases.

[49] Permitting the spouse of a U.S. citizen employed by certain U.S. corporations engaged in international commerce an
continued

exemption from the residence requirements for naturalization.

[50] *Button Depot, Inc. v. U.S. Dep't of Homeland Sec.*, 386 F. Supp. 2d 40 (C.D. Cal. 2005); *Hong Kong TV Video Program v. Ilchert*, 685 F. Supp. 712 (N.D. Cal. 1988); *Tongatapu Woodcraft Hawaii, Ltd. v. Feldman*, 736 F.2d 1305, 1308 (9th Cir. 1984).

[51] *Young China Daily v. Chappell*, 742 F. Supp. 552 (N.D. Cal. 1989).

[52] *In re Paoli R.R. Yard PCB Litig.*, 35 F.3d 717 (3d. Cir. 1994).

[53] *See Hong Kong TV*, 685 F. Supp. 712.

with, and as such adds little to satisfy the international recognition aspect . . . ."[54]

Note that the above decision used the word "most," and simply ignored the experts who had no connection whatsoever with the petitioner, university, or beneficiary.

The generally hostile reaction of USCIS and the AAO to expert testimony is inappropriate and contrary to the spirit that guides federal adjudications. Although there are no court cases involving the weighing of expert testimony for EB-1 petitions,[55] guidance can be found in the Federal Rules of Evidence and in cases addressing this issue in other areas of law. The Advisory Committee on Rules, Federal Rules of Evidence says:

> An intelligent evaluation of facts is often difficult or impossible without the application of some scientific, technical, or other specialized knowledge. The most common source of this knowledge is the expert witness, although there are other techniques for supplying it.[56]

In the scientific world, top researchers in the same field are typically few, and they usually know each other. The public and governments encourage researchers to share information and to collaborate in order to foster advances in science, engineering, and medicine. As a result, in many instances, researchers work together, especially if they are prominent figures in the field. The fact that these prominent researchers know or may have spoken at a conference on a panel with an EB-1 applicant is actually further proof of their international prestige and significance in the field.

While a professional expert opinion may hold less weight if biased, the content should not be rejected unless the author is suspected of fraudulent misrepresentation. Instances of out-and-out lying are very rare. The livelihood of those giving testimony depends on their reputation.

The Federal Rules of Evidence do not require complete lack of bias for expert testimony to be ad-

missible.[57] In fact, impartiality is not a requirement at all for being an expert witness.[58] An expert is one who can assist in understanding the evidence or determining the facts at issue. The admissibility of expert testimony is governed by Rule 702 of the Federal Rules of Evidence, which provides:

> If scientific, technical *or other specialized knowledge* will assist the trier of fact to understand the evidence or to determine a fact in issue, a witness qualified as an expert by knowledge, skill, experience, training, or education, may testify thereto in the form of opinion or otherwise.[59]

Although the Federal Rules of Evidence do not apply to administrative agencies, "the spirit of" the Supreme Court's decision in *Daubert v. Merrell Dow Pharmaceuticals, Inc.*,[60] which gives the rules for qualifying an expert witness in federal trials, "does apply to administrative proceedings."[61] The court in *Niam v. Ashcroft* pointed out:

> [B]ut it would be odd for an agency to adopt an even more stringent filter for expert testimony than that used by the courts for judicial proceedings, and there is no indication that the immigration service has done so. It would be particularly odd for that service to do so, given the great weight that the immigration judges and the Board of Immigration Appeals give to the anonymous country and asylum reports.[62]

In the same vein, the Seventh Circuit, in *Koval v. Gonzales*,[63] held that an immigration judge erred in excluding expert testimony when finding that a Ukrainian Mormon had not suffered persecution. The court found that it was an error for the immigration judge to exclude the testimony of the petitioners' expert while relying heavily on anonymous Department of State country reports.

There are indications that the California Service Center may begin to ignore the testimony from experts located by the petitioner using a commercial service. Again, there is no basis for such a broad-

---

[54] In this case, not all of the 17 expert letters were from the beneficiary's colleagues. With a motion and a few more expert letters, the petition was eventually granted.

[55] The court in *Hong Kong TV*, 685 F. Supp. 712, discussed uncontradicted expert testimony, but did not involve questions of the experts' bias. *See id.* at 712.

[56] Fed. R. Evid. 702, Advisory Committee's Note.

[57] *See* J. Weinstein & M. Berger, 4 *Weinstein's Federal Evidence* §§702-59 to 60 & n.38 (J. McLaughlin ed., 2d ed. 2002).

[58] *U.S. v. Williams*, 81 F.3d 1434, 1441 (7th Cir. 1996).

[59] Fed. R. Evid. 702 (emphasis added).

[60] 509 U.S. 579 (1993).

[61] *Koval & Vagil v. Gonzales*, 418 F.3d 798 (7th Cir. 2005).

[62] 354 F.3d 652, 660 (7th Cir. 2004).

[63] 418 F.3d at 798.

brush view. Courts balance competing policy objectives to determine expert disqualification.[64] However, experts should be allowed to pursue their trade, and parties should be permitted to select their own experts.[65] In *Chamberlain Group, Inc. v. Interlogix, Inc.*, the court stated, "There is no indication that Chamberlain's choice of Dr. Rhyne is in bad faith because he has served as Chamberlain's expert in six other proceedings."[66]

In *Henry Quentzel Plumbing Supply Co., Inc. v. Quentzel*,[67] the court held that occasional professional contacts between one of the arbitrators and an expert witness were insufficient to disqualify an arbitrator on ground of appearance of bias or partiality. The arbitrator, who was a specialist in forensic accounting, had past professional contacts with an expert witness and the accounting firm for which the witness worked. These contacts could not disqualify the arbitrator on the basis of appearance of bias or partiality because the occasional contacts merely involved serving with the witness on professional committees and educational panels in the past and serving as an unpaid consultant for the accounting firm.

In *Furstenberg v. U. S.*,[68] the Supreme Court discussed the issue of expert-witness testimony involving a narrow field of specialization, which is directly applicable to the narrow fields of many EB-1 cases. The court said:

> Furthermore, viewing an expert's participation on the Art Advisory Panel as creating personal bias might unnecessarily discourage distinguished experts from participation on the panel, to the ultimate detriment of the Internal Revenue Service and the tax system, or might reduce the availability of expert witnesses at trial. The record indicates that there are only a relatively small number of experts qualified to evaluate the works of certain artists.[69]

In *Matter of Nicole V.*,[70] the court found that an expert's relationship to the party offering her as a witness did not disqualify the expert from giving opinion evidence, and any bias the witness may have had could be addressed on cross-examination.[71]

Professors and experts are often in the best position to explain the significance of the applicant's research or discoveries. They provide evidence akin to eyewitness testimony. Where there is credible, persuasive, and fact-specific testimony, it must be considered. If the AAO really has questions about the expert's credibility or bias, an RFE can be used to request evidence to satisfy this concern.

The regulations do not require that visa petitions be supported by independent corroborative evidence. And, at least in the asylum field, the courts have consistently held that the applicant's credible testimony may be sufficient without corroborative testimony.[72]

Cumulative Weight of the Evidence

Facts of evidence must be considered individually as well as cumulatively. This basic concept of administrative law has been discussed extensively with respect to hardship waivers.[73]

Submission of New Evidence on Appeal

The AAO, unlike the BIA, reviews decisions de novo.[74] In the past, the AAO allowed new evidence to be submitted with an appeal or with counsel's brief. Recently, this policy has changed. Now, if a document was requested by an RFE from a service center and the document was not provided, the AAO will not accept it on appeal. This new policy will

---

[64] *Cordy v. Sherwin-Williams Co.*, 156 F.R.D. 575, 580 (D.N.J. 1994).

[65] *See Stencel v. The Fairchild Corp.*, 174 F. Supp. 2d 1082, 1083 (C.D. Cal. 2001).

[66] L. 653893, 4–5 (N.D. Ill. 2002); *see The Fairchild Corp.*, 174 F. Supp. 2d at 1082, n. 4 (absence of evidence of bad faith weighs against disqualification).

[67] 193 A.D.2d 678, 598 N.Y.S.2d 23 (2d. Dep't 1993).

[68] 595 F.2d 603 (Ct. Cl. 1979).

[69] *Id.* at 605.

---

[70] 71 N.Y. 2d 112, 518 N.E. 2d 914 (1987).

[71] *See also U.S. v. Kelley*, 6 F. Supp. 2d 1168, 1183 (D. Kan. 1998) (quoting 4 *Weinstein's Federal Evidence* §702.06[8] at 702-45 (1997)); *Grant Thornton, L.L.P. v. FDIC*, 297 F. Supp. 2d 880, 883–84 (S.D. W. Va. 2004).

[72] *See Bolanos-Hernandez v. INS*, 767 F.2d 1277, 1285 (9th Cir. 1985).

[73] *See Gutierrez-Centeno v. INS*, 99 F.3d 1529 (9th Cir. 1996); *Mattis v. INS*, 774 F.2d 965, 968 (9th Cir. 1985); *Matter of O–J–O–*, I&N Dec. 381 (BIA 1996); *Matter of Anderson*, 16 I&N Dec. 596 (BIA 1978); *Matter of Riccio*, 15 I&N Dec. 548 (BIA 1976).

[74] The AAO reviews I-129 nonimmigrant petitions, I-140 immigrant petitions, I-601 waivers, bond breaches, fiancé petitions, reentry permits, and other benefits. *See* Ira Kurzban, *Kurzban's Immigration Law Sourcebook* 825–26 (9th ed. 2004).

create serious problems because RFEs are often confusing and vague; sometimes it is impossible to know exactly what an RFE is requesting. You may believe that the documents presented in response to an RFE are sufficient. If the AAO examiner decides they are not, the AAO will bar you from providing new evidence on the issue. However, you can respond in a respectful manner by reiterating what the evidence shows, with specificity. For example, the following language is one way to briefly accept the onus of error, thus disposing the adjudicator to more closely consider your argument: "Apparently counsel did not clarify that . . . ." Then, immediately move to your substantive argument: "The applicant intended to demonstrate . . . See exhibit 2, which states that . . . ."

At times, the RFE in the petition being appealed will have misconstrued the law. If it does, remain firm in your argument, and point to the source of the law that you assert is correct. For example: "Although the RFE requested the applicant's federal tax returns, a USCIS memorandum establishes that a director may accept the statement of a financial officer."[75]

At a recent AILA conference, William R. Yates, former associate director of operations, USCIS, recommended against submitting "900-page RFE responses." He said that examiners cannot read that amount of material, and the needed documents cannot be identified. However, the change in the AAO evidence policy promotes the safe, over-prepared response. To protect the record for appeal, you may be forced to submit many more documents than normal to ensure that the appeal will not be denied because the response to the RFE was noncompliant.

CONCLUSION

When representing a client before the BIA, AAO, or a USCIS service center, it is important for an attorney to follow the general principles of advocacy. It is also important to know the specific techniques and procedures that are unique to each forum, and how to avoid certain mistakes when appearing before them. The authors hope that the suggestions in this article will assist both new and experienced counsel as they continue to represent clients before the various tribunals.

---

[75] See USCIS Memorandum (Yates), "USCIS Issues Guidance on Determination of Ability to Pay" (May 4, 2004), published on AILA InfoNet at Doc. No. 04051262 (posted May 12, 2004).

APPENDIX—PRINCIPLES OF STYLE IN LEGAL WRITING

Compelling, effective writing is a key skill for an attorney. To help the style-challenged, here are a few suggestions.

Avoid too many complex, compound sentences

If your sentence sounds like something written by Faulkner or Joyce or, worse, a native German speaker, it is probably too long. Look for ways to break the sentence into smaller sections. Another clue that a sentence is complex is if it has so many dependent clauses that the reader no longer remembers the subject by the end of the sentence. Sometimes writers use 20 words to say something that could be said in 8. The result is usually less persuasive.

For example, this sentence is long but not very persuasive:

"It could be said that in facts similar to those presented here that have been considered relevant to other asylum cases, the Respondent has raised sufficient evidence to allow the Court to conclude that he is eligible for asylum."

Instead, this sentence is shorter and more persuasive:

"Respondent presented sufficient evidence of past persecution—including her credible testimony, testimony from witnesses and an expert opinion—to require a grant of asylum."

Avoid the passive voice in general

But use the passive voice judiciously when it would create a clearer, more economical sentence. Sometimes, the passive voice is useful for a transition from one concept to another or to grapple with theoretical constructs that are not necessarily implicated by the facts of the case at bar. In those cases, the passive voice can be used because it is more economical. In all other instances, writing should be active, not passive.

Do not substitute nouns for verbs, or vice-versa

Doing so almost always slows a reader down or obscures the meaning of your writing. For example, the phrase "they inflicted persecution on him when they imposed a death sentence in a closed court" would be more active and concise if the nouns *"persecution"* and *"sentence"* became verbs: "They persecuted him when they sentenced him to death in a closed court." Legal language is especially prone to nominalizations, and some nominalizations cannot be fixed because they are integral to legal standards. For example, the nominalization "Request for Evidence" in *"The Service Center issued a Request for Evidence"* cannot be converted to "The Service Center requested evidence" because "Request for Evidence" is a legal term of art that should not be changed. At the same time, do not convert nouns into verbs merely because doing so would be easier, because it can obscure the meaning of your writing. For example, the noun "reference" has become a verb in the following sentence: *"Counsel references an Eighth Circuit case."* Revise the sentence by replacing the noun with an appropriate verb: *"Counsel refers to an Eighth Circuit case."*

Do not begin paragraphs with conjunctions; do not use conjunctions indiscriminately

Beginning paragraphs with "but," "therefore," "however," and the like not only looks ugly, it also weakens the persuasiveness of the writing. These words generally imply that something has come before the word that is necessary to complete your loop of logic. If that something is segregated in a previous paragraph, it interrupts the flow of the logic. It also visually interrupts the flow of the argument and can confuse the reader. The use of "however" or "therefore" is sometimes necessary to break up an overly long or complex sentence. In that case, conjunctions may be used, but they should not substitute for good transitions.

Ensure parallelism

Parallelism is the use of the same grammatical form or structure for ideas in a list or comparison.[76] For example, the following sentence has three ideas, two of which use past tense with a specific year, and one of which uses an "-ing" verb without a specific year: "The applicant entered the United States in 1986, adjusting status three years later, and became a citizen in 1992." One way to rewrite this sentence so that its structure is parallel would be as follows: "The applicant entered the United States in 1986, adjusted status in 1989, and became a citizen in 1992." The latter sentence is far easier to read and understand than the former sentence.

Connect your sentences

A reader will more quickly understand your writing if you link your sentences to each other by putting previously introduced information first, then adding new information. For example, if the first sentence reads "The car is blue," the second sentence should read "Blue cars are more difficult to see than yellow cars" because the idea of "blue cars" is previously introduced information that the reader already knows. "Yellow cars," on the other hand, is new information that the sentence introduces. The second sentence should not read "Yellow cars are easier to see than blue cars," because that sentence introduces the new idea of "yellow cars" at the beginning, and the reader cannot immediately connect that new information to the prior sentence.

Avoid tag words and phrases such as "clearly" or "in fact"

These words are almost always unnecessary. And they are almost always suspect. If an assertion is clear, this will be apparent from the manner in which it is presented—adding the word "clearly" accomplishes nothing. Usually, inclusion of this word also causes the adjudicator to suspect that the stated premise is *not* clear. The use of "in fact" carries similar implications and should be avoided for the same reason. It is appropriate, however, to use "in fact" to effectively counter a factual or legal misstatement by the court or the opposing side.

Apply verb-noun agreement

Sometimes a legal submission will contain sentences that are so long that by the time the writer gets to the verb it is no longer clear what the subject and direct object of the sentence are (or were). As a result, there are sentences where the conjugation of the verb does not match the relevant noun. Plural and singular nouns should be accompanied by the appropriate verb forms. Be very vigilant to avoid this common error.

Know the difference between the plural and the possessive

This grammatical error can be avoided by consulting a good style manual rather than relying on your computer's built-in grammar checker. If something sounds "funny," it's usually incorrect. Style manuals are a quick and effective source for checking.

Use words and acronyms consistently

Do not use different words for the same legal concept or party. Especially in the law, certain words are terms of art and therefore must be used consistently. In legal writing, using different words to express the same legal meaning is a sign of inconsistency, causes confusion, and is sometimes rewarded with an AWO (Affirmance Without Opinion). Acronyms are another tricky device in legal writing. Too many acronyms are not only confusing but make most readers crazy. Inconsistently applied acronyms are worse. It is very important to explain all acronyms and limit them to those commonly used in the field.

Do not repeat yourself

Legal submissions would be much shorter if lawyers did not constantly repeat themselves. So, do not repeat yourself. Again, do not repeat yourself. Be alert to repetition in everything you write. Repetition can occur because the same idea is phrased slightly differently, or because it is buried in an overly complex sentence. Either way, it should be avoided.

---

[76] Muriel Harris, *Prentice Hall Reference Guide to Grammar and Usage*, ch. 10 (4th ed. 2000).

Proofread

This is crucial, especially if you use templates for briefs, RFEs, or motions. There are certain errors that a spelling or grammar checker simply will not catch. Is the name and gender of your client correct? Did you choose the correct homonym (for example, "principal" versus "principle")? Did you include an errant apostrophe? Did you confuse the singular and plural? The list is endless, and the mistakes can only be discovered by reading and rereading your work. It is also very helpful to have someone else proofread your work.

Use formal language

Avoid contractions, colloquialisms, and slang. These words are not sufficiently formal for legal writing. Your writing should be elegant and flow easily, but it should never be casual.

Be careful with gender

Many courts now explicitly encourage counsel to use gender-neutral terms and avoid sexist language. Although the traditional male pronouns and male possessive ("he," "him," "his") may in some cases be preferred, you should consciously decide to use them, rather than subconsciously using them as the traditional default. You have several options in this regard, depending on the context in which the pronoun is used. Following are some of these options:

- *Use a plural noun.* Instead of "An asylum applicant establishes that he fears persecution when ...," try "Asylum applicants establish that they fear persecution when ..."

- ***Repeat the noun rather than using a pronoun.*** Instead of "An asylum applicant fears persecution on account of political opinion when he has expressed a political opinion ..." try: "An asylum applicant fears persecution on account of political opinion when the applicant has expressed a political opinion ..."

- *Use "he or she" instead of the male pronoun.* Instead of "An asylum applicant establishes that he fears persecution on account of his political opinion when ...," try "An asylum applicant establishes that he or she fears persecution on account of political opinion when ..." The downside to this method is that it is cumbersome. Although "s/he" is less cumbersome, do not use this because it is too informal for a legal submission.

- *Use the pronoun that fits the gender of your client.* If your client is a woman, use female pronouns when writing; if your client is a man, use male pronouns. However, do not vary the gender pronouns. Although interspersing the two kinds of gender pronouns is encouraged in other forms of writing, it can lead to confusion in legal submissions.

HABEAS CORPUS AND THE REAL ID ACT:
SOME CONSTITUTIONAL CONCERNS

*by Lisa S. Brodyaga**

INTRODUCTION

In *INS v. St. Cyr*,[1] the Supreme Court reaffirmed the availability of habeas corpus review of deportation orders.[2] The *St. Cyr* decision, handed down in 2001, also revealed that use of the Suspension Clause to guarantee such review continues to hang by a one-vote thread in the new Supreme Court. Other recent decisions[3] provide further evidence that the pendulum of constitutional protections for immigrants is on a downward trajectory.

The future of habeas corpus review of deportation orders, or meaningfully equivalent review in the courts of appeal, will likely turn on whether, and to what extent, the Supreme Court continues to hold that such review is constitutionally mandated. This paper discusses the history of habeas review of deportation orders prior to passage of the REAL ID Act in 2005, analyzes the current state of the law, identifies arguments that can be used to counter the limitations of REAL ID, and briefly looks to the future.

HABEAS REVIEW PRIOR TO THE REAL ID ACT

Availability of Habeas Review

Historically, noncitizens have been able to challenge deportation orders through habeas corpus proceedings in federal district court. Such review was considered to be constitutionally mandated. As the Supreme Court summarized in 1953 in *Heikkila v. Barber*:[4]

> Read against this background of a quarter of a century of consistent judicial interpretation, '19 of the 1917 Immigration Act, 39 Stat. 889, clearly had *the effect of precluding judicial intervention in deportation cases except insofar as it was required by the Constitution*. And the decisions have continued to regard this point as settled. *Kessler v. Strecker*, 307 U.S. 22, 34 (1939); *Bridges v. Wixon*, 326 U.S. 135, 149, 166, 167 (1945); *Estep v. United States*, 327 U.S. 114, 122, 123, n. 14 (1946); *Sunal v. Large*, 332 U.S. 174, 177, n. 3 (1947). Clearer evidence that for present purposes the Immigration Act of 1917 is a statute precluding judicial review would be hard to imagine. Whatever view be taken as to the breadth of §10 of the Administrative Procedure Act, the first exception to that section applies to the case before us. The result is that appellant's rights were not enlarged by that Act. *Now, as before, he may attack a deportation order only by habeas corpus.* (footnotes omitted) (emphasis added).

The extent to which *Heikkila* is settled law has been called into question with increasing intensity over the past decade. In *St. Cyr*, a bare majority upheld the fundamental premise of *Heikkila*, in an opinion by Justice Stevens, joined by Justices Kennedy, Souter, Ginsburg, and Breyer.

---

* **Lisa Brodyaga** is a graduate of Catholic University School of Law (1974); certified by the Texas Board of Legal Specialization (1981); co-founder of and volunteer attorney with Refugio Del Rio Grande, Inc., a nonprofit §501(c)(3) refugee camp with embedded law office on a 45-acre wilderness near San Benito, Tex. (1985 to present). Her current work focuses on lawful permanent residents facing removal as a result of AEDPA and IIRAIRA, primarily through federal litigation. (*See* www.refugiodelriogrande.tripod.com).

[1] *INS v. St. Cyr*, 533 U.S. 289 (2001).

[2] For purposes of this paper, the term "INS" refers to the various federal agencies involved in immigration litigation. The term "deportation order" covers orders of deportation, exclusion, and removal, unless the context clearly indicates otherwise. Much of the analysis is based on Fifth Circuit law, for two reasons: first, it is the circuit with which the author is most familiar, and second, because it has some of the most restrictive precedent in the country. If support can be found for an argument in the Fifth Circuit, it can probably be found elsewhere as well.

[3] *See, e.g., Reno v. American-Arab Anti-Discrimination Committee (AADC)*, 525 U.S. 471 (1999), and *Demore v. Kim*, 538 U.S. 510 (2003). While it reaffirmed the availability of habeas corpus to challenge detention, *Demore* held that the mandatory detention provisions of 8 USC §1226(c), INA §236(c) are constitutional, even as applied to lawful permanent residents, (LPRs).

[4] *Heikkila v. Barber*, 345 U.S. 229, 234–35 (1953).

Justice O'Connor, dissenting, expressed the view that, even if it were assumed that the Suspension Clause (Article I, Section 9, Clause 2), which generally prohibits suspension of the privilege of a federal writ of habeas corpus, guaranteed some minimum extent of habeas corpus review, the right asserted by the immigrant in *Heikkila* fell outside the scope of that review. Justice Scalia, joined by Chief Justice Rehnquist and Justice Thomas, and in pertinent part by Justice O'Connor, expressed the view that the Supreme Court and the courts below lacked jurisdiction to entertain the claims raised therein, as 8 USC §1252 unambiguously repealed the application of §2241 and all other provisions for judicial review of challenges to removal brought by certain criminal aliens, including that brought by St. Cyr.

Justice Stevens noted[5] that in *Heikkila*, the Court observed that the then-existing statutory immigration scheme had the effect of precluding judicial intervention in deportation cases except insofar as it was required by the Constitution, and that this allowed habeas review of questions of law concerning an alien's eligibility for discretionary relief. He therefore concluded that the ambiguities in the scope of the exercise of the writ at common law, and the suggestions in the Court's prior decisions as to the extent to which habeas review could be limited consistent with the Constitution, were such that INS's reading of the statute would present "difficult and significant" Suspension Clause questions. In a footnote, he commented as follows on the reading given by the dissent:[6]

> n. 24. The dissent reads into Chief Justice Marshall's opinion in Ex parte Bollman, 8 U.S. 75, 4 Cranch 75, 2 L. Ed. 554 (1807), support for a proposition that the Chief Justice did not endorse, either explicitly or implicitly. See post, at 14–15. He did note that "the first congress of the United States" acted under "the immediate influence" of the injunction provided by the Suspension Clause when it gave "life and activity" to "this great constitutional privilege" in the Judiciary Act of 1789, and that the writ could not be suspended until after the statute was enacted. 4 Cranch at 95. That statement, however, surely does not imply that Marshall believed the Framers had drafted a Clause that would proscribe a temporary abrogation of the writ, while permitting its

permanent suspension. Indeed, Marshall's comment expresses the far more sensible view that the Clause was intended to preclude any possibility that "the privilege itself would be lost" by either the inaction or the action of Congress. See, e.g., ibid. (noting that the Founders "must have felt, with peculiar force, the obligation" imposed by the Suspension Clause).

Notably, Immigration and Naturalization Service's (INS's) litigation position has evolved over time. Previously, INS also adhered to the fundamental premise of *Heikkila* that some form of review was constitutionally mandated, and focused its efforts on claiming that the scope of constitutionally protected review was far more limited than that available under §2241 and other statutes providing for habeas review. In *U.S. ex rel Marcello v. INS*,[7] the Fifth Circuit specifically found that the 1961 statute preserved habeas review.[8] The court further rejected INS's position that even if such review was available, the 1961 statute repealed all statutory grants of habeas jurisdiction and limited habeas to the constitutional core protected by the Suspension Clause.[9] The court expressly held that there is "little or no indication" in the 1961 Act that Congress intended to repeal or amend the habeas statute and restrict habeas review to the constitutional minimum.[10]

The litigation position of INS found support from some pre–*St. Cyr* circuit court decisions, such as *LaGuerre v. Reno*, where the court expressed doubt that the suspension clause requires preserving habeas corpus as a vehicle for challenging final orders of deportation in cases in which the jurisdiction of the immigration authorities over the alien is not in question.[11] The *LaGuerre* court noted that at the time the Constitution was enacted, habeas corpus was a limited remedy, which lay only to test the jurisdiction of whatever governmental body or officer was detaining the applicant. The court reasoned that although Congress thereafter authorized a much broader use of habeas corpus, "it cannot be that curtailing an optional statutory enlargement violates the suspension clause." As the Court concluded,

---

[5] *Id.* at 300.

[6] *Id.* at note 24.

[7] *U.S. ex rel Marcello v. INS*, 634 F.2d 964 (5th Cir. 1983).

[8] *Id.* at 968.

[9] *Id.* at 971.

[10] *Id.*

[11] *See, e.g., LaGuerre v. Reno*, 164 F.3d 1035, 1038–39 (7th Cir. 1998).

There can be no doubt that the applicants for habeas corpus in the present cases are detained pursuant to valid orders issued by the responsible authorities. The issue they wish to press—the issue of whether they are entitled to ask for discretionary relief from these orders—does not raise doubts about the jurisdiction of the Immigration and Naturalization Service over them.[12]

The Interaction of Direct and Habeas Review from 1952 until the REAL ID Act of 2005

Following passage of the Immigration and Nationality Act of 1952, judicial review of most deportation orders was channeled directly to the U.S. courts of appeal. Habeas review was limited to exclusion orders and cases where the person was in the actual, physical custody of INS.[13]

Once Congress provided for direct review in the courts of appeals, and given the doctrine that Congress can substitute a "collateral" remedy for habeas corpus so long as it is neither inadequate nor ineffective to test legality of the petitioner's detention,[14] issues arose as to when and under what circumstances habeas review of deportation orders was still available. These questions primarily involved two types of cases: (1) cases where evidence was required which was extrinsic to the record, and (2) cases where a timely petition for review had not been filed.

The Ability to Develop Evidence Extrinsic to the Record

Fifth Circuit precedent recognized that there would be instances where a remand was required to develop evidence.[15] The Fifth Circuit recently reiterated the vitality of *U.S. ex rel Accardi v. Shaughnessy,*[16] *Accardi* in dicta, *U.S. v. Caldeon-Pena.*[17]

---

[12] *Id.* at 1039.

[13] *See* 8 USC §1105a, enacted in 1952, and repealed in 1996. *See also Umanzor v. Lambert,* 782 F.2d 1299 (5th Cir. 1986).

[14] *See Swain v. Pressley,* 430 U.S. 372,381 (1977).

[15] *Garcia v. Boldin,* 691 F.2d 1172, 1182 (5th Cir. 1982) (Where "alleged unfairness is extrinsic to the record, a court of appeals may remand the case to the agency for further inquiry and findings. 28 USC §2347(c)"). *See also Osaghae v. INS,* 942 F.2d 1160 (7th Cir. 1991).

[16] *U.S. ex rel Accardi v. Shaughnessy,* 347 U.S. 260, 267–68 (1954).

[17] *U.S. v. Calderon-Pena,* 383 F.3d 254, 256 (5th Cir. 2004) ("reinstat[ing] that portion of the panel opinion, *United continued*

This included the discussion of *U.S. ex rel Accardi v. Shaughnessy.*[18]

Calderon-Pena was an unlawful re-entry case, under 8 USC §1326. The defendant asserted a due process violation because the immigration judge (IJ) failed to follow the requirement to advise him of the availability of discretionary relief. He equated this to *Accardi,* where the alien attacked the validity of the denial of his application for suspension of deportation, alleging that certain conduct by the Attorney General deprived him of rights guaranteed to him by the applicable immigration statute and regulations. Specifically, the petitioner in *Accardi* asserted that the Board of Immigration Appeals (BIA) had failed to exercise its discretion in denying his application for suspension of deportation, as was required under the regulations, and had instead denied the application only because he was included on a confidential list of people the Attorney General wanted deported. In considering Accardi's application for writ of habeas corpus, the court concluded that he had sufficiently alleged a due process interest in having INS follow its own regulations, and remanded to the district court with instruction to determine whether there had, in fact, been a prejudgment and, if so, to order a new administrative hearing. In *Calderon-Pena I,* however, the court distinguished *Accardi* as follows:

> Calderon-Pena does not cite, nor have we located, any cases applying Accardi in the criminal context; all examples of relief granted came either via direct appeal of an administrative ruling or by writ of habeas corpus. *In civil proceedings, Accardi is applied by ordering a new administrative hearing, and therefore courts do not require a showing of prejudice.* Here, we are not empowered to order, nor has Calderon-Pena requested, a new deportation hearing; rather, we may only dismiss the indictment for his subsequent illegal reentry. This is not a remedy contemplated by Accardi or its progeny. (emphasis added)

Unfortunately, both Supreme Court precedents[19] and *Calderon-Pena I* have been ignored by the Fifth

---

States v. Calderon-Pena, 339 F.3d 320, 323–25 (5th Cir. 2003), that rejected Calderon-Pena's attempt to collaterally attack his prior removal").

[18] *Ex rel Accardi,* 347 U.S. at 260 (remanding for hearing on allegation of due process violation, to wit, that BIA's denial of discretionary relief was influenced by non-record factors).

[19] In addition to *Accardi,* other Supreme Court cases contradict the claim that immigrants have no due process rights in *continued*

Circuit in recent cases, holding that there is no liberty interest in discretionary relief, and hence no entitlement to due process in the adjudication of such applications.

Exhaustion of Remedies

In the "good old days" (before the shift in Fifth Circuit precedent), the Fifth Circuit also followed the general habeas exhaustion principle that failure to file a petition for review with the court of appeals was excused where there was no "deliberate bypass" of direct review:

> [T]he government urges us to discern and apply to Marcello's attempt to obtain relief in this case, pursuant to 28 USC §2241, the exhaustion requirements that are applied in actions brought pursuant to sections 2254 (state criminal convictions) and 2255 (federal ones). Only when the alien has availed himself of the normal mode of appeal provided him by section 1105a, it is said, should the courts entertain a plea for the extraordinary relief of habeas corpus. There is force and reason in this contention as well; however, to apply it now would be to bar Marcello from any review whatever, the six-month period for an appeal having long passed. Absent a finding of deliberate bypass of the direct appeal, we do not believe such an outcome just or appropriate.[20]

The deliberate bypass test was later modified to "cause and prejudice."[21]

The Shift in Fifth Circuit Precedent

Over time, however, and probably due as much to changes in the composition of the court as in the governing jurisprudence, the Fifth Circuit became increasingly unwilling to follow its own precedent in such cases. For example, the holding of *Marcello* that in habeas proceedings under 28 USC §2241 exhaustion was not required, absent a deliberate bypass of statutorily provided remedies, was argued, and ignored, in *Goonsuwan v. Ashcroft*,[22] which held that the failure to file a motion to reopen with the BIA to assert ineffective assistance of counsel deprived the court of jurisdiction in habeas corpus to entertain a due process challenge on that basis. And recent cases holding that an immigrant cannot complain of due process violations with respect to applications for discretionary relief[23] ignore not only Fifth Circuit precedent[24] and Supreme Court authority such as *Accardi* and *Jay*, but also the line of cases finding interests in discretionary benefits to be constitutionally protected where rules and standards governed the exercise of discretion.[25]

The Illegal Immigration and Immigrant Responsibility of Act of 1996 (IIRAIRA)[26] also specifically restricted review under §1252 to the "administrative

---

the adjudication of applications for discretionary relief. *See, e.g., Jay v. Boyd*, 351 U.S. 345, 363 (1956) (alien is entitled to a "fair hearing" on application for suspension of deportation); and *Bridges v. Wixon*, 326 U.S. 135, 145 (1945) (emphasis added):

> Here the liberty of an individual is at stake. . . . That deportation is a penalty—at times a most serious one—cannot be doubted. Meticulous care must be exercised lest the procedure by which he is deprived of that liberty not meet the essential standards of fairness.

[20] *U.S. ex rel Marcello v. INS*, 634 F.2d 964, 971 (5th Cir. 1983). *See also Fay v. Noia*, 372 U.S. 391 (1963), involving a statutory exhaustion requirement, under 28 USC §2254.

[21] *See Keeney v. Tamayo-Reyes*, 504 U.S. 1, 5–6 (1992) (noting that the Court subsequently substituted "cause and prejudice" for the deliberate bypass standard in state procedural default cases), *Dretke v. Haley*, 541 U.S. 386, 392–93 (2004) (recognized an equitable exception to the procedural default bar when a habeas applicant can demonstrate cause and prejudice).

[22] *Goonsuwan v. Ashcroft*, 252 F.3d 383 (5th Cir. 2001).

[23] *See, e.g., Mireles-Valdez v. Ashcroft*, 349 F.3d 213, 214–15 (5th Cir. 2003). *See also Dave v. Ashcroft*, 363 F.3d 649, 652–53 (7th Cir. 2004) (immigrant cannot complain of ineffective assistance of counsel with respect to application for discretionary relief, for lack of protected interest in such an application); *Smith v. Ashcroft*, 295 F.3d 425 (4th Cir. 2002) (same).

[24] *See, e.g., Haitian Refugee Center v. Smith*, 676 F.2d 1023, 1039 (5th Cir. 1982) (finding constitutionally protected interest in the right to be heard on an application for discretionary relief, asylum, even though there is no protected right to receive such relief).

[25] *See Board of Regents v. Roth*, 408 U.S. 564, 577 (1972). By contrast, in *U.S. v. Copeland*, 376 F.3d 61 (2d Cir. 2004), the Second Circuit found a constitutionally protected right to apply for discretionary relief. It is anticipated that a petition for certiorari will be filed in a Fifth Circuit case dismissing a petition for review which involved particularly egregious facts, to wit, where an Accredited Representative forgot to timely file an application for cancellation under 8 USC §1229b(a) with the EOIR, even though he had paid the fee to INS well in advance of the deadline.

[26] Illegal Immigration Reform and Immigrant Responsibility Act of 1996 (IIRAIRA), Division C of the Omnibus Appropriations Act of 1996 (H.R. 3610), Pub. L. 104-208, 110 Stat. 3009.

record on which the order of removal is based," §1252(b)(4)(A), and eliminated the escape hatch relied upon in *Garcia v. Boldin* by providing that a court could "not order the taking of additional evidence under [28 USC] 2347(c)."

Remarkably, the only known case addressing this limitation was not one seeking review of a final order of removal or deportation.[27] Rather, it was a proceeding brought under 28 USC §1331, challenging the selective prosecution of several Palestinians on the basis of what would be, for U.S. citizens, conduct protected by the First Amendment. In *AADC*,[28] the government promised that, should the need for additional evidence arise in a future removal case, it would agree to a remand under 28 USC §2347(b).[29]

However, as correctly pointed out therein, this was an empty promise, as that section applies only where no hearing had been held. And even if the government were to honor its promise and agree to a remand, since the right to a hearing under the statute is a jurisdictional question, a court would be bound to raise it *sua sponte* and make a determination based on the statute, rather than on the position of the parties.

---

[27] There is, however, a recent Third Circuit case that simply ignores the limitation. In *Borges v. Gonzales*, 402 F.3d 398, 407 (3rd Cir. 2005), the court granted the petitioner's motion to supplement the record with what he described as "newly-discovered evidence of fraud—including altered documents," and instructed the BIA to consider this evidence on remand.

[28] *Reno v. American-Arab Anti-Discrimination Committee (AADC)*, 525 U.S. 471 (1999).

[29] 525 U.S. 488. 28 USC §2347(b), provides:

> (b) When the agency has not held a hearing before taking the action of which review is sought by the petition, the court of appeals shall determine whether a hearing is required by law. After that determination, the court shall—
>
> (1) remand the proceedings to the agency to hold a hearing, when a hearing is required by law;
>
> (2) pass on the issues presented, when a hearing is not required by law and it appears from the pleadings and affidavits filed by the parties that no genuine issue of material fact is presented; or
>
> (3) transfer the proceedings to a district court for the district in which the petitioner resides or has its principal office for a hearing and determination as if the proceedings were originally initiated in the district court, when a hearing is not required by law and a genuine issue of material fact is presented. The procedure in these cases in the district court is governed by the Federal Rules of Civil Procedure.

Barring further changes in the composition of the Supreme Court, *St. Cyr* offers some basis for hope that the Suspension Clause would still protect the right to habeas review of deportation orders, at least where any substitute procedures Congress has enacted, including the REAL ID Act, are demonstrably "inadequate or ineffective" to reach the issues raised by a given removal order.

THE REAL ID ACT OF 2005

Not surprisingly, many members of Congress were dissatisfied with the results in *St. Cyr*, particularly to the extent it provided what they considered to be an "extra layer" of review for criminal aliens, by permitting them to go first into a federal district court, in habeas corpus, and if unsuccessful there, to a courts of appeals. This is evident from the REAL ID Act of 2005,[30] in which Congress expressed its intent, in unambiguous language, to preclude habeas review of deportation orders, even as it shifted all review of questions of law and constitutional claims to the courts of appeals.

As added by REAL ID, 8 USC §1252(a)(2)(D) now provides:

> (D) Judicial review of certain legal claims. Nothing in subparagraph (B) or (C), or in any other provision of this Act (other than this section) which limits or eliminates judicial review, shall be construed as precluding review of constitutional claims or questions of law raised upon a petition for review filed with an appropriate court of appeals in accordance with this section.

Questions remain, however, as to whether the scope of review provided by REAL ID necessarily meets the test of *Swain v. Pressley*. While §1252(a)(2)(D) now permits "review of constitutional claims [and] questions of law," the battle is not over. As noted above, there is no provision under §1252(a) that would allow for remand for an evidentiary hearing in cases where an alleged constitutional violation does not appear on the face of the record. In addition, the Department of Homeland Security (DHS) is now arguing that only "substantial" or "colorable" constitutional claims are subject to review. While at first glance this may seem to be a petty dispute, it has enormous procedural ramifications. It allows the court to dismiss cases raising

---

[30] REAL ID Act of 2005, Emergency Supplemental Appropriations Act for Defense, the Global War on Terror, and Tsunami Relief, 2005, Division B, Pub. L. No. 109-13, 119 Stat. 231 (May 11, 2005) (REAL ID Act).

only constitutional claims on motion. Since the federal rules do not require that the court rule otherwise, this allows dismissal without giving any reasoning or justification. Further, the court issues the mandate simultaneously with its order when it dismisses a petition on motion. Dismissal on motion deprives the person of the ability to seek *en banc* reconsideration, and makes it extremely difficulty to seek certiorari, as there is no means of deciphering the reasoning of the court. [31]

ISSUES REMAINING UNDER REAL ID

Cases Where No Petition for Review Was Timely Filed

One issue to be explored is the fate of untimely filed petitions for review. In habeas cases there was no time limit, and such petitions could be filed virtually at any time, so long as the requisite custody existed. Following REAL ID, that option is gone. For example, in *Medellin-Reyes v. Gonzales,*[32] a lawful permanent resident (LPR) was ordered removed in 1997 but did not seek judicial review of the BIA until 2004, when he filed a habeas challenge to the order. Following REAL ID, the petition was transferred to the Seventh Circuit. The court noted that the last sentence of §1252(a)(2)(D) instructed the court of appeals to treat the transferred case as if it had been filed pursuant to a petition for review under such §242, "except that subsection (b)(1) of such section shall not apply." The court concluded:

> Subsection (b)(1) contains the time limit, which therefore "shall not apply." This means that all collateral proceedings pending on May 11, 2005, when the Real ID Act took effect, and transferred to courts of appeals under §106(c), must be treated as timely petitions for review, no matter how long it has been since the Board rendered its decision. Collateral proceedings filed on or after May 11, however, will be dismissed outright; the window for belated judicial review has closed.[33]

It does not even appear that equitable tolling will be available, given that the 30-day limit is jurisdictional. In the Eleventh Circuit, the court stated:

> We do not consider the merits of the BIA's final order of removal against Dakane issued on March 11, 2004, for lack of jurisdiction. ... Since the statutory limit for filing a petition for review in an immigration proceeding is "mandatory and jurisdictional," it is not subject to equitable tolling. *See Stone v. INS,* 514 U.S. 386, 405, 131 L. Ed. 2d 465, 115 S. Ct. 1537 (1995) (construing the former 90-day period for filing a petition for review under the INA §106(a)(1), 8 USC §1105a(a)).[34]

An almost infinitesimal ray of hope can be seen in *Nahatchevska v. Ashcroft:*[35]

> The filing of a timely petition for review is "mandatory and jurisdictional" and is "not subject to equitable tolling." *Stone v. INS,* 514 U.S. 386, 405, 131 L. Ed. 2d 465, 115 S. Ct. 1537 (1995). Nor does this case present "unique circumstances" sufficient to excuse petitioner's untimeliness. *See Thompson v. INS,* 375 U.S. 384, 387, 11 L. Ed. 2d 404, 84 S. Ct. 397 (1964); *Osterneck v. Ernst & Whinney,* 489 U.S. 169, 179, 103 L. Ed. 2d 146, 109 S. Ct. 987 (1989) (noting that "Thompson applies only where a party has performed an act which, if properly done, would postpone the deadline for filing his appeal and has received specific assurance by a judicial officer that this act has been properly done.").

More likely to be of assistance is the suggestion made in *Asere v. Gonzales,*[36] where the Seventh Circuit pointed to one possible escape from this dilemma, to wit, through a motion to reopen, wherein the 90-day time limit *is* subject to equitable tolling:

> Though this case is disappointing, all hope may not be lost for Asere. Ordinarily, a motion to reopen must be filed no later than 90 [days] after the date on which the final administrative decision was rendered in the proceeding sought to be

---

[31] This practice is being challenged in a case in a petition for certiorari before the Supreme Court. *Galindo and Acosta v. Gonzales,* No. 05-1276.

[32] *Medellin-Reyes v. Gonzales,* 435 F.3d 721,723–24 (7th Cir. 2006).

[33] *Id.* A similar case is pending at the Fifth Circuit. *Iturbe-Covarrubias v. Gonzales,* No. 05-60566. It involves an LPR who was deported when DWI was still considered to be an aggravated felony. He returned illegally, and was prosecuted for unlawful re-entry, under 8 USC §1326. Relying on *Zala-*
continued

---

wadia v. Ashcroft, 371 F.3d 292 (5th Cir. 2004), he filed a habeas action challenging the removal order, which was transferred under REAL ID.

[34] *Dakane v. U.S. Att'y Gen.,* 399 F.3d 1269, 1272 (11th Cir. 2004).

[35] *Nahatchevska v. Ashcroft,* 317 F.3d 1226, 1227 (10th Cir. 2003).

[36] *Asere v. Gonzales,* 439 F.3d 378 (7th Cir. 2006).

reopened. 8 CFR §1003.2(c)(2). For Asere, that time has lapsed. However, we have held that the deadlines for motions to reopen are not jurisdictional, and are therefore subject to equitable tolling. *Pervaiz v. Gonzales*, 405 F.3d 488, 490 (7th Cir. 2005). We have also suggested that ineffective assistance of counsel is a possible basis for tolling the reopening deadline. *See id.*; *Mahmood v. Gonzales*, 427 F.3d 248, 251 (3d. Cir. 2005). As is all too evident, the failure to file a timely appeal of the BIA's January 25, 2005, decision was fatal. Based on this failure, Asere might have sufficient grounds to file a new motion to reopen to challenge the BIA's decision.[37]

See also *Infanzon v. Ashcroft*:[38]

We have recited these arguments at some length because they illustrate petitioner's lack of support for his claimed entitlement to equitable tolling and his complete failure, even when furnished with the road map to follow, to satisfy the requirements of *Lozada*. Indeed, it is petitioner's belated challenges, some made years after the events he testified to at the administrative proceedings, that underscore the need for adherence to the "high standard . . . necessary . . . [as] a basis for assessing the substantial number of claims of ineffective assistance of counsel that come before the Board." *Lozada*, 19 I&N Dec. at 639; *see Mickeviciute v. INS*, 327 F.3d 1159, 1161 n.2 (10th Cir. 2003) (noting that motion based on claim of ineffective assistance of counsel must be supported as outlined in *Lozada*); *Tang v. Ashcroft*, 354 F.3d 1192, 1196–97 (10th Cir. 2003) (noting no abuse of discretion by BIA's denial of motion to reopen where petitioner failed to comply with *Lozada*).

Motions to reopen are "disfavored," and are subject to review only for abuse of discretion, under which the immigrant bears a "heavy burden." As explained in *INS v. Abudu*:[39]

The reasons why motions to reopen are disfavored in deportation proceedings are comparable to those that apply to petitions for rehearing, and to motions for new trials on the basis of newly discovered evidence. There is a strong public interest in bringing litigation to a close as promptly as is consistent with the interest in giving the adversaries a fair opportunity to develop and present their respective cases.[40] (footnotes omitted)

As recently explained by the Fifth Circuit in *Altamirano-Lopez v. Gonzales*:

While this Court reviews a denial of a motion to reopen under a "highly deferential abuse-of-discretion standard," *Zhao v. Gonzales*, 404 F.3d 295, 303 (5th Cir. 2005), we review constitutional challenges de novo. *Soadjede v. Ashcroft*, 324 F.3d 830, 831 (5th Cir. 2003). Additionally, motions to reopen deportation proceedings are "disfavored," and the moving party bears a "heavy burden." *INS v. Abudu*, 485 U.S. 94, 107–08, 108 S. Ct. 904, 99 L. Ed. 2d 90 (1988).[41]

Moreover, under Fifth Circuit precedent, there is no "liberty interest," and therefore no right to due process, in the adjudication of a motion to reopen:

Because we determine that there is no liberty interest at stake in a motion to reopen, Altamirano cannot establish a due process violation. The decision to grant or deny a motion to reopen is purely discretionary. 8 CFR §1003.23(b)(1)(iv). Even if a moving party has established a prima facie case for relief, an IJ can still deny a motion to reopen. 8 CFR §1003.23(b)(3). As we stated in *Finlay v. INS*, "the denial of discretionary relief does not rise to the level of a constitutional violation even if [the moving party] had been eligible for it." *Finlay*, 210 F.3d 556, 557 (5th Cir. 2000); see also, *Assaad v. Ashcroft*, 378 F.3d 471, 475 (5th Cir. 2004) ("[Petitioner's] motion to reopen does not allege a violation of his Fifth Amendment right to due process because 'the failure to receive relief that is purely discretionary in nature does not amount to a deprivation of a liberty interest.'")[42] (citation omitted).

Therefore, while motions to reopen may be the only vehicle by which to attempt to salvage a case in which a petition for review was not timely filed, the extent to which such motions can be considered to not be "ineffective or inadequate" is open to debate.

A recent case dismissed by the Fifth Circuit for lack of jurisdiction illustrates a number of these principles. In that case, the petitioner, Alfonso, attempted to challenge a reinstatement order issued

---

[37] *Id.* at 381.

[38] 386 F.3d 1359, 1363 (10th Cir. 2004).

[39] *INS v. Abudu*, 485 U.S. 94, 107–08 (1988).

---

[40] *Id.* at 107.

[41] *Altamirano-Lopez v. Gonzales*, 435 F.3d 547, **4–5 (5th Cir. 2006).

[42] *Id.* at **7–8.

under 8 USC §1231(a)(5) on the grounds that he was a U.S. citizen. He had been deported twice, in 1993 and 2004. He re-entered across the Rio Grande River on May 23, 2005. He was again arrested by INS and charged with unlawful re-entry, under 8 USC §1226. The same day, Alfonso signed the form stating that he did desire to make a statement contesting reinstatement. Instead of giving him the opportunity to do so, INS immediately determined that he was subject to reinstatement. However, Alfonso was neither given a copy of the form embodying this determination nor advised that it had been made. He hired an attorney, and only then learned that because his mother is a U.S. citizen who was unmarried at the time of his birth, he had a very strong claim to have acquired U.S. citizenship through her. Through counsel, he filed an N-600 within 30 days of his arrest. During proceedings on the N-600, counsel was led to believe that the order of removal had not been reinstated, and that it would not be reinstated unless and until Alfonso's claim to U.S. citizenship had been adjudicated, and rejected. The existence of the May 23, 2005, determination was kept secret from his attorney. In fact, Alfonso was removed on August 6, 2005, after counsel had been led to believe that the N-600 would be approved and before it was actually denied. Counsel, believing that August 6, 2005, was the date of the reinstatement order, (he first obtained a copy of the May, 23, 2005, "determination" when the government filed its motion to dismiss), filed a petition for review on August 26, 2005.

Under 8 CFR §§241.8, 1241.8, there is no requirement that INS consider any claim to U.S. citizenship, although it does contemplate that the initial determination leading to the issuance of the Notice of Intent be based on an investigation of whether or not the conditions of reinstatement are met. Further, nothing in the regulations requires that the alien be served with a copy of the reinstatement order, or even notified of its existence.

Because Alfonso had requested the right to make a statement challenging reinstatement, he argued to the Fifth Circuit that his N-600 constituted his statement, and that it was improper to issue a reinstatement order prior to considering his statement. In the alternative, he argued that his N-600 should be viewed as a motion to reconsider the reinstatement order and that the denial of his N-600 should be construed as a denial of the motion to consider, under which theory his petition for review should be

viewed as a timely challenge to the denial of reconsideration.[43]

However, the Fifth Circuit simply granted INS's motion to dismiss and simultaneously issued the mandate. No attempt was made, either by INS or the court, to respond to Alfonso's arguments. He was, in effect, left with no remedy. There is no administrative record, and no opinion by the Fifth Circuit. Since the mandate was issued simultaneously with the order dismissing the petition, it was impossible to file a petition for en banc rehearing. And with no record or written opinion, the likelihood of success on a petition for certiorari would be slim to none.

Cases Where Additional Evidence May Be Required

Finally, one may confront cases where constitutional claims are made that require evidentiary support. Since neither the IJs nor the BIA can consider constitutional challenges,[44] few of us are used to thinking about such challenges in time to build an evidentiary record before the IJ. In fact, most IJs will not allow such evidence. This does not mean, however, that we should not think through our cases well enough to anticipate the constitutional challenges that might be relevant, and to make an "offer of proof" with respect to any facts necessary to support such a challenge. In cases where the IJ already had ruled when REAL ID was passed, it would probably be sufficient to make such an offer before the BIA.[45]

In some cases—for example, where the IJ terminated proceedings and the BIA reversed but, instead of remanding, ordered the person removed—this fact can be used to support the argument, as held by the Ninth Circuit in *Noriega-Lopez v. Ashcroft*,[46]

---

[43] *See Ponta-Garcia v. Ashcroft*, 386 F.3d 341 (1st Cir. 2004).

[44] *See Matter of Gonzales*, 21 I&N Dec. 937, 942 (BIA 1997).

[45] *See, e.g., Molina v. Sewell*, 983 F.2d 676, 680 (5th Cir. 1993), wherein an offer of proof before the BIA as to what evidence could have been submitted in support of a contention that the IJ erred in not advising the alien of his right to present evidence in an exclusion hearing, to show that he was not making an "entry," was deemed sufficient to establish prejudice from the IJ's failure to abide by the pertinent regulation.

[46] 335 F.3d 874 (9th Cir. 2003). This argument is based on the fact that 8 USC §1229a(a)(1)–(3), enacted in 1996, specifies that IJs shall conduct proceedings "for deciding the . . . deportability of an alien," and that this shall be the "exclusive procedure" for "determining whether an alien may be . . . removed from the United States."

that such an order is *ultra vires*. If the case was in habeas proceedings when the REAL ID Act was enacted and a record had been made in those proceedings, it is worth arguing that the court should consider any evidence and/or factual findings made therein.

The most difficult cases will be those where it is alleged that an irregularity occurred in the proceedings but is extrinsic to the record, as in *Accardi*. There, one can request a remand under 28 USC §2347(b), as INS promised could be done in *AADC*, or simply ask the court to supplement the record, as occurred in *Borges*. Failing this, the only option would be to simply file a habeas petition, citing directly to *Accardi*. At some point, this issue will have to be confronted. This author would, however, caution that this be tried only in the most compelling cases, on the theory that (from the government's perspective) "hard cases make bad law."

CONCLUSION

In conclusion, it is worth noting that the worst may be yet to come. There are proposals afoot in Congress to eliminate review even of questions of law and constitutional claims in some cases. We can only hope that so long as the five-member majority that gave us *St. Cyr* holds together, we might be able to successfully challenge such an amendment. However, the number of immigrants, and their families, who would suffer irreversible harm in the interim is incalculable. As it is, mandatory detention has had the effect of encouraging large numbers of LPRs who are in removal proceedings and have strong legal arguments and constitutional claims, to accept deportation, return illegally, and thereafter join the underground labor force. Since this vulnerable group would not benefit from any guest-worker program, it is important that we continue to fight the abuses that exist, and those still to come.

GETTING OUT: STRATEGIES FOR CHALLENGING UNLAWFUL DETENTION IN FEDERAL COURT

*by Jeff Joseph, Holly S. Cooper, and David W. Leopold**

Despite its innumerable other problems, the REAL ID Act of 2005[1] did not affect the federal court's powers to review unconstitutional detention. The federal courts have consistently held that habeas corpus review of detention decisions survives the jurisdictional-stripping provisions of §106(a) of the REAL ID Act.[2] Practitioners can, and should, continue to rely on writs of habeas corpus to challenge unconstitutional detention by the Department of Homeland Security (DHS).

The purpose of this article is to discuss recent developments in federal litigation of detention claims and provide arguments and strategies for federal challenges to unconstitutional detention.

I'M EXHAUSTED! SETTING YOURSELF UP FOR FEDERAL COURT REVIEW

The first step in a federal court challenge to unconstitutional detention does not occur in federal court. The first step in obtaining federal court review is before DHS and the immigration judge (IJ). Generally, federal courts require that an individual exhaust all administrative remedies mandated by law before seeking federal court redress for constitutional violations.[3]

Be aware, however, that in the detention context, there is no statutory exhaustion requirement for judicial challenges to DHS custody.[4] The Supreme Court in *McCarthy v. Madison* specifically provided that where Congress has not clearly required exhaustion, "sound judicial discretion governs."[5]

In determining whether judicial discretion is warranted, the court will consider: (1) whether available remedies provide a genuine opportunity for adequate relief; (2) whether irreparable injury may occur without immediate judicial relief; (3) whether administrative appeal would be futile; and (4) in certain instances, whether a plaintiff has raised a substantial constitutional question.[6] Before going into federal court, you will want to be able to demonstrate that at least one (if not all) of the factors is present in your case. Exhaustion may also be excused if "the interest of the individual in retaining prompt access to a federal judicial forum [outweighs] countervailing institutional interests favoring exhaustion."[7]

* **Jeff Joseph** is senior partner in the Joseph Law Firm, a full-service immigration law firm. Mr. Joseph is a past chair of the Colorado Chapter of AILA and is currently a member of the national board of governors of AILA. He is on the AILA National Immigration and Customs Enforcement Liaison Committee, as well as the AILA Amicus Committee, and Restrictionist Watch Committee. In 2004, Mr. Joseph received the Joseph Minsky Young Lawyer of the Year Award from AILA. He is an adjunct professor of immigration law at the University of Denver College of Law.

Holly Cooper graduated in 1998 from University of California, Davis School of Law, where she received the Martin Luther King, Jr. award for community service. At the Florence Immigrant & Refugee Rights Project, she initiated a pilot project for the hundreds of detained immigrant children in Arizona who were in removal proceedings without representation. Ms. Cooper is currently senior staff attorney working out of the Eloy Detention Center, where approximately 1,000 men are currently detained in DHS custody.

David Leopold practices removal defense and business and family immigration in Cleveland. He is AILA national treasurer (2006–07) and was an elected director on the AILA board of governors (2003–05). Mr. Leopold is former chair of the ICE Liaison Committee (2003–04) and of the AILA Due Process Committee (2002–03), and former member of the AILA General Counsel Liaison Committee (2004–05). He is a co-founder of the AILA/AILF Litigation Institute and served as Ohio Chapter Chair (2001–03).

[1] REAL ID Act of 2005, Emergency Supplemental Appropriations Act for Defense, the Global War on Terror, and Tsunami Relief, 2005, Division B, Pub. L. No. 109-13, 119 Stat. 231 (May 11, 2005) (REAL ID Act).

[2] *See, e.g.*, H.R. Rep. No. 109-72, at 300 (2005); *Hernandez v. Gonzales*, 424 F.3d 42, 42 (1st Cir. 2005); *Forbes v. Atty. Gen. of the United States*, No. 05-3659, 2006 WL 615984 (3d Cir. Mar. 13, 2006); *Gul v. Rozos*, No. 05-30327, 2006 WL 140540 (5th Cir. Jan 19, 2006); and *Armentero v. INS*, 412 F.3d 1088, 1099 (9th Cir. 2005).

[3] *McCarthy v. Madison*, 503 U.S. 140, 144 (1992).

[4] *Tam v. INS*, 14 F. Supp. 2d 1184, 1189 (E.D. Cal. 1998) ("Congress has not specifically mandated exhaustion before judicial review of [INS] custody determination").

[5] *McCarthy v. Madison*, 503 U.S. at 144.

[6] *Howell v. INS*, 72 F.3d 288, 291 (2d Cir. 1995).

[7] *McCarty v. Madison*, 503 U.S. at 146.

Despite the lack of a statutory requirement to exhaust, it is prudent to try to do so. File a written request for release with the field director for detention and removal and file a motion for bond determination with the IJ—even if you know that the field director will deny your request, or that the IJ will not entertain a bond motion. By getting a written order to that effect, you can demonstrate that you have exhausted your administrative remedies. When you file the habeas, attach as exhibits copies of your requests for release and bond motion and any written decisions.

If the issue is jurisdictional, *i.e.*, whether your client is subject to mandatory detention, and therefore whether the judge has jurisdiction to redetermine bond, file a motion for a *Matter of Joseph* hearing.[8] In *Matter of Joseph*, the Board of Immigration Appeals (BIA) held that the judge has jurisdiction to determine, in the first instance, whether someone is properly classified as subject to §236(c) and held under mandatory detention.[9] In other words, the IJ has jurisdiction to determine whether he or she has jurisdiction over an individual whom U.S. Immigration and Customs Enforcement (ICE) alleges is subject to mandatory detention. Although *Matter of Joseph* deals specifically with §236(c), argue that *Matter of Joseph* stands for the general proposition that IJs have jurisdiction to determine their jurisdiction over other bond decisions, such as whether someone is properly classified as an arriving alien.

Argue, too, that appeal of the bond issue to the BIA is not required because appeal would take a minimum of six months and since a final order of removal is likely to be issued before you receive a decision on the bond and the petitioner would remain in custody during that time, exhaustion is futile. Also, argue that appeal to the BIA would be futile because the habeas petition raises substantial constitutional questions that the BIA cannot address.

Finally, in your petition, lay out the irreparable harm that is caused by your client's continued detention. Argue that your client suffers irreparable injury every day in the form of loss of liberty. Argue that mandatory detention separates the family and penalizes your client for pursuing claims against deportation. It also causes your client to face the indefinite loss of income that may be necessary to support your client's family and deprives U.S. citizen family members of financial, physical, and emotional support.

SOMEBODY'S GONNA' GET SUED HERE! WHERE DO YOU FILE THE HABEAS PETITION?

One of the issues that will certainly be on the forefront of detention-related litigation in the next few years is where to file the habeas. Who is the custodian of your client? What is the proper venue? These are confusing questions today.

- Your client may have been arrested in Miami (Eleventh Circuit), detained and processed at Krome (Eleventh Circuit), transferred to Oakdale, Louisiana (Fifth Circuit) after the hurricane, but appear by video conference before a judge in Arlington (Fourth Circuit).

- A client convicted of first-time drug possession in Idaho (Ninth Circuit), where *Lujan-Armendariz* says that a first-time drug possession offense that is expunged pursuant to a state rehabilitative statute is not a conviction for immigration purposes, and your client is not removable. The Denver detention district has jurisdiction over Idaho, so your client is detained in Denver (Tenth Circuit). In the Tenth Circuit, your client is an aggravated felon with no relief available.

Where do you file the habeas? DHS has consistently argued that the "immediate custodian" rule should apply and that the only proper respondent to a habeas action is the field director with immediate physical control over your client. This is a very narrow and inflexible approach to habeas venue considerations, but it has been adopted by some circuit courts.[10]

The circuits have divided on whether a detained alien challenging removal must name the warden of the detention facility in a petition for habeas corpus, or whether the alien may name more senior officials such as the Attorney General or the Secretary of DHS.[11]

---

[8] *Matter of Joseph*, 22 I&N Dec. 799, 1999 WL 339053 (BIA 1999) *See* further discussion, *infra*.

[9] *Id.*

[10] *Roman v. Ashcroft*, 340 F.3d 314, 322 (6th Cir. 2003); *Vasquez v. Reno*, 233 F.3d 688, 693 (1st Cir. 2000); *Yi v. Maugans*, 24 F.3d 500, 507 (3d Cir. 1994).

[11] *Cf. Roman v. Ashcroft*, 340 F.3d 314, 320 (6th Cir. 2003); *Henderson v. INS*, 157 F.3d 106, 126 (2d Cir. 1998); *Kholyavskiy v. Achim*, 2006 U.S. App. LEXIS 9567 (7th Cir. Apr. 17, 2006) (the warden of the state and local facility is a *continued*

The Supreme Court in *Rumsfeld v. Padilla*,[12] applying the immediate custodian rule, held that Padilla's challenge to his detention as an enemy combatant at a naval brig in South Carolina under military custody was a "core challenge" to "present physical confinement" and that the proper respondent is the warden of the facility where the detainee is being held.[13] The Court also held that the habeas challenge may only be brought in the district court that has territorial jurisdiction over the detainee's immediate custodian.[14] Nevertheless, the Court specifically reserved applying the decision to immigration habeas petitions and left open the question of whether the immediate custodian rule applies in the immigration habeas context.[15]

On the other side of the equation, the Ninth Circuit adopted the "functional custodian" approach of *Armentero v. INS*.[16] Under this approach, the proper custodian is the Attorney General or Secretary of DHS, and the habeas can be filed in any jurisdiction because the Attorney General has the ultimate power to cause the petitioner to be present.

After analyzing five Supreme Court cases, culminating in *Braden v. 30th Judicial Circuit Court of Kentucky*,[17] the Ninth Circuit in *Armentero* concluded that, "read as a whole, the Supreme Court's pertinent case law indicates that the concept of custodian is a broad one that includes any person empowered to end restraint of a habeas petitioner's liberty, not just the petitioner's immediate on-site, immediate physical custodian."[18]

The court acknowledged the First Circuit decision in *Vazquez* and agreed that "while a petitioner's immediate physical custodian is typically a proper respondent in traditional habeas petitions, the statutory custodian requirement of 28 U.S.C. §2241 is sufficiently flexible to permit the naming of respondents who are not immediate physical custodians if practicality, efficiency, and the interests of justice so demand."[19] The court went on to state that the circumstances surrounding immigration-related detention of aliens demand such flexibility.[20] "Although held at the behest of federal authorities, immigration detainees are physically detained in a host of institutions, ranging from specialized immigration detention centers to federal prisons to state and local prisons and jails."[21] It also noted that "[i]mmigration detainees are frequently transferred among federal, state, and local institutions across the country."[22] The court then recognized many problems encountered by aliens who have been transferred and whose habeas petitions are constrained by the "immediate custodian" approach[23]: access to counsel, dismissal or frequent transfer of petitions for lack of personal jurisdiction over the respondent, *pro hac vice* rules of the transferee district, and overload of court dockets in those areas with large immigration detention facilities.[24]

Although DHS will raise the issue of forum shopping, the same argument can be raised against application of the immediate custodian rule. Because ICE routinely transfers immigration detainees to remote detention centers, permitting suit only in the district court of confinement gives the government complete control over where the action can be filed and thus, the circuit court law that will govern.

NO MORE *DEMORE*—
CHALLENGING THE APPLICATION
OF §236(c) IN FEDERAL COURT

In 1996, Congress considerably expanded the breadth of the mandatory detention provisions.[25] Currently under INA §236(c), most noncitizens with inadmissible or removable criminal offenses are confined in mandatory administrative detention before a final removal order. In *Kim v. Ziglar*, the Ninth Circuit found the mandatory detention provisions to be unconstitutional as applied to lawful

---

contract agent used by INS to act pursuant to INS detention standards and exercise control at the direction of INS; thus, the INS field director is a proper respondent); *Yang You Yi v. Maugans*, 24 F.3d 500, 507 (3d Cir. 1994) (the warden of the facility where the detainee is being held is the proper custodian); *Vazquez v. Reno*, 233 F.3d 688, 689 (1st Cir. 2000) (rejecting the Attorney General as a proper respondent).

[12] 542 U.S. 426 (2004).

[13] *Id.* at 438.

[14] *Id.* at 444.

[15] *Id.* at 436 n.8.

[16] 340 F.3d 1058 (9th Cir. 2003).

[17] 410 U.S. 484 (1973).

[18] *Armentero v. INS*, 340 F.3d at 1064.

[19] *Id.* at 1068.

[20] *Id.*

[21] *Id.*

[22] *Id.* at 1069.

[23] *Id.*

[24] *Id.*

[25] INA §236(c).

permanent residents.[26] It held that a permanent resident in removal proceedings is entitled to an individualized bond hearing and cannot be automatically detained without bond under INA §236(c). In *Demore v. Kim*, the Supreme Court reversed *Kim v. Ziglar*. The Supreme Court held that certain classes of lawful permanent residents may be detained without individualized bond hearings used to determine whether they posed a flight risk or danger to the community.[27]

This section will present arguments that you can raise to challenge the applicability and breadth of *Demore v. Kim*.

How Can I Challenge Mandatory Detention Under §236(c)?

The starting point for any analysis is determining whether the mandatory detention provisions apply to you or your client.

Was Your Client Released Before the Transitional Period Custody Rules Expired?[28]

First, the mandatory detention provisions should only apply to individuals who were released from physical criminal custody on or after October 9, 1998.[29] The logical extension should be that only release for a removable/inadmissible offense listed in INA §236(c) should subject a person to mandatory detention. Thus, if your client was released from physical custody before October 9, 1998, your client could be eligible for a bond hearing. Moreover, if your client was released from physical criminal custody on or after October 9, 1998, for a criminal offense that is not enumerated in INA §236(c), your client may also be eligible for a bond hearing.

Did Your Client Plead Guilty to a Criminal Offense Enumerated in INA §236(c) Before April 1, 1997?

INA §236(c) should not apply retroactively to individuals who pleaded guilty to a criminal offense before April 1, 1997, IIRAIRA's general effective date, but were released after October 8, 1998. At least one district court has found that §236(c) should not apply retroactively. In *Boonkue v. Ridge*,[30] the petitioner was convicted in 1994 for felony issuing checks with insufficient funds; probation was revoked in 1998, and he was released after serving his sentence in 1999, but was not detained by ICE until 2004.

Was Your Client Given Only Probation for the Criminal Offense?

Mandatory detention should not apply to persons sentenced to probation only after October 8, 1998, because "release" in that statute means release from physical confinement.[31]

Was Your Client Released from Criminal Custody Only to Later Be Taken Into ICE Custody?

Mandatory detention provisions should only apply to persons taken into DHS custody immediately upon release from criminal incarceration for an offense enumerated in §236(c).[32]

Does the American Baptist Church v. Thornburgh Settlement Protect Your Salvadoran or Guatemalan Client from Mandatory Detention?

Most lawyers are unaware that the *American Baptist Church v. Thornburgh* settlement may exempt a client from mandatory detention.[33] Paragraph 17 of the settlement states,

> The INS may only detain class members, eligible for relief under paragraph 2, who are otherwise subject to detention under current law and who: (1) have been convicted of a crime involving moral turpitude for which the sentence actually imposed exceeded a term of imprisonment in ex-

---

[26] 276 F.3d 523 (9th Cir. 2001).

[27] 538 U.S. 510 (2003).

[28] On October 9, 1998, the legislative authority expired for the exercise of discretion to release noncitizens under the Transition Period Custody Rules (TPCR) of IIRAIRA §303(b)(2).

[29] *Matter of Adeniji*, 22 I&N Dec. 1102 (BIA 1999); *Matter of West*, 22 I&N Dec. 1405 (BIA 2000).

[30] 2004 WL 1146525 (D. Or. 2004).

[31] *Matter of Nguyen*, A25 404 392 (BIA 2000); *In re West*, 22 I&N Dec. 1405 (BIA 2000); *In re Adeniji*, 22 I&N Dec. 1102 (BIA 1999); *see also Tenrreiro v. Ashcroft*, 2004 WL 1354277 (D. Or. 2004), *order vacated on reconsideration on other grounds*, 2004 WL 1588217 (D. Or. 2004) (convicted of theft in 2003 and received probation with no incarceration).

[32] *Quezada-Bucio v. Ridge*, 03-CV-03668-ORD (Apr. 7, 2004 W.D. Wa.); *Tenreio v. Ashcroft*, 2004 WL 1354277 (D. Or. 2004), *order vacated on reconsideration on other grounds*, 2004 WL 1588217 (D. Or. 2004). *But see Matter of Rojas*, 23 I&N Dec. 117 (BIA 2001) (finding §236(c) could apply to individuals not immediately taken into custody after release but leaving open the issue of whether the offense had to be one enumerated in INA §236(c)).

[33] *American Baptist Church v. Thornburgh*, 760 F. Supp. 796 (N.D. Cal. 1991).

cess of six months; or (2) pose a national security risk; or (3) pose a threat to public safety.[34]

The distinction of *ABC* members under paragraph 17 is important because it appears to exempt members from mandatory detention. The paragraph categorically prohibits ICE from detaining class members unless they meet the criteria.[35]

Do the Mandatory Detention Provisions Apply to Your Client If You Are Challenging That Your Client Is Not Even Removable or Inadmissible?

Often detainees are challenging the premise that they are even removable. For example, a detainee may be claiming U.S. citizenship through acquisition or be challenging that the offense is removable as an aggravated felony. Persons in this situation should argue that they are entitled to a hearing pursuant to *Matter of Joseph*,[36] where they can show through a special hearing that they are not properly included in the mandatory detention category. A person who is denied a *Joseph* hearing should appeal to the BIA to exhaust his or her administrative remedies (unless exhaustion is not required) to then pursue a federal challenge to the *Joseph* finding.[37]

Although the BIA found in *Joseph* that the noncitizen had to show that DHS was "substantially unlikely" to establish the charges, advocates and pro se detainees should argue that the proper standard is "likelihood of success on the merits of the charge."

Also, *Demore v. Kim* left open the possibility that a lawful permanent resident who has not yet conceded removability could still challenge detention. The majority appeared to give considerable weight to Kim's alleged concession of deportability.

In *Tijani v. Willis*,[38] the Ninth Circuit avoided deciding the constitutional issue and interpreted the authority conferred by INA §236(c) as applying only to expeditious removal of criminal aliens. "Two years and four months of process is not expeditious; and the foreseeable process in this court, where the

government's brief in the appeal has not yet been filed, is a year or more."[39]

The concurring opinion by Judge Tashima strongly criticized *Joseph* and held that the *Joseph* standard was egregiously unconstitutional because it placed the burden on the defendant to prove that he should not be physically detained, making the burden all but insurmountable.[40] The court found that §236(c) should apply to mandatory detention more narrowly, holding that only immigrants who could not raise a "substantial argument" against their removability should be subject to mandatory detention.[41] The opinion criticized *Joseph* for establishing a system of detention by default.[42]

Finally, if your client is claiming U.S. citizenship by birth, derivation, or acquisition, you should challenge the applicability of §236(c) through a *Joseph* hearing or a writ of habeas corpus.

What If My Client Is Detained for an Unreasonable Period Under §236(c) and There Is No Final Order or the Order Is Stayed?

In the seminal case of *Ly v. Hansen*,[43] the Sixth Circuit granted a petition for a writ of habeas corpus and construed the pre-removal detention statute §236(c) to include an implicit requirement that removal proceedings be concluded in a reasonable time. Ly was detailed for about 18 months while his removal proceedings were pending.

Does a Stay of Removal in the District Court or Circuit Court of Appeals Affect Ability to Be Released?

In *Lawson v. Gerlinski*,[44] the petitioner secured a stay of removal while challenging his removal order in circuit court. The petitioner simultaneously pursued a writ of habeas corpus in district court. The court found that the price for securing a stay of removal should not be prolonged incarceration. Where detention becomes prolonged, special care must be exercised so that confinement does not continue beyond the time when the original justifications for custody are no longer tenable.

---

[34] *Id.* at 804.

[35] *But see ABC* Settlement Wire 15 (Apr. 24, 1991) (*see* 68 *Interpreter Releases* 910 (July 22, 1991) (stating that *ABC* members convicted of aggravated felonies are subject to the mandatory detention provisions of the Immigration Act).

[36] 22 I&N Dec. 799 (BIA 1999).

[37] *See* discussion, *supra*.

[38] 430 F.3d 1241 (9th Cir. 2005).

[39] *Id.* at 1242.

[40] *Id.* at 1246.

[41] *Id.*

[42] *Id.* at 1244.

[43] 351 F.3d 263 (6th Cir. 2003).

[44] 332 F. Supp. 2d 735 (M.D. Penn 2004).

In *Oyedeji v. Ashcroft*,[45] the court found that a noncitizen with removable convictions who filed a stay of removal and a petition for review challenging his removal could be released. The court found petitioner's convictions did not conclusively establish that he was a danger to the community or a flight risk. Further, the court found the alien's incarceration for more than four years after he petitioned for the stay of removal was unreasonable.

In *Haynes v. DHS*,[46] the court ordered DHS to provide petitioner with a meaningful review pursuant to 8 CFR §241.4(i). The petitioner had filed a petition for review and stay of removal. Petitioner challenged his prolonged confinement by filing a writ of habeas corpus. DHS argued that his stay of removal tolled the 90-day removal period. The court, however, found the DHS position inconsistent with the constitutional command that liberty be taken away only for appropriate reasons and only after the individual was afforded meaningful opportunity to be heard.

In *Parlak v. Baker*,[47] the court granted the habeas petition where the detained noncitizen, who had not been convicted of a crime inside the United States, claimed that his eight-month detention violated due process. The court stated that, given the legal intricacies surrounding petitioner's removal, it would very likely take years for a final determination of his status, and it could not ignore the fact that petitioner was facing a significant period of detention for an indeterminate time. The prospect of prolonged detention, the court found, amounted to a violation of due process.

In *Diomande v. Wrona*,[48] the court granted the petition for writ of habeas corpus, finding that detention where removal proceedings had been pending for 21 months violated due process.

In *Uritsky v. Ridge*,[49] the court found that detention of a 19-year-old lawful permanent resident for almost one year while removal proceedings and Service appeal was pending was not justified by "sufficiently compelling government need."[50]

REMOVE ME OR RELEASE ME. CHALLENGING POST-REMOVAL DETENTION UNDER *ZADVYDAS*

When Does the 90-Day Removal Period Start Counting?

Typically, the issuance of a final administrative order by the IJ or the BIA triggers the removal period during which the alien is subject to mandatory detention pending removal within 90 days.[51] Since mandatory detention of aliens post-removal is statutorily limited to the 90-day period, it is important to analyze whether the period has been triggered, because if it has not, your client is arguably entitled to apply for reasonable bond.[52]

INA §241(1)(B) offers clear guidance. It provides that the removal period begins on the *latest* of the following: (1) the date the order of removal becomes administratively final; (2) if a court orders a stay of removal, the date of the court's final order; or (3) if the alien is detained or confined (except under an immigration process), the date the alien is released from detention or confinement.[53] The statute also provides that the removal period is stayed if the alien fails to apply for a travel document or obstructs the deportation process.[54]

If the alien is subject to a final administrative order, the removal period is deemed to have commenced on the date that the BIA issued its decision. But, as most practitioners know, it is common DHS practice in nondetained cases to begin counting the 90-day period only after the alien is taken into custody for execution of the removal order. For example, if a noncitizen is subject to an old order of deportation or removal and detained at an adjustment interview, ICE will begin counting the 90 days as of the date of the alien's arrest.

A challenge to this practice will usually be of little use since ICE is likely to obtain a travel document within the 90-day period, and release through an independent arbiter is remote at best. However, you may want to consider challenging ICE's practice of commencing the counting of the 90-day period where removal is unlikely or impossible.

---

[45] 332 F. Supp. 747 (M.D. Penn. 2004).

[46] 2005 U.S. Dist. LEXIS 13662 (M.D. Penn. 2005).

[47] 374 F. Supp. 2d 551 (E.D. Mich. 2005).

[48] 2005 U.S. Dist. LEXIS 33795 (E.D. Mich. 2005).

[49] 286 F. Supp. 842 (E.D. Mich. 2003).

[50] *But see Sanusi v. INS*, 100 Fed. App. 49 (2d Cir. 2004); *Suarez v. Acting Director*, 2004 WL 1811494 (W.D. N.Y.

continued

2004) (finding 90-day period does not start until after the final decision on appeal).

[51] INA §241(a).

[52] *Id.*

[53] INA §241(a)(1)(B).

[54] INA §241(a)(1)(C).

The argument in such cases is that the statute clearly states that the removal period commenced upon issuance of the final administrative order, not arrest of the alien. Therefore, so you should argue, the 90-day period has run and the noncitizen is eligible for release. This might lead to the alien's earlier release.

There do not appear to be any administrative or judicial decisions analyzing this question, but the Supreme Court decision in *Zadvaydas v. Davis*,[55] which holds that a six-month period of post–removal-order detention is presumptively reasonable, may cause a federal district court to take pause before considering release.

If a noncitizen is not removed from the United States within the 90-day removal period, the statute provides that the noncitizen be released subject to an order of supervision.[56] The removal period, however, may be extended for many reasons, including flight risk or failure to cooperate with the removal order. This does not mean that if your client is denied release at 90 days, he or she must remain in indefinite detention. The Supreme Court in *Zadvydas v. Davis* read an implicit limitation into the statute's post–removal-period detention provision, which it defined as "the period reasonably necessary to bring about [the individual's] removal."[57] The Court allowed provided for six months for the government to effectuate removal unless the noncitizen's removal was reasonably foreseeable.

What About Those Who Are from Countries That Won't Take Them Back or Accept Them?

Many individuals with a final order of removal may be awaiting travel documents from their embassies that may not be forthcoming. The majority of individuals in this situation are from Vietnam, Laos, Iran, and Iraq, or native stateless Palestinians. Any of these individuals could be physically deported to their countries, but often the embassies refuse travel document requests or the country may have no diplomatic relationship with the United States. Practitioners should be cautioned, however, that lengthy delays in issuance of a travel document do not necessarily mean that your client will not eventually be physically removed.

In 2005, the Supreme Court extended the *Zadvydas* decision to inadmissible aliens in *Clark v. Martinez*, which involved two Mariel Cubans found inadmissible due to prior convictions in the United States.[58] In *Jama v. Immigration and Customs Enforcement*, the Supreme Court also held that noncitizens may be removed to a country without advance consent from that country's government.[59] The Court refused to read an acceptance requirement into the removal statute when Congress had not indicated such in the plain language. The country at issue in *Jama* was Somalia.

In *Ali v. Ashcroft*,[60] the Ninth Circuit ruled that where there is no functioning government to receive a national, immigration authorities cannot carry out a valid removal order. The Ninth Circuit upheld the district court's certification of a nationwide habeas and declaratory class composed of all persons in the United States who were subject to orders of removal to Somalia. It further upheld the district court order that the named petitioners be released from detention because there was no significant likelihood of removal in the reasonably foreseeable future. The injunction should be valid post-*Jama*.

What if ICE Is Refusing to Release the Client After the Removal Period Because It Says the Client Is Mentally Ill or Specially Dangerous Under 8 CFR §§241.14, 1241.14?

In *Thai v. Ashcroft*,[61] the Ninth Circuit held that the Supreme Court's construction of §241(a)(6) did not authorize the continued and potentially indefinite detention of an alien based on a determination that the alien's mental illness made him specially dangerous to the community. The court also held that the danger of criminal conduct by an alien was not automatically a matter of national security as that term was used in *Zadvydas*.

What If the Client is in the Post-Removal Period, Has a Petition for Review Pending, and Has Received a Stay of Removal?

The applicability of the removal period is also at issue when a noncitizen has filed a petition for review and the circuit court has issued a stay of removal. The

---

[55] *Zadvydas v. Davis*, 533 U.S. 678 (2001).

[56] INA §241(a)(3).

[57] *Zadvydas*, 533 U.S. 678.

[58] 125 S. Ct. 716 (2005).

[59] *Jama v. Immigration Customs and Enforcement*, 125 S. Ct. 694 (U.S. 2005).

[60] 346 F.3d 873 (9th Cir. 2003).

[61] No. 03-35626 (9th Cir. May 3, 2004); *See also Tran v. Gonzales*, CV-02202 (W.D. La. Jan. 24, 2006) (following *Thai*).

statute clearly provides that if the final administrative order is judicially reviewed *and* if a court issues a stay, the removal period does not begin until the court issues a final order.[62] Therefore, the removal period has not yet begun and the alien's detention is governed by INA §236, which governs custody decisions prior to the removal period.[63] Only after judicial review is complete does the removal period begin and INA §241(a)(2), the mandatory detention period governing the removal period, come into play.

Nevertheless, ICE's practice is to continue to detain petitioners even where the court of appeals has issued a stay of removal, presumably on the theory that the stay is an action which "interferes" with removal under §241(a)(1)(C).[64] However, most federal courts have generally rejected this analysis and held that if the case is being judicially reviewed and the court enters a stay, the mandatory detention provision of the 90-day removal period does not apply.[65] Therefore, practitioners whose clients have sought judicial review *and* obtained a stay from the court should strenuously argue that their client is not subject to detention. Since the client is under a final administrative order, INA §236—which governs pre-order detention—arguably does not apply. Since a stay has been issued, the detention provisions of the 90-day removal period do not apply. While not precisely applicable because it covers supervision of noncitizens "after the 90-day period," INA §241(a)(3) may provide guidance for the release of noncitizens who have been granted stays of removal or deportation while their cases are being judicially reviewed.

Alternatively, practitioners might argue that detention is governed by INA §236, which provides

that "the Attorney General…may release the alien on bond of at least $1,500."[66]

The proper court in which to test the detention issue raised by a noncitizen under a final order of removal is in habeas proceedings in the federal district court. While the REAL ID Act divested the district courts of jurisdiction to entertain challenges to removal orders, its provisions did not disturb district court jurisdiction over challenges to unlawful detention.[67]

But once the habeas is granted, who hears the bond motion? Since the noncitizen is under a final administrative order, there is no clear jurisdiction in the immigration courts. While there is nothing to prevent the court from remanding the matter to the agency for a bond hearing, the order may be met with confusion by an IJ who does not clearly understand his or her jurisdiction to consider bond where the noncitizen is under a final order of removal.

Unfortunately, the state of the law is of little help. It could be argued that INA §236 controls the detention because the removal period has not yet been triggered. The applicable standard for release, therefore, is set forth in the statute and case law.[68] Practitioners might alternatively argue that there is a gap in the law; INA §236(c) controls pre–final order

---

[62] INA §241(a)(1)(B)(ii).

[63] *See generally Demore v. Kim,* 538 U.S. 510 (2003).

[64] At least one circuit court has accepted this analysis. *See Akinwale v. Ashcroft,* 287 F.3d 1050, n.4 (11th Cir. 2002).

[65] *See Bejjani v. Ashcroft,* 271 F.3d 670 (6th Cir 2001) (because of a court-ordered stay, removal period did not begin until the date of the court's final order. Thus, INS did not have authority to detain); *Clavis v. Ashcroft,* 281 F. Supp. 2d 490, 493 (E.D.N.Y. 2003) ("Because the court entered a temporary stay of deportation, up to this point petitioner has remained in INS custody pursuant to Section 236"); and *Milbin v. Ashcroft,* 293 F. Supp. 2d 158, 161 (D. Conn. 2003) ("Until this decision is filed, Milbin continues to be subject to mandatory detention under 236(c), as the Court's stay order…remains in effect.") *But cf. De La Teja v. United States,* 321 F.3d 1357, 1362–63 (11th Cir. 2003).

[66] The government will likely respond, in part, by asserting that the final administrative order divested the noncitizens of his or her lawful permanent resident status, citing INA §101(a)(20), which defines "lawfully admitted for permanent residence" as "the status of having been lawfully accorded the privilege of residing permanently in the United States as an immigrant in accordance with the immigration laws, such status not having changed." The entry of a final administrative order, so the government will likely assert, changes a legal permanent resident's status. 8 CFR §1.1 provides that lawful permanent residency status terminates upon entry of a final administrative order. However, the BIA has held that if a person appeals the BIA's decision and it is overturned, that person never lost legal permanent resident status. *See Matter of Farinas,* 12 I&N 467 (BIA 1967) (holding that a person not properly found deportable remains a lawful permanent resident).

[67] *Supra* note 2.

[68] INA §236(a) provides that "an alien may be arrested and detained pending a decision on whether the alien is to be removed from the United States … pending such decision, the Attorney General … may release the alien on … bond of at least $1,500." BIA precedent also strongly favors release of a noncitizen in removal proceedings. *Matter of Patel,* 15 I&N Dec. 666 (BIA 1976) (an alien should not be detained or required to post bond unless he is a national security threat or flight risk).

cases, and INA §241 applies to cases post–final order. Since the noncitizen has been granted a stay of removal, INA §241(a)(1)(B) places him or her in a statutory gap between the two provisions. Therefore, since neither detention provision directly applies, and since the client is under a final administrative order, the court might look for guidance to INA §241(a)(3), which governs release after the removal period, for guidance. Under these circumstances, 8 CFR §241.4(e), which sets forth factors for release, could be applied by analogy.

For practical purposes, it might makes sense to move the district court to hear the merits of bond itself. Practitioners should argue to the court that it has the inherent power to release a habeas applicant on bond.[69] The government will likely assert, at least about in the context of noncitizens convicted of criminal offenses, that its authority to detain an alien under a final administrative order, which is set forth in INA §241(a)(6), is entitled to de minimis review;[70] that the scope of review of its discretionary decisions in the immigration context is extremely limited;[71] that detention of a noncitizen for up to six months is presumptively reasonable;[72] and that detention thereafter is appropriate so long as removal is reasonably foreseeable.[73] Further, the government will likely attack the district court's inherent authority to release as a limited power "to be exercised in special cases only."[74]

Yet, neither the statute nor the case law suggests that DHS can hold a noncitizen pending judicial review unless the person proves his or her case is "special." The "special circumstances," so the practitioner should argue, apply where an individual files a habeas application and collaterally attacks a criminal conviction. In that context, the applicant will usually not be released from detention unless there

are "special circumstances or a high probability of success." The Supreme Court has made it clear, however, that a different standard applies to civil detention.[75]

WELCOME TO THE UNITED STATES, HERE ARE THE HANDCUFFS: CHALLENGING THE DETENTION OF ARRIVING ALIENS

Generally, an IJ is divested of jurisdiction for an arriving alien in a bond hearing.[76] Challenge the denial of a bond hearing for returning lawful permanent resident aliens who are being treated as arriving aliens because of IIRAIRA's new definition of admission. The categorical denial to lawful permanent resident aliens of the right to a bond hearing may raise serious constitutional issues.

One also could challenge the lack of proper notice for a person seeking admission on an advance parole. In *Shahwan v. Chertoff*,[77] the district court found that where an alien was granted advance parole and the immigration authorities failed to warn him of the prospect of detention without the possibility of bond, such notice would be insufficient. As a result, the court remanded the case to the IJ for a bond hearing. The petitioner in this case was apprehended and categorized as an arriving alien because he had falsely represented himself as a U.S. citizen on a passport application.

Finally, in *Nadarajah v. Gonzalez*,[78] the Ninth Circuit found that detention for five years despite having prevailed at every administrative level of review and never having been charged with any crime would be counter to the *Zadvydas* and *Clark* holdings. In *Nadarajah*, DHS claimed the authority to indefinitely detain a person seeking admission and pursuing asylum under INA §235(b)(1)(B)(ii) and (b)(2)(A). The court disagreed and concluded that the statutes at issue permit detention only while removal remains reasonably foreseeable. Further, after a presumptively reasonable six-month detention, "once the alien provides good reason to believe that there is no significant likelihood of removal in the reasonably foreseeable future, the Government must respond with evidence sufficient to rebut that showing."

[69] *Ewing v. U.S.*, 240 F. 241 (6th Cir. 1917).

[70] *See Carlson v. Landon*, 342 U.S. 524 (1952); *Reno v. Flores*, 507 U.S. 292 (1993) (upholding the Attorney General's custody scheme for juvenile aliens because these rules met "the (unexacting) standard of rationality advancing some legitimate governmental purpose").

[71] *See Jean v. Nelson*, 727 F.2d 957 (11th Cir. 1984), *aff'd*, 472 U.S. 846 (1984)

[72] *Zadvydas v. Davis*, 533 U.S. 678, 678 (2001).

[73] *Id.* at 701.

[74] *Mapp v. Ashcroft*, 241 F.3d 221 (2d Cir. 2001) ("[A] habeas petitioner should be granted bail only in unusual cases, or when extraordinary or exceptional circumstances exist which make the grant of bail necessary to make the habeas remedy effective").

[75] *Aronson v. May*, 85 S. Ct. 3, 13 L.Ed.2d 6 (1964); *Yanish v. Barber*, 73 S. Ct. 1105, 97 L.Ed. 1637 (1953).

[76] 8 CFR §1003.19(h)(2)(i)(B).

[77] CV-044218 (N.D. Ca. 2005).

[78] 05-56759 (9th Cir. Mar. 17, 2006).

PRISON OF A DIFFERENT KIND: CHALLENGING THE DETENTION OF REFUGEES

In a disturbing nationwide trend, ICE appears to be apprehending refugees with criminal convictions (often nonremovable criminal convictions) and detaining them from 18 months to two years without filing a notice to appear. ICE detains the refugees for such lengthy periods because it compels them to submit adjustment of status applications to the local U.S. Citizenship and Immigration Services (USCIS) office and the processing times for such applications are well over a year for refugees. ICE claims authority for the detention because refugees are considered arriving aliens or INA §209 permits "custody" of a refugee seeking admission. Most IJs will conduct a bond hearing finding that refugees are not arriving aliens but are subject to the limits of INA §236(c) even though no removal proceedings are pending.[79] The BIA has found in many unpublished decisions that they have no jurisdiction over such custody because it falls under §209(a). Further, the BIA found in an unpublished case that they have no authority to review the legality of an arrest.

Advocates should distinguish between the terms "custody" and "detention." As §209 only permits "custody," argue that custody is a temporary arrest and does not authorize long-term detention.[80] Furthermore, even if §209 is accepted as a detention-authorizing statute, courts should be authorized to conduct individualized bond hearings. Additionally, it could be argued that holding refugees for indefinite periods without charges violates due process. Finally, the arriving alien categorization of unadjusted refugees should have no bearing on custody because 8 CFR §1003.19(h)(2)(i)(B) only divests IJs of jurisdiction over an arriving alien where removal proceedings are pending.

ICE'S TRUMP CARD: CHALLENGING THE AUTOMATIC STAY PROVISIONS OF 8 CFR §1003.19

Even if the IJ redetermines bond and gives your client a bond, the fight may not be over. The regulations provide that ICE may file an automatic stay of the IJ's decision in any case where the bond is initially set above $10,000 and the judge lowers the bond below $10,000.[81] ICE must file Form EOIR-43 with the Executive Office for Immigration Review seeking an automatic stay of the IJ's custody decision. Although the Supreme Court determined in *Demore v. Kim*[82] that mandatory detention during removal proceedings is constitutionally permissible, the Court was interpreting §236(c). However, the automatic stay comes into play in cases where the judge already has determined that the respondent is not subject to mandatory detention under INA §236(c) and should be released on bond.

Many district courts that have considered the constitutionality of the automatic stay provisions have found them to be unconstitutional.[83] The first challenge that can be raised is that the automatic stay is ultra vires, since there is no statutory authority for the stay regulation and the statute allows the Attorney General, by way of the IJ, to redetermine bond. ICE's exercise of the automatic stay provisions at 8 CFR §1003.19(i)(2) effectively allows it to bypass §236(a), which authorizes release, and to secure the mandatory detention of anyone regardless of whether they are subject to §236(c).[84]

---

[79] 8 CFR §1003.19(h)(2)(i)(B) (only divests IJs of jurisdiction over an arriving alien where removal proceedings are pending).

[80] *See* Legal Opinion No. 97-2, 1997 WL 33169234, Office of General Counsel, Legal Opinion on Whether a Personal Interview Is Required for All Refugee and Asylee Adjustment of Status Applications under INA §209 ("The crucial question here is whether the use of the term 'custody' requires the Service to take actual physical control over refugees adjusting status when their admissibility is determined. Current practice does not include the taking of this type of custody over a refugee, and it seems doubtful that Congress intended the Service to detain refugees applying for adjustment of status. Both in common usage and as a technical legal term, custody denotes many different types of control over a person short of physical restraint. Webster's Dictionary defines custody as 'judicial or penal safekeeping: control of a thing or individual with such actual or constructive possession as fulfills the purpose of the law or duty requiring it…'.Therefore, it is reasonable to interpret 'custody' in Section 209(a) to mean something other than physical restraint. It should be understood to mean sufficient control over an alien to carry out the purpose of Section 209(a).").

---

[81] 8 CFR §1003.19(i).

[82] 538 U.S. 510 (2003).

[83] *Zavala v. Ridge*, 310 F. Supp. 2d 1071 (N.D. Cal. 2004) (citing other cases).

[84] *Almonte-Vargas v. Elwood*, Civ. Act. No. 02-CV-2666, 2002 U.S. Dist. LEXIS 12387 (E.D. Pa. June 28, 2002) ("It is the operation of the appeal and automatic stay, and not §1226(c) that is technically responsible for her continued detention").

After an individualized hearing before an IJ on whether or not your client is a flight risk or a danger to the community, as required by longstanding BIA precedent,[85] and after assessing the positive and negative equities in the case, the IJ is in the best position to redetermine bond because as the trier of fact, he or she is in the best position to determine the flight risk and danger potential of the applicant, and such determination should not be unilaterally thwarted by ICE through an ultra vires regulation without statutory authority. "Due process is not satisfied where the individualized custody determination afforded to Petitioner was effectively a charade."[86] "In effect, the automatic stay provision renders the Immigration Judge's bail determination an empty gesture."[87]

The government's principal justifications for the automatic stay are to ensure the presence of criminal aliens at their removal proceedings and to protect the public from dangerous criminal aliens. Yet in some cases ICE invokes the automatic stay for cases in which the respondent has been living freely and crime-free in the community for decades.

Furthermore, 8 CFR §1003.19(i)(2) contains definite time requirements for the filing of the stay and appeal but *no* time limits for when the BIA or Attorney General must render a decision on the stay or appeal. This distinguishes the case from the Supreme Court decision in *Demore v. Kim*. The Court stated, "Congress . . . may require that persons . . . be detained for the brief period necessary for their removal proceedings."[88] The time limitation has been a consistent concern of the Court in addressing detention without bond.[89] The cases addressing the automatic stay confirm that the period can be more than six months.[90]

CONCLUSION

"Freedom from bodily restraint has always been at the core of the liberty protected by the Due Process Clause from arbitrary governmental action."[91] The authors hope that this article has given you some tools, arguments, and strategies for protecting your clients' liberty.

---

[85] *Carlson v. Landon*, 243 U.S. 524 (1952); *Matter of Patel*, 15 I&N Dec. 666 (BIA 1976); *Matter of Moise*, 12 I&N Dec. 102 (BIA 1967); *Matter of S–Y–L–*, 9 I&N Dec. 575 (BIA 1962).

[86] *Almonte-Vargas v. Elwood*, 2002 U.S. Dist. LEXIS 123897, at 5.

[87] *Ashley v. Ridge*, 2003 U.S. Dist. LEXIS 19335, at 16.

[88] *Demore v. Kim*, 538 U.S. 510 (2003).

[89] *Zadvydas v. Davis*, 533 U.S. at 690 ("a statute permitting indefinite detention would raise a serious constitutional problem"); *Reno v. Flores*, 507 U.S. 292, 314 (1993) (noting that juveniles would remain in custody only an average of 30 days, and that individual abuses would be remedied through habeas).

[90] *Ashley v. Ridge*, 2003 U.S. Dist. LEXIS 19335 (Aug. 19, 2003, to Oct. 29, 2003, when the Court vacated the stay); *Bezman v. Ashcroft*, 245 F. Supp. 2d 446 (July 31, 2002, to Feb. 21, 2003, when the Court vacated the stay); *Uritsky v. Ridge*, 2003 U.S. Dist. LEXIS 17698 (Apr. 3, 2003, to Sept. 29, 2003, when the Court vacated the stay); *Almonte-Vargas v. Elwood*, 2002 U.S. Dist. LEXIS 12387 (Feb. 27, 2002, to June 28, 2002, when the Court vacated the stay); *Grant v. Zemski*, 54 F. Supp. 2d 437, 439 (E.D. Pa. 1999) (noting that BIA appeals of detention decisions can take three to six months).

[91] *Foucha v. Louisiana*, 504 U.S. 71, 80 (1992).

PLYLER V. DOE, THE EDUCATION OF UNDOCUMENTED CHILDREN, AND THE POLITY

*by Michael A. Olivas**

It is hard to know how Supreme Court decisions will come to be regarded, but one thing is certain: none of them exists in a vacuum. Getting a case to federal or state court in the first place is a lightning strike, and very few make it all the way through the chute to the Supreme Court. Fewer still are genuinely memorable, even within the specialty area in which the case is situated. *Plyler v. Doe*[1] always stood for its resolution of the immediate issue in dispute: whether the State of Texas could enact laws denying undocumented children free access to its own public schools. But it also dealt with a larger, transcendent principle: how this society will treat its alien children. Thus, for the larger polity, *Plyler* has become an important case for key themes, such as fairness for children, how we guard our borders, how we constitute ourselves, and who gets to make these crucial decisions. To a large extent, *Plyler* may also be the apex of the Court's treatment of the undocumented, a concept that never truly existed until the 20th century.[2]

In this Chapter, I consider first how the controversy developed and was treated on the ground, in school districts in Texas. Second, once the case quickened, it took on unusual procedural dimensions that warrant discussion. After the various strands of the cases were consolidated, its actual litigation strategy required case management, with complex back-stage maneuvers essential to gaining traction for the parties. Because the decision itself is one with "epochal significance" for the undocumented population generally, in Peter Schuck's evocative characterization,[3] the third section dissects the case and examines some of the extensive commentary it prompted. Finally, as a postscript, I examine the path *Plyler*'s teachings followed, both in related Supreme Court cases on the same issue and in allied settings, such as debates over federal legislation that would have mimicked the Texas law struck down in *Plyler,* and in postsecondary education residency litigation and legislation. Understanding *Plyler*'s provenance ultimately sheds light on how important legal cases become recurring fugues, with themes that build and influence subsequent decisions and sometimes the polity at large.

* Copyright © 2005 Foundation Press. Reprinted with permission from M. Olivas, "Plyler v. Doe, the Education of Undocumented Children, and the Policy" 197–220 *Immigration Stories* (D. Martin & P. Schuck, eds., Foundation Press).

Michael A. Olivas is the William B. Bates Distinguished Chair in Law at the University of Houston Law Center, where he directs the UHLC Institute for Higher Education Law & Governance. He has held visiting teaching positions at the University of Wisconsin and the University of Iowa. He is an elected member of the American Law Institute and the National Academy of Education, the only person to hold membership in both organizations. He has served as chair of the Immigration Law Section of the AALS twice, and as chair of the Education Law Section three times.

Kristen D. Werner and Eric L. Munoz provided excellent research assistance on this project. In addition, the author wishes to thank Professors Richard Delgado and Kevin R. Johnson for expert comments, and Professors David A. Martin and Peter H. Schuck for their editorial assistance and for undertaking this book enterprise. The author acknowledges the extraordinary resources of the Green Library of Stanford University, and its Special Collections staff, particularly Roberto Trujillo (Head, Department of Special Collections and Frances & Charles Field Curator of Special Collections), Steven Mandeville-Gamble (Assistant Head and Special Collections Principal Manuscripts Processing Librarian), and Polly Armstrong (Public Services Manager). The MALDEF files gathered there are a treasure, and being in such a great reading room reminded the author of what all professors know—we lead a charmed and privileged life. Although this author agreed not to reveal the names of the several attorneys and other participants who talked about the *Plyler* case, thanks to all of them for their confidences.

ON THE GROUND IN TEXAS: UNDOCUMENTED SCHOOL ATTENDANCE AND THE LEGISLATIVE REACTION

In 1975, the State of Texas enacted section 21.031 of the Texas Education Code, allowing its public school districts (called "Independent School Districts" or ISDs in Texas) to charge tuition to undocumented children.[4] The Legislature held no hearings on the matter, and no published record explains the origin of this revision to the school code. Discussions with legislators from that time have suggested that it was inserted into a larger, more routine education bill, simply at the request of some border-area superintendents who mentioned the issue to their representatives.[5] The statute, in pertinent part, read:

(a) All children who are citizens of the United States or legally admitted aliens and who are over the age of five years and under the age of 21 years on the first day of September of any scholastic year shall be entitled to the benefits of the Available School Fund for that year.

(b) Every child in this state who is a citizen of the United States or a legally admitted alien and who is over the age of five years and not over the age of 21 years on the first day of September of the year in which admission is sought shall be permitted to attend the public free schools of the district in which he resides or in which his parent, guardian, or the person having lawful control of him resides at the time he applies for admission.

(c) The board of trustees of any public free school district of this state shall admit into the public free schools of the district free of tuition all persons who are either citizens of the United States or legally admitted aliens and who are over five and not over 21 years of age at the beginning of the scholastic year if such person or his parent, guardian or person having lawful control resides within the school district.[6]

Although they were entitled under this statute to do so, not all ISDs in the State chose to charge tuition. In a 1980 random survey prepared by Houston's Gulf Coast Legal Foundation once litigation commenced, six of the ISDs polled with more than 10,000 students reported that their districts would admit undocumented students without charge, six would charge tuition, eleven would exclude them entirely, while the rest did not respond or did not know how they would respond to such an occurrence.[7] For ISDs with enrollments under 10,000 students, seven would not charge tuition, five would charge tuition, three would exclude entirely, and sixteen did not know or did not respond. The State's largest district, Houston ISD (with over 200,000 students), and a smaller one, Tyler (with approximately 16,000 students) would allow them to enroll, but required parents or guardians to pay $1000 annually for each child. In addition, several of the school districts nearest the border reported they excluded these children from enrolling, whether or not tuition were paid, such as Ysleta ISD (near El Paso and across the border from Ciudad Juarez) and Brownsville ISD (across the border from Matamoros), as did the State's second largest district, Dallas ISD, many hundreds of miles from the border.

THE LITIGATION AND THE PRINCIPAL PLAYERS

Prologue

The first case to challenge 21.031 was *Hernandez v. Houston Independent School District,* filed in spring 1977 in state courts, by a local Houston attorney, Peter Williamson. The district court and the court of civil appeals rejected his due process and equal protection arguments against the statute.[8] In November, 1977, the appeals court held that such legislation was reasonable: "The determination to share [the State's] bounty, in this instance tuition-free education, may take into account the character of the relationship between the alien and this country."[9]

MALDEF's Role

While observers of thirty years ago recall some localized resistance across the state to the practice of charging the families tuition for what were generally referred to as "free public schools," the issue appears to have come onto the national radar in the late 1970s, prompted by a September 26, 1977 letter from Joaquin G. Avila, director of the San Antonio office of the Mexican American Legal Defense and Educational Fund (MALDEF). It was addressed to the MALDEF National Director for Education Litigation, Peter Roos, located at the organization's national headquarters in San Francisco, California. Avila wrote:

This statute was made effective on August 29, 1977. Basically, this statute seeks to regulate the number of students who move in with relatives to attend another school district. As the amended statute now provides (Section 21.031(a)), a student who lives apart from his parent, guardian, or other person having lawful control of him under an order of a court, must demonstrate that his presence in the school district was not based primarily on his or her desire to attend a particular school district. In other words, if a case of hardship can be established, a student will be able to attend the school district. Otherwise, the relatives will have to secure a court order of guardianship. This requirement will impose a hardship on those families who cannot afford an attorney to process a guardianship. So far we have not received any complaints only a request by Pete Tijerina, our first general counsel to launch a lawsuit.

What are your feelings on the constitutionality of such a provision. What would we have to show to demonstrate a disparate impact. Please advise at your earliest convenience.[10]

This letter contains the spores of the *Plyler* case (without referencing the *Hernandez* litigation that was underway in the state courts in Houston at the same time), even though Avila does not appear to have appreciated the full dimensions of the matter that had been flagged by MALDEF board member (and one of the organization's founders in the mid-1960s) Pete Tijerina. To Avila, the issue kicked up to San Francisco was whether the revised Texas statute improperly affected the residency of undocumented students, by requiring the parents or formal legal guardians to reside in the district. This was a related issue, but one far less essential to the algebra of undocumented school attendance than the tuition issue presented eventually in *Plyler,* especially for school districts in the interior, away from the border. Indeed, a year after *Plyler* ruled in favor of the schoolchildren, the exact issue Avila noted in his letter reached the Supreme Court in *Martinez v. Bynum,*[11] where it was resolved in favor of the school districts involved. By that time, however, the more fundamental and important threshold issue had been settled; all else was detail.

But this was not clear in 1977, when Peter Roos began to sniff out the full extent of the practice in Texas and other states. He looked especially at the Southwestern and Western states, where most undocumented families resided, where undocumented Mexican immigration was most pronounced (as opposed to undocumented immigration from other countries and other hemispheres), and where MALDEF concentrated most of its program activities. MALDEF was in search of an appropriate federal-court vehicle to consolidate its modest victories in the many small state-court cases it had taken on in its first decade of existence. Unlike the laser-like focus of its role model the NAACP Legal Defense Fund, which had strategically targeted desegregation as its reason for being, MALDEF had been somewhat behind the curve, in part due to its representation of ethnic and national-origin interests for Mexican Americans and in part due to the diffuse focus that derived from representing the linguistic, immigration, and even class interests of its variegated clients.

After all, Mexican Americans were not African Americans, although their histories of oppression and exclusion from American Anglo life were more similar than they were dissimilar. Historian Steven White has noted the origins of the different litigation theories employed by the two groups to combat school segregation:

> The . . . creation of MALDEF had less to do with the shift in thinking [about school desegregation strategies] than might be expected. The upheavals brought by the black civil rights struggle, the farm workers' movement, and antiwar protests inspired many disaffected Mexican-descended youths to adopt similar goals and direct action tactics—such as walkouts and other disruptive demonstrations—in order to combat the inequities they encountered. As a result, however, activists frequently found themselves sanctioned by school administrators or even law enforcement agencies. Instead of suing schools to change the rules of desegregation, therefore, MALDEF undertook a number of cases that established the new organization as something of an unofficial civil liberties bureau for militant Chicano students. Significantly, in these cases, MALDEF's attorneys did not argue—and in civil liberties cases had no reason to claim—that Mexican Americans were and ought to be considered a group distinct from Anglos. Nevertheless, MALDEF's early victories in this field helped to reestablish litigation as a tool for vindicating Mexican Americans' civil rights.[12]

My discussions with the various parties involved from the MALDEF side of this case clearly indicate that Roos and MALDEF President Vilma Martinez, a young Texas lawyer who had begun her civil rights career with the NAACP Legal Defense Fund, soon saw *Plyler* as the Mexican American Brown v. Board of Education: a vehicle for consolidating attention to the various strands of social exclusions that kept Mexican-origin persons in subordinate status. This case promised to decide issues affecting Mexican migrant workers, who had been in the American imagination due to the charismatic leadership of Cesar Chavez, head of the United Farm Workers union, who had organized a successful nationwide grape boycott.[13] It concerned education in Texas schools, long considered the most insensitive to Mexicans and Mexican Americans. It incorporated elements of school leadership and community relations, where the political powerlessness of Chicanos was evident even in geographic areas where they were the predominant population. The tuition dimension resurrected school finance and governance issues, which had earlier been raised by Chicano plaintiffs seeking to have the radically unequal school financing scheme in Texas declared unconstitutional. After initial success, they had lost in a controversial 1973 decision by the U.S. Supreme Court, San Antonio Independent School District v. Rodriguez.[14] The 5-4 ruling seemed designed to call a halt to any expansions in the use of the equal protection clause, and it specifically declared that education was not a fundamental right that would trigger strict scrutiny under that clause. And finally, *Plyler* implicated immigration status, often dividing families based merely on the side of the Rio Grande where the mother had given birth. *Plyler* even held out the promise to unite the class interests between immigrant Mexicans and the larger, more established Mexican American community in a way that earlier, important cases litigating jury selection, school finance, and desegregation had not been able to achieve.[15] Even though these cases all occurred in Texas over many years, and had even included some small victories, they had not appreciably improved the status of Chicanos or broken down the barriers for large numbers of the community.

In his pathbreaking study of Mexican American education litigation, historian Guadalupe San Miguel analyzed the law suits undertaken by MALDEF in Texas in the years 1970–1981, its earliest record.[16] It undertook 93 federal and state court cases in the state during those years, and compiled a substantial record across several areas: 71 cases in the area of desegregation (76.3%), four in employment (4.3%), three in school finance (3.2%), seven in political rights (7.5%), six in voting (6.5%), and two other education cases (2.2%). In addition, a number of the cases included collateral issues such as language rights and bilingual education.[17] As an example of these cases, MALDEF undertook *United States v. Texas*, a comprehensive assault upon the worst exclusionary practices by school districts, such as class assignment practices and inadequate bilingual education.[18] The judge in that district court decision noted with some bite: "Serious flaws permeate every aspect of the state's efforts. . . . Since the defendants have not remedied the serious deficiencies, meaningful relief for the victims of unlawful discrimination must be instituted by court decree."[19]

Over the years, MALDEF had joined forces with other Mexican American organizations, including more conservative groups such as the League of United Latin American Citizens (LULAC) and the GI Forum, organizations active over the years in assimilationist and citizenship issues and Latino military veteran issues. Thus, these national organizations, all founded in Texas to combat discrimination, merged their divergent interests in order to effect solidarity, and have since served as plaintiffs in cases filed by MALDEF.[20]

Just as Thurgood Marshall had traveled the South to execute the Legal Defense Fund's strategic approach toward dismantling segregated schooling and the American apartheid system, seeking out the proper cases and plaintiffs, Martinez, Roos, and other MALDEF lawyers and board members had been seeking just the right federal case. They wanted to have a larger impact than they could expect from dozens of smaller cases in various state courts in the Southwest. If Mexican American plaintiffs could not win the school finance case in *San Antonio Independent School District v. Rodriguez*, with such demonstrable economic disparities as had been evident in that trial, MALDEF needed to win a big one, both to establish its credibility within and without the Chicano community and to serve its clients. A case involving vulnerable schoolchildren in rural Texas being charged a thousand dollars for what was available to other children for free seemed to be that vehicle. The MALDEF lawyers found their Linda Brown in Tyler, Texas, where the brothers and sisters in the same family held different immigration status. Some had been born in Mexico, while those born in Texas held U.S. citizenship. Perhaps more importantly, they found their Earl Warren in federal district court judge William Wayne Justice, widely admired and reviled for his liberal views and progressive decisions.[21] Thus, in this small, rural setting in Tyler, Texas, the stage was set.

The *Plyler* Campaign

The first issue to arise after the case was filed was whether the children could be styled in anonymous fashion in the caption and conduct of the case, so that their identities and those of their families would not be divulged. Use of the actual names of the plaintiffs in the *Hernandez* case against the Houston schools had placed all of them at risk of deportation. In the Tyler case, even though Judge Justice permitted the case to proceed with "John Doe" plaintiffs, the risk persisted. The U.S. Attorney had apparently asked the Dallas district director of the Immigration and Naturalization Service (INS) to conduct immigration sweeps in the area, so as to intimidate the families into dropping their suit.[22] In response, Roos wrote to the head of the INS in Washington, requesting that he call off any planned raids and characterizing them as trial-tampering. As it happened, in this endeavor MALDEF enjoyed a run of luck, which is always an ingredient of successful trials. The INS Commissioner at the time was Leonel Castillo, a native of Houston and a prominent Mexican American politician with progressive politics, himself a former Peace Corps volunteer who was married to an immigrant.[23] At his direction, the INS ultimately made no such raids. After these initial skirmishes, Judge Justice issued a preliminary injunction on September 11, 1977, enjoining the Tyler ISD from enforcing 21.031 against any children on the basis of their immigration status.[24]

As a part of the overall trial strategy, Roos, Martinez, and other MALDEF officials began to press public opinion leaders to "support the schoolchildren" and to develop a backdrop of public acceptance of their immigration status. As an example, Roos wrote leaders of the National Education Association (NEA), the progressive national teachers union, in October, 1977, to request support and assistance; NEA later filed a brief and provided additional support to MALDEF.[25] In addition, MALDEF leaders traveled to meet with other Latino organizational leaders to enlist support and solicit resources, and to encourage legal organizations to file amicus briefs on behalf of the plaintiff children. They asked for people to write editorials and to host fundraisers. I recall being a law student in Washington, D.C., during this time and cutting class one night to attend a small fundraiser at a local hotel, an event sponsored by Latino organizations and Washington professionals.

On September 14, 1978, after a two day hearing, Judge Justice issued his opinion, striking down 21.031 as applied to the Tyler ISD. He found that the state's justifications for the statute were not rational and violated equal protection, and that the attempt to regulate immigration at the state level violated the doctrine of preemption, which holds immigration to be a function solely of federal law.[26] Immediately after, the state moved for leave to re-open the case, citing the decision's implications for other school districts in the state and seeking a chance to bolster the record. Observers have suggested that the state had simply underestimated the plaintiffs' case, inasmuch as the *Hernandez* case in state court had sustained the statute fairly readily. But Judge Justice overruled the motion, because the "amended complaint does not state a cause of action against any school district other than the Tyler Independent School District and since this court intends to order relief only against the Tyler Independent School District. . . ."[27]

Case Management by MALDEF

During the federal trial, the issue of *Plyler*'s potential impact upon other Texas school districts arose, as word had spread to dozens of other communities, sparking many companion lawsuits. The original *Hernandez* decision had not spawned similar state court litigation; MALDEF and others turned to the federal courts so as to avoid having to litigate in hostile state venues. MALDEF now confronted questions about how best to mesh its efforts, including its response to the *Plyler* appeals filed by the Tyler ISD and the State of Texas, with proceedings in other venues. Some of the issues became clearer when the State's largest school district, Houston ISD, faced a lawsuit in federal court in September, 1978, by a group of local attorneys and another California-based public interest law firm, with civil rights lawyer (and South African immigrant) Peter Schey as lead counsel. By this time, with the good news spreading from the Tyler case, four cases raising these issues had been filed in the Southern District of Texas, and two in the Northern District. Moreover, the Eastern District court that had just decided *Plyler* faced six additional cases after the ruling. Rather than just suing the particular ISDs, these suits included as defendants the State of Texas, the Texas Governor, the Texas Education Agency (the state agency that governed K–12 public education in the State), and its Commissioner. Eventually, all these cases were consolidated into In re Alien Children, which was tried in the Southern District of Texas in Houston, before Judge Woodrow Seals. Judge Seals held a 24-day trial.[28]

These sprawling cases presented an even broader assault upon the system, whereas *Plyler* had been narrowly focused upon 21.031 and the Tyler ISD. The various cases were brought by several different attorneys on many fronts, relying upon several theories, hoping that they could replicate the victory Roos had carved out in his Tyler case. At this point, it became crucial that the various parties coordinate, because the defendants had deep pockets, legions of deputy attorneys general and private counsel, and other advantages, most importantly the staying power to mow down the plaintiffs at the trial and appellate levels. True, Roos had convinced the United States to intervene in his case on the side of the alien schoolchildren, but over the long haul, the federal government could not be wholly relied upon in civil rights cases, as its interests could change, depending upon the administration in office.[29]

In May, 1979, after *Plyler* was decided at the trial level but before *In re Alien Children* was to go to trial, the local Houston counsel for the plaintiffs in the case before Judge Seals wrote Peter Roos, requesting that MALDEF consolidate its efforts into their case, which was more complex and comprehensive than the original case against the Tyler ISD. Roos responded to attorney Isaias Torres, a Texas native who had just graduated from law school and was working for the Houston Center for Immigrants, Inc., that MALDEF felt "quite strongly that consolidation would not be in the best interests of our mutual efforts."[30] After all, MALDEF had carefully selected Tyler as the perfect federal venue for arguing its case: progressive judge, sympathetic clients, a rural area where the media glare would not be as great. In addition, in Tyler the case could be made that excluding the small number of undocumented children (the practical effect of charging $1000 tuition to each) would actually lose money for the district, inasmuch as the State school funding formulae based allocation amounts upon head count attendance. In a large urban school district or a border school district, the fact questions and statistical proofs would be more complex and expensive to litigate for both sides.[31] Moreover, because the Tyler trial had been a case of first impression at the federal level, the State's legal strategy had not been as sophisticated as it would be in another similar trial. The *Hernandez* case in state court had not involved the full panoply of legal and social science expertise and financial support available to a national effort such as that mounted by MALDEF.

Roos noted to Torres that the State had tried to make a late-in-the-day correction for its ineffective original efforts by seeking the leave to re-open the record, a request that Judge Justice had denied. State counsel would not likely make that mistake again, and would mount a more aggressive strategy in their second go-around. Roos wrote: "While no doubt you have been incrementally able to improve upon our record [developed in the Tyler trial], consolidation would allow the state and other parties to buttress their record. I believe that one could only expect a narrowing of the present one-sidedness [of the trial record in MALDEF's favor]. Consolidation would play right into th[e] hands of [the State's attorney] Mr. Arnett."

Torres, on the other hand, worried that unless the cases were consolidated, the relief in *Plyler* might not extend beyond that small district. Tyler had folded, but what about Houston, Dallas, and the more important border districts? After all, Texas had over 1000 ISDs, and many of them had the same policies towards undocumented students as had Tyler; it was a state statute that gave them such permission. To this understandable concern, Roos indicated that his original strategy was aimed at winning once and then later applying it elsewhere, not joining up with other pending actions and thereby increasing the risk of losing on appeal: "Most importantly, I believe that once we have a Tyler victory, we will have started down a slippery slope which will make it impossible for the court to legally or logistically limit the ruling to Tyler." This approach mirrors that of the NAACP on the road to *Brown,* where Thurgood Marshall and his colleagues carefully picked their fights, each case incrementally building upon the previous litigation.[32] Indeed, MALDEF General Counsel Vilma Martinez had worked at the Legal Defense Fund with Marshall's former colleague and successor, Jack Greenberg; she clearly understood the value of an overarching strategic vision.

But Roos had yet another reason for declining to join in the consolidated cases: he had drawn ineffective opposing local counsel, and wished to press his momentary advantage. He wrote, in a remarkable and candid assessment: "A final, but important reason for believing consolidation unwise is, frankly, the quality of opposing counsel. Our [local] opposing counsel in Tyler is frankly not very good." He went on to say that this would likely not be the case in Houston, where the defense would include experienced attorneys from the specialized education law department of a major law firm, and where other districts would also contribute their efforts and resources. He added, "I believe it is our mutual interest to isolate the worst counsel to argue the case against us. Consolidation works against that. For the above-stated reasons, I would urge you not to seek consolidation. I just don't believe that it serves our mutual interest of getting this statute knocked out."[33]

The Results

Although Roos did not agree to combine forces at the crucial early stages, this issue was eventually taken out of his hands at the U.S. Supreme Court. At the request of the State of Texas, the Judicial Panel on Multidistrict Litigation eventually did consolidate a number of the cases—but significantly, not Plyler—into the *In re Alien Children* litigation, and notwithstanding Roos' doubts about whether the Houston plaintiffs would succeed, Judge Seals rendered a favorable decision on the merits on July 21, 1980.[34] The plaintiff schoolchildren prevailed in a big way, most importantly on the issues of whether the State of Texas could enact a statute to discourage immigration and whether equal protection applied to the undocumented in such an instance. Judge Seals determined that strict scrutiny applied because the law worked an absolute deprivation of education. Texas' concern for fiscal integrity was not a compelling state interest, and charging tuition to the parents or removing the children from school had not been shown to be necessary to improve education within the State. Most importantly, he concluded that 21.031 had not been carefully tailored to advance the state interest in a constitutional manner.

In the Fifth Circuit, meanwhile, Judge Justice's *Plyler* decision was affirmed in October, 1980, and in May, 1981, the U.S. Supreme Court agreed to hear the matter.[35] The Fifth Circuit issued a summary affirmance of the consolidated Houston cases a few months later, and the Supreme Court combined the Texas appeals of both cases under the styling of *Plyler v. Doe,* handing Peter Roos the lead vehicle over Peter Schey's cases.[36] Having developed fuller records and armed with Fifth Circuit wins, the two Peters worked out a stiff and formal truce, dividing the oral arguments down the middle, but with MALDEF's case leading the way.

Roos spent the time until the Supreme Court arguments shoring up political support. In March, 1979, he had written to Drew Days, the Assistant Attorney General for Civil Rights, urging the government to join the litigation. Later he persuaded the Secretary of Health, Education, and Welfare, Joseph Califano, to write the Solicitor General urging him to enter into the fray on the side of the children, which the government did. Other MALDEF letters went to state officials in California and elsewhere, requesting their support. After the Reagan administration took office in January of 1981, Roos wrote William Clohan, Under Secretary of the newly created Department of Education, to urge him to continue the actions of the Carter administration. Fortunately for Roos, the Reagan administration did not seek to overturn the lower court decisions, although it did not formally enter its amicus brief on the side of the plaintiffs (as had the Democrat lawyers), and it took no position on the crucial equal protection issue. In fact, the brief stressed the primacy of the federal government in immigration, a position that favored the schoolchildren.[37]

THE SUPREME COURT'S RULING

In June, 1982, the Supreme Court gave the schoolchildren their win on all counts, by a 5-4 margin. Justice Brennan, in his majority opinion striking down the statute, characterized the Texas argument for charging tuition as "nothing more than an assertion that illegal entry, without more, prevents a person from becoming a resident for purposes of enrolling his children in the public schools."[38] He employed an equal protection analysis to find that a State could not enact a discriminatory classification "merely by defining a disfavored group as non-resident."[39]

Justice Brennan dismissed the State's first argument that the classification or subclass of undocumented Mexican children was necessary to preserve the State's "limited resources for the education of its lawful residents."[40] This line of argumentation had been rejected in an earlier case, *Graham v. Richardson*, where the court had held that the concern for preservation of Arizona's resources one could not justify an alien-age classification used in allocating welfare benefits.[41] In addition, he relied on the findings of fact from the *Plyler* trial: although the exclusion of all undocumented children might eventually result in some small savings to the state, those savings would be uncertain (given that federal and state allocations depended primarily upon the number of children enrolled),[42] and barring those children would "not necessarily improve the quality of education."[43]

The State also argued that it had enacted the legislation in order to protect itself from an influx of undocumented aliens.[44] The Court acknowledged the concern, but found that the statute was not tailored to address it: "Charging tuition to undocumented children constitutes a ludicrously ineffectual attempt to stem the tide of illegal immigration."[45] The Court also noted that immigration and naturalization policy is within the exclusive powers of federal government.[46]

Finally, the state maintained that it singled out undocumented children because their unlawful presence rendered them less likely to remain in the United States and therefore to be able to use the free public education they received in order to contribute to the social and political goals of the United States community.[47] Brennan distinguished the subclass of undocumented aliens who had lived in the United States as a family and for all practical purposes, permanently, from the subclass of adult aliens who enter the country alone, temporarily, to earn money.[48] For those who remained with the intent of making the

United States their home, "[i]t is difficult to understand precisely what the State hopes to achieve by promoting the creation and perpetuation of a subclass of illiterates within our boundaries, surely adding to the problems and costs of unemployment, welfare, and crime."[49]

Prior to *Plyler*, the Supreme Court had never taken up the question of whether undocumented aliens could seek Fourteenth Amendment equal protection.[50] The Supreme Court had long held that aliens are "persons" for purposes of the Fourteenth Amendment,[51] and that undocumented aliens are protected by the due process provisions of the Fifth Amendment.[52] However, Texas argued that because undocumented children were not "within its jurisdiction,"[53] they were not entitled to equal protection. Justice Brennan rejected this line of reasoning, concluding that there "is simply no support for [the] suggestion that 'due process' is somehow of greater stature than 'equal protection' and therefore available to a larger class of persons."[54]

After the *Rodriguez* school finance decision, Justice Brennan had to walk a fine line to apply what amounted to scrutiny more demanding than the usual rational basis review. Although he rejected treating undocumented alienage as a suspect classification,[55] he concluded that the children were not responsible for their own citizenship status and that treating them as Texas law envisioned would "not comport with fundamental conceptions of justice."[56] He was more emphatically concerned with education, however, carefully elaborating the nature of the entitlement to it. While he reaffirmed the earlier *Rodriguez* holding that public education was not a fundamental right (undoubtedly to attract the vote of Justice Powell, the author of the *Rodriguez* majority opinion), he recited a litany of cases holding education to occupy "a fundamental role in maintaining the fabric of our society."[57] He also noted that "[i]lliteracy is an enduring disability,"[58] one that would plague the individual and society. These observations enabled him to establish "the proper level of deference to be afforded § 21.031." He concluded, in light of the significant ongoing costs, that the measure "can hardly be considered rational unless it furthers some substantial goal of the State"—subtle and nuanced phrasing that nudged the level of scrutiny to what would be characterized as intermediate scrutiny.[59] Chief Justice Burger's dissent, in contrast, stuck with the customary formulation, requiring only "a rational relationship to a legitimate state purpose."[60] As a result of Brennan's

careful construction, the Court rejected the claim, which the dissent had found persuasive, that the policy was sufficiently related to protecting the state's asserted interests.

Further, while the Court did not reach the claim of federal preemption,[61] it did draw a crucial distinction between what states and the federal government may do in legislating treatment of aliens.[62] The Court had upheld state statutes restricting alien employment[63] and access to welfare benefits,[64] largely because those state measures mirrored federal classifications and congressional action governing immigration. For example, in *DeCanas v. Bica*, the Supreme Court had held that a state statute punishing employers for hiring aliens not authorized to work in the United States was not preempted by federal immigration law.[65] In public education, however, Brennan wrote, distinguishing *DeCanas*, "we perceive no national policy that supports the State in denying these children an elementary education."[66]

REACTIONS

Much of the considerable scholarly response to the Court's reasoning in the case has evinced surprise that the majority went as far as it did in rejecting the state's sovereignty. Peter Schuck, for example, characterized the decision as a "conceptual watershed in immigration law, the most powerful rejection to date of classical immigration law's notion of plenary national sovereignty over our borders. . . . Courts are expositors of a constitutional tradition that increasingly emphasizes not the parochial and the situational, but the universal, transcendent values of equality and fairness immanent in the due process and equal protection principles. In that capacity, they have also asserted a larger role in the creation and distribution of opportunities and status in the administrative state. In *Plyler*, the Supreme Court moved boldly on both fronts."[67] Surveying the line of equal protection cases involving aliens from *Yick Wo* through *Graham* to *Plyler* and beyond, Linda Bosniak has summarized: "alienage as a legal status category means that the law of alienage discrimination is perennially burdened by the following questions: To what extent is such discrimination a legitimate expression, or extension, of the government's power to regulate the border and to control the composition of membership in the national community? On the other hand, how far does sovereignty reach before it must give way to equality; when, that is, does discrimination against aliens implicate a different kind of government power, subject to far more rigorous constraints? To what degree, in short, is the status of aliens to be understood as a matter of national borders, to what degree a matter of personhood, and how are we to tell the difference? These questions, I argue, shape the law's conflicted understandings of the difference that alienage makes."[68]

Although *Plyler*'s incontestably bold reasoning has not substantially influenced subsequent Supreme Court immigration jurisprudence in the twenty-plus years since it was decided, the educational significance of the case is still clear, even if it is limited to this small subset of schoolchildren—largely Latinos—in the United States. Given the poor overall educational achievement evident in this population, even this one success story has significance.[69] Again, the parallel to *Brown is* striking: *Brown*'s legacy is questioned even after fifty years, largely due to Anglo racial intransigence and the failure of integration's promise.[70]

POSTSCRIPT TO *PLYLER*—THE EDUCATION OF THE POLITY

In September of the same year, the Court denied petitions to rehear the case, and the matter was over.[71] More than five years had passed since the issue had first appeared on the MALDEF radar screen, and the extraordinary skills and disciplined strategy of Roos and Martinez had prevailed. Indeed, their overarching strategic vision had enabled them to avoid the many centripetal forces that threatened *Plyler* at every turn. To be sure, good fortune appeared to have intervened at all the key times: sympathetic clients with a straightforward story to tell confronting an unpopular state statute that never had had its own compelling story, flying under big-city legal radar and lucking into poor opposing local counsel, federal and state officials at the early stages who were responsive and helpful, continuity in federal support for the plaintiffs despite a change in the national administration, the ability to keep the Tyler case on track and for the Houston-based cases to prevail at their own speed and upon their own legs, and the right array of judges hearing the cases as they wended their way through the system. This issue could have foundered at any one of the many turns, winding up like *Rodriguez*, with a similar gravitational pull but a more complex statistical calculus and worse luck. But the considerable legal and political skills of the MALDEF lawyers served the schoolchildren well, as had lawyers of color and Anglo lawyers on the path to *Brown*.

Soon after *Plyler*, both Vilma Martinez and Peter Roos left MALDEF, she to a Los Angeles law firm

and he to the San Francisco-based public interest organization, META, where he continued education litigation on bilingual rights and immigrant rights. The original MALDEF San Antonio lawyer who had written the first *Plyler* memo, Joaquin Avila, succeeded Martinez as President and General Counsel. In 1996 he won a MacArthur Foundation "genius" fellowship after several years in private practice concentrating on voting rights; he now is a law teacher at Seattle University. Whatever became of the undocumented schoolchildren from Tyler, Texas? According to a newspaper story following up on them, nearly all of them graduated and, through various immigration provisions, obtained permission to stay in the United States and regularize their status.[72]

The U.S. Supreme Court soon took up a related case, *Martinez v. Bynum*,[73] and upheld a different part of section 21.031, which provided that the parents or guardians of undocumented children had to reside in a school district before they could send their children to free public schools. Although this was the element of the statute that first drew Avila's attention and started the ball rolling towards MALDEF's filing of the *Plyler* lawsuit, *Martinez* does not amount to a significant narrowing of *Plyler*, where the parents actually resided in the school districts, albeit in unauthorized immigration status. The student in *Martinez* was the U.S. citizen child of undocumented parents who had returned to Mexico after his birth and left him in the care of his adult sister, who was not his legal guardian. The Court in *Martinez* sustained Texas' determination that the child did not reside in the district and thus did not qualify for free public schooling there, ruling that *Plyler* did not bar application of appropriately defined bona fide residence tests. Interestingly, in *Plyler*'s footnote 22, the Court had indicated that the undocumented may establish domicile in the country, a much larger issue than that presented in *Martinez,* where the child's parents had not established the requisite residence in the district. That footnote elaborated: "A State may not . . . accomplish what would otherwise be prohibited by the Equal Protection Clause, merely by defining a disfavored group as nonresident. And illegal entry into the country would not, under traditional criteria, bar a person from obtaining domicile within a State."[74]

In 1994, an unpopular governor of California, Pete Wilson, revived his reelection campaign by backing a ballot initiative known as Proposition 187, which would have denied virtually all state-funded benefits, including public education, to undocumented aliens. Proposition 187 passed with nearly 60 percent of the vote and Wilson was re-elected, but the federal courts enjoined implementation of most of the ballot measure, relying prominently on *Plyler*.[75] During the congressional debates that eventually led to the enactment of the Illegal Immigration and Immigrant Responsibility Act of 1996, Representative Elton Gallegly (R.-Cal.) proposed an amendment that would have allowed states to charge tuition to undocumented students or exclude them from public schools. He was banking that, in the wake of such federal legislation, the courts would distinguish *Plyler* and sustain the state measure. The provision became quite politicized, receiving prominent support from Republican presidential candidate Robert Dole. Gallegly might have been right that the Constitution would not be read by the Court of the 1990s to nullify a federal enactment of the kind he proposed, but he never got a chance to find out, because *Plyler* proved to have considerable strength in the political arena. The Gallegly amendment drew heated opposition in Congress and in the media, and critics relied heavily on the values and arguments highlighted in *Plyler*—and often on the decision itself. After months of contentious debate, the amendment was dropped from the final legislation, and no provisions became law that restricted alien children's right to attend school. *Plyler* and the polity appear to have settled the question.[76]

Although *Plyler* had addressed the issue of public school children in the K–12 setting, questions arose almost immediately after the ruling about how far the decision could be extended, notably whether it would protect undocumented college students. Before long, Peter Roos was going for the long ball again, litigating postsecondary *Plyler* cases in California.[77] The cases have mostly denied relief, although the record is mixed. That history is for a companion volume, but I will say this: the ultimate irony is that in 2001, just after Governor George Bush left Texas to become President George Bush, the State enacted H.B. 1403, establishing the right of undocumented college students to establish resident status and pay in-state tuition in the State's public colleges.[78] In the 25 years since Texas had enacted 21.031, this was silent testimony to the idea that you reside where you live, quite apart from your immigration status. A dozen states have acted since the Texas innovation.[79] And in Congress, conservative Utah Senator Orrin Hatch co-authored the Development, Relief, and Education for Alien Minors (DREAM) Act.[80] If enacted, it would remove a provision from federal law that discourages states from providing in-state tuition status to undocumented college students, and would also allow the students the opportunity to regularize their federal immigration status—an enormous benefit that would go well beyond what a state could provide.[81] *Plyler* clearly is alive and well in its adolescence.

ENDNOTES

1. 457 U.S. 202 (1982).

2. The historian Mae M. Ngai, in a perceptive study concerning the history of undocumented immigration and the way in which different nationalities have been racialized by the immigration process, has concluded:

> [The process of how the nation constituted immigration] had an important racial dimension because the application and reform of deportation policy had disparate effects on Europeans and Canadians, on the one hand, and Mexicans, on the other hand. But, the disparity was not simply the result of existing racism. Rather, the processes of territorial redefinition and administrative enforcement informed divergent paths of immigrant racialization. Europeans and Canadians tended to be disassociated from the real and imagined category of illegal alien, which facilitated their national and racial assimilation as white American citizens. In contrast, Mexicans emerged as iconic illegal aliens. Illegal status became constitutive of a racialized Mexican identity and of Mexicans' exclusion from the national community and polity.

Her full-length book, Illegal Aliens and Alien Citizens: Immigration Restriction, Race, and Nation, 1924–1965, outlines these differentiated developments in considerable detail, and this background elaborates upon why "illegal alienage" has developed in immigration policy and practice as essentially a concept of guarding our Southern border (our "frontera") from undesirables. See also Mae M. Ngai, The Strange Career of the Illegal Alien: Immigration Restriction and Deportation Policy in the United States, 1924-1965, 21 L. AND HIST. REV. 145 (2003). See Note, Law, Race, and the Border: The El Paso Salt War of 1877, 117 HARV. L. REV. 941 (2004); Carl Gutierrez Tones, Rethinking the Borderlands: Between Chicano Culture and Legal Discourse (1995); Steven W. Bender, Greasers and Gringos: Latinos, Law, and the American Imagination (2003); Juan F. Perea, A Brief History of Race and the U.S.-Mexican Border: Tracing the Trajectories of Conquest, 51 UCLA L. REV. 283 (2003).

3. Peter H. Schuck, The Transformation of Immigration Law, 84 COL. L. REV. 1, 54 (1984).

4. Tex. Educ. Code Ann. § 21.031 (Vernon Supp.1981).

5. In the Houston case challenging this statute, the federal court trial judge found:

> The court cannot state with absolute certainty what the Legislature intended when passing the amendment to 21.031. Neither the court nor the parties have uncovered a shred of legislative history accompanying the 1975 amendment. There was no debate in the Legislature before the amendment was passed by a voice vote. There were no studies preceding the introduction of the legislation to determine the impact that undocumented children were having on the schools or to project the fiscal implications of the amendment.

In re Alien Children Education Litigation, 501 F. Supp. 544, 555, n.19 (1980). The record, such as it is, showed that the legislation likely arose after a Texas Attorney General Opinion held that prior to 1975, the Texas education law did not differentiate among children based upon their immigration status. Att'y Gen. Op. H-586 at 3 (1975).

6. Tex. Educ. Code Ann. § 21.031 (Vernon Supp.1981).

7. The *In re Alien Children* record included considerable statistical testimony, including the data in this paragraph, prepared by then-law student Laura Oren and Houston lawyer Joseph Vail; I found copies of the original hand-tabulated data in the Oren files on this subject. (Copies on file with author.) Both Professor Oren and Professor Vail are now my colleagues at the University of Houston Law Center, where both migrated after local law careers, including Professor Vail's later service as an immigration judge.

8. *Hernandez v. Houston Independent School District*, 558 S.W. 2d 121 (1977). The case was tried in Austin rather than Houston because of the administrative proceedings required to challenge the state administrative agency.

9. *Id.* at 125.

10. I found a copy of the letter in the Stanford University Green Library special Collections Room, MALDEF files. The concordance to these records is Theresa Mesa Casey and Pedro Hernandez, comps. and eds., Research Guide to the Records of MALDEF/PRLDEF (1996). The Avila-Roos letter was located in MALDEF, M0673, Box 115, Folder 5 (Avila to Roos, September 26, 1977). Additional files from early MALDEF work in Houston are available in the archives of the Houston Metropolitan Research Center (HMRC), particularly the Abraham Ramirez collection, used extensively by Guadalupe San Miguel, Jr. to explain earlier Houston school desegregation cases and bilingual education issues in his excellent study, Brown, Not White: School Integration and the Chicano Movement in Houston (2001). Ramirez was a local civil rights attorney who was affiliated with MALDEF in its early years, although he was not an employee. For additional studies of Houston schooling, see William H. Kellar, Make Haste Slowly: Moderates, Conservatives, and School Desegregation in Houston (1999); Angela Valenzuela, Subtractive Schooling: U.S.-Mexican Youth and the Politics of Caring (1999).

11. 461 U.S. 321 (1983). In order to stop this practice, Congress in 1996 enacted what is now INA § 214(m), 8 U.S.C. §1184(m).

12. Steven H. Wilson, Brown Over "Other White": Mexican Americans' Legal Arguments and Litigation Strategy in School Desegregation Lawsuits, 21 LAW AND HISTORY REVIEW 145, 193 (2003) (citations omitted). See Vicki L. Ruiz, "We Always Tell Our Children They Are Americans," Mendez v. Westminster and the California Road to Brown v. Board of Education, COLL. BD. REV. No. 200 (Fall, 2003), at 20; Margaret E. Montoya, A Brief History of Chicana/o School Segregation: One Rationale for Affirmative Action, 12 BERK. LA RAZA L. J. 159 (2001); Ian F. Haney Lopez, Race, Ethnicity, Erasure: The Salience of Race to LatCrit Theory, 85 CAL. L. REV. 57 (1998); Ian F. Haney Lopez, White by Law: The Legal Construction of Race (1996); Clare Sheridan, "Another White Race": Mexican Americans and the Paradox of Whiteness in Jury Selection, 21 L. AND HIST. REV. 109 (2003).

13. Richard Griswold de Castillo and Anthony Accardo, Cesar Chavez: The Struggle for Justice (2002).

14. 411 U.S. 1 (1973).

15. George A. Martinez, Legal Indeterminacy, Judicial Discretion, and the Mexican American Litigation Experience: 1930-1980, 27 U.C. DAVIS L. REV. 555 (1994). Mario T. Garcia, Mexican Americans: Leadership, Ideology, & Identity, 1930-1960 (1989). Gary A. Greenfield and Don B. Kates, Jr., Mexican Americans, Racial Discrimination, and the Civil Rights Act of 1866, 63 CALIF. L. REV. 662 (1975); Richard Delgado and Victoria Palacios, Mexican Americans as a Legally Cognizable Class Under Rule 23 and the Equal Protection Clause, 50 NOTRE DAME LAWYER 393 (1975); George J. Sanchez, Becoming Mexican American: Ethnicity, Culture and Identity in Chicano Los Angeles, 1900-1945 (1993); Christopher Arriola, Knocking On the Schoolhouse Door: *Mendez v. Westminster*, Equal Protection, Public Education and Mexican Americans in the 1940's, 8 LA RAZA L. J. 166 (1995); Neil Foley, The White Scourge: Mexicans, Blacks, and Poor Whites in Texas Cotton Culture (1997); Juan F. Perea, *Buscando* America: Why Integration and Equal Protection Fail to Protect Latinos, 117 HARV. L. REV. 1420 (2004).

16. Guadalupe San Miguel, "Let All of Them Take Heed": Mexican Americans and the Campaign for Educational Equality in Texas, 1910-1981 (1987).

17. *Id.* at 174 (Table 10); see Jorge C. Rangel and Carlos M. Alcala, De Jure Segregation of Chicanos in Texas Schools, 7 HARV. C.R.-C. L. L. REV. 307 (1972).

18. *United States v. Texas*, 506 F. Supp. 405 (E.D. Tex. 1981), rev'd, 680 F.2d 356 (5th Cir. 1982). It is not surprising that such anti-Mexican legislation and practices would have originated in Texas, a jurisdiction widely regarded to be officially inhospitable to its Mexican-origin population. See Arnoldo De Leon, They Called Them Greasers: Anglo Attitudes Toward Mexicans in Texas, 1821-1900 (1983); David Montejano, Anglos and Mexicans in the Making of Texas, 1836-1986 (1987).

19. 506 F. Supp. at 428.

20. For example, the *U.S. v. Texas* case was formally styled United States of America, Plaintiff, Mexican American Legal Defense Fund, LULAC, and G. I. Forum, Plaintiffs-*Intervenors v. State of Texas et al.*, Defendants. For histories of these organizations, see Carl Allsup, The American G. I. Forum: Origins and Evolution, Monograph No. 6, University of Texas Mexican American Studies (1982); Benjamin Marquez, LULAC: The Evolution of a Mexican American Organization (1993); Henry A. J. Ramos, The American GI Forum: In Pursuit of the Dream, 1948-1983 (1998); Laura E. Gomez, The Birth of the "Hispanic" Generation: Attitudes of Mexican-American Political Elites Toward the Hispanic Label, 75 LAT. AM. PERSP. 45 (1992); Suzanne Oboler, The Politics of Labeling: Latino/a Cultural Identities of Self and Others, 75 LAT. AM. PERSP. 18 (1992); Suzanne Oboler, Ethnic Labels, Latino Lives (1995).

21. For example, Judge Justice was the trial judge in *U.S. v. Texas*, in which he found Texas and the school districts to have been out of compliance with regard to school desegregation and English language instruction obligations under federal law. 506 F. Supp. 405 (E.D. Tex. 1981), rev'd, 680 F.2d 356 (5th Cir. 1982). For examples of his long record of progressive decisions, see John J. DiIulio, Governing Prisons (1987) (longstanding prison litigation). For this record, he earned an impeachment bill, H. Res. 168 (97th Cong.), introduced on June 24, 1981. See Frank R. Kemerer, William Wayne Justice: A Judicial Biography (1991).

22. The plaintiff in that early case was named Carlos Hernandez. See the letter from Peter Roos to Leone] Castillo (September 13, 1977), where he warns, "We have been informed that the local United States Attorney, John Hannah, has requested the Director of [the Dallas INS] to take steps to deport the plaintiffs in this case and possibly to conduct a sweep in the Tyler region." M0673, Box 115, Folder 5. This issue arose in a recent case in which undocumented college students in Virginia who brought an action concerning a state statute that denied state college access to undocumented students sought to file their case anonymously. The judge ruled against them on this issue. *Doe v. Merten*, 219 F.R.D. 387, 184 Ed. Law Rep. 843 (E.D. Va., 2004). And then he ruled against them on the larger issue, once alternative plaintiff organizations were enlisted as substitutes, holding that the State of Virginia could enact practices which denied undocumented students admission or residency status. *Equal Access Education v. Merten*, 305 F. Supp. 2d 585 (E.D.Va. 2004), and 325 F. Supp. 2d 655 (E.D. Va. 2004) (finding that students did not have standing, absent evidence that institution denied admission on perceived immigration status).

23. In the *Plyler* trial court case and at the Fifth Circuit, the U.S. Department of Justice and the U.S. Attorney intervened on the side of the schoolchildren. After he left office, Castillo returned to Houston. In 1983, he wrote in a Foreword to a special immigration issue of a law review: "the authors are all persons of recognized ability and concern. . . . [Among others, Isaias

Torres and Peter Schey] have all been involved in the daily battles of making the INA fit a particular individual's situation at a particular time. During the time that I served as Commissioner (1977-79), it was my privilege to be sued by some of these individuals. I knew that regardless of the outcome, the ultimate goal of justice for immigrants would prevail because effective advocates help cure improper procedures and faulty legislation." Leonel Castillo, Foreword, 5 HOU. J. INTL L. 191 (1983).

24. See *Doe v. Plyler*, 628 F.2d 448, 450 (5th Cir. 1980).

25. MALDEF files, M0673, Box 115, Folder 6 (Roos to Roy Fuentes, October 18, 1977). Roos was also trying at this time to address similar issues in California, as a series of letters in the MALDEF files revealed. He wrote California school districts that their attendance practices violated State guidelines for undocumented children: M0673, Box 61, Folder 8 (March 12, 1979); M0673, Box 62, Folder 1 (October 29, 1979); M0673, Box 62, Folder 1 (October 19, 1979).

26. *Doe v. Plyler*, 458 F.Supp. 569 (E.D. Tex. 1978).

27. Quoted in *In re Alien Children Educ. Litigation*, 501 F.Supp. 544, 552 (S.D. Tex. 1980).

28. *In re Alien Children Educ. Litigation*, 501 F. Supp. 544 (S.D. Tex 1980). The federal case became a veritable magnet, as various plaintiffs and defendants were added, requiring many pages of explanation for these procedural issues. A playbill would include: (1) from the Southern District: *Martinez v. Reagen*, C.A. No. H-78-1797, filed September 18, 1978; *Cardenas v. Meyer*, C.A. No. H-78-1862, filed September 27, 1978; *Garza v. Reagen*, C.A. No. H-78-2132, filed November 6, 1978; *Mendoza v. Clark*, C.A. No. H-78-1831, filed September 22, 1978; (2) from the Northern District: *Doe v. Wright*, C.A. No. 3-79--4440-D; (3) from the Western District: *Roe v. Holm*, MO-79-CA-49; *Coe v. Holm*, MO-78--CA--54. at the court termed "tag-along actions," originally filed in the Southern District were also consolidated: *Cortes v. Wheeler*, C.A. H-79-1926, filed September 20, 1979; *Rodrigues v. Meyer*, C.A. H-79-1927, filed September 20, 1979; *Adamo v. Reagen*, C.A. H-79-1928, filed September 20, 1979; *Arguelles v. Meyer*, C.A. H-79-2071, filed October 4, 1979. Six additional cases originally filed in the Eastern District of Texas were likewise consolidated: *Doe v. Sulphur Springs*, P-79-31-CA, filed October 29, 1979; *Doe v. Lodestro*,)3-79-618-CA, filed September 18, 1979; *Doe v. Ford*, TY-79-351-CA, filed September 28, 1979; *Roe v. Horn*, TY-79-338-CA, filed September 24, 1979; *Roe v. Como-Pickton*, P-79-234-CA, filed October 19, 1979; and *Poe v. Chappel Hill*, TY-79-449-CA, filed December 10, 1979.

Observers of this trial have reported that Judge Woodrow Seals committed an interesting gaffe during arguments when he asked, "whether anything of worldwide importance had ever been written in Spanish," or words to that effect. (Apparently he had not heard of the classic works by Miguel Cervantes, Octavio Paz, Juan Vasconcellos, Gabriel Garcia Marquez, Pablo Neruda, Sor Juana, or many other Latino or Latina writers.) Witnesses report that it was an electric moment, one he sensed, and after which he publicly apologized. See Juan R. Palomo, Judge Seals Calls Spanish Comment "Senseless, Dreadful," Houston Post, March 7, 1980, 3B.

29. See below, note 37 and accompanying text. A good example of this unreliability appeared in connection with a long-running dispute involving public colleges in Nashville, Tennessee. The U.S. Department of Justice supported the plaintiffs over the course of many years, and after working out the dispute among the many parties, the judge entered a final order that included racially specific remedies. Later, after the Reagan administration took office, the U.S. Department of Justice attempted to switch horses and get the court to strike down the agreement. The judge refused to accept this too-little-too-late intervention. *Geier v. Alexander*, 801 F. 2d 799 (6th Cir. 1986); see also *Geier v. Blanton*, 427 F. Supp. 644 (M.D.Tenn.1977). The original case finally wound down on June 18, 2004, when the issue of attorney fees was decided. *Geier v. Sundquist*, 372 F. 3d 784 (6th Cir. 2004).

30. Roos to Isaias Torres, May 17, 1979, MALDEF files, M0673, Box 61, Folder 10. In the interest of full disclosure, I note that Mr. Torres was a Georgetown University Law Center classmate of mine.

31. These were some of the problems that had doomed the educational finance case. See Michael Heise, State Constitutional Litigation, Educational Finance, and Legal Impact: An Empirical Analysis, 63 U. CINN. L. REV. 1735 (1995); Augustina H. Reyes, Does Money Make a Difference for Hispanic Students in Urban Schools?, 36 EDUC. AND URB. SOCIETY 353 (2003).

32. Mark V. Tushnet, The NAACP's Legal Strategy Against Segregated Education, 1925-1950 (1987); Mark V. Tushnet, Making Civil Rights Law: Thurgood Marshall and the Supreme Court, 1936-1961 (1994); Robert J. Cottrol, Raymond T. Diamond, and Leland B. Ware, Brown v. Board of Education: Caste, Culture, and the Constitution (2003); Amilcar Shabazz, Advancing Democracy: African Americans and the Struggle for Access and Equity in Higher Education in Texas (2004); William C. Kidder, the Struggle for Access from Sweatt to Grafter: A History of African American, Latino, and American Indian Law School Admissions, 1950-2000, 19 HARV. BLACK LETTER L. J. 1 (2003). For the history of earlier Mexican American trial strategies, see Lisa Lizette Barrera, Minorities and the University of Texas Law School (1950.1980), 4 TEX. HISP. J. L & POL'Y 99 (1998); Guadalupe Salinas, Mexican-Americans and the Desegregation of Schools in the South-west, 8 HOUS. L. REV. 929 (1971); Ricardo Romo, Southern California and the Origins of Latino Civil Rights Activism, 3 W. LEGAL LIST. 379 (1990); George Martinez, The Legal Construction of Race: Mexican-Americans and Whiteness, 2 HARV. LAT. L. REV. 321 (1997).

33. Roos to Torres, MALDEF files, M0673, Box 61, Folder 10, page two (May 17, 1979).

34. 501 F. Supp. 544 (S. D. Tex. 1980). His remarks about the Spanish language had occurred on the final day of the plaintiffs' testimony.

35. 451 U.S. 968 (1981) (noting probable jurisdiction in the *Plyler* litigation).

36. 452 U.S. 937 (1981) (noting probable jurisdiction in *In re Alien Children*). The procedural sequence is more fully explained in the *Plyler* merits decision, 457 U.S. at 207–10.

37. Although the Carter administration officials had actually supported MALDEF and the Houston children's attorneys in the earlier stages of the cases, including both the trial court and Fifth Circuit phases, the Reagan administration did not side with the appellee children when the cases finally made their way to the Supreme Court, filing instead only as amicus curiae. 1981 WL 390001. As examples of the support MALDEF tried to line up for its side, the MALDEF files include letters Roos wrote to Peter Schilla (Western Center on Law and Poverty, Sacramento, May 19, 1981), M0673, Box 63, Folder 6; Norella Beni Hall (May 14, 1981) (urging her support, but focusing upon education issue), M0673, Box 63, Folder 6; California Board of Education member Lorenza Schmidt (June 25, 1981), M0673, Box 63, Folder 7; Associate AG Drew Days (March 28, 1979), M0673, Box 61, Folder 8; and William Clohan, Undersecretary, U.S. Dept. of Education, May 20, 1981, M0673, Box 63, Folder 6. The files also include a letter from HEW Secretary Joseph Califano to the U.S. Solicitor General Wade McCree, urging the United States to enter the case on behalf of the children plaintiffs (July 17, 1979), M0673 Box 907, Folder 9. These letters and dozens more show the extent to which Roos and MALDEF sought and then shored up support for their clients.

38. 457 U.S. at 227.

39. *Id*.

40. *Id*.

41. 403 U.S. 365, 375 (1971).

42. *Doe v. Plyler*, 458 F. Supp. at 576–77.

43. 457 U.S. at 229.

44. *Id*. at 229–30.

45. *Id*. at 228.

46. *Id*. at 225–26.

47. *Id*. at 229–30.

48. *Id*. at 230.

49. *Id*. at 230.

50. No State shall . . . deprive any person of life, liberty, or property, without due process of law; nor deny to any person within its jurisdiction the equal protection of the laws." U.S. CONST. amend. XIV § 1.

51. *Yick Wo v. Hopkins*, 118 U.S. 356, 369 (1886) (stating that Fourteenth amendment provisions "are universal in their application to all persons within the territorial jurisdiction, without regard to any differences of race, of color, or of nationality").

52. *Wong Wing v. United States*, 163 U.S. 228 (1896).

53. 457 U.S. at 211.

54. *Id*. at 213. In the dissent, Chief Justice Burger concurred that the equal protection clause applies to undocumented aliens. *Id*. at 243.

55. 457 U.S at 219, n.19.

56. 457 U.S. at 220 (citing *Trimble v. Gordon*, 430 U.S. 762, 720 (1977), an important case applying greater scrutiny to classifications disadvantaging out-of-wedlock children).

57. 457 U.S. at 221 (citations omitted).

58. *Id*. at 222,

59. *Id*. at 223–24.

60. *Id*. at 248.

61. *Id*. at 210 n,8. In a postsecondary education alienage case decided soon after *Plyler*, *Toll v. Moreno*, the decision turned on preemption. 458 U.S. 1 (1982). See Michael A. Olivas, *Plyler v. Doe* and Postsecondary Admissions: Undocumented Adults and "Enduring Disability," J. L. & ED. 19 (1986).

62. 457 U.S. at 224–26.

63. *De Canas v. Bica*, 424 U.S. 351 (1976).

64. *Mathews v. Diaz*, 426 U.S. 67 (1976).

65. 424 U.S. 351, 356 (1976).

66. 457 U.S. at 226. This sentence became the focus of efforts to change federal law in 1996, led by Representative Elton Gallegly (R. Calif.), to incorporate an explicit provision authorizing exclusion of undocumented children from public schools. These efforts are discussed in the final part of this Chapter.

67. Peter H. Schuck, The Transformation of Immigration Law, 84 COL. L. REV. 1, 58 (1984).

68. Linda Bosniak, Membership, Equality, and the Difference That Alienage Makes, 69 N.Y.U. L. Rev. 1047, 1057 (1994). See also Kevin R. Johnson, Civil Rights and Immigration: Challenges for the Latino Community in the Twenty-First Century, 8 LA RAZA L. J. 42 (1995).

69. See Guadalupe San Miguel, "Let All of Them Take Heed": Mexican Americans and the Campaign for Educational Equality in Texas, 1910–1981 (1987); Jorge C. Rangel and Carlos M. Alcala, De Jure Segregation of Chicanos in Texas Schools, 7 HARV. C.R.-C. L. L. REV. 307 (1972); Gilbert G. Gonzalez, Chicano Education in the Era of Segregation (1990). While there is an increasing amount of attention to this complex history of Latino/a schooling, there is still much that needs attention by future scholars. And if there is too little we know about the schooling of Chicanos, we know less yet of the education litigation undertaken by Puerto Ricans or of other Latino populations. See Antonia Pantoja, The Making of a Nuyorican: A Memoir (2002).

70. For critiques of Brown, citing its promise and the failure of white communities to implement its holding, see, among others, Alex M. Johnson, Jr., Bid Whist, Tonk, and *United States v. Fordice*: Why Integrationism Fails African-Americans Again, 81 CAL. L. REV. 1401 (1993); Kimberle Williams Crenshaw, Race, Reform, and Retrenchment: Transformation and Legitimation in Antidiscrimination Law, 101 HARV. L. REV. 1331 (1988); Richard Delgado and Jean Stefancic, The Social Construction of *Brown v. Board of Education*: Law Reform and the Reconstructive Paradox, 36 WM. & MARY L. REV. 547 (1995); Jack M. Balkin, What *Brown v. Board of Education* Should Have Said (2001).

71. 458 U.S. 1131 (1982).

72. See Paul Feldman, Texas Case Looms over Prop. 187's Legal Future Justice: U.S. High Court Voided that State's '75 Law on Illegal Immigrants,but Panel has Shifted to the Right, L.A. Times Al (October 23, 1994). I thank Professor Maria Pabon Lopez for bringing this source to my attention.

73. 461 U.S. 321 (1983)

74. 457 U.S. at 227 n.22

75. *League of United Latin American Citizens v. Wilson*, 997 F.Supp. 1244 (C.D. Cal. 1997)

76. Stephen Legomsky, Immigration and Refugee Law and Policy 1162 (3rd ed. 2002); Thomas Alexander Aleinikoff, David A. Martin, Hiroshi Motomura, Immigration and Citizenship, Process and Policy 1166-69 (5th ed. 2003); see also 73 Interp. Rel. at 1111, 1209, 1255, 1281 (1996); Rebecca A. Maynard & Daniel J. McGrath, Family Structure, Fertility and Child Welfare in The Social Benefits of Education 125 (Jere Behrman & Never Stacey, eds. 1997); Sidney Weintraub, Francisco Alba, Rafael Fernandez de Castro, and Manuel Garcia y Griego, Responses to Migration Issues in Mexico-US Binational Migration Study Report 467 (United States Commission on Immigration Reform) (1997), available at *www.utexas.edu/lbj/uscir/binpapers/vl-5weintraub.pdf*, at 468 (last visited on September 10, 2004). For a thorough analysis of these issues and other restrictive legislative efforts, see Kevin R. Johnson, Public Benefits and Immigration: The Intersection of Immigration Status, Ethnicity, Gender, and Class, 42 UCLA L. REV. 159 (1995).

77. Roos later litigated such cases as *Leticia "A" v. Board of Regents of the University of California*, Tentative Decision, No. 588982-5 (Cal. Super. Ct. Alameda Cty., April 3, 1985); Judgment (May 7, 1985); Statement of Decision (May 30, 1985) (Leticia "A" I); Clarification (May 19, 1982) (Leticia "A" II). Peter D. Roos, Postsecondary Plyler, IHELG Monograph 91-7 (1991); Michael A. Olivas, Storytelling Out of School: Undocumented College Residency, Race, and Reaction, 22 HAST. CON. L. Q'TLY 1019 (1995).

78. Tex. Educ. Code Ann. § 54.052 (Vernon Supp.2001). See Clay Robinson, Budget Hits Include Judges' Pay Hike, Houston Chronicle (June 18, 2001), at IA (describing tuition, revenue bill details). For insomniacs in the reading public, see Michael A. Olivas, IIRIRA, The DREAM Act, and Undocumented College Student Residency, 30 J. COLL. & UNIV. L. 435 (2004).

79. Olivas, at Table One (cited in note 78).

80. S. 1545, 108th Cong. (2003).

81. Olivas at 461–63 (cited in note 78).

ASYLUM GRAB BAG: SEXUAL ORIENTATION, GANGS, CHILDREN, AND PRESENTATION OF BACKGROUND COUNTRY CONDITION EVIDENCE

by Salvador Colon, Hilary A. Han, and Mary E. Kramer[*]

Persecution based on "social group" membership is the most fluid ground within the "refugee" definition.[1] This article discusses the evolution of sexual orientation as a social group and moves on to the emerging category of gangs and the persecution perpetrated upon youths in Central and South America, including a look at the children left behind by a generation of successful immigrant parents. Finally, the article shifts to a discussion of evidence, specifically the successful presentation of background country condition documentation and expert witness testimony.

PERSECUTION BASED ON SEXUAL ORIENTATION

Almost 12 years ago, then-Attorney General Janet Reno designated as precedent a Board of Immigration Appeals (Board or BIA) decision, holding that homosexuals constitute a particular social group as defined in the refugee definition. As a result, gay men and lesbians who face persecution in their home countries have applied for and been granted asylum. Despite this fact, the notion that persecution on account of

one's sexual orientation is a valid basis for asylum is not yet universally accepted. The circuit courts have been slow to affirm the Attorney General's decision, and the BIA itself has been inconsistent in its application of the law. This portion of the article outlines some of the important precedent decisions in this area, and how those decisions affect gay men, lesbians, and transgender persons seeking asylum.

In *Matter of Toboso-Alfonso*,[2] the Attorney General designated as precedent a decision issued by the BIA on March 12, 1990. The applicant in that case was a native and citizen of Cuba who had suffered harm, and feared future harm, because he was a homosexual. The immigration judge (IJ) found the applicant credible, determined that homosexuals are a social group under the Immigration and Nationality Act (INA),[3] and granted him withholding of deportation.[4] On appeal to the Board, legacy Immigration and Naturalization Service (INS) argued that: (1) homosexual activity was a socially deviant behavior; and (2) the applicant had been harmed because of his activity, rather than his status as a homosexual.[5]

The Board affirmed the IJ's finding that homosexuality is an "immutable" characteristic and the judge's conclusion that gay men and lesbians constitute a particular social group, noting that INS had not challenged those findings.[6] Moreover, the BIA found that the harm the applicant faced was on account of his status as a gay man and not simply the enforcement of laws against particular homosexual acts.[7] As such, the Board upheld the grant of withholding of deportation.[8]

Since *Toboso-Alfonso*, the Board has not issued any precedent decisions relating to asylum based on

---

[*] **Salvador Colon** is a graduate of University of Houston Law Center, J.D. (1994); Loyola University, B.A., and is board-certified by the Texas Board of Legal Specialization in immigration and nationality law. Mr. Colon is licensed to practice in Texas, admitted to practice before the Texas Supreme Court, the U.S. District Court for the Southern District of Texas, and the Courts of Appeals for the Second, Fifth, and Ninth Circuits. *See www.lawyers.com/scolonpc.*

Hilary Han is a partner at Dobrin & Han, a Seattle immigration law firm. The firm represents noncitizens seeking asylum, lawful permanent residence, and naturalization before the Department of Homeland Security, and defends noncitizens facing removal in the administrative and federal courts.

Mary Kramer is a sole practitioner in Miami and past chair of the AILA South Florida Chapter. She presently serves as her chapter's liaison to Krome and other South Florida detention centers, and is a co–supervising attorney of the Legal Assistance Project. She also serves on the board of Catholic Charities Legal Services, Inc.

[1] Immigration and Nationality Act of 1952, Pub. L. No. 82-414, 66 Stat. 163 (*codified as amended at* 8 USC §§1101 *et seq.*), INA §101(a)(42).

[2] 20 I&N Dec. 819 (A.G. 1994).

[3] Immigration and Nationality Act of 1952, Pub. L. No. 82-414, 66 Stat. 163 (*codified as amended at* 8 USC §§1101 *et seq.*) (INA).

[4] *Toboso-Alfonso*, 20 I&N Dec. at 822.

[5] *Id.*

[6] *Id.* at 822–23.

[7] *Id.* at 823.

[8] *Id.*

sexual orientation. In particular, it has not cast doubt in any way upon *Toboso-Alfonso*'s central holding. As a result, noncitizens have been granted asylum on account of sexual orientation, both by asylum officers and IJs. Moreover, in assessing a potential client's asylum claim, it has become more and more common for immigration attorneys to inquire into whether sexual orientation was a basis for past harm or could be a basis for future harm. Thus, immigrants who never suspected that the harm they suffered could qualify them for lawful status are now asylees.

However, for an 11-year-old undisturbed Board precedent, the *Toboso-Alfonso* decision has remained relatively obscure. Courts of appeals have only recently begun to address claims of asylum based on sexual orientation, and they have not uniformly endorsed *Toboso-Alfonso* as might be expected. This has permitted U.S. Immigration and Customs Enforcement (ICE) and the Department of Homeland Security (DHS) to continue to argue that homosexuals do not constitute a particular social group, and for IJs to so find. In addition, although some gay, lesbian, and transgendered persons have applied for asylum, many others have remained unaware of their potential eligibility for lawful status in this country.

Only the Ninth Circuit has addressed this issue in detail, and its discussion of the issue has taken some time to evolve to the point of unequivocally affirming *Toboso-Alfonso*. Three Ninth Circuit decisions are important in this regard. In the first, *Hernandez-Montiel v. INS*,[9] the court reviewed the denial of asylum to a gay Mexican man. The well-reasoned decision modified the Ninth Circuit's definition of a particular social group and cited expert testimony to conclude that "gay men with female sexual identities in Mexico fall within that definition."[10]

Because the formulation of the particular social group in *Hernandez-Montiel* was so narrow, a much more important holding was lost to those who did not read the case in its entirety. In particular, before considering whether gay men with female sexual identities in Mexico are a particular social group, the court affirmed *Toboso-Alfonso* by finding generally that sexual orientation and sexual identity can be the basis for establishing the "on account of" requirement.[11]

Since the *Hernandez-Montiel* court's affirmation of *Toboso-Alfonso* was not as explicit as it could have been, there remained some question about the state of the law. Some IJs and practitioners were even under the impression that, after *Hernandez-Montiel*, only those gay men with female sexual identities could qualify for asylum.

The Ninth Circuit did not definitively clarify *Hernandez-Montiel* until 2005, in *Karouni v. Gonzales*.[12] The panel there noted that the *Hernandez-Montiel* court had suggested all homosexuals were members of a particular social group.[13] It then stated that, to the extent its case law had been unclear, it was affirming that *all* alien homosexuals are members of a particular social group.[14]

Karouni was important for one other reason. The panel rejected the government's argument that the petitioner had been persecuted on account of his homosexual acts, not because of his status as a homosexual.[15] In *Toboso-Alfonso*, the Board had rejected a similar argument, but on the ground that the applicant faced persecution because of his status, not because of his acts. The Ninth Circuit went further, holding that it did not matter whether the petitioner had been persecuted for his acts or status;[16] it found no appreciable difference between an individual being persecuted for being a homosexual and being persecuted for engaging in homosexual acts.[17]

The third Ninth Circuit decision of note was *Boer-Sedano v. Gonzales*.[18] The IJ had found that male homosexuals in Mexico were not of a particular social group, and the BIA affirmed.[19] The court cited *Karouni* in reversing the Board's finding,[20] again stating that "alien homosexuals constitute a particular social group."[21]

Three other courts of appeals have touched upon the issue of whether gay men and lesbians constitute

---

[9] 225 F.3d 1084 (9th Cir. 2000).

[10] *Hernandez-Montiel*, 225 F.3d at 1091–95.

[11] *Id.* at 1093–94.

[12] 399 F.3d 1163 (9th Cir. 2005).

[13] *Karouni*, 399 F.3d at 1172.

[14] *Id.* (emphasis in original).

[15] *Id.* at 1172.

[16] *Id.* at 1173.

[17] *Id.*

[18] 418 F.3d 1082 (9th Cir. 2005).

[19] *Id.* at 1087–88.

[20] That the agency reached this conclusion nine years after *Toboso-Alfonso* underscores the lack of clarity in the law (and the BIA's failure to follow its own case law).

[21] *Id.*

a particular social group. Each circuit court has assumed, or seemed to assume, that they fall within that protected ground. However, unlike the Ninth Circuit, none has explicitly affirmed *Toboso-Alfonso*. The Third Circuit came closest to doing so in *Amanfi v. Ashcroft*.[22] There, the petitioner claimed that he faced harm not because he was gay, but because he was incorrectly perceived as gay.[23] The Board had found that homosexuals are a particular social group, and the Third Circuit cited that finding approvingly.[24] However, the precise issue before the court was whether the petitioner could qualify for asylum based on his imputed homosexuality, a question the Third Circuit ultimately answered in the affirmative.[25]

Similarly, in *Joaquin-Porras v. Gonzales*,[26] the Second Circuit did not seem to question the notion that homosexuals are a protected group. However, it denied the petitioner's applications for asylum and withholding of removal on alternate grounds and never had to explicitly reach the issue. Finally, the Eighth Circuit, in a pair of precedent decisions, assumed without deciding that homosexuals constitute a particular social group.[27] Although neither panel found it necessary to reach the issue, Judge Heaney did in the dissenting opinion in *Kimumwe v. Gonzales*. Citing *Toboso-Alfonso*, he stated that it was beyond question that a person's sexual orientation may form the basis for a legitimate asylum claim.[28]

Judge Heaney's opinion is a correct statement of the Board's well-settled case law. Although courts of appeal have not uniformly affirmed that law, no precedent decision has cast any doubt on it. Hopefully, as more gay men and lesbians seek asylum, asylum adjudicators will become aware of *Toboso-Alfonso* and will follow it faithfully. When that day comes, there will be no need for courts of appeal to publish precedent decisions clarifying that homosexuals are a protected group.

PERSECUTION BY GANGS

In February 2006, the Salvadoran government issued a plea for U.S. help with its gang problem.[29] El Salvador pointed to its own cooperation in the U.S. wars on drugs and terrorism. If the plea sounds desperate, the desperation is not without foundation. The homicide rate in El Salvador has now surpassed that of Colombia.[30]

In 2005, 1,900 Salvadorans were deported from the United States because of criminal convictions, according to the Salvadoran government. In January 2006, 500 such deportations from the United States occurred. The result has been an increase in the murder rate in El Salvador from 34 per 100,000 inhabitants in 2003, to 55 murders per 100,000 inhabitants in 2005.[31] Between nine and 11 murders are reported per day—1,700 a year.[32]

Salvadoran authorities estimate that there are over 10,000 gang members in El Salvador, approximately 4,000 of them currently in prison.[33] Some sources place the number of gang members throughout Central America at 25,000.[34] Gangs are blamed for the unsolved rape and murder of more than 700 young women and girls in Guatemala since 2001. In Honduras, a young girl was beheaded in October 2003 in retaliation for the police killing of a gang member.[35]

The gangs appear to have an aggressive recruitment program that includes the murder of youths who refuse to join. For example, on January 22, 2006, members of the gang Mara 18 massacred seven youths at a soccer field in the city of Zacatecoluca, Department of La Paz.[36] Although one of them was reported to have been a gang member, the

---

[22] 328 F.3d 719 (3d Cir. 2003).

[23] *Amanfi*, 328 F.3d at 724.

[24] *Id.*

[25] *Id.* at 730.

[26] 435 F.3d 172, No. 03-4202, 2006 U.S. App. LEXIS 1570 (2d Cir. Jan. 18, 2006).

[27] *Kimumwe v. Gonzales*, 431 F.3d 319 (8th Cir. 2005); *Molathwa v. Ashcroft*, 390 F.3d 551 (8th Cir. 2004).

[28] *Kimumwe*, 431 F.3d at 323 n.2 (Heaney, J., dissenting).

[29] J. Dalton, "El Salvador pide a EE UU ayuda en el combate," *El País* (Feb.14, 2006) (Madrid) (hereinafter Dalton).

[30] B. Castillo, *Diario Co Latino* (Feb. 13, 2006) (San Salvador).

[31] Dalton, *supra* note 29.

[32] "Salvadoran Archbishop Urges Government Action on Violence," *Prensa Latina* (July 25, 2005) (Havana), translation provided by Resource Center of the Americas.org, www.americas.org/item_20932.

[33] *El Diario de Hoy*, (Jan. 23, 2006) (San Salvador).

[34] K. Lydersen, "Grim News in Central America: Wave of Gang Violence Grows," *Resource Center of the Americas.org*; www.americas.org/item_12 (Jan. 19, 2004) (hereinafter Lydersen).

[35] *Id.*

[36] *Id.*; *El Diario de Hoy, supra* note 33.

other seven were soccer players or soccer fans who had refused to join the gang.

In El Salvador, the government has responded with a zero tolerance program called *Mano Dura*, or Strong Hand. Responding to the soccer field murders, Salvadoran President Elías Antonio Saca has started an even stronger response, *Súper Mano Dura*.[37]

Some of the Salvadoran tactics should be familiar to those in the United States. Students are required to have clear backpacks, for example, so that teachers and authorities can easily see what the students are carrying into schools.[38] However, police response has become increasingly brutal, contributing to an atmosphere of lawlessness and violence. Margaret Swedish, director of the Religious Task Force on Central America and Mexico, reports that "some of the [Central American] countries have received more criminal aliens than they have people in prison in the country—they can't possibly absorb these people. As a result, police often resort to extra judicial executions of suspected gang members as a way to solve the problem."[39]

Despite these dismal statistics, the courts have so far not been receptive to asylum claims based on gang violence. *Escobar v. Alberto Gonzales*[40] held that Honduran street children do not constitute a particular social group. Escobar is a native of Honduras whose parents abandoned him at an early age. He lived with his maternal grandparents and other relatives who abused him. He then ran away at nine years old and was living on the streets doing odd jobs. The street gangs would steal from him and try to force him to steal. The police would not protect him; in fact, they would treat him as the gangs treated him.

Escobar then went to Mexico and was then able to contact his mother, and he came to the United States. The Third Circuit reviewed the Board's decision stating that "Honduran street children" is not a cognizable particular social group. They looked at *Fatin v. INS*,[41] which brings refugee law into conformance with the 1967 United Nations Protocol relating to the status of refugees. The Protocol defined refugee using the terms race, religion, nationality, and memberships in a particular social group. However, no guidance was given as to what a particular social group meant.

The court turned to *Matter of Mogharrabi*,[42] stating that "particular social group" was a group of persons all of whom share a common, immutable characteristic. The court noted that the main elements of the Honduran street children as a particular social group were poverty, homelessness, and youth. Thus, the court did not see any realistic differences between these children and those from Guatemala, Brazil, or other locations. The court sympathized with the situation, but said that the record did not contain evidence to support a finding that Honduras was different from any other developing country.

The court seemed to be missing one additional attribute: these were poor homeless youths *who happened to be persecuted by gangs*. The practitioner might wonder: is the problem the source country, or is it gangs? Does it really matter that gangs are running rampant and killing children in Guatemala, Brazil, or other locations? Could it not be said that union organizers in El Salvador are the same as union organizers in Guatemala? If so, could their persecution during the 1980s not also be dismissed under the *Escobar* rationale?

Lopez-Soto v. Ashcroft[43] is another somewhat confusing case. Lopez-Soto is Guatemalan. The Mara 18 gang was trying to recruit him, but he refused. When the gang threatened to kill him if he did not join, he fled to the United States with his cousin. His cousin was deported and killed by the Mara 18 when he returned. His older brothers were also killed by the Mara 18 because they had refused to join.

The court held that Lopez-Soto did not establish persecution *on account of* a cognizable social group. In this case, Lopez-Soto tried to use the family relationship as a particular social group. The court does recognize family as a particular social group. Upon reviewing the CAT claim, the court held that the government did not acquiesce to the gangs, but did recognize that the government is powerless to the Mara 18; the court denied the CAT claim as well.

However, in the dissenting opinion, Judge Michael noted that the Mara 18 started to target the

---

[37] *Id.*

[38] G. Varela, *El Diario de Hoy* (Jan. 27, 2006) (San Salvador).

[39] Lydersen, *supra* note 34.

[40] 417 F.3d 363 (3d Cir. 2005).

[41] 12 F.3d 1233 (3d Cir. 1993).

[42] 19 I&N Dec. 439 (BIA 1985).

[43] 383 F.3d 228 (4th Cir 2004).

family in 1990. The gang tried to recruit Lopez-Soto's brother; when he refused, he was killed. That was reported to the police and nothing was done. There was a similar situation with another brother. His cousin was killed by the gang. The gang even sent him a letter telling him how he would be killed like his brother if he did not join the gang.

The dissenting judge stated the following as the issue—what is the motive for the well-founded fear of persecution—and noted that the persecution need not be solely from the family membership but that if the illicit motive was due to the family relationship, it did not have to be the sole cause.

THE CHILDREN LEFT BEHIND

Of course, gangs are not the only problem confronting Central American children.

No doubt, there have always been minors coming to the United States. The legacy of the fictional Corleone family in *The Godfather* begins with a young Vito Corleone arriving from Italy after his family is killed by a gangster. However, a new and troubling demographic is coming into existence, and the immigration laws of this country are proving themselves hard-pressed to respond.

Many Central Americans have now lived in the United States in a Temporary Protected Status (TPS)[44] for many years, and a large number of these have even been able to adjust their status under NACARA.[45] Many of these protected immigrants left young children behind, often to be raised by their grandparents. The grandparents are now aging or dying, and the children have no one left who is willing or able to care for them.

The result has been that families that have taken care of the children all these years are now anxious to return the children to their parents in the United States. These children do not have the protection of past TPS grants and have no derivative NACARA benefits. Nor do their parents' asylum claims offer

derivative benefits, either because the asylum claims are abandoned or denied during NACARA proceedings, or they have become untenable because the parents can no longer show a fear of persecution.

If a child in ICE custody has relatives in the United States who have a lawful status, the child will usually be released to them. However, proceedings will not be terminated even if venue is changed.

Often these children are accompanied by relatives anxious to make sure they do not become separated from the children under any circumstances. Thus, the accompanying relatives or friends claim to be the parents of the children, in effect bringing the children in under a false identity. This creates problems because not only does it delay reunification with the real family, it puts in doubt any identity documents the family might produce.

Documents, particularly nationality documents, are very important. More and more, the Board is taking the position that if a document is or should be available, failure to produce it will result in denial of the claim.[46] In the view of the Board, submitting a fraudulent document so taints the application that asylum should be denied.[47]

When the children are placed in proceedings, the courts often pressure the children to accept voluntary departure. If the voluntary departure order is obeyed, the children are returned to the same desperate situation that forced them to come here in the first place. If the voluntary departure order is disobeyed, the children become fugitives from an order of deportation and are barred from future benefits for at least 10 years,[48] including any possibility of reopening proceedings.[49] Furthermore, the period of voluntary departure cannot be extended beyond 120 days.[50]

As counterintuitive as it sounds, when faced with this situation, perhaps the best decision is to accept a removal order, then request a stay of deportation from ICE. While the removal order would make the

---

[44] INA §244.

[45] The Nicaraguan Adjustment and Central American Relief Act, Pub. L. No. 105-100, *as amended by* Pub. L. No. 105-139, Pub. L. No. 106-386, and Pub. L. No. 106-554. Section 203 of NACARA permits eligible Guatemalans and Salvadorans who applied for benefits under the settlement agreed to in *American Baptist Churches v. Thornburg*, 760 F. Supp. 796 (N.D. Cal. 1991) to apply for lawful permanent residence using the old suspension of deportation (former INA §244(a)).

[46] *In re Y–B–*, 21 I&N Dec. 1136 (BIA 1998) (held that failure to produce documentation of a stay in a refugee camp should result in denial). *In re M–D–*, 21 I&N Dec. 1180 (BIA 1998) (denied asylum where no documentation as to identity and nationality was offered).

[47] *In re O–D–*, 21 I&N Dec. 1079 (BIA 1998).

[48] INA §240B(d).

[49] *In re Arie Shaar*, 21 I&N Dec. 541 (BIA 1996).

[50] INA §240B(a)(2)(A).

child inadmissible for 10 years,[51] the Attorney General may waive this ground of inadmissibility.[52]

EFFECTIVE PRESENTATION OF EVIDENCE—BACKGROUND COUNTRY CONDITIONS

Introduction

The key to any removal case is advance preparation; asylum cases are no exception. In addition to preparing a client to give detailed, coherent, and credible testimony, defense counsel can assist enormously by preparing a quality package of background documentation on country conditions. In addition, the presentation of an expert witness affidavit (for asylum interviews) and expert testimony (for asylum court) can assist enormously in providing interesting, corroborative background information on country conditions. Through research, presentation, and the testimony of an expert, counsel can turn a lackluster asylum case into a strong, compelling claim and make obviously a huge difference in the client's life.

The Law on Evidence of Country Conditions

In *Matter of S–M–J–*,[53] the BIA issued an important decision on presentation of corroborative evidence. The Board discussed not only background information on country conditions but also evidence particular to the individual's claim. In terms of background evidence on country conditions, the Board wrote that the applicant, government counsel, and the IJ are responsible for presenting reports, articles, and profiles from not only the State Department (DOS)—but also Amnesty International (which is specifically mentioned), other reputable organizations, and academic institutions.[54] Citing *Matter of Dass*,[55] the Board specifically identified the expert witness as a source of credible evidence on background country conditions.[56] If an applicant fails to present background information in support of the claim, the claim may be denied.[57] Again, however, both the court and government counsel have an obligation to supplement the record with country condition information.

The REAL ID Act[58] essentially codified the Board's directives in *Matter of S–M–J–* by requiring presentation of corroborative evidence to support an applicant's claim.

Counsel should be aware that significant, compelling background information may *make* the entire case in the absence of evidence linked directly to the individual:

(iii) In evaluating whether the applicant has sustained the burden of proving that he or she has a well-founded fear of persecution, the asylum officer or immigration judge shall not require the applicant to provide evidence that there is a reasonable possibility he or she would be singled out individually for persecution if:

(A) the applicant establishes that there is a pattern or practice in his or her country of nationality or, if stateless, in his or her country of last habitual residence, of persecution of a group of persons similarly situated to the applicant on account of race, religion, nationality, membership in a particular social group, or political opinion; and

(B) The applicant establishes his or her own inclusion in, and identification with, such group of persons such that his or her fear of persecution upon return is reasonable.[59]

Certainly based on the more stringent requirements of REAL ID, an applicant must establish *why* individualized evidence (*i.e.*, evidence specifically relevant to his or her case) is not available. The point here, however, is that strategic, thoughtful presentation of background evidence can make background country conditions the core of the claim (contingent, of course, upon the applicant's establishment that he or she is part of the particular group that is suffering a pattern and practice of persecution). The Board specifically noted this perspective, based on the regulation, in *Matter of S–M–J–*.[60]

---

[51] INA §212(a)(9)(A)(ii).

[52] INA §212(a)(9)(A)(iii).

[53] 21 I&N Dec. 722 (BIA 1997).

[54] *Matter of S–M–J–*, 21 I&N Dec. 722, 729 (BIA 1997) (citing *The Basic Law Manual, U.S. Law and INS Refugee/ Asylum Adjudications* (1994)).

[55] 20 I&N Dec. 120, 125 (BIA 1989).

[56] *Matter of S–M–J–*, 21 I&N Dec. at 731.

[57] *Id.* at 726.

[58] The Emergency Supplemental Appropriations Act for Defense, the Global War on Terror, and Tsunami Relief, Division B, Pub. L. No 109-13, 119 Stat. 231 (REAL ID Act of 2005).

[59] 8 CFR §§208.13(b)(2)(iii), 1208.13(b)(2)(iii).

[60] *Matter of S–M–J–*, 21 I&N Dec. at 730.

Practical Tips

So what does *S–M–J–* really mean in the reality of the immigration courtroom? Routinely, government counsel for ICE provides a copy of the latest *State Department Country Reports* to the court and the applicant. Unless ICE counsel takes an unusual interest in a case, he or she will rarely do more. Some good and interested IJs do maintain their own mini-library and refer to key articles by organizations such as Human Rights Watch and Amnesty International, but the real burden of the requirements of *S–M–J–* and REAL ID falls on asylum applicants and counsel. The evidentiary requirements regarding background country conditions should be viewed as an opportunity to win the case—not a burden.

The beauty of *S–M–J–* is that the courts *must* consider the background evidence. The courts *must* allow expert witnesses to testify. IJs are not at liberty to disallow a relevant expert witness (see discussion on experts below); they must consider well-presented information from a pertinent report or article. An IJ cannot (and the Board specifically states this in *S–M–J–*) cynically refuse to consider relevant background evidence because he or she already "knows so much" about the country, or hears so many similar claims each day. To insert one's own knowledge into the decision, without specifically referencing a source, is verboten by *S–M–J–*.[61]

Concise Presentation

Lest counsel lose an incredible opportunity to sway the case in his or her client's favor, pay careful attention to the actual presentation of background evidence. Some practitioners fall into a routine of submitting a bulk background package of material that is not referred to in the course of the case by anyone. This is a huge mistake. Each client's case is unique and deserves special attention. Counsel should carefully select articles[62] directly relevant to the claim, tab and index them, and then highlight by underlining or marking the relevant portions. Indeed, the index itself can summarize the article's relevance. For example:

"Paramilitaries Take Control of West Coast of Colombia," *Human Rights in South America Website* (Nov. 16, 2005).

> This article discusses the fact that the Autodefensas paramilitary group has been given free reign to organize and control certain small towns along the West coast of Colombia, including Casaslibres, the town that Respondent Martinez fled in 2004. The Government of Colombia signed this agreement at negotiations on January 1, 2005. At pages 4 through 6, Commander Cara Blanca of the 3rd Block of AUC is discussed in terms of atrocities which he is believed to have committed in and around Casaslibres. Commander Blanca is the individual who ordered the death of Respondent Martinez according to a list dated March 6, 2004.

In this way, the court is not bombarded by written information, and can "speed read" relevant portions (hopefully enticed to go back and review the report in its entirety after catching the written "soundbites"). In addition, to be truly considered in the record, counsel's pretrial statement or brief should cite to, and quote in whole portions, relevant documents. Depending on the flexibility of the IJ, counsel may refer to supporting articles during examination itself. Consider the following example from a hypothetical direct examination in court:

Counsel's question: What leads you to believe that police in Sao Paolo would arrest someone simply for being gay?

Respondent's answer: It was a regular occurrence. When I would go out with friends, to clubs, parties, restaurants, we always feared the police and took steps to conceal how we—well—felt, if we thought the police might be around. Three of my friends were arrested and beaten in just one year. They had done nothing wrong.

Counsel: Your honor, I'd like to briefly draw your attention to Exhibit 4-C, at page 5, which corroborates this testimony—indicating that police violence against gay persons reached an all-time high in 2005, with over 50 deaths being attributed to harassment and persecution of homosexuals by the police.

In the closing statement, counsel should be prepared to refer to portions of the articles that support the client's claim. This type of presentation—referencing key portions of relevant background material—places a burden on the court to mention the articles and state for the record why this information

---

[61] *Id.*

[62] An excellent resource on websites and nongovernmental organizations (and asylum law in general) may be found in R. Germain, *AILA's Asylum Primer*, 4th ed. (2005), *www.ailapubs.org*.

is or is not being considered in support of the claim. Based on *S–M–J–*, it is reversible error for a judge to deny a claim in contradiction of specific supporting information without citing *why* such information is not being taken into account or is otherwise discredited. On the other hand, if counsel does not at some point in the record of proceedings make mention of an article's relevance to the case (either in a pretrial brief, during the course of examination, or in closing), the Board is unlikely to criticize the court for disregarding it in a decision denying asylum.

USE OF EXPERT WITNESS TESTIMONY

Matter of S–M–J– provides as examples a variety of acceptable forms of background evidence, including expert testimony. In other words, it is counsel's choice. Use of the expert witness is a proud tradition in all areas of litigation. Why use an expert instead of simply submitting an article, or even the expert's own affidavit? The answer is that a live human being brings color and spark to the case—a good witness is far more compelling than words on paper. In addition, the weight to be given a witness who is subject to cross-examination by opposing counsel is stronger than that of an article (which is not subject to cross-examination). However, more important than the weight of evidence, an expert can bring the case to life, fill in the gaps, and help enormously in convincing a judge that asylum should be granted.

Federal Rules of Evidence

Although the Federal Rules of Evidence do not strictly apply to immigration court proceedings, there is no good reason why they should not be adhered to in terms of presenting a witness. At the very least, the Rules serve as guidelines, and guidelines are needed at times because there is confusion about the role of an expert. Although there are several rules relevant to the application of expert testimony, the specific rules regarding expert witnesses are found at Rules 701 through 706.

Qualification of the Expert

An expert's testimony must be relevant to be admissible.[63] It must also be reliable.[64] Counsel seeking to present an expert should notify the court in advance through the pretrial statement or a similar submission that incorporates a witness list, and the expert's curriculum vitae (CV) should be submitted in advance of the hearing.

An Important Tip: *Read* the CV before presenting it to the court. If it should be refined to include experience relevant to the particular case, counsel may speak to the expert about a case-specific CV. Revisions to a CV take a few minutes, but will determine the direction voir dire will take at the time of hearing.

As for voir dire, counsel should ensure that an informal voir dire "practice" has taken place in advance of the hearing, so the expert is prepared for cross-examination and questions from the court. If the expert is a professor, voir dire may include the current curriculum taught, classes taught the previous year, professional associations, scholarly writing and editing, trips to the country in question, and always—always—whether the expert has been qualified previously in an immigration court. (The judge will be hard-pressed to find someone is not an expert if his or her "neighbor" [the judge next door] found otherwise last week.)

In preparing an expert, provide the asylum application, all exhibits that have been presented to the court, and a review of relevant questions for the hearing. The expert should not meet the client unless counsel sees a specific need for this; talking to the client is not the role of an expert on background country conditions. The expert may, however, properly be asked by ICE counsel how much he or she is being paid; so prepare the witness for that somewhat unnerving financial compensation question.

Expert testimony presents scientific, technical, or specialized knowledge to help the trier of fact (the IJ) understand the evidence or determine a fact at issue.[65] In an asylum case, an expert witness may be an academic, an employee of a human rights organization, or an anthropologist or health care worker, for example, who can testify about events, groups, and activities in a certain country. Journalists would make good experts, but they are rarely willing to testify. Professors from colleges or universities are the obvious choice as experts, and in a pro bono or legal service agency's case, may be willing to offer their own services pro bono as well.

Another type of expert in an asylum case may be a psychologist or psychiatrist who can testify about an applicant's psychological condition following a traumatic experience, or a medical doctor who has

---

[63] Fed. R. Evid. 401.

[64] Fed. R. Evid. 701, 702.

[65] Fed. R. Evid. 702.

examined injuries, but these types of witnesses would be more factual than those testifying as to background country conditions.

There are many ways to locate a good expert. They are quoted in the press, they have published works, they can be recommended by colleagues—when in doubt, a good Google search on the topic of the case will generally reveal experts on the theme.[66]

An expert witness on country conditions is not a factual witness; he or she will often *not* have personal knowledge of events specifically affecting the particular applicant. Therefore, an expert witness should not be sequestered during the applicant's and other witness' testimony. Furthermore, an expert witness on background country conditions should not be expected to specifically research the particular claim; an expert is not a private investigator, and this sort of exercise would turn the expert into a factual witness.

Of specific importance is that an expert, unlike a factual witness, is indeed qualified to testify regarding the ultimate issue: is the applicant more likely than not to be persecuted? Rule 704 states that an expert's opinion on the ultimate issue is not objectionable because it is an opinion. *"Objection, calls for speculation"* has no place in regard to an expert's testimony. Thus, counsel should take full advantage of this point and toward the conclusion of direct examination, ask the all-important question:

> Professor, in your expert opinion, is Vladimir Rutskin likely to be persecuted by the Ukranian Secret Service on account of his political activities for the New Democratic Society if returned to the Ukraine?

Sources of Information Relied upon by the Expert

The judge and/or ICE counsel may properly ask for copies of all articles or sources of research relied upon for that specific hearing.[67] Certainly, an expert witness—for example, a professor—will have a healthy quantity of professional information and may not have specific articles or books to reference in support of testimony. Rather, the testimony represents a lifetime of study, teaching, travel, and contemplation (after all, that is what makes this person

an expert). But to the extent that key points on specific issues are made during an expert's testimony, or articles or data have indeed been reviewed for the particular case, the expert should be prepared to cite to the sources. Counsel may be asked to provide copies to the court. (If the court were to request copies, presumably they could be provided after the hearing; there is no need to come to court armed with three sets of copies of the expert's research.)

Expert Testimony versus Documentation on Background Conditions

Documentation on background conditions becomes less important if an expert is going to testify, but counsel should still present background articles and reports, for example, from agencies like Amnesty International, to supplement the record. Ensure that the expert is familiar with these documents, lest they become fodder for adverse cross-examination. In particular, since DOS's *Country Reports on Human Rights Practices* are routinely reviewed, remind the expert to review them before the hearing.

A Final Word on Experts

Experience teaches that the judge has the final word on the presentation of expert testimony, and each IJ may have different perspectives and rules about this. The dichotomy can be frustrating, but counsel must be flexible and learn to expect nuances among courtrooms. Some judges, for example, may desire a short voir dire; others may turn voir dire directly over to assistant chief counsel first. Some judges may not understand the nature of an expert witness and insist on sequestration. Other judges may make an expert wait in the waiting room while the respondent testifies, rather than giving the professional courtesy of testifying upon his or her arrival. Ultimately, the judge controls the presentation of all witnesses in the courtroom, and counsel should make his or her points, based on the rules of evidence, but ultimately, and politely, defer to the court's judgment.

What a judge cannot do, again based on *S–M–J–*, is refuse to hear relevant testimony from a qualified expert witness because—in the judge's mind—it is not "necessary," or the court is already omniscient on country conditions. In the end, everyone in the courtroom can enjoy the testimony of an interesting expert witness: a good expert will often come as a refreshing change to an otherwise humdrum day on a routine docket. Enjoy the experience of presenting a good expert.

---

[66] If a good expert is located out of state, counsel can file a motion to present the testimony by telephone. However, if financially and physically feasible, an expert witness should come to court to testify in person—a human face is always more compelling than a voice on the phone.

[67] Fed. R. Evid. 705.

BRIEF HISTORY OF LESBIAN, GAY, BISEXUAL, TRANSGENDER, AND HIV (LGBT/H ASYLUM) LAW

excerpted from LGBT/HIV Based Asylum Handbook: Winning Asylum, Withholding and CAT Cases Based on Sexual Orientation, Transgender Identity and/or HIV-Positive Status [*]

U.S. asylum law is derived from international agreements written after World War II which provide protection to people fearing or fleeing from persecution. The first agreement, the 1951 Convention Relating to the Status of Refugees, was drafted by the United Nations in response to the large migrations of people in the aftermath of the Second World War. The United Nations attempted to set forth an internationally agreed upon standard for who will be considered a refugee. The 1951 Convention, however, only applied to people who were refugees on the basis of events occurring before January 1, 1951. The United Nations incorporated the definition of refugee set forth in the 1951 Convention but expanded it to include future refugees in the 1967 U.N. Protocol Relating to the Status of Refugees.[1] The United States ac-

ceded to the 1967 Protocol in 1968. In order to bring U.S. law into compliance with its obligations under the Protocol, the United States enacted the Refugee Act of 1980, adopting essentially the same definition of refugee as set forth by the Convention. A refugee is defined as:

> "any person who is outside any country of such person's nationality or, in the case of a person having no nationality, is outside any country in which such person last habitually resided, and who is unable or unwilling to return to, and is unable or unwilling to avail himself or herself of the protection of that country because of persecution or a well-founded fear of persecution on account of race, religion, nationality, membership in a particular social group, or political opinion."[2]

An individual can be granted asylum if she is present in the United States and otherwise meets the definition of a refugee.[3] Refugee status can be based on either race, religion, nationality, membership in a particular social group, or political opinion. Of the five grounds on which a claim for asylum can be based, membership in a particular social group is the most open to interpretation and thus provides the best basis for claims of asylum based on sexual orientation and gender identity. Although there is no statutory definition of what suffices as membership in a particular social group, it has frequently been described as a group of persons who share a common, immutable characteristic that the members of the group cannot or should not be required to change.[4] In 1994, Attorney General Janet Reno declared as precedent the *Matter of Toboso-Alfonso* case in which a gay Cuban man was found to be eligible for withholding of removal on the basis of his

---

[*] This article contains excerpts from a book-length manual entitled *LGBT/HIV Based Asylum Handbook: Winning Asylum, Withholding and CAT Cases Based on Sexual Orientation, Transgender Identity and/or HIV-Positive Status*. Reprinted with permission. The Manual is available at *www.immigrationequality.org,* which was written by Immigration Equality and the Midwest Immigrant & Human Rights Center.

Immigration Equality is the only national organization whose mission is to end the discriminatory treatment of lesbian, gay, bisexual, transgender, and HIV-positive individuals under U.S. immigration law. Immigration Equality runs a pro bono asylum project, provides technical assistance to attorneys, maintains an informational website, and fields questions from LGBT and HIV-positive individuals and their loved ones from around the world. Additionally through education, outreach and advocacy, Immigration Equality works to change the laws that unfairly impact LGBT and HIV-positive immigrants.

The Midwest Immigrant & Human Rights Center (MIHRC), a program of Heartland Alliance for Human Needs and Human Rights, provides direct legal services to and advocates for impoverished immigrants, refugees, and asylum seekers. MIHRC has provided assistance to low-income immigrants since 1881. Through its National Asylum Partnership on Sexual Orientation, MIHRC has provided legal representation to immigrants and asylum-seekers who are seeking protection from human rights abuses due to their sexual orientation.

[1] U.N. Protocol Relating to the Status of Refugees, Jan. 31, 1967, 19 U.S.T. 6223, T.I.A.S. No. 6577, 606 U.N.T.S. 267 (1967).

[2] INA §101(a)(42)(A), 8 USC §1101(a)(42)(A).

[3] INA §208(a),(b)(1); 8 USC §1158(a),(b)(1).

[4] *Matter of Acosta*, 19 I&N Dec. 211, 233 (BIA 1985); Office of the United Nations High Commissioner for Refugees, Refugee Protection in International Law: UNHCR's Global Consultations on International Protection 313 (Erika Heller, Volker Türk & Frances Nicholson eds.) (2003), *available at* http://www.unhcr.ch/cgi-bin/texis/vtx/publ?id= 41a1b51c6.

membership in the particular social group of homo-sexuals.[5] This case was pivotal in establishing that a well-founded fear of persecution on the basis of one's sexual orientation is a valid basis on which to claim asylum status in the United States. More recently, the Ninth Circuit has affirmed that "*all* alien homosexuals are members of a 'particular social group.'"[6] The recognition of this basis for asylum is in accord with other countries which have granted asylum to gay and lesbian refugees.[7]

In the years after *Matter of Toboso-Alfonso*, courts have employed a more expansive definition of what constitutes a particular social group, including gender-based violence, such as female genital mutilation and domestic violence, as sufficient grounds for asylum.[8] Courts have also been more willing to recognize persecution based on sexual identity. Since *Toboso-Alfonso* there have been more than half a dozen precedential lesbian, gay, bisexual, transgender and/or HIV-positive ("LGBT/H") asylum cases.[9]

Although those who identify as transgender have not been explicitly found to be considered members of a particular social group, courts have recognized that gay men with female sexual identities constitute a social group and may be persecuted based on this identity.[10] While there has been no precedential decision recognizing women with male sexual identities as members of a social group, there have been numerous successful, non-precedential claims based on this ground.

Another significant ruling for LGBT/H people considers the intent of the person or persons who commit the persecution. Generally in asylum cases, the persecutor intends harm to the victim, however, courts have acknowledged that persecution can occur even when the persecutor has no intention to harm the victim, such as when a gay person is subjected to electroshock therapy to "cure" her sexual orientation.[11]

Persons living with HIV and/or AIDS face harsh and discriminatory policies when attempting to immigrate to the United States. Their entry as legal immigrants is barred unless they are legally married to, are the parent of, or are the unmarried son or daughter or lawfully adopted child of a U.S. citizen or legal permanent resident. For the purposes of asylum, however, there is the possibility that people facing HIV persecution in their own country may be considered members of a particular social group. In 1996, the Immigration and Naturalization Service (INS) Office of General Counsel issued a memorandum which recommended that the INS and the Executive Office for Immigration Review (EOIR) should grant asylum based on the social group category of HIV-positive individuals, assuming that the applicant in question meets all of the other elements required for asylum.[12] Although there are no precedential cases which recognize HIV status as creating membership in a particular social group, asylum has been granted in some cases where HIV persecution was an essential element of the application.[13]

---

[5] *Matter of Toboso-Alfonso*, 20 I&N Dec. 819 (BIA 1990).

[6] *Karouni v. Gonzales*, 399 F.3d 1163, 1172 (9th Cir. 2005). *See also Amanfi v. Ashcroft*, 328 F.3d 719, 727 (3d Cir. 2003) (noting concession of the BIA that homosexuals are a protected group). *But see Kimumwe v. Gonzalez*, 431 F.3d 319 (8th Cir. 2005) (denying asylum to a gay man from Zimbabwe and using language which seems to question whether homosexuality constitutes a particular social group).

[7] The International Gay and Lesbian Human Rights Commission reports that the governments of Australia, Belgium, Canada, Denmark, Finland, France, Germany, Ireland, Italy, the Netherlands, New Zealand, Thailand, and the UK have granted asylum on the basis of sexual orientation. *Available at www.iglhrc.org/site/iglhrc/content.php?type=1&id=78*.

[8] *See In re Kasinga*, 21 I&N Dec. 357, 358 (BIA 1996) (finding the threat of female genital mutilation as a sufficient basis for an asylum claim); *Gonzales v. Gutierrez*, 311 F.3d 942, 947 n.9 (9th Cir. 2002) (asylum granted on the basis of domestic violence).

[9] For an updated list of LGBT/H precedential asylum decisions, see *http://www.immigrationequality.org/template.php?pageid=204*. Note that this Manual uses the phrase LGBT/H throughout to discuss case law and strategy pertinent to members of any of these particular social groups. However, in working on an asylum case, it is important to specifically identify the particular social group to which the applicant belongs, for example, "lesbians," or "transgender women and people living with HIV."

[10] *Hernandez-Montiel v. INS*, 225 F.3d 1084 (9th Cir. 1997); *Reyes-Reyes v. Ashcroft*, 384 F.3d 782 (9th Cir. 2004).

[11] *Pitcherskaia v. INS*, 118 F.3d 641 (9th Cir. 1997).

[12] *See* Memorandum from INS Office of the General Counsel, David A. Martin, General Counsel, to all Regional Counsel, Legal Opinion: Seropositivity for HIV and Relief from Deportation (Feb. 16, 1996), *reported in* 73 *Interpreter Releases* 901 (July 8, 1996).

[13] *Matter of [ ]*, (IJ Dec. 20, 2000) (Baltimore, MD) (Gossart, IJ), *reported in* 78 *Interpreter Releases* 233 (Jan. 15, 2001) (HIV-positive married woman wins asylum as a member of the social group of married women in India based on evidence of ostracism and lack of appropriate medical care if she returned to her native country); *Matter of [ ]*, A71-498-940 (IJ

continued

In 1996, Congress passed the Illegal Immigration Reform and Immigrant Responsibility Act, which generally restricted access to asylum protection and greatly hindered the ability to obtain asylum status on the basis of sexual orientation. This legislation created additional bars to asylum, the most restrictive of which was the one year filing deadline. In order to be granted asylum, an applicant must file for asylum within one year of his or her arrival in the United States. This deadline has created unique hardships for LGBT/H asylum seekers because they are often unaware that their sexual orientation, gender identity, or HIV status can form the basis of an asylum claim and, are often afraid to disclose these intimate aspects of their identity to a government official given the persecution they faced in their own country.[14]

In May 2005, Congress passed the Real ID Act which imposes further limitations on the asylum process.[15] Under the revised law, asylum seekers must provide documents to corroborate their claims unless they can demonstrate to the adjudicator why the documents are unavailable or why the applicant cannot obtain them. The Real ID Act also makes it easier for an adjudicator to deny a claim based on lack of credibility by the asylum seeker. Now, if an asylum seeker makes an inconsistent statement, even if the statement is not directly related to the substance of the claim, the application can be denied on credibility grounds. An applicant also must now demonstrate that his or her protected characteristic was "at least one central reason" behind the persecutor's actions. It remains to be seen whether adjudicators will see the Real ID Act as a codification of existing case law, or whether they will apply a stricter standard to cases filed after May 2005.

In recent years there have been several precedential cases from federal Courts of Appeals on LGBT/H asylum cases.[16] LGBT/H status-based asylum law is an exciting and developing area of the law. As LGBT/H immigrants struggle for equality under U.S. immigration law, asylum continues to be one of the few areas of immigration law where the U.S. government gives LGBT/H foreign nationals the opportunity to begin a new and freer life in the United States.

****

PRECEDENTIAL LGBT/H ASYLUM CASES

With asylum cases in general, and LGBT/H cases in particular, there is not that much precedent that exists. The vast majority of cases are decided without any written opinion at the Asylum Office level. Even cases that go before Immigration Judges are mostly decided by oral opinion which is only transcribed if a party appeals. In any event, decisions by Asylum Officers and Immigration Judges do not have precedential value.

Similarly, the vast majority of BIA decisions are unpublished. To date there has been only one precedential LGBT/H BIA decision. In recent years, there has been an increasing number of LGBT/H decisions in the federal Courts of Appeals.

The following is a complete list of LGBT/H asylum cases as of the date of publication of this Manual.

- *Matter of Toboso-Alfonso* (BIA 1994) — 20 I&N Dec. 819 (BIA 1990) — the original case, designated as precedent in 1994, which established sexual orientation as "membership in a particular social group" and paved the way for asylum based on sexual orientation. Toboso-Alfonso was a gay man from Cuba who suffered various abuses at the hands of his government, including being forced to participate in a labor camp.

- *Pitcherskaia v. INS* (9th Circuit 1997) — 118 F.3d 641, 645 (9th Circ. 1997) — finding that even if the abuser does not intend harm to the victim, if the victim experiences the abuse as harm, this can rise to the level of persecution. In this case, the applicant was a lesbian from Russia who, among other abuses, had been forced to undergo electroshock therapy to "cure" her of her homosexuality.

Oct. 31, 1995) (New York, NY), *reported in* 73 *Interpreter Releases* 901 (July 8, 1996) (man from Togo granted asylum on the basis of his membership in the particular social group of individuals infected with HIV).

[14] Victoria Neilson & Aaron Morris, "The Gay Bar: The Effect of the One-Year Filing Deadline on Lesbian, Gay, Bisexual, Transgender and HIV-Positive Foreign Nationals Seeking Asylum or Withholding of Removal," 8 *N.Y. City L. Rev.* 601 (2005).

[15] REAL ID Act, Pub. L. No. 109-13, 119 Stat. 231 (May 11, 2005).

---

[16] *See* Section # 4 for a complete list of precedential LGBT/H asylum cases. *Ed. Note: See* full *Manual* for Section # 4.

- *Hernandez-Montiel v. INS* (9th Circuit 2000) — 225 F.3d 1088 (9th Cir. 2000) — finding that a gay man with a female sexual identity who suffered persecution in Mexico, largely because he was effeminate, qualified for asylum.

- *Amanfi v. Ashcroft* (3rd Circuit 2003) — 328 F.3d 719 (3d Cir. 2003) — finding that it is possible to proceed with an asylum claim based on persecution on account of imputed membership in a particular social group, in this case sexual orientation, even if the applicant is not actually gay. In this case the applicant, a man from Ghana who feared he would be ritually sacrificed, engaged in a homosexual act with another man, knowing that this would lead to his being spared the sacrifice. After he was spared, however, he was mistreated because the authorities believed he was gay. The Court recognized his imputed membership in a particular social group and remanded the case for further investigation on his claim of persecution.

- *Reyes-Reyes v. Ashcroft* (9th Circuit 2004) — 384 F.3d 782 (9th Cir. 2004) — reaffirming that a "gay man with a female sexual identity" belongs to a particular social group, and finding that if a government willfully turns a blind eye to severe physical abuse inflicted by non-government actors this can rise to the level of government acquiescence in torture so as to qualify for relief under the Convention against Torture treaty. In this case Reyes-Reyes was a gay man with a female sexual identity from El Salvador who had been kidnapped, beaten and raped by non-government actors because of his sexual orientation. The Court remanded for further proceedings on his CAT and withholding claims.

- *Molathwa v. Ashcroft* (8th Cir. 2004) — 390 F.3d 551 (8th Cir. 2004) — holding that the federal court lacked jurisdiction to review his claimed exception to the one year filing deadline for asylum and that Molathwa had failed to demonstrate that it was more likely than not that he would be persecuted because of his gay sexual orientation in his native Botswana.

- *Galicia v. Ashcroft* (1st Cir. 2005) — 396 F.3d 446 (1st Cir. 2005) — denying gay Guatemalan man's petition for review because he failed to show government involvement or lack of protection from past mistreatment he suffered by his neighbors.

- *Karouni v. Gonzalez,* (9th Cir. 2005) — 399 F.3d 1163 (9th Cir. 2005) — holding unequivocally that "*all* alien homosexuals are members of a "'particular social group'" and finding that Karouni, a gay, HIV positive man from Lebanon, had established a well founded fear of future persecution.

- *Boer-Sedano v. Gonzalez,* (9th Cir. 2005) — 418 F.3d 1082, (9th Cir. 2005) — holding that a gay Mexican man with AIDS who was sexually and physically abused by a Mexican police officer was statutorily eligible for asylum. The case also contains good language about the applicant's HIV status making internal relocation within Mexico impossible, as well as good language that return trips to the home country alone do not render an applicant ineligible for asylum.

- *Salkeld v. Gonzalez,* (8th Cir. 2005) — 420 F.3d 804 (8th Cir. 2005) — holding that gay man from Peru who did not personally suffer past persecution and who did not meet a one year filing deadline exception, failed to prove a clear probability of future persecution and therefore did not meet the standard for withholding of removal. The Court found it significant that Salkeld himself had never experienced physical violence, there are no laws against homosexuality in Peru, and there are some regions in Peru which are relatively safer for gay people than others.

- *Kimumwe v. Gonzalez,* (8th Cir. 2005) — 431 F.3d 319 (8th Cir. 2005) — terrible decision (with good dissent) holding that a gay man from Zimbabwe had not established past persecution although, among other things, he was jailed without charges for two months after having sex with another man at college. The Court found that he was jailed because of sexual misconduct, not homosexual identity. The Court also found that in spite of Mugabe's statements that homosexuals have no rights, and Zimbabwe's poor record on human rights, that Kimumwe had failed to prove a fear of future persecution.

****

THORNY ISSUES IN
LGBT/H ASYLUM CASES

Some asylum applications are relatively straightforward. The applicant is filing within one year of his last arrival in the United States, he has severe past persecution with documentation to corroborate the abuse, and he has never done anything wrong in the United States or in his native country. Cases such as this are relatively easy to work on, and with careful preparation have a strong chance of winning.

Often, however, clients are not so perfect. When asylum applications include facts which seem to undermine the claim, it is important to address these facts head on. Asylum Officers, Judges, and ICE attorneys will be looking for these issues and will confront your client with them. It is therefore best to have the applicant raise difficult issues first so that he can fully explain the circumstances of the bad fact. There are some issues in particular which arise frequently in LGBT/H asylum issues which require extra thought and preparation.

Marriage

It is essential to remember in preparing a sexual orientation-based asylum claim, that the first element which must be proven to the adjudicator is that the applicant really is lesbian or gay. This can be accomplished by including affidavits, letters and/or testimony from current and/or past romantic partners. Proof of sexual orientation can also be bolstered by including evidence that the applicant is involved in LGBT organizations. And, of course, the applicant's detailed and compelling written and oral testimony about romantic feelings are crucial.

But what if the applicant was or is married? Will this be fatal to a sexual orientation-based asylum application? The answer, as with most asylum issues, is, it depends. It is important when preparing the case to realize that this will be a significant issue and to prepare the client to talk about the marriage honestly.

Marriage in the Home Country

In many cases an asylum applicant will have married in her own country because her family forced her into the marriage, because she was hoping the marriage would work and she could "cure" her sexual orientation, or because she believed the marriage would provide her with a "cover" which would allow her to continue to seek same sex relationships with other women. In situations where the applicant tried to be married and the marriage failed because of the applicant's sexual orientation, the marriage (and possible divorce) itself can become part of the evidence of the applicant's sexual orientation. It is important, if possible, to corroborate the failure of the marriage, whether this is through a letter from the (ex)spouse, a letter from a friend or family member in whom the applicant confided, or a

letter from a therapist who tried to help save the marriage.

The longer the marriage lasted, and the deeper the commitment appeared to be, for example, if the couple had children, the more in depth the explanation the applicant should be prepared to give. Expert testimony from a psychiatrist or psychologist can be essential to a case where the applicant appeared to lead a heterosexual life in the past. It is important to remember that the asylum adjudicator is probably heterosexual and may need to be educated about the complex psychological components that make up a person's sexual orientation.

Marriage in the United States

If the applicant married a person of the opposite sex in the United States, he will be facing an even more difficult obstacle in his asylum application. It is possible that the applicant married an opposite sex spouse in the United States for the same reasons he might have done so in his own country: the hope of "overcoming" his gay feelings or the hope that he could appease his family. Of course, without the extreme societal pressures which may come to bear on the applicant in his own country, it is more difficult to explain why he would feel the need to marry in the United States where, at least in theory, gay people are free to pursue relationships with members of the same sex. In a situation where the applicant marries in the United States, it will be essential to have a mental health expert testify about the coming out process and the applicant's motivations for entering into the marriage.

An even more difficult situation arises when the applicant married a U.S. citizen or legal permanent resident for the purpose of obtaining a "green card" without truly intending the marriage to be bona fide. In dealing with this situation it is important to remember, first, that an asylum applicant must be truthful at all times. There is no more serious wrong an applicant for immigration status can commit than to intentionally fabricate information in an asylum application, so if the applicant never intended the marriage to be real, he must be truthful about this. Admitting that the applicant committed immigration fraud will probably mean that the applicant will be ineligible for asylum and will instead be focusing on his application for withholding of removal. In addition to meeting the elements of the refugee definition, a successful asylum application requires a "favorable exercise of discretion" (See Section # 3.4 of full *Manual*), and it is unlikely that an adjudicator will exercise this discretion if the applicant admits to having committed immigration fraud.

The other danger with admitting that the applicant previously submitted a fraudulent application is that the adjudicator may find that if the applicant lied to the government in the past in an effort to receive an immigration benefit, he may be doing so again with the current asylum application. It is important to work closely with a client in this difficult situation to make sure that he testifies with complete candor about the marriage and his motivations for entering into it so that the adjudicator believes his current testimony. It is also important to focus on corroborating the applicant's homosexual sexual orientation, as well as to provide other evidence of the applicant's good moral character so that the adjudicator can see that the fraudulent marriage was an aberration borne out of desperation rather than that the applicant is generally untrustworthy.

Bisexual Claims

One reason that an applicant may be married now or may have married in the past, may be that she identifies as bisexual rather than homosexual. There are no precedential asylum claims recognizing bisexuals as a particular social group. As with any other asylum claim, whether or not the claim of a bisexual applicant will succeed will be very dependent on the particular facts of the case.

If the applicant suffered past persecution because of bisexuality, there is a rebuttable presumption that she will suffer future persecution. If she is currently married to a man who would return with her to her country if she is removed, this change in circumstances may be sufficient for ICE to rebut the presumption of future persecution. On the other hand, if the applicant was known to have had same sex relationships in her country, and will be presumed to be a lesbian and face future persecution as a result, she could argue that the fact that she has had some relationships with men would not protect her from the abuse she would face in the future.

Asylum adjudicators often want the issues in cases to be black and white. It is not hard to imagine an asylum adjudicator taking the position that if the applicant is attracted to both sexes, she should simply "choose" to be with members of the opposite sex to avoid future persecution. In a case which is based on bisexual identity, it will be very important to include the testimony of a mental health expert who can describe for the adjudicator that bisexual individuals do not "choose" whether to fall in love with men or women any more so than anyone else "chooses" whom they fall in love with.

The Applicant Does Not "Look Gay"

While it is always necessary for an asylum applicant to prove that he actually is a member of the particular social group of homosexuals, it is especially important to focus on this element of the case if the applicant does not fit the stereotype of an "effeminate gay man" or a "masculine lesbian woman." Every adjudicator approaches an asylum application with his or her own biases. If the applicant "looks gay" to the adjudicator based on whatever stereotypes or "gaydar" the adjudicator brings to the interview or hearing, it is probably more likely that the applicant will win the case. There are several reasons for this.

First, most LGBT applicants cannot prove their membership in a particular group as clearly as other asylum applicants can prove, for example, their affiliation with a political party or their ethnic group. Asylum adjudicators are often fearful that an applicant has completely fabricated his claim simply to remain in the United States If, on a gut level, the adjudicator believes the applicant is gay or lesbian, it is much more likely that the adjudicator will believe other aspects of the case.

Second, even if the adjudicator does believe that the applicant is homosexual, the adjudicator will also question how the applicant's government or other members of society will know the applicant's sexual orientation such that he will be likely to suffer harm in his country. If the applicant is a "flaming queen" it may be easier for the adjudicator to picture the applicant being gay bashed on the street or abused by policemen than if the applicant looks like a professional athlete. If the adjudicator can't tell that the applicant is gay, the adjudicator may question how the applicant's countrymen could tell.

This is precisely the issue in the *Soto-Vega v. Ashcroft*,[17] a case which is currently pending in the Ninth Circuit. In *Soto-Vega*, the Immigration Judge found that although the applicant had suffered past persecution both by the police and the public in his native Mexico, the applicant did not "look gay" to the Judge, so he did not believe the applicant would suffer future persecution. The BIA affirmed the Judge's ruling without opinion, and the case is now

---

[17] *See www.lambdalegal.org/cgi-bin/iowa/news/press.html? record=1543.*

in federal court. Of course, having found past persecution, the applicant was entitled to a presumption of future persecution which the Judge's own informal observations should not have rebutted. The other important lesson from *Soto-Vega*, however, is how important it is to develop the record (which fortunately Soto-Vega's attorneys did) regarding the applicant's sexual orientation. In *Soto-Vega* a witness who was an expert on country conditions in Mexico for LGBT individuals, testified that according to cultural markers in Mexico, Soto-Vega was obviously recognizable as a gay man. This testimony in the record is a crucial part of Soto-Vega's appeal.

In cases where the applicant does not fit the U.S. stereotype of gay man or lesbian woman, the applicant's representative must make sure that the record contains as much corroborating evidence as possible that the applicant really is homosexual. (See Section # 20.2.1 of full *Manual*). The applicant must also be prepared to prove that she would be recognized as a homosexual person in her country and would face persecution as a result. Obviously, if she has already been persecuted in the past, this should be compelling evidence both that she was previously recognized as a lesbian and that her sexual orientation would be known in her country if she returns. Testimony from a country conditions expert that the applicant "looks homosexual" according to the cultural norms of her country can also be very important to the success of the case. It is also important to include other evidence of how the applicant's sexual orientation would become known. For example, in many cultures it is unheard of for a 30 year old man to be unmarried. In other societies the fact that two adults of the same gender are living in the same household would immediately subject them to scrutiny from their neighbors and the government. It is essential to get this evidence into the record, both through country condition reports and expert testimony.

Multiple Return Trips to Country of Origin

The classic factual scenario for an asylum seeker is that the applicant suffers some terrible incident of persecution in his country, flees his country as soon thereafter as possible, and seeks asylum in the United States shortly after arriving here. Cases with this fact pattern are certainly not uncommon, but frequently the realities of asylum seekers' lives don't fit so neatly with this paradigm.

Often LGBT/H individuals have no idea that their sexual orientation, transgender identity or HIV-

positive status could be grounds for seeking asylum in the United States Thus many LGBT/H individuals who visit the United States are careful to return to their countries before their authorized stay expires so that they won't lose the ability to return to the United States in the future. This is often especially true for individuals who are HIV-positive and visiting the United States regularly to obtain medication that is unavailable in their home countries.

If the applicant has returned to his home country after leaving the United States, the adjudicator will certainly want to know why the applicant fears for his safety in returning now when he returned of his own volition in the past. In many cases there was one final incident that occurred to the applicant or to someone the applicant knows which made the applicant realize once and for all that it would be unsafe to remain in his country. The representative should always discuss with the client what compelled him to flee to the United States permanently this last time.

The Ninth Circuit has recently addressed the issue of return trips to the home country after having been persecuted and reiterated that that Circuit has "never held that the existence of return trips standing alone can rebut th[e] presumption [of future persecution.]"[18] In *Boer-Sedano*, the applicant was a gay man with AIDS from Mexico who had suffered past sexual and physical abuse by a police officer because of his sexual orientation. The Court found that Boer-Sedano's several return trips to Mexico to gather enough income to relocate permanently in the United States did not render him ineligible for asylum.

As with most issues in asylum cases, whether or not an applicant's return trips to his country of origin are fatal to his asylum application will depend on the specific facts of the case. It is important for the representative to explore this topic fully with the client and prepare the applicant to explain the reason for the trips to the adjudicator. The applicant should also be prepared to explain (and if possible corroborate) any ways in which he modified his behavior while back in his country. For example, if he remained in his country for a brief time, he avoided gay meeting places and he rarely left his home, these facts may help an adjudicator understand why the applicant was able to escape harm on the trip home.

---

[18] *Boer-Sedano v. Gonzalez*, 418 F.3d 1082 (9th Cir. 2005).

Be careful, however, that these facts don't backfire into an adjudicator determining that if the applicant does not "flaunt" his homosexuality, he can avoid harm in his country. The applicant (and representative) should be prepared to argue that it is one thing to spend a couple of weeks avoiding the public eye and potential harm, but it is quite another thing to be forced into a life of celibacy to survive. In another recent 9th Circuit case, *Karouni v. Gonzales*, the Court addressed this issue, finding that it was unacceptable to saddle Karouni, a gay, HIV-positive man from Lebanon, with the "Hobson's choice of returning to Lebanon and either (1) facing persecution for engaging in future homosexual acts or (2) living a life of celibacy."[19] Thus the applicant should be able to explain why he would fear having to live in his country again, including his fear of persecution if he had a romantic partner or tried to find a romantic partner, even if he was able to escape harm on a brief visit.

Likewise, HIV-positive applicant may be able to demonstrate that they avoided harm on a brief trip to their home country by bringing enough medication to last for the trip. The applicant could argue that be avoiding seeking medical care (something that would be impossible to do if he returned to his country permanently) he was able to conceal his HIV-positive status.

Criminal Issues

The interplay between criminal law and immigration law is one of the most complicated areas in the complicated area of immigration law. As such, it is generally beyond the scope of this manual. However, anyone who is representing an asylum seeker must know a few basics about how criminal convictions can affect eligibility for asylum and withholding of removal. Applicants who meet the heightened standard for relief under the Convention against Torture cannot be removed to the country where they would face torture regardless of their criminal history in the United States, though they can face indefinite detention here if they are deemed to be a threat to the community.

The asylum applicant must answer questions on the I-589 about criminal convictions and arrests, so the representative must impress upon the applicant the importance of discussing past criminal activity openly. All asylum applicants are fingerprinted mul-

tiple times during the application process, and if the applicant was arrested in the United States, it is extremely unlikely that DHS would not know about the arrest.

Applicants for both asylum and withholding are considered statutorily ineligible if they have been convicted of a "particularly serious crime." For purposes of asylum applications, any conviction for an aggravated felony[20] will render the applicant statutorily ineligible.[21] For purposes of withholding of removal, if the applicant has been convicted of one or more aggravated felonies for which the aggregate term(s) of imprisonment are five years or more, he will be statutorily ineligible for having committed a "particularly serious crime."[22] Even if the applicant's aggregate prison term was under five years, the adjudicator can still make an individualized inquiry as to whether or not the conviction rose to the level of a "particularly serious crime" to determine whether or not the applicant is statutorily eligible.

Even if the applicant's conviction was for a crime that did not rise to the level of an aggravated felony, the conviction can lead to the denial of an asylum application. The leading case on determining whether or not a criminal conviction is a "particularly serious crime" is *Matter of Frentescu*.[23] Additionally, to qualify for asylum, an applicant must merit a favorable exercise of discretion. Thus, even if an asylum applicant's conviction is not found to be a "particularly serious crime" and does not render him statutorily ineligible for asylum, an adjudicator may still deny the application on discretionary grounds. If the applicant committed a crime, it will be crucial to the case for the applicant to fully explain the circumstances of the conviction and (if

---

[19] *Karouni v. Gonzales*, 399 F.3d 1163, 1173 (9th Cir. 2005).

[20] For a definition of aggravated felonies, see §101(a)(43). Aggravated felonies include but are not limited to: murder; rape; drug trafficking; certain firearms offenses; money laundering or crimes of fraud for amounts over $10,000; crimes of violence for which the term of imprisonment is at least one year; theft or burglary for which the term of imprisonment is at least one year; child pornography offenses; racketeering and gambling certain prostitution offenses; and certain alien smuggling offenses. INA §101(a)(43). It is important to understand that even crimes which are not considered felonies under state law can be considered aggravated felonies for immigration purposes.

[21] INA §208(b)(2)(B)(i).

[22] INA §241(b)(3)(B).

[23] 18 I&N Dec. 244 (BIA 1982).

possible) to express remorse and demonstrate rehabilitation.

If the applicant committed a "serious nonpolitical crime" in her own country or any other country outside the United States, she is also statutorily ineligible for asylum or withholding.[24] Again, it is important to question the applicant thoroughly about any criminal activity before she arrived in the United States. In many cases, the applicant may have faced arrest or conviction because of her sexual orientation. If the applicant is being prosecuted for engaging in a protected activity, such as having private, consensual sexual relations, such an arrest would not render the applicant ineligible for asylum and would actually be an important part of her claim.

Prior Government Employment

Another issue which a representative should explore with the applicant is whether or not he was employed by the government in his country of origin. In the classic paradigm of an asylum case, where an applicant was a political activist against a dictatorial government, it was reasonable to conclude that employment by that same government would undermine the claim. In most LGBT/H asylum cases, the primary problem that applicants have experienced from the government has been abuse by the police or military, or failure by the police to protect against harm from private individuals. Given this fact pattern, employment as a government clerk or the like should not render an applicant ineligible for asylum, but it may still be an issue which an adjudicator pursues. After all, if the applicant's claim is that the entire country is intolerant of sexual minorities, and sexual minorities face abuse and discrimination, why would the government hire a gay person? If the answer to this question is that the applicant kept his sexual orientation hidden from his employer, then an adjudicator might reasonably question how the police, individuals on the street, or other potential persecutors would be aware that the applicant was gay when those as close to him as his employer remained unaware. Again, the answers to these questions will be specific to the facts of the case, but it is an issue which the representative must prepare the applicant to discuss with the adjudicator.

Visa Waiver Program

If an applicant entered the United States without a visa under the Visa Waiver Program[25] (VWP), she is not entitled to an interview with an Asylum Officer. Instead, her application will be heard by an Immigration Judge in asylum only removal proceedings.[26] Most entrants under the VWP, a program which allows foreign nationals from low risk visa violating countries to enter the United States for up to 90 days without first applying for a tourist visa, come from Western Europe and would therefore not be seeking asylum in the United States The issue does arise at times, however, when the applicant has dual citizenship with a VWP country and enters the United States using the passport of the VWP country. Also, while Argentina has been removed from the VWP list, there are Argentine nationals who entered the United States under the VWP as it existed several years ago who may wish to seek asylum because of their sexual orientation.

Dual Nationality

If an asylum applicant has dual nationality, that is she is a citizen of more than one country and has the legal right to reside in and enjoy full citizenship rights in both countries, this can be a reason to deny the asylum application. The principle behind asylum applications in the United States is not that the application is a way to choose to live legally in the United States but rather that it is an application of last resort to avoid persecution. Thus, if the applicant has a safe alternative in another country, the United States can remove the applicant to that country. Therefore if an applicant is a dual citizen of Venezuela and Spain, it will be very difficult to win an asylum case in the United States since Spain now grants greater rights to gay and lesbian citizens than the United States does. On the other hand, if the applicant is a dual citizen of Venezuela and Colombia, the applicant may be able to prevail on an application based on persecution in Venezuela, but will also have to prove, through country conditions documentation, that Colombia is also an unsafe country for LGBT/H people.

---

[24] INA §§208(b)(2)(A)(iii) and 241(b)(3)(B)(iii).

[25] For more information on the VWP, see *http://travel.state.gov/visa/temp/without/without_1990.html*.

[26] 8 CFR §217.4(a)(1).

****

THE APPLICATION PROCESS AND WORKING WITH ASYLUM SEEKERS

There is no doubt that the work an attorney does on an asylum application can mean the difference between a successful application, or deportation of the client. Vital as the attorney's role is, however, it is ultimately the client's story which will win or lose the case. In many ways, your most important job is to build a relationship of trust with your client so that he feels free to tell his entire story to you and, ultimately, to the adjudicator.

A client-centered approach differs from traditional lawyering by stressing the central role of the client in her relationship with the attorney, and the client's active, intelligent participation in the preparation and representation of her claim. While not suspending a professional rapport, a client-centered approach encourages the attorney to consider the client's circumstances from the client's perspective and to respond to the client's legal issues (and non-legal concerns when appropriate) with human care and compassion. This approach helps both you and your client work together in a partnership more effectively, thereby ensuring client satisfaction, high quality legal services and even client empowerment. Client empowerment results not only when the client understands her relationship to the relevant law and its procedure, but when she assumes a central role and responsibility in preparing the case. Through this approach, the client becomes a critical agent in the process and in the potentially successful outcome of the case.

There are additional considerations that both you and your client should be aware of when beginning to explore an asylum claim. Asylum-seekers can be experts in their own culture, language and education, and particular concerns related to their experiences and fears of persecution in their homelands, and therefore, asylum-seekers can be valuable sources of information for the attorney. However, asylum-seekers' unfamiliarity with the United States's legal system compounded with experiences they may have had in their home countries, also can challenge the development of client-attorney rapport. Asylum-seekers often mistrust the law and lawyers, especially when their countries' legal systems are not independent and are riddled with corruption. Additionally, asylum-seekers may be unfamiliar with refugee law in the United States and its procedures. Given their intense fear of return and the possible psychological repercussions of their experiences, it is important that asylum-seekers and their attorneys understand how stress or trauma can affect asylum-seekers' memory, testimony and demeanor during the proceedings, which can adversely impact their claims.

Through a client-centered approach, you and your client can build mutual trust, respect and understanding and, in turn, facilitate the client's openness and cooperation with the legal representative. A client-centered approach can also assist LGBT/H immigrants who are unfamiliar with the grounds for asylum based and who may fear "coming out," especially to a foreigner (let alone a legal professional). This reluctance is understandable given societal homophobia, transphobia, HIV phobia and/or clients' perceptions that their sexual orientation, transgender identity or HIV-positive status is private fact not for a legal representative and immigration authorities to know. Indeed, many asylum-seekers may erroneously believe that being LGBT/H could lead to a denial of their claim.

You therefore need to take affirmative steps to create a safe space to ensure that the client trusts you, and feels comfortable to discuss her sexual orientation, gender identity and/or HIV status and related experiences in her homeland, and ensure her active participation in the case. There are certain methods that the attorney may use in interviewing, preparing and representing the client that provide for an effective demarcation of roles and a time-saving division of labor.

Recognizing and Respecting Client Individuality

An open, non-judgmental attitude that involves recognizing and respecting client individuality is the key to a successful relationship with LGBT/H clients through the proceedings because sexual minorities and people with HIV/AIDS are individuals as diverse as their heterosexual or HIV-negative counterparts. You should not make assumptions about your client's experiences based merely on stereotypical profiles such as appearance, dress and physical features; *e.g.*, gay men as effeminate and probably HIV-positive; lesbians as masculine. Questions laden with stereotypes or judgments not only might injure the client's self-esteem but might inhibit the client from trusting and working with you. Common stereotypes to avoid include: that a person's sexual orientation or HIV-status is the central defining feature of her identity; that homosexuals are promiscuous, lonely, self-hating people; that a homosexual no longer practices or believes in her religion since most religions reject homosexuality; that homosexuality is "caused" in men by overbearing, controlling mothers and absent fathers; that lesbians are trying to be men, or always dress in a masculine or androgynous manner; that an ostensibly "effeminate" character means that the male homosexual plays a woman's role in a romantic relationship; that in order to define herself as a transgender, a transgender individual must have had surgery or be contemplating medical interventions.

Regarding people with HIV/AIDS, there are many judgmental assumptions about how they contracted HIV (*e.g.*, that they contracted HIV through willful or reckless conduct); their celibacy (*e.g.*, that they should be celibate now); medical treatment regimens (*e.g.*, that they should be pursuing Western medical treatment and the protease inhibitor "cocktail"); social support needs (*e.g.*, that they should be involved in individual or group therapy). Additionally, there is the negative assumption that a client is somehow self-hating when he is not completely "out" about his sexual orientation, gender identity and/or HIV status to family, friends, employer, etc.

The diversity of how clients construct, understand and live their identities is the evidence that contradicts these stereotypes and judgmental perspectives. Through your conscious, close attention to your own communication and interaction with the client, you can evince an open, nonjudgmental attitude. This bolsters the client's trust, confidence and cooperation with you through all stages of case preparation and representation.

Setting the Stage for Client Trust, Confidence and Candor in the Initial Consultation

It is important in the initial consultation for you to set the stage for client trust, confidence and truthfulness by explaining the format of the consultation and the respective roles of the client and the attorney. You should stress that the consultation is confidential and no information will leave the office or be revealed to anyone including immigration authorities without the client's prior consent. You should also clearly caution the client that he must openly share all information in order for to represent him effectively. It is important that the client understands that you cannot assist him in putting forward anything that is untruthful in the application. Given your professional ethical responsibilities, you could face sanctions by immigration authorities, while the client could face deportation and the inability to obtain future immigration benefits in the United States if

any aspect of his claim is fabricated. *See* Section # 3.5 in full *Manual.*

Brief Explanation of Asylum Law, Its Extended Eligibility to Socially Marginalized Groups and Its Requirements

If you are taking a *pro bono* asylum case that has been screened through a non-profit organization, an attorney at the non-profit will already have had one or more consultations with the client and will have explained the asylum application process. Nevertheless, immigration law is complicated and an applicant may need to hear the same information several times before he fully understands it. You should therefore expect that the applicant may have basic questions about the asylum application process, and you should make every effort to understand the basics of the process before your first client meeting.

If the applicant asks you a question that you aren't sure how to answer, you should never "guess" the answer because if you are wrong the client will be misinformed and may find it hard to trust your answers in the future. Instead, explain that you are new to this area of law, that you don't know the answer right now, but you will research the question before your next meeting. The non-profit who referred the case to you may be able to answer your question easily or, in any event, should be able to steer you to the correct place to research the answer.

Overcoming Cultural Barriers

Even if you are an LGBT/H person yourself, remember that your client may come from a culture that is entirely different from ours. Your client may have limited literacy abilities or may have never been in a city before coming to the United States. Try to keep an open mind when meeting with your client and remember potential cultural barriers in your understanding of the client's experience. For example, your client may talk about his prior homosexual experiences in sexual terms without seeming to express strong emotional attachment to someone he "dated" for a long time. It is best to suspend judgment in your early meetings, and after you and your client have become more comfortable together, you can gently ask him questions about his feelings. In some cultures, the possibility of having a long-term, same sex relationship may be so taboo that it is difficult even for sexually active LGBT people to imagine the possibility of a true "partnership" with someone of the same sex.

Another area where your client may have difficulties is remembering dates. Clients frequently are not able to remember in what month an event happened or even what year. Since such gaps can create serious credibility problems, you may have to be creative about establishing a foundation for specific testimony. For example, occurrences may need to be tied to whether or not it was the rainy season or other events that the client can relate the occurrence to.

Another cultural barrier is the client's natural reticence about answering questions fully and honestly. Often, a client's only experiences in dealing with well-dressed interrogators sitting behind desks in business offices have been unpleasant and threatening. They may withhold information at first or may modify their story, or concoct one completely, based on their assumptions about what you want or expect to hear.

Dealing with Psychological and Medical Barriers

Finally, a more difficult and surprisingly prevalent problem may be the presence of psychological barriers, which make case preparation and presentation difficult. A substantial percentage of asylum seekers suffer from Post Traumatic Stress Disorder (PTSD) or other psychiatric disturbances, such as depression or anxiety as a result of what they have witnessed or suffered in their home country.

From the lawyer's point of view, these problems may manifest themselves in a variety of ways. For example:

- The client may simply block out an entire traumatic event, or significant parts of one. The client may have witnessed or endured something that would clearly make her eligible for asylum but may be unable to testify about it in any credible fashion, or even remember it at all;

- The client may be able to remember traumatic events and describe them to the attorney, but may find the experience so distasteful that he simply does not show up at the next appointment or resists efforts to go over the story again;

- The client may display inappropriate behavior or affect while talking about things that happened to her. The most obvious and best-known example is the tendency of many people to relate horrifying events in a flat, seemingly emotionless voice; or

- The client may be suffering from other problems, such as depression or substance abuse, related to or stemming from PTSD or other psychological condition.

It is often very helpful to the asylum seeker to seek professional mental health assistance during the asylum application process. Even if the applicant never thought that he needed counseling in the past, you can explain to him what an emotionally draining experience it is to apply for asylum. If the applicant has severe memory problems or her affect during testimony is flat, it can be crucial to the claim to have an affidavit from a mental health expert explaining the psychological causes of the client's difficulties in testifying.

If you are working with an HIV-positive client, it is also important to understand that her HIV illness may include neurological impairments. Many HIV medications also have severe side effects, and, again, it will be very important to have a letter from the applicant's doctor if, for example, side effects of the HIV medication include loss of memory or ability to focus.

****

WORKING WITH LGBT/H CLIENTS

If this is your first case working with a lesbian, gay, bisexual, transgender and/or HIV-positive client, you may be unsure of what questions are appropriate to ask and which are not. The basic rule, as with all aspects of asylum cases, is to be respectful, non-judgmental, and, for the most part, limit your questioning to issues that are relevant to the development of the case. If you are LGBT/H yourself, you may want to disclose this to your client if you believe this will make him feel more comfortable. On the other hand, you may feel comfortable not disclosing personal details of your life to your client. There is no right or wrong approach, but the more comfortable you feel with your client, the more comfortable you will make him feel to open up about the basis of his claim.

Remember that sexual orientation, gender identity and HIV status are all separate issues. An applicant may have claims based on more than one of these issues simultaneously, but you should treat each issue separately. Do not make assumptions. Just because and applicant is HIV-positive, doesn't mean that he's gay. Just because an applicant is transgender, doesn't mean that her romantic relationships are with men.

Working with Lesbian, Gay and Bisexual Clients

It is important to understand that every client is different. Some clients will be very open about their sexual orientation, while others may feel very reticent to talk about an aspect of their identity that they perceive to be a "problem." Follow your client's lead, make her feel comfortable, and understand that it will take time and several meetings before she begins to reveal information about her case.

It is often a good idea to use the same language that the client uses to describe herself. Thus if your client refers to herself as a "lesbian," you can ask her, "When did you first realize that you were a lesbian?" If she uses the word "gay," use the word "gay." If your client calls herself a lesbian, it is best not to refer to her as "homosexual" because this word often has negative clinical connotations.

Remember clients who come from different cultures which are not as open about sexual orientation issues may not use the same terms to talk about their sexuality. Thus, you may ask your client, "When did you come out as a lesbian?" and she may now know what this means. Use your common sense and don't leap to conclusions because your client expresses her sexuality in a way that's different from you (even if you are LGBT/H yourself).

If your client is bisexual, explore what this means to her. Sometimes clients from very homophobic cultures will self-identify as bisexual rather than homosexual even though they don't really have any interest in the opposite sex, because bisexuality seems less taboo than homosexuality. On the other hand, if your client has only had relationships with members of the opposite sex, and is not sure if she will ever act upon her attraction to women, it may be impossible to prove that she is a member of the particular social group of bisexuals. See Section # 11.2 of full *Manual* for more information about bisexual claims.

> ➤ *Practice pointer*: Avoid the terms "sexual preference" and "lifestyle." "Sexual preference" sounds like the client's orientation is not immutable, like she may "prefer" women to men, but that it is something which could, perhaps be changed. Likewise, "lifestyle" sounds like a choice. Deciding to live in a fancy apartment in Manhattan versus renting a more reasonable priced outer borough apartment is a "lifestyle" choice; falling in love with someone of the same sex is not.

Working with Transgender Clients

If you have never worked with a transgender client before, remember the basic rules, be respectful and non-judgmental. The term "transgender" can have different meanings to different people. For some, being transgender simply means not conforming to rigid gender norms, and thus some people, for example very butch lesbians, or effeminate gay men may identify as transgender although they do not believe that their bodies do not match their gender identity.

For others, the term "transgender" means that the individual feels that the anatomical sex with which she was born does not match her gender identity. Transgender people who feel this way often take medical steps to make their anatomy match their gender identity.

Transgender people often refer to the anatomical sex which was assigned to them at birth as their "birth sex." The process of taking medical steps, such as hormone therapy, electrolysis, and/or surgery, to give an outward appearance that matches gender identity, is often called "transitioning." When referring to a client's gender or sex after transitioning, the phrase "corrected gender" or "corrected sex" is often used.

When working on the asylum claim with your client, you'll want to ask her about any problems she had as a child. Maybe she was perceived as particularly effeminate and suffered mistreatment as a result. You'll want to find out when she first realized that she was transgender and when she began living as a female. You can also ask whether she's taken any medical steps to transition and whether she has any plans in the future to transition further.

Remember, most transgender people never have genital reassignment surgery. Surgery is expensive and rarely covered by health insurance. For transgender men (F→M) the surgical techniques are not as advanced as they are for transgender women. Gender identity is comprised of much more than just anatomy, and some transgender people never choose to undergo any medical steps to transition.

Also, remember that being "transgender" is not a third category of gender; transgender people, like non-transgender people, are either male or female. Don't refer to your client as a "transgender" person; refer to her as a transgender woman.

It is also important to understand that gender identity and sexual orientation are different aspects of a person's identity. Transgender individuals, like non-transgender individuals may consider themselves heterosexual, homosexual, or bisexual. Don't make assumptions about your client's sexual orientation based upon her gender identity. On the other hand, remember that even if your client identifies as heterosexual, he may be perceived as homosexual in his country and may fear persecution on this basis. For example, if an F→M transgender man had a relationship with a woman in his country in the past, people in his community may have considered the relationship lesbian, even if the applicant and his partner viewed the relationship as heterosexual.

Working with HIV-Positive Clients

If your client's case is based in whole or in part on his HIV-positive status, you'll need to get some information about his health. Remember HIV and AIDS are not synonymous; HIV is the virus which leads to AIDS. Your client can be HIV-positive without having full-blown AIDS. It is only after an individual has suffered an AIDS-defining symptom, or had his CD4 cell count fall below 200, that he is given an AIDS diagnosis. Once a person is diagnosed with AIDS, he will always be considered to have AIDS even if his CD4 cells rise and/or his symptoms go away. You should be prepared to educate the adjudicator about the difference between being HIV-positive and having AIDS. For information about AIDS-defining symptoms, see *http://www.health.state.ny.us/diseases/aids/facts/que stions/appendix.htm.*

You should find out when your client was diagnosed with HIV as this will generally be relevant to the case. Sometimes a recent HIV diagnosis can be used as an exception to the one year filing deadline. On the other hand, if your client was diagnosed with HIV in his own country, it will be important to elicit whatever information you can about problems he experienced as a result of his HIV.

How your client contracted HIV is generally not relevant to the case. Unless your client believes that he contracted HIV as a result of the persecution he suffered (for example being raped) there's probably no reason to question your client about how he may have been infected with HIV.

You should make sure that your client is currently receiving medical care, and if he is not, you should try to find an appropriate referral for him to do so. As the attorney in your client's asylum case, it is generally not appropriate for you to give your client medical advice, or to counsel him about HIV transmission. If you believe your client is not getting appropriate medical treatment or is engaging in unsafe behavior, you should refer him to an appropriate medical/social service professional. The nonprofit organization which referred you the case should be able to provide you with referrals.

You should talk with your client about any medical problems he's had as a result of his HIV, whether he's ever been hospitalized, and what medications, if any, he is currently taking. You should get a letter from his medical and/or social service professional detailing the course of his illness, what medications he is currently taking, and what would happen if the medications were no longer available.

Some states, such as New York, have very strict laws about revealing confidential HIV information. Before a medical or social service professional can speak with you about a case, your client will have to sign a specific HIV release form. Although attorneys are not strictly required to have a client sign such a release before disclosing his HIV information (for example to CIS), it is best practice to have your client sign the form. The form is available at *www.immigrationequality.org/uploadedfiles/HIV%2 0release-HIPAA%20compliant.pdf.*

****

PROCEDURE FOR RAISING CAT CLAIMS

Individuals seeking relief under the CAT must bring their claims before an Immigration Judge. The procedure for filing a claim under the CAT will differ depending on certain factors, including the status of an individual's case. If the applicant is filing for asylum, she should request relief under withholding of removal and CAT in her I-589 asylum application and should include the following information:

- The type of torture she is likely to experience if forced to return to her country;

- Any past instances of torture that she has experienced;

- Any past instances of torture experienced by close family members and associates; and

- Documentary support showing related human rights abuses by the government of her country, such as the U.S. State Department's Human Rights Country Reports, Amnesty International Reports, Human Rights Watch reports, and reports from other human rights monitoring groups.

If the applicant has already filed for asylum, but did not mention withholding of removal and CAT, she should supplement the application with the above information.

Remember that relief under the Convention Against Torture is not as beneficial as asylum or withholding. It is generally only applicants with serious criminal convictions who benefit from CAT. Thus, while most applicants file for asylum, withholding and CAT in the alternative, unless the applicant is statutorily ineligible for asylum or withholding, it is unlikely that the CAT claim will be a major part of her case.

LGBT/H CAT Case

While the regulations state that under CAT, torture is severe pain or suffering "inflicted by or at the instigation of or with the consent or acquiescence of a public official or other person acting in an official capacity,"[27] the Ninth Circuit has taken a broader view. In the case of *Reyes-Reyes v. Ashcroft*,[28] it finds that, "acquiescence" by the government included not addressing severe physical abuse inflicted by non-government actors. The case involved a transgender woman who was kidnapped, severely beaten, and raped by a group of men. In addition, she was also threatened by her abusers and feared retaliation if she reported the crimes. The court remanded the case for a reevaluation of both the CAT and the withholding of removal claims, finding that the Immigration Judge had misapplied the requirement for government involvement.

HIV and CAT

There have been at least two unpublished cases where attorneys have successfully demonstrated that an HIV-positive applicant who would be jailed upon being returned to his country of origin, meets the standard for CAT relief. In those cases, the Immigration Judges found that prison conditions in the applicants' countries of origin, Haiti and Cuba, were so atrocious, that a person living with HIV would likely die shortly after returning to his country. In the Haitian case, the applicant faced mandatory detention in Haiti because he would have been a criminal deportee. In the Cuban case, the applicant had deserted the Cuban army because he refused to serve in Angola, and therefore would have faced imprisonment.[29]

---

[27] 8 CFR §208.18(a)(1).

[28] *Reyes-Reyes v. Ashcroft*, 384 F.3d 782 (9th Cir. 2004).

[29] For more information on the Haitian case, see Victoria Neilson, "On the Positive Side: Using a Foreign National's HIV Positive Status in Support of an Application to Remain in the United States," *AIDS & Public Policy Journal*, Vol. 19, No. 1/2, *available at www.immigrationequality.org/uploadedfiles/AIDS%20&%20Public%20Policy%20Article.pdf*

"MAYBE YOU SHOULD," "YES, YOU MUST," "NO, YOU CAN'T": SHIFTING STANDARDS AND PRACTICES FOR ENSURING DOCUMENT RELIABILITY IN ASYLUM CASES

by Virgil Wiebe[*]

As the demand for corroborating evidence in asylum cases continues to rise, the question of the reliability of that evidence takes on ever-increasing importance.[1] This article addresses how the reliability of documentary evidence is evaluated at the various levels of the asylum process. With a growing concern by federal law enforcement about document fraud and its role in asylum claims,[2] advocates must be proactive in testing whether documents provided by clients are reliable pieces of evidence.

The article title summarizes the current state of affairs when it comes to how various adjudicators view the reliability of documentary evidence, such as whether or not an applicant for asylum must strictly adhere to the document authentication regimes found at 8 CFR §287.6. In the "Maybe You Should" camp, we find that the asylum offices of U.S. Citizenship and Immigration Services (USCIS) and some federal circuit courts of appeal do not require strict adherence to the rules of authentication found at 8 CFR §287.6, but look to other indicia of reliability. In the "Yes, You Must" camp, we have some immigration judges (IJ) and some other federal courts of appeal that support exclusion of evidence if authentication rules are not strictly followed. Finally, the Department of State (DOS) states that if you are an asylum applicant, then "No, You Can't" verify documents with investigations through consular offices overseas—at least not without the request coming directly from USCIS or the IJ.

The article unfolds as follows. General corroboration standards (pre– and post–REAL ID Act of 2005)[3] are briefly presented to provide an evidentiary context. Then, three basic methods of checking the reliability of documents are described: (1) Document authentication techniques; (2) Forensic document examination; and (3) Field investigation. Finally, current standards and practices of the Asylum Office, the immigration courts, and Board of Immigration Appeals (BIA), DOS, and varying federal courts of appeal are presented.

CORROBORATION: GET IT OR YOU'D BETTER HAVE A REALLY GOOD REASON WHY YOU DON'T HAVE IT

Congress codified standards for corroboration in asylum claims by passing the REAL ID Act in spring of 2005, with its requirement applying to applications filed after May 11, 2005. At INA[4]

[*] **Virgil Wiebe** is associate professor of law and director of clinical legal education at the University of St. Thomas School of Law (Minneapolis). He has been an active member for over a decade in the New York City, Maryland/D.C., and Minnesota/Dakotas AILA chapters, and was supervising attorney for New York City Interfaith Community Services, a nonprofit immigration services provider, from 1995 to 1999. Since 1999, Mr. Wiebe has been involved in law school teaching and clinical supervision at Georgetown, the University of Maryland, and the University of St. Thomas.

The author would like to thank Kathryn Weeks for her tireless research assistance. Others who contributed materials and ideas include Philip Schrag, Jaya Ramji-Nogales, Kathleen Lohmar Exel, Dick Zonneveld, Michael Armbrecht, Richard Breitman, Ben Casper, and Angela Bean.

[1] This article takes as its starting point an earlier work, V. Wiebe & S. Parker, "Asking for a Note from Your Torturer: Corroboration and Authentication Requirements in Asylum, Withholding, and Torture Convention Cases," 1 *Immigration & Nationality Law Handbook* 414 (AILA 2001–02) (updated and reprinted in *Immigration Briefings*, Oct. 2001). (hereinafter Wiebe & Parker, "Asking for a Note") The present article seeks to generally update but not exhaustively cover every issue raised there.

[2] *See, e.g.*, U.S. ICE Press Release, "11th Guilty Plea in Massive Asylum, Document Fraud Case" (Feb. 11, 2005), *www.ice.gov/graphics/news/newsreleases/articles/021105_1 1thguiltyplea.htm* (Detailing Operation Jakarta, a U.S. ICE-led fraud investigation into the illegal practices of Indonesian immigration brokers operating in Northern Virginia and Maryland, including the use of "counterfeit Indonesian documents, such as birth certificates, baptismal certificates and police reports.").

[3] Division B of the Emergency Supplemental Appropriations Act for Defense, the Global War on Terror, and Tsunami Relief Act, Pub. L. No. 109-13, 119 Stat. 231 (May 11, 2005).

[4] Immigration and Nationality Act of 1952, Pub. L. No. 82-414, 66 Stat. 163 (*codified as amended at* 8 USC §§1101 *et seq.*) (INA).

§208(b)(1)(B)(ii), Congress essentially enshrined in statute a rule arrived at by several circuits:

> In determining whether the applicant has met the applicant's burden, the trier of fact may weigh the credible testimony along with other evidence of record. Where the trier of fact determines that the applicant should provide evidence that corroborates otherwise credible testimony, such evidence must be provided unless the applicant does not have the evidence and cannot reasonably obtain the evidence.

The Second, Third, Sixth, and Eighth Circuits have applied a similar rule to pre–REAL ID cases.[5] The Eighth Circuit, in adopting that approach in 2004, restated the rule as follows:

> [A] particular decision denying asylum eligibility because of the absence of corroborating evidence cannot be sustained if the BIA failed to: (1) rule explicitly on the credibility of [the applicant's] testimony; (2) explain why it was reasonable in this case to expect additional corroboration; or (3) assess the sufficiency of [the applicant's] explanations for the absence of corroborating evidence.[6]

These circuits base their standard largely on the line of BIA cases culminating in *Matter of S–M–J–*.[7]

In contrast, the Ninth Circuit clearly has held "that an alien's testimony, if unrefuted and credible, direct and specific, is sufficient to establish the facts testified without the need for any corroboration."[8] It was perhaps to overrule the Ninth Circuit that Congress took the action that it did. In any event, the demands for corroboration have uniformly increased with the passage of the REAL ID Act.

The bottom line is that if you have, or can get, relevant and probative documents, you should submit them if you are largely confident in their reli-

ability.[9] If you cannot get such documents, you should explain why they are not available and the efforts undertaken to obtain them.

AN INTRODUCTION TO DOCUMENT RELIABILITY

Methods used to enhance the confidence of adjudicators in document reliability can be broadly classified as document authentication techniques—forensic document examination, field investigation, and document authentication. None, one, or a combination of these procedures might be used by any party (the asylum applicant or various elements of the government) in the asylum process. There is not a bright line necessarily between the three methods. For instance, what the author has broadly characterized below as "field investigation" often is used in conjunction with the other two methods described. Each of these techniques is described in some detail before moving on to how these techniques are viewed by adjudicators. The case law discussed at the end of the article provides instances of how the three methods often interact.

DOCUMENT AUTHENTICATION

Document authentication is not concerned with the underlying document so much as the signatures and seals on it. The process is based on reassuring the fact finder who receives the document that the person who issued the document was indeed authorized to do so by verifying their signatures. While much ink has been spilled in creating and maintaining these systems, they boil down to one or more persons looking at a signature, comparing it to one they have on file of a government official, and saying, "Yes, that's John Smith's signature." All of these processes require the services of foreign officials who are the representatives of a government being accused either of direct persecution or the inability to stop persecution. Turning over documents for verification to the very government being accused of persecutory acts raises serious questions about the confidentiality of asylum claims and the danger into which such a practice may put an applicant and his or her family. The confidentiality requirements of 8 CFR §§208.6, 1208.6 are discussed

---

[5] *See, e.g., Diallo v. INS*, 232 F.3d 279 (2d Cir. 2000); *Abdulai v. Ashcroft*, 239 F.3d 542 (3d Cir. 2003); *Dorosh v. Ashcroft*, 398 F.3d 379 (6th Cir. 2004); *El Sheik v. Ashcroft*, 388 F.3d 643, 647 (8th Cir. 2004), and their progeny.

[6] *El Sheik*, 388 F.3d at 647 (citations omitted).

[7] 21 I&N Dec. 722 (BIA 1997).

[8] *Ladha v. INS*, 215 F.3d 889, 899, 901 (9th Cir. 2000). *See also Dawoud v. Gonzales*, 424 F.3d 608, 612 (7th Cir. 2005) ("This court has often held that a credible asylum applicant . . . need not provide corroborating evidence in order to meet his burden of proof.").

[9] At least one circuit court believes that with the passage of the REAL ID Act, "the difference in approaches among the circuits with respect to the Board's corroboration rule will become a moot point." *Dawoud*, 424 F.3d at 613.

more fully below in the section on overseas field investigations, but they fully apply to all stages of the asylum process.

The regulations at 8 CFR §§287.6, 1287.6 lay out the two basic methods of document authentication: (1) the Chain Authentication Method; and (2) the Hague Convention Apostille Method.

Chain Authentication

The *Foreign Affairs Manual* (FAM) of the Department of State (DOS) provides a succinct definition of authentication:

> An authentication is a certification of the genuineness of the signature and seal or the position of a foreign official who has previously executed, issued, or certified a document so that a document executed or issued in one jurisdiction may be recognized in another jurisdiction. U.S. embassies and consulates maintain exemplars of the seals and signatures of host government officials against which documents presented for authentication can be compared. Originally, these were card files of signatures and seals. Many posts now maintain these exemplars electronically.[10]

The process is verifying the authenticity of the signature and/or stamps on a document, not necessarily the underlying authenticity of the document or contents in the document.[11]

8 CFR §287.6(b), 1287.6(b) provides guidance in immigration cases for the process in immigration cases of authenticating "official records" from countries not signatories to the Hague Convention.[12] The appendix to this article lists the countries that are parties to the treaty, and by process of elimination, you can determine if the country that is the source of the documents falls under the chain authentication regime.

The language of the regulation states that a U.S. consular officer "*must* certify the genuineness of the signature and the official position" of a foreign official in the chain of signatures.[13] While that language sounds mandatory, a closer look at DOS regulations governing the actions of consular officials charged with examining signatures and seals shows that there may be circumstances in which such certification is not required:

> If no specimen [of an official's seal and signature] is available to the consular officer, he should require that each signature and seal be authenticated by some higher official or officials of the foreign government until there appears on the document a seal and signature which he can compare with a specimen available to him. However, this procedure of having a document authenticated by a series of foreign officials should be followed *only where unusual circumstances,*

---

[10] 7 FAM 871(a) (Sept. 13, 2005), available at *http://foia.state.gov/masterdocs/07FAM/07M0870.PDF*. A more formal legal definition is found at 22 CFR §92.36:

> An authentication is a certification of the genuineness of the official character, i.e., signature and seal, or position of a foreign official. It is an act done with the intention of causing a document which has been executed or issued in one jurisdiction to be recognized in another jurisdiction. Documents which may require authentication include legal instruments notarized by foreign notaries or other officials, and copies of public records, such as birth, death, and marriage certificates, issued by foreign record keepers.

For more details on the actual steps consular officials are required to follow, see 22 CFR §§92.37, 92.39. *See also* 7 FAM 871 to 7 FAM 875.3 (2005), available at *http://foia.state.gov/masterdocs/07FAM/07M0870.PDF*.

[11] "Authentication conveys no judgment on the part of the authenticating officer of the validity or truth of the content of an authenticated document, but if circumstances warrant, you may include in the body of the certification a statement to the effect that 'For the content of the foregoing (or, annexed document) I assume no responsibility.'" 7 FAM 873(b) (2005), available at *http://foia.state.gov/masterdocs/07FAM/07M0870.PDF*.

[12] 8 CFR §§287.6(b), 1287.6(b) reads as follows:

> (1) In any proceeding under this chapter, an official record or entry therein, when admissible for any purpose, shall be evidenced by an official publication thereof, or by a copy attested by an officer so authorized. This attested copy in turn may but need not be certified by any authorized foreign officer both as to the genuineness of the signature of the attesting officer and as to his/her official position. The signature and official position of this certifying foreign officer may then likewise be certified by any other foreign officer so authorized, thereby creating a chain of certificates.

> (2) The attested copy, with the additional foreign certificates if any, must be certified by an officer in the Foreign Service of the United States, stationed in the foreign country where the record is kept. This officer must certify the genuineness of the signature and the official position either of (i) the attesting officer; or (ii) any foreign officer whose certification of genuineness of signature and official position relates directly to the attestation or is in a chain of certificates of genuineness of signature and official position relating to the attestation.

[13] 8 CFR §§287.6(b)(2), 1287.6(b)(2) (emphasis added).

or the laws or regulations of the foreign country require it.[14] (emphasis added)

It is important to determine what constitutes an "official record" before going to the expense and risk of trying to get a document authenticated. The CFR does not define "official records," but guidance can be taken from cases involving Fed. R. Civ. P. 44, a related federal regulation that uses the same language. An early case defined "official" as "work done by a person in the employment of the government in the course of the duties of his position," and "record" as "papers, demands, and writings made in the regular course of business."[15] Federal cases have found the following domestic and foreign records to be official records:

> federal government records, including internal memorandum; foreign vital statistics records, including government identification cards, birth certificates and birth records, military records, census records, government statements concern-

ing passport records, and records of proxy marriages; foreign government records, including Hong Kong immigration service records, secret decrees and ministerial orders, and ship manifests retained by immigration service; judicial records, including criminal records such as convictions, indictments, judgments, sentences, and commitments; U.S. Selective Service records; federal income tax returns, assessments, and Treasury Department computer printouts.[16]

How Do You Get a Document Authenticated Through a Consulate?

DOS maintains a helpful website on the general process of authentication.[17] Checking with the particular consulate in question is the most direct way to determine procedures and costs. A list of all U.S. embassies and consulates can be found on DOS's website.[18] Many, but not all, U.S. consulates have information about authenticating documents on their websites. A number of private fee-based services exist to assist persons in obtaining authentications through either method laid out in 8 CFR §§287.6, 1287.6.[19]

China: A Country-Specific Example of Chain Authentication Methods and Pitfalls for Asylum-seekers

Taking a somewhat unscientific approach to choosing countries to profile, the author looked at recent asylum data from the Executive Office for Immigration Review (EOIR). In fiscal year 2005, the top 10 countries in terms of asylum grants were China, Colombia, Haiti, Albania, Indonesia, India, Armenia, Ethiopia, Cameroon, and Guinea.[20] Of

---

[14] 22 CFR §92.37(a). Federal Rule of Civil Procedure 44 also contemplates that it may not be possible to authenticate a document according to the strict rules. A leading treatise on federal practice summarizes the challenges and alternatives as follows:

> [T]he rule makes provision for the unusual case in which it may be difficult or even impossible to satisfy the certification requirements of the amended rule. As the Advisory Committee Note points out, there may be no United States consul in a particular foreign country; the foreign official may not cooperate; or peculiarities may exist in the law or practice of a foreign country. To deal with these possibilities the final sentence provides the court with discretion to admit an attested copy of a record without a final certification, or an attested summary of a record with or without a final certification. The rule permits this to be done only if reasonable opportunity has been given to all parties to investigate the authenticity and accuracy of the documents, and if good cause for the exercise of that discretion has been shown. Presumably the requirement of good cause puts on the proponent of the evidence the burden of showing that he cannot prove the record by either of the first three methods made available by the rule. When such a showing has been made by the proponent of the evidence, it does not seem unfair to put the burden on the opposing party to show some question about the authenticity of the evidence.

Wright & Miller, *Federal Practice & Procedure* §2435 (2005) (citations omitted).

[15] *U.S. v. Aluminum Co. of America*, 1 F.R.D. 71, 75–76 (D.C.N.Y. 1939), *cited in* 9 C. Wright & A. Miller, *Federal Practice & Procedure*, §2432 (1995) and in Wiebe & Parker, "Asking for a Note," *supra* note 1, at 7.

[16] Wiebe & Parker, "Asking for a Note," *supra* note 1, at 7, summarizing cases cited in 9 C. Wright & A. Miller, *Federal Practice & Procedure* §2432, fn. 4 and §2435, fn. 1 (1995).

[17] DOS, Notarial and Authentication Services of U.S. Consular Officers Abroad, *http://travel.state.gov/law/info/judicial/judicial_2086.html* (visited Mar. 15, 2006).

[18] DOS, Websites of U.S. Embassies, Consulates, and Diplomatic Missions, *http://usembassy.state.gov* (updated Feb. 23, 2006).

[19] *See, e.g.*, T.I.S. Inc. International Visa Service, *www.visalady.com* (visited Mar. 15, 2006). This service is listed simply as an example, and does not constitute an endorsement by the author or AILA.

[20] China (3008, 25.63 percent), Colombia (1150, 9.8 percent), Haiti (653, 5.56 percent), Albania (608, 5.18 percent), Indonesia (374, 3.19 percent), India (310, 2.64 percent), Armenia (268, 2.28 percent), Ethiopia (264, 2.25 percent),

continued

those countries, four countries are signatories to the Hague Convention (Colombia, Albania, India, and Armenia), with the other six falling under the chain authentication method.[21] Many of the circuit court decisions discussed below address documents from several of these countries. Documents from China preoccupy judges at both the trial and appellate levels, and therefore, it makes sense to take a brief look at the authentication instructions at one of the four U.S. consulates in China.[22] Colombia serves as an example under the Hague Convention method below.

The U.S. consulate at Guangzhhou, China, lists procedures for authentication on its website.[23] The website includes the following information:

> As outlined in our Foreign Affairs Manual for documents originating in foreign jurisdiction, the consular certification is the end of the authentication chain for documents intended for use in the United States. To permit the authentication of the last signature by the consular officer: 1) a Chinese notary public office at city or county level must first notarize the documents; 2) The foreign affairs office (FAO) of the provincial govern-

ment, which has jurisdiction over the city where the documents were notarized, must then authenticate them; 3) The Consulate can then authenticate the signature of the foreign affairs official at the provincial level. The Consulate in Guangzhou can only authenticate the signatures of Chinese provincial-level foreign affairs officials within our consular district, which includes the provinces of Guangdong, Guangxi, Fujian and Hainan. The Consulate does not accept requests for authentication of documents by mail. Therefore, the applicant or his designated representative must appear at the Consulate in person, with the documents to be authenticated. . . . Please note that a consular authentication of a provincial FAO official's signature conveys no judgement [sic] on the part of the authentication officer as to the validity or truth of an authenticated document. Thus, the authentication of a provincial FAO officer's signature by a U.S. consular official is merely that: attestation to the veracity of the foreign official's signature. We make no claim to the veracity of the contents of the document.[24]

These instructions, on their face, raise many concerns for an asylum-seeker. Most notably, one (if not more) Chinese government officials must review and sign off on documents. In order to get those signatures, a person (possibly a family member or friend) would need to go to the various Chinese government offices. The documents must also be presented in person to the U.S. consulate. For persons in the United States, these hurdles raise obvious practical as well as safety concerns. Advocates have successfully argued that these barriers preclude the necessity of following authentication rules.[25]

Cameroon (263, 2.24 percent), Guinea (257, 2.19 percent), all others (4582, 39.04 percent). Executive Office of Immigration Review, Office of Planning, Analysis, and Technology, *FY 2005 Statistical Yearbook* (Feb. 2006) Fig. 15, at J1, *www.usdoj.gov/eoir/statspub/fy05syb.pdf.*

[21] See the appendix for a list of all countries party to the Hague Convention as of Jan. 16, 2006.

[22] The areas of Hong Kong and Macao, but not mainland China, are members of the Hague Convention. Status Table: Convention of 5 October 1961 Abolishing the Requirement of Legalisation for Foreign Public Documents (Jan. 16, 2006), *www.hcch.net/index_en.php?act= conventions.status &cid=41.* Websites relating to the authentication procedures of several other consulates with in countries with high numbers of asylum applicants are as follows: Embassy of the U.S., Port-au-Prince (Haiti), Public Services, *http://haiti.usembassy.gov/notaries.html* (visited Feb. 25, 2005); Embassy of the U.S., Addis Ababa (Ethiopia), U.S. Citizen Services, *http://addisababa.usembassy.gov/service. html* (visited Feb. 25, 2005); Consulate General of the U.S., Shanghai (China), Notaries, *www.usembassychina.org.cn/ shanghai/acs/linkfiles/NotarialServices.htm* (covering provinces of Shanghai, Anhui, Zhejiang and Jiangsu) (visited Feb. 25, 2006).

[23] Consulate General of the U.S., Guangzhhou (China), Information for Travelers: Information on Procedure for Authentication of Chinese Documents, *http://guangzhou .usconsulate.gov/authentication_of_chinese_documents.html* (visited Feb. 25, 2006).

[24] *Id.*

[25] *Liu v. Ashcroft,* 372 F.3d 529, 533 (3d Cir. 2004). "[A]sylum applicants can not always reasonably be expected to have an authenticated document from an alleged persecutor." *Id.* at 532. *Liu* is discussed in greater detail below. Professor Philip Schrag, of the Georgetown Center for Applied Legal Studies, has shared that their clinic

> had a Chinese religious persecution case a few years ago in which we needed to authenticate a record from a prison. We contacted the consulate in Beijing and asked what its procedure was for authenticating documents for immigration court. The consulate responded that to authenticate Chinese prison records, it would have to pass the records along for inspection and authentication by Chinese officials. Of course this procedure would have revealed that our client had applied for asylum in the US

continued

The Hague Convention Apostille Method

The 1961 Hague Convention Abolishing Requirement for Legalization of Foreign Documents[26] (Hague Convention) came into being to simplify the process of certifying documents by eliminating the final step of the chain authentication method. In the United States, the final step eliminated is the certification by a U.S. consular official.[27]

8 CFR §§287.6(c)(1), 1287.6(c)(1) lays out the requirements of the Hague Convention in the immigration context:

In any proceeding under this chapter, a public document or entry therein, when admissible for any purpose, may be evidenced by an official publication, or by a copy properly certified under the Convention. To be properly certified, the copy must be accompanied by a certificate in the form dictated by the Convention. This certificate must be signed by a foreign officer so authorized by the signatory country, and it must certify (i) the authenticity of the signature of the person signing the document; (ii) the capacity in which that person acted, and (iii) where appropriate, the identity of the seal or stamp which the document bears.

To decide if you must have a document certified with a Hague convention apostille (the final certification from the country of origin), you must first determine if the document qualifies as a foreign public document. According to 8 CFR §§287.6(c), 1287.6(c), the following are deemed to be public documents: "(i) Documents emanating from an authority or an official connected with the courts of tribunals of the state, including those emanating from a public prosecutor, a clerk of a court or a

process server; (ii) Administrative documents; [and] (iii) Notarial acts."[28]

How Do You Get a Document Authenticated by the Apostille Method?

The Hague Conference on Private International Law maintains a useful website on the Hague Convention, with multiple links to useful information. (Current parties to the treaty are listed in the appendix to this article.) One link on the website lists up-to-date contact information for competent authorities in each country empowered to issues apostilles.[29]

DOS also maintains a useful website that details what the Hague Convention is, how it operates, which states (*i.e.*, countries) are party to it, and whether the United States recognizes that a particular state party to the treaty is considered able to comply with the treaty. The website also lists the competent authorities in each country.[30]

Colombia: Example of the Apostille Method of Certifying Documents

Colombia is a major source of asylum claims in the United States and thus provides a good example to profile. The U.S. embassy in Colombia notifies visitors to its website that

Colombian documents that are going to be used in the United States require an apostille issued by competent authorities in Colombia. In Colombia, that authority is held by the Ministry of Foreign Relations . . . Documents legalized with the apos-

---

and could have risked retaliation against his relatives who were still in China. The immigration judge understood the risk and did not require authentication through the methods specified in the regulations.

E-mail from Philip Schrag to Virgil Wiebe concerning authenticating documents from China (Mar. 15, 2006).

[26] The Hague Convention Abolishing the Requirement of Legalization for Foreign Public Documents, Oct 5, 1961, 33 UST 883, can be found at *www.hcch.net*. The full text of the treaty can be found at *www.hcch.net/index_en. php?act=conventions.text&cid=41* (visited Mar. 15, 2006). The treaty is referred to in various circles as the Hague Convention, the Hague Apostille Convention, or Hague Legalization Convention.

[27] 8 CFR §§287.6(c)(2), 1287.6(c)(2).

[28] Foreign "public documents" therefore encompass a larger range of documents than "official records," as notarial acts are included as well. In the asylum context, if this approach is fully applied, notarized affidavits prepared by persons in the country of claimed persecution would be subjected to review by government officials. Ironically, this may be a situation where an attempt at chain authentication through the consulate of the notary's signature might be worth a try, assuming the consulate maintains a listing of such notaries and their signatures.

[29] Authorities: *www.hcch.net/idex_en.php?act= conventions. authorities&cid=41* (visited Mar. 15, 2006).

[30] U.S. Dep't of State, Hague Convention on Legalization of Foreign Public Documents, *www.travel.state.gov/law /legal/ treaty/treaty_783.html* (visited Mar. 15, 2006). *See also* U.S. Dep't of State, "What is an "Apostille," *www.travel.state.gov/law/info/judicial/judicial_2545.html* (visited Mar. 16, 2006).

tille of the Ministry do not need to be authenticated by a US consular official.[31]

Other routes to finding contact information include checking the Hague Convention Authorities website, which will lead you to the Office of Coordination of Legalizations and Apostille in the Colombian Ministry of Foreign Relations.[32] The Foreign Ministry of Colombia also maintains a detailed website dedicated to document authentication.[33] At that site, for instance, one is instructed that to get an apostille for a military-court judgment, the document must first have a signature recognized by the Tribunal Superior Militar at the Ministry of Defense before it is brought to the Foreign Relations Ministry.[34] It should go without saying that an asylum seeker, or a family or friend, might be hesitant about legalizing a document.

FORENSIC DOCUMENT EXAMINATION

Document examination involves taking a close scientific look at the document in question.[35] This is usually done by a professionally trained and licensed forensic document examiner who looks at how the document in question was made and/or altered using a variety of techniques (*i.e.*, review under microscopes and various light frequencies, paper and ink analysis, and handwriting analysis) and also, if possible, compares the document to a reference template that is known to be a true version. Examiners from the Department of Homeland Security (DHS) Forensic Document Laboratory (FDL) regularly examine documents for asylum cases and issue reports.[36] It is also possible for applicants to engage the services of private document examiners to do initial evaluations or to discredit adverse findings by the FDL. Potential experts might be contacted through various professional organizations.[37]

DOCUMENT VERIFICATION THROUGH FIELD INVESTIGATION

Field investigation involves inquiries into how the document was made by contacting or investigating the person and/or institution that presumably created the document. This again might be done by any party to the proceedings. U.S. consular officials at times undertake such investigations. U.S. Immigration and Customs Enforcement (ICE) has over 50 offices internationally, from which immigration fraud investigations may be conducted.[38] While bound by rules of confidentiality, this process involves risks to the asylum-seeker and their associates and families. ICE counsel may ask for an "Overseas Investigation" of a claim, and such investigation may involve delving into claims about documentation. The FDL may "assist field officers via the Photophone and Image Storage and Retrieval

---

[31] Autenticaciones, US Embassy, Bogota, Colombia, *http://bogota.usembassy.gov/wwwsc063.shtml* (visited Mar. 16, 2006) (Translation by author).

[32] *www.hcch.net/index_en.php?act=authorities.details &aid =363* (visited Mar. 16, 2006).

[33] Tramite: Legalización de documentos que van a surtir efecto en el exterior o vienen a surtir efecto en Colombia, Ministerio de Relaciones Exteriores de la Republica de Colombia, *http://portal.minrelext.gov.co/portal/webdrive r.exe? MIval=po_inicio.html* (updated Feb. 15, 2006).

[34] *Id.*

[35] "The examination of questioned documents consists of the analysis and comparison of questioned handwriting, hand printing, typewriting, commercial printing, photocopies, papers, inks, and other documentary evidence with known material in order to establish the authenticity of the contested material as well as the detection of alterations." American Board of Forensic Document Examiners, Frequently Asked Questions, *www.abfde.org/faqs.htm* (visited Mar. 17, 2006).

[36] The ICE Forensic Document Laboratory includes among its work the following:

> Forensic examination of disputed handwriting and hand printing; Forensic examination of any documents, foreign or domestic; Attempts to link multiple documents in one case through handwriting, stamp, and seal impressions, copy machines, or typewriters; Processing evidence for latent fingerprints in an attempt to identify the person(s) who handled documents and ink-to-ink fingerprint comparisons; Training and technical assistance in the detection of fraudulent documents; Document intelligence *Alerts* and other operational intelligence products; Assisting field officers via the Photophone and Image Storage and Retrieval System; Managing the FDL Library; [and] On-going liaison with other federal, state, local, and foreign government entities." ICE also claims that "most often the most persuasive 'evidence' guiding the judge or magistrate is the FDL Report of Findings.

ICE Fact Sheet, Forensic Documents Laboratory (Sept. 26, 2005), *www.ice.gov/graphics/news/factsheets/fdl_fs_080304.htm.*

[37] *See, e.g.*, Midwest Association of Forensic Scientists, *http://mafs.net/index.html* (visited Mar. 16, 2006); American Board of Forensic Document Examiners, *http://www.abfde.org* (visited Mar. 16, 2006); American Society of Questioned Document Examiners, *www. asqde.org* (visited Mar. 16, 2006).

[38] ICE Fact Sheet, ICE Office of Investigations (July 7, 2004) *www.ice.gov/graphics/news/factsheets/investigation_FS.htm.*

System,"[39] an example of how different methods of document investigatory methods complement one another.

If field investigations breach confidentiality provisions of the law, or are conducted in an unprofessional or slipshod manner, advocates may consider filing motions to preclude such reports from being introduced.[40]

The Government Must Observe Confidentiality Provisions When Conducting Overseas Investigations

8 CFR §§208.6, 1208.6 generally prohibits the disclosure of asylum-related information to third parties without the written consent of the applicant. While field investigations of asylum claims by U.S. government authorities are not completely prohibited by the regulation, memos issued by legacy Immigration and Naturalization Service (INS) and the current USCIS Asylum Division explicitly lay out the dangers involved in such investigations, including cautions to halt such investigations if confidentiality might be breached. According to a memo issued in 2001 by then INS General Counsel Bo Cooper:

(1) If an investigation cannot be accomplished without compromising the confidentiality of the application, the investigation should be abandoned and the investigator should inform the requestor of the investigation of this fact.

(2) Generally, confidentiality of an asylum application is breached when information contained therein or pertaining thereto is disclosed to a third party, and the disclosure is of a nature that allows the third party to link the identity of the applicant to: (1) the fact that the applicant has applied for asylum; (2) specific facts or allegations pertaining to the individual asylum claim contained in an asylum application; or (3) facts or allegations that are sufficient to give rise to a reasonable inference that the applicant has ap-

plied for asylum. If one or the other part of this link is missing, then no breach has occurred.[41]

The dangers to the asylum applicant were reiterated in a memo issued in 2005 by the Asylum Division of USCIS Office of Refugee, Asylum, and International Operations:

Public disclosure of asylum-related information may subject the claimant to retaliatory measures by government authorities or non-state actors in the event that the claimant is repatriated, or endanger the security of the claimant's family members who may still be residing in the country of origin. Moreover, public disclosure might, albeit in rare circumstances, give rise to a plausible protection claim where one would not otherwise exist by bringing an otherwise ineligible claimant to the attention of the government authority or non-state actor against which the claimant has made allegations of mistreatment.[42]

The Government Must Observe Competent Investigatory Practices in Conducting Overseas Investigations

Reports from overseas investigations should be subjected to careful scrutiny by advocates. In *Ezeagwuna v. INS*, the court harshly criticized a letter from DOS's Office of Country Reports and Asylum Affairs that summarily concluded that five documents submitted by a Cameroonian applicant were fraudulent.[43] The letter was based almost entirely on another letter supplied by a U.S. vice-consul for the U.S. Embassy in Cameroon. The court found that the IJ and the BIA based their decisions denying asylum largely on the basis of the DOS letter. The court raised four concerns about the letter. First, the letter did not satisfy its standards of "reliability and fairness" because of the manner in which it was procured and the long delay in providing it to opposing

---

[39] ICE Fact Sheet, Forensic Documents Laboratory, *supra* note 36.

[40] The author's thanks to Michael Armbrecht for sharing such a sample motion. *See In the Matter of A–D–*, Bloomington, MN, Respondent's Memorandum Opposing Consular Reports (Sept. 17, 2002) (on file with author).

[41] Memorandum for Jeffrey Weiss, Director, Office of International Affairs, from Bo Cooper, INS General Counsel (June 21, 2001), *reprinted in* 8 *Bender's Immigr. Bull.* 976 (June 1, 2003), at Appendix F.

[42] USCIS Asylum Division, Fact Sheet: Federal Regulations Protecting the Confidentiality of Asylum Applicants (June 3, 2005), *published on* AILA InfoNet at Doc. No. 05062440 (*posted* June 24, 2005). *See also* Joseph E. Langlois, Director, Asylum Division, Office of Refugee, Asylum and International Operations, "Fact Sheet on Confidentiality" (June 15, 2005), *published on* AILA InfoNet at Doc. No. 05062440 (*posted* June 24, 2005).

[43] *Ezeagwuna v. INS*, 325 F.3d 396 (3d Cir. 2003).

counsel. Second, the court found it to be "multiple hearsay of the most troubling kind," with the writer of the letter being "three steps away from the actual declarant." Third, the court criticized INS for trying to simply trade on the prestige of the State Department's letterhead. Finally, the court concluded that it had "absolutely no information about what the 'investigation' consisted of, or how the investigation was conducted."[44]

A failure to conduct investigations properly and thoroughly may form a basis for suppressing such evidence. The General Counsel of legacy INS laid out minimal standards for such reports, and advocates should use such standards to test overseas investigations reports:

> The content of the investigative report is critical if it is to effectively convey the information to the adjudicating official, be it an asylum officer or an immigration judge. . . . In the case of a fraudulent document, a comprehensive and, therefore, effective report will lead the adjudicator down the path taken by the investigator, and hopefully help the adjudicator reach the same conclusion. Such a report must contain, at a minimum:
>
> (i) the name and title of the investigator;
>
> (ii) a statement that the investigator is fluent in the relevant language(s) or that he or she used a translator who is fluent in the relevant language(s);
>
> (iii) any other statements of the competency of the investigator and the translator deemed appropriate under the circumstances (such as education, years of experience in the field, familiarity with the geographic terrain, etc.);
>
> (iv) the specific objective of the investigation;
>
> (v) the location(s) of any conversations or other searches conducted;
>
> (vi) the name(s) and title (s) of the people spoken to in the course of the investigation;
>
> (vii) the method used to verify the information;
>
> (viii) the circumstances, content and results of each relevant conversation or searches; and

> (ix) a statement that the Service investigator is aware of the confidentiality provision found in 8 C.F.R. §208.6.[45]

Advocates for Asylum-seekers May Submit Information from Their Own "Field Investigations"

Advocates should not overlook the opportunity to conduct their own "field investigations" in order to shore up the reliability of documents. You may be able to persuade a sympathetic local or international nongovernmental human rights organization to check into local practices on the production of documents such as identification cards, hospital records, and police and judicial records and submit the information to you by fax, e-mail, or affidavit. Experts on country conditions may well be informed about document production practices in the home country. In some cases, advocates have actually traveled to their client's home country to conduct first-hand investigation.

---

[44] *Id.* at 406–08.

[45] Memorandum for Jeffrey Weiss, Director, Office of International Affairs, from Bo Cooper, INS General Counsel (June 21, 2001), *reprinted in* 8 *Bender's Immigr. Bull.* 976 (June 1, 2003) at Appendix F.

> In proceedings before an immigration judge, for example, the quality of the investigative report can determine the report's admissibility as evidence and, if admitted, the weight the immigration judge will accord to it. A report that is simply a short statement that an investigator has determined an application to be fraudulent is of little benefit. Instead, the reports should lay a proper foundation for is conclusion by reciting those factual steps taken by the investigator that caused the investigator to reach his or her conclusion. In addition, the conclusion of the investigator should be stated in neutral and unbiased language.

Id. Advocates may also wish to consult Department of State rules on confidentiality surrounding Sensitive but Unclassified (SBU) information. 12 FAM 540, Sensitive But Unclassified Information (SBU) (2005), *http://foia.state.gov/masterdocs/12fam/12m0540.pdf.* "Sensitive but unclassified (SBU) information is information that is not classified for national security reasons, but that warrants/requires administrative control and protection from public or other unauthorized disclosure for other reasons" and includes "[d]epartment records pertaining to the issuance or refusal of visas, other permits to enter the United States, and requests for asylum" 12 FAM 541(a) and (b)(3)(2005), *http://foia.state.gov/master docs/12fam/12m0540.pdf.* "U.S. citizen direct-hire supervisory employees are ultimately responsible for access, dissemination, and release of SBU material. All employees will limit access to protect SBU information from unauthorized or unintended disclosure." 12 FAM 543(a)(2005), *http://foia. state.gov/masterdocs/12fam/ 12m0540.pdf.*

In cases where an applicant had to obtain improper travel documents in order to escape his or her country, you also may be faced with the situation of trying to prove that a document is either fraudulent or a facially reliable and legitimate document that was fraudulently obtained. Ironically, information about the illegal document industry in the country of origin, especially if such information comes from U.S. government reports, can be helpful in supporting the claim.

USCIS ASYLUM OFFICE GUIDANCE: "MAYBE YOU SHOULD GET DOCUMENTS VERIFIED IN SOME WAY, BUT WE UNDERSTAND IF YOU'VE GOT A GOOD EXPLANATION"

How Are Questionable Documents Treated by the Asylum Offices?

Persons who are not in removal proceedings nor considered arriving aliens may present their asylum claims "affirmatively" to an asylum officer from one of the eight asylum offices around the country. Asylum office procedures indicate that formal document verification is not normally an issue at the affirmative asylum stage unless the officer has reason to believe that a document that goes to the heart of the claim is fraudulent. When it does become an issue, the preferred method appears to be sending the document in question to the ICE Forensic Document Laboratory.

If an issue does arise, the preferred method by the asylum offices appears to be to submit the questioned documents to actual physical examination rather than request that the document be authenticated by the 8 CFR §287.6 procedures.

According to the *Asylum Office Procedures Manual*, an "applicant may present documents in support of his/her case during the interview," with no restriction on the amount or nature of documents.[46] Less weight is given to fax and photocopies of documents. "When the applicant presents an original document, the [Asylum Officer] copies the document (if copies are not submitted by the applicant), and writes on it, 'original seen and re-

turned.'"[47] The Asylum Office Basic Training Course materials state that:

> When applicants do provide documents, they may not be able to establish the authenticity of the documents. If the asylum officer is satisfied that the documents are genuine, the evidentiary value should not be discounted merely because the documents are not certified.[48]

If an asylum officer (AO) thinks that a document is fraudulent or was fraudulently obtained, the officer may request permission from the applicant to retain the document. If an applicant admits that a document is fraudulent, the officer is to take a sworn statement from the applicant.[49] At the same time, asylum officers are cautioned to "bear in mind that documents created in some developing countries may not look as polished as documents created in more developed countries."[50]

With the permission of the applicant, "an AO may retain a document of questionable authenticity for further analysis, such as forensic examination."[51] A refusal to turn over a document may be taken into

---

[46] Office of International Affairs, Asylum Division, *Affirmative Asylum Procedures Manual* (Feb 2003), at 19, *http://uscis.gov/graphics/lawsregs/handbook/AffrmAsyMan FNL.pdf* (hereinafter Aff. Asylum Proc. Man.). Certified English translations must accompany foreign language documents. *See* 8 CFR §103.2(b)(3) for translation requirements.

[47] Aff. Asylum Proc. Man., *supra* note 46, at 19.

[48] Immigration Officer Academy, Asylum Officer Basic Training Course, Asylum Eligibility Part IV: Burden of Proof, Standards of Proof, and Evidence (Nov. 30, 2001) at 12, *www.asylumlaw.org/docs/united_states/asylum _officer _training_eligibility4_112001.pdf* (hereinafter AOBTC Burden of Proof). Since 1990, legacy INS (and its successor USCIS) has dispensed with some of the authentication requirements for copies of public records required by 8 CFR §287.6, notably the need for U.S. consular chain authentication or the Hague Apostille. *See USCIS Adjudicators' Field Manual*, Chap 11.1(d) Submission of Supporting Documents and Consideration of Evidence: Evidentiary Standards (Dec. 2005), at *http://uscis.gov*. The *Field Manual* asserts that "the strict rules of evidence used in judicial proceedings do not apply in administrative proceedings," and therefore "a wide range of oral or documentary evidence may be used in a visa petition proceeding or other immigration benefit application proceeding." *Id.* Nonetheless, USCIS still maintains that "only the custodian of the record needs to certify a foreign public record in order for the foreign public record to be admissible." *Id.* This of course does not recognize that in the asylum context such an approach may still amount to asking one's persecutor for a certification of a document. The Asylum Officer Corps apparently has recognized this danger in its training materials.

[49] Aff. Asylum Proc. Man., *supra* note 46, at 19.

[50] AOBTC Burden of Proof, *supra* note 48, at 12.

[51] Aff. Asylum Proc. Man., *supra* note 46, at 19. An asylum office director may place a case on "hold" while a document is being analyzed and stop the 180-day EAD clock. *Id.* at 20.

account in what weight to give the document.[52] Documents submitted for analysis may be sent to the FDL or another fraudulent document or intelligence unit. It should be done "only if the AO/SAO believe that the analysis of such a document may affect the outcome of the decision."[53] If the FDL finds the document authentic or no determination is made, the document is to be returned. If the document is found to be fraudulent, the applicant is notified that the document will be retained.[54]

It should go without saying that submission of fraudulent documents by an applicant may affect eligibility for asylum[55] and that such submission "creates doubts regarding the applicant's overall credibility."[56] Asylum officers are nonetheless cautioned:

> The use of fraudulent documents is not always inconsistent with a credible claim, and the context in which the documents are used is critical to the credibility determination. Genuine refugees may need to use fraudulent identity or travel documents to escape persecution. There may also be cases in which an applicant with a genuine claim submits fraudulent documents because he or she is under the misimpression that documentation is required to receive asylum.

Therefore, an asylum officer may not automatically conclude that a claim is untrue because an applicant submits fraudulent documents. Rather, the asylum officer must inquire into the reason the fraudulent documents were submitted and evaluate the commission of fraud in light of the entire circumstances presented in the case.[57]

Such an approach arguably retains integrity even under the REAL ID Act, as credibility determinations may be made "[c]onsidering the totality of the circumstances and all relevant factors."[58]

Asylum Office Practice Pointers

The asylum offices do not formally require either compliance with 8 CFR §§287.6, 1287.6 or other forms of documents verification. One might therefore wrongly conclude that there is no need to carefully consider whether documents presented by a client should be submitted. Unless you have valid reasons for not authenticating documents under 8 CFR §§287.6, 1287.6 (such as exposing your client or her family to further persecution by the home country government), you should consider complying with the procedures in order to bolster confidence in the documents in question.

Advocates must also question clients about how they came into possession of certain documents. The pressure of increased corroboration requirements may lead clients to feel they have to come up with

---

[52] Aff. Asylum Proc. Man., *supra* note 46, at 20. According to the manual, requiring the document at this stage is not permitted. If the case is referred to immigration court, counsel for the government may request the immigration judge to order the document be turned over for analysis. *Id*. This appears to be somewhat at odds with the general application submission instructions for all affirmative filings for any type of immigration relief found at 8 CFR §103.2. 8 CFR §103.2(b)(5) reads as follows:

> Request for an original document. Where a copy of a document is submitted with an application or petition, the Service may at any time require that the original document be submitted for review. If the requested original, other than one issued by the Service, is not submitted within 12 weeks, the petition or application shall be denied or revoked. There shall be no appeal from a denial or revocation based on the failure to submit an original document upon the request of the Service to substantiate a previously submitted copy. Further, an applicant or petitioner may not move to reopen or reconsider the proceeding based on the subsequent availability of the document. An original document submitted pursuant to a Service request shall be returned to the petitioner or applicant when no longer required.

[53] Aff. Asylum Proc. Man., *supra* note 46, at 20. "Due to time constraints and FDL's policy of prioritizing the analysis of documents pertaining to detained and criminal aliens over cases submitted by an asylum office, submission of documents to the FDL should be done only if the AO or SAO believes that the analysis may impact on the outcome of the decision." *Id*. at 41.

[54] *Id*. at 20.

[55] *Id*. (citing to Joseph E. Langlois, INS Asylum Division. *Matter of O–D–*, 21 I&N Dec. 1079 (BIA 1998), Memorandum to Asylum Directors, Supervisory Asylum Officers and Asylum Officers (Washington, D.C., 29 Apr. 1998) and Joseph E. Langlois, INS Asylum Division. Discovery of fraudulent documents after the asylum interview, Memorandum to Asylum Directors, Supervisory Asylum Officers and Asylum Officers (Washington, D.C., 27 May 1998) (memos on file with author)).

[56] Immigration Officer Academy, Asylum Officer Basic Training Course, Credibility (Mar. 1999), at 20, www.asylumlaw.org/docs/united_states/asylum_officer_train ing_credibility_031999.pdf.

[57] *Id.*

[58] INA §208(b)(1)(B)(iii) (2005). *C.f.*, K. Jastram, "Considering the Circumstances: The Credibility of Prior Statements under the REAL ID Act," 10–17 *Bender's Immigr. Bull.* 2 (Sept. 2005).

some sort of documentation to bolster an otherwise solid claim. Advocates should ask how, when, where, why, and by whom the document in question was acquired. Advocates should also warn applicants that documents may very well be subjected to physical analysis, to authentication procedures, and to on-the-ground investigation by U.S. government in their home country.

IMMIGRATION COURTS AND THE BIA

On questions of documentation, the *Immigration Judge Benchbook* simply restates the requirements of 8 CFR §§287.6, 1287.6.[59] Some IJs take the position that official records or foreign public documents that are not authenticated accordingly must be excluded. Others take a broader view of authentication, acknowledging that officials from a country accused of persecuting its citizens might be inclined to claim that an asylum applicant's documents are fraudulent.[60]

The BIA has not clearly addressed the issue of document authentication in asylum cases in a precedential decision.[61] In an unpublished decision in 2003 in a case in Philadelphia, the BIA found the IJ had "improperly excluded" a number of documents from Albania due to a lack of authentication pursuant to 8 CFR §§287.6(b)(2), 1287.6(b)(2). Citing circuit case law, the BIA stated that the "procedure specified in 8 CFR §1287.6 is not a prerequisite to admissibility; it is merely one recognized method for authenticating documents." The case was remanded for consideration of the documents "after determining their proper weight, in conjunction with the re-

spondent's testimony and other documentary evidence."[62]

If you are located in a federal circuit that has not yet clearly ruled on whether or not document authentication regimes under 8 CFR §§287.6, 1287.6 must be followed (see below), you might consider citing the above case as support. While discouraged from doing so, advocates are not prohibited from citing nonprecedential BIA decisions in appeals to the BIA.[63]

DEPARTMENT OF STATE: "WE CAN'T HELP YOU WITH DOCUMENT *VERIFICATION*, BUT MAYBE WE CAN WITH DOCUMENT *AUTHENTICATION*"

DOS decided in 2003 that it would not respond to requests from private attorneys to verify documents in asylum cases through consular officers. In a 2005 letter to a private attorney, the Deputy Director of the Office of Country Conditions and Asylum Affairs wrote that

> [i]t has been standard practice for the Office of Country Reports and Asylum Affairs to forward document verification requests to overseas posts after an immigration judge or the Department of Homeland Security attorney has asked for the verification of certain key documents. This practice was recently reaffirmed in a State Department cable delivered to all diplomatic posts in December 2003. We do not conduct document verification requests made by individual attorneys due to our limited resources, both here and overseas, to handle such requests.[64]

In essence, the State Department will not conduct field investigations for private parties.[65]

---

[59] *Immigration Judge Benchbook*, at 11–14 (Oct. 2001), www.usdoj.gov/eoir/statspub/benchbook.pdf.

[60] For a discussion of unpublished IJ decisions, see Wiebe & Parker, "Asking for a Note," *supra* note 1, at 10–11. *See also Decision on a Motion in the Matter of [name not provided]*, Dallas, TX, Immig. Judge Deitrich Sims, Aug. 19, 2005, discussed in detail below.

[61] For a discussion of BIA decisions in a non-asylum context, see Wiebe & Parker, "Asking for a Note," *supra* note 1, at 11. In a one-child policy Chinese asylum case in 1993, the BIA noted that a village level committee notice fining the applicant for violating the policy had not been certified pursuant to 8 CFR §§287.6, 1287.6, but apparently did not exclude the notice nor comment on whether the rule was mandatory or permissive. *Matter of G–*, 20 I&N Dec. 764, 774, fn. 13 (BIA 1993).

[62] *In Re [name not provided]*, BIA Decision, June 2, 2003 (case on file with author, compliments of Joseph Hohenstein, counsel for respondent).

[63] *Board of Immigration Appeals Practice Manual*, §4.6(d)(ii) at 56, www.usdoj.gov/eoir/vll/qapracmanual/pracmanual/chap4.pdf (last revised June 15, 2004).

[64] Letter from LeRoy Potts, Deputy Director, Office of Country Conditions and Asylum Affairs, to Paul Zoltan, dated Sept. 27, 2005, *reprinted in* 10-21 *Bender's Immigr. Bull.* 20, at 1700–01 (Nov. 1, 2005) (hereinafter Potts Letter).

[65] In light of harsh criticism of some consular investigatory practices, this caution may be warranted on grounds other than limited resources. *See, e.g., Ezeagwuna v. INS*, 325 F.3d 396 (3d Cir. 2003) (criticizing field investigations conducted by U.S. staff in Cameroon).

Furthermore, the deputy director suggested that private attorneys submit such documents to USCIS or to an IJ, who would then ask that the document be verified.[66] This practice has been confirmed at various consular posts around the world.[67]

While a lack of resources is an understandable rationale for not providing such services, advocates should be wary of relying on the asylum office or the IJ forwarding the documents to DOS as the method for verifying the authenticity of a client's documents. Submitting the documents directly to DOS as a method of determining whether or not the documents are authentic (after evaluating the risks to the client, of course) is not the same as submitting the documents as evidence. By going through the adjudicator (asylum officer or IJ), you are asking the documents be admitted into evidence before knowing whether they are authentic. Unless you have a high degree of confidence in the documents, you risk a negative-credibility finding or even worse, a frivolous-filing finding.

At the same time, advocates should not take a refusal by DOS to conduct "document verification" in asylum claims (*i.e.*, field investigation) as a refusal to follow the formal chain authentication procedures available as a consular service for a set fee. If there are good reasons to follow the normal 8 CFR §§287.6, 1287.6 procedures without placing your client or their family and colleagues in danger, then

that process remains an option through many consulates. Along the same lines, if there are no concerns about approaching the designated authority in a Hague Convention country for an apostille, that should be considered.

CIRCUIT COURTS OF APPEAL SPLIT ON THE ISSUE

Since 2001, the number of circuit court cases directly addressing the issue of document authentication under 8 CFR §§287.6, 1287.6 in asylum cases has increased dramatically.[68]

Circuits Holding that Documents Need Not Necessarily Be Authenticated Under 8 CFR §§287.6, 1287.6

In 2001, the Ninth Circuit examined authentication requirements in *Khan v. INS*. There, in the case of a Bangladeshi asylum-seeker, the court overruled the IJ's decision to exclude documents for lack of 8 CFR §287.6(b) authentication. The Ninth Circuit remanded the case, stating that

[d]ocuments may be authenticated through any 'recognized procedure, such as those required by INS regulations or by the Federal Rules of Civil Procedure'" and that the "procedure specified in 8 CFR §287.6 provides one, but not the, exclusive method. It was error to exclude the official records based solely on the lack of consular certification.[69]

Other circuits soon followed. In *Georgis v. Ashcroft*, a copy of a letter from the Ethiopian Transitional Government Second Police Station that the applicant claimed corroborated the facts and circumstances of her husband's arrest was excluded in part because of a lack of authentication under 8 CFR §287.6. The Seventh Circuit stated that it was "uncertain whether the letter qualifies as an 'official record' within the meaning of 8 CFR §287.6, but

---

[66] Potts Letter, *supra* note 64.

> It is our policy only to respond to specific inquiries or request for document verification from the Citizenship and Immigration Services or from Executive Office for Immigration Review immigration court judges. If you would to have a U.S. embassy or consulate investigate the validity of a document, I would encourage you to submit the desired documents to the appropriate immigration judge. If the judge determines that there is a need to verify the authenticity of the document, it will be forwarded to our attention, and our office will respond accordingly to the request. *Id.*

[67] *See, e.g.*, Letter from U.S. Consul Paul Schultz, U.S. Embassy to Slovenia, to Dick A. Zonneveld, dated Nov. 22, 2005 (on file with author); Letter from U.S. Vice Consul Trina Saha, U.S. Embassy to Cameroon, to Dick A. Zonneveld, dated Jan 23, 2005 (on file with author). The letter from the U.S. embassy in Cameroon also states that the Office of Country Reports is "prohibited from divulging information to private attorneys in asylum matters." *Id.* This seems odd because the confidentiality regulations at 8 CFR §§208.6, 1208.6 are meant to protect applicants. Written consent of an applicant allows disclosure. Arguably such consent may be given by an applicant's legal representative.

[68] Lexis/Nexis searches ("287.6 and asylum") on March 16, 2006 in the federal case database yielded a total of only two cases before January 1, 2001, and 55 cases since that date (including precedential and nonprecedential decisions).

[69] *Khan v. INS*, 237 F.3d 1143, 1144 (9th Cir. 2001) (citing to *Espinosa v. INS*, 45 F.3d 308, 209–10 (9th Cir. 1995); *Chung Young Chew v. Boyd*, 309 F.2d 857 (9th Cir. 1962); *Iran v. INS*, 656 F.2d 469, 472 n.8 (9th Cir. 1981); *Hoonsilapa v. INS*, 575 F.2d 735, 738 (9th Cir. 1978)).

even if it does, §287.6 is not the only way that Georgis could authenticate the document."[70]

The Third Circuit, in 2004, held in *Liu v. Ashcroft*, that "8 CFR §287.6 is not an absolute rule of exclusion, and is not the exclusive means of authenticating records before an immigration judge."[71] There, a Chinese couple attempted to introduce evidence about abortions that had been done and testified that they were told by provincial officials that no authentication was performed at that level. The court concluded that "the Lius should have been allowed to attempt to prove the authenticity of the abortion certificates through other means, especially where (as here) attempts to abide by the requirements of §287.6 failed due to lack of cooperation from government officials in the country of alleged persecution."[72]

The First Circuit, in a case in which the asylum applicant was attempting to exclude German immigration records on the basis that they were not properly authenticated under 8 CFR §§287.6, 1287.6, similarly held that the provision was "one, but not the exclusive" method of authenticating documents.[73] In that case, the court stated that it was acceptable for the immigration court to allow into evidence the hearsay testimony of a German official

that the records came from official files because there was "nothing dubious" about the statement.[74]

Other Alternatives Under Federal Rules or "Recognized Procedures"

In looking at other alternatives mentioned in the cases above, advocates should turn to the Federal Rules of Evidence and the Federal Rules of Civil Procedure.[75] Both FRCP 44 and FRE 902(3) describe the chain authentication method. FRCP 44(a)(2) uses the term "foreign official records," as also found in 8 CFR §§287.6(b), 1287.6(b). FRE 902(3) uses the broader term "foreign public document," as found in the Hague Convention and 8 CFR §§287.6(b), 1287.6(c).

FRCP 44(b)(2) and FRE 902(3) offer the alternative of admitting for good cause the official record or official document in question without final certification if all parties have had an opportunity to investigate the authenticity of the document.[76]

---

[70] *Georgis v. INS*, 328 F.3d 962, 969 (7th Cir. 2003). *See also Shtaro v. Gonzales*, 435 F.3d 711 (7th Cir. 2006) (failure to authenticate Slovenian documents under 8 CFR §287.6 does not amount to presumptive proof of falsity).

[71] *Liu v. Ashcroft*, 372 F.3d 529, 533 (3d Cir. 2004). "[A]sylum applicants can not always reasonably be expected to have an authenticated document from an alleged persecutor." *Id.* at 532.

[72] *Id. See also Leia v. Ashcroft*, 393 F.3d 427, 435 (3d Cir. 2005) (Ukrainian applicant "had the right to present evidence explaining why authentication was impossible and it thus was an abuse of discretion for the IJ to refuse to consider [expert testimony] to the effect of the political situation on the ability of a dissident…to obtain government certification."); *Chen v. Gonzales*, 434 F.3d 212, 218 fn. 6 (3d Cir. 2005) (recognizing that 287.6 is not an exclusive rule, but stating that "in this case there is not only a lack of direct evidence of the abortion certificate's authenticity, but a lack of evidence which might explain the circumstances or context of the issuance of that certificate."); *Zhang v. Gonzales*, 405 F.3d 150 (3d Cir. 2005).

[73] *Yongo v. INS*, 355 F.3d 27, 30–31 (1st Cir. 2004) (citations omitted).

[74] *Id. See also Lin v. Ashcroft*, 371 F.3d 18, 22 (1st Cir. 2004) (17 documents had been submitted only six days prior to the hearing). "Given the undisputed government reports that the documents from the Fuzhou area of China are subject to widespread fabrication and fraud, it was reasonable for the IJ to require some type of authentication of the documents submitted by Lin. In this case no authentication was offered, or attempted through the minimal effort of having the official seals recognized by the American consulate in China." *Id.*

[75] For a discussion of the differences between the FRE and the FRCP on this issue, see Wiebe & Parker, "Asking for a Note," *supra* note 1, at 7–8, 11–3.

[76] FRE 44(a)(2)(2005) reads in relevant part:

> If reasonable opportunity has been given to all parties to investigate the authenticity and accuracy of the documents, the court may, for good cause shown, (i) admit an attested copy without final certification or (ii) permit the foreign official record to be evidenced by an attested summary with or without a final certification. The final certification is unnecessary if the record and the attestation are certified as provided in a treaty or convention to which the United States and the foreign country in which the official record is located are parties.

The final sentence anticipates an Apostille under the Hague Convention. FRE 902(3) reads in relevant part that "If reasonable opportunity has been given to all parties to investigate the authenticity and accuracy of official documents, the court may, for good cause shown, order that they be treated as presumptively authentic without final certification or permit them to be evidenced by an attested summary with or without final certification."

FRCP 44(c) should also not be overlooked. It states that "[t]his rule does not prevent the proof of official records or of entry or lack of entry therein by any other method authorized by law."

In a recent case before an IJ, a motion was made to authenticate official documents through the procedure described above with respect to the Bureau of Human Rights at the State Department, *i.e.*, requesting that the judge send the documents to the State Department, which would then forward them to the consulate in question. The motion was denied in part on the basis of *Khan*, which calls for alternative authenticating by any recognized procedures, such as through the Federal Rules of Civil Procedure. The judge stated that the "respondent has failed to make a diligent and good faith effort to authenticate foreign documents by other means other than 8 CFR §1287.6."[77] The Catch-22 here is that the request procedure from IJ to DOS is the very sort of "other method authorized by law" contemplated by FRCP 44(c).

The Second Circuit with an Internal Split: "Maybe You Should, Yes You Must"

In *Lin v. Gonzales*—a Chinese coerced abortion case—the Second Circuit found "that the IJ erred by rejecting the notarial birth certificate based on Cao's failure to authenticate it pursuant to 'regulation'." To reach this finding, the Court favorably cited the Third Circuit to the effect that 8 CFR §§287.6, 1287.6 is not the exclusive means of authentication and that "applicants can not always reasonably be expected to have an authenticated document from an alleged persecutor."[78]

In contrast, another Second Circuit panel, in *Borovikova v. U.S. Dep't of Justice*, upheld the IJ's finding that a Russian birth certificate was fraudulent, in part due to a failure to comply with 8 CFR §§287.6, 1287.6. Here we find an interplay between an overseas investigation report and the authentication rules at 8 CFR §§287.6, 1287.6. The U.S. embassy in Moscow issued a report describing inconsistencies in the birth certificate. The court found that "the Embassy Report was surely worthy of the IJ's attention" and that the "rebuttal evidence does not overcome the embassy report largely because the

documents petitioner offered had not been authenticated pursuant to applicable regulations" under 8 CFR §§287.6(b), 1287.6(b).[79]

In contrast to the attitude of the Third Circuit in *Ezeagwuna*, which criticized the government for trying to trade on the letterhead of the Department of State,[80] the *Borovikova* court relied almost exclusively on the report of an INS official stationed in Moscow whose credentials to examine documents were unknown. A letter from a Ukranian official stating that a birth certificate in petitioner's maiden name was registered in official records in Kiev was insufficient to authenticate the birth certificate,[81] in contrast to the *Yongo* case in the First Circuit, in which hearsay testimony from a German official served to authenticate official German records.[82]

Circuits Upholding IJ Decisions Excluding or Limiting the Weight of Documents based on Lack of Compliance with 8 CFR §§287.6, 1287.6

In an Eighth Circuit case, *Fongwo v.Gonzales*,[83] the IJ relied on the FDL review of identity documents, including a comparison of petitioner's passport with official Cameroon passports on file with INS to confirm that the asylum applicant was not who he claimed to be. Little weight was given to a second birth certificate with the name "Fongwo" because it was not authenticated in accordance with 8 CFR §§287.6, 1287.6. The Eighth Circuit upheld the IJ's finding that the applicant had filed a frivolous claim, but did not discuss at all the permissive or mandatory nature of 8 CFR §§287.6, 1287.6.[84] This case provides a good example in which one method of testing document reliability (forensic document examination) won the day when no countering evidence was presented by the other side.

---

[77] Decision on a Motion in the *Matter of [name not provided]*, Dallas, TX, Immigr. Judge Deitrich Sims, Aug. 19, 2005. (copy on file with author compliments of Paul Zoltan).

[78] *Lin v. Gonzales*, 428 F.3d 391, 404–05 (2d Cir. 2005).

[79] *Borovikova v. U.S. Dep't of Justice*, 435 F.3d 151, 158 (2d Cir. 2006). This conclusion was reached notwithstanding the submission of other evidence that tended to reinforce the legitimacy of the birth certificate in question. It may also be worthy of note that the Court criticized the applicant for not following 8 CFR §§287.6(b), 1287.6(b), even though the Russian Federation is a signatory to the Hague Convention, which would have required authentication under 8 CFR §§287.6(c), 1287.6(c).

[80] *Ezeagwuna v. INS*, 325 F.3d 396, 408 (3d Cir. 2003).

[81] *Borovikova*, 435 F.3d at 158.

[82] *Yongo v. INS*, 355 F.3d 27, 30–31 (1st Cir. 2004).

[83] *Fongwo v. Gonzales*, 430 F.3d 944, 946 (8th Cir. 2005).

[84] *Id.*

The Fifth Circuit in *Zhao v. Gonzales* reversed a decision denying asylum to a Chinese applicant who claimed persecution based on Falun Gong membership.[85] In that case, the applicant had submitted two unauthenticated police summons. The IJ had given the applicant time to authenticate them, and when he had not done so in the time allotted, the documents were excluded. The court of appeals did not comment specifically on the issue of whether such authentication was mandatory for admission of the documents.[86]

In a Tenth Circuit case, the IJ determined that "the medical certificate and the summonses . . . seem unreliable to this Court. Those documents were not authenticated as permitted under 8 CFR §287.6. The Court has no way of knowing whether these documents are authentic. There are no recognizable indicia of authenticity on those documents, which the Court can point to." The court of appeals stated, "given our deferential standard of review, we conclude that the IJ's determination that the records in question were not reliable and did not support Sviridov's claims is supported by substantial evidence and is substantially reasonable."[87]

CONCLUSION

The foregoing review of the procedures, practices and case law reveals two seemingly contradictory trends. On the one hand, the corroboration requirements for asylum-seekers continue to rise. On the other, a growing number of circuit courts are beginning to realize that strict adherence to authentication standards in the asylum context undermines the very nature of asylum law. While a growing flexibility is being adopted by various circuits, advocates should not take that as a sign that their preparation will be getting any easier. Courts will expect document authentication to be the default, absent compelling reasons to view a particular case otherwise.

---

[85] *Zhao v. Gonzales*, 404 F.3d 295, 300 (5th Cir. 2005).

[86] *Id.*

---

[87] *Sviridov v. Ashcroft*, 358 F.3d 722, 728 (10th Cir. 2004). *See also Woldemeskel v. INS*, 257 F.3d 1185 (10th Cir. 2001). In *Woldemeskel*, documents had been excluded by the IJ and BIA in part due to a lack of §§287.6, 1287.6 compliance. Because the court of appeals found that other reasons given for excluding the documents existed, it did not reach the issue of whether §§287.6, 1287.6 had to be followed. *Id.* at 1192, fn. 3.

APPENDIX

CONTRACTING STATES TO THE HAGUE CONVENTION AS OF JANUARY 16, 2006[88]

The Hague Conference lists state parties as "members" and "nonmembers." This designation applies to membership in the Hague Conference for Private International Law (the international organization that convenes countries to create and review a host of international agreements), not to whether a state is a party to a particular treaty.

Albania; Andorra; Antigua and Barbuda; Argentina; Armenia; Azerbaijan (with other contracting states that have not raised objections); Australia; Austria; Bahamas; Barbados; Belarus; Belgium; Belize; Bosnia and Herzegovina; Botswana; Brunei Darussalam; Bulgaria; People's Republic of China (Special Administrative Regions of Hong Kong and Macao only); Colombia; Cook Islands; Croatia; Cyprus; Czech Republic; Dominica; Ecuador; El Salvador; Estonia; Fiji; Finland; France; Germany; Greece; Grenada; Honduras; Hungary; Iceland; India (with other contracting states that have not raised objections); Ireland; Israel; Italy; Japan; Kazakhstan; Latvia; Lesotho; Liberia; Liechtenstein; Lithuania; Luxembourg; Malawi; Malta; Marshall Islands; Mauritius; Mexico; Monaco; Namibia; Netherlands; New Zealand; Niue; Norway; Panama; Poland; Portugal; Romania; Russian Federation; Saint Kitts and Nevis; Saint Lucia; Saint Vincent and the Grenadines; Samoa; San Marino; Serbia and Montenegro; Seychelles; Slovakia; Slovenia; South Africa, Spain, Suriname; Swaziland; Sweden; Switzerland; the former Yugoslav Republic of Macedonia; Tonga; Trinidad and Tobago; Turkey; Ukraine; United Kingdom of Great Britain and Northern Ireland; United States of America; Venezuela.

---

[88] Status Table: Convention of 5 October 1961 Abolishing the Requirement of Legalisation for Foreign Public Documents (Jan. 16, 2006), at *www.hcch.net/index_en.php?act=conventions.status&cid=41*.

NACARA FOR GUATEMALANS, SALVADORANS, AND FORMER SOVIET BLOC NATIONALS

by Mark Silverman and Linton Joaquin[*]

INTRODUCTION

Scope of This Article

This article, which is excerpted from Chapter 1 of the Immigrant Legal Resource Center's (ILRC) *Winning NACARA Suspension Cases*, analyzes section 203 of NACARA.

Suspension of Deportation Benefits Under NACARA—An Overview

The Nicaraguan Adjustment and Central American Relief Act (NACARA),[1] which was signed into law on November 19, 1997, provides significant benefits to Salvadorans, Guatemalans, and nationals of former Soviet bloc and Eastern European nations. The legislation gives them the opportunity to apply for suspension of deportation under rules that preceded IIRAIRA.[2]

This article provides an update on implementation of NACARA, drawing on the interim regulations[3] and on policy statements that legacy INS/DHS and the Executive Office for Immigration Review (EOIR) have issued to date. The interim rule contains important changes made in response to comments to the proposed rule. Most significantly, the interim rule establishes a streamlined procedure for processing cases of applicants who are class members in *American Baptist Churches v. Thornburgh*[4] (*ABC*), affording them a rebuttable presumption that they meet the "extreme hardship" requirement for suspension or special rule cancellation. The interim rule took effect on June 21, 1999.

FRAMEWORK FOR ANALYZING NACARA CASES

The NACARA statute is complicated, and the regulations add a further level of complexity. To assist practitioners in analyzing NACARA cases, the following four-step process, which can be divided into two parts, may be useful:

First, the practitioner analyzes his or her client's *NACARA* and then *suspension/cancellation eligibility*.

- *NACARA eligibility*: Is the person eligible to *apply* for suspension or special cancellation under *NACARA's more generous requirements*? Is the person eligible for the *rebuttable presumption of extreme hardship*?

- *Remedy*: Is the person eligible for NACARA Suspension or Special Rule Cancellation? Are there any suspension/cancellation eligibility issues?

Subsequent to that eligibility determination, there are additional considerations of where, when, and how to bring the case, including:

- *Application Procedures*: Is the person eligible for an asylum office adjudication?

- *Evaluation of the Case*: How strong is the case based on a *hardship claim*, as well as other suspension or cancellation requirements and information from the prior three steps? *Should the person be preparing to file for NACARA now, or should he or she wait?*

Each of these aspects of analyzing NACARA cases is discussed in detail below.

---

[*] Updated from an article published at *Immigration & Nationality Law Handbook* 1013 (2005–06 ed.)

Mark Silverman is the director of Immigration Policy with the Immigrant Legal Resource Center (ILRC) in San Francisco. **Linton Joaquin** is the executive director at the National Immigration Law Center (NILC) in Los Angeles. The authors gratefully acknowledge the contributions of Matti Surh, Cristina Fabie, Juan Osuna, Evelyn Cruz, Sarah Chester, Judy London, Angela Kelley, Dan Kesselbrenner, Shari Kurita, and Lisa Klapal.

[1] Nicaraguan Adjustment and Central American Relief Act, enacted as Title II of the District of Columbia Appropriations Act for fiscal year 1998, Pub. L. No. 105-100, 111 Stat. 2160 (Nov. 19, 1997).

[2] Illegal Immigration Reform and Immigrant Responsibility Act of 1996, Division C of the Omnibus Appropriations Act of 1996 (H.R. 3610), Pub. L. No. 104-208, 110 Stat. 3009.

[3] 64 Fed. Reg. 67856 (May 21, 1999).

[4] 760 F.2d 796 (N.D. Cal. 1991).

ANALYSIS OF NACARA CASES

Step One: Eligibility Requirements and the Rebuttable Presumption of Hardship

Under NACARA, certain individuals are potentially eligible to apply for suspension/cancellation of removal based on the more generous suspension of deportation standards that were in place before IIRAIRA took effect on April 1, 1997. The following groups of persons are eligible for suspension/cancellation benefits as NACARA principals and dependents, provided that they have not been convicted of an aggravated felony:

- *Salvadoran nationals*: (1) who first entered the United States on or before September 19, 1990 and registered for benefits under the *ABC* settlement agreement on or before October 31, 1991 (either by applying for temporary protected status (TPS) or by submitting an *ABC* registration),[5] unless apprehended at the time of entry after December 19, 1990,[6] or (2) who filed an application for asylum with legacy INS on or before April 1, 1990.[7]

- *Guatemalan nationals*: (1) who first entered the United States on or before October 1, 1990 and registered for *ABC* benefits on or before December 31, 1991,[8] unless apprehended at the time of entry after December 19, 1990, or (2) who filed an application for asylum with legacy INS on or before April 1, 1990.[9]

Filed with legacy INS. The interim regulation wisely clarifies that a person satisfies the eligibility prong of filing an asylum application with legacy INS on or before April 1, 1990, "either by filing an application with the Service or filing an application with the Immigration Court and serving a copy of that application on the Service."[10]

Filed an Application for Asylum is defined as the proper filing by a principal or "filing a derivative asylum application by being properly included as a dependent spouse or child in any asylum application *pursuant to the regulations and procedures in effect at the time of filing* of the principal or derivative asylum application."[11] For example, Lydia was properly included as a dependent (or derivative) applicant in her father's application in 1988. Therefore, Lydia is eligible to apply for NACARA because she filed an asylum application on or before prior to April 1, 1990.

Is the Person Eligible for the Rebuttable Presumption of Extreme Hardship? If person is in one of the categories described above, he or she is eligible for the rebuttable presumption of extreme hardship.[12] All Salvadorans and Guatemalans who are eligible for NACARA as principals are presumed to have established the requisite extreme hardship requirement because the regulations specifically provides the presumption to both groups of NACARA principals from those countries—those who registered for *ABC* either directly or via TPS, and those who applied for asylum on or before April 1, 1990.[13] Therefore, for purposes of the presumption, all NACARA-eligible principals from El Salvador and Guatemala are *ABC* class members whether or not they ever registered or applied for asylum pursuant to the *ABC* settlement. The Supplementary Information section of the NACARA regulations states that result of the unusual immigration history of the ABC class "is the creation of a large class of individuals who share certain strong predictors of extreme hardship."[14] These characteristics include the fact that *ABC* class members came to the United States on or before 1990 during a period of civil strife in El Salvador and Guatemala. They were entitled to special asylum adjudication procedures as a result of a settlement of litigation that alleged discriminatory treatment of Guatemalan and Salvadoran asylum applicants. There is a detailed discussion of the rebuttable hardship presumption in a separate section of this article.

---

[5] IIRAIRA §309(c)(5)(C)(i)(I)(aa), *amended by* NACARA §203(a)(1); 8 CFR §240.61(a)(1). Note: All references in the text and footnotes to the regulation are to the *interim* rule unless otherwise indicated.

[6] IIRAIRA §309(c)(5)(C)(i)(I), *amended by* NACARA §203(a)(1); 8 CFR §240.60; 8 CFR §240.61(a)(1).

[7] IIRAIRA §309(c)(5)(C)(i)(II), *amended by* NACARA §203(a)(1); 8 CFR 240.60; 8 CFR §240.61(a)(2).

[8] IIRAIRA §309(c)(5)(C)(i)(I)(bb), *amended by* NACARA §203(a)(1); 8 CFR 240.60; 8 CFR §240.61(a)(1).

[9] IIRAIRA §309(c)(5)(C)(i)(II), *amended by* NACARA §203(a)(1); 8 CFR §240.61(a)(2).

[10] 8 CFR §240.61(a)(2) (emphasis added).

[11] 8 CFR §240.60—definition of "*Filed an application for asylum*" (emphasis added).

[12] 8 CFR §240.64(d).

[13] 8 CFR §§240.61(a)(1) and 240.61(a)(2).

[14] For Supplementary Information section of the NACARA regulations, see 64 Fed. Reg. 27866, first column.

- ***Former Soviet Bloc Nationals.*** Aliens who entered the United States on or before December 31, 1990, and applied for asylum on or before December 31, 1991. At the time of application the individuals were nationals of the Soviet Union, Russia, any republic of the former Soviet Union, Latvia, Estonia, Lithuania, Poland, Czechoslovakia, Romania, Hungary, Bulgaria, Albania, East Germany, Yugoslavia or any state of the former Yugoslavia.[15] Former Soviet bloc nationals *are not* afforded the rebuttable presumption of hardship.

NACARA-eligible Dependents. The spouse or an unmarried child under 21 years of age of a person who is granted suspension under the NACARA provisions can also be granted NACARA benefits as long as the relationship between the spouse or child and principal exists at the time that the decision to grant the benefit is made.[16]

The rules are different for unmarried sons or daughters over 21 years of age. They must have entered the United States on or before October 1, 1990 and the relationship between the son or daughter and the parent granted the benefit must exist at the time that the decision to grant the benefit is made.[17]

Dependents Are Not Eligible for the Rebuttable Hardship Presumption. The interim regulations do not provide NACARA-eligible Salvadoran or Guatemalan dependents the presumption of extreme hardship which has been afforded to their parents or spouse (who are NACARA principals). For example, Pedro registered for TPS, and therefore is eligible for NACARA as well as the rebuttable presumption. His wife and child, age 14, are eligible for NACARA as dependents but will not be able to benefit from the rebuttable presumption.

Apprehended at the Time of Entry. Practitioners should note that *ABC* Salvadorans and Guatemalans apprehended at the *time of entry* after December 19, 1990 are not eligible for NACARA benefits.[18] However, Salvadorans and Guatemalans who qualify as dependents of a NACARA-eligible spouse or parent

or as persons who applied for asylum before April 1, 1990 are not subject to this bar.

The Supplementary Information states that the Department of Justice decided not to define "apprehended at time of entry" in the regulation. The Supplementary Information does, however, provide helpful information about legacy INS interpretation of this term at pg. 27860, stating, "The Service has issued and continues to provide policy guidance to its officers explaining that a class member who has been apprehended after the class member has effected an entry (consistent with the former "entry doctrine") cannot be considered to have been apprehended at the time of entry." For example, Juan, who was apprehended in 1991 *after crossing the border* illegally near San Ysidro, California, would not be barred from NACARA eligibility. The legacy INS/USCIS position is that the person must have been under legacy INS "supervision" from the time that he or she crossed the border until his or her apprehension by legacy INS.

VAWA II Eligibility. The VAWA II legislation[19] provides that spouses and children who have suffered abuse at the hands of the §203 NACARA principal may pursue their NACARA (I-881) applications independently.

Step Two: Eligible for Suspension or Special Rule Cancellation of Removal?

NACARA-eligible persons who are in deportation proceedings (which by definition were commenced prior to April 1, 1997) may apply for *suspension of deportation*,[20] even where those proceedings have been administratively closed. Individuals who were not placed in deportation or exclusion proceedings by this date may apply for "special rule" *cancellation of removal.*

Requirements for Suspension or Special Rule Cancellation Under NACARA. The applicant must meet the following additional requirements in order to qualify for suspension/cancellation under NACARA:

1. maintain continuous presence in the United States for seven years (§1.4(A));

2. possess good moral character (§1.4(D));

---

[15] IIRAIRA §309(c)(5)(C)(i)(V), *amended by* NACARA §203(a)(1); 8 CFR §240.61(a)(3).

[16] IIRAIRA §309(c)(5)(C)(i)(III), *amended by* NACARA §203(a)(1); 8 CFR §240.61(a)(4).

[17] IIRAIRA §309(c)(5)(C)(i)(IV), *amended by* NACARA §203(a)(1); 8 CFR §240.61(a)(5).

[18] IIRAIRA §309(c)(5)(C)(i)(I), *amended by* NACARA §203(a)(1); 8 CFR §240.61(a)(1).

---

[19] Violence Against Women Act of 1998, H.R. 3514, 105th Cong. (1998) (VAWA II).

[20] 8 CFR §240.65(a).

3. demonstrate that returning to the country of origin would result in extreme hardship to the applicant or to the applicant's child, spouse, or parent who is a U.S. citizen or lawful permanent resident (LPR); and,

4. merit a favorable exercise of discretion.[21]

These are the normal requirements for suspension of deportation, as it existed before IIRAIRA replaced this form of relief with the tougher cancellation of removal standards.

Practice Pointer: Be sure your client who is eligible to *apply* for NACARA (Step 1) also meets the requirements for NACARA Suspension/Cancellation (Step 2). For example, Carlos is a NACARA principal. His wife, Dora, entered the United States four years ago. Dora is eligible to *apply* for NACARA now because she is the spouse of a NACARA-eligible principal. (Step 1). Dora, however, does not *now* meet the requirements for NACARA special rule cancellation because she has been present in the United States for less than the required seven years. Carlos may apply for NACARA now. Dora should wait three more years when she will have accrued her seven years of continuous physical presence.

The eligibility requirements for NACARA suspension and cancellation are very similar, but in some aspects are *not identical*. Therefore, it is sometimes important to determine for which of the two forms of NACARA relief your client is eligible. The most important practical differences between the two are issues concerning *absences from the United States* and *bars* to relief.

Advance Parole. The rule states the deportation proceedings against NACARA-eligible individuals who departed and returned to the United States under a grant of advance parole while those deportation proceedings were pending are considered to have terminated as of the date of the person's departure from the United States.[22] This rule applies to persons who obtained advance parole pursuant to Deferred Enforced Departure. There is a different result for those who departed with advance parole pursuant to the original Salvadoran TPS program.[23]

By deeming the deportation proceedings of these individuals to have terminated as of their departure dates, the rule allows them now to apply for special rule cancellation of removal.

The following hypotheticals illustrate this point. Jorge was in deportation proceedings, which were administratively closed for TPS in 1991. He subsequently registered for Deferred Enforced Departure (DED), and on March 1, 1994, he left the United States and returned from El Salvador pursuant to a Service grant of advance parole three weeks later. His pending deportation proceedings were terminated on March 1, 1994, the date he left the United States pursuant to advance parole. He filed an *ABC* asylum application in 1995. Jorge may apply for NACARA special rule cancellation with the asylum office because he has accrued seven years of continuous physical presence since that date, and if his case is not granted, he will be able to apply again in front of an immigration judge in removal proceedings.

In another hypothetical, Juan had a deportation order entered in his case in 1988. He did not leave the United States at that time. He subsequently was granted TPS and DED. On February 10, 1993, he left the United States and returned to the United States 46 days later pursuant to advance parole granted pursuant to his DED status. His deportation order was executed when he left the United States pursuant to advance parole, and his deportation proceedings were terminated. He has an *ABC* asylum application pending with the asylum office. Juan may apply for NACARA with the asylum office. He does not need to file a motion to reopen with EOIR because there is no outstanding deportation order in his case. Juan has now accrued the necessary seven years of continuous physical presence in the United States since his return of March 26, 1993.

---

[21] IIRAIRA §309(f), *created by* NACARA §203(b).

[22] 8 CFR §240.70(h).

[23] The rule definitely applies to departures grants of advance parole pursuant to Deferred Enforced Departure (DED), which began on July 1, 1992, and those thereafter. There is a different result when the person left on advance parole pur-
continued

suant to the original TPS program. The Miscellaneous and Technical Immigration and Naturalization Amendments of 1991 (Pub. L. No. 102-232, 105 Stat. 1733 (MTINA)) expressly provides that individuals granted Temporary Protected Status (TPS) who leave the United States pursuant to a grant of advance parole, on their return "shall be inspected and admitted in the same immigration status the alien had at the time of departure." §304(c)(1). Thus, individuals with administratively closed deportation proceedings who had TPS status at the time they left the country should still be considered to have pending deportation proceedings, and should be eligible for NACARA suspension rather than special rule cancellation.

Eligibility to Apply for NACARA in Exclusion Proceedings. The discussion in the regulation concluded that persons in exclusion proceedings are not eligible for NACARA suspension of deportation because they are subject to a ground of inadmissibility rather than a ground of deportation. The DOJ also states in the rule that these persons are not eligible for cancellation of removal because they are in exclusion proceedings (which began prior to April 1, 1997).[24] Unfortunately, a recent circuit case decision supports this holding.[25] DOJ, however, does recognize that these individuals could become eligible should legacy INS/USCIS agree to terminate the exclusion proceedings and initiate removal proceedings. The transitional rules of IIRAIRA provide a simple way for legacy INS/USCIS to do this, by invoking removal rules in the exclusion proceedings under IIRAIRA §309(c)(2) (in cases where the hearing has not yet been held), or by terminating the exclusion proceedings and initiating removal proceedings under IIRAIRA §309(c)(3) (in cases where the hearing has been completed). In the interim rule, however, DOJ states that it has not decided to take this action at this time. We believe that the regulations should give effect to Congress's generous intent by providing for the use of these transitional rules in this manner, and urged the DOJ to take this position in the final rule or in implementing instructions to the field.

Continuous Physical Presence and Absences From the United States

An applicant for suspension/cancellation may still be eligible to apply under the NACARA provisions even though he or she left the United States and returned. The applicant, however, needs to establish continuous physical presence in the United States.

Duration of Absence—For both NACARA suspension and cancellation, a single absence of 90 days or less and aggregate absences of 180 days or less will not break the required continuous physical presence based on the *length* of the absence.

Suspension—The statute governing suspension of deportation specifies that "[a]n alien shall not be considered to have failed to maintain continuous physical presence in the United States... if the absence from the United States was brief, casual, and innocent and did not meaningfully interrupt the continuous physical presence."[26] The interim regulation confirms that the "brief, casual, and innocent" standard applies to absences of applicants whose deportation proceedings began before April 1, 1997.[27] The authors commend the Department for providing in the interim rule that any single absence of 90 days or less or an aggregate total of no more than 180 days shall be considered *brief*.[28]

A single absence of more than 90 days or aggregate absences of more than 180 days may still be considered *brief*, and therefore not to have broken the required continuous physical presence for suspension but not special rule cancellation. The rule for NACARA suspension cases states that "[f]or purposes of evaluating whether an absence is brief, single absences in excess of 90 days, or absences that total more than 180 days in the aggregate will be evaluated on a case-by-case basis."[29]

Special Rule Cancellation—The cancellation statute provides that if an applicant has been outside the United States for a period of more than 90 days during a single absence, or a cumulative total of 180 days or more, the absence will break the required continuous physical presence in the United States.[30] The interim rule brought the regulation in line with the statute by eliminating the requirement that an applicant demonstrate that an absence or absences were *brief* even where they satisfied the 90/180 day rule.

"Casual and Innocent" Absences—The NACARA applicant must still show that any single absence of 90 days or less was "casual and innocent" in nature. The interim regulation states that for both suspension and special rule cancellation, continuous physical presence is terminated whenever (1) a person leaves pursuant to a deportation or removal order; (2) a person leaves pursuant to an order of voluntary departure; or (3) where the "departure is made for purposes of committing an unlawful act."[31] Many practitioners believe that this rule is not

---

[24] In some instances, we believe that it would not be appropriate to place individuals returning to the United States with advance parole in exclusion proceedings. See, for example, the discussion of the effect of advance parole on individuals with TPS, *supra* note 23.

[25] *Sherifi v. INS*, 260 F.3d 737 (7th Cir. 2001).

[26] Former INA §244(b)(2).

[27] 8 CFR §240.64(b)(1).

[28] *Id.*

[29] 8 CFR §240.64(b).

[30] NACARA §203(b) amends IIRAIRA §309(f)(2) by incorporating the definition of continuous physical presence found in INA §240A(d)(2).

[31] 8 CFR §240.64(b)(3).

appropriate for special rule cancellation because the cancellation statute's objective test based on duration of the absence appears to replace the somewhat subjective "brief, casual, and innocent" test that was used to evaluate absences for suspension purposes.

Bars to NACARA Suspension and Cancellation Eligibility—For both NACARA suspension and special rule cancellation of removal, there is a much more restrictive eligibility standard that applies to individuals who are deportable because of criminal convictions or certain other enumerated grounds. These individuals must establish that they were continuously present in the United States for a period of 10 years *after* the commission of the crime or conduct that made them deportable, that the individual was of good moral character, and they must show that their deportation would cause "exceptional and extremely unusual hardship" to themselves or their spouse, parent, or child.[32]

This heightened standard applies to applicants for NACARA suspension if they are deportable because of criminal or security grounds under former INA §241(a)(2), (3), or (4).[33] This includes all of the criminal grounds of deportability[34], failure to register, having a conviction for falsification of documents, or being the subject of a civil document fraud final order,[35] and any of the national security or terrorist grounds of deportability.[36]

Similarly, applicants for special rule cancellation who are deportable or inadmissible under the criminal and security grounds are subject to the statute's heightened eligibility standards.[37] An applicant for special rule cancellation is subject to the heightened eligibility standards if he or she: (1) is inadmissible or deportable for a conviction or commission of a crime of moral turpitude;[38] (2) has two or more convictions (whether or not for crimes of moral turpitude) with aggregate sentences of five years;[39] (3) is

a drug trafficker,[40] or has a drug conviction,[41] or is a drug abuser or addict;[42] (4) is inadmissible for having engaged in prostitution within the last 10 years or having come to the United States to engage in prostitution (also applies to commercialized vice);[43] (5) is deportable as an aggravated felon;[44] (6) is deportable for a firearms conviction;[45] (7) is deportable for a conviction of domestic violence after September 30, 1996,[46] or a violation of a temporary protective order after September 30, 1996;[47] (8) is deportable for having falsely claimed U.S. citizenship in order to receive a benefit under any state or federal law after September 30, 1996, for having failed to register, or for either having been convicted for falsification of documents or having a civil document fraud final order[48]; or (9) is inadmissible or deportable as a threat to national security or as a terrorist and on related grounds.[49]

Importantly, these more restrictive eligibility standards only apply to individuals who are charged with and found to be deportable or inadmissible in removal or deportation proceedings for one of the specified criminal or security grounds.[50] Additionally, there are ways of overcoming some crime-related bars by obtaining post-conviction relief. The charts in Appendix 1-A summarize the ineligibility bars for suspension and special rule cancellation.

Good Moral Character

There are additional bars or potential problems in terms of satisfying the good moral character requirement for suspension and special rule cancellation. Establishing good moral character is a two-step

---

[32] Former INA §244(a)(2); IIRAIRA §309(f)(1)(B), *amended by* NACARA §203(b); 8 CFR §240.65(c).

[33] IIRAIRA §309(c)(5)(C), *amended by* NACARA §203(a); 8 CFR §240.65(c).

[34] Former INA §241(a)(2)

[35] Former INA §241(a)(3).

[36] Former INA §241(a)(4).

[37] IIRAIRA §309(f)(1)(A), *amended by* NACARA §203(b); 8 CFR §240.66(c).

[38] INA §§212(a)(2)(A)(i) and 237(a)(2)(A).

[39] INA §212(a)(2)(B).

[40] INA §212(a)(2)(C).

[41] INA §§212(a)(2)(A)(i)(I) and 237(a)(2)(B)(i).

[42] INA §237(a)(2)(B)(ii).

[43] INA §212(a)(2)(D).

[44] INA §237(a)(2)(A)(iii). Persons who have been convicted of an aggravated felony are completely ineligible for relief under NACARA. IIRAIRA §309(c)(i), *amended by* NACARA §203(a)(1).

[45] INA §237(a)(2)(C).

[46] INA §237(a)(2)(E)(i).

[47] INA §237(a)(2)(E)(ii).

[48] INA §237(a)(3).

[49] INA §§212(a)(3) and 237(a)(4).

[50] *Matter of Ching*, 12 I&N Dec. 710 (BIA 1968). *See also Matter of Fortiz-Zelaya*, Int. Dec. 3340 (BIA 1998) (finding that an alien must be charged with, and found, deportable as an aggravated felon to be barred from §212(c) relief).

process. First, the applicant establishes that he or she is not statutorily precluded from establishing good moral character.[51] Criminal convictions are the biggest concern in this area. Second, the asylum officer or immigration judge will determine in the exercise of his or her discretion whether the NACARA applicant is a person of good moral character.[52] Problems with taxes during the last seven years have emerged as the single biggest issue in terms of good moral character determinations. For example, Pedro has paid taxes for the last five years. Before that, he did not pay taxes when he was working for himself as a gardener. We recommended that Pedro, with the assistance of counsel, either demonstrate that he earned so little during those years that he was not required to file an income tax return, or file amended returns. However, even if Pedro does neither of these things, the asylum officer must weigh this against positive equities in making his or her discretionary determination. It is important to note that if an asylum officer intends to make a discretionary finding of a lack of good moral character, the case must first be reviewed by USCIS. USCIS has clarified that mistakes in filing taxes do not constitute evidence of lack of good moral character per se. Rather, it is critical to examine the intent of the applicant at the time he or she made a mistake in the submission of his or her income tax returns.

Other Bars Not Listed in the NACARA Statute

Section 240.65 of the rule would disqualify NACARA suspension applicants if they are "subject to any bars to eligibility in former §242B(e) of the Act," or "any other provision of law." Thus, for example, former §242B(e) contains four bars to relief that apply to aliens who: (1) failed to appear for their deportation hearings and were ordered deported in absentia; (2) failed to depart the United States within an authorized period for voluntary departure; (3) failed to appear for deportation; or (4) failed to appear for an asylum hearing. Where applicable, these bars preclude aliens from most forms of discretionary relief, including suspension of deportation, for a five-year period. Section 240.66 of the rule similarly applies the parallel bars of INA §§240(b)(7), 240B(d), and 240A(c) to applicants for special rule cancellation.

Many practitioners disagree with the rule's application of these bars to NACARA because the statute expressly indicates Congress's intent to permit all persons other than aggravated felons to apply for suspension or cancellation if otherwise eligible, notwithstanding bars to eligibility for applicants other than those defined by NACARA.[53] Those who are subject to the bars are in large part NACARA dependents, whose deportation proceedings occurred within the last five years, whereas the deportation proceedings and overstays of voluntary departure of most NACARA principals occurred long enough ago to shield them from these bars.

In some cases, the practitioner may not have sufficient information to know for certain whether the client is eligible for NACARA suspension or special rule cancellation. It is not essential to make that determination in those cases where it does not matter which of these two NACARA remedies is appropriate.

Step Three: Application Procedures for NACARA

Introduction

The procedures for NACARA suspension/cancellation rules differ depending for the most part on whether an eligible individual has an application for asylum pending before legacy INS/USCIS.

Traditionally, only immigration judges grant suspension. Under NACARA, legacy INS/USCIS asylum officers will adjudicate the initial suspension applications for the majority of NACARA beneficiaries. Approximately 240,000 *ABC*-registered class members had asylum applications pending with legacy INS/USCIS.

Almost all *NACARA principal beneficiaries* who currently have asylum applications pending with legacy INS/USCIS will be able to apply for suspension with the asylum office. Asylum officers have been authorized by the Attorney General to consider certain applications for suspension under

---

[51] INA §101(f).

[52] See INA §101(f) for what constitutes establishing good moral character.

[53] "Notwith*standing any limitation imposed by law* on motions to reopen removal or deportation proceedings (except limitations premised on an alien's conviction of an aggravated felony. . .) any alien who has become eligible for cancellation of removal or suspension of deportation as a result of the amendments made by §203 of the Nicaraguan Adjustment and Central American Relief Act may file one motion to reopen removal or deportation proceedings to apply for cancellation of removal or suspension of deportation." IIRAIRA §309(g), *enacted by* §203(c) of NACARA (emphasis added).

NACARA.[54] This includes all persons who submitted an *ABC* asylum application, which is still pending at the asylum office as well as most others who have pending affirmative asylum applications.[55] The only NACARA-eligible persons with pending asylum applications at the asylum office who may not apply for suspension from legacy INS/USCIS are those who registered for *ABC* benefits but then filed an affirmative asylum application *after* the *ABC* deadline.[56]

An individual with a pending *ABC* application who has been placed in deportation or removal proceedings still may apply to legacy INS/USCIS but only if an immigration judge or the Board of Immigration Appeals (BIA) has administratively closed the case to permit the person to apply for NACARA or *ABC* asylum.[57]

The group of NACARA-eligible persons who *are not entitled to an asylum office* adjudication but may present their suspension case to an *immigration judge* includes people who did not submit an asylum application but are eligible for NACARA because they are either: (1) persons who had registered for TPS; (2) persons who registered for *ABC* benefits but did not submit timely asylum applications; or (3) persons who initially filed for asylum with legacy INS/USCIS or EOIR but their cases are not now pending at the asylum offices.[58] For example, if a person initially applied for asylum with legacy INS/USCIS, but his or her asylum application is or was pending with EOIR, and he or she did not file an *ABC* asylum application with an asylum office, his or her NACARA suspension application may be adjudicated only by EOIR.

Under the rule, an exception will be made for NACARA-eligible *dependents* where the (parent or spouse) principal is eligible for adjudication of his or her suspension application at the asylum office or whose NACARA suspension case has been granted by the asylum office.[59] Returning to a previous ex-

ample, if Pedro, who had previously filed a timely *ABC* asylum application, is granted NACARA suspension by the immigration judge, then his wife, Maria, and daughter, Deborah, both NACARA *dependents* will have to get into removal proceedings in order to file an I-881 (NACARA) because Pedro's I-881 was *not granted by the asylum office*. A better strategy would be for Pedro to seek administrative closure of his deportation case so that the entire family could file their I-881s at the Asylum Office. Dependents who have been placed in proceedings will be able to have their EOIR cases administratively closed and joined with the principal's NACARA case at the asylum office.[60]

Application Process to the Asylum Office

The regulation's description of the procedure for NACARA applications submitted to the asylum office is similar in many respects to the procedure for affirmative asylum applications.[61] The applicant files the I-881 application with the appropriate service center. After the application is filed, the applicant must comply with fingerprinting requirements.[62] After USCIS has received a "definitive response" from the FBI that the background check has been completed, USCIS will send the applicant a notice of the date, time, and place of a scheduled interview.[63] If the applicant decides to pursue his or her asylum application as well as the application for suspension or cancellation, the asylum officer will elicit information relating to eligibility for both forms of relief.[64] A different asylum officer will adjudicate the asylum application than the officer who does the NACARA interview in order to comply with the *ABC* settlement. USCIS recommends that the applicant bring a copy of the application and the originals of any supporting documents to the interview. At the interview, the applicant may be represented by an attorney or other representative, in which case the representative must submit a Form G-28, Notice of Entry of Appearance.[65]

---

[54] 8 CFR §240.62(a).

[55] *Id.*

[56] Legacy INS/USCIS has permitted a very small number of registered *ABC* class members who did not file for asylum on time to submit an application now where legacy INS/USCIS determines that it failed to send those persons the "Notice 5" which was required by the settlement.

[57] 8 CFR §240.62(b)(1).

[58] 8 CFR §240.62(b).

[59] 8 CFR §240.62(a)(4).

---

[60] 8 CFR §240.62(b)(2)(iii).

[61] *See also* "INS, EOIR Issue Proposed Rule for Second Group of NACARA Beneficiaries," *reprinted in* 75 *Interpreter Releases* 81649 (Dec. 7, 1998).

[62] 8 CFR §240.67(a).

[63] *Id.*

[64] 8 CFR §240.67(b)(1).

[65] 8 CFR §240.67(b)(2).

An applicant who is not fluent in English must bring an interpreter to the interview.[66] The applicant's attorney or representative may not serve as interpreter, nor may any witness in the case. Applicants who have asylum applications pending with USCIS cannot use employees of their country of nationality as interpreters. USCIS considers that failure to bring a competent interpreter to the interview, without good cause, may be considered a failure to appear for the interview, which may result in dismissal of the application or referral to immigration court.

The proposed rule required applicants who failed to appear for fingerprinting or interviews to show good cause in order to reschedule. The interim rule recognizes that this provision conflicts with the treatment of rescheduling of interviews in the *ABC* settlement agreement. Accordingly, the interim rule allows applicants to reschedule their interviews if they have a reasonable excuse. The request to reschedule should be submitted in writing before the interview date, or immediately thereafter if the reason for missing the interview could not be foreseen. Under the interim rule, applicants who fail to appear for fingerprint appointments must show a reasonable excuse in the same manner as those who fail to appear for NACARA interviews. USCIS recognizes that if the notice of fingerprinting or interview was not mailed to a current address that the applicant provided to USCIS, this constitutes a reasonable excuse.

Practitioners should advise clients to create a record that they attempted to inform USCIS of changes of address and to otherwise comply with application requirements.[67]

The Decision

The applicant is required to return in person to the asylum office to receive the decision unless the asylum officer renders a decision on the day of the interview.[68] If the applicant is not fluent in English, he or she must bring an interpreter to this appointment. In practice, asylum officers have been approving most cases at the time of the interview.

Legacy INS/USCIS has determined that before an applicant may be granted suspension of deportation or cancellation of removal, the applicant must be found to be deportable (or, in removal cases, deportable or inadmissible). The Supplementary Information to the

rule states that "since asylum officers are not authorized to make determinations regarding inadmissibility or deportability in most contexts," applicants will be required to concede inadmissibility or deportability before USCIS can grant them relief. Accordingly, the rule provides that if USCIS has made a preliminary determination to grant suspension or cancellation, the applicant will be notified in writing of that decision and asked to sign an admission of deportability or inadmissibility.[69] If the applicant refuses to concede deportability or inadmissibility, the case will be referred to immigration court.[70]

The asylum officer is to refer the case to immigration court if he or she determines that the applicant is not "clearly eligible" for suspension or cancellation.[71] Further, if the asylum officer refers the case to immigration court, he or she must provide to the applicant written notification of the reasons for the decision.[72] If USCIS grants suspension or cancellation and adjusts the applicant to permanent residence, USCIS may notify the applicant that it intends to dismiss the asylum application without prejudice unless the applicant notifies the agency in writing within 30 days of the notice that he or she would like to pursue that application.[73]

If the asylum officer determines that an applicant is eligible for both suspension or cancellation and asylum, USCIS will grant the suspension or cancellation application and adjust the applicant to permanent residence. USCIS will also grant the applicant asylum, an action that allows the applicant to immediately apply to bring immediate family members to the United States. If the asylum officer determines that the applicant is eligible for asylum but not suspension or cancellation, USCIS will grant asylum and dismiss the suspension or cancellation application without prejudice.[74] The rule provides that if the asylum officer determines that an *ABC* class member is not eligible for suspension, cancellation, or asylum, USCIS will place the applicant in removal or deportation proceedings or move to re-calendar or resume any proceedings that previously were administratively closed.[75] We believe this rule also applies

---

[66] 8 CFR §240.67(b)(3).

[67] 8 CFR §240.68.

[68] 8 CFR §240.70(a).

[69] 8 CFR §240.70(b); 8 CFR §240.70(c).

[70] 8 CFR §240.70(d)(3).

[71] 8 CFR §240.70(d)(1).

[72] *Id.*

[73] 8 CFR §208.14(f).

[74] 8 CFR §240.70(e).

[75] 8 CFR §240.70(f)(2).

to other NACARA applicants where the asylum officer determines that they are not eligible for these forms of relief.

Report on Asylum Office Adjudications, Which Began in the Fall of 1999

USCIS statistics confirm an asylum office approval rate of 95.23 percent as of December 31, 2003. USCIS (including legacy INS) has granted 83,340 applications as of December 31, 2003. USCIS expects to complete NACARA interviews of pending cases by 2006. Persons in deportation or removal proceedings continue to be able to apply for NACARA suspension/cancellation with EOIR, or in many situations, to administratively close their EOIR cases in order to file with the asylum office.

Fees

The fee is $275 for a single individual applying with USCIS, and family cap of $550 for a family applying all at the same time with USCIS. The fee for applying with immigration court is $155.[76] Individuals who have already filed a suspension application and paid the fee to the immigration court, and who have their cases closed to pursue an application with legacy INS/USCIS, still must pay the USCIS fee. Each applicant 14 years of age or older will also have to be fingerprinted, even if he or she previously submitted fingerprints with an asylum application— the current fee for fingerprinting is $70.

Practice Tip on Fees: In some cases, but not many, practitioners should advise family members to apply for NACARA separately even though they will pay more in fees than if they took advantage of the family cap. For example, Salvador is applying for NACARA cancellation even though his case has some problems. The attorney advises Salvador that his three children who qualify as NACARA *dependents* (the oldest of whom is 14), not apply unless Salvador's case is granted even though this will cost the family an additional $550 in fees. If they apply at the same time (to take advantage of the family fee cap) and Salvador's case is denied, the children will also be placed in removal proceedings.

Motions to Reopen

If an applicant had a final order of deportation, or removal or voluntary departure and has become eligible for suspension as a result of NACARA, he or she was entitled to file a special NACARA motion to reopen by September 11, 1998.[77] The Department of Justice issued a final rule, which required the submission of supplementary material (including the suspension application) within 150 days of the effective date of the interim rule, which was June 21, 1999. Therefore, the NACARA applications in these cases must have been submitted by about November 17, 1999.

An applicant is not required to file a motion to reopen, however, if he or she was in deportation proceedings before an IJ or the BIA, and there has been no final order of deportation (or voluntary departure) in the case. For example, many cases were administratively closed (usually those of TPS applicants or those pursuant to the *ABC* settlement).

Persons with final orders who missed these deadlines must get the local ICE district counsel to agree to file a joint motion to reopen. Legacy INS General Counsel Paul Virtue's memorandum of February 8, 1999 instructed trial attorneys that "[I]n assessing whether to join in a motion to reopen, attorneys should bear in mind the ameliorative purposes of NACARA and should seek to ensure that those who appear to be eligible for relief have an opportunity to have their claim adjudicated on the merits."[78] Unfortunately, a number of ICE district counsel offices have not complied with either the letter or spirit of this very reasonable policy memorandum.

Obtaining Work Authorization

Most Central Americans who are eligible for suspension under NACARA may already have work authorization as *ABC* or asylum applicants. For those who do not, the regulation provides that applicants for NACARA are eligible to apply for and be granted employment authorization. They may apply for work authorization at the time they file a suspension or cancellation application with USCIS or EOIR.[79]

---

[76] *See* 69 Fed. Reg. 20527 (Apr. 15, 2004), "USCIS Fee Increases to Take Effect April 30," *published on* AILA InfoNet at Doc. No. 04041463 (*posted* Apr. 14, 2004); "Chart of New USCIS Fees (Amended 4/22/04)," *published on* AILA InfoNet at Doc. No. 04041664 (*posted* Apr. 16, 2004).

[77] IIRAIRA §309(g), *amended by* NACARA §203(c).

[78] Memorandum from Paul W. Virtue, legacy INS General Counsel (Feb. 8, 1999), *reproduced in Winning NACARA Suspension Cases* (ILRC), available at *www.ilrc.org/pubdesc.html#winnacara*, Appendix 8.B, second paragraph.

[79] 8 CFR §274a.12(c)(10), 1274a.12(c)(10).

*The Hardship Requirement
and the Rebuttable Presumption*

The DOJ established a rebuttable presumption of extreme hardship for *ABC* class members in response to over 400 comments to the proposed rule. The interim rule retains the requirement of a case-by-case determination of extreme hardship without the presumption for other NACARA-eligible persons. We suggest the following three-part approach to evaluating your client's hardship claim.

Rebuttable Presumption

First, in Step One, you will have already determined whether the rebuttable presumption applies in your client's case. The presumption applies to *all* NACARA-eligible principals from El Salvador and Guatemala. They "shall be presumed to have established that deportation or removal from the United States would result in extreme hardship to the applicant" or to his or her U.S. citizen or lawful permanent resident (LPR) spouse, parent or child.[80]

Second, if your client will have the benefit of the hardship presumption, then you must decide whether there is any risk that this is one of the few cases in which the presumption might be rebutted where "the evidence in the record establishes that it is more likely than not that neither the applicant nor a qualified relative would suffer extreme hardship."[81] Legacy INS/ICE has the burden of proof to rebut the presumption.[82] If the asylum officer determines that the presumption is rebutted, the applicant "will again be considered to have a presumption of extreme hardship before the Immigration Court."[83] Not one case has resulted in rebuttal at the presumption by the asylum office as of February 1, 2002.

The regulation states that in making a determination on whether the presumption is rebutted, "the adjudicator shall consider relevant factors, including those listed in 8 CFR §240.58," which are discussed below. Further, in seeking to overcome the hardship presumption, legacy INS/ICE has the burden of proving that it is more likely than not that neither the applicant nor a qualifying relative would suffer extreme hardship.[84]

The Supplementary Information describes in more detail the limited circumstances in which the presumption might be rebutted. After describing on pg. 27865–66 the shared characteristics of the *ABC* class that serve as strong predictors of the likelihood of extreme hardship (such as length of stay in the United States, especially with employment authorization and legal status, and having fled "circumstances of civil war and political violence in their homelands"), the Supplementary Information states on pg. 27866 (third column, last paragraph):

The lack of one or more factors will not lead to a conclusion that the presumption has been overcome. Instead, adjudicators will evaluate an application on the basis of whether, given the presumption, the application contains evidence of factors associated with extreme hardship (as set forth in §240.58). *Generally, the presumption will be overcome only under two circumstances.* First, the presumption might be overcome in those cases where there is no evidence of factors associated with extreme hardship (for example, an applicant who has no family in the United States, no work history, and no ties to the community). Second, evidence contained in the record could significantly undermine the basic assumptions on which the presumption is based. For example, if an individual has acquired significant resources or property in his or her home country, the individual and his or her qualified family members may be able to return without experiencing extreme hardship, in the absence of other hardship factors in the case (such as a serious medical treatment for which there is no treatment in the home country) (emphasis added).

The Supplementary Information also provides useful information about the application process in these cases. Applicants for whom hardship is presumed are required to answer a series of "yes or no" questions on the I-881 application form regarding extreme hardship. They will not initially be required, however, to attach documentary evidence to support his or her hardship claim. Applicants should provide narrative explanation of hardship.[85]

Revisiting an earlier example, Pedro is presumed to meet the hardship requirement because he qualifies as a NACARA principal—in his case, by having registered for TPS. He has worked in the United

---

[80] 8 CFR §240.64(d)(1).

[81] 8 CFR §240.64(d)(2).

[82] 8 CFR §240.64(d)(3).

[83] 8 CFR §240.64(d)(4).

[84] 8 CFR §240.64(d)(3).

---

[85] *See* Chapter 7 of the *Winning NACARA Suspension Cases* manual.

States for over 10 years and lives with his wife Maria, and daughter Deborah, age 14, both of whom entered the United States unlawfully after 1991. Pedro filed a timely *ABC* asylum application in 1995, in which his wife and daughter were included. The presumption of hardship should not be rebutted in his case because there is evidence of at least one hardship factor in his case—a work history. His family in the United States—even if without legal status—should also count as a hardship factor. In addition, he may have community ties, such as the shared experience of sending money home to El Salvador and having fled civil war or repression, but these additional factors should not be necessary according to the supplementary information because he has demonstrated *one* hardship factor. Assuming there are no other difficult issues in the case, Pedro and his attorney decide to begin collecting documents and information, so that Pedro can file for NACARA.

No Rebuttable Presumption

The third part of the approach is only necessary for those NACARA-eligible persons who do not benefit from the rebuttable presumption. These persons have the burden of demonstrating that they meet the extreme hardship requirement. They are either NACARA dependents or former Soviet bloc nationals. Returning to the prior example, Pedro's wife Maria, and daughter Deborah, are eligible for NACARA as dependents but are not eligible for the hardship presumption. Therefore, the practitioner must evaluate the strength of their hardship claims based on factors noted in the interim regulation (as well as case law and sometimes local practice).

It is useful to divide the factors into four categories. First, the rule identifies factors that may be relevant in evaluating whether extreme hardship to the applicant or qualified relative would result from deportation or removal. The Supplementary Information at pg. 27866 notes that the "predictive characteristics" which are often present in cases of *ABC* class members may be present in other cases, stating, "Accordingly, the rule will provide that evidence of an extended stay in the United States without fear of deportation and with the benefit of work authorization shall be considered relevant to the determination of whether deportation will result in extreme hardship." These characteristics are found in the regulation's list of hardship factors at (5) and (13) as reproduced below.

Second, there are factors which are also often present in the cases of *ABC* class members but were not specifically discussed in the Supplementary Information. These include (7), (9), (10), and (12). Third, other *positive* factors include (1), (2), (3), (6), and (8). Fourth, there are two *negative* hardship factors, which are (11) and (14). It should be noted that family ties in an applicant's home country (11) may be considered a negative factor in and of itself, but the psychological impact resulting from the inability to continue to provide financial support for those close family members is a very important positive hardship factor (9).

The hardship factors listed in the regulation include:[86]

(1) The age of the alien, both at the time of entry to the United States and at the time of applying for suspension;

(2) The age, number, and immigration status of the applicant's children and their ability to speak the native language and adjust to life in another country;

(3) The health condition of the alien or the alien's child, spouse, or parent, and the availability of any required medical treatment in the country to which the alien would be returned;

(4) The alien's ability to obtain employment in the country to which the alien would be returned;

(5) The length of residence in the United States;

(6) The existence of other family members who will be legally residing in the United States [this factor will apply in *all* cases of NACARA dependents];

(7) The financial impact of the alien's departure;

(8) The impact of a disruption of educational opportunities;

(9) The psychological impact of the alien's deportation or removal;

(10) The current political and economic conditions in the country to which the alien would be returned;

(11) Family and other ties to the country to which the alien would be returned;

---

[86] 8 CFR §1240.58(b). The 14 factors are listed in the same order and with the same enumeration here as they are in the rule.

(12) Contributions to and ties to a community in the United States, including the degree of integration into society;

(13) Immigration history, including authorized residence in the United States; and

(14) The availability of other means of adjusting to permanent resident status.

The rule also includes a number of other factors that may apply in addition to, or instead of the above factors, for cases where the applicant seeks suspension or cancellation as an abused spouse, child, parent of an abused child, or child of an abused parent. These provisions relate to suspension or cancellation applicants who filed under the Violence Against Women Act (VAWA),[87] for individuals who were battered or subjected to extreme cruelty by a U.S. citizen or permanent resident spouse or parent. Legacy INS/USCIS agreed to include in the interim rule the same hardship factors for VAWA suspension and cancellation cases that the agency has accepted in determining the existence of "extreme hardship" in VAWA self-petition adjustment cases.

Returning to our example, the attorney for Maria and Deborah (wife and daughter of Pedro) analyzes their hardship claims. As with *all* NACARA dependents at the time of their interviews, both will have a LPR parent or spouse (Pedro) in the United States because that is a requirement for their NACARA eligibility (6). In this case, the hardship to Pedro, who is now an LPR, if his wife or daughter is sent to El Salvador instantly becomes an extremely compelling hardship argument. The practitioner now examines the factors referred to in the rule's discussion of the rebuttable presumption. Maria obtained employment authorization in 1996 as a derivative of Pedro's *ABC* asylum application, and therefore, has "evidence of an extended stay in the United States without fear of deportation and with the benefit of work authorization" which the Supplementary Information specifically mentions as relevant to non-presumption cases. She would face an inability to obtain full employment in El Salvador (4). The practitioner also determines that both possess the following factors from the second group, which are often also present in *ABC* cases: (7) financial impact of their departure to El Salvador; (9) psychological impact of their forced removal, *including the psycho-*

logical impact on Maria if she is no longer able to send money to help support her relatives; (10) the extremely difficult economic (and social) conditions in El Salvador presently; and (12) integration and ties in the United States, including participation in church, school, friends, and employment. The practitioner then looks at the applicability of the other factors, deciding that the fact that Deborah entered the United States at age six (1), her inability to adapt to life in El Salvador (2), and the disruption to her education since she is now in high school here (8), are particularly relevant.

The fact that their hardship claims becomes much stronger once Pedro wins his case make it highly probable that they will be able to establish the requisite extreme hardship.

**Step Four: Case Evaluation—
Preparing to File for NACARA Now?**

Practitioners should be evaluating all their potential NACARA suspension cases in order to advise clients on whether it is preferable to file now or to wait to see how applicants in similar situations fare. In most cases, it is in the interest of the clients with the rebuttable presumption to file now. In addition, the practitioner should synthesize his or her analysis from the prior three steps outlined in this article to complete the case evaluation.

Returning again to a previous example, the practitioner determines that his or her client, Pedro, is *NACARA-eligible* because he registered for TPS and therefore *ABC*, and he will be accorded the rebuttable hardship presumption. In step two, the practitioner determines that Pedro may apply for *cancellation* rather than suspension because deportation, exclusion, or removal proceedings have never been commenced against him. In step three, the practitioner determines that Pedro will be permitted to first apply for NACARA with the asylum office because he filed a timely *ABC* application which is still pending at that office. Therefore, if the asylum office does not grant Pedro's application, he will be able to apply again before EOIR.

In step four, the entire analysis comes together to determine whether Pedro should prepare to file for NACARA as soon as possible or whether he should wait. Per discussion of the first two steps in the analysis, there are no eligibility problems for Pedro. Analyzing the strength of his extreme hardship claim in the previous section, Pedro should easily meet the hardship requirement because the rebuttable presumption applies to his case, and there is no

---

[87] Violence Against Women Act of 1994, Pub. L. No. 103-322, 108 Stat. 1902–1955 (codified at 8 USC §§1151, 1154, 1186a note, 1254, 2245) (VAWA).

evidence to rebut it. Therefore, Pedro should begin preparation of his NACARA cancellation application now. There is one circumstance in which Pedro or someone in his situation may decide it is better not to apply for NACARA now—for example, if his wife has been here less than seven years and has filed a derivative asylum application. If Pedro's NACARA application is granted, and he does not pursue asylum, USCIS will end his wife's asylum application, as well as her employment authorization. In addition, the asylum office would have discretion to issue a Notice to Appear to the wife.

Evaluating Cases: Dividing Them Into Three Groups

Prospective NACARA cases may be evaluated by classifying them into one of three groups. The first two categories essentially comprise a rating system based on the likelihood that a client will win NACARA suspension. Most clients who will be afforded the rebuttable presumption of hardship should be placed in Group One. Some other cases, even if not particularly strong, will also be in the first group if there is an urgent need to file the application soon—especially those persons with children who may "age out." The first group of cases are those in which you advise your client to file for NACARA now.

There will be a second group of cases that practitioners are not as certain will prevail. The practitioner will revisit these cases once there is a track record of NACARA suspension adjudications by the local asylum office and the immigration court. Clients who will not be afforded the rebuttable presumption because they are not *ABC* class members and whose hardship cases are not strong will be in this category. There will be other cases in which there may be difficult issues of good moral character, especially involving taxes and criminal convictions, or continuous physical presence. Practitioners should keep in mind these are not static categories. For example, some clients who do not benefit from the presumption and have apparently mediocre hardship cases will bring in letters from schools, churches, employers, etc. which will strengthen their cases.

Practitioners must keep tabs on all NACARA-eligible clients, including those with weaker cases for whom no NACARA applications will be filed in the near future. There is no deadline for suspension/cancellation applications pursuant to §203 of NACARA to determine when it is appropriate to file the I-881 application. However, once a particular asylum office is keeping up with current affirmative applications for NACARA along with their asylum workload, it will

begin adjudicating *ABC* asylum cases again. A practitioner in almost all cases should avoid his or her client being called for a *ABC* asylum interview *before* the practitioner has filed the NACARA suspension or cancellation application. To illustrate this, let's assume that Carlos Cuidadoso has decided based on his attorney's advice not to file for NACARA cancellation at the beginning of the program. The practitioner keeps tabs on progress of adjudications at the asylum office, and in 2002 becomes aware that the local office is beginning to adjudicate *ABC* cases again. The practitioner assists Carlos in submitting his NACARA cancellation application so that it is on file with the asylum office before Carlos is called for his *ABC* interview there.

The third group consists of a small number of cases in which there is a *legal issue as to eligibility* for NACARA that has not yet been resolved by the DOJ or the federal courts.

Reinstatement of Removal Is No Longer a Bar to NACARA Eligibility

Persons who are subject to reinstatement of removal are no longer in this third group. For example, what if a client was deported in 1985, and returned unlawfully three months later? The "LIFE Act Amendments,"[88] enacted in December 2001, states that a person who is otherwise eligible for NACARA suspension or special rule cancellation "shall not be barred from applying for such relief by operation of section 241(a)(5)" of the INA.[89] Prior to this amendment, legacy INS/USCIS took the position that this individual was subject to reinstatement of removal pursuant to INA §241(a)(5) because he or she had returned to the United States unlawfully after a deportation (or removal) order, and that the reinstatement of his or her prior deportation order makes him or her ineligible for NACARA—as well as any other relief under the INA except for withholding of removal. The client's attorney correctly concluded that it was too risky to submit an application at that time. Based on the change in the law, the attorney now correctly decides to submit the I-881 application. A legacy INS memo by Joseph E. Langlois, Director of the Asylum Division, dated February 22, 2001, instructs Service/USCIS officers that they may now process NACARA (I-881) applications.[90]

---

[88] Pub. L. No. 106-554, 114 Stat. 2763.

[89] New section 309(h) of IIRAIRA, *added by* section 1505 of the LIFE Act Amendments.

[90] See *Interpreter Releases* (Mar. 5, 2001), beginning on page 444 for a discussion of this and another INS memo on LIFE's elimination of reinstatement of removal as a bar to NACARA.

continued

ADDITIONAL PRACTICE CONSIDERATIONS FOR NACARA SUSPENSION

There are a number of additional issues relating to NACARA cases that practitioners should be aware of.

First, practitioners should take initial steps to obtain documentation for *all* NACARA suspension cases, including ones that they will not be filing now. Practitioners should submit a FOIA request for every client for whom he or she does not have a complete legacy INS/USCIS and EOIR file. We also recommend submitting fingerprints with the fee of $18 directly to the FBI, Identification Division, Washington, D.C. 20537-9700, requesting a copy of your client's record. Practitioners or their clients should also submit requests to the Internal Revenue Service (IRS) for IRS computer printouts of the person's tax records, as is permitted by the I-881. Practitioners should also advise clients to begin obtaining letters and other evidence to demonstrate their eligibility for NACARA suspension, especially the continuous presence requirement and where there is no rebuttable presumption, the extreme hardship requirement. We recommend that practitioners provide clients with letters to give to teachers, priest and ministers, employers, and others that explain the need for letters.

It is always a good idea to request criminal background checks early in order to be informed and help the client consider all options. If the client has a conviction that may block NACARA eligibility or make the person deportable, practitioners should consider the possibility of eliminating the conviction through postconviction relief. Postconviction relief is an order issued by the criminal court system where the person was convicted, ruling that the conviction no longer exists for certain purposes. In immigration proceedings, only certain types of postconviction relief will work on certain convictions. At least in immigration cases within the Ninth Circuit, if the person has been convicted in any state of only one offense of simple possession of a controlled substance, any state "expungement" or "deferred adjudication" will eliminate the conviction.[91]

For all other types of offenses—for example, second possession of a drug, shoplifting, or possession of a firearm—a simple expungement will not work. The conviction must be vacated for cause.[92] Vacating a conviction for cause is an expensive and difficult process that requires an attorney, but many people win these cases. Even if you are not an attorney specializing in postconviction relief, you can help the client gain valuable time by helping him or her to gather all court records pertaining to the conviction, so that a postconviction relief specialist can review the case to see if there is hope of eliminating the conviction.

Third, practitioners should identify cases that involve children who will be turning 21 years of age in the next few years. Anyone with children who are in the United States, who are not LPRs, and who are 17 years of age or older will need to ensure that they do not "age out." This point is illustrated below.

Fourth, practitioners should make a determination as to whether their clients should pursue asylum even if they are granted NACARA suspension. This point is illustrated below.

Fifth, we recommend that practitioners preparing NACARA cases use one of the computer forms programs. In addition to being more efficient now, this will also permit the practitioners to create I-130 visa petitions for applicable relatives of the successful NACARA client, and prepare his or her citizenship application five years later.

Children Turning 21

Anyone with children who are in United States, are not LPRs, and are 17 years of age or older should see an attorney to be sure that the children will not lose their NACARA eligibility by aging out.

The provisions for eligibility as a NACARA dependent for children, unmarried sons and daughters as well as spouses is contained in §203(a)(1) of NACARA, which amended IIRAIRA §309(c)(5)(C)(i). There are two important facts to determine the NACARA eligibility of the child of a NACARA-eligible parent: (1) the child's age at the time the parent is granted NACARA suspension/cancellation and (2) the date the child (including those over 21) entered the United States. If the child is under 21 at the time of the parent's NACARA grant, it does not matter when he or she entered the United States. If the son or daughter is age 21 or older at the time of the grant, he or she must have entered the

---

For those with the *Winning NACARA Suspension Cases* manual, see Appendix 1.H for a more detailed explanation.

[91] *See Lujan-Armendariz v. INS*, 222 F.3d 728 (9th Cir. 2000) (partially overruling *Matter of Roldan*, 22 I&N Dec. 512 (BIA 1999)). *Roldan* is applied outside of the Ninth Circuit. *Matter of Salazar*, 23 I&N Dec. 223 (BIA 2002).

[92] *See Matter of Pickering*, 23 I&N Dec. 621 (BIA 2002).

United States on or before October 1, 1990. For example, Samuel is granted NACARA relief on November 1, 1999. The ages of his children on that date are: Mario, 15 (entered the United States in 1991); Miguel, 22 (entered the United States in 1989); and Luisa, 23 (entered the United States in 1991). Mario, 15, is eligible for NACARA because even though he entered after October 1, 1990, he is under 21. Miguel is eligible because even though he is over 21, he entered the United States before October 1, 1990. Luisa is not eligible because she was over 21 when legacy INS granted her father's NACARA application, *and* entered the United States after October 1, 1990.

Practitioners should push cases in which the children are approaching 21 years of age (or even 17 or 18) where the child entered the United States after October 1, 1990. The language of the statute limits the benefits of the NACARA suspension/cancellation to dependents (spouses and offspring) who have accumulated seven years of continuous physical presence. However, there is no requirement that the dependent have acquired the seven years at the time the principal NACARA applicant is granted suspension.

To illustrate, consider the example of "Hilda," who is 19 years of age and entered the United States without inspection in January 1991. Her parents are *ABC* asylum applicants. NACARA provides that a child in Hilda's situation can obtain NACARA special rule cancellation if she is under 21 years of age when her parent is granted cancellation. Hilda's attorney therefore advises Hilda's parent to expedite the adjudication of her parent's NACARA cancellation case so that Hilda is still under 21 years of age at the time the IJ grants. Hilda has the option of filing her I-881 at the same time her parents submit their applications because she has more than seven years of continuous physical presence in the United States.

If 19-year-old Hilda had been in the United States since the beginning of 2001, the attorney would still advise the parents to push the NACARA cancellation case, because Hilda must be under 21 years of age when one of her parents is granted cancellation but she *does not have to be eligible for NACARA herself at that time.* The attorney files the parents' I-881 applications when Hilda is still 19. When Hilda turns 20, the attorney first writes the person in charge of NACARA at the local asylum office, pointing out that the parents need their interview before Hilda "ages out." Hilda's parents are granted suspension when Hilda is still 20, and therefore she will be able to apply for NACARA cancel-

lation in 2008 (when she is 26) because she will have acquired seven years of continuous physical presence by that time.

What if Hilda is 22 years of age? Under amended IIRAIRA §309(c)(5)(C)(i)(IV), she is not eligible for NACARA benefits because she entered the United States after October 1, 1990. Her parent upon winning NACARA suspension should consider filing a 2B family visa petition for Hilda, and also joining the campaigns for legalization.

Asylum as well as Suspension?

NACARA applicants will be able to apply for both asylum and suspension. Clients, with the help of their attorneys, need to decide if they wish to obtain *asylum as well as suspension/cancellation.* The Department of Justice is to be commended for clarifying in its regulation that a person who has been granted adjustment pursuant to NACARA suspension/cancellation may also pursue his or her asylum application.[93] In some cases, it may be in the client's interest to be granted asylum as well as adjustment pursuant to suspension/cancellation.

Situations in which asylum should be pursued even if the client is granted suspension/cancellation include the following: (1) the applicant has a spouse or minor child in his or her home country, or in the United States, who could obtain legal status as a derivative asylee (through Form I–730) once the applicant wins asylum; or (2) the applicant needs public benefits to which he or she will be entitled (at least for a period of time) as an asylee but to which he or she is not entitled as an LPR who did not obtain that status as an asylee or refugee. Persons need to inform the asylum office that they wish to pursue their asylum case in this situation within 30 days of the grant of adjustment to lawful permanent residence status,[94] although we recommend notifying the asylum office at the time the client receives his notice of the I-881 interview.

Any client for whom asylum is beneficial should also pursue NACARA suspension/cancellation. The advantage of suspension is that a person will obtain LPR status immediately once suspension is granted. There will be a wait of several years before a person who only is granted asylum becomes a LPR. This is especially important for applicants who want to file

---

[93] 8 CFR §208.14(f), 1208.14(f).

[94] *Id.*

immigrant visa petitions for relatives for whom they are unable to file an I–730 derivative asylee petition (*e.g.*, children who are married or over the age of 21).

Where Dependent Is Part of Asylum Case But Has Not Been Here Seven Years

In some limited circumstances where a person's dependent spouse or child is listed on the asylum application but has not yet been in the United States for seven years, the person might decide to delay filing for NACARA. For example, Juan is eligible for NACARA. His wife, Maria, and daughter Deborah, who is now 10 years old, entered the United States in 2001, and were added to his pending ABC asylum case at that time. Let us assume that Juan's asylum case is weak. Once the asylum office grants Juan's NACARA case, he decides not to pursue his asylum case.

How will this affect his wife and daughter? First, once Juan's asylum application is withdrawn, Maria and Deborah will no longer be entitled to employment authorization as asylum applicants and they do not qualify for NACARA because they have not been in the United States for seven years. Juan, based on advice from counsel, may decide *not* to apply for NACARA now so that his asylum application will remain pending and his wife may continue to have employment authorization.

The practitioner should also determine what is the *local* procedure of her asylum office in this situation in terms of the dependent wife and daughter once the principal's asylum application has been withdrawn. Asylum offices have had discretion in this area. We understand that many offices have a policy of not pursuing the asylum applications of the wife and daughter under these circumstances. On the other hand, if the local asylum office has a policy of scheduling the asylum interview of the wife and daughter, this is likely to result in a referral of the asylum case to EOIR with a Notice of Appear in removal proceedings. Maria and Deborah are not eligible for NACARA because they have not been here for seven years. Assuming that their asylum case is weak, they are likely to be subject to an order of either removal or voluntary departure in removal proceedings.

CONCLUSION

NACARA was a response to concerns that many individuals who have spent many years in the United States would be adversely affected by IIRAIRA's stringent changes. The authors commend the Department of Justice for creating interim regulations, which further the goals of the legislation, especially the rebuttable presumption of extreme hardship requirement.[95]

---

[95] The Immigrant Legal Resource Center (ILRC) sends regular e-mail alerts on NACARA issues. To subscribe to this free service, please go to *www.ilrc.org* and click on "listserves." The ILRC hopes to continue providing these services. To obtain more information or send a donation to help continue this NACARA technical assistance project, please contact: ILRC, 1663 Mission Street, Suite 602, San Francisco, CA 94103.

Appendix 1-A (Part I)

Bars to NACARA Seven-Year
Special Cancellation of Removal

	Grounds of deportation that don't bar NACARA eligibility	Grounds of deportation barring NACARA eligibility	Grounds of inadmissibility barring NACARA
Immigration Violations			
Inadmissible/excludable at entry	§237(a)(1)(A)		
Present in violation of the law	§237(a)(1)(B)		
Violated status	§237(a)(1)(C)		
Termination of conditional residency	§237(a)(1)(D)		
Alien smuggling	§237(a)(1)(E)		
Marriage fraud	§237(a)(1)(G)		
Criminal Offenses			
Crimes involving moral turpitude		§237(a)(2)(A)*	§212(a)(2)(A)(i)(I)* [g]
Aggravated Felony		§237(a)(2)(A)(iii)	
Multiple criminal convictions			212(a)(2)(B)* [g]
High speed flight		§237(a)(2)(A)(iv)*	
Drug trafficker			§212(a)(2)C* [g]
Drug conviction		§237(a)(2)(B)(I)*	§212(a)(2)(A)(i)(II)* [g]
Drug abuser or addict		§237(a)(2)(B)(ii)*	§212(a)(2)(A)(i)(II)*
Firearm convictions		§237(a)(2)(C)*	
Miscellaneous crimes (espionage, Selective Service, sabotage)		§237(a)(2)(D)*	
Domestic violence and violations of protection orders		§237(a)(2)(E)*	
Prostitution or commercialized vice			§212(a)(2)D* [g]
Asserted immunity from prosecution			§212(a)(2)E*
Failure to register as an alien and conviction for falsification of documents		§237(a)(3)*	
Security and related grounds		§237(a)(4)	§212(a)(3)
Within 5 years of entry has become a public charge	§237(a)(5)		
Unlawful voting	§237(a)(6)		

*These grounds do not bar applicants from applying under the ten-year cancellation provision of NACARA.

Also: [g] = ground of inadmissibility is also a statutory preclusion to establishing **good moral character** (GMC) if within last 7 years. The applicant may be statutorily barred or determined not to have the requisite GMC based on other reasons not enumerated in this chart. The GMC bar for drug convictions does not apply to simple possession of 30 grams or less of marijuana.

Notes: Present without being admitted or paroled (previously "entry without inspection") is a ground of inadmissibility—§212(a)(6)(A). It is **not** a bar to NACARA eligibility. Persecution of others, a bar to restriction on removal for persons who have—§241(b)(3)(B)(i), is also a bar to NACARA.

Created by Cristina Fabie and Mark Silverman, ILRC

Appendix 1-A (Part II)

Bars to NACARA Seven-Year Suspension

	Grounds of deportation which don't bar NACARA eligibility**	Grounds of deportation barring NACARA eligibility**
Immigration Violations		
Inadmissible/excludable at entry	§241(a)(1)(A)	
Present in violation of the law	§241(a)(1)(B)	
Violated status	§241(a)(1)(C)	
Termination of conditional residency	§241(a)(1)(D)	
Alien smuggling	§241(a)(1)(E)	
Marriage fraud	§241(a)(1)(G)	
Criminal Offenses		
Crimes involving moral turpitude		§241(a)(2)(A)(i)*
Aggravated felony		§241(a)(2)(A)(iii)
Multiple criminal convictions		§241(a)(2)(A)(ii)*
High speed flight	***	
Drug conviction		§241(a)(2)(B)(i)*
Drug abuser or addict		§241(a)(2)(B)(ii)*
Firearm convictions		§241(a)(2)(C)*
Miscellaneous crimes (espionage, Selective Service, sabotage)		§241(a)(2)(D)
Domestic violence, and violations of protection orders	***	
Failure to register as an alien and conviction for falsification of documents		§241(a)(3)(B)*
Document fraud		§241(a)(3)(C)*
Security and related grounds		§241(a)(4)* [not for (4)(D)]
Within 5 years of entry has become a public charge	§241(a)(5)	

 * These grounds do not bar applicants from applying under the ten-year suspension provision of NACARA.

 ** These section numbers are given as they were prior to the enactment of IIRAIRA; however, they still apply to NACARA suspension of deportation cases.

 *** These grounds were added by IIRAIRA and therefore should not apply to NACARA suspension of deportation cases.

Note: The applicant may fail to meet the Good Moral Character requirement for other reasons not listed on this chart.

Notes: Persecution of others, a bar to restriction on removal for persons who have—§241(b)(3)(B)(i), is also a bar to NACARA special rule cancellation, but it does not appear to be a bar to suspension of deportation.

Created by Mark Silverman and Lisa Klapal, ILRC

APPENDIX 2

We would like to thank Bryan Christian of USCIS's Asylum Division for providing this information in February, 2004. We have not changed Mr. Christian's text, but have reformatted it slightly.

The following is a summary of NACARA 203 statistics from the beginning of the program in 1999 to the end of the last calendar year.

> • From 6/21/1999 to 12/31/2003, U.S. Citizenship and Immigration Services, (USCIS, formerly INS) received 131,688 applications for relief under Section 203 of NACARA.
>
> • We granted 83,340 applications, dismissed 2,676 applications, referred 3,245 cases to the immigration court, and rescinded 13 granted applications.
>
> • The 83,340 granted applications represent 95.23% of total adjudicated applications (87,516).
>
> • As of 12/31/2003, there were 42,427 applications pending.

Given current and projected filing trends and productivity targets, we expect to complete the NACARA program within the next two years.

Note from ILRC: This would mean that NACARA interviews of currently pending applications would be completed by about February of 2006. There will be additional persons applying because NACARA dependents (and some principals for whom continuous physical presence had been broken subsequent to their initial qualifying entry) will become eligible in the future as they acquire the requisite seven years of continuous physical presence.

THE ABCS OF WORKING WITH IMMIGRANT CHILDREN TO OBTAIN SPECIAL IMMIGRANT JUVENILE STATUS FOR THOSE ABUSED, NEGLECTED, OR ABANDONED

*by Anne Chandler, Judy Flanagan, and Kathleen A. Moccio**

Within a legal framework famous for its lack of procedural or substantive safeguards for the interests of children, there is a narrow exception for abused, neglected, or abandoned children, Special Immigrant Juvenile Status (SIJS). In INA §101(a)(27)(J), Congress carved out a special visa that permits certain abused, neglected, or abandoned children to avoid return to their country of origin—not that it is easy to obtain the coveted visa that is often a direct route to legal permanent residency. Congress set out multiple bureaucratic and legal hurdles, including the requirement that the juvenile pass through state court to obtain a "dependency order" from a state judge.[1] Though it is crudely drafted by Congress and laborious to obtain, the special immigrant juvenile visa provides hope for advocates attempting to keep children from returning to violent family households or to a life on the streets. This article attempts to guide the reader through the medley of federal and state institutions and introduce terminology and administrative guidance for when a child seeks permanent legal residency by way of a special immigrant juvenile visa.

BACKGROUND ON DEMOGRAPHICS

Over the last decade, a rising number of children have entered the United States every year without a visa or other valid document. Official U.S. Department of Homeland Security (DHS) numbers from fiscal year 2004 show that 122,122 immigrants under the age 18 were apprehended.[2] This staggering number does not include children apprehended by Detention and Removal officials once they have reached the interior of the United States or children who made it to U.S. soil undetected.

About one-third of the children apprehended by U.S. Customs and Border Patrol (CBP) enter the United States unaccompanied by a family member or legal guardian.[3] Some of these children are attempting to reunite with a family member already inside the United States. Others know no one within the United States. Whether or not they have family ties in the United States, these juveniles are labeled "unaccompanied alien children."[4] Once apprehended, they enter a bureaucratic maze without navigation tools or an attorney or guardian ad litem to help them through.

---

* Anne Chandler is the supervising attorney at the University of Houston Law School Immigration Clinic. Her practice focuses on detained clients with political asylum and related claims. Ms. Chandler served as the immigration attorney for the YMCA International of Houston and as a bilingual teacher (Spanish) in the Alief School District. She is a 1998 cum laude graduate of the University of Houston Law Center where she served on the *Houston Law Review*, received a Distinguished Service Award, won the Joan Glantz Garfinkel Scholarship for civil liberties research, and served as president of the Public Interest Law Organization.

Judy Flanagan is a sole practitioner in Phoenix who has practiced immigration law exclusively since 1998, after stints as a city prosecutor, legal aid attorney, and hearing officer with the Arizona Department of Juvenile Corrections. Ms. Flanagan received her undergraduate degree from the University of California, Berkeley, and her law degree from The John Marshall Law School in Chicago. She loves to contra dance.

Kathleen Moccio is vice chair of AILF's Board of Trustees and a member of AILA's Board of Governors. She has experience in employment, family, and asylum immigration matters. Currently, Ms. Moccio is working to develop support for pro bono work within the field of immigration. Her work includes recruiting volunteers and developing trainings for the National Center for Refugee and Immigrant Children, a co-venture between AILA and the U.S. Committee for Refugees and Immigrants.

[1] Immigration and Nationality Act of 1952, Pub. L. No. 82-414, §101(a)(27)(J), 66 Stat. 163 (codified as amended at 8 USC §§1101 et seq.) (INA); *see also* 8 CFR §204.11.

[2] Department of Health and Human Services, Administration for Children & Families, Office of Refuge Resettlement, Division of Unaccompanied Children's Services (DUCS) (hereinafter ORR/DUCS Fact Sheet).

[3] Department of Homeland Security, Office of Inspector General, "A Review of DHS's Responsibilities for Juvenile Aliens," OIG-05-45 (Sept. 2005) (hereinafter OIG Juvenile Report).

[4] An unaccompanied alien child is a child who: (a) has no lawful immigration status in the United States; (b) has not attained 18 years of age; and (c) with whom: (i) there is no parent or legal guardian in the United States; or (ii) no parent or legal guardian in the United States available to provide care and physical custody. 6 USC §279(g)(2).

When apprehended by CBP and found to be "Other-than-Mexican" (OTM),[5] the unaccompanied alien child is transferred to the Detention and Removal Office (DRO) of U.S. Immigrant and Customs Enforcement (ICE). DRO processes and transports the unaccompanied child to a shelter and other housing option managed by the Division of Unaccompanied Children's Services (DUCS) of the Health and Human Services Office of Refugee Resettlement (ORR).[6] In fiscal year 2005, 6,847 unaccompanied alien children were placed in ORR care.[7] Most of them were males ages 15 through 17, but a surprising 10.5 percent were under the age of 12.[8] Roughly 27 percent were girls.[9]

Once in ORR custody, the vast majority of unaccompanied children appear before an immigration judge (IJ) of the Executive Office for Immigration Review (EOIR).[10] Like their adult counterparts, unaccompanied children in ORR care have a right to an attorney but *at no expense* to the government.[11] Some unaccompanied minors find pro bono counsel through the National Center for Immigration and

Refugee Children after ORR has released them to a qualified and willing sponsor.[12] Others remain in ORR care throughout their removal proceedings because they cannot identify a qualified sponsor or a sponsor they can identify is unwilling to appear.

WORKING WITH ABUSED, NEGLECTED, OR ABANDONED CHILDREN— EXPECT THE UNEXPECTED

Interviewing and preparing children to testify is inherently different from working with adults. Children's perceptions of the world, their attention span, their susceptibility to offering the answer they assume is expected, and their understanding of the legal system heavily influence the information they are likely to give in an interview.[13] Even when the interviewing technique is child-appropriate, the child's developmental stage and the physiological affects of trauma may hinder the child's ability to give detailed, coherent answers to questions. For physiological reasons, including actual changes in their brains and bodies, traumatized children are often incapable of detailing their stories in the way our legal system expects.[14] Other children, though equally traumatized by abuse or neglect, are physiologically able to recount their stories in detail and consistently.[15] The greater the violence, specifically interpersonal violence and violence that cannot be controlled, the more likely it is the children will be unable to recount their stories.[16] The services of a forensic psychologist or psychiatrist may be vital to document why a child is unable or unwilling to process information or detail past facts.

Children in detention are interviewed by many people—from CBP, ICE, and ORR officials and U.S. Marshal Office to social workers and medical personnel. Often the child does not understand the role of the interviewer. When interviewing detained

---

[5] OIG Juvenile Report, *supra* note 3, at 12. CBP officials turn unaccompanied children of Mexican origin around at the border as part of the ICE Secure Border Initiative.

[6] *See* § 462 of the Homeland Security Act of 2002, Pub. L. No. 107-296, 116 Stat. 2135, *published* on AILA InfoNet at Doc. No. 02120240 (*posted* Dec. 2, 2002). DHS and ORR also have joint obligations under the settlement agreement that followed the Supreme Court's decision in *Reno v. Flores*, 507 U.S. 292 (1993). The *Flores* agreement directs that when a child is in the custody of the federal government, the child will be treated with dignity, respect, and special concern for the particular vulnerabilities of children. The agreement favors release to custodians where consistent with public safety, the safety of the juvenile, and the need for the juvenile to appear for immigration proceedings. Juveniles are only released to a responsible adult.

[7] ORR/DUCS Fact Sheet, *supra* note 2.

[8] *Id.*

[9] *Id.*

[10] Soon after the Illegal Immigration Reform and Immigrant Responsibility Act of 1996 (IIRAIRA) (Division C of the Omnibus Appropriations Act of 1996 (H.R. 3610), Pub. L. No. 104-208, 110 Stat. 3009) was implemented, INS issued a memorandum that generally exempts unaccompanied minors from expedited removal. The memorandum instructs federal agents to place unaccompanied minors in normal removal proceedings under INA §240. "Unaccompanied Minors Subject to Expedited Removal," Memorandum from Office of Programs, INS (Aug. 21, 1997). *See* 74 *Interpreter Releases* 1367 (Sept. 8 1997).

[11] INA §240(b)(4).

---

[12] 8 CFR §§236.3, 1236.3 (detention and release of detained juveniles under 18 years of age).

[13] J. Bhabha and W. Young, "Through a Child's Eyes: Protecting the Most Vulnerable Asylum Seekers," 75 *Interpreter Releases* 757 (June 1, 1998).

[14] H. Sadruddin, N. Walter & J. Hidalgo, "Human Trafficking in the United States: Expanding Victim Protection Beyond Prosecution Witnesses," 16 *Stan. L. & Pol'y Rev.* 379, 398–401.

[15] *Id.* at 399.

[16] S. Rachmen, "Foreword," in *Post-Traumatic Stress Disorders: Concepts and Therapy* (Wm. Yule, ed., 1999).

children, attorneys are but one more adult face among many who have inquired about the child's family history and motive for coming to the United States.[17] The child may not want to speak to you. You have the advantage of not wearing a uniform or a badge, but you have the disadvantage that the child may be only willing to share with you a false history offered by a smuggler hired to help the child cross a dangerous border.[18] Encouraging a child to step out of a false history and to trust you is arduous. Considerable guidance for advocates striving to communicate affectively with children can be found in written standards from the United Nations High Commissioner for Refugees and the American Bar Association on interviewing unaccompanied children.[19]

It is obviously important for the child to honestly detail as much personal history as possible. It is equally important that a child who is detained inform you of the information he or she has already given to government officials, including ORR caseworkers and therapists because these records are generally available to the ICE officers who are considering whether to allow the child to proceed with obtaining SIJS.[20]

The notes and reports of ORR caseworkers and therapists are part of the record DHS consults when deciding whether a child's claim of abuse, neglect, or abandonment is credible. A predominant reason why DHS denies children the opportunity to seek SIJS is the child's failure to adequately explain inconsistent or incomplete statements made over time.

GETTING THROUGH STATE COURT

Detained Children First Need Consent From ICE to Proceed with SIJS Relief

In 1997, Congress amended the definition of "special immigrant juvenile" by requiring that the Secretary of DHS (formerly the Attorney General) consent to juvenile court dependency jurisdiction.[21] In the case of detained children, the statute says:

> no juvenile court has jurisdiction to determine the custody status or placement of an alien in the actual or constructive custody of the Attorney General unless the Attorney General specifically consents to such jurisdiction.[22]

The 1997 amendment requiring consent for detained juveniles was passed ostensibly to limit SIJS beneficiaries to those who needed relief from abuse or neglect, rather than to enable SIJS applicants to obtain permanent resident status.[23] Despite the passage of this amendment in 1997, no regulations have been promulgated to implement the consent portion

---

[17] It is important to keep in mind that detained children may have been recently traumatized by U.S. government officials. The Florence Immigration and Refugee Project reports: "Children apprehended and held in temporary facilities across the Southwest by Border Patrol have been severely and deliberately mistreated. These children are being handcuffed, forced to sleep on the floor without blankets or pillows, denied medical treatment, and verbally and physically abused." *Available at www.firrp.org/children.asp* (*last visited* Mar. 18, 2006).

[18] As explained by psychologist Marie Hessle who worked with separated children in Europe, "I have seen many children living with false histories, and if they can tell their real story, in my experience, it is almost always worse than the false one." "A Gap in their Hearts: The Experience of Separated Somali Children," IRIN Web special, UN Office for the Coordination of Humanitarian Affairs (Jan. 2003), *available at www.irinnews.org/webspecials/Somalichildren/Chapter3/c3Intro.asp.*

[19] United Nations High Commissioner for Refugees, "Community Services Guidelines, Working with Unaccompanied Children: A Community-based Approach," 2d ed., revised May 1996; American Bar Association, "Standards for the Custody, Placement and Care; Legal Representation; and Adjudication of Unaccompanied Alien Children in the United States," pp. 16–27.

[20] Detained children must obtain specific consent from ICE to proceed with SIJS relief before proceeding with a state dependency order. Please see the following section "Getting to and Through State Court."

[21] INA §101(a)(27)(J)(iii), *as amended* November 27, 1997, by Pub. L. No. 105-119, §113, 111 Stat. 2440.

[22] *Id.*

[23] *See F.L. v. Tommy Thompson,* 293 F. Supp. 2d 86, 96 (D.D.C. 2003) (noting that the "legislative history of the 1997 amendment to [8 USC] §1101 indicates that the requirement of Attorney General consent was imposed as a precondition to juvenile court jurisdiction in an effort to ensure that SIJ applicants have a special need to remain in the United States and do not use the process simply to gain an immigration benefit. The Conference Report on the Amendment states, 'the language has been modified in order to limit the beneficiaries of this provision to those juveniles for whom it was created, namely abandoned, neglected, or abused children, by requiring the Attorney General to determine that neither the dependency order nor the administrative or judicial determination of the alien's best interest was sought primarily for the purpose of obtaining the status of an alien lawfully admitted for permanent residence, rather than for the purpose of obtaining relief from abuse or neglect.' H.R. Rep. No. 105-405, at 2981 (1997), 1997 WL712946, at 130."; *see also M.B. v.Quarantillo,* 301 F.3d 109, 115–16 (3d Cir. 2002)).

of the statute. The SIJS regulations, approved before the 1997 amendment, do not address criteria for consent.[24] The lack of guidance creates serious complications if you are representing children who may be in "constructive" custody because an incorrect determination of the child's status will result in denial of the SIJS petition.[25] To glean whether consent is required, look to case law, policy memoranda,[26] and public statements of DHS officials.[27]

DHS has issued three interoffice memoranda on SIJS. The latest, the May 27, 2004, Yates Memorandum (Yates memo), states that it consolidates and supersedes all previous guidance issued by legacy Immigration and Naturalization Service (INS).[28] DHS guidance states:

> In the case of juveniles in custody due to their immigration status (either by US Immigration and Customs Enforcement (ICE) or by the Office of Refugee Resettlement (ORR)), the specific consent must be obtained *before* the juvenile may enter juvenile court dependency proceedings; failure to do so will render invalid any order issued as a result of such proceedings.[29]

The Yates memo goes on to state:

> This memorandum addresses only those eligibility issues relating to the actual adjudication of the petition for special immigrant juvenile classification and the application to that of adjustment of status. It does not address eligibility criteria relating to 'specific consent.'

Even though the Yates memo purports to supersede all prior guidance, it specifically declines to discuss the standard for specific consent. Therefore, advocates may be well advised to look to the 1999 Cook Memorandum (Cook memo), which provides a two-part test for specific consent.[30] The Cook memo states that the district director, in consultation with district counsel, should grant specific consent to juvenile court jurisdiction if: (1) it appears that the juvenile would be eligible for SIJS if a dependency order is issued; and (2) in the judgment of the district director, the dependency proceeding would be in the best interest of the juvenile.[31] Several courts have held that the Cook memo gives sufficient guidance for review of agency abuse of discretion under the Administrative Procedures Act (APA).[32]

The Cook memo indicates that requests for consent must be in writing and directed to the district director (of then-INS, now USCIS) with jurisdiction over the juvenile's place of residence. Current practice, however, is for consent requests to be sent to John Pogash, National Juvenile Coordinator, ICE, U.S. DHS, with copies to the local USCIS district director, the local chief counsel of ICE, and the USCIS juvenile coordinator.[33]

---

[24] 8 CFR §204.11.

[25] *See* USCIS Memorandum, William R. Yates, "Memorandum #3—Field Guidance on Special Immigrant Juvenile Status Petitions" (May 27, 2004), *published on* AILA InfoNet at Doc. No. 04062168 (*posted* June 21, 2004) (hereinafter Yates Memorandum). "The adjudicator must be satisfied that the petitioner obtained specific consent from ICE where necessary. If specific consent was necessary but not timely obtained, a juvenile court dependency order is not valid and the petition must be denied."

[26] *Id.*; *see also* INS Memorandum, Thomas E. Cook "Special Immigrant Juveniles—Memorandum #2: Clarification of Interim Field Guidance" (July 9, 1999), *published on* AILA InfoNet at Doc. No. 99100690 (*posted* Oct. 6, 1999) (hereinafter Cook Memorandum).

[27] AILA Teleconference Tape on Special Immigrant Juvenile Status, December 1, 2005 (Chris Nugent, for example, noted in a recent exchange with a colleague on the Center for Constitutional and Human Rights's Special Immigrant Rights listserve that John Pogash was explicit during the AILA call that specific consent is not required when a child has been released from ORR custody).

[28] Yates Memorandum, *supra* note 25.

[29] *Id.* at p. 1.

[30] Cook Memorandum, *supra* note 26; *see also* discussion in Appendix K of S. Kinoshita & K. Brady, *Special Immigrant Juvenile Status For Children Under Juvenile Court Jurisdiction* (2005) (manual available as a free download from the Immigrant Legal Resource Center's website, *www.ilrc.org*).

[31] Cook Memorandum, *supra* note 26, at 2.

[32] *M.B. v. Quarantillo*, 301 F.3d 109, 113 (3d Cir. 2002) (the Cook memo and the SIJS regulation, 8 CFR §204.11, supply "some law to apply," thus allowing judicial review); *A.A.-M v. Alberto Gonzales*, C05-2012C, 2005 WL 3307531 at 2–3; *Zheng v. Pogash*, Civ. Action No. H-06-197, page 4, fn. 4 (S.D. Tex. filed Feb. 23, 2006). *See also Yue Yu v. Brown*, 36 F. Supp. 2d 922 (D.N.M. 1999) (INS has nondiscretionary duty to process special immigrant juvenile applications, though it has discretion in the ultimate decision whether to grant LPR status).

[33] John Pogash's phone number is (202) 732-2913. "Pogash is charged with reviewing and deciding all specific consent requests." *Zheng*, Civ. Action No. H-06-197. Earlier, the D.C. District Court determined that DHS, rather than the Office of Refugee Resettlement (ORR), retains authority to grant consent to juvenile court jurisdiction in SIJS cases.

continued

According to statements at continuing education conferences, ICE's position is that a child is in "constructive custody" if the U.S. government is paying for the child's care.[34] To make this determination, contact ORR and the facility where the child is held to find out about the child's placement. Even when the facts are known, it can still be difficult to determine whether consent is required. For instance, foster care arrangements can be quite complex. What appears to be a state placement may in fact be funded by ORR. Given the lack of clear guidance, practitioners are vulnerable to incorrectly determining that consent is not required. This uncertainty results in practitioners contacting ICE, the very agency that has authority to grant consent and is at the same time moving to deport the child, to offer its opinion on whether consent is required.

MAKING THE CASE FOR CONSENT

In SIJS cases where a dependency order has not yet been ordered, the child is in DHS custody, and DHS consent will be required, typically there will not have been any investigation by a state child welfare agency, and the advocate will need to establish that the child has been abused, neglected, or abandoned. [35] If the abuse, neglect, or abandonment occurred in the United States, obtaining proof generally is fairly straightforward. However, if the abusive conduct occurred in the foreign country, advocates will need to be creative in putting together solid evidence. The challenge is often magnified by the fact that the client may be in danger of aging out, so it is necessary to gather documentation as quickly as possible.

The Yates memo provides a useful checklist of documentation requirements for SIJ petitions, but the checklist really contemplates the filing of the petition after consent has been obtained.[36] That memo does not outline documentation requirements

for establishing abuse, neglect or abandonment, but the Cook memo indicates that "[e]vidence that a dependency order was issued on account of 'abuse, neglect, or abandonment'…is crucial to obtaining the Attorney General's consent to the dependency order."[37] Hence, it is important to incorporate a common-sense set of documents in the initial consent request. It is useful to think of what would have to be done to document an asylum applicant's case.

A starting point is a detailed affidavit from the client to establish what happened. It often takes numerous interviews of the child to establish rapport and gain the child's trust. Painful details about the past may not be revealed immediately, so again, if aging-out is an issue, start interviewing the client immediately. The child's affidavit should contain information about the parents and why it would not be in the child's best interests to return to the home country.

Typically, the client may be interviewed by DHS or an ORR social worker or caseworker, often before he or she meets the advocate. It is advisable to request a copy of the client's file with all client statements, intakes, evaluations, and incident reports. Compare the information gathered from the client with the statements or reports prepared by DHS or ORR or the private agency. If necessary, make a Freedom of Information Act (FOIA) request to DHS or ORR to obtain these records. Given that it is taking more than six months to get a response on an FOIA request, you may need to make arrangements to view DHS or ORR files separately.

If physical abuse is at issue and there are visible injuries or scars or ongoing pain, obtaining a forensic medical exam is advisable. Photographs of any visible injuries or scars can be used to document the case. Hospital or other medical records and copies of prescriptions for medication used for treatment may be useful in establishing abuse.

Psychological abuse can be established with an evaluation by a mental health professional, such as a psychiatrist, psychologist, social worker, or other therapist. If a psychological condition is diagnosed, supplement the record with a copy of the description of the condition from the American Psychiatric Association's Diagnostic and Statistical Manual.[38] Obtain any previous records, such as reports from therapists.

F.L. v. Tommy Thompson, 293 F. Supp. 2d 86 (D.D.C. 2003).

[34] AILA Teleconference Tape from December 1, 2005.

[35] Where the child is not in DHS custody and a dependency order has already been obtained, the state child welfare agency (Child Protective Services) will have already established such proof, *e.g.,* by police or Child Protective Services agency investigation. Most unaccompanied minors in DHS or ORR custody will be recent entrants to the United States, and there will be no existing evidence of harm in the United States.

[36] Yates Memorandum, *supra* note 25.

[37] Cook Memorandum, *supra* note 26, at 3.

[38] American Psychiatric Association, *Diagnostic and Statistical Manual of Psychological Disorders* (rev. 2000).

Working with professionals who have received training on the issues to be addressed in SIJS or other immigration cases will make your job much easier.

If a parent or guardian is deceased, obtain a death certificate. Barring that, you will need affidavits from the client and family members or friends as to the circumstances of the parent's death. Gather any police reports of abuse or any child welfare agency reports.

You must have evidence of the child's age.[39] The SIJS regulation states that "documentary evidence of the alien's age, in the form of a birth certificate, passport, official foreign identity document issued by a foreign government, such as a Cartilla or a Cedula, or other document which in the discretion of the director establishes the beneficiary's age" must be submitted in support of the petition.[40] The document, if not in English, must be translated.

The advocate must establish that it is not in the best interests of the minor child to return to his or her home country.[41] Although the SIJS statute clearly indicates that the juvenile court must make this determination, in consent cases it is wise to include best interest evidence with the request to DHS.[42] In addition to evidence documenting the abuse, abandonment or neglect, the request for consent should be supplemented with information about home country conditions using such documents as State Department Country Reports and Consular Travel Warnings and any articles about the client's home country that discuss health and medical conditions, education, or child welfare statistics there. Provide as much evidence as possible of services available in the United States that are not available or are limited or inaccessible to the client in the home country, such as general health care, physical therapy, special education, psychiatric services, and specialized health care needs (for clients with autism or developmental disabilities, for example). The unavailability or unwillingness of family members in the home country to care for the minor child can be documented with the child's affidavit or perhaps even from family members themselves.

FORCING THE DECISION

Obtaining specific consent can take months. Requests often languish even though the child beneficiary is precariously close to aging out of SIJS eligibility.[43] Aging out may occur at 18, 19, or 21, depending on when a particular state court loses jurisdiction over juveniles.[44] Obtaining DHS consent, then, can become a major battle when a client will soon be aging out. For a detained 17-year-old child in removal proceedings who is SIJS-eligible in Arizona, for example, the advocate must develop the evidence to establish that the child has been abused, abandoned, or neglected; track down a birth certificate and submit this evidence to DHS requesting consent, continuing to follow up on the request; obtain consent or, if consent is not granted, head to federal court for a temporary restraining order and preliminary injunction; file a dependency proceeding in juvenile court; obtain service of process on parents in the dependency action; obtain the juvenile court order after hearing; file the SIJS petition and assure that DHS schedules the child for fingerprinting; attend an interview on the SIJS petition; and then head back to immigration court for an IJ to adjudicate the Adjustment of Status petition—all before the client turns 18.[45]

ICE often denies consent,[46] without interviewing the child, conducting an evidentiary hearing, or setting forth any adverse evidence.[47] Furthermore, the

---

[39] 8 CFR §204.11(d)(1).

[40] Id.

[41] INA §101(a)(27)(J)(i) (administrative or judicial body must determine that it "would not be in the alien's best interest to be returned to the alien's or parent's previous country of nationality or country of last habitual residence").

[42] The Cook Memorandum, supra note 26, indicates that evidence showing that it would not be in the juvenile's best interest to be removed from the United States "is crucial to obtaining the Attorney General's consent to the dependency order."

[43] See section on aging out, infra.

[44] INS (now DHS) regulations limit SIJS eligibility to those children who are under 21 years of age, 8 CFR §204.11(c)(1), and "continue to be dependent upon the juvenile court and eligible for long-term foster care, such declaration, dependency or eligibility not having been vacated, terminated, or otherwise ended." 8 CFR §204.11(c)(4). See also 8 CFR §205.1(3)(iv), automatically revoking SIJ classification upon the child's ceasing to be dependent on state court.

[45] Ariz. Rev. Stat. §8-201(6) (Arizona defines a child or juvenile as an individual under the age of 18 years); Ariz. Rev. Stat. §8-202 (juvenile court jurisdiction over a child is retained until the child becomes 18 years of age).

[46] At a February 13, 2006, preliminary injunction hearing in U.S. District Court, DHS stated that "not many of the requests [for specific consent] are granted." Zheng v. Pogash, Civ. Action No. H-06-197 (S.D. Tex. filed Feb. 23, 2006).

[47] See A.A.-M v. Alberto Gonzales, Case No. C05-2012C, 2005 WL 3307531 (W.D. Wash. Dec. 6, 2005) (DHS denial

continued

minor child has no right to review or rebut adverse witnesses, and DHS often uses evidence not disclosed to the minor or counsel.[48] DHS affords no right to appointed counsel, guardians ad litem, or interpreters in the consent process. SIJS-eligible minors have no right to have consent requests decided by a neutral and detached decision-maker or under defined and consistent legal standards.[49] Further, there is no right to an administrative appeal from an adverse consent decision.[50]

Constitutional as well as APA[51] challenges to the INS and DHS practice of denying consent to juvenile court jurisdiction for SIJS-eligible children have been raised in federal court.[52] In two early SIJS cases, the courts concluded that INS did not issue arbitrary or capricious decisions or abuse its discretion in denying consent to juvenile court jurisdiction.[53] In *M.B. v. Quaran-*

tillo,[54] conflicting evidence as to the child's birth date, country of birth, whether his parents had been killed, and whether his aunt had abused him led the court to find that INS could have reasonably decided that it would have been impossible for the minor to obtain corroborating documents, and hence INS refusal to consent to juvenile court jurisdiction was reasonable since consent "would have amounted to endorsing an exercise in futility."[55] In *Yeboah v. U.S. Dept. of Justice*,[56] the court found subject matter jurisdiction to review an INS consent decision under the APA,[57] but determined that INS did not abuse its discretion in weighing the "conflicting evidence of abandonment versus deliberate design on the part of the father to create permanent residence status" for the minor.[58]

In a Washington District Court case, *A.A.-M v. Alberto Gonzales*,[59] a case in which the child's credibility was dispositive, the district court found abuse of discretion where DHS denied consent without ever having interviewed the child.

A Texas District Court recently held that DHS acted arbitrarily and capriciously in denying consent to a 17-year-old Chinese boy whose father abandoned him after having him smuggled into the United States by "Snakeheads" at the age of 14 and agreed to have his son work off the $60,000 smuggling fee.[60] The court rejected the DHS argument

---

of consent, made based on dispositive credibility determinations but without a single interview of the child, constitutes an abuse of discretion).

[48] *See Perez-Olano v. Alberto Gonzalez*, Case No. CV-05-3604 DDP (RZx) (Dist. Ct. CD Ca. filed 2005).

[49] Contrast this with the protections afforded asylum applicants who have the right to a nonadversarial interview by specially trained asylum officers on their asylum claims. 8 CFR §208.1(b), §208.9(b).

[50] *See Zheng*, Case No. H-06-197, p. 10. DHS regulations do allow an appeal to the USCIS Associate Commissioner, Examinations, from a denial of SIJ status, 8 CFR §204.11(e), but there are no such regulatory provisions for appeal of a DHS denial of consent to juvenile court jurisdiction.

[51] 5 USC §§701 (2000) *et seq*.

[52] Challenges to an agency's procedures on constitutional grounds may properly be brought in federal court to prevent insulation of INS policies and procedures from review. *Gete v. INS*, 121 F.3d 1285, 1291–93 (9th Cir. 1997); *Blazina v. Bouchard*, 286 F.2d 507, 511 (3d Cir. 1961) (applicants for INS benefits have a right to have their applications considered); *F.L. v. Tommy Thompson*, 293 F. Supp. 2d 86, 92 (D.D.C. 2003) ("protection of the INS applicant's right to agency consideration of his petition requires that the agency with legal authority to grant or deny consent evaluate plaintiff's request and issue a response"); *Zheng*, Case No. H-06-197, at 12 (internal INS memoranda provide sufficient guidelines by which to review consent denial under the APA). The Center for Human Rights and Constitutional Law in Los Angeles has brought a class action in federal court to challenge DHS's long-standing arbitrary failure to timely adjudicate statutorily eligible minors' applications for SIJS classification and for adjustment of status. *Perez-Olano*, Case No. CV-05-3604 DDP (RZx).

[53] *M.B. v. Quarantillo*, 301 F.3d 109 (3d Cir. 2002); *Yeboah v. U.S. Dept. of Justice*, 345 F.3d 216 (3d Cir. 2003).

---

[54] 301 F.3d at 113.

[55] This decision underscores the need to nail down the facts in a special consent case. In this case, the child had documents in his possession from a proceeding before the Italian Labor & Immigration Department in which he gave his date of birth as June 25, 1982. *Id*. at 110–11. However, he told INS at an initial interview that he was born on July 25, 1984. *Id*. INS then proceeded to have a dentist x-ray the plaintiff's teeth and wrist, and the dentist "opined that plaintiff was more than 18 years of age." *Id*. at 111.

[56] 345 F.3d 216.

[57] *Yeboah* held that the standard of review is abuse of discretion under the APA, 5 USC §706(2)(A) ("stating that an agency action may be overruled if 'arbitrary, capricious, an abuse of discretion, or otherwise not in accordance with the law'"). *Id*. at 224.

[58] *Id*. at 220–21.

[59] Case No. C05-2012C, 2005 WL 3307531 (W.D. Wash. Dec. 6, 2005).

[60] *Zheng v. Pogash*, Case No. H-06-197, pp. 7–9, 22 (S.D. Tex. filed Feb. 23, 2006). The *Zheng* court noted that even DHS had conceded that Zheng's situation involved neglect. *Id*. at 14–15, 18.

that the REAL ID Act[61] precluded judicial review of discretionary decisions like specific consent decisions and granted a preliminary injunction ordering DHS to provide specific consent.[62] The court found that DHS's denial of consent may be reviewed under the APA because Zheng had no other remedy for review and the court had "sufficient agency guidelines by which to review DHS's decision."[63]

STATE COURT DEPENDENCY PROCEEDINGS

To qualify for SIJS, a child must be declared dependent on a juvenile court or be placed under the custody of an agency or department of a state. The court must also deem the child eligible for long-term foster care due to abuse, neglect, or abandonment. Finally, there must be a finding that it would not be in the child's best interest to be returned to his or her home country or last country of residence.[64]

Round 1—The State Judge

The process to obtain a dependency order varies from state to state. In some states, probate courts issue dependency orders; in others, it is the family courts. In some jurisdictions, juvenile delinquency proceedings can establish dependency.[65] Immigration practitioners pursuing special immigrant juvenile status must know the laws and procedures of the particular state venue with authority to issue the dependency order.[66] The findings necessary to obtain SIJS status are not necessarily the same as those for dependency proceedings. Therefore, some state judges resist issuing an order that contains the language the INA wants. Working with an experienced family law attorney can be helpful in developing an approach that meets both state dependency federal immigration requirements. Before heading into

state court, practitioners representing a child who is not in removal proceedings should determine whether there is a risk the state will turn the child over to DHS to initiate proceedings.

Round 2—USCIS

Successfully obtaining a state court dependency order is a critical first step to obtaining SIJS,[67] but there are two more hurdles to clear before a juvenile can obtain permanent resident status. USCIS must approve a Special Immigrant Juvenile Petition, Form I-360, and the child must also obtain approval of the Application for Adjustment of Status, Form I-485.

Filing the I-360

Form I-360 may be filed by any person, including the child beneficiary.[68] Children who are not in removal proceedings file the I-360 and I-485 concurrently at the local USCIS office that has jurisdiction over the child's place of residence. Children in proceedings file the I-360 with the local USCIS office.[69] USCIS guidance provides that the special immigrant juvenile petition must be supported by a

- court order declaring dependency on the juvenile court or placing the juvenile under (or legally committing the juvenile to) the custody of an agency or department of a state;

- court order deeming the juvenile eligible for long-term foster care due to abuse, neglect, or abandonment (*i.e.*, a determination that family reunification is no longer a viable option);

- determination from an administrative or judicial proceeding that it is in the juvenile's best interest not to be returned to his or her country of nationality or last habitual residence; and

- proof of the juvenile's age.[70]

---

[61] INA §252(a)(2)(B)(ii). The REAL ID Act, portions of which amend the INA, is part of the Emergency Supplemental Appropriations Act for Defense, the Global War on Terror, and Tsunami Relief. *See* Pub. L. No. 109-13, 119 Stat. 231 (May 11, 2005).

[62] *Zheng*, Case No. H-06-197, at 2–3, 12–16.

[63] *Id.* at 11 (referring to John Pogash, National Juvenile Coordinator, ICE).

[64] INA §§101(a)(27)(J)(i), 101(a)(27)(J)(ii).

[65] Practitioners need to be careful that a delinquency order does not also unnecessarily raise grounds of inadmissibility.

[66] Practitioners may encounter such diverse issues as who can bring a state dependency action on behalf of a detained child to problems with serving notice of the action on the child's parents.

[67] Before filing for SIJS, the attorney should carefully review the child's eligibility. Information in a Special Immigrant Juvenile's application is not confidential. Filing an application for an ineligible child who is not in removal proceedings could result in USCIS using the information to start removal proceedings against the child. If a child is already in removal proceedings, there is little harm in filing an SIJS application.

[68] 8 CFR §204.11(b)(1).

[69] Practitioners representing children in removal should consider seeking administrative closure. If the court does not grant closure, IJs often are willing to continue a child's case to enable USCIS to adjudicate a special immigrant juvenile petition. If there is a final order of removal, filing a special immigrant petition will not stay removal.

[70] *Supra* note 26.

The regulations, while listing the types of documents that may establish the child's age, recognize that children may not have birth certificates, passports, or other foreign identity documents and specifically provide that other documents can be used.[71] Because the child's age is critically important, practitioners should make every effort to obtain the child's birth certificate and document in detail the efforts expended.[72] If the birth certificate cannot be located, other records that may establish age are baptismal certificates, affidavits, school records, and census records.[73] If none of these are available, obtain an expert medical opinion on age or argue that the state court finding of fact regarding the child's birth date is sufficient. Given the time it takes to obtain foreign documents or find alternative verifications of age, an attorney who accepts a SIJS case should immediately begin obtaining evidence of the child's age.

To adjudicate the petition, USCIS reviews the evidence to determine whether the court's order was issued primarily for the purpose of obtaining immigration relief, rather than relief from abuse or neglect or abandonment (*i.e.*, is the petition bona fide?). Thus, it is important that the order contain enough findings of fact to show that the court made an informed decision in finding the child was in need of relief due to abuse, neglect, or abandonment.[74] Crafting an order with factual information that supports a finding of abuse, neglect, or abandonment can be very helpful in reducing the chances USCIS will ask for additional evidence the disclosure of which violates state confidentiality laws.[75] In responding to a request for additional evidence in support of a Special Immigrant Juvenile Petition, you must be familiar with the state law pertaining to the disclosure of juvenile records.

Sometimes a child will have a protective order that does not contain enough findings of fact to determine the basis for the order. In those instances, obtain an affidavit from the court or the state agency or department in whose custody the child has been placed.[76] An affidavit from the child's social worker that summarizes the evidence presented to the court may also establish that the order was issued primarily to protect the child from abuse, neglect, and abandonment.

Once the adjudicator acknowledges that the petition is bona fide, it meets the statutory requirement for "express consent."[77] Approval of the petition itself thus serves as a grant of express consent.[78]

Keeping the Approval Alive

Approval of an SIJS petition may be revoked if the child reaches 21 before the approval of lawful permanent resident status, marries, ceases to be eligible for long-term foster care, or ceases to be under juvenile court jurisdiction.[79]

It is often difficult to convince a juvenile court to retain jurisdiction of the case until permanent residency is granted. For instance, children who are adopted or placed in guardianship must continue to be dependent upon the juvenile court even though many courts terminate jurisdiction once the adoption is final.[80] Likewise, many juvenile courts routinely terminate jurisdiction once the child reaches 18. You will need to work with the juvenile court to ensure that it retains jurisdiction after a child reaches age 18 or an adoption or guardianship is in place. State practices vary. Some judges have issued guidance suggesting that the juvenile court retain jurisdiction past the age of 18 for children who may be eligible for SIJS relief. Other courts are amenable to retaining jurisdiction if the attorney files a motion with the court. Practitioners need to be familiar with local family law and the juvenile court and be willing to pursue creative options for the court to retain jurisdiction until permanent residence is approved.

If it proves impossible to retain state court jurisdiction past the age of 18, the practitioner must request that USCIS expedite processing of the child's

---

[71] 8 CFR §204.11(d)(1).

[72] DOS's *Foreign Affairs Manual* provides detailed information about the availability of foreign birth certificates and on how to obtain them.

[73] *See* 8 CFR §204.1(g)(2), which lists the types of secondary evidence acceptable in family cases.

[74] DHS has instructed adjudicators that they "generally should not second-guess the court rulings or question whether the court's order was properly issued," *supra* note 50.

[75] Some child advocates counsel attorneys not to provide USCIS with documentation supplementing the findings in the court order. Practitioners should support the order with the May 27, 2004, Yates Memorandum, *supra* note 25.

[76] *Supra* note 26.

[77] *Id.* Express consent is statutorily required for all SIJS applicants. Detained children must also obtain specific consent.

[78] *Id.*

[79] 8 CFR §204.11(c). Please note the statute does not include the regulatory requirement that children remain unmarried.

[80] While adopted children and those placed in guardianship need to remain under the court's jurisdiction, the regulations provide that these children continue to be considered eligible for long-term foster care. *See* 8 CFR §204.11(a).

petition and application for permanent residency. USCIS offices are to provide expedited processing of cases at risk for aging out.[81]

The Application for Permanent Residence

The application for permanent residence must be supported by:

- a birth certificate or other proof of identity;[82]

- a medical examination result;

- two ADIT-style photographs;

- Form G-325A Biographic Information, if the applicant is over 14;

- certified copies of the disposition for any arrests;

- for a child seeking a waiver of inadmissibility, Form I-601 and supporting documentation showing the waiver should be granted for humanitarian purposes, family unity, or the public interest;

- because SIJS applicants are deemed paroled into the United States, it is not necessary to show lawful entry, but it is prudent to include with the I-485 filing proof of entry or a copy of the statute and DHS guidance.[83]

Children applying for lawful permanent residence are eligible for employment authorization. It is important to obtain this authorization even if the child does not intend to work because the employment authorization document (EAD) gives a child an identity document and the ability to apply for a Social Security number.

Just as it is critical that the juvenile court retain jurisdiction until the application for permanent residence is granted, the application must be granted by the time the child reaches 21.[84] Obtaining timely biometric clearances can be problematic. DHS guidance directs adjudicators to expedite cases that are in danger of aging out.[85] You also might look for other options available to expedite biometric processing. One such option is to file a nonfrivolous asylum application.

Eligibility for Lawful Permanent Residence

Children applying for SIJS are eligible to adjust status in the United States even if they entered without inspection or have failed to maintain status in the United States.[86] It is important to recognize that not all grounds of inadmissibility apply to special immigrant juveniles. Specifically, they are exempt from inadmissibility for likelihood of becoming a public charge, lack of labor certification, and failure to possess a valid visa.[87] Most grounds of inadmissibility that apply to special immigrant juvenile applicants can be waived for humanitarian purposes, family unity, or when it is in the public interest.[88] There are, however, a few grounds of inadmissibility that are not waivable. They are found in INA §§212(a)(2)(A), (B), and (C)[89] and INA §§212(a)(3)(A), (B), (C), and (E). Because unaccompanied children often speak to numerous officials who are responsible for handling detained children,[90] if the child is in removal proceedings, you might consider filing for SIJS even if the child cannot adjust because it offers an opportunity to present information about the child's circumstances that may lead to other avenues of relief.[91] Conversely, it is unwise to file a SIJS petition for an ineligible child who is not in removal proceedings because doing so puts the child at risk, since there are no confidentiality protections to stop USCIS from sharing information with ICE.

ALTERNATIVE FORMS OF RELIEF

An unaccompanied minor who has been abused, neglected, or abused by parents or legal guardians may have other immigration relief available, such as the T visa[92] for victims of "trafficking," a U visa, protection under Violence Against Women Act, or asylum.

---

[81] *Supra* note 26.

[82] Evidence that establishes age for the I-360 does not necessarily establish identity for the I-485. For instance, a medical examination may prove the child's age but is not sufficient to prove identity.

[83] *Supra* note 26.

[84] Senator Feinstein's recently passed bill would require the application for permanent residence to be approved by the time a child turns 18.

[85] *Supra* note 26.

[86] Children applying for SIJS are deemed to be paroled into the United States. *See* INA §245(h)(1).

[87] *See* INA §245(h)(2)(A).

[88] *See* INA §245(h)(2)(B).

[89] Except for a single instance of simple possession of 30 grams or less of marijuana.

[90] It is extremely important to review the child's records to ensure they do not contain information that may give USCIS reason to believe the child has been involved with drug trafficking.

[91] In addition to the forms of relief discussed in the following sections, consider relief such as administrative closure and deferred action.

[92] INA §§101(a)(15)(T); Trafficking Victims Protection Act of 2000, Division A of Pub. L. No. 106-386, 114 Stat. 1464 (Oct. 28, 2000); Victims of Trafficking and Violence Protection Act; H.R. Conf. Report No. 106-939; 8 CFR §214.11; 67 Fed. Reg. 4784 (Jan. 31, 2002); Torture

continued

T Visa

The term "trafficking" is a misnomer. The T visa does not protect the majority of children that are held hostage, raped, beaten, or otherwise brutalized by someone hired to help the child cross the U.S. border. If the child cannot demonstrate that someone used "force, fraud or coercion" to induce him or her to perform sexual or labor services, the child is not a victim of "trafficking." Human trafficking, more precisely termed human slavery, nevertheless finds its way onto the walls of ORR detention centers that are commonly covered with unaccompanied children's artwork depicting the misery of their journeys. Traffickers often employ a broad range of techniques to coerce abused, neglected, or abandoned children to escape from their misery to a promised land. The Trafficking Protection Act of 2000 is replete with vivid language explaining that vulnerable victims, such as children, fall prey to "rape and other forms of sexual abuse, torture, starvation, imprisonment, threats, psychological abuse, and coercion" to perform profitable services for another.[93] If a child describes any instances of entrapment in "commercial sexual exploitation such as prostitution, or labor exploitation in sweatshops, domestic servitude, construction sites, and agricultural settings,"[94] explore eligibility for a T visa alongside the efforts to obtain SIJS.

U Visa

Many children in the United States are traumatized by forms of family violence occurring miles from U.S. borders. Other children are victims of rape, incest, assault, sexual exploitation, false imprisonment, and other violent crimes that either occurred on U.S. soil or within a large smuggling or trafficking ring of the type investigated or prosecuted by U.S. law enforcement. Children in the latter situation are likely to be eligible for a U visa.[95] A U visa permits a child victim who has

"suffered substantial physical or mental abuse" to remain legally in the United States for three years with the possibility of obtaining permanent residency. To submit an application for a U visa, an applicant 16 years of age or older must submit a certificate from a federal, state, or local qualifying official (such as, but not limited to, a law enforcement officer, prosecutor, or judge) stating that the applicant "has been helpful, is being helpful, or is likely to be helpful." Children under 16 need not possess key information about the crime or cooperate with law enforcement. They may be eligible for a U visa if a "parent, guardian, or next friend" has been helpful, is being helpful, or is likely to be helpful to a federal, state, or local law enforcement official investigating or prosecuting the crime. Children who are 16 or 17 are treated as adults and must possess key information about the crime and cooperate with law enforcement.[96]

Violence Against Women Act (VAWA)

A child[97] who has resided with an abusive parent in the United States may be eligible for VAWA benefits.[98] VAWA benefits are available for children who have resided with an abuser in the United States in two different situations: (a) when a child's parent was abused by a U.S. citizen or permanent resident spouse, even though the child was not abused; or (b) if the child was directly abused by a U.S. citizen or

---

Victims Protection Reauthorization Act of 2003; Pub. L. No. 108-193, 117 Stat. 2875 (Dec. 19, 2003), H.R. 2620.

[93] 8 CFR §214.11.

[94] U.S. Dept. of Justice et al., "Assessment of U.S. Government Activities to Combat Trafficking in Persons" (2004).

[95] In November 2000, Congress mandated the issuance of U visas to encourage victims of crime to cooperate with law enforcement. INA §101(a)(15)(U). To date, the U visa is still nonexistent. In this regulatory vacuum, an internal agency memorandum directs the agency to grant certain qualified applicants interim benefits of deferred action, employment authorization, parole, and stays of removal. INS Memorandum, Cronin, Acting Ex. Assoc. Comm. Programs HQINV 50/1, "Victims of Trafficking and Violence Protection Act of

continued

2000 (VTVPA) Policy Memorandum #2—"T" and "U" Nonimmigrant Visas" (Aug. 30, 2001), *published on* AILA InfoNet at Doc. 02011734 (*posted* Jan. 17, 2002). Applications for deferred action and employment authorization as interim relief are filed with the USCIS Vermont Service Center. USCIS Letter and Memorandum, William R. Yates, Assoc. Dir. Operations, "Centralization of Interim Relief For U Nonimmigrant Status Applicants" (Oct. 8, 2003), *published on* AILA InfoNet at Doc. No. 03101420 (*posted* Oct. 14, 2003); USCIS Updates Guidance on U Nonimmigrant Applications, 83 *Interpreter Releases* 163 (Jan. 23, 2006).

[96] INA §101(a)(15)(U).

[97] As more precisely defined in case law and regulations, a child for VAWA purposes is an unmarried person less than 21 years of age who is: (a) legitimated child; (b) a stepchild; (c) a child legitimated under the law of the child's residence or under the law of the father's residence; (d) an illegitimate child; (e) a child adopted while under the age of 16; (f) a child who is an orphan. INA §204(a); 8 CFR §204; INA §240(A).

[98] *See* The Violence Against Women and Department of Justice Reauthorization Act of 2005 (Pub. L. No. 109-162) (Jan. 5, 2006); INA §204(a)(1)(A); 8 CFR §294.2 (self-petitioning provisions for battered spouses or children). *See also* INA §204(A); 8 CFR §1240.65 (Special Rule Cancellation of Removal).

legal permanent resident parent. Crudely defined, abuse under VAWA constitutes physical abuse or psychological abuse amounting to "extreme cruelty." For VAWA purposes, a child must be unmarried, under 21, and a person of "good moral character."[99] If a child informs you that the abusive stepparent, adoptive parent, or biological parent is a not a resident or citizen, more research may be necessary before concluding that the child is ineligible for VAWA benefits. Many individuals acquire and derive U.S. citizenship without their knowledge. The complexity of U.S. citizenship laws make it imperative for children's attorneys to be creative in their investigation into whether an abusive parent acquired or derived citizenship without the child's knowledge or, in many instances, without the abusive parent's knowledge.

Asylum

When a child fears returning to his or her homeland, consider whether the child is eligible for asylum,[100] withholding of removal,[101] or relief under the United Nations Convention Against Torture.[102] To qualify for these three forms of relief from deportation to the country of harm, child applicants, like their adult counterparts, must meet the definition of a refugee in the INA.[103] Often child asylum claims are not necessarily related to a child's age. In other cases, age is central to the claim. Child soldier conscription, child abuse, incest, bonded or dangerous child labor, child slavery, infanticide, child marriage, gang recruitment, and violence against street children are examples of cases where a child's age is a central element of the case.[104] Whatever the situation, U.S. law shamefully

fails to embrace the guiding principle in the 1989 Convention on the Rights of the Child that a child has a unique legal personality and that the best interest of the child should be taken into account when adjudicating a child's asylum claim.[105] Despite this cold reality, the DHS Guidelines for Children's Asylum Claims,[106] EOIR Guidelines for Immigration Court Cases Involving Unaccompanied Alien Child,[107] and the UNCHR Handbook[108] provide considerable ammunition for arguing that the asylum definition must be interpreted through a window that acknowledges a child's unique vulnerabilities and cognitive abilities to comprehend and process information.

CONCLUSION

There are many factors and strategies to consider in representing children who may be eligible for SIJS, including issues of state law as well as federal immigration law. This article is a guide for practitioners who are exploring possible eligibility for a child and the procedural steps involved to pursue an SIJS case. Be prepared to enlist the assistance of professionals in other disciplines, including state juvenile law, social work, and psychology, to adequately represent a child seeking SIJS.

---

[99] Children under the age of 14 are presumed to be of good moral character and are excused from submitting police clearance letters with self-petitions.

[100] The definition of "refugee" is found at INA §101(a)(42); INA §208.

[101] INA §241(b)(3); 8 CFR §1208.16.

[102] United Nations Convention Against Torture and Other Cruel, Inhuman or Degrading Treatment or Punishment, subject to any reservations, understandings, declarations, and provisos contained in the U.S. Senate resolution of ratification of the Convention, as implemented by §2242 of the Foreign Affairs Reform and Restructuring Act of 1998 (Pub. L. No. 105-277, 112 Stat. 2681, 2681–821); 8 CFR §§1208.16–1208.18.

[103] INA §§101(a)(42), 208.

[104] What groups constitute a "particular social group" is a matter of considerable controversy and uncertainty. Memorandum from INS to Asylum Officer Corps on Guidelines for Children's Asylum Claims (Dec. 10, 1998) at 20–27 (hereinafter Guidelines for Children's Asylum Claims).

[105] The Convention on the Rights of the Child, adopted by the U.N. General Assembly, November 20, 1989, entered into force on September 2, 1990. *See www.unicef.org/crc/status.htm.* UNHCR, "Guidelines on Policies and Procedures in Dealing with Unaccompanied Children Seeking Asylum" (1997), *www.unhcr.ch/cgi-bin/texis/vtx/publ/opendoc.pdf?tbl=PUBL& id=3d4f91cf4* (hereinafter UNHCR Guidelines). For example, EOIR instructs that the "best interest of the child" should be nothing more than a "factor that relates to an immigration judge's discretion in taking steps to ensure that a child-appropriate hearing environment is established, allowing a child to freely discuss the elements and details of his or her claim." U.S. Department of Justice, Executive Office for Immigration Review, Interim Operating Policies and Procedures Memorandum 04-07: "Guidelines for Immigration Court Cases Involving Unaccompanied Alien Children," memorandum from the Office of the Chief Immigration Judge (Sept. 16, 2004), *published on* AILA InfoNet at Doc. No. 04100568 (*posted* Oct. 5, 2004) (hereinafter EOIR Children Guidelines); *see, e.g., Lukwago* v. *Ashcroft,* 329 F.3d 157, 170 (3d Cir.2003).

[106] Guidelines for Children's Asylum Claims, *supra* note 104 (citing UNHCR Handbook ¶52). The harm a child fears or has suffered may be relatively less than that of an adult and still qualify as persecution. INS Guidelines, at 19 (citing UNHCR Handbook ¶52).

[107] EOIR Child Guidelines, *supra* note 105.

FAMILY IMMIGRATION ISSUES: LOVE CONQUERS ALL?

by Jan H. Brown[*]

INTRODUCTION

One of the philosophical underpinnings of U.S. immigration laws is family unification; in principle, the system is dedicated to uniting husbands with wives and children with parents. Regrettably, due to understaffing, underfunding, and security concerns, cases often cannot be processed as quickly as a family would desire or as quickly as the law allows.

Pursuant to the Immigration and Nationality Act (INA),[1] certain family members related to either U.S. citizens or lawful permanent residents (LPR) may enter the United States and remain as lawful permanent residents. The best category to be in is the immediate relative category (*see* INA §201(b)(2)(A)(i)):

- The parents of a U.S. citizen son or daughter who is at least 21 years old;

- A child (a person under the age of 21 and unmarried at the time the petition is filed) of a U.S. citizen (*see* INA §201(f));

- A widow or widower of a U.S. citizen, provided that the marriage was in existence for at least two years before the U.S. citizen died, and that the petition is filed within two years of the spouse's death (INA §§201(b)(2)(A)(i), 204(a)(1)(A)(ii));

- A battered spouse or child, subject to extreme cruelty or battered by the U.S. citizen spouse or parent (*see* INA §204(a)(1)(A)(iii)(I)(bb)).

PROCESSING DELAYS—QUOTAS

There are no legal impediments to a grant of permanent residence for those in the immediate relative categories regarding the granting of permanent resident status to the beneficiaries once the petition and application processes have been completed. In the best of all possible worlds, persons in these cate-

gories should be able to obtain permanent residence promptly. However, this is not the case in large jurisdictions such as New York City.

There are also preference categories where there are legal impediments to the prompt granting of permanent residence status. Unlike immediate relative cases, only a limited number of visas are allocated to each category.

The preference categories are based on supply and demand. No one can obtain permanent residence before a priority date becomes current. The priority date is the date on which a Form I-130 is filed (*see* 22 CFR §42.53(a), 9 FAM 42.53 N.1).

The preference categories, the filing dates after which immigrant visas may be approved, and the number of annual visas issued per category are listed in the State Department Visa Bulletin.[2]

First Preference: Unmarried sons and daughters of citizens, including sons and daughters of U.S. citizens over 21 years of age and their children: 23,400 visas annually, plus any numbers not required for fourth preference.

Second Preference: Spouses, children, and unmarried sons and daughters of permanent residents: 114,200 visa annually, plus the number (if any) by which the worldwide family preference level exceeds 226,000 and any unused first preferences numbers:

- Spouses and children: 77 percent of the overall second preference limitation, of which 75 percent are exempt from the per-country limit.

- Unmarried sons and daughters (21 years of age or older): 23 percent of the overall second preference limitation.

Third Preference: Married sons and daughters of citizens: 23,400 visas annually, plus any numbers not required by first and second preferences. Includes married sons and daughters of U.S. citizens, regardless of age, and their spouses and children.

---

[*] **Jan Brown** is a principal in the Law Offices of Jan H. Brown, P.C., in New York City. He is chair of the Immigration and Nationality Committee of the New York State Bar Association, International Law and Practice Section. Mr. Brown often lectures and writes on immigration topics.

[1] Immigration and Nationality Act of 1952, Pub. L. No. 82-414, 66 Stat. 163 (*codified as amended at* 8 USC §§1101 *et seq.*) (INA).

[2] *See http://travel.state.gov/visa.*

Fourth Preference: Brothers and sisters of adult citizens: 65,000 visas annually, plus any numbers not required by the first three preferences.

India, Mexico, China (mainland), and Philippines have their own priority dates. It is evident that there can be a substantial wait before a beneficiary can receive a benefit under these categories.

Sometimes an oblique attack on the problem is the best strategy. For example, if an LPR parent can naturalize, an adult unmarried son or daughter would jump from category 2B to category 1, thus saving potentially three years or more of waiting.

If a beneficiary or a potential beneficiary is in a failed marriage, a speedy divorce can help improve the beneficiary's chances of receiving permanent residence or, in the case of a son or daughter of a permanent resident, create the opportunity, since married children of LPRs cannot be sponsored at all by their LPR parents. Likewise, a practitioner may want to warn a beneficiary that, no matter how hard Cupid has struck, it might be wiser not to get married until the immigration processing is completed. For example, a first preference beneficiary will automatically drop to the third preference upon marriage. (See 8 CFR §204.2(i) on automatic conversions from category to category). Likewise, a child of a U.S. citizen who marries is converted from the immediate relative to the third preference category.

While love may conquer all, Father Time can certainly slow the process down and take some of the gloss off a marriage. A strategy that some people employ is to enter the United States as an unmarried son or daughter and then marry. Regrettably, this would put the new spouse in category 2A, spouse of a permanent resident—which would entail either a period of great separation or a period where the new LPR would be spending much money on travel to the old country to see the spouse. Such are the problems immigrants encounter—and such are the weaknesses in the family unification philosophy as implemented.

PROCESSING DELAYS— BUREAUCRATIC INERTIA

Processing can be delayed by bureaucratic complications. Among them is the fact that, since cases in some jurisdictions can take well over a year to process, various applications have to be updated and renewed. At a New York State Bar Association seminar in March of 2004, the Ombudsman of U.S. Citizenship and Immigration Services (USCIS),

Prakash I. Khatri, said he estimates that 75 percent of the entire workload of USCIS concerns adjustment of status on family cases and derivative forms and procedures, such as employment authorizations, advance paroles, and security clearances. He has estimated that the average case requires a USCIS official to take action on all or part of an application at least eight times. All of this can slow down and complicate the process. Since, for example, advance parole, employment authorization, and security checks all expire in 12 to 15 months, they must be renewed if adjustment takes longer than that, as it often does.

Additionally, many people contact USCIS to inquire about the status of their long-pending cases or the status of the derivative applications such as employment authorization; responding would mean that personnel are used in an unproductive way. After all, advising an alien that an application is still pending does not help get files adjudicated. Long waits and multiple procedures also increase the likelihood that a file will be misplaced. Or the bureaucrat assigned to a case may retire, die, or be reassigned, leaving the file in limbo until a new adjudicator rescues it. USCIS is working to remedy the situation in several ways.

Recognizing this problem, the Department of Homeland Security (DHS) on July 30, 2004, published an interim regulation that amends 8 CFR §274a.[3] USCIS now has the authority to issue Employment Authorization Documents (EADs) for periods greater than one year, as was previously the case. This new regulation recognizes that the system is overburdened. However, USCIS has not implemented this much-needed reform, perhaps, in the author's opinion, because of the potential for revenue loss.

With InfoPass, USCIS's Internet appointment system, a person whose employment authorization request is pending for more than 90 days can go online and obtain an appointment within two weeks to be processed for employment authorization (*see* 8 CFR §274a.13(d)). The system is also useful to obtain a status report on a pending case or for any other request requiring an entry into a USCIS facility. InfoPass means that long lines outside federal buildings are disappearing, and both the alien and USCIS functionaries have an easier time adjudicating applications.

---

[3] 69 Fed. Reg 45555, *published on* AILA InfoNet at Doc. No. 04072962 (*posted* July 29, 2004).

Sometimes the processing of I-130 petitions in particular can be frustratingly slow. To alleviate backlogs in other areas, USCIS has recently changed its policies and will now not adjudicate a pending I-130 petition "until a visa number becomes available." While this will allow USCIS to allocate its overburdened resources to the adjudication of other types of petitions, regrettably, beneficiaries awaiting approval of I-130 petitions may suffer in two ways. First, since the stated policy of USCIS is to not adjudicate a relative petition until a visa number is available, there are likely to be additional delays before the petition is actually adjudicated even after a visa number is available. Under current policies, if a preference category is backlogged seven years, when the seven years are up, the I-130 would have been adjudicated. Under the new policy, only then would the I-130 adjudication process begin, causing additional frustrations and delays to the family. Perhaps more serious to the beneficiary than an additional need for patience is the fact that an approved petition potentially gives a beneficiary more rights than does a pending petition in the case of the death of the petitioner.[4]

The death of the petitioner is grounds for automatic revocation of a petition unless USCIS determines that there are humanitarian reasons why the petition should not be revoked.[5] The Attorney General may, on humanitarian grounds, permit certain relatives to meet the affidavit of support requirement under INA §213A(f)(5) when the petitioning relative has died. If the petition has not been approved, but is merely pending when the petitioner dies, the beneficiary may not use humanitarian arguments to get the petition approved.[6]

PERMANENT RESIDENCE THROUGH MARRIAGE—ALL YOU NEED IS LOVE?

Adjustment of Status or Consular Processing

There are two ways to obtain permanent residence for the spouse of a U.S. citizen or LPR.

In the adjustment of status process, an application is filed by an alien in the United States who is either the spouse of a U.S. citizen and who was inspected and admitted or paroled into the United States, or who is the spouse of an LPR who has maintained lawful nonimmigrant or parole status and for whom a visa is currently available.[7]

Today, I-485 adjustment of status applications are filed at the National Benefits Center, which performs all pre-interview processing, including background security checks. Hopefully this will ease the burden on local USCIS offices, though they still must interview applicants and adjudicate the case.

The advantage of the adjustment of status route is that the alien spouse may remain in the United States and obtain employment authorization while the application is pending, and the parties' attorney can attend the interview.

The alternate way permanent residence may be pursued is through consular processing. This choice is attractive for aliens who are outside the United States and in situations where it may be more desirable for the alien to be interviewed without the petitioning spouse, as may be the case in an unstable marriage; petitioning spouses sometimes fail to appear for the adjustment interview, to the alien's extreme detriment. Another advantage of consular processing is that scheduling an interview may be faster than with USCIS. If speed is a consideration, the practitioner should compare the processing times of the local USCIS office with jurisdiction over the alien's place of residence with the delays at the consular posts at which the alien might apply for an immigrant visa.

The primary disadvantage of consular processing is that many posts do not allow attorneys to attend the interview. Moreover, consular decisions are not subject to judicial or administrative review, as a domestic adjustment application is.[8]

Love Conquers All?

These are the kinds of problems that may occur in marriage cases:

The Problem Interview

In the Second Circuit, if an interviewer is not satisfied that a marriage is bona fide, the case is referred for a secondary interview, pursuant to *Stokes v. INS*, 393 F. Supp. 24 (S.D.N.Y. 1975). This interview is recorded, and the parties may be separated so that both can be asked the same questions. There are no right or wrong answers—only same or different.

[4] *See* 8 CFR §§205.1(a), 1205.1(a).
[5] 8 CFR §§205.1(a)(3)(i)(C), 1204.1(a)(3)(i)(C).
[6] *See Abboud v. INS*, 140 F.3d 843 (9th Cir. 1998).
[7] *See* INA §245; 8 CFR §§245.2(a)(5)(ii), 1245.2(a)(5)(ii).
[8] *See* INA §104(a)(1).

In the other circuits, the parties are not protected by this decision, and interviewers can separate the parties at the initial (and often only) interview in the quest for the bona fides of the marriage. Thus, practitioners outside the Second Circuit must prepare their clients for intensive, often aggressive, grilling.

Advance Parole

The ability to leave the United States and return is often the Holy Grail for an alien long separated from family and friends in the home country. Regrettably, for a person who has been unlawfully present in the United States for more than six months, advance parole can be a time bomb that will explode by the time of the adjustment interview. Pursuant to INA §212(a)(9)(B), a person who leaves the United States after six months of unlawful presence is barred from the United States for three years. After one year of unlawful presence, this bar climbs to 10 years. An alien who has used advance parole will be allowed to return to the United States to finalize the adjustment of status application, but unless a waiver of excludability is filed, per INA §212(a)(9)(B)(v), and extreme hardship to a qualifying spouse or parent is established, the adjustment will be denied and the alien barred for the applicable penalty period. An alien who can avoid a departure from the United States until after becoming an LPR avoids this problem entirely.

The Battered Spouse

Regrettably, marriages, even without the pressures of a USCIS interview, collapse, or just limp along, like a wounded bird.

Congress has recognized that some petitioning spouses were taking advantage of their alien companions, who had to make the Hobbesian choice of leaving the marriage and thus losing the opportunity to obtain residence, or remaining, often to the detriment of their health and welfare, while the quest for permanent residence proceeded. The passage of INA §204(a)(1) ameliorated this problem. It is necessary to establish that the alien spouse or child resided with the petitioner; that the alien spouse entered the marriage in good faith, and that the alien was the subject of battery or extreme cruelty.[9]

This section of the law is surprisingly generous in the standards it sets, in that it applies to aliens who in good faith entered into void marriages, such as bigamous marriages.[10]

Also, an alien whose spouse has died may still file as an abused spouse under the Violence Against Women Act of 1994, provided that the petition is filed within two years of the abusing spouse's death.[11] This is a much more generous standard than the nonabused widow's special immigrant petition process, which requires, as a condition precedent, two years of marriage before the death of the U.S. citizen spouse.[12]

An alien otherwise subject to the unlawful presence bar may overcome this impediment upon a showing that the unlawful presence was substantially connected to the domestic abuse.

An abused spouse may qualify for adjustment in spite of an entry without inspection. Even a subsequent remarriage will not defeat an abused spouse petition according to the Violence Against Women Act.[13]

CONDITIONAL RESIDENCE AND ITS REMOVAL

According to the Immigration Marriage Fraud Amendments of 1986,[14] a marriage now results only in the granting of "conditional residence and not permanent residence," unless the marriage was entered into two years or more before the granting of immigrant status (see INA §216). This is one area of the law where processing delays work to the benefit of the beneficiary. If not approved until after the marriage has been extant for over two years, then LPR status should be granted upon approval.

If not, the alien shall be required to file a new application within three months immediately before the second anniversary of the grant of conditional residence on Form I-751. Preferably, this form will be used as a joint petition that is signed by both the beneficiary and the petitioner spouse.[15] When the

---

[9] See 8 CFR §204.2(c)(2).

[10] See INS Memorandum, Johnny N. Williams, Executive Associate Commissioner, Immigration Services Division, HQADN/ 70/8 (Aug. 21, 2002), published on AILA InfoNet at Doc. No. 02091042 (posted Sept. 10, 2002).

[11] See http://uscis.gov/graphics/howdoi/battered.htm, for guidelines.

[12] 8 CFR §204.2(b)(1).

[13] See http://uscis.gov/graphics/howdoi/battered.htm.

[14] Immigration Marriage Fraud Act of 1986, Pub. L. No. 99-639, 100 Stat. 3537 (IMFA).

[15] See 8 CFR §§216.4(a)(1), 1216.4(a)(1).

parties file this joint petition, they should submit documentation establishing that they have been sharing their lives in a bona fide marital relationship. Historically, joint petitions with substantial documentation of the marital relationship have resulted in approvals without an interview, at least in New York City. However, according to reported observations, this policy appears to be changing; more and more parties are being scheduled for interviews, regardless of the strength of their documentation.

Since many marriages deteriorate or fail entirely within this two-year period, it is often necessary for a waiver to be filed, also using Form I-751 but signed only by the alien, during the same 90-day window mentioned. Once Form I-751 is filed, the alien's status is automatically extended for one year, affording the conditional resident the opportunity to continue to work in the United States and to travel out of and into the United States without the need for further documentation. Regrettably, due to processing delays, there is no certainty that the application to remove the conditions will be adjudicated within this one-year period. An alien who wishes to obtain further permission to work or travel must be inconvenienced by a trip to a USCIS office to obtain a stamp in his or her passport extending employment and travel authorization while the application is pending. This regrettably not only inconveniences the applicant; it further taxes the overburdened USCIS as staff resources have to be allocated to this process. Unfortunately, there is no automatic procedure in place to extend a person's status beyond the one year granted when Form I-751 is filed.

If the petitioning spouse is unable or unwilling to sign the petition to remove the conditions on residence, the alien can submit the form with only the alien's signature. If the spouse is either deceased or the marriage is terminated through divorce or annulment, the applicant must document that the marriage, while in existence, was bona fide through, *e.g.*, photographs, financial records, leases, wills, employment records, and insurance documents. However, if the marriage is still in existence, but the petitioner spouse is unavailable because the parties are separated, the conditional resident must not only document that the marriage was bona fide but also must establish that extreme hardship would accrue as a result of removal from the United States. Extreme hardship, including economic hardship, can be shown by examining country conditions in the alien's homeland and the impact upon the alien and other lawfully present, close family members both in

the United States and abroad. Only hardship that arose during the two-year conditional resident period should be cited.

Ironically, for removal of the conditions, it is better for two persons to be divorced rather than merely estranged; the requirements for removal of conditions are much more stringent in the latter case than in the former. This is a strange situation in that our government espouses "family values," yet here prefers divorce to a situation where reconciliation might be possible.

The former USCIS policy of allowing an alien to indicate on the form "marriage terminated" when in fact a divorce was only anticipated or pending is no longer in effect.[16] Formerly, as long as a divorce decree could be produced before the application was adjudicated, the application could have been approved in that category. It was not necessary that a divorce be finalized before Form I-751 was filed. Now, an alien who has initiated a divorce that is not finalized must present documentation to qualify under the extreme hardship waiver. Fortunately, the application can be amended when the divorce is granted to request the waiver on the basis of marriage termination, obviating the hardship requirement.

An interview should be anticipated for all cases where a waiver is filed and often where the petition is jointly filed. At the interview, the parties should be prepared to establish the bona fides of the marriage during all or part of the two-year conditional residence period, as well as any additional grounds, such as extreme hardship. This process is certainly prejudicial to a person whose marriage collapses soon after the grant of conditional residence, since there might not be much proof available to demonstrate the marital relationship.

CONCLUSION

While love may not conquer all, a good understanding of the vicissitudes of the immigration process is likely to ensure the successful outcome of an application for permanent residence and help clients understand the time and effort that will be required to complete the process.

---

[16] *See* USCIS Memorandum, William Yates, USCIS Acting Associate Director of Operations, "Filing a Waiver of the Joint Filing Requirement Prior to Final Termination of the Marriage" (Apr. 10, 2003), *published on* AILA InfoNet at Doc. No. 03050643 (*posted* May 6, 2003).

YES, SAME-SEX COUPLES CAN GET MARRIED IN FOUR COUNTRIES AND MASSACHUSETTS—NO, THEY *STILL* ARE NOT I-130 ELIGIBLE

*by Noemi E. Masliah and Lavi S. Soloway**

INTRODUCTION

"Public recognition and sanction of marital relationships reflect society's approbation of the personal hopes, desires and aspirations that underlie loving, committed conjugal relationships."[1] This hopeful phrase is the rationale for the 2003, Ontario Court of Appeals decision invalidating the common law definition of marriage that had restricted the union to one man and one woman, and reformulating it to include "the voluntary union for life of two persons to the exclusion of all others."[2] Further, as the Massachusetts Supreme Judicial Court wrote in its opinion removing the exclusion of marriage for same-sex couples in that state based on the constitutional principles of respect for individual autonomy and equality under law, "Marriage is a vital social institution. The exclusive commitment of two individuals to each other nurtures love and mutual support; it brings stability to our society."[3] It is true that the rationale behind these progressive rulings inspires optimism in those seeking to end discrimination against gays and lesbians in marriage in the United States. Similarly inspiring have been developments in recent years leading to the legalization of same-sex marriage in the Netherlands, Belgium, and Spain. The reality is, however, that the legal effect of these developments does not transcend national and state borders. In the context of U.S. federal law, including immigration law, social change continues with "all deliberate speed."[4]

When same-sex marriage became a reality in the four countries and one U.S. state described above, the burning question for many was whether a U.S. citizen (USC) or legal permanent resident (LPR) who married a person of the same sex in one of those four countries or in the state of Massachusetts[5]

* **Noemi Masliah** is a partner in the New York City law firm of Masliah & Soloway, PC. She received her B.A. in French and Spanish literature from Queens College, New York, and J.D. from the Benjamin N. Cardozo School of Law, Yeshiva University. She has been exclusively engaged in the practice of immigration law since 1980, and has spoken frequently on a broad range of immigration topics. She is a member of AILA's Liaison Committee with the Vermont Service Center. Ms. Masliah served as co-chair of the Board of Directors of Lambda Legal Defense and Education Fund, Inc. from 1995 to 1997. One of the founders of the Lesbian and Gay Immigration Rights Task Force, now called Immigration Equality, Ms. Masliah is one of the co-authors of the Uniting American Families Act (formerly the Permanent Partners Immigration Act). A daughter of Holocaust survivors, Ms. Masliah emigrated from Cuba in 1962 and became a naturalized U.S. citizen in 1967.

Lavi Soloway is a partner in the New York City law firm of Masliah & Soloway, PC. He received his B.A. in history at the University of Toronto, and J.D. from Benjamin N. Cardozo School of Law, Yeshiva University. Born in Canada, he was a founding member of the Lesbian and Gay Immigration Rights Task Force, now called Immigration Equality, and served as the chair of its board of directors and as its National Coordinator from 1994 to 2001. Mr. Soloway has participated in numerous panels and conferences speaking on gay immigration issues and has been quoted in many newspaper and magazine articles across the nation on issues impacting lesbian, gay, and HIV+ immigrants. He has won numerous cases of political asylum for lesbian, gay, transgender, and HIV+ applicants. Mr. Soloway assisted in drafting the Uniting American Families Act (formerly the Permanent Partners Immigration Act) and has counseled hundreds of lesbian and gay bi-national couples. He became a naturalized U.S. citizen in 2004.

The authors thank Daniel J. Parisi, former associate at Masliah & Soloway, PC, for his contributions to the researching and writing of this article, and Matthew W. Walding, associate at Masliah & Soloway, PC, for his contributions to the 2006 update of this article.

[1] *Halpern v. Toronto*, 172 O.A.C. 276 (June 10, 2003).

[2] *Id.*

[3] *Goodridge v. Massachusetts Department of Public Health*, 798 N.E. 2d 941 (2003).

[4] *Alexander v. Holmes County Bd. of Educ.*, 368 U.S. 1218, 1219 (1969) (Black, J., citing *Brown v. Bd. of Educ.*, 349 U.S. 294, 301 (1955) referring to Court's use of "all deliberate speed" as a "soft euphemism for delay").

[5] As a practical matter, it is not currently certain whether nonresidents of Massachusetts may avail themselves of the legal recognition of a same-sex marriage in that state. In *Cote-Whitacre v. Department of Public Health*, No. SJC-9436 (Mass. Sup. Ct.), a case currently pending before the Massachusetts Supreme Judicial Court, the plaintiffs are seeking to bar the application of a 1913, state law blocking nonresident couples from marrying in Massachusetts. The law prohibits marriage clerks from issuing a marriage license to couples whose marriage would not be valid in their home state, and prior to the legalization of same-sex marriage in
continued

would be deemed to be legally married in the United States for federal law purposes.[6] For immigration lawyers, the question contained an additional layer: whether a USC or LPR in a same-sex relationship with a foreign national would be able to marry in one of these jurisdictions and thereby petition the U.S. Citizenship and Immigration Services (USCIS)[7] to have his or her spouse immigrate as an alien relative. The answer to both of these questions is a resounding and unfortunate "no." While additional countries and states may eventually legalize same-sex marriages or recognize such marriages performed in other jurisdictions, such legalization has no necessary bearing on the decisions and actions of U.S. state[8] and federal government[9] bodies, including USCIS.[10]

The discussion in this article will be limited to our negative response in the immigration context.

Massachusetts, the law had not been enforced for decades. The Massachusetts Supreme Judicial Court heard the case in the fall of 2005; its decision is still pending.

[6] C. Kraus, "Canadian Leaders Decide to Propose Gay Marriage Law," *N.Y. Times*, June 18, 2003, at A1.

[7] For the purposes of this article, the legacy Immigration and Naturalization Service (INS) and the Bureau of Citizenship and Immigration Services (BCIS) will be referred to in their most recent incarnation—U.S. Citizenship and Immigration Services (USCIS).

[8] Currently, Massachusetts is the only state in the United States to recognize same-sex marriage. Vermont and Connecticut recognize legal civil unions between same-sex partners, and California, New Jersey, Hawaii, and Maine recognize legal domestic partnerships between same-sex partners. The following 17 states have enacted state constitutional amendments banning same-sex marriage: Alaska, Arkansas, Georgia, Kentucky, Louisiana, Michigan, Missouri, Mississippi, Montana, Nebraska, North Dakota, Nevada, Ohio, Oklahoma, Oregon, Texas, and Utah. State constitutional amendments banning same-sex marriage will be on the 2006 ballot in Alabama, Arizona, California, Tennessee, and Wisconsin. *See www.marriageequality.org* (last visited Mar. 10, 2006).

[9] *See* Defense of Marriage Act, Pub. L. No. 104-199, 110 Stat. 2419 (1996), discussed in more detail below.

[10] *See* USCIS Memorandum, William R. Yates, Acting Associate Director for Operations, "Spousal Immigrant Visa Petitions (*AFM* Update AD 02-16)," *published on* AILA InfoNet at Doc. No. 03072915 (*posted* Mar. 20, 2003), discussed in more detail below.

STATE OF RELEVANT JURISPRUDENCE: FROM *HOWERTON* TO *LAWRENCE*

The issue of whether a USC or an LPR can file an I-130 petition for a same-sex spouse has a limited jurisprudence. In a 1982, case involving the denial of an I-130 petition filed by a bi-national gay couple married in Colorado, the Ninth Circuit determined that under §201(b) of the Immigration and Nationality Act of 1952 (INA),[11] a spouse must be a person of the opposite gender.[12] The court in *Howerton* determined that Congress's specific intent in including the word "spouse" in the INA and its subsequent amendments was to exclude same-sex partners.[13] Without deciding the validity of the underlying Colorado marriage, the court explicitly declined to expand this definition of the term "spouse."[14]

At the time the *Howerton* court sustained the denial of that couple's petition, there was no foreign jurisdiction in which gay couples could legally marry. However, the rationale applied in *Howerton* would likely apply today to a Canadian same-sex marriage in which one spouse is a USC. Nothing in the intervening period has reversed the legislative intent behind the INA with respect to the definition of marriage. (In fact, as the authors discuss in the section "Defense of Marriage Act," *infra*, congressional intent has been reinforced in this regard in recent years.) *Howerton* continues to control the meaning of "spouse" and will likely form the basis of any future decision invalidating a Canadian same-sex marriage offered for immigration purposes.

Even without *Howerton*, there are other obstacles. A same-sex marriage may be deemed to violate public policy, and a marriage that is against public policy may not be the basis for immigration even if the marriage is valid in the country where it was celebrated. This public policy exception has been applied in cases where the marriages involved incest[15] or polygamy,[16] and it presents a very real ob-

---

[11] Immigration and Nationality Act of 1952, Pub. L. No. 82-414, 66 Stat. 163 (*codified as amended at* 8 USC §§1101 *et seq.*).

[12] *See Adams v. Howerton*, 673 F.2d 1036, 1038 (9th Cir. 1982).

[13] *Id.* at 1040.

[14] *Id.*

[15] *Matter of Zappia*, 12 I&N Dec. 439 (BIA 1967) (holding that an incestuous marriage between cousins in the state of Georgia was void as against public policy).

stacle to a USC or an LPR attempting to obtain spousal immigration benefits on behalf of his or her same-sex partner or spouse.

Although the U.S. Supreme Court's 2003, decision in *Lawrence v. Texas*,[17] striking down a Texas statute criminalizing homosexual sodomy is a critical step forward in the pursuit of gay and lesbian equality, there is no guarantee that this liberal trend will prevail and thereby impact current U.S. immigration laws with respect to same-sex couples. While Justice Kennedy's majority opinion in *Lawrence* that "[w]hen sexuality finds overt expression in intimate conduct with another person, the conduct can be but one element in a personal bond that is more enduring"[18] may seem to be a harbinger of future success in the struggle for gay rights, the *Lawrence* decision may be, for now, a high-water mark in the quest for legal equality in the United States.[19] If the trend is toward a more inclusive future, this move will likely be a slow one punctuated by periodic setbacks in the coming years, given the current make-up of the U.S. Supreme Court.

In order to appreciate the "deliberate speed" of this trend, we must look at the development of sexual orientation and the law in the United States to its current state. In 1986, in *Bowers v. Hardwick*, the U.S. Supreme Court decided the constitutionality of a Georgia law criminalizing consensual sodomy.[20] In *Bowers*, the Court determined that the appropriate test for deciding whether a right was constitutionally protected was whether that right was "deeply rooted in this Nation's history and tradition."[21] The Court explicitly stated that it would not be persuaded by changing trends in the law in the individual states.[22] Moreover, as the dissenting justices noted, the Court was so preoccupied with not validating any aspect of

homosexual relationships that it upheld a law that criminalized sodomy between both homosexuals and heterosexuals.[23] Although the Court in *Lawrence* overruled its decision in *Bowers*,[24] *Bowers* was binding precedent for 17 years that generally gave cover to a jurisprudential and legislative climate in which gays and lesbians were treated as second-class citizens. For almost two decades, the Supreme Court was impervious to changing social values and to the ongoing struggle for gay and lesbian legal equality.

In its evolution toward the more expansive view of privacy and personal autonomy expressed in the *Lawrence* decision, the Supreme Court did take an intermediate step. In 1996, a full 10 years after its *Bowers* decision, the Court in *Romer v. Evans*[25] revisited the issue of gay and lesbian legal equality. Here, the Court invalidated an amendment to the Colorado Constitution that prevented "all legislative, executive or judicial action at any level of state or local government designed to protect . . . gays and lesbians."[26] The Court, finding that the amendment's specific purpose was to make homosexuals "unequal to everyone else,"[27] concluded that a state could not take a proactive step to deny homosexuals access to the political process without a "legitimate purpose."[28] Even with this extremely deferential constitutional standard, which has rarely formed the basis for invalidating a law, the Court found the Colorado constitutional amendment invalid.

In the immigration context, then, it may appear that this jurisprudential trend, taken to its conclusion, should result in a finding that to deny a same-sex married couple the definition of "spouse" does not serve a "legitimate purpose." Notwithstanding Justice Scalia's dissent in *Lawrence*,[29] this is an unlikely result at this point in our history because of the obstacles, cultural and legal, that continue to prevail.

---

[16] *Matter of H–*, 9 I&N Dec. 640 (BIA 1962) (holding that a polygamous Jordanian marriage valid in Jordan is void in the United States as against public policy).

[17] 539 U.S. 558 (2003).

[18] *Id.*

[19] *See Standhardt v. Arizona*, 77 P.3d 451 (Ct. App. Ariz. 2003) (holding that *Lawrence v. Texas* does not require finding a constitutionally protected right to homosexual marriage).

[20] *Bowers v. Hardwick*, 478 U.S. 186 (1986).

[21] *Id.* at 194.

[22] *Id.* at 196 (White, J., declaring that the Court would not consider the changing social mores or the fact that the 25 states had invalidated similar sodomy laws).

[23] *Id.* at 219 (Blackmun, J., dissenting).

[24] *Lawrence*, 123 S. Ct. at 2484 (declaring that *Bowers v. Hardwick*, 478 U.S. 186, 194 (1986) was wrongly decided and that its holding must be rejected).

[25] 517 U.S. 620 (1996).

[26] *Id.* at 624.

[27] *Id.* at 635.

[28] *Id.*

[29] *Lawrence*, 539 U.S. at 586 (Scalia, J., dissenting) (stating that the majority's holding ends all "morals legislation" including legislation against "fornication, bigamy, adultery, adult incest, bestiality, and obscenity").

DEFENSE OF MARRIAGE ACT

If federal courts are ever given the opportunity to rule on a challenge to a denial of an I-130 petition submitted by a same-sex couple, they may do little more than cite the Defense of Marriage Act (DOMA)[30] to sustain the denial. DOMA provides, in pertinent part, that a marriage is defined as a union between a man and a woman for all federal law purposes.[31] DOMA would seemingly end the prospects of a same-sex marriage as the basis of a spousal immigrant visa petition. This would be as true for a foreign same-sex marriage as for a same-sex marriage legally solemnized in the United States, such as a Massachusetts same-sex marriage. The U.S. government is under no legal obligation to give effect to a foreign marriage between persons of the same sex. In fact, at its enactment, DOMA was specifically intended as a bar to recognizing foreign same-sex marriages.[32] While the United States commonly does give effect to foreign heterosexual marriages, it does so based on notions of comity, or international good will, not under any legal obligation (absent a specific treaty).[33]

THE 2003 YATES MEMO, THE 2004 YATES MEMO, AND IN RE: LOVO-LARA

Despite the possibility of judicial review and intervention, USCIS issued a memorandum in 2003 regarding spousal immigrant visa petitions.[34] The 2003 Yates Memo contained uncompromising language regarding foreign marriages considered offensive to public policy in the United States.[35] Citing DOMA, the memo strongly confirmed that petitions based on same-sex marriages are to be denied. Moreover, USCIS rejected the notion that a marriage between "opposite" sex partners can be valid if one of the parties to the marriage is a post-operative transsexual.[36] Here, the memo stated that since Congress has not addressed the issue of whether the change in sex is recognized for federal law purposes, USCIS is therefore forced to conclude that this is a same-sex marriage and ineligible for I-130 petition purposes under DOMA.[37] The 2003 Yates Memo also cited the *Howerton* decision and reiterated that "defining marriage under immigration law is a question of Federal law, not state law."[38]

Just over a year later, USCIS issued a second memorandum touching on the adjudication of I-130 spousal immigrant petitions filed by or on behalf of a transsexual person.[39] In the 2004 Yates Memo, USCIS's position that I-130 petitions filed by or on behalf of a post-operative transsexual should be denied was expanded to include I-130 petitions filed by or on behalf of an individual who "claims to be a transsexual, regardless of whether [he or she] has undergone sex reassignment surgery."[40] The 2004 Yates Memo continued to justify this exclusion based on the fact that, absent a controlling federal law on this point, USCIS had no legal authority to recognize a person's change of sex.

The Board of Immigration Appeals (BIA) effectively overturned the holding of the 2004 Yates Memo in the case *In re: Jose Maurico Lovo-Lara*.[41] This case involved the denial of an I-130 petition filed by a post-operative transsexual USC on behalf

---

[30] Defense of Marriage Act, Pub. L. No. 104-199, 110 Stat. 2419 (1996).

[31] *Id.*

[32] D. Dunlap, "Congressional Bills Withhold Sanction of Same-Sex Unions," *N.Y. Times*, May 9, 1996, at B15 (quoting Representative Bob Barr (R-GA), "[DOMA] does not outlaw gay marriage," but by withholding federal tax, welfare, pension, health, immigration and survivors' benefits, the bill denies gay couples many of the civil advantages of marriage).

[33] Moreover, the proposed Federal Marriage Amendment to the U.S. Constitution (FMA) would define marriage as a union between a man and a woman and also would incorporate the limiting language of the Defense of Marriage Act. The FMA was first proposed by Rep. Marilyn Musgrave in 2002. While the FMA currently is not believed to have enough congressional support to pass and be sent to the states for ratification, its support has continued to grow each year.

[34] USCIS Memorandum, William R. Yates, Acting Associate Director for Operations, USCIS, "Spousal Immigrant Visa Petitions (*AFM* Update AD 02-16)," *published on* AILA
continued

InfoNet at Doc. No. 03072915 (*posted* Mar. 20, 2003) (hereinafter the 2003 Yates Memo).

[35] *Id.*

[36] *Id.* at §J.

[37] *Id.* at §I.

[38] *Id.*

[39] USCIS Memorandum, William R. Yates, Associate Director for Operations, USCIS, "Adjudications of Petitions and Applications Filed by or on Behalf of, or Document Requests by, Transsexual Individuals," *published on* AILA InfoNet at Doc. No. 03072915 (*posted* Apr. 16, 2004) (hereinafter the 2004 Yates Memo).

[40] *Id.*

[41] 23 I&N Dec. 746 (May 18, 2005).

of her foreign national husband. The couple was married in North Carolina after the petitioner effectively and legally changed her sex from male to female, and North Carolina recognized as legal the marriage of a post-operative transsexual and a person of the opposite sex.[42] The BIA found that it was compelled to sustain the petitioner's appeal and approve the underlying I-130 petition because the marriage was valid under North Carolina law, there was no federal law addressing the issue of transsexualism, and, lastly, DOMA and its legislative history were explicitly limited in scope to the subject of same-sex marriage.[43] Further, the BIA's decision questioned the legitimacy of DHS's reliance on the chromosomal patterns of the petitioner to determine her sex, particularly in light of the debate within the medical community concerning the legitimacy of relying on chromosomal patterns for this purpose.[44]

While the BIA's decision in *Lovo-Lara* is an example of an expansive interpretation of immigration law in the very limited scope of the facts of the case involving a post-operative transsexual in a state that recognizes a legal change of sex, the fact remains that the 2003 Yates Memo's holding still prohibits the approval of an I-130 petition filed by or on behalf of a same-sex spouse.

SAME-SEX MARRIAGES AND ETHICAL CONSIDERATIONS OF FILING AN I-130 PETITION

In addition to the domestic legal obstacles precluding the approval of an I-130 petition based on same-sex marriage, there are practical factors that affect the lives of our clients as well. It may be ill-advised to recommend marriage in a jurisdiction that

recognizes same-sex marriage to a bi-national gay or lesbian couple considering the option.[45] Assuming the foreign partner is able to leave and return to the United States, there are many reasons why an I-130 petition should not be filed. Such a filing could be found to be fraudulent, essentially because, although the couple is in fact married, the petitioner and the beneficiary are not "married" under U.S. law. However, their lack of intent to deceive or misrepresent their marital status makes this charge unlikely. It is more probable that such a filing will be considered frivolous since it is not approvable, given that the marriage between two persons of the same sex does not create an immediate relative spousal relationship under current federal law.

A much more compelling reason to deter gay and lesbian clients from filing I-130 petitions is that they will surely obtain only denials. If appealed, the denial of a petition is almost certain to be sustained on the numerous grounds cited in this article. At this time, such a ruling at the appellate level would be devastating for the future of litigation in this area and could set back the greater movement for equality for lesbian and gay persons.

Finally, filing such a petition would provoke only false expectations and be a waste of your clients' money (itself a potential ethical issue) and energy, and may also make the foreign national vulnerable to the issuance of a Notice to Appear if he or she has failed to maintain legal status.

UNITING AMERICAN FAMILIES ACT (FORMERLY THE PERMANENT PARTNERS IMMIGRATION ACT)

The Uniting American Families Act (UAFA)[46] is recently introduced legislation constituting the best hope for bi-national same-sex couples. First introduced by Representative Jerrold Nadler (D-NY) on Valentine's Day in February 2000 as the Permanent Partners Immigration Act, this bill would amend the INA to add the words "permanent partner" wherever the INA contains the word

---

[42] *Id.*

[43] *Id.* (holding that "[t]here is no indication that the DOMA was meant to apply to a marriage involving a postoperative transsexual where the marriage is considered by the State in which it was performed as one between two individuals of the opposite sex").

[44] *Id.* The BIA's decision referred to a much more complex and accurate set of factors that medical experts consider to be determinative of sex, including: (1) Genetic or chromosomal sex—XX or XY; (2) Gonadal sex—testes or ovaries; (3) Internal morphologic sex—seminal vesicles/prostate or vagina/uterus/fallopian tubes; (4) External morphologic sex —penis/scrotum or clitoris/labia; (5) Hormonal sex— androgens or estrogens; (6) Phenotypic sex (secondary sexual features)—facial and chest hair or breasts; (7) Assigned sex and gender of rearing; and (8) Sexual identity.

[45] While a Canadian marriage between a USC and her foreign same sex spouse will not confer a benefit for immigration purposes, it may be used as an indication of immigrant intent and thus complicate future entries for a visitor or a student. Attorneys should advise clients about this issue if they express an intention of marrying in Canada.

[46] H.R. 3006, 109th Cong. (2005); S. 1278, 109th Cong. (2005).

"spouse."[47] The UAFA defines a "permanent partner" as an individual 18 years of age or older; in a committed, intimate relationship with another individual 18 years of age or older; who is financially interdependent with that other individual; not married to or in a permanent partner relationship with any other person.[48] This bill would bring the United States in line with the 17 other countries that recognize same-sex couples for immigration purposes.[49] Reintroduced last year in the House of Representatives and the Senate, UAFA has the support of 10 senators and 93 representatives.[50] The American Immigration Lawyers Association and other organizations that promote fairness in our immigration laws urge the passage of UAFA. This is the first piece of legislation to grant same-sex couples recognition under federal law, and it does so without giving legal effect to same-sex marriages. Although this bill is far from having enough support for passage, it is encouraging to note that most of its declared support came after 9/11, a period when Congress grew increasingly sensitive to criticism that it was too expansive in enacting immigration laws. UAFA has now been referred to the Judiciary Committee in both houses of Congress.[51] While this bill may not be an immediate solution to a client's present situation, UAFA remains a pragmatic, non-political option, and advising clients and colleagues to contact their congressperson to encourage sponsorship of UAFA is a proactive step that can be taken to move toward making same-sex partner immigration a reality. Given the unlikelihood of same-sex marriage rights gaining recognition in the immigration context in the near future, the enactment of UAFA is the best prospect for making family reunification, a principal goal of our immigration laws, a reality for the tens of thousands of couples in this situation.

---

[47] *Id.*

[48] *Id.* at §2.

[49] Australia, Belgium, Brazil, Canada, Denmark, Finland, France, Germany, Iceland, Israel, the Netherlands, New Zealand, Norway, South Africa, Spain, Sweden, and the United Kingdom. *See www.immigrationequality.org* (last visited Mar. 10, 2003).

[50] *See http://thomas.loc.gov* (last visited Mar. 10, 2003).

[51] *Id.*

STOPPING TIME AND IGNORING THE REALITY OF AGING: THE SIMPLE BEAUTY OF THE CHILD STATUS PROTECTION ACT

by Royal F. Berg and Ronald H. Ng[*]

In its purest form, immigration law is about families, preserving them, reuniting them, and fighting for them. The concept of family permeates all aspects of immigration law, from the basic I-130 petition, to finding a way for the son of an executive of a multi-national corporation to stay in the United States. Family plays a role in asylum and waiver adjudications, and whether a child will be allowed to stay with his or her parents, or be faced with the perils of undocumented status and the horror of deportation.

For years, immigration lawyers struggled with the institutional inefficiencies of the (former) Immigration and Naturalization Service (INS), to try to have applications adjudicated before a child would "age out," *i.e.*, turn 21 years old. Turning 21 meant changing classifications and often losing the right to adjust status and delaying immigration. The authors also had the difficult task of explaining to their Filipino clients that naturalization would mean the waiting period for a visa for an unmarried son or daughter would lengthen. This forced a Hobson's choice for the lawful permanent resident (LPR) parent: between naturalizing and thereby delaying the immigration of a unmarried child, but permitting a petition for a married child, or not naturalizing and allowing for the immigration of an unmarried son or daughter sooner, but precluding the petition for a married son or daughter, and denial to the parent of the other myriad of benefits of U.S. citizenship.

The Child Status Protection Act (CSPA),[1] though not eliminating all of the stresses of the practice of immigration law, went a long way to reducing our ulcers and delaying the inevitable onslaught of grey hair. A brilliant solution to the harsh realities of the pragmatics of immigration law, CSPA allowed for the stoppage of time and the naturalization of a petitioning parent without jeopardizing the immigration possibilities of an unmarried son or daughter.

The article will explore this wonderful piece of legislation and review the government memos that have addressed it.

THE STATUTE

The CSPA was enacted to provide "age-out" protections to children who would otherwise have no longer qualified as children for immigration purposes upon turning 21 years old. CSPA benefits both children who are direct beneficiaries of relative immigrant visa petitions filed on their behalf and children who are the derivative beneficiaries of relative or employment preference immigrant visa petitions, applications for asylum or refugee status, and diversity immigrant applications, by allowing them to retain classification as a "child," even if they have reached the age of 21.

The reason that "age-out" protection is needed is because a "child" is defined in §101(b)(1) of the Immigration and Nationality Act (INA) to mean, generally, an unmarried person under 21 years of age. This definition has not been altered by CSPA. However, CSPA changes the rules for determining a person's age, allowing a person who may chronologically be over the age of 21 to continue to be considered to be under 21 for purposes of eligibility for immigration benefits.

[*] **Royal Berg** is an elected director of AILA's Board of Governors. He served as chair of the Greater Chicago Chapter of AILA and chair of the Immigration and Naturalization Law Committee of the Chicago Bar Association. Mr. Berg also served for three years as chair of AILA's liaison with the Executive Office for Immigration Review. He is a recipient of the Chicago AILA Chapter's Joseph Minsky Beacon of Light Award and the Chicago Bar Association's Edward Lewis Award, honoring him for his pro bono work.

Ronald Ng is an attorney with the Law Offices of Kenneth Y. Geman & Associates in Chicago.

The authors wish to express their appreciation to Kenneth Y. Geman, without whose assistance this article would not have been possible. The authors also wish to acknowledge the excellent practice advisories on CSPA by M. Kenney of AILF: "Aging Out: Recent Developments Related to the Child Status Protection Act and Other Provisions," *published on* AILA InfoNet at Doc. No. 05022464 (*posted* Feb. 24, 2005) and "The Child Status Protection Act Updated," *published on* AILA InfoNet at Doc. No. 04031261 (*posted* Mar. 12, 2004).

[1] Child Status Protection Act of 2002, Pub. L. No. 107-208, 116 Stat. 927 (Aug. 6, 2002), *published on* AILA InfoNet at Doc. No. 02080740 (*posted* Aug. 7, 2002).

The lack of the age-out protections provided by CSPA, especially with the lengthy processing times and delays by legacy INS, had very harsh results under the prior law. Before CSPA, individuals had to remain under the age of 21 years old throughout each stage of the processing in order to continue to qualify as a "child" for purposes of immigration benefits. If adjustment of status or issuance of an immigrant visa could not be completed in time, individuals who were under the age of 21 when processing first began lost their eligibility to obtain lawful permanent residence as a derivative child through their parents upon reaching 21. They were then placed into a lower preference category with a substantially longer wait for visa availability. A derivative asylee who did not adjust status before turning 21 was required to file an asylum application as a principal asylum applicant in order to adjust status.

CSPA added or amended various provisions of the INA to establish special rules for determining the age of a child for immigration purposes. These special rules allow a child to retain eligibility for derivative classification, irrespective of the child's actual age as determined from date of birth. The extent of the age-out protections that CSPA provides varies, depending on the preference category of a child (or parent) and the type of application that is involved. As the February 14, 2003, memorandum of Johnny N. Williams, Executive Associate Commissioner of the Office of Field Operations of legacy INS acknowledged, "it is impossible to anticipate and address every possible scenario" involving CSPA.[2]

The changes in law made in CSPA set or lock in the age of the child according to a specific event or point in time, earlier than the date of adjustment of status or immigrant visa issuance. Depending on the category of the child, this specific event is the date of the filing of the I-130 Petition for Alien Relative, the date of the naturalization of a parent who was an LPR when the I-130 Petition for Alien Relative was first filed with U.S. Citizenship and Immigration Services (USCIS), the date on which an immigrant visa first becomes available minus the number of days that it took USCIS to adjudicate the petition, or the date that the parent filed an application for asylum or refugee protection.

Under CSPA, the child continues to be a "child" for purposes of immigration benefits, provided that the child does not marry and any procedures specifically required by CSPA for the child to lock in his or her age are followed.

The rules are relatively simple and straightforward for children who are immediate relatives of U.S. citizens and derivative asylees and refugees, but much more complicated for children of LPRs and successful diversity visa program applicants. Section 6 of CSPA also provides for the automatic conversion into the family first preference category of a beneficiary of a petition under INA §203(a)(2)(B), upon the naturalization of the petitioning parent before the beneficiary obtains lawful permanent residence.

Child of a U.S. Citizen

Children of U.S. citizens are covered by CSPA §2, which amended the statute by adding INA §201(f). This statutory provision locks in the age of a child of a U.S. citizen, using the child's age on the date that the U.S. citizen parent filed the I-130 Petition for Alien Relative on behalf of the child with USCIS. With regard to CSPA §2, the September 20, 2002, Williams memorandum states:

> The Service will now use the date of the filing of a Form I-130, Petition for Alien Relative, to determine the age of a beneficiary adjusting as the child of a United States citizen (USC). For example, if a Form I-130 is filed for the child of a USC when the child is 20, that child will remain eligible for adjustment as an IR-2 or as an IR-7, even if the adjustment does not occur until the child turns 21, provided the child remains unmarried.[3]

---

[2] The Feb. 14, 2003, memorandum (HQADN 70/6.1.1) was the second to be issued on CSPA by Executive Associate Commissioner Williams. *See* INS Memorandum, "The Child Status Protection Act—Memorandum Number 2" (Feb. 14, 2003), *published on* AILA InfoNet at Doc. No. 03031040 (*posted* Mar. 10, 2003) (hereinafter Feb. 14, 2003, Williams memorandum).

Williams also issued a Sept. 20, 2002, memorandum on CSPA. *See* INS Memorandum, "The Child Status Protection Act" (Sept. 20, 2002), *published on* AILA InfoNet at Doc. No. 02092732 (*posted* Sept. 27, 2002.) (hereinafter Sept. 20, 2002, Williams memorandum).

[3] Sept. 20, 2002, Williams memorandum, *supra* note 2. Although an immediate relative child could still lose eligibility for this classification, if he or she marries during a lengthy delay in adjudication, the Feb. 14, 2003, Williams memorandum takes the unreasonable position that "[f]or immediate relative adjustments, as the age is locked in on the date of filing, no expediting should ever be needed."

INA §201(f)(2) also provides that, if a parent who is an LPR at the time of filing of the I-130 petition subsequently naturalizes, the age of the child shall be determined using the child's age on the date that the parent becomes a U.S. citizen. If the child is under the age of 21 on the date that his or her parent naturalizes, the child will be automatically converted into the immediate relative category. The September 20, 2002, Williams memorandum states:

> The Service will now use the child's age on the date of the parent's naturalization to determine whether the child will be eligible for immediate relative status. For example, if a lawful permanent resident (LPR) files a Form I-130 for her 16-year old daughter and then naturalizes when the daughter is 20, that daughter will remain eligible for adjustment as an IR-2 or as an IR-7, even if the adjustment does not occur until after she turns 21.[4]

In addition, a married child whose marriage is terminated while he or she is under the age of 21 also receives benefits under CSPA §2. He or she will qualify as an immediate relative child for immigration purposes, with his or her age being fixed on the date of the termination of the marriage:

> Section 2 of the CSPA also amends the Act to allow married children of USCs to use their age on the date of the termination of their marriage when determining under which immigrant category to adjust. For example, if a USC files a Form I-130 for his 18 year-old married son and that son subsequently obtains a divorce prior to turning 21, that son will be classifiable as an IR-2 or as an IR-7, even if the adjustment does not occur until after he turns 21.[5]

Unmarried Son or Daughter of an LPR and Derivative Beneficiaries—Accompanying or Following to Join Provision in INA §203(d)

Determining the "age" of a child of an LPR in the family second preference category and the "age" of derivative children is much more complex. The age of a child in this category is not fixed by a single event, such as the filing of the I-130 Petition for Alien Relative or the naturalization of the parent. Rather, CSPA §3, entitled "Treatment of Certain Unmarried Sons and Daughters Seeking Status as Family-Sponsored, Employment-Based, and Diver-

sity Immigrants," establishes a mathematical formula that is to be used to determine the age of a child classified under INA §203(a)(2)(A) as the unmarried son or daughter of an LPR and a derivative child of a parent who is a family-sponsored, employment-based, or diversity immigrant. This section of CSPA amends the INA by adding §203(h).

Under the mathematical formula, the number of days that the visa petition was pending adjudication by USCIS is subtracted from the age of the child on the date that a visa number becomes available to the child (or the child's parent). Each of the terms in the mathematical formula has a specific interpretation.

There is a "visa available" when the priority date of the child or the child's parent is current. This is determined by reference to the U.S. Department of State's (DOS) monthly *Visa Bulletin*. Both USCIS and DOS have stated in their policy guidance that they will consider the date a visa becomes available to be the first day of the month for which the *Visa Bulletin* shows the child's priority date as being current.[6]

If a visa is available when the petition is approved, USCIS will consider the visa availability date for purposes of the mathematical formula in CSPA §3 to be the date the petition is approved.[7]

In those cases where visa availability retrogresses after the child has applied for adjustment of status based upon a then-current priority date, USCIS will note the earlier visa availability date and use that date to calculate the child's age under CSPA §3 when the priority date again becomes current. The Feb. 14, 2003, Williams memorandum states on page 3:

> If a visa availability date regresses, and an alien has already filed a Form I-485 based on an approved Form I-130 or Form I-140, the Service should retain the Form I-485 and note the visa availability date at the time the Form I-485 was filed. Once the visa number again becomes available for that preference category, determine

---

[4] Sept. 20, 2002, Williams memorandum, *supra* note 2, at 2.

[5] *Id.*

[6] *See* Feb. 14, 2003, Williams memorandum, *supra* note 2, at 2–3 ("The date that a visa number becomes available is the first day of the month of the Department of State (DOS) Visa Bulletin, which indicates availability of a visa for that preference category.").

[7] *See* Feb. 14, 2003, Williams memorandum, *supra* note 2, at 3 ("The date that a visa number becomes available is the approval date of the immigrant petition if, according to the DOS Visa Bulletin, a visa number was already available for that preference category on that date of approval.").

whether the beneficiary is a "child" using the visa availability date marked on the Form I-485. If, however, an alien has not filed a Form I-485 prior to the visa availability date regressing, and then files a Form I-485 when the visa availability date again becomes current, the alien's age should be determined using the subsequent visa availability date.[8]

The period that a petition was "pending" means the period between the date the petition was properly filed and the date that the petition was approved. The February 14, 2003, Williams memorandum states:

> The "period that a petition is pending" is the date that it is properly filed (receipt date) until the date an approval is issued on the petition.

For a derivative child of a diversity immigrant, on the other hand, a "petition" is considered to be pending from the first day of the diversity visa program mail-in period for the year in which the diversity immigrant was selected to the date that the notification letter of selection for further processing under the diversity visa program was received. The February 14, 2003, Williams memorandum states on page 4:

> For the purpose of determining the period during which the "petition is pending," Service officers should use the period between the first day of the DV mail-in application period for the program year in which the principal applicant has qualified and the date on the letter notifying the principal alien that his/her application has been selected (the congratulatory letter). That period should then be subtracted from the derivative alien's age on the date the visa became available to the principal alien.

It is important to note that the locking in of a child's age according to the mathematical formula in CSPA §3 *does not occur automatically*. Rather, CSPA §3 requires the child to have "sought to acquire the status of an alien lawfully admitted for permanent residence" within one year of a visa becoming available to the child. Only if the child seeks LPR status within one year of a visa becoming available is the child's age locked in according to the mathematical formula established by CSPA §3.

Footnote 3 of the February 14, 2003, Williams memorandum indicates that USCIS interprets "hav-

ing sought to acquire lawful permanent resident status" to mean, in the case of a child who is presently in the United States, the filing of an application for adjustment of status. DOS has taken the position, for a person who is processing for an immigrant visa, that a DS-230 Part I must be submitted for the requirement of "having sought to acquire lawful permanent resident status" within one year of visa availability to be met.[9] Paragraph 17 of the DOS cable states:

> In cases where the principal applicant's case goes through visa processing rather than adjustment of status, a better interpretation would be to measure the date on which the applicant first seeks to acquire LPR status as the date on which the applicant submits the completed DS-230, Part I. Therefore, if a preference or DV visa applicant submits the DS-230, Part I within one year of visa availability, then the applicant would be eligible for CSPA benefits, assuming the CSPA otherwise applies to the case.

If the child is a derivative on a petition for a parent, a DS-230 Part I covering the principal is insufficient to establish that the derivative sought to acquire LPR status within one year:

> In cases involving derivatives, it is not enough that the principal may have taken the required steps within the one-year time frame—the derivative him/herself must have taken those steps (or the principal must have taken the required step specifically for the derivative, acting as the derivative's agent). Therefore, if the applicant seeking CSPA benefits is a derivative, then the determining factor is the submission of a completed DS-230, Part I, that specifically covers the derivative. The submission of a DS-230 Part I that covers the principal will not serve to meet the requirement.

Where the parent has already adjusted status in the United States, the date that the parent files an I-824 Application for Action on An Approved Application or Petition for the child to follow-to-join will be considered the date the child seeks to acquire lawful permanent residence for purposes of the mathematical formula in CSPA §3. The DOS cable states at paragraph 22:

---

[8] Feb. 14, 2003, Williams memo, *supra* note 2, at 3.

---

[9] *See* DOS Cable, "Child Status Protection Act: ALDAC #2" (Jan. 17, 2003), *published on* AILA InfoNet at Doc. No. 03020550 (*posted* Feb. 5, 2003).

The requirement that the preference or DV applicant submit the DS-230, Part I within one year of visa availability shall apply only in cases where the principal applicant was processed for a visa at a consular post abroad. If the principal applicant adjusted status in the U.S. and a derivative is applying for a visa abroad to follow-to-join, then the date on which the derivative will be considered to have sought LPR status for purposes of satisfying CSPA Section 3 will generally be the date on which the principal (acting as the derivative beneficiary's agent) filed the Form I-824 that is used to process the derivative's following to join application. Therefore, in cases involving a derivative seeking to follow to join a principal who adjusted in the U.S., the derivative can benefit from the CSPA if the principal filed a Form I-824 for the beneficiary within one year of a visa becoming available (i.e., within one year of the case becoming current or petition approval, whichever is later).

The DOS cable recognizes that there may be cases in which "some other concrete step" may have been taken besides the filing of an I-824 and advises that "posts should submit such cases to the Department (CA/VO/L/A) for an advisory opinion."

As of this writing, the Board of Immigration Appeals (BIA) has only issued one decision on CSPA. That decision, while excellent, is unpublished and not precedent.[10] In *Kim*, the Board held that the CSPA §3 requirement of having "sought to acquire lawful permanent resident status" within one year of a visa being available was satisfied where the beneficiary's parents consulted an attorney regarding the filing of an adjustment of status application for their daughter within the one-year period, but the adjustment of status application was not filed by the attorney until 17 months after eligibility.

In removal proceedings in that case, the immigration judge had initially denied Ms. Kim's adjustment application on the ground that she did not qualify as a derivative beneficiary of her father's employment-based visa petition because she had not "sought to acquire" LPR status within one year. The IJ interpreted "sought to acquire" to mean the filing of the I-485 Application to Register Permanent Residence or Adjust Status, rejecting the argument by Ms. Kim that her parents had retained counsel to prepare their

applications for permanent residence within one year of the visa petition being approved. The BIA reversed, stating:

> We find that the Immigration Judge's interpretation of the statute, although reasonable, should not apply in the instant case. This Board has held that in interpreting a statute we look first to the precise language of the statute. . . . Congress chose to use the words "sought to acquire" rather than "filed" in section 203(h)(1)(A) of the Act. The plain meaning of seek or "sought" includes "to try to acquire or gain" or "to make an attempt." Merriam-Webster's Collegiate Dictionary 1124 (11th Ed. 2003). The term "acquire" is defined as "to gain possession or control of; to get or obtain." Black's Law Dictionary 25 (8th ed. 2004). In other words, the alien must "make an attempt or get or obtain" status as a lawful permanent resident within one-year of such availability. By contrast, the plain meaning of "file" is "to deliver a legal document to the court clerk or the record custodian for placement in the official record." Black's Law Itinerary 660 (8th Ed. 2004). See e.g. 8 C.F.R. 204.1(b)–(d)(2004) (the DHS requirement for filing a visa petition).[11]

The BIA, citing *Matter of M/V Seru*,[12] noted that it is not bound by DOS or DHS cables, and therefore, was not constrained by the narrow interpretation of either the February 14, 2003, Williams memorandum or the DOS cable. The Board determined that under the rules of statutory construction and the congressional intent as expressed in the legislative history of CSPA, "sought to acquire" has a broader meaning than "to file." The Board stated:

> we conclude that Congress intended the term "sought to acquire" lawful permanent residence at section 203(h)(1)(A) to be broadly interpreted within the context of the statute, and not limited to the filing of the application. Under the facts of this case, where the record demonstrates that the alien's parents had hired counsel to prepare the application for adjustment of status within a year of the approval of the employment based visa petition, the application for adjustment of status to lawful permanent residence was actually filed within a reasonable time thereafter, and the alien child was still under the age of 21 at the time the application for adjustment was filed, we find that

---

[10] *Matter of Kim*, File No. A77-828-503 (BIA Dec. 20, 2004).

[11] *Id.* at 2–3.

[12] 20 I&N Dec. 595 (BIA 1992).

the respondent "sought to acquire" lawful permanent residence within a year of her eligibility for such status. To conclude otherwise would undermine the very purpose and intent of the statute, which was to protect an alien child from "aging out" due to "no fault of her own."[13]

While *Kim* is not a precedent decision, the arguments and findings contained therein can and should be used before DOS and the Department of Homeland Security (DHS), and the Executive Office for Immigration Review. Also important to cite is *Padash v. INS*,[14] in which the Ninth Circuit held that CSPA should be interpreted expansively, and *INS v. St. Cyr*,[15] for the holding that immigration laws are to be interpreted so as to favor the alien. The congressional history of CSPA is also helpful and should be cited. As noted by the Board in *Kim*:

> The clear congressional intent in enacting the CSPA was to "bring families together." 148 Cong. Rec. H4989-01, H49991, July 22, 2002, statement by Rep. Sensenbrenner.[16] Congress desired to "provide relief to children who lose out when [the administrative agency] takes too long to process their adjustment of status applications." *Id* at H4992, statement by Rep Gekas.[17]

---

[13] *Kim*, at 4.

[14] 358 F.3d 1161 (9th Cir. 2004).

[15] 533 U.S. 289, 121 S. Ct. 2271 (2001).

[16] Representative Sensenbrenner's (R-WI) full statement regarding the purpose of CSPA to which the BIA cites in *Kim* was:

> Bringing families together is a prime goal of our immigration system. H.R. 1209 facilitates and hastens the reuniting of legal immigrants' families. It is family-friendly legislation that is in keeping with our proud traditions. I urge my colleagues to support this bill.

[17] Rep. Gekas stated:

> H.R. 1209, "the Child Status Protection Act," allows the children of U.S. citizens whose visa petitions were filed before they reached 21, but turn 21 before their adjustment of status applications are processed, to adjust status without having to wait for years. Pursuant to the bill, they will still be considered minor children of U.S. citizens, thus avoiding the first preference backlog. This bill protects the children of American citizens whose opportunity to receive a visa quickly has been lost because of INS delays. It will also apply to those rare cases where a child "ages out" overseas during the usually more expeditious State Department visa processing. The bill was modified in the Senate *to provide relief to other children who lose out when the INS takes too long to process their adjustment of status applications*—such as the children of permanent residents and of asylees

continued

The overriding concern was that alien children "through no fault of their own, lose the opportunity to obtain immediate relative status." H.R. Rep 107-45, H. Rep. No. 45, 107th Cong., 1st Sess. 2001, reprinted in 2002 U.S.C.C.A.N. 640, 641 (Apr. 20, 2001) 2001 WL 406244 (Leg. His.).[18]

In practice, the protections that CSPA §3 provides to children of LPRs and derivative beneficiaries of preference petitions have been inadequate in many cases. The long waiting periods for an immigrant visa number to become available in the family second preference classification and the retrogression in the employment preference categories, combined with the shortened processing times for many petitions, mean that many children continue to be at risk of aging out. Under the formula in CSPA §3, very little time is subtracted from the chronological age of the child, which, in many cases, is much higher by the time that a visa does become available. Another limitation is that beneficiaries are in many cases unaware when their priority date has become current so as to trigger the beginning of the one-year period during which immigrant status must have been sought in order to receive the benefits of the calculation in CSPA §3.

An improvement on CSPA would be that the age of the child would lock in when the I-130 Petition for Alien Relative was filed. This would be similar to the rule for derivative children of applicants for asylum and refugee status and the children of U.S. citizens.

Derivative Child of an Asylee or Refugee

The general rule for the derivative child of an asylee or refugee is that the age of the child is locked in on the date the parent files the I-589 Application for Asylum or the I-590 Registration for Classification as a Refugee.

USCIS guidance on the provisions for derivative asylees and refugees in CSPA §§4–5 can be found in two memoranda. The first is an August 7, 2002, memorandum of Joseph E. Langlois, Director of the Asylum Division, on processing derivative refugees and asylees under CSPA (HQIAO 120/12.9) (Lan-

---

and refugees. I want to commend Senator Feinstein for these changes.

(Emphasis added.)

[18] *Kim*, at 4.

glois memorandum).[19] The second is the more comprehensive August 17, 2004, memorandum of William R. Yates, Associate Director for Operations, entitled "The Child Status Protection Act—Children of Asylees and Refugees" (HQOPRD) (Yates memorandum).[20] The Yates memorandum states:

> For asylum and refugee applications pending on or after August 6, 2002, continued eligibility for derivative status is determined based on the child's age at the time the parent filed the Form I-589, Application for Asylum and Withholding of Removal, or Form I-590, Registration for Classification as Refugee.

The age of a derivative child of an asylee or refugee who qualifies for age-out protection under CSPA §4 or §5 will remain locked in for all purposes until the derivative child has adjusted status. The Yates memorandum states that the derivative child "will retain classification as a child for purposes of the initial asylum or refugee determination, for any subsequent Form I-730 Refugee/Asylee Relative Petition, and/or for the Section 209 adjustment."

The Yates memorandum indicates that the derivative child must be listed on the I-589 or I-590 prior to adjudication of the parent's application in order to be eligible for continued classification as a child under CSPA. In addition, a child who ages out before the August 6, 2002, enactment date of CSPA derives no benefits *unless* an application for one of the covered benefits was pending on that date. The Yates memorandum clarifies that USCIS will apply a very broad definition of "pending": "if all necessary steps for issuing travel documents to the derivative child or following to join child (such as approval of the Form I-730, the overseas interview, or completion of all security checks) were not completed on or before August 6, 2002, the case is considered to be 'pending.'"[21]

Opting-Out When Mom Naturalizes

CSPA §6 provides for the automatic conversion into the family first preference category of an unmarried son or daughter who is the beneficiary of a petition filed in the family second preference category in INA §203(a)(2)(B) upon the naturalization of the petitioning parent. As discussed in the March 23, 2004, memorandum of Joe Cuddihy, USCIS Director of International Affairs (Cuddihy memorandum), CSPA §6 also permits a person who is eligible for automatic conversion to "opt out" and be processed as an immigrant in the family first preference.[22] A beneficiary will want to "opt out" where the visa availability dates in the second preference category for an unmarried son or daughter are actually earlier or more current than the first preference.

At the time the Cuddihy memorandum was issued, only beneficiaries from the Philippines fell within this category. The Cuddihy memorandum instructs that beneficiaries from the Philippines wishing to opt out of automatic conversion under CSPA §6 must file a request in writing, addressed to the Officer in Charge at the U.S. Embassy in Manila. The Cuddihy memorandum states:

> If the beneficiary's request is approved, the beneficiary's eligibility for family-based immigration will be determined as if his or her parent had never naturalized and they will remain a second preference alien.

DHS takes the position that the opt-out provision in CSPA §6 applies only to a petition that was initially filed for an unmarried son or daughter under INA §203(a)(2)(B). According to Cuddihy,

> section 6 of the CSPA applies only to "a petition under this section initially filed for an alien unmarried son or daughter's classification as a family-sponsored immigrant under section 203(a)(2)(B)." Thus, this opt-out provision applies only to beneficiaries whose initial Form I-130, Petition for Alien Relative, was filed based on their being the unmarried son or daughter of an LPR. Therefore, if a Form I-130 was filed by an LPR on behalf of his or her child when the child was under 21 years of age, the child attained the age of 21,

---

[19] INS Memorandum, Joseph E. Langlois, Director of the Asylum Division, "H.R. 1209—Child Status Protection Act" (Aug. 7, 2002), *published on* AILA InfoNet at Doc. No. 02090531 (*posted* Sept. 5, 2002) (hereinafter Langlois memorandum).

[20] USCIS Memorandum, William R. Yates, Associate Director for Operations, "The Child Status Protection Act—Children of Asylees and Refugees" (HQOPRD 70/6.1) (Aug. 17, 2004), *published on* AILA InfoNet at Doc. No. 04091561 (*posted* Sept. 15, 2004) (hereinafter Yates memorandum).

[21] *Id.* at 2.

[22] USCIS memorandum, Joe Cuddihy, USCIS Director of International Affairs, "Section 6 of the Child Status Protection Act" (HQOPRD 70/6) (Mar. 23, 2004), *published on* AILA InfoNet at Doc. No. 04032615 (*posted* Mar. 26, 2004) (hereinafter Cuddihy memorandum).

and then the parent naturalized, section 6 of the CSPA could not be utilized by this beneficiary.

To V or Not To V?

CSPA does not refer or apply to nonimmigrant "V" visas. Following a decision by the U.S. Court of Appeals for the Ninth Circuit, however, USCIS has decided to eliminate the "age-out" restrictions in the regulations applicable to V visa beneficiaries.

The federal regulations on V visas had provided that a child could not be admitted in V classification or be granted an extension of V status beyond his or her 21st birthday.[23] The Ninth Circuit invalidated this provision and held that it was in conflict with the statute and congressional intent in *Akhtar v. Burzynski*.[24] Subsequent to this ruling, USCIS decided to apply *Akhtar* on a nationwide basis.[25]

Effective Date

CSPA is—unfortunately, with very limited exceptions—not retroactive. CSPA generally does not protect anyone who had already aged out prior to August 6, 2002, unless he or she falls within one of the exceptions in CSPA §8. These exceptions relate to cases "pending" as of August 6, 2002. In addition to someone who ages out on or after August 6, 2002, CSPA will apply to someone who aged out before August 6, 2002, if the petition was pending on or after August 6, 2002 or the petition was approved before August 6, 2002, but no final determination has been made on the application for an immigrant visa or application for adjustment of status based on the approved petition.[26]

DOS has indicated that it will not consider a decision on an application for an immigrant visa to be a final determination, if the refusal occurred between August 6, 2001 and August 5, 2002.[27] The June 2003, DOS cable states:

> In such cases, if the alien's visa application was refused between August 6, 2001 and August 5, 2002, the refusal will not be considered a 'final determination' and the CSPA may be applied to the case.

In contrast, a refusal prior to August 6, 2001 *is* a "final determination" unless the refusal was pursuant to INA §221(g)[28] or the applicant applied for a waiver and the waiver application was pending on August 6, 2002.

CONCLUSION

Immigration lawyers are at our finest when we fight for families. While many of the tools we have historically used have been taken from us, CSPA provides us with new ways to help our clients keep their families together—a welcome change from the many anti-immigrant provisions enacted by Congress over the last 10 years.

---

[23] *See* 8 CFR §214.15(g).

[24] 384 F.3d 1193 (9th Cir. 2004).

[25] *See* USCIS Memorandum, Terrance M. O'Reilly, Director, Field Operations, "Adjudication of Form I-539 for V-2 and V-3 extension" (Jan. 10, 2005), *published on* AILA InfoNet at Doc. No. 05020460 (*posted* Feb. 4, 2005).

[26] Specifically, CSPA §8 states:

> The amendments made by this Act shall take effect on the date of the enactment of this Act and shall apply to any alien who is a derivative beneficiary or any other beneficiary of—
>
> (1) a petition for classification under section 204 of the Immigration and Nationality Act (8 USC 1154) approved before such date but only if a final determination has not been made on the beneficiary's application for an immigrant visa or adjustment of status to lawful permanent residence pursuant to such approved petition;

> (2) a petition for classification under section 204 of the Immigration and Nationality Act (8 USC 1154) pending on or after such date; or

> (3) an application pending before the Department of Justice or the Department of State on or after such date.

[27] *See* DOS cable, "Child Status Protection Act: ALDAC #4 —What Constitutes a 'Final Determination' on an Application Adjudicated Prior to the Effective Date of CSPA?" (May 17, 2003), *published on* AILA InfoNet at Doc. No. 03060243 (*posted* June 2, 2003).

[28] *Id.* Paragraph 5 states, however, that an INA §221(g) refusal may be considered to be a final determination if the case was "ultimately terminated under INA 203(g) for failure to make reasonable efforts to overcome [the] 221(g) refusal. A 203(g) termination will be considered a 'final determination.'"

continued

VIOLENCE AGAINST WOMEN ACT (VAWA) SELF-PETITIONS

by Julie E. Dinnerstein[*]

INTRODUCTION

Twenty years ago, if you met an immigrant victim of family violence who was being sponsored for lawful permanent resident (LPR) status by a family member, there was little that could be done to help that victim pursue immigration status on her[1] own. Today, after years of legislative amendments to the Immigration and Nationality Act (INA)[2] for victims of domestic violence,[3] spouses, children, and now, in

some cases, parents who suffer abuse at the hands of U.S. citizen (USC) and LPR family members have options that allow them to pursue immigration status on their own. This article will guide you through one of the most common options, the Violence Against Women Act (VAWA) self-petition on Form I-360, and identify resources and support for you and your client in this work.[4]

It is critical to remember that the VAWA self-petition described in this article is available only to certain family members of abusive USCs and LPRs. Those who have been abused by noncitizens in other immigration statuses[5] or without any immigration status will not be able to file VAWA self-petitions as a step along the path to obtaining LPR status. These battered immigrants may be eligible for other forms of immigration relief for victims of domestic violence that are beyond the scope of this article.[6]

---

[*] **Julie Dinnerstein** is the deputy director for Immigration Policy and Training at the New York Immigration Coalition. She also teaches immigration law at the School of Professional Studies at the City University of New York (CUNY). Prior to joining the Coalition, she served for six years as the Director of the Immigration Intervention Project at Sanctuary for Families. Ms. Dinnerstein is a graduate of Columbia College and Columbia Law School.

[1] Victims of domestic violence may be male or female, and immigration options for victims of domestic violence are open to both male and female victims. Nonetheless, the vast majority of victims of intimate partner domestic violence are women (*see, e.g.*, National Coalition Against Domestic Violence Facts, *available at www.ncadv.org/files/DV_Facts.pdf* (last viewed Mar. 15, 2006)), and the majority of immigrants who have availed themselves of protection under the Violence Against Women Act (VAWA) are spouses (as opposed to children) of abusive U.S. citizens (USCs) or lawful permanent residents (LPRs) (according to adjustment statistics in Office of Immigration Statistics, Department of Homeland Security, 2004 Yearbook of Immigration Statistics, Table 5 (Jan. 2006), *available at http://uscis.gov/graphics/shared/statistics/yearbook/Yearbook2004.pdf.*)

[2] Immigration and Nationality Act of 1952, Pub. L. No. 82-414, 66 Stat. 163 (*codified as amended at* 8 USC §§1101 *et seq.*) (INA).

[3] *See* Section 701 of the Immigration Act of 1990, Pub. L. No. 101-649, 104 Stat. 4978 (Nov. 29, 1990) (IMMACT90) (allowing conditional resident victims of domestic violence to petition to remove conditions without the abusive sponsoring spouse or parent); Subtitle G—Protections for Battered Immigrant Women and Children of Title IV, the Violence Against Women Act of the Violent Crime Control and Law Enforcement Act of 1994, Pub. L. No. 103-322, 108 Stat. 1796 (Sept. 13, 1994) (hereinafter VAWA) (creating VAWA self-petitions for immigrant spouses and children of abusive USC/LPR spouses and parents and VAWA suspension for immigrant spouses and children of abusive USC/LPR spouses and parents in deportation proceedings); Title V, Battered Immigrant Women Protection Act of 2000 of the Victims of Trafficking and Violence Protection Act of 2000, Pub. L. No. 106-386, 114 Stat. 1464 (Oct. 28, 2000) (herein-

continued

after VAWA 2000) (improving access to VAWA self-petitioning); and Title VIII, Protection of Battered and Trafficked Immigrants of the Violence Against Women and Department of Justice Reauthorization Act of 2005, Pub. L. No. 109-162, 119 Stat. 2960 (Jan. 5, 2006) (hereinafter VAWA 2005).

Every five years, when VAWA is due for reauthorization, many people express concerns that VAWA self-petitioning will disappear. There is nothing to fear for VAWA immigration remedies. While certain programs or funding sources may be disappear, the VAWA amendments to the INA are permanent.

[4] This article will focus on just one of the remedies available to immigrant victims of domestic violence seeking an alternative route to LPR status for family members of abusive USCs and LPRs—VAWA self-petitions. Charts attached as appendices to this article provide additional information about other alternatives.

[5] Note that the one exception to the rule that the abuser must be a current or former USC or LPR is found at INA §106, added by §814(c) of VAWA 2005. Under this provision, abused spouses of A, E-3, G, and H visas may obtain employment authorization benefits.

[6] For an overview of the many different remedies now available to immigrant victims of domestic violence, including gender-based asylum, T and U visas, see Julie E. Dinnerstein, "Immigration Options for Immigrant Victims of Domestic Violence," 38 *Clearinghouse Review* 427 (Sept.–Oct. 2004).

PLACING IMMIGRATION REMEDIES FOR DOMESTIC VIOLENCE VICTIMS IN CONTEXT: A BRIEF REVIEW OF IMMIGRATION AND THE FAMILY

Under U.S. immigration law, USCs and LPRs have the option to sponsor their family members for lawful permanent residence. The importance of the family-sponsorship category should not be underestimated. Of the 946,142 noncitizens granted permanent resident status in the United States in FY 2004, 621,236, or 65.6 percent, were granted to those who received residence through a family-sponsorship category.[7] This percentage, a relatively consistent one over the years, indicates that we privilege family ties over other reasons—education, skills, humanitarian, and luck (*i.e.*, the diversity visa lottery)—when we decide which noncitizens we will allow to join us as permanent members of our American society.

The critical role of the USC or LPR family sponsor is best understood through a review of the family sponsorship process—a process that, from a structural perspective, is *always* bifurcated. As an initial matter, the USC or LPR must establish his or her own immigration status and the qualifying familial relationship with the noncitizen. This process is done through the filing of a Petition for Alien Relative on Form I-130 (the Relative Petition). The Relative Petition is filed by the USC or LPR, called the petitioner. The family member who is not an LPR or USC and who would stand to benefit were the petition approved is called the beneficiary. With the Relative Petition, it is the petitioner, not the beneficiary, who is in the driver's seat.

Separately, either through the adjustment of status process here in the United States or through consular processing abroad, the intending immigrant applies for LPR status. Some relatives, called "immediate relatives,"[8] are not subject to a statutory cap as to the number who may immigrate each year and may apply for lawful permanent residence either concurrently with the filing of the Relative Petition (if in the United States), or as soon as the Relative Petition is adjudicated (if applying from overseas). In contrast to immediate relatives, those who are deemed "preference relatives"[9] are *not* immediately eligible to apply for LPR status. Instead, they must wait in line until their priority date (the filing date that becomes the intending immigrant's placeholder on line) is "current." The term "current" is used to indicate that the intending immigrant has reached the front of the line. Only at that point, anywhere from about four years to 23 years (under current family backlogs),[10] depending on the preference category and country of origin of the noncitizen, can the noncitizen *apply* for LPR status.

Throughout the entire process, from the initial filing of the Relative Petition until the final grant of residency, the petitioner has the option to withdraw the petition. This is true whether the waiting is a matter of just a few months from initial filing to grant of residency, as it might be for an immediate relative in Vermont filing an adjustment of status application with the Relative Petition, or whether the noncitizen waits decades in the Philippines after the filing of the Relative Petition for the chance to apply for residency through consular processing.

Once lawful permanent residence is granted, the U.S. government generally bows out of following familial relationships and, for the most part, the ongoing status of the family relationship will not affect the immigration status of the newly minted LPR.

---

[7] N. Rytina, "U.S. Legal Permanent Residents" (DHS Pulbications June 2005), available at *http://uscis.gov/graphics/shared/statistics/publications/FlowReportLegalPermResidents2004.pdf*.

[8] The term "immediate relative" means the spouse of a USC, the unmarried child under 21 of a USC or the parent of a USC who is 21 or over. INA §201(b)(2)(A)(i).

[9] Preference relatives are divided into the following categories:

- Unmarried sons and daughters, 21 or over, of USCs (Preference Category 1);
- Spouses and unmarried children under 21 of LPRs (Preference Category 2A);
- Unmarried sons and daughters, 21 or over of LPRs (Preference Category 2B);
- Married sons and daughters of USCs (Preference Category 3); and
- Siblings of USCs (Preference Category 4).

INA §203(a).

[10] For the most up-to-date information on the length of the wait, see the current Visa Bulletin *available at* the U.S. Department of State's website at *http://travel.state.gov/visa/frvi/bulletin/bulletin_1360.html*. For a discussion of the backlogs, see the National Immigration Forum's website for the article *Immigration Backlogs are Separating American Families, available at www.immigrationforum.org/desktopDefault.aspx?tabid=153*.

The major exception[11]—an exception that accounts for roughly 20 percent of family-sponsored immigrants[12]—is conditional permanent resident status granted to spouses and children of USCs (and LPRs)[13] under the following circumstances:

- the spousal relationship that forms the basis of the grant of permanent residency is less than two years old at the time of grant;[14]

- the parent-child relationship that forms the basis of the grant of permanent residency is less than two years old at the time of grant;[15] or

- the noncitizen entered the United States on a fiancé(e) visa.[16]

Conditional permanent resident status, accorded for a period of two years, generally requires the original petitioner and the conditional resident to apply jointly to remove the condition in the 90-day window prior to the two-year anniversary of the grant of residency.[17] The idea behind conditional permanent resident status—which gives federal immigration authorities two separate opportunities separated by at least two years to review the bona fides of the underlying marital relationship leading to immigration status—is to root out immigration marriage fraud.[18] Even with conditional permanent resident status, once the condition is removed, any further changes in family composition will not affect the residency status of the family-sponsored immigrant.

Familial relationships also play a determinative role in cancellation of removal cases. Where the U.S. government has initiated removal proceedings, a noncitizen may avoid removal and be granted LPR status upon a showing of "exceptional and extremely unusual hardship" to the noncitizen's USC or LPR "spouse, parent, or child."[19]

There is a logic to the central role of the USC or LPR anchor relative (*i.e.*, the USC or LPR relative upon whom the intending immigrant's claim is based)—whether petitioner in the family-based immigration process or anchor relative in a cancellation case. While the U.S. government does not follow the fate of a particular family forever, where a USC or LPR loses interest in having the noncitizen family member around, or, in the case of removal, cannot demonstrate extreme suffering at the loss of the noncitizen family member, the U.S. government generally has no particular reason to grant an immigration preference to the noncitizen based on a family relationship.

It is in this context of valuing family (and the general lack of interest in noncitizen family members of USCs and LPRs where the USC or LPR has lost interest in family unity) that we can understand the variations of this process created for domestic violence victims. As a society, we have a competing value, the value of protecting family members from domestic violence. This competing value sometimes trumps our practice of granting benefits only to noncitizens whose USC or LPR family members still supports their quest for permanent immigration status in the United States. The remainder of this article will explore how this competing value—protecting domestic violence victims—plays out.

---

[11] Another exception is the opportunity provided to spouses of U.S. citizens to naturalize after three years in permanent resident status. INA §319(a).

[12] *See* Office of Immigration Statistics, Dep't of Homeland Security, 2004 Yearbook of Immigration Statistics, Table 5 (Immigrants admitted by type and class of admission: fiscal year 2004) (Jan. 2005, *available at http://uscis.gov/graphics/shared/statistics/yearbook/Yearbook2004.pdf* (approximately 22 percent of family-based admissions were for conditional residents)); Office of Immigration Statistics, Dep't of Homeland Security, 2003 Yearbook of Immigration Statistics, Table 5 (Immigrants admitted by type and class of admission: fiscal year 2003) (Sept. 2004), *available at http://uscis.gov/graphics/shared/statistics/yearbook/YrBk03Im.htm* (approximately 19 percent of family-based admissions were for conditional residents).

[13] Spouses and children of LPRs, like USCs, can be granted conditional residence. *See generally* INA §216; *see also* INA §§216(g)(1)(C), 216(g)(2). In practice, however, as the backlogs for spouses and children of LPRs are longer than two years, spouses and children of LPRs are not currently being granted conditional status. Should the backlogs move more quickly, spouses and children of LPRs would be eligible for conditional permanent residence.

[14] *See generally* INA §216; *see also* INA §216(g)(1)(A).

[15] *See generally* INA §216; *see also* INA §§216(g)(1)(A), 216(g)(2).

[16] *See generally* INA §216; *see also* INA §§101(a)(15)(K), 214(d), 216(g)(1)(A), 216(g)(2), and 245(d).

[17] INA §216(d)(2).

[18] *See* S. Ignatius & E. Stickney, *Immigration Law and the Family*, §5.2 (Thomas/West 2005).

[19] INA §240A(b)(1)(D).

IMMIGRATION OPTIONS FOR VICTIMS OF VIOLENCE AT THE HANDS OF ABUSIVE USC AND LPR FAMILY MEMBERS

An Overview

While some options for domestic violence victims relate specifically to the forms of violence that they have suffered and the circumstances surrounding that violence rather than any familial relationship with a USC or LPR,[20] three immigration remedies—Violence Against Women Act (VAWA) self-petitions on Form I-360, battered spouse or child waivers on Form I-751,[21] and VAWA cancellation on Form EOIR 42B—are all variations on immigration benefits granted to noncitizens who are, but for the violence, similarly situated in happy families.[22] Depending on the noncitizen's current immigrant

status and procedural posture, she may be eligible to file for one or more of these remedies. This article focuses on the most common of these remedies, the VAWA self-petition on Form I-360.

A Word on Terminology

The term "VAWA self-petitioner" may be used for a noncitizen seeking immigration relief in the form of:

- adjustment of status;
- removal of conditions on residence;
- cancellation of removal; or
- suspension of deportation;

as the spouse, child, and in some cases, parent of an abusive

- USC;
- LPR;
- Person eligible for relief under the Cuban Refugee Adjustment Act of 1966;[23]
- Person eligible for relief under the Haitian Refugee Immigration Fairness Act of 1988 (HRIFA);[24] or
- Person eligible for relief under the Nicaraguan Adjustment and Central American Relief Act (NACARA).[25]

A recent amendment to the INA codifies this broad definition.[26] In addition, VAWA legislation has created additional remedies for victims of trafficking and certain crimes, including domestic violence.[27]

This article will use the phrase "VAWA self-petitioner" narrowly to describe those filing Special Immigrant Petitions on Form I-360, as opposed to those seeking battered spouse or child waivers, VAWA cancellation, U visas, or T visas.

---

[20] Gender-based asylum claims under INA §208, T visa claims under INA §101(a)(15)(T) and INA §214(o), and U visa claims under INA §101(a)(15)(U) and INA §214(p) do not specifically correlate to any forms of immigration relief to similarly situated noncitizens who are in happy family situations.

[21] A flow chart, originally created by Shira Galinsky, then a paralegal at Sanctuary for Families and now an attorney with South Brooklyn Legal Services, and reprinted with permission, attached as Appendix B, identifies which forms to use with VAWA self-petitions and battered spouse/child waivers.

[22] Charts at Appendix C delineate some of the major similarities and differences and at Appendix D compare and contrast VAWA self-petitions, battered spouse/child waivers, and VAWA cancellation.

Note that due to space limitations, not all variations of VAWA self-petitions will be discussed. Specifically, the following VAWA self-petition remedies are *not* discussed in this article:

VAWA self-petitioning relief under:

- the Nicaraguan Adjustment and Central American Relief Act (NACARA) (NACARA, as amended, §202(d)(1));
- Pub. L. No. 89-732 (8 USC §1255 note) (commonly known as the Cuban Adjustment Act) (see the first section of the Cuban Adjustment Act, as amended);
- the Haitian Refugee Immigration Fairness Act of 1998 (8 USC §1255 note)—spouse and children of HRIFA (HRIFA §902(d)(1)(B)) applicants.

VAWA employment authorization under INA §106, added by §814(c) of the Violence Against Women and Department of Justice Reauthorization Act of 2005, Pub. L. No. 109-162, 119 Stat. 2960 (Jan. 5, 2006), available to spouses of those granted nonimmigrant visas under the following provisions: INA §§101(a)(15)(A), 101(a)(15)(E)(iii), 101(a)(15)(G), and 101(a)(15)(H).

[23] Pub. L. No. 89-732.

[24] Pub. L. No. 105-277.

[25] Pub. L. No. 105-100, 111 Stat. 2160, Tit. II, Div. A (Nov. 19, 1997), *as amended by* Pub. L. No. 105-139, 111 Stat. 2644 (Dec. 2, 1997).

[26] Section 811 of VAWA 2005 (*codified at* INA §101(a)(51)).

[27] *See* codification at INA §§101(a)(15)(T), 101(a)(15)(U), 214(o), and 214(p).

A Few Preliminary Thoughts on Working With Domestic Violence Victims

When you begin working with a domestic violence victim, it is important to remember that your client may well be in danger. Every year in the United States, intimate partner "violence results in nearly 20 million injuries and nearly 1,300 deaths."[28] As an immigration lawyer, your role is to provide neither false assurances nor domestic violence counseling. Rather, refer your client to a domestic violence service provider[29] who can guide your client through safety planning for herself and her children, assess other needs that she may have, and make appropriate recommendations. Ideally, if you work regularly with domestic violence victims, you can develop a collaborative practice across professional disciplines.[30] For most immigration attorneys, however, who may work only occasionally with domestic violence victims, remembering that clients may need not just a sympathetic ear nor a straightforward legal service, but professional expertise from domestic violence service providers is key to ensuring the client's well-being and thus the attorney's ability to provide effective legal counsel.

The heart of any immigration case for an immigrant victim of domestic violence is her story. This is a story you will need to understand in excruciating detail. You will be able to explore your client's experiences effectively only if you can gain her trust and set up a working attorney-client relationship. As Dorchen A. Leidholdt has pointed out:

> Your first interview with your client is crucial. If she feels that you are untrustworthy, judgmental, or unable to relate to her experience, she will censor herself and you will not get the information you need to represent her effectively. . . . [A]n attorney-client relationship predicated on trust . . . may not be easy to achieve,

however, particularly since she is emerging from a relationship in which her trust has been repeatedly betrayed.[31]

When interviewing your client, be careful with "why" questions, such as:

- Why did he hit you?
- Why did you ever marry him?
- Why did you stay with him?

Such questions may seem straightforward ones designed to bring out basic facts of the case. To a domestic violence survivor, however, these kinds of questions may sound like victim-blaming and make it harder for your client to work with you in gathering the information for your case that you will need. Instead, try to ask more open-ended questions. You may need to schedule more time to interview a domestic violence survivor than you would need for other clients.

Also be aware that your client's description of her experiences may change over time. What may seem like a contradictory story to you may instead be the product of an emerging ability to recount her experiences, a deepening comfort in her own relationship with you, and the confusion that may be present with a trauma survivor. Accept that the relating of facts may not be as constant as you might like in the initial telling, but be sure that by the time you submit the VAWA self-petition, everything within the petition is consistent.

Learning about the dynamics of domestic violence can help you both to consider some of what your client may be going through and to better direct client and witness interviews, and evidence-gathering efforts. The Power and Control Wheel,[32] modified to emphasize some of the experiences of immigrants, offers an excellent starting point. The categories of abuse identified in the Wheel include isolation, emotional abuse, economic abuse, intimidation, using citizenship and residency privilege, threats, using children, and sexual abuse. Each of these issues can serve as a catalyst for exploration and discussion with your client. A number of websites also can help you to quickly introduce yourself

---

[28] Center for Disease Control and Prevention, Department of Health and Human Services, Costs of Intimate Partner Violence Against Women in the United States, 19 (Mar. 2003).

[29] If you are not familiar with domestic violence service providers in your area, you can start with a call to the national domestic violence hotline 1-800-799-SAFE (7233) or 1-800-787-3224 (TTY).

[30] The author's former employer, Sanctuary for Families, is an excellent example of collaborative service provision. At Sanctuary for Families, lawyers and social workers together serve victims of domestic violence through legal services, counseling, and a network of domestic violence shelters. *See* www.sanctuaryforfamilies.org.

[31] D. Leidholdt, "Interviewing Battered Women," *in Lawyer's Manual on Domestic Violence Representing the Victim* 11, 11 (eds. J. Goodman & D. Leidholdt) (2005 4th ed.), *available at* www.courts.state.ny.us/ip/womeninthecourts/DV-Lawyers-Manual-Book.pdf.

[32] Attached as Appendix A.

to the topic of domestic violence.[33] A brief introduction to domestic violence, however, cannot substitute for the expertise of a domestic violence professional. Whenever possible, immigration lawyers should work in collaboration with experts in the field of domestic violence.

The VAWA Self-Petition

A VAWA self-petition is a variation on a Relative Petition. Instead of allowing a USC or LPR family member to control the process, a noncitizen herself may act independent of familial involvement and go through the entire process—both the petitioning and the application for residence—without the involvement of the abusive family member. VAWA self-petitioning is open to close family members: the parents,[34] spouses, and unmarried children under 21[35] of USCs (immediate relatives), as well as to spouses and unmarried children under 21 of LPRs.[36] The idea is to put the noncitizen in the same place in the immigration process as she would have been had her USC or LPR family member not been abusive.[37]

The VAWA self-petition simply replaces the Relative Petition both conceptually and, if a Relative Petition has been filed, practically, in that:

- the VAWA self-petitioner keeps the same place on line (the priority date) of a Relative Petition filed under Preference Category 2A (whether or not the Relative Petition has been withdrawn);[38] and

- if an application for adjustment of status is already pending, and the Relative Petition has not already been withdrawn or denied, no new application for LPR status is required.[39]

The criteria for a VAWA self-petition[40] may be summarized as follows:

- Good faith marriage to a USC or LPR (for marriage-based VAWA self-petitions, not parent/child-based ones);

- Qualifying relationship
  - legally valid marriage to a USC or LPR;
  - qualifying bigamy to a USC or LPR;
  - recognized parent/child relationship where abusive parent is USC or LPR; or
  - recognized parent/son or daughter relationship where abusive son or daughter is USC;

- Abuse
  - physical battery; or
  - extreme cruelty;

---

[33] *See, e.g.,* the National Coalition Against Domestic Violence, at *www.ncadv.org,* 2005, and the many website resources listed at *www.ncadv.org/resources/ExternalLinks_68.html.*

[34] Section 816 of VAWA 2005 amended the INA so that noncitizen parents of abusive USC sons or daughters may now file VAWA self-petitions. INA §204(a)(1)(A)(vii).

[35] Section 805 of VAWA 2005 amended the INA so that noncitizens who were children of abusive USCs and LPRs also may now file VAWA self-petitions until their 25th birthdays if there is a connection between the abuse suffered and the failure to file before turning 21. INA §204(a)(1)(D)(v).

[36] *See* INA §204(a)(1)(A)–(D); see also attached Appendix D, for a more detailed break-out of relevant statutory and regulatory provisions.

[37] There are some additional benefits granted to VAWA self-petitioners. Upon the approval of a VAWA self-petition, these benefits include, but are not limited to, employment authorization (INA §204(a)(1)(K)) and deferred actions status. *See* INS Memorandum, Michael D. Cronin, Acting Exec. Assoc. Comm'r, to Vermont Service Center, File No. HQ/ADN70/6.1P, "Deferred Action Determinations for Self-petitioning Battered Spouses and Children" (Sept. 8, 2000), *available at www.asistaonline.org/AllPolicyMemoranda.html* and *reproduced in* 77 *Interpreter Releases* 1432 (Oct. 2, 2000) (hereinafter Cronin Memorandum, Sept. 8, 2000). With respect to certain children, see INA §204(a)(1)(D)(i)(II) (granting some VAWA self-petitioning and derivative children ongoing deferred action and employment authorization after their 21st birthdays, after approval of VAWA self-petitions but before adjustment to LPR status); the ability to adjust status, regardless of entry without inspection, unlawful pres-
continued

ence or visa overstay (INA §245(a) and (c)); and distinct rules for motions to reopen that take into account domestic violence (§825 of VAWA 2005, codified at various sections of the INA).

[38] 8 CFR §204.2(h)(2). *See also* Interim Rule Implementing the Self-Petitioning Provisions and Instructions for Processing Self-Petitions, at 2–3, attached to INS Memorandum, T. Alexander Aleinikoff, INS Exec. Assoc. Comm'r, to all INS offices, File No. HQ 204-P, "Implementation of Crime Bill Self-Petitioning for Abused or Battered Spouses or Children of U.S. Citizens or Lawful Permanent Residents" (Apr. 16, 1996), *available at www.asistaonline.org/AllPolicyMemoranda.html* (hereinafter Aleinikoff Memorandum, Apr. 16, 1996).

[39] Id.

[40] INA §204(a)(1)(A)–(D). *See also* 8 CFR §204.2(c) (spouses) and 8 CFR §204.2(e) (children); note that while, at the time of this writing, 8 CFR §204.2(c)(1)(i)(G) and 8 CFR §204.2(e)(1)(i)(G) indicate that a VAWA self-petitioner also must establish extreme hardship upon return to her home country, this requirement has been eliminated by §1503 of the Victims of Trafficking and Violence Protection Act of 2000, Pub. L. No. 106-386 (Oct. 28, 2000). VAWA self-petitioning criteria are detailed in a chart at Appendix D.

- Joint residence; and
- Good moral character.

In addition:

- if the marriage has been terminated within the past two years, the VAWA self-petitioner must demonstrate a connection between the divorce and the abuse;[41] and
- if the abusive anchor relative has lost USC or LPR status within the last two years, the VAWA self-petitioner must demonstrate a connection between the loss of status and the abuse.[42]

While the standard for evidence that U.S. Citizenship and Immigration Services (USCIS) must consider—"any credible evidence"[43]—is generous, each and every element must nonetheless be carefully established.

The VAWA Self-Petitioner's Statement

The starting point for a VAWA self-petition is the domestic violence victim and her story. She is a naturally qualified expert in her own life; quite fre-quently, she has become an expert on the abuser as well. The most important part of any VAWA self-petition is the story of the VAWA self-petitioner in her own words. You will begin your work on the VAWA self-petition, therefore, by drafting a detailed account of your client's life story. Your client's life began before she met her abuser, and the narrative you present to USCIS should, too. You also should give a little bit of background information about who your client was and how she became that way. Your client's experiences must come alive and make sense through a stack of papers to a person sitting at a desk in an office near the Canadian border.[44]

The client's story should be told in natural language, not legalese. If you find yourself writing "attached hereto" or "as described herein" or "on or about" or "see Exhibit D," you will know that you have gone off the path and have a little rewriting to do. Consider the following two descriptions of the same event:

Description A

On or about February 7, 1998, at approximately 7:00 pm, while Petitioner was stirring hot food over a gas stove, Respondent placed his left hand on the upper right arm of Petitioner, used his right hand to grab a hot metal cooking implement from Petitioner's right hand. Respondent then pressed the hot metal cooking implement against Petitioner's face, to wit, her right cheek, creating a red burn mark that left a permanent scar. Respondent then dropped the metal cooking implement and grabbed a serrated butcher knife, approximately 2 inches wide and 12 inches long, and held it to the base of her throat for approximately 30 seconds and uttered words which, in sum and substance, indicated that Respondent would kill Petitioner were she to ever leave him. *See* Police Report, dated Feb. 8, 1998, attached hereto as Exhibit Q.

Description B

It is hard to remember all of the times that Steve attacked me. One of the worst attacks I remember early on must have been during the second or third winter after we were married—after one of the many times that Steve was fired from one job

---

[41] *See* INA §§204(a)(1)(A)(iii)(II)(aa)(CC)(ccc) (USC) and (B)(ii)(II)(aa)(CC)(bbb) (LPR). *See also* INS Memorandum, Stuart Anderson, Exec. Assoc. Comm'r, to Michael Pearson, Exec. Assoc. Comm'r, File No. HQADN/70/8, "Eligibility to Self-Petition as a Battered Spouse of a U.S. Citizen or Lawful Permanent Resident Within Two Years of Divorce" (Jan. 2, 2002), *available at www.asistaonline.org/AllPolicy Memoranda.html* and *published on* AILA InfoNet at Doc. No. 03100649 (*posted* Oct. 6, 2003).

[42] INA §§204(a)(1)(A)(iii)(II)(CC)(bbb) (spouse of USC who lost status in connection with domestic violence); §204(a)(1)(A)(iv) (child of USC who lost status in connection with domestic violence); 204(a)(1)(B)(ii)(II)(CC)(aaa) (spouse of LPR who lost status in connection with domestic violence); and 204(a)(1)(B)(iii) (child of LPR who lost status in connection with domestic violence). *See also* USCIS Memorandum, Michael Aytes, Acting Assoc. Director, Domestic Operations, to Regional Directors, District Directors, Officers-in-Charge, Administrative Appeals Office Director, File No. HQ 70/8, "Eligibility to Self-Petition as a Battered Spouse or Child of a U.S. Citizen or Lawful Permanent Resident Within Two Years of the Abuser's Loss of Status; Revisions to *Adjudicator's Field Manual* (AFM) Chapter 21.4(q) (*AFM* Update AD05-12)" (Oct. 31, 2005), *available at www.asistaonline.org/AllPolicyMemoranda.html* and *published on* AILA InfoNet at Doc. No. 05110961 (*posted* Nov. 9, 2005) (hereinafter Aytes Memorandum, Oct. 31, 2005).

[43] INA §204(a)(1)(J). While any credible evidence shall be considered, no "adverse determination" can be made "using information furnished solely by" the abusive USC or LPR or a member of that abuser's household. 8 USC §1367(a)(1); *see also* IIRAIRA §384, as amended by VAWA 2005.

[44] All VAWA self-petitions are handled by the Vermont Service Center located in St. Albans, Vermont, around 50 miles south of the Canadian border.

or another. I was cooking dinner and all of a sudden, out of nowhere, Steve was grabbing a hot metal spoon and hitting my face with it. He then grabbed a butcher knife and held it to my throat. He screamed that he would kill me if I ever tried to leave him. I think I spent most of the night sobbing on the kitchen floor. To this day, I have a scar on my face from that burn.

Description A is typical of the kind of language you might see in a petition submitted to Family Court. Description B, in contrast, tells a story from the point of view of the person who was attacked. The client's statement that you will draft should resemble Description B.

Your client's statement will address each of the elements of the VAWA self-petition. Regardless of what other supporting documentation is or is not available, keep in mind that your client's detailed, sworn statement is not only evidence, but one of the most important documents you will submit.

Establishing That Your Client Meets the VAWA Self-Petitioning Criteria

Unfortunately, at the time of this writing, the regulations relating to VAWA self-petitioning were last updated in 1997.[45] The regulations, therefore, until they are revised—and revisions are expected out this summer[46]—are to be ignored where they contradict the current statute. Among the most noteworthy differences between the current statute and the regulations is the hardship-upon-return-to-the-home country requirement described in 8 CFR §204.2(c)(1) and 8 CFR §204.2(e)(1), which was eliminated by §1503 of the Victims of Trafficking and Violence Protection Act of 2000, signed into law on October 28, 2000 as Pub. L. No. 106-386, 114 Stat. 1464.

Good Faith Marriage

With respect to cases based on marriage, your client will need to explain why she married her abusive partner, an element usually not required in other kinds of domestic violence legal cases (*e.g.*, divorce, criminal prosecution, and protective order), and why that marriage made sense. While falling in love after a period of dating might be a common scenario (at least in romance novels), family pressure, arranged marriage, desire for economic stability for oneself and one's children, and accidental pregnancy are also common and valid reasons from an immigration perspective, for a decision to marry. However, the more your client's experience differs from a theoretically typical American marriage experience, the more explaining you will need to do. Differences in age, religion, and ethnicity also raise red flags for immigration officers who must discern between good faith marriages and marriage fraud; be sure to address any such differences head-on. Ultimately, if the marriage was made in good faith, there must be a way to explain it. Your job is to find the way to do so.

A number of additional documents, where available, should also be included to support your client's claim of good faith marriage. Examples of additional documents include joint financial documents, birth certificates of children in common, abortion or miscarriage records during the relationship, pictures, videos, cards, e-mails, and statements from people who know the couple. Incidental records from a common life together—from emergency contact lists in employment or school records to junk mail—should be included as evidence.

The abusive husband's ex-wives and ex-girlfriends often can provide support not only for abuse but for good faith marriage. If a VAWA self-petitioner knows her husband's ex-partners, it adds to the sense that the VAWA self-petitioner is someone deeply involved in the life of her husband. Surprisingly, the abuser's family and friends can often provide supportive statements. Even where they have little or no knowledge of the abuse, they should not be discounted out of hand as sources of statements in support of the good faith nature of the relationship.

Above all, do not take the good faith nature of the relationship for granted. It is a critical component of any VAWA self-petition based on a marital relationship.

---

[45] *See* 62 Fed. Reg. 60769, 60771 (Nov. 13, 1997).

[46] Section 828 of VAWA 2005 requires that "[n]ot later than 180 days after the date of enactment of this Act, the Attorney General, the Secretary of Homeland Security, and the Secretary of State shall promulgate regulations to implement the provisions contained in the Battered Immigrant Women Protection Act of 2000 (title V of Public Law 106-386), this Act, and the amendments made by this Act." As VAWA 2005 was enacted on January 5, 2006, regulations are expected on July 5, 2006 (as July 4, 2006, the 180-day mark, is a federal holiday).

Qualifying Relationship[47]

Your client should describe the marriage itself and why (in layman's terms) she believes the marriage to be valid. If the qualifying relationship is a parent/child or parent/son or daughter relationship, the VAWA self-petitioner should describe that relationship, even where it may seem self-explanatory (as in a biological relationship where a birth certificate is provided).

VICTIM OF BIGAMY

A legally valid marriage is not always required; bigamy is not, per se, a barrier to immigration relief.[48] Where a client knows that she is the victim of bigamy, she should describe the circumstances relating to the bigamy and her knowledge of it. One VAWA self-petitioner found out that she was the victim of bigamy when she went to City Hall to obtain a copy of her marriage certificate in preparation for filing a VAWA self-petition. The clerk told her that her husband appears to have married another woman only two weeks before the VAWA self-petitioner's own marriage. The VAWA self-petitioner described her experiences in detail.[49] Another VAWA self-petitioner, separated from her husband for several years, found out upon joining him in America that he had another wife. While she was never sure if he had married the other woman before or after her own marriage or if her husband remained married to the other woman, she disclosed all that she had been able to ascertain.[50] In both cases, these women's VAWA self-petitions were approved.

Even in cases where it seems unlikely that bigamy was committed, but the VAWA self-petitioner's spouse has been previously married and she does not have proof that her spouse was previously widowed or divorced, she may need to avail herself of the same protections afforded to those who know they have been victims of bigamy. The VAWA self-petitioner without proof of the death or divorce of all previous spouses must explain in great detail why she believes that her spouse was, in fact, widowed or divorced.

DIVORCE

If your client has divorced within the last two years, she may still file a VAWA self-petition if she "demonstrates a connection between the legal termination of the marriage within the past 2 years and battering or extreme cruelty."[51] Regardless of the grounds for divorce or annulment, or the lack thereof (*i.e.*, no fault divorces), your client herself must explain in her own words this connection. While it should not be too difficult to explain why a relationship plagued by domestic violence resulted in a divorce, you cannot neglect the simple act of providing the VAWA self-petitioner's explanation.

Where you have an opportunity to influence the timing, it is preferable to file the VAWA self-petition prior to the issuance of a final divorce decree, thereby avoiding the need to explain the connection between the divorce and the domestic violence.

Immigration Status of the Abusive Spouse, Parent, Son, or Daughter

If you have copies of birth certificates, Green Cards, naturalization records, or U.S. passport pages that establish the immigration status of the abuser, you are lucky. Be sure to include such documents. If the abuser is (or was) an LPR, a naturalized USC, or has previously filed a petition with federal immigration authorities, USCIS can look up the abuser's immigration status.[52] If the abusive relative is a USC born in the United States, you must look to the law

---

[47] *See* INA §§204(a)(1)(A)(iii)(II)(aa)(BB) (USC) and (B)(ii)(II)(aa)(BB) (LPR); *see also* INS Memorandum, Johnny N. Williams, Exec. Assoc. Comm'r, to Regional Directors, Deputy Exec. Assoc. Comm'r, INS, File No. HQADN/70/8, "Eligibility to Self-Petition as an Intended Spouse of an Abusive U.S. Citizen or Lawful Permanent Resident" (Aug. 21, 2002), *available at* www.asistaonline.org/AllPolicyMemoranda.html and *published on* AILA InfoNet at Doc. No. 02091042 (*posted* Sept. 10, 2002) (hereinafter Williams Memorandum, Aug. 21, 2002).

[48] See id.

[49] This VAWA self-petitioner is a client of the author's former employer, Sanctuary for Families, and the account is based on the author's personal knowledge of the case.

[50] *Id.*

[51] INA §§204(a)(1)(A)(iii)(II)(aa)(CC) (USC) and (B)(ii)(II)(aa)(CC)(bbb) (LPR); *see also* INS Memorandum, Stuart Anderson, Exec. Assoc. Comm'r, to Michael Pearson, Exec. Assoc. Comm'r, File No. HQADN/70/8, "Eligibility to Self-Petition as a Battered Spouse of a U.S. Citizen or Lawful Permanent Resident Within Two Years of Divorce" (Jan. 2, 2002) (hereinafter Anderson Memorandum, Jan. 2, 2002).

[52] *See* 8 CFR §204.1(g)(3) ("If a self-petitioner . . . is unable to present primary or secondary evidence of the abuser's status, the Service will attempt to electronically verify the abuser's citizenship or immigration status from information contained in Service computerized records. Other Service records may also be reviewed. . . .").

of the state in which the USC was born to see if your VAWA self-petitioning client, by virtue of her legal relationship with the abusive USC, is eligible to obtain a copy of the birth certificate.[53]

In New York, spouses and children are not per se eligible to obtain a copy of the birth certificates of their spouses or parents.[54] However, on repeated occasions, attorneys in New York State have successfully obtained copies of birth certificates for the purposes of obtaining supporting evidence for VAWA self-petitions through bringing court cases seeking a judicial order to receive the birth certificate.

Keep in mind that if the abuser has lost immigration status within the last two years and that loss of status can be connected to the domestic violence, then your client will still be eligible to file a VAWA self-petition.[55]

Abuse (Either Physical Battery or Extreme Cruelty)

Talking about abuse that one has suffered is never easy, but it is something that the VAWA self-petitioner will need to do. If your client has not previously talked about the abuse, she may have an especially hard time describing what has happened. As she discusses what has happened to her, she might cry or she might even laugh. Alternatively, she may nonchalantly describe her experiences without displaying any emotion at all. As with victims of other forms of trauma, you cannot predict how a client will behave as she recounts what has happened to

her. Nonetheless, in order to prepare her VAWA self-petition, you must help your client to articulate what she has suffered.[56]

Sometimes, people do not realize that some of the bad things that have happened to them are forms of abuse. For example, isolation from friends and family, economic control, or forced sex are all common in domestic violence, but victims of these behaviors often do not realize the relevance of such behaviors as part of a pattern of abuse. It may be useful to sit with your client and review the Power and Control Wheel;[57] ask her if she has experienced any of the things that are described in the wheel.

Police reports, court records, protection orders, and other documents indicating involvement with government authorities are helpful, but they are not required. If your client never attempted to avail herself of government protection orders, you should explain why. If records do exist, do *not* simply include them without carefully reviewing such documents with your client. Government records are frequently inaccurate and often contain internally inconsistent information such as "crime victim reported verbal harassment; was taken to the hospital." Immigration officers will go through all the evidence submitted in connection with the VAWA self-petition with a fine-tooth comb, looking for any inconsistencies, and government records are often a treasure-trove for contradictory information. As with all evidence that you submit, review police and court documents with your client, and be sure to correct or explain any inconsistent information.

If the VAWA self-petitioner knows ex-girlfriends, ex-wives, and other family or friends who have suffered violence at the hands of her abuser, you may be able to get evidence (such as records from child protective service agencies, public records, or statements from these other victims). Forget that this kind of information would never make it into a court of law. If you can establish the abuser's violence toward others, it tends to support your client's claim that the abuser was violent against her.

In addition to violence against people, consider any violence against animals. Those who abuse family members often also abuse animals, particularly

---

[53] Asista has gathered information about state laws relating to birth certificates. This information is available at *www.asistaonline.org/legalresources/I-360Self-Petitiondocs/ Obtaining_Birth_Certificates.pdf.*

[54] *See* N.Y. Pub. Health Law §4174(1)(b) ("The commissioner or any person authorized by him shall . . . issue certified copies or certified transcripts of birth certificates only (1) upon order of a court of competent jurisdiction, or (2) upon specific request therefor by the person, if eighteen years of age or more, or by a parent or other lawful representative of the person, to whom the record of birth relates, or (3) upon specific request therefor by a department of a state or the federal government of the United States").

[55] INA §§204(a)(1)(A)(iii)(II)(CC)(bbb) (spouse of USC who lost status in connection with domestic violence); §204(a)(1)(A)(iv) (child of USC who lost status in connection with domestic violence); 204(a)(1)(A)(vii)(I) (parent of USC son or daughter who lost status in connect with domestic violence); 204(a)(1)(B)(ii)(II)(CC)(aaa) (spouse of LPR who lost status in connection with domestic violence); and INA §204(a)(1)(B)(iii) (child of LPR who lost status in connection with domestic violence); *see also* Aytes Memorandum, Oct. 31, 2005, *supra* note 42.

[56] With young child victims or other victims suffering from debilitating abuse that prevents them from communicating, it may be possible to rely on a mental health or other medical expert to provide information on the abuse.

[57] Attached hereto as Appendix A.

the pets belonging to victimized family members.[58] Information about violence to pets should also be included.

Mental health and domestic violence workers also can provide useful statements, but like police records, they are by no means a requirement. Ask such providers not to focus so much on diagnoses like post-traumatic stress disorder (PTSD) and depression, but rather why, in the worker's professional opinion, he or she believes that your client has suffered domestic violence. A detailed description of the basis of that conclusion, rather than the finding itself, is what is most likely to be helpful.

Records that indicate other professionals have acknowledged your client is a domestic violence victim (keeping the domestic violence victim's address confidential on school records, admission to a domestic violence shelter, emergency public housing transfer, etc.) are also helpful. Records that indicate other people met your client, believed she was a domestic violence victim, and treated her accordingly can go a long way in supporting your client's own description of her experience.

Sometimes other people can provide statements that alone do not establish abuse, but taken together with a VAWA self-petitioner's statements can help to paint the picture of an abusive relationship. One VAWA self-petitioner, for example, had co-workers who knew she had to leave at 5:00 pm on the dot every day from an office where people tended to leave anywhere from a few minutes to an hour after the technical end of the day. Her co-workers had thought it odd that she insisted her husband would be worried as she ran out the door. As the VAWA self-petitioner explained in her own statement, her husband stood at the door waiting for her to come home and punished her for any perceived lateness. While the co-workers knew nothing of what awaited the VAWA self-petitioner upon the end of her journey home each day, they were able to attest to her hurried departures from work that differed remarkably from those of her colleagues.[59]

Remember that physical abuse is *not* required by statute and that extreme cruelty can provide the basis for a VAWA self-petition. As the Ninth Circuit in the landmark case *Hernandez v. Ashcroft*[60] noted, "Congress clearly intended extreme cruelty to indicate nonphysical aspects of domestic violence. Defining extreme cruelty in the context of domestic violence to include acts that 'may not initially appear violent but that are part of an overall pattern of violence.'"

The key idea here is that lack of perceived hard evidence in the way of police reports or court records should never prevent an immigrant victim of domestic violence from seeking relief as a VAWA self-petitioner. Rather, it is your job as your client's lawyer to recount your client's story and identify and include any supporting evidence that may be available.

Joint Residence

Your client needs to indicate each and every place she has lived with her spouse. Although the joint residence requirement relates only to the period during which the couple is legally married (or, in the case of bigamy, the VAWA self-petitioner believes herself to be legally married), do not neglect to talk about any co-habitation that pre-dates (or post-dates) a legal marriage. If your client has had non-traditional living arrangements (living with family members or in homeless shelters, for example), her detailed, clear account of joint residence is particularly critical.

Supporting evidence beyond your client's statement may not be readily available. While joint leases and mortgage statements are ideal, such documents frequently do not exist. Pull together whatever documents may exist (*e.g.*, junk mail, pay stubs, school records, and police reports) that may tie both the VAWA self-petitioner and the abuser to the same address.

Good Moral Character

Good moral character, not mentioned in the INA provisions relating to USC- and LPR-initiated Relative Petitions, is a statutory requirement for the approval of a VAWA self-petition.[61] If your client has no arrest record and does not fall within the class of persons described in INA §101(f), there is little that

---

[58] *See, e.g.*, Animal Cruelty/Domestic Violence Fact Sheet produced by the Humane Society and available at *www.hsus.org*.

[59] This VAWA self-petitioner is a client of the author's former employer, Sanctuary for Families, and the account is based on the author's personal knowledge of the case.

[60] 345 F.3d 824, 839 (9th Cir. 2003).

[61] INA §§204(a)(1)(A)(iii)(II)(bb); 204(a)(1)(A)(iv); 204(a)(1)(B)(ii)(II)(bb); 204(a)(1)(B)(iii); and §204(a)(1)(A)(vii)(II).

your client must state other than that she is a person of good moral character and provide police records from her places of residence for the last three years documenting her lack of a criminal record.[62] As the regulations explain:

> Primary evidence of the self-petitioner's good moral character is the self-petitioner's affidavit. The affidavit should be accompanied by a local police clearance or a state-issued criminal background check from each locality or state in the United States in which the self-petitioner has resided for six or more months during the 3-year period immediately preceding the filing of the self-petition. Self-petitioners who lived outside the United States during this time should submit a police clearance, criminal background check, or similar report issued by the appropriate authority in the foreign country in which he or she resided for six or more months during the 3-year period immediately preceding the filing of the self-petition. If police clearances, criminal background checks, or similar reports are not available for some or all locations, the self-petitioner may include an explanation and submit other evidence with his or her affidavit.[63]

Despite the three-year period noted in the regulations and the promise that "[a] self-petitioner's claim of good moral character will be evaluated on a case-by-case basis, taking into account the provisions of

section 101(f) of the Act and the standards of the average citizen in the community,"[64] practitioners have noticed USCIS's increasingly stringent interpretation of this provision. Any VAWA self-petitioner who has been arrested (even if charges were eventually dismissed) or may otherwise fall within INA §101(f) will need to provide in-depth explanations. Specifically, if the act that is the basis of a conviction (or even an arrest) is one that could lead to a finding that the petitioner lacks good moral character, she will need to demonstrate that "the act or conviction [on which the potential finding of lack of good moral character is based] was connected to the alien's having been battered or subjected to extreme cruelty."[65]

There appear to be various aspects of USCIS's approach that could be challenged in federal court. First, it is doubtful a finding that a self-petitioner is lacking in good moral character, based solely on conduct prior to the regulatory period, would be upheld, at least under current case law in the Ninth Circuit.[66] Yet, VAWA self-petitions are routinely denied for conduct that occurred several years prior to the filing of a VAWA self-petition.[67] Second, case law suggests that an adverse determination on good moral character *cannot* be made on a criminal charge alone as opposed to a conviction or an admission of facts sufficient for a conviction,[68] yet VAWA cases are sometimes denied based on charges, rather than convictions, admissions, or other evidence suggesting that the VAWA self-

---

[62] If your client has lived in several jurisdictions within the United States, you may wish to obtain a record from the Federal of Bureau of Investigations (FBI) that should show any arrests throughout the United States as well, in some cases, past interactions with federal immigration authorities. Instructions for obtaining an FBI record are as follows:

> The subject of a record in the system may obtain a copy thereof by making a request in writing with the envelope and the letter clearly marked "Privacy Act Request." The request must include the requester's full name, date of birth and place of birth, a certified check or money order in the amount of $18 made payable to the Treasurer of the United States, and a set of rolled-inked fingerprint impressions placed upon fingerprint cards or forms commonly utilized for applicant or law enforcement purposes by law enforcement agencies. The requester must also provide a return address for transmitting the information. Such requests for access to information must be addressed to the Federal Bureau of Investigation, CJIS Division, Attn: SCU, Mod. D-2, 1000 Custer Hollow Road, Clarksburg, WV 26306. *See* *http://foia.fbi.gov/firs552.htm.*

[63] 8 CFR §204.2(c)(2)(v) (self-petitioning spouses); 8 CFR §204.2(e)(2)(v) (self-petitioning children).

[64] 8 CFR §204.2(c)(1)(vii) (self-petitioning spouses); 8 CFR §204.2(e)(1)(vii) (self-petitioning children).

[65] INA §204(a)(1)(C); *see also* USCIS Memorandum, William R. Yates, Assoc. Director, to Paul E. Novak, Director, Vermont Service Center, File No. HQOPRD 70/8.1/8.2, "Determinations of Good Moral Character in VAWA-Based Self-Petitions" (Jan. 19, 2005), and the attachments thereto, available at *www.asistaonline.org/AllPolicyMemoranda.html* and *published on* AILA InfoNet at Doc. No. 05012561 (*posted* Jan. 25, 2005).

[66] *See, e.g., Santamaria-Ames v. INS,* 104 F.3d 1127, 1131 and 1133, n.8 (9th Cir. 1996) (while "conduct predating the regulatory period . . . may be considered . . . in determining naturalization eligibility," such "conduct prior to the regulatory period" cannot "be the sole basis for finding lack of good moral character").

[67] This statement is based on the experiences of clients at the author's former employer, Sanctuary for Families.

[68] *See Billeke-Tolosa v. Ashcroft,* 385 F.3d 708 (6th Cir. 2004); *Matter of Grullon,* 20 I&N Dec. 12 (1989).

petitioner did in fact engage in criminal acts.[69] At the time of this writing, the author is unaware of any federal court challenges to USCIS's severe interpretation of the good moral character requirement. Litigation, however, may be required to bring USCIS's practice with respect to good moral character findings in VAWA self-petitions in line with good moral character case law in other areas of immigration.

Privacy Protection

Many victims of domestic violence may fear that abusive family members will try to interfere with their immigration filings, either by providing negative information to USCIS or by seeking to obtain copies of documents filed with USCIS. You can assure your clients that the law protects the privacy of their filings and does not deny petitions based solely on information provide by abusers and their family members.[70] Be aware, however, that in practice, USCIS does occasionally make mistakes and accidentally provides limited information (such as receipts and notices of interview) to abusive family members.

Eligibility for Lawful Permanent Residence

If your client is an immediate relative (the spouse, child, or parent of a U.S. citizen), is present in the United States, and is filing a VAWA self-petition, she may simultaneously file an Application for Adjustment of Status on Form I-485 (the application for LPR status; also known popularly as "Green Card" status, "the Adjustment Application"). Similarly, if your client is a preference relative (spouse or child of an LPR), has a current priority date based on a Relative Petition previously filed by the abusive anchor relative,[71] and is present in the United States, she is immediately eligible to file an Adjustment

Application. If, however, your client is the spouse or child of an LPR and does not have a current priority date, she must wait until her priority date becomes current before filing an Adjustment Application.

Should your client's abusive relative become a U.S. citizen, her petition is, by operation of law, "deemed reclassified," and she is immediately eligible to file for permanent residence as the approved VAWA self-petitioning spouse, child, or parent of a U.S. citizen.[72] You should write to the Vermont Service Center and ask for a new approval notice indicating that the VAWA self-petitioner is an immediate relative, not a preference relative. If you have proof of the change of status of the abusive relative, it is useful to include it. However, even if you have no proof, the VAWA Unit at the Vermont Service Center can look up the abusive relative's naturalization. In addition to mailing a letter, it is a good idea to call the VAWA voicemail at (802) 527-4888 and alert them to your request.

If your client is abroad, upon approval of the VAWA self-petition, she is eligible to apply for lawful permanent residence through consular processing if she is the spouse, child, or parent of a U.S. citizen or has a current priority date based on a previously filed Relative Petition. Otherwise, she must wait outside the United States until her priority date becomes current or her abusive LPR family member becomes a U.S. citizen and, only at that point will she be eligible to apply for lawful permanent residence through consular processing.

Note that the approval of a VAWA self-petition does not negate the grounds of inadmissibility listed in INA §212(a), which prevent the grant of LPR status. Therefore, some approved VAWA self-petitioners may never be eligible to apply for lawful permanent residence. However, some—but by no means all—grounds of inadmissibility may not be applicable or may be waived under special rules for battered immigrants.[73]

In a similar vein, some VAWA self-petitioners may benefit from special rules that, under some circumstances, allow them to apply to reopen previous removal proceedings,[74] even where they have failed to depart pursuant to orders of voluntary departure.[75]

---

[69] This statement is based on the experiences of clients at the author's former employer, Sanctuary for Families.

[70] 8 USC §1367; see also IIRAIRA §384, as amended by VAWA 2005 §817; see also INS Memorandum, Paul W. Virtue, INS Acting Exec. Assoc. Comm., to all INS offices, File No. 96act. 036, "Non-Disclosure and Other Prohibitions Relating to Battered Aliens: IIRAIRA §384" (May 5, 1997), reprinted in 2 Bender's Immigr. Bull. 502 (June 15, 1997) and available at www.asistaonline.org/AllPolicyMemoranda.html.

[71] See Interim Rule Implementing the Self-Petitioning Provisions and Instructions for Processing Self-Petitions, at 2–3, attached to Aleinikoff Memorandum, Apr. 16, 1996, supra note 38. Note that priority dates can be found on the State Department's website at http://travel.state.gov/visa/frvi/bulletin/bulletin_1360.html.

[72] INA §204(a)(1)(D)(v)(II).

[73] See, e.g., INA §§212(a)(6)(A)(ii); 212(a)(9)(B)(iii)(IV); 212(a)(9)(C)(ii); 212(g)(1)(C); 212(h)(1)(C); 212(i)(1).

[74] INA §§240(c)(6)(C)(iv); 240(e).

[75] INA §240B(d)(2).

Upon reopening, VAWA self-petitioners may file Adjustment Applications with the immigration judge (IJ) (if currently eligible for adjustment), file motions to terminate so that they can file Adjustment Applications with USCIS, or seek VAWA cancellation before the IJ.

Filing

Send your VAWA self-petition (and any accompanying submissions to USCIS) to the Vermont Service Center at the following address:

> U.S. Citizenship and Immigration Services
> Attention: Violence Against Women Act
> (VAWA) Unit
> Vermont Service Center
> 75 Lower Welden Street
> St. Albans, VT 05479

Working to ensure proper treatment of your submission in the mailroom at the Vermont Service Center is an independent challenge. Be sure to take a big red marker and write "VAWA" on the cover letter and "VAWA" on the outside envelope. This should help ensure that the mailroom sends your submission to the appropriate place. Additionally, if you are submitting multiple petitions/applications (for example, an Application for Employment Authorization Document (EAD) on Form I-765 (EAD Application, also known as a work permit application and an Adjustment Application)), the VAWA self-petition itself should go in one inner envelope marked "VAWA self-petition," and each additional application should go in a separate inner envelope marked, in big red letters, "Employment Authorization Document Application submitted in connection with VAWA self-petition" and "Adjustment of Status Application submitted in connection with VAWA self-petition." Mark *both* sides of the inner envelope with these notations.

Similarly, if your client is requesting a fee waiver, you should write "fee waiver requested" in red on both sides of each envelope, as well as on the face of the relevant petition/application itself.[76] In addition to these markings on the envelopes and pe-

titions or applications with a big red marker, write the words "fee waiver requested" in red on the physical request for a fee waiver itself, and place a big post-it on the front of each petition or application indicating that the filer is seeking a fee waiver. If, as frequently happens, despite your best efforts, the package is returned for lack of payment (as opposed to a specific denial of the request for a fee waiver), take a red marker (and, by now, you may realize that you should have several handy) and write something like "No! Adjudicated fee waiver request!" on the blue notice returned to you indicating lack of payment. Place the blue notice with your handwritten direction, place a rubber band around the entire returned package, and send back to the Vermont Service Center. This practice of resubmission could take a couple of attempts, but eventually your fee waiver will be adjudicated.

If your client is eligible to file an Adjustment Application, she can file it (with biographic information on Form G-325A and yet another Notice of Appearance on Form G-28) in the Vermont Service Center along with her VAWA Self-Petition.

If an Adjustment Application is currently pending, based on a Relative Petition filed by the abusive relative, there is no requirement that a new Adjustment Application be filed.[77] However, depending on the District in which you practice, it may be difficult to ensure that the District: (1) has notice that a VAWA self-petition has been filed; (2) will not deny the pending Adjustment Application should the abusive relative withdraw the Relative Petition on file;[78] (3) will hold open the Adjustment Application until the VAWA self-petition is adjudicated; and (4) will reschedule the VAWA self-petitioner for an interview once the VAWA self-petition is adjudicated. In New York City, for example, many advocates simply refile Green Card Applications with the Vermont Service Center because of the challenges involved in matching the new VAWA self-petition and the pending Adjustment Application file and ensuring timely adjudication of the pending Adjustment Application after the VAWA self-petition has been approved. You need to know both federal immigration policy—no new Adjustment Application is required

---

[76] For additional information on eligibility for fee waivers, see USCIS Memorandum, William R. Yates, Assoc. Director, to Service Center Directors, Regional Directors, District Directors, File No. HQ70/5.5, "Field Guidance on Granting Fee Waivers Pursuant to 8 CFR 103.7(c)" (Mar. 4, 2004), available at *http://uscis.gov/graphics/lawsregs/handbook/ FeeWaiverGd3404.pdf*.

[77] Interim Rule Implementing the Self-Petitioning Provisions and Instructions for Processing Self-Petitions, at 3, *attached to* Aleinikoff Memorandum, Apr. 16, 1996, *supra* note 38.

[78] This practice is somewhat common, even though the practice was explicitly rejected by INS. *See id.*

if a previous Adjustment Application based on a previously filed Relative Petition by the abusive relative remains pending)[79]—and what actually happens in the District where you practice.

All relevant forms are available at *www.uscis.gov*. At a minimum, you will submit a VAWA self-petition on Form I-360,[80] along with a Notice of Appearance on Form G-28, and supporting evidence. Along with your submission, you should submit a cover letter, indicating the documents you are including, an index, and a cover memo describing why your submission meets the criteria.[81]

If you are filing an Adjustment Application, you may also wish to file an Application for Waiver of Grounds of Excludability on Form I-601 (Excludability Waiver),[82] if such a waiver will be required, and an Application for Action on an Approved Application or Petition on Form I-824 (Following-to-join Petition), if the applicant's children currently live abroad and will be following to join the applicant after the adjudication of her Adjustment Application.[83]

If your client does not currently have an EAD, you will wish to include in your filing with the Vermont Service Center an EAD Application (again, with yet another Notice of Appearance on Form G-28, in a separate inner envelope marked in red, on both sides, with the phrase "EAD application filed with VAWA self-petition" and "fee waiver requested," as appropriate). If the EAD Application is based on the concurrent filing of an Adjustment Application, the EAD Application can be filed based on 8 CFR §274a.12(c)(9) (which, in practical terms, means that you write in "(c)(9)" in response to question number 16 on the EAD Application). The EAD may be issued well before the adjudication of VAWA self-petition itself.

If, however, your client is not immediately eligible to file an Adjustment Application, your client may still wish to file an EAD Application concurrently with her VAWA self-petition. If your client is not currently in removal, exclusion, or deportation proceedings and does not have a prior removal, exclusion, or deportation order, the Vermont Service Center will automatically grant deferred action to the VAWA self-petitioner upon the approval of the VAWA self-petition.[84] This grant of deferred action can (and at the time of this writing, does) serve as a basis for granting an EAD pursuant to 8 CFR §274a.12(c)(14) (which means that you write "(c)(14)" in response to question number 16 on the EAD Application).

Note that under legislative changes passed in VAWA 2005, approved VAWA self-petitioners are now authorized to work incident to status.[85] Accordingly, procedures for obtaining documents evidencing employment authorization are likely to change in the near future.

---

[79] *Supra* note 77.

[80] Note that Form I-360 is used for a variety of case types. Only fill out questions relevant to the VAWA self-petition and ignore, for example, sections relating to Amerasian children or children applying for Special Immigrant Juvenile Status.

[81] *See* samples, available at *www.probono.net/ny/family*, a free service that allows attorneys and accredited representatives access to a host of resources. The immigration section is maintained by attorneys at Sanctuary for Families. Sample cover letters, indices, and cover memos can be found at this website.

[82] Note that many practitioners choose *not* to file Excludability Waivers at the time of filing Adjustment Applications if they believe that the law is not clear as to whether an Excludability Waiver will be required. In such instances, it is common practice to prepare and bring an Excludability Waiver to the adjustment of status interview where the Adjustment Application is adjudicated and file at the time of interview, if USCIS deems such a filing necessary. The suggestion to file an Excludability Waiver with the Adjustment Application in the Vermont Service Center is not meant to argue against such a practice but rather, in situations in which a practitioner determines that an Excludability Waiver will definitely be required, it may be advisable to file the Excludability Waiver concurrently in the Vermont Service Center.

[83] Children of VAWA self-petitioners are not required to file separate petitions but are automatically included, by operation of law, in their parents' VAWA self-petitions. A child of a VAWA self-petitioner physically present in the United States files an Adjustment Application in his or her own right and an EAD Application in his or her own right, but no separate petition. In order to seek benefits for a child of a VAWA self-petitioner who lives abroad, a Following-to-Join Petition can
continued

be filed with the Adjustment Application (but not before) and once the VAWA self-petitioner's Adjustment Application has been approved, the child can then consular process and enter the United States as a lawful permanent resident.

[84] *See* Cronin Memorandum, Sept. 8, 2000, *supra* note 37, and INS Memorandum, Michael D. Cronin, Acting Assoc. Comm'r, Office of Programs, to all Regional Directors, File Number HQ204-P, "Deferred Action for Self-petitioning Battered Spouses and Children with Approved I-360 Petitions" (Dec. 22, 1998), available at *www.asistaonline.org/AllPolicyMemoranda.html*.

[85] INA §204(a)(1)(K) ("Upon the approval of a petition as a VAWA self-petitioner, the alien—(i) is eligible for work authorization; and (ii) may be provided an "employment authorized" endorsement or appropriate work permit incidental to such approval.").

Post-Filing

Should you receive any requests for evidence (RFEs), you should provide prompt responses. Even if you believe that you have already answered the question or provided information, you should repeat your previous explanations, provide again requested information, and wherever possible, elaborate on previously given information and provide additional documents. Should you have questions for the Vermont Service Center's VAWA Unit, you can contact the VAWA Voicemail at (802) 527-4888. Note that only calls made by those with Notices of Appearance on file will be returned.

Post-Approval

If your client is present in the United States and has already filed an Adjustment Application concurrently with her VAWA self-petition, then, upon approval of her VAWA self-petition, she will simply wait until the time of her Adjustment interview to have her Adjustment Application processed. Waiting time varies from District to District. If your client has not received an Adjustment interview before the expiration of her EAD, she should file a renewal EAD approximately 100 days before the expiration date. The renewal should be filed with the Vermont Service Center based on deferred action, or, after new procedures are put in place for VAWA self-petitioners, based on eligibility to work incident to VAWA self-petitioner status. By filing with the VAWA Unit of the Vermont Service Center rather than following procedures for obtaining an EAD based on a pending Adjustment Application, the VAWA self-petitioner reminds the VAWA Unit to renew her deferred action status.

If your client is in the United States and is the spouse of an LPR and does not have a current priority date, she can renew her EAD each year with the Vermont Service Center. When she becomes eligible to file an Adjustment Application, she can do so at the National Benefits Center.

As noted above, approved VAWA self-petitioners outside the United States have no basis for entering the United States, but rather must apply for LPR status at consulates abroad. Only those whose anchor relatives are U.S. citizens or those with current priority dates are eligible to file such applications. As noted above, approved VAWA self-petitioners are subject to grounds of inadmissibility, including the three- and ten-year bars, as well as bars for previous removal or unauthorized re-entry.[86]

Also noted above are the special rules for VAWA self-petitioners to apply for relief post–removal orders and post-grants of voluntary departure.[87]

Adjustment Interview

In due time, an Adjustment Application should result in an adjustment of status interview where the VAWA self-petitioners request for LPR status itself is adjudicated. Many District Adjudications Officers (DAOs) are unfamiliar with VAWA self-petitions, and you may need to educate the DAO. Common areas of misunderstanding are described below.

First, many DAOs do not realize that many common barriers to adjustment described in INA §245(a) and INA §245(c)—entry without inspection (EWI), unlawful work, visa overstay, or other civil immigration violations—do not apply to VAWA self-petitioners.[88] As DAOs are often not comfortable reading and interpreting the law directly, trying to review the finer points of language in INA §245(a) and INA §245(c) is unlikely to be helpful. Instead, bring a copy of the directions to Supplement A to Form I-485, a form frequently filed, along with a $1,000 fine, for Adjustment Applicants who would normally be prevented from adjusting status due to the strictures of INA §245(a) and INA §245(c), but who qualify for an exemption from these limitations due to meeting criteria listed in INA §245(i). The instructions to the form explicitly state that those who "[h]ave an approved Form I-360, Petition for Amerasian, Widow(er), Battered or Abused Spouse or Child, or Special Immigrant, and are applying for adjustment

---

[86] INA §212(a)(10)(ii). *See also* §813(c) VAWA 2005, stating that it is the "sense of Congress" that the Secretary of the Department of Homeland Security, the Attorney General, and the Secretary of the Department of State should "particularly consider exercising" discretion in allowing VAWA self-petitioners and certain other victims of violence to reapply for admission to the United States.

[87] *See* INA §§240(c)(6)(C)(iv); 240(e); and 240B(d)(2).

[88] *See* INA §§245(a) (referencing VAWA self-petitioners eligible for adjustment with the following language: "the status of any other alien having an approved petition for classification under subparagraph (A)(iii), (A)(iv), (B)(ii), or (B)(iii) of section 204(a)(1)" of the INA); and 245(c) (exempting VAWA self-petitioners from list of those prohibited from adjusting with the following language: "Other than an alien having an approved petition for classification under subparagraph (A)(iii), (A)(iv), (A)(v), (A)(vi), (B)(ii), (B)(iii), or (B)(iv) of section 204(a)(1)" of the INA).

as a special immigrant juvenile court dependent, or as a special immigrant who has served in the U.S. armed forces, or as a battered or abused spouse or child" are not required to file Supplement A to Form I-485. Although the connection may not be obvious to the beginning practitioner, the DAO is likely to readily understand that those who are not required to file Supplement A to Form I-485 are eligible to adjust to LPR status without regard to the just-described restrictions of INA §245(a) and INA §245(c).

Second, many DAOs may not realize that the Affidavit of Support, required for most Adjustment Applicants being sponsored by family members,[89] does not apply to VAWA self-petitioners.[90] Likewise, some DAOs may not realize that public benefits received by VAWA self-petitioners in connection with their efforts to escape domestic violence cannot be held against Adjustment Applicants when determining whether they may be barred from adjusting on public charge grounds.[91] Unlike the potential confusion over INA §245(a) and INA §245(c), which can usually be dispelled with the display of the instructions to Supplement A to Form I-485, there is no way around engaging in a discussion of the actual text of the law on this issue.

Third, some DAOs will seek to readjudicate the VAWA self-petition, questioning the approved VAWA self-petitioner about the facts of her case and the evidence submitted. As neither a DAO nor anyone else at the District level has authority to revoke an approved VAWA self-petition,[92] a readjudication of the underlying VAWA self-petition is neither necessary nor possible during the adjustment interview. A copy of the relevant memo on VAWA revocation[93] may be shown to a DAO, or the DAO's supervisor, should any questions arise. Experience suggests that this particular point may be difficult to communicate successfully on the spot and may lead to delayed adjudication of the Adjustment Application. Should the problem arise frequently, local prac-

titioners may wish to seek a meeting with the Section 245 Unit (the unit responsible for adjudicating Adjustment Applications) to review USCIS policy with respect to the adjudication and revocation of VAWA self-petitions.

Four, some DAOs do not realize that children of VAWA self-petitioners who are the current (or former) spouses of U.S. citizens are automatically included as derivatives on the VAWA self-petition of their parent.[94] This confusions stems from the contrast between the VAWA self-petitioning process in which derivative children are always included in the VAWA self-petition of the spouse of an abusive U.S. citizen and the petitioning process for immediate relatives in which a U.S. citizen must file separate petitions for a spouse and each child.

Naturalization

The final benefit received by VAWA self-petitioners is early eligibility to naturalize. VAWA self-petitioners are eligible for naturalization three years after becoming lawful permanent residents.[95]

RESOURCES

No single article can provide you with all the information you will need to prepare a VAWA self-petition or represent a domestic violence victim in other immigration case types. Throughout the process of representing noncitizen victims of domestic

---

[89] INA §§212(a)(4)(C)(ii); 213A.

[90] INA §212(a)(4)(C)(i).

[91] See INA §212(s) (instructing those determining inadmissibility under INA §212(a)(4) "not to consider any benefits" received as "qualified aliens" under 8 USC §1641(c)).

[92] See INS Memorandum, Johnny N. Williams, Exec. Assoc. Comm'r, to Regional Directors and Deputy Exec. Assoc. Comm'r, File No. HQADN/70/9, "Revocation of VAWA-Based Self-Petitions (I-360s)" (Aug. 5, 2002), available at www.asistaonline.org/AllPolicyMemoranda.html.

[93] Id.

[94] 8 CFR §204.2(c)(4) ("[a] child accompanying or following-to-join the self-petitioning spouse may be accorded the same preference and priority date as the self-petitioner without the necessity of a separate petition").

[95] INA §319(a). See also USCIS Memorandum, William R. Yates, Assoc. Director of Operations, to Regional Directors, District Directors, Officers-in-Charge and Administrative Appeals Office Director, File No. HQOPRD 70/33.1, "Clarification of Classes of Applicants Eligible for Naturalization under Section 319(a) of the Immigration and Nationality Act (INA), as amended by the Victims of Trafficking and Violence Protection Act of 2000 (VTVPA), Pub. L. 106-386" (Jan. 27, 2005), available at www.asistaonline.org/AllPolicyMemoranda.html, www.uscis.gov/graphics/lawsregs/handbook/Sec319a012705.pdf, and published on AILA InfoNet at Doc. No. 05020760 (posted Feb. 7, 2005); and INS Memorandum, William R. Yates, Deputy Exec. Assoc. Comm'r, Office of Field Operations, Immigration Services Division, to Regional Directors, District Directors, Officers-in-Charge, Service Center Directors, File No. HQISD 70/33, Policy Memo #89, "Instructions Regarding the Expanded Meaning of Section 319(a)" (Oct. 15, 2002), available at www.asistaonline.org/AllPolicyMemoranda.html and published on AILA InfoNet at Doc. No. 02103143 (posted Oct. 31, 2002).

violence, you may wish to seek assistance from experienced practitioners and Internet resources. The New York Immigration Coalition, (212) 627-2227, and Sanctuary for Families, (212) 349-6009, both provide free technical assistance to practitioners. Should you need to contact the VAWA Unit at USCIS directly, with respect to a VAWA self-petition that has already been filed, you may contact the VAWA voicemail at (802) 527-4888. Calls will only be returned to practitioners who have Notices of Appearance on file.

Web resources are available at *probono.net*, at *www.probono.net/index.cfm*.[96] Immigration is also available from Asista, at *www.asistaonline.org* and from the National Immigration Project at *www.nationalimmigrationproject.org/DVPage/DomesticViolencePage.html*. These sites provide limited access to nonmembers. There is also a national listserve for VAWA practitioners. One can subscribe by e-mailing to *VAWAexperts-subscribe@yahoogroups.com*. For an excellent resource guide to gender-based asylum, see the Center for Gender and Refugee Studies' website at *http://cgrs.uchastings.edu*.

---

[96] Membership on *probono.net* is free, but password protected, as it is a website meant for legal practitioners, not members of the public seeking assistance in preparing pro se applications. Practitioners simply request a password and explain that they are admitted to practice law or are accredited representatives.

APPENDIX A—POWER AND CONTROL WHEEL

This version of the Power and Control wheel, adapted with permission from the Domestic Abuse Intervention Project in Duluth, Minnesota, focuses on some of the many ways battered immigrant women can be abused.

APPENDIX B—FORMS FLOW CHART*: I-751 OR I-360+

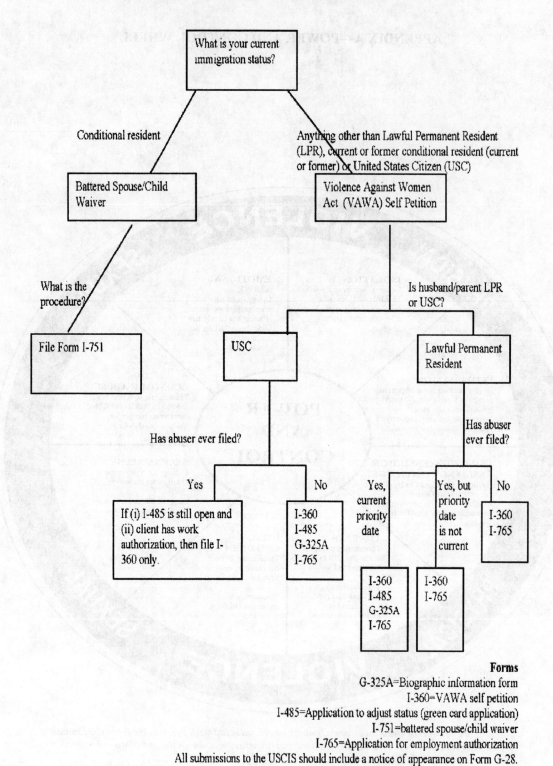

Forms

G-325A=Biographic information form
I-360=VAWA self petition
I-485=Application to adjust status (green card application)
I-751=battered spouse/child waiver
I-765=Application for employment authorization
All submissions to the USCIS should include a notice of appearance on Form G-28.
All forms are available on the USCIS website, www.uscis.gov

---

* Initially created by Shira Galinsky and reprinted with permission.

APPENDIX C

Family-Related and Domestic Violence-Related Immigration Options:
Some Similarities and Differences

	VAWA Self Petition on Form I-360	Relative Petition on Form I-130
Petitioner	The intending immigrant herself files the VAWA self-petition and controls the process.	The USC or LPR family member files the Relative Petition and may withdraw any time up until the moment permanent resident status is granted.
Immigration status of anchor relative at time of filing	• USC • LPR • former USC where immigration status lost in the previous two years because of domestic violence[97] • former LPR where immigration status lost in the previous two years because of domestic violence[98] or deceased USC • deceased USC spouse where death occurred in the last two years[99]	• USC[100] • LPR
Effect of pre-filing termination or non-existence of marital relationship	• *Pre*-filing, a divorce will not prevent eligibility for filing a VAWA self-petition where the divorce takes place in the two years immediately preceding the filing, and there is a connection between the divorce and the domestic violence[101] • *Pre*-filing lack of marital relationship due to previously unknown bigamy does not change eligibility for a VAWA self-petition[102]	Prevents eligibility.

Continued

---

[97] INA §§204(a)(1)(A)(iii)(II)(aa)(CC)(bbb) (spouse of former USC); 204(a)(1)(A)(iv) (child of former USC).

[98] INA §§204(a)(1)(B)(ii)(II)(aa)(CC)(aaa) (spouse of former LPR); 204(a)(1)(B)(iii) (child of former LPR).

[99] INA §204(a)(1)(A)(iii)(II)(aa)(CC)(aaa) (widowed spouse of deceased USC).

[100] *NB*: Although noncitizens whose spouses have died may not file Relative Petitions, they are eligible to self-petition as widows. INA §201(b)(2)(A)(i).

[101] INA §§204(a)(1)(A)(iii)(II)(aa)(CC)(ccc)(USC) and (B)(ii)(II)(aa)(CC)(bbb) (LPR); *see also* Anderson Memorandum, Jan. 2, 2002, *supra* note 51.

[102] *See* INA §§204(a)(1)(A)(iii)(II)(aa)(BB) (USC) and (B)(ii)(II)(aa)(BB) (LPR); *see also* Williams Memorandum, Aug. 21, 2002, *supra* note 47.

	VAWA Self Petition on Form I-360	**Relative Petition on Form I-130**
Ongoing familial relationship with USC or LPR anchor relative	• *Post*-filing loss of status by anchor relative does not affect the validity of the VAWA self-petition[103] • *Post*-filing divorce from anchor relative does not affect the validity of the VAWA self-petition[104] • *Post*-filing death of anchor USC relative does not affect the validity of the VAWA self-petition[105] • *Post*-approval remarriage or marriage of VAWA self-petitioner[106] • *Post*-lack of marital relationship due to previously unknown bigamy does not change validity of VAWA self-petition[107]	The Relative Petition will be automatically revoked[108] upon: • Loss of immigration status of the petitioner • Divorce between petitioner and beneficiary • Marriage of beneficiary where marriage ends beneficiary's eligibility as an immediate or preference relative • Aging-out[109] • Death of petitioner[110]
Employment authorization	Upon approval of the I-360, the approved VAWA self-petitioner is eligible to work incident to status.[111]	The approval of the I-130 grants no employment authorization benefits.[112]
Lawful presence in the United States	Upon approval of the I-360, a VAWA self-petitioner is allowed to remain in the United States (if already present) and is granted deferred action, making her lawfully present.[113]	The approval of an I-130 does not grant a non-citizen the right to be in the United States.[114]
Derivative children	Derivative children are included by operation of law for *both* immediate relatives and preference relatives.	Derivative children are included by operation of law *only* for preference relatives.

Continued

---

[103] INA §§204(a)(1)(A)(vi) (spouses and children of USCs); 204(a)(1)(B)(v)(I) (spouses and children of LPRs).

[104] *Id.*

[105] INA §204(a)(1)(A)(vi).

[106] INA §204(h).

[107] *See* INA §§204(a)(1)(A)(iii)(II)(aa)(BB) (USC) and (B)(ii)(II)(aa)(BB) (LPR); *see also* Williams Memorandum, Aug. 21, 2002, *supra* note 47.

[108] 8 CFR §205.1.

[109] Some children are protected from aging out upon turning 21 under INA §§201(f) or 203(h).

[110] Under certain circumstances, USCIS may choose to allow a beneficiary of a Relative Petition to obtain LPR status after the death of the petitioner (called humanitarian reinstatement). *See* 8 CFR §205.1(a)(3)(i)(C); *see also* INA §§212(a)(4)(C)(ii), 213A(f).

[111] INA §204(a)(1)(K).

[112] *But cf.* INA §101(a)(15)(V) and INA §214(q) (a limited exception for Preference Category 2A I-130 beneficiaries who had pending or approved I-130s before Dec. 21, 2000).

[113] *See* Cronin Memorandum, Sept. 8, 2000, *supra* note 37; with respect to certain children, *see* INA §§204(a)(1)(D)(i)(II) and (IV).

[114] *But cf.* INA §§101(a)(15)(V) and 214(q) (a limited exception for Preference Category 2A I-130 beneficiaries who had pending or approved I-130s before Dec. 21, 2000).

	VAWA Self Petition on Form I-360	Relative Petition on Form I-130
Age-Out Protections	• Protected by the provisions of the Child Status Protection Act (CSPA),[115] • Children of USCs allowed to petition up to age 25 as if they were children under 21 if there is connection between late-filing and domestic violence.[116]	Protected by the provisions of the Child Status Protection Act (CSPA)[117]
Good moral character	Good moral character is required of all VAWA self-petitioners, and the statute provides no limit on the time period that federal immigration authorities may consider good moral character.[118]	There is no good moral character requirement.
Adjustment of Status	Approved VAWA self-petitioners are eligible to adjust status under INA §245(a), regardless of entry without inspection (EWI) or any of the prohibitions to adjustment enumerated in INA §245(c), including unlawful employment or visa overstay. INA §245(i) and the fines paid pursuant to that provision are irrelevant to VAWA self-petitioners.	• Immediate relatives cannot adjust status under INA §245(a) if they entered without inspection and are not eligible for relief under INA §245(i). • Preference relatives cannot adjust status under INA §245(a) if they entered without inspection or are prevented from adjustment under INA §245(c) for such acts as unlawful employment, visa overstay, or any other delineated act if they are not eligible for relief under INA §245(i).
	Petition to Remove Conditions on Residence (Battered Spouse/Child Waiver) on Form I-751	**Petition to Remove Conditions on Residence (Joint Petition) on Form I-751**
Petitioner	Only the conditional resident is a petitioner.[119]	The spouse or parent who initially filed the Relative Petition on Form I-130 files as a petitioner jointly with the conditional resident[120]
Effect of death of spouse/parent	None	Death creates a separate ground for waiving joint-filing requirement.
Effect of Divorce	None	Divorce creates a separate ground for waiving joint-filing requirement.

Continued

---

[115] Pub. L. No. 107-208, 115 Stat. H.R. 1209 (Aug. 6, 2002); children covered by VAWA legislation are explicitly included by Sec. 805(b) of the Violence Against Women and Department of Justice Reauthorization Act of 2005, Pub. L. No. 109-162, 119 Stat. 2960 (Jan. 5, 2006).

[116] INA §204(a)(1)(D)(v).

[117] Pub. L. No. 107-208, 115 Stat. H.R. 1209 (Aug. 6, 2002).

[118] INA §§204(1)(A)(iii)(II)(bb) (spouses of USCs); 204(1)(A)(iv) (children of USCs); 204(1)(B)(ii)(II)(bb) (spouses of LPRs); 204(1)(B)(iii) (children of LPRs). Self-petitioners are required to provide affirmative evidence of good moral character for the three-year period immediately prior to filing. 8 CFR §204.2(c)(2)(v) (spouses of USCs and LPRs) and 8 CFR §204.2(e)(2)(v) (children of USCs and LPRs). Despite the seeming three-year limitation on looking back at good moral character, in the author's experience as an attorney at Sanctuary for Families, the author found that the Vermont Service Center routinely denies VAWA self-petitions based on lack of good moral character for conduct that occurred prior to the three-year period. Whether or not such denials are lawful (*see, e.g., Santamaria-Ames v. INS*, 104 F.3d 1127, 1131 and 1133, n.8 (9th Cir. 1996) (holding that while "conduct predating the regulatory period . . .may be considered . . . in determining naturalization eligibility," such "conduct prior to the regulatory period" cannot "be the sole basis for finding lack of good moral character")) is unclear, but to the author's knowledge, such denials have not yet been challenged in federal court.

[119] INA §216(c)(4)(C).

[120] INA §216(c)(1)(A).

	VAWA Self Petition on Form I-360	**Relative Petition on Form I-130**
Employment authorization	Employment authorization is incident to status as a conditional resident;[121] such status continues automatically during the pendency of the Battered Spouse/Child Waiver.[122]	Employment authorization is incident to status as a conditional resident;[123] such status continues automatically during the pendency of the Joint Petition.[124]
Lawful presence in the United States	Lawful presence is incident to status as a conditional resident; such status continues automatically during the pendency of the Battered Spouse/Child Waiver.[125]	Lawful presence is incident to status as a conditional resident; such status continues automatically during the pendency of the Joint Petition.[126]
Ability to travel in and out of the United States	Traveling in and out of the United States is incident to status as a conditional resident; such status continues automatically during the pendency of the Battered Spouse/Child Waiver.[127]	Traveling in and out of the United States is incident to status as a conditional resident; such status continues automatically during the pendency of the Battered Spouse/Child Waiver.[128]
Derivative children	Derivative children are included *only* if they received conditional status concurrently or within 90 days of the parent receiving such status.[129]	Derivative children are included *only* if they received conditional status concurrently or within 90 days of the parent receiving such status.[130]
Time to file	A Battered Spouse or Child Waiver may be filed at any time.[131]	90 days prior to the two-year anniversary of the grant of status.[132]
	Application for Cancellation of Removal and Adjustment of Status for Certain Nonpermanent Residents on Form EOIR 42B for certain domestic violence victims (VAWA Cancellation)	**Application for Cancellation of Removal and Adjustment of Status for Certain Nonpermanent Residents on Form EOIR 42B (10-year Cancellation)**
Applicant	Noncitizen facing removal	Noncitizen facing removal

Continued

---

[121] 8 CFR §274a.12(a)(1) ("An alien who is a lawful permanent resident (with or without conditions pursuant to section 216 of the Act), as evidenced by Form I–551 issued by the Service. An expiration date on the Form I–551 reflects only that the card must be renewed, not that the bearer's work authorization has expired").

[122] 8 CFR §216.4(a)(1).

[123] 8 CFR §274a.12(a)(1) ("An alien who is a lawful permanent resident (with or without conditions pursuant to section 216 of the Act), as evidenced by Form I–551 issued by the Service. An expiration date on the Form I–551 reflects only that the card must be renewed, not that the bearer's work authorization has expired").

[124] *Id.*

[125] 8 CFR §216.4(a)(1).

[126] *Id.*

[127] *Id.*

[128] *Id.*

[129] 8 CFR §216.4(a)(2).

[130] *Id.*

[131] The explicit requirement that a petition to remove conditions must be filed within the 90-day window prior to the two-year anniversary of the grant of conditional status described in INA §216(d)(2) applies only to joint petitions filed pursuant to INA §216(c)(1). This point is frequently lost on both mailroom staff and adjudications officers, but nonetheless is the law. Sanctuary for Families has successfully filed Battered Spouse Waivers on behalf of noncitizens even after such status has been affirmatively terminated by federal immigration authorities and as late as a dozen years past the initial two-year grant of conditional permanent resident status.

[132] INA §216(d)(2).

	VAWA Self Petition on Form I-360	**Relative Petition on Form I-130**
Immigration status of anchor relative at time of filing	<ul><li>USC;</li><li>LPR;</li><li>former USC;</li><li>former LPR;</li><li>deceased USC;</li><li>deceased LPR[133]</li></ul>	<ul><li>USC; or</li><li>LPR[134]</li></ul>
Relationship with anchor relative	<ul><li>Current spouse;</li><li>Former spouse;</li><li>Current parent;</li><li>Former parent;</li><li>USC/LPR (current or former) with whom the applicant has a child in common where USC/LPR abused child.</li></ul>	<ul><li>Current spouse;</li><li>Current parent;</li><li>Current child</li></ul>
Effect of death of anchor spouse/parent/child	None	Ends eligibility
Effect of divorce from anchor relative	None	Ends eligibility
Employment authorization	Employment is eligible to apply for authorization during the pendency of the application.[135]	Employment is eligible to apply for authorization during the pendency of the application.[136]
Nature of required hardship	Extreme hardship[137]	Exceptional and extremely unusual hardship[138]
Who must suffer the hardship?	<ul><li>VAWA cancellation applicant;</li><li>Child;</li><li>Parent[139]</li></ul>	<ul><li>Current USC/LPR spouse;</li><li>Current USC/LPR parent;</li><li>Current USC/LPR child[140]</li></ul>
Derivative children	None	None
Effect of age or current marital status of applicant whose anchor relative is a parent	None	None
Good moral character	Required for three years prior to application.	Required for 10 years prior to application

---

[133] The conclusion that current immigration status is *not* a requirement is based on the use of the phrases "is or was a United States citizen," INA §240A(b)(2)(A)(i)(I) and "is or was a lawful permanent resident," INA §240A(b)(2)(A)(2)(i)(II). In addition, the repeated use of the present progressive "has been" throughout INA §240(2) suggests that past actions alone may be the basis for eligibility.

[134] The conclusion that current immigration status is required for 10-year cancellation is based on the language of INA §240A(b)(1)(D), which states there must be hardship to a qualifying relative "who *is* a citizen of the United States or an alien lawfully admitted for permanent residence." (emphasis added)

[135] 8 CFR §274a.12(c)(10).

[136] *Id.*

[137] INA §240A(b)(2)(A)(v). Note that special hardship factors for those seeking VAWA suspension of deportation (and presumably, by analogy, VAWA cancellation) are listed at 8 CFR §1240.58(c).

[138] INA §240A(b)(1)(D).

[139] INA §240A(b)(2)(A)(v).

[140] INA §240A(b)(1)(D).

APPENDIX D

Information on VAWA Self-Petitions, Battered Spouse/Child Waivers, and VAWA Cancellation

	VAWA Self Petition	**Battered Spouse/Child Waiver**	**VAWA Cancellation**
Statute	Generally, INA §204(a)(1)(A)–(D),[141] specifically, • INA §204(a)(1)(A)(iii)—spouse of USC • INA §204(a)(1)(A)(iv)—child of USC • INA §204(a)(1)(A)(v)—spouse or child of USC employee of U.S. Government or member of the uniformed services where family jointly resided abroad • INA §204(a)(1)(A)(vii)—parent of USC • INA §204(a)(1)(B)(ii)—spouse of LPR • INA §204(a)(1)(B)(iii)—child of LPR • INA §204(a)(1)(B)(iv)—spouse or child of LPR employee of U.S. Government or member of the uniformed services where family jointly resided abroad.	INA §216(c)(4)(C)	INA §240A(b)(2)

Continued

---

[141] Although beyond the scope of this article, VAWA self-petitioning relief is available for abused spouses and children of those eligible for relief under:

▪ the Nicaraguan Adjustment and Central American Relief Act (NACARA) (NACARA, *as amended*, §202(d)(1));

▪ Pub. L. No. 89-732 (8 USC §1255 note) (commonly known as the Cuban Adjustment Act) (see the first section of the Cuban Adjustment Act, *as amended*);

▪ the Haitian Refugee Immigration Fairness Act of 1998 (8 USC §1255 note)—spouse and children of HRIFA (HIRIFA §902(d)(1)(B)) applicants

In addition, under INA §106, added by §814(c) of the Violence Against Women and Department of Justice Reauthorization Act of 2005, Pub. L. No. 109-162, 119 Stat. 2960 (Jan. 5, 2006), employment authorization, but no other benefit, is available to spouses of nonimmigrant visa holders in the following categories:

▪ INA §101(a)(15)(A);

▪ INA §101(a)(15)(E)(iii);

▪ INA §101(a)(15)(G); and

▪ INA §101(a)(15)(H).

	VAWA Self Petition	Battered Spouse/Child Waiver	VAWA Cancellation
Regulations[142]	• 8 CFR §204.2(c)—spouse of USC or LPR • 8 CFR §204.2(e)—child of USC or LPR • No regulations at the time of this writing for parent of a USC	8 CFR §216.5	• 8 CFR §1003.47 (filing in proceedings generally) • 8 CFR §1240.20; • 8 CFR §1240.21; • 8 CFR §1240.58
Status of Applicant	• No immigration status (including those who entered without inspection (EWI)) • Nonimmigrant visa • Abuser never petitioned • Approved I-130 • Adjustment pending	• Conditional Resident	• Person must be in removal proceedings and may have any immigration status other than USC

Continued

---

[142] As of March 26, 2006, the regulations have not been updated to reflect the Battered Immigrant Women Protection Act of 2000 incorporated into the Victims of Trafficking and Violence Protection Act of 2000, Pub. L. No 106-386, 114 Stat. 1464 (Oct. 28, 2000) (VAWA 2000) or Title VIII, Protection of Battered and Trafficked Immigrants of the Violence Against Women and Department of Justice Reauthorization Act of 2005, Pub. L. No. 109-162, 119 Stat. 2960 (Jan. 5, 2006) (VAWA 2005). Both VAWA 2000 and VAWA 2005 made significant changes to the options available for immigrant victims of domestic violence under the INA. To the extent that regulations—most recently amended, in relevant part (as of the time of this writing) on Nov. 13, 1997, at 62 Fed. Reg. 60769, 60771 (VAWA self-petitions), on Dec. 21, 1998, at 63 Fed. Reg. 70313, 70315 (battered spouse/child waivers) and on May 21, 1999, at 64 Fed. Reg. 27856, 27875 (VAWA cancellation)—contradict the statute, the statute itself controls.

Mindful that regulations have not previously been promulgated in a timely manner, §828 of VAWA 2005 requires that "[n]ot later than 180 days after the date of enactment of this Act, the Attorney General, the Secretary of Homeland Security, and the Secretary of State shall promulgate regulations to implement the provisions contained in the Battered Immigrant Women Protection Act of 2000 (Title V of Public Law 106-386), this Act, and the amendments made by this Act. As VAWA 2005 was enacted on January 5, 2006, regulations are expected on July 5, 2006 (as July 4, 2006, the 180-day mark, is a federal holiday.)

	VAWA Self Petition	**Battered Spouse/Child Waiver**	**VAWA Cancellation**
Status of Abuser	• USC; • LPR; • former USC where immigration status lost in the previous two years because of domestic violence[143] • former LPR where immigration status lost in the previous two years because of domestic violence or deceased USC[144] • deceased USC where death occurred in the last two years	• USC • LPR[145] • deceased USC • deceased LPR	• USC; • LPR; • former USC; • former LPR; • deceased USC; • deceased LPR
Relationship between abuser and domestic violence victim	• Spouse • Ex-spouse (divorced within the last two years due to domestic violence)[146] • Intended spouse (but not legally a spouse solely because of bigamy of which domestic violence victim was unaware)[147] • Child (includes single young adult sons and daughters of USCs between the ages of 21 and 25 who, due to the domestic violence, filed after their 21st birthdays[148]) • Parent of USC	• Spouse; • Ex-spouse; • Child; • Child of ex-spouse; • Widow/Widower • Son or daughter (who was child at time he or she became a conditional resident)	• Spouse; • Ex-spouse; • Child; • Child of ex-spouse; • Widow/Widower; • Son or Daughter

Continued

---

[143] INA §§204(a)(1)(A)(iii)(II)(CC)(bbb) (spouse of USC who lost status in connection with domestic violence), §204(a)(1)(A)(iv) (child of USC who lost status in connection with domestic violence), 204(a)(1)(A)(vii)(I) (parent of USC son or daughter who lost status in connect with domestic violence); *see also* Aytes Memorandum, Oct. 31, 2005, *supra* note 42.

[144] INA §§204(a)(1)(B)(ii)(II)(CC)(aaa) (spouse of LPR who lost status in connection with domestic violence) and 204(a)(1)(B)(iii) (child of LPR who lost status in connection with domestic violence); *see also* Aytes Memorandum, Oct. 31, 2005, *supra* note 42.

[145] Since Preference Category 2A is currently backlogged more than two years, spouses of LPRs will receive permanent residency without condition at time of the approval of application for permanent resident status.

[146] *See* INA §§204(a)(1)(A)(iii)(II)(aa)(CC)(ccc)(USC) (citizen) and (B)(ii)(II)(aa)(CC)(bbb) (LPR); *see also* Anderson Memorandum, Jan. 2, 2002, *supra* note 51.

[147] *See* INA §§204(a)(1)(A)(iii)(II)(aa)(BB) (USC) and (B)(ii)(II)(aa)(BB) (LPR); *see also* Williams Memorandum, Aug. 21, 2002, *supra* note 47.

[148] INA §204(a)(1)(D)(v).

	VAWA Self Petition	Battered Spouse/Child Waiver	VAWA Cancellation

Elements	• Legal and valid marriage (or non-marriage due to bigamy that is no fault of the self-petitioner)
	• Good faith marriage (for self-petitioning spouses)
	• Joint residence in the United States (or abroad where abuser is an employee of the U.S. Government or member of the U.S. armed services)
	• Good moral character
	• Qualifying abuse:
	  ➢ Physical battery; or
	  ➢ Extreme cruelty
		• Good faith marriage
		• Qualifying abuse:
		  ➢ Physical battery; or
		  ➢ Extreme cruelty
			• Either:
			  ➢ Legal and valid marriage (or non-marriage due to bigamy that is no fault of the self-petitioner); *or*
			  ➢ child in common where USC or LPR parent engages in qualifying abuse against USC or LPR child
			• Good faith marriage (if claim is based on marriage rather than abused child in common)
			• Good moral character
			• Three years' physical presence
			• Extreme hardship to the noncitizen, the noncitizen's child, or the noncitizen's parent
			• Qualifying abuse:
			  ➢ Physical battery; or
			  ➢ Extreme cruelty

Effects of Divorce	For spouses, must have occurred within the two years prior to filing and only where there is a connection between the domestic violence and the divorce.[149]	No direct effect, but creates additional ground for waiver.[150]	None
Effects of marriage or remarriage	*After* self-petition is approved, the approved petition remains valid • Upon remarriage of self-petitioning former spouse; • Upon marriage of self-petitioning child[151]	No effect	No effect
Forms	I-360	I-751	EOIR-42B G-325A

Continued

---

[149] INA §§204(a)(1)(A)(iii)(II)(aa)(CC)(ccc) (USC) and (B)(ii)(II)(aa)(CC)(bbb) (LPR); *see also* Anderson Memorandum, Jan. 2, 2002, *supra* note 51.

[150] INA §216(c)(4)(B).

[151] INA §204(h).

	VAWA Self Petition	Battered Spouse/Child Waiver	VAWA Cancellation

Where to file	VAWA Unit
	Vermont Service Center
	75 Lower Weldon Street
	St. Albans, VT 05479
		The Service Center with jurisdiction over the state of residence of the battered spouse/child waiver petitioner.[152]	Original to:
			• Immigration Judge
			  ➢ Include all supporting materials in addition to the forms.
			Copies to:
			• USCIS Texas Service Center[153]
			  PO Box 85246
			  Mesquite, Texas 75185-2463
			  ➢ Include two separate checks or money orders, one for the application fee and the other for the biometric fee;
			  ➢ Include an additional original G-325A;
			  ➢ Do *not* include supporting materials.
			• ICE Counsel where noncitizen is in proceedings
			  ➢ Include copies of all supporting materials in addition to the forms.

Cost	**BEWARE THAT COSTS ARE SUBJECT TO CHANGE. PRIOR TO SUBMITTING ANY FILING, YOU MUST CONSULT THE RELEVANT WEBSITE (***http://uscis.gov/graphics/formsfee/forms/index.htm***) FOR VAWA SELF-PETITIONS AND BATTERED SPOUSE/CHILD WAIVERS and ***www.usdoj.gov/eoir/formslist.htm*** for VAWA cancellation)**		
	$190	$205 (biometrics)	$100 + $70

---

[152] Should the Vermont Service Center cover the jurisdiction where the battered spouse/child waiver petitioner resides, the submission should be sent to the VAWA Unit, which will adjudicate it; should the battered spouse/child waiver petitioner be in proceedings, follow the submission procedures described for cancellation of removal applications.

[153] As the time of this writing, all applications for cancellation of removal applications are being sent to the Texas Service Center, per instructions effective April 1, 2005. As the procedures are in flux, please be sure to contact your local court and review 8 CFR §1003.47 and the interim rule promulgated at Background and Security Investigations in Proceedings Before Immigration Judges and the Board of Immigration Appeals, 70 Fed. Reg. 4743 (Jan. 31, 2005).

APPENDIX E[1]—CHECKLIST

**DOCUMENTS THAT MAY BE HELPFUL IN PREPARING
A VAWA SELF PETITION OR BATTERED SPOUSE/CHILD WAIVER:
A LIST OF SUGGESTIONS, NOT REQUIREMENTS**

Battered Immigrant's Identity and Immigration Status:
___Birth certificate(s) of battered immigrant woman and children
___Passport(s) of battered immigrant woman and children
___I-94 Card(s) of battered immigrant woman and children, if any
___All documentation previously submitted to or received from the immigration service

Evidence of Abuser's Citizenship or Lawful Permanent Resident Status (Self-Petitions only)
- For U.S. Citizens:
___Abuser's birth certificate
___Abuser's naturalization certificate, if any
___Abuser's passport

- For Lawful Permanent Residents:
___Abuser's Permanent Resident Card ("green card")
    (other possibilities: knowledge of abuser's alien registration number)
___Abuser's passport

Legal Marriage (Self Petitions only):
___Divorce decree(s), annulment decree(s), or death certificate(s) from prior marriages of
    both battered immigrant woman and abuser
___Marriage certificate of battered immigrant woman and abuser

Joint Residence in the U.S. (Self Petitions Only):
___Battered immigrant woman's affidavit[2]
___Credit card bills, letters, cards, and any mail addressed to one or both spouses at the address
___Joint bank accounts listing address
___Employment records
___Utility receipts (gas, electric, water, cable, phone)
___School records
___Hospital or medical records

---

1   Adopted from a checklist developed by Hilary Sunghee Seo and Carolien Hardenbol of the Immigration Intervention Project at Sanctuary for Families' Center for Battered Women's Legal Services and is reprinted with permission.

2   The battered immigrant should not be asked to draft her own affidavit – an attorney or law graduate should do so based on her statements and any notes she can provide.

___Leases, deeds, mortgages, rent receipts, letters from landlord, superintendent, or neighbors
___Insurance policies
___Affidavits[3] by persons who knew battered immigrant woman and abuser lived together

Good Faith Marriage:
___Battered immigrant woman's affidavit[4]
___Proof that one spouse is listed on other spouse's insurance policies, leases, income
    tax forms, bank accounts, car title
___Proof of other major purchases made as a couple
___Photos taken of wedding; photos taken during relationship before and after marriage
___Correspondence between spouses both before and after marriage, or between
        friends or   family members
___Emergency contact lists at place of employment that lists spouse as contact
___Birth certificates of children of battered immigrant woman and spouse
___Affidavits[5] of persons who knew battered immigrant woman and abuser as a
        married couple

Evidence of Physical Abuse or Extreme Cruelty:
- *Physical Abuse:*
___Battered immigrant woman's affidavit[6]
___Reports from police, judges and other court officials.
___Reports and affidavits[7] from medical personnel, school officials, clergy, social workers, and
        other social service agency personnel
___Orders of protection or other court findings of abuse
___Documentation that battered immigrant woman sought assistance for abuse, such as record of
        residence in battered women's shelter, or participation in battered women's support group
___Affidavits[8] from family, friends, and neighbors with knowledge of abuse

---

3   Your client and those providing supporting affidavits should not be asked to draft affidavits. Ask
     your client to make a list of those who know about her situation, including friends, family
     members, colleagues and professionals familiar with her case, such as advocates, counselors,
     doctors, and clergy people. You should approach the list of people she gives you to see if they
     would be willing to speak briefly with an attorney and then sign a confidential statement drafted by
     you.

4   See Note 1.

5   See Note 2.

6   See Note 1.

7   See Note 2.

8   See Note 2.

Good Moral Character *(Self Petitions only):*

___Police clearance or state-issued background check from each locality where battered immigrant woman has lived for six months or more in the past three years*

Forms

___ Battered Spouse/Child Waiver: I-751 and G-28 (a Notice of Appearance on Form G-28 printed on blue paper accompanies every form submitted on behalf of client, except for the G-325A)

___ Self Petition: I-360 and G-28. In addition, some or all of the following: G-325A, I-485, I-765, I-824, I-765

Additional information:

1. *All documents in foreign languages must be translated into English and accompanied by certificates of translation. Note that there is no such thing as an "official" translation of immigration documents. Anyone competent to translate can do so simply by stating in writing that he or she certifies that the translation is complete and correct and that the translator is competent to translate the foreign language into English.*

2. *Copies of all documents will be accepted, but affidavits and letters in support of self-petitions should be submitted as originals when possible.*

This check-list is not exhaustive and has been created solely as an initial reference guide.

INTERNATIONAL ADOPTION—A BASIC GUIDE TO THE THREE VISA CATEGORIES

by Daniel E. Marcus and Irene A. Steffas, with contributions from Boyd F. Campbell[*]

To cover the broad topic of adoption for immigration purposes, a practitioner must first look at the Immigration and Nationality Act (INA)[1] at §§101(b)(1)(E)(i), (F)(i), and (G)(i). There is a different definition set forth in each section. The goal of this piece is to introduce the two main sections, §§101(b)(1)(E)(i) and (F)(i), currently in use, and a new section now being drafted, (G)(i).

In short, INA §101(b)(1)(E)(i) defines an adopted child as a child who has been residing with the adoptive parent or parents for two years and has been in their legal custody for two years. INA §101(b)(1)(F)(i) defines an orphan as a child who

---

[*] **Daniel Marcus** is president of Globman & Marcus, P.C. of Hartford, Conn., a firm that has practiced exclusively in immigration law since 1946. Mr. Marcus is a 1981 graduate of Union College, cum laude, and a 1984 graduate of the Suffolk University Law School. Mr. Marcus is a past chapter chair of AILA's Connecticut Chapter and served as a member of AILA's EOIR Committee. Mr. Marcus is listed in *The Best Lawyers in America* for his work in the field of immigration law.

Irene Steffas practices law with the Steffas Law Center in Marietta, Ga. In 2004, the American Academy of Adoption Attorneys recognized her with the President's Award for Dedicated and Extraordinary Service to the Academy and Improving Adoption Law. In 2003, Ms. Steffas represented the Department of State at a World Congress on Inter-Country Adoptions in Barcelona, where nine countries made presentations regarding the Hague Adoption Convention and how each country regulates specific components of the treaty. The Steffas Law Center represents adoption agencies, adoptive parents, and children before DOS, USCIS, and AAO; additionally, the Center represents children in special immigrant juvenile (SIJ) and citizenship cases, as well as adult adoptees in pursuit of citizenship.

Boyd Campbell has practiced immigration and nationality law and private international law in Montgomery, Ala., since 1988. He is a veteran AILA mentor in the areas of intercountry adoption, Ls, Es, and religious visas. Mr. Campbell was appointed Alabama's first practicing civil law notary by the Alabama Secretary of State in August 2001. Alabama and Florida are the only two states in the nation with laws establishing the office of civil law notary.

[1] Immigration and Nationality Act of 1952, Pub. L. No. 82-414, 66 Stat. 163 (codified as amended at 8 USC §§1101 *et seq.*) (INA).

---

lost his or her parents within the terms of the INA.[2] INA §101(b)(1)(G)(i) defines a child who has been adopted pursuant to the Intercountry Adoption Act of 2000, also known as the Hague Convention, but will not be in force in the United States until at least July 2007.

Even an experienced immigration attorney can confuse the requirements and procedures of the three INA sections. It is imperative to read the INA, the regulations, and the *Foreign Affairs Manual* (FAM) when deciding which avenue to pursue.

For a broad picture of international adoption procedures, familiarize yourself with 8 USC §§1101, 1151–54, and 1434. Also become familiar with the regulations in 8 CFR §§204.2(d)(2)(vii)–(e)(1), 204.2(f)(2)(iv), and 204.3(a)–(k)(4). There are many twists and turns within each definition and regulation.

ADOPTED CHILDREN

For adoption purposes, INA §101(b)(1)(E)(i) defines child as "an unmarried person under twenty-one years of age" who is:

a child adopted while under the age of sixteen years if the child has been in the legal custody of, and has resided with, the adopting parent or parents for at least two years or if the child has been battered or subject to extreme cruelty by the adopting parent or by a family member of the adopting parent residing in the same household: Provided, That no natural parent of any such adopted child shall thereafter, by virtue of such parentage, be accorded any right, privilege, or status under this Act; or

(ii) subject to the same proviso as in clause (i), a child who:

(I) is a natural sibling of a child described in clause (i) or subparagraph (F)(i);

---

[2] A 1995 *Immigration Briefings* article is still one of the best reviews of the international adoption process. See K. Sullivan, "Intercountry Adoption: A Step-by-Step Guide for the Practitioner," 95-09 *Immigration Briefings* (Sept. 1995).

(II) was adopted by the adoptive parent or parents of the sibling described in such clause or subparagraph; and

(III) is otherwise described in clause (i), except that the child was adopted while under the age of 18 years;

One of the most common issues in an adoption case is proof of two years' residency/legal custody.[3] The two years' residency may occur before or after the adoption.[4] The residency can occur at any time but must be for a full two years.[5] The custody and residency requirement can be fulfilled simultaneously.[6]

The legal custody and residency requirements can be satisfied if the child has resided with one of the adoptive parents. Further, legal custody requires either a final adoption decree or an official document in the form of a custody award by a court or recognized government entity. Less formal documents, such as sworn affidavits, are insufficient.[7]

A determination from a proper state court that prospective adoptive parents are the legal guardians of the child to be adopted is, in our experience, acceptable by both U.S. Citizenship and Immigration Services (USCIS) and U.S. embassies as proof of legal custody. Therefore, when considering an adoption in the United States, obtaining guardianship first (while the adoption is pending) is wise to start the two-year clock ticking.

The adopted child petition is filed on Form I-130, but cannot be submitted until the two years of legal and physical custody have been met. If the child is in the United States and otherwise eligible to adjust under INA §245, the I-130 can be filed concurrently with an I-485.

Documents that can be used to prove the two-year residency requirement include school records, medical records, dental records, and tax returns listing the child as a dependent (to be listed on a U.S. tax return, the child should have a taxpayer identification number). This list is not exhaustive, and a practitioner has an opportunity to be creative in obtaining documents to satisfy this requirement.

Finally, the adoption must occur before the child is 16. Adoption after the child's 16th birthday will not be given retroactive effect.[8] However, a court order entered *nunc pro tunc* is evidence of proper adoption before the child's 16th birthday.[9] If a family adopts a child who is the natural sibling of another adopted child and the adoption occurs at the same time as or after the adoption of the first child, the second child can be under the age of 18 instead of 16.[10] USCIS defines "natural sibling" for purposes of this act as children "sharing one or both biological parents."[11]

The following fact patterns may help clarify the adopted child provisions. Keep in mind that the provision is relatively rare and is often confused with the more common category of orphan, discussed next.

How facts impact procedure and outcome:

▪ **Two years legal custody and joint residency**: A couple in India adopts a 2-year-old child; the adoption is finalized when the child is 2. When the child is 5, the State Department issues the family a visa to come to the United States as H-1B nonimmigrants. They plan to work for three years and then return to India. Their child comes to the United States with them. In this scenario, a child who was 4 years old when he was adopted (with less than two full years of legal or physical custody) would not be able to come to the United States, even as a nonimmigrant, because he does not meet the definition of child under INA §101(b)(1)(E)(i).[12]

It is not uncommon for consular officers to issue dependent visas for adopted children on the misunderstanding of the definition of "child" under INA §101(b)(1)(E)(i). Some consular posts will issue a

---

[3] *Matter of Repuyan*, 19 I&N Dec. 119 (BIA 1984) (addressing issue of residency for adoption).

[4] *See* 8 CFR §204.2(d)(2)(vii)(C); *Matter of M*, 8 I&N Dec. 118 (BIA 1958).

[5] *Matter of Lee*, 11 I&N Dec. 911 (BIA 1966).

[6] Pub. L. No. 99-653, §2 (Nov. 14, 1986).

[7] INS Memorandum, Puleo, Asst. Comm., Adjudications (Feb. 17, 1989), *reprinted in* 66 *Interpreter Releases* 260 (Mar. 1989).

[8] *Matter of Cariaga*, 15 I&N Dec. 716, 717 (BIA 1976).

[9] *Allen v. Brown*, 953 F. Supp. 199 (N.D. Ohio 1977).

[10] *See* INA §101(b)(1)(E)(ii).

[11] INS Memorandum, Pearson, Exe. Assoc. Comm. HQADN 70/8.3 (Nov. 13, 2000), *reprinted in* 78 *Interpreter Releases* 336, 353–56 (Feb. 5, 2001).

[12] If the adopted parents had a court order granting them custody, they could accrue the two-year period from the date of that court order. An affidavit is not sufficient; they must have a court order establishing custody.

B-2 visa for the adopted child for the duration of the principal visa holder's stay. This is similar to the practice of issuing B-2 visas for domestic partners.

- **Two years' legal custody and joint residency**: U.S. citizens who are missionaries in Ghana adopt a 5-year-old child in Ghana. After five years, they wish to return to the United States with their adopted child. They may do so under INA §101(b)(1)(E)(i), because the child meets the USCIS definition of child. Compare this to the case of a U.S. businessman working in Chile; he and his wife adopt a 2-year-old. After one year in Chile, his company wants to transfer him back to the United States. This child is not allowed to immigrate because he does not meet the definition of child under INA §101(b)(1)(E)(i). Yet a child who was an orphan can immigrate under the F definition discussed in the next section.

- **Two years' legal custody and joint residency**: U.S. citizens residing in the United States adopt a 12-year-old noncitizen child under state law. After the adoptive parents have two years' legal custody, the adopted parents may apply to USCIS for the child's permanent residency status using Forms I-130 and I-485. The child qualifies as an immediate relative of a U.S. citizen by meeting the statutory definition of child under INA §101(b)(1)(E)(i).

- **Children who enter with inspection**: A child entered the United States as a tourist. She has a passport and proof of inspection (an I-94 Arrival/Departure Document). Although the child's passport and visa are good for 10 years, USCIS only granted two months of authorized stay on the I-94 card. If the period of authorized stay expires, the child is out of status but does not accrue unlawful presence as a minor.[13] However, if the child were to leave the United States, there would be no way for her to re-enter as an adopted child. After satisfying the four technical requirements under INA §101(b)(1)(E)(i), including a finalized adoption by U.S. citizen parents, the results are the same as example three: legal permanent residency. *Note*: Practitioners should be careful in advising clients on this issue. U.S. citizen parents should not use the B-2 visa as a vehi-

cle for bringing the child to the United States for adoption.

- **Children entering without inspection**: The child is an undocumented alien. After satisfying the four requirements under INA §101(b)(1)(E)(i), the parents may file a family petition for the child. However, since there is no proof of legal entry, the child entered without inspection (EWI) and must return to her country of origin f to obtain legal permanent residency status through consular processing (or if applicable, file for adjustment under INA §245(i)). The U.S. consulate abroad will adjudicate the case for legal permanent residency status.

- **Child adopted by non–U.S. citizens**: A child enters the United States with USCIS inspection and is later adopted by parents who are legal permanent residents, not U.S. citizens. After the child meets the four requirements of INA §101(b)(1)(E)(i), his parents file an I-30 with USCIS. Because the parents are not U.S. citizens, a visa is not immediately available for the child, who must wait for an immigrant visa to become available. Advice to this client will need to include consideration of unlawful presence if the child turns 18 before a visa becomes available, and the Child Status Protection Act if the child turns 21 before receiving an immigrant visa.

- **Child over 21 adopted by U.S. citizens residing abroad**: U.S. citizens who are working and residing in Germany adopt a 3-year-old child from the Ukraine. The child lives with her parents in early childhood and later attends Swiss boarding schools. At the *age of 35*, the child wants to immigrate to the United States. Can she? Yes, since the adoption occurred before the child's 16th birthday, the second step of immigration can be done at any later time. Note, her parents are U.S. citizens; though the adult child will not qualify as an immediate relative, she will be family-sponsored first preference or single or third preference if married.

Practice Pointers Regarding the Adopted Child Definition of INA §101(b)(1)(E)

- The child does not have to meet the technical definition of orphan of §101(b)(1)(F). For example, the child may have two married living parents who consent to the adoption.

- The two years of joint residency can accrue before or after the adoption. There need simply be

---

[13] INA §212(a)(9)(B)(i)(I) states the 3-year bar on admission; INA §212(a)(9)(B)(i)(II) states the 10-year bar on admission; INA §212(a)(9)(B)(iii)(I) states the exception for minors.

24 months of residency before applying to USCIS.

- The two years' legal custody can accrue before or after the adoption. There need simply be 24 months of custody before applying to USCIS.

- To meet the legal custody requirement, a court order is needed as evidence of the grant of legal custody.

- To establish two years of physical custody before the adoption, a court order of guardianship is needed; affidavits alone are insufficient. Health insurance cards, school records, medical billing statements, and tax returns make excellent evidence.

- You can establish two years of legal custody after the adoption with the final order of adoption.

- It is not sufficient to file a petition of adoption before the child's 16th birthday. The adoption must be finalized before that birthday (or the 18th in the case of a sibling adopted along with a child under 16).

- The petition to USCIS can be made at any time during the child's life, once the four statutory requirements are satisfied.

- There is no requirement that a child be in lawful immigration status while he or she accrues the two years' custody or residence in the United States.

- Generally, USCIS will not initiate deportation proceedings for a child who is adopted by USC parents and residing illegally or out of status in the United States (though if the child becomes an aggravated felon under the immigration definition, USCIS will bring removal proceedings).

- Even illegal children are entitled to an education through the public school system.[14]

- A child who has lived with U.S. citizen parents all his or her life but was not adopted has no status unless there is a final decree of adoption before his or her 16th birthday.

ORPHAN PETITION

INA §101(b)(1)(F) provides that:

(i) a child, under the age of sixteen at the time a petition is filed in his behalf to accord a classification as an immediate relative under section 201(b) of this title, who is an orphan because of the death or disappearance of, abandonment or desertion by, or separation or loss from, both parents, or for whom the sole or surviving parent is incapable of providing the proper care and has in writing irrevocably released the child for emigration and adoption; who has been adopted abroad by a United States citizen and spouse jointly, or by an unmarried United States citizen at least twenty-five years of age, who personally saw and observed the child prior to or during the adoption proceedings; or who is coming to the United States for adoption by a United States citizen and spouse jointly, or by an unmarried United States citizen at least twenty-five years of age, who have or has complied with the preadoption requirements, if any, of the child's proposed residence: Provided, that the Attorney General is satisfied that proper care will be furnished the child if admitted to the United States: Provided further, that no natural parent or prior adoptive parent of any such child shall thereafter, by virtue of such parentage, be accorded any right, privilege, or status under this Act; or

(ii) subject to the same provisos as in clause (i), a child who:

(I) is a natural sibling of a child described in clause (i) or subparagraph (E)(i);

(II) has been adopted abroad, or is coming to the United States for adoption, by the adoptive parent (or prospective adoptive parent) or parents of the sibling described in such clause or subparagraph; and

(III) is otherwise described in clause (i), except that the child is under the age of 18 at the time a petition is filed in his or her behalf to accord a classification as an immediate relative under section 201(b).

Initially, note that an orphan petition cannot be processed to completion inside the United States. Although a child may theoretically be adopted in the United States, USCIS must first approve an I-600 application, which is the form filed for the classification of an orphan. It is then forwarded to the U.S. embassy in the country where the child resides. A child who qualifies as an orphan and is living with adoptive parents in the United States will have to leave the United States to be processed as an orphan. In order to avoid this problem, even though the child may qualify as an orphan, the child should be processed as an adopted child under §101(b)(1)(E)(i).

---

[14] *Plyler v. Doe*, 457 U.S. 202 (1982).

8 CFR §204.3(k)(3) provides that a child who has been paroled into the United States and has not been adopted there is eligible for the benefits of an orphan petition when all the requirements of INA §§101(b)(1)(F)(i), 204(d), and (e) have been met. A child in the United States either illegally or as a non-immigrant, however, is ineligible for the benefits of an orphan petition.

Note that an I-600 petition for an orphan must be filed before the child's 16th birthday, and the child must be adopted before that birthday. However, limited exceptions to this rule permit an I-600 petition to be filed after the child is 16. An I-130 petition for an adopted child does not have to be filed before the child's 16th birthday so long as the child was adopted before that birthday.

Further, under 8 CFR §204.3(f)(2), an orphan can be granted an immigrant visa even if the adoption is not final until the child enters the United States if :

that an orphan who is coming to be adopted in the United States if he or she will not be or has not been adopted abroad, or if the unmarried petitioner or both the married petitioner and spouse did not or will not personally see the orphan prior to or during the adoption proceedings abroad, and/or if the adoption abroad will not be, or was not, full and final. If the prospective adoptive parents reside in a State with preadoption requirements and they plan to have the child come to the United States for adoption, they must submit evidence of compliance with the State's pre-adoption requirements to the Service. Any pre-adoption requirements which by operation of State law cannot be met before filing the advanced processing application must be noted. Such requirements must be met prior to filing the petition, except for those which cannot be met by operation of State law until the orphan is physically in the United States. Those requirements which cannot be met until the orphan is physically present in the United States must be noted.

This provision allows a child to come to the United States to be adopted if the petitioner(s) is not able to go abroad to participate in the adoption process. This is an exception to the requirement that a child must be adopted before he or she can be brought to the United States as an orphan.

Before undertaking an orphan petition, it is crucial to study the definition of "orphan." Section 204.3(b) of 8 CFR specifies abandonment by both parents, desertion by both parents, disappearance of both parents, incapability of providing proper care by both parents, loss of both parents, or separation from both parents, sole parent, and surviving parent. Many orphan cases involve situations that qualify as orphan under the regulation even though both natural parents are not deceased. Often, one of the parents is deceased and the other (sole or surviving parent) has either abandoned or deserted the child or is incapable of providing proper care.

The most difficult of the definitions to satisfy is that of a sole parent who is incapable of providing proper care consistent with the standards of the foreign sending country. 8 CFR §204.3(b) states:

[S]ole parent means the mother when it is established that the child is illegitimate and has not acquired a parent within the meaning of section 101(b)(2) of the Act. An illegitimate child shall be considered to have a sole parent if his or her father has severed all parental ties, rights, duties, and obligations to the child, or if his or her father has, in writing, irrevocably released the child for emigration and adoption. This definition is not applicable to children born in countries which make no distinction between a child born in or out of wedlock, since all such children are considered to be legitimate. In all cases, a sole parent must be incapable of providing proper care as that term is defined in this section.

Foreign countries that have government adoption agencies or boards often will provide reports on the adopted child's living conditions and means of support. If these agencies conclude that the sole parent cannot provide proper care consistent with local standards, USCIS will accept the determination.

As a result of Public Law 104-51, 109 Stat. 467, which President Clinton signed into law on November 15, 1995, and which became effective immediately, the definitions of child under INA §101(b)(1) and of parent or father under INA §101(b)(2) were changed. These changes allow a child to be considered as having a "sole parent" (the birth mother) if:

- The child was born out of wedlock; and

- The child has not been legitimated under the law of the child's residence or domicile or under the law of the natural (birth) father's residence or domicile while the child was in the legal custody of the legitimating parent or parents; and

- The child has not acquired a stepparent; and

- The natural father has disappeared or abandoned or deserted the child or has in writing irrevocably released the child for emigration and adoption.

Because of this change, it not necessary to determine whether a child born out of wedlock is regarded as legitimate or illegitimate under the laws of the foreign sending country. However, if the natural father has ever had sole or joint legal custody of the child, it will still be necessary to determine whether the child may have been legitimated under the law of the child's or the father's residence or domicile. The marriage of the child's birth parents will legitimate a child born out of wedlock in most countries. In countries where all children are regarded as legitimate at birth, a child who has been acknowledged or recognized by the natural father before the child was 18 and in the legal custody of the father or the natural parents may be regarded as legitimated.

Another problem in orphan petitions is fulfilling the requirement of abandonment by both parents or a single parent where there is only one. As defined by 8 CFR §204.3(b), abandonment by both parents means:

The parents have willfully forsaken all parental rights, obligations, and claims to the child, as well as all control over and possession of the child, without intending to transfer, or without transferring, these rights to any specific person(s). Abandonment must include not only the intention to surrender all parental rights, obligations, and claims to the child, and control over and possession of the child, but also the actual act of surrendering such rights, obligations, claims, control, and possession. A relinquishment or release by the parents for a specific adoption does not constitute abandonment. Similarly, the relinquishment or release of the child by the parents to a third party for custodial care in anticipation of, or preparation for, adoption does not constitute abandonment unless the third party (such as a governmental agency, a court of competent jurisdiction, an adoption agency, or an orphanage) is authorized under the child welfare laws of the foreign-sending country to act in such a capacity. A child who is placed temporarily in an orphanage shall not be considered to be abandoned if the parents express an intention to retrieve the child, are contributing or attempting to contribute to the support of the child, or otherwise exhibit ongoing parental interest in the child. A child who has been given uncondition-

ally to an orphanage shall be considered to be abandoned.

Again, to satisfy the legal definition of abandonment it is useful to contact the adoption agency in the specific country, if there is such an agency, to execute a statement from the natural parents that will address all of the requirements in this definition. Similarly, to prove desertion, disappearance, loss of parents, or separation from parents, it is also useful to have the adoption agency execute the necessary statements. If an adoption agency does not exist in the specific country, affidavits can be obtained from family members attesting to abandonment or desertion by parents, disappearance of both parents, loss of both parents, and separation from both parents. However, USCIS or the U.S. embassy may deem these affidavits to be self-serving.

Common orphan adoption situations involving the orphan definition:

- **Sole surviving parents and directed placements**: Often it can be established that a child is an orphan because he has a sole surviving parent; the other parent may be deceased or have deserted the child, disappeared, or been separated or become lost from the family. U.S. law permits a sole surviving parent to make a directed placement[15] only when that parent cannot support the child in accordance with the standard of living of the home country. Good examples are: (a) a parent who is incarcerated; (b) a parent who is terminally ill; (c) a parent who cannot support the child financially because of an overwhelming burden—poverty and unemployment are not enough. The poverty must exceed the average for other children in the home country.

- **Two-parent families**: A child who has two parents who are very poor will not qualify as an orphan unless both parents abandon[16] the child to a recognized child-placing entity in the home country and that entity has the authority to decide who adopts the child.

When two parents are married and caring for the child, it is simply impossible to classify that child as an orphan and have a family member adopt the

---

[15] It is not sufficient that the U.S. law permits the directed placement, but the law of the child's home country must also permit a directed placement.

[16] "Abandon," as defined in 8 CFR §204.3 is commonly referred to as voluntary relinquishment.

child. Only a sole surviving parent may make a directed placement. Under the Hague Treaty and the InterCountry Adoption Act, discussed below, a child may qualify as an orphan. Hence, a child not qualifying as an orphan under INA §101(b)(1)(F) may qualify as an orphan under INA §101(b)(1)(G).

It is good practice to explore the circumstances of a case to see if it can be established that the child is an orphan. For example, the child has a mother and a father, but the mother disappeared when the child was 4 months old. If there is a court finding that the mother disappeared (after a legitimate search was made for her), the father can be a sole surviving parent. To orchestrate such a case, it is imperative to have good communications with a foreign attorney.

The Child's Home Country's Law

It is paramount to seek *knowledge* about the foreign country's adoption laws and sentiments toward adoptions whenever you are considering an orphan adoption. First, go to the Department of State website: *www.travel.state.gov*; near the bottom is a section called *Children and Family* with three subsections. Click on *International Adoption*; once you are on that page, look to the left of the screen; click on *Country Specific Information*. Find the country (the list is alphabetical) and click on it to read a basic summary of the country's international adoption procedures.

Another step in determining feasibility is to send an e-mail inquiring about the process to the child's home country. Go again to *www.travel.state.gov*. On the bottom left you will see *Links to U.S. Embassies & Consulates Worldwide*. Some consulates will simply tell you that your inquiry is premature; others offer extensive assistance that will give you the tools you need to evaluate the feasibility of the case.

The third and most important way to determine the law of a foreign country is to ask your client to locate an attorney or adoption agency in the specific country. We ask that the attorney have e-mail or fax and, if possible, speak English.

Knowledge of the foreign country's laws is crucial to ensuring that the adoptive parents are not circumventing that country's adoption procedures.

A second piece of the puzzle is the relinquishment procedure of the foreign country. For example, some countries permit *a parent* to surrender a child directly to adoptive parents. Other countries require that the surrender be only to certain approved governmental agencies. Knowing this in advance can prevent a fatal error.

Past bad precedents haunt current visa issuance. For example, treaties are the basis on which visas are issued to children for *medical treatment*. The foreign countries allow children to leave with the understanding that after the children receive medical treatment they will be returned to their country of origin. This mechanism is often abused to circumvent adoptive parents having home studies and to avoid compliance with the strict orphan definitions. In the very near future, much tighter controls over both tourist and medical waiver visas are likely.

Of concern among all countries is the fear that vulnerable birth parents will surrender their children for profit. Whatever steps can be taken to establish that an adoption is legitimate will help a case. In countries where there is great suspicion of adoption, the consulate will take great measures to investigate cases. The U.S. consulate in Guatemala *routinely* requires DNA testing in all cases to verify that the person signing the consent for adoption is in fact the biological parent. However, in countries like the Dominican Republic, where local sentiment is positive about adoption, the U.S. consul is more relaxed in granting orphan visas. [This is not to say they are lax; they simply do not view *every* case as suspect.]

In determining the foreign law, be ready to do a lot of networking. Also understand that what was the law yesterday may no longer be the law today. It is recommended that the attorney making the request put forth the facts of the case instead of asking broad questions. Local congressional offices can be very helpful in tracking down this type of information. Often, a congressional office will take a constituent's case to the Library of Congress, thus expediting the process and reducing costs. The opinion from the Library of Congress should then be sent to the American consulate where the child is located. Other resources to tap into when evaluating foreign adoption laws are law school professors in the foreign country.

Can a Relative Be Adopted as an Orphan?

Another common problem in the adoption and orphan context is whether a relative can be adopted. There is no general bar in the INA regarding the adoption of a relative; the only bar is when a natural parent gives up rights to a child for that child to be adopted: A child who obtains lawful permanent resident status through adoption generally may not petition for his or her natural parents. The only exception is when the adoption decree of the child has been lawfully terminated and the natural parent's relationship has been re-established. USCIS will inquire into the bona fides of an adoption, particularly where adoptive parents are relatives of natural parents.[17] Where the adoptive child continues to reside with natural and adoptive parents, the burden is on the adoptive parents to establish that they exercise primary parental control.[18] This primary parental control can be satisfied by showing that the adoptive parents are listed as the parents on the child's school records, medical records, or dental records.

Practice Pointer: It can be very helpful when a home study is required to work with the adoption agency so that the home study meets the requirements of the INA and 8 CFR §204.3.[19] Some district offices and suboffices maintain lists of approved home study agencies, but most do not. These agencies are usually quite proficient in preparing reports. Further, adoption agencies often will process an orphan adoption to completion: they will both procure the adoption pursuant to INA requirements and process the immigration work. Attorneys tend to be called when there is an identified, nonagency adoption, or the orphan petition becomes unusually complicated.

HAGUE ADOPTION CONVENTION
§101(b)(1)(G)(i)

Many countries, concerned about their citizens adopting children from beyond their homelands, have identified problems with intercountry adoptions. These concerns climaxed with the troubles of the Romanian adoptions of the early 1990s.[20] Some would argue that those tribulations were a catalyst for the Hague Adoption Convention. The Hague[21] addressed these concerns and, in 1993, a multilateral treaty was drafted—the

Convention on Protection of Children and Co-operation in Respect of InterCountry Adoption. The legislation is genuinely intended to promote the welfare of children who cannot be raised in their country of origin while protecting the interests and personal situations of both birth and prospective adoptive parents.[22]

Legislative History

In 1994, the United States became a signatory to the Hague Adoption Convention. Since then, five bills[23] have been submitted to Congress in attempts to ratify it. One bill, the InterCountry Adoption Act of 2000, was passed in 2000. After the ratification, the State Department, together with many adoption interest groups, began the tedious process of hammering out detailed regulations. However, the more than 300 agencies that compose the Joint Council on InterCountry Services and the tragedy of 9/11 have caused serious delays. Originally, a consulting group was hired to sift through all the opinions and comments. Proposed regulations were issued in September 2003, but the comment period was extended. In the summer of 2005, the regulations were sent from the State Department to OMB. On February 15, 2006, final regulations were issued in 22 CFR §96.

What we know: the State Department will allow 18 months so that all agencies wishing to be accredited or approved can do so. Therefore, we can anticipate the United States will not be *en force* with the treaty until July 2007.

Application of the Hague Adoption Convention

Ratification of the Hague Adoption Convention will affect certain adoptions but not all. Compare the following situations: A couple from the United States adopts a child from Romania: the United States is not *en force* with the Convention but Romania is. Result: adoption falls outside the Convention. Another example: A French couple adopts a

---

[17] *Matter or Marques*, 20 I&N Dec. 160 (BIA 1990).

[18] *Matter of Cuello*, 20 I&N Dec. 94 (BIA 1989); 8 CFR §204.2(d)(2)(vii)(B).

[19] The home study requirements of 8 CFR §204.3 should be reviewed carefully to ensure compliance with regulations.

[20] Due to the lack of procedures and laws in Romania, the country temporarily shut down intercountry adoptions in the early 1990s. Once they formulated the laws, the chaos ended and adoptions resumed.

[21] The Hague is the capital city of the Netherlands. Often the Hague Tribunal is simply referred to as The Hague. The Tribunal was founded in 1899 as the Permanent Court of International Arbitration. In 1922, it became the Permanent Court of International Justice and since 1945, it selects the nominees for election to the United Nations International Court of Justice.

---

[22] Memorandum by Professor Joan Heifetz Hollinger in *The Post*, Issue 27, April 2000. *See also* Department of State: *http://travel.state.gov/adoption_info_sheet.htm*, or *www.jcics.org /Hague.html*.

[23] In 1998, the Clinton Administration sponsored a bill: it died when no one introduced it in Congress. In the first session of the 106th Congress (1999), Senator Helms sponsored S. 682 and Congressman Burr sponsored a mirror bill in the house, H.R. 2342; additionally, a bipartisan group of Representatives introduced H.R. 2909 (sponsored by Rep. Gilman). In the second session, an amendment in the nature of a substitute was offered to H.R. 2909: this bill will be referred to as the InterCountry Adoption Act of 2000.

child from Brazil; both countries have ratified the treaty. Therefore, the procedures of the Convention must be followed.

Once the United States is *en force* with the Convention, adoptions from China will not be affected because China is not *en force* with the Convention. At one time, most adopted children coming to the United States came from countries that had not ratified the Convention. However, as time has passed, more and more countries have accepted it.[24]

Central Authority

The treaty establishes a Central Authority, which is a federal-level clearinghouse. The Central Authority is to intercountry adoptions what ICPC (the Interstate Compact on the Placement of Children) is to interstate domestic adoptions. The InterCountry Adoption Act of 2000/S. 682 assigns the Central Authority to the Department of State, whose Office of Children's Issues will function as the Central Authority. This expands the role and power of the State Department, but not as significantly as one might imagine.

Currently, the State Department, together with USCIS, approves intercountry adoptions on a federal level. This is done routinely as I-600s are approved and embassies review final adoption decrees before visas are issued. The InterCountry Adoption Act expands the authority of the State Department by scrutinizing the stability and procedures of agencies and attorneys facilitating intercountry adoptions. Currently, while states regulate adoption agencies and attorneys, state regulations focus on domestic and intrastate adoptions. Now, for the first time, agencies and attorneys handling intercountry adoption will be monitored and regulated if they place children from the United States to foreign countries or arrange for U.S. families to adopt children from countries that are *en force* with the Convention.

Approval/Accreditation

In its function as the Central Authority, the State Department will *approve* attorneys, facilitators, and child-placing agencies incorporated for profit. Although minimum standards are set out in the Inter-Country Adoption Act, exact requirements will be set out in regulations. Not-for-profit licensed child-placing agencies will be *accredited* after meeting minimum standards.

Numerous organizations and government entities are making recommendations for the *standards for approval* and *standards for accreditation*. The issues will be addressed, negotiated, and drafted into regulations. The requirements for approval and accreditation will be based on the actual Hague Adoption Convention. Therefore, the requirements will cover business procedures, fiscal strength and management, maintenance of records, and standing with a state's licensure authorities.

Ultimately, all attorneys and agencies that provide intercountry adoption services or facilitate an intercountry adoption will need either approval or accreditation from the Central Authority. Attorneys who merely provide legal advice are exempt from approval. Read the regulations carefully to determine where you might cross the line from advising to facilitating an adoption. The Central Authority will ensure that all agencies, *not-for-profit* and *for-profit*, as well as attorneys, follow the standards established by the Hague Adoption Convention.

The Central Authority will be responsible for, but will not necessarily administer, the following services. First, it will approve or accredit the party that is providing services to the adoptive parents and the child. Second, it will issue to the prospective adoptive parents a certificate after all other requirements of the law have been met.[25] This will occur after a child-placing agency licensed by an individual state grants a home study that gives a favorable recommendation to prospective adoptive parents. In this step, individual state requirements will be carefully followed. Third, the Central Authority will verify that a child is *free for adoption*.[8] This will cover such issues as termination of parental rights, compliance with state and federal laws, validity of the adoption decree or guardianship order, and compliance with the laws of the child's home country.

Initially, there was concern that the federal government was overreaching and interfering with the states' ability to govern adoptions, but this framework actually reinforces state adoption codes. Compare the

---

[24] For an up-to-date list of countries that have signed the Hague Convention, see the following website, *http://hcch.e-vision.nl/index_en.php?act=conventions.status&cid=69*.

[25] InterCountry Adoption Act of 2000, §301(1).

[26] *Free for adoption* is a legal term signifying that there is no legal impediment to finalizing a child's adoption. For example, due diligence has been used to locate and identify the birth father, the putative father registry has been checked, and parental rights were not surrendered under duress.

Central Authority function of the Hague Adoption Convention to the function of the Interstate Compact on the Placement of Children. Both systems ensure the following: (1) state adoption laws are strictly followed; (2) adoptive parents have a valid home study that favorably recommends them as adoptive parents; and (3) they must be accountable for the child's financial and medical needs. The Central Authority will monitor and hold agencies and attorneys accountable for children adopted internationally. Furthermore, the Central Authority will oversee and account for adopted children *emigrating* from and *immigrating* to the United States.

Accrediting Entities

The State Department has so far designated the following entities to accredit not-for-profit agencies: The Council on Accreditation and the State Offices of Licensure for Connecticut, Colorado, New Mexico, Utah, and Vermont.

Children Emigrating from the United States

Perhaps surprisingly, each year children leave the United States to be adopted. Infertility and the desire to adopt are worldwide. At present, there is no mechanism to account for the number of children who annually leave the United States or to assess how these children fare after adoption. Once the United States ratifies and implements the Hague Adoption Convention, a method to monitor emigrating adopted children will be in place.

For emigrating children, the accredited agency or approved person providing the adoption service will verify that the adoptive parents are certified by the their home country, that the adoption complies with state and federal laws, and that medical and family histories of these children are properly maintained.[27]

Although no statistics exist, a "guesstimate" is that fewer than 1,000 children emigrate from the United States each year. The Hague Adoption Convention will provide statistics, accountability, and safeguards for them.

Finally, the new §101(b)(1)(G) will read as follows:

(G) a child, under the age of sixteen at the time a petition is filed on the child's behalf to accord a classification as an immediate relative under Section 201(b), who has been adopted in a foreign state that is a party to the Convention on Protec-

tion of Children and Co-operation in Respect of Intercountry Adoption done at The Hague on May 29, 1993, or who is emigrating from such a foreign state to be adopted in the United States, by a United States citizen and spouse jointly, or by an unmarried United States citizen at least 25 years of age –

(i) if -

(I) the Attorney General is satisfied that proper care will be furnished the child if admitted to the United States;

(II) the child's natural parents (or parent in the case of a child who has one sole or surviving parent because of the death or disappearance of, abandonment or desertion by, the other parent), or other persons or institutions that retain legal custody of the child, have freely given their written irrevocable consent to the termination of their legal relationship with the child, and to the child's emigration and adoption;

(III) In the case of a child having two living natural parents, the natural parents are incapable of providing proper care for the child;

(IV) The Attorney General is satisfied that the purpose of the adoption is to form a bona fide parent-child relationship, and the parent-child relationship of the child and the natural parents has been terminated (and in carrying out both obligations under this subclause the Attorney General may consider whether there is a petition pending to confer immigration status on one or both of such natural parents); and

(V) In the case of a child who has not been adopted –

(aa) the competent authority of the foreign state has approved the child's emigration to the United States for the purpose of adoption by the prospective adoptive parents or parent; and

(bb) the prospective adoptive parent or parents has or have complied with any preadoption requirements of the child's proposed residence; and

(ii) Except that no natural parent or prior adoptive parent of any such child shall thereafter, by virtue of such parentage, be accorded any right, privilege or status under this act.

---

[27] InterCountry Adoption Act of 2000/S. 682, §303.

PROBLEM COUNTRIES

The following countries have either completely barred intercountry adoptions or placed severe restrictions on them:

Azerbaijan: Adoptions resumed in August 2004 after an April 2004 suspension to investigate adoption practices. As of February 2006, only three American families have completed adoptions. Many families face continual bureaucratic delays.

Belarus: Virtually all intercountry adoptions have ceased since October 4, 2004, when Belarusian President Aliaksandr Lukashenko asked his cabinet to look into international adoptions. The government of Belarus has not suspended or made any provision for completing adoptions that were in the pipeline before October 2004.

Cambodia: Cambodian adoptions have been suspended since December 21, 2001. A joint USCIS-DOS task force has been examining how the Cambodian government can provide assurances that baby-selling and other fraud has been eliminated, but there is likely to be no report for the foreseeable future. Prospective parents are strongly urged to consider having their cases redirected for adoption in another country, such as Thailand.

Romania: On December 22, 2005, Romania's prime minister rejected appeals by the United States and European governments to allow foreigners to adopt about 1,000 Romanian children. About 200 U.S. families and 800 European families had filed paperwork before 2004, when Romania passed laws that effectively banned all foreign adoptions, except for close relatives of the child. Romania banned foreign adoption in 2004 under pressure from European lawmakers who accused Romanian authorities of corruption in the adoption system.

Ukraine: President Yushchenko on January 31, 2006, signed the law giving interim authority over adoptions to the Ministry of Education's National Adoption Center (NAC) until a new adoption authority is established under the Ministry of Family, Youth, and Sports. This law goes into effect upon its publication in Parliament's official newspaper, *Holos Ukrainy*, which should already have occurred. The NAC has full authority to process adoptions in Ukraine until May 1, 2006, the date by which the new adoption central authority must be established. The NAC has stated that it is resuming normal processing not only of suspended cases but also of cases that had been previously scheduled through the end of January. The NAC has not yet released a notice to

the international adoption community explaining details about processing of adoptions during the transition period.

United Kingdom: As of December 31, 2005, any child who has been abandoned to an orphanage cannot be adopted by foreigners. The Local Authority for the district or shire (equivalent to the government adoption agency) with jurisdiction over the orphanage will retain an interest in the orphan, even after an adoption is finalized, until the time the orphan becomes a lawful permanent resident. This also holds true if the orphan is placed in foster care. Therefore, an English orphan is not free to be adopted if it is either in an orphanage or foster care.

Vietnam: On June 21, 2005, the United States and Vietnam signed agreements that laid the groundwork for recommencement of intercountry adoptions between the two countries after a two and one–half-year hiatus. The agreement entered into force on September 1, 2005, and on January 25, 2006, the Embassy in Hanoi issued the first orphan immigrant visa under the new agreement to a Vietnamese child adopted by an American family. Vietnam now requires all U.S. embassy adoption service providers (ASPs) desiring to operate in Vietnam to be licensed by the Vietnamese Ministry of Justice's Department of International Adoptions (DIA). The DIA has indicated that, with extremely rare exceptions, it will accept adoption applications ("dossiers") ONLY through licensed ASPs. Prospective parents considering adopting from Vietnam should consult the adoption page of the website for the U.S. embassy in Hanoi (*http://vietnam.Usembassy. gov/orphan_visa.html*) where the embassy posts the names of American ASPs that have been licensed.

CONCLUSION

If the requirements for an adoption under either INA §101(b)(1)(E)(i) or §101(b)(1)(F)(i) cannot be fulfilled, you may look to INA §101(a)(27)(J) to obtain a special immigrant juvenile (SIJ) visa for a child who is in the United States. This type of work is complicated and beyond the scope of this article. The SIJ category applies to children under 21, and essentially requires that the child be dependent on a juvenile court in the United States and eligible for long-term foster care, and that there be a determination by the juvenile court that it would not be in the child's best interest to be returned to the country of his or her nationality. There are other requirements for this visa, so INA §101(a)(27)(J) and 8 CFR §204.11 should be examined closely, as well as USCIS memoranda on the subject.

INTERCOUNTRY ADOPTIONS FROM INDIA

by Anil Malhotra and Ranjit Malhotra[*]

INTRODUCTION

This article briefly discusses the intercountry adoption procedure for children from India. At the outset, it is important to emphasize that at present, there exists no general law on adoption of children governing non-Hindus and foreigners. Adoption is permitted by statute among Hindus, and by custom among some other communities. While an adoption deed can be given to certain governmental agencies, there is a three-month period for revocation. In addition, when an adoption deed is given to a relative, extensive evidence of compliance with the Hindu Maintenance and Adoption Act of 1956 should be gathered, including photos of the ceremony, affidavits of witnesses, and show a change in custody.

---

[*] **Anil Malhotra** has been a practising Advocate at the Punjab and Haryana High Court, Chandigarh, India since September 1983. Mr. Malhotra regularly appears as Counsel in the Supreme Court of India at New Delhi and before other courts, commissions, boards, and tribunals within India. He holds bachelor of science and bachelor of laws (Professional) degrees from the Punjab University, Chandigarh, and was enrolled as an Advocate in India in 1983. He attained his LL.M degree from the University of London in November 1985. For over 20 years, Mr. Malhotra has had extensive exposure in handling civil, matrimonial, criminal, and overseas litigation on behalf of nonresident Indians residing abroad. He also has represented a large number of overseas clients in Indian courts and has been regularly opining on matters of Indian law in cases arising in related matters in foreign jurisdictions. Mr. Malhotra may be reached at *malhotrasunilindia@yahoo.co.in*.

Ranjit Malhotra the first Indian lawyer to be awarded the prestigious Felix Scholarship to read for the LL.M. degree at the School of Oriental and African Studies, University of London and obtained his degree with merit in 1993, specialising in immigration laws and South Asian family laws. An India-based lawyer handling substantial international work, Mr. Malhotra is a member of number of associations, including the International Bar Association (also serving as regional representative for India of the IBA migration and nationality law committee), the Immigration Law Practitioners Association, and the American Immigration Lawyers Association. He is one of the principal authors in the recently published book titled *Acting for Non-resident Indian Clients*. The same has been published by Jordan Publishing Limited, UK. His firm, Malhotra & Malhotra Associates, is on the panel of lawyers for five major embassies in New Delhi. Mr. Malhotra may be reached at *malhotraranjitindia@rediffmail.com*.

At present, non-Hindus and foreigners can only be guardians of children under the Guardian and Wards Act 1890. In actual practice, foreign nationals wishing to adopt children from India first obtain guardianship orders from the District Court or the High Court, as the case may be, within whose territorial jurisdiction the child is residing. This is with a view to adopt formally under the legal system of the country of their habitual residence.

HISTORY

The Indian Ministry of Welfare, pursuant to certain guidelines issued by the Supreme Court of India in a public interest litigation petition, *Laxmi Kant Pandey v Union of India* (AIR 1984 SC 469), framed guidelines governing intercountry adoptions. This case was monitored by the Supreme Court from time to time until 1991, when the court scrupulously reviewed the existing procedure and practices followed in intercountry adoptions. The main objective was to prevent trafficking of children and protect the welfare of adopted children.[1]

Justice Bhagwati (in AIR 1987 SC 232 at p. 240, para 12) incorporated a vital note of clarification, as follows:

> We would, therefore, direct that in case of a foreigner who has been living in India for one year or more, the home-study report and other connected documents may be allowed to be prepared by the recognized placement agency which is processing the application of such foreigner for guardianship of a child with a view to its eventual adoption and that in such a case the Court should not insist on sponsoring of such foreigner by a social or child welfare agency based in the country to which such foreigner belongs nor should a home-study report in respect of such

---

[1] *See also Laxmi Kant Pandey v. Union of India* (AIR 1986 SC 272) (bond for guardian should ordinarily be waived); *Laxmi Kant Pandey v. Union of India* (AIR 1987 SC 232) (guardian judge need not insist on security or a cash deposit or bank guarantee; bond from a recognized Indian placement agency should be sufficient; agency may in turn take a corresponding bond from the sponsoring social or child welfare agency in the foreign country).

foreigner be required to be obtained from any such foreign social or child welfare agency, the home study report and other connected documents prepared by the recognized placement agency should be regarded as sufficient.

After the implementation of the initial guidelines in 1989, it was felt necessary to revise them. Accordingly, a taskforce comprising a cross-section of representatives of adoption agencies under the chairmanship of former Chief Justice of India, Mr. Justice PN Bhagwati, was constituted on 12 August 1992. The taskforce submitted its report on 28 August 1993, and the Indian Government accepted its recommendations. Accordingly, the Government of India circulated revised guidelines in 1994 (hereinafter the Guidelines) to regulate matters relating to the adoption of Indian children. These guidelines were published by the Government in the Gazette of India on 20 June 1995, and are discussed below.

It may, however, be pertinent to point out that the high court in *Anokha v. State of Rajasthan* ((2004) 1 Hindu Law Reporter 351) has held that the above guidelines would not be applicable where the child is living with his or her biological parent(s) who have agreed that he or she is to be given in adoption to a known couple who may be of foreign origin. The court in such cases has to deal with the application under section 7 of the Guardian and Wards Act 1890 and dispose of the same after being satisfied that the child is being given in adoption voluntarily with the parents being aware of the implications of adoption, *i.e.*, that the child would legally belong to the adoptive parents' family; that the adoption is not induced by any extraneous reasons, such as the receipt of money; that the adoptive parents have produced evidence in support of their suitability; and finally that the arrangement would be in the best interest of the child.

Much more recently, the Supreme Court of India has again reiterated the guidelines in case of adoption of children by foreign parents, as originally laid down in the case of *Lakshmi Kant Pandey vs. Union of India*, AIR 1984 SC 469. While emphatically following these guidelines in *St. Theresa's Tender Loving Care Home and others vs. States of Andhra Pradesh* 2006(1) Hindu Law Reporter 122, the apex Court pointed in para 10 at page 128 of the judgment:

> While making the requisite and prescribed exercise it has to be kept in mind that the child is a precious gift and merely because he or she for various reasons is abandoned by the parents that cannot be a reason for further neglect by the society. . . .

PROCEDURE TO BE FOLLOWED IN INTERCOUNTRY ADOPTION

In the first place, para 2.14 of the Guidelines stipulates that every application from a foreigner wishing to adopt a child must be sponsored by a social or child welfare agency recognized or licensed by the government of the country in which the foreigner is resident. Furthermore, the agency should be recognized by the Central Adoption Resource Agency (CARA) set up under the aegis of the Indian Ministry of Welfare. CARA is the principal monitoring agency of the Indian Government handling all affairs connected with national and intercountry adoptions.

No application by a foreigner to adopt a child should be entertained directly by any social or child welfare agency in India working in the areas of intercountry adoption or by any institution or centre to which the children are committed by the Juvenile Court. The reasons behind this directive have been summed up by MN Das in his book *Guardians and Wards Act* (Eastern Law House, 14th ed, 1995) at pp 80–81:

> Firstly, it will help to reduce, if not eliminate altogether, the possibility of profiteering and trafficking in children, because if a foreigner were allowed to contact directly agencies or individuals in India for the purpose of obtaining a child in adoption, he might, in his anxiety to secure a child for adoption, be induced or persuaded to pay any unconscionable or unreasonable amount which might be demanded by the agency or individual procuring the child. Secondly, it would be almost impossible for the court to satisfy itself that the foreigner who wishes to take the child in adoption would be suitable as a parent for the child and whether he would be able to provide a stable and secured family life to the child and would be able to handle trans-racial, transcultural and trans-national problems likely to arise from such adoption, because, where the application for adopting a child has not been sponsored by a social or child welfare agency in the country of the foreigner, there would be no proper and satisfactory home study report on which the court can rely. Thirdly, in such a case, where the application of a foreigner for taking a child in adoption is made directly without the intervention of social or child welfare agency, there would be no authority or agency in the country of the foreigner who could be made responsible for supervising the progress of the child and ensuring that the child is adopted at the earliest in accordance with

law and grows up in an atmosphere of warmth and affection with moral and material security assured to it.

Paragraph 2.15 of the Guidelines provides that where there is no recognized foreign agency in a particular country, then the concerned government department or ministry of that country may forward the applications and related documents of the prospective adoptive parents to CARA. CARA will, in turn, examine and send those papers to the recognized Indian placement agencies indicated in the application. A list of Statewide placement agencies entitled to process adoption applications of Indian and foreign parents, including nonresident Indians, has been circulated by the office of CARA, New Delhi.

It is also mandatory for the enlisted foreign agency to send a copy of the application, as well as the prescribed documents including the home study report, to CARA. These documents have to be duly notarized by a notary public whose signature is additionally duly attested either by an officer of the Ministry of External Affairs or the Ministry of Justice or the Ministry of Social Welfare of the foreigner's country of habitual residence or by an officer of the Indian Embassy or High Commission or consulate in that foreign country.

HOME STUDY REPORT

Paragraph 2.14 of the Guidelines categorically and emphatically enumerates the required contents of the home study report, which should include the following information:

- social status and family background;
- description of the home;
- standard of living as it appears in the home;
- current relationship between the husband and wife;
- current relationship between the parents and children (if there are any children);
- development of any already adopted children;
- current relationship between the couple and the members of each other's family;
- employment status of the couple;
- health details, such as clinical tests, hearing condition, past illness (medical certificate);
- economic status of the couple;
- accommodation for the child;
- schooling facilities;
- amenities in the home;
- reasons for wanting to adopt an Indian child;
- attitude of grandparents and relatives toward the adoption;
- anticipated plans for the adoptive child;
- legal status of the prospective adoptive parents.

Mere receipt of the application as well as other original documents will not entitle the Indian placement agency to proceed with the case; it can proceed only after obtaining a "no objection certificate" from CARA.

Paragraph 2.14 further states that CARA should endeavor, as far as possible, to ensure that this no objection certificate be issued within a reasonable period of time, *e.g.*, five weeks from the date of receipt of the certified copies of the application and other relevant documents.

Once it has received the original application and the original documents from the enlisted foreign agency, the Indian placement agency will then register the name of the prospective foreign parents in the appropriate register.

The placement agency will then proceed to examine carefully the home study report of the prospective foreign adoptive parents and start the exercise of matching the home study report with the child study report. When it arrives at the conclusion that a child can be placed with that particular family, it will have to ensure that the child concerned is cleared by the Voluntary Coordinating Agency (VCA) for intercountry adoption. It is pertinent to mention that there exist separate VCAs in every state in India.

Thereafter, the Indian placement agency will send the child study report, the photograph of the child, and the medical report to the sponsoring foreign agency for approval by the prospective adoptive parents. After obtaining the approval of the child by the prospective adoptive parents, the Indian placement agency will apply to CARA for clearance of the child.

It is at this stage that CARA will have to ensure that the placement agency has put in adequate efforts for finding an Indian family for the said child. CARA, after going through the information furnished by the placement agency and the VCA, will immediately give clearance to the agency. The VCA clearance is mandatory.

The Supreme Court of India, in Karnataka State Council for *Child Welfare v. Society of Sisters of*

Charity St. Gerosa Convent (AIR 1994 SC 658), held that the rationale behind finding Indian parents or parents of Indian origin is to ensure the children should grow up in Indian surroundings so that they retain their culture and heritage. This is definitely an issue that has a bearing on the question of the welfare of the children. The best interest of the children is the main and prime consideration.

GUARDIANSHIP ORDER

The recognized Indian placement agency thereafter will process the case with the local court in the jurisdiction, to seek the grant of guardianship of the child to the prospective foreign adoptive parents.

Once again, the Indian scrutinizing agency must, at this stage, inspect all the documents and advise the competent court that the intercountry adoption is in the best interests of the child. The court will grant the guardianship of the child to the foreign parents within the stipulated time as laid down by the Supreme Court of India.

On the basis of the court guardianship order, the placement agency must apply to the regional passport office for an Indian passport for the child. Thereafter, the entry clearance/visa has to be obtained from the Embassy/High Commission of the country where the child is to live. After this rigorous procedure has been carried out, the child leaves India together with the prospective adoptive parents or with an escort, as the case may be, for the country of the prospective adoptive parents.

The Gujarat High Court in a progressive judgment in *Jayantilal v. Asha* (AIR 1989 Gujarat 152) upheld the validity of guardianship orders in favor of two Norwegian couples appointed as guardians of Hindu children. The court held (at p. 156, para 12):

> if the biological parents have died rendering the child an orphan then the society owes a duty to the child that at least a semblance of comfort and care which the biological parents could have provided will be provided to the child, if some people from howsoever distant a corner of this planet, come forth to do so. In such a case a petty contention like the change of religion or culture of the child can hardly stand in the way of the court in sanctioning inter-country adoption. Unfounded and imaginary apprehensions also are of little consequence and once the court is assured that there is no possibility of the child being abused which assurance can flow from the independent agencies which are ordained for the pur-

pose then nothing can and need prevent the court from sanctioning an inter-country adoption.

Thus, the procedure described above and the supervisory role of the court serves as a double-check on intercountry adoptions. Not only does this dual process ensure a check against suspected child abuse, but at the same time, it also removes hypertechnical objections to facilitate the conclusion of the adoption process and enable the adopted child to leave the country with his or her adoptive parents without further bureaucratic delays.

The Allahabad High Court in *Jagdish Chander Gupta v. Dr Ku Vimla Gupta* ((2004) 1 Hindu Law Reporter 282) held that, under section 9 of the Guardian and Wards Act 1890, the application for guardianship of a minor shall be made to the district court having jurisdiction in the place where the minor ordinarily resides. The supervisory role of the court in placing the welfare of the minor as the primary consideration is best reflected in the following words of the court (at p. 285, para 16):

> It should not be lost sight of and must be emphasized that in custody cases, a child has not to be treated as a chattel in which its parents have a proprietary interest. It is a human being to whom the parents owe serious obligations. One's own self interest sometimes clouds his perception of what is the best for those for whom he or she is responsible. It takes a very high degree of selflessness and maturity—which is for most of the people probably unattainable degree for a parent/proposed guardian to acknowledge that it might be better for the child to be brought up by someone else.

REQUIREMENT BEFORE THE COURT

Paragraph 2.18 of the Guidelines provides that, where an application is made to the court by prospective adoptive parents, or by an Indian placement agency on behalf of such parents, for the appointment of such parents as guardians of the child with a view to taking the child in adoption, the certificate of no objection from CARA shall be produced along with the application. If no response has been made by CARA to the application for taking the child in adoption within the time-limit specified in the Guidelines, the application shall be accompanied by an affidavit made by the placement agency stating that the requirements of the Guidelines have been fulfilled in regard to obtaining the certificate of no objection from CARA.

Handicapped Children and Children Requiring Medical Attention

Paragraph 2.14 of the Guidelines especially relates to handicapped children and children requiring urgent medical attention. It is stated that "the requirement of obtaining a 'no objection certificate' from CARA will also apply in case of handicapped children and children needing urgent medical attention which the social or child welfare agency looking after the child cannot provide within the country, siblings and also children above the age of six years."

The recognized placement agency, soon after the admission of such a child, without waiting for foreign prospective adoptive parents to be located, shall submit an application, together with information about the child, to CARA for issue of a no objection certificate. CARA will ordinarily issue a no objection certificate, such as in the case of handicapped/special needs children, within a period of one week from the date of receipt of information about the child from the placement agency. Simultaneously, the placement agency would be allowed to send the referral of such a child to the foreign agency of its choice and, after the approval of the child by any foreign parents, the placement agency concerned could follow the procedure laid down in the judgment of the Supreme Court of India.

At this stage, the scrutinizing agency should carefully examine all the documents furnished by the foreign agency in this regard and advise the competent court in coming to the conclusion as to whether it would be in the interest of the child to be given in adoption to foreign parents. The recognized Indian placement agency should obtain a certificate in this regard from the relevant chief medical officer of the government hospital prior to processing the case. Details of such children, together with a copy of any certificate(s) issued by the chief medical officer, where required, should be sent at the end of each month to CARA by the placement agency.

Documents Required from Foreign Adoptive Parents and Overseas Social or Child Welfare Agency for Intercountry Adoption

Adoption Application

Experience of dealing with the Ministry of Welfare suggests that the documentation should be compiled meticulously in order to avoid bureaucratic delays. The following documents must be submitted by the foreign adoptive parents. It will be noted that the Indian requirements are quite similar to those prescribed in various appendices of RON 117 issued by the British Home Office:

- home study report under para 2.14 of the new Guidelines;

- recent photographs of the adoptive family;

- marriage certificate of the foreign adoptive parents;

- declaration concerning the health of the foreign adoptive parents;

- certificate of medical fitness of the foreign adoptive parents duly certified by a medical doctor;

- declaration regarding financial status, together with supporting documents including employer's certificate, wherever applicable;

- employment certificate of the foreign adoptive parents, if applicable;

- income tax assessment order(s) of the foreign adoptive parents;

- bank references for the foreign adoptive parents;

- particulars of properties owned by the prospective adoptive parents;

- joint declaration tendered by the foreign adoptive parents stating willingness to be appointed guardians of the child;

- undertaking from the social or child welfare enlisted agency sponsoring the foreigner to the effect that the child would be legally adopted by the foreign adoptive parents according to the law of the country within a period not exceeding two years from the time of arrival of the child;

- undertaking from the foreign adoptive parents to the effect that the child would be provided with the necessary education and upbringing according to status of the adoptive parents;

- undertaking from the recognized foreign social or child welfare agency that the report relating to the progress of the child along with his or her recent photograph would be sent quarterly during first two years and half-yearly for the next three years in the prescribed pro forma through the relevant Indian diplomatic post;

- power of attorney conferred by the intending parents in favor of the social or the child welfare agency in India that will be required to process the case. Such power of attorney should also authorize the lawyer in India to handle the case on behalf of the foreign adoptee parents, if they are not in a position to come to India;

- certificate from the recognized foreign social or child welfare agency sponsoring the application to the effect that the adoptive parents are permitted to adopt a child according to the laws of their country;

- undertaking from the recognized foreign social or child welfare agency to the effect that, in case of disruption of the adoptive family before the legal adoption has been effected, it will take care of child and find a suitable alternative placement for the child with prior approval of CARA;

- undertaking from the recognized foreign social or child welfare agency that it will reimburse all expenses to the concerned Indian social or child welfare agency as fixed by the competent court toward maintenance of the child and the processing charge fees.

It is important to reiterate that all the above certificates, declarations, and documents in support of the application should be duly notarized by a notary public whose signature should be duly attested either by an officer of the Ministry of External Affairs, the Ministry of Justice, or the Ministry of Social Welfare of the country of the foreign adoptive parents or by an officer of the Indian Embassy or the High Commission or Consulate in that country.

DOMESTIC LAW

Having elaborated the law and procedure relating to intercountry adoptions, brief reference is now made to the domestic law governing adoptions by Hindus.

The principal law relating to adoption in India by Hindus only is contained in the Hindu Adoptions and Maintenance Act 1956 (HAMA 1956).

Requisites of a Valid Adoption

Section 6 stipulates four conditions for a valid adoption, namely:

- the person adopting has the capacity, and also the right, to take in adoption;

- the person giving the child in adoption has the capacity to do so;

- the person adopted is capable of being taken in adoption; and

- the adoption is made in compliance with the other conditions mentioned in chapter 2 of HAMA 1956.

Section 6(iv) requires that the adoption should be made in compliance with other conditions men-

tioned in chapter 2 of HAMA 1956. In other words, for the adoption to be valid, the provisions of Sections 7 to 11 must be satisfied. Section 7 deals with the capacity of a male Hindu to take in adoption; and section 8 with the capacity of a female Hindu to take in adoption. Section 9 qualifies persons capable of giving children in adoption; section 10 categorizes those persons who may be adopted; and section 11 enumerates other conditions for a valid adoption. Thereafter, section 12 elaborates the effects of a valid adoption.

Other Conditions for a Valid Adoption

Section 11 of HAMA 1956 stipulates other vital conditions for a valid adoption, and is reproduced below.

11. Other conditions for a valid adoption

In every adoption, the following conditions must be complied with:—

(i) if the adoption is of a son, the adoptive father or mother by whom the adoption is made must not have a Hindu son, son's son or son's son's son (whether by legitimate blood relationship or by adoption) living at the time of adoption;

(ii) if the adoption is of a daughter, the adoptive father or mother by whom the adoption is made must not have a Hindu daughter or son's daughter (whether by legitimate blood relationship or by adoption) living at the time of adoption;

(iii) if the adoption is by a male and the person to be adopted is a female, the adoptive father is at least twenty-one years older than the person to be adopted;

(iv) if the adoption is by a female and the person to be adopted is a male, the adoptive mother is at least twenty-one years older than the person to be adopted;

(v) the same child may not be adopted simultaneously by two or more persons;

(vi) the child to be adopted must be actually given and taken in adoption by the parents or guardian concerned or under their authority with intent to transfer the child from the family of its birth [or in the case of an abandoned child or child whose parentage is not known, from the place or family where it has been brought up] to the family of its adoption:

Provided that the performance of datta homam shall not be essential to the validity of adoption.

Effects of a Valid Adoption

Section 12 specifically deals with the legal effects of an adoption made in accordance with the provisions of HAMA 1956. It can be pointed out that section 12 of HAMA 1956 satisfies the requirements of cl (ix) of para 310 of HC 395 of the current British Immigration Rules governing adoption. This clause in very harsh terms states that the adopted child "has lost or broken his ties with his family of origin."

As to the legal effects of a valid adoption, it is important to cite certain decisions of the Supreme Court of India. It was held by the Supreme Court of India in *Smt Sitabai v. Ramchandra* (AIR 1970 SC 343) (at p. 348, para 6):

> The true effect and interpretation of ss 11 and 12 of Act No 78 of 1956 therefore is that when either of the spouses adopts a child, all the ties of the child in the family of his or her birth become completely severed and these are all replaced by those created by the adoption in the adoptive family.

Similarly, it was held by the Supreme Court in *Kartar Singh v. Surjan Singh* (AIR 1974 SC 2161) (at p. 2163, para 7):

> The words in section 11(vi) "with intent to transfer the child from the family of its birth to the family of its adoption" are merely indicative of the result of the actual giving and taking by the parents or guardians concerned referred to in the earlier part of the clause. Where an adoption ceremony is gone through and the giving and taking takes place, there cannot be any other intention.

More recently, the Supreme Court of India in *Chandan Bilasini v. Aftabuddin Khan* ((1996) 1 Hindu Law Reporter 79, SC) held (at p. 81, para 6):

> Section 12 of the Hindu Adoptions and Maintenance Act clearly provides that an adopted child shall be deemed to be the child of his adoptive father or mother for all purposes with effect from the date of the adoption and from such date all ties of the child in the family of his or her birth shall be deemed to be severed and replaced by those created by the adoption in the adoptive family.

Finally, section 15 of the HAMA 1956 underlines the irrevocability of the validly performed adoption by stating that it cannot be cancelled or renounced. Therefore, under Indian law, once a legitimate adoption is obtained, in accordance with the procedure established by law, the margin for interference is minimal, except in certain exceptional circumstances.

Registered Adoption Can be Challenged

Section 16 of the HAMA 1956 reads as follows:

16. Presumption as to registered documents relating to adoption

Whenever any document registered under any law for the time being in force is produced before any court purporting to record an adoption made and is signed by the person giving and the person taking the child in adoption, the court shall presume that the adoption has been made in compliance with the provisions of this Act unless and until it is disproved.

In an important ruling concerning adoption by Hindus, *Jai Singh v. Shakuntala* (2002 (3) SCC 634), the Supreme Court of India has recently held that, though a document registering an adoption should be treated as final proof of adoption, it could still be challenged in a court of law if evidence to the contrary was put forward.

The apex court, in interpreting the statutory intent of section 16 of the HAMA 1956, said that the presumption about the registered document relating to adoption "cannot be an irrebuttable presumption." Justices Umesh C Banerjee and Brijesh Kumar held (at pp. 636 and 637, para 2):

> 2. The section thus envisages a statutory presumption that in the event of there being a registered document pertaining to adoption there would be a presumption that adoption has been made in accordance with law. Mandate of the statute is rather definite since the legislature has used "shall" instead of any other word of lesser significance. Incidentally, however, the inclusion of the words "unless and until it is disproved" appearing at the end of the statutory provision has made the situation not that rigid but flexible enough to depend upon the evidence available on record in support of adoption. It is a matter of grave significance by reason of the factum of adoption and displacement of the person adopted from the natural succession—thus onus of proof is rather heavy. Statute has allowed some amount of flexibility, lest it turns out to be solely dependent on a registered adoption deed. The reason for inclusion of the words "unless and until it is disproved" shall have to be ascertained in its proper perspective and as

such the presumption cannot but be said to be a rebuttable presumption. Statutory intent thus stands out to be rather expressive depicting therein that the presumption cannot be an irrebuttable presumption by reason of the inclusion of the words just noticed above. . . .

In the above-mentioned ruling, the Supreme Court also concurred with the similar tenor of law laid down by the Punjab and Haryana High Court in *Modan Singh v. Sham Kaur* (AIR 1973 P&H 122).

Clearly, the ruling in *Jai Singh* will be of immense help to immigration officers of foreign missions/consulates/embassies in India in weeding out suspect adoption immigration applications lodged from within the applicant's own family designed to circumvent immigration controls.

PROBLEMS FACED IN INTERCOUNTRY ADOPTION

At present, non-Hindus and foreign nationals can only be guardians of children under the Guardian and Wards Act 1890. They cannot adopt children. The child loses out by being deprived of the benefits of a valid adoption. There have been disturbing press reports about "greedy social activists." Sharma Vinod, in his article *Indian child losing out in adoption mart*,[2] pointed out that at the root of the problem is certain placement agencies' desire for financial gain and their propensity to extort money from childless foreigners. In the same report, it was pointed out that in practice, the paperwork is complex. The system is not working because of long delays at the different levels of scrutiny. Moreover, India has not ratified the Hague Convention on the Protection of Children and Co-operation in Respect of Intercountry Adoption (29 May 1993). As pointed out by the Bhagwati Panel, the political and other rights of the Indian child with foreign adoptive parents can be best assured through bilateral pacts under the Convention.

Additionally, according to in-vitro fertilization experts in New Delhi, the number of infertile couples from foreign countries opting for in-vitro fertilization is increasing. Low-cost and hi-tech treatment in India is helping nonresident Indian couples to realize their dreams of natural parenthood. Nonresident Indian couples are reluctant to opt for adoption for two major reasons. First, religious and social factors are a major issue. Secondly, it has been high-lighted that cumbersome adoption and immigration laws make it very difficult to take the child to the United Kingdom or the United States, after the adoptive child is chosen from the homeland.[3]

In a hard-hitting editorial opinion, titled *Maternity for Hire*,[4] it has been noticed that a new trend is emanating. India, after becoming a hub for medical tourism, is entering another new platform. India is emerging as a sought-after destination for surrogate mothers. Desperate childless NRI couples are rushing to India to rent a womb. Anand, in Gujarat, has seen as many as 14 commercial in vitro fertilization surrogacy cases in the last two years. It is a disturbing trend. A woman's womb is not a piece of real estate to be rented out. Going through such a commercial pregnancy, a woman undergoes considerable physical and psychological trauma.

This article sadly and rightly so laments:

It is particularly sad because there are over 12 million orphaned children in India who need parents. And another 44 million destitute children who are denied the warmth of a family. If only people could transcend the desire to have a baby that is genetically theirs, India would be the logical place where childless couples could seek parental happiness through adoption. Research shows that parental love has less to do with biological ties and more with shared experiences, and that adoptive parents love their children as much as biological parents. But our adoption figures don't go beyond a few thousand per year. Playing spoilsport is a 115-year-old Act—the Guardians and Wards Act—which does not allow Muslims, Christians, Jews and Parsis to become a child's adoptive parents. They can only be a "guardian." Even the more liberal Hindu Adoption and Maintenance Act, 1956, does not allow non-Hindus to adopt a Hindu child. The adoption process is tedious and hemmed in by all sorts of unnecessary restrictions. It is ironical that in a country with so many children without a home, there's a long waiting list of couples wanting to adopt. We urgently need to change the laws, make the process less cumbersome and allow India to become a popular adoption destination.

Surrogacy has indeed arrived in India. In their day-to-day practice, the authors are confronted with

---

[2] *The Hindustan Times*, 9 Sept. 1997.

[3] For details, see S. Jyoti, *How Egg-citing! NRIs Eye Desi Donors*, The Times of India, 29 Aug. 2003.

[4] Published in *The Times of India*, New Delhi/Chandigarh Ed., 24 Feb. 2006.

queries from foreign lawyers as to the legal position relating to surrogacy arrangements. Here, it would be pertinent to briefly elaborate as to the legal position in this regard.

The Law as Applicable in India as to the Legal Parentage of Children Born In that Jurisdiction as a Result of a Surrogacy Arrangement

In India at the moment, we do not have any legislation on legal parentage as a result of surrogacy arrangements. At the moment, in India, we have the Registration of the Births and Deaths Act, 1969, which does not contain any provision regarding parentage as a result of a surrogacy arrangement. The said enactment laid down by the Parliament of India came into force on 31 May 1969. Surrogacy parentage was not an issue at the time the said legislation came into being. Neither have there been any amendments or additions with regard to any surrogacy issues in the said enactment pertaining to the registration of births and deaths in the Indian jurisdiction.

As far as legislation on surrogacy is concerned, draft surrogacy proposals were going through the Parliament at some stage. The current position in this regard is not very clear. Guidelines dealing with Artificial Reproductive Technologies (ART) have been prepared by an expert committee of the Indian Council of Medical Research in association with the National Academy of Medical Sciences (India), which could in the future become a part of the final draft of a proposed legislation. The preface to the Guidelines as circulated in March 2004 specifically points out that "[t]here are no guidelines for the practice of ART, accreditation of infertility clinics and supervision of their performance in India. This document aims to fill this lacuna and also provide a means of maintaining a national registry of ART clinics in India."

For this purpose, the National Guidelines for accreditation, supervision, and regulation of ART clinics in India have been framed. These guidelines provide a foundation for the proposed legislation relating to this field of law. These guidelines state that the surrogate mother is under no circumstances considered to be the legal mother.

Para 3.5.4 of the said Guidelines provides that in cases where the surrogate mother is biologically unrelated to the child, the birth certificate shall have the name of the genetic parents. Therefore, if the genetic parents are the Commissioning parents, who have contributed their genetic material for the unborn child, they shall be automatically recorded as

the legal parents, if DNA tests prove the same. No adoption procedure needs to be followed by the genetic parents under such circumstances. Para 3.5.4 of the said Guidelines reads as follows:

> **3.5.4—A surrogate mother carrying a child biologically unrelated to her must register as a patient in her own name.** While registering she must mention that she is a surrogate mother and provide all the necessary information about the genetic parents such as names, addresses, etc. She must not use/register in the name of the person for whom she is carrying the child, as this would pose legal issues, particularly in the untoward event of maternal death [in whose names will the hospital certify this death?]. **The birth certificate shall be in the name of the genetic parents.** The clinic, however, must also provide a certificate to the genetic parents giving the name and address of the surrogate mother. All the expenses of the surrogate mother during the period of pregnancy and post-natal care relating to pregnancy should be borne by the couple seeking surrogacy. The surrogate mother would also be entitled to a monetary compensation from the couple for agreeing to act as a surrogate; the exact value of this compensation should be decided by discussion between the couple and the proposed surrogate mother. An oocyte donor can act as a surrogate mother.

However, in terms of the above-mentioned Guidelines, in cases where the surrogate mother also donates her egg, the commissioning parents/infertile couple will have to legally adopt the child, and it is only after this legal procedure has been complied with, then the infertile couple become the legal parents of the child born through such an arrangement. This fact will also have to be recorded in the birth certificate issued to such a child.

Furthermore, where the genetic material is supplied by third party donors, in such cases, the birth certificate issued to the child will initially have the names of the genetic parents. Here, it would become mandatory for the infertile couple to legally adopt the child so born, before they can be referred to as the legal parents of such a child.

In order to avoid conflicts at a later stage, the said Guidelines categorically state that once the child has been legally adopted by the infertile couple, then the third party donor and the surrogate mother shall relinquish all parental rights connected with the child. Para 3.5.5. of the said Guidelines mandates as follows:

3.5.5—A third-party donor and a surrogate mother must relinquish in writing all parental rights concerning the offspring and vice versa.

However, it is submitted that the law relating to surrogacy in India is in its prenatal stage, and unfortunately at the moment, there is no legislation in existence prescribing a code of practice governing the moral, ethical, and legal aspects of such surrogate arrangements. Hence, the said Guidelines only have persuasive value at this moment in time.

Conflict of Laws

During the time as counsel dealing with adoption applications at the British High Commission, New Delhi, the authors have quite frequently encountered a conflict of laws situation where nonresident Indians, who have been residing abroad for several decades, adopt children from within their own family. The preference for adoption by immediate blood relatives is a common South Asian phenomenon.

The unsuspecting adoptive parents duly comply with the requirements of the HAMA 1956 for taking the child in adoption. The adoption deed is proudly presented to the immigration authorities; and this is where the trouble begins. The UK immigration authorities completely disregard the Indian adoption deed, and they are legally justified in doing so under the Adoption (Designation of Overseas Adoptions) Order 1973, SI 1973/19.

Under the 1973 Order, if a child has been legally adopted from a country whose adoption orders are recognized as valid under UK law, *i.e.*, from a "designated" country, then the parents may apply for the child to join them in the United Kingdom as their adopted child.

If the child has not been legally adopted from a "designated" country, or the adoption is from a country whose adoption orders are not recognized as valid in UK law, *i.e.*, the child is from a "non-designated" country, entry clearance will have to be obtained for the child to travel to the United Kingdom for adoption through the English courts. India is specified as a "non-designated" country under the 1973 Order.

The adoptive parents, then, are confronted with a refusal by the immigration authorities on the ground that the adoption deed is not valid under the 1973 Order, although there has been due compliance with the provisions of HAMA 1956. The only avenues available to the parents are to challenge the refusal by way of appeal or to lodge a fresh application.

The real dilemma in such a situation is to set back the clock to satisfy the requirements of British immigration law. How can a nonresident Indian adoptive couple obtain a guardianship order from a local court once a formal irrevocable adoption process has taken place? Certainly, a guardianship order is on no better footing than a valid adoption under HAMA 1956. This is a proposition, which, sooner or later, will have to be tested by the British courts.

Rather, it has been done so by the Court of appeal in a judgment, upholding a judgment under the provisions of HAMA, 1956. But, the central plank to uphold the validity of such an adoption is on the basis of right to family life. This judgment of immense significance has been analyzed by the authors' co-author Rambert De Mello in their book titled *Acting for Non-resident Indian Clients*.[5] De Mello's analysis is as follows:

Recently, the Court held that the bias against Indian adoption custom was wrong and that it was a breach of the right to family life and discriminatory to refuse an adopted child entry clearance to the United Kingdom by giving less weight to an adoption effected by customary law in India and which was recognized as valid there, on the ground that it was not a recognized practice in English law: *Singh v ECO Delhi* [2004] EWCA Civ 1075.

(1) The main principle arising for consideration in *Singh* was whether an adoption which does not meet the requirements of relevant international instruments should invariably be a reason for according little weight to it in determining whether family life exists or not. The adoption of the boy in the case of *Singh* was valid in India but not recognized in the United Kingdom.

(2) The Court concluded that such a rigid and formulaic approach is not justified and that the failure to satisfy the requirement of relevant international instruments will vary from case to case, and that of considerable importance will be the nature of the departure from the provisions of a relevant instrument. If the departure is one of substance rather than procedure and goes to the heart of the safeguards that the instrument is intended to promote, then it may well be appropriate to give the adoption order little weight ([2004] EWCA Civ 1075 at [33]).

---

[5] Jordan Publishing Limited, First Edition, 2004, at pp. 221–22.

(3) In this case much might be said of the fact that the children had not been adopted and that their biological link with their natural parents was fluid, continuing and developing.

(4) The principles enunciated in Singh which are relevant in determining whether family life exists between an adopted child and adoptive parents are equally applicable in a situation which needs to resolve whether there is family life existing between a child and his natural parents who are separated from each other.

(5) The best interests of the child will be relevant and may well be determinative at the stage at which the court has to decide the extent to which respect should be given to family life or whether interference with family life is justified under Art 8.2 ([2004] EWCA Civ 1075 at [34] per Dyson LJ, at [68] per Munby J).

(6) The potential for development of family life is relevant in determining whether family life already exists and this is not confined to cases involving children and their natural parents; unless some degree of family life is already established, the claim to family life will fail and will not be saved by the fact that at some time in the future it could flower into a full-blown family life or that the applicants have a genuine wish to bring this about ([2004] EWCA Civ 1075 at [38]).

(7) The fact is that many adults and children, whether through choice or circumstance, live in families more or less removed from what until comparatively recently would have been recognized as the typical nuclear family—the Convention is a living instrument ([2004] EWCA Civ 1075 at [63]–[64] per Munby J). The law must adapt itself to these realities (at [65]). There is no bright line test that the law can set. The infinite variety of the human condition precludes arbitrary defining.

(8) The existence or non-existence of family life is a question of fact depending upon the real existence in practice of close personal ties—a close personal relationship which has sufficient constancy and substance to create de facto family ties—the parents' cohabitation with the child will often be highly significant but this is not decisive ([2004] EWCA Civ 1075 at [79]).

(9) The fact that the parents do not see their children frequently is not fatal to establishing family life; one must be cautious before setting too high a benchmark for the existence of family life certainly where there is the constancy and commitment which a parent has shown towards his child ([2004] EWCA Civ 1075 at [90]).

It is strange, that this judgment has not got due recognition in the academic and the professional arena. This judgment should be publicized vigorously, so that prospective adoptive parents residing overseas can take due benefit of this path-breaking judgment. No doubt, this ruling is indeed laudable for building the edifice of the right to family life to recognize an adoption made in India under the provisions of HAMA, 1956, which is otherwise in direct conflict with the provisions of British immigration law as contained in HC 395.

Likewise, the American Embassy and numerous European embassies at New Delhi also outright refuse to accept the above-mentioned adoption deeds under the provisions of HAMA 1956. Hence, only guardianship orders are acceptable. These can be obtained only by lodging guardianship petitions under the provisions of the Hindu Minority and Guardianship Act, 1956 in the court of the guardian judge, in whose jurisdiction the minor child is residing. It is like a full blown trial. It is very difficult to obtain guardianship orders. These petitions have to be supported by exhaustive documentation as to the background and standing of the proposed overseas adoptive parents. Sometimes, it can be a time-consuming exercise, and it is very difficult in such a situation for the foreign couple to spend long periods of time in India awaiting custody orders. With these custody orders, the adoption ultimately takes place in the foreign country of habitual residence of the adoptive parents. In India, there is no exclusive law of adoption for foreigners or nonresident Indians.

Furthermore, adoptions within the family fold are not encouraged, while adoption applications by foreigners seeking to adopt children from orphanages and welfare homes are likely to receive positive treatment.

The noose of British immigration law has been further tightened by changes to HC 395, which were given effect by HC 538, and came into force on 1 April 2003. Reference in this regard is drawn to the observations of Richard McKee, a prominent Immigration Appeals Adjudicator:

Now HC 538 has not only lifted the restriction on third party support, but it has introduced a provision for de facto adoption. For all adopted children coming from countries whose adoption orders (if they have such things) are not recognized in the UK, the adoptive parents must have been living abroad, having assumed the role of the child's parents, for at least 18 months, of which the last 12 must have been spent living together with the child. This is to show a genuine transfer of parental responsibility. The expectation that the adoptive parents be married has now been dropped.[6]

The most worrying issue about these changes is that it is next to impossible for nonresident Indian couples to come and spend one complete calendar year with the adoptive child in India. Certainly, no UK employer or any other overseas employer would grant such long leave to any employee. However, more positively, senior level expatriates posted in India could possibly comply with the time requirement stipulated by the newly introduced provisions of HC 538.

CONCLUSION

There has been a growing demand for a general law of adoption enabling any person, irrespective of his or her religion, race, or caste, to adopt a child. There is now a clear case for overhauling the existing adoption law in India.

As far as the mechanics of intercountry adoption are concerned, all the major embassies in India are more than stringent in dealing with adoption applications. The refusal rates are very high. There is no room at all for compassion. The hurdles are almost insurmountable, causing lot of hardship to childless nonresident Indian couples.

The question that now remains to be answered is as to how successful the revised Guidelines discussed in this article have been. Sadly, the answer can be found in a very recent Andhra Pradesh High Court judgment, *John Clements v. All Concerned* (AP) ((2003) 2 Hindu Law Reporter 331). The court lamented (at pp 331, paras 59–61):

> 59. Para 2.14 of the guidelines envisages that no application by foreigner for taking a child in adoption should be entertained directly by any social child welfare agency in India working in the areas of inter-country adoption or by any institution or centre or Home to which children are committed by the Juvenile Court. The very next paragraph says "the original application along with original documents as prescribed by the Supreme Court of India would be forwarded by the foreign enlisted agency to a recognized placement agency in India".

> 60. Taking advantage of the inconsistency in the guidelines and ignoring the judgment of the Supreme Court the foreign enlisted agencies started directly approaching the placement agencies in India and are trying to take the Indian children in adoption with their connivance and active support of VCA and CARA officials, who are simply putting their seal of approval on these adoptions without bothering whether the procedure prescribed for intercountry adoption of a child is followed or not. With the result, trafficking in female children is going on unabated in violation of the guidelines given by the Supreme Court.

> 61. After the present scam came to light, the Government of Andhra Pradesh issued the Andhra Pradesh Orphanages and other Charitable Homes (Supervision and Control) Rules in GO Ms No 16, dated 18.04.2001. In para 11 (VII) of the said GO it is stated that "relinquishment" of child by "biological parents" on family grounds of poverty, number of children, unwanted girl child will not be permitted. Such children should not be admitted in Homes or "Orphanages" and, it admitted, the license and recognition of Home or Orphanage shall be cancelled or withdrawn.

Therefore, it can be concluded that, although there is no doubt that CARA is doing good work in its policing role, the negative media feedback has definitely not escaped judicial notice.

Lastly, the authors' experience reveals that guardian judges, especially in small towns and cities in India, who deal with such cases, are not particularly conversant with the interpretation of the inter-country adoption Guidelines discussed in this article. Therefore, in sum and substance, it can be stated that a uniform but strict procedure must be evolved that can be easily followed and adhered to both in letter and spirit. No doubt, procedural hurdles and legal formalities are necessary to prevent abuse of the process, but separate and intricate adoption and immigration procedures often leave foreign adopting parents in confusion over differing interpretations. Therefore, if the adoption process and procedures are overhauled so that they conform to a uniform pattern, it may make the process more convenient, less cumbersome, and easier to follow. All of this would be in the best interests of the child, which is undoubtedly the paramount consideration, and at the same time, would allow both the letter and spirit of law to be adhered to. Considered changes are thus urgently required in the field of intercountry adoption from India.

---

[6] For details, see R. McKee, "New immigration rules" [2003] 17.2 IA & NL 127–29.

"SHOULD I STAY OR SHOULD I GO?"

by Dyann DelVecchio, Cyrus D. Mehta, Shannon M. Underwood, and Paul W. Virtue[*]

INTRODUCTION

This article will articulate the differences between filing an adjustment of status (AOS) application with U.S. Citizenship and Immigration Services (USCIS) using Form I-485 and pursuing Consular Processing (CP) through a participating consular post of the U.S. Department of State (DOS).

The first part of the article will set forth the advantages and disadvantages of each process and offer practice pointers on how to choose the best op-

[*] **Dyann DelVecchio**, a partner at Seyfarth Shaw LLP in Boston, represents corporations, educational institutions, hospitals, and research institutions seeking to obtain visas for professionals, managers, and executives. Ms. DelVecchio is a cum laude graduate of Middlebury College and Northeastern University School of Law and served for two years as a law clerk to the Justices of the Massachusetts Superior Court. Proficient in several languages, she has co-authored a number of articles on immigration law and served on AILA's national Department of Labor Liaison Committee, its F-1 Student Committee (also as chair), and its Vermont Service Center Liaison Committee.

Cyrus Mehta, a graduate of Cambridge University and Columbia Law School, is the managing member of Cyrus D. Mehta & Associates, P.L.L.C., in New York City. Mr. Mehta is the chair of the Board of Trustees of AILF, recipient of the 1997 Joseph Minsky Young Lawyers Award, and a Fellow of the Academy of Business Immigration Lawyers. He also is secretary of the Association of the Bar of the City of New York and is past chair of the Committee on Immigration and Nationality Law of that Association. Mr. Mehta has received an AV rating from Martindale-Hubbell and is also listed in the *International Who's Who of Corporate Immigration Lawyers*.

Shannon Underwood is an associate attorney with the Law Offices of Carol L. Edward, P.S., in Seattle. She received her J.D. from the University of Colorado at Boulder and has practiced immigration law exclusively since 2001.

Paul Virtue is a partner in the Washington office of Hogan & Hartson, LLP. He is listed as a *Leader in Their Field* by *Chambers U.S.A.*, and is a frequent speaker and author on immigration topics. Before joining Hogan & Hartson, he was general counsel and executive associate commissioner for Programs of INS. Mr. Virtue is a member of the boards of trustees of AILF and the National Immigration Forum. He received his law degree from West Virginia University College of Law in 1982.

The authors wish to thank Jennifer Rogers, currently a second-year law student at New York Law School, for her invaluable assistance.

tions for the client. The second part will analyze how AOS or CP will impact the client's ability to take advantage of certain benefits, such as protecting a minor child from "aging out" and obtaining work authorization and travel permission. The third part will explore ways for the client to apply for AOS so as to avoid the statutory bars to re-entry into the United States. The fourth part will discuss strategies to overcome denial of the adjustment application.

AOS VS. CP

Informing Both Clients

In approaching the crucial decision of whether to process a permanent residence application in the United States through AOS or abroad through CP, thoughtful practitioners will apprise their foreign national clients of the merits and challenges of each approach. In employment-based cases, where a U.S. business entity is the sponsor and the attorney has a dual representation role, it is essential that this dialogue include both the employer and the foreign national. In far too many instances, beneficiaries have been pushed toward one approach or another, and their attorneys have not given them or their U.S. sponsors the information needed to make informed decisions.

In employment-based cases, the decision to file a request via AOS or CP is generally articulated on Form I-140 filed with the USCIS regional service center. In family-based cases, it is generally articulated when Form I-130 is submitted.

Diagnostic Questions

At the beginning, certain diagnostic questions should be asked to trigger the dialogue necessary to determine whether the foreign national—and, in employment cases, the foreign national and the sponsor—would be best served by filing through AOS or through CP:

- Does the foreign national—or his or her dependents—wish to obtain an employment authorization document (EAD) or advance parole (AP)?

- How likely is it that the foreign national will seek I-485 portability?

- Is the foreign national maintaining a residence in the United States?

- Even with a U.S. residence, will business or personal matters require the foreign national to be outside the United States for the foreseeable future?

- Does the foreign national/prime beneficiary have dependent family members who are resident and will immigrate from abroad?

- Would the foreign national face the three- or ten-year bars under IIRAIRA if he or she were to leave the United States?

- How important is it to you and your clients to preserve your rights to appeal and to file a motion to reopen?

- How important is it to the foreign national and the employer that the case be processed as speedily as possible?

- Will the U.S.-based employer permit the foreign national to spend the amount of time outside the United States necessary to complete consular processing at this particular post?

Benefits of Adjustment of Status in a Nutshell

There are a number of benefits and rights that flow to the applicant with filing the I-485 but not with CP filing.

Employment Authorization and Advance Parole

When the I-485 is filed, and in the same package, the applicant may also file Form I-765 to obtain an EAD and Form I-131 to obtain AP travel permission. The applicant's spouse and minor children are also eligible for these benefits. Often obtaining the EAD is in the employer's interest because it can obviate the need for costly extensions of the H-1B, L-1, or other nonimmigrant work visa. If the filings are timed correctly, particularly where the employer has several I-485s in process, the employer can find major cost savings.

I-485 Portability

The importance of preserving eligibility for I-485 portability[1] will hinge on the foreign national's degree

of job satisfaction, career prospects, and the perceived long-term strength of the company (*e.g.*, whether it is ripe for acquisition, bankruptcy, dissolution, or other changes that could make I-485 portability a "lifesaver" for the beneficiary). If, for example, the beneficiary might face termination in the future, the company is likely to be acquired, or the company's current fortunes portend an uncertain future, it generally makes sense to file the I-485 at the earliest possible opportunity to trigger the ticking of the six-month portability "clock."[2] Absent a retrogression, if USCIS fails to process the I-485 within 180 days and the applicant secures a generically similar employment opportunity, he or she may obtain the Green Card in spite of a job change. This safety net is not available to applicants who pursue CP.

Ability to Adjust Under §245(i) or §245(k)

Eligible applicants who file the I-485 can take advantage of the "forgiveness" provisions—§245(i) and §245(k) of the Immigration and Nationality Act (INA). For instance, §245(i) waives all disqualifying conditions to adjustment status under §245(a). A great number of applicants are still considered "grandfathered" under §245(i) due to the LIFE Act provisions[3] that sunset on April 30, 2001, and §245(k) protects employment-based applicants who either failed to maintain lawful status for 180 days or fewer, or who engaged in authorized employment or otherwise violated the terms and conditions of admission for 180 days or fewer.

Benefits Locked In

Even if the processing queue should retrogress (*see* Visa Bulletin at *http://travel.state.gov/visa/ frvi/ bulletin/bulletin_1360.html*), the filing of an I-485 during a month when the priority date is *current* permits the applicant to continue to obtain benefits

---

[1] Section 204(j) of the Immigration and Nationality Act (INA), Pub. L. No. 82-414, 66 Stat. 163 (*codified as amended at* 8 USC §§1101 *et seq.*), preserves the validity of the underlying employment-based petition or labor certification if the I-485 application is pending for 180 days or more and the noncitizen applicant changes jobs or employers in the same or similar occupation. *See also* USCIS Memorandum, William R. Yates, Associate Director for Operations, "Interim Guidance for Processing Form I-140 Employment-Based Immigrant Petitions and Form I-485 and H-1B Petitions Affected by AC21"
continued

(May 12, 2005), *published on* AILA InfoNet at Doc No. 05051810 (*posted* May 18, 2005) (hereinafter AC21 Memo).

[2] The offer of employment at the time of filing the employment-based I-140 petition and the I-485 must be bona fide, which means that at the time of the filing, the employer must have intended to employ the beneficiary and the beneficiary must have intended to undertake employment upon adjustment. *See* AC21 Memo, *supra* note 1.

[3] *See* LIFE Act Amendments, Pub. L. No. 106-554 (§§1502(a)(1)(B) and (D) Dec. 21, 2000), extended the protection of INA §245(i) to April 30, 2001, for persons who were present in the United States on Dec. 21, 2000, when the amendments were enacted. *See also* discussion of §245(i), *infra*.

such as EAD and AP. This is true even if the processing queue should *retrogress*.

Motions to Reopen/Ability To Litigate

Filing the I-485 preserves the applicant's right to file a motion to reopen or to litigate the case in removal proceedings and thereafter on appeal. Generally, CP does not allow for appeal or review of the consular officer's decision.

Benefits of Consular Processing in a Nutshell

The benefits of CP are certainly fewer, but many individuals choose to pursue it to save time. The decision will in part depend on what your clients value. If they value a quicker processing time, are willing to forego the opportunity to qualify for benefits such as the EAD/Advance Parole and I-485 portability, prefer the convenience of processing through their home country, or have dependent family members resident in the consular district, CP may well be the right choice.

Speed

In almost all situations, filing for permanent residence through CP will take less time, often significantly less time, than processing the I-485. However, it is absolutely essential to be aware of the current as well as projected CP processing times at the post in question before committing to this option. It is also necessary to understand and factor in the interplay between USCIS, National Visa Center (NVC), and DOS. Processing times and actual filing protocols vary wildly among the posts, with severe backlogs particularly in high-population, high-fraud consular posts or posts subject to terrorist attacks. Consult the website, *www.travel.state.gov*, for processing times, and if you are in any doubt, contact the post directly. You should also consult AILA's *Visa Processing Guide*, written by trusted and seasoned AILA members, as well as consular staff.

Convenience

Even where the foreign national is maintaining a residence in the United States, if the foreign national beneficiary's main residence is abroad, it almost always makes sense to pursue CP. Also, if the prime beneficiary is living in the United States but has dependent residents abroad, it often makes sense to process the entire family via CP.

Dual Processing

The visa petition forms (I-130 and I-140) require that the petitioner "elect" CP or AOS for the princi-

pal beneficiary. Is it possible for a client to pursue both CP and AOS at the same time by filing Form I-824, Application for Action on an Approved Application or Petition, to request CP when Form I-485 is already pending? The former Immigration and Naturalization Service (INS) said "no" in a revision to its *Adjudicator's Field Manual* issued in August 2000.[4] The revision reads in pertinent part as follows:

> When an alien with a pending I-485 files a Form I-824 requesting that the visa petition be forwarded to a consulate, the alien or the attorney of record will be notified that the I-824 will be treated as a request to withdraw the I-485. In accordance with 8 CFR §103.2(b)(8) the notice will provide the alien a response time in which to advise the Service on how they wish to proceed. The I-485 is to be terminated by written notice if the alien chooses to pursue consular processing or fails to respond within the time granted. This notice will also advise the alien of the termination of any employment authorization granted under 8 CFR §274a.12(c)(9). The I-824 is then to be approved, and the visa petition forwarded to the NVC for processing.

> Likewise, if the Service receives a *duplicate* immigrant visa petition requesting consular processing, and the alien has a pending I-485, the Service will notify the alien or the attorney of record that the duplicate petition will be treated as a request to withdraw the I-485, [and] as above, provide a response time in which to advise the Service on how they wish to proceed. The I-485 is to be terminated by written notice if the alien wishes to pursue consular processing or fails to timely respond. This notice will advise the alien of the termination of any employment authorization granted under 8 CFR §274a.12(c)(9). The visa petition along with the duplicate is then to be forwarded to the NVC for processing.[5]

---

[4] *See* INS Memorandum, Michael Cronin, Acting Exec. Assoc. Comm., HQ 70/23.IP, "Prohibition on Concurrent Pursuit of Adjustment of Status and Consular Processing (AD00-15)" (Aug. 8, 2000), *published on* AILA InfoNet at Doc. No. 00101803 (*posted* Oct. 18, 2000) (hereinafter INS Memorandum); *see also* INS Adjudications Liaison Minutes (03/01), *published on* AILA InfoNet at Doc. No. 01061932 (*posted* June 19, 2001).

[5] *Adjudicator's Field Manual* §23.2(2). The redacted version of the *Adjudicator's Field Manual* found on the USCIS website, *http://uscis.gov/lpbin/lpext.dll/inserts/afmredacted/afm95-redacted-1?f=templates&fn=document-frame.htm#afm-95-redacted-begin-95-redacted*, does not contain the August 2000 revision.

However, some practitioners challenge this conclusion, arguing that USCIS does not have jurisdiction over consular processing, rendering the *Field Manual* revision ultra vires.[6] With this interpretation, dual processing is at least theoretically possible. But even practitioners who proffer the interpretation acknowledge that "a number of practitioners . . . consider dual processing to be extremely risky," due to USCIS's treatment of such cases.[7]

While some posts will create an immigrant visa application file with a receipt notice for Form I-824, they will not adjudicate a visa application in such a case until they receive the petition from the NVC, thus, foreclosing the prospect of pursuing CP and AOS concurrently. However, a DOS cable encourages posts to process cases on the basis of an I-797 Notice of Approval, and the beneficiary must provide the original I-797 notice of approval of an I-140 petition, a copy of the I-140 petition, a receipt for the I-824, and evidence that the applicant was last resident in the host country of the post.[8]

AOS/CP, CSPA, AND THE ABILITY TO WORK AND TRAVEL

Child Status Protection Act

The Child Status Protection Act (CSPA)[9] was enacted to address the problem of children who "age out" as a result of USCIS delays in processing visa petitions and asylum and refugee applications. The INA defines a "child" as an unmarried individual under 21 years of age.[10] CSPA explains how to determine the age of a child for purposes of eligibility to adjust status or re-

ceive an immigrant visa at a consulate abroad. Application of CSPA to a given case can be complex, especially if the case involves the effective date of the INA.[11] The authors discuss CSPA briefly here as its application to a given case may weigh in favor of CP or AOS, depending on the circumstances.

Before CSPA was enacted, an application by a child for permanent residency as a direct or derivative beneficiary of a visa petition or grant of asylum/refugee status would be approved only if adjudicated before the child turned 21. Upon turning 21, a child would "age out," losing the status of a child. Due to agency backlogs and other delays, many children aged out before their cases were complete. CSPA was enacted to "lock in" the age of the child at an earlier date in the process, thus preserving the status of "child" for those who otherwise would have aged out.

CSPA Age Calculation

Under CSPA, the age of an immediate relative child of a U.S. citizen will be calculated as of the date the parent files the I-130 Petition for Alien Relative. Thus, if a U.S. citizen mother files an I-130 petition for an unmarried daughter who is 20, the daughter will retain the status of a "child" even if the visa petition or adjustment of status application is not adjudicated until she is 24.[12]

In cases involving the child of a lawful permanent resident (LPR), or the derivative of a family-based, employment-based, or diversity visa, the beneficiary's age will be locked in on the date that the priority date of the approved visa petition becomes current, less the number of days that the petition was pending—but only if the beneficiary seeks to acquire the status of an LPR within one year of the date the visa number became available. Thus, if an I-130 that was filed in 2002 when the beneficiary was 18 years old was approved in 2003, and the priority date became available in 2005 after she turned 21, the child's age would be locked in at 20 years

---

[6] *See* J. Pederson and M. Funk, "Strategic Lawyering at Consular Posts," *Immigration & Nationality Law Handbook* 649, 654–55 (AILA 2005–06 ed.).

[7] *Id.* at 655.

[8] *See* DOS Cable, 00 State 180792 (Sept. 2000), *published on* AILA InfoNet at Doc. No. 00092773 (*posted* Sept. 27, 2000). The cable indicates that attorney certification of the I-140 petition is not necessary, although it may still be a good idea to certify the copy of the I-140 petition at posts where fraud is high. It is also a good idea to check the procedures at specific posts. For example, the U.S. Consulate in Mumbai, India, *http://mumbai usconsulate.gov*, allows beneficiaries of approved employment-based first preference (EB-1) and second preference (EB-2) petitions to request CP even if they have a pending AOS application in the United States.

[9] Pub. L. No. 107-208, 116 Stat. 927 (Aug. 6, 2002), *published on* AILA InfoNet at Doc. No. 02080740 (*posted* Aug. 7, 2002).

[10] INA §101(b)(1).

[11] *See* R. Berg & R. Ng, "Stopping Time and Ignoring the Reality of Aging: The Simple Beauty of the Child Status Protection Act," elsewhere in this volume. *See also* Practice Advisory, M. Kenney, "Updated Practice Advisory on The Child Status Protection Act" (Mar. 8, 2004), *publsihed on* AILA InfoNet at Doc. No. 04031261, and Practice Advisory, M. Kenney, "'Aging Out': Recent Developments Related to the Child Status Protection Act and Other Provisions" (Feb. 24, 2005), *published on* AILA InfoNet at Doc. No. 05022464 (*posted* Feb. 24, 2005).

[12] CSPA §2; INA §201(f).

(*i.e.*, 21 less the one year the petition was pending) for eligibility for permanent resident status. If the LPR parent naturalizes after filing an I-130 for a child in the 2A preference category, the beneficiary's age will be locked in as of the date of naturalization. A child who is under age 21 on date of naturalization, the child will be protected.[13]

AOS vs. CP for CSPA Cases

A possible reason for recommending adjustment of status over consular processing for a derivative beneficiary may be the interpretation that USCIS has given to the date of availability of a visa number in cases of visa retrogression. According to the CSPA memoranda, if a visa availability date retrogresses after the beneficiary has filed an application for AOS (Form I-485) based upon an approved visa petition, USCIS will retain the I-485 and make a note of the visa availability date at the time the I-485 was filed. When a visa number again becomes available, USCIS will calculate the beneficiary's age by reference to the earlier visa availability date that it marked on the I-485.[14] The memo advised that the agency will not follow this practice where the I-485 had not been filed when the visa availability date retrogressed. The absence of similar guidance from DOS may be reason to recommend the AOS option where visa retrogression may be an issue.

The child's age will only lock in if the beneficiary has sought to acquire the status of a lawful permanent resident within one year of the date of visa availability. For a child beneficiary who is adjusting status, USCIS indicates that the date the child seeks to acquire LPR status is the date the I-485 is filed.[15]

DOS has advised that where the principal applicant was processed for a visa at a consular post, the date a child seeks to acquire LPR status is the date Form DS-230, Part I is submitted by the child or a by the child's parent on the child's behalf. It is not enough, according to DOS, for the principal to have sought LPR status within one year of visa number availability.[16] Where no record of Part I of the visa packet for a derivative child exists at the post, DOS requires the derivative beneficiary to provide alternate proof.

When the principal is adjusting status in the United States and the derivative will be applying abroad for a follow-to-join visa, the derivative will be considered to have sought LPR status on the date the principal filed Form I-824 to initiate the child's follow-to-join application. Because filing Form I-824 is not the only way to initiate this process, a DOS revised cable instructs visa-issuing posts to seek an advisory opinion where some other "concrete" step was taken to initiate a child's follow–to-join application. DOS does not define what constitutes a "concrete" step. Accordingly, the authors recommend that Form I-824 be filed along with the principal's Form I-485 in these cases where a derivative child will apply for a "follow to join" visa abroad.

Work Authorization and Travel

Work Authorization

The desire to work in the United States will often drive the client's decision for AOS or CP.

The beneficiary of an immigrant visa petition who is residing legally in the United States may already have authorization to work. Examples of such authorization are a nonimmigrant employment visa (*e.g.*, H or L status) or authorization as the result of temporary protected status (TPS).[17] These individuals will be able to continue working whether they opt for AOS or CP. However, if the independent manner through which work is authorized ceases, an EAD can only be secured if an AOS application is pending.[18] There is no avenue to seek work authorization if one has chosen to CP for an immigrant visa petition.

Even where the primary beneficiary of an employment-based immigrant visa petition has work authorization based on proper maintenance of H or L status, AOS over CP can create considerable advantages. Derivative family members can receive work

---

[13] CSPA §2; *see also* INS Memorandum, Johnny N. Williams, Exec. Assoc. Comm., HQADN 70/6.1.1, "Child Status Protection Act" (Sept. 20, 2002), *published on* AILA InfoNet at Doc. No. 02092732 (*posted* Sept. 27, 2003), and INS Memorandum, Johnny N. Williams, Exec. Assoc. Comm, HQADN 70/6.1.1, "The Child Status Protection Act– Memorandum Number 2," (Feb. 14, 2003), *published on* AILA InfoNet at Doc. No. 03031040 (*posted* Mar. 10, 2003) (hereinafter CSPA memoranda).

[14] For an argument that the same rationale should be applied to lock in the age of the child when I-140 and I-485 are filed concurrently even before approval of the I-140, see T. Fox-Isicoff & H. R. Klasko, "The Child Status Protection Act–Is Your Child Protected?," 80 *Interpreter Releases* 973 (July 21, 2003).

[15] *See* CSPA memoranda, *supra* note 13.

[16] *See* "DOS Issues Revised Cable on Child Status Protection Act," *published on* AILA InfoNet at Doc. No. 03020550 (*posted* Feb. 5, 2003).

[17] *See* INA §244(a)(1)(B).

[18] 8 CFR §§274a.12(c)(9), 1274a.12(c)(9).

authorization while their cases are being processed. Also, the ability to receive an EAD after filing the AOS application can significantly decrease the costs of maintaining and extending the nonimmigrant status of the primary beneficiary.

An individual who is in lawful H or L status while the I-485 is pending will not lose non-immigrant status by filing Form I-765, Application for Work Authorization.[19] However, using an EAD to leave the employer who sponsored the H or L visa would violate that nonimmigrant status.[20] Using the EAD for employment with a separate employer while the individual is on H-1B status through another employer would also violate nonimmigrant status; a derivative spouse will not be able to maintain H-4 status while working on an EAD.[21] Though an individual is considered to be maintaining lawful status while an adjustment application is pending, he or she is protected during this time only if the adjustment is approved. If nonimmigrant status lapses while the I-485 is pending, the individual will be considered out of status as of the date the nonimmigrant visa lapsed if the adjustment application is denied and will not be able to file for extension of the H or L visa status that had previously lapsed.[22] Hence, there is always an incentive to maintain the client's underlying nonimmigrant status rather than relying solely on an EAD while the adjustment application is pending.

If the client opts to rely on work authorization through AOS, it is important to advise him or her about delays in obtaining and renewing the EAD. An application for an EAD, Form I-765, may be filed with the adjustment application or at any time after the government receives the adjustment application. USCIS is required to adjudicate the I-765 within 90 days of receipt.[23] After 90 days, USCIS

must issue the applicant an interim EAD valid for up to 240 days.[24] The applicant may request the interim EAD at a local USCIS office.[25] Since USCIS can take over three months to process an EAD request, the applicant must carefully strategize the filing of the initial EAD and extension applications to avoid any gaps in permission to work. Continued employment is not authorized until an EAD is issued.

Travel

The client's need to travel in and out of the United States can further affect whether it is more prudent to pursue AOS or CP. Unless the beneficiary has an independent ability to travel in and out of the United States (such as an H or L visa), permission to travel will only be granted during AOS through AP, and there is no independent basis for travel permission during CP.

An individual who has filed an adjustment application under INA §245 will be considered to have abandoned the application upon leaving the United States unless he or she was granted AP before leaving the United States[26] or otherwise has the legal ability to travel while in H or L status (*see* below). Note, however, that an individual who enters the United States on advance parole is not considered *admitted* under the INA.[27] An applicant whose last entry into the United States was on AP will be treated as seeking admission and therefore subject to the grounds of inadmissibility found in INA §212 at the time of the adjustment adjudication.[28] For example, if departure from the United States caused the unlawful presence bars to trigger,[29] the individual will be found inadmissible; to adjust status, he or she must either qualify for a waiver of the three- or ten-year bar or wait for three or ten years to pass to seek admission.[30] Although the individual might be able to gain entry into the United States upon AP, he or she will be found inadmissible at the time of adjudication.[31]

---

[19] *See* INS Memorandum, Michael Cronin, Acting Assoc. Comm., Office of Programs, "Amended INS Memo on H/Ls Traveling on Advance Parole," *published* on AILA InfoNet at Doc. No 00052603 (*posted* May 26, 2000) (hereinafter Cronin Memo).

[20] *Id.*

[21] An L-2 spouse can obtain an EAD under INA §212(c)(2)(E) and should work under this EAD to preserve L-2 status. For application procedure, see INS Memorandum, William R. Yates, Deputy Exec. Assoc. Comm. Field Operations, HQ 70/6.2.5, 6.2.12 (Feb. 22, 2002*), reprinted in* 79 *Interpreter Releases* 338, 343–46 (Mar. 4, 2002).

[22] It may be possible for the employer to file a new nonimmigrant visa petition for CP if the noncitizen client does not face the three- or ten-year bars; *see infra.*

[23] 8 CFR §§274a.13(d), 1274a.13(d).

---

[24] *Id.*

[25] It is important to request an appointment for an EAD through the InfoPass system well in advance of the 90 days because some offices are unable to issue appointments soon enough.

[26] 8 CFR §§245.2(a)(4)(ii)(B), 1245(a)(4)(ii)(B). Applicants for Advance Parole must file Form I-131, 8 CFR §223.2(a).

[27] INA §101(a)(13)(B).

[28] 8 CFR §§245(a)(4)(ii)(B), 1245(a)(4)(ii)(B).

[29] *See* INA §§212(a)(9)(B)(i)(I)–(II).

[30] *Id.*

[31] *See* INS Memorandum, Paul W. Virtue, Acting Exec. Assoc. Comm., Office of Programs, "Advance Parole for

continued

To qualify for a waiver of the unlawful presence bars under INA §212(a)(9)(B)(v), the applicant must be the spouse, son, or daughter of a U.S. citizen or lawful permanent resident who would suffer extreme hardship if the individual is denied admission into the United States.[32]

An applicant who is subject to the bars may not need to spend the three or ten years outside the United States; it could be argued that the applicant could spend this time within. Specifically, the language of both prongs of INA §212(a)(9)(B)(i) states that an alien will be inadmissible if he or she "*seeks admission* within 3 (or 10) years of the date of such alien's departure or removal from the United States."[33] Nothing in the language of this section suggests that one has to wait the three or ten years outside the United States. Thus, if an applicant has triggered the three-year bar after leaving the United States on AP, and the adjustment interview occurs after three years, it can be argued that he or she will not be inadmissible under INA §212(a)(9)(B)(i)(I).

An individual with a pending adjustment application will not need AP to travel if he or she is in lawful H-1 or L-1 status, is returning to same employer authorized by the H or L visa, and is in possession of a valid visa.[34] However, an individual with an H or L visa is also eligible to seek AP, and entry as a parolee does not preclude the individual from later receiving an extension of H or L status; the grant of an extension will have the effect of admitting the alien and terminating his or her status as a parolee.[35] An individual who has both a grant of AP and a valid H or L visa has the option to choose the status under which to be admitted.[36] Given the delays in obtaining nonimmigrant visas at most posts, an individual in valid H or L status may quickly travel back to the United States on AP without jeopardizing nonimmigrant status. Presumably, a derivative of such an applicant could still seek an H-4 or L-2 visa at a consular post. Spouses and dependants of an H or L beneficiary are eligible for the same period of admission in H-4 or L-2 status as the principal beneficiary;[37] the fact that the applicant entered on AP should still allow him or her to retain nonimmigrant status. It is hoped that consular officials will recognize the Cronin Memo.

AOS AND UNLAWFUL STATUS

It is vital for a noncitizen who is not in status to be able to adjust status to permanent residence within the United States. Unless that can be done, the individual would have to leave the United States to pursue an immigrant visa at an overseas consular post. That could trigger either the three- or ten-year bar of inadmissibility.[38] Thus, it would make no sense for that person to initiate the Green Card process through a labor certification or some other family- or employment-based petition if he or she would not be able to adjust status here and would have to leave and trigger the bars. An individual who cannot avoid CP must be carefully advised whether the bars would trigger, and if so, the possibility of obtaining a waiver against the bars.

INA §245 governs eligibility for adjusting status to permanent residence within the United States.[39] Essentially, the noncitizen must have been "inspected and admitted or paroled into the United States" and must also be the beneficiary of an approved immigrant visa petition under INA §204(a)(1). This would include a family, employment, religious worker, or investor petition and a diversity visa (from the Green Card lottery).

Furthermore, status cannot be adjusted if the applicant has accepted unauthorized employment, been in unlawful status, or failed to maintain continuously

---

Alien Unlawfully Present in the United States for More than 180 days" (Nov. 26, 1997), *published on* AILA InfoNet at Doc. No. 97120290 (*posted* Dec. 2, 1997); *see also* INS Advisory, "INS on Travel While Change/Adjustment is Pending," *published on* AILA InfoNet at Doc. No. 00112902 (*posted* Nov. 29, 2000).

[32] INA §212(a)(9)(B)(v).

[33] *Id.*

[34] 8 CFR §245.2(a)(4)(ii)(C).

[35] *See* Cronin Memo, *supra* note 19.

[36] *Id.*

[37] 8 CFR §§214.2(h)(9)(iv), (l)(7)(ii).

[38] As noted, INA §212(a)(9)(B)(i) imposes a three-year bar on a person who has been unlawfully in the United States for more than 180 days and a ten-year bar to a person who has accrued unlawful presence in the United States for more than one year. A noncitizen is unlawfully present in the United States "after the expiration of the period of stay authorized by the Attorney General or is present in the United States without being admitted or paroled." INA §212(a)(9)(B)(ii). For details on which status constitutes "unlawful presence," see INS Memorandum, Paul W. Virtue, Acting Exec. Assoc. Comm, "INS on Unlawful Presence" (Sept. 19, 1997), *published on* AILA InfoNet at Doc. No. 97092240 (*posted* Sept. 22, 1997).

[39] *See also* 8 CFR §§245.1, 1245.1.

a lawful status since entry into the United States.[40] There are other bars to adjustment of status. For instance, alien crewmen or aliens admitted in transit without a visa also cannot adjust status.[41]

On the other hand, there are several exceptions, particularly for those who are in violation of their status in the United States:

Immediate Relatives

Immediate relatives who have been sponsored by U.S. citizen relatives—spouses, minor children, and parents[42]—may still be able to adjust status even if they have failed to maintain lawful status or have taken unauthorized employment. However, even this group of individuals must have been "inspected and admitted or paroled" into the United States to be eligible for adjustment of status despite subsequently violating their status. An immediate relative of a U.S. citizen who originally entered the United States without inspection would still not be eligible to adjust status.

Note that a fiancée or fiancé of a U.S. citizen on a K-1 visa or a spouse of a U.S. citizen on a K-3 visa, pursuant to INA §101(a)(15)(K), can only adjust status through the citizen who filed the K visa petition.[43] Hence, that individual could not adjust status based on a marriage to a U.S. citizen who was not the sponsor of the K visa petition.

Crewmen and aliens on transit visas are ineligible even if they are immediate relatives of U.S. citizens.

Battered Immigrants

Battered spouses and children who are beneficiaries of approved Form I-360 self-petitions are eligible for adjustment of status regardless of any violations of their status and of the manner of entry.[44] This exception applies to battered immigrants applying under both the immediate relative category and the family second preference.[45]

Technical Exceptions

INA §245(c) excuses status violations "through no fault of his own or for technical reasons." The regulations of USCIS limit the technical exceptions to the following:

- Inaction of another individual or organization designated by regulation to act on behalf of an individual and over whose actions the individual has no control, if the inaction is acknowledged by that individual or organization (as, for example, where a designated school official or an exchange program sponsor did not notify USCIS of continuation of status as required, or did not forward a request for continuation of status to USCIS);

- A technical violation resulting from inaction of USCIS (as, for example, where an applicant establishes that he or she properly filed a timely request to maintain status that USCIS has not yet acted on that request);

- A technical violation caused by the physical inability of the applicant to request an extension of nonimmigrant stay from USCIS either in person or by mail (as, for example, an individual who is hospitalized with an illness at the time nonimmigrant stay expires and that is verified by a letter from the physician or hospital);

- A technical violation resulting from USCIS's application of the maximum five/six-year period of stay for certain H-1 nurses only if the applicant was reinstated to H-1 status in accordance with the terms of Public Law 101-656 (Immigration Amendments of 1988).[46]

These exceptions have been construed narrowly. The first does not apply if the sponsor delayed in filing the documents, the Department of Labor did not approve the labor certification in time, or the noncitizen was unable to file the adjustment application in time because the priority date was not current. It would only apply if the school or exchange visitor sponsor did not take timely action, which resulted in the F or J visa-holder's violation, and the designated official acknowledged that.

It may, however, be possible for a V-2 or V-3 visa-holder to assert the first exception, if the person was earlier not able to extend his or her status beyond the age of 21 but can now do so as a result of a reversal in USCIS policy.[47]

---

[40] INA §245(c)(2).

[41] INA §§245(c)(1), (c)(3).

[42] INA §201(b)(2)(A)(i).

[43] INA §245(d).

[44] INA §§245(a), (c).

[45] Id.

---

[46] 8 CFR §§245.1(d)(2), 1245.1(d)(2).

[47] In *Akhtar v. Burzynski*, 384 F.3d 1193 (9th Cir. 2004), the court held that 8 CFR §214.15(g), terminating V-2 or V-3 nonimmigrant status before the child's 21st birthday, was

continued

The second exception applies when a noncitizen files an asylum application before his or her visitor visa expires and then files for adjustment of status while the asylum application is pending.[48] Even if the asylum application is denied, the individual can still adjust status so long as the application was filed before the denial.[49] This is true even if the asylum application is not granted at a USCIS Asylum Office, the noncitizen is placed in removal proceedings, and applies for adjustment of status before an immigration judge (IJ).[50] On the other hand, the exception may not apply if an adjustment application was filed while a timely request for extension of nonimmigrant status was pending.[51]

The third exception is self-explanatory, and the fourth no longer applies.

INA §245(i)

INA §245(i), on the other hand, allows a person to apply for adjustment of status even if he or she entered without inspection, overstayed, or worked without authorization. Under this provision, a person who has violated immigration status would still be able to adjust to permanent residence if a fee of $1,000 accompanied the filing and as long as this person (including the spouse and children) is the

beneficiary of a labor certification or petition filed under INA §204 on or before April 30, 2001.

INA §245(i) previously sunset on January 14, 1998, but was revived under the LIFE Act amendments to cover any application filed on or before April 30, 2001.[52] Under the latest amendment, if a person filed after January 14, 1998 and before April 30, 2001, he or she had to be physically present in the United States on or before December 21, 2000, to take advantage of §245(i).

Interestingly, INA §245(i) waives all the disqualifying conditions to adjusting status in §245(a), requiring an entry with inspection or parole, and §245(c). Thus, under §245(i), a person who entered without inspection can still adjust status if he or she meets all of the other conditions. Moreover, the disqualifications in §245(c) are also not relevant, such as being an alien crewman or on a transit visa, if an individual is eligible under §245(i). But a K visa-holder would still not be able to take advantage of §245(i) if he or she is adjusting through a citizen spouse who was not the sponsor of the K visa.

Although the latest version of §245(i) again sunset on April 30, 2001, it still can be a boon for non-citizens who are considered grandfathered under this provision.[53] For a person to be grandfathered, the labor certification or petition should have been "approvable as filed," which means "that, as of the date of the filing of the qualifying immigrant visa petition under INA §204 or qualifying application for labor certification, the qualifying petition or application was properly filed, meritorious in fact, and non-frivolous ["frivolous" being defined herein as patently without substance]."[54] If a petition or application that was approvable as filed is later withdrawn, denied, or revoked due to circumstances that arose after the time of filing, it would still preserve the noncitizen's eligibility to adjust status under a different application or petition.[55]

On March 9, 2005, USCIS issued an important memo[56] clarifying who can be grandfathered under

---

contrary to congressional intent to reunite families when it enacted the LIFE Act. *See also* USCIS Press Release, "USCIS Announces New Policy Regarding V Status Extensions" (Mar. 16, 2005), which announced that *Akhtar* would be applied nationwide and those whose extension requests had been denied solely because they were over 21 could file new V extension applications.

[48] *See Matter of [name and file number not provided]* (AAU Dec. 23, 1993), *digested in* 71 *Interpreter Releases* 257 (Feb. 14, 1994).

[49] *See* Letter from Edward H. Skerrett, Chief, Immigration Branch, INS Adjudications, to attorney Ronald J. Tasoff, HQ 245-C (Apr. 6, 1994), *reproduced at* 71 *Interpreter Releases* 634, 641 (May 9, 1994).

[50] One of the authors, Cyrus D. Mehta, was able to successfully argue this over the government's objections before an IJ in New York.

[51] *See* Memorandum, Janice Podolny, Chief, Inspections Law Division, Office of General Counsel, HQCOU 90/15, "Interpretation of 'Period of Stay Authorized by the Attorney General' in determining 'unlawful presence' under INA section 212(a)(9)(B)(ii)" (Mar. 27, 2003), *published on* AILA InfoNet at Doc. No. 03042140 (*posted* Apr. 21, 2003) (noncitizen is not considered to be in lawful status while timely extension or change of status application is pending even though he or she may not be unlawfully present).

[52] Pub. L. No. 106-554, 114 Stat. 2763.

[53] 8 CFR §§245.10, 1245.10.

[54] 8 CFR §§245.10(a)(3), 1245.10(a)(3).

[55] *Id.*

[56] *See* USCIS Memorandum, William R. Yates, Assoc. Dir. for Operations, HQOPRD 70/23.1, "Clarification of Certain Eligibility Requirements Pertaining to an Application to Adjust Status under Section 245(i) of the Immigration and Nationality Act" (Mar. 9, 2005), *published on* AILA InfoNet at Doc. No. 05031468 (*posted* Mar. 14, 2005).

§245(i). It is noteworthy because it clarifies that there is no restriction on the number of times a noncitizen may seek to adjust status under §245(i). In the past, USCIS often took the position that a noncitizen could file under §245(i) only once.

The memo also clarifies the circumstances under which a derivative spouse or child can grandfather under §245(i). If a spouse was already married to an alien who was the beneficiary of a labor certification or immigrant visa petition filed on or before April 30, 2001, the spouse would be independently grandfathered under §245(i) even if the marriage was later terminated. Thus, the derivative spouse could file an adjustment application on a wholly independent basis separate from the spouse's immigrant visa petition. The same principle applies to a derivative child. The memo, on the other hand, distinguishes between a spouse who was married to a grandfathered alien before April 30, 2001, and one who marries such an alien after April 30, 2001. In the latter situation, the spouse cannot independently grandfather and is limited to filing an adjustment of status application under §245(i) as a derivative of the spouse who has been grandfathered. The memo notes that the qualifying relationship must continue to exist at the time the principal alien adjusts status in order for the spouse or child to obtain the derivative benefit.

According to the memo, if an "after-acquired" spouse—one who married a grandfathered alien after April 30, 2001—subsequently divorces, such a spouse is not considered to be grandfathered and may not file for adjustment of status under §245(i) either independently or as a dependent of the principal alien.

INA §245(k)

Another useful, though limited exception is INA §245(k). This provision may only be used by a beneficiary of an employment-based petition under the first, second, and third preferences, or the beneficiary of a religious worker petition who is seeking to adjust status. Unlike §245(i), which waives all disqualifications under §245(a) and (c), §245(k) only waives the disqualifications listed in §§245(c)(2), (c)(7), and (c)(8).[57] Section 245(k) triggers if:

(1) the alien on the date of filing an application for adjustment of status, is present in the United States pursuant to a lawful admission;

(2) the alien, subsequent to such lawful admission has not, for an aggregate period exceeded 180 days—

(A) failed to maintain, continuously, a lawful status;

(B) engaged in unauthorized employment; or

(C) otherwise violated the terms and condition of the alien's admission.[58]

A noncitizen who is present in the United States "pursuant to a lawful admission" and "on the date of filing an application for adjustment of status" has not violated status or engaged in unauthorized employment for more than 180 days would be eligible to adjust status.

Although there has not been much interpretation on §245(k), it has now been confirmed that the 180-day period starts running after the last "lawful admission."[59] Prior violations of status would therefore not count toward the 180 days that begin after the "lawful admission."

It is debatable whether §245(k) trumps any violations that occur after the adjustment application has been filed or whether the 180 days continue to run after the adjustment application has been filed. Suppose the adjustment application is filed 170 days after the noncitizen has violated status. Then, subsequent to the filing, the noncitizen continues to work without authorization for 11 more days. If the 11 days were to be added to the 170 days, §245(k) would no longer protect the noncitizen.

There is a strong basis for arguing that the 180-day period stops running when the application is filed based on the statutory language "on the date of filing an application for adjustment of status is present in

---

[57] INA §245(c)(7) disqualifies a noncitizen who seeks adjustment of status under the employment-based preferences and is not in a lawful nonimmigrant status. INA §245(c)(8) disqualifies a noncitizen who was employed in an unauthorized capacity or who has otherwise violated the terms of a nonimmigrant visa. These provisions apply to a noncitizen even after the filing of an adjustment of status application. For example, if the individual works without an EAD while *continued*

the application is pending, INA §245(c)(8) would disqualify him or her from adjusting to permanent residence.

[58] INA §§245(k)(1), (k)(2).

[59] The USCIS Chief Counsel advised AILA that for purposes of §245(k), an adjustment applicant needs to demonstrate maintenance of status only from his or her last entry up to the date the adjustment application is filed. However, the question of maintenance of status after the filing and the applicability of §245(k) were not addressed. *See* "USCIS Chief Counsel Addresses Maintenance of Status Under 245(k)," *published on* AILA InfoNet at Doc. No. 04060767 (*posted* June 7, 2004).

the United States."[60] As noted earlier,[61] unauthorized employment after the adjustment application is filed would disqualify the noncitizen pursuant to §245(c)(8)—but §245(k) explicitly exempts the application of (c)(7) and (8), which triggers even after the filing of the application. In sum, one could argue that the 180-day period stops at the point the application is filed, and if there is a violation after the filing, §245(k) waives that as well.

Unfortunately, USCIS has not agreed with this interpretation. In an AILA/USCIS liaison meeting on October 28, 2004, USCIS advised that any unauthorized employment post-filing due to a gap in the issuance of the EAD would count toward the 180 days; thus, an applicant who goes over the 180-day period could still be precluded from adjusting status.[62]

CP Despite Facing the Bars

In the event that a noncitizen who has accumulated unlawful presence is not eligible for the statutory exceptions or the waivers under §245(i) or §245(k), he or she should only be advised to CP if the three- or ten-year bars are not applicable. If they are applicable, a waiver is available for the three- and ten-year bars under §212(a)(9)(B).

First, the statute provides that the period of unlawful presence shall not accrue while the noncitizen is a minor, has a bona fide application for asylum pending and has not been employed without authorization, or is a beneficiary of family unity protection.[63] Time spent by battered women and children in violation of the terms of a nonimmigrant visa shall not accrue as unlawful presence if there is a substantial connection between the violation and the abuse.[64] Section 212(a)(9)(B)(iv) further provides that a noncitizen who has been lawfully admitted or paroled and who filed a nonfrivolous application for a change or extension of status before the expiration of the valid period of stay will have the period of unlawful presence tolled for 120 days while the application is pending, as long as

the noncitizen was not employed without authorization before or during the pendency of the application.[65]

Second, §212(a)(9)(v) provides for waiver of the three- and ten-year bars for the spouse, son, or daughter of a U.S. citizen or permanent resident, based on extreme hardship to the citizen or lawful permanent resident spouse or parent. Note that extreme hardship to a U.S. citizen *child* cannot serve as the basis for waiver. The waiver is available at the sole discretion of the Attorney General, whose decision is not subject to judicial review.

Finally, a client facing a three-year bar under INA §212(a)(9)(B)(i)(I) and unable to file for AOS, can try to initiate removal proceedings so as to make it a voluntary departure[66] and, thus, escape the three-year bar. That person can CP and re-enter the United States as an LPR. INA §212(a)(9)(B)(i)(I) only applies to the individual who voluntarily departs *before* proceedings commence. Thus, one who voluntarily departs after proceedings begin will not be subject to the three-year bar.[67]

REMEDIES UPON DENIAL OF APPLICATION FOR AOS

This section will summarize the options for relief if the I-485 application is denied before the client has to resort to CP. Although federal court litigation through declaratory judgments and mandamus actions may also be an option, a discussion on that is beyond the scope of this article.[68]

---

[60] INA §245(k)(1).

[61] 8 CFR §§245.10(a)(3), 1245.10(a)(3).

[62] *See* Question 3 of the October 28, 2004, AILA/USCIS Liaison Minutes, *published on* AILA InfoNet at Doc. No. 05012163 (*posted* Jan. 21, 2005).

[63] INA §§212(a)(9)(B)(iii)(I)–(III).

[64] INA §212(a)(9)(B)(iii)(IV). As noted, a battered spouse can also adjust status without using the INA §245(i) waivers, because battered spouses are exempt from the bars to adjustment of §§245(a) and (c).

[65] This provision has been interpreted to mean that a timely application for extension or change of status will toll unlawful presence until the application is denied. *See* INS Memorandum, Michael A. Pearson, Exec. Assoc. Comm, Office of Field Operations, HQADN70/21.1.24-P, "Period of Stay Authorized by the Attorney General after 120-day tolling period for purposes of Section 212(a)(9)(B) of the Immigration and Nationality Act" (Mar. 3, 2000*), published on* AILA InfoNet at Doc. No. 00030774 (*posted* Mar. 7, 2000).

[66] INA §240B.

[67] *See* Letter from Pearl Chang, Branch Chief, Residence and Status Services Branch, to attorney Elliot Lichtman, HQ 70/21.1.16 (Mar. 23, 1998), *published* on AILA InfoNet at Doc. No. 98032490 (*posted* Mar. 24, 1998). The same reasoning does not apply to the ten-year bar, INA §212(a)(9)(B)(i)(II), because it does not have similar language with respect to departure before the proceedings begin. The ability to escape the three-year bar but not the ten-year bar has been upheld in *Cervantes-Ascencio v. INS*, 326 F.3d 83 (2d Cir. 2003).

[68] *See* AILF Practice Advisories on Federal Court Review at *www.ailf.org*.

Motions to Reopen or Reconsider

There is no right to appeal if the adjustment application is denied, although it is possible to file a motion to reopen or reconsider. Upon denial, the applicant has 30 days to file a motion to reopen or reconsider.[69] If the applicant can show that the delay was reasonable and beyond his or her control, USCIS has discretion to accept motions to reopen beyond the 30 days.[70] The motion to reopen or reconsider should be filed at the office that made the last decision on the application. In support of a motion to reopen, the applicant must demonstrate facts not previously available that support approval.[71] A motion to reconsider must establish that the denial was based on an incorrect application of the law or USCIS policy with regard to the evidence in the record at the time of the denial.[72]

Since a motion to reopen or reconsider could take over a year in some USCIS districts, the applicant may also opt file a new I-485 application. Though filing both a motion to reopen or reconsider and refiling the I-485 application can be burdensome, it is the only way to receive continuing work extensions and travel authorization. A pending I-485 may also help prevent further accrual of unlawful presence. If, on the other hand, the motion to reopen or reconsider leads to approval of the originally filed I-485, the subsequent application can be withdrawn.

A good example for filing such a motion is where the district adjudications officer failed to consider a financial document such as a tax return to support the Affidavit of Support, Form I-864, or where such a document has only become available since denial.

Renewal Before an Immigration Judge

The adjustment application can also be renewed before an IJ during removal proceedings.[73] Removal proceedings are initiated after an application is denied, although some districts do not have the resources to bring removal proceedings. Although the IJ has exclusive jurisdiction over an I-485 application and accompanying waivers, he or she has no jurisdiction over the immigrant visa petition.[74] The Board of Immigration Appeals (BIA) has recently held that this lack of jurisdiction extends to the application of INA §204(j),[75] dealing with I-485 portability.

Consular Processing

Finally, an applicant who is unsuccessful in AOS will want to explore the CP option. He or she will need to file Form I-824 requesting that USCIS notify the consulate in his or her home country of the approved immigrant visa petition. CP may be considered if the applicant was found to be in violation of status and is unable to seek the protection of §§245(i) or 245(k). Of course, if the applicant also faces other grounds of inadmissibility, the practitioner should consider whether the client is eligible for waivers. For instance, if the applicant was denied for fraud or misrepresentation under §212(a)(6)(C)(i) during AOS and he or she does not have a qualifying relative to apply for the waiver,[76] CP will be futile. It would be best to contest the charge of fraud or misrepresentation in removal proceedings before an IJ if there is an arguable basis for doing so.

CONCLUSION

The practitioner must take a comprehensive view of CP and AOS when advising the client, including possible remedies if the application is denied. If the client can only CP or AOS, the practitioner's job becomes that much easier. The challenge is far greater when the client can both CP and AOS; it is hoped that this article offers insight on how the practitioner can best advise a client. Finally, if the client is unable to readily AOS or CP, the insightful practitioner may still be able to find ways to make AOS or CP a reality, while cautioning the client about the attendant pitfalls and risks.

---

[69] 8 CFR §103.5(a)(1)(i).

[70] *Id.*

[71] 8 CFR §103.5(a)(2). The motion to reopen must be supported by affidavits or other documentary evidence.

[72] 8 CFR §103.5(a)(3).

[73] 8 CFR §§245.2(a)(1)(i)–(ii), 1245.2(a)(1)(i)–(ii). Denial of the application of a paroled alien allows for the renewal of the application during removal proceedings only if the application was properly filed after the applicant's inspection and admission into the United States, and the later absence from and return to the United States was under the terms of advance parole. *Id.*

[74] *Matter of Velarde-Pacheco*, 23 I&N Dec. 253 (BIA 2002).

[75] *In re Perez Vargas*, 23 I&N Dec. 829 (BIA 2005).

[76] INA §212(i) allows the applicant to waive inadmissibility under INA §212(a)(6)(C)(i) upon a showing of extreme hardship to a spouse or parent who is either a U.S. citizen or a lawful permanent resident.

PRIORITY DATES: MORE IMPORTANT THAN EVER

by Jeffrey A. Devore and Xiomara M. Hernández[*]

FINDING A PLACE IN LINE

The priority date system, while simple on its face, is one of the most complicated areas of immigration law. While immediate relatives are not subject to preference allocation, all other immigrants are. An early priority date can shave years off an alien's wait for an immigrant visa. This article offers useful tips and tricks for the immigration practitioner.

A Review of Terms

The Immigration and Nationality Act (INA)[1] defines the term "child" for immigration purposes as an unmarried person under 21 years old who meets specified criteria for legitimacy or adoption.[2] For example, a stepchild is considered a child and an immediate relative if he or she is under the age of 18 at the time the parents marry.[3] In some contexts where Congress intended to extend benefits to offspring without regard to age or marital status, the INA refers instead to "sons and daughters."[4] The terms "parent," "father," and "mother" are also defined under the INA for immigration purposes.[5]

The term "immediate relative" means the children and spouse of any U.S. citizen and the parents of a U.S. citizen who is at least 21 years old. This definition does not include sons and daughters as defined in the INA.[6] An alien married to a U.S. citizen for at least two years at the time of the citizen's death is classified as an immediate relative if the alien spouse files an immediate relative petition within two years after the date of the citizen's death and does not remarry before admission.[7] Immediate relatives, along with certain other special categories of aliens, are entitled to immigrant visas without regard to annual or per-country restrictions.[8]

The spouse or children of an alien admitted with a family-based, employment-based, or diversity-based immigrant visa also may be issued an immigrant visa in the same category if "accompanying or following to join" the spouse or parent.[9] These dependents are referred to as "derivative beneficiaries." The alien they accompany or follow to join is known as the "beneficiary" or "principal alien."

The distinction between accompanying and following to join is unimportant in determining priority dates, but an alien can only "accompany" within six months of the principal's entry.[10] In contrast, there is no statutory time period during which a following-to-join alien must apply for a visa and seek admission.[11] However, a following-to-join alien must do so while still entitled to the dependent classification being sought. For example, a following-to-join child would have to seek admission before marrying or reaching 21.[12]

[*] Updated from an article by J. Devore and M. O'Sullivan at 1 *Immigration & Nationality Law Handbook* 344 (AILA, 2002–03 ed.).

Jeffrey Devore is a shareholder in Devore & Devore, P.A., with offices in Palm Beach Gardens and Boca Raton. He received his B.S. in computer science from Bowling Green State University, and his J.D. from the Thomas M. Cooley Law School in Lansing, Mich. He is board-certified in immigration and nationality law by the Florida bar and is admitted to practice before the U.S. District Court for the Southern District of Florida and the Eleventh Circuit Court of Appeals. Mr. Devore is a past chair of the South Florida Chapter of AILA, and presently serves on the AILA National Texas Service Center Liaison and USCIS Technology Workgroup Committees.

Xiomara Hernández is an associate at Devore & Devore, P.A. Ms. Hernández received her B.S. in political science from Santa Clara University in 1996, and her J.D. from Cornell Law School in 2000. Ms. Hernández is presently cochair of the Legal Assistance Project and the Young Lawyers Division liaison for the South Florida Chapter of AILA.

[1] Immigration and Nationality Act of 1952, Pub. L. No. 82-414, 66 Stat. 163 (codified as amended at 8 USC §§1101 et seq.) (INA).

[2] INA §101(b).

[3] INA §101(b)(1)(B).

[4] INA §203(a)(1); 22 CFR §40.1(q).

[5] INA §101(b)(2).

[6] A son or daughter of a U.S. citizen would be classifiable under the 1st or 3rd preference.

[7] INA §201(b)(2)(A)(i).

[8] INA §201(b)(1)(A).

[9] INA §203(d).

[10] 22 CFR §40.1(a)(1).

[11] 9 *Foreign Affairs Manual* (FAM), N.7.1 to 22 CFR §40.1.

[12] *Id. See also Matter of Hernandez-Puente*, 20 I&N Dec. 335 (BIA 1991) (holding that adjustment of status cannot be granted *nunc pro tunc* under INA §245).

Annual Allocations

Each fiscal year (October 1 to September 30) a fixed number of immigrant visas is allocated to the family-based, employment-based, and diversity visa categories, and there is a limit as to how many may be distributed to each country. The eligibility of an alien to apply for lawful permanent residence at a consulate or adjust his or her status before the U.S. Citizenship and Immigration Services (USCIS) or the Executive Office for Immigration Review (EOIR) is determined by his or her immigration category and priority date.

Previously, the annual visa limit for the four family-sponsored preferences was fixed at 216,000 and for employment-sponsored preferences at 54,000. However, the Immigration Act of 1990 (IMMACT90)[13] created a numerical formula to determine the family preference limit each year. The maximum number of family-based lawful permanent resident (LPR) visas is now 480,000 visas per fiscal year.[14] Immediate relatives (spouse, parents, or unmarried minor children of a U.S. citizen) are exempt from numerical limits but are a principal factor in this calculation.

Since October 1, 1991, the number of family-sponsored preference immigrants worldwide is determined by subtracting from 480,000 from the number of immediate relatives who were issued immigrant visas or whose status was adjusted to permanent residence in the previous fiscal year, plus the total children who were admitted without a visa, *i.e.*, those born after an accompanying parent was issued an immediate relative visa or born to an LPR during a temporary visit abroad.[15]

IMMACT90 fixed a minimum or "floor" of 226,000 for family-based preference categories,[16] apportioned among the family-sponsored preference categories as follows:

- First (unmarried sons or daughters of U.S. citizens): 23,400 (10.35 percent)

- Second (spouses, children, and unmarried sons or daughters of LPRs): 114,200 (50.53 percent); subdivided between:

  - (2A) spouses and children, 77 percent;

  - (2B) sons/daughters (21 years old and above), 23 percent

- Third (married sons or daughters of citizens): 23,400 (10.35 percent)

- Fourth (brothers and sisters of citizens): 65,000 (28.77 percent).

If the worldwide annual limit exceeds the 226,000 minimum, all additional numbers will be added to the second preference figure.[17] Numbers that cannot be used in one preference will fall to the next. Petitions for classification in the family-based preference categories or as an immediate relative are filed using a Petition for Alien Relative (Form I-130). Other forms are used for other immigrant categories.

The annual limit in the employment-based preferences is fixed at 140,000.[18] Distribution of employment-based visas is as follows:

- First preference (priority workers): 40,000 (28.6 percent)[19]

- Second preference (professionals holding advanced degrees or persons of exceptional ability): 40,000 (28.6 percent)[20]

- Third preference (skilled workers, professionals, and other workers): 40,000 (28.6 percent)[21]

- Fourth preference (certain special immigrants): 10,000 (7.1 percent)[22]

- Fifth preference (employment creation): 10,000 (7.1 percent).[23]

Unused employment-based first preference numbers fall to second, and unused second preference numbers to third. There is no provision for additional numbers to fall into the fourth or fifth preferences but any unused fourth or fifth preference numbers "fall up" to first preference.[24] Immigrant visa petitions requesting classification in the EB-1, EB-2, and EB-3 categories are filed using an Immigrant Petition for Alien Worker (Form I-140).

---

[13] Immigration Act of 1990 (IMMACT90), Pub. L. No. 101-649, 104 Stat. 4978; 20 CFR Part 655.700.

[14] INA §201(c)(1).

[15] INA §211(a).

[16] 67 *Interpreter Releases* 1355 (Dec. 3, 1990); 67 *Interpreter Releases* 1394 (Dec. 10, 1990).

[17] INA §203(a).

[18] INA §201(d).

[19] INA §203(b)(1).

[20] INA §203(b)(2).

[21] INA §203(b)(3).

[22] INA §203(b)(4).

[23] INA §203(b)(5).

[24] INA §203(b)(1).

Chargeability

The country to which a beneficiary or applicant's permanent resident visa will be charged is crucial, particularly if a country is oversubscribed. A country is considered oversubscribed if its visa demand is more than the per-country limitation. The Department of State's monthly *Visa Bulletin* details immigrant visa availability.[25] An alien's place of birth, not country of citizenship, determines the country whose numerical limit will be charged.[26] This can lead to unusual situations. For example, persons born in a territory now controlled by a different country are charged if possible to the country that controlled the territory when they were born. Thus, a Pakistani immigrant born before Pakistan was carved out of India is subject to India's limits and must wait in line with millions of Indians.

To prevent separation of immediate relatives, the chargeability rules are by law softened to allow a family member's visa to be cross-chargeable to the country to which his or her spouse or parent is chargeable (also called "derivative" chargeability).[27] Thus, an alien spouse and children born in a country like the Philippines, for which all immigrant visas are severely backlogged, may still immigrate if the principal has a preference category that is available under, say, the Australian allocation and the cross-chargeability is necessary to prevent family separation. These derivative beneficiaries are charged to the preference category of the principal applicant.[28]

More noteworthy is the fact that an accompanying alien, though not one following to join, can confer cross or alternate chargeability on the principal.[29] For example, if an FB-4 beneficiary, who was born in a country for which no FB-4 visa numbers are currently available, is accompanied to the United States by his wife who was born in a third country, he may be issued an FB-4 visa chargeable to that third country if FB-4 numbers are available for it.[30]

RECAPTURING OLD PRIORITY DATES IN FAMILY-BASED CASES

Establishing a Priority Date

The priority date determines when an alien in a preference category is eligible to apply for permanent residence. For family-based cases, the priority date is the date a U.S. citizen properly files an I-130 with USCIS for his or her unmarried son or daughter (first preference), married son or daughter (third preference), or brother or sister (fourth preference), or an LPR files an I-130 for a spouse or unmarried son or daughter (second preference).[31] Although a petition might not be approved for years after it was filed, upon its approval, the petition's beneficiary is entitled to a priority date that was the date of filing.[32]

The relationship between a petitioner and a beneficiary can and often does change, as can the status of each. Relative petitions are valid "for the duration of the relationship to the petitioner and of the petitioner's status as established in the petition."[33] But under the INA, "children" grow up to become "sons or daughters,"[34] LPRs become citizens, marriages end, and petitioners die.

Change in Relationship

When there is a change in the relationship between the petitioner and beneficiary, or a change in the beneficiary's status is required by the particular classification, a priority date may be preserved, and a new preference classification established, without filing a new petition if the immediate succeeding petitioner/beneficiary relationship is one that would have initially supported a petition. The following examples illustrate situations where priority dates are retained or lost when, because of a change in the status of the beneficiary or petitioner, a petition must be converted to another category or revoked:

- 1st to 3rd. A U.S. citizen has an approved petition for her unmarried daughter under the first preference. The daughter later marries before being admitted as an immigrant. The petition is automatically regarded as approved under the third preference as of the date of marriage, with the original priority date retained.[35]

---

[25] See *http://travel.state.gov/visa/frvi/bulletin/bulletin_1360.html*.

[26] INA §202(b); 22 CFR §42.12(a).

[27] INA §202(b); 22 CFR §42.12(b)–(e); 9 FAM 42.12, N.2.

[28] INA §203(d).

[29] 9 FAM 40.1, N.8; 9 FAM 42.12, N.2.

[30] *Id.*

[31] 8 CFR §204.1(a); 22 CFR §42.53(a).

[32] 8 CFR §204.1(c); 22 CFR §42.53(a)

[33] 8 CFR §204.2(h)(1).

[34] *See* section titled A Review of Terms.

[35] 8 CFR §204.2(i)(1)(i).

- 3rd to 1st or Immediate Relative. A U.S. citizen has an approved petition for her married daughter under the third preference. If the daughter obtains a divorce, she will be considered to have first preference approval as of the date of the divorce, with the original priority date retained.[36] If the daughter is under 21, she will be considered an immediate relative and no longer subject to preference allocation.[37]

- 2nd to 1st or Immediate Relative. An LPR who has an approved petition to classify her unmarried daughter under the second preference is naturalized as a U.S. citizen. If the daughter is over 21, she will be considered the beneficiary of an approved first preference petition with the same priority date as the properly filed second preference petition.[38] If the daughter is under 21, she is deemed the beneficiary of an approved immediate relative petition.[39]

- 2nd to 1st to 3rd. If the daughter in the previous example marries after the petitioner's naturalization, she is deemed the beneficiary of a third preference petition with the same priority date as the original second preference petition.[40] When she obtains an immigrant visa or adjusts status, her new spouse, and their children who accompany or follow to join her, would be entitled to third preference classification with the priority date the daughter obtained when the original second preference petition was filed.[41]

- Immediate Relative to preference. An approved petition by a U.S. citizen for a child is accorded immediate relative status with no priority date. A priority date was not necessary because immediate relatives are not subject to numerical restrictions. However, when the beneficiary ceased to be a child because he or she reached the age of 21 or married, the beneficiary would be considered to be approved for preference status under either the first or third preference with the same priority date as the date the petition for immediate relative classification was filed.[42]

- Immediate Relative or preference to self-petition. A battered spouse or child who is the beneficiary of a visa petition filed on his or her behalf by the abuser can transfer the visa petition's priority date to his or her own self-petition without regard to the current validity of the visa petition.[43]

When the change of relationship or status of the immediate succeeding relationship is not one that will support a petition, no new preference is established and the priority date is lost, even if a later status change would support a petition. For example:

- 2nd to 3rd. The beneficiary of an approved second preference petition would benefit as the beneficiary of a third preference petition if he or she married *after* the petitioner's naturalization (see earlier example). But the beneficiary would lose the preference and the original priority date if he or she married *before* the petitioner naturalized, because the marriage of a second preference beneficiary results in the automatic revocation of the petition filed in his or her behalf—the second preference is available only to unmarried sons or daughters of LPRs; there is no preference category for married sons or daughters of LPRs.[44]

- Petitioner's loss of status. If a petitioner is denaturalized or loses status as an LPR through deportation, removal, or rescission, the beneficiary is no longer entitled to preference status.[45]

- Death of the petitioner. This automatically revokes any preference status unless the Attorney General in his discretion determines that revocation would be inappropriate.[46]

MAKING THE WAIT MORE BEARABLE

Who Is Eligible for a V Visa?

Congress has finally recognized that spouses and children of LPRs have an often agonizing wait before they are reunited with family members. With

---

[36] 8 CFR §204.2(i)(1)(iii).

[37] *Id.*

[38] 8 CFR §204.2(i)(3).

[39] *Id.* When a beneficiary turns 21 for immigration purposes is now often determined by the Child Status Protection Act (CSPA), discussed *infra. See also* R. Berg & R. Ng, "Stopping Time and Ignoring the Reality of Aging: The Simple Beauty of the Child Status Protection Act," elsewhere in this volume.

[40] 8 CFR §204.2(i)(1)(i).

[41] INA §203(d).

[42] 8 CFR §204.2(i)(2).

[43] 8 CFR §204.2(h)(2).

[44] 8 CFR §§205.1(a)(3)(i)(I), 1205.1(a)(3)(i)(I).

[45] 8 CFR §§205.1(a)(3)(i)(J), 1205.1(a)(3)(i)(J).

[46] 8 CFR §§205.1(a)(3)(i)(C), 1205.1(a)(3)(i)(C).

the passage of the LIFE Act,[47] Congress created the V visa, allowing the spouse and children of an LPR to enter the United States and obtain employment authorization while they await an immigrant visa. Unfortunately, while helpful, the V visa has limited application.

There are two basic requirements that must be satisfied for an alien to obtain a V visa:

1. The LPR spouse or parent must have filed an immigrant visa petition (I-130) on or before December 21, 2000, under the F2A preference category; and

2. The I-130 must have been pending for three years or more or the petition has must have been approved and three years passed since the date of filing in either of the following circumstances:

   a. An immigrant visa number is not yet available to the beneficiary; or

   b. If an immigrant visa number is available, the beneficiary's application for an immigrant visa abroad or application for adjustment of status is still pending.

An eligible spouse of an LPR will be classified as V-1, an eligible child as V-2. The child of either, if eligible to accompany or follow to join the principal alien, will be classified as V-3.[48]

However, the LIFE Act explicitly limited the benefits of the V visa to beneficiaries who had an immigrant visa petition filed on their behalf on or before December 21, 2000. Those whose immigrant visa petitions were filed after that date are ineligible for V visas, as are adult children of LPRs.[49]

The regulations have an age-out provision: a child's V-2 or V-3 status terminates the day before his or her 21st birthday.[50] In 2004, the Ninth Circuit invalidated the age-out provision as contrary to con-gressional intent.[51] On May 16, 2005, the Department of Homeland Security (DHS), acquiescing to the Ninth Circuit's decision, announced that the age-out provision no longer applies to aliens who were *previously* granted V-2 or V-3 status.[52] Consequently, an alien who is physically present in the United States and was previously granted V-2 or V-3 status can now apply for an extension of that status if his or her application for extension had been denied because he or she had aged out. An alien who did not even apply for an extension of V-2 or V-3 status because he or she had aged out also may apply to extend the status.[53] An alien in V-2 or V-3 status now may extend that V status until he or she becomes an LPR, but will lose V-2 or V-3 status if he or she marries because he or she will no longer meet the statutory definition of a child.[54]

Application Procedure

Alien Beneficiary in the United States

The alien beneficiary must file an Application to Change Nonimmigrant Status (Form I-539) with USCIS but need not be lawfully present to request a change to V status.[55]

An alien applying for V nonimmigrant status should submit proof of filing of the immigrant petition that qualifies him or her for V status (*e.g.*, a priority date on or before December 21, 2000). This may include a copy of the Notice of Action (Form I-797C), a Notice of Approval (Form I-797B), or a receipt from a local USCIS office. If official notices are not available, USCIS will consider other forms of evidence, such as correspondence with USCIS about a pending petition.[56]

If an alien who appears to be eligible for V nonimmigrant status is currently in removal, deportation or exclusion proceedings, the practitioner should file

---

[47] Legal Immigration Family Equity Act (LIFE), Pub. L. No. 106-553, 114 Stat. 2762, Title XI of HR 5548 (Dec. 21, 2000), H. Rep. No. 106-1005 at 185; 2000 H.R. 4942 and LIFE Act Amendments, Pub. L. No. 106-554, 114 Stat. 2763, Title XV, Division B, of H.R. 5666 (Dec. 21, 2000), H. Rep. Conf. 106-1033; 146 Cong. Rec. S11850-02 (daily ed. Dec. 15, 2000–Senator's Joint Memorandum).

[48] 8 CFR §214.15(a).

[49] INA §101(a)(15)(V).

[50] 8 CFR §214.15(g).

[51] *Akhtar v. Burzynski*, 384 F.3d. 1193 (9th Cir. 2004), *published on* AILA InfoNet at Doc. No. 04102260 (*posted* Oct. 22, 2004).

[52] Memo, O'Reilly, Director Field Operations, USCIS, (Jan. 10, 2005), *published on* AILA InfoNet at Doc. 05020460 (*posted* Feb. 4, 2005).

[53] U.S. Department of Homeland Security, Press office, Press Release, "USCIS Announces New Policy Regarding V Status Extensions," May 16, 2005, *published on* AILA InfoNet at Doc. No. 05051761 (*posted* May 17, 2005).

[54] *Id.*

[55] 8 CFR §248.1(b).

[56] 8 CFR §214.15(f)(2).

a motion with the immigration court or Board of Immigration Appeals (BIA) (whichever venue is appropriate) to administratively close the proceedings in order to allow the alien to pursue the application for V nonimmigrant status with USCIS. If the court or BIA finds that the alien appears to be eligible for V status, the proceedings will be closed. If USCIS later finds that the alien is ineligible for V status, it may file a motion to recalendar the proceedings.[57] The wording of this regulation would appear to preclude the U.S. Immigration Customs Enforcement's (ICE) Office of the Chief Counsel from requiring that an application to change status be approved before administratively closing the proceedings.

The LIFE amendments did not contain any special provisions for reopening proceedings where an alien is already subject to a final order or removal, deportation, or exclusion. It would therefore appear that the rules on motions to reopen before the court[58] and the BIA[59] would apply. Both have time and numerical limitations on the filing of motions to reopen.

The regulations do, however, provide for an exception to a motion to reopen filed jointly with the Office of the Chief Counsel. Therefore, practitioners should contact that office to ask whether it will join them in a motion. If USCIS is unwilling to do so, the practitioner may wish to simply file the motion anyway, arguing a change in the law has made relief available. Since the *INS v. St. Cyr*[60] decision, the immigration courts and BIA have been more liberal in granting such motions.

Alien Beneficiary Outside of the United States

An alien applicant outside the United States must apply for a V visa at a U.S. consulate abroad. The regulations do not require that USCIS approve the alien's V visa petition or application before he or she applies for a visa. The applicant must apply at the consular post designated as the processing post in the underlying immigrant visa petition.[61]

The Department of State has interpreted the phrase an "application for a visa remains pending"

to mean that an alien has applied for an immigrant visa (*i.e.*, has personally appeared before a consular officer and submitted all forms, documents, and fees required) but no decision has been made to issue a visa or refuse the application.[62] In practice, most immigrant visa cases are either granted or refused on the day of interview, so once an alien is interviewed about the immigrant visa application, he or she will no longer be eligible for a V visa.

Termination of V Status

An alien's V status automatically terminates 30 days after any of the following:

1. The denial, withdrawal, or revocation of the I-130 filed on behalf of the alien;[63] or

2. The denial or withdrawal of the alien's application for an immigrant visa;[64] or

3. The denial or withdrawal of the alien's application for adjustment of status to that of a lawful permanent resident;[65] or

4. The V-1 spouse's divorce from the LPR becomes final;[66] or

5. An alien in V-2 or V-3 status marries.[67]

When a V-1 or V-2 alien's status is terminated, the status of any dependents in V-3 status is also terminated.[68] However, if the denial of the immigrant visa petition is appealed, the alien's V nonimmigrant status does not terminate until 30 days after any administrative appeal is dismissed.[69]

If the LPR petitioner who filed the I-130 naturalizes, V status for any spouse or children terminates at the end of the current admission period,[70] but the alien spouse and child will be considered immediate relatives[71] and eligible for adjustment of status.

---

[57] 8 CFR §214.15(l).

[58] 8 CFR §1003.23.

[59] 8 CFR. §1003.2.

[60] 533 U.S. 289 (2001), *published on* AILA InfoNet at Doc. No. 01062601 (*posted* July 2, 2001).

[61] 22 CFR §41.86(d).

[62] 22 CFR §41.86(a).

[63] 8 CFR §214.15(j)(1)(i).

[64] 8 CFR §214.15(j)(1)(ii).

[65] 8 CFR §214.15(j)(1)(iii).

[66] 8 CFR §214.15(j)(1)(iv).

[67] 8 CFR §214.15(j)(1)(v).

[68] 8 CFR §214.15(j)(2).

[69] 8 CFR §214.15(j)(3).

[70] 8 CFR §214.15(k).

[71] INA §201(b).

RETENTION OF PRIORITY DATES
IN EMPLOYMENT-BASED CASES

For years, most aliens immigrating through an employment-based category did not have to wait long to apply for permanent residence because the priority dates for the employment-based categories were current. Unfortunately, those days are all but over. In October 2005, the State Department's *Visa Bulletin* announced that the annual numerical limits for employment-based categories would be reached; causing a retrogression of visa numbers in the various categories. Since an immigrant visa cannot be issued unless the applicant's priority date is current, the retrogression of visa numbers means that aliens immigrating through the employment-based categories, particularly from India and China, have to wait a lot longer before they can apply to adjust their status or apply for an immigrant visa at the consulate abroad. Thus, establishing or retaining a priority date for these aliens is essential.

Establishing a Priority Date

As set forth in 8 CFR §204.5(d), the priority date in employment-based cases is the date the Department of Labor (DOL) accepts the labor certification application for processing. If no labor certification is required, the priority date is the date the I-140 is properly filed with USCIS.[72]

Recapturing an Old Priority Date for the Employee

The priority date remains with the job until the alien's I-140 is approved. An individual who loses the job offer while the labor certification is pending or before the I-140 is approved will lose the priority date of that labor certification or I-140. If, however, the alien loses the job offer or changes jobs *after* the I-140 is approved, the alien, not the employer, retains the old priority date.[73]

Under 8 CFR §204.5(e), employees can retain the original priority date of an approved I-140 and apply it to any petition later approved for employment-based first, second, or third preference.[74] The regulations do not require that the later job be in the same preference category as the original labor certification or I-140. It is only necessary that the job fall within one of the employment-based preferences (first, sec-ond, or third).[75] However, if the job requires a labor certification, the alien will have to obtain a new labor certification to recapture the priority date of the first I-140 petition.

To recapture the priority date, an alien must submit a copy of the I-140 approval notice from the original job with the subsequent I-140 and labor certification (if the new job requires it) and request recapture of the earlier priority date. The USCIS approval notice of the later petition will have the priority date of the original I-140 as the priority date.

For example, Mr. Patel is the beneficiary of an approved labor certification and visa petition filed by the Greencard County Library on January 1, 1995. After waiting five years for his priority date to become current, the library has to cut personnel and Mr. Patel is informed that his services are no longer needed. If Mr. Patel obtains an offer of employment from a new employer, he can retain his January 1, 1995, priority date, so long as the new employer obtains a new labor certification and visa petition on his behalf—whether or not the new job is the same as the one Mr. Patel had with Greencard County Library. Thus, it is always worth asking the alien, particularly during times of retrogression, if a labor certification and visa petition was ever filed on his or her behalf in the past. If the alien has a priority date under INA §§203(b)(1)–(3) but the priority date is currently backlogged, check to see whether he or she may qualify for one of the other categories and recapture the date.

Retention of the Priority Date for the Employer

The employer retains the priority date until the employment-based petition is approved. Thus, if Mr. Patel quits his job with the Greencard County Library while certification is pending, the library can use that labor certification to file a visa petition for another alien to work in the job that has been certified. The new beneficiary must have met the requirements of education and experience specified on the certification at the time the original labor certification was filed (and the priority date established).[76]

---

[72] 8 CFR §204.5(d).

[73] 8 CFR §204.5(e).

[74] INA §§203(b)(1), (2), or (3).

[75] 8 CFR §204.5(e).

[76] On February 13, 2006, the Department of Labor published a proposed rule that would eliminate substitution of labor certification beneficiaries and impose a 45-day validity period on approved labor certifications. 71 Fed. Reg. 7656 (Feb. 13, 2006), *published on* AILA InfoNet at Doc. No. 06021312 (*posted* Feb. 13, 2006).

The practitioner must file the original labor certification with the I-140 for the new beneficiary with proof of the required experience and ask to substitute the new beneficiary in the abandoned certification. If successful, the new beneficiary will be given the priority date of the old certification.

For example, ABC Exports files a labor certification for its financial manager, Ms. Lopez, on January 1, 1995. The certification is approved but Ms. Lopez leaves before ABC Exports files the I-140 petition for her. ABC Exports then hires Mr. Cardoza as financial manager and files an I-140 petition for him with the labor certification it originally obtained for Ms. Lopez. If USCIS approves the substitution of beneficiaries, Mr. Cardoza will get Ms. Lopez's priority date of January 1, 1995.

Since the priority date remains with the job until the visa petition is approved, it is always worth asking if the employer ever filed a labor certification for the position in the past. If so, the employer may be able to use the old certification to sponsor a new employee.

Because the regulations provide that a labor certification is valid indefinitely[77] unless invalidated by fraud,[78] employers should be advised to retain any approved labor certifications that were abandoned because the intended beneficiary has changed jobs. The employer can use that abandoned certification when another beneficiary is found to fill the certified job. Keep in mind that this is only possible if the new beneficiary possesses the required education and experience on the date that labor certification was accepted for processing.

The substitution of beneficiaries can be very useful to shorten the immigration process for an H-1B who is running out of time or an employee who has aging-out children.

Promoted Workers or Those Transferred to Another Location

Individuals whose jobs change due to a promotion or a transfer can also retain their old priority dates. Unfortunately, they still need to obtain a new labor certification if the new job requires one. If it does not (as with the employment-based first preference), the individual could skip the second labor certification. In either case, the first priority date is recaptured when the second visa petition is approved

I-140 Portability Under the American Competitiveness in the Twenty-First Century Act

In §106(c) the American Competitiveness in the Twenty-First Century Act of 2000 (AC21)[79] establishes that the beneficiary of an approved I-140, who has filed an I-485 that has been pending for more than 180 days, can transfer or "port" the approved I-140 application to a new employer. Thus, an alien whose I-485 is affected by retrogression can change jobs so long as the new position is the "same or similar" to the position in the initial I-140.[80]

For example, California Gallery Inc. files a labor certification in 1999 on behalf of an employee, Mr. O'Malley, as a market research analyst that is approved. On April 20, 2001, the gallery files an I-140 on behalf of Mr. O'Malley, who concurrently files an I-485. Four years later, on April 20, 2005, USCIS approves the I-140 petition but does not adjudicate the I-485. In the meantime, Florida Gallery Inc. offers Mr. O'Malley a position as a market research analyst. Since Mr. O'Malley is the beneficiary of an approved I-140 and his I-485 has been pending more than 180 days, he can port his I-140 to his new employer, so long as he will be performing the "same or similar" duties as those described in the initial I-140 filed by California Gallery Inc.

For purposes of I-140 portability under AC21, a job will be considered the same or similar as long as the duties of the new position are the same as or similar to the duties described in the ETA 750A or the initial I-140.[81] USCIS adjudicators may also consider the *Dictionary of Occupational Titles* (DOT) code or the Standard Occupational Classification (SOC) code assigned to the position in the initial I-140 and compare it to the new position to determine whether it is the same or similar.[82]

Accordingly, AC21 §106(c) allows an alien who has an approved I-140 but whose I-485 application is affected by retrogression to change jobs without jeopardizing the pending I-485. The portability provision also facilitates the petitioning process for employers of aliens who are eligible for porting because the employer is not

---

[77] *Id.*

[78] 20 CFR §656.30.

[79] American Competitiveness and Workforce Improvement Act of 1998, Pub. L. No. 105-277, 112 Stat. 2681 (div. C, title IV).

[80] Memo, Yates, Assoc. Dir. for Operations, HQPRD70/6.2.8-P (May 12, 2005), *published on* AILA InfoNet at Doc. 05051810 (*posted* May 18, 2005).

[81] *Id.*

[82] *Id.*

required to file a new petition with USCIS. For the most part, the new employer need only submit a job offer letter because there is no requirement that the new employer show an ability to pay.[83]

Under AC21 §106(c), an alien can port on an unapproved I-140, so long as it was filed concurrently with the I-485 application and the I-485 has been pending for more than 180 days. However, the alien must be advised that although he or she can take a new job, the initial I-140 must still be approved. If the initial I-140 is denied, the I-485 and portability request will also be denied because "there never was an approved I-140 from which to port."[84] Aliens who port on a pending I-140 thus assume certain risks. For example, USCIS may issue a Request for Evidence (RFE) for the initial I-140 and the previous employer may not respond. It is therefore necessary to advise clients of the possible ramifications of porting on a pending I-140.

No Retention of Priority Date
If No Visa Petition Approval

If the visa petition is denied or the approval is revoked, the individual will lose the priority date[85] and cannot recapture it even if a the same employer files a later petition the same employee in the same job.

The Impact of INA §245(i)[86]

USCIS has stated that multiple beneficiaries will not be grandfathered under §245(i)[87] but only the alien who was the beneficiary of the labor certification filed before April 30, 2001. Thus, although a new beneficiary may be substituted into an abandoned labor certification filed under §245(i), the new beneficiary will not be grandfathered, even though he or she may gain the benefit of that priority date.

CHILD STATUS PROTECTION ACT

The Child Status Protection Act (CSPA) amends the INA to allow a child to retain "child" status for immigration purposes despite "aging out" (turning 21). CSPA became effective on August 6, 2002.[88] Because it is not retroactive, it applies only to aliens who aged out on or after August 6, 2002.[89] Someone who aged out earlier may be covered under CSPA in the following two circumstances:

- The alien had a petition pending on August 6, 2002; or,

- The petition was approved and an immigrant visa or adjustment application was filed on or before August 6, 2002, and no final determination was made before August 6, 2002.[90]

CSPA benefits immediate relatives by locking in the age of the beneficiary as of the date the I-130 petition is properly filed.[91] Thus, if a U.S. citizen mother files an I-130 for her 20-year old daughter, the daughter retains child status and can immigrate as an immediate relative even if her adjustment application is not adjudicated until she is 23.

The CPSA age of children who immigrate as the child of an LPR or a derivative beneficiary of a family-based petition is calculated by subtracting the age of the child on the date the priority date becomes current less the number of days the I-130 petition is pending (the date the of the I-130 approval minus the date the I-130 was properly filed). If the age is locked in at less than 21, the alien retains the child status and may obtain permanent residence as a child, provided he or she remains unmarried. Note that the CSPA age is not locked-in unless the alien applies for an immigrant visa or adjustment of status within one year of the immigrant visa becoming available.[92]

CSPA also allows a child who is the derivative beneficiary of an employment-based petition to retain child status despite having turned 21.[93] The CSPA age is calculated by determining the age of the child when the priority date becomes current and subtracting the number of days the I-140 was pending (approval of the I-140 minus the date the I-140 was properly filed). As in the family-based cases, the alien must apply for an immigrant visa or adjustment of status within a year of visa availability.

---

[83] *Id.*

[84] *Id.*

[85] 8 CFR §204.5(e).

[86] INA §245(i).

[87] 8 CFR §245.10(j); 66 Fed. Reg. 16383 (Mar. 26, 2001).

[88] Child Status Protection Act, Pub. L. No. 107-208, 116 Stat. 927 (Aug. 6, 2002).

[89] *Id* at §8. *See also* Memo, Williams, Exec. Assoc. Comm. Office of Field Operations, INS, HQADN 70/6.1.1 (Feb. 14, 2003), *published on* AILA InfoNet at Doc. No. 03031040 (*posted* Mar. 10, 2003).

[90] CSPA §8.

[91] CSPA §2.

[92] CSPA §3.

[93] *Id.*

The calculation for determining the CSPA age is directly affected when priority dates retrogress. Where the visa availability date retrogresses and an I-485 is pending, USCIS will not be able to adjudicate the I-485. USCIS will retain the file and write the priority date that was current when the I-485 was filed. When the priority date becomes current for the alien's preference category, USCIS will calculate the alien's CSPA age by using the visa availability date noted on the I-485 in its calculation.[94] However, if an alien is the beneficiary of an approved I-130 or I-140 but has not filed an I-485 when his or her priority date retrogresses, USCIS will use the subsequent visa availability date to determine CSPA age.[95] Since the CSPA calculation depends on how long the I-140 is pending and the retrogression of priority dates will usually be much longer than the number of days the I-140 will be pending, most children will not qualify for CSPA protections and practitioners will need to look to other alternatives.

CONCLUSION

The priority date system determines when a client is eligible to apply to become an LPR. It is therefore crucial that every practitioner understand how the priority date system works. Regardless of whether your client is applying to adjust status or for an immigrant visa at the consulate abroad, what he or she wants most is to get a Green Card as soon as possible. Sometimes things happen that can speed up the client's priority date, such as the petitioner in a family-based case becoming a U.S. citizen. Similarly, sometimes things happen that cause delays, such as the retrogression of visa numbers. This article has sought to provide practitioners with alternatives to assist their clients in reaching or at least retaining a priority date so that they may obtain their goal of becoming lawful permanent residents.

---

[94] Williams memo, *supra* note 89.

[95] *Id.*

PULLING THE RABBIT OUT OF THE HAT
USING WESTERN HEMISPHERE PRIORITY DATES TO MOVE BUSINESS AND FAMILY-BASED IMMIGRATION

by Kathrin S. Mautino[*]

In this era of backlogs in every family-based preference category and of increasing backlogs in employment-based categories, it is important for practitioners to be familiar with all the legal tools for advancing the cases of their clients. Along with the provisions for cross-chargeability, the old Western Hemisphere Priority Date (WHPD) program is one of the often overlooked tools in the workshop.[1] While it does not solve priority date issues for every client, it is still useful for the potential immigrant population. This article will review the WHPD program and offer practical guidance on moving a case forward when an early priority date is found.

HISTORICAL BACKGROUND

Before 1921,[2] there were no numerical restrictions on immigrants. By 1924, the "national origins" quota system was imposed, favoring immigrants from Western European countries.[3] However, no quotas at all were imposed on nationals of independent countries of the Western Hemisphere, such as Canada, Mexico, Brazil, and Peru.

The 1952 Act[4] continued the national origins quota system, including the absence of quotas on Western Hemisphere natives. It was not until the numerical system was completely changed in 1965 that restrictions were placed on natives of independent Western Hemisphere countries.[5] Backlogs soon developed because the government wrongly charged Cuban citizens eligible to adjust through a different law to the Western Hemisphere quota.[6]

The Western Hemisphere numerical cap went into effect on July 1, 1968. It differed greatly from the numerical preference system familiar to immigration practitioners today, or for that matter the separate numerical restrictions then in place for the rest of the world. All Western Hemisphere immigrants, regardless of the qualifying method of immigration, were placed in the same category.[7]

In 1976, new laws moved the Western Hemisphere countries into the established preference system,[8] but a savings clause preserved the old priority date for individuals who qualified and registered to immigrate before January 1, 1977.[9] This savings clause still allows certain individuals almost instant immigration to the United States today.[10]

THE 1976 SAVINGS CLAUSE

Individuals who registered under the WHPD system retain that priority date until they use it. The priority date can be used in conjunction with *any* properly approved visa petition filed on behalf of the alien, including both family and employment-based petitions. The petition is deemed to have been filed on the Western Hemisphere date previously obtained.[11] Often individuals who have a WHPD are also covered by Immigration and Naturalization Act

---

[*] **Kathrin Mautino** is a partner with Mautino and Mautino in San Diego, where her practice focuses on immigration and nationality law. She is one of fewer than 200 attorneys certified as a specialist in immigration and nationality law by the state bar of California. Ms. Mautino writes and speaks frequently on immigration-related issues to local, regional, and national groups.

[1] *See generally* R. Mautino, "Save the Western Hemisphere Priority Date Program," 71 *Interpreter Releases* 513–21 (April 18, 1994).

[2] The Act of May 19, 1921, 42 Stat.5, contained the first immigration quota.

[3] Act of May 26, 1924, 43 Stat. 153.

[4] Immigration and Nationality Act of 1952, Pub. L. No. 82-414, 66 Stat. 163 (codified as amended at 8 USC §§1101–1524) (INA).

[5] Act of October 3, 1965 sec. 21(e), Pub. L. No. 89-236, 79 Stat. 911.

[6] Cuban Adjustment Act of November 2, 1966, Pub. L. No. 89-732, 80 Stat. 1161.

[7] U.S. Dept of State, 9 *Foreign Affairs Manual* (FAM) N.5.5 to 22 CFR §42.53.

[8] Immigration and Nationality Act Amendments of 1976, Pub. L. No. 94-571, 90 Stat. 2703, 2707.

[9] *Id*. at §9(b). *See generally* 53 *Interpreter Releases* 411–12 (Dec. 16, 1976).

[10] 9 FAM N.5.5 to 22 CFR §42.53.

[11] *Id*.

(INA) §245(i), which gives them a second form of relief from some of the harsher consequences of our present laws.

HOW PRIORITY DATES WERE ESTABLISHED

Between 1968 and 1976, individuals established eligibility for immigration by showing the consular officer that (1) they had a labor certification, (2) they were exempt from the labor certification requirement, or (3) the labor certification did not apply to them.[12] How individuals registered to immigrate varied by category and will be discussed in detail below.

Though most of the immigration categories that existed between 1968 and 1976 are similar to immigrant categories available today, there were some important differences. Spouses, parents, and children of U.S. citizens and lawful permanent residents were exempt from the labor certification requirement. Therefore, parents of American citizens could register to immigrate, as could parents of lawful permanent residents.

Immediate Relatives

Immediate relatives were exempt from numerical limitation and labor certification requirements, as they are today. Unlike present law, however, derivative beneficiaries of the immediate relative were granted derivative priority dates.[13] The priority date was the date on which the I-130 was filed.

Other Relatives of U.S. Citizens

In order to bring in other relatives, a U.S. citizen filed Department of State Form FS-497 with proof of the qualifying relationship with the U.S. consular office. The date the FS-497 was received there became the priority date, which was normally stamped on the form itself by the consulate.

Relatives of Lawful Permanent Residents

Parents, spouses, and children of lawful permanent residents qualified to immigrate to the United States, so in theory a permanent resident could file the same Form FS-497. For some unknown reason, however, lawful permanent residents were required to file Form I-550 (verification of lawful permanent residence) with INS. Again, the date INS received the I-550 became the priority date. INS then forwarded the approved form to the appropriate consular office.

Labor Certifications and Persons Who Would Not Be Employed

An approved labor certification or a showing that the applicant was on the Department of Labor's Schedule A[14] constituted registration for immigration. The priority date was the date the labor certification was filed, or the date on which the consular officer received the documentation supporting Schedule A classification.[15]

Investors and others who would not be employed in the United States filed Form FS-497 and supporting documents with the consular officer. Again, the priority date was the date on which the consular official was accepted and approved the FS-497.

Derivative Family Members

As is the case today, spouses and children were eligible to immigrate with the principal applicant. The spouse and legitimate unmarried minor children received the same priority date as the principal.[16] The spouse retained the priority date even if the marriage was later terminated.[17] The children retained the priority date even after marriage or reaching age 21.[18]

Children Born After WHPD Registration

Children who were born to a marriage that existed at the time a priority date was established were also entitled to that priority date.[19] Thus, a child can have a priority date that precedes his or her date of birth. These children, too, retain the priority date even after marriage or reaching age 21.

---

[12] 22 CFR §42.61(a) (1970). *See generally* 34 Fed. Reg. 4964 (Mar. 7, 1969).

[13] *See Barajas v. Shultz*, No. 87-0870-E-(IEG) (S.D. Cal. Filed June 15, 1987), *reported in* 65 *Interpreter Releases* 617 (June 13, 1988).

[14] 20 CFR §656.10 (1970).

[15] 22 CFR §42.62(b)(1) (1970). *See generally* 34 Fed. Reg. 4964 (Mar. 7, 1969).

[16] 22 CFR §42.62(d) (1970).

[17] 9 FAM N.6.1 to 22 CFR §42.53.

[18] 9 FAM N.5.5, 6.1 to 22 CFR §42.53.

[19] 9 FAM N.5.5, 6.2 to 22 CFR §42.53; 22 CFR 42.62(d) (1970).

After-Acquired Spouse of a Permanent Resident

Normally, a spouse acquired after a priority date cannot benefit from it,[20] but there was one exception: If the couple married outside the United States while the permanent resident was temporarily absent from the United States, the spouse acquired as his or her priority date the date of the marriage.[21] A child born to that marriage, immigrating alone, received his or her date of birth as the priority date.

On August 31, 1978, TL-930 cancelled the part of the *Foreign Affairs Manual* that provided this benefit. It is unclear how this cancellation affects otherwise eligible children who were born after January 1, 1977.

COMMON EXAMPLES OF WHPD REGISTRATION

Most practitioners do not believe that WHPDs could possibly apply to their clients, but there are some common situations where WHPDs are available and can be used.

Husband Immigrates and Leaves Wife and Children in Home Country

This was a common situation especially along the U.S./Mexico border. Although a significant number of Mexican citizens came to the United States as nonimmigrant workers, many also applied to immigrate, either through a job offer or a qualifying relative. For various reasons, they often decided that the children and the caregiving spouse would stay in Mexico. Because there was a marriage that existed when the principal immigrated, the spouse and all children of that marriage, including later-born children, receive a WHPD. In theory, if the spouse and children could have immigrated with the principal, generally they received a WHPD registration.

Illegitimate children could not immigrate with the principal applicant. Thus, children from a "second family" were not given the benefit of a WHPD registration even if they were listed on the consular forms. Generally, illegitimate children had to be legitimated before they could be considered part of the family for derivative WHPD purposes. Legitimation is a matter of local law; practitioners are urged to research the law of the country at the time of the

potential WHPD registration to determine if derivative benefits flowed to illegitimate children.

Also, children who had reached 21 or who married before the parent's WHPD was established did not derive registration through the immigration of the parent.

Wife Applies to Immigrate but Did Not Meet the Public Charge Provisions

A failure to complete the immigration process did not cancel the priority date. Individuals who applied to immigrate and were found not to qualify for some reason generally did not lose the priority date. Similarly, individuals who changed their minds and decided not to immigrate after they were registered retained their priority date.

It is different situation where the immigration process was not completed because of a fraudulent relationship between the petitioner and beneficiary. In that situation, the visa registration would normally be voided ab initio, so there would be no priority date.

Derivative children and spouse received a WHPD even where they were not listed as immigrating with the parent/spouse.

Husband Files I-550 for Wife Only

This situation arises both in the stepparent/stepchild relationship and where, for whatever reason, it was decided to leave children at home in the care of other relatives. Here, the children receive WHPDs as the derivative beneficiaries of the mother, even if the mother does not immigrate to the United States.

Where the beneficiary is the father, his legitimate children also would derive a WHPD, though normally illegitimate children would not unless the father had taken action to legitimate them before the WHPD was set.

Wife Files an I-550 for Husband and an I-550 for a Child

It is possible for an individual to receive more than one WHPD registration. In this situation, the child would receive a direct registration due to the I-550 filed on his or her behalf, and a second registration as the derivative of the I-550 filed on behalf of the husband.

Remember, an individual retains a WHPD until it is used. Only when an individual immigrates using a WHPD is that priority date extinguished. Thus, individuals who did immigrate before 1977 cannot re-use

---

[20] 9 FAM N.6.3 to 22 CFR §42.53.

[21] 9 FAM N.2.3 to 22 CFR §42.62 (TL-801) (Sept. 20, 1971) *quoted in* 71 *Interpreter Releases* 515–16 (Apr. 18, 1994).

their registration if they abandoned their residency status. However, children especially had more than one priority date because of their status as a derivative in a parent's application.

Husband Immigrates When Single and Later Marries

The "after-acquired" spouse received a WHPD if the permanent resident (1) married the spouse outside the United States while (2) temporarily away from the United States. In other words, the permanent resident had to have a residency in the United States at the time of the marriage. Individuals who commuted from Mexico or Canada did not maintain permanent residency in the United States and their spouses generally did not benefit from the WHPD provision. Again, the WHPD for the spouse was the date of marriage to the permanent resident.

Note again that the WHPD survives the death of the marriage. If the permanent resident spouse later died or if the parties divorced or otherwise terminated the marriage, the nonresident spouse maintained the date of marriage as the priority date.

A stepchild or a child born to the parties before their marriage and accompanying the spouse would also receive the date of the marriage as the WHPD. For children born to the marriage later, their date of birth would be the WHPD registration date if they did not immigrate as their parent's derivative. It is still an open question whether a child born to an otherwise qualifying marriage after the Department of State revoked the regulation in 1978 would receive any benefit.

Applicant Had a Labor Certification Approved When Single but Married Before Immigrating

As is the law today, the family of a principal applicant is entitled to immigrate by either accompanying the principal or following to join him or her. As is also the law today, as long as the marriage took place before the principal immigrated, the spouse and children received the same priority date as the principal. Again, if the family remained outside the United States, any after-born children of the marriage also received the priority date of the principal, so their priority date may predate their date of birth.

Son or Daughter Registers Father

Unlike the law today, derivative beneficiaries of an immediate relative also received a WHPD. Thus, where an adult child who was a U.S. citizen petitioned for the father, the father's spouse would re-

ceive the same WHPD, as would other legitimate children of the father (including stepchildren).

Remember that the spouse of a parent may or may not be the other parent of the petitioning son or daughter. If the child's parents never married, or if their marriage terminated before the child filed the petition, no derivative benefits would flow to the other biological parent. In that situation, the child would have to file a separate petition for the other biological parent in order to establish a WHPD.

Here again, it is possible for an individual to receive multiple priority dates. A son or daughter who petitioned to immigrate both parents individually would have registered both parents twice (assuming the parents were married to each other). Each parent would receive a WHPD through the direct registration by the child and a derivative registration through the spouse. Other qualifying children (legitimate, unmarried, and under 21) would also receive two derivative registrations, one through each parent.

Parent of U.S. Citizen Registers to Immigrate

Under the law at the time, parents of minor U.S. citizens could register to immigrate, as could parents of lawful permanent residents without needing the cooperation of the qualifying relative. Thus, if a child was born in the United States on Monday (making that child a United States citizen), the parents could go to an American consulate on Tuesday and register to immigrate. The parent would file form FS-497 with proof of the relationship to the U.S. citizen child. Again, as discussed above, there would be derivative registrations for the spouse of the registered parent and other legitimate unmarried minor children.

Parent Immigrates Before There Was a Western Hemisphere Limitation

Numerical limitations on Western Hemisphere immigrants began in 1968, and it might be logical to assume that WHPDs could not be established before then. However, State Department regulations allowed individuals who registered for immigration before 1968 to retain their original priority dates in the WHPD category. In effect, the rules for WHPD registration remained the same.

EXAMPLES OF WHPDS TODAY

Although individuals who applied to immigrate before 1977 still appear in my office, the vast majority of WHPDs involve derivative registrants who were unaware of their registration and their own family members. Quite often, these are children of individuals who registered but either never completed the immigration process or who never sought to bring in the children. Some case histories show how WHPD registration can appear today.

Child of a Marriage That Existed at the Time of Immigration

José Juan had applied for "late amnesty" and just recently received a denial from the AAO. He owns his own trucking business and wonders if he, his wife, Alma, and two children, age 14 and 12, can apply for permanent immigration or possibly E visas through the company. In the course of our conversation, Alma mentions that her father had immigrated in 1958. Alma's father and mother had married in 1954. Alma is one of seven children born between 1956 and 1970. Alma was born in 1963. One of Alma's sisters had become a naturalized U.S. citizen, as had one of José Juan's brothers. José Juan's brother had filed a 4th preference family petition on behalf of José Juan on April 20, 2001. Alma's father died in 1980.

After discussing the matter, Alma goes to her mother's house and starts digging through old papers. She discovers her father's permanent resident card, showing an admission date of May 1, 1958.

Analysis: Alma is entitled to a WHPD of at least May 1, 1958, because she was born to a marriage that existed when her father immigrated. Her actual priority date is earlier, because it would be the date that a FS-497, labor certification, or petition was filed and approved on behalf of her father. However, since documentation of the earlier priority date would be difficult to find, the State Department allows for the use of the date of immigration as the priority date for derivative beneficiaries.[22] As all family and employment-based categories have visa cut-offs well after 1977, the use of a later date of immigration does not hurt Alma and her family.

The State Department says that WHPDs cannot be cross-charged to another spouse,[23] but, this view is not supported by Board of Immigration Appeals precedent[24] and has been successfully challenged by immigration practitioners. Nevertheless, to avoid

conflict with the U. S. Citizenship and Immigration Services (USCIS), even though José Juan had a pending I-130, Alma's sister prepared a new petition and filed it concurrently with the I-485s for José Juan, Alma, and their two children. José Juan's §245(i) eligibility did, of course, cover the whole family and they were able to adjust in the United States.

Note that all of Alma's brothers and sisters are entitled to WHPDs, as are their spouses and unmarried minor children. As this example shows, quite often WHPDs can help a large family group.

Child of an After-Acquired Spouse

Agustin had gone to a "visa fixer" who promised him that he qualified for permanent resident status because he had lived in the United States for 10 years and his father was a lawful permanent resident. The visa fixer surrendered Agustin and many of his friends to the USCIS to initiate removal proceedings and allow Agustin to apply for suspension of deportation. Although Agustin met the minimum qualifications, his father actually resided in Mexico and did not rely on Agustin for financial support. Many of Agustin's friends who went to the visa fixer did not qualify for suspension but were nonetheless surrendered to USCIS.

The visa fixer was a fraud, and the Border Patrol had talked to Agustin and his friends about serving as witnesses against her after her arrest. The Border Patrol urged Agustin to accept a grant of voluntary departure from the immigration judge and leave. The Border Patrol would then parole Agustin into the United States and give him a work permit for the length of the trial. Agustin wondered if that was a good idea. As he was subject to unlawful presence bars and had a weak basis to apply for a waiver (his permanent resident father was not dependent on Agustin), it clearly was not a good idea.

Further discussion with Agustin elucidated the following: Agustin's father had immigrated to the United States in 1960 while he was single. In 1962, he married Agustin's mother in Mexico, residing with her for about six months. He then returned to the United States, where he worked picking crops throughout the state of California. He wrote numerous love letters to his new bride, which she kept. Agustin was born in 1968. In 1969, Agustin's father filed an I-550 to bring in Agustin's mother. However, she was unable to meet the public charge provisions and so never completed the immigration process.

---

[22] *See generally* 9 FAM N.6.4 to 22 CFR §42.53.

[23] 9 FAM N.4.3 to 22 CFR §42.53.

[24] *See Matter of Ponce De Leon*, 14 I&N Dec. 106 (BIA 1972), *Matter of Ascher*, 14 I&N Dec. 271 (BIA 1973).

Analysis: Agustin is entitled to two WHPDs. First, because his father married his mother outside the United States and then returned to reside within the United States, Agustin is entitled to a WHPD of his birthdate. It is not likely that the government would dispute that Agustin's father resided in the United States because many of the love letters sent to his wife were from Northern California—a difficult distance to commute daily from Mexico. The second WHPD occurred when Agustin's father filed the I-550 for Agustin's mother in 1969 because Agustin was a derivative in his mother's petition.

Agustin was in the United States illegally. Although he had a sister who was naturalized, she did not file an I-130 until after the §245(i) expired. Our firm decided to rely on the second WHPD registration because the local district counsel agreed that I-550 clearly was a petition that qualified under 245(i).[25] Although the regulations state that a petition under current law is deemed to have been filed at the time of the WHPD,[26] it is not clear that a present WHPD-based petition would qualify under §245(i). With the cooperation of local district counsel, we were able to have the I-130 adjudicated locally and filed with the immigration court, whereupon the immigration judge granted adjustment of status.

Multiple Registrations

Ana entered the United States as a visitor but has overstayed her I-94 card by several years. She recalls that as a child in the 1970s, she and her family lived in the Los Angeles area. Her family returned to their native Peru after her father was seriously injured in an accident. She and her family members applied for copies of their immigration files through Freedom of Information Act requests. They show that Ana's father came to the United States several times and finally immigrated in 1972. As soon as he

arrived, Ana's father filed I-550s on behalf of Ana's mother and each of the children, including Ana. Ana, her mother, and two brothers immigrated in 1973 and returned to Peru in 1976. Ana's parents had married in 1968.

Analysis: Ana received a WHPD through her father when he immigrated in 1972. She also received one directly when the I-550 was filed on her behalf in 1973 and she received a derivative registration through the I-550 filed on behalf of her mother.

A WHPD continues until it is used.[27] When Ana immigrated in 1973, one of those registrations was used. However, she continues to have two WHPDs that she may use today. One of her brothers was born in Los Angeles during the family's stay and he was willing to file an I-130 on Ana's behalf. Again, because the I-550 counts as a petition for §245(i) purposes,[28] Ana, her husband, and three minor children were able to adjust status within the United States.

Invalid Visa Petition

Pedro and Sofia entered the United States illegally in 1972 with their two children. A third child was born in San Diego in 1973. They hired a visa fixer to help them with their legal status. The visa fixer should have filed Form FS-497 with proof of their relationship to the U.S. citizen child, but he was a crook, and he filed four I-130 petitions with legacy INS. INS accepted the petitions and denied each one in written opinions dated December 6, 1974. The denials were proper because the parents did not qualify as immediate relatives—they were not parents of an adult U.S. citizen—and the siblings did not qualify because no preference categories applied to the Western Hemisphere at that time.

Analysis: Pedro, Sofia, and the two children are entitled to a 1974 WHPD. The State Department regulations at the time stated that a priority date was established when an individual submitted "evidence to establish that: . . . (ii)[t]he applicant has a relation to a U.S. citizen or resident alien which statutorily exempts him from the provisions of 212(a)(14)."[29] In this case, the State Department agreed that the parties had submitted sufficient evidence of a rela-

---

[25] INA §245(i) and the supporting regulations allow an individual who is a beneficiary of a petition for classification under INA §204 and qualifying spouses and children to pay a penalty fee and adjust status within the United States. The 1969 INA §204 included as eligible immigrants "any alien lawfully admitted for permanent residence claiming that an alien is entitled to preference status by reason of the relationship described in §203(a)(2) [spouses, parents, unmarried sons or unmarried daughters of lawful permanent residents]." INA §204 (1969). Local district counsel and the immigration judge agreed that Agustin met the requirements of present INA §245(i).

[26] 9 FAM N.5.5 to 22 CFR §42.53.

[27] 9 FAM N.4.1 to 22 CFR §42.53.

[28] *See* note 25, *supra.*

[29] 22 CFR §42.62(b)(2)(ii) (1974); INA §212(a)(14) required intending immigrants to have an approved labor certification application.

tionship to a U.S. citizen (the child born in the United States) to satisfy the regulation.

PRACTICAL PROBLEMS AND SOLUTIONS

The first problem facing individuals who believe they qualify for a WHPD is finding proof of the WHPD. Some individuals find old documents in a dusty box hidden away in a relative's closet. Copies of old permanent resident cards, entry stamps in passports, appointment notices at consulates, and similar documents are generally sufficient to establish a WHPD registration. Where no such documents can be found, a request under the Freedom of Information Act can lead to discovery of useful documentation. FOIA requests can take several months, especially if the requestor cannot provide an alien number, social security number, or other identifying information. Certainly, if a family was involved in prior immigration, FOIA requests should be filed on behalf of as many family members as possible. Especially if you suspect that the individual registered at an American Consulate overseas, you should make FOIA requests to the Department of State or the appropriate consulate in addition to the requests to the USCIS.

At other times, you may be able to find indirect evidence of a WHPD. Permanent resident cards with an entry classification of O1 or SA1 through SA8 all indicate a likely WHPD registration. Date of entry as a permanent resident is also an important clue. Keep in mind, however, that some individuals who entered after 1977 may nonetheless have a WHPD. Because those who qualified under the *Silva* program by definition had a WHPD, those who have evidence of *Silva* registration have evidence of a WHPD.[30]

Once you have the evidence of the WHPD, what do you do with it? If the individual is already in the United States and eligible to adjust status, you can file a concurrent I-130/I-485 with the Chicago lock-box or a concurrent I-140/I-485 with the appropriate service center. Expect the package to be returned at least once, because the contractors in the mail room are not normally trained in WHPD issues. In some districts, the local USCIS office is willing to accept and forward family-based WHPD cases for processing at the lock-box, in effect vouching for your

analysis. USCIS headquarters in Washington, D.C., has made an effort to have at least one individual familiar with WHPDs in its office. Practitioners should encourage the local or regional USCIS office to contact headquarters for confirmation of the WHPD program. If the local office cannot or will not help, AILA liaison or a federal court mandamus action may be necessary.

If the individual is outside the United States or does not wish to adjust status, the I-130 or I-140 is filed with the appropriate service center. Again, the contractors in the mail room are unlikely to understand why, for example, a new family-based 4th preference petition or an employment-based 3rd preference petition has a current priority date. Liaison or federal court action is essential to ensure that the service center does not delay adjudication of the petition. In this author's experience, the service centers will adjudicate the petition but refuse to assign a priority date, stating that the State Department has greater expertise with WHPDs.

If a petition has been filed, approved, and forwarded to the National Visa Center before evidence of the WHPD was available, normally a letter with copies of the supporting documentation is sufficient to get an earlier priority date assigned.

It is not enough that an individual has a WHPD. That person must also have a visa petition on which to attach the WHPD. Individuals who do not qualify for family-based or employment-based immigration cannot immigrate solely because they have a WHPD. However, in many families, there is a relative who can petition for the individual. Perhaps a sister or brother immigrated through some other method and has been naturalized. Sometimes, a parent who immigrated before 1977 (thus providing the WHPD registration) is still alive and able to file a family-based petition. In some circumstances, it may be simpler to file a combined I-130/I-485 petition than to get a labor certification approved and then file an I-140/I-485 combination. Of course, WHPDs can be used with I-140s as well as I-130s.

CONCLUSION

WHPDs are an important tool to help individuals promptly immigrate to the United States. A few simple questions can discover a potential WHPD:

- Did you ever register to immigrate to the United States?

- Did your parents ever apply to immigrate before 1977?

---

[30] *Silva v. Bell*, No. 76C 4268 (N.D. Ill. Oct. 10, 1978). Class members were allowed to remain in the United States after recaptured visas were exhausted. *See Marquez-Medina v. INS*, 765 F.2d 673, 675, n. 2 (7th Cir. 1985).

- Were your parents married at that time?
- Did either of your parents spend a lot of time in the United States before 1977?
- Where were you born?
- What about your spouse—do any of these questions apply to him or her?

The questions themselves take less than two minutes to ask. If the answers are positive, the next step is to see what evidence of the WHPD can be found and to decide on a strategy for filing the visa petition and possible adjustment of status. As far as your client is concerned, you have just PULLED THE RABBIT OUT OF THE HAT.

DOL PROPOSES DRASTIC CHANGES TO THE LABOR CERTIFICATION PROGRAM

by Mitchell L. Wexler and Careen B. Shannon[*]

On February 13, 2006, the Employment and Training Administration (ETA) of the U.S. Department of Labor (DOL) published a notice of proposed rulemaking (NPRM)[1] that would implement drastic changes to the labor certification program. The title of the proposed rule, "Labor Certification for the Permanent Employment of Aliens in the United States; Reducing the Incentives and Opportunities for Fraud and Abuse and Enhancing Program Integrity"—as well as the fact that the e-mail address to which comments were to be sent was *fraud.comments@dol.gov*—reveals the motivation behind this initiative: to reduce fraud. The comment period closed in April 2006. The rule, if adopted in its current form, will have a profound effect on employers' use of the labor certification process.

The proposed rule has four components: (1) elimination of the ability of employers to ask DOL to permit them to substitute beneficiaries on pending or approved labor certifications; (2) implementation of a 45-day validity period on labor certifications; (3) a ban on the sale, barter, purchase, and certain payments related to labor certifications; and (4) proposals related to debarment and program integrity. This article discusses all four of these issues to varying degrees, but focuses primarily on substitution.

ELIMINATION OF SUBSTITUTION

Background

Under current law, a labor certification is valid indefinitely, but is limited to the specific job opportunity for which the application was filed, to the specific foreign national named on the application, and to the area of intended employment listed on the application.[2] Changes in the location of the employer or job site or in the nature of the job itself typically require that a new labor certification application be filed, although there are exceptions. For example, if the new location of the employer or the job site is within the same area of intended employment,[3] or if a change in the job duties is not a material change, the original labor certification and, by extension, the original priority date may be retained, so long as the employer notifies U.S. Citizenship and Immigration Services (USCIS) when it files the Form I-140 Petition for Immigrant Worker on the foreign national's behalf. In addition, no new labor certification need to be filed if the new employer is a "successor in interest" to the original employer and can document to USCIS's satisfaction that it has assumed all the rights, duties, and obligations of the original employer.

Under provisions of the American Competitiveness in the 21st Century Act (AC21),[4] a foreign national whose application for adjustment of status to permanent residence[5] has been pending for at least 180 days can change jobs within the same company, or can move to another job with another employer, and still pursue his or her adjustment application, so long as the new job is in "the same or similar occupational classification" as the job that was described on the original labor certification. In essence, the employee is permitted to substitute employers. If DOL's NPRM becomes final in its current form, however, employers would be precluded from substituting employees, at least according to DOL (though DOL itself acknowledged in the preamble to the NPRM that the effect of its proposed rule on

[*] **Mitchell Wexler** is a partner in the firm of Fragomen, Del Rey, Bernsen & Loewy in Irvine, California.

Careen Shannon is of counsel to the firm in the New York office.

The authors would like to thank Nadia Yakoob, an associate in our San Francisco office, for her assistance.

[1] *See* "Labor Certification for the Permanent Employment of Aliens in the United States; Reducing the Incentives and Opportunities for Fraud and Abuse and Enhancing Program Integrity," 71 Fed. Reg. 7655 (Feb. 13, 2006).

[2] 20 CFR §656.30(c)(2). Note that the authors' discussion is limited to non–Schedule A applications. For Schedule A applications, different rules apply. *See* 20 CFR §656.30(c)(1).

[3] *See, e.g.*, 20 CFR §§656.3, 656.30(c)(2).

[4] *See* Immigration and Nationality Act of 1952, Pub. L. No. 82-414, 66 Stat. 163 (*codified as amended at* 8 USC §§1101 *et seq.*) (INA), §§204(j), 212(a)(5)(A), *as added or amended by* AC21, Pub. L. No. 106-313, §106(c), 114 Stat. 1251 (2000).

[5] *See* INA §245.

USCIS's current practice of permitting substitutions upon the filing of an I-140 is ambiguous.)[6]

For many years, DOL has permitted an employer to substitute employees by replacing the original beneficiary of an approved labor certification with another foreign national. This practice was premised on the notion that a labor certification relates to the availability of U.S. workers for the job and is not dependent on the particular beneficiary named by the employer in the application as the person to whom the job has been offered. DOL removed the ability of employers to substitute one foreign national for another on an approved labor certification in an interim final rule that became effective on November 22, 1991.[7] That rule amended 20 CFR §656.30 to provide that the validity of a labor certification is limited to "the alien for whom certification was granted." DOL's elimination of its substitution procedure was immediately challenged in federal court,[8] and the rule was stricken because the court found DOL had violated the Administrative Procedures Act (APA) by failing to provide adequate notice of the rule change or an opportunity for comments.[9] Accordingly, the original rule was restored as of December 1, 1994.

To solve the rulemaking violation, DOL needed to publish a new proposed rule setting forth its reasons for eliminating the substitution procedures and soliciting public comment on the proposed change. For more than a decade, it did not do so. In May 1995, DOL did issue a field memorandum that set out interim procedures for substitution,[10] but this memorandum was later superseded when legacy Immigration and Naturalization Service (INS) and DOL agreed to transfer responsibility for approving substitutions in approved labor certifications to INS in March 1996.[11] Nonetheless, certain state workforce agencies (SWAs) and certifying officers (COs) continued to permit substitution on an informal basis on applications that were pending in those offices.

INS's (now USCIS's) practice is that an employer may substitute one foreign beneficiary for another on an approved labor certification by filing an I-140 petition on behalf of the foreign national to be substituted.[12] The substituted foreign national must have met all of the minimum education, training, and/or experience requirements, as stated on the employer's portion of the labor certification application, at the time the original application was filed. If USCIS determines that the substituted foreign national met the requirements as of the date the application was originally filed, the I-140 is approvable and will be processed like any other I-140 petition. The priority date in this scenario is the date when the original labor certification was filed.[13]

DOL has now published a new notice of proposed rulemaking that would eliminate substitution of beneficiaries on pending or approved labor certifications.[14] Substitution would be prohibited as of the effective date of a final rule resulting from the NPRM and would apply to all pending permanent labor certification applications and to approved certifications not yet filed with USCIS, whether the application was filed under the current PERM regulation pertaining to labor certifications or under the prior regulation. The NPRM also would revise 20 CFR §656.30(c) to provide that a certification resulting from an application filed under the current or prior regulation related to permanent labor certifications is only valid for the alien named on the original labor certification application.

Impact on Business

From an employer's perspective, the elimination of the ability to substitute beneficiaries on labor certification applications would significantly diminish workforce flexibility, increase costs, and in some cases, might even drive jobs offshore. Elimination of substitution also would have a serious negative impact on many foreign workers, particularly those whose path toward permanent residence has been blocked due to the historically lengthy processing

---

[6] *See* 71 Fed. Reg. 7655, 7659.

[7] *See* 56 Fed. Reg. 54920 (Oct. 23, 1991).

[8] *Kooritzky v. Martin*, Civ. No. 91-3011-LFO (D.D.C., filed Nov. 20, 1991).

[9] *Kooritzky v. Reich*, 17 F.3d 1509 (D.C. Cir. 1994).

[10] Field Memorandum No. 37-95 from Barbara Ann Farmer, Administrator, DOL Office of Regional Management, "Interim Procedures for Substituting Alien Beneficiaries on Approved Labor Certifications" (May 4, 1995), *reproduced in* 6 *AILA Monthly Mailing* 456 (1995), 72 *Interpreter Releases* 678–82 (May 15, 1995).

[11] *See* INS Memorandum, Louis Crocetti, INS Associate Commissioner, "Substitution of Labor Certification Benefi-
continued

ciaries," File No. HQ 204.25P (Mar. 7, 1996), *reproduced in* 73 *Interpreter Releases* 444 (Apr. 8, 1996).

[12] *Id.*

[13] 8 CFR §204.5(d).

[14] *See* 71 Fed. Reg. 7655.

backlogs at DOL and USCIS and, more recently, by priority date cut-offs imposed by the U.S. Department of State (DOS). In some cases, the proposed rule might even work to contravene congressional intent in seeking to ameliorate the effects of such delays. While DOL has a clear interest in combating fraud, the handful of prosecutions cited in the preamble to the proposed rule should be weighed against the hundreds of thousands of labor certifications that have been approved since the inception of the labor certification program. The relatively small number of prosecutions would not seem to merit such a wholesale change in labor certification practice.[15]

If DOL adopts its proposed rule, the majority of employers will lose the benefits of substitution due to the misdeeds of the few. Substitution has enabled U.S. businesses to retain highly skilled workers in whom they have invested considerable time and money, which ultimately benefits employers, employees, and DOL. In some cases—where the shortage of qualified U.S. workers is particularly acute—the authors would even argue that substitution has benefited the national economy as a whole.

Substitution has been critical in a time of backlog in immigrant visa priority dates. In light of the fact that many prospective employment-based immigrants are subject to priority date backlogs that could last for many years,[16] a principal benefit of substitution historically, and again in recent years, has been to enable employers to avoid the pitfalls of immigrant visa cut-off dates and retrogression for essential foreign employees who are not yet at the adjustment-of-status stage of the permanent residence application process and who may not be eligible for a post–sixth-year H-1B extension. Substitution in these cases allows the foreign national to benefit from an earlier priority date, which, in many cases, also may be the only reason the person does not need to leave the United States altogether.

Substitution also has aided employers in retention and recruitment, and is currently used in a number of different situations. For example, when a foreign national leaves the employer and the employer has already made a substantial investment in recruitment and in the labor certification process itself, and where no qualified U.S. workers are available, substitution allows the employer to hire another qualified foreign worker—or to effect an internal transfer of an existing foreign worker—without the need to assume the expense of advertising and recruiting again in order to sponsor that foreign national for permanent residence.

This often occurs when the foreign national has been working in H-1B status for another employer, perhaps one that was not sponsoring the person for permanent residence, and the promise of sponsoring the employee for permanent residence was an important incentive for the foreign national to change employers. Aside from the savings in cost and time, an employee who is reaching the end of his or her six-year period of stay in H-1B status might only be eligible to extend that status if he or she is the beneficiary of a labor certification that has been pending for 365 days. Accordingly, filing a new labor certification application for that employee is not a viable option, whereas substitution on an application that has been pending for 365 days or longer is an option. Similarly, an existing employee for whom the organization has only recently decided to move forward with the labor certification—perhaps due to an inability to find qualified U.S. workers in the local labor market—also can benefit from substitution.

Substitution is often used in situations where a company is restructuring. In some instances of corporate restructuring—such as those involving an acquisition or a merger where the new corporate entity is a successor-in-interest to the previous employer—an existing labor certification may still be used on behalf of the named beneficiary, so long as the job duties are unchanged and the job site is in the

---

[15] DOL cites a total of five instances in which the federal government has prosecuted cases resulting from employers, agents, or attorneys seeking to profit fraudulently on the substitution of beneficiaries on approved labor certifications and applications. *See* 71 Fed. Reg. 7655, 7657 (Feb. 13, 2006).

Granted, there may be others, and at least one of the cited these cases was particularly egregious: one attorney filed approximately 2,700 fraudulent applications with DOL that he later sold to foreign nationals for at least $20,000 each so they could be substituted for the named beneficiary. Ironically, the attorney prosecuted in that case, *U.S. v. Kooritzky*, No. 02-502-A (E.D. Va.), is the same Kooritzky whose federal court challenge to DOL's 1991 interim rule eliminating substitution caused that rule to be invalidated.

[16] For example, as of this writing, the priority date for a third preference employment-based petition filed on behalf of a person born in India is March 1, 2001; for a person born in Mexico, the priority date is April 1, 2001; for all others, the date is May 1, 2001. DOS's monthly Visa Bulletin is available at *http://travel.state.gov/visa/frvi/bulletin/bulletin_1360.html*.

same area of intended employment.[17] In many cases, however, a corporate restructuring may cause some long-time employees to be transferred to a different job, a different division or office in a new location, or an entirely new company. In those cases, employers have often relied on substitution in order to ensure that foreign employees who may already have been waiting for several years are not disadvantaged by being put at the beginning of the processing queue. In these cases, where the employer is in possession of approved labor certifications for the new job or new location that were originally filed for employees who later resigned, the newly transferred or reassigned employee can be substituted on the existing labor certification. While the authors recognize that with more efficient processing under PERM, DOL foresees that lengthy processing backlogs will be a thing of the past, this goal has not yet been achieved.

Substitution also can be helpful in certain cases when a foreign national has a child nearing the age of 21 who will "age out" of eligibility for permanent residence as a derivative family member of the foreign worker, since the ability to substitute labor certification beneficiaries speeds up the overall application process.

Permitting employers to substitute beneficiaries on pending or approved labor certifications is a benefit to DOL as well. Where the employer has already documented that there are no qualified U.S. workers available, substitution on an application keeps DOL from using its resources to adjudicate a new application for the same job.

In any event, DOL's proposal to limit the validity of an approved labor certification to the alien named on the original application cannot, in and of itself, preclude USCIS from allowing an employer to substitute beneficiaries on an approved labor certification that is timely filed in support of an I-140 petition with USCIS. Accordingly, unless USCIS publishes a companion rule to DOL's NPRM (which had not been done as of this writing), it is uncertain what effect DOL's absolute ban on substitution will have on the existing substitution procedure at USCIS, except to the extent that the 45-day validity period (discussed below) will impose its own limitations.

LABOR CERTIFICATION VALIDITY AND FILING PERIOD

The proposed rule would amend the regulation at 20 CFR §656.30(b) to provide that an approved labor certification must be filed in support of an I-140 petition with USCIS within 45 calendar days of the date DOL grants certification.[18] For those labor certifications granted before the effective date of a final rule resulting from the proposed rule, employers would have 45 calendar days from the final rule's effective date to file the labor certification with USCIS in support of an I-140 petition.

A 45-day validity period is impractical, unreasonably short, and such a radical departure from previous practice that it will seriously disrupt employers' current immigration programs. It also fails to account for the fact that DOL is essentially penalizing employers for a problem that it has itself been instrumental in creating.

DOL asserts in the preamble to the regulations that the current indefinite validity of approved labor certifications has created a "black market" for such documents, and that the federal government has prosecuted several cases involving the sale of fraudulent applications or certifications. DOL also suggests that over time, the likelihood that a certified job opportunity still exists as it appeared on the original application becomes more doubtful, and the labor market test and the prevailing wage determination become less accurate or stale.

DOL fails to consider that it has been the government's processing delays, rather than the deliberate delay by employers or attorneys, that has increased the supply of older approved labor certifications. It is true that with the speedy processing of most PERM cases, substitution should not be needed to accommodate long wait times to the same extent as has been the case for the last several years. Nonetheless, even if an approved labor certification is filed in support of an I-140 petition with USCIS within the proposed 45-day period, it may still be subject to delays at USCIS, as well as long waits in many cases due to immigrant visa retrogression. A 45-day deadline would impose a major burden on employers, while doing little to alleviate the use of allegedly stale labor certifications.

There are a number of reasons why the 45-day period is unreasonably short. First, employers are

---

[17] *See, e.g.,* 20 CFR §§656.3, 656.30(c)(2).

[18] 71 Fed. Reg. 7655, 7658 (Feb. 13, 2006).

currently experiencing considerable delays in many cases from the date a labor certification application is certified in the online PERM system and the date they receive the actual paper approval in the mail. Such delays can range from a few days to several months, but typically seem to average at least three weeks. Even a three-week delay would amount to nearly half of the 45-day period. In addition, as of this writing, some employers have been receiving approvals in the mail without the blue certified ETA 9089 form. While the authors assume that most glitches of this nature will be fixed or addressed in some fashion—for example, in response to this problem, DOL issued a "Frequently Asked Questions" (FAQ) document setting out procedures for requesting a duplicate labor certification when filing the I-140 petition with USCIS[19]—other glitches are likely to occur in the future that would further contribute to delay in employers receiving PERM approvals. Even assuming USCIS continues to exercise its discretion to accept an incomplete filing in these types of situations, processing of the I-140 would undoubtedly be delayed as employers are forced to supplement filings, and USCIS is forced to process an increased volume of mail related to I-140 petitions.

There also are often logistical obstacles to the quick turnaround time between receipt of an approved certification and the filing of an I-140, not the least of which is the preparation and signing of the I-140 form. While best case scenarios would provide for preparation of the I-140 and all supporting documentation in advance, some processing steps cannot be taken until after approval. For example, the PERM rule requires employers, beneficiaries, and attorneys to sign the actual labor certification after the application is approved. Moreover, there are frequently unanticipated obstacles that make the 45-day period unrealistic. Business or vacation travel may make either the employee or a key manager or human resources contact at the employing company unavailable to review and sign the necessary paperwork during the 45-day window. The release of certain corporate documents may require board approval, or a company may have certain time-consuming sign-off requirements that must be fulfilled prior to the filing of an I-140.

USCIS requires that beneficiaries of I-140 petitions submit employment verification letters from former employers listed on the labor certification application. While the best practice is to collect all documents in support of both the I-140 prior to filing the labor certification application, in many cases, employees experience delays in securing employment letters, and employers proceed with filing the labor certification immediately for other legitimate reasons, such as ensuring that the employee will be eligible for later post–sixth year H-1B extensions should they prove necessary. There are many reasons that an employee may experience delays in obtaining employment confirmation letters: (1) the former employer may have gone out of business; (2) the employee may have left on bad terms; (3) the employee's former supervisor may no longer be with the company; (4) the employer may be located in a foreign country, making it difficult to obtain the requisite documentation; or (5) the employment may have occurred so long ago that the former employer cannot easily access its records of the individual's employment. All of these are legitimate reasons that foreign workers are often unable to obtain employment verification letters from former employers quickly. Thus, a 45-day window is insufficient in many cases for this purpose.

Because USCIS permits the concurrent filing of an I-140 and I-485 when a visa number is available, an even greater amount of preparation time is required before filing the I-140. Preparing an I-485 application for adjustment of status often involves compiling detailed biographical information about not only the principal beneficiary but about multiple family members as well. Birth certificates and marriage certificates need to be obtained, and medical examinations need to be scheduled. Since medical exam results can expire, it may not be advisable to schedule exams prior to the approval of a labor certification. While DOL to date has had a relatively good record of adjudicating most PERM cases on a timely basis, many cases still fall outside DOL's estimated processing time frames. Moreover, applications pending at one of the Backlog Elimination Centers (BECs) may still take over 18 additional months, even given DOL's most optimistic projections.[20] Accordingly, a 45-day filing window may

---

[19] *See* "PERM FAQ Set Round 8" (Mar. 20, 2006), *available at http://ows.doleta.gov/foreign/pdf/perm_faqs_3-20-06.pdf* and *published on* AILA InfoNet at Doc. No. 06032716 (*posted* Mar. 27, 2006).

[20] *See* notice on DOL's Foreign Labor Certification website, which, as of this writing, has a notice stating: "Backlog will be eliminated 9/30/07: 19 Months Remaining," *www.plc.doleta.gov* (last visited Apr. 13, 2006).

effectively eliminate the possibility of concurrent filing of the I-140 and I-485, which, in turn, is likely to cause processing delays at USCIS since the I-485 will have to be filed separately from the I-140.

Another issue arises when an employer may wish to postpone filing an I-140 petition for an individual in Trade NAFTA (TN) or F-1 status until he or she has obtained an extension of stay or has changed status to H-1B. Except for persons holding valid H-1B or L-1 status, USCIS has offered some inconsistent signals on how the filing of an I-140 might impact future extensions of nonimmigrant status, particularly where there is an issue of the immigrant's intent. For instance, in the case of TN status under the North American Free Trade Agreement (NAFTA), legacy INS declared in a policy memorandum nearly a decade ago that the filing of an I-140 should not make an individual ineligible to receive an extension or grant of TN status.[21] However, the U.S. Department of Homeland Security (DHS) does not necessarily apply this policy consistently at service centers and ports of entry, and most immigration attorneys advise their clients to wait until after an extension is granted prior to filing an I-140. This is perfectly appropriate and a best practice, given the ambiguity in the law. A 45-day deadline would in many cases preclude this.

Note also that USCIS is in the process of creating a new e-filing system in which both employer-petitioners and employee-beneficiaries will need to provide extensive information prior to filing any immigration-related petitions or applications.[22] This system would require all parties to any immigration-related application or petition—including both employers and employees in the employment-based context—to take the time to ensure the accuracy of all information prior to submission. Both employers and foreign nationals may need to seek the advice of counsel on the appropriate way to answer certain questions. Given that there are many gray areas in immigration law and practice, and wrong answers

may result in a finding of inadmissibility, completion of the online registration forms could take time and conceivably cut into the 45-day period. Again, the immigration process is very costly, in terms of both time and money, and prior to the time that a case is even certified by DOL, it would be inappropriate to require or expect that all work resulting in the completion of a Form I-140 or joint I-140/485 filing should be complete.

For all of the reasons outlined above, a 45-day expiration period would require employers to make significant modifications to how they administer their immigration programs and would result in prejudice to those employers and employees who are unable to file an I-140 petition within that time frame. In the past, DOL has conceded that labor market conditions do not change abruptly.[23] The government itself only updates its wage surveys twice a year, allows use of PERM recruitment for up to six months, and presides over a backlog that has at times reached back more than five years. Based on comments that DOL has received in response to publication of the proposed rule, there is some hope that DOL might extend the validity period to something more reasonable, such as 180 days or one year. Still, any limitation on the validity of labor certifications will have a significant impact on the ability of employers to benefit from the time and expense involved in securing those certifications.

PROHIBITION ON SALE, BARTER, PURCHASE, AND RELATED PAYMENTS

There is no question that, to the extent that labor certifications may have become commodities for sale on the black market, it is reasonable for DOL to wish to ban the sale, barter, or purchase of labor certification applications or approved labor certifications. However, prohibiting employers from seeking or receiving payment of any kind, from any source, is overbroad. In addition, it may impermissibly intrude on the attorney-client relationship.

The proposed rule would provide, in a new 20 CFR §656.12(a), a complete ban on the sale, barter, and purchase of labor certification applications and

---

[21] *See* INS Memorandum, Yvonne M. Lafleur, Chief, Business and Trade Services, Benefits, "Lifting of I-94s from Approved TN Canadian NAFTA Applicants" (June 18, 1996), *reproduced in* "INS Discusses TN Eligibility of Beneficiaries of Approved I-140s," 72 *Interpreter Rele*ases 970 (July 22, 1996) and *published on* AILA InfoNet at Doc. No. 96061891 (*posted* June 18, 1996).

[22] *See* USCIS's five separate 45-day notices of information collection, *published at* 70 Fed. Reg. 77171–74 (Dec. 29, 2005).

[23] *See* DOL Memorandum, Dale Ziegler, Chief of the Division of Foreign Labor Certification, to All Regional Certifying Officers, "Clarification of Reduction in Recruitment (RIR) Policy in an Environment of Increased Layoffs" (May 28, 2002), *published on* AILA InfoNet at Doc. No. 02060703 (*posted* June 7, 2002).

certifications.[24] The rule also would add a provision at 20 CFR §656.12(b) that would ban payments from foreign workers or other third parties, directly or indirectly, of the employer's attorney's fees and costs related to preparing, filing, and obtaining a permanent labor certification.[25] DOL's reasoning is that "[e]mployers, not aliens, file a permanent labor certification application and, therefore, these employer costs are not to be paid or reimbursed in any way by the alien beneficiary."[26]

Because of the significant expense involved in sponsoring a foreign national for permanent residence, many employers enter into some kind of reimbursement agreement with sponsored employees. For example, such an agreement might provide that if an employee resigns within one year of being granted permanent residence based on an employment-based application, the employee must reimburse the employer a certain percentage of the costs the employer incurred. Given the significant expense that employers typically bear when sponsoring an employee for permanent residence, and given that the long-term benefit of permanent residence accrues to the employee personally as well as to the employer, it seems reasonable for employers to seek some kind of reimbursement if the employee resigns soon after earning permanent residence based on employment.

Agreements that seek reimbursement if a foreign employee resigns upon being granted permanent residence are consistent with the public policy underlying the labor certification program, namely, that such applications are for prospective, long-term employment in positions for which it has been established that there are no qualified, willing, or able U.S. workers available. When employees leave the employment of the sponsoring employer upon obtaining permanent residence, this contravenes the very purpose of the labor certification program. It is therefore not unreasonable for employers to seek reimbursement of some or all of the expenses incurred in connection with the permanent residence application process.

Other observers have suggested that because dual representation is often an inevitable part of immigration practice, "[t]he technical distinction insisted upon by DOL does not reflect the reality that attorneys routinely provide advice regarding rights and obligations under the immigration law to both employers and employees."[27] Given this reality, it is not unreasonable for employees and employers to share the cost of such legal advice. DOL's proposal to ban all alien payments also ignores the reality that many small businesses and nonprofit organizations that are unable to find qualified U.S. workers may be unable to afford any of the costs associated with the process of sponsoring a foreign national for permanent residence, though they may be quite willing and able to hire a foreign national so long as he or she bears the expense involved in obtaining labor certification and filing all of the subsequent petitions and applications with USCIS. By prohibiting a sponsored foreign national from paying any costs associated with the filing of a labor certification application, DOL is essentially prohibiting such persons from retaining counsel, and this may arguably constitute a violation of free speech under the First Amendment of the Constitution.[28]

ENFORCEMENT PROVISIONS

The authors cannot really argue against DOL's proposal to clarify its current policies and procedures related to fraud, including adding procedures for debarment from the permanent labor certification for fraud or willful misrepresentation. However, to the extent that there have been instances of fraudulent labor certification applications, many involving fictitious employers or fictitious job offers, the PERM regulation already promulgated by DOL[29] addresses this through procedures designed to verify the bona fides of the employer and the job offer.

CONCLUSION

For the reasons discussed above, the authors believe that in its zeal to combat fraud, DOL's Employment and Training Administration may be eviscerating the very program it is charged with administering. It may also be advocating for changes that could hurt the U.S. economy more than help it.

---

[24] See 71 Fed. Reg. 7655, 7658, 7662 (Feb. 13, 2006).

[25] Id.

[26] Id. at 7658.

[27] C. Velez, "DOL Proposal to Prohibit Payment of Legal Fees by Foreign National Beneficiaries of Labor Certification Applications is Bad Policy and Violates the First Amendment" (Mar. 3, 2006), available at www.cyrusmehta.com/news_cyrus.asp.

[28] Id.

[29] See "Labor Certification for the Permanent Employment of Aliens in the United States; Implementation of New System," 69 Fed. Reg. 77326 (Dec. 27, 2004).

LABOR CERTIFICATIONS AND THE LAW OF RECRUITMENT

by Rómulo E. Guevara[*]

INTRODUCTION

The labor certification system has undergone a complete overhaul in the last 15 months. The old traditional and Reduction in Recruitment (RIR) system had become bogged down in extensive processing delays due to high case volume, insufficient resources, and an increase in fraudulent filings. Beginning on March 28, 2005, the new, streamlined Permanent Electronic Review Management (PERM) system was launched. PERM was designed to eliminate fraud and to significantly reduce processing times through an automated electronic filing system. Replacing a system that typically took five years after filing for labor certification approvals, PERM has reduced adjudications to as little as two days or, at most, a few months.

However, backlog of pre-PERM cases that is currently in the Backlog Elimination Centers (BEC) remains sizeable. The Department of Labor (DOL) projects the backlog will end in 2007, although DOL's earlier projections of end dates had to be extended. It is likely that with its limited resources, DOL may extend the end of BEC's backlog past 2007.

With these two divergent labor certification systems, the law of recruitment remains the common element. Although PERM requires additional recruitment steps, the rules that govern how candidates are evaluated remain virtually unchanged. To date, there have been no PERM appeals decided on recruitment issues. The first PERM appeal was only docketed in March 2006, to which AILA was invited to submit an amicus brief.[1]

This article explores the law of recruitment and the general principles that apply to both systems with regard to the second and third employment-based categories, which require labor certification. The analysis is based on case law established by the (then newly established) Board of Labor Certification Appeals (BALCA) through its early en banc decisions of the late 1980s and early 1990s. Each decision has a long line of cases following it or distinguishing it based on case-specific distinctions. To include all those subsequent cases would be outside the scope of this article. The purpose here is to provide a springboard for research on a particular sub-area of the law of recruitment that may be relevant to the reader's case.

STATUTORY AND REGULATORY SCHEME

Labor certification originates from §212(a)(5)(A) of the Immigration and Nationality Act (INA),[2] which states that certain aliens seeking permanent employment are ineligible for visas or admission unless a labor certification is obtained. The section reads:

(i) Any alien who seeks to enter the United States for the purpose of performing skilled or unskilled labor is inadmissible, unless the Secretary of Labor has determined and certified to the Secretary of State and the Attorney General that—

(I) there are not sufficient workers who are able, willing, qualified (or equally qualified in the case of an alien described in clause (ii)) and available at the time of application for a

[*] **Rómulo Guevara** is a senior attorney with Littler, Mendelson, Bacon, & Dear, PLLC (*www.littlerglobal.com*) in Phoenix, where he specializes in business immigration law for large corporate clients. He is a member of the AILA Board of Publications, the YLD National Steering Committee, and the Planning Committee for the AILA National Conference in 2007. He is also a member of the Immigration Committee of the Hispanic National Bar Association (HNBA). Mr. Guevara frequently contributes articles analyzing the latest developments in immigration law to a wide variety of immigration law journals. He also has lectured at conferences for AILA and *ILW.com*, and has served as associate editor on recent AILA publications, including AILA's *Immigration Practice Toolbox* (2d. ed. 2006). He graduated from Hofstra University School of Law in 1996 and has been practicing immigration law since 1997. He is originally from El Salvador.

[1] *See* "Update on PERM and BALCA," *published on* AILA InfoNet at Doc. No. 06031661 (*posted* Mar. 16, 2006). The issue in the pending appeal is whether DOL abused its discretion in denying a PERM case based on an advertisement that was placed on a Sunday, but a Monday date was incorrectly entered on the form. BALCA is asked to decide whether or not this is "harmless error." This will be the first "test" case subject to the appellate process under PERM.

[2] Immigration and Nationality Act of 1952, Pub. L. No. 82-414, 66 Stat. 163 (*codified as amended at* 8 USC §§1101 *et seq.*) (INA).

visa and admission to the United States and at the place where the alien is to perform such skilled or unskilled labor, and

(II) the employment of such alien will not adversely affect the wages and working conditions of workers in the United States similarly employed.

A foreign national coming to the United States to perform skilled or unskilled labor is deemed *inadmissible* by default unless a labor certification is approved on his or her behalf. The labor certification "tests" the labor market to see if there are qualified U.S. workers available to perform the duties of the job opportunity. If there are U.S. workers available, no labor certification can be approved. However, if no U.S. workers are available and if the foreign national fits the qualifications listed on the application form, certification is granted. The test of the labor market is processed through a recruitment campaign that involves advertisements in newspapers of wide circulation, trade journals (if relevant), job websites, radio and television announcements, and various other sources. Depending on which system the case is filed under, the employer would prepare a recruitment report with proof of the recruiting and the responses received, if any, and why the candidates who did apply do not qualify for the proffered position.

The regulations that pertain to labor certification can be found at 20 CFR §656. These detail what is required in terms of case preparation and procedures. Although PERM substantially altered the substantive and procedural content of the labor certification program, cases still pending as traditional or RIR filings will be adjudicated under the old regulatory scheme.

Traditional Labor Certifications

Traditional filings under the old system were filed without recruitment data. Only Forms ETA 750 Parts A and B were submitted. DOL would review the case and make objections to the job duties or the academic and/or experience requirements. Once this phase had reached a consensus, DOL would coordinate the ad campaign, supervise recruitment efforts with the employer, and monitor the receipt of candidates responding to the recruiting campaign. Every candidate who applied would be directed to the employer for review and/or interview. The employer would then submit a documented report (along with proof of the recruitment used) detailing why each candidate who was directed to the employer by DOL

did not qualify for the job opportunity. If the reasons for rejection were deemed lawful, certification would be granted. If not, DOL would issue a Notice of Findings (NOF), in essence an intent to deny based on specific problems in the case. The employer was provided 35 days to rebut the findings. If the rebuttal was successful, certification followed. If not, denial would follow, with rights to appeal to BALCA.

As of this writing, there are a good number of traditional cases still pending at the BECs, which means that practitioners must still be well-versed in this old version of labor certification process.

Reduction in Recruitment (RIR) Waiver

In 1997, DOL encouraged employers to conduct good faith recruitment prior to filing the labor certification application. Under General Administration Letter (GAL) 1-97, employers could conduct recruitment within six months of filing of the labor certification and submit the recruitment evidence and the recruitment report with Forms ETA 750 Parts A and B. If DOL deemed the case to fall within the guidelines of GAL 1-97, supervised recruitment was waived and the Reduction in Recruitment would be granted, and certification promptly issued.

With the re-emergence of INA §245(i) in December 2000, DOL experienced an unprecedented rate of filings, which culminated in the §245(i) eligibility expiration date of April 30, 2005. This backlog gave rise to the establishment of BECs and revamping of the labor certification system to what exists today.

PERM

Under PERM, the regulations focus on fraud prevention in its procedures and substantive requirements. PERM imposes harsher penalties for failure to document proper recruitment. However, similar to the old system, the law remains the same with regard to how candidates are evaluated. Case law governs what constitutes good faith recruitment and the proper rejection of U.S. workers.

GOOD FAITH RECRUITMENT EFFORTS

Recruitment under the labor certification system can be very frustrating to employers, foreign nationals, and attorneys alike. Although DOL has attempted to create a system that reflects "real-world" recruitment, the reality is that it is not very "real." Where most positions accept a combination of duties or a variety of skills, DOL tends to rule that such duties are "unduly restrictive" or that the combination of duties is impermissible. Actual perceptions and evaluations of candidates can be proper reasons for rejecting a candidate in the real world, but not in the labor certification system.

The basic principles of the regulations include the concept that a U.S. worker is considered able and qualified for the job opportunity if the worker can perform the duties involved in a normally acceptable manner, by education, training, experience or similar combination, as customarily performed by other U.S. workers.[3] In order to protect the interest of all U.S. workers, the regulations require that the job opportunity be open to any qualified U.S. worker.[4] If U.S. workers apply for a position offered to a foreign national, rejection of U.S. workers may occur only for lawful, job-related reasons.[5]

APPLICABLE CASE LAW

What follows are cases that developed the general principles governing this complex area of immigration practice—involving: (1) sufficiency of documentation; (2) foreign national's involvement; (3) timely contact of the U.S. worker; (4) a candidate's travel expenses; and (5) the alternative publication requirement.

Sufficiency of Documentation

In pursuing labor certification, it is important that a company be able to demonstrate it has made a good faith effort to find U.S. workers and be able to document that effort. A good case to read in this area is *M.N. Auto Electric Corp.*[6] At the heart of what constitutes good faith recruitment efforts is not the actual contact of U.S. workers but the sufficiency of these reasonable contact efforts. The preferred practice is that candidates who respond to an advertisement in the case be contacted by certified mail, return receipt requested. This is not a DOL requirement, but it is a good practice pointer for practitioners to properly document the reasonableness of the recruitment efforts.

Employers can request detailed telephone records to show the number of attempts to contact candidates by highlighting the call transaction on the telephone records. If these records are not available, the employer should document it attempted to obtain such records.[7] It also is permissible to document contact efforts through interview sheets summarizing the telephone calls with candidates and also through follow-up letters.[8] Where a candidate expresses lack of interest in the advertised position and the employer submits his or her interview notes, in addition to a subsequent letter confirming the same, certification should be granted.[9]

There is a string of en banc decisions in which BALCA found that employers did not sufficiently document their recruitment efforts. In one case, an employer was denied certification because it failed to show the frequency of contact attempts, the methods of the attempts, and alternative means of communication.[10] In another case, the employer only submitted a simple affidavit indicating that candidates rejected the job by telephone, while others were contacted but never appeared for the interview. Certification was denied for insufficient proof of good faith recruitment.[11] Certification also was denied in a case where the employer did not substantiate its efforts to contact applicants, and U.S. workers submitted questionnaires to DOL stating they had not been contacted by the employer.[12]

Practice Pointer: The law affords an employer the opportunity to show that its overall recruitment efforts were made in good faith, even where certified mail return receipts were not used. DOL will give bare assertions very little weight in evaluating a case for certification. It is important to document all communications with candidates as detailed above.

---

[3] 20 CFR §656.24(b)(2)(i).

[4] Under the pre-PERM regulations, the relevant rule was at 20 CFR §656.20(c)(8). Now, a similar rule is found at 20 CFR §656.10(c)(8).

[5] 20 CFR §656.21(b)(6) (under the old regulations); 20 CFR §656.10(c)(9) (under PERM).

[6] *M.N. Auto Electric Corp.*, 2000-INA-165 (Aug. 8, 2001) (en banc).

[7] *Cf. Diceon Electronics, Inc.*, 1988-INA-253 (Apr. 18, 1989) (en banc).

[8] *Yedico International, Inc.*, 1987-INA-740 (Sept. 30, 1988) (en banc).

[9] *Komfort Industries, Inc.*, 1988-INA-402 (May 4, 1989) (en banc).

[10] *Yaron Development Co., Inc.*, 1989-INA-178 (Apr. 19, 1991) (en banc).

[11] *Medical Designs, Inc.*, 1988-INA-159 (Dec. 19, 1988) (en banc).

[12] *Carriage House Realtors, Inc.*, 1987-INA-739 (Apr. 5, 1989) (en banc).

Foreign National's Involvement

As a general matter, the foreign national cannot be involved in the recruitment phase. Such involvement irreparably taints the labor certification process.[13] The foreign national cannot participate in the review of résumés, or in the contact or interview of candidates.

An ethical dilemma can arise in this instance with regard to dual representation. The foreign national may believe the attorney (whom in many cases he or she has hired) is not representing him or her zealously, by not permitting him or her to review the résumés or be present at the candidate interviews. Labor certification is an employer-owned process. An attorney must weigh his or her obligations under dual representation carefully.[14]

Practice Pointer: Although ethical dilemmas may arise in the course of representation, a balanced approach is the key element. Practitioners must take care to identify when a conflict in representation necessitates one party to seek independent counsel. Candidates must be timely contacted to show good faith recruitment, but the foreign national cannot be involved in recruitment, so as to not taint the process.

Finally, an employer cannot "create" a position after a qualified U.S. worker applies for the advertised position, in order to keep the proffered position open for labor certification purposes.[15]

Timely Contact of U.S. Worker

As a general principle, employers must contact candidates within a reasonable time after receipt of the résumé so as to indicate to the candidates that the job opportunity is truly open to them.[16] The Board, in *Creative Cabinet & Store Fixture Co.*,[17] also stated, "an employer remains under the affirmative duty to commence review and make all reasonable attempts to contact applicants as soon as possible" and that "a delay is likely to result in workers becoming disinterested in the [job] opportunity," equating to a lack of good faith in the recruitment.[18]

Where an employer left the United States for a month and did not delegate recruitment responsibilities while abroad, the eventual contact of the candidate will be deemed untimely.[19] It is improper for an employer to place the burden of contact on the U.S. worker because the employer must show he or she is actively recruiting qualified workers.[20] Similarly, an employer cannot discourage U.S. workers by making it difficult to schedule an interview.[21]

What if there is a misunderstanding about the time and date of an interview with a candidate? BALCA has found there was no intentional misunderstanding about the time of an interview. The Board remanded the case for interview of the candidate and ordered that if the candidate were no longer available, re-advertisement would be required.[22]

Where there are multiple contact numbers, the employer must attempt to contact the candidate wherever possible—if one of the telephone numbers is the candidate's current employment location, the employer can write the candidate a letter if such telephone contact would be a sensitive matter.[23] An employer cannot leave a message with a candidate's spouse so as to relieve the employer of its burden to attempt to contact the candidate directly.[24]

Candidate's Travel Expenses

If the job is a professional position not limited to the local area, an employer is obligated to mitigate the financial hardship of the candidate if an in-person

---

[13] *Master Video Productions, Inc.*, 1988-INA-419 (Apr. 18, 1989) (en banc).

[14] For an excellent discussion on dual representation, see C. Mehta, "Finding the 'Golden Mean' in Dual Representation," *Immigration & Nationality Law Handbook* 29 (AILA 2005–06 ed.)

[15] *Amger Corporation*, 1987-INA-545 (Oct. 15, 1987) (en banc).

[16] *Loma Linda Foods, Inc.*, 1989-INA-289 (Nov. 26, 1991) (en banc) (majority believes the focus is not on intent, but on the probable effect on U.S. workers; the dissent strongly argues that intent plays a key role in the analysis).

[17] *Creative Cabinet & Store Fixture, Co.*, 1989-INA-181 (Jan. 24, 1990) (en banc).

[18] *Id.*

[19] *Leonardo's*, 1987-INA-581 (Nov. 20, 1987) (en banc).

[20] *Viva of California*, 1987-INA-583 (Nov. 20, 1987) (en banc).

[21] *Budget Iron Work*, 1988-INA-393 (Mar. 21, 1989).

[22] *Bolton Electric, Inc.*, 1988-INA-192 (Dec. 22, 1988) (en banc). *Cf. Suniland Music Shoppes*, 1988-INA-93 (Mar. 20, 1989) (en banc) (interview at the wrong location based on employer's poor coordination).

[23] *Bruce A. Field*, 1988-INA-333 (May 26, 1989) (en banc).

[24] *Dove Homes, Inc.*, 1987-INA-680 (May 25, 1988) (en banc); *Switch, U.S.A., Inc.*, 1988-INA-164 (Apr. 19, 1989) (en banc); *Diceon Electronics, Inc.*, 1988-INA-253 (Apr. 18, 1989) (en banc); *Bay Area Women's Resource Center*, 1988-INA-379 (May 26, 1989) (en banc).

interview is requested.[25] In this instance, the employer cannot refuse to interview the candidate by telephone as an alternative.[26] Mitigation of this requirement can include the reduction of the applicant pool to only the most qualified individuals for in-person interviews.[27]

Alternative Publication Requirement

DOL can require an employer to advertise in an alternative publication if it can describe why such an action will yield additional qualified U.S. workers.[28] But DOL's authority is not "unbridled" in this regard.[29]

REJECTION OF U.S. WORKERS

This is a highly contested area for obvious reasons. During an economic downturn, the number of responses to advertisements will no doubt increase dramatically. Some employers might be tempted to steer the recruitment process away from what the law requires, usually stemming from a natural inclination in favor of the foreign national whom the employer is sponsoring.

Practice Pointer: Employers must be carefully counseled to understand the logic of the labor certification system and how the test of the labor market fits into the employment-based immigration process. The cases that follow can be very useful in guiding an employer away from the common pitfalls in this area of law.

Assessment of Availability

When is a U.S. worker deemed to be available for labor certification purposes? If a worker is not available at the time recruitment is made but is available at a later time, can this candidate be deemed available for labor certification purposes? The Board held in *Adry-Mart, Inc.*[30] that the availability of a worker is assessed as of the time of recruitment. In this case, the candidate was not available due to scheduled surgery. The certifying officer (CO) ruled that the candidate was available after the recovery from surgery and that the employer should have deemed him a qualified worker. BALCA disagreed, stating that at the time of recruitment, the candidate was not available and, thus, could not be considered for the job opportunity.

Sufficiency of Documentation

As a general matter, the employer bears the burden of both production and persuasion in demonstrating to the satisfaction of DOL that U.S. workers were rejected for a lawful reason.[31] The employer is required to document the lawful reasons for the rejection of U.S. workers. Bare assertions are not permitted.[32] Supporting evidence is required where the employer simply states that a candidate was not interested in the job opportunity.[33] Similarly, if an employer asserts without further explanation that a candidate was rejected for poor communication skills, certification will be denied.[34] In addition, cursory notations for the rejection of U.S. workers do not meet the "specificity" requirement.[35]

Qualification Standards

The basic principles in this area were established by panel decisions. For instance, in *Matter of Concurrent Computer Corp.*[36] and *Matter of Hong Kong Royale Restaurant*,[37] BALCA held that where the job requirements are not unduly restrictive and the applicant does not meet these requirements, rejection is

---

[25] *American Export Trading Co.*, 1988-INA-220 (June 15, 1990) (en banc); *Hipoint Development, Inc.*, 1988-INA-340 (May 31, 2989) (en banc). *See also Warmtex Enterprises*, 1988-INA-403 (June 28, 1989) (panel) (en banc review denied, 1988-INA-403 (Oct. 31, 1989)). The denial of en banc review was affirmed by *Warmtex Enterprises v. Martin*, 953 F.2d 1133 (9th Cir. 1992).

[26] *Id.*

[27] *Lin & Associates, Inc.*, 1988-INA-7 (Apr. 14, 1989) (en banc).

[28] *Intel Corporation*, 1987-INA-570 and 571 (Dec. 11, 1987) (en banc). *See also Alpine Electronics of America*, Inc., 1988-INA-107 (Mar. 14, 1989) (en banc); *Peking Gourmet*, 1988-INA-323 (May 11, 1989); *National Institute for Petroleum and Energy Research*, 1988-INA-535 (Mar. 17, 1989) (en banc).

[29] *Id.*

[30] *Adry-Mart, Inc.*, 1988-INA-243 (Feb. 1, 1989) (en banc).

[31] *Cathay Carpet Mills, Inc.*, 1987-INA-161 (Dec. 7, 1988) (en banc).

[32] *Custom Card d/b/a Custom Plastic Card Company*, 1988-INA-212 (Mar. 16, 1989) (en banc).

[33] *Id.*

[34] *Hughes Aircraft Company*, 1988-INA-325 (Mar. 21, 1989) (en banc).

[35] *U.S.A. Manufacturing, Inc.*, 1988-INA-373 (May 1, 1989 (en banc) (Employer's explanation simply stated 'No import/export experience, only clerical.' and 'Documentation clerk experience.')

[36] *Matter of Concurrent Computer Corp.*, 88-INA-76 (Aug. 19, 1988).

[37] *Matter of Hong Kong Royale Restaurant*, 88-INA-60 (Oct. 17, 1988).

proper. Conversely, in *Matter of Fritz Garage*[38] and *Matter of Vanguard Jewelry Corp.*,[39] the Board held that a U.S. worker may not be rejected for not meeting job requirements not stated on the form.

However, where unstated job duties are implied, such duties will be treated as if they had been stated on the form. The principle here is that certain duties are not stated because they are obvious and likely to be met by anyone applying for the job opportunity. This was the case in *Veterans Administration Medical Center*,[40] where the job requirement at issue was "proficiency in the English language."

But does the U.S. worker need to be as qualified as the foreign national? For instance, if the foreign national has a master's degree in a relevant field and five years of experience, but the job only requires a master's degree and two years of relevant experience, can a U.S. worker be rejected for having the required degree and experience but not the additional three years experience that the foreign national possesses? BALCA has ruled in the negative. Even though an employer may wish to hire a more qualified worker, a U.S worker needs to meet only the minimum requirements of the job opportunity as specified on the application form.[41]

Obligation of Certifying Officer

BALCA also places an obligation on the CO to address or contest an employer's summary rejection of U.S. workers in a timely manner, or BALCA will reverse denial and/or remand for further processing. In one case, the Board reversed denial where the CO failed to raise the issue of improper rejection of a U.S. worker and also failed to state why the employer's rejection of a U.S. worker was unlawful.[42] In another case, the Board overruled the CO's finding that there were qualified U.S. workers where the CO did not address the employer's explanations in the recruitment report and rebuttal, and where no challenge was issued to the employer's requirement

for education and experience.[43] In yet another case, BALCA objected to the CO's failure to challenge the employer's listed coursework requirements, which had been disclosed throughout the life of the case, until the final determination. In this case, the CO's denial was deemed inappropriate and untimely. Consequently, the employer's rejection of the U.S. worker became lawful.[44]

Unchallenged Job Requirements

Similarly, where the CO does not challenge any of the job requirements as unduly restrictive, a U.S. worker may be rejected for not meeting such minimum requirements.[45] The rationale here is that if any of the job qualifications are not challenged, an employer may rely on such qualifications in reviewing candidates' eligibility.[46] As will be discussed in the next section, the Board appears to have limited this rule in subsequent panel cases under the theory that this principle should apply only where it is clear the candidate lacks the qualifications sought.

Employer's Duty to Further Investigate

Of course, if the candidate meets the job requirements, rejection is improper.[47] If a candidate, however, appears to be qualified, the employer is required to investigate further under the *Gorchev & Gorchev* standard.[48] If a candidate's résumé does not expressly state suitable qualifications for all of the duties in the job opportunity, but only lists broad qualifications, it is incumbent upon the employer to further investigate through an interview or other means to determine if the candidate meets the job requirements.[49] Similarly, where a candidate's résumé is ambiguous as to all the required qualifications, the employer must investigate

---

[38] *Matter of Fritz Garage*, 88-INA-273 (Aug. 17, 1988).

[39] *Matter of Vanguard Jewelry Corp.*, 88-INA-273 (Sept. 20, 1988).

[40] *Veterans Administration Medical Center*, 1988-INA-70 (Dec. 21, 1988) (en banc).

[41] *Exxon Chemical Company*, 1987-INA-615 (July 18, 1988) (en banc); *Veterans Administration Medical Center*, 1988-INA-70 (Dec. 21, 1988) (en banc); *Paperlera Del Plata, Inc.* 1990-INA-53 (Jan. 31, 1992) (en banc).

[42] *New Consumer Products*, 1987-INA-706 (Oct. 18, 1988) (en banc).

[43] *Lee & Chiu Design Group*, 1988-INA-328 (Dec. 20, 1988) (en banc).

[44] *Concurrent Computer Corp.*, 1988-INA-76 (Aug. 19, 1988) (en banc).

[45] *Euclid Chemical Co.*, 1988-INA-398 (May 4, 1989) (en banc); *Datagate, Inc.*, 1987-INA-582 (Feb. 17, 1989) (en banc).

[46] *Anonymous Management*, 1987-INA-672 (Sept. 8, 1988) (en banc).

[47] *Quality Products of America, Inc.*, 1987-INA-703 (Jan. 31, 1989) (en banc).

[48] *Gorchev & Gorchev Graphic Design*, 1989-INA-118 (Nov. 29, 1990) (en banc); *Creative Cabinet & Store Fixture, Co*, 1989-INA-181 (Jan. 24, 1990) (en banc); *Adry-Mart, Inc.*, 88-INA-243 (Feb. 1, 1989) (en banc).

[49] *Nancy, Ltd.*, 1988-INA-358 (Apr. 27, 1989) (en banc).

in order to make an informed decision regarding the applicant.[50]

The *Gorchev & Gorchev* standard[51] also was applied in *Dearborn Public Schools*,[52] where a choral director was sought with a state teacher's license, a master's degree for music educators, and three years of experience. The candidate in question had a PhD in music education and a variety of experiences ranging over 20 years. The employer rejected the applicant without interview. The Board imposed on the employer a duty to further investigate. Based on the candidate's qualifications, it was possible that through an interview, the specific qualifications could have been explored to determine if the candidate met the minimum job requirements. The Board stated:

> A resume is just that: a summary; an introductory overview highlighting an applicant's background of qualification. It is not a temple to be worshiped as the fount of all knowledge about an applicant's qualifications. Under the *Gorchev & Gorchev* standard, an employer truly seeking a qualified U.S. applicant would have contacted [a candidate as in this instance] and her references to inquire further about her qualifications.[53]

Finally, where a candidate states career objectives that may not be within the employer's business, the employer may not make unilateral findings against the candidate's interest or ability to perform the duties without further inquiry.[54]

"Fortuitous Cure"

As a general rule, an improper rejection of a U.S. worker cannot be cured fortuitously by a subsequent attempt to correct the error. There is a long line of cases on point. A general sample of en banc decisions follows.

Basically, the Board framed the issue as follows: it "is not whether the [candidates] are still available for the position five months after it was offered, but rather whether the applicants were lawfully rejected in the first place."[55] Where there are belated efforts

to contact U.S. workers, a later lack of interest in the job does not cure the earlier failure to timely contact.[56] Similarly, an employer cannot attempt to cure an initial failure to timely contact a candidate at a Notice of Findings (NOF) or post-NOF stage of the case.[57] Where there is an initial unlawful rejection but a subsequent contact and lawful rejection, the CO must examine the appropriateness of the initial rejection to make sure it was not unlawful. If it is unlawful, this would taint even the second lawful rejection.[58] The same principle will hold true under a PERM audit.

Lack of Experience in a Particular Job Duty

In order to have proper grounds to reject a U.S. worker for lack of experience, the employer must specify those requirements because the law will not imply them.[59] Under the old system, if a particular job duty that the candidate lacked was absent from ETA Form 750 Part A, items 14 and 15, the employer could not reject the candidate for lack of experience in this duty.[60] The objective of items 14 and 15 of the form "is to notify the C.O. of employer's minimum requirements so that the C.O. may, if necessary, challenge the stated requirements as unduly restrictive or as not the actual minimum."[61]

In the Fifth Circuit, the governing case is *Ashbrook-Simon-Hartley v. McLaughlin*.[62] After *Ashbrook*, a number of cases were remanded for consideration under the standards established therein.[63] However, BALCA has not extended *Ashbrook* outside the Fifth Circuit.

---

[50] *Creative Cabinet*, 1989-INA-181 (Jan. 24, 1990) (en banc).

[51] 1989-INA-118 (Nov. 29, 1990) (en banc).

[52] 1991-INA-222 (Dec. 7, 1993) (en banc).

[53] *Id.*

[54] *National Semiconductor*, 1988-INA-301 (Mar. 3, 1989) (en banc).

[55] *Done-Rite, Inc.*, 1988-INA-341 (Mar. 2, 1989) (en banc).

[56] *Suniland Music Shoppes, Inc.*, 1988-INA-93 (Mar. 20, 1989) (en banc).

[57] *Carriage House Realtors*, 1987-INA-739 (Apr. 5, 1989) (en banc); *Custom Plastic Card Company*, 1988-INA-212 (Mar. 16, 1989) (en banc).

[58] *See Kennedy Research, Inc.*, 1988-INA-350 (Dec. 21, 1989) (en banc); *see also Nancy Ltd*, 1988-INA-358 (Apr. 27, 1989) (en banc).

[59] *Universal Energy Systems, Inc.*, 1988-INA-5 (Jan. 4, 1989) (en banc).

[60] *Chromatochem Inc.*, 1988-INA-8 (Jan. 12, 1989) (en banc).

[61] *Bell Communications Research, Inc.*, 1988-INA-26 (Dec. 22, 1988) (en banc) (citation omitted).

[62] *Ashbrook-Simon-Hartley v. McLaughlin*, 863 F.2d 410 (5th Cir. 1989).

[63] *Omega Contractor, Inc.*, 1988-INA-37 (Apr. 25, 1989) (en banc); *Motorola, Inc.*, 1988-INA-47 and 160 (Apr. 18, 1989)

continued

Verification of Employment

A candidate may be lawfully rejected if he or she fails to respond to an employer's reasonable requests for verification of educational credentials and prior employment history.[64]

Tests, Salary, and the Overqualified

Employers are permitted to use tests and questionnaires to assess the qualifications of candidates as long as these are used to determine the applicant's knowledge rather than as a term or condition of employment. Therefore, tests and questionnaires can be used in the same way that questions are used in an interview.[65]

Where the salary offered is low, the candidate's expressed dissatisfaction with the low salary is not sufficient ground for lawful rejection by an employer. Salary can be used as a means to reject U.S. workers only if the position is actually offered to the candidate and the candidate rejects it based on the low salary.[66]

Subjective Grounds for Rejection

An overqualified candidate cannot be rejected simply on the employer's subjective assertion about the candidate's likelihood of dissatisfaction in a job for which he or she is overqualified.[67] Similarly, where the candidate is related to an employer's competitor, this fact alone cannot be the basis of lawful rejection. The employer must use documentation, such as affidavits from prior employers, for example, stating that the security of the business would be compromised by the hiring of the candidate.[68]

BALCA has maintained consistent rulings on subjective grounds for rejection of U.S. workers. For instance, in *Empire Marble Corp.*,[69] the Board refused to permit the rejection of a candidate simply because the employer perceived him as only a "paper man" who made the employer feel uncomfortable and not confident in him. In *K Super KQ-1540 A.M.*,[70] rejection of a U.S. worker was deemed unlawful where the job of radio announcer was not given to the U.S. worker on the basis that the foreign national possessed a better radio voice.

The lack of communications skills has also found its way into litigation. Rejection is improper where a U.S. worker is unable to understand the employer's heavily accented English. The Board found this to be more of an orientation issue than a specific skill.[71] Finally, in *Impell Corporation*,[72] the CO spoke to the rejected U.S. worker and found that there was no problem in communications; the rejection on the basis of lack of English fluency was improper.

CONCLUSION

The law of recruitment is a key element in a labor certification case. Whether it is under the old system or under the new, practitioners must be up-to-date on the nuances in this area of law. Most of the issues are case-specific and require careful review and analysis. There has been no shortage of BALCA cases addressing common fact patterns. The cases discussed in this article form the foundation from which the current interpretation of law has emerged. Practitioners must examine these cases and their progeny in order to identify the themes and variations that may be useful in the cases before them.

(en banc); *Veterans Administration Medical Center*, 1988-INA-70 (Dec. 21, 1988) (en banc).

[64] *A-Ghazali School*, 1988-INA-347 (May 31, 1989) (en banc) (quoting *In re Sunee Kim's Enterprises*, 87-INA-713 (Jul. 22, 1988)).

[65] *Allied Towing Service*, 1988-INA-46 (Jan. 9, 1989) (en banc).

[66] *Impell Corporation*, 1988-INA-298 (May 31, 1989) (en banc).

[67] *Metroplex Distributors*, 1988-INA-249 (May 22, 1989) (en banc) (an accountant applied for a bookkeeper's position and the employer improperly assumed subjectively the candidate would be bored in a lesser position).

[68] *Paperlera Del Plata, Inc.*, 1990-INA-53 (Jan. 31, 1992) (en banc).

[69] *Empire Marble Corp.*, 1988-INA-360 (Feb. 28, 1989) (en banc).

[70] *K Super KQ-1540 A.M*, 1988-INA-397 (Apr. 3, 1989) (en banc).

[71] *Carriage House Realtors*, 1987-INA-739 (Apr. 5, 1989) (en banc).

[72] 1988-INA-298 (May 31, 1989) (en banc).

PERM STRATEGIES AND AD HOC RULES FOR BENEFICIARIES WITH THREE-YEAR BACHELOR'S DEGREES

*by Ronald Y. Wada**

INTRODUCTION

The purpose of this article is to shed light on the elusive ad hoc rules that appear to govern the adjudication of I-140 petitions for beneficiaries who hold three-year bachelor's degrees from non-American universities. By understanding the history of unpublished Administrative Appeals Office (AAO) decisions in this area, we can gain insight on how to structure PERM applications to minimize risks to the Green Card applications for beneficiaries who hold such degrees. The AAO has made an issue of three-year bachelor's degrees through a series of unpublished, nonprecedent decisions. While unpublished AAO decisions do not, in theory, carry precedential weight, it has become apparent that the U.S. Citizenship and Immigration Services (USCIS) service centers have followed the AAO's interpretations of degree equivalencies, making the AAO's interpretations de facto precedents. Since AAO nonprecedent decisions are not published, they are not available in a searchable form[1]; they are also highly case-specific, and are a poor vehicle for stating general adjudication standards or policies.[2] Practitioners

have solicited policy interpretations of the governing regulations from USCIS and have received letters in response, but USCIS service centers as well as the AAO have not followed the interpretation set forth in those letters. The result is that many practitioners remain understandably confused about what the rules are, and how to structure a PERM application that best serves the interests of both the employer petitioners and the beneficiary employees.[3]

A word of caution: the "ad hoc rules" presented here are based on unpublished decisions by service centers and the AAO. They are like shifting sands and are subject to change without notice, yet their impact and influence cannot be ignored when drafting either amendments to pending reduction in recruitment (RIR) applications or new PERM applications.

BACKGROUND

Three-Year Bachelor's Degrees in the EB-2 Category

The issue of whether a three-year bachelor's degree is equivalent to a U.S. bachelor's degree can be traced back to an EB-2 class action.[4] The *Chintakuntla* litigation was brought against the Immigration and Naturalization Service (INS) because INS was denying EB-2 I-140 petitions for beneficiaries who held a bachelor's degree followed by five years of progressive experience, in contradiction to its own regulation at 8 CFR §204.5(k)(2).[5] The regulation at 8 CFR §204.5(k)(2) allows for two types of

---

* **Ron Wada** is senior counsel in the San Francisco office of Berry, Appleman & Leiden, LLP. He has served as chair of the AILA Amicus Committee from 2003 to 2005, and is currently a member of the AILA USCIS Liaison Committee. He is a member of the editorial board of *Bender's Immigration Bulletin* and has authored numerous articles on business immigration and removal defense issues. Mr. Wada received AILF's 1997 Edward L. Dubroff Award for Outstanding Scholarship in the field of immigration law.

[1] The AAO has, based on FOIA considerations, been posting unpublished decisions at *http://uscis.gov/graphics/lawsregs/admindec3/index.htm*; however, these decisions are not indexed or searchable and one must laboriously plow through much irrelevant material to find the occasional pearl.

[2] Nonprecedential AAO decisions are poor vehicles for stating adjudication standards or policies because USCIS service centers and even the AAO are not bound to follow them in other decisions, they may be highly case-specific, and they are not announced, distributed, or made publicly available in any convenient format. Only after many similar decisions are issued, and such decisions are shared among practitioners, does it become obvious that a de facto policy is being created and applied.

[3] The AILA USCIS Liaison Committee is engaged in continuing discussions with USCIS on this issue. A guidance memorandum may be forthcoming, but as of this writing, USCIS has not provided any information on either the timing or content of such a memorandum.

[4] *Chintakuntla v. INS*, Case No. 99-5211 (N.D. Cal. 2000).

[5] *See* R. Wada, "Court Issues Permanent Injunction in EB-2 Class Action Suit," 5 *Bender's Immigr. Bull.* 449 (May 15, 2000); R. Wada, G. Surmaitis & W. Leiden, "*Chintakuntla et al. v. INS*—An Interim Report on the EB-2 Class Action Litigation," 5 *Bender's Immigr. Bull.* 386 (May 1, 2000). While the three-year degree was not at issue in *Chintakuntla*, the litigation appears to have prompted the AAO to find a new basis for denying EB-2 petitions.

advanced degree equivalency: (1) a beneficiary can qualify if he or she holds a "foreign equivalent degree" to the U.S. advanced degree required on Form ETA-750 Part A; or (2) if a master's degree is required, a U.S. bachelor's degree or foreign equivalent degree plus five years of progressive, post-baccalaureate experience may be substituted for a master's degree.[6] The latter definition of equivalency has been the principal source of misunderstanding and confusion.

It is well established that legacy INS, and now the AAO and USCIS, have the authority to determine whether a beneficiary of the approved labor certification meets the job requirements set forth by the employer and approved by the Department of Labor.[7] Prior to the *Chintakuntla* litigation, INS had routinely accepted degree equivalency evaluations prepared by qualified education evaluators; after the litigation, it became more commonplace for INS to substitute its judgment for the expert opinions provided by qualified credential evaluators.[8] In essence, if an employer (or attorney) was not skillful in specifying the degree requirement for a position in the labor certification application, INS would exercise

its discretionary judgment about what degree would be sufficient to satisfy an employer's stated job requirement, and would do so in the narrowest possible fashion.

INA §203(b)(2) merely states that the second preference category is reserved for "members of the professions holding *advanced degrees or their equivalent*," but the implementing regulation adopted by INS limits the definition of equivalency to "a *foreign equivalent degree*."[9] This subtle turn of phrase in the regulation makes all the difference.[10] It is the cornerstone of the AAO's position on three-year bachelor's degrees that has led to the confusion and frustration that continues to this day.

Applying its regulatory language, INS required that the beneficiary possess, in the strictest possible sense, the foreign equivalent degree—not a combination of degrees or coursework or experience—in order to be qualified for the position described in the labor certification. Thus, in cases where a beneficiary possessed the equivalent of an advanced degree as required by statute, the more limiting language of the implementing regulation controlled the decision. While it seems obvious that the more generic language in the statute more accurately reflects real-world hiring practices, to date, legacy INS/USCIS has not indicated any desire to modify either its regulation or its interpretation of that regulation on this point.

In the absence of any workable policy guidance from USCIS on this issue, practitioners have devised expedient work-around formulations such as "bachelor's degree or academic equivalent," or "bachelor's or equivalent," together with a definition of what was meant by the phrase, "or equivalent", that was tied to the definition of equivalency provided for H-1B nonimmigrants qualifying for "specialty occupations" at 8 CFR §214.2(h)(4)(iii)(D). Although awkward, this latter formulation made sense because

---

[6] *See* 8 CFR §204.5(k)(2) ("Advanced degree means any United States academic or professional degree or a foreign equivalent degree above that of baccalaureate. A U.S. baccalaureate degree or a foreign equivalent degree followed by at least five years of progressive experience in the specialty shall be considered the equivalent of a master's degree. If a doctoral degree is customarily required by the specialty, the alien must have a United States doctorate or a foreign equivalent degree.").

[7] *See Mandany v. Smith*, 696 F.2d 1008, 225 U.S. App. D.C. 53 (DC Cir. 1983) and subsequent cases.

[8] In particular, it was during the post-litigation resolution of cases presented by *Chintakuntla* class members that the AAO first applied its rationale for denying EB-2 petitions involving beneficiaries from India who held three-year bachelor's degrees —if the employer specified that a bachelor's degree was required for a position, the AAO presumed that the employer meant "a U.S. bachelor's degree or a foreign equivalent degree," and then concluded that the three-year bachelor's degree was not a foreign equivalent degree, contrary to any educational credential evaluation stating otherwise. In fairness, the reliability of a particular education evaluation may be difficult to assess and it is not unfair for USCIS to question the validity of an education evaluation in some cases; however, legacy INS/USCIS has never established its credentials for evaluating an individual's education, and, therefore, for it to deny a petition by substituting its own judgment for that of an ostensibly qualified education evaluator without even requesting a second opinion borders on arbitrary and capricious action.

[9] *Compare* INA §203(b)(2) ("In general.—Visas shall be made available . . . to qualified immigrants who are members of the professions holding advanced degrees or their equivalent . . . "), *with* 8 CFR §204.5(k)(2): Definitions. As used in this section: Advanced degree means any U.S. academic or professional degree or a foreign equivalent degree above that of baccalaureate.

[10] *See, e.g., Matter of [name not provided]* (AAO, Jan 20, 2004), *available at http://uscis.gov/graphics/lawsregs/admindec3/b5/2004/jan2004_02b5203.pdf.* ("Both evaluators have found that the beneficiary possesses the equivalent of a bachelor's degree, rather than "a foreign equivalent degree.")

(1) it was consistent with most employers' actual job requirements, and (2) most employees for whom employers were filing applications for labor certification had met the requirements for and held H-1B status. The only problem with this work-around is that it does not define a position that qualifies for classification as EB-2 because even with five years of progressive, post-baccalaureate experience, the degree equivalency does not match the very limited definition of advanced degree under 8 CFR §204.5(k)(2).

Recent AAO Decisions Regarding EB-2 Degree Equivalency

The AAO position on three-year bachelor's degrees has been most clearly articulated in an unpublished 2004 decision:

> After reviewing section 121 of the Immigration Act of 1990, and the Joint Explanatory Statement of the Committee of Conference, legacy INS specifically noted that both the Act and the legislative history indicate that an alien must have at least a bachelor's degree:
>
> . . .
>
> Because neither the Act nor its legislative history indicates that bachelor's or advanced degrees must be United States degrees, the Service will recognize foreign equivalent degrees. But both the Act and its legislative history make clear that, in order to qualify as a professional under the third classification or to have experience equating to an advanced degree under the second, *an alien must have at least a bachelor's degree.* (Emphasis in original.)[11]

There is no provision in the statute or the regulations that would allow a beneficiary to qualify under section 203(b)(2) of the Act with anything less than a full baccalaureate degree. Although the preamble to the publication of the final rule specifically dismissed the option of equating 'experience alone' to the required bachelor's degree, the same reasoning applies to accepting an equivalence in the form of multiple lesser degrees, professional training, incomplete education without the award of a formal degree, or any other level of education deemed to be less than the 'foreign equivalent degree' to a United States

baccalaureate degree. Whether the equivalency of a bachelor's degree is based on work experience alone or on a combination of multiple lesser degrees, the analysis results in the 'equivalent' of a bachelor's degree rather than a 'foreign equivalent degree.' In order to have experience and education equating to an advanced degree under section 203(b)(2) of the Act, the beneficiary must have a single degree that is the 'foreign equivalent degree' to a United States baccalaureate degree. As noted in the federal register, persons who claim to qualify for an immigrant visa by virtue of education or experience equating to bachelor's degree will qualify for a visa pursuant to section 203(b)(3)(A)(i) of the Act as a skilled worker with more than two years of training and experience. In addition, a combination of degrees which, when taken together, equals the same amount of coursework required for a U.S. baccalaureate degree does not meet the regulatory requirement of a foreign equivalent degree.[12]

In the same decision, we find the apparent source of the AAO's position on three-year bachelor's degrees from India:

> A United States baccalaureate degree is generally found to require four years of education. *Matter of Shah*, 17 I&N Dec. 244 (Reg. Comm. 1977). According to India's Department of Education, the nation's education degree structure provides for both three-year and four-year bachelor's degree programs. After 12 years of primary and upper primary school, a bachelor's degree in the arts, commerce, or the sciences may be earned after three years of higher education. A bachelor's degree in a professional field of study, such as agriculture, dentistry, engineering, pharmacy, technology, and veterinary science, generally requires four years of education. *See generally* Government of India, Department of Education, *Higher Education in India, Academic Qualification Framework–Degree Structure,* (last updated October 1, 2001), available at *www.education. nic.in/htmlweb/higedu.htm* (printed copy incorporated into the record of proceeding). If supported by a proper credentials evaluation, a four-year baccalaureate degree from India could reasonably

---

[11] 56 *Fed. Reg.* 60897, 60900 (Nov. 29, 1991).

[12] *Matter of [name not provided]* (AAO Jan. 20, 2004) at 6, available at *http://uscis.gov/graphics/lawsregs/admindec3/b5 /2004/jan2004_02b5203.pdf.*

be deemed to be the 'foreign equivalent degree' to a United States baccalaureate degree. However, in *Matter of Shah,* the Regional Commissioner declined to consider a three year Bachelor of Science degree from India as the equivalent of a United States baccalaureate degree because the degree did not require four years of study. *Matter of Shah* at 245.[13]

The AAO's reasoning as expressed in this decision contains critical logical leaps and inferences about what Congress meant, and ultimately rests on a close parsing of the language of 8 CFR §204.5(k)(2), and not on any purported legislative history. The regulation and the AAO interpretation of it is by no means mandated by the plain language of the governing statute, 8 USC §1153(b)(2)(A), which defines the immigrant visa category as "members of the professions holding advanced degrees or their equivalent." It is inconceivable that Congress would have had the expertise or foresight to make a distinction between a four-year U.S. bachelor's degree and a foreign three-year bachelor's degree. Thus, the de facto AAO and USCIS policy on three-year bachelor's degrees relies on a combination of the restrictive regulatory language adopted by INS years ago and on apparently simplistic assumptions about degree equivalency that bear no resemblance to either actual equivalent education or what employers accept as part of their real-world employment practices.

A Noteworthy Exception

On January 9, 2004, the AAO issued a nonprecedent decision in a case filed at the California Service Center (CSC), reversing the CSC's denial of an EB-2 petition where the degree requirement on Form ETA-750 Part A was "Master's or equivalent" in computer science, and the beneficiary presented an education evaluation stating that he held the foreign equivalent to a bachelor's degree in mechanical engineering plus evidence that he had "well over a

decade of . . . experience in the field of computer science."[14] The AAO noted as follows:

> The director denied the petition, stating '[t]he labor certification does not state that the equivalent of a Bachelor's degree or any other level of education will satisfy the requirement.' The director noted that the beneficiary holds a degree in Mechanical Engineering, rather than in Computer Science, and that the record contains no evidence that the beneficiary's college education included any computer courses.
>
> . . .
>
> [I]t is not unusual for an individual to pursue a bachelor's degree in one field, and a master's degree in a different field. The labor certification does not indicate that all of the candidate's education must have been in computer science; only that the 'Master's degree or equivalent' be in that field. The regulations indicate that five years of progressive post-baccalaureate experience is functionally equivalent to a master's degree for the purposes of the classification sought . . . we find that the petitioner has overcome this ground for denial by demonstrating that the beneficiary's post-baccalaureate experience in computer science is equivalent to a master's degree in that field.

Thus, the AAO has, at least in this decision, affirmed that the phrase, "or equivalent" means something more than "foreign equivalent degree," and includes as a minimum a U.S. bachelor's degree or a foreign equivalent degree *in any field* plus five years of progressive post-baccalaureate experience in the field sought (here, computer science). While the particular fact situation presented in this case appears to be rare, the AAO's decision is a curious departure from the narrow interpretation of an employer's job requirements applied by INS/USCIS in other cases involving degree equivalency issues.

The essential distinction here appears to be that the beneficiary actually held a foreign equivalent bachelor's degree, thus removing it from the scope of the AAO's carefully crafted position on three-year bachelor's degrees. It is ironic that the AAO in this decision draws upon real-world information to justify its decision ("[I]t is not unusual for an individual to pursue a bachelor's degree in one field, and

---

[13] *Id.* at 5. Note that the AAO's characterization of *Matter of Shah* is not quite accurate—the Commissioner's conclusion was that "the petitioner has failed to establish that his [bachelor's degree] is equivalent to a U.S. bachelor's degree . . . ." *Matter of Shah* at 245. This leaves open the possibility that *Matter of Shah* can be overcome in situations where equivalency can be demonstrated.

[14] *Matter of [name not provided]*, California Service Center (AAO Jan. 9, 2004), available at *www.lexisnexis.com/practice areas/immigration/pdfs/web493.pdf.*

a master's degree in a different field."), while it chooses to ignore the real world in all decisions involving three-year bachelor's degrees.

In sum, the denial of EB-2 petitions involving three-year bachelor's degrees (at least from India) is based on the following line of reasoning:

- The employer, as stated on box 13 of Form ETA 750 (or line H.4 or H.8 of Form ETA 9089), requires a bachelor's degree for the position described in the approved labor certification.

- USCIS interprets the entries "BS," "BA," or "bachelor's" in box 13 to mean a U.S. baccalaureate degree or a foreign equivalent degree, because that is the only equivalency allowable under the regulations at 8 CFR §204.5(k)(2).

- USCIS has authority to determine whether a beneficiary of the approved labor certification meets the job requirements set forth by the employer and approved by the Department of Labor.[15]

- The beneficiary's three-year bachelor's degree standing alone is not equivalent to a U.S. bachelor's degree; the regulation allows for "a foreign equivalent degree"—not a combination of degrees or diplomas, but a single degree. Therefore, in the absence of a master's degree, no amount of supplementary education after the bachelor's degree will be sufficient to meet the regulatory definition of what is required to qualify for EB-2.

Practice Tip: The AAO decisions do not address cases where the beneficiary holds a three-year bachelor's degree but also holds an advanced degree (*i.e.*, a master's degree, PhD, or advanced professional degree such as M.D.). Thus, if the position requires an advanced degree (master's degree, PhD, or other advanced degree) and the beneficiary holds the required U.S. degree or a foreign equivalent degree, the beneficiary is not attempting to qualify for the position based on a three-year bachelor's degree, and it should be irrelevant. Nevertheless, there have been unconfirmed reports of scattered denials for EB-2 petitions in this situation.[16] Unfortunately, broad generalizations are not possible because of the

variety of degree combinations that exist, and each case must be carefully evaluated.[17]

Practice Tip: For the purpose of designing a PERM application where the beneficiary is attempting to qualify based on a three-year bachelor's degree, the AAO position as articulated in its nonprecedent decisions appears to be twofold: (1) a position that requires anything other than a U.S. bachelor's degree or a foreign equivalent degree followed by at least five years of progressive, postbaccalaureate experience in the professional field will not qualify for EB-2; and (2) if the position requires a U.S. bachelor's degree or foreign equivalent degree, a three-year bachelor's degree from India will not meet this requirement, regardless of what supplementary diplomas or experience the beneficiary may have.

Three-year Bachelor's Degrees in the EB-3 Category

Key Differences Between the EB-3 Category and the EB-2 Category

Until recently, USCIS had continued to approve EB-3 petitions for positions requiring a bachelor's degree as long as the beneficiary held the equivalent of the required U.S. bachelor's degree based on education alone—*e.g.*, a three-year bachelor's degree and a one-year postgraduate diploma in a relevant field was acceptable for EB-3.[18]

---

[15] *See Mandany v. Smith*, 696 F.2d 1008, 225 U.S. App. D.C. 53 (DC Cir. 1983), and subsequent cases.

[16] The author posted an inquiry on the AILA InfoNet message board soliciting information or documentation on any case with this fact pattern that has been denied. Despite numerous "hits," no responses were received.

[17] For example, it seems unlikely that either USCIS or a qualified credential evaluator would find that a two-year bachelor's degree followed by a two-year master's degree program would equate to a U.S. master's degree; whereas completion of a three-year bachelor's program followed by a three-year master's degree program provides a much more credible basis for a finding that the beneficiary possesses a foreign equivalent master's degree. On the borderline between these extremes is the three-year bachelor's degree followed by a two-year master's degree—the Nebraska Service Center reports that it is "currently awaiting guidance from headquarters on this issue." *See* NSC Liaison Q&A of April 19, 2006, No. 8, *published on* AILA InfoNet at Doc. No. 06050966 (*posted* May 9, 2006).

[18] A legacy INS Operations Instruction, Section 204.4, paragraph five, addresses degree equivalencies in EB-3 adjudications as follows:

Instances when a request for an advisory evaluation would be appropriate are where a diploma does not confer a degree recognizable as a baccalaureate or higher degree in this country and a petitioner or applicant asserts that the diploma represents the equivalent of a specified degree in the United States, or when there is

continued

Similar degree equivalency language is used in regulations governing EB-3 for individuals qualifying as a "member of the professions."[19] However, the EB-3 visa category is more broadly defined at INA §203(b)(3) to include "skilled workers, professionals, and other workers." Professionals are defined as "[q]ualified immigrants who hold baccalau-reate degrees and who are members of the professions," whereas skilled workers are defined as "[q]ualified immigrants who are capable, at the time of petitioning for classification under this paragraph, of performing skilled labor (requiring at least 2 years of training or experience), not of a temporary or seasonal nature, for which qualified workers are not available in the United States."

Thus, the key difference between the EB-3 and EB-2 categories is that the EB-3 category includes both professionals and skilled workers, and it is the expansive statutory definition of the EB-3 category that allows flexibility for accommodating positions where an employer may accept a variety of education and experience backgrounds.[20]

The pitfall created by the AAO for three-year bachelor's degrees in the EB-2 category may also appear in the EB-3 category depending on how the employer's job requirement is expressed in the labor certification. To accommodate three-year bachelor's degrees, the now-standard labor certification specification of job requirements for positions destined for the EB-3 category is "bachelor's or equivalent," where "equivalent" is defined by the employer somewhere on Form ETA 750 (usually in box 15, where there is enough space on the form to include a clarifying definition), or on Form ETA-9089 (in box H.14). If equivalency is defined in terms other than "a foreign equivalent degree" that would allow alternative qualifications, the EB-3 petition may not be approvable as "a member of the professions," but it can still be approved as a "skilled worker." The difference is more semantic than substantive, since both subcategories are lumped together in the EB-3 category, and the result should be the same, an approved EB-3 I-140.

But what happens with a naked "bachelor's or equivalent" requirement in the EB-3 category? While USCIS has the authority to determine whether a beneficiary meets the job requirement set forth by the employer-petitioner on the approved labor certification, can USCIS take the additional step of applying its own interpretation of the employer's job

---

> any reason to doubt that a diploma conferring a degree is equivalent to a similar degree in the United States. When an evaluation is needed the request shall be made on Form I-72 and the following paragraph shall be inserted on the form:
>
> Your petition and supporting documents are being returned. It has been determined after review that an advisory evaluation of the beneficiary's credentials must be obtained before a decision can be made. This evaluation is necessary to determine the level and major field or educational attainment described in the supporting documents in terms of equivalent education in the United States. The Immigration and Naturalization Service does not endorse or recommend evaluators. Many private individuals, organizations and educational institutions provide this service. An acceptable evaluation should:
>
> (i) **Consider formal education only, not practice experience.**
> (ii) State if the collegiate training was post-secondary education, i.e., did the applicant complete the U.S. equivalent of high school before entering college?
> (iii) Provide a detailed explanation of the material evaluated, rather than a simple conclusory statement.
> (iv) Briefly state the qualifications and experience of the evaluator providing the opinion.

This instruction implies that any combination of formal education that did not involve practical experience could be used as the basis for degree equivalency, and based on the author's experience this was the policy that was followed for EB-3. Based on anecdotal communications with practitioners, it appears that over the past year or more, USCIS service centers have begun ignoring the Operations Instructions and denying EB-3 petitions where the labor certification required a "bachelor's degree or equivalent" and the beneficiary held the equivalent education but not a single source degree. Since Operations Instructions are not statements of agency policy per se, and individual case decisions and nonprecedential AAO decisions are scattered and are not published, it is difficult to document when such a quasi-adjudication standard is changed, except by informal anecdotal communications with practitioners. The work-around is to require a "bachelor's degree or equivalent" and define specifically what is meant by "equivalent" directly on the labor certification application.

[19] See 8 CFR §204.5(l)(2) ("Professional means a qualified alien who holds at least a United States baccalaureate degree or a foreign equivalent degree and who is a member of the professions.")

---

[20] The AAO has acknowledged that beneficiaries holding the equivalent of a bachelor's degree may qualify for EB-3. *See Matter of [name not provided]* (AAO Jan 20, 2004), at 6 ("persons who claim to qualify for an immigrant visa by virtue of education or experience equating to bachelor's degree will qualify for a visa pursuant to section 203(b)(3)(A)(i) of the Act as a skilled worker with more than two years of training and experience.").

requirements to conclude that a beneficiary is not qualified for the position and therefore deny the EB-3 I-140 petition? Does USCIS have the authority to impose its interpretation of an employer's job requirements where the specification shown on the labor certification is ambiguous?

Grace Korean United Methodist Church v. Chertoff

In *Grace Korean United Methodist Church v. Chertoff*[21] (*Grace Church*), the federal district court, District of Oregon, addressed this point. The church filed an EB-3 I-140 petition based on an approved labor certification that specified an education requirement of a "B.A. or equivalent" in theology. The beneficiary had a bachelor's degree in home economics and two years of seminary education toward a bachelor's degree in theology, and many years of experience. No definition of "or equivalent" was provided on the ETA 750. The I-140 was denied by the Nebraska Service Center; the subsequent appeal and two motions to reopen were subsequently denied by the AAO, which held to its position that the labor certification requires a candidate with a specific degree, and that the beneficiary did not possess that degree. In essence, the Nebraska Service Center and the AAO interpreted the phrase "or equivalent," as stated on the approved labor certification, to mean "foreign equivalent degree," and refused to accept the petitioner's definition that was offered in its motions. The district court held that

> [n]either the statute nor the implementing regulations require an actual degree for approval under this classification . . . [b]ecause Congress did not require a degree for classification as a 'skilled worker,' defendants' requirement that [the beneficiary] possess an actual degree is contrary to the plain language of the statute and the clear Congressional intent . . . *CIS does not have the authority or expertise to impose its strained definition of 'B.A. or equivalent' on that term as set forth in the labor certification* . . . If any agency has the power to define the job qualifications set forth in a labor certification, it is the DOL, the agency responsible for reviewing and adjudicating the labor certification.[22] (Emphasis added.)

Grace Church thus supports the more general proposition that USCIS does not have the authority to impose its interpretation of an employer's job requirements where those requirements are ambiguous and subject to more than one interpretation.

This conclusion is consistent with a previous INS guidance memorandum for adjudicating EB-2 petitions in response to the *Chintakuntla* EB-2 class-action litigation. That memorandum was published in the *Federal Register* as part of the settlement in *Chintakuntla*.[23] In the memorandum, INS stated that if the employer fails to specify whether the five years of experience must be progressive or must be post-baccalaureate, adjudicators should not deny the petition, but should "request a supplemental statement clarifying whether the position requires five years of post-baccalaureate experience that is truly progressive in nature."[24]

Practice Tip: Attorneys continue to report EB-3 I-140 cases being denied by USCIS service centers even when the "bachelor's or equivalent" formulation is used. As of this writing, the Nebraska Service Center has declined to follow the *Grace Church* decision and is therefore continuing to deny EB-3 I-140 petitions with the naked "or equivalent" formu-

---

It is the employer, working under the supervision and direction of OED and DOL that establishes the requirements for employment. CIS looks to education and experience requirements in the labor certification to determine whether the applicant falls within the skilled worker or professional classification. . . It is the responsibility of the employer, not CIS, to establish the criteria for the open position. It is undisputed that the Church intended the language 'B.A. or equivalent' to include degree equivalency based on education and experience, because it drafted the labor certification with [the beneficiary] in mind. It is also not in dispute that [the beneficiary] possessed the equivalent of a bachelor's degree in theology based on her unique combination of education and relevant experience.

The court held that the Service 'decision to deny Plaintiffs' I-140 immigrant visa petition on the grounds that plaintiff [ ] did not have a foreign degree equivalent to a B.A. in Theology was arbitrary, capricious, and an abuse of discretion. The court vacates Defendants' decision and orders Defendants to approve the Church's I-140 immigrant visa petition on behalf of Park.'

[23] 65 Fed. Reg. 41093 (July 3, 2000).

[24] *Id.* at 41096. The court's conclusion is also consistent with the precedent decision in *Matter of Silver Dragon Chinese Restaurant*, 19 I&N Dec. 401, 406 (Comm. 1986) ("[USCIS] may not ignore a term of the labor certification, nor may it impose additional requirements.")

---

[21] *Grace Korean United Methodist Church v. Chertoff*, Case No. CV. 04-1849-PK (Dist. Ore., Nov. 3, 2005).

[22] The court went on to explain:

continued

lation where the beneficiary does not hold a single-source bachelor's degree.[25] Thus, it remains crucial to include a definition of equivalency on the Form ETA 750 or 9089. In this situation, it may be helpful to submit documentation of the AAO's position as expressed in *Matter of X– (name redacted)*[26] to the service center either with the original petition or as part of a motion to reconsider/appeal.

WHAT ABOUT NON-INDIAN THREE-YEAR BACHELOR'S DEGREES?

As mentioned earlier, unpublished AAO decisions are a poor way of setting policy that affects the adjudication of many I-140 petitions. In most of the AAO decisions on this topic, the AAO refers to three-year degrees generically, implying that its interpretation of the regulation applies to all foreign three-year bachelor's degrees. However, all of the denials appear to be for three-year bachelor's degrees from India, despite the fact that three-year bachelor's degrees are common at universities in Canada, Western Europe, and Australia. In these countries it is common for students on an academic track to complete 13 years of grade school and secondary school education prior to admission to a bachelor's degree program, one year more than is typically required for admission to U.S. bachelor's degree programs.[27] In this scenario, the bachelor's degree should be equivalent to a U.S. bachelor's degree because the additional year was completed as a prerequisite to entry to the bachelor's program. This is analogous to a person in the United States who completes one year of education at a community college and transfers credits to a college and completes the final three years at the degree-conferring college or university.[28]

As suggested in *Matter of (name redacted)* (AAO Jan. 20, 2004), the AAO has evidence that three-year bachelor's degrees from India are not equivalent to U.S. four- year degrees, and if similar evidence were available for three-year degree programs in other countries, those degrees would also be found to be not equivalent to U.S. bachelor's degrees. The absence of reported denials involving three-year degrees from non-Indian universities suggests that the AAO and the USCIS service centers are presumptively accepting three-year degrees from non-Indian universities as equivalent to U.S. bachelor's degrees. For EB-2 cases involving beneficiaries with non-Indian three-year bachelor's degrees, practitioners would be wise to collect documentation of the degree program showing that thirteen years of primary and secondary education are required for admission to the program before attempting an EB-2 I-140.

WHAT ABOUT THOSE USCIS OPINION LETTERS FROM EFREN HERNANDEZ?

Efren Hernandez, Director, Business and Trade Services, USCIS Office of Adjudications, has issued two letters in response to inquiries from immigration attorneys, purporting to interpret USCIS degree equivalency requirements in the EB-2 category;[29]

---

[25] *See* NSC Q&A from the AILA Northwest Regional Immigration Law Conference (3-9-06), Item #15, *published on AILA InfoNet at Doc. No. 06032964* (March 29, 2006). ("With regard to the *Grace Church* decision, the NSC is not following the finding by the court.")

[26] As quoted earlier, the AAO stated that "persons who claim to qualify for an immigrant visa by virtue of education or experience equating to a bachelor's degree will qualify for a visa pursuant to section 203(b)(3)(A)(i) of the Act as a skilled worker . . . ." The decision is available online at *http://uscis.gov/graphics/lawsregs/admindec3/b5/2004/jan20 04_02b5203.pdf.*

[27] Since these cases are being approved without question, documentation supporting this essential fact has not been produced.

[28] The AAO has expressed agreement with this type of equivalency in commentary accompanying a nonprecedential decision:

> We do not find that our interpretation would disqualify an individual who obtained an associates degree at a community college and subsequently received a baccalaureate degree at a university. If the university awarded the baccalaureate degree after less than four years, it would be because it allowed the student to transfer his or he community college credits towards the four year degree that the university normally awards. Thus, the final degree, and not a combination of degrees would be a baccalaureate degree.

Matter of Divine, Inc., A96 146 275 (AAO July 17, 2003), n.1.

[29] On January 7, 2003, in response to a written inquiry on this question submitted by one attorney, Efren Hernandez, Director, Business and Trade Services, stated as follows:

> You ask whether the reference to "a foreign equivalent degree" in 8 CFR 204.5(k)(2) means that the foreign equivalent advanced degree must be in the form of a single degree. Despite the use of the singular "degree," it is not the intent of the regulations that only a single foreign degree may satisfy the equivalency requirement.

continued

however, the AAO has undermined the authority of these letters by advising service centers in unpublished decisions that the Hernandez letters are not statements of USCIS policy and are not binding on service center decisions.[30] With guidance such as this from the AAO, it is no surprise that USCIS service centers have declined to follow the interpretation offered in the Hernandez letters.

SUMMARY OF "AD HOC RULES" FOR DRAFTING PERM APPLICATIONS

The highly dispersed and case-specific information that now exists makes it difficult to discern what rules to apply when drafting PERM applications.[31] Until official guidance is made available by USCIS, the "ad hoc rules" that appear to be in effect

> Provided that the proper credential evaluations service finds that the foreign degree or degrees are the equivalent of the required U.S. degree, then the requirement may be met.

Efren Hernandez III, Letter to Mr. Aron Finkelstein, Jan. 7, 2003, *published on* AILA InfoNet at Doc. No. 03041544 (*posted* Apr. 15, 2003).

Again on July 23, 2003, in response to another written inquiry on this question, Mr. Hernandez stated as follows:

> You ask if the completion of a three-year university course of study resulting in a bachelor's degree, followed by the completion of a PONSI-recognized postgraduate diploma program may be deemed to be the equivalent of a four-year U.S. bachelor's degree. In my opinion such a combination may be deemed the equivalent of a four-year U.S. bachelor's degree. . . an alien in this scenario may combine that equivalent degree with five years of progressive experience in the specialty in order to satisfy the "advanced degree" requirements of INA §203(b)(2)(A) and 8 CFR §204.5(k)(2).

Efren Hernandez, Letter to Ms. Naomi Schorr, July 23, 2003.

Unfortunately, these opinion letters appear to have had little impact where it counts since subsequent to the issuance of these letters the AAO and the service centers have continued to deny cases involving beneficiaries who happened to have graduated from a university that offered only three-year bachelor's degree programs regardless of what additional education they completed to supplement their bachelor's degree programs, in contradiction to the interpretation offered by Hernandez.

[30] *See, e.g., Matter of X– (name redacted)* (AAO Jan 20, 2004) ("[T]he letter from the Office of Adjudications is not persuasive . . . the letter's reasoning would be [*sic*] lead to results directly contrary to the regulations, statute, and the intent of Congress . . . .")

[31] USCIS has indicated that a guidance memo is under development; such a memo, if ever released, may help clarify its policy in this area.

based on available unpublished AAO decisions may be summarized as follows for EB-2 and EB-3:

Ad Hoc Rules for EB-2

- If an employer requires an advanced degree (master's, PhD, M.D., etc.) and the intended beneficiary holds the required advanced degree or a foreign equivalent degree, the beneficiary should qualify for the position; if the beneficiary also has an underlying three-year bachelor's degree from India, the service center may question whether the advanced degree is in fact a foreign equivalent degree.[32]

- If an employer accepts a bachelor's degree followed by five or more years of progressive experience in the relevant field, and the intended beneficiary holds a three-year bachelor's degree from India, the beneficiary will not qualify for EB-2 regardless of how much supplemental education (such as a one-year or two-year postgraduate diploma) the beneficiary may possess. The bachelor's degree is not equivalent to a US bachelor's degree; the postgraduate diploma is not equivalent to a U.S. bachelor's degree, and the two together won't equate to a U.S. bachelor's degree under the AAO interpretation.

- If the beneficiary possesses a three-year degree from a non-Indian university, *e.g.*, from Canada, UK, France, Germany, Australia, etc., it appears that the service centers presume that the bachelor's degrees are equivalent to U.S. bachelor's degrees. Substantively, the bachelor's degree should be equivalent to a U.S. bachelor's degree where the education system includes a 13th year of secondary education making it analogous to a person in the United States who completes one year of education at a community college and transfers credits to a four-year college and com-

[32] The foreign equivalent degree meets the requirements of the regulation at 8 CFR §204.5(k)(2). This should be true regardless of whether the master's program required two or three years to complete. *See* NSC Liaison Q&A no. 8 *supra* note 177 (NSC requesting clarification from headquarters where beneficiary has a three year bachelor's degree and a two year master's degree). In more doubtful cases (*e.g.*, a three-year bachelor's degree followed by a one-year master's degree, or a two-year bachelor's degree program followed by a two-year master's degree program), most credential evaluators will not issue an advanced-degree equivalency, so the prudent attorney should require a detailed and authoritative education evaluation to support the master's degree equivalency before going forward with the case.

pletes the final three years at the degree conferring college or university.[33]

- Acceptance into or certification by a professional organization, such as the Institute of Chartered Accountants, is not a foreign equivalent degree of any kind.[34]

- Work experience cannot be counted toward satisfying a bachelor's degree requirement in the EB-2 category; however, a beneficiary with five years of progressive, post-baccalaureate experience in the relevant field can qualify for EB-2 even if the beneficiary's bachelor's degree is in another field.[35]

- Combining a master's degree requirement with an alternative requirement that is less than a master's degree or less than a bachelor's degree followed by five years of progressive experience will not qualify for the EB-2 category; regardless of whether the beneficiary has the proper qualifications as defined by the regulation, USCIS may conclude that the position does not qualify for EB-2 because the employer will accept someone for the position whose qualifications do not meet the equivalency standard set forth at 8 CFR §204.5(k)(2).[36]

Ad Hoc Rules for EB-3

- If an employer specifies a "bachelor's degree" as the job requirement in the labor certification application, and the beneficiary holds a U.S. bachelor's degree or a foreign equivalent degree (*i.e.*, not a three-year bachelor's degree from India), then the I-140 petition should be approved as a "professional."

- If an employer specifies a "bachelor's degree" as the job requirement in the labor certification application, and the beneficiary holds a three-year bachelor's degree from India, the beneficiary will not qualify for the position, and the I-140 petition will probably be denied. Historically, a beneficiary in this position who had the equivalent of a U.S. bachelor's degree by virtue of also holding a one-year postgraduate diploma or similar education could still qualify, but this appears to be inconsistent with the AAO's interpretation of the regulatory language that, as in the EB-2 category, impliedly requires a single-source degree.

- If an employer (1) specifies a "bachelor's degree or equivalent" as the job requirement in the labor certification application, (2) defines what is meant by the phrase "or equivalent" in a manner that is different from "a foreign equivalent degree," and (3) the beneficiary meets the job requirement, then the I-140 petition should still be approvable for EB-3 as a "skilled worker" rather than as a "professional."

---

[33] This "ad hoc rule" is based on the absence of any reported denials of EB-2 or EB-3 petitions for beneficiaries holding three-year bachelor's degrees from non-Indian universities. In addition, the AAO has expressed agreement with the "transfer or credits" type of equivalency in commentary accompanying a nonprecedential decision:

> We do not find that our interpretation would disqualify an individual who obtained an associates degree at a community college and subsequently received a baccalaureate degree at a university. If the university awarded the baccalaureate degree after less than four years, it would be because it allowed the student to transfer his or he community college credits towards the four year degree that the university normally awards. Thus, the final degree, and not a combination of degrees would be a baccalaureate degree.

Matter of Divine, Inc., A96 146 275 (AAO July 17, 2003).

[34] *Id.* Again, the key difference is equivalent education instead of "a foreign equivalent degree."

[35] *See Matter of [name not provided]* (AAO Jan. 9, 2004), discussed earlier as "a notable exception."

[36] *See, e.g.*, 2006 Midwest AILA Conference NSC Update Q&A of April 7, 2006, *published on* AILA InfoNet Doc. No. 06041860 (*posted* Apr. 18, 2006):

> 9. We had a liaison inquiry recently where the petitioner's requirements for the permanent position were a Master's in computer science, plus one year experience
> *continued*

or a bachelor's in computer science, plus three years experience was required. In an RFE, NSC stated that "As the Labor Certification will accept less than a master's or a bachelor's plus five years of post baccalaureate progressive experience, category d [meaning the EB-2 category] is not appropriate." Please discuss the NSC's rationale for this position.

According to regulation, to qualify for classification under 203(b)(2) the position must require a person with an advanced degree. Title 8 of the CFR, §204.5(k)(2) defines "Advanced Degree" as "any United States academic or professional degree or a foreign equivalent degree above that of baccalaureate. A United States baccalaureate degree or a foreign equivalent degree followed by **at least five years** of progressive experience in the speciality shall be considered the equivalent of a master's degree" (emphasis added in original). Therefore, since the Labor Certification clearly indicates that a baccalaureate with three years experience is acceptable the position does not require an individual holding an advanced degree and is ineligible for petitioning under 203(b)(2).

- Work experience can be counted toward a bachelor's degree requirement in the EB-3 category if the employer specifies that a "bachelor's degree or equivalent" is required for the position, and then defines what equivalency it will accept (*e.g.*, "employer will accept educational equivalency as determined by a qualified credentials evaluator in accordance with 8 CFR §214.2(h)(4)(iii)(D)"), the I-140 petition should be approvable in the EB-3 skilled worker category.

Practice Tip: When preparing a PERM application for a beneficiary who holds a three-year bachelor's degree, practitioners should carefully review the beneficiary's educational background and where necessary request precise language from the credential evaluator. Because the typical credential evaluation that is produced today states equivalencies in ambiguous terms, it may be useless in situations involving three-year bachelor's degrees. For example, an evaluation that lumps all of a beneficiary's education and experience together to conclude that the beneficiary holds the equivalent of a bachelor's degree may have been sufficient to support an H-1B petition, but it will not be sufficient to support an EB-2 petition because it will not be clear that the equivalency is based on a single-source degree, and it will not be clear whether some of the work experience was counted toward the degree equivalency.[37] For beneficiaries who have a master's degree and a three-year bachelor's degree, the credential evaluation should isolate the evaluation of the beneficiary's master's degree from other education and experience and clearly state that the beneficiary's master's degree is a foreign equivalent degree to a U.S. master's degree. For beneficiaries who hold a three-year bachelor's degree from a non-Indian university, it would be ideal if the credential evaluation discussed the additional (*e.g.*, 13th) year of preparation required for admission to the degree program.

DRAFTING PERM JOB SPECIFICATIONS ON FORM ETA-9089

Before attempting to draft a PERM job specification on Form ETA-9089, it is best to decide whether the ultimate I-140 petition will be filed as EB-2 or EB-3 so that the proper "ad hoc rules" can be applied. The new Form ETA-9089 does not provide for the specification of educational equivalencies per se. The employer must specify the minimum education level required for a position by checking the appropriate box in item H.4 (or H.8A, if this is an alternate requirement). For example, to indicate that a bachelor's degree or equivalent is required, the options are to (1) check "bachelor's" and provide additional clarification in item H.14, "Specific skills or other requirements" (or H.8B, for an alternate requirement), or (2) check "other" and explain what is meant in item H.4-A.[38]

Whatever is specified in section H regarding job requirements, care must be taken to ensure that the beneficiary's qualifying education as described at item J.11, and the supporting documentation that will be filed with the I-140 petition, matches the employer's specification at H.4 (or H.8).

CONCLUSION

In order to properly draft a PERM application involving a beneficiary with a three-year bachelor's degree, it is necessary to understand how USCIS will interpret that application when it reaches a service center as the basis of an I-140 petition. The "ad hoc rules" presented here are an attempt at formulating interim practice guidelines based on available but unpublished AAO decisions that appear to form the basis of USCIS service center decisions. The AILA USCIS Liaison committee is engaged in a continuing dialog with USCIS officials to encourage USCIS to clarify, as well as modify, the adjudication standards for degree equivalencies to be applied by USCIS service centers. The "ad hoc rules" stated here may evaporate if and when a guidance memorandum is issued.

---

[37] *See, e.g.*, NSC Liaison Q&A #8 *supra* note 17("a simple credential evaluation stating that the degree is equivalent may not be sufficient. It should be supported by a detailed explanation of how that conclusion was made and the transcripts of the beneficiary's schooling to support the explanation and to document where the evaluator found the coursework equating a four-year degree.")

[38] While it appears that either method should work, the reported experience is not sufficient as yet to determine if there is a best method for expressing the employer's education requirement. The author's preference is to check "bachelor's" and include the equivalency language in H.14 in hopes of minimizing delays in DOL adjudication of the 9089.

THE REVIVAL OF SCHEDULE A, GROUP II: IS "EXCEPTIONAL" IN VOGUE?

by Rita Kushner Sostrin[*]

IS "EXCEPTIONAL" TRENDY AGAIN?

The world of high fashion has taught us that style trends are cyclical, and what seems to have gone out of fashion will eventually make its comeback. Be it platform shoes or oversized "Jackie O" sunglasses, styles disappear for a while but sooner or later return to runways and magazine covers. Has the immigrant visa classification of Schedule A, Group II followed in the footsteps of fashion, coming full circle and returning from obscurity with a newly found power to defy immigrant visa backlogs? Is it merely a fleeting trend that, after a brief reappearance, will again collect dust? Or is Schedule A, Group II a classic that is here to stay?

After the enactment of the Immigration Act of 1990 (IMMACT90),[1] Schedule A, Group II[2] quickly became a rarely utilized, nearly forgotten immigrant visa classification that was replaced by the creation of the EB-1 priority worker category.[3] Most aliens who could claim super powers were covered by the EB-11 for individuals of extraordinary ability[4] and the EB-12 for outstanding professors and researchers.[5] Yes, Schedule A, Group II was sometimes used in those limited instances where a petitioner wished to take advantage of its two-criteria standard, but the alien was neither a professor nor a researcher. Or, perhaps, the professor or researcher alien lacked the necessary three years of experience[6] or a permanent job offer[7] and thus could not make use of the EB-12 category. Nevertheless, while EB-12 did not always accommodate all who had a sponsoring employer, the rest could usually claim extraordinary abilities under EB-11.

Immigration law publications openly acknowledged the redundancy of the Schedule A, Group II immigrant classification. In his book, *Kurzban's Immigration Law Sourcebook*, Ira Kurzban called it "unnecessary in light of EB-1."[8] A number of articles discussing employment-based preference categories, when giving Schedule A, Group II a token mention, spoke of its superfluous nature.[9] There was even an entire article written on the sole issue of whether or not Schedule A, Group II had "a reason to exist."[10] Thus, Schedule A, Group II was tossed aside, like an old shoe, by the immigration bar. There was simply no real justification to use Schedule A, Group II with its confusing two sets of regulations, overlapping legal standards, and needless Department of Labor (DOL) forms. This was the case until the start of the era of immigrant visa retrogression, which brought back Schedule A, Group II.

In its November 2005 Visa Bulletin, the Visa Office of the U.S. Department of State (DOS) announced that, as of October 1, 2005, it had established cut-off

Rita Kushner Sostrin is senior counsel at Wolfsdorf Immigration Law Group, one of the largest immigration firms in Los Angeles, and the seventh largest in the United States. She is listed in *An International Who's Who of Corporate Immigration Lawyers* and is a frequent speaker and author on employment-based immigration law topics. Ms. Kushner Sostrin's practice is focused on immigration of academics and international medical graduates, and she represents several major academic institutions, hospitals, and scientific laboratories around the United States. She is currently serving her third term on AILA's CSC Liaison Committee.

The author wishes to thank Colleen Croal, Sandra Goldstein, and David Hackett for their assistance with this article.

[1] Immigration Act of 1990, Pub. L. No. 101-649, 104 Stat. 4978.

[2] INA §212(a)(5)(A)(ii)(II).

[3] INA §203(b)(1); 8 USC §1153(b)(1).

[4] INA §203(b)(1)(A); 8 USC §1153(b)(1)(A).

[5] INA §203(b)(1)(B); 8 USC §1153(b)(1)(B).

[6] 8 CFR §204.5(i)(3)(ii).

[7] 8 CFR §204.5(i)(3)(iii)(A)–(C).

[8] *See Kurzban's Immigration Law Sourcebook* 753 (9th ed.). Visit *www.ailapubs.org* to order and to see a table of contents of the tenth edition.

[9] *See* P. Webber, "Strategies for Avoiding Labor Certification," 93-12 *Immigration Briefings* (Dec. 1993); A. Cherazi *et al.*, "Employment-Based Petitions Exempt from Labor Certification," *Immigration & Nationality Handbook* 291 (AILA 2005–06 Ed.).

[10] F. Retman, "Schedule A, Group II: A Reason to Exist," *Immigration Options for Academics & Researchers*, 185 (AILA 2005). See *www.ailapubs.org* for more information about this book.

dates for the first and second employment-based immigrant visa preferences for China and India.[11] Since that time, when priority dates retrogressed as far back as 1999, only limited forward movement on visa processing has been observed. This has subjected Chinese and Indian aliens with extraordinary and outstanding abilities and whose work is in the national interest, and who would usually use the first or second employment-based immigrant visa preferences, to long delays in obtaining visas.

As a result, today, Schedule A, Group II has, once again, gained recognition and popularity, for it has become a streamlined way to obtain immigrant visas for those individuals who would normally opt for one of the EB-1 or EB-2 categories, currently subject to visa retrogression. The Emergency Supplemental Appropriations Act provided for 50,000 additional visas for the Schedule A category, including both Groups I and II.[12] Qualified individuals who would otherwise have to wait several years now have a direct path to permanent residence, thanks to Schedule A.

THE DOL LEGAL STANDARD

Through the Schedule A, Group II category, DOL allows petitioners to seek an immigrant visa on behalf of aliens of exceptional ability in the sciences or arts (including performing arts), and university teachers, by bypassing the process of labor certification.[13] DOL refers to this procedure as precertification to the effect that the alien's admission would not adversely affect the U.S. workforce and, consequently, would not require a labor certification. Since DOL's Schedule A application allows for pre-certification only and does not provide an alien with an immigrant visa, the petitioner must also qualify its beneficiary for an immigrant visa through either the second or third employment-based immigrant visa preferences. In other words, a petitioner must meet two sets of regulations—those of DOL and those of U.S. Citizenship and Immigration Services (USCIS)—in order to gain approval of a Schedule A, Group II petition.

Schedule A, Group II is an employer-sponsored classification and is unavailable to self-petitioners.

It explicitly covers only those aliens who possess exceptional abilities in the sciences and the arts, including the performing arts,[14] and excludes individuals who excel in other fields, such as athletics, from getting an immigrant visa through this classification. DOL defined the term "exceptional ability" as "recognized outstanding performance well above the standard for professional competence in the occupation."[15] A "science" or an "art" is defined as a field in which "colleges and universities commonly offer specialized courses leading to a degree."[16] It could therefore be argued that aliens working in the fields of business or education, included in the EB-1 regulations,[17] could be eligible for Schedule A, Group II because colleges and universities grant degrees in these fields. The regulations specify that an alien need not have received such a degree to qualify for the Schedule A, Group II occupation.[18] Hence, a prodigy painter who has not received a formal education in the fine arts could qualify for a Schedule A, Group II, provided that he or she meets the requisite legal standard.

The Legal Standard for Arts and Sciences

According to DOL regulations, an alien can qualify for an immigrant visa if he or she satisfies a three-prong test by demonstrating: (1) widespread acclaim and international recognition accorded by recognized experts; (2) documentation confirming that the alien's work during the past year did, and the alien's intended work will, require exceptional ability; and (3) confirmation that the alien meets at least two of the seven regulatory criteria.[19]

Prong One: Widespread Acclaim and International Recognition Accorded by Recognized Experts

The first prong of the Schedule A, Group II standard is reminiscent of the EB-1. It is, in fact, similar to a combination of the EB-11's "sustained

---

[11] http://travel.state.gov/visa/frvi/bulletin_2712.html.

[12] Emergency Supplemental Appropriations Act for Defense, the Global War on Terror, and Tsunami Relief, 2005, Pub. L. No. 109–13, 119 Stat. 231.

[13] 20 CFR §§656.5(b); 656.15(d).

[14] The PERM regulation extended Schedule A, Group II eligibility to performing artists who were excluded in the original DOL regulations. 69 Fed. Reg. 77391 (Dec. 27, 2004).

[15] Employment and Training Admin., U.S. Dep't of Labor, Technical Assistance Guide No. 656: Schedule A (TAG); 9 FAM 40.41, Exhibit I.

[16] 20 CFR §656.5(b)(1).

[17] 8 CFR §204.5(h)(1).

[18] 20 CFR §656.5(b)(1).

[19] 20 CFR §656.15(d)(1).

acclaim"[20] and EB-12's "international recognition."[21] DOL regulations, however, specifically address the type of evidence that must be submitted in order to meet this prong. The regulations ask for testimony from "recognized experts," which should be in the form of reference letters. While reference letters are normally submitted in support of a beneficiary's claim of original contributions, Schedule A, Group II analysis additionally requires that reference letters address the claim of widespread acclaim and international recognition. This can be achieved either by a separate set of letters from recognized experts or by presenting letters that cover all bases.

Ideally, the petitioner will submit reference letters from a diverse group of recognized experts who know the alien through his or her widespread acclaim and international recognition. To confirm the international reputation of the beneficiary, reference letters should come from experts in different countries or should speak of the beneficiary's accomplishments in more than one country. Practitioners should be aware that USCIS pays careful attention to the credentials of referees. In a 2001 decision, the Administrative Appeals Office (AAO) rejected the argument that an alien's petition was supported by experts from around the world because most of the experts, although then currently living and working in different international locations, were the beneficiary's former compatriots. The AAO ruled that "[t]he dispersal of the beneficiary's former collaborators to several countries does not make the beneficiary's reputation 'international' in any meaningful sense."[22]

It is important also to ensure that the experts who write letters on an alien's behalf understand the high benchmark of proof and utilize appropriate language that assists the case. Some modest cultures in Europe, Africa, and Asia consider "competent" to be a high form of praise. Yet such language would be destructive to any claim of "exceptional" ability or attempt to show widespread acclaim and international recognition. USCIS could use such evidence against the alien, arguing that even the alien's own supporters describe him or her only as competent, not exceptional. Likewise, any reference to an alien as a "promising" scientist or artist will be regarded

as a statement rejecting his or her eligibility, since one who is "promising," by definition, has not yet made it.

It is common for USCIS to question the objectivity of reference letters, particularly when they are written by individuals who personally know the beneficiary. We frequently see language such as "the reference letters are predominantly written by the beneficiary's collaborators, mentors or supervisors and, as such, their probative value is limited by these previous relationships." However, it is the author's opinion that, in addition to submitting some letters from experts who do not personally know the alien, practitioners can argue that letters from some referees who know the beneficiary should also be admissible. What is really at issue here is whether they qualify as "recognized experts," as required by the regulations.[23] If they do, USCIS cannot dismiss statements of top scholars, who are considered industry experts and who submitted support letters in that capacity, as biased merely because they may have worked with the alien. It is simply inaccurate to presume that all recognized experts would be willing to issue compromised reference letters just to accommodate a colleague. In fact, it can be argued that collaboration of the referees with the beneficiary only confirms the elite professional circles with which the beneficiary affiliates.

Legacy Immigration and Naturalization Service (INS) has acknowledged in a number of AAO decisions that expert testimony must be accorded evidentiary weight in petitions evaluating outstanding or extraordinary ability,[24] and the same reasoning should apply to Schedule A applications. Further, the examiner cannot substitute his or her judgment for that of experts, nor can the examiner ignore evidence that clearly satisfies a category.[25] Reference letters confirming widespread acclaim and international recognition issued by recognized experts should satisfy this prong, regardless of whether they personally know the alien.

---

[20] 8 CFR §204.5(h)(3).

[21] 8 CFR §204.5(i)(3)(i).

[22] Matter of [name not provided], EAC-99-081-50490 (AAO Apr. 13, 2001).

[23] 20 CFR §656.15(d)(1).

[24] In Matter of [name not provided], LIN-02-015-53361, (AAO Jul. 15, 2002), an appeal was sustained because INS failed to consider all evidence submitted in support of a petition, specifically citing expert reference letters. In Matter of [name not provided], LIN-02-243-52670, (AAO Feb. 28, 2003), the AAO likewise concluded that the beneficiary satisfied a regulatory criterion by providing letters from experts about the value of his work.

[25] Muni v. INS, 891 F. Supp. 440, 444 (N.D. Ill. 1995).

Prong Two: Confirmation that the Alien's Work During the Past Year Did, and Intended Work Will, Require Exceptional Ability

There are three parts to this prong, all of which must be satisfied: (1) the alien has at least one year of experience; (2) his or her work during the past year required exceptional ability; and (3) his or her future work will continue to require exceptional ability.

Demonstrating one year of experience is the easy part. A letter from an employer will meet this portion of the regulations. A more complicated scenario would arise if an alien with at least one year of experience has taken a year off and has done no work, exceptional or otherwise, during the *past* year. In that situation, it is advisable to gain the requisite experience in a nonimmigrant status before applying for Schedule A, Group II.

The second and third parts of this prong examine whether the alien's work during the past year required, and his or her future work will continue to require, exceptional ability. This is in direct conflict with the EB-11, which asks the beneficiary only to demonstrate that he or she will work in the area of extraordinary ability,[26] but does not mandate that the alien's job require extraordinary ability. Similarly, in a 2002 decision, the AAO sustained an appeal of an O-1 case that presented this issue.[27] The AAO cited the supplementary information from the regulations and confirmed that there is no statutory support for the requirement that the alien must be coming to the United States to perform services that require extraordinary ability.

This is not so, however, for exceptional aliens seeking to qualify under Schedule A, Group II. They must show both that their past year's work and future work can be performed only by a person with exceptional skills. Both can be demonstrated by the reference letters from recognized experts required by prong one. This is where a letter from the beneficiary's employer should be given particular credence, since the employer is in the best position to

assess whether exceptional abilities are required to perform the beneficiary's job. Additionally, publications about an alien's work or any other documents confirming the uniqueness of his or her work would be helpful to satisfy this regulation.

Furthermore, the regulations do not specifically state that the alien's one year of exceptional work experience must be in the same field in which he or she seeks pre-certification. What if the alien's work during the past year required exceptional ability in one field, but his or her future work will require exceptional ability in another field due to a career change? It appears that this could be allowed under the current version of the regulations. However, DOL's clarification in its Technical Assistance Guide, which accompanied its pre-PERM regulations, suggested otherwise. It stated that Schedule A, Group II is intended for aliens of exceptional ability "… who have been practicing their science or art during the year prior to application and who intend to practice *the same* science or art in the United States"[28] (emphasis added). Practitioners should also keep in mind that most of the seven regulatory criteria of the third prong require that the alien's accomplishments be "in the field in which certification is sought."

Prong Three: Confirmation that the Alien Meets at Least Two Regulatory Criteria

Acceptable proof of "exceptional ability," required in prong three of the DOL regulations, is defined as documentation in at least two of the following seven groups:

- *Receipt of internationally recognized prizes or awards for excellence in the field for which certification is sought.*[29]

This criterion asks exclusively for "internationally recognized" awards, thus significantly limiting the beneficiary's options, as nationally recognized awards would be inadmissible. However, the definition of "internationally recognized" is not provided by the regulations. Would a GRAMMY Award, the most coveted national music award in the United States, be considered acceptable? GRAMMY Awards have been issued by The Recording Academy for nearly 50

---

[26] 8 CFR §204.5(h)(5); INA §101(a)(15)(O)(i).

[27] *Matter of [name not provided]*, LIN-02-184-53385 (AAO Sep. 17, 2002). The AAO said: "After careful consideration, the Service agrees that there is no statutory support for the requirement that an O-1 alien must be coming to the U.S. to perform services requiring an alien of O-1 caliber. 59 Fed. Reg. 41820 (August 15, 1994). In review, the director applied an incorrect legal standard."

[28] Employment and Training Admin., U.S. Dep't of Labor, Technical Assistance Guide No. 656: Schedule A (TAG); 9 FAM 40.41, Exhibit I.

[29] 20 CFR §656.15(d)(1)(i).

years, honoring achievements in the recording arts and supporting the music community. It can be argued that the GRAMMY, while a national award, is certainly recognized internationally as one of the top U.S. music awards and, therefore, satisfies this criterion. The GRAMMY argument is an easy one to make, given this award's prestige. However, similar logic can be applied to other, less obvious, national awards for excellence.

- *Membership in international associations, in the field for which certification is sought, which require outstanding achievements of their members, as judged by recognized international experts.*[30]

Here, exceptional aliens seeking to qualify under Schedule A, Group II are again restricted to holding memberships only in "international associations." Therefore, membership in the U.S. National Academy of Sciences, for example, may not be sufficient for a Schedule A, Group II beneficiary, despite that members are elected into the academy based on their "distinguished and continuing achievements in original research."[31] Once again, creative lawyering is important in order to meet this criterion where an alien is a member of prestigious professional organizations that, on first glance, appear to be national.

- *Published material in professional publications about the alien, about the alien's work in the field.*[32]

This criterion calls for published material in "professional publications" only and omits any mention of major trade publications or other major media.[33] A front-page article on the alien in *The Los Angeles Times* or an interview as an expert on *The Today Show* is unlikely to satisfy this criterion because neither *The Los Angeles Times* nor *The Today Show* would qualify as "professional publications." Note that published material must be "about the alien" or "about the alien's work." It is not specifically required that the publication be strictly about the alien him- or herself, as materials about his or her work would

suffice. It follows that even published material that does not mention the beneficiary by name but discusses his or her work would qualify. This is helpful to those exceptional aliens who avoid personal celebrity and prefer to promote their work instead.

- *Evidence of participation on a panel, or individually, as a judge of the work of others in the same or in an allied field.*[34]

Artists usually demonstrate this criterion by showing that they have participated in judging professional competitions or contests. For academics, service as a reviewer or editor of professional journals will be sufficient to meet this standard. Note that it is not necessary to show that the beneficiary was selected to act as a judge on account of his or her exceptional abilities. Simply showing that an alien has served as a judge of others' work should satisfy this criterion.[35]

- *Evidence of original scientific or scholarly research contributions of major significance in the field.*[36]

There are two components to this criterion. The alien must show that his or her professional contributions are "original" and also that they are of "major significance." For instance, although many patented inventions are considered original,[37] they do not necessarily lead to commercially successful products or scientific methodologies that considerably influence the field. Such original contributions would not satisfy this regulatory criterion of Schedule A, Group II because they would not meet the "major significance" component.

---

[30] 20 CFR §656.15(d)(1)(ii).

[31] See the National Academy of Sciences website at *www.nas.edu/nas* for membership criteria.

[32] 20 CFR §656.15(d)(1)(iii).

[33] 8 CFR §204.5(h)(3)(iii).

[34] 20 CFR §656.15(d)(1)(iv).

[35] *Buletini v. INS*, 860 F. Supp. 1222, 1229 (E.D. Mich. 1994), specifically addresses this regulatory criterion and confirms that the alien did not have to prove that his selection as a judge was as a result of his extraordinary abilities.

[36] 20 CFR §656.15(d)(1)(v).

[37] Over the years, legacy INS/USCIS has made conflicting statements regarding whether or not patents are considered "original." In one AAO decision, INS opined that "[t]he granting of a patent documents that an invention or innovation is original..." *Matter of [name not provided]*, LIN-02-298-52969 (AAO Mar. 12, 2003). A year later, however, the AAO contradicted itself by saying "the simple grant of a patent does not signify that the petitioner has made an original contribution to his field of endeavor." *Matter of [name not provided]* (AAO Apr. 13, 2004).

It is also noteworthy that this Schedule A, Group II criterion only asks for "scientific or scholarly research" contributions and leaves out artistic contributions. It may be inferred from this drafting of the regulation that DOL does not expect artists to produce evidence relating to the original contributions criterion, unless they are also scholars in their respective fields. This begs a bigger question: Does DOL believe that artists do not make original contributions of major significance? Picasso certainly argued otherwise when he said "[d]rawing is no joke. There is something very serious and mysterious about the fact that one can represent a living human being with line alone and create not only his likeness but, in addition, an image of how he really is."[38]

■ *Evidence of authorship of published scientific or scholarly articles in the field in international professional journals or professional journals with international circulation.*[39]

International circulation is required for publications authored by exceptional aliens, and professional publications with only national circulations would not qualify. It is also apparent that, as in the "original contributions" criterion, there is no mention of aliens who work in the field of the arts. The regulation calls for "scientific or scholarly" articles in "professional journals" and omits any mention of articles in artistic professional journals or in the major media. An interior designer who published an article about his award-winning project in *Architectural Digest*, one of the leading international publications in the field of interior design, would not be able to satisfy this criterion.

Despite USCIS's frequent attempts to place the additional condition that the articles be well regarded or that the journals that publish them be of a high rank, the law imposes no such requirements. USCIS regularly remarks that, because all researchers are expected to publish, an alien seeking to qualify as extraordinary, outstanding, or exceptional must show that his or her publications establish national or international acclaim or international recognition. This is simply incorrect. National or international acclaim and recognition are demonstrated through satisfying the required number of regulatory criteria, depend-

ing on the visa classification. The alien should not be required to demonstrate it through meeting the singular criterion of "authorship of scholarly articles." It is important to keep in mind, however, that the journals that publish the alien's articles be "professional." In other words, publications in peer-reviewed journals will meet this requirement.

■ *Evidence of the display of the alien's work, in the field, at artistic exhibitions in more than one country.*[40]

Again, this criterion requires artistic exhibitions with an international reach. Additionally, it emphasizes that the exhibitions must be artistic and not in any other field. USCIS has been adamant about not allowing scientists and academics to use presentations at professional conferences as admissible evidence for this criterion.[41] Some practitioners have been getting around this requirement by arguing that "display of work at scholarly exhibitions" is sufficiently comparable to the "display of work at artistic exhibitions." In both cases, the alien showcases his or her work to an audience, the alien can participate by invitation only, and invitations to display work are granted based on merit of achievement. USCIS, however, has been routinely rejecting this position.

The Legal Standard for Performing Arts

PERM regulations added the performing arts to the list of eligible fields for the Schedule A, Group II category.[42] This standard appears to be slightly lower than that for the sciences and nonperforming arts, since it combines the prong of "widespread acclaim and international recognition" with the criterion of "international prizes and awards," resulting in only two required prongs. To qualify for Schedule A, Group II in the field of performing arts, a petitioner must satisfy a two-prong test by demonstrating: (1) that the alien's work during the past year did, and the alien's intended work will, require exceptional ability; and (2) that the alien has exceptional ability by meeting some of the enumerated regulatory criteria.[43] The regulations are silent about

---

[38] H. Clark, *Picasso: In His Words* 76 (1993).

[39] 20 CFR §656.15(d)(1)(vi).

[40] 20 CFR §656.15(d)(1)(vii).

[41] *Matter of [name not provided]* (AAO Apr. 13, 2004), stating that "[t]he wording of this criterion strongly suggests it is for visual artists such as sculptors and painters."

[42] 20 CFR §§656.5(2); 656.15(d)(2).

[43] 20 CFR §656.15(d)(2).

exactly how many criteria a performing artist must meet to be considered exceptional, and it could be assumed that meeting just one would suffice. Those criteria are:

- documentation of current widespread acclaim and international recognition, and receipt of internationally recognized prizes and awards for excellence;[44]

- published material by or about the alien, such as critical reviews or articles in major newspapers, periodicals, or trade journals;[45]

- evidence of earnings commensurate with the claimed level of ability;[46]

- playbills and star billings;[47]

- confirmation of the outstanding reputation of theaters, concert halls, night clubs, and other establishments where the alien has appeared or is scheduled to appear;[48]

- confirmation of the outstanding reputation of theaters or repertory companies, ballet troupes, orchestras, or other organizations where the alien has performed during the past year in a leading or starring capacity.[49]

It is noteworthy that aliens in the performing arts were excluded by the original Schedule A regulations. This is because DOL had concluded that performing artists of exceptional ability were already available in the United States and were having difficulty finding permanent employment.[50] Today, DOL has a different view of performing artists of exceptional ability and has added this field of endeavor to the Schedule A, Group II regulations.

ADDITIONAL DOL REQUIREMENTS

"International" Legal Standard

Nearly all regulatory criteria of the Schedule A, Group II classification require international recognition of the alien and stipulate that each criterion should be supported by evidence of such recognition "in the field in which certification is sought." These requirements make the Schedule A, Group II unavailable to aliens with acclaim on a national level allowed under the EB-11 regulations,[51] or to those who received most of their accolades in another field.

Although it is clear that "exceptional ability" in this context requires international recognition and is "far above average in the field,"[52] some practitioners argue that applying the highest standard, that the individual must reach the very top of his or her field, is too restrictive. However, USCIS clarified this issue in a recent Interoffice Memorandum by confirming that "Congress intended for the 'extraordinary ability' classification to be comparable to DOL's 'exceptional ability' standard in Schedule A, Group II."[53] It then went on to state that the standard of exceptional ability of the USCIS regulations under the second preference[54] is "less restrictive" than the exceptional ability standard of DOL. In other words, it is clear that DOL's "exceptional ability" should be addressed like USCIS's "extraordinary ability," while DOL's and USCIS's "exceptional ability" standards are, in fact, different.

Go figure.

Form ETA-9089

The petitioner must file a signed, uncertified Form ETA-9089,[55] in duplicate, together with Form I-140 and the rest of the evidence, with USCIS. The ETA-9089 must be submitted in paper form, not electronically.

When completing the ETA-9089, it is advisable to state in item H-12, which calls for information

---

[44] 20 CFR §656.15(d)(2)(i).

[45] 20 CFR §656.15(d)(2)(ii).

[46] 20 CFR §656.15(d)(2)(iii).

[47] 20 CFR §656.15(d)(2)(iv).

[48] 20 CFR §656.15(d)(2)(v).

[49] 20 CFR §656.15(d)(2)(vi).

[50] Employment and Training Admin., U.S. Dep't of Labor, Technical Assistance Guide No. 656: Schedule A (TAG); 9 FAM 40.41, Exhibit I.

[51] 8 CFR §204.5(h)(3).

[52] *Matter of Medical University of South Carolina*, 17 I&N 266 (R.C. 1978); *Matter of Tagawa*, 13 I&N Dec. 13 (DD 1967).

[53] USCIS Interoffice Memorandum, "Current Processing of Pending Forms I-140 for a Schedule A/Group I or II Occupations Missing Evidence of Compliance with U.S. Department of Labor (DOL) Notification/Posting Requirements and Guidance Effective March 28, 2005, Pursuant to New DOL Regulations at 20 CFR Part 656 Regarding the New Process for Blanket Labor Certification for Schedule A," Yates, Assoc. Dir. Operations, HQPRD70/8.5 (Sep. 23, 2005), *published on* AILA InfoNet Doc. No. 05101267 (*posted* Oct. 12, 2005)

[54] 8 CFR §204.5(k)(2).

[55] 20 CFR §656.17.

about special skills or requirements, that the job requires exceptional ability in the alien's field. This is to ensure that the information listed in Form ETA-9089 is aligned with the regulatory prerequisite that the alien's intended work require exceptional ability.[56] Likewise, if the petitioner is seeking to qualify under the second preference immigrant visa by claiming an advanced degree,[57] Form ETA-9089 should list the advanced degree in item H-4 as an educational requirement for the job.

If the case is approved, a copy of the Form ETA-9089 will be forwarded to the Chief of the Division of Foreign Labor Certification.[58]

Posting Notice Requirement

The employer is required to provide notice of filing the Application for Permanent Employment Certification.[59] Notice must be given to the appropriate bargaining unit representative or, if there is no such representative, it must be posted in a visible location at the place of the alien's employment for at least 10 consecutive business days.[60] Additionally, if the employer normally uses other methods of in-house media to recruit for similar positions, the posting should be published in all such in-house media. Once the posting is completed, it must be filed with the rest of the petition.

The notice must be posted between 30 and 180 days prior to filing of the petition.[61] In other words, USCIS would have sufficient grounds to deny a Schedule A, Group II application if the posting notice is dated more than 180 days or less than 30 days prior to filing.

Prevailing Wage Determination

Under the new PERM regulations, the employer must pay a Schedule A, Group II applicant a prevailing wage, and a wage determination issued by the state workforce agency (SWA) must be submitted with the application.[62] The alien's wage must be at least 100 percent of the prevailing wage.[63] Once again, to ensure the SWA's proper determination of

the prevailing wage for the alien's position, it should be indicated that the job requires exceptional abilities. The same applies to the educational requirements. If the alien beneficiary seeks a second preference immigrant visa as a member of the professions holding an advanced degree,[64] the degree requirement should be listed in the prevailing wage request.

MEETING THE USCIS REQUIREMENTS

Once the DOL requirements of the Schedule A, Group II classification are satisfied, pre-certification may be granted. However, since Schedule A, Group II is not an immigrant visa, but an alternative to a labor certification, it is not sufficient alone and should be accompanied by an immigrant visa petition. A beneficiary wishing to obtain pre-certification under these provisions must qualify either for the second or third preference employment-based category in order to receive an immigrant visa.

Second Preference Employment-Based Immigrant Visa

In practice, most beneficiaries who are able to successfully claim exceptional abilities hold advanced degrees, making it easy for them to meet the requirements of the second preference. Under this category, an employer may file an immigrant visa petition if the beneficiary holds an advanced degree or has exceptional abilities.[65] Note that the law only requires one or the other, and those aliens who hold a master's degree or above would make the grade.[66] Alternatively, a beneficiary may show that he or she holds a baccalaureate degree followed by at least five years of progressive experience in the field, which should also meet the requirement of an "advanced degree."[67] To qualify under this provision, the employer must demonstrate that the job requires an advanced degree.[68] Should a doctoral degree be required by the alien's profession, than he or she

---

[56] 20 CFR §656.15(d)(1).

[57] 8 CFR §204.5(k)(1).

[58] 20 CFR §656.15(f).

[59] 20 CFR §656.10(d).

[60] *Id.*

[61] 20 CFR §656.10(d)(3)(iv).

[62] 20 CFR §656.15(b)(i).

[63] H-1B Reform Act of 2004, Pub. L. No. 108-447.

[64] 8 CFR §204.5(k)(1).

[65] *Id.*

[66] INA §203(b)(2); 8 CFR §204.5(k).

[67] 8 CFR §204.5(k)(2).

[68] 8 CFR §204.5(k)(4)(i). *See also* INS Memorandum, "Educational and Experience Requirements for Employment-Based Second Preference (EB-2) Immigrants" (Mar. 20, 2000), *published on* AILA InfoNet at Doc. No. 0032703 (*posted* Mar. 27, 2000).

must possess a doctorate in order to satisfy this requirement.[69] Thus, if the alien qualifies as a member of the professions holding an advanced degree, there is no reason to meet the exceptional ability standard of the USCIS regulations. However, in those rare instances where the beneficiary does not possess, at minimum, a bachelor's degree and five years of experience, or holds less than the Ph.D. required by the job, it will be necessary to go to the second part of the test and demonstrate exceptional abilities.

USCIS regulations define exceptional ability as "a degree of expertise significantly above that ordinarily encountered in the sciences, arts, or business."[70] Curiously, USCIS added the field of business, despite the fact that DOL limited its scope to the sciences or arts.[71] Meeting this standard of exceptional ability is accomplished by presenting evidence of at least three of the following six criteria[72]:

- degree, diploma, or certificate from a college, university, or other institution of learning relating to the area of exceptional ability;

- confirmation of at least 10 years of full-time experience in the occupation;

- license to practice the profession or certification for a particular profession;

- evidence of a salary or remuneration that demonstrates exceptional ability;

- membership in professional associations; or

- evidence of recognition for achievements and significant contributions to the field by peers, governmental entities, or professional or business organizations.

Additionally, the petitioner must establish the prospective benefit requirement of the EB-2 classification.[73] Aliens of exceptional ability must show that they will "substantially benefit prospectively" the United States. The regulations are silent about this statutory prerequisite and provide no guidance as to documentation requirements in this regard. A district court in *Buletini v. INS* analyzed the prospective benefit requirement in the context of the EB-1 statute and concluded that legacy INS/USCIS should assume that "persons of extraordinary ability working in their field of expertise will benefit the United States."[74] In other words, according to *Buletini*, if an extraordinary alien will work in his or her field of expertise, it is reasonable to assume that he or she will substantially prospectively benefit the United States. Legacy INS has also opined that "[o]rdinarily, the 'substantial benefit' criterion is met through satisfying the other statutory requirements" and that "there may be very rare instances where an extraordinary alien's admission may be damaging or detrimental to the interests of the United States."[75] Therefore, as long as the alien meets the other requirements for extraordinary ability, the prospective benefit of his or her work is implied, with rare exceptions.

The same reasoning could be applied to exceptional aliens. In order to be eligible for the Schedule A, Group II pre-certification, USCIS must conclude that the alien qualifies as "exceptional" by satisfying at least two of the seven regulatory criteria of prong three. Therefore, by following the *Buletini* logic that prospective benefit is satisfied by proving extraordinary abilities, proof that the alien does in fact possess exceptional abilities should be sufficient to meet the prospective benefit requirement for this visa preference category. In other words, if it is confirmed that the alien has exceptional abilities and is working in his or her field of expertise, it should follow that the alien's work will benefit the United States.

Third Preference Employment-Based Immigrant Visa

Given that the standard of exceptional ability for the EB-2 is lower than that for the Schedule A, Group II,[76] an alien who has met the DOL regulations for exceptional ability should have no problem meeting the USCIS requirements. However, nothing mandates that the second preference be used, and the petitioner may choose to qualify under the third preference, if necessary. This may apply to an individual working in the arts who does not meet two of the most commonly utilized criteria, namely, a college degree and 10 years of experience. As such, a famous movie producer who meets at least two of the DOL regulations (*i.e.*, evidence of international awards and evidence of publications about the alien), may not

---

[69] 8 CFR §204.5(k)(4)(i).

[70] 8 CFR §204.5(k)(2).

[71] 20 CFR §656.5(b).

[72] 8 CFR §§204.5(k)(3)(i)(A)–(F).

[73] INA §203(b)(2)(A).

[74] *Buletini v. INS*, 860 F. Supp. 1222, 1229 (E.D. Mich. 1994).

[75] Letter, Skerrett, Chief, Imm. Branch, Adjudications, HQ 204.23-C (Mar. 8, 1995).

[76] *Supra* note 53.

qualify for at least three of the second preference regulations, since most of these regulations do not reflect the reality of who succeeds in Hollywood.

In that situation, the petitioner may opt to use the third preference employment-based visa designed for skilled workers, professionals, and other workers as the appropriate immigrant visa vehicle.[77] The regulations of the third preference specifically allow the petitioner to apply for the Schedule A designation in lieu of submitting a labor certification.[78]

CONCLUSION

Schedule A, Group II is back in fashion. In the past several months, it has become the necessary and much-needed bridge to permanent residence for Indian and Chinese nationals of exceptional abilities who are now faced with lengthy delays due to immigrant visa retrogression. Our country has been suffering from a chronic shortage of scientists and must rely on foreign nationals in order to fill our hospitals, universities, and scientific laboratories.

William A. Wulf, Ph.D., president of the National Academy of Engineering of the National Academies, reported to the U.S. House of Representatives' Subcommittee on Immigration, Border Security, and Claims Committee on the Judiciary:

"One third of all U.S. Ph.D.s in science and engineering are now awarded to foreign born graduate students. We have been skimming the best and brightest minds from across the globe, and prospering because of it; we need these new Americans even more now as other countries become more technologically capable."[79]

Over the years, we have been benefiting from the extraordinary, outstanding, and exceptional abilities of numerous foreign nationals who chose to work in this country on a permanent basis. Today, with visa retrogression posing a major obstacle, Schedule A, Group II has provided an important avenue by adding visa numbers and allowing those aliens who would be subjected to years of waiting to qualify for permanent residence.

So, is Schedule A, Group II in vogue again? Is it, as they say in high fashion, "the new black"? Coco Chanel once said, "I want to create classics," and in 1926, with the little black dress, she did.[80] And while it may look plain and redundant, the little black dress will never go out of style. Rather than being "the new black," Schedule A, Group II may have emerged as the "little black dress" of immigration law. It is not a trend, but rather a classic that is a solid backup when other options are not current.

---

[77] 8 CFR §204.5(l)(1).

[78] 8 CFR §204.5(l)(3).

[79] "Sources and Methods of Foreign Nationals Engaged in Economic and Military Espionage: Hearings before the Subcomm. on Immigration, Border Security, and Claims Comm. on the Judiciary," 109th Cong., 1st Sess. (2005) (testimony of William A. Wulf) (the importance of foreign-born scientists and engineers to the security of the United States), also found at *www7.nationalacademies.org/ocga/testimony/Importance_of_Foreign_Scientists_and_Engineers_to_US.asp.*

[80] *www.chanelamour.com.*

SCHEDULE A, GROUP II CHART

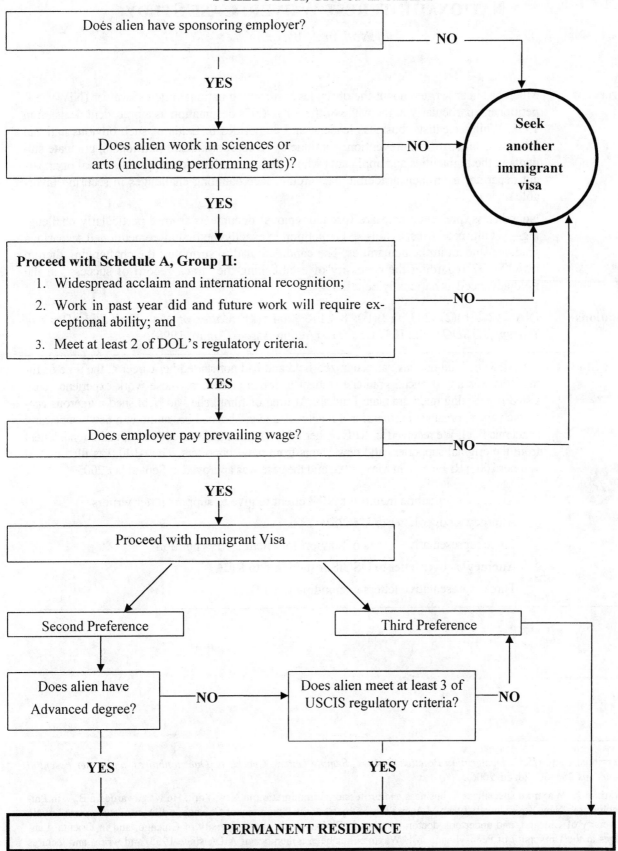

NATIONAL INTEREST WAIVER: CASE STUDY

by Nathan A. Waxman[*]

Overview Much has been written about the obstacles confronting national interest waiver (NIW) self-petitioners, particularly in the wake of the *NYSDOT*'s designation as a precedent decision in 1998. While scientists, business leaders, and authorities in fields of such obvious national interest as bioterrorism prevention, continue to be appropriate self-petitioners, graduate students in the humanities and applicants whose prospective service represents a real or apparent departure from their academic background face daunting challenges in securing favorable review.

Nonetheless, presented here are (pseudonymous) documents from a particularly challenging—yet ultimately successful—NIW petition in exactly the first aforementioned scenario: a graduate student in the humanities. The candidate had to surmount the challenging dictum in *NYSDOT* regarding the necessity of establishing the "track record of success" in the field advanced as nationally beneficial.

Citations INA §§203(b)(2), 203(b)(2)(B); 8 CFR §204.5(k); *Matter of New York State Dep't of Transp. [NYSDOT]*, 22 I&N Dec. 215 (Acting Assoc. Comm. 1998).

Case Study I "Darya Rivic" did not have a recognized field and had not started her career at the time of filing. She was an advanced graduate student in urban aesthetics whose work experience consisted of teaching undergraduate English. At time of filing, she had published numerous academic papers, organized professional meetings, and established her name in a newly emerging academic field. We received an RFE on her initial petition and responded with additional letters from the original supporters and new letters from new supporters. The I-140 was filed in November 2003; RFE came in May 2005; and the case was approved in September 2005.

Documents

Attorney's guideline memo for NIW client to give to support-letter writers

Attorney's cover letter to USCIS

Three representative letters of support for client's NIW petition

Attorney's cover letter to USCIS responding to RFE

Three representative letters responding to RFE

---

[*] Reprinted from *AILA's Immigration Practice Toolbox: Sample Letters, Checklists, Questionnaires, and Other Essential Documents* 253–80 (2d. ed. 2006).

Nathan A. Waxman specializes in business and professional immigration in New York. He was awarded a B.A. in Philosophy from New York University, an M.A. in Philosophy from the University of Chicago, a J.D. cum laude from Loyola University of Chicago, and undertook doctoral studies in Philosophy at the University of Chicago, and in Oriental Languages at the University of Pennsylvania. Mr. Waxman has been a member of AILA since 1985, and writes and lectures extensively on business and academic immigration topics.

[Attorney's guideline memo for NIW client to give to support-letter writers]

Guidelines to Writing a Letter Supporting
Ms. Darya Rivic's National Interest Waiver (Self-Sponsorship) Green Card Petition

Darya Rivic is applying to U.S. Citizenship and Immigration Services (USCIS) for permanent U.S. residence. Ms. Rivic is seeking residence (*i.e.*, her "green card") through a mechanism devised by Congress 12 years ago that enables talented individuals to sponsor themselves for permanent residence circumventing the complicated, traditional methodologies involving the securing of an appropriate organizational or employer sponsorship through complicated Labor Department procedures. The benefit of expediting the permanent residence would be of inestimable value to her career as a scholar, writer, and performer and would emancipate her from the usual limitation of pre–green card employment to particular employers—many of whom have in recent years been less cooperative, trying to avoid complicated interactions with the immigration authorities.

Ultimately, Ms. Rivic must prove she meets the following three conditions to warrant her receipt of permanent residence through the national interest waiver.

1. That her work is in an area of substantial importance. The challenge here is unifying her various activities and accomplishments into a recognizable field of endeavor. After extensive collaborative discussion, we believe the best unifying description of Ms. Rivic's multifaceted activities is "Urban Aesthetics." While this is not a universally commonplace designation for a field, we believe this is the best of the numerous characterizations we have reviewed (*e.g.*, Urban Planning, Cultural Studies, Performance Studies, Architecture, Tourist Studies, American Studies)—all of which we considered but rejected as excessively narrow to encompass her varied activities.

2. That the impact of Ms. Rivic's activities is national in scope despite the focus of her writings and lectures on New York City. While New York is admittedly a microcosm of the nation as a whole, the application will be reviewed by middle-level bureaucrats in rural Northern Vermont. Therefore, the broader potential and scope of her work must be emphasized.

3. Most critically, that Ms. Rivic's endeavors somehow significantly "exceed the norm" of accomplishment of others in her field (making it especially critical that we establish that, although not conventionally recognized as such, "Urban Aesthetics" constitutes a valid description of an area of endeavor representing the collaborative efforts of people in a number of traditionally recognized disciplines, such as Urban Planning, Cultural Studies, Performance Studies, Architecture, Tourist Studies, and Architecture) and that they have impacted others in her field, within and outside of New York. It is critical to recognize that contributors to "Urban Aesthetics" may themselves be primarily practitioners of more traditionally recognized disciplines and that "Urban Aesthetics" constitutes an emerging hybrid analogous to such previously unrecognized by now established fields as Computer Science, History of Religions, or Women Studies.

Our collective presentation of Ms. Rivic's application will focus on a depiction of her as an urban aesthetician who focuses on the city not just as a built environment but as a lived experience. Her interest in how residents and visitors alike personalize public space—how they make the city their own— encompasses the studies of what people do in the urban environment and of how they remember/recall the experience of the city, through writing, performance, and model making. Her accomplished history of international publication—including essays, poetry, and scholarly papers—and performance in Bulgaria and the United States reflects these interests. Likewise, so does her academic exploration of the notion of the city as a dynamic public art form and the concept of the city as archive, with special reference to the 1939/1940 World's Fair model of New York City as a dynamic memory palace capturing the histories of the city.

In order for Ms. Rivic's petition to succeed, we need to assemble an authoritative collection of letters from senior, well-established, and highly regarded leaders in her field of work, documenting her ". . . past record of specific prior achievement which justifies projections of future benefit to the national interest" and confirming that she can ". . . in some capacity . . . serve the national interest to a substantially greater extent than the majority of her colleagues." The letters must also ". . . demonstrate to some degree her influence on her field of employment as a whole."

It is important to define her specialty within the field of urban studies in such a way that she can be accurately characterized as having had significant impact on her specialty field. It would be best to downplay the fact that she is currently a graduate student and instead focus on her publications and presentations and on her contributions to public discussions of urban planning issues.

Please discuss the innovative leadership role Ms. Rivic has taken in her work in this field and emphasize she has had impact on the field itself and on other workers in it. Please also discuss the importance of her research and her leadership role in the field. Please focus your letter on some aspect of her work that has relevance to planning for and understanding critical issues of urban planning and space and on how she is uniquely and remarkably well-qualified to play a novel, critical role the field. It would be helpful if you would discuss her work vis à vis your own and comment on any impact her work has had on yours.

It is important to focus more on Ms. Rivic's special qualities, perceptions, or research tools that make her so well-suited to doing the research and writing she has done than to focus on the shortage of qualified scholars/writers in her field. Defining what differentiates her from other people researching and writing about the urban environment and doing it in a way that "speaks to" USCIS may be a bit challenging.

USCIS wants to hear that her work will benefit this country beyond the immediate locale where she works. Wherever possible, please emphasize that she has published in nationally and internationally prominent publications and that the classes she has taught have introduced her way of seeing and thinking about the city to students from all over the country.

It would be accurate to point out that the meaning of the city, its individual buildings and structures, and its use of public space have assumed an even greater collective significance to the American public in the period since the destruction of the World Trade Center buildings. Hardly a day goes by without a national newspaper or national newscast covering some aspect of how New York City—and, in fact, the entire country —will use the space previously occupied by the WTC. The "meaning" of those buildings and of the attacks on them and the role of city structures and spaces in preserving and recording memories are very much on the collective mind these days. Ms. Rivic's work—especially in that it relates to NYC—speaks to these concerns.

It is also important to characterize her as being distinguished among her peers, which could encompass people working in many different areas of scholarship, public planning, and performance: urban specialists, urban planners, poets, artists, museum and monument curators, and so forth.

Several aspects of what USCIS is looking for are counterintuitive. USCIS does not want to hear there is a shortage of urban planners or monument curators. Such language reinforces the immigration authority's perception that Ms. Rivic should employ the default mechanism of labor certification, rather than obtain a waiver of the burdensome labor certification mechanism. It is appropriate, however, to distinguish Ms. Rivic from the others in the field by saying that she is "widely recognized as playing a foundational/highly innovative/trail-blazing role" or that she is "unquestionably in the forefront of this field of study/investigation." Comparative descriptions are excellent, as USCIS needs demonstration that Ms. Rivic can be expected to ". . . serve the national interest to a substantially greater extent than the majority of her colleagues."

While hyperbole should be avoided, USCIS responds well to extremely hyperbolic statements of a type that make some academic people uneasy. Please remember that this is not a peer-review situation, these letters are *not* going to your colleagues, and they are destined for a folder that will be one of many passing by an overworked USCIS officer who has little patience for anything but the most extreme, unambiguous language. These are not conventional "letters of recommendation." Ms. Rivic is applying to USCIS for a green card, not for a job or a grant. The point of your letter is not to provide a balanced appraisal of her as a potential employee, colleague, or grant recipient.

USCIS is more interested in past and present accomplishments than in future potential. It is much better to say, for example, that "I am confident that Ms. Rivic will continue to enrich this country's collective understanding of its urban spaces, buildings, and activities" than to say "Ms. Rivic has enormous potential in the field of urban studies and I am confident that she will realize that potential."

Another surprise to many supporting-letter writers is that USCIS places more reliance on letters from independent commentators, from people who have not worked directly with Ms. Rivic and/or who have no personal interest in her acquisition of permanent residence. In some instances where a national interest petitioner has only presented letters from her mentors, senior collaborators, classmates, and employers, USCIS has specifically discredited the aggregate testimony as being biased. Therefore, we have suggested that Ms. Rivic seek letters of support from people with whom she has not worked or studied. If you have not worked with her directly, it is important that you make the point unambiguously and say that your comments on her accomplishments are based on her reputation, her standing in a community to which you both belong, her public presentations and articles, etc.

Because USCIS needs to know that Ms. Rivic's support letters are being written by senior, well- established, respected leaders in her field, we need a copy of your curriculum vitae (CV), an article about you, or a copy of your entry in "Who's Who" or your Web page or some other biographical reference. It is also appropriate to mention in your letter any points of your own special personal distinction.

Please state clearly the connection between you and Ms. Rivic or between your work and hers. If you are discussing work she did in collaboration with other people, please focus on her unique and distinguishable role.

The following are two sample letters that suggest some possible and alternative wordings. If you follow one of the drafts, please modify it and "make it your own," rewording it and adding details based on your own experience. Feel free to contact me by phone, fax, or e-mail if you have any questions about the letter in general or about Ms. Rivic's letter in particular. I would appreciate it very much if you would fax or e-mail me the working draft of your letter so that I might suggest any changes that would strengthen it.

Once you have printed the letter on letterhead and signed it, please mail it to me at the address below. It should *not go directly to USCIS*. I will send USCIS all the letters in a packet with Ms. Rivic's other petition materials.

Please note the sample letters that follow are just that—samples—and are not intended to serve as final drafts. Please mix, match, and rearrange the elements, drawing on different letters and on your own experience with Ms. Rivic.

Thanking you in advance for your cooperation.

Daphne Kaniss,
Senior legal assistant
to Nathan Waxman
404 Park Avenue South,
New York, NY 10009
Phone: (212) XXX-XXXX
Fax: (212) XXX-XXXX
dsk@waxlaw.com

[Please provide the requested information, modify the details as appropriate, add anything you feel should be in the letter, and then e-mail or fax a copy of your letter to me before you print it on letterhead. I will review your draft and make sure it will help Ms. Rivic's petition, without raising any of the red flags that slow down processing of this type of petition. Once I have reviewed the letter, I will give you the "go ahead" to print it on letterhead and mail or fax the hard copy to me, along with a copy of your CV and/or article about yourself or your organization and your role in it. *Do not send the letter directly to USCIS.* Please feel free to call, fax, or e-mail me if you have any questions. Thank you for your help.

Daphne Kaniss, Senior legal assistant to Nathan Waxman, 404 Park Avenue South, New York, NY 10009. Phone: (212) XXX-XXXX. Fax: (212) XXX-XXXX. E-mail: *dsk@waxlaw.com*]

[Sample draft letter from someone who has worked with Ms. Rivic]

USCIS / DHS
Vermont Service Center
75 Lower Welden St.
St. Albans, VT 05479

Dear **[Immigration Officer / Director / Immigration Adjudicator]**:

I am **[writing / pleased to write / submitting]** this letter in **[support / endorsement]** of the **[application / request / petition]** of Ms. Darya Rivic for permanent residence in the United States, in the category of National Interest Waiver. I am **[describe your position and your professional relationship to Ms. Rivic, and give any additional information that accredits yourself, your institution, or your own professional contributions.]** The projects that my organization focuses on **[describe your focus, especially as it relates in some way to Ms. Rivic's work]**.

I have known Ms. Rivic **[or I have been familiar with Ms. Rivic's work]** since **[year you met her]**, when we **[met at / corresponded about / collaborated on** . . . (Describe Ms. Rivic's contributions to the work in your group, or to your specialty field, emphasizing any innovative, cutting-edge, ground-breaking projects she led. Please be sure to mention any articles or reports she wrote or contributed to and describe any instances of her work receiving special recognition. Focus on the practical, national interest value of her work: how it did or could result in new ways of understanding and planning the use of urban spaces. Please include some comments on both the potential social impact of her work and on its impact on her professional field and colleagues.)**]**

I **[respectfully / enthusiastically / earnestly]** **[urge / encourage / ask]** you to **[approve / facilitate approval of / grant]** Ms. Rivic's petition for U.S. permanent residence, as her truly **[exceptional / outstanding skills / talents]** will clearly continue providing high-value benefits to the American people.

Sincerely,

[Name]

[Sample draft letter from an independent commentator]

Vermont Service Center
USCIS
Department of Homeland Security
St. Albans, VT 05479

Dear Immigration Officer:

Ms. Darya Rivic has asked me to comment on the significance and national interest value of her **[publication and research in . . .]** Although she and I have never **[worked together / collaborated]**, I have reviewed her published reports and extensively discussed her work with her and her colleagues. Based on my __ years of experience as a **[describe your own position and work]**, I feel that I am well-qualified to evaluate Ms. Rivic's contributions to **[fill in the details]**.

Ms. Rivic's interests overlap with mine in the area of **[. . .]**, and/but my group has taken a **[different / similar / analogous]** approach to solving this problem. We are focusing on **[. . .]**.

At a time in history when the values and important symbolic buildings of the United States are under attack and facing renovation in a social environment of questioning and uncertainty, I **[respectfully / heartily / enthusiastically / unhesitatingly / unreservedly]** **[urge / encourage]** your office to approve Ms. Rivic's permanent residence petition promptly, as I have no doubt that she has a major continuing role in the rebuilding of the physical and spiritual/psychological restructuring of this country.

Sincerely,

[Name]

[Attorney's cover letter to USCIS]

Nov. 3, 2003

Director
U.S. Citizenship and Immigration Services
Vermont Service Center
75 Lower Welden St.
St. Albans, VT 05479

Re: I-140 Petition of Ms. Darya Rivic seeking Employment Second Preference Classification as an Advanced Degree Professional Alien Performing Services Prospectively in the National Interest; and concurrently submitted I-485 application seeking Adjustment to Lawful Permanent Resident Status

Dear Director:

Enclosed please find the I-140 petition of the above referenced national of Bulgaria who is seeking EB-2 classification as an advanced degree professional. As confirmed by the attached letter from recognized experts in the field, Ms. Rivic's past, present, and prospective leadership role as an innovative urban aesthetician unquestionably serves the national interest.

Please note that the above-captioned I-140 petition is accompanied by the petitioner's application for Adjustment of Status pursuant to recent regulatory revision.

Ms. Rivic's qualifies for National Interest Waiver classification under §203(b)(2) of the Immigration and Nationality Act, which states that "visas should be made available to qualified immigrants who 'because of their exceptional ability in the sciences, arts, or business will substantially benefit prospectively the national economy, cultural or educational interests, or welfare of the United States."

Ms. Rivic's 1998 M.A. in Performance Studies from Gotham University and her status as an advanced dissertation candidate at that university qualify her as an advanced degree professional, thereby qualifying her for eligibility to document the national interest value of her achievements, under INA §203(b)(2)(B), and the Miscellaneous and Technical Immigration and Naturalization Amendments of 1991, Pub. L. No. 102-232, 105 Stat. 1733 (MTINA). Moreover, her distinguished record of accomplishment and documented track record of professional recognition conclusively demonstrate that she is already serving U.S. national interests to a **significantly** greater extent than other contributors to the nascent multidisciplinary field of Urban Aesthetics.

Indeed, the enclosed testimonial and documentary evidence unambiguously establish that Ms. Rivic is internationally regarded as a seminal figure in laying the foundations for the worldwide recognition of Urban Aesthetics as a socially and intellectually critical discipline, essential to the new millennia in its amelioration of the social, economic, and aesthetic ills engendered by the uncontrolled acceleration of urban growth in the past century.

Ms. Rivic's eligibility for national interest waiver classification under INA §203(b)(2)(B)(i) is premised upon her documented stature as a scholar, teacher, and writer in the rapidly expanding multifaceted field of Urban Aesthetics, whose contribution has substantially contributed to legitimizing Urban Aesthetics as a recognized academic and applied discipline and whose profoundly original, groundbreaking research has served to crystallize the contours of Urban Aesthetics as an invaluable component of the ensemble of disciplines contributing to the betterment of urban life in our country.

We respectfully urge that the enclosed statements from an extraordinarily diverse panoply of indisputably qualified authorities in the broadest range of disciplines constituting Urban Aesthetics corroborate the profound significance of Ms. Rivic's accomplishments to date and establish that she meets, and indeed exceeds, the rigorous standards set forth in the AAU's precedent decision, *New York State Department of Transportation v. INS*.

The aforementioned supporting statements, primarily emanating from neutral and unbiased international authorities, in conjunction with the enclosed documentary evidence substantiating Ms. Rivic's extraordinary record of publication, presentation, and propagation of original and socially beneficial ideas of immediate relevance to the improvement of the quality of urban life in the United States, manifestly establish her satisfaction of each of the three "legs" of the *NYSDOT* formulation. A brief synopsis of her qualification under *NYSDOT* follows:

1. **The benefits of Ms. Rivic's expertise are national in scope and will not adversely affect the interests of other regions of the country.**

Ms. Rivic's highly diverse work product of theoretical and applied publication focuses upon easily applied methodologies and remedies for improving the quality of urban life in cities of all sizes throughout the United States.

While much of Ms. Rivic's writing has targeted New York as a paradigm of American urbanization, the immediate and long-term impact of her far-reaching reconceptualization of the aesthetic dimension of urban land use and the social valuation of public spaces is indisputably non-local in scope, equally and as easily applicable to a pristine New England community such as St. Albans as to the exponentially larger metropolises of Los Angeles, Chicago, and Boston. Moreover, the improvement of public life in any one American city serves as an exemplary model likely to inspire similar positive transformations of life in other U.S. cities.

2. **Ms. Rivic's accomplishments clearly represent an area of substantial intrinsic merit that is important to the national interests of the United States, and the benefits of her service unquestionably further the national interest of maintaining the integrity and quality of urban life in the United States.**

Ms. Rivic's contributions to enriching the quality of urban life in our country are far from speculative. Tangible illustrations of her strikingly original thinking about the city include her conceptualization of the city as a dynamic, constantly evolving system, metaphorically analogous to a performance whose main characters are its residents; the recognition of the city's organic capacity to heal and regenerate itself, as exemplified by Ms. Rivic's moving and insightful commentary on the necessity of cautious and publicly beneficial redevelopment of the World Trade Center site; her innovative analyses of the profound social, economic, and public security benefit of urban decentralization over the established 20th-century preference for urban over-centralization. In addition to these concrete contributions to the betterment of urban life in America, the enclosed evidence confirms Ms. Rivic's achievement of equally stellar theoretical and aesthetic insights as illustrated by her illuminating recognition of the role of personal memory in collectively reclaiming and transforming the city, further exemplified by her nationally commended development and innovative teaching of the previously unrecognized genre of "city writing."

Finally, Ms. Rivic's crowning intellectual contribution to the enrichment of her discipline, and inevitably to the betterment of urban life throughout the United States, is her strikingly original application of the Classical/Renaissance model of the "memory palace" to her metaphoric reconceptualization of the city as a dynamic, interactive museum-without-walls, enabling occupants and visitors alike to deconstruct the traditional dichotomization between observer and participant in the city's unfolding history. Moreover, Ms. Rivic's analysis of urban scale models, such as the Panorama of New York in the Queens Museum of Art, enriches our appreciation of the complexity and interrelatedness of the diversity of public spaces, private edifices, and intra-urban unifying structures such as parks and bridges in a matter previously inconceivable to the average urban dweller or visitor.

Ms. Rivic's writings have paved new ground in recognizing the previously neglected potential for urban regeneration afforded by the use of scale models in enabling the public to appreciate the interconnectedness of the city's diverse economic and structural components.

3. **The enclosed evidence documents Ms. Rivic's establishment of tangible and theoretical contributions to the national welfare, significantly above that necessary to prove the "prospective national benefit" required of all aliens seeking to qualify as "exceptional."**

The unambiguous consensus of the multinational authorities submitting expert opinions from the broadest range of Urban Aesthetics's ensemble of constituent disciplines, including Performance Studies, Cultural Studies, Urban Studies, Architecture, and Urban Planning, leaves no doubt as to the superiority of Ms. Rivic's contribution to her field. A cursory review of these opinions readily confirms this conclusion and establishes the petitioner's eligibility for the requested benefit.

4. **The documentation persuasively demonstrates that the national interest would be adversely affected if a labor certification were required of Ms. Rivic and that it would be contrary to the national interest to potentially deprive prospective employers of her services by making available to U.S. workers the position she seeks.**

Ms. Rivic's petition is supported by unambiguous testimony and conspicuous samples of her impressive record of publication. The incipient nature of Urban Aesthetics constitutes the ideal scenario for a meritorious national interest waiver petition, in that Ms. Rivic's demonstrated combination of research, teaching, and writing (both expository and creative) clearly contemplate a career of self-employment. As such, it is difficult to conceive of an appropriate labor certification petitioner whose requirements for employment could plausibly justify the diversity of theoretical, artistic, and didactic activities comprising Ms. Rivic's extraordinary record of contribution to date. Accordingly, it is virtually inconceivable that the granting of the requested petition for waiver of the labor certification requirement could stand to deprive a minimally qualified U.S. worker of an employment opportunity. On the contrary, the overwhelming weight of the submitted evidence substantiates the proposition that U.S. workers and their families stand only to benefit from granting Ms. Rivic the opportunity to permanently improve the quality of life in our country.

5. **Ms. Rivic is not seeking a national interest waiver based on a shortage of qualified workers in the field of Urban Aesthetics.**

As indicated, the supporting evidence amply confirms Ms. Rivic's status as a critical and seminal figure in the genesis and crystallization of the socially and economically beneficial field of Urban Aesthetics. Her eligibility is not premised on the labor market unavailability of "minimally qualified" U.S. workers in her field but on her indisputable stature as a national figure substantially contributing to that field.

We trust that the enclosed evidence will readily confirm Ms. Rivic's eligibility for the requested National Interest Waiver.

In support of the enclosed I-140, and in satisfaction of applicable regulations, we submit the following documentation:

1. Form G-28 Attorney Appearance Form

2. I-140

3. ETA 750-B

4. I-140 filing fee of $195

5. Copies of Ms. Rivic's 1998 Master's degree from Gotham University in New York City and her 1996 B.A. from the American University in Bulgaria.

6. A copy of Ms. Rivic's abbreviated résumé, listing her publications, professional activities, and academic awards.

7. Twelve letters from highly qualified academics and practitioners in fields overlapping with Urban Aesthetics (Performance Studies, Urban Studies, Cultural Studies, Architecture, Art History, Urban Planning, Visual Arts, and Museum Studies). The letter writers work in cities as diverse as

New York, Los Angeles, and Davis in the United States, Bristol in the United Kingdom, Sofia in Bulgaria, and Melbourne in Australia. Thus, they represent the developers of this new discipline on three continents: North America, Europe, and Australia. The supporters—professors, editors, city planners, and architects—are affiliated with leading universities (Gotham University, University of Bristol, University of Melbourne, Pratt Institute, The University of California at Davis), major cultural institutions (The Queens Museum of Art, The Lower Manhattan Cultural Center, and Center for Land Use Interpretation), and urban planning organizations (The New York Department of City Planning, Department of Urban Planning in the University of Architecture, Civil Engineering, and Geodesy in Sofia, and J. Kent Walker Design, Los Angeles).

(a) **Marna Johnson**, Associate Professor of Global Studies Director of Culture Center, Prell Institute, Boston, Massachusetts (CV enclosed).

(b) **William Nichols**, Professor and Chair of Urban Studies, University of Bristol, Bristol, UK; Editor of the *International Journal Tourist Studies* (CV enclosed).

(c) **Gloria Silver, Ph.D.**, University Professor and Professor of Performance Studies, Gotham University, New York (CV enclosed).

(d) **Wilson Coleridge, Ph.D.**, Director of Center for Land Use Interpretation, Los Angeles, California, Lecturer, Curator (CV enclosed).

(e) **Daniel Steinberg, MFA, MA** (Art History and Visual Arts), Executive Director, Queens Museum of Art, New York City (CV enclosed).

(f) **Willard Luchinsky, MA, MLS**, Collection Development, Librarian of the Social and Behavioral Sciences, The University of California, Davis; Editor of the academic journal *X-Cp: Cross Cultural Poetics*, U.S. (CV enclosed).

(g) **Elwood MacTavish, Ph.D.**, Senior Lecturer in Architecture, Faculty of Architecture, Building, and Planning, The University of Sydney, Sydney, Australia (CV enclosed).

(h) **Charles Starks, MA** (City and Regional Planning), New York City Department of City Planning, New York (CV enclosed).

(i) **George Fitzgerald, Ph.D.**, Professor of Art and Public Policy and Associate Dean, Gotham University, New York (CV enclosed).

(j) **Albert Tarkov, MA**, Architect and Associate Professor, Urbanism (Urban Planning), The University of Architecture, Civil Engineering, and Geodesy, Sofia, Bulgaria (CV enclosed).

(k) **Nora Dublin, MA** (Museum Studies), Associate Director of Visual and Media Arts, Lower Manhattan Cultural Council, New York City (CV enclosed).

(l) **Gabriel Marquez**, Architect and Designer, S. Gabriel Marquez Design, Los Angeles, California (CV enclosed).

8. Nine of Ms. Rivic's most recent publications in Urban Aesthetics, appearing in distinguished, peer-reviewed journals, distributed internationally and nationally, including *Tourist Studies* (published in the United Kingdom) and *The Journal of American and Comparative Cultures, Genre,* and *Streetnotes: X-Cultural Poetics,* and *The African Language Center* (published in the United States).

(a) "The Ideology of Architecture: the Boulevard, the Cathedral of Light, and the Low Overpass." *Genre: Imagined Cities*, United States, In print. Fall 2003. Acceptance letter and information about the publication is included.

(b) "My Heart's in the Small Lands: Touring the Miniature City in the Museum." *Tourist Studies*, United Kingdom, Vol. 2, Number 3, December 2002. Information about the publication is included.

(c) "The Miniature Metropolis as Memory Palace." *Journal of American and Comparative Cultures: Studies of Civilization*, United States, Fall and Winter 2002. Information about the publication is included.

(d) "Blackout," "Rain in the City," "1/yr," "Paris," "9/28/01." Five poems in *Streetnotes, X-Cultural Poetics*, United States, Summer 2003.

(e) "Roller-blading: Documenting the City." *Streetnotes, X-Cultural Poetics*, Summer 2002. Information about the electronic journal and archived copy of contributor lists, documenting both Ms. Rivic's history of contribution and the six-year history of the publication.

(f) "Screams and Bridges." *Streetnotes, X-Cultural Poetics*, Summer 2002.

(g) Five poems in *Streetnotes, X-Cultural Poetics*, Summer 2003.

(h) Four poems in *Streetnotes, X-Cultural Poetics*, Summer 2002.

(i) "Antoine Tempe: Catching the Poetry of Everyday Urban Life." Photography review and interview in *African Language Center*, *www.africanlanguagecenter.com*, September 2002. This is one of Ms. Rivic's numerous contributions to the electronic publication documenting the urban experience of West African artists in New York City.

9. Documentation of recent professional and academic conferences at which Ms. Rivic has presented papers or participated in panel discussions.

(a) "Remains of the Fair," accepted paper for PCA/ACA (Popular Culture Association/American Culture Association) annual conference, to be held in San Antonio, Texas, April 7–10, 2004.

(b) "Robert Moses: The Belated Master Plan," accepted paper for Empire and Imperial Cultures Conference, CSU Stanislaus, to be held February 2004.

(c) "My Heart's in the Small Lands: Touring the Miniature City in the Museum," at Researching New York, panel on Envisioning the City, November 20–21, 2003, Albany, New York.

(d) "My Heart's in the Small Lands: Touring the Miniature City in the Museum," MAP/ACA (Mid-Atlantic Popular/American Culture Association) Conference, panel on Urban Culture, November 7–9, 2003, Wilmington, Delaware.

(e) "Performing the City: The Visual Medium, the Master Plan, and the Everyday," at the Popular Culture in America/American Culture Association Annual Conference, April 16–19, 2002, New Orleans, Louisiana.

(f) "9/11 From A to Z," for Sound Off, at the Performance Studies International Conference, April 11–14, 2002, Gotham University. New York, New York.

(g) "The Miniature Metropolis as Memory Palace," at the Popular Culture in America/American Culture Association Annual Conference, March 13–16, 2002, Toronto, Canada.

(h) "Toy-City Writings," at the Memory Matters: The Relationship between Memory and Catastrophe Symposium, Nov. 11, 2002, Gotham University, New York, New York.

10. Documentation of how Ms. Rivic is influencing the field of Urban Aesthetics and the work of other leading figures working in the field.

   (a) E-mail communication from Lauren Schloss, Director of Education, Queens Museum of Art, confirming the museum's interest in Ms. Rivic's writing an essay on the Panorama of the City of New York," the main Queens Museum exhibit, for the museum's new brochure.

   (b) E-mail from Dr. William Nichols, editor of *Tourist Studies*, asking Ms. Rivic to review an article for the publication.

   (c) E-mail communication from Willard Luchinksy, MA , MLS, editor of *Xcp: Streetnotes*, asking for Ms. Rivic's help in soliciting papers for an upcoming issue of *Streetnotes* with a thematic focus inspired by her ideas. Also included is the Call for Papers for this issue of the publication.

   (d) E-mail communication from Matthew Coolidge, Director of the Center for Land Use Interpretation, in Los Angeles, California, expressing interest in Ms. Rivic's work on World's Fairs for an exhibit at the center that he directs.

11. Exhibits A1 through A13 pursuant to Ms. Rivic's concurrently filed I-485 and accompanying documents.

   The enclosed documentation supports our belief that Ms. Darya Rivic exemplifies the extraordinarily talented and productive professional whose continued presence enriches this country and whom Congress intended to welcome when it created the national interest waiver.

Please note that Ms. Rivic is in valid F-1 status at Gotham University, in New York City, and is eligible to file adjustment of status concurrently in St. Albans, Vermont. Please send all notices to the office of the undersigned.

Respectfully submitted,

Nathan A. Waxman
Encl.

[Three representative letters of support for client's NIW petition]

July 15, 2003

Bureau of Citizenship and Immigration Services
Vermont Service Center
75 Lower Welden St.
St. Albans, VT 05479

Dear Immigration Officer:

It is with great pleasure that I write this letter of endorsement for Ms. Darya Rivic, whose request for permanent resident status in the United States, in the category of National Interest Waiver, I wholeheartedly support. Ms. Rivic is an exceptional individual with impeccable credentials and a remarkable international record of publications and public appearances.

Ms. Rivic is a brilliant Urban Aesthetician whose groundbreaking insights in the field of Urban Aesthetics have affected, and will continue to affect, numerous fields such as Cultural Studies, Architecture, Tourist Studies, American Studies, Anthropology, Urban Planning, Geography, and Theater Studies. Her career as a performer, writer, academic, tour guide, urban analyst, and scholar has brought national attention to her ideas and observations about cities and city life in the growing field of Urban Aesthetics. Ms. Rivic's boundless imagination and perceptive intelligence are directly responsible for a new and exciting understanding of urban America and its future development.

I write confidently about Ms. Rivic's accomplishments as an Urban Aesthetician myself with a long career in the field of global urbanism. I have written extensively about Urban Aesthetics in Africa, the Caribbean, Asia, and Europe. I have published four books and over two dozen articles. As the Director of the Culture Center at the internationally renowned Prell Institute in Boston, Massachusetts, I can attest to Ms. Rivic's brilliance and significant impact in the fields mentioned above.

As a nationally recognized and internationally established scholar, I have long been impressed by Ms. Rivic's grasp of the globalizing condition of urban life. I have personally been influenced by Ms. Rivic's innovative ideas regarding urban spatial developments and her thoughts on revitalizing New York City. I have drawn upon the depth and breadth of her knowledge in the fields of Performance Studies, Urban Aesthetics, Cultural Studies, Anthropology, and Tourist Studies to fuel the curricula at Prell Institute. Most importantly, I continue to find Ms. Rivic's contributions of critical importance to the future of our perceptions about American cities. New York City needs Ms. Rivic. Our nation needs people like Darya to help us heal and move ahead with our lives. Ms. Rivic is New York—that great experiment of the American imagination.

Ms. Rivic is an exceptional American without having become a formal American. I have known of her work in the field of urban studies for over six years. Ms. Rivic's writings and presentations, recognized nationally and internationally, combine history, theory, and practical working models for a humanistic approach to the development of American cities. This is the kind of individual the United States needs urgently at this time. We need someone who understands the history of the United States and cares about its future enough to offer fresh, insightful, and innovative approaches to rethinking the idea of how we live in cities today.

A quick glance at Ms. Rivic's curriculum vitae attests to an extraordinary engagement with public life in the United States through her work with museums, public performances, journalistic writings, public presentations of scholarly work, tour guiding, and her exhaustive work as historian of New York City. This stellar career is proof itself of an individual of exceptional merit and potential whose accomplishments to date are original, pathbreaking, and nationally influential. Of particular note is her outstanding research on the Panorama of the City of New York which sheds light on key experiments in American urbanism and offers innovative ideas on the notion of the city. Some key thoughts of Ms.

Rivic's that have impacted the national discourse on urban aesthetics are the notion of the city as a dynamic public art form and the concept of the city as archive. Both of these ideas are powerful and evocative. They have generated a wealth of discussion around the notion of the interactive city, showing how central Ms. Rivic has been to the proliferation of interest in her theories and their practical application in the United States.

Darya Rivic's multidimensional, generative ideas offer immediate solutions to difficult problems ailing cities in the United States today. As an active urban theorist who has seen Ms. Rivic present her work on numerous occasions in international seminars, colloquia, professional associations, and public venues such as museums, I consider her to be the future of American Urban Aesthetics. It is critical that we recognize individuals of Ms. Rivic's stature, with the ebullience, talent, brilliance, experience, imagination, passion, and skills to strengthen our society's ailing cities.

Ms. Rivic's long and distinguished career as an urban aesthetician is a confirmation of her ability to continue to enrich the U.S.'s cumulative understanding of its urban future. Ms. Rivic's ability to deal with print, media, and the Internet as forums for her long-term goal of changing urban aesthetics in the United States further strengthens her case as a versatile and agile individual with exceptional abilities in diverse forums to affect change.

I submit this letter with the hope that Ms. Rivic's case impresses you as much as she has convinced me and my colleagues nationally. She is a gifted individual of extraordinary accomplishments and stellar credentials. It has been a great honor to write this letter for such a delightful and impressive individual with a great heart for America and the dedication it takes to be an urban American. Ms. Rivic comes with my highest accolades and recommendations. I wholeheartedly endorse granting this individual the status she seeks. Ms. Rivic is a gift to the United States. Let her shine and continue to show us how to love our cities.

Yours sincerely,

Marna Johnson
Associate Professor of Global
Studies
Director of Culture Center
Prell Institute
Boston, Massachusetts

U.S. Citizenship and Immigration Services
Vermont Service Center
Immigration Authorities
St. Albans, VT 05479

Dear Immigration Officer:

Ms. Darya Rivic has asked me to comment on the significance and national interest value of her publication and research into Urban Aesthetics. Although she and I have never collaborated—nor even met—I have reviewed her published reports and extensively discussed her work with her and her colleagues. More specifically, as Editor of the international journal *Tourist Studies* and as Professor holding the Chair of Urban Studies at the University of Nottingham, United Kingdom, I have also recently considered and accepted for publication an academic paper she has written.

Based on 15 years of experience as an academic working in the urban field and having held senior professorial positions in Australia, Norway, and the UK, I am well-qualified to evaluate Ms. Rivic's contributions to Urban Aesthetics, a field of growing significance as the city moves from a place of industry and residence to a place of performance, arts, lifestyle, culture, and consumption. The more cities evolve in this way, the more cities and nations need to develop a corps of highly trained writers and scholars who creatively develop the necessary sensibilities, skills, techniques, and training. These are rare gifts, and this creative talent needs to be nurtured, rewarded, and employed if the contemporary city and nation are to benefit from current opportunities.

With these thoughts in mind, I have absolutely no doubt that Ms Rivic is an exceptional talent in her area of specialty. Moreover, she is considerably more able than the majority of others I have seen and read from your country. Darya's interests overlap with mine in the area of Urban Aesthetics although my research team has taken an analogous approach to understanding the aestheticization of cities. We are focusing on the anthropology of contemporary city life from a post-humanist viewpoint applying the work of Latour, Haraway, and Law, whereas I see Ms Rivic's work arising from an application of the fertile field of performativity.

I was particularly struck by the value of her work in demonstrating the significance of the tourism industry of the city for inhabitants of the city themselves. This was a singularly original perception and written in such a way as will forge further debate, policy formation, and positive social and cultural benefits, and it was on this basis that her paper was accepted for publication. Is this not precisely what we need from our top writers and scholars? During the review of her paper, I became convinced that other important scholars working in the area should take a look at the work of this fine scholar. My fellow reviewers included American, European, and Australasian scholars. The resounding opinion from them was, without exception, "original, important, and brilliant!!" All of the external reviewers' reports were similarly mantled in superlatives: here was a great scholar and writer who could not only work effectively for the good in a city such as New York, but also apply this knowledge to cities throughout the United States and the world. She has made a considerable impact in this field, and I was very pleased with the international feedback we received concerning her analysis of New York. Her work outshone that of other scholars presenting articles in the same and similar fields.

Practically, her work identifies clear and inspirational ways in which the city can be lived to greater effect by its inhabitants, thereby improving their lives and the health of society. Her work also provides a clear and practical guide to those involved in creating and regenerating cities. Ms. Rivic has made huge strides in her field and has established herself as a major national and international player in Urban Aesthetics. The United States should continue to benefit from the unique, brilliant, and community-minded work of this candidate.

Sincerely,
Professor William Nichols

To Whom It May Concern:

It is my pleasure to write in support of Darya Rivic's Green Card Petition. I have known Ms. Rivic for more than five years, during which time I have had the opportunity to follow her work closely. I can attest to her excellence as a scholar and her national and international reputation in the fields of urban history and urban aesthetics, in which she is doing pioneering work. Urban aesthetics involves the study of how the city's built environment gives form to meaning and value, not only in line with the intention of architects and planners, but also as a result of those who live in the city and make it their own. The fundamental question that urban aesthetics addresses—this is central to Ms. Rivic's work—is how people make cities livable.

I have been working on the aesthetics of everyday life in cities for the last 35 years. My work includes attention to tourism, from a performance studies perspective, in relation to heritage and museums. I serve on the editorial boards of important journals in these fields, have published on these subjects (my most recent book was published this year by University of California Press), serve on the boards and consult for such organizations as the Smithsonian Institution, City Lore; New York Center for Urban Folk Culture, and museums in Europe, Canada, New Zealand, Australia, Vietnam, and the United States. In 2003, I was named Distinguished Humanist by Ohio State University. I am thus in a good position to assess Ms. Rivic and her work.

Consistent with the most recent and important trends in fields related to her work, Ms. Rivic is exploring the urban environment through the ways in which it is represented and experienced, historically and at present, not only thanks to enlightened planning, but also thanks to the efforts of ordinary people in their everyday lives. While focusing on New York City, Ms. Rivic brings a broad and comparative international perspective to her work, which draws on her studies of Paris, Berlin, and Montreal, among other cities.

Ms. Rivic is blessed with a brilliant and original mind. Her formidable research skills, which combine indefatigable energy and great resourcefulness in finding sources and working imaginatively with them, are matched by her elegance and eloquence as a writer. Not surprisingly, her work has already attracted considerable attention. She has participated in national and international conferences and contributed her work to the leading journals in the field, including the *Journal of American and Comparative Cultures* and *Tourist Studies*, among others. Most recently, in acknowledgment of her deep knowledge of New York City, her expertise in urban aesthetics, and her superb communication skills, the Queens Museum of Art invited her to conduct guided tours of the largest architectural scale model in the world, The Panorama of the City of New York, which was originally created for the 1939–1940 New York World's Fair at the behest of Robert Moses, mayor of New York.

In a word, Ms. Rivic is absolutely exceptional in how she conceptualizes the city and brings empirical research to bear on her imaginative ideas. Through the field of Performance Studies, which was created at Gotham University and has spread in the United States and abroad, she is bringing a unique perspective to the city as a public art form, a site of memory, and lived in as well as livable space. Her work offers insight into the nature of city life that will provide an unusual and productive basis for those concerned with planning and policy. Moreover, Ms. Rivic is an extraordinary teacher and has been conveying her ideas through her teaching, which has been highly praised by students and colleagues alike for her commitment and talent in communicating her ideas and exciting undergraduates encountering an approach like hers for the first time.

Given her stellar track record of research, publication, contributions to conferences, and excellent teaching—and the far-reaching implications of her work in urban form and aesthetics—Ms. Rivic is most worthy of receiving a green card. She has already made important contributions to her field and will continue to do so.

Sincerely,
Gloria Silver
University Professor and Professor of Performance Studies

[Attorney's cover letter to USCIS responding to RFE]

June 25, 2005

Director
U.S. Citizenship and Immigration Service
Vermont Service Center
75 Lower Welden St.
St. Albans, VT 05479-0001

Re: **I-797 Request for Evidence regarding Rivic**
      I-140 File Number EAC 040xxxxxxx
      Petitioner/Beneficiary Rivic, Darya

Dear Director:

This memorandum is submitted in response to the enclosed I-797, dated March 31, 2005. It is respectfully urged that your office review the evidence previously submitted in support of the original petition and consider the enclosed documentation of Ms. Darya Rivic's accomplishments and unquestionable eligibility for waiver of the statutory labor certification requirement. Please note that, while we are not providing additional copies of documentation already submitted, we are enclosing documentation that directly answers issues raised by the I-797.

Your enclosed I-797 appropriately acknowledges that Ms. Rivic's field of endeavor, Urban Aesthetics, has substantial intrinsic merit. It also acknowledges that she ". . . has made original contributions, as is to be expected from an advanced degree student, and the beneficiary's professors and others in the fields of cultural studies, architecture, tourist studies and urban planning clearly hold these contributions in high regard." The I-797 questions the national scope and extent of the benefits of Ms. Rivic's work, her impact on her academic field, and the impact on the interests of the nation if she were required to undergo the labor certification process.

While we believe that the materials originally submitted in support of Ms. Rivic's November 2003, petition did indeed address all the concerns raised in the I-797, we submit here letters from eight additional independent stakeholders in fields that come within the ambit of Ms. Rivic's considerable sphere of influence, and we submit further objective documentation of her accomplishments and impact as an urban aesthetician.

To address the impact and influence of Ms. Rivic's work, we include copies of her recent publications in peer-reviewed, national, and scholarly journals; documentation of her participation at national conferences, as a chairperson of multiple panels and as a peer-reviewed speaker, and as a consultant to numerous cultural organizations; and copies of e-mail exchanges between Ms. Rivic and her colleagues throughout the United States. The extent and depth of Ms. Rivic's contributions to the field of urban aesthetics is readily apparent from this enclosed documentation.

Your inquiry regarding the adverse effect of requiring the beneficiary's labor certification on the national interest may be answered succinctly: It would be enormously to the detriment of the United States and its population were Ms. Rivic to be required a labor certification as a precondition to her obtaining permanent residence. As the enclosed letters and documentation show, since she received her EAD in 1994, she has been doing distinguished, highly-regarded work in several distinct areas of employment, all of which are interconnected and related to her academic specialization, but none of which is a full-time, permanent position. She requires a waiver of the labor certification requirement in order to continue pursuing the academic teaching and public arts organization consulting she has done for the past three years.

Ms. Rivic's academic and public interest contributions and accomplishments of the past two years include the following:

She has published articles in peer-reviewed, national, scholarly journals

- "Public Places/Private Spaces," Tisch School of the Arts Writing Workshop in *Street as Method*, a special issue of *StreetVibes, X-Cultural Poetics* (Winter 2004).

- "The Ideology of Architecture in Paris, Berlin, and New York: the Boulevard, the Cathedral of Light, and the Low Overpass." Genre: Imagined Cities. Vol. 24 (2004).

- "City in the Sky: The Rise and Fall of the World Trade Center." Book review in peer-reviewed, national scholarly journal Women and Performance, special issue on Falling (Sept. 2004).

- "Design and Discipline: The Legend of an Urban Park." GR Journal for the Arts, Sciences, and Technology" Montreal, Canada (2005).

She has contributed an article to a textbook compiled by New York University

"My Heart's in the Small Lands: Touring the Miniature Metropolis in the Museum" in Writing the Essay, Art in the World, the World Through Art: Tisch School of the Arts Core Curriculum, Gotham University, 2005–2006, ed. by Darlene A. Forrest, Randy Martin, and Pat C. Hoy II, McGraw-Hill Companies (2005).

She has participated in national academic conferences, as a session chair and as a presenter.

Chair

- Chaired eight sessions of the Urban Culture Area for the Mid-Atlantic Popular Culture/American Culture Association (MAPACA) Conference in Buffalo, New York of the Urban Culture with more than 30 presenters (more than in any other area) from around the United States and Europe in November 2004.

Panelist

- Mid-Atlantic Popular Culture/American Culture Association (MAPACA) Annual Conference, panel on Urban Culture, Wilmington, Delaware (Nov. 2003).

- Researching New York, panel on Envisioning the City, Albany, New York (Nov. 2003).

- Pace Institute for Environmental and Regional Studies (PIERS), Pace University, New York (Apr. 2004).

- 25th Conference on New York State History, Skidmore College, Saratoga Springs, New York (June 2004).

- "Performing Place: The Walking, Talking, and Pointing of the Urban Tour Guide," Pace Institute of Environmental and Regional Studies (PIERS) Conference Proceedings: Senses of Place: Urban Narratives as Public Secrets, Pace Center for Environmental and Regional Studies (PIERS), Pace University, New York. Vol. 4 (2004).

- Forum on Forms of Seeing Symposium (a year-long gathering of scholars in the visual arts), Institute of Fine Arts, Gotham University, New York (Apr. 2005).

- CTRL Conference, Montreal, Canada (Oct. 2004).

- Mid-Atlantic Popular Culture/American Culture Association (MAPACA) Annual Conference, panel on Urban Culture, Buffalo, New York (Nov. 2004).

- Pace Institute of Environmental and Regional Studies (PIERS) Annual Conference, Pace University, New York (June 2005).

Workshop Leader

- Organized and led a workshop of 10 participants from the United States, Europe, and Australia on "Writing the City" as part of the Urban Culture Area of the Mid-Atlantic Popular Culture/American Culture Association (MAPACA) (Nov. 2004).

Public appearances in forums of national scope

- Contributed to "Street as Method," an Internet forum of teachers who use the street in their classrooms (*X-Cp: Cross Cultural Poetics*, Winter 2003).

- Interviewed on WKCR Radio "Art Attack" Program, a forum for urban art and research (Mar. 2005).

- Interviewed for a project presented at UnionDocs, an arts collaborative dedicated to the exploration of the documentary form (Mar. 2005).

Provided consultation to leading urban forums, institutes, and organizations

- *Saveur Magazine* (Apr. 2004).

- The Swiss American Film Festival (May 2004).

- The Queens Museum of Art, Panorama Improvement Project (Spring 2005, Summer 2004).

- The Van Alen Institute (Dec. 2004).

- Soundwalks (Mar. 2005).

- The National Geographic Channel, documentary on Grand Central Terminal (May 2005).

Served as a peer reviewer for international scholarly journals

- *Tourist Studies* (since June 2003).

- *Women and Performance* (Aug.2003, special issue on Falling).

We submit here 12 letters (four from people who submitted letters supporting her original petition and eight from people who have not written before) which outline in detail the ways in which Ms. Rivic's contributions have impacted on her field. The eight new letters come from people who know Ms. Rivic professionally and who comment on their perception of her work and its impact. Several letters address the scope and significance of the academic publications in which she has published her work. Please note that the work Ms. Rivic has done since she filed her original petition have all grown directly out of her earlier work and should be regarded as an expansion of it.

These letters collectively address all the issues raised in the I-797:

- Her impact *has been shown to far exceed* that of other practitioners in the field of endeavor.

- She *has compiled a substantial record* as a scholar whose publications and presentations have been recognized for their significant impact and importance to the field of urban aesthetics.

- The publications in which her articles have appeared *are* nationally recognized.

- Her published articles *have had significant impact* on the field of Urban Aesthetics.

- Her work *has garnered attention* to a higher degree than the work of others in the field.

- She *has played a distinguished leadership role* in the field of urban aesthetics, and her work has resulted in *findings of major significance to her field.*

- Her scholarly findings and concepts *have been widely implemented in many locations outside of New York City*.

- The evidence clearly indicates that *her expertise has already benefited* institutions, corporations, and professional firms that have had no direct contact with her and *have never retained her services*.

- The enclosed letters ***unquestionably refute your conclusion*** that ". . . the record simply offers no indication that" Ms. Rivic's ". . . contributions to the fields of cultural studies, architecture, tourist studies and urban planning are generally acknowledged as representing major advances in the field, significantly beyond the capabilities of the majority of her colleagues in the field."

- Ms. Rivic has submitted, as you requested, ". . . additional opinions from independent national experts in the fields of cultural studies, architecture, tourist studies, urban planning, geography or other fields who oversee programs of national importance who deem the beneficiary's work in the national interest."

Enclosed please find the original I-797 and following documentation demonstrating Ms. Darya Rivic's unquestionable qualifications for a waiver of the statutory labor certification requirement:

1. **Comments from four people who wrote letters supporting her original petition.**

   a. Gloria Silver, Ph.D., University Professor and Professor of Performance Studies, Gotham University, New York.

   b. Morton Coleridge, Director, Center for Land Conversion, Los Angeles, California.

   c. Willard Luchinksy, MA, MLS, editor of *X-CP: Cross Cultural Poetics: Streetnotes*, Behavioral and Social Sciences Librarian, University of California, Davis

   d. George Amberfine, MFA, Executive Director, Queens Museum of Art, Queens, New York.

2. **Letters from eight people who have not previously written in support of Ms. Rivic's national interest waiver petition.**

   a. Jacqueline Morris, Master of landscape architecture/Regional Planning, President, Principal, Owner, Morris Associates (planning, urban design, and landscape architecture firm), Boulder, Colorado; CV enclosed.

   b. Charles Starks, Master of City Planning, senior urban planner, AICP, PP, Starks, Sutterfield, Wilson Associates, Inc. (Planning and Real Estate Consultants), New Jersey and New York, résumé enclosed.

   c. Tom Kitts, Ph.D., President of Mid-Atlantic Popular Culture/American Culture Association, Chair of Division of English and Speech, St. John's University, Brooklyn, New York; CV enclosed.

   d. Tanya Kash, film producer, Partisan Pictures for the National Geographic Channel; résumé enclosed.

   e. Vanessa Sharp, Founts Media and Red Harpoon, founding employee, Creative Development Manager, Urban Dramaturge; résumé and press materials.

   f. Heidi Alpart, radio and film producer, PAQ Films, Berlin and New York, résumé enclosed.

   g. Anouk Radiguet, MA, Education and Preservation Dep't, Toronto Museum of Contemporary Art; résumé enclosed.

   h. Rolf Landrich, Ph.D., professor emeritus, Sociology Department, Swedenborg College, Anderson, Wisconsin; CV enclosed.

3. **Copies of Ms. Rivic's recent publications in peer-reviewed, national, scholarly journals.**

- "Public Places/Private Spaces," Tisch School of the Arts Writing Workshop in *Street as Method*, a special issue of *StreetVibes, X-Cultural Poetics* (Winter 2004).

- "The Ideology of Architecture in Paris, Berlin, and New York: the Boulevard, the Cathedral of Light, and the Low Overpass." *Genre: Imagined Cities*. Vol. 24 (2004).

- "City in the Sky: The Rise and Fall of the World Trade Center." Book review in peer-reviewed, national scholarly journal *Women and Performance*, special issue on Falling (Sept. 2004).

- "Design and Discipline: The Legend of an Urban Park." *GR Journal for the Arts, Sciences, and Technology*, Montreal, Canada. (In print, 2005).

4. Copy of Ms. Rivic's textbook article contribution

- "My Heart's in the Small Lands: Touring the Miniature Metropolis in the Museum" in Writing the Essay, Art in the World, the World Through Art: School of the Arts Core Curriculum, Gotham University, 2005–2006, ed. by Martha C. McFarland, Mauro Palazzo, and Matthew Beaupre, McGraw-Hill Companies (2005).

5. Evidence of Ms. Rivic's participation in national conferences

- As Chair of eight sessions of the Urban Culture Area for the Mid-Atlantic Popular Culture/American Culture Conference in Buffalo, New York of the Urban Culture with more than 30 presenters (more than in any other area) from around the United States and Europe in November 2004.

As a panelist at:

- MAPACA Annual Conference, panel on Urban Culture, Wilmington, Delaware (Nov. 2003).

- Researching New York, panel on Envisioning the City, Albany, New York (Nov. 2003).

- Pace Institute for Environmental and Regional Studies (PIERS), Pace University, New York (Apr. 2004).

- 25th Conference on New York State History, Skidmore College, Saratoga Springs, New York (June 2004).

- "Performing Place: The Walking, Talking, and Pointing of the Urban Tour Guide," PIERS Conference Proceedings: Senses of Place: Urban Narratives as Public Secrets, Pace Center for Environmental and Regional Studies, Pace University, New York. Vol. 4 (2004).

- Forum on Forms of Seeing Symposium (a year-long gathering of scholars in the visual arts), Institute of Fine Arts, Gotham University, New York (Apr. 2005).

- CTRL Conference, Montreal, Canada (Oct. 2004).

- MAPACA Annual Conference, panel on Urban Culture, Buffalo, New York (Nov. 2004).

- Pace Institute of Environmental and Regional Studies (PIERS) Annual Conference, Pace University, New York (June 2005).

6. Information about the scholarly publications in which Ms. Rivic's articles have appeared, in response to the I-797's request for same.

7. Copies of e-mails from Ms. Rivic's colleagues and peers, responding to her published articles and scholarly presentations, and seeking her consultation services.

The evidence submitted previously and enclosed here resoundingly confirms Ms. Rivic's past and on-going contributions to the national interest and affirms the reasonable expectation that she will continue to make such contributions. The evidence supports the assertion that she is an outstanding example of the exceptionally talented person whose immigration the national interest waiver was intended to expedite.

We respectfully urge you to approve her petition expeditiously so that she can continue her work and enrichment of urban life in this country.

Please direct all notices to the office of the undersigned, as the attorney of record in this matter.

Respectfully submitted,

Nathan A. Waxman
Attorney for Petitioner/Beneficiary

[Three representative letters responding to RFE]

June 4, 2005

USCIS, Vermont Service Center
75 Lower Welden St
St Albans, VT 05479
Attn: Immigration Adjudicator

Dear Madam/Sir:

I would like to voice my wholehearted and professional support for Ms. Darya Rivic's National Interest Waiver petition in the field of Urban Aesthetics that is unjustly in dispute. I am a leader in the field of Urban Aesthetics myself: As a founding employee and director of urban affairs and tourism consulting in the country's most innovative and fastest-growing company, Founts Media, which unites the potentials of art, travel, entertainment, and technology in an effort to redefine the urban landscape and reinvent the business of urban tourism; a co-inventor of the widely recognized global public art project Red Harpoon, and a renowned scholar of urban studies. Although a resident of New York City, I work around the world as an urban tourism consultant and city-focused artist, with a long history of contracts, projects, and lectures in such places as San Francisco (Intel Berkeley Urban Research Labs), Miami (Art Basel Miami Beach 2004), Boston (Massachusetts Institute of Technology and Boston Cyberarts Festival), Copenhagen, Berlin, Seoul, and Mexico City. I can, therefore, provide an expert opinion regarding Ms. Rivic's case.

For many years I have been deeply engaged with Ms. Rivic's distinguished ideas in Urban Aesthetics, even though I only met Ms. Rivic in person recently. In Founts Media, we conceive and implement innovative products and projects globally that engage residents and visitors directly in their perception of their communities and environment. We work directly with tourism councils, municipal governments, the world's leading technology firms such as Ericsson, and creatively engage national brands to improve the life and value of America's great urban centers. Red Harpoon, our first flagship project, has been adopted in 18 countries and 158 cities worldwide. I have been a leader in focusing our growth in urban communities, and in this aspect of our work, I have frequently referenced Ms. Rivic's work in company strategy sessions and creative brainstorming meetings. She has significantly enriched our understanding of the importance of creating cutting-edge urban initiatives that are integrated into the community in a dynamic, interactive, and inclusive manner. Her emphasis on the relationship between planning and community—(visible in her widely circulated articles in the prominent scholarly publications *Genre: Imagined Cities*, *Tourist Studies*, *X-Cp: Cross Cultural Poetics: StreetVibes* and through her public presentations in national forums such as the Popular Culture/American Culture Association)—can be directly witnessed in my choices to always incorporate users in the creative process.

It is beyond question that Ms. Rivic stands out as a truly unique contributor to the field. She has significantly influenced the way American cities and cities around the world perceive themselves and intelligently plan a wide variety of tourist initiatives. Tourism is now the single largest industry in the world. Urban tourism in recent years has gained astounding momentum as a source of vital revenue and community value throughout the United States. It is precisely professionals such as Ms. Rivic who are necessary for this country to capitalize on this very important trend and to create the most lively, inspiring cities and communities possible. Her exceptional achievements have not only deeply affected me but have had enduring influence, surpassing that of others working in the same discipline, on numerous professionals throughout North America.

Ms. Rivic has successfully produced work that moves beyond mere local specifics to make invaluable general insights with profound relevance on professionals throughout the United States and around the world. She has taught us how to utilize technology and forward-thinking visioning to improve the future lives of urban inhabitants. Her remarkable appreciation of scale models, memories, and everyday experiences has allowed us to expand our understanding of psychogeography, mapping, and new technologies, such as GIS (Geographic Information Systems). Most recently, Ms. Rivic's ideas have concretely enriched our global urban project, Red Harpoon, which fundamentally addresses the aesthetics of the urban environment as it seeks to engage everyday people in the lives of their cities. Red Harpoon is both a vital tool for tourism—and a featured project by Lonely Planet, the world's largest travel media company—and artistic exploration. Ms. Rivic's thinking about the interplay between fiction and reality in her analysis of the scale model of New York directly influenced the creative thinking of me and my colleagues in inventing Red Harpoon. The project allows anybody to inject their personal memories, subjective fantasies, historical observations, and emotions onto the cityscape, much as Ms. Rivic describes the experience of visitors to the scale model. This unique synthesis of the fictional and real that Red Harpoon achieves and that is a direct result of Ms. Rivic's work, has since been written about by such recognized national publications as *Wired*, *The Boston Globe*, *The Miami Herald*, *The Oakland Tribune*, *Public Art Review*, *NPR*, *NY1 News*, and *Metro News*, among countless others. Internationally, the project has received attention from most of Europe's largest newspapers, such as *El Mundo*, *Politiken*, *Liberation*, *Le Figaro*, *De Volkskrant*, *Politiken*, and *RAI*.

Clearly, the outcome of Ms. Rivic's intellectual efforts is tangible, and the scope of her work indisputably national. Further evidence of her far-reaching influence are her indispensable contributions to UnionDocs, a documentary arts collaboration, of which I am the artistic director. In our exploration of urban issues, we chose to incorporate Ms. Rivic's work along with such other prominent authors as Dolores Hayden, Sudhir Venkatesh, and Lawrence Lessig. We will integrate her work in a live performance piece this summer at the Volksbühne in Berlin, one of Europe's most highly acclaimed theaters, during an international urban arts festival. Moreover, my frequent encounters with Ms. Rivic's writings directly inspired the philosophy and method of viewing the urban environment in my recently published book, *The Colors of Berlin*. This publication is the product of a funded project about urban art in Berlin, where I founded the gallery and artist group Cornu with two German architects. Our work has been exhibited at the German Architecture Center in Berlin, Museum of Contemporary Art Denver, Van Alen Institute in Manhattan, and architekturgalerie am weißenhof in Stuttgart. The book was released by Prestel, one of the world's leading publishers in the fields of architecture, photography, and urban arts, and will be distributed throughout the United States, Europe, and Asia.

Ms. Rivic's ideas have already helped improve our lives in cities nationwide. The fact that her work is so vital to the urban tourist industry—what is now one of the country's largest sources of employment and wealth and one of the most promising sectors for the future—lends the approval of her application particular urgency.

Thank you for considering my testimony.

Sincerely,

Vanessa Sharp
Founding employee, Creative
Development Manager, Urban
Dramaturge—Founts Media
Co-Founder—Red Harpoon

May 30, 2005

Anouk Radiguet
Museum of Modern Art
Toronto, ONT
Canada

Dear Immigration Adjudicator:

I am writing to provide an informed opinion with regard to Ms. Darya Rivic's petition for the National Interest Waiver in the field of Urban Aesthetics. I understand her petition has been challenged by your office, which questions Ms. Rivic's central contribution to the emergence of this new discipline and to expanding its field of study throughout the United States. I was most surprised at your accusation that Ms. Rivic's work has principally focused on New York City.

In direct response to this claim, I first came across Ms. Rivic and her work when I participated in the Mid-Atlantic Popular Culture/American Culture Conference in Buffalo last November. The area in which I took part, Urban Culture, was entirely organized and chaired by Ms. Rivic and consisted of eight panels and 30 participants each addressing issues of urban culture in cities across the United States. I had not heard of Urban Aesthetics until this point. Fascinated by Ms. Rivic's presentation and the brilliant framework that she created for our Urban Culture panels in Buffalo, I actively sought to better understand this new discipline and came to realize the exceptional role that Ms. Rivic has played in its emergence. I encountered her inspirational writings and innovative approaches in influential North American journals such as *Cross-Cultural Poetics: StreetVibes*, *Genre: Imagined Cities*, *Journal of American and Comparative Cultures*, *Tourist Studies*, and *GR Journal for the Arts, Sciences, and Technology*, the latter published here in Montreal.

Because Urban Aesthetics must be considered not only as a field of study, but also as a methodological approach germane to issues of urban life, tourism, and the collective and individual experience of memory and space in the city, the idea that Ms. Rivic's work is specific to New York is simply baseless. I am an art historian working in the Education and Conservation Department at the Toronto Museum of Modern Art. I now use Ms. Rivic's groundbreaking ideas of the roles that museums play within a city's collective imagination and how they serve as tools in the tourist industry when writing exhibition catalogue entries that are read by Toronto's cosmopolitan public and by tourists, who represent 65 percent of the museum's visitors.

Due to the homogenizing tendencies of the international economic markets and artistic centers, it is increasingly important for museums to articulate a sense of local aesthetics. Ms. Rivic's renegotiation of theories of urban landscape through aesthetics offers a crucial methodological approach for museums in the important role they play in promoting a sense of place. These practices can certainly be adopted by museums in cities within and beyond the political borders of the United States.

To question Ms. Rivic's exceptional academic contribution to your country as a whole is absurd. I hope that a more informed and diligent reconsideration of her achievements will lead to an approval of Ms. Rivic's petition.

Sincerely,

Anouk Radiquet

June 1, 2005

USCIS, Vermont Service Center
75 Lower Welden St
St Albans, VT 05479

Dear Immigration Adjudicator:

Please allow me to provide an expert opinion and enthusiastic support for Ms. Darya Rivic's National Interest Waiver petition that was recently unnecessarily challenged by your office. Although I barely know Ms. Rivic in person, I have often read and applied her enlightening concepts on Urban Aesthetics, and I have no hesitation in stating that she stands out as a professional who has tangibly influenced the extent to which American cities view themselves as community engagement places and deploy public spaces as vehicles for civic unification and enrichment. Furthermore, her work has been influential in inspiring me and numerous other urban planners, landscape architects, and writers throughout the United States. Please realize that Ms. Rivic's exceptional achievements significantly exceed the achievements of others in her field because they have permanently affected other professionals' work far beyond New York City and are recognized nationally and internationally.

As the president and primary owner of the nationally recognized landscape architecture and urban design firm of Morris Associates in Boulder, Colorado, I am in the position to expertly evaluate the body of Ms. Rivic's diverse work, published in the influential scholarly journals *GR Journal for the Arts, Sciences, and Technology*, *Genre: Imagined Cities*, *Tourist Studies*, *Cross-Cultural Poetics: StreetVibes*, and *The Journal of American and Comparative Cultures*, and its continuing influence upon the culture of our cities and parks nationwide. The work of Morris Associates centers on urban and regional planning as well as landscape architecture and therefore links to Ms. Rivic's discipline in many respects. We plan and design parks, open spaces, urban plazas, and streetscapes throughout America and constantly seek to create places that strengthen communities and enhance the quality of life and visitor experiences for people from many walks of life. We have worked throughout America with projects currently in the states of Nevada, Oregon, Florida, New York, Colorado, Idaho, Utah, Wyoming, and Montana.

I was introduced to Ms. Rivic's work in Urban Aesthetics by a prominent colleague of mine who works worldwide and have since had the pleasure to experience the significant ways in which it has enriched my understanding of the importance of creating urban infrastructures and park and open space systems that are integrated into the community in a dynamic, interactive, and inclusive manner as opposed to the outdated post-war paradigm of the nuclear city with diminishing concentric gradations of public spaces. Our projects seek to implement many of Ms. Rivic's ideas with careful yet consistent revitalization of cities through the introduction of walkable spaces and the creation and revitalization of urban parks according to the multiple needs of diverse user groups.

Ms. Rivic's exceptional intellectual achievement of integrating the classical and renaissance concept of the city as an exclusionary and segregated place and the value of urban models for organizing the optimization of civic involvement has revolutionized our theoretical and practical understanding of the ideal way to plan and develop public spaces. While all of our projects strive to integrate Ms. Rivic's ideas, I will use one that clearly exemplifies our integration of her ideas into our work. This project recently won an American Society of Landscape Architecture award and focuses on the revitalization of an expansive park in Denver, Colorado that was unattractive, underutilized, and divided neighborhoods. The new plan included numerous public meetings and strived to address local residents' needs. Park facilities such as playgrounds, picnic sites, seating areas, and community gardens are concentrated directly adjacent to different neighborhoods; a frisbee golf course, designed for youth, spans the length of the park; community-related park facilities and local art are shown at transit stops and neighborhood connectors, such as a regional, multiuse trail; large, artful bridges and restful overlooks with views into and across the park are planned. The first phase of the plan is currently being implemented so all age groups will have easy access to the area, attractive spaces will be created and youth will have facilities that reflect their needs and desires.

Ms. Rivic's contribution to the country is very special. As an urban aesthetician, concentrating on the understanding of the city as a vehicle for the healthy integration of diverse populations and public appreciation, she has drawn upon classical, modern, and postmodern empirical and theoretical studies to synthesize a highly original and readily applicable model of low-cost, high public benefit spatial utilization. To deprive Ms. Rivic of the opportunity to continue her nationally beneficial, clearly tangible work in the United States would truly be damaging to Americans, coast to coast.

The loss of Ms. Rivic's services would be all the more tragic in light of their economic benefit: As a private scholar and consultant, Ms. Rivic has already materially contributed to the amelioration of urban spaces at absolutely no cost to the American tax payer. Should her petition be denied, all of us lose a public benefactor of inestimable value. Accordingly, I trust that sober reflection and reconsideration will motivate your recognition of Ms. Rivic's phenomenal achievements to date and her many future contributions still to come.

Sincerely,

Jacqueline Morris
President, Principal, and Owner

EB-5 IMMIGRANT INVESTORS

by Stephen Yale-Loehr[*]

OVERVIEW

Congress created the fifth employment-based preference (EB-5) immigrant visa category in 1990 for immigrants seeking to enter to engage in a commercial enterprise that will benefit the U.S. economy and create at least 10 full-time jobs.[1] The basic amount required to invest is $1 million, although that amount may be $500,000 if the investment is made in a "targeted employment area."[2] Of the approximately 10,000 numbers available for this preference each year, 3,000 are reserved for entrepreneurs who invest in targeted employment areas.[3] A separate allocation of 3,000 visas is set aside for entrepreneurs who immigrate through a regional center pilot program discussed below.

The statutory requirements of the EB-5 visa category are onerous. At most only about 1,000 people a year have immigrated in this category, just one-tenth of the visas available.[4] The former Immigration and Naturalization Service (INS) (now U.S. Citizenship and Immigration Services (USCIS)) made it even harder to qualify in this category by issuing four precedent decisions in 1998 that significantly restricted eligibility for EB-5 status.[5] Since then, the Administrative Appeals Office (AAO) has issued numerous nonprecedent decisions that further tighten the screws on EB-5 cases.[6]

In 2002, Congress enacted a law designed to help certain stranded immigrant investors hurt by the 1998 decisions.[7] Those provisions are discussed in detail below. As of the end of March 2006, regulations to implement the 2002 law have not been published.[8]

---

[*] Updated from an article by Mr. Yale-Loehr published at *Immigration & Nationality Law Handbook* 311 (2005–06 ed.). Copyright © 2006 Stephen Yale-Loehr. All rights reserved.

Stephen Yale-Loehr (*syl@millermayer.com*) is co-author of *Immigration Law and Procedure*, the leading immigration law treatise, published by LexisNexis/Matthew Bender. He also teaches immigration law and refugee law at Cornell Law School, and is of counsel at Miller Mayer (*www.millermayer.com*) in Ithaca, N.Y. Mr. Yale-Loehr co-writes a bi-monthly column on immigration law for the *New York Law Journal*, and chairs AILA's Business Visa Committee. He is a member of AILA's Investor Committee, and used to be the co-editor of *Interpreter Releases* and the executive editor of *Immigration Briefings*. He graduated from Cornell Law School in 1981 *cum laude*, where he was editor-in-chief of the *Cornell International Law Journal*. Mr. Yale-Loehr thanks Lindsay Schoonmaker, a research assistant at Miller Mayer, for her assistance in updating this article.

[1] INA §203(b)(5), 8 USC §1153(b)(5). For a detailed treatment of the EB-5 immigrant investor category, see 3 C. Gordon, S. Mailman, & S. Yale-Loehr, *Immigration Law and Procedure* §39.07 (rev. ed. 2006).

[2] INA §203(b)(5)(C)(ii), 8 USC §1153(b)(5)(C)(ii).

[3] INA §203(b)(5)(B)(i), 8 USC §1153(b)(5)(B)(i).

[4] Office of Immigration Statistics, U.S. Dep't of Homeland Security, 2004 Yearbook of Immigration Statistics 14-15 (2006) (Table 4).

[5] *Matter of Soffici*, 22 I&N Dec. 158, 19 Immigr. Rep. B2-25 (Assoc. Comm'r, Examinations 1998); *Matter of Izummi*, 22 I&N Dec. 169, 19 Immigr. Rep. B2-32 (Assoc. Comm'r, Examinations 1998); *Matter of Hsiung*, 22 I&N Dec. 201, 19 Immigr. Rep. B2-106 (Assoc. Comm'r, Examinations 1998); *Matter of Ho*, 22 I&N Dec. 206, 19 Immigr. Rep. B2-99 (Assoc. Comm'r, Examinations 1998).

[6] *See generally* H. Joe, R. Oh, S. Smalley, & S. Yale-Loehr, "More AAO EB-5 Decisions," 7 *Bender's Immigration Bulletin* 251 (Mar. 1, 2002); 6 *Bender's Immigration Bulletin* 945 (Sept. 15, 2001) (summaries of four AAO EB-5 decisions); L. Stone, W. Mason, B. Stern Wasser, & S. Yale-Loehr, "Immigrant Investors Strike Out Again at AAO," 6 *Bender's Immigration Bulletin* 709 (July 15, 2001); S. Park & S. Yale-Loehr, "More Bad News from the AAO for Immigrant Investors," 6 *Bender's Immigration Bulletin* 309 (Mar. 15, 2001); L. Stone, R. Oh, & S. Yale-Loehr, "Recent AAO Decisions Continue Trend of Limiting Immigrant Investor Visas," 5 *Bender's Immigration Bulletin* 1031 (Dec. 15, 2000); B. Palmer, "Recent EB-5 Denials," 4 *Bender's Immigration Bulletin* 1139 (Dec. 1, 1999); 4 *Bender's Immigration Bulletin* 810 (Aug. 15, 1999) (summaries of four AAO EB-5 denials). Some AAO EB-5 decisions are available at *uscis.gov/graphics/lawsregs/admindec3/B7/index.htm* (last visited Feb. 20, 2006).

[7] 21st Century Department of Justice Appropriations Authorization Act, Pub. L. No. 107-273, 116 Stat. 1758 (2002). The immigrant investor provisions are in §§11031–37. The conference committee report is H.R. Conf. Rep. No. 107-685 (2002).

[8] USCIS has published interim field guidance pending publication of the regulations. Memorandum from William R. Yates, BCIS Acting Assoc. Dir. for Operations, to all BCIS offices, "Amendments Affecting Adjudication of Petitions for Alien Entrepreneur (EB-5)," File No. HQ40/6.1.3 (June 10, 2003), *reprinted in* 8 *Bender's Immigration Bulletin* 1179 (July 1, 2003), *published on* AILA InfoNet at Doc. No. 03061744 [hereinafter Yates Memo].

In 2003, Congress asked the U.S. Government Accountability Office (GAO) to study the EB-5 program.[9] The GAO report concluded that the program has been under-used for a variety of reasons, including the rigorous application process and the failure to issue regulations implementing the 2002 law.[10] The report found that even though few people have used the EB-5 category, EB-5 participants have invested an estimated $1 billion in a variety of U.S. businesses.[11]

STATUTORY REQUIREMENTS

The Regular Program

Immigration and Nationality Act (INA) §203(b)(5)[12] provides a yearly maximum of approximately 10,000 visas for applicants to invest in a new commercial enterprise employing at least 10 full-time U.S. workers. To qualify under the EB-5 category, the new enterprise must: (1) be one in which the person has invested (or is in the process of investing) at least $1 million (or at least $500,000 if investing in a "targeted employment area," discussed below) after November 29, 1990; (2) benefit the U.S. economy; and (3) create full-time employment for at least 10 U.S. workers. Moreover, the investor must have at least a policy-making role in the enterprise.

The Pilot Program

To encourage immigration through the EB-5 category, Congress created a temporary pilot program in 1993.[13] The pilot program directs the Attorney General and Secretary of State to set aside 3,000 visas each year for people who invest in "designated regional centers." The pilot program has been renewed several times, and is currently due to expire September 30, 2008.[14]

The pilot program does not require that the immigrant investor enterprise itself employ 10 U.S. workers. Instead, it is enough if 10 or more jobs will be created directly or indirectly as a result of the investment.[15] This program also differs from the regular EB-5 provisions in that it permits private and governmental agencies to be certified as regional centers if they meet certain criteria.[16] (*See* Appendix, "Designated Regional Centers," *infra*).

Qualified Immigrants

Outside of the investment and employment requisites, the statute does not specifically address who may be a qualified applicant. USCIS appears to preclude corporate or other nonindividual investors from this category. However, two or more individuals may join to make an EB-5 investment. A single new commercial enterprise may be used for investor/employment-creation classification by more than one investor, provided that: (1) each petitioning investor has invested (or is actively in the process of investing) the required amount; and (2) each investment results in the creation of at least 10 full-time positions for qualifying employees.[17] In fact, a new commercial enterprise may be used for investor/employment-creation classification even though there are several owners of the enterprise, including persons not seeking classification, if: (1) the source(s) of all capital invested is (are) identified; and (2) all invested capital has been derived by lawful means.[18] The lawful source of funds issue is discussed in more detail in "Legal Acquisition of Capital," *infra*.

The New Commercial Enterprise

There are two basic requirements for showing a new commercial enterprise. First, the enterprise must be "new," *i.e.*, formed after November 29, 1990.[19]

---

[9] Basic Pilot Program Extension and Expansion Act of 2003, Pub. L. No. 108-156, §5, 117 Stat. 1944.

[10] U.S. Government Accountability Office, No. GAO-05-256, "Immigrant Investors: Small Number of Participants Attributed to Pending Regulations and Other Factors" (Apr. 2005), available at *www.gao.gov/new.items/d05256.pdf* (last visited Feb.14, 2006).

[11] *Id*. at 1.

[12] 8 USC §1153(b)(5).

[13] Departments of Commerce, Justice, and State, the Judiciary, and Related Agencies Appropriations Act of 1993, Pub. L. No. 102-395, §610, 106 Stat. 1828; S. Rep. No. 102-918 (1992).

[14] Basic Pilot Program Extension and Expansion Act of 2003, *supra* note 9, §4(b) (extending EB-5 pilot program five years to Sept. 30, 2008).

[15] 21st Century Department of Justice Appropriations Authorization Act, *supra* note 7, §11037(a)(3).

[16] 8 CFR §204.6(m)(3).

[17] 8 CFR §204.6(g)(1).

[18] *Id*.

[19] *See, e.g., Matter of [name not provided]*, EAC-91-184-50136, 12 Immigr. Rep. B2-51 (AAU Aug. 12, 1993) (denying petition as investment made before Nov. 29, 1990;

continued

Second, it must be a "commercial" enterprise. Any for-profit entity formed for the ongoing conduct of lawful business may serve as a commercial enterprise. This includes sole proprietorships, partnerships (whether limited or general),[20] holding companies, joint ventures, corporations, business trusts, or other entities publicly or privately owned.[21] This definition would even include a holding company and its wholly owned subsidiaries, if each such subsidiary is engaged in a for-profit activity formed for the ongoing conduct of a lawful business. However, the term "new commercial enterprise" does not include non-commercial activity, such as owning and operating a personal residence or nonprofit enterprise.[22]

Creating an Original Business—According to a 1998 precedent decision, an EB-5 petitioner had to have a hand in the creation of the enterprise and must be present at the enterprise's inception.[23] This posed particular problems for people investing in partnerships. The partnership will usually be created and then the general partner will seek individuals to invest as limited partners. Under the legacy INS's interpretation, such investors could not qualify for EB-5 classification because they were not partners at the establishment of the original partnership. In 2002, Congress eliminated the "establishment" requirement for EB-5 investors.[24] Instead of proving that they have "established" a commercial enterprise themselves, investors now need only show that they have "invested" in a commercial enterprise.

Buying an Existing Business—By reorganizing or restructuring an existing business, an investor may create a "new commercial enterprise" and therefore qualify for a visa. The statute and regulations provide little insight into what degree of restructuring or reorganization must be done to establish a new enterprise. The AAO has held that simply changing the legal form of the enterprise does not satisfy this re-quirement.[25] There is only one known case where the AAO agreed the business was sufficiently restructured or reorganized.[26]

Regardless of the forms used to create a new enterprise, the focus of the law is on the creation of at least 10 new employment opportunities. Investments creating a new enterprise but failing to create 10 new jobs will also fail to qualify for EB-5 classification.

Expanding an Existing Business—An investor also can create a new enterprise by expanding an existing business. Only an expansion resulting in an increase of at least 40 percent in the net worth of the business or in the number of employees of the business will satisfy the visa requirements.[27] This could require the investor to create more than 10 new jobs to qualify for a visa. The larger the business that the investor expands, the more onerous his or her burden to qualify for a visa under this standard. However, an investor need not show that his or her investment alone caused the 40 percent increase.[28] The AAO has insisted that proof of expansion of the company requires audited financial statements concerning the company's former net worth at the time of investment.[29]

Pooling Arrangements—The regulations specifically allow immigrant investors to pool their investments with others seeking EB-5 status.[30] Each investor must invest the applicable statutory amount. All of the new jobs created by the new commercial

investor's documentation of "expanded business" deemed insufficient). *See also* Yates Memo, *supra* note 8, at ¶2.

[20] The 21st Century Department of Justice Appropriations Authorization Act, *supra* note 7, clarifies that a "commercial enterprise" may include a limited partnership. *Id.* §11036(b)(3).

[21] 8 CFR §204.6(e) (definition of commercial enterprise).

[22] *Id.*

[23] *Matter of Izummi*, 22 I&N Dec. 169, 198, 19 Immigr. Rep. B2-32 (Assoc. Comm'r, Examinations 1998).

[24] 21st Century Department of Justice Appropriations Authorization Act, *supra* note 7, §11036(a)(2). *See also* Yates Memo, *supra* note 8, at ¶1.

[25] *Matter of Soffici*, 22 I&N Dec. 158, 166, 19 Immigr. Rep. B2-25 (Assoc. Comm'r, Examinations 1998) ("A few cosmetic changes to the decor and a new marketing strategy for success do not constitute the kind of restructuring contemplated by the regulations, nor does a simple change in ownership.").

[26] *Matter of [name redacted]*, (AAO July 11, 2001) (approved case involved the "restructuring" of a horse breeding business into a new business for horse breeding and training).

[27] 8 CFR §204.6(h)(3). *See also* Yates Memo, *supra* note 8, at ¶2.

[28] Memorandum from T. Alexander Aleinikoff, INS General Counsel, to Louis D. Crochetti, Jr., Acting Assoc. Comm'r for Examinations, "Whether a Pool of Alien Immigrant Investors Can Create a New Commercial Enterprise by Expanding an Existing Business by at Least 40%," HQ 204.27-C (Jan. 31, 1995), *reprinted in* 73 *Interpreter Releases* 1625 (Nov. 18, 1996).

[29] *Matter of [name not provided]*, WAC-99-010-50117 (AAO Dec. 15, 2000).

[30] 8 CFR §204.6(g).

enterprise will be allocated among those within the pool seeking permanent investor visas.[31]

The AAO has injected a restriction on pooling investments by requiring the petitioner to show that *every* investor in the partnership identify the source of their funds and prove that they were derived by lawful means.[32] This evidentiary hurdle makes it almost impossible for members in a partnership to qualify for EB-5 status.

"Engaging" in a New Commercial Enterprise

The statute requires an EB-5 applicant to enter the United States to engage in a new commercial enterprise.[33] To qualify, an investor must maintain more than a passive role in the new enterprise upon which the petition is based. The regulations require an EB-5 immigrant to be involved in the management of the new commercial enterprise.[34] The petitioner must either be involved in the day-to-day managerial control of the commercial enterprise or manage it through policy formulation. The regulations state that if the EB-5 petitioner is a corporate officer or board member, or, in the case of a limited partnership, is a limited partner under the provisions of the Uniform Limited Partnership Act (ULPA), he or she satisfies the requirement of engaging in the management of the new commercial enterprise.[35] The AAO, however, has found that merely calling the investor a limited partner pursuant to the ULPA in a partnership agreement does not automatically mean that the person is involved in the management of the new commercial enterprise.[36]

"Investing" or "Actively in the Process of Investing" "Capital"

The statute requires an EB-5 petitioner to have invested or be in the process of investing. Although the statute explicitly states that an EB-5 petitioner may be "in the process" of investing the required capital,[37] USCIS requires the entire capital amount to be already invested and at risk in the commercial enterprise at the time the I-526 petition is filed. This interpretation appears to contravene the statute.

The term "invest" means to contribute capital. A contribution of capital in exchange for a note, bond, convertible debt, obligation, or any other debt arrangement between the entrepreneur and the new commercial enterprise does not constitute a contribution of capital and will not constitute an investment.[38]

The regulations define "capital" as cash and cash equivalents, equipment, inventory, and other tangible property.[39] According to USCIS, retained earnings cannot count as "capital."[40]

Capital does not include loans by the petitioner or other parties.[41] Indebtedness secured by assets owned by the entrepreneur may be considered capital, provided the investor is personally and primarily liable for the debts and the assets of the enterprise

---

[31] *See generally* H.R. Klasko, "Pooled Investment Arrangements: Unraveling the Controversy," 2 *Immigration & Nationality Law Handbook* 107 (1998–99 ed.) [hereinafter Klasko]; A.J. Vasquez-Aspiri, "The Role of Commercial Organizations in the EB-5 Employment Process," 2 *Bender's Immigration Bulletin* 813 (Oct. 15, 1997).

[32] *See, e.g., Matter of [name not provided]*, WAC-98-106-51072, slip op. at 20 (AAO July 6, 2000); *Matter of [name not provided]*, WAC-98-106-51583, slip. op. at 22 (AAO Sept. 11, 2000). This requirement is discussed further *infra*.

[33] INA §203(b)(5)(A), 8 USC §1153(b)(5)(A).

[34] 8 CFR §204.6(j)(5).

[35] *Id. See also* 73 *Interpreter Releases* 48, 55 (Jan. 10, 1996).

[36] *See, e.g., Matter of [name not provided]*, WAC-98-111-53508, slip op. at 23 (AAO Mar. 20, 2000) ("Despite the superficial language in the limited partnership agreement referring to the ULPA and to 8 CFR §204.6(j)(5)(iii), it is clear that the petitioner here does not in fact have the rights normally granted to limited partners under the ULPA.").

---

[37] INA §203(b)(5)(A)(i), 8 USC §1153(b)(5)(A)(i). *See also* 8 CFR §204.6(j)(2) (allowing an investor to be "actively in the process of investing the required amount of capital"). Indeed, even the regulations governing removal of an EB-5 investor's conditional resident status two years later acknowledge that an investor may not have invested all of his or her money by then. The regulations simply require an investor to provide evidence that the alien "invested or was actively in the process of investing the requisite capital." 8 CFR §216.6(a)(4)(ii).

[38] *See* 8 CFR §204.6(e) (definition of "invest").

[39] *Id.* (definition of "capital").

[40] Letter from Efren Hernandez, Chief, USCIS Business and Trade Branch, to Stephen Yale-Loehr, File No. HOOPRD 70/6.2.8 (June 4, 2004), available at *www.usa-immigration.com/litigation.htm* (last visited Feb. 14, 2006). *See also Kenkhuis v. INS*, No. 3:01-CV-2224-N, 2003 U.S. Dist. LEXIS 3334 at *6 (N.D. Tex. Mar. 6, 2003) ("[t]he definition of 'invest' . . . requires an infusion of new capital, not merely a retention of profits of the enterprise"); *De Jong v. INS*, No. 6:94 CV 850 (E.D. Tex. Jan. 17, 1997).

[41] *Matter of Soffici*, 22 I&N Dec. 158, 19 Immigr. Rep. B2-25 (Assoc. Comm'r, Examinations 1998).

upon which the petition is based are not used to secure any of the indebtedness.[42]

Indebtedness typically consists of a promissory note signed by the petitioner that specifies a payment schedule to the new commercial enterprise. Absent fraud, a signed promissory note that is secured by the petitioner's personal assets constitutes a contribution of capital by the petitioner.[43] The issuer of the promissory note, *i.e.*, the investor, is considered to be "at risk" if the petitioner is clearly obligated to make all the required payments on the note and there are no "escape" clauses. The investor cannot receive any bond, note, or other debt arrangement from the enterprise for the capital contributed to it. This includes any stock redeemable at the holder's request. All capital is valued at fair market value in U.S. dollars at the time it is given.[44]

Debt arrangements are extremely complicated. A prudent practitioner must do careful research and analysis to determine current USCIS positions and policies on this issue.[45]

Benefiting the U.S. Economy

The statute requires that investments "benefit the U.S. economy" to qualify the investor for an EB-5 visa or status.[46] The statute provides no guidance on which investments benefit the economy. This silence means USCIS adjudicators are left to their subjective interpretations of the investment and its relative benefits when reviewing the petition. Arguably, the petitioner has benefited the economy by merely meeting the employment and investment requirements of the visa classification. However, because the statute specifically identifies the "benefit" element as distinct from other components of the visa, it appears that the applicant must independently show that the enterprise, in the conduct of its business, will

benefit the U.S. economy. Therefore, a consulting firm exclusively serving customers abroad with no return benefit to the U.S. economy (other than employing the requisite number of workers), might not support an EB-5 petition. In contrast, showing that the new enterprise provides goods or services to U.S. markets should satisfy this requirement.

Federal regulation of foreign investments is extensive. Some regulations restrict foreign investments in aviation, banking, shipping, communications, land use, energy resources, and government contracting. Additionally, Congress has imposed several disclosure and data requirements on foreign investments.[47] An investment may not be deemed beneficial to the U.S. economy if it runs afoul of any statutory limitation on foreign investment.

Creating or Saving Jobs

To qualify for EB-5 status, an investment normally must create full-time employment for at least 10 U.S. citizens, lawful permanent residents, or other immigrants lawfully authorized to be employed in the United States.[48] Neither the investor nor the investor's spouse and children count toward the 10-employee minimum.[49] Nonimmigrants are also excluded from the count. The "other immigrants" provision means that conditional residents, temporary residents, asylees, refugees, and recipients of suspension of deportation or cancellation of removal may all be considered employees for EB-5 purposes.

The regulations define an "employee" for EB-5 purposes as an individual who (1) provides services or labor for the new commercial enterprise and (2) receives wages or other remuneration directly from the new commercial enterprise.[50] This definition excludes independent contractors.[51]

The EB-5 pilot program does not require the investment to directly create 10 U.S. jobs. Instead, pilot program investments only require an indirect

---

[42] 8 CFR §204.6(e) (definition of "capital").

[43] *Matter of Hsiung*, 22 I&N Dec. 201, 19 Immigr. Rep. B2-106 (Assoc. Comm'r, Examinations 1998).

[44] *Matter of Izummi*, 22 I&N Dec. 169, 192–93, 19 Immigr. Rep. B2-32 (Assoc. Comm'r, Examinations 1998) (finding that investor failed to show how bank accounts in Japan were in trust or otherwise secured the note, as required by 8 CFR §204.6(e), and that the note was not readily enforceable and was in any event not now worth its face value payable over six years).

[45] *See generally* W. Cook, "Somewhere, Over the Rainbow . . . Lies the EB-5 Pot of Gold," 3 *Bender's Immigration Bulletin* 1205 (Dec. 1, 1998); Klasko, *supra* note 31.

[46] INA §203(b)(5)(A)(iii), 8 USC §1153(b)(5)(A)(iii).

[47] For a comprehensive summary of the regulations, see Marans, Williams, Griffin, & Pattison, *Manual of Foreign Investment in the United States* (3d ed. 2004); *United States Law of Trade and Investment* (B. Kozolchyk & J. Molloy eds., 2000).

[48] INA §203(b)(5)(A)(iii), 8 USC §1153(b)(5)(A)(iii).

[49] *Id.*

[50] 8 CFR §204.6(e) (definition of "employee").

[51] *Id.*

creation of jobs and an improvement of the local economy.[52]

The Types of Jobs—The jobs created must be full-time. This means employment of a qualified employee in a position that requires a minimum of 35 working hours per week, regardless of who fills the position.[53] Job-sharing arrangements, where two or more qualifying employees share a full-time position, will also serve as full-time employment if the hourly requirement per week is met.[54] Job-sharing does not include combinations of part-time positions even if when combined such positions meet the hourly requirement per week.[55]

When the Jobs Must Exist—The law is unclear about when new jobs must exist. The statutory language is prospective and therefore does not require jobs to exist at the time of initial investment or before the I-526 petition is filed. USCIS does not require retention of employees until a reasonable time after conditional visa issuance. In fact, a petitioner may support a petition with a comprehensive business plan demonstrating a need for at least 10 employees within the next two years. The business plan need only indicate the approximate dates during the following two years when the employees will be hired. The temporary vacancy of a position during the two-year conditional period does not disqualify an investor, as long as good-faith attempts to re-staff the position are made.

Where the Jobs Must be Located—When enacting the EB-5 program, Congress took an affirmative step toward creating jobs in the geographic areas that need them most. The statute sets aside 3,000 of the approximately 10,000 EB-5 visas available annually for foreign citizens who invest in "targeted employment areas."[56] The statute defines a "targeted employment area" as a rural area or an area that has experienced high unemployment of at least 150 percent of the national average.[57] An area not within a metropolitan statistical area (as designated by the Office of Management and Budget) or the outer boundary of any city or town having a population of 20,000 or more is considered a rural area.[58] Each state notifies USCIS which state agency will apply these guidelines, and determines targeted employment areas for that state.[59]

Troubled Businesses—Special rules govern investments in "troubled" businesses. A troubled business is one that has been in existence for at least two years, has incurred a net loss for accounting purposes during the 12- or 24-month period before the petition was filed, and the loss for such period is at least equal to 20 percent of the business's net worth before the loss.[60] To establish an investment in a troubled business, the petitioner must show that the number of existing employees will be maintained at no less than the pre-investment level for at least two years. Thus, this provision includes a significant incentive in that it does not require the creation of 10 new jobs. Instead, it requires only that the business maintain the number of existing employees during the conditional status period.[61] As a caveat, if the troubled business does not remain afloat for two years after the investment, the investor might lose his or her conditional residency status.

EB-5 PROCEDURES: INITIAL EVIDENCE

The regular EB-5 program and the pilot program have similar requirements to begin the process. The distinction between the two processes is that the former requires the petitioner to submit all of the described evidence; the latter requires the designated regional center to certify that the investor has met its criteria.

In either case the investor files for EB-5 classification using Form I-526. The petition must be signed by the investor, not someone acting on his or her behalf. If the EB-5 commercial enterprise will primarily do business in a location within the ordinary jurisdiction of the Vermont or Texas Service Centers, the petition is filed with the Texas Service Center; otherwise it is filed with the California Service Center.[62]

---

[52] *Id.*

[53] 21st Century Department of Justice Appropriations Authorization Act, *supra* note 7, §11031(f). *See also* Yates Memo, *supra* note 8, at ¶ 4.

[54] 8 CFR §204.6(e) (definition of "full-time employment").

[55] *Id.*

[56] INA §203(b)(5)(B), 8 USC §1153(b)(5)(B).

[57] INA §203(b)(5)(B)(ii), 8 USC §1153(b)(5)(B)(ii).

[58] INA §203(b)(5)(B)(iii), 8 USC §1153(b)(5)(B)(iii).

[59] Several states have websites that can help determine whether a particular area in the state qualifies as a "targeted employment area" for EB-5 purposes. *See, e.g., www.labor.ca.gov/ calBIS/cbfederalvisaprog.pdf* (last updated June 2005) (last visited Feb. 14, 2006).

[60] 8 CFR §204.6(e) (definition of troubled business).

[61] 8 CFR §§204.6(h)(3), 204.6(j)(4)(ii).

[62] *See* 63 Fed. Reg. 67,135 (Dec. 4, 1998).

Initial Evidence for the Regular EB-5 Program

The following paragraphs detail the evidence that should be submitted with an I-526 petition for EB-5 classification under the regular program.

The New Commercial Enterprise—To qualify for EB-5 classification an investor must show that an investment has been made in a qualified commercial enterprise. The applicant should include:

- An organizational document for the new enterprise, including articles of incorporation, certificates of merger and consolidation, or partnership agreements;

- A business license or authorization to transact business in a state or city; and

- For investments in an existing business, proof that the required amount of capital was transferred to the business after November 29, 1990, and that the investment has increased the net worth or number of employees by 40 percent or more.[63]

Capitalization—To show that the petitioner has invested (or is actively in the process of investing) the required amount of capital, the petition must be accompanied by evidence that the petitioner has placed the required amount of capital "at risk." A mere intention to invest will not demonstrate that the petitioner is actively in the process of investing. The investor must show actual commitment of the required amount of capital. Such evidence may include:

- Bank statements showing deposits in the U.S. account of the enterprise;

- Evidence of assets purchased for use in the enterprise;

- Evidence of property transferred from abroad;

- Evidence of funds invested in the enterprise in exchange for stock, except for stock redeemable at the holder's request; or

- Evidence of debts secured by the investor's assets and for which the investor is personally and primarily liable.[64]

The AAO has held that merely putting cash into the corporate account of a business does not show that the capital is "at risk" for the purpose of gener-

ating a return.[65] The AAO has also held that the full amount of the required capital must be expended by the enterprise directly toward job creation; otherwise that capital is not at risk of loss.[66] Based on these statements, it is difficult to know what a petitioner must do to show that the money is truly at risk.

Legal Acquisition of Capital[67]—The regulations require filing the following types of documentation to establish that capital used in the new enterprise was acquired by legitimate means:

- Foreign business registration records;

- Personal and business tax returns, or other tax returns of any kind filed anywhere in the world within the previous five years;

- Documents identifying any other source of money; or

- Certified copies of all pending governmental civil or criminal actions and proceedings, or any private civil actions involving money judgments against the investor within the past 15 years.[68]

Although the regulations list these requirements in the disjunctive, meaning that submission of any one type of document should suffice, the AAO requires investors to submit tax returns for the previous five years.[69] This interpretation makes it harder for investors to qualify for EB-5 status, and appears to violate the regulations.

The regulations further define "capital" as only those assets acquired through lawful means.[70] The AAO has held that money earned or assets acquired

---

[63] 8 CFR §204.6(j)(1).

[64] 8 CFR §204.6(j)(2).

[65] *See Matter of [name not provided]*, file no. redacted (AAO July 7, 2000).

[66] *See, e.g., Matter of [name redacted]*, WAC-98-194-50913 (AAO Aug. 16, 2002). For a good discussion of the immigration agency's overly restrictive interpretation of the "at risk" requirement, see L. Stone, "Immigrant Investment in Local Clusters: Part II," 80 *Interpreter Releases* 937, 941–45 (July 14, 2003) [hereinafter Stone].

[67] For an in-depth discussion of the requirement that an investor's capital be from a lawful source, see Stone, *supra* note 66, at 946–50; L. Stone & S. Yale-Loehr, "Evidence of Source of Capital in Immigrant Investor Cases," 6 *Bender's Immigration Bulletin* 972 (Oct. 1, 2001).

[68] 8 CFR §204.6(j)(3).

[69] *See, e.g., Matter of [name not provided]*, file no. redacted, slip op. at 12 (AAO July 7, 2000) ("In addition, the petitioner has not submitted his corporate and personal tax records for at least the five years preceding filing the petition as required by 8 CFR §204.6(j)(3).").

[70] *See* 8 CFR §204.6(e) (definition of "capital").

while in the United States in an unlawful status are not considered lawful means to acquire capital.[71] This interpretation goes far beyond Congress' original concern to prevent drug smugglers or other criminals to use their ill-gotten gains to be able to obtain permanent residents status in the United States through the EB-5 category.

Creating Employment—To show that a new commercial enterprise will create at least 10 full-time positions for qualified employees, the petition must be accompanied by:

- Photocopies of relevant tax records, Forms I-9, or similar documents for 10 qualifying employees; or

- A comprehensive business plan showing the need for at least 10 qualifying employees, and when the employees will be hired.[72] The plan should include a description of the business; the business' objectives; a market analysis including names of competing businesses and their relative strengths and weaknesses; a comparison of the competition's products and pricing structures; a description of the target market and prospective customers; a description of any manufacturing or production processes, materials required and supply sources; details of any contracts executed; marketing strategy including pricing, advertising, and servicing; organizational structure; and sales, cost and income projections and details of the bases therefore. In addition, specifically with respect to employment, the business plan must set forth the company's personnel experience, staffing requirements, job descriptions for all positions, and a timetable for hiring.[73]

Troubled Business—To show that a new enterprise, established through capital investment in a troubled business, meets the statutory requirement, the petition must show that the number of existing employees will be maintained at no less than the pre-investment level for a period of at least two years. The applicant should include photocopies of the I-9

forms, tax records or payroll documents, and a comprehensive business plan.[74]

Managerial Capacity of the Investor—An EB-5 immigrant must be involved in the management of a new commercial enterprise to qualify for a visa. The petitioner must either be involved in the day-to-day managerial control of the enterprise, or manage it through policy formulation. These requirements may be evidenced by:

- A comprehensive job description for the position occupied by the investor. The petitioner's title should also be indicated;

- Evidence that the petitioner is a corporate officer or on the board of directors; or

- Evidence that the petitioner is involved in direct management activities or policymaking activities of a general or limited partnership. A limited partner must also show that he has rights, powers and duties commensurate with those normally granted under the Uniform Limited Partnership Act (ULPA).[75] The AAO, however, has found that merely calling the investor a limited partner pursuant to the ULPA in a partnership agreement does not automatically mean that the person is involved in the management of the new commercial enterprise.[76]

Designation of a High Unemployment Area—The state government may designate a particular geographic or political subdivision as an area of high unemployment (at least 150 percent of the national average rate). Evidence of such designation may be provided with Form I-526. Such evidence should include:

- Boundaries of the subdivision;

- The date of the designation; and

- The methods by which the statistics were gathered.[77]

The Investment Must Benefit the U.S. Economy—This requirement has not been fully defined in the

---

[71] *See, e.g., Matter of [name not provided]*, file no. redacted, slip. op. at 12 (AAO July 7, 2000); *Matter of [name not provided]*, file no. redacted, slip. op. at 12 (AAO July 11, 2000); *Matter of [name not provided]*, WAC-98-106-51583, slip. op. at 22 (AAO Sept. 11, 2000).

[72] 8 CFR §204.6(j)(4)(i).

[73] *Matter of Ho*, 22 I&N Dec. 206, 19 Immigr. Rep. B2-99 (Assoc. Comm'r, Examinations 1998).

[74] 8 CFR §204.6(j)(4)(ii).

[75] 8 CFR §204.6(j)(5).

[76] *See, e.g., Matter of [name not provided]*, WAC-98-111-53508, slip op. at 23 (AAO Mar. 20, 2000) ("Despite the superficial language in the limited partnership agreement referring to the ULPA and to 8 C.F.R. §204.6(j)(5)(iii), it is clear that the petitioner here does not in fact have the rights normally granted to limited partners under the ULPA.").

[77] 8 CFR §204.6(i).

regulations. Letters from local government officials, chambers of commerce, or regional development agencies should satisfy the requirement and should be included with the petition.

Creation of Employment in a Targeted Employment Area—To show that the new commercial enterprise has created, or will create, employment in a targeted employment area, the petition must be accompanied by:

- For a rural area, evidence that the new commercial enterprise is not located within any standard metropolitan statistical area, or within any city or town having a population of 20,000 or more; or

- For a high unemployment area, evidence that the metropolitan statistical area, or the county in which a city or town with a population of 20,000 or more is located, in which the new commercial enterprise is principally doing business has experienced an average unemployment rate of 150 percent of the national average rate; or a letter from the state in which the new commercial enterprise is located which certifies that the area has been designated as a high unemployment area.[78]

Pilot Program

An investment under the EB-5 pilot program must be made in a commercial enterprise located within a "regional center," defined as "any economic unit, public or private, which is involved with the promotion of economic growth, including increased export sales, improved regional productivity, job creation, or increased domestic capital investment."[79]

A center seeking USCIS approval must submit a proposal showing how it plans to focus on a geographical region within the United States and to achieve the required growth by the means specified.[80]

The proposal must show "in verifiable detail how jobs will be created indirectly through increased exports," as well as the amount and source of capital committed and the promotional efforts made and planned.[81] The Appendix at the end of this article contains a list of designated regional centers.

Relatively few of the approved regional centers, however, are actually functioning.

Just as INS/USCIS has made it more difficult to obtain immigrant status under the regular EB-5 program, so too the agency has become more restrictive in reviewing applications for regional center designation under the pilot program. Many applications for regional center designation have remained pending for more than three years. In 2000, the INS issued five decisions on regional center applications, denying or remanding all of them.[82] The decisions set forth restrictive new requirements to qualify as a regional center.[83]

To counteract this trend, in 2002 Congress amended the EB-5 regional center designation provisions.[84] Under the 2002 law, USCIS should approve applications for EB-5 regional center status as long as the applications are based on a general prediction concerning: (1) the kinds of commercial enterprises that will receive capital from investor; (2) the jobs that will be created directly or indirectly as a result of the investment of capital; and (3) the other positive economic impacts that will result from the investment of capital.[85]

Assuming a regional center application has been approved, an applicant seeking EB-5 status under the pilot program must make the qualifying investment (*i.e.*, the amount required under the basic program) within an approved regional center. However, the requirement of creating at least 10 new jobs is met by a showing that as a result of the new enterprise, such jobs will be created directly or indirectly.[86]

To file an I-526 form under the pilot program, attach a copy of the INS or USCIS letter designating the regional center. The petitioner's new commercial enterprise must be within the area specified in that letter. If the commercial enterprise is involved directly or indirectly in lending money to job-creating businesses, it may only lend money to businesses

---

[78] 8 CFR §204.6(j)(6).

[79] 21st Century Department of Justice Appropriations Authorization Act, *supra* note 7, §11037(a)(2).

[80] 8 CFR §204.6(m)(3).

[81] *Id.*

[82] *See generally* L. Stone, "INS Decisions Cloud Future of Investor Pilot Program," 6 *Bender's Immigration Bulletin* 233 (Mar. 1, 2001).

[83] *Id.*

[84] 21st Century Department of Justice Appropriations Authorization Act, *supra* note 7, §11037.

[85] *Id.* §11037(a)(3). For a good analysis of the kinds of economic benefits EB-5 regional centers could potentially create, see L. Stone, "Immigrant Investment in Local Clusters: Part I," 80 *Interpreter Releases* 837 (June 16, 2003).

[86] 8 CFR §§204.6(j)(4)(iii), 204.6(m)(7).

located within targeted employment areas to take advantage of the lesser capital requirement ($500,000).[87] The businesses receiving the loans must be within the geographic limits of the regional center if the enterprise is to qualify under the pilot program. Otherwise the enterprise is not promoting economic growth through "improved regional activity" as required by the regulations.[88]

In 2003 Congress gave USCIS discretion to "give priority" to EB-5 petitions filed through a regional center.[89] To date USCIS has not acted on this statutory authorization.

EB-5 PROCEDURES: REMOVING THE CONDITIONS

Assuming USCIS approves an investor's I-526 petition under either the regular or pilot program, he or she becomes a conditional resident for two years. The procedure to remove the conditions is analogous to that followed by people who obtain conditional residence through marriage to a U.S. citizen or lawful permanent resident.[90] An immigrant investor's petition to remove the conditions should be filed on Form I-829 with the relevant service center.[91] It must be accompanied by evidence that the individual invested or was in the process of investing the required capital, and that the investment created or will create 10 full-time jobs. The individual also must show that he or she "sustained the actions required for removal of conditions" during the person's residence in the United States. An entrepreneur will have met this requirement if he or she has "substantially met" the capital investment requirement and has continuously maintained this investment during the conditional period.[92]

Failure to File Form I-829

An immigrant investor in conditional resident status must submit Form I-829 to the appropriate service center within the 90-day period immediately preceding the second anniversary of his or her admission to the

United States as a conditional permanent resident.[93] Failure to do so will result in automatic termination of the conditional resident's status and initiation of removal proceedings.[94]

Adjudication of Form I-829 by a Service Center

Initial Review of Form I-829—An immigration service center may (1) approve an I-829 petition without review, (2) issue a request for further evidence, or (3) refer it for an adjudication (with or without the interview) by a district office.[95]

Approval of Form I-829 by the USCIS Service Center—A service center may approve an I-829 petition if the petition establishes the requirements for removing the conditions outlined above. If approved, the service center director will remove the conditions on the conditional resident's status as of the second anniversary of his or her admission as a conditional resident.[96] The approval notice will instruct the conditional resident to report to the appropriate district office for processing for a new permanent resident card (Form I-551). At the district office, the conditional resident will surrender any permanent resident card previously issued and receive interim documents valid for 12 months in the form of either a temporary I-551 stamp in his or her unexpired foreign passport, or a Form I-94 containing a temporary I-551 stamp and his or her photograph.[97]

Request for Further Evidence—A service center may also issue a request for further evidence (RFE). An RFE must be based on a determination by the service center director that the conditional resident must provide further documentation or answer certain questions in writing.[98] If the questions cannot be answered in writing, the petition must be referred for

---

[87] *Matter of Izummi*, 22 I&N Dec. 169, 19 Immigr. Rep. B2-32 (Assoc. Comm'r, Examinations 1998).

[88] *Id.*

[89] Basic Pilot Program Extension and Expansion Act of 2003, *supra* note 9, §4(a)(2).

[90] *See* INA §216, 8 USC §1186a.

[91] 8 CFR §§216.6, 1216.6.

[92] 8 CFR §§216.6(a)(4), 1216.6(a)(4).

[93] 8 CFR §§216.6(a)(1), 1216.6(a)(1).

[94] 8 CFR §§216.6(a)(5), 1216.6(a)(5); Memorandum from Michael A. Pearson, INS Executive Associate Comm'r, to all INS field offices, "EB-5 Field Memorandum No. 9: Form I-829 Processing" (Mar. 3, 2000), *published on* AILA InfoNet at Doc. No. 00060702 (*posted* June 7, 2000) (amending INS Adjudicators Field Manual §25.2) [hereinafter I-829 Memo]. *See also* L. Stone, "Removal of the Conditions on Permanent Residence for Immigrant Investors," *in* AILA 2005–06 *Immigration & Nationality Law Handbook* 329 (Stephanie L. Browning et al. eds., 2005).

[95] *Id.*

[96] 8 CFR §§216.6(d)(1), 1216.6(d)(1).

[97] I-829 Memo, *supra* note 94.

[98] *Id.*

an interview. An RFE will not be issued if the petition is clearly deniable on grounds other than those for which the RFE might be issued. A conditional resident has 12 weeks to respond to an RFE.[99] Upon receipt of the RFE, the service center director must either approve or refer the Form I-829 petition to the district office.[100]

Determination that Referral to District Office is Appropriate—A service center will refer the petition to a district director if the initial review of the petition or the response to a request for additional evidence reveals that (1) the requirements for removal of conditions have not been met and the case should be denied without an interview, or (2) an interview is necessary to approve or deny the petition.[101]

A petition will be denied without an interview if the service center determines that there is no material issue of fact in dispute and that the petition does not meet the requirements of the law and the regulations.

Adjudication of Form I-829 by the District Office

Approval of Form I-829 by the District Director—A district office may approve an I-829 petition if it is satisfied that the petition satisfies the requirements for removing the condition outlined above.[102]

Denial of Form I-829 by the District Director—A district director must deny an I-829 petition if the petition does not establish the requirements for removing the condition. There is no appeal from this decision. The conditional resident may seek review of the district director's decision in removal proceedings.[103]

Status of Conditional Residents While I-829 is Pending

Immigrant investors remain in valid status while their I-829 petition is pending. Their status is supposed to be extended automatically in one-year increments until USCIS acts on the petition. During that time they are authorized to travel.[104] Practitioners have complained, however, that many offices are unaware of this procedure. Extending conditional resident status, obtaining re-entry permits, and

proving authorization to travel can be particularly difficult for spouses and children of EB-5 investors.

USCIS issued a memo in January 2005 intended to help conditional residents with pending or denied I-829 petitions that might benefit from the 2002 law discussed below.[105] The memo instructs USCIS adjudicators to extend conditional resident status for affected EB-5 petitioners. The memo also instructs agency officials to assist pending I-829 petitioners with travel and parole requests.[106]

TERMINATION OF EB-5 STATUS

The statute provides three separate grounds for terminating an EB-5 investor's status during the two-year conditional period.[107] Immigrant status will be terminated if USCIS determines that:

- The investment in the new commercial enterprise was to evade the immigration laws of the United States.[108] This provision requires termination only if the investment of the enterprise was "solely" to evade immigration laws. This suggests that if the investment was made with legitimate intentions, in addition to an intention to fraudulently procure permanent resident status, termination would not be proper;

- The investor failed to invest (or was not in the process of investing) the requisite capital, or failed to sustain the investments during the two-year conditional period;[109] or

- The individual was otherwise not conforming to the requirements of the employment-creation status provisions of INA §203(b)(5).[110] This catch-all provision is dangerous because it does not define the conduct giving rise to termination of status. USCIS could potentially apply this provision broadly to terminate the investor status of an applicant for any infraction of the section.

---

[99] 8 CFR §103.2(b)(8).

[100] I-829 Memo, *supra* note 94.

[101] *Id.*

[102] *Id.*

[103] 8 CFR §§216.6(d)(2), 1216.6(d)(2); I-829 Memo, *supra* note 94.

[104] I-829 Memo, *supra* note 94.

[105] Memorandum from William R. Yates, USCIS Assoc. Director for Operations, to all USCIS offices, "Extension of Status for Conditional Residents with Pending or Denied Form I-829 Petitions Subject to Public Law 107-273 (Jan. 18, 2005), *published on* AILA InfoNet at Doc. No. 05012167 (*posted* Jan. 21, 2005), *reprinted in* 10 *Bender's Immigration Bulletin* 236 (Feb. 15, 2005).

[106] *Id.*

[107] INA §216A(b), 8 USC §1186b(b).

[108] INA §216A(b)(1)(A), 8 USC §1186b(b)(1)(A).

[109] INA §216A(b)(1)(B), 8 USC §1186b(b)(1)(B).

[110] INA §216A(b)(1)(C), 8 USC §1186b(b)(1)(C).

Fortunately, however, it does not appear that USCIS has ever invoked this provision to terminate the status of an immigrant investor.

An EB-5 investor admitted under the pilot program is also subject to the same conditions and restrictions.

DETERRING FRAUDULENT INVESTMENTS

In enacting the EB-5 program, Congress expressed concern about the possibility of fraudulent investments. To deter such fraud, establishing a commercial enterprise for the purpose of "evading any provision of the immigration laws" is a felony punishable by up to five years imprisonment.[111] One reason Congress provided for two-year conditional permanent residency status for EB-5 investors is to aid in this deterrence. This two-year continuum for business activity and investment requires a significant investment and is a strong deterrent to fraud. Nonetheless, should fraud be discovered by USCIS before the two-year conditional period ends, the investor's status will be terminated.[112] So far it appears that USCIS has not prosecuted any EB-5 investors for fraud.[113]

EB-5 PETITIONS: THEORY vs. REALITY

The statutory and regulatory provisions discussed above are onerous.[114] For this reason, immigration through the EB-5 category has never approached the maximum of about 10,000 a year. Yet the legacy INS radically restricted the EB-5 program even further in 1998 by issuing four precedent AAO decisions that made it even harder to obtain EB-5 status.[115]

A complete discussion of the four precedent decisions is beyond the scope of this article. Below is a summary of the changes created by the four decisions.[116] The post-1998 requirements are listed first; prior law or policy is listed in italics.[117]

Post-1998: Promissory note valued at fair market value.

Pre-1998: Promissory note valued at face value.

Post-1998: Promissory note must generally be paid after two years.

Pre-1998: No limit on term of promissory note.

Post-1998: Security for promissory note needs to be perfected under the UCC.

Pre-1998: Security does not need to meet UCC perfected security interest requirements.

Post-1998: Bank accounts cannot be used as security.

Pre-1998: Bank accounts can be used as security.

Post-1998: Reduce the fair market value of promissory note by "considerable expense and effort" to execute on foreign assets.

Pre-1998: Promissory note valued at face value.

---

[111] INA §275(d), 8 USC §1325(d).

[112] INA §216A(b)(1), 8 USC §1186b(b)(1).

[113] For an interesting case, rife with intrigue, fraud, and shady dealings surrounding two EB-5 promoters, see *United States v. O'Connor*, 158 F. Supp. 2d 697 (E.D. Va. 2001). Individual EB-5 investors appear to have been victims, not perpetrators, of the fraud. *See also* Serova v. Teplen, No. 05 CIV.6748 (HB), 2006 U.S. Dist. LEXIS 5781 (S.D.N.Y. Feb. 16, 2006) (EB-5 investor claims her attorney failed to represent her adequately, in part by failing to disclose that he also represented the company in which she invested).

[114] For current information on litigation and other developments surrounding EB-5 provisions, see the EB-5 Litigation Document Web page at *www.usa-immigration.com/litigation.htm* (last visited Feb. 14, 2006).

[115] *Matter of Soffici*, 22 I&N Dec. 158, 19 Immigr. Rep. B2-25 (Assoc. Comm'r, Examinations 1998); *Matter of Izummi*, 22 I&N Dec. 169, 19 Immigr. Rep. B2-32 (Assoc. Comm'r, Examinations 1998); *Matter of Hsiung*, 22 I&N Dec. 201, 19 Immigr. Rep. B2-106 (Assoc. Comm'r, Examinations 1998); *Matter of Ho*, 22 I&N Dec. 206, 19 Immigr. Rep. B2-99 (Assoc. Comm'r, Examinations 1998). *See generally* W. Cook, "Somewhere, Over the Rainbow…Lies the EB-5 Pot of Gold," 3 *Bender's Immigration Bulletin* 1205 (Dec. 1, 1998).

[116] Note that the requirements established by these cases may be applied retroactively, even if they contravene practices established by earlier unpublished decisions or other guidance. *See Golden Rainbow Freedom Fund v. Ashcroft*, 24 Fed. Appx. 698, 2001 U.S. App. LEXIS 25482 (9th Cir. Nov. 26, 2001). *See also R.L. Inv. Ltd. Partners v. INS*, 86 F. Supp. 2d 1014 (D. Haw. 2000), *aff'd*, 273 F.3d 874 (9th Cir. 2001). *But see Chang v. United States*, 327 F.3d 911 (9th Cir. 2003) (ruling that retroactive application of the newly established requirements is impermissible if the applicant was granted conditional residency before the new requirements came into effect); *Sang Geun An v. United States*, No. C03-3184P (W.D. Wash. Feb. 16, 2005) (following *Chang*). at *www.lexisnexis.com/practiceareas/immigration/pdfs/web 641.pdf* (last visited Feb. 20, 2006).

[117] Thanks to H. Ronald Klasko, who drafted this list of changes and allowed them to be reprinted here.

Post-1998: No redemption provisions can be agreed to before end of conditional residence and before conclusion of payments on promissory note.

Pre-1998: Redemption provisions can be agreed to so long as redemption does not occur until after promissory note has been paid in full.

Post-1998: Third party guarantees to investor prohibited.

Pre-1998: Third party guarantee allowed unless backed by government obligation.

Post-1998: Amounts attributable to expenses to start new commercial enterprise must be deducted from capital contribution.

Pre-1998: Start-up costs and expenses included in amount of capital contribution.

Post-1998: New ownership and new corporation are not sufficient to establish new commercial enterprise.

Pre-1998: Restructuring or reorganization sufficient to establish new commercial enterprise.

Post-1998: All of the activities must benefit the targeted geographical area to count indirect employment.

Pre-1998: The qualifying investment must be within the approved regional center; there is no separate requirement to prove benefit solely to the regional center.

Below is a summary of additional restrictive interpretations created by the AAO in nonprecedent decisions:

Post-1998: Money earned or assets acquired while in the United States in an unlawful status are not considered lawful means to acquire capital.

Pre-1998: Drug smugglers or other criminals cannot use their ill-gotten gains to obtain permanent resident status in the United States through the EB-5 category; nothing specified about others illegally in the United States.

Post-1998: All investors in the partnership must identify the source of their funds to prove that they were derived by lawful means.

Pre-1998: Only the petitioning investor must identify the source of his or her funds in the

partnership to prove that they were derived by lawful means.

Post-1998: Merely injecting cash into the corporate account of a business does not show that the capital is "at risk" for the purpose of generating a return.

Pre-1998: Injecting cash into a corporate account could show that the capital is "at risk" for the purpose of generating a return.

2002 AMENDMENTS

Investors who were hurt by the changes the immigration agency made in 1998 lobbied Congress for relief. Eventually, in 2002 Congress enacted changes to the EB-5 program as part of a Justice Department authorization bill.[118] To qualify under the new law, an investor must have filed a petition for EB-5 classification (Form I-526) and had it approved between January 1, 1995 and August 31, 1998.[119] The law took effect November 2, 2002.

Section 11031(c) of the 2002 law sets forth procedures to determine whether investors can have their conditions removed. The government must decide three things: whether (1) the I-829 petition contains any material misrepresentations; (2) the investment created or saved 10 jobs; and (3) the investor has substantially complied with the investment requirement ($1 million or $500,000).[120] Investments in regional centers or in troubled businesses count.[121] The law gives investors a choice of three dates by which to measure their compliance: (1) the date the I-829 petition was filed; (2) six months after the I-829 petition was filed; or (3) the date the government makes its determination under the new law.[122]

If the investor meets the jobs and investment requirements and has not made a material misrepresentation, the government will remove the conditional resident status and the investor and family

---

[118] 21st Century Department of Justice Appropriations Authorization Act, *supra* note 7, §§11031–37. *See generally* S. Yale-Loehr, "Congress Helps Stranded Immigrant Investors," 7 *Bender's Immigration Bulletin* 1306 (Nov. 1, 2002). *www.millermayer.com/new/bibeb5bill.html* (last visited Feb. 14, 2006)

[119] 21st Century Department of Justice Appropriations Authorization Act, *supra* note 7, §§11031(b)(1), 11032(b).

[120] *Id.* §11031(c)(1)(A).

[121] *Id.* §11031(c)(1)(B), (C).

[122] *Id.* §11031(c)(1)(D).

members will become permanent residents as of the second anniversary of the date they became conditional residents.[123] If the government finds against an investor on any of the three grounds, the government must notify the investor, and provide the investor with an opportunity to submit evidence to rebut the adverse determination.[124] If the investor loses on the jobs or investment requirement, the government will continue the investor's conditional resident status for additional two years.[125] During that time the investor can try to meet those requirements.

If the government finds that the investor made a material misrepresentation, the government will terminate the investor's conditional resident status.[126] The investor can appeal to the Board of Immigration Appeals and then seek judicial review.[127] During administrative or judicial review proceedings the investor and his or her family members remain in conditional resident status.[128]

Most investors are unlikely to persuade the government that they fully met the capital investment and jobs creation requirement. The new law gives them an additional two years to make another investment. During that time they can combine investments made earlier with new investments to show that altogether they invested the total amount required.[129] This includes investments in limited partnerships.[130]

An investor must file another I-829 during the 90 days preceding the new two-year anniversary.[131] Failure to file will normally terminate a conditional resident's status.[132] There is a good cause exception.[133]

Assuming an investor files another I-829 petition, the government has 90 days to decide three things: whether (1) the I-829 petition has any material misrepresentations; (2) the investment created or saved 10 jobs; and (3) the investor has substantially complied with the investment requirement ($1 million or

$500,000).[134] The investor can aggregate money invested before and jobs created or saved from the initial investment.[135] Investments in regional centers or in troubled businesses count.[136]

If the investor meets the job creation and investment requirements and has not made a material misrepresentation, the government will remove the conditional resident status of the investor and family members. They will become permanent residents as of the second anniversary of the date their conditional resident status was continued.[137] If the government finds against an investor on any of the three grounds, the government must notify the investor, who may attempt to rebut the adverse facts.[138] If the investor loses, the government will terminate the investor's conditional resident status.[139]

Section 11032 of the 2002 law provides similar procedures for EB-5 investors whose I-526 petitions were approved, but who never became conditional residents because the INS never acted on their adjustment of status applications or because they remained overseas. This section defines an eligible individual as an investor who filed an I-526 petition that was approved between January 1, 1995, and August 31, 1998, and who then timely filed an adjustment of status application or applied for an immigrant visa overseas. Investors are not eligible if they are inadmissible or deportable on any ground.[140]

If INS revoked the I-526 petition on the ground that the investor failed to meet the capital investment requirement, that revocation is to be disregarded.[141] If the adjustment of status application or immigrant visa application overseas was not pending on November 2, 2002, the date of enactment, it is to be treated as reopened if: (i) it is not pending because the government claims the investor never complied with the capital investment requirement; or (ii) the investor left the United States without advance parole.[142] If an investor applied for adjustment of status

---

[123] Id. §11031(c)(1)(E).

[124] Id. §11031(c)(1)(F)(i).

[125] Id. §11031(c)(1)(F)(ii).

[126] Id. §11031(c)(1)(F)(iii).

[127] Id. §11031(c)(1)(F)(iv).

[128] Id.

[129] Id. §11031(c)(2)(A).

[130] Id.

[131] Id. §11031(c)(2)(C)(i).

[132] Id. §11031(c)(2)(D).

[133] Id. §11031(c)(2)(C)(ii).

[134] Id. §11031(c)(2)(E).

[135] Id.

[136] Id.

[137] Id. §11031(c)(2)(F).

[138] Id. §11031(c)(2)(G)(i).

[139] Id. §11031(c)(2)(G)(ii).

[140] Id. §11032(b).

[141] Id. §11032(c)(1).

[142] Id. §11032(c)(2)(A).

in the United States but is now overseas, the government will establish a process to let them return to the United States if necessary to obtain adjustment.[143]

The government was supposed to approve adjustment of status applications for eligible investors by May 1, 2003, 180 days after enactment.[144] However, that has not happened yet, because USCIS has not yet published regulations to implement the 2002 law. The investors will eventually be in conditional resident status. Such investors must file an I-829 petition within two years of becoming a conditional resident.[145] The determinations and process are similar for both §11031 and §11032 investors. For example, the government must credit the investor with funds invested and jobs created or saved both before and after November 2, 2002, the date of enactment.[146] This section gives investors a choice of two dates by which to measure their compliance: (1) the date they filed their adjustment of status application; or (2) the date the government decides the I-829 petition.[147]

Finally, the new law states that a noncitizen who was admitted on a conditional basis by virtue of being the child of an EB-5 investor shall still be considered a child for purposes of the new law, even if they turn 21 or marry.[148]

CONCLUSION

Qualifying a person for EB-5 status is one of the most complicated subspecialties in immigration law. A sophisticated knowledge of corporate, tax, investment, and immigration law are all required. Moreover, the four 1998 precedent AAO decisions and subsequent nonprecedent decisions have made it even harder to obtain approvals of EB-5 petitions. Investors must discard normal investment opportunities in favor of investments structured to meet the unrealistic requirements of the precedent decisions. Attorneys, in turn, must proceed at their peril in advising clients. In many cases it may be more practicable for investors to come to the United States through other visa categories such as the E-2 inves-

tor, L-1 intracompany transferee, or EB-1-3 multinational executive or manager routes.

Nevertheless, things may be looking up for the EB-5 category. In September 2004, USCIS held a public meeting to discuss EB-5 issues.[149] Over 100 people attended the meeting. At the meeting, top USCIS officials promised to place more attention on the EB-5 program. They followed up that promise in January 2005 by establishing a new Investor and Regional Center Unit (IRCU) at USCIS headquarters. The IRCU provides oversight for EB-5 policy and regulatory development, field guidance, and training. According to USCIS, establishing the IRCU will "strengthen and protect the integrity of the [EB-5] program while promoting the intent of Congress to encourage investment and increase employment within the United States."[150]

The new USCIS memo and the September 2004 meeting may mark a major leap forward in USCIS policy toward the EB-5 visa category.[151] The possible changes hold the promise of making the EB-5 process more user-friendly in terms of processing times and responsiveness to investors' concerns. USCIS officials now say that they want to meet the needs of the business community so that the EB-5 category can be more effectively used. Time will tell whether that goal is met.

---

[143] *Id.* §11032(c)(2)(B).

[144] *Id.* §11032(a).

[145] *Id.* §11032(e).

[146] *Id.* §11032(e)(2).

[147] *Id.* §11032(e)(3).

[148] *Id.* §§11031(e), 11032(f).

[149] *See* Stephen Yale-Loehr, "USCIS Vows to Improve EB-5 Immigration Investor Program," 10 *Bender's Immigration Bulletin* 169 (Feb. 15, 2005).

[150] USCIS Memorandum, William R. Yates, USCIS Assoc. Dir. for Operations, to all USCIS offices, "Establishment of an Investor and Regional Center Unit," File No. HQPRD 70/6.2.8 (Jan. 19, 2005), available at *uscis.gov/graphics/lawsregs/handbook/EB5Unit011905Pub.pdf* (last visited Feb. 14, 2006), *published on* AILA InfoNet at Doc. No. 05012663 (*posted* Jan. 26, 2005), *reprinted in* 10 *Bender's Immigration Bulletin* 195 (Feb. 15, 2005).

[151] *See generally* S. Mailman & S. Yale-Loehr, "Immigrant Investor Green Cards: Rise of the Phoenix?," *N.Y.L.J.*, Apr. 25, 2005, at 3, *reprinted in* 10 Bender's Immigration Bulletin 801 (May 15, 2005) and at *www.millermayer.com/EB5NYLJ0405.html*.

APPENDIX:
DESIGNATED REGIONAL CENTERS[152]

World Trade Center/Greenville-Spartanburg Inc.
315 Old Boiling Springs Road
Greer, SC 29650

Beacon U.S. Studios Inc.
5610 Sanderling Way
Blaine, WA 98230

City of New Orleans
Mayor's Economic Development Department
1300 Perdido Street, Suite 8E10
New Orleans, LA 70112

North Country Alliance
One Lincoln Boulevard
Rouses Point, NY 12979

Aero-Space Port International Group
512 Strander Boulevard
Tukwila, WA 98188

North Texas Commission
P.O. Box 610246
DFW Airport, TX 75261

Legacy Project
1100 Spring Street, Suite 600
Atlanta, GA 30309

Abacus, LLC
740 6thh St., NW, Suite 302
Washington, DC 20001-3798
www.eb-5investors.com/

American Export Partners
180 East Bay Street, Suite 300
Charleston, SC 29401-2123
E-mail: *info@tenstate.com*

Danou Enterprises
World Trade Center Detroit/Windsor
1251 Fort Street
Trenton, MI 48183

Pueblo Economic Development Corporation
P.O. Box 5807
Pueblo, CO 81002

GV Development
7525 W. Highway 68
P.O. Box 10430
Golden Valley, AZ 86413-2430

Unibex Global Corporation
1201 Eleanor Avenue
Las Vegas, NV 89106

State of Hawaii, Department of Business,
Economic Development & Tourism
P.O. Box 2359
Honolulu, HI 96804

Atlanta International Center for Academic [sic] and Athletics
1131 Alpharetta Street
Roswell, GA 30075

The Gateway Freedom Fund
(a/k/a Golden Rainbow Freedom Fund)
c/o American Life Inc, 3223 3rd Ave South
Seattle, WA 98134
www.amlife.us/visa.html

West Rand Gold Trust
P.O. Box 2222
Ridgecrest, CA 93556

Miami Chinese Community Center, Ltd.
331 NE 18th Street
Miami, FL 33132

CKS Western Inc. World Trade Center
620 W. Graham Drive
Lake Elsinore, CA 92530

Empirical Entertainment
6255 Sunset Boulevard, Suite 2000
Hollywood, CA 90028

State of Vermont
Agency of Commerce and Community Development
109 State Street
Montpellier, VT 05609-0501

Trading Partners International of California LLC
2677 N. Main Street, Suite 930
Santa Ana, CA 92705

CMB Export LLC
Corona Professional Center
400 S. Ramona Avenue, Suite 212AA
Corona, CA 91719

Alameda Trade Center
c/o Lowe Enterprises Commercial Group
1818 East 7th Street, Suite 200
Los Angeles, CA 90021

Matrix International, LLC
P.O. Box 22891
Seattle, WA 98122

---

[152] Memorandum from Jacquelyn A. Bednarz, Acting INS Ass't Comm'r for Programs, "Designation of Regional Centers Under the Immigrant Investor Pilot Program," HQ 7C/6.2.5 (July 31, 1998).

California Consortium for Agricultural Export
c/o Spencer Enterprises Inc.
4974 East Clinton, Suite 200
Fresno, CA 93727
www.ccax.com/[153]

Philadelphia Industrial Development Corporation
2600 Centre Square West
1500 Market Street
Philadelphia, PA 19102-2126
www.canamenterprises.com[154]

South Dakota International Business Institute
711 East Wells Avenue
Pierre, SD 57501-3369
www.sd-exports.org/dairy2002/regional.htm[155]

Iowa Department of Economic Development
200 East Grand Avenue
Des Moines, IA 50309
www.extension.iastate.edu/ag/staff/info/
ianewfarmfamily.pdf[156]

Capitol Area Regional Center
1801 K Street, NW, Suite 201-L
Washington, DC 20006[157]

Redevelopment Agency of the City of Vernon
4305 Santa Fe Avenue
Vernon, CA 90058[158]

---

[153] Approved February 27, 2002. Available at www.ccax.com/pdf/CCAERegionalCenterApproval.pdf (last visited Feb. 14, 2006).

[154] Approved February 28, 2003. Available at www.canamenterprises.com/ins_approval_letter.pdf (last visited Feb. 14, 2006). Amended April 23, 2004. Amendment available at www.usa-immigration.com/litigation.htm (last visited Feb. 14, 2006).

[155] Approved April 8, 2004. Available at www.usa-immigration.com/litigation.htm (last visited Feb. 14, 2006).

[156] Approved December 10, 2004. Available at www.usa-immigration.com/litigation.htm (last visited Feb. 14, 2006).

[157] Approved Nov. 25, 2005.

[158] Approved Dec. 27, 2005. Available at www.usa-immigration.com/litigation.htm (last visited Feb. 14, 2006).

HOW MUCH IS ENOUGH?
DOCUMENTING THE ABILITY TO PAY IN RELIGIOUS WORKER CASES

Updated by James D. Eiss and Danielle Rizzo[*]

INTRODUCTION

Special immigrant religious worker cases present a petitioner and counsel with a variety of evidentiary challenges in establishing entitlement to permanent resident status for the religious worker. One factor often overlooked is the need to establish the petitioner's ability to pay the religious worker's salary. Religious workers, unlike most employment-based immigrants, need not be paid a prevailing wage.[1] As a result, religious organizations have more flexibility than businesses to offer a salary within its ability to pay. However, just as every employment-based I-140 petition must include evidence of the petitioner's ability to pay, the religious organization must submit evidence of the ability to pay with the special immigrant religious worker's I-360 petition. A "religious organization" (which includes churches, synagogues, mosques, and other places of worship) faces unique difficulties in proving its ability to pay that businesses do not. This article addresses these concerns and provides religious entities with guidance in successfully establishing an ability to pay a religious worker's salary.

MEETING THE REQUIREMENTS OF THE REGULATION

Generally

The requirement to establish the petitioner's ability to pay is found at 8 CFR §204.5(g)(2):

---

[*] Updated from an article by Melanie R. Nezer and Joel Pfeffer appearing at *Immigration & Nationality Law Handbook* 165 (AILA 2005–06 ed.)

James D. Eiss is a former INS officer who has been practicing immigration law in the Buffalo area for the past 16 years.

Danielle Rizzo is a third-year law student and has been a paralegal at the Law Offices of James D. Eiss for the past five years.

Mr. Eiss and Ms. Rizzo co-authored the article, "R-1 Admissions at the Canadian Border: How DHS's Organizational Structure Affects Admission of Foreign Nationals at Ports of Entry," *Immigration Options for Religious Workers* 23 (AILA 2005).

[1] This does not exempt special immigrant religious workers from the public charge ground of inadmissibility found in INA §212(a)(4).

Any petition filed by or for an employment-based immigrant that requires an offer of employment must be accompanied by evidence that the prospective United States employer has the ability to pay the proffered wage. The petitioner must demonstrate this ability at the time the priority date is established and continuing until the beneficiary obtains lawful permanent residence. Evidence of this ability shall be either in the form of copies of annual reports, federal tax returns, or audited financial statements. In a case where the prospective United States employer employs 100 or more workers, the director may accept a statement from a financial officer of the organization which establishes the prospective employer's ability to pay the proffered wage. In appropriate cases, additional evidence, such as profit/loss statements, bank account records, or personnel records, may be submitted by the petitioner or requested by the Service.

The regulation requires an offer of employment and evidence that the employing entity has the ability to pay the proffered wage continuing until the time the beneficiary obtains lawful permanent resident status. The regulations state that this evidence "*shall*" consist of any of the following: an annual report; a federal income tax return; or an audited financial statement.

Many religious organizations face difficulties in submitting one of these three types of evidence. The regulation places a heavy burden on churches that are exempt from filing federal income tax returns and that are not likely to prepare audited financial statements for any other purpose. The cost of preparing audited financial statements poses a significant burden on many religious organizations, without a corresponding benefit. The question arises as to how the two sentences following the requirement that the employer "shall" provide one of these three types of evidence modify this requirement.

What Do "Shall" and "Additional" Mean?

The regulation permits some flexibility in the type of evidence required. It contains three sentences describing the type of evidence required to prove ability to pay. The first sentence states that the evidence "shall be" in the form of either annual reports, federal tax returns, or audited financial statements. The second sentence appears to make a discretionary exception to this rule. It states that where the employer employs 100 or more workers, the director "may accept" a statement from a financial officer of the organization which establishes ability to pay. The third sentence appears to create an additional discretionary exception to this rule. It states that in appropriate cases, additional evidence may be submitted by the petitioner or requested by U.S. Citizenship and Immigration Services (USCIS). The regulations are ambiguous because there are no clear instructions on how the second and third sentences modify the first sentence.

There are three different logical interpretations of the combination of these three sentences, as follow:

(1) Petitioners must submit an annual report, federal tax return, or financial statement in support of every immigrant petition, and alternative forms of evidence of any type are only accepted on a discretionary basis and *in addition to* one of the first three types of evidence.

(2) Petitioners are required to submit an annual report, federal tax return, or financial statement unless they have more than 100 employees, in which case, upon the discretion of the USCIS, a statement from a financial officer can be submitted *in lieu of* one of the first three types of evidence. Any other alternative forms of evidence are accepted only on a discretionary basis and *in addition to* one of the first three types of evidence.

(3) Petitioners are required to submit an annual report, federal tax return, or financial statement unless an alternative type of evidence is appropriate.

Much has been made of the fact that the regulations classify the alternative types of evidence as "additional" evidence. Legacy INS/USCIS has interpreted it to mean that "additional evidence" should only be considered after petitioner has already submitted an annual report, federal income tax return, or audited financial statement.[2] However, the word "additional" can be read to expand the list of types of acceptable evidence in appropriate cases— one or more of which the petitioner "shall" submit.

What Additional Evidence Can I-360 Petitioners Provide?

Beyond the examples of additional evidence listed in the regulations, W-2 statements also demonstrate the payment of wages, and bank statements reflect an employer's income. It is possible, however, that these documents would be insufficient without a general discussion of petitioner's assets, income, and expenses. Normally, USCIS does not accept budgets, operating statements, or balance sheets prepared by petitioner without an audit letter from a certified public accountant.[3] Nevertheless, there is indication from AILA Liaison Minutes that USCIS will accept self-prepared financial statements if they are supported by further verifiable evidence that demonstrates the petitioner's ability to pay.[4]

This evidence may include bank statements and payroll information for an extended period of time submitted in conjunction with an explanation and evidence of petitioner's ongoing fundraising activities, expenses, and other obligations. Volunteer workers should be listed among the petitioner's assets, particularly if petitioner's net assets are not substantially greater than the offered salary. If congregants provide free building maintenance and upkeep, the petitioner should be able to show that no reserve funds are needed for capital improvements and overhead, freeing funds for the offered wage.

The practitioner clearly has an obligation to advocate to the adjudicating officer that petitioner has the ability to pay and can demonstrate a track record of fundraising that supports both the salary and its regular ongoing operations. If the adjudicating officer has any reservations about the petitioner's ability to pay, the adjudicator may issue either a denial or a request for evidence (RFE) to clarify petitioner's ability to pay.

THE YATES MEMO

On May 4, 2004, William Yates issued a memorandum entitled, "Determination of Ability to Pay Under 8 CFR 204.5(g)(2)."[5] The Memorandum (not to be confused with the now rescinded Yates RFE Memorandum

---

[2] *See, e.g.,* "INS Written Answers to AILA's Liaison Questions," *published on* AILA InfoNet at Doc. No. 02080642 (*posted* Aug. 6, 2002) (hereinafter Liaison Questions).

[3] *See Matter of [name not provided]*, EAC 98-078-50543 (AAO, Jan. 10, 2000), and *Matter of [name not provided]*, EAC 98-064-51100 (AAO June 9, 2000).

[4] Liaison Questions, *supra* note 2.

[5] USCIS Memorandum, "Determination of Ability to Pay Under 8 CFR 204.5(g)(2)" (May 4, 2004), *published on* AILA InfoNet at Doc. No. 04051262 (*posted* May 12, 2004) (hereinafter the Memorandum).

of the same date) establishes an analytical framework for adjudicators to apply in determining whether petitioners have the ability to pay the proffered wage. It states that petitioners "*must* submit" an annual report, federal income tax return, or audited financial statements, which the memo collectively dubs "initial evidence." If one of the three types of "initial evidence" is not submitted with the petition, adjudicators are instructed to issue an RFE. The memo then states that USCIS adjudicators are not required to accept, request, or RFE for "additional financial evidence," and that acceptance of these documents is discretionary.

The analytical framework set up by the memorandum is flawed in two key respects. First, the term "initial evidence" does not appear anywhere in the regulations except as a general heading for 8 CFR §204.5(g). The section entitled "Initial Evidence" encompasses the entire section on ability to pay, including the subset of "additional evidence." This supports the reading that the word "additional" in the regulation is used to expand the list of acceptable types of initial evidence in appropriate cases.

Second, the regulations do not state that acceptance of "additional evidence" is discretionary. To the contrary, the regulations state that the director "may accept" the statement of a financial officer for an organization that employs over 100 people; but, it states that additional evidence "may be submitted by the petitioner or requested by the Service." Officers have discretion as to whether or not to request additional evidence, but not as to whether to accept such evidence when submitted. What is discretionary is the determination of whether the additional types of evidence are "appropriate." As with all elements of the request for an immigration benefit, petitioner bears the burden of proof. Petitioner must therefore prove the "appropriateness" of the documents. However, the regulations do not state that acceptance of the evidence is discretionary.

While the memorandum is flawed in its analysis of the types of acceptable evidence of ability to pay, it does provide clear and helpful guidance on what constitutes ability to pay. The memo supports a positive ability to pay determination when the petition meets one of three tests: net income (that petitioner's net income is equal to or greater than the proffered wage); current assets (that petitioner's net assets are equal to or greater than the proffered wage); or employment of the beneficiary (that petitioner employs the beneficiary and has paid or is paying the proffered wage).

Furthermore, it is not clear whether the Yates memo applies to I-360 petitions. It has been rumored that in a July 2004, liaison meeting with community-based organizations, USCIS stated the memorandum is limited to I-140 petitions and that guidance regarding the ability to pay will be issued at a future date with regard to I-360 petitions. On its face, the memo only purports to apply to only ability to pay determinations in the I-140 context. Nowhere are I-360 petitions mentioned. However, 8 CFR §204.5(g) applies to all employment-based immigrant petitions, including I-360 petitions. Adjudicators could therefore reasonably conclude that the memo also applies in the I-360 context. It is not yet clear whether there is more flexibility for religious petitioners in documenting the ability to pay. Anecdotal evidence from practitioners indicates that adjudications on the issue of ability to pay in the I-360 context are inconsistent.

Petitioners should submit evidence with respect to all three tests, if possible. Evidence of net income can include, as indicated above, self-prepared financial statements and budgets, bank statements, federal and/or state payroll tax forms, and a general discussion of fundraising activities, along with evidence of the church's ongoing expenses. The petitioner should also include an explanation of why the church is not required to file a federal income tax return.

Petitioners should submit evidence of the church's assets, which include any building owned by the church and evidence of any mortgage or other debt associated with the church generally or the building specifically. A statement from a real estate broker regarding the value of church buildings will help to establish petitioner's equity. Photographs of the building are useful in establishing both the nature of the church itself and the church building as a capital asset. Finally, if petitioner has employed the beneficiary, petitioner should submit evidence of payment of the worker's wages.

AAO DECISIONS

The Administrative Appeals Office (AAO) has denied cases where it concluded that petitioner had not established it had the ability to pay the proffered wage at the time of filing the petition or at the time the RFE was issued.[6] Because the regulation specifically provides that ability to pay must be established at the time the petition is filed and continuing thereafter until the case is approved, petitioners should be careful to include a relevant financial statement for a reasonable period of time preceding the time of filing. If USCIS issues an RFE,

---

[6] *See Matter of [name not provided]*, LIN 02-009-50271 (AAO July 1, 2004).

petitioner should provide financial information that spans the time between the filing date and the date petitioner submits the response to the RFE, if possible.

In another decision,[7] the AAO considered an audited financial statement showing nearly $3 million in net assets as satisfactory for meeting the ability to pay. While most religious worker petitioners will not be in a position to provide such documentation, formal real estate appraisals together with affidavits confirming the petitioner's liabilities can be sufficient to establish financial net worth.

In an unpublished decision, the AAO initially denied a petition on the basis that the church failed to establish its ability to pay the proffered salary. The service center issued an RFE on issues unrelated to ability to pay, and in response, the church submitted unaudited financial statements for a period of two years. USCIS found the submitted documents were insufficient to show an ability to pay, even though those documents were submitted for an entirely different purpose. The church appealed to the AAO, which denied the appeal. On motion for reconsideration, the AAO reopened the case and approved the petition on the basis that the record contained evidence that the church had employed the beneficiary for almost three years. Citing the Yates memorandum dated May 4, 2004, the AAO stated that USCIS adjudicators should make a positive ability to pay determination when the record contains credible, verifiable evidence that the petitioner has paid or currently is paying the proffered wage. For additional AAO cases, please refer to "Summary of AAO Decisions on 'Religious Visas,'" appearing elsewhere in this *Handbook*.

CONCLUSION

Although a church may have limited financial documentation available to prove its ability to pay, the Yates memorandum dated May 4, 2004[8] does not necessarily preclude submission of alternate forms of evidence, in lieu of annual reports, federal tax returns, or audited financial statements to prove ability to pay. Evidence that the beneficiary's salary has been paid, such as cancelled checks, W-2 forms, and tax returns, are powerful evidence of petitioner's ability to pay. If petitioner does not employ the beneficiary at the time the petition is filed, self-prepared, unaudited financial statements coupled with financial evidence of income, expenses, and assets may be sufficient to overcome the burden to establish the petitioner's ability to pay.

ABILITY TO PAY CHECKLIST: RELIGIOUS WORKER VISA PETITIONS

Initial Evidence

- ❏ Annual report; or
- ❏ Tax return; or
- ❏ Audited financial statement; or
- ❏ Statement of financial officer (only for cases where petitioner employs 100 or more workers).

If none of the required *initial evidence* is available, petitioner may provide *documentation in lieu of initial evidence*. However, this evidence must present a complete picture of the church's financial position. Documentation of petitioner's assets, income, and expenses should be submitted in cases where initial evidence is available.

Documentation in Lieu of Initial Evidence

- ❏ Profit/Loss statements
- ❏ Bank account records
- ❏ Personnel records
- ❏ Federal and/or state payroll tax forms
- ❏ W-2s
- ❏ Self-prepared financial statements
  - Budget
  - Operating statements
  - Balance sheets
- ❏ Documentation of fundraising activities
- ❏ Documentation of volunteer contributions
- ❏ Assets
  - Buildings owned by petitioner
  - Mortgage statement, other debt
  - Real estate broker's assessment of value of buildings owned by petitioner
- ❏ Photographs of property owned by petitioner

---

[7] *Matter of [name and number not provided]* (AAO Jan. 30, 2003).

[8] The Memorandum, *supra* note 5.

SUMMARY OF AAO DECISIONS ON "RELIGIOUS VISAS"

by Rodney M. Barker and Dhara Sharma[*]

In 2005, U.S. Citizenship and Immigration Services (USCIS) posted about 129 additional decisions of the Administrative Appeals Office (AAO) on special immigrant religious workers from each of the four USCIS service centers.[1] Five themes run through all the decisions. These themes are:

- The satisfaction of the *two-year period of experience* required under the statute:

  - The work experience must be in the vocation or occupation and not just any vocation or occupation.

  - Students cannot satisfy the statutory requirement that the beneficiary has been continuously carrying on the religious work for at least two years, although a person taking "continuing education" studies that do not prevent him or her from the required full-time religious work may be alright.

  - Volunteer work will not satisfy the statutory requirement that the beneficiary has been continuously carrying on the religious work for at least two years.

  - Proper documentation is required to show that the beneficiary meets the statutory requirement of the two-year period of continuous experience.

- The *ability to pay the proffered wage* as of the date of filing the petition must be established with proper documentation.

- The *qualifying job/traditional religious function* is established by the actual duties, not just the title of the position.

- The *valid job offer* must be for permanent, full-time work.

- The petitioner must establish its eligibility for *tax-exempt status according to the Internal Revenue Code* as of the time of filing the petition as a religious organization.

ESTABLISHING THE TWO-YEAR PERIOD OF EXPERIENCE REQUIRED IMMEDIATELY PRIOR TO FILING PETITION

For this category, the regulations at 8 CFR §204.5(m)(3)(ii)(A) require the petitioner to establish that the beneficiary has been engaged continuously in a qualifying religious vocation or occupation for two full years immediately preceding the filing of the petition. For this element to be met, it is important to remember that the case law, interpreting the intent of Congress, has developed to mean that the work must have been full-time, salaried employment.[2]

Work experience. In order to satisfy the two-year work experience requirement, many of the AAO cases tell us that the beneficiary must have worked in *the* vocation or occupation and not just in *a* vocation or occupation.[3] Therefore, the petitioner must show

---

[*] **Rodney Barker** is a principal of Barker, Epstein & Loscocco in Boston. He served as chair of the New England Chapter of AILA (1992–93). He is currently a member of AILA's Religious Worker Committee.

Dhara Sharma is currently working as an associate attorney at Barker, Epstein & Loscocco. She received her JD from Suffolk University Law School in 2004.

[1] These decisions covered the period of January to May 2005. *See www.uscis.gov.*

[2] In *Matter of [name not provided]*, LIN-03-202-50617 (AAO Apr. 27, 2005), the AAO summarized the development of the case law. It stated that according to INA §101(a)(27)(C)(iii),

> the religious worker must have been carrying on the religious vocation, professional work, or other work continuously for the immediately preceding two years. . . . Under prior law, . . . [t]he term "continuously" was interpreted to mean that one did not take up any other occupation or vocation. *Matter of B*, 3 I&N Dec. 162 (CO 1948).

Later decisions concluded that if the worker received no salary for the religious work, the assumption was that he or she would be required to earn a living by obtaining other employment. The AAO concluded that

> [i]n line with these past decisions and the intent of Congress, it is clear, therefore that to be continuously carrying on the religious work means to do so on a full-time basis. That the qualifying work should be paid employment, not volunteering, is inherent in those past decisions.

[3] *See Matter of [name not provided]*, WAC-02-058-53343 (AAO Mar. 3, 2005); *Matter of [name not provided]*, EAC-02-282-52919 (AAO Mar. 3, 2005); *Matter of [name not provided]*, WAC-03-221-52867 (AAO Feb. 28, 2005); and

continued

evidence that the beneficiary's work experience was in the same job as the proffered position.

Practice Pointer: Submit a list of duties for the previous employment and a list of duties for the proffered position to show evidence that the work experience was in the same job.[4]

Students. As in many previous cases, the AAO stated again that a person in training for a vocation or occupation is not "working" in that vocation or occupation, and therefore cannot fulfill the work experience requirement.[5] Additionally, the AAO clarified its position on whether a beneficiary can fulfill this requirement if he or she is concurrently working in the religious vocation/occupation while also a student. In denying the petition, the AAO in *Matter of [name not provided]*, LIN 03-202-50617 (AAO Apr., 27 2005) stated that a "detrimental fact" to the petitioner's claim of the beneficiary's continuous employment was the fact that she was a student during much of the requisite period.[6] The reason the AAO does not look favorably upon beneficiaries trying to establish the two-year work experience requirement if they were also studying during the qualifying period, is that it raises questions as to whether the beneficiary's religious work was the principal activity.[7] However, interestingly enough, in another decision, the AAO approved the petition on behalf of the beneficiary even though the beneficiary was a student.[8] The petitioner in this case filed a motion to reopen with the AAO after it had previously denied the petition. The petitioner's counsel noted, on motion, that the AAO cited no source that would indicate that graduate studies inevitably interrupt the continuity of an alien's ministerial work, and that the beneficiary "only pursued master's degree studies to enrich his base of knowledge in the field of religion." In approving the case, the AAO reasoned that "the beneficiary's salary, documented by canceled checks in the record, did not diminish after he began his studies, as one might expect if his hours of service had been curtailed, and the evidence, therefore, is consistent with the assertion that the beneficiary's graduate studies represent 'continuing education,' rather than "full-time studies that left the beneficiary unable to fulfill his ministerial duties."

Volunteer. The AAO has affirmed many times that a volunteer cannot meet the two-year period of experience requirement. The AAO has interpreted "continuously carrying on religious work" to mean that it must be full-time work.[9] The AAO's interpretation also leads it to conclude the qualifying work should be paid employment, and not volunteer work, because if the religious worker is not paid, the assumption is that he or she is engaged in other "secular employment." In *Matter of [name not provided]*, SRC-00-276-50885 (AAO Apr. 27, 2005), the self-petitioner argued that he need not be employed in a paid position because he was engaged in a vocation. Although this is generally true, the AAO denied the petition, reasoning that the self-petitioner's argument was unsubstantiated where the record contained his tax returns and W-2s showing he has clearly been paid a salary for a portion of the qualifying period. The AAO stated that his situation was not similar to that of a nun or priest who lives in an unsalaried environment. Further, the AAO addressed the attorney's argument that circumstances beyond the self-petitioner's control—namely, his immigration status—prevented him from salaried employment. The AAO stated that it was not out of his control because it was his choice to remain in the United

---

Matter of [name not provided], WAC-97-192-50646 (AAO Feb. 01, 2005).

[4] *See Matter of [name not provided]*, EAC-02-282-52919 (AAO Mar. 3, 2005).

[5] *Matter of [name not provided]*, SRC-01-156-60086 (AAO Mar. 3, 2005). The AAO determined that the beneficiary had been in training under the auspices of the petitioning organization for the two years prior to filing, and training for the position is not considered working in that position.

[6] In this case, the AAO stated that the beneficiary had not been "carrying on such vocation" as required by §101(a)(27)(C)(iii); rather, she had been undergoing training and continuing her studies. The AAO concluded that part-time ministerial work by a student is not continuous experience as a minister.

[7] *See Matter of [name not provided]*, EAC-02-282-52919 (AAO Mar. 2, 2005). In this case, the petitioner only submitted partial copies of the beneficiary's Form 1040 income tax returns for the qualifying period. Both tax returns reflected that the beneficiary requested a $1,000 Hope and Lifetime Learning Credit based on payment of tuition and related expenses for her own higher education. This raised questions as to whether the beneficiary's religious work was her principal activity.

---

[8] *Matter of [name not provided]*, EAC-01-178-52582 (AAO Jan. 26, 2005).

[9] *Matter of [name not provided]*, SRC-01-173-51841 (AAO Feb. 3, 2005). The AAO stated that the AAO's previous decisions, prior case law, and the intent of Congress make it clear that to be continuously carrying on the religious work means to do so on a full-time basis.

States to await the approval of his R-1 nonimmigrant visa rather than return home to continue his work while waiting for the approval. In *Matter of [name not provided]*, WAC-03-266-53307 (AAO Jan. 31, 2005), the beneficiary had been working as a volunteer for a portion of the two-year period, and the AAO denied the petition because petitioner has not proved the two-year experience requirement, among other things. In this case, although petitioner provided a copy of a check "purportedly issued" to the beneficiary as a "remuneration/love gift" in the amount of $11,091.66, the AAO found there was no evidence the beneficiary actually received and cashed this check. The AAO further noted that regardless of this, it "[does] not consider this check as evidence of the beneficiary's employment when the petitioners clearly state that the beneficiary's work was voluntary." However, the AAO has given room for an exception to the general rule that a volunteer cannot meet the work experience requirement. In *Matter of [name not provided]*, SRC-01-173-51841 (AAO Feb. 03, 2005), the AAO stated that

> in the rare case where volunteer work might constitute prior qualifying experience, the petitioner must establish that the beneficiary, while continuously and primarily engaged in the traditional religious occupation, was self-sufficient or that her financial well being was clearly maintained by means other than secular employment.

In this case, counsel stated the beneficiary supported herself through monies from her own funds in Colombia and monetary assistance from her father, enabling her to purchase the apartment where she was residing. She also received money contributions from friends for the spiritual assistance she offered them. However, the AAO noted that the record did not reflect the frequency of the contributions or the amount she received, nor did petitioner submit evidence of the personal funds. Therefore, the evidence was not sufficient to establish that she was maintained by means other than secular employment.

Proper Documentation. It is important to show that the beneficiary meets the two-year experience requirement through proper documentation. The AAO has repeated its position that it would look at tax returns and W-2s to confirm full-time employment.[10] Furthermore, the AAO looks at other evidence, such as cancelled checks or pay vouchers to substantiate the beneficiary's employment.[11] The AAO has been clear that there are no exceptions to the documentation requirement. In *Matter of [name not provided]*, SRC-96-257-50620 (AAO May 26, 2005), although petitioner's counsel explained that petitioner was a small church and did not have payroll records, audits, and so forth, the AAO denied the petition, stating that regardless of petitioner's size, petitioner must still meet the requirements by providing documentary evidence that the work had been continuous, full-time, paid employment. The AAO stated that petitioner should have at least provided a work schedule showing that the beneficiary's duties were full-time. In another AAO case, as evidence of full-time paid work, petitioner submitted a work schedule for its full-time religious workers, which reflected a total of 55 hours.[12] Petitioner also submitted copies of Form 1099-MISC for the two years, indicating non-employee compensation and also copies of canceled checks. Although the AAO agreed with the director's conclusion that the beneficiary was an independent contractor, it disagreed with the director's reasoning that because the beneficiary worked as an independent contractor for the petitioner, it could not establish that the beneficiary had worked continuously in the religious occupation for two full years preceding the filing of the visa petition. The AAO established that the beneficiary can in fact use self-employment to show two years' work experience. In *Matter of [name not provided]*, EAC-01-231-55270 (AAO Jan. 26, 2005), not only was the AAO dissatisfied with the lack of evidence provided, but it found that the evidence submitted did not support the assertion that beneficiary met the two-year work experience requirement. The petitioner in this case sought to classify the beneficiary as a religious instructor. In this case, where the beneficiary was paid by mosque members whose children the beneficiary taught and the mosque exercised supervisory control over the religious work, the AAO agreed the "exact payment mechanism is not as important as the work that the beneficiary performed for the petitioner." However, the AAO asserted that petitioner still has the burden of showing that the beneficiary was compensated as claimed. The AAO in this case carefully scrutinized and analyzed the evidence provided to see if the beneficiary

---

[10] *See Matter of [name not provided]*, WAC-01-218-51517 (AAO Feb. 28, 2005).

[11] *Matter of [name not provided]*, LIN-02-094-51196 (AAO Feb. 3, 2005).

[12] *Matter of [name not provided]*, SRC-03-073-51355 (AAO Jan. 26, 2005).

actually met the two-year work requirement. The petitioner provided affidavits showing the beneficiary was working for a family and was being paid by them. The AAO stated that the affidavits were vague because they did not specify the days and hours the beneficiary worked. Additionally, the AAO commented on petitioner's assertion that during the qualifying period, the beneficiary provided instruction until almost 11:00 pm every weeknight to their three children (ages 2, 4, and 6 years old) during the qualifying period. In denying the petition, the AAO noted that it "[is] not required to presume that children so young would even be awake at 11:00 pm, let alone capable of comprehending meaningful religious instruction." The AAO denied the petition, finding that there was no actual documentation of payments issued to the beneficiary during this time, and there was insufficient information to conclude that the beneficiary worked full-time during the qualifying period.

Practice Pointer: As evidence that the beneficiary's work experience has been paid, full-time work for the two years, provide concrete documentation such as tax returns and W-2s or audited financials and cancelled checks or pay stubs as proof of receipt. If the experience has been unpaid, submit detailed proof as to how the beneficiary was able to survive financially without interrupting the full-time religious work.

ABILITY TO PAY THE PROFFERED WAGE

8 CFR §204.5(g)(2) states that the prospective employer offering the employment must show that it has the ability to pay the proffered wage at the time the priority date is established and continuing until the beneficiary obtains lawful permanent residence. This means that the AAO will consider the financial status at the date of filing the petition.[13] Furthermore, the AAO will only look at evidence of the petitioning employer's ability to pay, regardless of the payment arrangements for the beneficiary.[14] 8 CFR

§204.5(g)(2) states that the evidence required to show ability to pay can be in the form of petitioner's tax returns, audited financials, or audited reports. Other evidence can be submitted in addition to, but not in lieu of, the above-mentioned documents, and unavailability of these types of documents creates a "presumption of ineligibility."[15] Furthermore, it is not enough for petitioner merely to submit the required documentation to meet the financial ability to pay requirement. The information contained in that report must demonstrate the petitioner has sufficient assets and/or income to pay the beneficiary's salary, and to pay it consistently.[16] In one case, the AAO considered petitioner's assets when making a decision on its ability to pay.[17] The AAO first considered petitioner's "building and grounds" and bus, and stated these were not liquid assets that were readily convertible into cash to pay the beneficiary's salary. The AAO further noted that even if they are sold, the question arises as to the next payments. The AAO also stated that the remaining liquid assets did not appear sufficient to pay the beneficiary's salary for the remainder of the year, and that the net income is not "sufficient enough to replenish those assets for the next year's payments." Similarly, in another case, petitioner submitted unaudited finan-

---

[13] *Matter of [name not provided]*, EAC-01-202-53177 (AAO Jan. 26, 2005), in which the AAO denied the petition filed on May 1, 2001, because the petitioners were unable to provide any evidence of its financial status as of that date.

[14] *Matter of [name not provided]*, EAC-01-231-55270 (AAO Jan. 26, 2005). In this case, the petitioner indicated that client families directly paid the beneficiary his wage. Regardless of the fact that their payments fell short of the prevailing wage, the AAO stated that the regulations plainly require that the *prospective employer* should be able to pay the prof-
continued

---

fered wage and that there is no provision stating that the employer need not show its ability to pay if some other entity pays the beneficiary instead.

[15] *See Matter of [name not provided]*, WAC-02-058-53343 (AAO Mar. 3, 2005); *Matter of [name not provided]*, EAC-02-282-52919 (AAO Mar. 3, 2005); *Matter of [name not provided]*, WAC-03-221-52867 (AAO Feb. 28, 2005); *Matter of [name not provided]*, WAC-97-192-50646 (AAO Feb. 1, 2005).

[16] *Matter of [name not provided]*, EAC-03-038-52172 (AAO Jan. 25, 2005).

[17] *Matter of [name not provided]*, EAC-03-038-52172 (AAO Jan. 25, 2005). The audited report showed that throughout the year, the petitioner's income exceeded its expenses by $1,050.80. The AAO notes that the audit report only indicated one salary payment labeled "pastoral salary." Although the petitioner claimed that this included two months of the beneficiary's salary along with the senior pastors, the AAO stated that the record contained no documentary evidence confirming that the payments to two people would be consolidated "in what is otherwise a meticulously itemized statement." Furthermore, the AAO pointed out that even if the beneficiary did receive the two months' salary, the liquid assets were insufficient to show proof of future payments. The AAO finally notes that the inadequacy of the petitioner's assets and earnings is compounded when it considers that petitioner has also filed petitions for two other workers in addition to the beneficiary.

cials that showed a profit of only $3,035. Although petitioner submitted a projection statement showing that it would make a net profit of $24,535, the AAO said that because these values were predictions rather than a report of actual revenues and expenses, it carried negligible weight.[18]

However, it is important to note that proof the petitioner has paid the beneficiary in the past carries much weight when the AAO is determining the ability of petitioner to pay the proffered wage. Interestingly, the AAO approved the petition in *Matter of [name not provided]*, EAC-03-262-50061 (AAO May 23, 2005), a case where petitioner submitted unaudited financials and a bank statement. Although this is generally insufficient for showing the ability to pay, the AAO concluded that because the record had sufficient credible evidence that the petitioner employed the beneficiary throughout the two years immediately prior to the filing and had compensated the beneficiary with a stipend and room and board, this was sufficient to establish the ability to pay that stipend and give room and board. Similarly, in *Matter of [name not provided]*, EAC-01-178-52582 (AAO Jan. 26, 2005), counsel stated on motion that "at the time of filing the petition, the Church had offered to pay [the beneficiary] an annual salary of $18,700, plus a housing allowance. . . . The Church has always had the ability to pay [the beneficiary] the designated compensation." The AAO pointed out that the record contains canceled checks and W-2s to show petitioner had paid the beneficiary during the two previous years, and it concluded that given the information that petitioner has in fact paid the beneficiary, it could not conclude that petitioner was unable to pay the wage. The AAO further noted the Associate Director of Operations, William R. Yates's memorandum, stating that "CIS adjudicators should make a positive ability to pay determination . . . when the record contains credible verifiable evidence that the petitioner . . . has paid or currently is paying the proffered wage."[19]

QUALIFYING RELIGIOUS JOB/TRADITIONAL RELIGIOUS FUNCTION

If the beneficiary will be working in a religious occupation, petitioner must establish that the position qualifies as a religious occupation.[20] The regulations define "religious occupation" as an activity relating to a "traditional religious function."[21] Similar to its previous decisions, the AAO stated again that USCIS interprets this to mean that petitioner must demonstrate the duties of the job are directly related to the religious creed of the denomination, the position is defined and recognized by the governing body of the denomination, and the position is traditionally a permanent full-time, salaried occupation within the denomination.[22]

Religious job. In *Matter of [name not provided]*, EAC-02-043-54254 (AAO Jan. 25, 2005), the AAO states that the fact the proffered position of "Literature Evangelist' is traditionally not voluntary and is a paid position, is not—in and of itself—enough to show the position is a religious occupation. The AAO found petitioner had not shown that the beneficiary received any compensation for the prayer and discussion, but rather the income appeared to derive entirely from sales-based commissions. Therefore, the AAO concluded that those religious duties did not constitute an occupation and, furthermore, that the job was not permanent as it was contingent upon weekly performance.[23] In another case, although

---

[18] *See Matter of [name not provided]*, EAC-01-231-55270 (AAO Jan. 26, 2005).

[19] *Matter of [name not provided]*, EAC-01-178-52582 (AAO Jan. 26, 2005) (citing to Memorandum from William R. Yates, Associate Director of Operations, "Determination of Ability to Pay under 8 CFR 204.5(g)(2)" (May 4, 2004)). This memorandum is available on AILA InfoNet at Doc. No. 04051262 (*posted* May 12, 2004).

[20] INA §101(a)(27)(C) defines the term "special immigrant" as it applies to religious workers and states that the immigrant has to be coming to the United States for one of three reasons: (1) carrying on the vocation of a minister; (2) to work in a professional capacity in a religious vocation or occupation; or (3) to work in a religious vocation or occupation.

[21] 8 CFR §204.5(m)(2).

[22] *See Matter of [name not provided]*, WAC-03-147-54566 (AAO May 20, 2005). AAO notes that the statute is silent on what constitutes a "religious occupation," and the regulation states that it is an activity relating to a "traditional religious function," which term is not specifically defined by the regulations. The regulations provide a list of examples, however, and those examples reveal that not all employees of a religious organization are considered to be engaged in a religious occupation for the purpose of special immigrant classification and notes that the lists of nonqualifying positions are those whose duties are primarily administrative or secular in nature.

[23] The AAO points out that the regulations specifically exclude fundraisers from the definition of "religious occupation."

petitioner identified the beneficiary's job title with that found in the regulation as a qualifying occupation, the AAO looked at the actual duties of the position, reasoning that it is the job duties rather than the title that will determine eligibility.[24] In *Matter of [name not provided]*, WAC-03-122-53068, the AAO found that the Christian book editor position qualified as a religious job because the beneficiary would be responsible for the actual content of the religious publication and was not just a proofreader or binder, and therefore, the work with religious material was not incidental, but the primary focus of the position.[25]

Occupation within the Denomination. The AAO states in another instance that the beneficiary's title is not conclusive evidence it qualifies as a religious job. Specifically, in one case, the AAO stated that petitioner must establish the position qualifies as a religious occupation within the denomination—merely assigning a position a title that on the surface is a religious occupation as defined elsewhere does not raise the position to the level of religious occupation within the denomination.[26] Furthermore, in one case, the AAO concluded the fact that petitioner served and operated as a church without the beneficiary's full-time and paid service did not support petitioner's assertion that the position was a traditional religious function within petitioner's denomination.[27] In *Matter of [name not provided]*, WAC-02-186-53114 (AAO Mar. 7, 2005), the AAO approved the petition where petitioner submitted first-hand documentation to demonstrate that the Southern Baptist Convention, of which petitioning church

was a member, considered "church music" to be an advanced liturgical activity, rather than merely a peripheral function to be performed by a parishioner who happens to be able to sing or play musical instruments.[28] If proof is required from the denomination, the AAO stated that someone with authority must speak.[29] According to the AAO, what the authorities say is extremely important. In *Matter of [name not provided]*, WAC-03-143-54324, where the religious authorities declared beneficiary was no longer a monk, the AAO said that regardless of what the beneficiary considers himself to be, he is no longer authorized clergy qualified to perform the duties of his position.

Practice Pointer: Provide a detailed description of the beneficiary's proffered duties, preferably with a weekly schedule showing the time allotted to each duty—make sure that the greatest proportion of the work is religious in nature and not merely administrative.

THE JOB OFFER

As in previous cases, the AAO has reiterated its position that petitioner needs to make a clear statement of the time requirement per day, and that employment of fewer than 35 hours a week is not full-time employment.[30] In *Matter of [name not provided]*, SRC-01-010-52023 (AAO Jan. 26, 2005), the AAO stated that although petitioner's letter of support claimed the beneficiary would be working full-time and listed the duties, petitioner provided no evidence regarding the school for which it was hiring the beneficiary, such as the number of students or teachers involved or other evidence that it would be a full-time and a permanent position. Addition-

---

[24] *Matter of [name not provided]*, EAC-02-282-52919 (AAO Mar. 3, 2005). In this case, although the position offered was that of a "Religious Instructor," the AAO did not find this reflected in the duties.

[25] Furthermore, the AAO noted that the "reversal of the director's decision did not, in any way, rest on counsel's argument that the prior approval of an R-1 nonimmigrant petition estops the Citizenship and Immigration Services from denying a subsequent immigrant petition."

[26] *See Matter of [name not provided]*, WAC-03-10051669 (AAO Feb. 28, 2005).

[27] *See Matter of [name not provided]*, WAC-03-154-54174 (AAO Jan. 31, 2005). The AAO found the petitioner offered nothing to show that the religious denomination considers the beneficiary's duties to be a traditional religious function, routinely assigned to a full-time paid employee, rather than tasks usually delegated to a part-time worker or volunteer from the congregation. Rather, the facts indicate the beneficiary was an unpaid volunteer.

[28] The director had determined that the beneficiary's duties were secular and typically delegated to volunteers from the congregation rather than paid employees. Although the AAO approved the petition, it notes that even though the petitioners submitted evidence showing the position met the requirements in this case, it was not stating "that every pianist, organist or choir member in a Southern Baptist church qualifies for immigration benefits as a religious worker. The individual facts of each proceeding must be taken into consideration."

[29] *See Matter of [name not provided]*, WAC-03-249-54639 (AAO Jan. 26, 2005). The AAO disagrees with the Director's interpretation of *Matter of Varughese*, 17 I&N Dec. 399 (BIA 1980), that the claim must come from "a Superior Principal of the denomination in the United States."

[30] *Matter of [name not provided]*, WAC-03-147-54566 (AAO May 20, 2005).

ally, in one case, the AAO denied the petition because petitioner's support letter stated that petitioner wanted to hire the beneficiary for three years.[31] The AAO concluded that this was not a permanent job offer because the "Act at section 101(a)(15)(R) excludes immigrant aliens who seek to enter the United States for a period of employment of five years or less."

WORKING FOR THE TAX-EXEMPT, BONA FIDE RELIGIOUS ORGANIZATION

Tax exempt status. As in previous cases, the AAO in *Matter of [name not provided]*, EAC-01-232-57152 restated that petitioner must show that it is tax-exempt by the Internal Revenue Service (IRS), either individually exempt or as group. In the alternative, petitioner can provide documentation proving that it would be eligible for tax exemption by the IRS.[32] The AAO in *Matter of [name not provided]*, EAC-01-231-55270 (Jan. 26, 2005), maintained that petitioner must show tax exemption at the time of filing the petition. In this case, petitioner gave the IRS approval of tax-exempt status after it filed the petition, but the AAO opposed the director's decision and concluded petitioner did in fact meet the regulation requirements because it had filed its documents with the IRS *before* filing the petition. The AAO reasoned that the regulations do not require the IRS approval has to be given by the date of filing—only that petitioner was eligible as of that date.

Tax-Exempt as a Religious Organization. Section 204.5(m)(3)(i) of 8 CFR requires petitioner to submit evidence that the organization qualifies as a nonprofit organization either by submitting documentation that it is exempt in accordance with §501(c)(3) of the Internal Revenue Code of 1986 (IRC) as it relates to religious organizations, or such documentation as required by the IRS to establish such eligibility. In *Matter of [name not provided]*, EAC-02-282-52919 (AAO Mar. 3, 2005), the AAO

explained that petitioner submitted documentation showing its tax-exempt status derived from the section of the IRC as it pertains to schools and not to churches. The AAO clarifies that qualification under the Code that pertained to schools can be religious or non-religious, and therefore, the burden of proof is on petitioner to show the reason it is tax-exempt is because of its "religious character, rather than from its status as an educational institution." The AAO stated that an organization can establish this by submitting documentation establishing the religious nature, such as brochures, calendars, flyers, and other literature describing the religious purpose and nature of the activities of the organization. In denying this case, although the AAO did not dispute that religious activities took place at the organization, it concluded that petitioner emphasized its educational rather than religious character when it applied for tax exemption.

Working for the Bona Fide Religious Organization. The statute requires the alien must be seeking entry into the United States to work for a bona fide religious organization. In *Matter of [name not provided]*, SRC-03-073-51355 (AAO Jan. 26, 2005), where the beneficiary had worked as an independent contractor, the AAO found this was not qualified employment. The AAO reasoned that because the alien is self-employed, she is not working for a religious organization as required by the statute.[33]

CONCLUSION

These cases demonstrate that for a permanent residence filing for a religious worker, it is essential to show the beneficiary has two years' full-time experience, the position offered is a traditional religious function, and the proffered job is full-time. The organization must also show it has the ability to pay the salary and that it is tax-exempt based on its religious nature. Furthermore, it is important to remember that concrete documentation is vital to the success of any case.

---

[31] *See Matter of [name not provided]*, LIN-02-094-51196 (AAO Feb. 3, 2005).

[32] 8 CFR §204.5(m)(3)(i) states the petitioner must submit evidence that the organization qualifies as a nonprofit organization either by showing it is exempt from taxation in accordance with §501(c)(3) of the Internal Revenue Code of 1986 as it relates to religious organizations or, alternatively, it can provide documentation proving that it would be eligible for tax exemption by the IRS under §501(c)(3) of the Code.

---

[33] INA §101(a)(27)(C).

EMPLOYMENT VERIFICATION SYSTEMS—
WHERE ARE WE AND WHERE ARE WE GOING?

by Eileen M.G. Scofield, Newton J. Chu, Leigh N. Ganchan, and Austin T. Fragomen, Jr.[*]

States all over the country, as well as the federal government, are seeking to create and implement employment verification systems as a means of "correcting" the "illegal immigration" problem that currently exists in the United States. There is a perception by many that a simple magic wand can be waved over some large database, and it will immediately be able to tell employers who is legally in the

[*] **Eileen Scofield** is a frequent international and national public speaker and published author of numerous articles primarily on business-related immigration. She has held numerous positions over her 21 years of practice with bar associations and AILA. Ms. Scofield also is a member of numerous organizations that advise Congress on business and immigration issues, such as the National I-9 Coalition. She heads a national practice with Alston & Bird, a 700-plus attorney firm, with offices in D.C., New York, Atlanta, Charlotte, and Raleigh.

Newton Chu serves as the resident director in the Hilo, Hawaii office of Torkildson, Katz, Fonseca, Moore & Hetherington. He has practiced immigration law for over 25 years. He currently practices in the area of immigration law and employment law representing management. A graduate of the University of Hawaii, Manoa, and the Antioch School of Law, Mr. Chu is a frequent lecturer on immigration and employment law issues in Hawaii.

Leigh Ganchan is board-certified in immigration and nationality law, by the Texas Board of Legal Specialization and was selected as one of Houston's Top Lawyers for 2005. Her employment-based practice features I-9 compliance planning and litigation, and health care professional immigration. She has authored many articles on employment eligibility verification, serves on the AILA/USCIS Benefits Liaison Committee, and participated on the AILA/Texas Service Center Liaison Committee for many years. Formerly an INS Assistant District Counsel, she is now a senior associate with Epstein Becker Green Wickliff & Hall in Houston.

Austin T. Fragomen, Jr. is chairman of Fragomen, Del Rey, Bernsen & Loewy LLP. Mr. Fragomen has served as staff counsel to the U.S. House of Representatives subcommittee on immigration, citizenship and international law and as an adjunct professor of law at New York University School of Law. He has testified before Congress on a range of immigration issues. He is vice-chair of the board of directors of the Center for Migration Studies, member of the board of CLINIC, and chair of the Practising Law Institute's Annual Immigration Institute. He also is the co-author of the *Immigration Handbook* series. He attended Georgetown University (B.S.) and Case Western Reserve University (J.D.).

United States and who is not. Unfortunately, for those of us who deal daily, if not hourly, with employment-related legal issues, particularly with regard to foreign born workers, we know and understand that databases created by the different government agencies not only fail to contain that information, but also fail to talk to each other. As a matter of fact, due to some of our privacy provisions, these systems may never talk to each other, but unfortunately, politicians continue to claim that employer verifications systems will solve the "illegal immigration" problem.

The following is a summary of a variety of issues related to this particular area—so widespread and broad that the authors have included a series of questions and then material seeking to answer these questions. Employment verification systems and the databases upon which they depend and the laws that seek to use them seem to change quite rapidly. Therefore, by the time of publication, some of this information may have already been amended. The authors, thus, recommend that you continue to look to the AILA InfoNet for updated and current information.

EMPLOYMENT VERIFICATION PROGRAM—WHERE ARE WE AND WHERE ARE WE GOING?

By way of background, right now under current federal law, the I-9 system of paperwork verification is the nation's sole mandatory employment eligibility verification program. There are, though, additional programs used to seek to verify work authorization. First is the Social Security Number Verification System (SSNVS); second, the Basic Pilot Program; and third, there is another program called SAVE, but it is not available to employers, only to government agencies.

The SSNVS is a Web-based version of other systems where employers can verify new employees' Social Security numbers against the Social Security Administration (SSA) database for preparing IRS W-2 forms. This system, though, specifically states that information provided by the SSA should not be used to verify an employee's immigration status.

The Basic Pilot Program is a voluntary Web-based verification system. First introduced in 1996, it seeks to verify employment eligibility by using information provided by the employee on the I-9 form and runs a query through the SSA and U.S. Citizenship and Immigration Services (USCIS)/Department of Homeland Security (DHS) databases. The Basic Pilot Program system, when updated and current, works well. Unfortunately, though, if the program database cannot ascertain the legal status of the individual, based on all the documentation inputted or on the information inputted by the government, potential employees have to generally wait eight days or so to get the inconsistency resolved.

The SSA and DHS have sought to improve the Basic Pilot Program by increasing the accuracy of the existing Homeland Security records, expediting data entry for new lawful permanent residence and arriving nonimmigrants, and for valid work authorization. Data errors do continue to exist with Basic Pilot Program, and in cases where the answer cannot be secured immediately via the Internet, there are often delays in hiring and questions related thereto.

Looking forward, however, new legislation seeks to create a new and improved employment verification system. According to the Chairman's Mark, Comprehensive Immigration Reform Act of 2006, introduced February 28, 2006, Senator Arlen Specter (R-PA) has created a compilation of many of the pending immigration bills and consolidated them into a single act. Naturally, there will be a great deal of discussion, and perhaps this bill will be amended and/or passed before the AILA Annual Conference, but as of the writing of this article, the following is a summary of some of the key employer verification provisions of the bill.

Title III of this legislation, Increased Worksite Enforcement and Penalties, as under the Immigration Reform and Control Act of 1986,[1] prohibits the hiring, recruiting, or referring an alien with knowledge or with reason to know the alien's illegal status. In addition, a company that continues to employ an unauthorized alien on its own through contracts or subcontracts is subject to violation of the law.

Also, the proposed law states that in a civil enforcement context, if it has been determined that an employer has hired more than 10 unauthorized aliens within a calendar year, the rebuttal presumption is created that the employer knew or had reason to know that such aliens were unauthorized. The key point with regard to this section, though, is that an employer who voluntarily uses the electronic employment verification system (Basic Pilot Program) under current terms has a good faith defense to any of these charges.

This legislation creates a new certificate of compliance with regard to an employer's formal assurance that the employer is, in fact, in compliance with immigration laws or that it has developed a plan to come in compliance. This provision allows DHS to rely on an employer's self-assessment and self-certification, rather than launching a formal DHS investigation.

There is a new document verification system whereby employers must take reasonable steps to verify that employees are authorized to work and that the employer attests under penalty of perjury that they have verified the identity and work authorization of employees by examining the documents. Finally, there is a standard of compliance with regard to the examination of the documents. This standard is similar to the current standard already in place with regard to I-9 verification process.

Similarly, the employee has an obligation to attest in writing to be legally authorized to work in the United States. The employer must now retain a copy of the attestation made by any such employee.

Senator Specter wants the basic program to be converted into the electronic employment verification system (EEVS). Under section (d), the Commissioner of Social Security, the Secretary of Homeland Security, must implement an EEVS system via the existing Basic Pilot Program. The EEVS will work through both a toll-free number and an electronic media. The Secretary of Homeland Security will keep a record of inquiries and responses to allow for an audit capability. Under this system, EEVS should be a bit tighter and faster than the current basic program because the response must be made within three days and, again, like the basic program, during a tentative nonconfirmation period, the employer may not terminate the employee based on a lack of work authorization. There is language in the statute that requires the system to be operated with maximum reliability, ease of use, and by privacy safeguards. The SSA's portion of this program will continue to compare names with alien identification and authorization numbers to confirm or deny work authorization.

Section (d)(3) outlines the employer requirements with regard to participation in the EEVS.

---

[1] Immigration Reform and Control Act of 1986, Pub. L. No. 99-603, 100 Stat. 3359 (partially codified in scattered sections of the INA) (IRCA).

Most importantly is to know that this EEVS will be a roll-out system. Within two years after enactment, employers with more than 5,000 employees must participate in the EEVS. All employers must participate within a five-year window. Eventually, under subsection d(6), an employer's failure to comply with the EEVS requirements shall be treated as a violation of the law, and such failure to comply shall be treated as presumed violations of the prohibition against the hiring of unauthorized aliens. So, therefore, within five years, all employers will be required to use the EEVS system, and the failure to do so will be a presumption of unauthorized employment of illegal aliens.

Subsection (d)(8) protects from civil and criminal liability an employer who relies in good faith on the information provided through the EEVS confirmation system. This provision is extremely important when it comes to the ability to avoid class actions such as the one that has currently been brought against Mohawk and that was previously brought against Tyson Foods in Tennessee a few years ago.

Eventually, under subsection (d)(11), the Secretary of Homeland Security may establish and require fees for employers participating in EEVS. The fees will be designed to help recover the cost of the system. In addition, under another subsection, the Secretary of Homeland Security is required to provide a report to Congress within one year of enactment on the capacity, integrity, and accuracy of EEVS.

Under subsection (e) of this section, the law provides that Homeland Security can still seek evidence and documentation with regard to compliance under these provisions. DHS also can issue pre-penalty notices if it believes there has been a violation. Mitigation continues to include good faith compliance and participation in EEVS. The criminal penalties for pattern and practice hiring will be $10,000 for each unauthorized worker and imprisonment for up to six months or both. The Attorney General can bring a civil action to seek such penalties.

Finally, on a few last compliance issues, employers are prohibited from requiring prospective or current employees to post a bond against liability arising from the employer's violation of the section. The legislation bars noncompliant employers from eligibility for federal contracts and directs that all funds paid for civil penalties be placed into an employer compliance fund that shall be used for enhancing and enforcement of employer compliance. There are other miscellaneous provisions not addressed here.

THE I-9 FORM: CHANGING THE FORM BUT NOT THE RULE

In an attempt to assist employers with the I-9 document review mandate, IIRAIRA[2] provided for a reduction in the number of documents acceptable for the employment eligibility verification process. The goal of this provision was to establish a condensed list of easily identifiable documents, as opposed to the current list of some 30 documents. On September 30, 1997, Immigration and Naturalization Service (INS) published an interim rule, amending the documents acceptable under List A, but made no changes to Lists B and C. The interim rule eliminated four documents from List A: (1) certification of U.S. citizenship (Form N-560 or N-561); (2) certificate of naturalization (Form N-550 or N-570); (3) re-entry permit (Form I-327); and (4) refugee travel document. However, in spite of this rulemaking event, INS never changed the I-9 form to reflect the reduced list of acceptable List A documents. Given that most employers would remain unaware of the interim rule and would likely continue to rely on the list as it appears on Form I-9, INS indicated that it would not impose civil penalties on employers who mistakenly continued to accept the documents that had been removed by the interim rule.[3]

In February 1998, INS published a proposed rule that made sweeping changes to the I-9 form and employment verification procedures.[4] These changes provided solutions to many of the problems associated with employment eligibility verification and on the whole, would render the process much easier for employers. Unfortunately, this proposed rule has never been finalized.

USCIS (formerly INS) issued what was expected to contain the long-awaited revisions to Form I-9 in May 2005. However, the only detectable changes were the replacement of outdated references to the Department of Justice (DOJ) and INS with references to DHS, and the addition of a fourth box in section 1 where employees could choose to indicate that they are "nationals" of the United States.[5] On

---

[2] Illegal Immigration Reform and Immigrant Responsibility Act of 1996, Division C of the Omnibus Appropriations Act of 1996 (H.R. 3610), Pub. L. No. 104-208, 110 Stat. 3009 (IIRAIRA).

[3] Note that the USCIS website indicates "Interim changes made on September 30, 1997 are currently in effect." *http://uscis.gov/graphics/howdoi/faqeev.htm.*

[4] 62 Fed. Reg. 5287 (Feb. 2, 1998).

[5] This change may have been intended to address a deficiency in the I-9 form that allowed some individuals who

continued

June 21, 2005, DHS announced that it is "rebranding" the I-9 form to reflect the transfer from DOJ to DHS. Without explanation, DHS replaced the "new" I-9 form from May 2005 with a different version of the I-9 form that again combines U.S. "citizen or national" into a single selection, but that reflected none of the changes provided for in the 1997 and 1998, rulemaking events. The government continues to promise to introduce a new Form I-9 that incorporates substantive changes based on the previous rulemakings;[6] however, it is far from clear when this will happen.[7] With regard to the *Handbook for Employers*, intended to provide a step-by-step explanation of what employers must do to meet their employment eligibility verification responsibilities under the law,[8] USCIS has no current plans to update the information contained therein.[9]

---

falsely claimed U.S. citizenship to obtain Green Cards. However, as long as the I-9 form contains only three boxes to choose from, it appears the government will continue to favorably adjudicate otherwise approvable adjustment of status applications where the alien has checked the referenced "citizen or national" block of the I-9 in the absence of other specific evidence of a false claim to US citizenship. *See* "AILA/TSC Liaison Questions & Answers," *published on* AILA InfoNet at Doc. No. 01041902 (*posted* Apr. 19, 2001).

[6] Press Release, "DHS Issues Rebranded Form I-9" (June 21, 2005).

[7] GAO Report to Congress, Immigration Enforcement: Weaknesses Hinder Employment Verification and Worksite Enforcement Efforts, GAO-05-813 (Aug. 2005) (recommending that DHS set a target time frame for completing the Department's review of the Form I-9 process and issuing final regulations on the process) (hereinafter GAO Report to Congress). In response to an AILA request to provide more underlying information regarding *Federal Register* Notices associated with changes to USCIS forms and regulations, USCIS has agreed to put a link in the notices that take the reader directly to the proposed or affected regulation or form. This might prove useful in monitoring future changes to the I-9 form. *See* "AILA-USCIS Liaison Meeting Minutes" (Sept. 22, 2005), *published on* AILA InfoNet at Doc. No. 05120941 (*posted* Dec. 9, 2005) (hereinafter AILA-USCIS Minutes, Sept. 22, 2005).

[8] INS *Handbook for Employers*, Instructions for Completing Form I-9 (M-274) (Nov. 21, 1991), available at *www.uscis.gov*.

[9] AILA-USCIS Minutes, Sept. 22, 2005, *supra* note 7. USCIS proposes that employers look to Office of Business Liaison employer bulletins for updated information. *See* USCIS Employer Information Bulletin 102, The Form I-9 Process in a Nutshell (Oct. 7, 2005) (noting that the bulletin's purpose is to supplement the 1991 version of the *Handbook for Employers* and the 1991 version of the Form I-9 and its instructions.).

CITIZENS VERSUS NATIONALS— NATIONALITY ISSUES FOR FORM I-9 PURPOSES

Form I-9 asks the potential employee to attest, under penalty of perjury, that he or she is a citizen or national of the United States.[10] The answer for most U.S. citizens is easy, but how many people or employers (let alone lawyers) know what a "national" of the United States is? The question rarely comes up unless you have clients who hail from, or employ, people from the Pacific basin.

Nationality Basics

According to the U.S. State Department (DOS), "[v]ery few persons fall within this category since, as defined by the INA, all U.S. citizens are U.S. nationals but only a relatively small number of persons acquire U.S. nationality without becoming U.S. citizens."[11] The answer to this baffling question on Form I-9 can be found if you read §101(a)(21–22) and §308 of the INA[12] together. Section 101(a)(21) defines the term "national" as a "person owing permanent allegiance to a state.[13] State is defined in the INA as any of the 50 states, plus the District of Columbia, Puerto Rico, Guam, and the Virgin Islands.[14] Section 101(a)(22) of the INA sets forth that all U.S. citizens are also nationals of the United States. However, a national is also "a person who, though not a citizen of the United States, owes permanent allegiance to the United States."[15] Further, INA §308 confers U.S. nationality, but not U.S. citizenship, on persons born in or having ties with "an outlying possession of the United States."[16] The

---

[10] Form I-9 (rev. Nov. 21, 1991), Section 1.

[11] U.S. State Department website, *http://travel.state.gov/law/citizenship/citizenship_781.html*.

[12] Immigration and Nationality Act of 1952, Pub. L. No. 82-414, 66 Stat. 163 (*codified as amended at* 8 USC §§1101 *et seq.*) (INA).

[13] The term "national" means a person owing permanent allegiance to a state.

[14] The term "State" includes the District of Columbia, Puerto Rico, Guam, and the U.S. Virgin Islands.

[15] The term "national of the United States" means: (A) a citizen of the United States; or (B) a person who, though not a citizen of the United States, owes permanent allegiance to the United States.

[16] INA §308:

Unless otherwise provided in section 301 of this title, the following shall be nationals, but not citizens of the United States at birth:

continued

statute sets forth the requirements that one needs to meet in order to be determined to be a national of such outlying possessions. According to INA §308, the persons eligible for this status, in addition to those mentioned above, include persons born abroad to two American noncitizen national parents, or persons born abroad to one alien parent and one noncitizen national parent. The statute also includes a residency requirement of the parents of the child prior to birth in order to transmit such nationality.[17]

Additional research reveals that the only "outlying possessions" as defined in INA §101(A)(29) are American Samoa and Swains Island.[18] Since there are no other statutes that define any other territories or any of the states as outlying possessions, we are limited to these two areas. However, the United States has a number of other insular possessions, such as Wake Island, which according to case law, are not foreign territory.[19] Apparently by inadver-

tence, these islands are not within the designation of "outlying possessions" as defined in the INA even though aliens coming from these areas ostensibly are not coming from a foreign port or place. However, they are excluded from the definition of the United States for immigration purposes, even though they are not regarded as foreign.

Proof of Nationality

If you determine that your client is a "national" but not a U.S. citizen, what do you advise your client to do? If you research this area of law, you will learn that INA §341(b) provides that you can make an application to the Secretary of State for a Certificate of noncitizen National Status. If you present sufficient proof of nationality, but noncitizen status, you would then take an oath of allegiance much like any petition for naturalization.[20]

However, if you inquire with DOS, you will learn that since the it has received so few requests for such certificates, it never created such a noncitizen national certificate. DOS will then direct those who would ordinarily be eligible for the nonexistent certificate to "apply for a U.S. passport that would delineate and certify their status as a national but not a citizen of the United States." DOS would instruct you as follows: "If a person believes he or she is eligible under the law as a non-citizen national of the United States and the person complies with the provisions of 8 USC 1452(b)(1) and (2), he/she may apply for a passport at any Passport Agency in the United States." When applying, applicants must execute a Form DS-11 and show documentary proof of their noncitizen national status as well as their identity.[21]

Quasi-Nationals

There also are other persons eligible to work in the United States who are not citizens or nationals, but subject to certain treaties, are eligible to live, work, and travel within the United States indefinitely. No, these are not citizens of Canada or Mexico, but Pacific Islanders such as the citizens of the

(1) A person born in an outlying possession of the United States on or after the date of formal acquisition of such possession;

(2) A person born outside the United States and is outlying possessions of parents both of whom are nationals, but not citizens, of the United States, and have had a residence in the United States, or one of its outlying possessions prior to the birth of such person;

(3) A person of unknown parentage found in an outlying possession of the United States while under the age of five years, until shown, prior to his attaining the age of twenty-one years, not to have been born in such outlying possessions; and

(4) A person born outside the United States and its outlying possessions of parents one of whom is an alien, and the other a national, but not a citizen, of the United States who, prior to the birth of such person, was physically present in the United States or its outlying possessions for a period or periods totaling not less than seven years in any continuous period of ten years—

(A) during which the national parent was not outside the United States or its outlying possessions for a continuous period of more than one year, and

(B) at least five years of which were after attaining the age of fourteen years.

The proviso of section 301(g) shall apply to the national parent under this paragraph in the same manner as it applies to the citizen parent under that section.

[17] *See U.S. v. Shiroma*, 123 F. Supp. 145 (D. Hawaii 1954).

[18] The term "outlying possessions of the United States" means American Samoa and Swains Island.

[19] Wake Island is not foreign territory. *See U.S. v. Paquet*, 131 F. Supp. 32 (D. Hawaii 1955), *Petition of Willess*, 146 F.
continued

Supp. 216 (D. Hawaii 1956) (however, Wake Island was deemed foreign for purposes of naturalization benefits).

[20] INA §341(b)(1): "A person who claims to be a national, but not a citizen, of the United States may apply to the Secretary of State for a certificate of non-citizen national status. Upon—(1) proof to the satisfaction of the Secretary of State that the applicant is a national, but not a citizen, of the United States."

[21] *http://travel.state.gov/law/citizenship/citizenship_781.html.*

Republic of the Marshall Islands, the Federated States of Micronesia, and Palau. These Pacific Islands may enter the United States and its territories and possessions, engage in employment, and establish residence (as nonimmigrants), without a nonimmigrant visa or a labor certification.[22]

Originally, these were Pacific islands controlled by Japan. At the conclusion of World War II, the United States acquired rights of dominion over these islands that were called the Pacific Trust Territory. The United States did not have full sovereignty over the Pacific Trust Territory even though it was clearly an American occupancy much like the Philippines.[23] Additionally, for immigration purposes, the Trust Territory was not a part of the United States and was regarded as a foreign port or place, and many Hawaiian court decisions have followed this analysis.[24]

During the past 20 years, the United States has conducted negotiations to resolve numerous issues and to terminate the Trusteeship Agreement. The ultimate goal of the United States was to provide autonomy for the inhabitants of the Trust Territory and allow them to decide their own future political status. Currently, there are agreements with four separate island groups within the Trust Territory. In 1986, these agreements were approved by Congress, and, thereafter, the United Nations declared that the United States had fully discharged its obligations under the original Trusteeship Agreement.[25]

The 1986, action created three new Associated States known as the Federated States of Micronesia (FSM), the Republic of the Marshall Islands (RMI), and the Republic of Palau (RP). The United States drafted and concluded Compacts of Free Association with each of these three new nations. These Compacts set forth the political, economic, military, and other terms of their relationship with the United States. Only the Republic of Palau has yet to approve its Compact. The most pertinent feature of these Compacts for immigration and employment law purposes is that it allows citizens of the three countries the right to enter, reside, and be employed in the United States indefinitely.[26]

In 1976, the fourth island group in the former Trusteeship, the Northern Mariana Islands, elected to become the Commonwealth of the Northern Mariana Islands. In the signed Covenant of Political Union, it conferred U.S. citizenship on the indigenous inhabitants of the Marianas and prescribes limited applicability of the immigration and nationality laws of the United States. As set forth in §302 of Pub. L. No. 94–241, certain inhabitants of the Commonwealth of the Northern Mariana Islands, who became U.S. citizens by virtue of Article III of the Covenant, are eligible to opt for noncitizen national status.[27]

More recently, on December 7, 2003, President George W. Bush signed legislation approving the amended Compacts of Free Association (CFA) with FSM and RMI. These Compacts went into effect on May 1, 2004 for RMI, and June 30, 2004, for FSM. After those dates, RMI and FSM citizens will no

---

[22] 8 CFR §212.1(d), §1212.1(d), *as amended*, 66 Fed. Reg. 37429, 37432 (July 18, 2001). This provision gives effect to provisions of §141(a) of the Compact between the United States of America and Marshall Islands and the Federated States of Micronesia, 48 USC §1901 note, and of §141(a) of the Compact between the United States of America and Palau.

[23] *See U.S. v. Shiroma*, 123 F. Supp. 145 (D. Hawaii 1954).

[24] *See Application of Reyes*, 140 F. Supp. 130 (D. Hawaii 1956); *Aradanas v. Hogan*, 155 F. Supp. 546 (D. Hawaii 1957); *see also Matter of A–*, 7 I&N Dec. 128 (1956).

[25] Presidential Proclamation 5564 (Nov. 3, 1986), *reproduced in* 63 *Interpreter Releases* 1069–70 (Nov. 19, 1986); North, "Sweeping Immigration Changes for U.S. Territories," 64 *Interpreter Releases* (Jan. 12, 1987).

[26] 8 CFR §212.1(d), §1212.1(d):

Citizens of the Freely Associated States, formerly Trust Territory of the Pacific Islands.

Citizens of the Republic of the Marshall Islands and the Federated States of Micronesia may enter into, lawfully engage in employment, and establish residence in the United States and its territories and possessions without regard to paragraphs (14), (20) and (26) of section 212(a) of the Act pursuant to the terms of Pub. L. 99-239. Pending issuance by the aforementioned governments of travel documents to eligible citizens, travel documents previously issued by the Trust Territory of the Pacific Islands will continue to be accepted for purposes of identification and to establish eligibility for admission into the United States, its territories and possessions.

[27] Section 302 of Pub. L. No. 94-241:

Any person who becomes a citizen of the United States solely by virtue of the provisions in Section 301 [applying to those born in or residing in the Northern Mariana Islands] may within six months after the effective date of that Section or within six months after reaching the age of 18 years, whichever date is later, become a national but not a citizen of the United States by making a declaration under oath before any court established by the Constitution or laws of the United States or any other court of record in the Commonwealth in the form as follows 'I _____ being duly sworn, hereby declare my intention to be a national but not a citizen of the United States.'

longer be exempt from passport requirements for travel to the United States and therefore require passports for entry. However, the amended Compacts preserved the right for RMI and FSM citizens to nonimmigrant admission without visa and allowance of employment eligibility. While 8 CFR §274a.12(a)(8), §1274a.12(a)(8), requires citizens of RMI and FSM to obtain an employment authorization document (EAD) as evidence of their eligibility to work in the United States, these new Amended Compacts now provide that a person admitted to the United States from the FSM or RMI under the CFA "shall be considered to have the permission of the Government of the United States to accept employment in the United States."

Thus, for Form I-9 purposes, an unexpired RMI or FSM passport with unexpired I-9 evidencing admission under the compact (or the compact as amended) shall be considered to be documentation establishing identity and employment authorization under "List A" documents. Therefore, citizens of FSM and the RMI no longer need an EAD to work in the United States. However, because the Republic of Palau has not yet approved the amended Compact, citizens of RP will continue to need to apply for and receive an EAD to work in the United States.[28]

WHAT CONSTITUTES NOTICE OF UNAUTHORIZED EMPLOYMENT?

An employer is liable under IRCA for knowingly hiring a foreign national who is unauthorized to work, or for continuing to employ a foreign national after learning that he or she is not work-authorized. The employer's liability is not limited to those situations in which it has actual knowledge of an employee's lack of work authorization. The employment authorization regulations define knowledge to include "not only actual knowledge but also knowledge which may be fairly inferred through notice of certain facts and circumstances which would lead a person, through the exercise of reasonable care, to know about a certain condition."[29]

The following scenarios are instances in which constructive knowledge may be found under current regulations:

▪ The employer does not complete Form I-9;

▪ The employer does not properly complete Form I-9, such as where the employer fails to enter an expiration date for an EAD;

▪ The employer fails to reverify the foreign national's employment eligibility after an employment eligibility document has expired.[30]

More difficult are the situations in which the employer obtains information that may indicate the employee is not authorized to work in the United States. In such situations, the employer generally has a duty to inquire further about the employee's status, while taking care not to run afoul of IRCA's employment discrimination provisions. Though not every constructive notice scenario can be described in this article, some commonly arising situations are as follows:

▪ The employee submits conflicting documentation during initial verification;

▪ The employee submits documents that appear to be forged or tampered;

▪ The employee states that he or she is work-authorized until a specific date, but presents acceptable documentation that does not include the expiration date of the authorization;

▪ The employer receives information from government enforcement personnel that an employee's documentation may not be valid;

▪ The employer receives information through other workplace sources that an employee is not authorized for employment, e.g., through a verification service such as the Basic Pilot program or through information from another employer.

A crucial issue for employers who obtain information that would indicate an employee's lack of work authorization is how to go about following up with the worker. Under prior law, requests for more or different documents during the I-9 verification procedure or refusals to honor acceptable documentation could be considered an unfair immigration-related employment practice, whether or not the employer's action was based on a good faith effort to comply with IRCA's employer sanctions provision. The 1996, revisions to IRCA modified this provision and provide that an employer's request for more documents or refusal to honor tendered documents is not unlawful unless made for the purpose or with the

---

[28] USCIS Employer Information Bulletin 106 (Mar. 16, 2005).

[29] 8 CFR §274a.1(l)(1).

[30] Id.

intent of discriminating against an individual on the basis of national origin or citizenship status.[31]

When following up situations such as those listed above, the employer should adhere to some general guidelines. The employer should never specify which documents it wants to see to establish identity or work eligibility. It should never require presentation of a document issued by USCIS, either during verification or reverification procedures. If the employee specifies an expiration date for his or her employment eligibility, but offers an employment eligibility document that does not contain an expiration date (e.g., a Social Security card), the employer should not request additional information or documents. If an employee has presented acceptable documentation for verification purposes, the information should be reverified only if the employee has listed an expiration date for employment eligibility on Form I-9. During the reverification, the employer should not require the employee to furnish a document issued by USCIS that shows an extended expiration date, and should accept any document offered by the employee, as long as it appears on the list of acceptable I-9 documents. Further reverification procedures should be conducted only if, upon initial reverification, the employee presents an EAD with an expiration date.

Where the employer receives information that raises the possibility of unauthorized employment, further investigation must be handled carefully. In general, the employer should not make further inquiries about employment eligibility, or request or require additional documentation based on mere rumor or hearsay, without more. Information received from the government may require further investigation. For example, if information is received from U.S. Immigration and Customs Enforcement (ICE) that the employee has not properly completed Form I-9 (e.g., where an inaccurate alien registration number has been provided), follow-up is required. Further inquiry is required when the employee offers a document that contains obvious signs of forgery or tampering, or where the name or descriptive information contained in the document does not relate to the employee. Likewise, follow-up is required where the employee presents a receipt showing an application for an acceptable I-9 document.

In general, the employer must develop a consistent approach to dealing with situations in which there is a duty to inquire further. Employers should remember that they are not expected to ferret out all unauthorized workers from the workplace. Therefore, when an employee presents documents evidencing employment eligibility from an acceptable list of documents, those documents are prima facie proof of the employee's eligibility to work in the United States. Absent clear evidence to the contrary, such as notification from enforcement personnel that the documents are invalid or a contradictory statement from the employee or obvious fraud, the employer need not inquire further about the employment eligibility of the employee.

Employers also should be aware of recent cases indicating that using third-party contractors to hire unauthorized workers may not shield them from IRCA liability. In 2005, in a widely publicized case, Wal-Mart Stores agreed to an $11 million settlement arising out of allegations that it had knowingly used the services of undocumented workers hired by independent contractors.[32] More recently, the Supreme Court has agreed to hear *Mohawk Industries, Inc. v. Williams*,[33] in which a class of workers at a carpet and rug manufacturing company has filed a civil lawsuit under the Racketeer Influenced and Corrupt Organizations (RICO) statutes, alleging that its employer, Mohawk, had conspired with a staffing agency to hire undocumented Chinese foreign nationals to take the place of legally authorized workers and had formed a racketeering enterprise to that end. Oral argument before the Court was held on April 26, 2006.

DEALING WITH SOCIAL SECURITY ISSUES

The most common Social Security issue that arises in the context of employment eligibility verification is the Social Security Administration (SSA) "no match" letter. No-match letters are periodically sent to employers to inform them that employee name and Social Security Number (SSN) information does not match the SSA's records. The typical no-match letter, titled "Employer Correction Request," generally explains that discrepancies exist between SSA's database and employee information provided by the employer on the W-2 form, and requests that employers respond to the letter with corrections "within 60 days." A list of mismatched SSNs is typically attached to the letter, along with information on making corrections. Receipt of a no-match letter raises immigration issues that should

---

[31] INA §274A(b)(6); 28 CFR §44.200(a)(3).

[32] *See* "Wal-Mart to Pay $11 Million in Lawsuit on Illegal Workers," *N.Y. Times*, Mar. 19, 2005.

[33] *Mohawk Industries Inc. v. Williams*, 411 F.3d 1252, *cert. granted*, 126 S. Ct. 830 (2005).

be carefully heeded by employers. In particular, an SSN mismatch may raise IRCA compliance issues, in particular, whether the affected employee is in fact authorized to work in the United States. Receipt of the no-match letter should not by itself prompt an employer to suspect that the affected employee is working without authorization. However, agency guidance suggests that employers who receive no-match letters have an obligation under INA §274A to follow up with affected employees.[34]

The SSA no-match makes clear that it "makes no statement about your employee's immigration status." Employers are further warned that the letter is not, by itself, a basis for taking any adverse action against an employee, such as termination, suspension, or discrimination. Legacy INS shared this view, stating in a 1997 letter that notice of a discrepancy between wage reporting information and SSA records does not by itself put the employer on notice that the employee is not authorized to work, and is not actual notice of an employer's lack of work authorization.[35]

Receipt of an SSA no-match letter should not be ignored, however; employers should take reasonable steps to try to resolve discrepancies. With respect to the possibility of unauthorized employment, the no-match letter should be considered with other circumstances to determine whether there is actual or constructive notice that an employee is not authorized to work. For example, in addition to the no-match letter, the employer may also receive information from another source, such as another employee, that a worker identified in the no-match letter is in fact not authorized to work. In such a case, the totality of circumstances might rise to actual or constructive notice of unauthorized employment.

Follow-up activity should be considered carefully. Receipt of a no-match letter does not authorize the employer to demand that the employee show his or her EAD or other immigration document. In fact, once an employer has received an employee's status documents for initial completion of Form I-9, rechecking immigration documents is prohibited by IRCA. Employees should be given an opportunity to rectify errors in their name or SSN, since mismatches are commonly due to name changes after marriage or divorce, as well as clerical errors. However, follow-up activity may yield information constituting actual or constructive notice of unauthorized employment. In such cases, further review of the employee's work eligibility is warranted, but any such investigation must be conducted in a consistent, nondiscriminatory manner, as discussed above.

THE CHANGING ROLE OF THE DRIVER'S LICENSE

The state driver's license is one of the most frequently selected List B identity documents when it comes to completing Form I-9. However, the REAL ID Act of 2005[36] may change that by making it difficult, if not impossible, for many individuals to obtain a state driver's license. The REAL ID Act provides that as of May 2008, a state driver's license cannot be accepted by federal agencies for any official purpose unless it meets the requirements of the Act. This would likely include the "official federal purpose" of the use of a driver's license to complete Form I-9.

Once the 1998 proposal[37] is in place, there will only be three List B identity documents, one of which is a state-issued driver's license.

Driver's license applicants must present documents that prove their identity, date of birth, citizenship or immigration status, Social Security number, legal name, and physical residence. Then, the Department of Motor Vehicles (DMV) must verify the authenticity of these documents (which include birth certificates, court documents, Social Security cards, U.S. and foreign passports, immigration documents, and other proof of physical residence, such as utility bills and bank statements) with the agency that issued them. Verification whether electronic or manual is likely to be slow. Denials, delays, and repeated trips to the DMV will be the norm. Certain nonimmigrants must receive only temporary licenses that will have to be renewed more often. Accordingly, even U.S. citizens may encounter difficulties trying to obtain their driver's licenses in a timely manner to complete an I-9 for a new job.

---

[34] *See* letter from William Ho-Gonzalez, Office of the Special Counsel for Unfair Immigration-Related Employment Practices, U.S. Department of Justice, to Carl G. Borden, (Dec. 16, 1993).

[35] *See* letter from INS General Counsel David A. Martin, to Bruce R. Larson (Dec. 23, 1997), *reproduced in 76 Interpreter Releases* 203 (Feb. 9, 1998).

[36] Division B of the Emergency Supplemental Appropriations Act for Defense, the Global War on Terror, and Tsunami Relief Act, Pub. L. No. 109-13, 119 Stat. 231 (May 11, 2005).

[37] 62 Fed. Reg. 5287 (Feb. 2, 1998).

On February 10, 2006, the Texas Department of Public Safety (DPS) changed the list of acceptable documents for issuance of a Texas driver's license. One particularly vexing consequence of this change resulted in the refusal of driver's license to many foreign nationals even though they were in valid nonimmigrant visa status, such as holders of J-1, H-1B, and F-1 visa statuses (except those with work authorization cards). After focused advocacy efforts of various interested groups (NAFSA: Association of International Educators and AILA), state officials provided temporary relief in the form of a DPS memo advising that DPS supervisors may accept a valid foreign passport with a valid visa or valid I-94 card.[38] The memo also provided a general reminder that in Texas, any person who has never had a Social Security card, or who is not eligible to obtain one, can sign a waiver with the Department and be issued a license. Although it may be changed based on future REAL ID implementation, for now the Texas DMV Commission plans to post for public comment its recommended language for a new administrative rule that will allow the combination of documents respective to legal status to be presented for identification. The posting of the rule will also allow for further comment prior to any final acceptance.

CATCH IT IF YOU CAN: THE INTERNAL AUDIT

One of the most rewarding situations an attorney can have is being involved preparing a large corporation for an I-9 audit. Imagine being locked up in a room for days with several human resource managers sorting through thousands of Form I-9s. The relatively simple and straightforward Form I-9 can create the most horrific of nightmares when you review them carefully for legal compliance. As we instruct all corporate clients, it is imperative to conduct an I-9 self-audit on an annual basis at the very minimum. The Form I-9 is deceptively simple, but fraught with potential problems. The Form's potential problems multiply when employers use different managers or employees with varying degrees of training to complete them. If you can save your client potentially thousands of dollars in civil monetary penalties, while teaching management to correctly complete Form I-9, your reward will be having a very satisfied client.

What Is Involved in a Self-Audit

The authors recommend that you follow a procedure that would mirror a government compliance audit. An audit begins with a request to see not only the I-9s, but also the payroll records for the company that lists all current and terminated employees within a certain period of time. The auditor will then determine what I-9s should be made available for inspection.

Therefore, once you obtain the list of the employees, it is important to first make sure that you have an I-9 for all current employees. These I-9s should be kept in a separate file outside of the employees' personnel files—the reason is that I-9s are only kept for inspection by ICE officials or Department of Labor audit teams and should not be available for everyone to see. From an employment law perspective, the I-9 contains information that, if alleged to be used to make an adverse employment decision, could create the foundation of protected category discrimination. Federal and state laws uniformly prohibit discrimination based on age, ethnicity, national origin, citizenship status, and race, and an I-9 form contains information that could be used in a discriminatory manner.

Once you match up all the I-9s with the employee names, you will learn which I-9s are missing. You will also learn which I-9s are for terminated employees. I-9s for terminated employees should be segregated and placed in separate folders or binders. Since I-9s are required to be kept for employees for three years from the date of hire, or one year after termination, whichever is longer, those I-9s that do not fall within these time periods should be destroyed. Additionally, the authors find it useful to write a destruction date on the top of terminated employees' Forms I-9.

Once the binders for current and terminated employees are established, the authors generally recommend following a procedure to systematically inspect each individual I-9 to check for errors and omissions. This includes checking the completion date of the I-9 along with the hire date, and looking for expired or temporary work authorizations that require reverification.

Self-audits are a great training tool, as errors or omissions will indicate specific procedural problems, and can determine areas for additional training of personnel.

Common Mistakes in Preparing Form I-9

Section 1:

- The Employee did not sign or date the form

---

[38] Memo in possession of the authors.

- The Employee did not complete Section 1 on the date of hire
- The Employee did not check one of the three boxes regarding status
- The Employee checked the wrong box
- The Employee did not list an Alien Number, Admission Number, or expiration date

Section 2:

- The Employer did not sign Section 2
- The Employer did not date Section 2
- The Employer did not fill in the date of hire
- The Employer did not complete Section 2 within three business days of hire
- The Employer photocopied the employee's documents but did not complete the form
- The Employer signing the Form is not the same person who saw the original documents
- The Employer accepted unacceptable documents (e.g., hospital birth certificates, foreign birth certificates)
- The Employer accepted documents that did not "reasonably relate" to the employee (e.g., different names, dates of birth)
- The Employer accepted too many documents (items on list A, B, and C), which can lead to a discrimination charge against the Employer
- The Employer keeps copies of documents for some employees, but not all (there is no requirement to keep copies, but the Employer's policy should be consistently applied for all employees)

Section 3: The Employer Did Not Reverify Form I-9 When Required

- The Employer did not complete the information required in Section 3
- The Employer did not sign Section 3

Self-Audit Corrections

The authors advise employers not to use "whiteout" to make corrections on Forms I-9. Such forms are originally completed containing certifications by both the employee and employer. Thus, a later modification must be additionally signed or initialed and dated by the person making the correction, whether it be the employee or employer. An additional notation such as "corrected during self-audit, date" has been accepted by federal auditors.

APPLICATION QUESTIONS— IS IT SAFE TO ASK THAT?

A significant cause for concern for employers is the issue of pre-hire inquiries into a job applicant's work-authorized status and need for future immigration sponsorship. The Department of Justice's Office of Special Counsel (OSC) has issued some guidelines on these issues.[39]

Pre-Hire Inquiries Generally

In general, an employer may institute a policy that limits hiring to those persons with current employment authorization. Under IRCA, the employer need not consider for employment any person who is not already work-authorized. OSC maintains that an employer may permissibly ask a job applicant whether he or she is currently authorized to work in the United States. If the applicant answers in the affirmative, the employer should not inquire into the basis of the employment eligibility, i.e., whether the employee is a U.S. citizen, lawful permanent resident, or a nonimmigrant foreign national with time-limited work authorization. If the applicant answers in the negative, the employer can permissibly inquire further regarding the applicant's current immigration status.[40] Such prehiring inquiries should have minimal risk, because an individual who answers "no" to the question, whether he or she is authorized to work in the United States, is not protected against discrimination under IRCA. Nevertheless, the employer should inquire further about immigration status only if its policy contemplates hiring some persons without current employment authorization (i.e., those who will require the employer's sponsorship). Otherwise, the employer can safely eliminate all such persons from employment consideration without any further inquiry.

Pre-Hire Inquiries and Limited Hiring Policies

Some employers wish to institute policies that limit hiring to those persons who have protected status under citizenship discrimination laws, i.e., U.S. citizens, lawful permanent residents, temporary residents, refugees, and asylees.[41] Such policies are

---

[39] See, e.g., Office of Special Counsel Opinion Letter of April 20, 1993 (concerning pre-employment inquiries by employers); U.S. Equal Employment Opportunity Commission Opinion Letter of June 17, 1993 (concerning pre-employment inquiries and prehiring completion of Form I-9).

[40] See, e.g., Office of Special Counsel Opinion Letter of August 6, 1998.

[41] 28 CFR §44.101(c).

generally permitted, but employers may not limit hiring to a subgroup of the protected class, *i.e.*, U.S. citizens and permanent residents only.[42]

The type of pre-hire inquiry discussed above is appropriate when an employer has a policy of recruiting any individual, regardless of current employment eligibility, or if the employer is willing to hire any individual with current employment eligibility. The inquiry is not sufficient, however, if the employer wants to limit hiring to those persons who are protected individuals under IRCA's citizenship discrimination provision. In asking questions to distinguish between those persons protected by IRCA and those who are not, the employer must keep in mind that OSC has not given the same type of explicit approval to such inquiries. In addition, the employer must be sensitive at all times to avoid national origin discrimination. The Equal Employment Opportunity Commission (EEOC) has not given a definitive opinion on the national origin discrimination implications of such inquiries. Because the EEOC reviews employer policies for disparate impact, and is not limited to cases in which it can establish intentional discrimination, the employer must review such inquiries carefully with employment counsel before instituting a limited hiring policy. In all cases, the employer should not ask the question "Are you a U.S. citizen?" The employer may not permissibly distinguish between U.S. citizens and other protected individuals under IRCA. Obtaining this information before the hiring decision is made leaves the employer open to discrimination charges by rejected job applicants.

Pre-Hire Sponsorship Inquiries

Another pre-hire concern of employer is whether the prospective employee will require sponsorship for an employment visa either at the time of hire or in the future. This information is important because it affects cost and timing issues that must be considered in the hiring decision. Merely asking a prospective employee whether he or she is currently work-authorized will not elicit the necessary information to make this determination, since the authorization may be temporary and require future sponsorship for extensions. In such circumstances, OSC has endorsed the following set of questions: (1) "Are you legally authorized to work in the United States?" and (2) Will you now or in the future require sponsorship for employment visa

status (*e.g.*, H-1B status)?"[43] OSC does not recommend that applicants be asked to specify their citizenship status in the context of the employment authorization process. Questions such as "Explain the basis of your current employment authorization" should be avoided because a rejected applicant may rely upon such an inquiry to allege later that the employer considered the information in making the hiring decision, and discriminated based on citizenship status.[44]

DEFENDING AGAINST INVESTIGATIONS

ICE's approach to worksite enforcement operations has markedly changed, ostensibly on account of widespread use of counterfeit documents[45] that make it difficult for ICE agents to prove that employers knowingly hired unauthorized workers, and set and collect fine amounts from employers.[46] Most indicative of this change is the dramatic decrease in the number of notices of intent to fine[47] issued to employers for knowingly hiring unauthorized workers or improperly completing Forms I-9.[48] Therefore, as a response to these difficulties, ICE now considers the pursuit of civil settlements with employers preferable to the administrative fines process.

Employers are now more likely to face a full-scale federal investigation including criminal search warrants authorizing seizure of business, financial and personnel records, as well as computers maintained by the

---

[43] *See, e.g.*, Office of Special Counsel Opinion Letter of August 6, 1998.

[44] *Id.*

[45] In its 1997 report to Congress, the U.S. Commission on Immigration Reform noted that the widespread availability of false documents made it easy for unauthorized aliens to obtain jobs in the United States. In 1999, GAO reported that large numbers of unauthorized aliens have either fraudulently used valid documents that belong to others or presented counterfeit documents as evidence of employment eligibility. GAO, "Significant Obstacles to Reducing Unauthorized Alien Employment Exist," GAO/GGD-99-33 (Apr. 1999) (citing GAO, "Immigration Reform: Employer Sanctions and the Question of Discrimination," GAO/GGD-90-62 (Mar. 29, 1990)).

[46] GAO Report to Congress, *supra* note 7.

[47] 8 CFR §274a.9(d) (the proceeding to assess administrative penalties under §274A of the INA is commenced when the Service issues a Notice of Intent to Fine (NIF) on Form I-763.) Upon service of the NIF, an employer has 30 days to contest the NIF and to ask for a hearing before an Administrative Law Judge (ALJ).

[48] *See* GAO Report to Congress, *supra* note 7, noting a decline in the number of notices of intent to fine from 417 in FY 1999 to three in FY 2004.

---

[42] 28 CFR §44.200(b)(2). *See also* Office of Special Counsel Opinion Letter of September 20, 1988.

employer.[49] ICE agents conducting the worksite enforcement operation also are likely to be accompanied by enforcement agents from other federal agencies, as well as state and local law enforcement officers.[50] At the close of the investigative phase, employer sanctions efforts are more likely to be driven by a U.S. Attorney in Federal District Court than the traditional ICE agent and trial attorney before an administrative law judge.[51]

The nature of sanctions and settlement agreements is also changing. Employers who plead guilty to criminal immigration charges can face significant criminal forfeiture sanctions.[52] Criminal forfeiture occurs when, after the owner is convicted of a crime, it is demonstrated that the property has a sufficient relationship to the criminal activity to justify depriving the owner of his or her property rights.[53] Since criminal forfeiture is justified as a criminal punishment (it is imposed in a criminal proceeding directed against an individual for his or her alleged misconduct), a defendant in a criminal forfeiture prosecution is entitled to all the procedural protections associated with the criminal process.[54] Immigration counsel would be well-advised to work closely with qualified criminal counsel under these circumstances.

Even where the United States concludes that federal criminal proceedings are not appropriate, the terms of the ensuing civil settlement agreement can be comprehensive. Settlement amounts are reaching unprecedented levels.[55] ICE widely publicized its conclusion of a consent decree that directed the employer to pay $11 million through the U.S. Attorney's Office to the Treasury Forfeiture Fund.[56] The government also seeks wide-ranging injunctive relief designed to ensure a partnership aimed at effective enforcement of these immigration laws. Consent decrees can include permanent injunctions from knowingly hiring, recruiting, and continuing to employ aliens who are not legally authorized to work within the United States; and directives to employers to establish a means to verify that independent contractors also are taking reasonable steps to comply with immigration laws in their employment practices and cooperate truthfully with any investigation of these matters, to train employees of their legal obligations to prevent the knowing hiring, recruitment, and continued employment of unauthorized aliens while complying with pertinent antidiscrimination laws, to establish an internal corporate policy and procedures for employment eligibility verification, and to cooperate in any ongoing investigations of other employers involved in the case.[57]

Heartened by the large forfeiture amounts and comprehensive decrees, ICE is likely to continue to pursue this approach to worksite enforcement and sanctions. In fact, ICE emphasizes that it will continue to conduct important enforcement operations at traditional worksites, especially where the agency suspects egregious criminal employer violations or cases in which there is a nexus to other violations such as alien smuggling, alien harboring, money laundering, fraud, or some form of worker exploitation.[58]

---

[49] Press Release, "Homeland Security Secretary Michael Chertoff Announces Six-Point Agenda for Department of Homeland Security" (July 13, 2005), published on AILA InfoNet at Doc. No. 07071365 (posted July 13, 2005).

[50] "120 arrested on immigration violations at Wal-Mart site," S. Armour & D. Leinwand, USA TODAY, Money section (Nov. 17, 2005) (ICE was assisted by the U.S. Department of Labor, the Social Security Administration, Pennsylvania State Police and the Schuylkill County sheriff); ICE News Release, "56 Illegal Aliens Arrested By ICE at Construction Site" (Feb. 22, 2006) (Carthage Police Department and Jasper County Sheriff's Department assisted ICE with executing this criminal search warrant).

[51] Press Conference with Secretary of Homeland Security Michael Chertoff, Assistant Secretary for Immigration and Customs Enforcement Julie Myers, and U.S. Attorney Glenn Suddaby (Apr. 20, 2006); see "News Release: DHS unveils comprehensive immigration enforcement strategy for nation's border," published on AILA InfoNet at Doc. No. 06042160 (posted Apr. 21, 2006).

[52] Contractors who actually hired the laborers for work inside stores for the world's largest retailer agreed to plead guilty to criminal immigration charges and together pay an additional $4 million in fines.

[53] T. Reed, American Forfeiture Law: Property Owners Meet The Prosecutor, Cato Policy Analysis No. 179 (Sept. 29, 1992).

[54] Id.

[55] The $11 million civil settlement alone is approximately four times larger than any other single payment received by the government in an illegal alien employment case. C. Bartels, "Wal-Mart Escapes Criminal Charges in Case," ABC News Online, Money section (Mar. 18, 2005).

[56] Id. Federal officials said the fine money would go to the Treasury Forfeiture Fund and will be spent on "promoting future law enforcement programs and activities in this field by U.S. Immigration and Customs Enforcement."

[57] ICE News Release about terms of Wal-Mart settlement agreement.

[58] ICE Fact Sheet, Oct. 20, 2005.

A Proactive Approach to DOL Audits—Bingo Revisited

by Alan Tafapolsky, Neil S. Dornbaum, Peter T. Shiron, Jr., and Andrew L. Wizner[*]

PROLOGUE

There was once a time when multi-pronged governmental audits were rare. Today, however, a Department of Labor (DOL) audit is often accompanied by investigations by numerous other federal agencies, including the Department of Homeland Security's (DHS) U.S. Immigration and Customs Enforcement (ICE), the Federal Bureau of Investigation (FBI), and other sub-agencies of the Department of Labor's (DOL) Employment Standards Administration, such as the Office of Federal Contract Compliance. While this article is focused on the H-1B audit under DOL's Wage and Hour Administration, the impact of other agencies and their enforcement statutes should not be ignored, and in fact should be expected when the government comes knocking.

RICO,[1] in this context, is an important enforcement statute utilized by federal agencies, including ICE, to bring pressure to bear on unknowing employers. The epilogue of this article explores the RICO statute and its potential application to employers of foreign nationals in the United States. DOL audits should not longer be viewed in a vacuum. They must now be seen in a larger context where private actions can lead to powerful federal enforcement measures on employers.

INTRODUCTION

The corporate world knows that on any given day it is better to be proactive than reactive. While "be-

ing proactive," for some may appear to be an empty business mantra reserved for a game of "corporate bingo,"[2] for those companies subject to a DOL Wage and Hour Administrator (WHA) audit,[3] the words are a sacred philosophy. A proactive approach to DOL H-1B audits includes fastidious maintenance of Labor Condition Application (LCA) public access files;[4] a system of regularly scheduled self-audits;[5] the assemblage of a well-prepared audit team; an assessment of initial exposure and, if necessary, an effort at self-correction. Seizing the initiative before the WHA auditor's letter arrives is a "heads-up" approach to being prepared for an audit. It is, however, only the beginning.

Once the initial audit letter[6] is received by a company, a proactive approach to the DOL investigation includes anticipating the target of investigation and preparing answers to initial and follow-up questions for the first meeting. Timely and efficient production of documents required by the WHA investigator also will help the company create a positive impression at the beginning of the investigation.[7] During the investigation, a cooperative, controlled approach to providing information required to move the investigation along creates a positive synergy between the company and the investigator. Putting the investigator in a positive mindset about the investigation can

---

[*] **Alan Tafapolsky** is a partner in the San Francisco and Los Angeles-based business immigration law firm of Tafapolsky & Smith LLP.

Neil Dornbaum is a partner in the Newark firm of Dornbaum & Peregoy, which limits its practice to immigration law with special emphasis on employment-based immigration.

Peter Schiron, Jr. is an assistant general counsel with Deloitte & Touche USA LLP in New York City, where he provides strategic legal advice and counseling to the organization on a wide range of immigration and employment law matters, with a specific focus on business immigration and global employment issues.

Andrew Wizner is a partner in the Hartford, Conn. firm of Leete, Kosto & Wizner, which limits its practice to immigration law.

[1] Racketeer Influenced and Corrupt Organization (RICO) statute, 18 USC §§1961 *et seq.*

[2] Corporate Bingo is the game of bingo using "corporate speak" instead of numbers to fill out the grid. The game is attached to this article as a benefit for the reader.

[3] The Wage and Hour Administrator's authority to investigate and enforce the Labor Condition Application (LCA) provisions of the H-1B program are found at 20 CFR §655.800.

[4] The contents of the public access file are enumerated at 20 CFR §655.760.

[5] For an excellent treatment of utilization of self-audits as a means of being proactive, see A. Paparelli & J. Burkemper, "Skeletons in the Closet: LCA Audits in The Age of H-1B Uncertainty," 73 *Interpreter Releases* 745 (June 3, 1996) (hereinafter Paparelli & Burkemper).

[6] Sometimes referred to as the "29 Question Letter" because it usually contains 29 questions.

[7] Cooperation in the production of documents and records is mandated by the regulations at 20 CFR §655.800(c), but expeditious production of documents is more of a "proactive strategy."

be as important as the actual substantive compliance of the company on wage-hour issues. Finally, a company's employees, both U.S. workers and H-1B workers, should be educated[8] about the process of the investigation, including potential interviews conducted by an investigator.

Taking a proactive approach to LCA compliance for WHA audits, both before an investigation occurs, and after one begins, accomplishes two important overall goals. Being in substantial compliance before a complaint is filed affords a company the confidence to deal directly and efficiently with the WHA investigator after the investigation begins. Providing relevant information to the WHA investigator in a timely manner is a "win-win." It fast-tracks the audit process while allowing the WHA investigator to obtain the information necessary to fully resolve any complaint. Additionally, self-correcting areas of noncompliance during the investigative process shifts the burden of implementing "remedies"[9] from the WHA investigator to the company. Leveraging the audit process to self-remediate makes the auditor's job simpler and easier and, at the same time, demonstrates the commitment of the employer toward future compliance.[10]

WHY BE PROACTIVE?

The bottom line is that a WHA H-1B audit can result in serious damage to your company or the company you represent. The list of enforcement mechanisms is diverse in scope and impressive in magnitude. If you "run the numbers," they include the "super-penalty" of $35,000[11] for certain displacement violations; criminal penalties of up to $10,000 and/or

five years of imprisonment for misrepresentation of a material fact on a filed LCA;[12] civil money penalties from $1,000 up to $5,000 per count;[13] debarment from the H-1B nonimmigrant program for a period of from one to three years;[14] the assessment of back wages;[15] and injunctions and other civil remedies as the WHA determines to be appropriate.[16] Legal penalties are not the end of the havoc a WHA investigation can wreak. Investigations can last from two months to several years, and their impact can seriously impede business operations and injure workplace morale. The length and extent of the investigation also can hit a company's legal budget with expenditures running into the tens of thousands of dollars in legal costs. Finally, if the press or the media get wind of the allegations alleged in the WHA investigation, regardless of the company's culpability, it creates a "lose-lose" scenario.

WHO IS VULNERABLE?

These days, almost all WHA investigations are complaint-driven.[17] Complaints can be made by either "aggrieved parties" or "non-aggrieved" parties who possess facts of sufficient detail to allow the Secretary of Labor to make a determination that there is "reasonable cause" of the violations of regulations found at 20 CFR §655.805. Any company that hires H-1B workers is therefore vulnerable. The H-1B companies most susceptible to a complaint are those who have had recent lay-offs, are under investigation of other agencies of the federal government related to employment conditions, or are being sued by individuals or a class of company employees. Most companies either fit this profile at present, or will sometime in the future.

PUBLIC ACCESS FILES AND SELF-AUDITS

Most companies believe that if their public access files are complete, and the company is paying

---

[8] The company and counsel should be careful to educate employees about the process of a WHA investigation but not to "coach" employees about the substance of their answers. Coaching potential interviewees will, without question, create antagonism between the WHA investigator and the company. Additionally, an employer should be extremely careful not to give the WHA investigator reason to believe that it is trying to retaliate against complainants or coerce employees in violation of 20 CFR §655.801.

[9] As set forth at 20 CFR §655.810.

[10] An employer's commitment to future compliance is a factor to be considered in determining the amount of civil money penalties to be assessed against an employer. 20 CFR §655.810(c)(6).

[11] As set forth in 20 CFR §655.810(b)(3) for displacement of a U.S. worker 90 days before or after the filing of an H-1 petition and a violation of 20 CFR §§655.805(a)(2)–(9).

[12] 20 CFR §655.805(a)(1); 18 USC 1001; see also 18 USC §1546.

[13] 20 CFR §655.810(b).

[14] 20 CFR §655.810(d).

[15] 20 CFR §655.810(a).

[16] 20 CFR §655.810(f).

[17] Unlike the mid-1990s, when many random audits were conducted, most WHA investigations occur as a result of a complaint of an aggrieved party (20 CFR §655.715), and process (20 CFR §655.806). There are also investigations of complaints of non-aggrieved parties.

the wage stated on the LCA, they need not fear an audit. Nothing could be further from the truth. Compliance with the paperwork and record-keeping provisions of the regulations found at 20 CFR §655.760 is a required element of a WHA audit, but it is not by any means the entire scope of the investigation. In order to be completely prepared for a WHA investigation, a self-audit should accompany a review and remediation of public access files. It is worth revisiting an article entitled "Skeletons in the Closet," authored by Angelo Paparelli and Ira Burkemper in 1996, to fully appreciate the benefits of a self-audit.[18] Self-audits that mirror the process of a real WHA audit allow a company to assess its complete legal exposure. Additionally, by stepping on the base of true liability, a game plan for remediation[19] can be leveraged long before DOL has set foot in the door. Paparelli and Burkemper suggest that self-audits be performed with the assistance of an objective observer such as outside immigration counsel or a professional consulting organization.[20] The authors agree with that advice from the simple perspective that is important advice, for it is more difficult to detect one's own imperfections than it is to identify the weaknesses of others. Paparelli and Burkemper use the term "voluntary audit" rather than "self-audit" to emphasize the importance of bringing a neutral third-party professional into the process as a strategic fit. Using an outside auditor to pull wage-hour skeletons out of the closet—and help bury them—can help a company prepare completely for a real WHA audit. A total quality self-audit, therefore, employs an impartial, independent professional to prepare for the real thing.

CREATE THE TEAM

The outsourced auditing professional should be matched with in-house immigration specialists, human resource managers, payroll and benefits specialists, and in-house legal personnel to create the perfect audit team. Many companies also retain outside employment counsel to preemptively resolve WHA issues that do not involve H-1B immigrants.[21] Finally, a criminal lawyer should be consulted if the company has been "out of the loop" in its compliance with wage-hour law.

GAP ANALYSIS

Any confident player of corporate bingo knows that "gap analysis"[22] is an euphemism for comparing company performance against an ideal standard, and then assessing the "gaps" or "shortcomings." Self-audits are the perfect opportunity for gap analysis. The company simply goes down a list of real-world, wage-hour compliance standards and matches the company's performance against those standards. An abbreviated list of items follows:

- Are H-1B workers paid what similarly situated U.S. workers are paid? Are H-1B workers earning the prevailing wage?[23]

- Are H-1Bs in same job occupation doing something other than U.S. workers are in the same position?

- Prevailing wages: are surveys valid?[24] Explain why different surveys might be used for different positions. Does the prevailing wage match what is put on the LCA?

- Are H-1B workers provided a copy of their LCA?[25] When?

---

[18] Paparelli & Burkemper, *supra* note 5.

[19] While taking steps to cure LCA and wage-hour defects does not technically cure violations, WHA, as a matter of practice, has considered a company to be in substantial compliance and not assessed civil penalties for past deficiencies. *See* Paparelli & Burkemper, *supra* note 5, at 746 n.4, 748–49 & nn.19–24 (quoting DOL officials on the subject of self-remediation). Complete remediation in certain circumstances may include back pay to H-1B workers if they have not been paid the appropriate compensation under the regulations.

[20] *Id.* at 750. Professional immigration consultants who are also legal professionals can impartially assist in conducting the audit. Salmon Consulting is one of the companies that supplies audit consultation by practicing lawyers in the San Francisco Bay Area. Salmon Consulting, 1430 Francisco Street, Suite 4, San Francisco, CA 94123.

---

[21] This can include, inter alia, the payment of overtime wages when required, minimum-wage compliance, and the employment of minors. Outside employment counsel also is important in providing advice on how to maintain H-1B compliance but not run afoul of state and federal discrimination laws.

[22] Gap analysis has morphed from its initial applications in biological science and engineering to the more general definition provided above.

[23] 20 CFR §§655.731(a)(1) and (2).

[24] Does the survey meet the independent authoritative source standard set forth in 20 CFR §655.731(b)(3)(iii)(C)?

[25] 20 CFR §655.734(a)(3).

- Postings? How many? Where posted? Is there a collective bargaining agreement in place? If so, are union notifications effected?[26]

- Are all of the contents of the public access file prepared and identifiable for each employee: signed and certified LCA, documentation of wage rate, actual wage memo, prevailing wage, evidence of postings/notice, summary of benefits, sworn statement for employers utilizing Sec. 401, lists of exempt employees, and evidence of recruitment of U.S. workers for dependent companies?[27]

- Are documents retained for the appropriate period?[28]

- Has there been any parking or benching of H-1B employees?[29]

- Are business expenses for H-1B employees paid by employer?[30]

- How are H-1B employees paid when they are away from the LCA-listed worksite (per diem versus actual expenses)?[31]

- Are H-1Bs placed at secondary sites?[32]

- What deductions are made from paychecks other than statutory deductions?[33]

- Are the fringe benefits that H-1B employees receive the same as those of other employees?[34]

- What is the pay period?[35]

- Is there a penalty/liquidated damages provision when an H-1B terminates before the end of his or her contract?[36]

- If dependent, is company complying with recruitment and nondisplacement provisions?[37]

- Are LCAs overloaded?[38]

- Are H-1Bs/LCAs withdrawn?[39]

The above list of regulatory compliance issues requires the production and preparation of certain records in order to complete the self-audit process. Those should include:

- Preparation of public access files;

- Preparation of payroll records;

- Preparation of list of similarly situated workers;

- Preparation of employee count and H-1B count;

- H-1B materials: I-129 petitions and letters of support;

- Preparation of benefits materials; and

- Location listing of H-1B employees.

Using these materials and focusing on the above-listed regulatory compliance issues, it is suggested that the audit take place from one week to one month from the time the decision to conduct the self-audit takes place. This period mirrors the amount of time the company will have to react and prepare for a real WHA audit. Best practices require that company compliance is benchmarked against perfect compliance to fully assess legal exposure.

MY COMPANY DOESN'T HAVE THE BANDWIDTH

If your company cannot conduct an audit on each of the issues listed above because it lacks the resources, then "think outside the box"—a different game plan is required. The bottom line is that if the WHA investigator decides to play hardball and implement enforcement measures against a company, he or she will focus on the following big five:

- Pay issues: Are H-1B workers being paid prevailing wage or what similarly situated U.S. workers are being paid, whichever is higher?

- Are H-1B employees and U.S. workers being similarly treated?

- LCA specificity—are areas of employment, start dates, and job titles accurate?

- Are there displacement issues?

---

[26] 20 CFR §§655.734(a)(1)(i) and (ii).

[27] Detailed requirements found in 20 CFR §§655.760(a)(1)–(10).

[28] 20 CFR §655.760(c).

[29] 20 CFR §655.731(c)(7)(i).

[30] 20 CFR §655.731(c)(9)(iii)(C).

[31] 20 CFR §655.735(b)(3).

[32] 20 CFR §655.735.

[33] 20 CFR §655.731(c)(9). For an excellent detailed treatment on the question of authorized versus nonauthorized deductions, see J. Evans, "The Authorized Deductions Toolbox," *Immigration Briefings* 02-07 (July 2002).

[34] *See* 20 CFR §§655.731 and 655.732, and enforcement remedies under 20 CFR §655.810(a).

[35] 20 CFR §655.731(c)(4).

[36] 20 CFR §655.731(c)(10).

[37] 20 CFR §655.738.

[38] A term the WHA investigators use when the list of people on Blanket LCAs exceeds the number of positions certified.

[39] 20 CFR §655.731(c)(7)(ii).

- Are public access files being kept in substantial compliance?

A limited self-audit would benchmark the above areas of compliance and provide a reasonable measure of the company's overall liability should a real WHA audit occur.

WHAT NEXT—REMEDIATION (THE MR. ROGERS APPROACH)

A proactive approach to WHA audits does not stop when areas of noncompliance are revealed. The areas of noncompliance should be remediated. But how? There are no regulations on correcting areas of noncompliance. The authors suggest the "Mr. Rogers approach"—"make believe."[40] Mr. Rogers has a land of "make believe" where children watch the behavior of puppets and people, and morality lessons are learned. Though the land of "make believe" is not the real world, the authors suggest that the company go there, and make believe it is setting up a perfect wage-and-hour world. If public access files are missing postings, they should be reposted at the appropriate place, for the appropriate time. If an H-1B worker is not being paid the "required wage,"[41] back wages should be paid until the H-1B wages are "on line." If an H-1B worker is not working at a geographic location covered by an existing LCA, a new LCA and H-1B petition should be filed, and back wages, if appropriate, should be assessed. Though an initial act of noncompliance cannot be cured, remediating the defect once it is discovered is the appropriate action to take.[42] The alternative, "the hide your head in the sand" approach, is a recipe for disaster. In Mr. Rogers' terms, "Can you say 'willful violator'"?[43]

THE REAL THING— PROCESS OF A WHA AUDIT

Assuming you have completed a self-audit on your company and taken appropriate corrective actions, you are empowered. You have knowledge of the company's weaknesses and strengths in the realm of wage-hour compliance. Do you just sit on that knowledge? No. A proactive approach would take this knowledge and communicate it to the wage-hour investigator so that the parties are on the "same page." Communication, whether it is with your spouse, child, political representative, or wage-hour investigator, is the grease on the wheel of life. Does this mean a company should communicate every piece of information it knows about its wage-hour compliance at or before an initial meeting? Not necessarily. The timing and flow of the communication to the wage hour investigator also is important. The process of a WHA audit occurs in three stages, of which there are many sub-stages. They are:

- the initial meeting;
- the investigation; and
- the final meeting.

The Initial Meeting

As soon as an audit letter is received, you should contact the WHA investigator to create a mutually convenient time to schedule the initial meeting. As suggested above, the meeting should be set with enough time to allow the company to prepare adequate answers to the audit letter and to prepare records for DOL inspection. If a self-audit has not been performed recently, it suggested that a "quick and dirty" one be conducted to assess the company's weaknesses and strengths. The meeting should not, however, be postponed for so long as to frustrate the WHA investigator's need to inspect the current condition of the company. A range of between one week and three weeks[44] may be reasonable, depending on the size of the company and the extent of the audit.

During this first contact, a protocol for communication should be implemented. If the company is being represented by outside immigration counsel, all communication and documentation should be channeled through counsel. This allows the company and counsel to keep a check on the flow of documentation and information that go to the WHA investigator. Using one spokesperson and one conduit of information will militate against duplicated requests for information. It also allows the company to maintain an accurate and ongoing working file for the audit.

---

[40] Mr. Rogers, a/k/a Fred Rogers, is a children's television icon and his land of make-believe was one of the author's favorite getaways.

[41] 20 CFR §655.715.

[42] The corrective measures taken may not exculpate the company but will certainly minimize its overall exposure in civil penalties. *See* 20 CFR §655.810(c)(4) ("efforts made by the employer to comply" can lower the amount of penalty assessed.)

[43] 20 CFR §655.736(f).

---

[44] A company should note, however, that pursuant to 20 CFR §655.760, public access files must be made available to the public, including the WHA investigator, within one working day from the date of filing the labor condition application.

The initial meeting is usually tense, as the WHA investigator takes oral testimony from the company's audit team, or team spokesperson, in response to the audit letter. The WHA investigator usually prepares a written statement to be signed by the company, to document responses. A dramatic moment usually occurs when the investigator asks the company to sign the written statement after testimony. A company may, on the advice of counsel, choose to sign a statement with the caveat "to the best of my knowledge the answers are true and accurate." Or it may choose not to sign any written statement but to orally maintain the veracity of the statement. The signing of the statement creates a possible piece of evidence against the company in the event that material misrepresentations[45] have been made. On the other hand, the signing of the statement may set a positive tone and tenor to the investigation. Some WHA investigators make the decision to sign the initial statement a prerequisite to the company having a copy of the initial statement. A proactive approach to the audit usually favors the signing of the initial statement as long as it accompanied by a "to the best of our knowledge" prefix.

The Investigation

The WHA investigator must gather necessary information to conduct a complete and thorough audit. This includes the inspection of evidence such as labor condition public access files, payroll and benefits records, immigration files, and other evidence pertinent to the investigation. Once this information has been provided, the onus is on the WHA investigator to transcribe information relevant to the case. To the extent that information can be provided to the investigator in an organized and coherent fashion, the investigator's job is facilitated and expedited. For example, a company can choose to provide payroll and similarly situated U.S. worker information in the form of computer records or spreadsheets.[46] This will allow the investigator to easily and quickly manipulate and peruse the data. Providing information in an ordered fashion is one way of taking a proactive approach to the investigation.

A WHA investigator usually conducts interviews of both H-1B workers as well as U.S. workers during the course of the investigation. It is natural for most employees to be scared of an investigator; hence, many employees will attempt to avoid the interviews altogether. A proactive approach requires educating company employees about the general purpose of the audit and the reason interviews are conducted. The company also should arrange interviews for the investigator so that the process can be completed in a manner that is least disruptive to business operations. The company must keep in mind, however, that an employee should not be coached on what to say to an investigator. While the WHA investigator will prefer that interviews with employees be conducted in private, it is normal for counsel to be present in the interviews of managers or executives of the company.

Being proactive during the course of the investigation creates a cooperative synergy between company and investigator and keeps the "big mo"[47] rolling. Retaining that momentum into the final meeting should be the goal for any proactive company.

Report Card—The Final Meeting

During the course of the investigation, the company or the investigator may uncover areas of noncompliance. Self-remediation with the guidance of the WHA investigator is the proactive approach. If the company's compliance is improved during the course of the audit, a WHA investigator is less likely, in the final meeting, to assess high civil money penalties[48] and may only order those remedies that will make employees whole.[49]

The final meeting is the last chance for the company to show interest in wage-hour compliance. The company is usually given a chance to assess its past performance in abiding by wage-hour regulations. The company, if it has had weaknesses, should acknowledge them, and accept reasonable penalties. A company should proactively seek out the advice of the WHA investigator as to how it can maintain wage-hour compliance moving into the future. WHA investigators may provide practical guidance as to how to comply with changing enforcement priorities of DOL. The investigators may also provide valuable insight as to what rules, policies, and procedures may be changing in the near future.

The final meeting ends with a written assessment of the company's compliance with WHA regula-

---

[45] 20 CFR §655.805.

[46] Excel, Lotus, and Quattro Pro are examples of spreadsheets that can provide information to the WHA investigator in an easy-to-use format.

[47] Corporate speak for "momentum."

[48] Under 20 CFR §655.810(b).

[49] Under 20 CFR §655.810(a).

tions. The company is often given a chance to explain or dispute areas of noncompliance at this time. If the company's arguments have merit, the WHA investigator may choose not to assess formal remedies.[50] Being ready to present the company's sophisticated legal argument in a nonconfrontational manner is part of being proactive. In areas where the company's noncompliance is indisputable, being contrite and promising immediate self-remedies is the proactive approach to avoiding a formal order. Whatever the result, having the company seize the initiative in demonstrating its commitment to wage-hour compliance is the recommended strategy.

BINGO

In our "real-time" world, a company must multitask certain action items to be proactively prepared for a WHA audit. A results-driven campaign for a successful audit includes careful maintenance of LCA public access files and the conduct of periodic self-audits followed by efforts at self-remediation. When faced with an actual audit, the company should work proactively with the WHA investigator to help complete the investigation and, at the same time, bring the company into complete wage-hour compliance. At the end of the day, if you prepare well for an audit, and then manage the expectations of the WHA investigator, your audit will . . . "BINGO" . . . be over before you know it.

EPILOGUE

Employers potentially face liability based on emerging theories of law brought by the government as well as private citizens vested with a private right of action. While DOL audits are one type of investigation, they often either trigger or accompany a cacophony of federal inquiries into a specific employer of foreign nationals. Nowhere is the concurrent investigation by various federal agencies into an employer's hiring of foreign nationals as stark or as infamous as the Wal-Mart case.

Government Enforcement of
I-9 Regulations and Independent Contractors

In an unprecedented settlement, Wal-Mart entered into a consent decree on March 18, 2005, with ICE that required the company to pay $11 million in civil penalties for engaging independent contractors who pro-

vided illegal workers[51] for janitorial services at Wal-Mart stores. ICE conducted a nationwide investigation that resulted in allegations of employment of illegal workers by these cleaning companies. ICE agents raided 612 Wal-Mart stores in more than 21 states and discovered more than 250 undocumented workers.[52]

The Wal-Mart investigation sends a strong message to employers that the government will seek to hold them liable for employment of undocumented workers even when the employer retains an independent contractor. Employers should be aware of whom their contractors bring to the worksite. Contractors should be required to furnish the employer with I-9 forms for the employer to audit. In fact, the Wal-Mart consent decree requires the company to establish a means to verify that independent contractors also are taking reasonable steps to comply with the employment verification requirements.

RICO Claims

Some individuals who claim economic and other damages resulting from violations of the Immigration and Naturalization Act (INA)[53] have begun to act in the role of private attorneys general. In a series of recent cases, they have invoked the Racketeer Influenced and Corrupt Organizations Act (RICO), which Congress amended in 1996 to allow claims based on violations of the INA.

RICO provides for a private right of action when taken by a "person injured in his business or property by reason of a violation of section 1962 of [Title 18]."[54] The law states that it is "illegal for any person employed by or associated with any enterprise engaged in, or the activities of which affect, interstate or foreign commerce, to conduct or participate, directly or indirectly, in the conduct of such enterprise's affairs through a pattern of racketeering activity"[55] The 1996 amendments to RICO expanded the definition of "racketeering activity" to include "any act which is indictable under the Immigration and Nationality Act, §274 (relating to bringing in and harboring certain aliens), §277 (relating to aiding or assisting certain aliens to enter the United

---

[50] Pursuant to the requirements of 20 CFR §655.815.

[51] 82 *Interpreter Releases* 491.

[52] 80 *Interpreter Releases* 1691.

[53] Immigration and Nationality Act of 1952, Pub. L. No. 82-414, 66 Stat. 163 (*codified as amended at* 8 USC §§1101 *et seq.*) (INA).

[54] 18 USC §1964(c).

[55] 18 USC §1962(c).

States), or §278 (relating to importation of aliens for immoral purpose) if the act indictable under such section of the INA was committed for the purpose of financial gain"[56] A plaintiff must "satisfy four elements of proof: (1) conduct (2) of an enterprise (3) through a pattern (4) of racketeering activity."[57]

The claims advanced in these cases generally rely on theories of economic harm to current or former employees or commercial competitors of companies that employ illegal workers. Generally, these claims are based on the premise that employers have kept labor costs low by unlawfully expanding the labor force through predicate violations of the INA.[58]

For example, in the first reported decision, a cleaning service brought suit against its competitor alleging that the hiring of undocumented aliens placed it at a competitive disadvantage.[59] On appeal of a dismissal pursuant to Federal Rule of Civil Procedure 12(b)(6), the Second Circuit held that the plaintiffs properly stated a claim involving a direct proximate relationship between its injury and its competitor's RICO violations by alleging that the defendant's knowing hiring of hundreds of illegal immigrants at low wages allowed it to underbid the plaintiff for lucrative contracts in the highly competitive and price-sensitive cleaning services industry.[60] The Sixth Circuit made a similar ruling in a case brought by former employees at a poultry processing plant who sued their former employer and plant owner alleging that use of illegal aliens depressed their wages.[61] Similarly, the Ninth Circuit dismissed a 12(b)(6) motion in the case of employees of two fruit orchard and packing companies who alleged their employers underpaid them by conspiring to hire undocumented workers at below-market wages.[62]

Aside from the challenge of marshalling proof regarding the proximate causation issue, plaintiffs in these cases faced other obstacles. At least two courts have questioned whether plaintiffs have properly identified the "enterprise" responsible for their injuries. RICO requires plaintiffs to establish "conduct of an enterprise," that the enterprise had a common goal, and that the defendant participated in or managed the enterprise itself.[63] The Seventh Circuit affirmed the dismissal of a RICO action brought by employees of an Illinois meat processing facility against their employer, in part, due to their defective allegation that the offending enterprise consisted of the employer, a group of recruiters who located undocumented aliens, and immigrant-welfare organizations that referred known illegal workers to the employer.[64] The court reasoned that this alleged "association in fact"[65] did not have a common purpose because each member had differing objectives: the employer sought to pay less to its employees, the recruiters wanted to increase their commissions, and the immigrant-welfare organizations simply desired to assist their members.[66]

Finally, the Supreme Court granted certiorari in a case where the sole question before the Court was whether the defendant corporation and its agents can constitute an "enterprise" under RICO in light of the settled rule that a RICO defendant must "conduct" or "participate in" the affairs of some larger enterprise and not just its own affairs.[67] In that case, current and former employees of a carpet and rug manufacturer alleged that their employer depressed their wages by knowingly employing hundreds of undocumented workers through an enterprise consisting of the employer and third-party temporary agencies and recruiters. The case was argued before the Supreme Court on April 26, 2006.

It remains to be seen whether plaintiffs in these cases will ever collect the treble damages permitted by RICO. At this stage, it appears that these plaintiffs have survived motions to dismiss but have not had their day in court to prove their allegations. Nonetheless, employers should be aware that there is a movement afoot by individuals who seek to stand in the government's place to claim injuries resulting from the employment of illegal aliens.

---

[56] 18 USC §1961(1)(F).

[57] *Williams v. Mohawk Industries*, 411 F.3d 1252, 1256 (11th Cir. 2005), *cert granted*.

[58] *Id.* at 1261.

[59] *Commercial Cleaning Serv. v. Colin*, 271 F.3d 374 (2d Cir. 2001).

[60] *Id.* at 379.

[61] *Trollinger v. Tyson Foods, Inc.*, 370 F.3d 370 (6th Cir. 2004).

[62] *Mendoza v. Zirkle Fruit Co.*, 301 F.3d 1163 (9th Cir. 2002).

[63] *Mohawk Industries, Inc. v. Williams*, 411 F.3d 1252, 1257 (11th Cir. 2005).

[64] *Baker v. IBP, Inc.*, 357 F.3d 685 (7th Cir. 2004).

[65] RICO defines enterprise to include a "group of individuals associated in fact although not a legal entity." 18 USC §1961(4).

[66] *Baker*, 357 F.3d at 691.

[67] *Mohawk Industries, Inc.*, 411 F.3d 1252.

Corporate Bingo

Do you keep falling asleep in meetings and seminars? What about those
long and boring conference calls? Here is a way to change all of that!

Synergy	Strategic Fit	Gap Analysis	Best Practice	Bottom Line
Revisit	Bandwidth	Hardball	Out of the Loop	Benchmark
Value-Added	Proactive	Win-Win	Think Outside the Box	Fast Track
Result-Driven	Empower [or] Empowerment	Knowledge	Base	Total Quality [or] Quality Driven Touch Base
Mindset	Client Focus[ed]	Ball Park	Game Plan	Leverage

SECURITY CLEARANCES AND TECHNOLOGY LICENSES

*by Mark J. Newman and Michael H. Gladstone**

As practicing immigration attorneys, we have seen the increasing difficulties faced by foreign nationals in obtaining visas to work for companies engaged in sensitive technologies. Since 9/11, the U.S. government has increased its focus on security issues, including the issuance of visas and in the admission of such individuals. We also have learned to advise clients, well in advance, of the requirements for obtaining security clearances and the potential significant delays at consulates in obtaining such clearances. Terms such as Visas Donkey and Visas Mantis have become part of our daily vocabulary.

This article deals with the procedures for obtaining security clearances and the related and potentially more significant issues of obtaining required licenses from the Department of Commerce (DOC) and the Department of State (DOS). The goals behind these laws is simple—to prevent the export of controlled and classified technology or items to unapproved foreign countries or foreign nationals. In actual practice—how, when, and where these regulations are triggered—are much less clear. This article provides the practitioner with a workable approach to dealing with the acquisition of these licenses.

* **Mark Newman** heads the immigration law group at Troutman Sanders in Atlanta. He served as chair of the Atlanta District Director's Liaison Committee of AILA. He co-chaired the ABA/Prentice Hall Seminar on the 1990 Immigration Act in Atlanta. Mr. Newman has spoken to audiences abroad about U.S. immigration and co-authored Immigration Law and Practice in Florida. He also has keynoted the October 2003 AILA Law Conference in Washington, D.C., and co-authored a recently published article in *Ethics in a Brave New World*. Mr. Newman received his undergraduate degree in 1976 from Princeton University and his law degree in 1979 from the University of Miami School of Law.

Michael Gladstone, a partner at Troutman Sanders LLP in Richmond, practices immigration law, product liability, and civil litigation matters. Admitted to the Virginia Bar, Mr. Gladstone received a J.D. from the University of Richmond and a B.S. from University of Virginia. He is a member of AILA; Richmond and Virginia bar Associations; Virginia Association of Defense Attorneys; Defense Research Institute; Virginia Trial Lawyers Association; and International Association of Defense Attorneys.

LEGAL SOURCES OF TECHNOLOGY PROTECTION AND SECURITY IN THE UNITED STATES

Two independent sets of regulations primarily control the export of sensitive technology to other countries, or their nationals: the Export Administration Regulations (EAR) 15 CFR Parts 730–772 and the International Traffic in Arms Regulations (ITAR), 22 CFR Parts 120–130. These regulations are administered by DOC and DOS, respectively.

The general goal of both regulatory schemes is to prevent "export" of controlled and classified technology or items to unapproved foreign countries or foreign nationals.[1] The export of technology includes "release" to a foreign national, broadly defined to include mere availability of the technology for visual inspection by the foreign national or oral disclosure to him or her.[2]

Under EAR, any release in a foreign country of technology or software subject to EAR, or any release of technology or source code subject to EAR to a foreign national, generally constitutes an export.[3] The release of technology or software is defined as "[v]isual inspection by foreign nationals of U.S.-origin equipment and facilities . . . Oral exchanges of information in the United States or abroad . . . The application to situations abroad of personal knowledge or technical experience acquired in the United States."[4]

Relative to foreign persons, "export" under ITAR is defined as "[d]isclosing (including oral or visual disclosure) or transferring technical data to a foreign person, whether in the United States or abroad; or . . . Disclosing (including oral or visual disclosure) or transferring technical data to a foreign person, whether in the United States or abroad."[5] Given the breadth of what can constitute an export by release, the implications for a company that operates numerous divisions or subsidiaries, some of which

---

[1] 15 CFR §§734.2(b)(2)(ii) and 736.1, 2; 22 CFR §120.

[2] 15 CFR §734.2(b)(2) and (3); 22 CFR §120.17(4).

[3] 15 CFR §734.2(b)(2).

[4] 15 CFR §734.2(b)(3)(i–iii).

[5] 22 CFR §120.17a (4–5).

may involve implicated technology and some of which do not, are clear. A company should address issues concerning internal physical, interdivision, inter-subsidiary, and computer system security, and should implement a compliance plan to address the risk of a foreign national in an uncontrolled area of the business coming into contact with a controlled part of the business and its data and equipment, or having discussions with other employees over controlled technology or articles. If it does not do so, the company may be deemed at substantial risk for allowing a "release" to a foreign national even though the foreign national does not work directly on controlled articles or technology.

The article will discuss the immigration implications of this possible "export," including the risk of being denied permission to hire a foreign national, and a delay or refusal of a visa for the foreign national. But apart from the immigration implications, if a company adopts a compliance program that adheres to U.S. law and international conventions applicable to the company's business, including export regulations, and that applies those requirements to the operations of the business at all pertinent levels, it will be dramatically better positioned to make strategic planning decisions with confidence, avoid disruption of its business, and make disclosures and credibly respond to government inquiries, than a business without such a plan.

In addition to EAR and ITAR, there are additional regulations and statutes that authorize other departments of the U.S. government to exercise control over much broader issues, but that also include control over trade involving protected or restricted articles and technologies. These are typically implicated in immigration situations when the visa candidate is from a country under embargo or sanctions, or involves a specifically prohibited technology or article. Examples of such regulations are those enforced by the Treasury Department's Office of Foreign Asset Control at 31 CFR Part 500, and regulations promulgated pursuant to the President's authority under the International Emergency Economic Powers Act (IEEPA), 50 USC §§1701 *et seq.*, or relative to embargoes imposed before 1977 under the Trading with the Enemy Act, 50 USC app. §§1–44. Additional agencies exercising authority over specific kinds of exports are listed in supplement 3 to 15 CFR Part 730, and include the Drug Enforcement Administration (DEA), the Food and Drug Administration (FDA), the Department of Interior (DOI), the Department of Energy (DOE), and the Nuclear Regulatory Commission (NRC). DEA regulates certain chemicals and drug precursors.

Scope of EAR and ITAR

The scope of the articles and technologies covered by the two schemes is defined in EAR by the Commercial Control List and Commerce Country Chart, 15 CFR Parts 774 and 738, and in ITAR by U.S. Munitions List (USML), at 22 CFR Part 121. Technology in the public domain, or which is publicly available, is not covered by USML or EAR.[6] Broadly speaking, EAR is concerned with "dual-use" technologies (those having both civilian and military applications), while ITAR focuses on dedicated military articles and technology. Generally speaking, characteristics of EAR make it less rigid than ITAR, but an analysis of the coverage, control, and licensing requirements ought to be performed for every nonimmigrant (NIV) foreign national whose job requirements present the potential of a deemed export of controlled technology. A detailed step-by-step procedure for evaluating a given technology or item under EAR is provided at 15 CFR Part 732. The Office of Defense Trade Control (ODTC) retains the authority to determine USML coverage of an article or technology, and ITAR provide no use instructions in so far as determining USML coverage. USML is, however, much shorter, less complex, and easier to survey for potential coverage than EAR.

It is possible to obtain an advisory opinion concerning the applicability of EAR to specific technology and whether a license is required.[7] Such advisory opinions are not binding on DOC.[8] Under ITAR, an advisory opinion regarding technology coverage and the likelihood of a grant of a Foreign National Employment License (FNEL) or Technology Assistance Agreement (TAA) is also obtainable, but it also is noted that "[t]hese opinions are not binding on the Department of State and are revocable."[9]

Classification of Articles/Technology Under ITAR

ODTC determines whether a given article or service is covered by USML, and thus, whether a license is required for export of the article or service

---

[6] 15 CFR §734; 22 CFR §120.10, 11.

[7] 15 CFR §734.6.

[8] 15 CFR §748.3.

[9] 22 CFR §126.9.

to a foreign country or foreign national.[10] A person need not be registered with ODTC to obtain classification of a specific article or service. If the article or service is deemed to be covered by USML, the exporter, manufacturer, or furnisher of services must register with ODTC.[11] Registration must occur before ODTC will consider an application for a TAA involving a foreign national or an FNEL. Appeal of the decision of ODTC is available within the Office of the Center for Defense Trade.[12] Disputes over governmental jurisdiction over an article or service are resolved among DOS, Department of Defense (DOD), and DOC according to "established procedures."[13] USML is extensive and captures virtually any technology that has been productively applied to a lethal or defensive military purpose.

Classification of Articles or Technology Under EAR

Classification of goods as to their coverage or control under EAR is not exclusively relegated to DOC in the same manner that determination of coverage by USML is to DOS. A private business is encouraged, therefore, to determine for itself whether or not its product or technology is subject to or controlled by EAR, such that an export license is required for lawful export of the product or technology.[14] Companies making such a determination are, however, responsible for any mistake or misclassification they might make. Even if a license is not required, controlled items are still subject to the applicable export clearance procedures and record-keeping requirements contained in 15 CFR Parts 758 and 762, respectively.

EAR provide detailed instructions for evaluating whether a given article or technology is subject to and controlled by the scheme.[15] The analysis path for a given article or technology is complex. Supplement No. 2 to 15 CFR Part 732 provides an eight-step analysis to determine whether a given article or technology is subject to EAR. Every step is guided by extensive regulatory provisions. Once it is determined that an article or technology is subject to EAR, one must next determine whether the article or

technology is controlled or "classified" by EAR—Supplement No. 1 to 15 CFR Part 732 provides a decision tree for evaluating whether an article or technology is controlled, requires a license for a given country, and is covered by license exceptions. At each step of the way, extensive and complex regulations govern the analysis.

A short enumeration of a few possible outcomes under this scheme provides a glimpse into the complexity of the analysis. For example, articles and or technology may be subject to EAR, but not controlled, thus requiring no export license unless there is an embargo on the destination or end user, or some other prohibited aspect of the transaction is prohibited.

Technology or an article may be controlled but subject to a license exception, obviating the need for an export license. An article or technology subject to and controlled by EAR may require a license for export to every country or only to some (or may be totally prohibited). Certain articles and technologies are much more sensitive and trigger increased license scrutiny, such as items and technology linked to nuclear uses, missiles, and encryption technology. The same is true for destination countries, where traditional allies of the United States in Western Europe (and modern U.S. allies) suffer fewer relative restrictions across all technology categories and sub-groups than do others. End uses, and users, also play an important part in the analysis, as does the question of whether articles, technology, or services pertaining to, for example, wholly foreign origin items involve a "proliferation activity."

EAR also contain the requirements of the Chemical Weapons Convention at 15 CFR Part 745. This portion of EAR is an additional sub-scheme that must be followed by exporters of chemicals covered by the convention, as listed in 15 CFR Part 745, Supplement No. 1. Advance notification of export and end-use certificate reporting are required by the convention. Thus, covered items have an additional layer of regulatory scrutiny.

Permission for Foreign Nationals to Receive Controlled Technology or Articles

Both EAR and ITAR focus on technology released to "foreign nationals" as defined by the INA anti-discrimination statute.[16] The practical effect is that a company cannot lawfully employ a covered

---

[10] 22 CFR §120.4.

[11] *Id.*

[12] 22 CFR §120.4(g).

[13] 22 CFR §120.4(f).

[14] 15 CFR §730.8.

[15] 15 CFR Part 732 and supplements 1 and 2 to Part 732.

[16] INA §274B(a)(3); 15 CFR §734.2; 22 CFR §120.16.

person in a position where the release of controlled technology is intended, or likely, without prior receipt of the export license/FNEL/TAA relative to the employment. This definition means generally that NIV holders are subject to the licensing requirements of EAR and ITAR. Release of such technology to a foreign national in the United States is referred to as a "deemed export."[17]

Neither an export license nor an FNEL/TAA is required, however, for release of controlled but unclassified technology where the employee is a lawful permanent resident (LPR) of the United States or a "protected person" under the anti-discrimination provisions of the INA, *e.g.*, LPRs, refugees, or asylees.[18] Such persons are expressly excluded from coverage under both schemes. Citizenship discrimination may occur, however, where authorized by statute or government contract. LPRs may, therefore, be treated as foreign nationals where classified technology is involved.[19] Separate ITAR rules apply to classified articles and technology.[20]

Release or "deemed export" of controlled items or technologies to NIV holders is permitted where an export license is granted by the Bureau of Industry and Security (BIS) for the EAR-covered technology and items, or a TAA or FNEL is issued by the Directorate of Defense Trade Controls (an office of DOS), relative to technology or items covered by ITAR.[21] The process of granting or refusing an export license or TAA/FNEL is a distinctly separate activity from visa adjudication. Severe civil and criminal penalties apply to violations.[22]

The lead time reported by DOC and DOS for export license or FNEL/TAA action is 90 days or more for BIS and 60 days or more for DOS.[23]

Both regulatory schemes require information regarding the immigration status of the foreign national employee under consideration in order to consider the application or request for an export license or FNEL/TAA and to link the period of the employment approval, if granted, to the duration of the foreign national's immigration status. Neither scheme seems to contemplate the prospect that a prospective foreign national employee may not yet have received a visa.[24] Others have recommended, however, "prophylactic" application for the export license or FNEL/TAA for presentation with the visa application.[25]

Technology Protection and Immigration

Notwithstanding U.S. Citizenship and Immigration Services's (USCIS) approval of nonimmigrant or immigrant status for a foreign national, all temporary visitors and permanent residents must be admissible in order to receive their nonimmigrant visa or immigrant visa. Where the Department of Homeland Security (DHS)/Customs and Border Protection (CBP), or DOS consular officer (conoff), has reasonable grounds to believe a foreign national seeks to enter the United States to engage, in any way or to any extent, in the violation or evasion of laws prohibiting the export of goods, technology, or sensitive information, the foreign national may be deemed inadmissible and refused a visa or entry.[26] The discretion of the DOS/conoff is very broad in determining inadmissibility for purposes of visa adjudication and regarding factual conclusions, it is virtually inalterable.[27]

---

[17] F. Debusk & D. Fisher-Owens, "Non-military Technology for Foreign Nationals," *Immigration Law Today*, at 18 (Sept./Oct. 2003) (hereinafter Debusk & Fisher-Owens, "Non-military Technology").

[18] INA §274B(a)(3); 15 CFR §734.2, *www.bis.coc. gov/deemedexports/deemedexportsfaqs.html*, question 5; 22 CFR §20.16.

[19] INA §274B(a)(2)(C).

[20] 22 CFR §125.3,7.

[21] 15 CFR §736.1, 2; 22 CFR §125.1, 2.

[22] 15 CFR §764.3; 22 CFR §120.27 (citing 12 separate U.S. criminal statutes).

[23] Debusk & Fisher-Owens, "Non-military Technology," *supra* note 17, at 20.

[24] Bureau of Export Administration, Office of Chemical and Biological Controls and Treaty Compliance, Guidelines for Preparing Export License Applications Involving Foreign Nationals, at 2 (block 19) (supplied through BIS at *www.bis.doc.gov/licensing/applying4lic.htm*); U.S. Department of State, Directorate of Defense Trade Controls, Guidelines for Completion of a Form DSP-5 Application, Request for Permanent Export of Unclassified Defense Articles and Related Unclassified Technical Data, at 11–12 (supplied through DOS at *http://pmdtc.org/docs/DSP_5_guidelines.pdf*).

[25] Debusk & Fisher-Owens, "Non-military Technology," *supra* note 17, at 16, 22; *see also* T. Walsh, "The Technology Alert List, Visas Mantis and Export Control: Frequently Asked Questions," *Immigration Briefings*, at 6 (Aug. 2004) (hereinafter Walsh, "Technology Alert List").

[26] INA §212(a)(3)(A).

[27] I. Kurzban, *Kurzban's Immigration Law Sourcebook*, at 685 (10th ed. 2006) (no judicial review, limited access to reconsideration of denial or its legal basis).

To facilitate identification of inadmissible foreign nationals on these grounds for inadmissibility, DOS promulgated the Technology Alert List (TAL) for use by conoffs. The TAL is so broad that it covers almost any modern technical field. Where a conoff believes—and this may amount to no more than intuitive suspicion—that a controlled or classified technology is implicated, the visa-seeking foreign national may be subjected to extensive delay—up to three months or more—while a background check known as a "Mantis" inquiry is performed on the individual. The quick version of a Mantis inquiry is called an "Eagle Mantis," and allows completion of the visa adjudication after 10 days. The slow version, requiring express DOS authorization of the individual, is called "Donkey Mantis" and is typically reported to require about 90 days. For some countries (*e.g.,* Cuba) though, the Donkey Mantis has been reported to have taken as long as a year. Though typically regarded as a U.S. ally, even Israel is identified by the United States as a country where technology proliferation is a concern; thus, no quick resolution of a technology-implicating visa application should be expected for its citizens.[28]

Since it is only over the last several years that inadmissibility under INA §212(a)(3)(A) (relative to evasion of technology protection rules) has become a significant issue for conoffs, there is little law or guidance available on how to satisfy DOS/conoffs that a NIV or IV candidate does not seek to enter the United States in order to evade U.S. technology protection laws once technology security issues are implicated under TAL. Commentators have observed that the seminal DOS memo regarding the use of TAL fails to provide conoffs and counsel with clear direction concerning use of the list, and that DOS guidelines signal a bureaucratic shift toward obtaining checks in all but the most obvious cases in order to err on the side of caution.[29]

PRACTICE POINTERS

There are ways to improve the chances of visa approval when sensitive technology is implicated. DOS guidance to conoffs regarding use of TAL directs them to determine whether the applicant intends to engage in "advanced" research or studies or a business related to the critical fields list, and whether the issues of inadmissibility under INA §212(a)(3)(a) are possibly implicated. The conoffs are further instructed to seek as much detail as possible concerning the applicant's background, proposed activities, travel plans, current and prospective employment positions, addresses and contact information for his or her U.S. employer/host, points of contact, the person/organization funding the travel, details regarding the specific technology involved, the applicant's destination after the U.S. admission, and how the applicant will use his or her technological knowledge.[30]

Conoffs are urged to insist on documentation of this information and to require other documents as well, such as complete résumés, publication lists, project descriptions, and corporate reports. The guidance further urges the referral of cases for Donkey Mantis or Eagle Mantis review. Even though the conoffs need not instigate such reviews in every technology case, "conoffs should use caution in adjudicating all such cases. Only when conoffs believe (3)(a) clearly does not apply should the case be processed to conclusion without seeking the department's opinion."[31]

Where possible, visa applicants also should supply documentation that the technology is in the public domain or is found in regularly taught academic courses. The applicant and his or her foreign and U.S. employers should be alerted to the prospect of detailed inquiries from the consular post. These inquiries could include direct questioning of the U.S. employer concerning its compliance with export control laws.[32] An employer's credibility respecting compliance with technology-protection regulations may be enhanced where the employment terms include basic conditions often included in an export license. The employer's ability to demonstrate and document to DOS that it has a regulatory compliance plan to avoid violations of U.S. export control and technology protection laws is crucial. An example is the typical license condition requiring written disclosure of all additional license conditions to the foreign national, including the foreign national's duty and affirmation not to disclose, transfer, or re-export controlled technology. Additional conditions

---

[28] Debusk & Fisher-Owens, "Non-military Technology," *supra* note 17, at 20–22; Walsh, "Technology Alert List," *supra* note 25, at 14.

[29] *Id. See* Walsh, "Technology Alert List," *supra* note 25, at 5.

[30] State Dept. Updates Guidance on Technology Alert Checks (Mar. 4, 2003), pgs. 3–4.

[31] *Id.,* pgs. 3–4, emphasis added.

[32] *Id. See* Walsh, "Technology Alert List," *supra* note 25, at 6.

of this sort regularly require affirmation by the foreign national of receipt, understanding of, and agreement to abide by the regulatory compliance plan of the employer and acknowledgement of firewalls set up by the compliance plan relative to other activities of the business not covered by the specific export license or FNEL/TAA applicable to the foreign national.[33] The credibility of both the employer and its job candidate is enhanced if the employer can demonstrate in the foreign national's job description that compliance with all company technology control laws and licenses (where applicable), and all company compliance programs, are conditions for the job, along with eligibility for a license (where applicable). Making eligibility for employment licensing under applicable regulations a published condition of employment also diffuses any suggestion of discriminatory intent when the question of national origin necessarily arises for such a candidate.

A letter promulgated by the U.S. Embassy in Tel Aviv, Israel, advises that certain measures should be taken by persons applying for a visa to travel to the United States on sensitive scientific or technological business in order to facilitate the evaluation by DOS/conoff of the effect of technology protection regulations on the visa application, and thus, adjudication of the visa application. Instructions are given specifically for foreign nationals whose U.S. employer is directly in the service of a U.S. government contract (processing time will probably be normal), and for foreign nationals whose employers have had U.S. government contracts in the past (processing may be delayed). Notably, foreign nationals seeking to enter the United States for business on a sensitive scientific or technological topic with a company that has no previous contractual relationship with the U.S. government are advised that they "will definitely require additional administrative processing under U.S. government regulations." This processing may take 2 to 4 months. Such applicants are advised that "[a]s always, the more information that can be provided, the sooner the visa can be adjudicated." No details are provided in the letter concerning the sort of information that would speed the process.

The Tel Aviv Embassy also has posted a web page addressing "All Applicants with a Technical Background who are Requesting Work or Study Visas,"[34] offering more specific instructions for establishing "admissibility" where EAR and ITAR apply. This posting specifically calls for the production at visa processing of:

- Letters, in English, from the current and prospective U.S. employer or host;

- Where relevant, a copy of the U.S. government contract being served by the applicant's work or visit to the United States, or the Technical Assistance Agreement applicable to the work or visit;

- Detailed and specific technical information concerning the work/visit; and

- Detailed information from the U.S. employer/host, such as regarding the purpose of the visit, the nature of the project and specific subject areas to be addressed, the dates and locations of meetings and activities, and the contact name and phone numbers of the U.S. participants.

The posting also suggests that where the applicant is traveling in service of an active contract or subcontract between the applicant's employer/host and the U.S. government that a confirmation letter be obtained from the Defense Contract Management Agency before the visa interview takes place. Applicants are advised that even with this information, the adjudication could take up to three months, and that nonrefundable airline tickets should not be purchased until after receipt of the visa.

CONCLUSION

Some attorneys urge filing a "prophylactic" application for an export license FNEL/TAA for foreign nationals, so that the approval may be presented at the time of visa application. But there appears to be no certain means of obtaining a binding opinion regarding issuance of an export license or FNEL/TAA so that an employer might avoid the cost of immigration filings for a foreign national as to whom the export license/FNEL would be denied. Petitions to USCIS for immigrant or nonimmigrant approvals are therefore totally at the employer's risk for later visa delay or refusal based on security inadmissibility grounds, and where NIV holders are concerned, later denial of an export license or FNEL/TAA. If classified technology is involved, IV applicants are subject to ITAR licensing requirements equally susceptible to refusal or revocation.

---

[33] Peters *et al.*, "Foreign Nationals in U.S. Technology Programs: Complying with Immigration, Export Control, Industrial Security and other Requirements," *Immigration Briefings*, at 13 (Oct. 2000).

[34] *http://isreal.usembassy.gov/publish/mission/consular2/technical.html*.

B-1 BUSINESS VISITORS

updated by Teri A. Simmons, Warren R. Leiden, and Lincoln Stone[*]

INTRODUCTION

Global businesses and businesspersons have an ongoing need to transact business internationally with minimal restrictions. Key company personnel must have the flexibility to travel to foreign countries to conduct business affairs, often on short notice. For the foreign national businessperson entering the United States, the nature of the business activity and the duration of the intended stay will determine available visa options. Immigration lawyers must be familiar with the laws, regulations, informal policy directives, and other guidance relating to business visitors in order to properly advise clients regarding available options. Furthermore, since officers at different consulates and ports of entry retain substantial discretion and enforce the law differently, immigration lawyers must familiarize themselves regarding local interpretations, procedures, and prejudices.

The B-1 business visitor visa allows businesspersons to enter the United States on relatively short notice. This article provides an overview of this classification.

AUTHORITY

Statutory Authority

The Immigration and Nationality Act of 1952[1] (INA) defines an individual in B nonimmigrant classification as:

An alien (other than one coming for the purpose of study or performing skilled or unskilled labor or as a representative of foreign press, radio, film, or other foreign information media coming to engage in such vocations) having a residence in a foreign country, which he has no intention of abandoning and who is visiting the United States temporarily for business or temporarily for pleasure.[2]

Visitors for business use the B-1 visa classification.

Regulatory Authority, Agency Guidelines, and Policy Considerations

B-1 visa applicants must be prepared to clear two separate stages of inquiry. The first stage of inquiry occurs upon application for a visa with the U.S. embassy or consular office. U.S. consular officers review these applications and are likely to use Department of State (DOS) regulations and the *Foreign Affairs Manual* (FAM) as sources of authority or reference.[3] The second stage of inquiry occurs upon inspection for admission at a U.S. port of entry or pre-flight inspection station. Officers of U.S. Customs and Border Protection (CBP)[4] inspect and admit arriving persons.

---

[*] Updated from L. Burgess, S. Cohen & M. Koestler, "B-1/B-2 Myths and Realities," 2 *Immigration & Nationality Law Handbook* 91 (2004–05 ed.) and "B-1 Business Visitors and TN Nonimmigrants," *Immigration & Nationality Law Handbook* 429 (2005–06 ed.).

Teri Simmons is a partner with the Atlanta law firm Arnall Golden Gregory, where she directs the International and Immigration Departments. A former chair of the Atlanta Chapter of AILA, Ms. Simmons is currently serving as the chair of the Atlanta Sister Cities Commission and as the president of the Georgia Indo American Chamber of Commerce. She speaks on immigration law frequently in the United States and Germany.

Warren Leiden is a partner in the San Francisco office of Berry Appleman & Leiden LLP, a corporate immigration law firm. Mr. Leiden is a member of the Board of Governors of AILA, and he serves on the national steering committee of the national business immigration coalition Compete America.

Lincoln Stone is a partner of Stone & Grzegorek LLP in Los Angeles. Mr. Stone is chair of AILA's Committee on Investor Visas, and he is a Commissioner on the Immigration & Nationality Law Advisory Commission, State Bar of California Board of Legal Specialization.

---

[1] Pub. L. No. 82-414, 66 Stat. 163 (*codified as amended at* 8 USC §§1101–1537).

[2] Immigration and Nationality Act of 1952, Pub. L. No. 82-414, 66 Stat. 163 (*codified as amended at* 8 USC §§1101 *et seq.*) (INA), §101(a)(15)(B).

[3] 22 CFR §41.31; 9 FAM 41.31. Note that the FAM is not a set of regulations and is more properly considered a reference source.

[4] Effective March 1, 2003, the Immigration and Naturalization Service (INS) transitioned into the Department of Homeland Security (DHS). Functions previously handled by the INS (and several other federal agencies) are now split among three bureaus within the Border and Transportation Security Directorate. U.S. Customs and Border Protection (CBP) assumed responsibility for enforcing customs and

continued

CBP officers may utilize not only DOS regulations and the FAM, but also Department of Homeland Security (DHS) regulations, Operations Instructions (OI), and the internal *Inspector's Field Manual* (IFM).[5] CBP management asserts that its inspectors are trained on all sources, including the more expansive FAM.

U.S. consular officers must balance two competing mandates when reviewing visa applications: (1) facilitating U.S. policy objectives, which include the promotion of international travel and the free movement of all individuals to the United States for cultural, social, and economic purposes;[6] and (2) serving as the initial gatekeeper to the United States by screening all visa applicants for eligibility with consideration for the general presumption that all applicants are intending immigrants, not mere visitors,[7] as well as the rationale that the requirements of the B-1 visitor classification should protect the U.S. labor force from "business visitors" who actually would perform work in the United States.[8] CBP officers perform a similar function at the port of entry. They also serve as a check against incorrect or corrupt visa issuance.

Application of the pertinent authorities is hardly a uniform practice from consulate to consulate. Various factors affect a given consulate's visa issuance policies, such as a high rate of fraud or overstays for a particular nationality, poor economic

conditions in the country, and the unreliability of government-issued documents. Moreover, up-to-date information on the status of security advisory opinions (SAOs) currently required for citizens of predominantly Muslim countries is critical, as the processing of such security clearances could significantly impact the timing of visa issuance.

Consulates in countries whose citizens are eligible to enter the United States under the Visa Waiver Program (VWP) are often especially skeptical of B-1 visa applications and require applicants to present concrete evidence regarding why they cannot conduct their business visit within 90 days.[9] Other consulates, such as those located in India, are particularly suspicious that highly educated computer professionals will in fact go to work once in the United States and therefore require an abundance of evidence to show that the professionals are not intending to work, and that the benefit of their visit will be to a company in India or otherwise abroad. This suspicion is particularly pointed in the absence of H-1B visa quota numbers.

As is true for all visa issuance, the applicant's prior immigration history is relevant to the consular officer's decision of whether to grant the requested visa. If an applicant has ever been refused entry into the United States, it is unlikely that he or she will be approved for a B-1 visa. Likewise, if an applicant has spent a great deal of time in the United States in B-1 status or under the VWP, consular officers will likely suggest that the applicant seek a visa authorizing employment.

Since the assumption is that the applicant is entering the United States for legal purposes, a visa will obviously be denied when the consular officer knows or has reason to believe that the applicant will engage in unlawful criminal conduct.[10]

THREE BASIC REQUIREMENTS OF THE B-1 CATEGORY

According to the statute, the B-1 visa is suited to the visitor who has an unabandoned foreign residence; intent to visit only temporarily; and intent to engage only in permitted business activities.

---

immigration laws at and between the 307 ports of entry. The U.S. Immigration and Customs Enforcement (ICE) assumed responsibility of enforcement of customs and immigration laws in the interior United States. U.S. Citizenship and Immigration Services (USCIS) assumed responsibility of immigration benefits, including adjudication of family- and employment-based petitions, issuance of employment authorization documents, asylum and refugee processing, naturalization, and implementation of special status programs such as Temporary Protected Status (TPS).

[5] *See* DHS regulations, 8 CFR §214.2(b). Although the OI is available for public review, the IFM is not.

[6] *See* 9 FAM 41.31 N.5—"Importance of Facilitating International Travel."

[7] INA §214(b); 9 FAM 41.31 N.5.

[8] *See, e.g., Matter of Lawrence*, 15 I&N Dec. 418 (BIA 1975) (Canadian who manages U.S. real estate business is ineligible for B-1); *Matter of Neill*, 15 I&N Dec. 331 (BIA 1975) (mechanical engineer who provides professional consulting services in the United States is ineligible for B-1); *See also, Matter of Hira*, 11 I&N Dec. 824 (BIA 1966, Att'y. Gen. 1966) (citing U.S. Supreme Court ruling that entry for "business" does not include entry to perform labor).

[9] The Visa Waiver Program (VWP) allows citizens of certain countries to visit the United States for a period not to exceed 90 days. INA §217(a). No extension may be granted. 8 CFR §214.1(c)(3)(i).

[10] 9 FAM 41.31 N.4.1.

Unabandoned Foreign Residence

The first requirement for B-1 classification is proof of an unabandoned foreign residence, considered the principal actual dwelling place in fact.[11] The focus of the inquiry should be the applicant's intent. If, at the conclusion of the contemplated visit, the applicant intends to resume (or establish) a residence abroad, the applicant is eligible for the visa. The residence need not be the exclusive residence of the applicant; it may be shared with another individual.[12] The residence need not be the applicant's former residence, but instead may be a residence the applicant intends to establish in the future.[13] Where the applicant already owns a residence in the United States, or is the beneficiary of an immigrant petition, the applicant should be able to demonstrate eligibility for the B-1 visa by presenting other evidence indicating the residence abroad is the principal place of abode to which the applicant will return at the end of the temporary visit.

Entry for a Temporary Period

The second requirement for B-1 classification is proof that the proposed entry is for a temporary period.[14] Before issuing a B-1 visa, the consular officer must be satisfied that the intended stay has a time limitation and is not indefinite.[15] Where the proposed stay is potentially limitless, the B-1 classification is inappropriate.[16] The applicant may prevent such an inference by presenting evidence of specific and realistic plans for the visit, adequate financial resources to carry out the purpose of the visit and to depart, and evidence of meaningful business, family, and other connections that are a strong inducement to depart the United States at the conclusion of a temporary visit.[17] The "mere suspicion" that an applicant may be induced to remain permanently in the United States is, in itself, insufficient to warrant visa refusal if the applicant's present intent is to return to a foreign residence.[18]

Permitted Business Activities

The third and perhaps most contentious requirement of B-1 classification is proof that the proposed temporary visit is solely for purposes of engaging in permitted business activities.[19] B-1 business visitors may be admitted for the purpose of engaging in business, but not for the purpose of local employment or labor for hire.[20] The contentiousness stems from the occasional difficulty in distinguishing between permissible business activities and impermissible labor or employment. The FAM instructs that the primary focus should be whether the principal place of business and actual accrual of profits are in the foreign country.[21]

Activities of a commercial or professional nature permitted under the B-1 business visitor status include, but are not limited to:[22]

- Engaging in commercial transactions (which do not involve gainful employment);
- Negotiating contracts;
- Consulting with business associates;
- Litigating;
- Participating in scientific, educational, professional or business conventions, conferences or seminars; and
- Undertaking independent research.

PROVING ELIGIBILITY FOR THE B-1 VISA

In support of an application for the B-1 visa, the applicant should:[23]

- Have adequate funds available to avoid his or her unlawful employment in the United States;
- If presenting assurances of financial support from sponsoring relatives or friends in the United States, show compelling ties that would lend credence to the sponsor's undertaking;

---

[11] 9 FAM 41.31 N.1.1(1), N.2.1.

[12] 9 FAM 41.31 N.2.1.

[13] 9 FAM 41.31 N.2.2.

[14] 9 FAM 41.31 N.1.1(2).

[15] 22 CFR §41.31(a)(1); 9 FAM 41.31 N.3.1.

[16] *Matter of Lawrence*, 15 I&N Dec. 418 (BIA 1975).

[17] 22 CFR §41.31(a)(3); 9 FAM 41.31 N.3.2, N.3.4.

[18] 9 FAM 41.31 N.2.3.

---

[19] 9 FAM 41.31 N.1.1(3).

[20] 22 CFR §41.31(b)(1).

[21] 9 FAM 41.31 N.7 (citing *Matter of Hira*, 11 I&N Dec. 824 (BIA 1966, Att'y. Gen. 1966)).

[22] 9 FAM 41.31 N.8.

[23] 9 FAM 41.31 N.3.1-4.2. A useful analysis is presented in A. Paparelli & S. Wehrer, "The Incredible Rightness of 'B'ing—Prudent and Practical Uses for the B-1 and WB Business Visitor Categories," 2 *Immigration & Nationality Law Handbook* 105 (2000–01 ed.).

- Present specific and realistic plans for the entire period of the contemplated visit;

- Establish with reasonable certainty that the departure from the United States will take place upon completion of the temporary visit. The period of time projected for the visit must be consistent with its stated purpose;

- Not express the proposed period of stay in terms of remaining for the maximum period allowable by U.S. authorities;

- Demonstrate sufficient ties to his or her home country, such as permanent employment, meaningful business or financial connections, close family ties, or other commitments that indicate a strong inducement to return abroad. The FAM states that questionable cases cannot be resolved by the applicant's offer to leave dependents abroad.[24] Despite this note, consular officers may well be persuaded to issue a visa if dependents are remaining in the home country, and the authors advise submitting such evidence as part of the application; and

- Show adequate provision for support of any dependents while the applicant is in the United States if the applicant is the family's principal wage earner.

B-1 STATUS FOR WORKERS IN THE UNITED STATES

Although normally excluded from entering the United States to perform skilled or unskilled labor, applicants who intend to work may be issued B-1 visas and be admitted into the United States in valid B-1 status if they fall into one of the following categories:

- Ministers on evangelical tour, ministers of religion who exchange pulpits with American counterparts, members of religious denominations entering the United States temporarily to perform missionary work, and members of charitable organizations, and participants in voluntary service programs;[25]

- Members of boards of directors of U.S. corporations may enter the United States to attend a meeting of the board or to perform other functions derivative of board membership;[26]

- Personal or domestic servants of U.S. citizens residing abroad or temporarily assigned to the United States;[27]

- Personal or domestic servants of certain aliens in nonimmigrant status;[28]

- Certain yacht crewmen and coasting officers;[29]

- Certain professional athletes;[30]

- Investors seeking an investment in the United States that would qualify them for E-2 nonimmigrant classification, as long as they do not perform productive labor or actively participate in the management of the business prior to being granted E-2 status;[31]

- Horse racing personnel, such as jockey, sulky driver, trainer, or groomer;[32] or

- Outer Continental Shelf employees.[33]

OTHER BUSINESS ACTIVITIES CLASSIFIABLE AS B-1

While the following categories generally may be classified under another nonimmigrant class (*e.g.*, E, H, F), consular officers may issue B-1 visas for the following classes of visitors as well:

- Commercial or industrial workers coming to the United States to install, service, or repair commercial or industrial equipment or machinery purchased from a company outside the United States, or to train U.S. workers to perform such services. However, in such cases, the contract of sale must specifically require the seller to provide such services or training, and the visa applicant must possess specialized knowledge essential to the seller's contractual obligation to perform the services or training, and must receive no remuneration from a U.S. source.[34] U.S. consulates and ports of entry have become increasingly

---

[24] 9 FAM 41.31 N.3.1.

[25] *See generally* 9 FAM 41.31 N.9, 9.1-1 to 9.1-5.

---

[26] 9 FAM 41.31 N.9.2.

[27] 9 FAM 41.31 N.9.3-1, 9.3-2.

[28] 9 FAM 41.31 N.9.3-3.

[29] 9 FAM 41.31 N.9.5, 9.6.

[30] 9 FAM 41.31 N.9.4.

[31] 9 FAM 41.31 N.9.7.

[32] 9 FAM 41.31,N.9.8.

[33] 9 FAM 41.31 N.9.9.

[34] 9 FAM 41.31 N.7.1.

critical of applicants seeking B-1 visas and/or entry under this category and often require the presentation of documentation evidencing the applicant's specialized knowledge, source of remuneration, and particularly, a copy of the contract requiring the provision of services.

- In the building or construction industry, only applicants coming to the United States for purposes of supervising or training other workers engaged in building or construction work may be classified as B-1 visitors. Those who actually perform building or construction work, whether onsite or in-plant, are precluded from admission in B-1 status;[35]

- Applicants coming to the United States merely and exclusively to observe the conduct of business or other professional or vocational activity, provided they pay the expenses for their visit.[36] Consulates and U.S. ports of entry also have become increasing critical of applicants seeking a B-1 visa and/or entry into the United States for purposes of observing the conduct of a business, often questioning whether practical, on-the-job training is a component of the assignment.

- Foreign airline employees working in an executive, supervisory, or highly technical capacity, where there is no applicable E visa treaty;[37] and

- Certain foreign medical school students pursuing an elective clerkship at a U.S. medical school hospital.[38]

This list is not exhaustive. Counsel should be alert to new FAM instructions, as well as occasional memoranda released by DHS agencies.[39]

B-1 IN LIEU OF H-1B OR H-3

In certain circumstances, applicants eligible for H-1B or H-3 status may be issued B-1 visas.[40] U.S. companies desiring to bring overseas workers to the United States on short notice, for brief periods of stay, to assist with important technical projects, or to

participate in training programs, have often utilized these B-1 classifications. The B-1 professional or trainee cannot receive a salary or other remuneration from a U.S. source except for an expense allowance or reimbursement for incidental expenses.[41] In the case of a B-1 trainee, the applicant must present evidence that the training is not available in his or her home country, that the training will benefit his or her career abroad, and that the training neither includes productive employment nor displaces a U.S. worker.[42]

The four-decade-old practice of issuing B-1 in lieu of H-1B visas has been under fire since the passage of the Immigration Act of 1990 (IMMACT 90).[43] IMMACT 90 was the basis for proposed INS regulations that would have established new criteria regarding the "B-1 in lieu of H-1B" provision.[44]

INS/USCIS views the H-1B cap and labor condition attestation requirements as a clear statement by Congress that the working conditions of U.S. workers are to be safeguarded. In its separate proposed regulation, the State Department stated that some foreign employers are "job shops" functioning essentially as employment agencies, particularly in the computer industry.[45] Under the INS/USCIS proposed rule, the following criteria would have to be met to qualify for admission as a B-1 in lieu of H-1B:

- The foreign firm must be regularly engaged in business of a commercial nature (*i.e.*, not merely set up to transfer employees to the United States);

- There may be no direct or indirect payment of the applicant's salary by the U.S. company;

- The foreign company must maintain control over the applicant's employment, including location of work and hours;

- All proprietary work product of the applicant must belong to the applicant or foreign firm; and

- In the case of a purchase contract between a U.S. company and a foreign firm, the purchase must

---

[35] 8 CFR §214.2(b)(5); 22 CFR §41.31(b); 9 FAM 41.31 N.10.1.

[36] 9 FAM 41.31 N.10.4-2-2.

[37] 9 FAM 41.31 N.10.2.

[38] 9 FAM 41.31 N.10.4-1.

[39] See 9 FAM 41.31 N.10.1–10.8-3, for a listing of other acceptable B-1 categories.

[40] *See* 9 FAM 41.31 N.8; OI 214.2(b).

[41] *Id.*

[42] 9 FAM 41.31 N.11.9.

[43] Pub. L. No. 101–649, 104 Stat. 4978 (1990).

[44] *See* 58 Fed. Reg. 40024–30 (July 26, 1993); 58 Fed. Reg. 58982–88 (Nov. 5, 1993). For a complete discussion of the proposed criteria, see 71 *Interpreter Releases* 149–55 (Jan. 24, 1994).

[45] 58 Fed. Reg. at 40026–27.

involve a "physical product" and not activities of a "service nature."

Neither DOS nor INS/USCIS has published a final rule, and theoretically, the "B-1 in lieu of H-1B" visa remains available to this day.[46] Practically, though, the strategy has not worked effectively, with the exception of entry granted to short-term business visitors from large, well-known companies.

BUSINESS VISITORS UNDER (NAFTA)[47]

Citizens of Canada and Mexico seeking temporary entry, who otherwise meet the existing requirements under INA §101(a)(15)(B), including but not limited, to requirements regarding the source of remuneration, will be admitted as business visitors under the North American Free Trade Agreement (NAFTA).[48] NAFTA expands the range of appropriate B-1 activities to include research and design, marketing, sales, and other activities that otherwise would not be permitted unless the person holds a working visa.

A business visitor is permitted to enter the United States pursuant to NAFTA if the purpose of the visit is in one of the following phases of the normal business cycle:[49]

- Research and Design—technical, scientific, and statistical researchers;

- Growth, Manufacture, and Production—harvester owner supervising a harvesting crew; purchasing and production management personnel;

- Marketing—market researchers and analysts; trade fair and promotion personnel;

- Sales—sales representatives and agents negotiating contracts; buyers;

- Distribution—transportation operators; customs brokers;

- After-Sales Service—installers, repair and maintenance personnel, and supervisors possessing specialized knowledge essential to the seller's contractual obligations;

- General Service—professionals, management, financial services, public relations, and tourism personnel.

Significantly, Canadian visitors (including business visitors) do not require a visa to enter the United States.[50] To gain U.S. admission, Canadians and Mexicans seeking status as business visitors should present proof of citizenship in the case of Canadian applicants, and valid entry documents such as a passport and visa, or Mexican border crossing card, in the case of Mexican applicants.[51] In addition, the NAFTA business visitor should present a description of the purpose of the entry, as well as evidence demonstrating that he or she is engaged in one of the occupations or professions set forth in Appendix 1603.A.1 to Annex 1603 of NAFTA.[52] Canadians and Mexicans engaged in an occupation or profession not listed in Appendix 1603.A.1 to Annex 1603 will not be precluded from temporary entry if they otherwise meet the existing requirements for admission as prescribed by the Attorney General.[53]

Thus, for example, a businessperson employed by a Mexican or Canadian company may enter the United States to conduct preliminary market research prior to the time when that company incorporates in the United States, or for the purpose of attending a trade fair.[54] Again, the business visitor should carry a letter from the foreign employer explaining the purpose of the visit.

A Canadian computer professional, for instance, may enter the United States if he or she has proprietary knowledge of his or her employer's systems, and if the employer has a contract with a U.S. company requiring "post-sales" service. This Canadian should have a company letter describing this specialized knowledge and a copy of the pertinent contract.[55] While this remains the law, entry from Canada under this category has become more and more difficult without a Trade NAFTA (TN) visa or other visa authorizing U.S. employment.

---

[46] *But see* Memorandum, "Business Visitor Field Guidance," WRINS 70/20, *published on* AILA InfoNet at Doc. No. 03040190 (*posted* Apr. 1, 2003) (indicating that OI 214.2(b) should be disregarded; applicant may be disqualified from admission as a B-1 visitor if coming to perform services that are inherently part of the U.S. labor market or for which a U.S. worker would have to be hired).

[47] Codified in relevant part at INA §214(e).

[48] 8 CFR §214.2(b)(4).

[49] 8 CFR §214.2(b)(4)(i)(A)–(G).

[50] 8 CFR §§212.1(a)(1), 1212.1(a)(1).

[51] 8 CFR §§212.1(c), 1212.1(c).

[52] 8 CFR §214.2(b)(4).

[53] 8 CFR §214.2(b)(4)(ii).

[54] 8 CFR §214.2(b)(4)(i)(C).

[55] 8 CFR §214.2(b)(4)(i)(F).

VISA APPLICATION, ADMISSION, EXTENSION, AND CHANGE OF STATUS

The applicant for a B visa submits to the U.S. consulate Forms DS-156, DS-157 (if required), a valid passport, required photos, the Machine Readable Visa (MRV) fee, and reciprocity fees applicable to specific nationalities. The visa will be issued for the maximum of 10 years, with multiple entries during those 10 years. The visa will be issued for less than 10 years and for limited entries in accordance with reciprocity schedules set by agreements between the United States and the country of the applicant's nationality. The consul also has discretion to issue a visa for less than the maximum time allowed.

The visa then is used to enter the United States. When admitted, the foreign national is given Form I-94 endorsed with the class and period of admission. Visitors who use a visa to enter the United States are subject to the US-VISIT[56] program at the port of entry.

USCIS regulations stipulate the limitations on the period of admission.[57] A B-1 visitor may be admitted for no more than one year. The actual period of admission granted by the inspecting officer should be a "period of time which is fair and reasonable for completion of the purpose of the trip."[58] Too often, this is just 30 days or even shorter.

On the other hand, B-2 visa holders are typically admitted for six months.[59] As a consequence, applicants who indicate they are entering the United States to engage in permissible business activities under the business visitor category, and then to go on vacation, are typically admitted for six months.

A B visitor may apply to USCIS on Form I-539 for extensions of stay in six-month increments.[60] An extension of stay may not be approved if the extension was filed after the previously accorded status expired, except that failure to file the extension before the previously accorded status expired may be excused at the discretion of USCIS when the following is found: (1) the delay was due to extraordinary circumstances; (2) the delay was beyond the control of the applicant; (3) the delay was commensurate with the circumstances; (4) the applicant has not otherwise violated status; (5) the applicant remains a bona fide nonimmigrant; and (6) the noncitizen is not subject to deportation or removal proceedings.[61]

An extension may not be approved for an applicant who has failed to maintain status.[62] An applicant is in authorized status but is not lawfully present after the initial period of admission expires while an extension is pending. If the extension is granted, lawful presence will relate back to the timely filing of the extension application.[63] A second extension filed after expiration of the initial period of admission, while an extension is pending but prior to the approval of that extension, will not extend the period of lawful presence if the first extension is not granted.[64]

A B visitor may file to change to most other nonimmigrant visa statuses so long as the applicant is not violating status and the application for change of status is timely filed. As in the case of an untimely extension application, an untimely request for a change of status may be excused if: (1) the delay is due to extraordinary circumstances; (2) the delay is beyond the control of the applicant; (3) USCIS finds the delay commensurate with the circumstances; (4) the applicant has not otherwise violated status; (5) the noncitizen remains a bona fide nonimmigrant; and (6) the noncitizen is not subject to deportation or removal proceedings.[65]

When requesting changes of status, however, it is imperative for the applicant to prove that he or she did not intend to engage in the activity requested in the application for a change of status at the time when he or she initially applied for the B-1 visa at a consulate abroad and then entered the United States in B-1 status. Changes of status sought shortly after U.S. entries are subject to heightened scrutiny in this regard and could pose a danger of ultimate visa denial at a consulate abroad.

---

[56] U.S. Visitor and Immigrant Status Indicator Technology Program, 69 Fed. Reg. 467 (Jan. 5, 2004).

[57] 8 CFR §214.2(b).

[58] OI 214.2(b).

[59] 8 CFR §214.2(b)(2).

[60] 8 CFR §214.2(b)(1).

[61] 8 CFR §214.1(c)(4).

[62] Id.

[63] INS Memorandum, Janice Podolny, "Interpretation of 'Period of Stay Authorized by Attorney General' in determining 'unlawful presence' Under INA Section 212(a)(9)(B)(ii)" (Mar. 27, 2003), published on AILA InfoNet at Doc. No. 03042140 (posted Apr. 21, 2003).

[64] Id.

[65] 8 CFR §248.1(b)(1).

CONCLUSION

B-1 business visitors are vital to U.S. participation in the global economy. In order to properly counsel clients, the immigration lawyer must know the definitions of "business," "commerce," and "employment" under the INA, as well as regulations, agency, local consular, port, and court interpretations. Practitioners must familiarize themselves with the specific regulatory criteria for B-1 applicants used by consular officers and CBP inspectors, and outlined in the FAM and the CBP Operations Instructions respectively.

But more than this, practitioners must now apply a real world analysis to cases in an attempt to predict whether an officer will admit an applicant without a visa that permits employment. This is particularly important in light of the consequences of refused entry, which can include incarceration and barriers to future entries. In this analysis, we must ask the real world question—"Is the applicant a temporary business visitor, or is he or she really working in the United States to the benefit of a U.S. employer?" If the answer falls on the side of U.S. employment, the applicant should be advised to seek a nonimmigrant status that permits employment.

E-1 Nonimmigrant Status

by Henry J. Chang[*]

INTRODUCTION

During 2005, the United States exported goods and services worth $1.27 trillion to other countries.[1] During that same year, it imported foreign goods and services worth $1.99 trillion.[2] Many of the foreign entities responsible for this trade are entitled to seek treaty trader (E-1) status under the Immigration and Nationality Act (INA).[3]

The E-1 classification is an underutilized non-immigrant category often overshadowed by the more common treaty investor (E-2) classification. However, E-1 status may be a preferred option for many foreign entities. It is available to individual traders and also key employees, provided that they possess the nationality of an eligible country.

This article discusses the eligibility requirements for E-1 treaty traders.

AUTHORITIES

Immigration and Nationality Act (INA) §101(a)(15)(E)(ii)

An E-1 nonimmigrant is defined as an alien entitled to enter the United States under provisions of a treaty of commerce and navigation between the United States and the foreign state of which he or she is a national, and the spouse and children of any such alien if accompanying or following to join him or her, solely to carry on substantial trade, including trade in services or trade in technology, principally between the United States and the foreign state of which he or she is a national.

Title 22, Code of Federal Regulations; 22 CFR §41.51

The treaty trader regulations of the Department of State (DOS) appear at 22 CFR §41.51.

Title 8, Code of Federal Regulations; 8 CFR §214.2(e)

The treaty trader regulations of U.S. Citizenship and Immigration Services (USCIS) are at 8 CFR §214.2(e).

Vol. 9, Foreign Affairs Manual; 9 FAM 41.51

Another extremely useful authority is 9 FAM 41.51, which contains interpretive notes relating to treaty trader eligibility. Although the FAM is not binding on consular officers, it is a valuable source of guidance for practitioners. Where relevant, the FAM should be cited in visa cases filed with consular posts abroad and in change-of-status or extension-of-stay cases filed with USCIS.

KEY CONSIDERATIONS

Overview

According to DOS regulations, an alien is eligible for E-1 treaty trader status if the alien qualifies under the provisions of INA §101(a)(15)(E)(i) and:

- will be in the United States solely to carry on trade of a substantial nature, which is international in scope, either on the alien's behalf or as an employee of a foreign person or organization engaged in trade, principally between the United States and the foreign state of which the alien is a national (consideration being given to any conditions in the country of which the alien is a national which may affect the alien's ability to carry on such substantial trade); and

- intends to depart from the United States upon the termination of E-1 status.[4]

This is consistent with the language contained in the FAM and USCIS regulations.[5]

---

[*] **Henry Chang** is a partner with the firm of Chang & Boos (*www.americanlaw.com*) in its Toronto office. He is a member of the State Bar of California and the Law Society of Upper Canada. Mr. Chang obtained his Bachelor of Laws from Osgoode Hall Law School (Toronto) in 1990, and has practiced exclusively in the field of immigration law for more than 13 years. Mr. Chang held the position of Canadian Chapter Chair of AILA (1996–98, 2000–02, and 2004–06).

[1] *www.census.gov/foreign-trade/statistics/highlights/annual.html.*

[2] *Id.*

[3] Immigration and Nationality Act of 1952, Pub. L. No. 82-414, 66 Stat. 163 (*codified as amended at* 8 USC §§1101 *et seq.*) (INA).

[4] 22 CFR §41.51(a).

[5] 9 FAM 41.51 N.1.1; 8 CFR §214.2(e)(1).

Existence of Treaty

INA §101(a)(15)(E) requires the existence of a treaty of Friendship, Commerce, and Navigation (FCN) between the United States and another country in order for the E visa classification to be granted to nationals of that country. Similarly, the term "treaty country" is defined in DOS regulations as a foreign state with which a qualifying FCN or its equivalent exists with the United States.[6] A treaty country also includes a foreign state that is accorded treaty visa privileges by specific legislation other than the INA.[7]

A list of treaties or the equivalent in effect between the United States and other countries, which give rise to E visa eligibility, appears in the FAM.[8] This list also is reproduced at the end of this article as Exhibit A. The most recent additions to the list of eligible countries are Chile[9] and Singapore.[10]

Some treaties allow a national of a treaty country to seek E-2 status but not E-1 status; other treaties may contain specific restrictions on E-1 eligibility.[11] To determine whether a particular foreign national will be eligible for E-1 status, a practitioner should refer to the list contained in the FAM and, if necessary, the text of the treaty itself.

Nationality

To qualify for E-1 status, the treaty trader must possess the nationality of the treaty country.[12] In most cases, it should be easy to establish nationality. In certain situations, however, it can be difficult.

The nationality of an individual treaty trader is determined by the authorities of the foreign state of which the alien is a national.[13] In unclear cases, practitioners should examine the nationality laws of the treaty country and the language of the relevant treaty in order to determine whether the individual qualifies for E-1 status. For example, in treaty countries where the doctrine of jus sanguinis exclusively applies, an individual born within the country's jurisdiction may not be a national of that country.

The nationality of a business is determined by the nationality of the individual owners of that business.[14] The country of incorporation is irrelevant to the nationality requirement for E visa purposes.[15] In order to qualify, at least 50 percent of the business must be owned by nationals of the relevant treaty country.[16] If the E-1 business is in turn owned by another company, at least 50 percent of the parent company must be owned (directly or indirectly) by nationals of the relevant treaty country.[17] When a company is equally owned and controlled by nationals of two different treaty countries, employees of either nationality may obtain E visas to work for that company.[18]

In the case of an owner holding dual citizenship (other than U.S. citizenship), the owner and all E visa employees of the company must possess the nationality of the same eligible country, and hold themselves out as nationals of that country for all E visa purposes involving that company, regardless of whether they also possess the nationality of another E visa country.[19] An E-1 employer must either maintain the status of an E-1 treaty trader or, if not in the United States, be classifiable as an E-1 treaty trader.[20]

Just as a citizen of the United States cannot be issued a visa or other documentation as an alien, a dual national having both treaty nationality and U.S. citizenship cannot qualify for E-1 status or act as an

---

[6] 22 CFR §41.51(a)(5).

[7] *Id.* An example of such legislation is the North American Free Trade Agreement Implementation Act, Pub. L. No. 103-182, 107 Stat. 2057 (Dec. 8, 1993).

[8] 9 FAM 41.51, Exhibit I. The list of treaty countries now appears online at *http://travel.state.gov/visa/reciprocity/ list_of_treaty_countries.htm.* The list mistakenly omits the availability of E-1 for citizens of Poland.

[9] U.S.-Chile Free Trade Agreement Implementation Act, Pub. L. No. 108-77 (effective Jan. 1, 2004).

[10] U.S.-Singapore Free Trade Agreement Implementation Act, Pub. L. No. 108-78 (effective Jan. 1, 2004).

[11] For example, "A Convention to Regulate Commerce Between the Territories of the United States and of His Britannick Majesty," July 3, 1815, *entered into force* July 3, 1815, 8 Stat. 228; TS 110; 12 Bevans 49, permits nationals of the United Kingdom to seek E-1 (and E-2) status, but applies only to British territory in Europe (the British Isles (except the Republic of Ireland), the Channel Islands and Gibraltar) and to "inhabitants" of such territory. This term, as used in the Convention, means "one who resides actually and permanently in a given place, and has his domicile there."

[12] 22 CFR §41.51(a)(6); 9 FAM 41.51 N.2.

[13] *Id.*

[14] *Id.*

[15] 9 FAM 41.51 N.3.2.

[16] 22 CFR §41.51(a)(2)(ii); 9 FAM 41.51 N.3.1.

[17] 9 FAM 41.51 N.3.1.

[18] 9 FAM 41.51 N.3.3.

[19] *Id.*

[20] 22 CFR §41.51(a)(2).

E-1 employer.[21] In addition, despite having the necessary nationality, a permanent resident of the United States cannot qualify for E-1 status.[22]

When a corporation is sold exclusively on a stock exchange in the country of incorporation, the nationality of the corporation is presumed to be the location of the exchange.[23] However, where a corporation's stock is exchanged in more than one country, it is much more difficult to rely upon this presumption. In such cases, the applicant must satisfy the consular officer with the best evidence available that the business meets the nationality requirement.[24] If it can be shown that at least 50 percent of the total outstanding shares are traded on the stock exchange in the country of incorporation, it should be possible to apply the presumption in order to establish that the company is at least 50 percent owned by nationals of that country.

The nationality requirement is fairly easy to satisfy when the treaty business is at least 50 percent owned by treaty nationals. However, nationality problems will arise when the treaty business is less than 50 percent-owned by treaty nationals. In such cases, the attorney may need to restructure the treaty business in order to satisfy the nationality requirement.

One possible solution is to sell an appropriate amount of shares from the nontreaty national to the treaty national. As payment for the shares, the treaty national could then execute a loan agreement with an option for the nontreaty national to later repurchase the shares at the original price. This option could be exercisable only after the expiration date of the treaty national's visa or upon certain earlier events such as the treaty national's departure from the business, or his or her insolvency. This strategy should satisfy the nationality requirement while also protecting the interests of the nontreaty national.

While there is no guarantee that a particular consulate will accept the above solution, especially where the option agreement is disclosed, it does appear to meet the requirements contained in the INA, DOS regulations, USCIS regulations, and the FAM.

If an option agreement becomes necessary to establish eligibility, the practitioner should have his or her client fully consider the implications thereof (*i.e.*, its effect in case of a disagreement among the parties, the death of one of the parties, or other circumstances that might arise) before entering into such an arrangement.

Under common law, a trust is not a separate legal entity from the trustee; the trustee is the legal owner of trust assets. If this principle were applied, a nontreaty national beneficiary could become eligible for E-1 status simply by placing the investment funds in a trust and hiring a treaty-national trustee to administer it. However, DOS has confirmed that it will look to the beneficiaries, rather than to the trustee, when determining the nationality of the treaty business.[25]

Meaning of "Trade"

Definition

The term "trade" is defined as the existing international exchange of items of trade for consideration between the United States and the treaty country.[26] This definition refers to several specific requirements:

- Trade must be in existence;
- Trade entails exchange;
- Trade must involve qualifying items of trade; and
- Trade must be international.

Trade Must Be in Existence

As stated above, a future intention to engage in trade is not sufficient; the alien must already be engaged in trade.[27] However, existing trade includes successfully negotiated contracts, binding upon the parties, which call for the immediate exchange of items of trade.[28] Such contracts alone would appear to meet the requirement of existing trade, without the need for documentation of previous exchanges. However, a single binding contract may not be sufficient to meet the substantiality requirement (discussed below), unless the contract contemplates numerous transactions over time.

---

[21] 22 CFR §40.2(a).

[22] 9 FAM 41.51 N.14.1. *See also* Letter from H. Edward Odom, DOS Chief, Advisory Opinions Division, *reproduced in* 71 *Interpreter Releases* 1379 (Oct. 7, 1994).

[23] 9 FAM 41.51 N.3.2.

[24] *Id.*

[25] Verbally confirmed by Stephen Fischel, Director of Legislation, Regulations and Advisory Assistance for the DOS Visa Office, during the 1999 AILA Annual Conference.

[26] 22 CFR §41.51(a)(7); 9 FAM 41.51 N.4.

[27] 22 CFR §41.51(a)(7).

[28] 22 CFR §41.51(a)(7); 9 FAM 41.51 N.4.2.

Trade Entails Exchange

As stated above, DOS regulations require an actual exchange of items of trade.[29] This exchange must be traceable and identifiable, and title to the trade item must pass from one treaty party to the other.[30]

The requirement that title pass does not necessarily mean that property rights must be transferred, at least in the case of services or intangible goods. The concept of title does not easily apply to trade in services. Although the concept of title may apply to intangible goods, many transactions involving intellectual property contemplate licensing of property rights rather than the transfer of title. Despite the inability to pass title, such activities are considered valid exchanges for E-1 purposes.[31]

An exchange of a good or service for consideration must flow between the two treaty countries. But the fact that proceeds from services performed in the United States may be placed in a bank account in the treaty country does not necessarily indicate that a meaningful exchange has occurred if the proceeds do not support any business activity in the treaty country.[32] As a result, E-1 treaty trader status may not be applicable to a sole proprietor who lives in the United States, who personally provides his or her services to U.S. clients while in the United States, and who maintains little or no business presence in the treaty country.[33]

Nevertheless, it should be possible to establish a qualifying exchange by documenting the alien's business presence in the treaty country. This documentation may include evidence of:

- a corporate entity in the treaty country;
- payment of income tax (relating to the international exchange) in the treaty country;
- a commercial lease for premises in the treaty country; and
- employees in the treaty country.

However, the extent to which the alien will be required to document his or her business presence abroad will vary from post to post.

Trade Must Involve Qualifying Items of Trade

According to DOS regulations, items that qualify for trade under the E-1 category include, but are not limited to, goods, services, technology, monies, international banking, insurance, transportation, tourism, communications, and some news gathering activities.[34] USCIS regulations contain a similar list, also mentioning data processing, advertising, accounting, design and engineering, and management consulting.[35] DOS regulations and the FAM indicate that representatives of foreign information media must first be considered for classification under INA §101(1)(15)(I) before being considered for E-1 status.[36]

DOS regulations do not define the meaning of goods or services. USCIS regulations define goods as "tangible commodities or merchandise having extrinsic value" and services as "legitimate economic activities, which provide other than tangible goods."[37]

Although it was once believed that trade in professional services could not support E-1 classification,[38] there is currently no doubt that trade in any service, professional or otherwise, may support an application for E-1 status. The Immigration Act of 1990 (IMMACT90)[39] specifically added trade in services to the definition contained in INA §101(a)(15)(E)(ii).

To constitute trade in a service for E-1 purposes, the provision of that service by an enterprise must be the purpose of that business, and the service itself must be the saleable commodity that the enterprise sells to clients.[40] Essentially, any service item commonly traded in international commerce would qualify.[41]

---

[29] 22 CFR §41.51(a)(7).

[30] *Id.*

[31] The definition of "items of trade" at 22 CFR §41.51(a)(8) includes "technology." In any event, trade in intangible goods almost always involves trade in services as well, which will clearly qualify as trade.

[32] 9 FAM 41.51 N.4.2.

[33] In this situation, the alien also may fail to satisfy the requirement that trade be "international" (discussed below).

[34] 22 CFR §41.51(a)(8).

[35] 8 CFR §214.2(e)(9).

[36] 22 CFR §41.51(a)(4); 9 FAM 41.51 N.4.5.

[37] 8 CFR §214.2(e)(9). USCIS's definition of goods is too narrow since it fails to include intangible goods. However, as stated above, the trade in intangible goods almost always involves trade in related services.

[38] *Matter of Hartikainan*, No. A26-547-687, at 2 (Assoc. Comm'r, Exam. Dec. 30, 1983).

[39] Pub. L. No. 101-649, §204, 104 Stat. 4978.

[40] 9 FAM 41.51 N.4.5.

[41] *Id.*

International Trade

According to the FAM, the purpose of FCN treaties is to develop international commercial trade between the two countries.[42] Development of the domestic market without international exchange does not constitute trade in the E-1 visa context.[43] The traceable exchange in goods or services must be between the United States and the other treaty country.[44]

An interesting question arises where the items of trade involve goods manufactured in a nontreaty country that are subsequently purchased by a treaty national and shipped to the treaty country. It is at least arguable that the sale of these goods by the treaty national to a U.S. national will qualify as trade for the purposes of E-1 eligibility, since title to the goods still passes from one treaty party to the other as required by the regulations.[45] Many FCNs specifically describe what goods will be eligible for preferred treatment.[46] As treaty trader eligibility also arises from these FCNs, it seems unlikely that an E-1 application could be supported by trade in goods that do not qualify under the relevant treaty. Practitioners faced with such a situation should review the applicable FCN to determine whether the goods being traded are eligible under the treaty before filing an application or petition for E-1 status.

No Requirement that the
Trader Be a For-Profit Entity

The FAM states that the treaty enterprise operated by an E-2 treaty investor must be "a real and active commercial or entrepreneurial undertaking, producing some service or commodity."[47] Because the investment is required to be a commercial enterprise, it must be for profit.[48] Nonprofit entities are therefore ineligible to seek E-2 visas.[49] However, this requirement does not appear to apply to E-1 applicants. Even nonprofit corporations may be eligible as E-1 treaty traders if they otherwise satisfy the eligibility requirements.

Although the FAM states that trade for E-1 purposes involves the commercial exchange of goods or services in the international marketplace, it does not require the E-1 enterprise itself to be a for-profit commercial undertaking.[50] If the trade itself involves a commercial exchange (trade in exchange for consideration), it should be acceptable for the E-1 trader to be a nonprofit corporation.

Trade Is Substantial

In order to qualify for E-1 status, the relevant trade must be considered substantial. DOS regulations define the term "substantial trade" as follows:

> [T]he quantum of trade sufficient to ensure a continuous flow of trade items between the United States and the treaty country. This continuous flow contemplates numerous exchanges over time rather than a single transaction, regardless of the monetary value. Although the monetary value of the trade item being exchanged is a relevant consideration, greater weight is given to more numerous exchanges of larger value. In the case of smaller businesses, an income derived from the value of numerous transactions which is sufficient to support the treaty trader and his or her family constitutes a favorable factor in assessing the existence of substantial trade.[51]

The above definition is consistent with the language contained in the FAM and USCIS regulations.[52]

An applicant who is able to establish only one transaction will clearly not qualify for E-1 status. In such cases, it may be advisable to delay filing the E-1 application until a sufficient number of transactions have occurred. However, a single binding contract that calls for numerous traceable and identifiable exchanges over an extended period of time may still qualify as substantial trade, even if no previous exchanges have taken place, if it establishes that a continuous flow of trade items is likely to occur.

The volume of trade appears to be much more important than the monetary value of each transaction. Although a single transaction of high monetary value will be insufficient to establish substantial trade, evidence of numerous small transactions may

---

[42] 9 FAM 41.51 N.4.3.

[43] *Id.*

[44] *Id.*

[45] 22 CFR §41.51(a)(7); 8 CFR §214.2(e)(9).

[46] For example, specific rules of origin appear in Chapter Four of the North American Free Trade Agreement (NAFTA).

[47] 9 FAM 41.51 N.9.

[48] *Id.*

[49] *Id.*

---

[50] 9 FAM 41.51 N.4.5.

[51] 22 CFR §41.51(a)(9).

[52] 8 CFR §214.2(e)(10); 9 FAM 41.51 N.6.

be sufficient to establish the requisite international trade.[53]

DOS's definition of "substantial trade" makes specific reference to a small business owner's ability to support herself and her family.[54] If income from the trading activity can support the treaty trader and her family, this constitutes a favorable factor in assessing the existence of substantial trade.[55] Similar language also appears in USCIS regulations and the FAM.[56]

This policy is in contrast to the marginality criteria applied in E-2 cases,[57] where income that is only sufficient to support the treaty investor and his or her family is considered a negative factor, as it suggests that the business is a marginal one.[58]

DOS regulations specifically permit the consular officer to consider any conditions in the treaty country that may affect the alien's ability to carry on substantial trade.[59] A similar provision also appears in the USCIS regulations.[60] Where conditions such as currency restrictions in the alien's home country will adversely affect his or her ability to engage in trade, the consular post may be willing to accept a lower level of trade as being substantial. However, the preamble to USCIS regulations states that, at some point, country conditions can become so restrictive that treaty eligibility will be denied. For example, citizens of Iran continue to be eligible for treaty trader status. However, the sanctions imposed by Executive Order 12959[61] make it essentially impossible for Iranians to qualify for such status.

The preamble to USCIS regulations, published in 1997, also provide some guidance regarding evidence that can be used to document substantial trade. It states that substantial trade may be demonstrated by evidence from many sources, including, but not limited to, bills of lading, customs receipts, letters of credit, insurance papers documenting

commodities imported, purchase orders, carrier inventories, trade brochures, and sales contracts.[62]

Principally Between the United States and the Treaty Country

DOS regulations indicate that principal trade between the United States and the treaty country exists when over 50 percent of the volume of international trade of the treaty trader is conducted between the United States and the treaty country of the treaty trader's nationality.[63] The remainder of the trade in which the alien is engaged may be international trade with other countries or domestic trade.[64]

Trade between the United States and the treaty country is measured as a percentage of the trader's total international trade. Therefore, domestic trade within the treaty country is not considered. However, domestic U.S. trade is specifically counted as non–qualifying trade in the calculation. A foreign corporation that engages in 60 percent domestic trade within the treaty country, 21 percent international trade between the treaty country and the United States, 10 percent international trade between the treaty country and other foreign countries, and 9 percent domestic trade within the United States, should still qualify. Although trade between the treaty country and the United States is only 21 percent of its total trade, it is actually 52.5 percent of the foreign corporation's *international* trade (domestic U.S. trade is treated as non–qualifying international trade for the purposes of this calculation).

The FAM confirms that corporations, but not branch offices, are to be treated as separate legal entities for the purposes of calculating principal trade.[65] In other words, a U.S. corporation carrying on principal trade between the United States and the treaty country may qualify even though it is owned by a foreign parent that engages exclusively in trade with third countries. However, because a branch office is not a separate legal entity, activities of the parent will be considered when measuring trade. If an alien intends to engage in considerable domestic trade or trade with third countries, he or she may wish to do so using a separate corporation.

---

[53] 9 FAM 41.51 N.6b.

[54] 22 CFR §41.51(a)(9).

[55] *Id.*

[56] 8 CFR §214.2(e)(10); 9 FAM 41.51 N.6b.

[57] 22 CFR §41.51(b)(10); 9 FAM 41.51 N.11.

[58] *Id.*

[59] 22 CFR §41.51(a)(1).

[60] 8 CFR §214.2(e)(1).

[61] 60 Fed. Reg. 24755–59 (May 9, 1995).

[62] 62 Fed Reg. 48138–55 (Sept. 12, 1997), *reproduced in* 74 *Interpreter Releases* 1390 (Sept. 15, 1997).

[63] 22 CFR §41.51(a)(10). *See also* 8 CFR §214.2(e)(11).

[64] 9 FAM 41.51 N.7.

[65] 9 FAM 41.51 N.7.1.

As long as the treaty trader conducts trade principally between the United States and the treaty country, the duties of the E-1 employee need not be similarly apportioned.[66] For example, if a U.S. subsidiary of a foreign corporation is engaged principally in trade between the United States and the treaty country, it is not material that the E-1 employee is also engaged in third country or intra-U.S. trade or that the parent firm's headquarters abroad is engaged primarily in trade with other countries.[67]

E-1 Employees

General Requirements for Employees

As mentioned above, an alien employee of a treaty trader may be classified E-1 if the employee is in or is coming to the United States to engage in duties of an executive or supervisory character or, if employed in a lesser capacity, the employee has special qualifications that make the services to be rendered essential to the efficient operation of the enterprise.[68] Employees of treaty traders seeking E status also must have the same nationality as their employer.[69]

To support an E-1 application filed on behalf of an alien employee of a treaty trader, the employer must be:

- a person having the nationality of the treaty country, who is maintaining the status of treaty trader if in the United States, or if not in the United States, would be classifiable as a treaty trader; or

- an organization at least 50 percent owned by persons having the nationality of the treaty country who are maintaining nonimmigrant treaty trader status if residing in the United States or if not residing in the United States who would be classifiable as treaty traders.[70]

In other words, where the employer is residing in the United States in some capacity other than E-1, it is not possible to seek E-1 treaty trader status on behalf of employees. The same applies in the case of a corporate employer where more than 50 percent of the individuals who own the employer are residing in the United States in some category other than E-1.

Executive or Supervisory Character

Executive or supervisory duties grant the employee ultimate control and responsibility for the enterprise's overall operation or a major component thereof.[71] An executive position provides the employee great authority to determine the policy and direction of the enterprise.[72] A supervisory position grants the employee supervisory responsibility for a significant proportion of an enterprise's operations and does not generally involve the direct supervision of low-level employees.[73]

In order to qualify as an executive or supervisory employee, the executive or supervisory element of the employee' position must be a principal and primary function of the position and not an incidental or collateral function.[74] E status generally would be appropriate, for example, if the position principally requires management skills or entails key supervisory responsibility for a large portion of a firm's operations and only incidentally involves routine substantive staff work.[75] Conversely, if the position chiefly involves routine work and entails supervision of low-level employees, the position could not be termed executive or supervisory.[76]

In determining whether the proposed position is executive or supervisory, consular officers will consider the title of the position, its place in the company's organizational structure, the duties of the position, the degree to which the applicant will have ultimate control and responsibility for the company's overall operations or a major component thereof, the number and skill levels of the employees the applicant will supervise, the level of pay, and whether the applicant possesses qualifying executive or supervisory experience.[77]

The weight given to a particular factor will vary from case to case.[78] For example, the position title of "vice president" or "manager" might be useful in assessing the supervisory nature of a position if the applicant were coming to a major operation having

---

[66] 9 FAM 41.51 N.7.2.

[67] *Id.*

[68] 22 CFR §41.51(a)(2).

[69] 9 FAM 41.51 N.14.1.

[70] 22 CFR §41.51(a)(2).

[71] 22 CFR §41.51(a)(11).

[72] *Id.*

[73] *Id.*

[74] 22 CFR §41.51(a)(2); 9 FAM 41.51 N.14.2.

[75] 9 FAM 41.51 N.14.2.

[76] *Id.*

[77] *Id.*

[78] *Id.*

numerous employees.[79] However, if the applicant were coming to a small two-person office, such a title in and of itself would be of little significance.[80]

In the case of a small business, the company may only have a few employees and the manager may be required to perform some routine staff work in addition to traditional managerial duties. The concept of a "functional manager," which is recognized in USCIS regulations for L-1A multinational managers,[81] is not expressly recognized for the E-1 classification. However, there is also no specific requirement that an E-1 supervisory employee manage any subordinate workers. The definition of "supervisory character" states only that it does not involve the direct supervision of low-level employees.[82] A similar limitation applies to L-1A multinational managers as well.[83] Therefore, a functional manager may be considered a supervisory employee within the E-1 context, even though he or she does not directly manage any subordinate employees.

Essential Skills

General

The applicant bears the burden of establishing at the time of application not only the need for the special qualifications that he or she offers but also the length of time that such skills will be needed.[84] In general, the E-1 classification is intended for specialists and not for ordinary skilled workers.[85]

Special qualifications are those skills and/or aptitudes that an employee in a lesser capacity brings to a position or role that are essential to the successful or efficient operation of the enterprise.[86] The essential nature of the alien's skills to the employing firm is determined by assessing the degree of proven expertise of the alien in the area of operations involved, the uniqueness of the specific skill or aptitude, the length of experience and/or training with the firm, the period of training or other experience necessary to perform effectively the projected duties,

and the salary that the special qualifications can command.[87]

Whether the special qualifications are essential will be assessed in light of all the circumstances at the time of each visa application, on a case-by-case basis.[88] In assessing the specialized skills and their essentiality, the consular officer should consider such factors as:

- degree of proven expertise of the alien in the area of specialization;
- uniqueness of the specific skills;
- function of the job to which the alien is destined; and
- salary such special expertise can command.[89]

The availability of U.S. workers is another factor in assessing the degree of specialization the applicant possesses and how essential the worker would be to the successful operation of the business.[90] This consideration is not a labor certification test, but a measure of the degree of specialization of the skills in question and the need for such skills.[91] As an example, the FAM mentions a TV technician coming to train U.S. workers in new TV technology not generally available in the U.S. market.[92] If the essential skills question cannot be resolved on the basis of initial documentation, the consular officer might ask the firm to provide statements from such sources as chambers of commerce, labor organizations, industry trade sources, or state employment services as to the unavailability of U.S. workers in the skill areas concerned.[93]

There is no requirement that an "essential" employee have any previous employment with the treaty enterprise.[94] Previous employment is a factor only when the needed skills can only be obtained by that employment.[95] The focus is on the company's need for the essential skills and the alien's possession of those skills.[96] Companies may need specific

---

[79] *Id.*

[80] *Id.*

[81] 8 CFR §214.2(l)(1)(ii)(B). Functional managers are not required to directly supervise any employees.

[82] 22 CFR §41.51(a)(11)(ii).

[83] 8 CFR §214.2(l)(1)(ii)(B).

[84] 9 FAM 41.51 N.14.3-1.

[85] *Id.*

[86] 22 CFR §41.51(a)(12).

[87] *Id.*

[88] *Id.*

[89] 9 FAM 41.51 N.14.3-2.

[90] *Id.*

[91] *Id.*

[92] *Id.*

[93] *Id.*

[94] 9 FAM 41.51 N.14.3-4.

[95] *Id.*

[96] *Id.*

skills to operate even though they do not have employees with those skills currently on their payroll.[97]

These criteria are similar, but not identical, to those applied in the context of L-1B cases of workers with specialized knowledge. In the L-1B context, "specialized knowledge" means knowledge possessed by an individual of the petitioning organization's product, service, research, equipment, techniques, management, or other interests and its application in international markets, or an advanced level of knowledge or expertise in the organization's processes and procedures.[98] This definition clearly differs from the concept of an essential skill worker because it emphasizes knowledge of the petitioning organization that is gained while working with that organization abroad.

There are two distinct types of essential skills workers: (1) short-term essential skills workers; and (2) long-term essential skills workers. Each is briefly discussed below.

Short-Term Need

In the case of short-term essential workers, the employer may need the skills for only a relatively short period of time (one or two years) when the purpose of the employee's admission relates to start-up operations (of either the business itself or a new activity of the business) or to the training and supervision of technicians employed in manufacturing, maintenance, and repair functions.[99] Ordinarily, skilled workers can qualify as essential employees but this almost always involves workers needed for start-up or training purposes.[100]

A new business or an established business expanding into a new field in the United States might need employees who are ordinarily skilled workers for a short period of time.[101] Such employees derive their essentiality from their familiarity with the overseas operations rather than the nature of their skills.[102] Their specialization of skills lies in their knowledge of the peculiarities of the operation of the

employer's enterprise, not in the skill held by the applicant.[103]

In such cases, an employer is expected to train U.S. workers to replace these employees within a relatively short period of time, usually within one or two years.[104] A consular officer may, at the time of the original application, set a time frame within which the business must replace such foreign workers with locally hired employees.[105] Short-term essential skills workers are therefore in a less desirable position than L-1B specialized knowledge workers, who are not required to demonstrate that U.S. workers will be trained to replace them.[106]

To illustrate the above, it may be useful to consider *In Re: X*.[107] In that case, the treaty investor employee sought an extension of stay for its E-2 employee as a "tatami service specialist" in a Japanese restaurant. The employer described her position as follows:

> The gourmet cuisine and service in a "Tatami" room is the most highly specialized, intricate and important in Japanese gastronomy, and requires intimate familiarity with the Japanese arts of the tea ceremony and flower arrangement. Because of her four years of experience, and her high level of linguistic proficiency, acquired at the Tokyo Foreign Language School, is uniquely qualified for her position.

> One year of training was required for the applicant to learn how to perform the duties of her position, and she earned $29,705 per year.

Relying upon the guidance contained in the FAM, the Administrative Appeals Unit (AAU) stated that applicant had to demonstrate that she was either: (1) a highly trained and specially qualified technician; or (2) a start-up employee of a new enterprise whose essentiality was based on her familiarity with the overseas operations of the employer rather than on the nature of her skills. The AAU concluded that the applicant was not a technician or a highly trained employee. She had not been shown to have any familiarity with an overseas operation of

[97] *Id.*

[98] 8 CFR §214.2(l)(1)(ii)(D).

[99] 9 FAM 41.51 N.14.3-1.

[100] 9 FAM 41.51 N.14.3-3.

[101] *Id.*

[102] *Id.*

[103] *Id.*

[104] 9 FAM 41.51 N.14.3-1. *See also* 8 CFR §214.2(e)(18)(ii).

[105] 9 FAM 41.51 N.14.3-3.

[106] L-1B specialized knowledge workers rarely have difficulty extending their status up to the five-year maximum described in INA §214(c)(2)(D).

[107] 11 Immig. Rptr. B2-79 (AAU 1993).

her employer in the United States, and the employer's business operation was not a new enterprise. The absence of a training program intended to replace the alien with a U.S. worker was also considered a negative factor. The AAU concluded that she was an ordinary skilled worker and denied her extension of stay.

The situation might have been different if, for example, the employee (although an ordinary skills worker) had previously worked for the employer's foreign operation, the U.S. operation was considered a new enterprise, and the employer had a training program in place designed to eventually replace the employee.

Long-Term Need

Long-term essentiality may be established in connection with continuous activities in such areas as product improvement, quality control, or the provision of a service not generally available in the United States.[108] If an applicant establishes that he or she has special qualifications and, on a long-term basis, these qualifications are essential for the efficient operation of the treaty enterprise, the training of U.S. workers as replacement workers is not required.[109] It should therefore be possible for such an employee to remain in the United States, in E-1 status, for an indefinite period of time.

The precedential decision relating to long-term essential skills workers is *Matter of Walsh and Pollard*.[110] The employees in that case were automotive design engineers from Britain who were coming to the United States (pursuant to a contract between the treaty investor and General Motors) for the purpose of redesigning General Motors's line of cars in a smaller, more European fashion. It was established that a worker with an engineering degree would still require approximately 10 years of training to become an automotive design engineer and that there were not sufficient numbers of U.S. automotive design engineers to fill the present needs of the automotive industry. The Board of Immigration Appeals (BIA) concluded that the employees were long-term essential skills workers and the treaty investor was not expected to replace the employees with U.S. workers in the future.

Labor Disputes (Citizens of Canada, Mexico, Chile, and Singapore Only)

Because of specific language contained in the North America Free Trade Agreement (NAFTA), citizens of Canada and Mexico are not entitled to E-1 classification if there is a strike or lockout in progress in the course of a labor dispute in the occupational classification at the place or intended place of employment, unless such alien establishes, pursuant to the regulations, that the alien's entry will not affect adversely the settlement of the strike or lockout or the employment of any person who is involved in the strike or lockout.[111] A similar restriction also applies to citizens of Chile and Singapore because of specific language contained in their respective treaties.[112]

Applicant Intends to Depart the United States When E-1 Status Terminates

To qualify for E-1 status, the alien must intend to depart from the United States upon the termination of his or her status.[113] However, an applicant does not have to establish either an intention to remain in the United States for a specific temporary period of time or the existence of a residence in a foreign country that the applicant does not intend to abandon.[114] The applicant's expression of an unequivocal intent to return when the E-1 status ends is normally sufficient, in the absence of specific evidence to the contrary.[115] This intent can normally be expressed by way of a written statement submitted with the E-1 visa application.

A limited form of dual intent is recognized for E-1 nonimmigrants. DOS's position is that an applicant who is the beneficiary of an immigrant petition may still be eligible for E-1 status by showing that he or she will not remain in the United States to adjust his or her status to lawful permanent resident or otherwise remain in the United States regardless of the legality of his or her status.[116] USCIS's position is that an application for initial admission, change of status, or extension of stay in E-1 classification may not be denied solely on the basis of an approved request for permanent labor certification or a filed or

---

[108] 22 CFR §41.51(a)(12)(ii).

[109] 9 FAM 41.51 N.14.3-3.

[110] 20 I&N Dec. 60 (BIA 1988).

[111] INA §214(j)(1); *see also* 22 CFR §41.51(a)(13).

[112] INA §214(j)(2).

[113] 22 CFR §41.51(a)(1)(ii).

[114] 9 FAM 41.51 N.15.

[115] *Id.*

[116] *Id.*

approved immigrant visa preference petition.[117] In addition, an applicant who has already filed an application for adjustment of status should still be able to file for an extension of E-1 status after that date.[118]

This clearly shows that an E-1 nonimmigrant may be the beneficiary of a labor certification, immigrant petition, or have an adjustment of status application pending, and still remain eligible for E status. However, it is important to remember that DOS will not issue a new E visa to an alien who is seeking adjustment of status rather than an immigrant visa.

Notwithstanding the above, INA §214(b) applies to E-1 aliens. A prior overstay or violation of status while in the United States can imply that the alien does not intend to depart from the United States upon termination of his or her status. It may be difficult to overcome such an inference. The best way to deal with this situation is to establish that the violation or overstay was brief and/or inadvertent.

PROCEDURAL CONSIDERATIONS

How, Where, and What to File

Consular Processing versus Change of Status

Most E-1 cases will originate at consular posts abroad, since they do not require prior petition approval from USCIS. USCIS may adjudicate an E-1 petition, but only when an alien is seeking a change of status or an extension of stay from within the United States.[119] However, an alien who acquires E-1 status through a change of status or extension of stay will require an E-1 visa to re-enter the United States after travel abroad, unless the alien is eligible for automatic visa revalidation after travel solely to contiguous territory for 30 days or less.[120]

Visa applicants who acquired E-1 status through a change of status in the United States will find that most consular posts do not simply issue E-1 visas based on a prior USCIS adjudication. Instead, most require the alien to submit a new application to the consular post along with completed forms, fees, and supporting documentation; the alien will essentially apply twice for the same benefit. For this reason, it is usually preferable to apply initially through a consular post.

Nevertheless, there are situations where a change of status or extension of stay may be more appropriate. If the alien is already in the United States and needs to commence business immediately, it may be faster to obtain a change of status to E-1 using the premium processing program and then seek an E-1 visa at a later date, when the alien is able to travel abroad. Similarly, where the alien's E-1 case is not strong enough to risk a consular application, it may be safer to simply seek a change of status and then obtain extensions of stay until the business has grown to an acceptable level. While USCIS will not always be less demanding, certain consular posts are notorious for being unreasonably strict in their legal interpretations. An alien who would otherwise be required to submit an application to one of these posts may find it preferable to take his or her chances with USCIS instead, especially if the alien intends to rely upon one or more precedent decisions of the BIA, which are binding on USCIS but not on consular posts.

Canadian citizens are normally visa-exempt for nonimmigrant entries.[121] However, this visa-exemption does not apply to Canadians entering as E-1 aliens.[122] Also, since the visa exemption applies to all other nonimmigrant classifications (except for K nonimmigrants[123]), a Canadian citizen who changes status to E-1 from within the United States will not have a prior visa with which to seek automatic revalidation.[124]

Third Country National E-1 Cases

Due to the complexity of the issues involved, many consular posts abroad will not accept E-1 visa applications from third country nationals. An E-1 applicant who wishes to apply outside of their country of citizenship or residence should first check to see if the application will be accepted.

Even if such an application is accepted, a third country national may still face increased difficulty in

---

[117] 8 CFR §214.2(e)(5).

[118] INS Memorandum, Paul Virtue, Acting Executive Commissioner, HQ 70/6.2.5, 70/6.2.9 (Aug. 5, 1997), *reprinted in* 74 *Interpreter Releases* 1226–29 (Aug. 11, 1997).

[119] Effective December 4, 1998, all petitions and applications relating to classification under the E-1 or E-2 categories must be filed with either the Texas or California Service Centers. *See* 63 Fed. Reg. 67135–36 (Dec. 4, 1998).

[120] 22 CFR §41.112(d).

[121] 8 CFR §§212.1(a), 1212.1(a).

[122] 8 CFR §§212.1(l), 1212.1(l).

[123] 8 CFR §§212.1(h), 1212.1(h).

[124] 22 CFR §41.112(d) requires the alien to be in possession of an expired nonimmigrant visa.

establishing certain relevant facts. For example, it may be harder to establish the existence of trade between the United States and the treaty country or the alien's intention to return to the treaty country upon termination of his or her E-1 status.

What to File

An E-1 application normally consists of a Form DS-156 executed by each visa applicant (including dependents), Form DS-157 (executed by each male between 16 and 45[125]), Form DS-156E, a document's brief containing sufficient supporting documentation to establish E-1 eligibility, and the Machine-Readable Visa fee for each applicant (currently $100).

Incidental Activities While in E-1 Status

E-1 treaty traders are entitled to engage in incidental activities so long as their primary purpose for coming to the United States is to engage in qualifying trade.[126] However, these incidental activities are limited to those activities in which any visitor could engage. In addition, because dependents of E-1 treaty traders are permitted to attend school,[127] it is probable that the principal alien will also be permitted to do so.

However, a treaty investor or treaty employee may only engage in employment that is consistent with the terms and conditions of his or her status and the activity forming the basis for the E-1 treaty status.[128] The one exception is employment with a subsidiary of the treaty enterprise. Performing work for subsidiaries of a common parent enterprise or organization will not be deemed to constitute a substantive change in the terms and conditions of the underlying E-1 treaty employment if, at the time the E-1 treaty status was determined, the applicant presented evidence establishing:

- The enterprise or organization, and any subsidiaries thereof, where the work will be performed; the requisite parent-subsidiary relationship; and that the subsidiary independently qualifies as a treaty organization or enterprise under this paragraph;

- In the case of an employee of a treaty trader, the work to be performed requires executive, supervisory, or essential skills; and

- The work is consistent with the terms and conditions of the activity forming the basis of the classification.[129]

Period of Visa Validity, Admission Period, and Extensions of Stay

The maximum validity period for an E-1 visa will depend upon reciprocity with the country of the alien's nationality. The maximum visa-validity period for each country is shown in the reciprocity schedules that appear in the FAM, but in many cases will be five years.[130]

In order to determine the maximum period of admission in the United States, one must refer to USCIS regulations. According to these regulations, an E-2 nonimmigrant (including dependents) may be admitted for an initial period of not more than two years at a time.[131] This is the period that will be shown on the alien's Form I-94. However, because the validity period of the visa has no relationship to the period of admission, the alien may seek a two-year period of admission even if his or her visa is due to expire within a shorter period of time.

Even if the alien enters the United States one day before his or her visa is due to expire, the immigration officer at the port of entry should issue a Form I-94 for a period of two years. However, if the alien subsequently leaves the United States prior to the expiration of his or her Form I-94, he or she will not be re-admitted for the remainder of his or her status without a valid visa (since a visa is required for admission to the United States). This can still be useful in light of the long delays in adjudicating E visa applications at consulates abroad.

USCIS regulations limit the total period of stay permitted for essential-skills employees who are needed in the start-up of an enterprise.[132] With limited exceptions, it is presumed that employees of treaty enterprises with special qualifications who are responsible for start-up operations should be able to complete their objectives within two years. Absent

---

[125] DOS Cable No. 006020 (Jan. 11, 2002), *reprinted in* 79 *Interpreter Releases* 118 (Jan. 21, 2002), *published on* AILA InfoNet at Doc. No. 02011134 (*posted* Jan. 11, 2002).

[126] 9 FAM 41.11 N.3.1.

[127] 8 CFR §248.3(e)(2); 9 FAM 41.11 N.5.2.

[128] 8 CFR §214.2(e)(8)(i).

[129] 8 CFR §214.2(e)(8)(ii).

[130] 9 FAM Appendix C. The reciprocity tables currently appear online at *http://travel.state.gov/visa/reciprocity/index. htm.*

[131] 8 CFR §214.2(e)(19).

[132] 8 CFR §214.2(e)(20)(ii).

special circumstances, such employees may not be eligible to obtain an extension of stay after this limit has been reached.

Dependents of E-1 Treaty Traders

The spouse and dependent children (unmarried and under age 21) of an E-1 treaty trader are entitled to the same classification as the principal alien.[133] The nationality of a spouse and child is not material to their eligibility.[134]

Such treaty dependents are permitted to engage in incidental activities, such as tourism[135] or attending school.[136] As a result of legislation enacted in 2002, dependent spouses of E-1 nonimmigrants who have been admitted in E-1 status may now apply for an open-market employment authorization document (EAD).[137] These EADs permit dependent spouses holding E-1 status to work for any employer. However, the legislation does not extend employment eligibility to dependent children of the principal alien.

SPECIAL PROVISIONS FOR EMPLOYEES OF THE TAIPEI ECONOMIC AND CULTURAL REPRESENTATIVE OFFICE (TECRO)

The United States does not have official relations with Taiwan and does not recognize Taiwan as an independent sovereign state. As a result, representatives of Taiwan are not entitled to receive A[138] or G[139] nonimmigrant visas.[140] The Taipei Economic and Cultural Representative Office (TECRO) is the instrumentality provided for in Section 10 of the Taiwan Relations Act[141] (TRA) to represent Taiwan in the United States in the absence of diplomatic relations.[142] Representatives of Taiwan employed by TECRO (and their dependents) are entitled to receive E-1 nonimmigrant visas.[143]

Persons possessing a Taiwan passport who are assigned for more than 90 days to TECRO offices in the United States, their dependent spouses, and unmarried sons and daughters are issued E-1 visas.[144] Other immediate family members (*e.g.*, parents or parent-in-law) who are members of the same household are not entitled to E-1 dependent visas but may be issued B-2 visas.[145] Personal employees of TECRO personnel may also be issued B-1 visas.[146]

As in the case of A and G applicants, TECRO E-1 applicants are exempt from the requirement to submit a Form DS-157 with their visa application.[147] However, consular officers still retain the right to require a Form DS-157 from any applicant seeking any visa classification.[148]

Dependent children of E-1 aliens who reach the age of 21 normally become ineligible for E-1 dependent status.[149] However, according to TRA §4(a), children of TECRO employees may continue to seek E-1 dependent status even after they reach the age of 21.[150] They may be issued E-1 dependent visas provided that they continue to meet the definition of "immediate family,"[151] which includes unmarried sons and daughters of the principal alien or spouse who:

- are related to the principal alien or spouse by blood or adoption;

- are not members of some other household; and

- will reside regularly in the household of the principal alien.

An alien spouse or unmarried son or daughter of a TECRO employee may apply for an open-market employment authorization.[152] However, the alien must fall within the definition of "dependent," which includes the following immediate family members habitually residing in the same household as the principal alien:

---

[133] 22 CFR §41.51(b)(3).

[134] *Id.*

[135] 9 FAM 41.11 N.3.1.

[136] 8 CFR §248.3(e)(2); 9 FAM 41.11 N.5.2.

[137] Pub. L. No. 107-124 (Jan. 16, 2002).

[138] INA §101(a)(15)(A).

[139] INA §101(a)(15)(G).

[140] 9 FAM 41.22 PN.1.1.

[141] Pub. L. No. 96-8.

[142] Reciprocity Schedule for Taiwan, available at *http://travel.state.gov/visa/reciprocity/Country%20Folder/T/Taiwan.htm* (hereinafter Reciprocity Schedule for Taiwan).

[143] 9 FAM 41.22 PN.1.1.

[144] Reciprocity Schedule for Taiwan, *supra* note 142.

[145] *Id.*

[146] *Id.*

[147] 9 FAM 41.22 PN.1.2.

[148] *Id.*

[149] INA §101(b)(1).

[150] 9 FAM 41.22 PN.1.3a.

[151] 9 FAM 41.22 PN.1.3b.

[152] 8 CFR §274a.12(c)(2); 9 FAM 41.22 PN.4.

- spouse;
- unmarried children under the age of 21;
- unmarried sons or daughters under the age of 23 who are in full-time attendance as students at post-secondary educational institutions;[153] or
- unmarried sons or daughters who are physically or mentally disabled to the extent that they cannot adequately care for themselves or cannot establish, maintain, or re-establish their own households.[154]

Employees of TECRO and their dependents are admitted for duration of status (D/S).[155] Dependents of TECRO employees who are deemed to be out of status because an immigration officer annotated their Form I-94 with an expiration date instead of "D/S" may apply for reinstatement to E-1 status.[156] In order to request reinstatement, TECRO must submit the following to the DOS Visa Office through the American Institute in Taiwan (AIT):

- applicant's passport, valid for at least six months;
- currently valid Form I-94 (reinstatement will not be considered where the applicant's Form I-94 has already expired); and
- letter from TECRO requesting that the Form I-94 be annotated to read "D/S."[157]

CONCLUSION

The E-1 treaty trader category is clearly a valuable nonimmigrant option for certain foreign companies (and their employees) and individual aliens who trade in goods or services. Despite the popularity of the E-2 investor category, practitioners should always consider the E-1 when the alien's nationality suggests entitlement to treaty classification.

---

[153] *See also* 9 FAM 41.22 PN.4.1.

[154] 8 CFR §214.2(a)(2).

[155] 9 FAM 41.22 PN.2.

[156] 9 FAM 41.22 PN.3.

---

[157] *Id.*

EXHIBIT A—LIST OF TREATY COUNTRIES

COUNTRY	CLASSIFICATION	Effective Date
Albania	E-2	January 4, 1998
Argentina	E-1	December 20, 1854
Argentina	E-2	December 20, 1854
Armenia	E-2	March 29, 1996
Australia	E-1	December 16, 1991
Australia	E-2	December 27, 1991
Austria	E-1	May 27, 1931
Austria	E-2	May 27, 1931
Azerbaijan	E-2	August 2, 2001
Bahrain	E-2	May 31, 2001
Bangladesh	E-2	July 25, 1989
Belgium	E-1	October 3, 1963
Belgium	E-2	October 3, 1963
Bolivia	E-1	November 9, 1862
Bolivia	E-2	June 6, 2001
Bosnia and Herzegovina[11]	E-1	November 15, 1882
Bosnia and Herzegovina[11]	E-2	November 15, 1882
Brunei	E-1	July 11, 1853
Bulgaria	E-2	June 2, 1994
Cameroon	E-2	April 6, 1989
Canada	E-1	January 1, 1993
Canada	E-2	January 1, 1993
Chile	E-1	January 1, 2004
Chile	E-2	January 1, 2004
China (Taiwan)[1]	E-1	November 30, 1948
China (Taiwan)[1]	E-2	November 30, 1948
Colombia	E-1	June 10, 1848
Colombia	E-2	June 10, 1848
Congo (Brazzaville)	E-2	August 13, 1994
Congo (Kinshasa)	E-2	July 28, 1989
Costa Rica	E-1	May 26, 1852
Costa Rica	E-2	May 26, 1852
Croatia[11]	E-1	November 15, 1882
Croatia[11]	E-2	November 15, 1882

Czech Republic[2]	E-2	January 1, 1993
Denmark[3]	E-1	July 30, 1961
Ecuador	E-2	May 11, 1997
Egypt	E-2	June 27, 1992
Estonia	E-1	May 22, 1926
Estonia	E-2	February 16, 1997
Ethiopia	E-1	October 8, 1953
Ethiopia	E-2	October 8, 1953
Finland	E-1	August 10, 1934
Finland	E-2	December 1, 1992
France[4]	E-1	December 21, 1960
France[4]	E-2	December 21, 1960
Georgia	E-2	August 17, 1997
Germany	E-1	July 14, 1956
Germany	E-2	July 14, 1956
Greece	E-1	October 13, 1954
Grenada	E-2	March 3, 1989
Honduras	E-1	July 19, 1928
Honduras	E-2	July 11, 2001
Iran	E-1	June 16, 1957
Iran	E-2	June 16, 1957
Ireland	E-1	September 14, 1950
Ireland	E-2	November 18, 1992
Israel	E-1	April 3, 1954
Italy	E-1	July 26, 1949
Italy	E-2	July 26, 1949
Jamaica	E-2	March 7, 1997
Japan[5]	E-1	October 30, 1953
Japan[5]	E-2	October 30, 1953
Jordan	E-1	December 17, 2001
Jordan	E-2	December 17, 2001
Kazakhstan	E-2	January 12, 1994
Korea (South)	E-1	November 7, 1957
Korea (South)	E-2	November 7, 1957
Kyrgyzstan	E-2	January 12, 1994
Latvia	E-1	July 25, 1928
Latvia	E-2	December 26, 1996
Liberia	E-1	November 21, 1939
Liberia	E-2	November 21, 1939
Lithuania	E-2	November 22, 2001
Luxembourg	E-1	March 28, 1963
Luxembourg	E-2	March 28, 1963

Macedonia, the Former Yugoslav Republic of (FRY)	E-1	November 15, 1882
Macedonia, the Former Yugoslav Republic of (FRY)	E-2	November 15, 1882
Mexico	E-1	January 1, 1994
Mexico	E-2	January 1, 1994
Moldova	E-2	November 25, 1994
Mongolia	E-2	January 1, 1997
Morocco	E-2	May 29, 1991
Netherlands[6]	E-1	December 5, 1957
Netherlands[6]	E-2	December 5, 1957
Norway[7]	E-1	January 18, 1928
Norway[7]	E-2	January 18, 1928
Oman	E-1	June 11, 1960
Oman	E-2	June 11, 1960
Pakistan	E-1	February 12, 1961
Pakistan	E-2	February 12, 1961
Panama	E-2	May 30, 1991
Paraguay	E-1	March 7, 1860
Paraguay	E-2	March 7, 1860
Philippines	E-1	September 6, 1955
Philippines	E-2	September 6, 1955
Poland	E-1	August 6, 1994
Poland	E-2	August 6, 1994
Romania	E-2	January 15, 1994
Senegal	E-2	October 25, 1990
Singapore	E-1	January 1, 2004
Singapore	E-2	January 1, 2004
Slovak Republic[2]	E-2	January 1, 1993
Slovenia[11]	E-1	November 15, 1882
Slovenia[11]	E-2	November 15, 1882
Spain[8]	E-1	April 14, 1903
Spain[8]	E-2	April 14, 1903
Sri Lanka	E-2	May 1, 1993
Suriname[9]	E-1	February 10, 1963
Suriname[9]	E-2	February 10, 1963
Sweden	E-1	February 20, 1992
Sweden	E-2	February 20, 1992
Switzerland	E-1	November 8, 1855
Switzerland	E-2	November 8, 1855
Thailand	E-1	June 8, 1968
Thailand	E-2	June 8, 1968

Togo	E-1	February 5, 1967
Togo	E-2	February 5, 1967
Trinidad & Tobago	E-2	December 26, 1996
Tunisia	E-2	February 7, 1993
Turkey	E-1	February 15, 1933
Turkey	E-2	May 18, 1990
Ukraine	E-2	November 16, 1996
United Kingdom[10]	E-1	July 3, 1815
United Kingdom[10]	E-2	July 3, 1815
Yugoslavia[11]	E-1	November 15, 1882
Yugoslavia[11]	E-2	November 15, 1882

[1] **CHINA (TAIWAN).** Pursuant to Section 6 of the Taiwan Relations Act, (TRA), Pub. L. No. 96-8, 93 Stat, 14, and Executive Order 12143, 44 F.R. 37191, this agreement, which was concluded with the Taiwan authorities prior to January 1, 1979, is administered on a nongovernmental basis by the American Institute in Taiwan, a nonprofit District of Columbia corporation, and constitutes neither recognition of the Taiwan authorities nor the continuation of any official relationship with Taiwan.

[2] **CZECH REPUBLIC AND SLOVAK REPUBLIC.** The Treaty with the Czech and Slovak Federal Republic entered into force on December 19, 1992; entered into force for the Czech Republic and Slovak Republic as separate states on January 1, 1993.

[3] **DENMARK.** The Treaty, which entered into force on July 30, 1961, does not apply to Greenland.

[4] **FRANCE.** The Treaty, which entered into force on December 21, 1960, applies to the departments of Martinique, Guadeloupe, French Guiana, and Reunion.

[5] **JAPAN.** The Treaty, which entered into force on October 30, 1953, was made applicable to the Bonin Islands on June 26, 1968, and to the Ryukyu Islands on May 15, 1972.

[6] **NETHERLANDS.** The Treaty, which entered into force on December 5, 1957, is applicable to Aruba and Netherlands Antilles.

[7] **NORWAY.** The Treaty, which entered into force on September 13, 1932, does not apply to Svalbard (Spitzbergen and certain lesser islands).

[8] **SPAIN.** The Treaty, which entered into force on April 14, 1903, is applicable to all territories.

[9] **SURINAME.** The Treaty with the Netherlands, which entered into force December 5, 1957, was made applicable to Suriname on February 10, 1963.

[10] **UNITED KINGDOM.** The Convention, which entered into force on July 3, 1815, applies only to British territory in Europe (the British Isles except the Republic of Ireland), the Channel Islands, and Gibraltar and to "inhabitants" of such territory. This term, as used in the Convention, means "one who resides actually and permanently in a given place, and has his domicile there." In order to qualify for treaty trader or treaty investor status under this treaty, the alien must be a national of the United Kingdom. Individuals having the nationality of members of the Commonwealth other than the United Kingdom do not qualify for treaty trader or treaty investor status under this treaty.

[11] **YUGOSLAVIA.** The U.S. view is that the Socialist Federal Republic of Yugoslavia (SFRY) has dissolved and that the successors that formerly made up the SFRY—Bosnia and Herzegovina, Croatia, the Former Yugoslav Republic of Macedonia, Slovenia, and the Federal Republic of Yugoslavia—continue to be bound by the treaty in force with the SFRY at the time of dissolution.

MAKING SENSE OF THE FAM NOTES ON TREATY INVESTOR VISAS

*by Paul W. Ferrell**

INTRODUCTION

One way to learn how something works is to take it apart and put it back together again. Try to improve or redesign it and you can learn even more. Those are the premises behind this exercise in tinkering. The text I have chosen is the set of notes in the *Foreign Affairs Manual* (FAM) relating to treaty investor visas. I parsed the E-2 regulation (22 CFR §41.51), the current FAM notes, and prior versions of current notes and by doing so got a sense of how the present system evolved. The requirements for E-2 visas have not always been the same and, conversely, the requirements are not what they used to be. If a practitioner does not review the notes regularly, it is easy to cite from memory a requirement or interpretation that has been dropped or rewritten.

The explanatory notes in the FAM are meant to offer guidance to consular personnel on the meaning of the law and regulations applicable to the adjudication of visa applications. Yet, anyone reading the current version of the FAM notes on E-2 visas could be forgiven for wishing for an equally official source that explains the explanation. What, for example, is a consular officer to make of the instruction that, when determining whether an investment is "substantial," he or she, "must view the proportionate amount of funds invested, as evidenced by the proportionality test, in light of the nature of the business and the projected success of the business?"

The current FAM notes are unintelligible in part because too many words are used and in part because there are too few. After reading the extensive and repetitive explanation of the proportionality test, I was left with the feeling that the author of the notes was struggling to convince him or herself of the meaning of the test and how it is meant to be applied. There are a number of instances in which the notes simply repeat the wording of the regulation without any attempt to elucidate or offer real-world

examples that might assist in applying the regulation. For example, FAM §41.51, Note 10.5 states that, "An element of judgment to be factored into the requirement of substantial investment concerns an assessment of the extent of the investor's commitment to the successful operation of the project in view of the amount invested." How does an investor evidence sufficient commitment to success over and above committing the funds required by the proportionality test? There is no guidance.

The current version of the treaty visa notes in the FAM can trace its origin to a memorandum published in the Visa Bulletin in March of 1982 (Vol. 5, No. 20). This memorandum, peppered with citations to BIA and federal court decisions, distilled and restated requirements taken from a wide variety of sources and provided a cogent statement of principles. Although some of the principles stated in the 1982 memorandum have been superseded by the 1997 regulation, the 1982 memorandum is a model of clarity compared to the current version of the FAM notes.

When the Department of State published the first comprehensive treaty trader and investor visa regulation in 1997, the FAM notes could have been rewritten to interpret and explain the coherent set of rules duly promulgated under the Administrative Procedures Act. Sadly, this opportunity was missed. Instead, the FAM notes published after 1997 have been an inartful blend of language taken piecemeal from the pre-1997 notes mixed in with some of the language and terminology from the regulation. In my opinion, the rewrites from 1997 onward have made the law less intelligible and have increased the likelihood that consular officers could impose their own requirements on petitions in an attempt to make sense of ambiguous terms and phrases.

It does not help that the notes use inconsistent terms instead of sticking to those used in the regulation. For example, the notes variously refer to "the applicant", "the alien", and "the investor" and use the terms "funds" and "capital" interchangeably. The notes also use the terms "value" and "cost" interchangeably even though they are not synonyms. (The regulation uses the term "cost" when defining "substantial amount of capital" at 22 §CFR §41.51(n).)

* **Paul Ferrell** is an attorney in the London office of Andrews Kurth LLP. He is a member of the Florida bar and has practiced U.S. immigration and nationality law in London since 1983. His previous unsolicited advice to the Visa Office was "The Corporate Alien and Treaty Visa Nationality," 7 *Geo. Immigr. L.J.* 283 (June 1993).

The following rewritten version is not an attempt to propose new interpretations or to modify the substantive requirements. My guiding principle has been to reconcile the interpretive notes with the regulations and to simplify them by removing superfluous or confusing language when possible. To the extent that the regulations themselves are opaque, the proposed notes remain unclear since I have not attempted to provide explanations or examples that are not supported by the regulations or the existing notes. For example FAM §41.51, Note 10.2(c) contains the sentence, "Unverified and unaudited financial statements based exclusively on information supplied by an applicant are normally insufficient to establish the nature and status of an enterprise." I chose to leave this statement intact even though it has been the basis for many aggravating requests from consular officers for audited financial statements from newly-formed businesses. The sentence appears in a note discussing how to determine the cost of a newly-created enterprise. How it helps in determining the cost of a newly-created enterprise is anybody's guess since very few such enterprises will have financial statements, audited or otherwise. Perhaps it means financial projections. Also, the use of the words "nature and status" is peculiar. How do financial statements, audited or otherwise, establish the "nature" of the business? And, what is the "status" of a business and why is it important in the determination of the value of a newly-created enter-prise? Substituting the word "state" for "status" would make more sense, but why is the sentence there at all?

Scorn for the use of unverified and unaudited financial statements can be traced to a principle set out in the 1982 Visa Bulletin memorandum under the heading "Burden of Proof" and cited the BIA decision in *Matter of Shaw*, 15 I&N Dec. 794 (1976). The original version reads, "unverified and unaudited financial statements based exclusively on information supplied by an applicant do not normally satisfactorily establish the affairs of an enterprise." This earlier version is a rule of evidence requiring verified and audited financial statements in every application. I interpret the current placement of the reworded version of the caution, in a note that only addresses new enterprises, as an attempt to limit its application.

What follows is my personal revision of those FAM notes dealing with qualifying for an E-2 visa as an investor, except those relating to nationality. The current official version of each note and my editorial comments (in italics) are in the left column; each of my revised notes sits opposite the originals on the right-hand side. I have no doubt that readers will be able to come up with better versions and my hope is that it provokes at least a few to attempt the exercise.

PROPOSED REVISION OF THE FAM NOTES ON TREATY INVESTOR VISAS

41.51 N8 APPLICANT MUST HAVE INVESTED OR IN PROCESS OF INVESTING

41.51 N8.1 Concept of "Investment" and "In Process of Investing"

The consular officer must assess the nature of the investment transaction to determine whether a particular financial arrangement may be considered an "investment" within the meaning of INA 101(a)(15)(E)(ii). The core factors relevant to a post's analysis of whether the applicant actually has invested, or is in the process of investing, in an enterprise are discussed below.

41.51 N8 APPLICANT MUST HAVE INVESTED OR BE IN THE PROCESS OF INVESTING

41.51 N8.1 Meaning of "Has Invested or Is in the Process of Investing"

The consular officer must assess the nature of the financial transaction or transactions presented by the applicant to determine whether each may be considered an "investment" or whether the applicant is actively in the process of investing within the meaning of INA 101(a)(15)(E)(ii) and 22 CFR Sec. 41.51 (b) and (l). The considerations relevant to a post's assessment are discussed below.

41.51 N8.1-1 POSSESSION AND CONTROL OF FUNDS

The alien must demonstrate possession and control of the capital assets, including funds invested. If the investor has received the funds by legitimate means, e.g., savings, gift, inheritance, contest, etc. and has control and possession over the funds, the proper employment of the funds may constitute an E-2 investment. (It should be noted, however, that inheritance of a business does not constitute an investment.) Furthermore, the statute does not require that the source of the funds be outside the United States.

Comment: The regulation defines investment in terms of "capital" that can take the form of funds or other assets. The current notes' use of the term "funds" as a substitute for "capital" suggests that the investment of "funds" is in some way superior to the investment of other assets. The reference to inherited businesses has been moved to Note 41.51 N8.1-2 because its justification lies not in whether the investor possesses and controls inherited capital, but rather whether he or she has actually "placed" the capital at risk. See 22 CFR §41.51(l).

41.51 N8.1-1 POSSESSION AND CONTROL OF CAPITAL

The applicant must be in possession and have control over the capital invested. The applicant must have received the capital by legitimate means and must demonstrate possession and control of the capital prior to its investment. Acquisition of the capital through savings, by gift, inheritance, or by winning a contest are all legitimate means of acquiring the capital invested. Acquisition of the investment capital by borrowing funds or by leasing assets is also permitted, but capital acquired by these methods will be treated differently than capital acquired by other means (See 9 FAM 41.51 Note 8.2). Neither the statute nor the regulations require that the source of the capital be outside the United States.

41.51 N8.1-2 INVESTMENT CONNOTES RISK

a. The concept of investment connotes the placing of funds or other capital assets at risk, in the commercial sense, in the hope of generating a financial return. (E-2 investor status shall not, therefore, be extended to non-profit organizations.) If the funds are not subject to partial or total loss if business fortunes reverse, then it is not an "investment" in the sense intended by INA 101(a)(15)(E)(ii). If the funds' availability arises from indebtedness, these criteria must be followed:

(1) Indebtedness such as mortgage debt or commercial loans secured by the assets of the enterprise cannot count toward the investment, as there is no requisite element of risk. For example, if the business in which the alien is investing is used as collateral, funds from the resulting loan or mortgage are NOT at risk, even if some personal assets are also used as collateral.

(2) On the other hand, loans secured by the alien's own personal assets, such as a second mortgage on a home, or unsecured loans, such as a loan on the

41.51 N8.1-2 INVESTMENT CONNOTES PLACING CAPITAL AT RISK

a. The definition of "investment" at 22 CFR 41.51 (l) requires that capital, including funds and other assets, be placed at risk in the commercial sense with the objective of generating a profit. The applicant's capital must be subject to partial or total loss if the business fails.

Since the applicant must "place" the investment capital at risk, the inheritance of a business by the applicant does not constitute an investment. The definition also excludes non-profit organizations from treaty investor status since they do not have profit as a business objective.

b. The applicant must demonstrate possession of and control over the capital invested or being invested.

c. If the capital invested has been borrowed by the applicant then it will only be considered as "at risk" if the loan is either unsecured, in other words a loan on the applicant's personal signature alone, or if the loan is secured by the personal assets of the applicant, such as the applicant's dwelling or other

alien's personal signature, may be included, since the alien risks the funds in the event of business failure.

b. In short, at risk funds in the E-2 context would include only funds in which personal assets are involved, such as personal funds, other unencumbered assets, a mortgage with the alien's personal dwelling used as collateral, or some similar personal liability. A reasonable amount of cash, held in a business bank account or similar fund to be used for routine business operations, may be counted as investment funds. (See 9 FAM 41.51 N8.1-3 below for contrast with uncommitted funds.)

41.51 N8.1-3 FUNDS MUST BE IRREVOCABLY COMMITTED

a. To be "in the process of investing" for E-2 purposes, the funds or assets to be invested must be committed to the investment, and the commitment must be real and irrevocable. As an example, a purchase or sale of a business which qualifies for E-2 status in every respect may be conditioned upon the issuance of the visa. Despite the condition, this would constitute a solid commitment if the assets to be used for the purchase are held in escrow for release or transfer only on the condition being met. The point of the example is that to be in the process of investing the investor must have, and in this case would have, reached an irrevocable point to qualify.

b. Moreover, for the alien to be "in the process of investing", the alien must be close to the start of actual business operations, not simply in the stage of signing contracts (which may be broken) or scouting for suitable locations and property. Mere intent to invest, or possession of uncommitted funds in a bank account, or even prospective investment arrangements entailing no present commitment, will not suffice.

41.51 N8.2 CONSIDERATION OF OTHER FINANCIAL TRANSACTIONS, PROPERTY OR PROPERTY RIGHTS AS "INVESTMENTS"

41.51 N8.2-1 Payments for Leases or Rents as Investments

Payments in the form of leases or rents for property or equipment may be calculated toward the investment in an amount limited to the funds devoted to that item in any one month. However, the market value of the leased equipment is not representative of the investment and neither is the annual rental cost (unless it has been paid in advance) as these rents are generally paid from the current earnings of the business.

41.51 N8.2-2 Value of Goods or Equipment as Investment

The amount spent for purchase of equipment and for inventory on hand may be calculated in the investment total. The value of goods or equipment transferred to the United States (such as factory machinery shipped to the United States to start or enlarge a plant) may be considered an investment.

The alien, however, must demonstrate that the goods or machinery will be put, or are being put, to use in an ongoing commercial enterprise. The applicant must establish that the purchased goods or equipment are for business, not personal purposes.

41.51 N8.1-3 CAPITAL MUST BE IRREVOCABLY COMMITTED

a. Mere intent to invest, the possession of uncommitted funds in a bank account, the signing of contracts in anticipation of the start of business operations, or any other form of prospective investment are not sufficient. The applicant has the burden of establishing that the capital has been irrevocably committed to the investment enterprise.

b. The definition of investment permits the use of any legal mechanism that irrevocably commits the funds to the enterprise but conditions the commitment on the applicant's being issued an E-2 visa. An escrow agreement in which the applicant commits funds to the purchase of a business by transferring them to a third party, on condition that the funds will be released to the seller when an E-2 visa is issued is an acceptable commitment of capital if the only condition to be met before the funds are irrevocably transferred to the seller is the issuance of the E-2 visa.

41.51 N8.2 QUALIFYING CAPITAL

a. Funds spent to purchase a business are considered qualifying capital when calculating the total investment, as are amounts actually spent for the purchase of equipment or inventory.

b. Funds spent for the rental of property or equipment may be considered as qualifying capital but only to the extent of the amount allocated to such rent in any one month. The annual rental cost (unless paid in advance) of leased property or equipment may not be considered as qualifying capital since such future costs are generally paid from the operating income of the enterprise.

c. The value of any goods or equipment transferred to the United States and committed to the investment enterprise may also be added to determine the total investment. The applicant must establish that the goods or equipment are for business and not personal use. The value of leased equipment cannot be considered as qualifying capital.

d. The rights to intangible or intellectual property such as patents or copyright may also be considered as qualifying capital and the value of such property, to the extent that it can reasonably be determined may be calculated as part of the investment. If there is no established market value for such property, the value of the publishing or manufacturing contracts generated by the property may be used. If that value is not available, then the opinions of experts in the field are acceptable and may be submitted for consideration.

41.51 N8.2-3 Intangible Property

Rights to intangible or intellectual property may also be considered capital assets to the extent to which their value can reasonably be determined.

Where no market value is available for a copyright or patent, the value of current publishing or manufacturing contracts generated by the asset may be used. If none exist, the opinions of experts in the particular field in question may be submitted for consideration and acceptance.

Comment: The notes lack a focus and have no readily discernable nexus to the regulation. What they have in common is that each attempts to distinguish capital that can be counted in the application of the proportionality test from capital that, though invested in the business world sense, cannot be counted.

41.51 N9 BONA FIDE ENTERPRISE

The investment must be in a business that is a real and active commercial or entrepreneurial undertaking that will produce some service or commodity. Investments in undeveloped land, stocks or other assets held simply for their potential to appreciate in value do not qualify as an investment. Further, the applicant must be close to the start of actual business operations and not simply at the stage of creating an organization on paper, signing contracts (that may be broken), or scouting for suitable premises.

41.51 N9 COMMERCIAL ENTERPRISE MUST BE REAL AND ACTIVE

The enterprise must be a real and active commercial or entrepreneurial undertaking, producing some service or commodity. It cannot be a paper organization or an idle speculative investment held for potential appreciation in value, such as undeveloped land or stocks held by an investor without the intent to direct the enterprise. The investment must be a commercial enterprise, thus it must be for profit, eliminating non-profit organizations from consideration. (See 9 FAM 41.51 N8.1 above.)

Comment: The regulation sets out "bona fide enterprise" as a defined term, so it seems strange that FAM uses its definition as a heading for the requirement rather than using the term itself.

41.51 N10 INVESTMENT MUST BE SUBSTANTIAL

41.51 N10.1 General

The purpose of requiring the investment of a substantial amount of capital is to ensure both that the applicant is sufficiently committed to the successful operation of the enterprise and that sufficient funds have been committed to the enterprise to give it a reasonable chance of success.

41.51 N10 INVESTMENT MUST BE SUBSTANTIAL

41.51 N10.1 General

The purpose of the requirement is to ensure to a reasonable extent that the business invested in is not speculative, but is, or soon will be a successful enterprise as the result of the exercise of sound business and financial judgment. The rules regarding the amount of funds committed to the commercial enterprise and the character of the funds, primarily personal or loans based on personal collateral, are intended to weed out risky undertakings and to ensure that the investor is unquestionably committed to the success of the business. Consequently, the consular officer must view the proportionate amount of funds invested, as evidenced by the proportionality test, in light of the nature of the business and the projected success of the business.

Comment: At the heart of the mystery surrounding E-2 visas is the eternal truth that the Department of State never has and never will define "substantial" as either a set dollar amount or as the product of a mathematical formula that would reach the same result regardless of who applied it. Instead, the definition at bottom requires an analysis of how much of the invested capital came from the applicant's "pocket" and how much was borrowed. The assertion that the regulation is there to "weed out risky undertakings" overstates the importance of the financing element in the analysis of whether a business is more or less risky. The risk level of a busi-

ness venture is determined by a combination of factors including the nature of the business and whether sufficient capital has been committed to the business. A properly capitalized business is less risky than one that is undercapitalized regardless of whether the capital was raised by borrowing.

41.51 N10.2 INTERPRETATIONS OF "SUBSTANTIAL" INVESTMENT

a. A substantial amount of capital for E-2 visa purposes constitutes that amount that is:

(1) Substantial in a proportional sense, (the application of the proportionality test): i.e., in relationship to the total cost of either purchasing an established enterprise, or creating the type of enterprise under consideration;

(2) Sufficient to ensure the treaty investor's financial commitment to the successful operation of the enterprise; and

(3) Of a magnitude to support the likelihood that the treaty investor will successfully develop and direct the enterprise. No set dollar figure constitutes a minimum amount of investment to be considered "substantial" for E-2 visa purposes.

b. This requirement is met by satisfying the "proportionality test". The test is a comparison between two figures. The amount of qualifying funds invested, and the cost of an established business or, if a newly created business, the cost of establishing such a business.

(1) The amount of the funds or assets actually invested must be from qualifying funds and assets as explained in 9 FAM 41.51 N7 above.

(2) The cost of an established business is, generally, its purchase price, which is normally considered to be the fair market value.

(3) The cost of a newly created business is the actual cost needed to establish such a business to the point of being operational. The actual cost can usually be computed as the investor should have already purchased at least some of the necessary assets and, thus, be able to provide cost figures for additional assets needed to run the business. For example, an indication of the nature and extent of commitment to a business venture may be provided by invoices or contracts for substantial purchases of equipment and inventory; appraisals of the market value of land, buildings, equipment, and machinery; accounting audits; and records required by various governmental authorities.

Comment: This seems to contradict the "breakable contracts" rule stated in note 41.51 N8.1-3 by giving evidentiary value to invoices or contracts without specifying that the funds they represent must be irrevocably committed.

c. If the consular officer questions these figures, he or she may seek additional evidence to help establish what would be a reasonable amount. Such evidence may include letters from chambers of commerce or statistics from trade associations. Unverified and unaudited financial statements based exclusively on information supplied by an applicant normally are insufficient to establish the nature and status of an enterprise.

41.51 N10.2 DETERMINING WHETHER AN INVESTMENT IS SUBSTANTIAL

The regulation defining "substantial amount of capital" requires the application of the proportionality test. In this test two figures are compared: the amount of qualifying capital invested (See 9 FAM 41.51 N8.1 and N8.2) and the total cost of the enterprise.

As long as the applicant meets all of the other requirements for an E-2 visa, the total cost of the enterprise is not by itself relevant nor can it be used to determine that an applicant does not qualify for an E-2 visa.

41.51 N10.3 VALUE OF BUSINESS DETERMINED BY NATURE OF BUSINESS

The value (cost) of the business is clearly dependent on the nature of the enterprise. Any manufacturing business, such as an automobile manufacturer, might easily cost many millions of dollars to either purchase or establish and operate. At the extreme opposite pole, the cost to purchase an on-going commercial enterprise or to establish a service business, such as a consulting firm, may be relatively low. As llong as all the other requirements for E-2 status are met, the cost of the business per se is not independently relevant or determinative of qualification for E-2 status.

Comment: The use of the words "nature of the enterprise" creates an ambiguity. Does the note mean that an existing business has one nature and a newly created enterprise another? Or is the phrase to be read in its more usual sense, namely the category of business engaged in. The first two sentences of the note seem to indicate that "nature" means category, but this interpretation would mean that the note is there to make the trivial point that some businesses cost more than others.

41.51 N10.3 DETERMINING THE TOTAL COST OF THE ENTERPRISE

a. When the applicant has purchased an established business, the total cost of the business is generally the purchase price, normally the fair market value of the business.

b. When the applicant is creating a new business, the total cost of the business is the actual capital needed to establish such a business and to bring it to the point that it can operate and produce some service or commodity.

(1) Since the applicant must show that the capital has been irrevocably committed to the investment enterprise, evidence of the total cost of the business will take the form of invoices, contracts for the purchase of equipment or inventory, or appraisals of the market value of land, buildings, machinery or equipment.

(2) If the consular officer questions the applicant's estimate of the actual capital needed to establish his or her enterprise, he or she may seek additional evidence to help establish a reasonable amount. This evidence could include letters or statistics from chambers of commerce or trade organizations. Unverified and unaudited financial statements based exclusively on information supplied by an applicant are normally insufficient to establish the nature and status of enterprise.

41.51 N10.4 PROPORTIONALITY TEST

The amount invested in the enterprise should be compared to the cost (value) of the business by assessing the percentage of the investment in relation to the cost of the business. If the two figures are the same, then the investor has invested 100% of the needed funds in the business. Such an investment is substantial. The vast majority of cases involve lesser percentages. The proportionality test can best be understood as a sort of inverted sliding scale. The lower the cost of the business the higher a percentage of investment is required, whereas, a highly expensive business would require a lower percentage of qualifying investment. There are no bright line percentages that exist in order for an investment to be considered substantial. Yet, as stated above, the lower the cost of the business the higher the percentage of qualifying investment is anticipated. Thus, investments of 100 percent or a higher percentage would normally automatically qualify for a small business of $100,000 or less. Yet, a business of this size involving two equal partners or joint ventures may prove qualification for E-2 status. At the other extreme, an investment of $10 million or a $100 million business would likely qualify, based on the sheer magnitude if the business itself.

41.51 N10.4 THE PROPORTIONALITY TEST

The proportionality test applies an inverted sliding scale. The regulation in essence states that, as the total cost of the enterprise becomes smaller, the qualifying capital figure must increase as a proportion of that total cost. The proportionality test is most obviously met whenever the applicant has invested qualifying capital equal to 100% of the total cost of the business. At the other extreme, an investment of qualifying capital equal to 10% of the value of an enterprise costing $100 million would likely qualify as substantial.

41.51 N10.5 FINANCIAL COMMITMENT

Another element of the definition of "substantial" is a requirement that the amount of capital invested must be sufficient to ensure that the applicant will be committed to the successful operation of the business.

41.51 N10.5 INVESTOR'S COMMITMENT

An element of judgment to be factored into the requirement of substantial investment concerns an assessment of the extent of the investor's commitment to the successful operation of the project in view of the amount invested.

41.51 N11 ENTERPRISE MUST BE MORE THAN MARGINAL

The alien must not be investing in a marginal enterprise solely for the purpose of earning a living. An applicant is not entitled to E-2 classification if the investment, even if substantial, will return only enough income to provide a living for the applicant and family. There are various ways to help in determining whether an investment is marginal, in the sense of only providing a livelihood for the applicant.

(1) First, look to the alien's income from the investment. If the income derived from the business exceeds what is necessary to support self and family, then this, too, meets the test.

Comment: The note does not mention future capacity when measuring the income derived and therefore does not conform to the regulation's definition of marginality at 22 CFR §41.51(o).

(2) If the first test is not met, and it becomes necessary to consider other factors, one can look to the economic impact of the business. The business must have the capacity, present or future, to make a significant economic contribution. The projected future capacity should generally be realizable within five years from the date the alien commences normal business activities. It is recommended that applicant's submit a reliable business plan to verify the capacity to realize a profit within a maximum five years.

Comment: Here the notes reach their nadir by substituting, or more probably, allowing a spell checker to substitute, "articulates" for the word "activities" as used in the regulation. (22 CFR §41.51(o)).

41.51 N12 CONTROLLING INTEREST

An equal share of the investment in a joint venture or an equal partnership of two parties, generally does give controlling interest, if the joint venture and partner each retain full management rights and responsibilities. This arrangement is often called "Negative Control". With each of the two parties possessing equal responsibilities, they each have the capacity of making decisions that are binding on the other party. The Department has determined that an equal partnership with more than two partners would not give any of the parties control based on ownership, as the element of control would be too remote even under the negative control theory.

Comment: This note misstates the definition of negative control. Control is "negative" in a 50/50 split of ownership precisely because each party does not have the capacity of making decisions that are binding on the other party.

41.51 N12.1 Requirements for Investor to Develop and Direct and Have Controlling Interest

In all treaty investor cases, it must be shown that nationals of a treaty country own at least 50 percent of an enterprise. It must also be shown, in accordance with INA 101(a)(15)(E)(ii), that a national (or nationals) of the treaty country, through ownership or by other means, develops and directs the activities of the enterprise. The type of enterprise being sought will determine how this requirement is applied.

41.51 N11 ENTERPRISE MUST BE MORE THAN MARGINAL

The applicant must not be investing an enterprise solely for the purpose of earning a living. An applicant is not entitled to E-2 classification if the investment, even if substantial, will return only enough income to provide a living for the applicant, spouse and children. The regulation provides two tests for determining whether an enterprise is marginal.

a. If the enterprise has the present or future capacity to generate an income that will exceed a minimal living for the applicant and his or her family then the enterprise is not marginal.

b. If the enterprise does not meet the first test then it may still qualify if it has the present or future capacity to make a significant economic contribution. The projected future capacity should generally be realizable within five years from the date that the applicant commences normal business activities. The applicant should submit a credible business plan to show that the enterprise will have the capacity to make a significant economic contribution within a maximum of five years.

41.51 N12 APPLICANT MUST SEEK ENTRY TO DEVELOP AND DIRECT

The regulations require that the applicant be seeking entry solely to develop and direct the enterprise. This requirement has two components.

a. First, the applicant must be in a position to exercise control of the enterprise through ownership or some other means.

(1) If the applicant owns at least 50 percent of the enterprise, the requirement is satisfied. A joint venture or a partnership consisting of two persons or entities is permissible since it gives a controlling interest to each joint owner or partner in the sense that each has "negative control." Since all decisions regarding the operation of the enterprise must be unanimous, neither partner is in a position to act without the other.

(2) Any arrangement that divides the ownership of the enterprise equally among more than two persons or entities would generally not give any one of the owners control of the enterprise. Nevertheless modern business practices constantly introduce new structures and an applicant owning a minority share in the enterprise may be still be able to satisfy the requirement by demonstrating that he or she possesses managerial control though some other means.

(3) When an enterprise meets the nationality requirement (9 FAM 41.51 N2) but the ownership of does not permit any one treaty country individual to

Comment: This note serves no particular purpose other than to state the princi-ple that, regardless of how control is exercised, 50 percent of the enterprise must still be owned by treaty country nationals. What does the "type of enterprise be-ing sought" mean? Does it mean that the requirement is to be applied differently if the enterprise is a hair salon as opposed to an automobile manufacturer?

41.51 N12.2 Owner to Demonstrate Development and Direction of Enterprise

In instances in which a sole proprietor or an individual who is a majority owner wishes to enter the United States as an "investor" or send an employee to the United States as his and/or her personal employee, or as an employee of the U.S. enterprise, the owner must demonstrate that he or she personally develops and directs the enterprise. Likewise, if a foreign corporation owns at least 50 percent of a U.S. enterprise, and wishes its employee to enter the U.S. as an employee of the parent corporation, or as an employee of the U.S. business, the foreign corporation must demonstrate it develops and directs the U.S. enterprise.

41.51 N12.3 Visa Holder to be Employee of U.S. Enterprise

a. In instances in which treaty country ownership may be too diffuse to permit one individual or company to demonstrate the ability to direct and develop the U.S. enterprise, the owners of treaty country nationality must:

(1) Show that together they own 50 percent of the U.S. enterprise; and

(2) Must demonstrate, that at least collectively, they have the ability to develop and direct the U.S. enterprise.

b. In these cases an owner may not receive an 'E' visa as the "investor", nor may an employee be considered to be an employee of an owner for 'E' visa purposes. Rather, all "E" visa recipients must be shown to be an employee of the U.S. en-terprise coming to the U.S. to fulfil the duties of an executive, supervisor, or es-sentially skilled employee.

Comment: The title of the note is misleading. The point of the note is that some owners of the business may be issued visas as employees, not that all visa holders must be employees of the enterprise.

41.51 N12.4 Control by Management

As indicated, a joint venture or an equal partnership involving two parties, could constitute control for E-2 purposes. Modern business practices constantly intro-duce new business structures, however. Thus, it is difficult to list all the qualifying structures. If an investor (individual or business) has control of the business through managerial control, the requirement is met.

The owner will have to satisfy the consular officer that the investor is developing and directing the business.

demonstrate control, the enterprise may still qualify, even though none of the owners would qualify for an E-2 visa as "the investor." In these cases individ-ual owners of the enterprise may qualify for E-2 visas as employees of the enterprise, provided that they are seeking to enter the United States to serve as executives, supervisors or essentially skilled employees.

b. Second, the applicant must demonstrate the intent to enter the United States for the purpose of actually developing and directing the enterprise.

CHALLENGES IN REPRESENTING NONIMMIGRANT PROFESSIONALS: A ROUNDTABLE Q&A WITH PRACTITIONERS

by Janet L. Henner, Eleanor Pelta, and Tarik H. Sultan[*]

INTRODUCTION

The speed and efficiency of international communication in the business world is unparalleled today. The Internet and wireless communication have provided professionals in all fields new opportunities to collaborate across great distances. However, globalization has also increased the need for greater and more expeditious global mobility of professionals. This, in turn, has added a new layer of complexity, as well as urgency, to the legal issues surrounding the transfer of professionals into the United States. Below, three practitioners tackle some common issues that arise in H, Trade NAFTA (TN), and E-3 visa practice.

---

[*] **Janet Henner** is an associate in the New York office of Fragomen, Del Rey, Bernsen & Loewy. Prior to joining Fragomen, Ms. Henner served as an Attorney-Advisor and Deputy Secretary to BALCA at the U.S. Department of Labor, Office of Administrative Law Judges. She is active in both the national and local New York Chapter of AILA, having served on several committees. Ms. Henner is a frequent lecturer on business immigration topics, particularly labor certifications, at immigration conferences for several business and educational organizations, including the American Council on International Personnel, *ILW.com*, and the New York Chapter of AILA.

Eleanor Pelta is a partner in the Labor and Employment Law Practice and Managing Director of Morgan Lewis Resources. Her practice focuses on immigration and nationality law. She is an elected director of the AILA Board of Governors, as well as a trustee of AILF. She coauthored the book, *At the Crossroads: Immigration Issues for Tax and Payroll Professionals*, with Donna Kepley, and has authored several articles on immigration law and has been featured as a keynote speaker at immigration law seminars across the country.

Tarik Sultan is a shareholder in the firm of Wolf & Sultan P.C. in Tucson. He has served on the national board of governors for AILA, as well as on numerous national liaison committees with the Departments of Labor and Justice. His practice is focused in all areas and aspects of immigration law, with a particular emphasis in employment-based visas and employer sanctions defense. Mr. Sultan is listed in *The Best Lawyers in America* for immigration law.

EDUCATIONAL ISSUES

1. What is the best way to prepare an H-1B petition, where there is a baccalaureate degree, but it is not related to the specialty occupation?

There are several common scenarios in which this occurs. In one scenario, the baccalaureate degree is in a general related field, but is not considered by U.S. Citizenship and Immigration Services (USCIS) to be sufficiently related to the position offered to support the granting of the H-1B visa. For example, Requests for Evidence (RFEs) are common where a foreign national possesses a degree in mathematics, physics, or chemistry, and the position is in the computer science field. Another variation on this, which often causes difficulty in the processing of an H-1B, is the situation in which the foreign national possesses a general bachelor's or master's degree in business, and the position is in a business subspecialty such as finance, accounting, or marketing. In some cases, the beneficiary has a degree completely unrelated to the specialty occupation, such as a degree in French literature as a background for a position in finance.

It is clear from the regulations, and from standard H-1B practice, that eligibility for an H-1B is like an equation. On the employer side, the employment offered must, at a minimum, require not only a baccalaureate degree, but a specific baccalaureate degree related to the field of endeavor. The employer may demonstrate that the degree is a requirement by showing that:

- the degree is common to the industry in similar position.

- the position's complexity or uniqueness warrants a degree.

- the employer normally requires a degree for the position.

- the nature of the duties is highly specialized and complex such that the level of knowledge required to perform the duties is normally associated with at least a baccalaureate degree.[1]

---

[1] 8 CFR §214.2(h)(4)(iii)(A).

On the beneficiary side of the "H-1B equation," he or she must hold a U.S. baccalaureate degree (or higher degree) or a foreign degree determined to be equivalent to the U.S. baccalaureate degree that is "required by the specialty occupation."[2]

Alternatively, the beneficiary may "[h]ave education, specialized training, and/or progressively responsible experience that is equivalent to the completion of a U.S. baccalaureate or higher degree in the specialty occupation, and have recognition of expertise in the specialty through progressively responsible positions directly related to the specialty." A beneficiary may show equivalence to a college degree by a number of means under the regulations, including the results of a recognized college-level equivalency examination or special credit program, evidence of certification or registration from a nationally recognized professional association or society for the specialty known to grant certification of competence in the specialty, or, most commonly, the equivalent in experience and/or education to a four-year baccalaureate degree program. Under the "3=1" rule, three years of specialized training and/or work experience equals one year of university-level education.

Frequently, USCIS's view on the type of degree required for a particular specialty occupation appears exceedingly narrow. During the late 1990s, when there was a widely acknowledged shortage of technology workers, legacy Immigration and Naturalization Services (INS) service centers liberally tended to accept a wide variety of science and technology degrees as a background for occupations in computer science. Today, notwithstanding the fact that sophisticated computer applications are used in all of those disciplines, employers who petition for beneficiaries with degrees in physics, mathematics, or chemistry must be prepared for a RFE, asking how the degree relates to the occupation.

Clearly, close examination of transcripts for courses involving the use of technology and a discussion of the computer applications learned in these courses may be helpful in constructing a response. If the transcript is heavy on such courses, it may be worthwhile to seek an opinion from an educational evaluator as to whether the beneficiary had sufficient courses for a "double major" or a degree in the scientific discipline, with emphasis on the technology aspects.

Another route that may prove helpful is to look at the situation from the employer side of the equation, rather than the beneficiary side. In other words, you may be able to demonstrate that a broader range of specific degrees is acceptable for the occupation. Here, websites of various university departments that confer similar degrees may be helpful. Many university departments, in describing their disciplines, list the types of occupations for which a degree in that discipline is standard preparation. The physics or math department of several major universities may advertise that a degree from that department is excellent preparation for a career in computer science. Similarly, it is worthwhile to look at the websites of professional associations as well. The American Institute of Physics website, *www.aip.org*, has a wealth of data regarding the types of occupations in which a person with a baccalaureate degree in physics might be employed. The website of the American Chemical Society, *www.chemistry.org*, offers similar information regarding positions for chemistry graduates.

Although the degree may not appear directly related to the position, sometimes there are special duties that require the particular degree. For example, many financial analysts must have a specific background in the industry that they follow and analyze. A degree in pharmacology or biochemistry may be appropriate for a position analyzing pharmaceutical companies for an investment company.

Where a foreign national possesses a general degree, such as a degree in business administration, USCIS may issue an RFE, stating that the degree is not sufficiently specific for the position offered by the employer. One way to avoid such a request is to determine whether the employer requires some specific experience along with the degree. For example, employers of business analysts often require either a degree in business with some experience in computer science, or a degree in a computer science discipline with experience in business. Alternatively, the beneficiary's transcript may be reviewed to determine whether there is an emphasis in a particular area, such as finance, marketing, or operations.

Notwithstanding the fact that many U.S. employers prefer graduates with liberal arts degrees, obtaining approval for an H-1B is more challenging where the beneficiary possesses a degree that is completely unrelated to the position offered. In this situation, a beneficiary has the greatest chance of success when he or she possesses experience in the field. Often an unrelated degree, along with six years of specialized

---

[2] 8 CFR §214.2(h)(4)(iii)(C)(2).

experience, can be evaluated as a degree with a second major in the area of specialization. Where the four-year degree includes some coursework in the specialty, it is sometimes possible to have a degree plus three years' experience in the specialty evaluated as a baccalaureate with a second major.

2. In an H-1B case, what issues are presented where the beneficiary has a three-year baccalaureate degree, deemed equivalent to a four-year U.S. degree?

The regulations governing H-1B petitions do not require four years of college-level education. Rather, they require the equivalent of a U.S. baccalaureate degree. Notwithstanding these rules, USCIS frequently issues RFEs where a beneficiary possesses a three-year foreign degree evaluated to be the equivalent of a U.S. baccalaureate degree. Occasionally, the RFE will state that USCIS simply does not give the evaluation any weight whatsoever.

Typically three-year degrees that are equivalent to four-year U.S. baccalaureate degrees come from jurisdictions in which there is a 13th year of high school that is equivalent to the first year of college, such as the United Kingdom and some parts of Canada. In addition, there are many Indian three-year degrees that constitute the equivalent of a four-year U.S. baccalaureate degree because of the intensity of study, the level of courses taken, and the lack of summer breaks.

A common approach to an H-1B petition involving a three-year degree is a detailed evaluation showing how the degree is equivalent of a four-year degree. Alternatively, education from a different college-level institution may be added to obtain the equivalent of a four-year degree. Here, a formal educational evaluation is highly advisable. However, short-term certification courses, such as technology courses, usually do not qualify as a fourth year of university-level education.

Finally, three years of education, plus three years of professional experience in the specialty, can usually be deemed equivalent to a four-year degree, although it is advisable to have a formal evaluation to document this. In addition to the formal evaluation, it is crucial to submit job letters documenting the experience, with detailed descriptions of the duties performed.

Note that for labor certification purposes, a three-year degree plus additional education or experience that equates to a four-year degree will not be acceptable to classify a beneficiary into the second em-ployment-based preference category, under the "Bachelor's plus five" category. Both USCIS and the Administrative Appeals Office (AAO) currently adhere strictly to an interpretation of the regulations that requires a four-year degree from one educational institution for this purpose.

Moreover, for EB-3 purposes, where the employer is willing to accept a combination of education and experience or education from different institutions in lieu of a baccalaureate degree, the employer should indicate this clearly on Form ETA 9089, in Item H-14. If this is not made clear, it is possible that the I-140 may be denied, as some service centers interpret the phrase "foreign equivalent" on the ETA 9089 to mean the foreign equivalent to four years of study at one educational institution.

3. To what extent must a baccalaureate degree be specifically or directly related to a TN occupation? For example, must a Computer Systems Analyst have a computer science degree or diploma?

While there is some "give" in terms of the types of degrees required for TN occupations, the paramount concern in preparing a TN application—particularly a TN for a Canadian national—is that the adjudicator has a limited amount of time to make a decision on the case. Therefore, the most successful applications will be those applications that demonstrate the clearest tie between the degree and the position.

That being said, anecdotally, there is more flexibility in some areas than in others. For example, the field of engineering, a very broad category under the North American Free Trade Agreement (NAFTA), includes software engineers.[3] There is a range of engineering degrees that could potentially qualify an individual to perform the duties of a software engineer. These include electrical and electronics engineers, and computer engineers. Moreover, in a TN application for an engineer, the field of engineering studied often need not match the job duties exactly, but should at least match the industry. Thus, for example, a TN applicant with a degree in chemical engineering may be working as a plant engineer in charge of a chemical plant or a chemical manufacturing process. Similarly, a TN applicant with a degree in mechanical engineering may qualify for a

---

[3] INS Memorandum, Cronin, Acting Ex. Assoc. Comm., Office of Programs, HQINS 70/6.2.23, *reprinted in* 77 *Interpreter Releases* 1550, 1556–57 (Oct. 30, 2000).

position in overseeing the installation of complex machinery as well as positions involving the design of machinery.

Another category in which there has been some flexibility is that of economist. For this position, adjudicators have accepted degrees in finance, business with an emphasis in finance or economics, and international relations, with an emphasis in economics. The key is to use the support letter to tie the degree to the duties of the position.

The category of Computer Systems Analyst does not require a baccalaureate degree, but allows for a post-secondary diploma or post-secondary certificate (both evidencing two years of post-secondary education from an accredited institution in Canada or Mexico) plus three years of experience. In this category, there has also been some flexibility in adjudications. Diplomas in computer science, computer systems analysis, management information technology, software development, and computer information technology have all been found acceptable.

It is important to note that equivalencies that rely upon multiple educational institutions or work experience to reach a baccalaureate degree are not permitted for TN purposes. In addition, a degree that is not from a U.S., Canadian, or Mexican institution must be accompanied by a formal educational evaluation.

4. What type of educational background is required to qualify for an E-3 visa?

The rules for the E-3 with respect to education background appear to be identical to the rules for the H-1B. There are no regulations yet for adjudications of E-3 applications. However, it may be instructive to review the way in which many consulates adjudicate blanket L-1B specialized knowledge professional application. Some consular officers routinely reject blanket L-1B applicants who possess a degree not directly or precisely related to the field in which they will work. For example, there are rejections of L-1Bs who will work in the computer science field and have degrees in electronics. Similarly, one cannot qualify for a blanket L-1B if one possesses the equivalent of a baccalaureate degree under the 3=1 rule. Whether consular officers will go the same route with respect to the degree requirement for E-3 visas remains to be seen.

COMPENSATION

5. In what instances, if ever, is the amount of compensation relevant in a TN application?

There are no regulatory provisions or agency guidance that address the level of compensation with regard to TN applications.

As there is presently no labor condition application (LCA) requirement for either a Mexican or Canadian TN,[4] it can be assumed that the amount of compensation is not dispositive with respect to a TN application in the same sense that is for an H-1B or H-1B1 petition, or an E-3 application. Since an LCA is not required, the employer does not have to make any attestations with respect to wages, working conditions, strike/lockout or work stoppage, or posting notices to its workers. However, since evidence of arrangements for remuneration must be presented to the immigration or consular officer adjudicating the application,[5] the amount of compensation may well be taken into consideration when making a determination with respect to the bona fides of the applicant's intent to engage in prearranged business activities at a professional level. For example, an inordinately low level of compensation may raise concerns that the position is not really an acceptable TN profession.[6] Conversely, an exorbitantly high level of compensation could raise questions pertaining to the TN applicant's ownership or control over the employing entity,[7] as well as the applicant's intent to enter the United States temporarily while maintaining his or her foreign residency.

Level of compensation aside, Mexican and Canadian applicants for TN status must still present evidence setting forth the arrangements for remu-

---

[4] The requirement for Mexican citizens to obtain certified LCAs sunset on December 31, 2003.

[5] 8 CFR §214.6(d)(3)(ii)(E).

[6] See Appendix 1603.D.1 at 8 CFR §214.6(c) for the list of acceptable TN professions.

[7] Ownership or control may be an issue because the regulations specifically prohibit self-employment. *See* 8 CFR §214.6(b).

> Engage in business activities at a professional level . . . does not authorize the establishment of a business or practice in the United States in which the professional will be, in substance, self-employed. A professional will be deemed to be self-employed if he or she will be rendering services to a corporation or entity of which the professional is the sole or controlling shareholder or owner. *Id.*

neration for the services to be rendered.[8] Accordingly, the source of remuneration may be an important factor. For example, a Management Consultant should either be an independent consultant or the employee of a consulting firm under contract to a U.S. entity, or the consultant, if a salaried employee of a non–management consulting firm should be in a supernumerary, temporary position.[9]

6. In what instances, if ever, may a TN, H-1B, H-1B1, or E-3 be on foreign payroll?

The Immigration and Nationality Act (INA)[10] and regulations are silent with respect to the ability to compensate TN, H-1B, H-1B1, or E-3 foreign nationals from a non–U.S. payroll.

TRADE NAFTA (TN)

It should be possible for a Canadian or Mexican TN to receive his or her compensation from a non–U.S. payroll; however, this position may not be as crystal clear in the case of the Mexican TN as it is for a Canadian TN.[11]

Since the elimination of the LCA requirement and numerical limitation on Mexican TNs, the same rules that apply to Canadians essentially apply to Mexicans; therefore, being employed by a Mexican entity and being paid by that entity should be permissible as long as the person is entering to provide legitimate TN services.[12]

The regulations governing the documentation to be presented to a consular officer (in the case of a

Mexican citizen) or a U.S. Customs and Border Protection (CBP) officer (in the case of a Canadian citizen) contained at 8 CFR §214.6(d)(3)(ii), provide that "a letter from the prospective employer(s) in the United States or from the foreign employer" must be presented to prove that the applicant is seeking entry to the United States to engage in business activities for a U.S. employer or entity at a professional level. The TN regulations do not separately define the term "employer" nor do the TN regulations set forth the source of a TN applicant's remuneration. Definitions for "employer" and "employment" may be found at 8 CFR §274a.1(g) and (h). These definitions are silent on whether the source of remuneration is a factor in determining who is an employer or whether there is employment.

Interestingly enough, the regulations contained at 8 CFR §214.6(h)(1) that provide for the filing of a TN extension of stay at a service center, state that "*[t]he United States employer* of a citizen of Canada or Mexico in TN status or a United States entity, in the case of a citizen of Canada or Mexico *in TN status who has a foreign employer*, may request an extension of stay by filing a form I-129[.]" (Emphasis added.) Almost in amplification of the regulations pertaining to the documentation to be submitted upon initial entry or grant of initial TN visa, this section specifically provides that a TN nonimmigrant may have a foreign employer, and only mandates that the I-129 petition to extend TN stay be filed by a U.S. employer or U.S. entity.

Additionally, 8 CFR §214.6(h)(2), which addresses re-admission in TN status at the border, provides that "[t]he application for admission " of a Canadian citizen seeking re-admission at the border in TN status "shall be supported by a new letter from the United States employer or the foreign employer" and a Mexican citizen seeking re-admission at the border "must present a valid passport and nonimmigrant TN visa when applying for readmission[.]" The Mexican citizen is not required to bring a letter from an employer (either U.S. or foreign) because the Mexican citizen would have already presented this to a U.S. consular officer in the context of the initial TN nonimmigrant visa application, and, therefore, only has to present a valid passport and TN visa.

The Department of State (DOS) *Foreign Affairs Manual* (FAM) also seems to support the conclusion that both Mexican and Canadian TN nonimmigrants may be paid from a non–U.S. payroll. The FAM specifically notes the prohibition of self-employment;

---

[8] 8 CFR §214.6(d)(3)(ii)(E).

[9] *See* INS Memorandum, James A. Puleo, INS Assistant Commissioner (Oct. 4, 1989), *reproduced in* 67 *Interpreter Releases* 639, 654.

[10] Immigration and Nationality Act of 1952, Pub. L. No. 82-414, 66 Stat. 163 (*codified as amended at* 8 USC §§1101 *et seq.*) (INA).

[11] AILA's *Immigration Practice and Procedure Under NAFTA and Other Free Trade Agreements* (3d ed. 2006) indicates that citizens of Mexico may qualify for Trade NAFTA (TN) status to work for a U.S. employer, while Canadian citizens also may qualify if they are employed by a Canadian employer and seek to enter the United States to provide pre-arranged services on behalf of a U.S. employer. (the LCA requirement and quota for Mexican TNs sunset on December 31, 2003). Note that there is a distinction between the source of payroll and the employer, *e.g.*, a person can be employed by a U.S. employer and be on a foreign payroll.

[12] See Appendix 1603.D.1 at 8 CFR §214.6(c) for the list of acceptable TN professions.

however, it otherwise appears open-ended with respect to the source or amount of remuneration.[13]

One argument in support of permitting a TN non-immigrant to remain on a foreign payroll is to draw the distinction between who the employer is and who is paying the salary. Arguably, the employer should be considered the entity that controls the TN's activities, which does not necessarily have to be the entity that pays the salary. If the TN is in fact working for, and taking direction from the U.S. company, and just happens to continue to be paid through the payroll of the Mexican affiliate, it should not mean that the person has a foreign employer. It can be argued that the TN has a U.S. employer, and therefore, the U.S. company could still legitimately offer the letter of employment. This is consistent with 9 FAM §41.54, Note 9 and Note 9.1, which, although appearing in the L visa section, are based on BIA case law and, therefore, have been used by DOS to define employer-employee issues for all visa categories:

> 9 FAM §41.54, Note 9 Employer-Employee Relationship
>
> The essential element in determining the existence of an "employer-employee" relationship is the right of control, that is, the right of the employer to order and control the employee in the performance of his or her work. Possession of the authority to engage or the authority to discharge is very strong evidence of the existence of an employer-employee relationship.

> 9 FAM §41.54, Note 9.1 Source of Remuneration and Benefits Not Controlling
>
> The source of the beneficiary's salary and benefits while in the United States (i.e., whether the beneficiary will be paid by the U.S. or foreign affiliate of the petitioning company) is not controlling in determining eligibility for L status. In addition, the employer-employee relationship encompasses a situation in which the beneficiary will not be paid directly by the petitioner, and such a beneficiary is not precluded from establishing eligibility for L classification.

If, however, the Mexican TN continues to be controlled by the Mexican company that is paying the salary (which typically happens in cases where the foreign company has a contract with a U.S.

company to provide a service and the TN applicant employed by the foreign entity goes to the United States to carry out the foreign company's contractual obligations to the U.S. company), then the specific question arises as to whether a Mexican TN can have a foreign employer, or must a Mexican TN have a U.S. employer.[14] There is no clear answer to this. The revised TN FAM notes, however, do not appear to distinguish between Mexicans and Canadians.

9 FAM §41.59, Note 7 Evidence of Professional Employment

(TL:VISA-604; 01-22-2004)

> The applicant must present evidence sufficient to satisfy the Immigration or Consular Officer of intent to engage in prearranged business activities for a U.S. employer(s) or entity(ies) at a professional level. *This evidence may be in the form of an employment letter from a U.S. or foreign employer*, or contract providing a detailed description of the business activities which the individual will be engaged in, and should state the following:
>
> (1) Activity in which the alien shall be engaged;
>
> (2) Purpose of entry;
>
> (3) Anticipated length of stay;
>
> (4) Educational qualifications or appropriate credentials demonstrating professional status;
>
> (5) Evidence of compliance with the Department of Homeland Security (DHS) regulations, and/or state laws; and
>
> (6) Arrangements for remuneration (Emphasis added).

It is not clear whether this FAM Note reflects a conscious decision by DOS to change the rules for Mexicans to align them with the rules for Canadians, in light of the termination of the LCA and petition requirements, or whether DOS just took the language that had been used for Canadians without giving it much thought. The consul presumably will refer to the FAM Note, however, without questioning whether it is right. Since the FAM Note indicates

---

[13] *See* 9 FAM 41.59 N.3.2.

[14] In such instances, the NAFTA B-1, for either a Canadian or Mexican citizen, may be more appropriate. See 8 CFR §214.2(b)(4) *et seq.*, for a list of appropriate NAFTA B-1 occupations and professions.

that a letter from a foreign employer is acceptable, it is likely the consul would issue the TN visa on that basis. However, the document checklist used by U.S. consular officials in Mexico, which has been updated since the LCA requirement was dropped for Mexican citizens, includes information about the U.S. employer including tax identification number, which may imply the Mexican TN visa applicant must be seeking admission in order to work for a U.S. employer. Given this potentially conflicting information, there may be an unknown risk for a Mexican seeking re-admission to the United States in such circumstances, or in filing an extension with USCIS.[15]

H-1B, H-1B1, AND E-3

For H-1B nonimmigrants, while there is no explicit forbiddance of a foreign company paying the employee's salary, there is the requirement of an employer-employee relationship, and 8 CFR §214.2(h)(4)(ii), defines a United States employer to be:

a person, firm, corporation, contractor, or other association, or organization in the United States which:

1. Engages a person to work within the United States;

2. Has an employer-employee relationship with respect to employees under this part, as indicated by the fact that it may hire, pay, fire supervise, or otherwise control the work of any such employee; and

3. Has an Internal Revenue Service Tax identification number.

Yvonne LaFleur, former Chief, Business and Trade Services Branch of legacy Immigration and Naturalization Service opined in a July 22, 1996, correspondence to a practitioner, that the regulations cited above only require the U.S. employer control the alien, but there is no requirement that the U.S. employer pay the alien's salary.[16] It is noteworthy that the regulatory definition of employer has not changed since 1996. Further, James Norris, Chief of Department of Labor's Division of Foreign Labor Certification, commented in an August 21, 1996, memorandum, that third parties are not prohibited from reimbursing an attesting employer for payments it made to an H-1B nonimmigrant, nor do the regulations prevent a third party from making payments to an attesting employer that, in turn, are paid to an H-1B nonimmigrant as wages paid for purposes of satisfying DOL's H-1B regulations.

Accordingly, it should be permissible to pay an H-1B worker from a foreign payroll, as long as the employer ensures that LCA, prevailing wage, as well as U.S. tax considerations are taken into account.[17]

The H-1B, H-1B1, and E-3 categories all require that an employer obtain a certified LCA prior to filing the petition with USCIS or lodging the application with a U.S. consulate abroad. Because of the LCA requirement, the issue may not be whether an employer can legally pay such a nonimmigrant on a foreign payroll. Rather, as indicated above, it may be whether it is practical for an employer do so and still be in compliance with the LCA.

The first LCA requirement regarding wages requires that an employer attest that, for the entire period of authorized employment, the required wage rate that will be paid will be the greater of the actual wage rate or the prevailing wage. This wage requirement includes the employer's obligation to offer benefits and eligibility for benefits provided as compensation for services to these nonimmigrants on the same basis, and in accordance with the same criteria, as the employer offers to U.S. workers. Given the fluctuation in foreign exchange rates, it

---

[15] AILA's *Immigration Practice Under NAFTA and Other Free Trade Agreements* (3d ed. 2006) indicates that citizens of Mexico may qualify for TN status to work for a U.S. employer, while Canadian citizens also may qualify if they are employed by a Canadian employer and seek to enter the United States to provide pre-arranged services on behalf of a U.S. employer. It may be that the LCA requirement that used to exist for Mexican citizens implied a requirement that the Mexican TN worker be employed by a U.S. entity. Since the LCA requirement for Mexican TNs sunset on December 31, 2003, this interpretation may be questionable. It is also noteworthy that the document checklist used by U.S. consular officials in Mexico, updated since the LCA requirement was dropped for Mexican citizens, includes information about the U.S. employer including tax identification number, which may imply the Mexican TN visa applicant must be seeking admission in order to work for a U.S. employer.

[16] Yvonne LaFleur, former Chief, Business and Trade Services Branch, INS, July 22, 1996, correspondence to a practitioner, 73 *Interpreter Releases* 1045, *published on* AILA InfoNet at Doc. No. 96052499.

[17] For a more detailed discussion on this, see H. Gordon, "DOL's LCA Rule: The Good, The Bad, and The Intrusive," *Fourth Annual AILA New York Chapter Immigration Law Symposium Handbook* 148 (2001).

could be difficult, if not unworkable, for an employer to satisfy the first LCA requirement if the foreign national is on a foreign payroll. Similarly, the ability to value and compare benefits packages could be an impossible task.

That being said, the American Competitiveness and Workforce Improvement Act of 1998 (ACWIA)[18] may have resolved the issue of whether or not an H-1B worker can be paid from a foreign source. In certain situations, multinational employers may choose to permit H-1B workers to remain on their home country benefits plan, instead of offering U.S. benefits. Specifically, if an H-1B worker is in the United States for fewer than 90 consecutive days, the worker may remain on the home country benefits plan.

FULL-TIME V. PART-TIME AND MULTIPLE EMPLOYERS

7. Must H-1B, TN, and E-3 workers work full time? May they work lawfully for multiple employers? What is the procedure for obtaining approval for a part-time or multiple employer situation under each nonimmigrant classification?

H-1B professional workers may work full-time or part-time. If they are employed part-time, the employer must indicate on the I-129 nonimmigrant petition the approximate number of hours per week the employee will be expected to work. In this situation, it is most common to indicate the wage as an hourly rate rather than an annual salary.

Part-time employment is also allowable in the TN classification.[19] The number of hours should be indicated in the TN application packet submitted at the port of entry (if Canadian) or the U.S. consulate (if Mexican). If the applicant is seeking approval of the TN status through the Nebraska Service Center, the number of hours should be indicated on the I-129 nonimmigrant petition.

Similarly, there is nothing in the E-3 regulations issued by DOS nor in the recently issued CBP memorandum[20] restricting E-3 employment to full-

time. The part-time nature of the employment would be indicated on the labor condition application, as well as in the visa application packet submitted to the U.S. consulate abroad.

With regard to the issue of multiple employers, an H-1B professional worker may work for multiple employers, but each employer must file an I-129 nonimmigrant petition. Likewise, each I-129 petition must accurately identify the number of hours the employee will be working for that respective employer.

Similarly, TN professional workers may have multiple employers in TN status. The TN worker may add employers by filing an I-129 nonimmigrant petition with the Nebraska Service Center.[21]

With regard to the E-3 classification, there is nothing in the E-3 regulations issued by DOS nor in the recently issued E-3 CBP memorandum[22] restricting the number of employers; anyone attempting to work for more than one employer in E-3 status should first attempt to secure an I-129 nonimmigrant petition approval through the Vermont Service Center.

CHALLENGING OCCUPATIONS

8. What is the best way to prepare an H-1B petition where there is a potential that the position may not be considered a specialty occupation? Some challenging occupations in the past have included sales managers, marketing professionals, graphic designers, and web developers. Can an RFE be avoided when submitting an H for such occupations?

As the global economy evolves, so too do we see an evolution in the type of customary requirements for professional-level positions. From time to time, practitioners find themselves having to educate USCIS and justify real-world requirements for the proffered position. In recent years, problems have been reported in securing approvals for marketing occupations, editorial positions, graphic designers, software design engineers, programmers, and other new economy jobs.[23]

---

[18] American Competitiveness and Workforce Improvement Act of 1998, Pub. L. No. 105-277, 112 Stat. 2681 (div. C, title IV) (ACWIA).

[19] 9 FAM 41.59 N.10.

[20] CBP Memorandum, Michael J. Hrinyak, "New Nonimmigrant Visa Classification: E-3" (Sept. 19, 2005), *published continued*

on AILA InfoNet at Doc. No. 06040712 (*posted* Apr. 7, 2006) (hereinafter Hrinyak memorandum).

[21] 9 FAM 41.59, N11.

[22] Hrinyak memorandum, *supra* note 20.

[23] As an example, the Administrative Appeals Office ruled that the position of Webographer was a specialty occupation *continued*

Part of the problem lies in the subjective definition of "specialty occupation," at INA §214(i)(1):

an occupation that requires theoretical and practical application of a body of highly specialized knowledge, and the attainment of a bachelor's (or higher) degree in a specific specialty (or its equivalent) as a minimum for entry into the occupation in the United States.

As discussed above, there are four regulatory criteria for determining whether a position is a "specialty occupation."[24] First, is a bachelor's degree or higher (or equivalent) normally the minimum requirement for entry into the particular position? Second, is the degree requirement common in the industry in parallel positions among similar organizations or alternatively is the position so complex or unique that a degree is required? Third, does the employer normally require a degree or equivalent for the position? Fourth, is the nature of the specific duties so specialized and complex that the knowledge required to perform the duties is usually associated with the attainment of a degree.

Under the regulations, in order for the position to be considered a "specialty occupation," the employer must demonstrate that one of the above four criteria is satisfied. However, best practices would compel the practitioner to document as many or all of the criteria that apply in each case.

First of all, bear in mind the job title does not control whether the position will be deemed a "specialty occupation." The USCIS adjudicator will look to the actual job duties, while considering the skills required to perform those duties, in making the determination. A job may be entitled an "Engineer," but if the duties are in the nature of a technician, it will not be considered a specialty occupation.

Second, the adjudicator must be convinced that the degree is actually required for the position, and not merely preferred. This may be done through the *Occupational Outlook Handbook* (OOH), O*NET guidance, industry documentation, and the submission of other online job openings for similar positions showing that the degree is customarily required. Remember that factors such as company size and geographic location are acceptable in meeting the "similar company" standard.

Third, clearly identify which criteria apply in your case. If it is unclear to the USCIS adjudicator which, if any, of the criteria apply, it may result in a denial or an RFE.

9. Why are TNs for Management Consultants and Scientific Technicians so difficult? What are the best techniques to create approvable applications for these positions?

The short answer on why these two TN categories are so difficult is that they are the two types of TNs that do not require a degree and are open to a degree of subjective scrutiny on the part of the CBP or USCIS officer adjudicating the application.

With regard to the Scientific Technician/Technologist classification, even legacy INS recognized that this category "has been problematic for all of the parties to NAFTA."[25] To qualify, the applicant must convince the inspector or consular officer that he or she: (1) possesses theoretical knowledge of any of the following disciplines: agricultural sciences, astronomy, biology, chemistry, engineering, forestry, geology, geophysics, meteorology or physics; and (2) has the ability to solve practical problems in any of those disciplines, or the ability to apply principles of any of those disciplines to basic or applied research.

The DHS *Inspector's Field Manual* (IFM) explicitly recognizes that Scientific Technician/Technologists do not customarily have a bachelor's degree.[26] The NAFTA Appendix itself does not give substantial guidance on how to demonstrate the above standard. Instead, since November 2002, the IFM has instructed adjudicators to use the following criteria in evaluating these applications:

1. Individuals for whom scientific technicians/technologists wish to provide direct support must qualify as a professional *in their own right* in one of the above-listed fields.

2. A general offer of employment by such a professional is not sufficient, by itself, to qualify for admission as a Scientific Technician/Technologist. The offer must demonstrate

---

in the nature of a graphic designer. *Matter of Image Plant,* EAC 00-247-50368 (AAO Feb. 15, 2002) (VSC).

[24] 8 CFR §214.2(h)(4)(iii)(A).

[25] INS Memorandum, Johnny N. Williams, "Field Guidance on the Admission of Scientific Technicians/Technologists under the North American Free Trade Agreement" (Nov. 7, 2002), *published on* AILA InfoNet at Doc. No. 02121331 (*posted* Dec. 13, 2002) (hereinafter Williams memorandum on Scientific Technicians/Technologists).

[26] IFM §15.5(f)(2)(A).

that the work of the applicant will be inter-related with that of the supervisory professional. That is, the work of the applicant must be managed, coordinated and reviewed by the professional supervisor, and must also provide input to the supervisory professional's own work.

3. The applicant's theoretical knowledge should have been acquired through the successful completion of at least two years of training in a relevant educational program. Such training may be documented by presentation of a diploma, a certificate, or a transcript accompanied by evidence of relevant work experience.

4. U.S. authorities will rely on the DOL Occupational Outlook Handbook to establish whether proposed job functions are consistent with those of a scientific or engineering technician/technologist. Applicants should not be admitted to perform functions that are primarily associated with other job titles.

5. Persons in construction trades (welders, boilermakers, carpenters, electricians, etc.) do not qualify in this classification.[27]

Unfortunately, this "clarification" seems to have only further restricted the number of approvals in a category that clearly was meant to be interpreted liberally by the drafters of NAFTA. Note in particular that criteria (1) requires that the applicant document the professional and educational qualifications of the person he or she is coming to support in the United States.

The other TN category subjected to the highest levels of suspicion and scrutiny is that of management consultants. With regard to this category, in the early years of the NAFTA, most ports of entry viewed the "bachelor's degree or 5 years experience" liberally, as they had under the former U.S.-Canada Free Trade Agreement. In the late 1990s, however, there was a dramatic shift as legacy INS more narrowly interpreted the types of positions that would qualify for the TN management consultant category.

If the applicant is basing his or her eligibility on experience, verification letters of the person's experience is ideal, either through employers or client companies, rather than relying solely upon the applicant's résumé. According to INS guidelines, the management consultant "should not be assuming an existing position, replacing someone in an existing position, or filling a newly created permanent position . . . the management consultant should either be an independent consultant or the employee of a consulting firm under contract to a U.S. entity or the consultant, if salaried, should be in a supernumerary temporary position."[28] The requirement of demonstrating a supernumerary, temporary position to the satisfaction of a CBP port officer is not easy and leaves this category open to the whims of the adjudicator. Obviously, if a consulting agreement exists, that should be included in the application packet to document the nature of the employment as an independent consultant.

Further guidance is found in the IFM, stating that management consultants "provide services which are directed toward improving the managerial, operating, and economic performance of public and private entities by analyzing and resolving strategic and operating problems and thereby improving the entity's goals, objectives, policies, strategies, administration, organization, and operation."[29] Thus, in preparing a TN management consultant application, the practitioner should take care to that the applicant is not endowed with executive or managerial authority, but is rather coming to analyze the management of the company and recommend improvements.

DUAL INTENT

10. Should a TN always be moved to H-1B status prior to initiating permanent residence? What are the ground rules?

Initially, it was unclear whether TN visa status required nonimmigrant intent or whether it allowed for dual intent in the nature of H-1B and L visa classifications. Unfortunately, in its final rule, legacy INS rejected the position urged by AILA that dual intent should apply in the TN classification.[30] Thus, the area of concern became whether the filing or approval of a labor certification or immigrant visa petition might constitute a basis for denying a TN admission or extension of stay application.

The safest course where an employer intends to pursue permanent residency for a TN employee is to

---

[27] *See* Williams memorandum on Scientific Technicians/Technologists, *supra* note 25.

[28] *See* IFM section on NAFTA TN admissions.

[29] IFM §15.5(f)(2)(G).

[30] 63 Fed. Reg. 1331, 1333 (Jan. 9, 1998).

change the employee's status to H-1B, if possible. This in turn allows the employee to lawfully maintain the intention to reside permanently in the United States while pursuing labor certification and/or an immigrant petition.

However, not all TN professionals qualify for H-1B status—perhaps the most notable exception being registered nurses. For persons in this situation, the TN professional should be advised of the nonimmigrant intent issues, and at a minimum, postpone filing of any Schedule A I-140 immigrant petition and adjustment of status until at least 60 days have elapsed from his or her admission. In this way, the foreign national will not fall under the presumption of misrepresentation under the 30/60-day rule.

Another school of thought is to pursue the immigrant visa through consular processing rather than adjustment of status. In this way, the applicant may take the position that all TN entries are of a nonimmigrant intention, and the foreign national intends to return abroad before declaring his or her immigrant intent to the U.S. consulate when applying for the immigrant visa.

As a practical matter, the filing of the I-140 is more problematic where a TN applicant applies for an extension while remaining in the United States, as the I-129 form specifically asks whether an immigrant visa petition has been filed for the beneficiary. This question is generally not raised when a TN applicant applies at the border. Of course, if it is raised, the applicant must answer the question honestly. However, as discussed above, the fact that an I-140 alone has been filed for the TN beneficiary may not be conclusive evidence of permanent intent especially where consular processing is planned.

11. What are the intent requirements for E-3 and H-1B1 (Chile and Singapore) visa-holders?

H-1B1 (Chile and Singapore Free Trade Agreements[31]) professional workers must have nonimmigrant intent in order to maintain status. The E-3 (Australia) specialty occupation worker classification is more nuanced. These workers must maintain an intention to depart the United States upon the expiration of termination of E status. However, an application for initial admission, change of status, or extension of stay in E-3 may *not* be denied solely on the basis of an approved request for permanent labor certification or a filed or approved immigrant visa preference petition.[32]

MAXIMUM STAY

12. We know that the American Competitiveness in the 21st Century Act of 2000 (AC21, Pub. L. No. 106-313), as amended by the 21st Century Department of Justice Appropriations Authorization Act (H.R. 2215), provides H-1B extensions for those for whom a labor certification was filed 365 days prior to the max-out date (§106 of AC21), and for those with approved I-140 petitions impacted by visa unavailability (§104 of AC21). But may an AC21 "extension" be filed when the beneficiary is not in the United States?

Beneficiaries of H-1B petitions must be physically present in the United States at the time of the filing of the extension of stay.[33] This is true for a non–post-sixth year extension, as well as an extension of stay based upon either §104 or §106 of AC21. On a similar note, an extension of stay may not be approved for an applicant who failed to maintain the previously accorded status, or where such status expired before the application or petition was filed, with certain exceptions.[34] This being said, a floor statement made by Senator Patrick Leahy (D-VT) when AC21 was passed on October 3, 2002, implies that Congress intended for an extension of stay to be permissible under AC21 where the foreign national was not physically in the United States.

The conference report also contains another important immigration provision to permit H-1B aliens who have labor certification applications caught in lengthy agency backlogs to extend their status beyond the sixth-year limitation or, if they have already exceeded such limitation, *to have a new H-1B petition approved so they can apply for an H-1B visa to return from abroad or otherwise re-obtain H-1B status.*[35] Despite this comment, USCIS still would likely take

---

[31] *See* U.S.-Chile Free Trade Agreement Implementation Act (Pub. L. No. 108-77) and the U.S.-Singapore Free Trade Agreement Implementation Act (Pub. L. No. 108-78).

[32] USCIS Memorandum, Michael Aytes, "Processing Guidelines for E-3 Australian Specialty Occupation Workers and Employment Authorization for E-3 Dependent Spouses" (Dec. 15, 2005), *published on* AILA InfoNet at Doc. No. 05121590 (*posted* Dec. 15, 2005).

[33] *See* 8 CFR §214.2(h)(15)(i).

[34] *See* 8 CFR §214.1(c)(4).

[35] 148 Cong. Rec. S11063 (daily ed. Nov. 14, 2002) (emphasis added).

the position that it is not possible to file a post–sixth-year extension when the beneficiary is not in the United States in H-1B status. An April 24, 2003, guidance memorandum issued by William R. Yates, then USCIS Acting Associate Director for Operations[36]—although a bit cryptic—seems to indicate that extensions are available only to foreign nationals who are present in the United States and eligible for an extension. This issue may be clarified in future USCIS-AILA liaison meetings or through regulations in AC21 yet to be issued by USCIS.

13. Where a foreign national has spent six years in H-1B status, may he or she change status to H-4 and remain here with an H-1B spouse?

The status of a dependent of an H-1B nonimmigrant is derivative of and, therefore, linked to the status of the principal H-1B nonimmigrant.[37] The field guidance referenced above clarifies that a derivative family member who has maxed out of H-1B status may be granted H-4 status, but he or she

would not be permitted to extend his or her H-1B status pursuant to the principal's permanent residence case or the principal's eligibility grounds under AC21. Unless the dependent is independently eligible for an extension of H-1B status, he or she would be limited to H-4 classification.

14. Why are Mexican citizens issued three-year visas? Does this mean they can stay in the United States for three years rather than one year at a time?

Mexican citizens are issued three-year multiple entry TN visas because of DOS's visa reciprocity schedule. However, admission in TN status may not be for more than one year. The period of admission is governed by 8 CFR §214.6(e), which states that "[a] citizen of Canada or Mexico who qualifies for admission under this section shall be provided confirming documentation (Form I-94) and shall be admitted under the classification symbol TN *for a period not to exceed one year.*" (Emphasis added.)

---

[36] USCIS Memorandum, William R. Yates, "The Significance of a Prior CIS Approval of a Nonimmigrant Petition in the Context of a Subsequent Determination Regarding Eligibility for Extension of Petition Validity" (Apr. 23, 2004), *published on* AILA InfoNet at Doc. No. 04050510 (*posted* May 5, 2004).

[37] *See* 8 CFR §214.2(h)(9)(iv).

MAKING DO: AC21 IN A REGULATORY VACUUM

by Naomi Schorr[*]

INTRODUCTION

There's a famous line from the Godfather III: "Just when you think you're out, they pull you back in." Now, *there's* a sentiment that resonates in me. Just when I thought I was through writing about AC21,[1] I find myself drawn right back in, attracted to this subject matter by obsessive forces apparently beyond my control.

We have no regulatory guidance yet, but too much has happened on the AC21 front for me to walk away just now. For one, the cap[2] on H-1B petition approvals was reached for fiscal year 2006 on August 10, 2005, almost two months before the fiscal year even began,[3] making it even more important to find every which way to fit into one of the cap exemptions. For another, the USCIS has recently issued guidance on a number of AC21 questions,

both in written memoranda and in statements at conferences of the American Immigration Lawyers Association (AILA). And finally, the USCIS Administrative Appeals Office (AAO) has rendered a number of decisions addressing important adjustment portability questions.

So, I decided to write two more AC21 articles. This one, written in a question and answer format, focuses on H-1B issues. A later one will examine the AAO decisions on adjustment portability. Although it may seem that some of the questions broached in this article have been raised by me before, this article actually takes up where the others[4] left off. It draws upon recent comments made about AC21 by government officials at meetings and conferences, and it introduces new issues and questions, made particularly important in the face of immigrant visa retrogression in a number of employment-based preference categories.[5]

WHAT IS AN INSTITUTION OF HIGHER EDUCATION?

At least four statutory provisions of H-1B law that refer to "institutions of higher education": exemptions from the H-1B cap;[6] exemptions from the H-1B training fee (also referred to as the ACWIA fee);[7] calculation of prevailing wages for those employed by institutions of higher education;[8] and the

---

[*] **Naomi Schorr** (nschorr@kramerlevin.com) is Special Counsel at Kramer Levin Naftalis & Frankel LLP in New York City, where she practices in the firm's Business Immigration Group. Copyright © 2005 Naomi Schorr. All rights reserved. An earlier version of the article appeared in 10 Bender's Immigr. Bull. 1712 (Nov. 15, 2005). The author thanks Stephen Yale-Loehr for editing this article.

[1] The American Competitiveness in the Twenty-First Century Act (AC21), Pub. L. No. 106-313, 114 Stat. 1251 (October 17, 2000).

[2] With certain exceptions, the total number of aliens who may be issued H-1B visas or otherwise provided H-1B status during any fiscal year is limited to 65,000. INA § 214(g)(1)(A)(vii), 8 U.S.C. § 1184(g)(1)(A)(vii).

[3] The announcement that the cap for fiscal year 2005 was reached on Aug. 10, 2005, appeared on the website of the U.S. Citizenship and Immigration Services (USCIS). The notice is available at http://uscis.gov/graphics/publicaffairs/newsrels/H-1Bcap_12Aug05.pdf (last visited Oct. 1, 2005). The cap for fiscal year 2005 was reached on Oct. 1, 2004, the first day of the fiscal year, and the cap for fiscal year 2004 was reached on Feb. 17, 2004. USCIS determined that the "final receipt date" for fiscal year 2006 numbers was August 10, 2005, and that any petitions received on that date would be subject to a random selection process. *Id.* For petitions received on the "final receipt date," USCIS applied a computer-generated random selection process that selected the exact number of petitions from the day's receipts needed to meet the congressionally mandated cap. After random selection, any remaining H-1B petitions that did not receive a FY 2006 number and were not otherwise exempt were rejected and returned along with the filing fee(s). *Id.*

[4] The other articles that I have authored or co-authored on AC21 issues are, Naomi Schorr, *A Capital Idea! All Governmental Research Organizations Are Exempt from the H-1B Cap*, 10 Bender's Immigr. Bull. 951 (Jun. 15, 2005); Naomi Schorr and Nathan Waxman, *So Quick Bright Things Come to Confusion: AC21 and the H-1B Cap*, 9 Bender's Immigr. Bull. 700 (Jun. 1, 2004) [hereinafter *So Quick*]; Naomi Schorr and Stephen Yale-Loehr, *Still Crazy After All These Years: AC21 in 2003*, 9 Bender's Immigr. Bull. 483 (Apr. 15, 2004); and Naomi Schorr and Stephen Yale-Loehr, *Buying Time: Practice Strategies for H-1B Workers Coming to the End of the Line and Related Issues*, 8 Bender's Immigr. Bull. 453 (Mar. 15, 2003).

[5] The current issue of the Visa Bulletin of the U.S. Department of State is *available at* http://travel.state.gov/visa/frvi/bulletin/bulletin_1360.html.

[6] INA § 214(g)(5)(A), 8 U.S.C. § 1184(g)(5)(A).

[7] INA § 214(c)(9), 8 U.S.C. 1184(c)(9).

[8] INA § 212(p)(1)(A), 8 U.S.C. § 1182(p)(1)(A).

583

additional exemption from the H-1B cap for up to 20,000 foreign nationals awarded master's or higher degrees from U.S. institutions of higher education.[9] The last provision was brought about by the L-1 Visa and H-1B Visa Reform Act.[10] It's time to get a better understanding of what these institutions are.

Question 1: INA § 214(g)(5)(A) exempts from the H-1B cap those who are employed at an institution of higher education as defined by § 101 of the Higher Education Act of 1965 (HEA).[11] What is that definition?

Answer: Just to set the record straight, let's first look at the statutory provision at hand, INA § 214(g)(5), 8 U.S.C. § 1184(g)(5):

(5) The numerical limitations contained in paragraph (1)(A)[12] shall not apply to any nonimmigrant alien issued a visa or otherwise provided status under section 101(a)(15)(H)(i)(b) who--

(A) is employed (or has received an offer of employment) at an institution of higher education (as defined in section 101(a) of the Higher Education Act of 1965 (20 U.S.C. 1001(a)), or a related or affiliated nonprofit entity;

(B) is employed (or has received an offer of employment) at a nonprofit research organization or a governmental research organization; or

(C) has earned a master's or higher degree from a United States institution of higher education (as defined in section 101(a) of the Higher Education Act of 1965 (20 U.S.C. 1001(a)), until the number of aliens who are exempted from such numerical limitation during such year exceeds 20,000.

Section 101(a) of the HEA, 20 U.S.C. § 1001(a) defines an institution of higher education as an educational institution in any State that -

(1) admits as regular students only persons having a certificate of graduation from a school providing secondary education, or the recognized equivalent of such a certificate;

(2) is legally authorized within such State to provide a program of education beyond secondary education;

(3) provides an educational program for which the institution awards a bachelor's degree or provides not less than a 2-year program that is acceptable for full credit toward such a degree;

(4) is a public or other nonprofit institution; and

(5) is accredited by a nationally recognized accrediting agency or association, or if not so accredited, is an institution that has been granted preaccreditation status by such an agency or association that has been recognized by the Secretary for the granting of preaccreditation status, and the Secretary has determined that there is satisfactory assurance that the institution will meet the accreditation standards of such an agency or association within a reasonable time.

Question 2: On the face of it, the definition of institution of higher education at § 101(a)(3) of the HEA seems to exclude schools that offer *only* degrees that are *higher* than a bachelor's degree. For example, the definition does not seem to include medical colleges or "stand alone" law schools that are not affiliated with bachelor's degree-granting universities and award only M.D. or J.D. degrees, but not bachelor's degrees. Does that mean that employment at those schools and at their related and affiliated nonprofit entities is not exempt from the H-1B cap? And are graduates of those schools not eligible for one of the additional 20,000 H-1B visas?

Answer: Schools that offer only degrees that are higher than bachelor's degrees are institutions of higher education under the HEA and are H-1B cap exempt, and their graduates *are* eligible for one of the 20,000 H-1B numbers. The regulations governing the education laws[13] refine the definition of institution of higher education to include those public or private nonprofit educational institutions that provide an educational program for which they award an "associate, baccalaureate, *graduate, or professional degree*."[14] Therefore, almost all post-

---

[9] INA § 214(g)(5)(C), 8 U.S.C. § 1184(g)(5)(C).

[10] The L-1 Visa and H-1B Visa Reform Act was included in Division J, Title IV of the Consolidated Appropriations Act, 2005, signed into law on December 8, 2004, Pub. L. No. 108-447. Among its provisions was an amendment to INA § 214(g)(5), adding subsection (g)(5)(C).

[11] Pub. L. No. 87-328. The Act was reauthorized in 1998 by Pub. L. No. 105-244.

[12] INA § 214(g)(1)(A) limits the number of new H-1B petitions approvals to 65,000 annually.

[13] 34 C.F.R. § 600.1 et seq.

[14] 34 C.F.R. § 600.4(i) (emphasis added). The regulations at 34 C.F.R. Part 600 govern institutional eligibility for and

continued

secondary degree-granting institutions are institutions of higher education, and are cap-exempt, as are their "affiliated" or "related" nonprofit entities.

Question 3: What about schools that are proprietary? Are private, for-profit institutions of higher education exempt from the H-1B cap?

Answer: It seems that these schools are not exempt from the cap. As we have seen, INA § 214(g)(5) exempts from the cap institutions of higher education as defined in § 101(a) of the HEA. To qualify under that section, an institution must be "public" or "nonprofit." For-profit schools, then, are cap subject. According to one source, there are more than 4,500 of these for-profit colleges in the United States.[15] None would seem to be eligible for the cap exemption provided by INA § 214(g)(5).

Question 4: The statutory provision adding 20,000 new H-1B numbers, INA 214(g)(5)(C), also refers to the definition of institution of higher education as provided by § 101(a) of the HEA. Does that mean that a foreign national who earns a master's degree at a proprietary, for-profit school is not eligible for one of these numbers?

Answer: Strictly speaking, a graduate of a proprietary, for-profit school is not eligible for one of

those 20,000 visas since the school does not fit within the definition of institution of higher education that is found at § 101(a) of the HEA.

Question 5: Are you saying that for-profit schools do not benefit from the special prevailing wage rules, from the exemption from the H-1B training fee provision, from the cap-exemption provisions, and from the provision exempting from the cap 20,000 H-1B numbers for graduates with advanced degrees?

Answer: Based on a strict reading of the law, they do not qualify, although I'm aware of no instances in which this issue has been raised by USCIS.

Question 6: The definition of institution of higher education in the HEA provides that the school must be in a "State." Suppose my client was awarded a master's degree by the University of Puerto Rico? Does he qualify for one of the 20,000 additional H-1B visas, and if he were employed at that university, would he be cap-exempt?

Answer: The regulations governing the education laws define "State" as a State of the Union, American Samoa, the Commonwealth of Puerto Rico, the District of Columbia, Guam, the Virgin Islands, the Commonwealth of the Northern Mariana Islands, the Republic of the Marshall Islands, the Federated States of Micronesia, and the Republic of Palau.[16] So, yes, he qualifies.

Question 7: Does the institution of higher education have to be physically located and providing instruction in a state, or is it enough to be incorporated in a state, or accredited by a U.S. regional accrediting body? I have a client who recently earned a master's degree from the American University of Beirut. Does he qualify?

Answer: That is a little unclear, but it seems that he does not qualify. In further defining institution of higher education, a regulatory provision states that an institution is "physically located in a State if it has a campus or other instructional site in that State."[17] That would seem to bar the American University of Beirut, assuming it has no instructional site in a state. Mind you, the statute itself does not require that the school be "physically located" in a state, only that it be an educational institution "in

---

participation in the student financial assistance programs authorized under title IV of the HEA, e.g., the Federal Pell Grant Program and the Federal Work Study Program. 64 Fed. Reg. 58,608 (Oct. 29, 1999) (supplementary information to final rule). However, in correspondence with the Office of the General Counsel of the U.S. Department of Education (DOE), the author was advised that in 34 C.F.R. § 600.4, the DOE has interpreted § 101(a)(3) of the HEA, 20 U.S.C. § 1001(a)(3), to include schools that award a professional degree, such as a medical or law degree, without regard to whether the institution is affiliated with an undergraduate university. Specifically, in 34 C.F.R. § 600.4(a)(4)(i), the DOE has interpreted that schools that award professional degrees are within the scope of HEA § 101(a)(3). That regulation interprets the general definition of "institution of higher education," and its application is not limited to title IV student aid programs. *See, e.g.,* Massachusetts School of Law at Andover v. American Bar Association, 914 F. Supp. 688 (D. Mass. 1996) (state action brought by stand-alone law school was able to be removed by defendant to federal court because school is institution of higher education within meaning of HEA).

[15] Doug Lederman, *Rough Ride for Career Colleges*, Inside Higher Education, March 2, 2005, available at http://www.insidehighered.com/news/2005/03/02/congress3_2 (last visited Oct. 4, 2005). Examples of for-profit institutions of higher education include DeVry University and the University of Phoenix.

---

[16] 34 C.F.R. § 600.2.

[17] 34 C.F.R. § 600.4(b).

any State." The regulation adds the requirement that it be "physically located" in a state.

Question 8: What about institutions like the University of Maryland, which operates all over the world?[18] If a foreign national earns a master's degree abroad at that university, would he qualify for one of the 20,000 H-1B numbers?

Answer: According to the regulatory definition, that person should qualify. Although he studied at an American university abroad, that university clearly has "a campus or other instructional site" in a state.

Question 9: What about online study? Would someone qualify for one of the 20,000 new H-1B visas if he was awarded a master's degree by a U.S. institution of higher education while sitting at home in Denmark, all the while taking courses online?

Answer: If the school met the HEA's definition of institution of higher education, it would seem he would qualify. When asked about this, a senior official of USCIS agreed: "The statute just speaks to the degree from a U.S. institution; it doesn't say anything about where you actually physically studied most of the time."[19]

Question 10: I have a client who's earned sixty credits beyond his bachelor's degree and has completed all the requirements for a Ph.D. degree, except his dissertation. Would he qualify for one of the 20,000 H-1B numbers?

Answer: The statute specifies that the person must have "earned" a master's or higher degree, and if your client didn't pick up his master's degree on the way to the doctorate, I believe that the USCIS would deny the petition.

Question 11: I'm a little confused by something. For many years, the U.S. Department of Labor (DOL) has had "special handling" labor certification provisions for "college and university teachers." Is

the definition of "colleges and universities" the same as "institutions of higher education"?[20]

Answer: No. The definition of institution of higher education is *not* the same as the definition of college and university. This takes a little explaining, and is best understood by reviewing what the DOL itself had to say about the differences.

In 1998, the DOL issued a regulation[21] that permitted the prevailing wages for researchers in "colleges and universities" to be established by comparing those wages to what was paid to researchers in similar facilities in the area of intended employment, rather than by comparing wage surveys across industries. (Note that the DOL permitted this disparate treatment for those employed *not* by "institutions of higher education," but by "colleges and universities.")

Several commenters on the proposed regulation[22] suggested that instead of using the term "colleges and universities," the DOL should use the term "institution of higher education," as defined by the HEA.[23] The DOL declined to adopt the HEA defini-

---

[18] Information about the university and its overseas operations is available at http://www.umuc.edu/ip/umucfacts_02.html (last visited Oct. 2, 2005).

[19] Comments of Efren Hernandez, USCIS Branch Chief, Business and Trade on the panel, "Surviving the H-1B Blackout" at the 2005 Annual Conference of AILA (conference tape no. 21) [hereinafter Comments of Efren Hernandez].

[20] The special handling provisions are retained in the PERM regulations at 20 C.F.R. § 656.18.

[21] The rule, found for a while at 20 C.R.F. § 656.40(c), was issued on March 20, 1998, to counter the harsh effects of *Matter of Hathaway Children's Services*, 91-INA-388 BALCA LEXIS 1 (Feb. 4, 1994). 63 Fed. Reg. 13,756 (March 20, 1998). In *Hathaway*, the Board of Alien Labor Certification Appeals held that prevailing wages, even for nonprofit entities, were to be determined by using wage data obtained by surveying employers across industries in the area of intended employment, not simply by comparing like entities in the area of employment. The rule was "trumped" by the passage of the American Competitiveness and Workforce Improvement Act (ACWIA) in October 1998, Pub. L. No. 105-277, 112 Stat. 2681. Section 415(a) of ACWIA amended the INA by adding § 212(p)(1)(A), which provides:

> In computing the prevailing wage level for an occupational classification in an area of employment for purposes of subsections (n)(1)(A)(i)(II) and (a)(5)(A) in the case of an employee of—
>
> > (A) an institution of higher education (as defined in section 101(a) of the Higher Education Act of 1965), or a related or affiliated nonprofit entity; . . . .

[22] The proposed rule was published in 61 Fed. Reg. 17,610 (Apr. 22, 1996). The comments about the definition of institution of higher education received in response to that proposed regulation were discussed in the supplementary information to the final rule. 63 Fed. Reg. at 13,762-63.

[23] 63 Fed. Reg. at 13,762. In March 1998, when the final rule was published, the definition of "institution of higher education" was found in § 1201(a) of the HEA. Later in 1998, as a result of the Higher Education Amendments of 1998, Pub. L.

continued

tion, finding it to be inappropriate for the labor certification program and inconsistent with the definition of "colleges and universities" it had used for many years in administering the special handling provisions.[24] The DOL explained its position this way:

> The Department has reviewed the definition of institutions of higher education in section 1201(a)[25] of the Higher Education Act and has

---

105-244, the definition of "institution of higher education" was changed somewhat, and renumbered at § 101(a) and (b) of the HEA. Earlier, from 1965 to 1968, the definition of "institution of higher education" was found at § 801(a) of the HEA. Since enactment in 1965, the HEA has always defined an institution of higher education as a "public or other nonprofit institution," except for purposes of financial assistance programs. In that case, the definition includes for-profit educational institutions.

[24] 63 Fed. Reg. at 13,762.

[25] The DOL referred to § 1201(a) of the Higher Education Act, which at the time the regulation was issued in March 1998, defined "institution of higher education" as follows:

> The term "institution of higher education" means an educational institution in any State which (1) admits as regular students only persons having a certificate of graduation from a school providing secondary education, or the recognized equivalent of such a certificate, (2) is legally authorized within such State to provide a program of education beyond secondary education, (3) provides an educational program for which it awards a bachelor's degree or provides not less than a two-year program which is acceptable for full credit toward such a degree, (4) is a public or other nonprofit institution, and (5) is accredited by a nationally recognized accrediting agency or association, or if not so accredited, is an institution that has been granted preaccreditation status by such an agency or association that has been recognized by the Secretary for the granting of preaccreditation status, and the Secretary has determined that there is satisfactory assurance that the institution will meet the accreditation standards of such an agency or association within a reasonable time. Such term also includes any school which provides not less than a one-year program of training to prepare students for gainful employment in a recognized occupation and which meets the provisions of clauses (1), (2), (4), and (5). Such term also includes a public or nonprofit private educational institution in any State which, in lieu of the requirement in clause (1), admits as regular students persons who are beyond the age of compulsory school attendance in the State in which the institution is located. For purposes of this subsection, the Secretary shall publish a list of nationally recognized accrediting agencies or associations which he determines, pursuant to subpart 2 of part G of subchapter IV of this chapter, to be reliable authority as to the quality of the education or training offered.

continued

---

determined that it is **not appropriate** for the labor certification program. The definition proposed by commenters is not consistent with the definition of "college or university" that has been used for many years in administering the special handling provisions in the regulations established for college and university teachers. Unlike the definition of "colleges and universities" used in administering the permanent labor certification program, section 1201(a) of the Higher Education Act includes business and vocational schools **and is limited to public or other nonprofit institutions**. A directive dated January 13, 1984, from Bryan T. Keilty, then ETA's Acting Administrator for Regional Management, to all regional administrators, in relevant part, defined "college or university" as follows:

> "College or university" means an educational institution: (A) which admits as regular students only individuals having a certificate or diploma of graduation from high school, or the recognized equivalent of such a certificate or diploma; (B) which is legally authorized by the Federal and/or State Government(s) to provide a program of education beyond high school; and (C) which provides an educational program for which it awards a baccalaureate (bachelor's) or higher degree, or provides a program which is acceptable for such a degree. This would include those junior or community colleges which award associate degrees, but which teach courses which can be credited toward a baccalaureate degree at another college or university.

The Department has concluded it cannot change the definition of "college or university" used for the past 14 years in administering the permanent labor certification program without complying with the notice and comment requirements of the Administrative Procedure Act.[26]

Question 12: Do you mean to tell me that the DOL has not adopted the same definition of institution of higher education used by the legacy Immigration and Naturalization Service (INS), and now the USCIS?

The HEA was itself amended later in 1998, and what had been § 1201(a) of the Act, became § 101(a) and (b).

[26] 63 Fed. Reg. at 13,762-63 (emphasis added). The DOL did not want to exclude private, for-profit educational institutions from its coverage, and it did not want to include business and vocational schools.

Answer: Yes and no. For special handling purposes, the DOL uses the same definition of "colleges and universities" that it has used since 1984. But for prevailing wages purposes, the DOL now uses the definition found at § 101(a) of the HEA. Though it first held to the "colleges and universities" definition for its March 1998 rule regarding the calculation of prevailing wages for researchers at colleges and universities, that rule quickly became outdated when, later in 1998, Congress passed ACWIA.[27] In doing so, Congress statutorily mandated a different computation of prevailing wages for all employees, not just researchers, in "institutions of higher education," or a related or affiliated nonprofit entity, or nonprofit research organization, or a Governmental research organizations.[28]

There is nothing in the legislative history of either ACWIA or AC21 that provides a clue to what Congress was thinking—if it was thinking—when it adopted the definition of "institution of higher education" found in § 101(a) of the HEA for H-1B cap exemption, fee exemption, and prevailing wage determinations purposes. For once, the DOL should be applauded for digging its heels in and keeping its definition of colleges and universities for the special handling provisions. It's *this* definition, which includes for-profit schools, which should've been used by Congress, not the HEA definition.

After all, what possible difference should it make if a professor teaches at Pennsylvania State University or the University of Phoenix? Shouldn't both be exempt from the H-1B cap? And why should it matter if a student is awarded a master's degree by Oklahoma State University rather than by DeVry University, or by an acupuncture college? Even the DOL, not the most generous agency in interpreting the law, did not want to limit the rules governing prevailing wages for educational institutions to apply only to nonprofit institutions of higher education, so why should the CIS make this distinction?[29]

A U.S. MASTER'S OR HIGHER DEGREE IN WHAT?

Question 13: INA § 214(g)(5)(C) is rather clear: To qualify under that provision, a foreign national must have earned a master's or higher degree from a U.S. institution of higher education. I know that, under normal H-1B requirements, a university degree has to be related to the job, and usually must be required by the employer. What about the advanced degree under this provision? A plain reading does not seem to require that the advanced degree be related to the position or required by the petitioner. Is my reading correct?

Answer: When asked for his views on this matter, a senior official of USCIS agreed that the advanced degree need not be required by or related to the position:

> If the job [in marketing] requires a baccalaureate in a specific field and the individual, for example, has a bachelor's degree in marketing and has a master's in English, the master's in English from a U.S. institution would make him exempt from the cap.[30] It would really not relate to the adjudication of the I-129 with the exception of the cap issue. If, however, you require a master's in marketing, that would be a different situation [if the person had a master's in English].[31]

---

[27] *Supra,* note 21.

[28] Section 415(a) of ACWIA amended the INA by adding § 212(p), which provides:

> (1) In computing the prevailing wage level for an occupational classification in an area of employment for purposes of subsections (a)(5)(A), (n)(1)(A)(i)(II) and (t)(1)(A)(i)(II) in the case of an employee of--
>
> (A) an institution of higher education (as defined in section 101(a) of the Higher Education Act of 1965), or a related or affiliated nonprofit entity; or
>
> (B) a nonprofit research organization or a Governmental research organization, the prevailing wage level shall only take into account employees at such institutions and organizations in the area of employment.

[29] As we've seen in the discussion *supra* at notes 21-24 and accompanying text, the DOL did not think it appropriate to have a bifurcated prevailing wage regulation, one for nonprofit educational institutions, the other for for-profit schools. It was the DOL that advocated the inclusion of for-profit schools in the special prevailing wage regulation it published in March 1998. See *supra* note 26 and accompanying text.

[30] What the speaker meant was not an exemption from the cap, but eligibility for one of the 20,000 H-1B numbers for those earning a master's or higher degree from a U.S. institution of higher education.

[31] Comments of William R. Yates at the April 4, 2005, monthly meeting of the New York Chapter of AILA [hereinafter Yates New York Comments]. A tape of the panel discussion is on file with the author. *Accord,* Comments of Efren Hernandez, *supra* note 19 (nothing in the statute says the master's degree has to be related to the job in any way, as long as the bachelor's degree is, nor that it be required by the job).

In other words, and in harmony with the general rules governing H-1B petition adjudication, if you have a master's degree from a U.S. institution of higher education, you qualify for one of the 20,000 additional H-1B numbers, as long as *either* the bachelor's degree *or* the master's degree is related to the position. Of course, if a position *does* require a master's degree, the beneficiary better have it. For example, if a drug rehabilitation center requires a counselor to have a master's degree in social work, the case will not work under normal H-1B law if the foreign national has a master's degree in French.

Question 14: INA § 214(g)(5)(C) reserves 20,000 H-1B visas for those who have earned a master's or higher degree from a U.S. institution of higher education. What about a juris doctor (J.D.) degree. Does that qualify? It's not a master's degree, for sure. Is it "higher" than a master's degree?

Answer: The question of what qualifies as a master's or higher degree was recently answered in a USCIS memorandum, which directed adjudicators to consider the place that the claimed degree holds on the academic hierarchy of degrees. To qualify as advanced, the degree must be one for which a bachelor's degree in any field is required in order to receive the advanced degree. Thus, a J.D. and an M.D. degree would qualify, since both are at least one level higher than a bachelor's degree.[32]

NONPROFIT ENTITIES AFFILIATED WITH OR RELATED TO INSTITUTIONS OF HIGHER EDUCATION

Question 15: What does the statute mean when it speaks of nonprofit organizations that are "affiliated" with or "related" to institutions of higher education?[33]

Answer: There are no regulations to explain what is meant by "affiliated" or "related" nonprofit entities in the cap-exempt realm, but those terms are given some definition in the regulations that spell out which entities are relieved from paying the additional H-1B training fee. In that context, 8 C.F.R. § 214.2(h)(19)(iii)(B) provides a fee exemption for:

> [a] nonprofit entity (including but not limited to hospitals and medical or research institutions) that is connected or associated with an institution of higher education, through shared ownership or control by the same board or federation operated by an institution of higher education, or attached to an institution of higher education as a member, branch, cooperative, or subsidiary.

There appears to be an error in punctuation in the regulatory language quoted above, with an important comma omitted. Here's how the language appears in the supplementary information to the DOL's regulations implementing its ACWIA regulations:

> An affiliated or related nonprofit entity. A nonprofit entity (including but not limited to hospitals and medical or research institutions) that is connected or associated with an institution of higher education, through shared ownership or control by the same board or **federation,** operated by an institution of higher education, or attached to an institution of higher education as a member, branch, cooperative, or subsidiary.[34]

The DOL claims that it worked with the INS in developing the definitions of "affiliated or related," found in the Service's 1998 interim final regulation implementing the additional H-1B training fee added by ACWIA.[35] It's interesting that the DOL's version of that definition, with the comma inserted between the words "federation" and "operated" appears to be the correct version, because it's the only way the phrase makes sense. The comma, of course, changes the meaning of the phrase, and extends exemptions to those nonprofit entities that are "operated" by an institution of higher education. But note, too, that this regulation covers only the ACWIA fee, and there is no reason why its narrow embrace should be adopted by USCIS in the cap exemption realm when

---

[32] Memorandum from Michael Aytes, Acting Associate Director Domestic Operations, USCIS, *AFM Update: Chapter 31: H-1B Cap Exemption for Aliens Holding a Master's or Higher Degree from a U.S. Institution*, HQPRD70/23.12, AD06-24 (May 2, 2006), *available at* http://www.aila.org/infonet (document no. 06050876) (last visited May 9, 2006). The memorandum advises adjudicators to consider more than the "simple nomenclature" of the degree. A degree, the memorandum claims, may be titled as "Doctor of ___" but in fact, may not be a graduate degree at all. The example provided is that of Doctor of Chiropractic, which is an "entry-level" degree, not requiring a bachelor's degree prior to obtaining it.

[33] For additional discussion about the terms "affiliated" and "related," see *So Quick, supra* note 4, at 702-04.

[34] 65 Fed. Reg. 80,110, 80181 (Dec. 20, 2000) (emphasis on the word "federation" and the comma that follows it added).

[35] 64 Fed. Reg. 628, 650 (Jan. 5, 1999) (supplementary information to the proposed ACWIA regulation). ("The Department is consulting with the INS on the definitional issues. . . .")

that agency finally gets around to issuing AC21 regulations.

Question 16: In the supplementary information to the interim regulations[36] that first implemented the additional H-1B training fee,[37] the INS claimed that it was "drawing on generally accepted definitions"[38] of the terms, "affiliate" and "related."[39] What are those "generally accepted" definitions?

Answer: According to Black's Law Dictionary, which the INS and DOL seem to have consulted (as evidenced by the use of some of the precise terms from the dictionary's definition), "affiliate" is defined this way: "Signifies a condition of being united; being in close connection, allied, associated, or attached as a member or branch."[40]

The INS was rather selective in which part of the definition it included in its regulation, focusing only the language after the "or": "attached to an institution of higher education as a member, branch, cooperative, or subsidiary."[41] The Service seemed to have decided to exclude the language preceding the "or": "being in close connection, allied, associated." Had it adopted the entire "generally accepted definition," a broad spectrum of arrangements and a wide variety of entities would clearly be entitled to the fee exemption, and through the borrowing of concepts, to the cap exemption, and for the favorable method of determining prevailing wages.

And why focus only on "affiliated"? Congress didn't limit cap exemptions only to nonprofit entities "affiliated" with institutions of higher education; it also exempted those nonprofit entities that are "related" to institutions of higher education. So, what does "related" mean? Turning again to Black's, we find: "Standing in relation; connected; allied; akin."[42] And what does "relate" mean? "To stand in some relation; to have bearing or concern; to pertain;

refer; to bring into association with or connection with."[43]

Since the INS said that in seeking to define the terms "affiliated" and "related," it was "drawing on generally accepted definitions of the terms,"[44] let the USCIS take note that the generally accepted definitions of those terms are broad and inclusive, and cover a wide variety of arrangements entered into between institutions of higher education and other nonprofit entities. This broader interpretation should guide the USCIS in its AC21 rulemaking.

EMPLOYED "AT"

Question 17: The argument has been made that the H-1B cap exemption applies so long as a foreign national is employed "at," not necessarily employed "by," an institution of higher education or a related or affiliated nonprofit entity, or employed "at" a nonprofit research organization or a governmental research organization.[45] Consider this example. A medical fellow in pathology has been employed by a public hospital for two years in H-1B status. That hospital is a major affiliate of a university's medical college. On June 30, her fellowship will be over, and on July 1, she will become part of a private, for-profit practice group of pathologists "at" the hospital. She will be doing exactly the same work that she did before July 1, but for reasons of hospital organization, billing, insurance, and other related matters, her technical employer on July 1 will be the practice group, which is *not* nonprofit. Can this physician continue to be H-1B cap-exempt?

Or consider this example: The Texas Medical Practice Act prohibits the corporate practice of medicine.[46] Under that law, hospitals generally are precluded from employing physicians directly for

---

[36] 63 Fed. Reg. 65,657 (Nov. 30, 1998).

[37] Enacted as title IV of the Omnibus Consolidated and Emergency Supplemental Appropriations Act for Fiscal Year 1999, Pub. L. No. 105-277, 111 Stat. 2681, 2681-641.

[38] 63 Fed. Reg. at 65,658.

[39] The INS also said it was borrowing from the regulations of the Small Business Administration (SBA) at 13 C.F.R. § 121.103. For a discussion of how the SBA defines "affiliation," see *So Quick, supra* note 4, at 702-03.

[40] Black's Law Dictionary 54 (5th ed. 1979) (emphasis added).

[41] 8 C.F.R. § 214.2(h)(19)(iii)(B).

[42] Black's, *supra* note 40, at 1158.

[43] *Id.*

[44] 63 Fed. Reg. at 65,658.

[45] This argument was put forward in *So Quick, supra,* note 4, at 704-5.

[46] See, Texas Occupations Code § 151.002(a)(13), which defines "practicing medicine" to include the diagnosis, treatment or offer to treat a disorder or injury by a person who "directly or indirectly charges money or other compensation for those services," and Texas Occupations Code § 164.052(a)(17), which provides that a physician commits a prohibited act if he "directly or indirectly aids or abets the practice of medicine by a person, partnership, association, or corporation that is not licensed to practice medicine by the board."

Answer: Take a look at Part C, item 5, of the H-1B Data Collection and Filing Fee Exemption Supplement to the I-129:

> Has the beneficiary of this petition been previously granted status as an H-1B nonimmigrant in the past 6 years and not left the United States for more than one year after attaining such status?

For the employee in your case who left the United States but came back within the past twelve months, the answer to this question is "yes." If the "yes" box is completed, the person will be deemed to be cap exempt. So far, the USCIS seems to agree that the one who came in during the time is not subject, but the other one is. This is an exchange that took place between the author and a senior USCIS official:

> Q. So two guys are sent abroad for 15 months. One of them comes back for a week after four months and then another week after eight months. He can answer the I-129 honestly, that he hasn't been gone for a full year, so he's not cap subject but the other one is.
>
> A. That's correct, he's not cap subject but the other one is, in that scenario.
>
> Q. So, do you think that makes sense?
>
> A: Now you're asking me if I think the laws Congress passes makes sense. Not necessarily.[56]

That the person who remained out for the full fifteen months is subject to the H-1B cap was confirmed by another senior USCIS official, who states that at least for now, that's the position the agency is taking.[57]

Practice pointer: If cap issues are of concern to an employer, it must make certain that H-1B workers assigned abroad return to the United States for even a day during that assignment, and not log in a continuous absence of one year. If, of course, the H-1B worker is assigned for a year or longer to the employer's overseas operations, a different result may ensue, with the possibility of a an L-1A or L-1B petition approval, and a new period of seven or five years presence.

---

[56] Exchange between the author and William R. Yates at the April 4, 2005 meeting of the New York Chapter of AILA, *supra* note 31.

[57] Comments of Efren Hernandez, *supra* note 19.

Question 20: If an entity is eligible for a cap exemption, must it claim it? For example, suppose a systems analyst is offered a one-year position by a university, but the systems analyst would rather draw from one of the 65,000 numbers to preserve his eligibility to change to a cap-subject employer later on. Can that be done? We understand that the petitioner must answer the questions on the H-1B data collection form accurately, and must state that it is an institution of higher education, and thus cap-exempt. But can it write on the form that it is *not* claiming the exemption for this case?

Answer: The USCIS has said that if exempt, an entity must claim the exemption. For matters of equity alone, the agency reasons, one who is eligible for the exemption should not be permitted to "take" a cap number from a person who is not exempt from the cap.[58] In other words, if you're a cap-exempt employer, you must claim the cap exemption, if for no other reason than to preserve numbers for those subject to the cap.

Despite this, I've seen a number of cases in which a cap-exempt petitioner did not claim the exemption, including a nonprofit medical facility closely affiliated with a medical school. Perhaps the petitioner was unaware that it could claim the exemption. There had been claims by some that Veterans Affairs medical centers, also closely affiliated with institutions of higher education, should claim the exemption, but the agency insists they are not eligible.[59] To date, there appear to be no instances in

---

[58] Remarks of senior USCIS operations official on the panel, "Surviving the H-1B Blackout," *supra* note 19.

[59] In the realm of the H-1B "training fee" regulation, 8 C.F.R. § 214.2(h)(19)(iii), the Office of the General Counsel of the Veterans Health Administration (VHA) insists that the VHA is not fee-exempt. Included in the USCIS fee-exemption regulation are nonprofit entities affiliated with or related to institutions of higher education. To qualify as "nonprofit," the entity must meet the definition in Internal Revenue Code § 501(c)(3), (c)(4), or (c)(6), and, as the opinion points out, the VHA does not. The opinion, Request for a Legal Opinion Regarding the New Filing Fee for Nonimmigrant Workers (Aug. 1, 2001), is on file with the author. In Employment Standards Administration v. Dallas VA Medical Center, 98-LCA-3 (DOL Oct. 30, 2003) the DOL held that for prevailing wage purposes, the Dallas VA did not qualify for the special rules available to governmental research organizations under INA § 212(p) and 20 C.F.R. § 755.731(a)(2)(viii) because its "primary mission" is not research. The opinion is available at http://www.oalj.dol.gov/public/ina/decsn/981ca03b.htm. This does not necessarily mean that VA medical centers are subject to the H-1B cap.

continued

which the USCIS looked behind the I-129 data collection form when the petitioner checked the box stating that it is *not* affiliated with an institution of higher education. (Note, however, that the USCIS has sent out requests for evidence when the petitioner claims that it *is* so affiliated.)

PHYSICIANS

Question 21: Are J-1 physicians who have obtained INA § 214(l) waivers from the two-year home residence requirement imposed by INA § 212(e)[60] exempt from the H-1B cap for all purposes?

Answer: There's a lot in that question, so let's respond to it one step at a time. First, some background.

Of all of the statutory exemptions from the numerical limitations of INA § 214(g)(1), the one enacted for physicians is the only one that unconditionally "runs to" the H-1B employee, rather than to the employee together with employing entity. For example, an exemption from the cap is provided by INA § 214(g)(5)(A), but only if the person will be employed at an institution of higher education or its affiliated or related nonprofit entity. There has never been such a limitation for physicians.

When Congress first enacted a cap-exempt statute for "Conrad 30" physicians in § 114 of AC21, that law provided:

> The numerical limitations contained in section 102 of this title shall not apply to any nonimmigrant alien granted a waiver that is subject to the limitation contained in paragraph (1)(B) of the first section 214(l) of the Immigration and Nationality Act (relating to restrictions on waivers).

Under a plain reading of the statute, that provision applied to all Conrad 30 physicians who were changing status from J-1 to H-1B while in the United States, to those physicians who were instead applying for an H-1B visa abroad, to those physicians who were extending status in the United States, and to those physicians who were seeking

concurrent H-1B employment, normally in the same health professional shortage area as the "waiver" facility.

Then, in December 2004, Congress passed a new law, which sought to *broaden* the H-1B cap exemption to cover not just Conrad 30 physicians, but those physicians receiving *federal* interested government agency waivers.[61] The newly enacted law, which does not seem to repeal AC21 § 114, amends INA § 214(l)(2)(A), which until now has simply provided:

> Notwithstanding section 248(2),[62] the Attorney General may change the status of an alien who qualifies under this subsection and section 212(e) to that of an alien described in section 101(a)(15)(H)(i)(b).

The new law added the following to § 214(l)(2)(A):

> Section 214(l)(2)(A) of the Immigration and Nationality Act (8 U.S.C. 1184(l)(2)(A)) is amended by adding at the end the following: "The numerical limitations contained in subsection (g)(1)(A) shall not apply to *any alien whose status is changed under the preceding sentence*, if the alien obtained a waiver of the 2-year foreign residence requirement upon a request by an interested Federal agency or an interested State agency.

Question 22: Well, does that mean that to benefit from the cap exemption, the physician must change his status in the United States?

Answer: Based on some preliminary responses from USCIS, it is probably safe to assume that, by referring to physicians who "change status," the new legislation merely reiterates that J-waivered physicians are *permitted*, but *not required*, to change status under INA § 248, and, whichever route they choose—change of status or application for an H-1B visa at a consulate—they are still cap-exempt. Here's what a senior USCIS official said about this issue:

At various AILA conferences, USCIS officials have stated that if a governmental agency has substantial research components, it could, indeed, be deemed to be cap exempt. A case can be made that, because of the extensive research that it conducts, the VHA qualifies for the exemption. The same argument could be applied to training fee exemptions and to prevailing wage issues.

[60] INA § 212(e), 8 U.S.C. § 1182(e).

[61] INA § 214(l)(2)(A) was amended by Pub. L. No. 108-441, Act of Dec. 3, 2004, § 1(b), 118 Stat. 2630.

[62] INA § 248, 8 U.S.C. § 1258 is the provision that permits change of nonimmigrant status in the United States, but also lists those nonimmigrants ineligible for a change of status. § 248(2) bars a change of status for "an alien classified as a nonimmigrant under subparagraph (J) of section 101(a)(15) who came to the United States or acquired such classification in order to receive graduate medical education or training."

The J waiver physician can alternatively pursue O-1 or even national interest waiver adjustment as a status under which to complete the years of service in an underserved area that constitute the only condition subsequent to obtaining the waiver. *The special mention of H-1B is just to allow change of status as the procedural vehicle which is otherwise prohibited for any alien who has enjoyed J-1 status as an FMG.*[63]

Question 23: Can we assume that, like AC21 § 114, the new legislation includes in the cap exemption those physicians who are not just taking up H-1B status for the first time, but those who are extending H-1B status? I know that the law provides the benefit of the cap exemption to those physicians going from J-1 to H-1B status, but are those extending H-1B status beyond year three also cap exempt? After all, many of these physicians in health professional shortage areas are employed by entities that would not themselves qualify for the cap-exemption. Many work at for-profit practices, and many are employed by entities having no affiliation with institutions of higher education. Can the physician continue to be cap exempt after his three-year waiver period is over if he is employed by a medical facility not otherwise cap exempt?

I'm asking because most physicians are not accorded lawful permanent resident (LPR) status before their three years of waiver service is up. Those applying under the special national interest waiver (NIW) provisions,[64] where the service obligation is five years, are not eligible for LPR status until the service obligation is complete, and often those physicians prefer to remain in H-1B status rather than working under an employment authorization document. This is particularly important now, as many physicians will not be permitted to file adjustment of status applications (with requests for interim benefits) because of the per country limitations on immigrant visas.

But even with non-NIW physicians, J-waivered physicians have to wait until their three years of service obligation is complete to file an adjustment application. As a practical matter, most have to extend

their H-1B status to finish up their three years, since it's virtually impossible to get the three-year H term to coincide exactly with the three-year waiver term. It is critically important for those physicians who serve in medically underserved areas to be able to extend their H-1B status to continue to render services in areas of the country most affected by physician shortages.[65]

And what happens after the service obligation is complete? Suppose my J-waivered physician client has just finished three years of service in a health professional shortage area in Texas, and he's now been offered a position with a for-profit private practice group in Chicago. Is he still exempt from the H-1B cap, or does he have to wait until October 2006 to take the new job?

Answer: The USCIS has said that it believes that J-waivered physicians are exempt for *all* purposes, including the three-year service obligation period, extensions of status beyond three years, concurrent H-1B employment, change of H-1B employers, and for employment after the three-year service obligation is complete. The USCIS also has said that the cap-exemption applies whether the doctor changes to H-1B status in the United States or applies for an H-1B visa at a consular post abroad.[66]

Question 24: How is the data collection form completed for J-waivered physicians after the first petition has been filed and approved? Part C of the form asks: "Is the beneficiary of this petition a J-1 nonimmigrant alien who received a waiver of the 2-year foreign residency requirement described in section 214(l)(1)(B) or (C) of the Act?"

At the time of the extension or concurrent employment, the beneficiary is an *H-1B*, not a J-1 nonimmigrant. His J-1 status is a thing of the past, so how do I complete the form?

And, what do I do in this case? My physician client wants to change employers after his three-year service obligation is complete. Currently, he's employed by a hospital that is a major affiliate of a

---

[63] Yates New York Comments, *supra* note 31 (emphasis added).

[64] INA § 203(b)(2)(B)(ii), 8 U.S.C. 1153(b)(2)(B)(ii) provides a mechanism for certain physicians serving in health professional shortage areas or in Veterans Affairs facilities to gain LPR status through that employment.

[65] I thank AILA member Rosanne Mayer, a partner at Miller Mayer LLP in Ithaca, N.Y., for providing me with the context in which H-1B cap issues arise for J-waivered physicians and for writing a portion of this question.

[66] Comments of Efren Hernandez, *supra* note 19. Though not stated as clearly, this view was also expressed by William R. Yates at the April 4, 2005, monthly meeting of the New York Chapter of AILA, *supra* note 31.

medical college, and is thus cap-exempt. Choice 6 on the data collection form asks:

> If the petition is to request a change of employer, did the beneficiary previously work as an H-1B for an institution of higher education, an entity related to or affiliated with an institution of higher education, or a nonprofit research organizations or governmental research institution. . . .

If I check "yes" to that question, which I must, won't the USCIS determine that my client had not yet been counted against the cap, and then subject him to the cap on the change of employer petition?

Answer: Though not in written guidance, the USCIS has advised that when the data collection form asks, "Is the beneficiary of this petition a J-1 nonimmigrant alien who received a waiver of the 2-year foreign residency requirement described in section 214(l)(1)(B) or (C) of the Act?" you should answer "no," because the beneficiary is not *then* a J-1 nonimmigrant. Instead, you will need to write some qualifying language on the data collection form, explaining that the physician *had been* a J-1 physician who received a waiver, and is therefore still exempt from the cap.[67]

AC21 § 104(C) AND IMMIGRANT VISA RETROGRESSION

Section 104(c) of AC21 provides that if immigrant visa numbers become unavailable, and an H-1B worker is thus unable to adjust his status to permanent resident, he can get extensions of H-1B status beyond the normal six years. The statute states:

> One-Time Protection Under Per Country Ceiling—Notwithstanding section 214(g)(4) of the Immigration and Nationality Act (8 U.S.C. 1184(g)(4)), any alien who—
>
> (1) is the beneficiary of a petition filed under section 204(a) of that Act for a preference status under paragraph (1), (2), or (3) of section 203(b) of that Act; and
>
> (2) is eligible to be granted that status but for application of the per country limitations applicable to immigrants under those paragraphs,

may apply for, and the Attorney General may grant, an extension of such nonimmigrant status un-

til the alien's application for adjustment of status has been processed and a decision made thereon.

Question 25: To benefit under this provision, does the I-140 immigrant visa petition have to be *approved,* or is it enough that the petition was *filed*?

Answer: In two memoranda, the immigration agency has insisted that to benefit under this provision, the I-140 petition must first be *approved.*[68]

Question 26: But the statute doesn't say that the petition has to be approved. It just talks about a petition that was *filed*.

Answers: What this statute means is not immediately apparent, and arguments can be made to support both claims: that an approved petition is required before one can benefit under § 104(c); and that a filed, not necessarily an approved petition, is all that's required to benefit. Let's review both sides, starting with the argument that an immigrant visa petition must first be approved.

ANSWER A: AN APPROVED PETITION IS REQUIRED

Reason 1:

AC21 § 104(c) says two things that seem to be at odds with each other. In § 104(c)(1), it says that the H-1B worker must be the beneficiary of a petition

---

[67] Remarks of senior USCIS operations official on the panel, "Surviving the H-1B Blackout," *supra* note 19.

[68] Memorandum from William R. Yates, Associate Director for Operations, USCIS, *Interim Guidance for Processing Form I-140 Employment-Based Petitions and Form I-485 and H-1B Petitions Affected by the American Competitiveness in the Twenty-First Century Act of 2000 (AC21) (Public Law 106-313),* HQPRD 70/6.2.8-P (May 12, 2005) [hereinafter Yates Memorandum] at 10, *reprinted at* 10 Bender's Immigr. Bull. 996 (App. G) (June 15, 2005), *available at* http://uscis.gov/graphics/lawsregs/handbok/AC21interm051205.pdf (last visited Oct. 26, 2005), http://www.aila.org/infonet (document no. 05051810) (last visited Sept. 25, 2005) ("an approved I-140 petition is required in order for an alien to qualify for an extension beyond the 6-year limit under [AC21] § 104(c)"); Memorandum from Michael D. Cronin, Acting Executive Associate Commissioner, Office of Programs, INS, to Michael A. Pearson, Executive Associate Commissioner, Office of Field Operations, *Initial Guidance for Processing H-1B Petitions as Affected by the "American Competitiveness in the Twenty-first Century Act" (Public Law 106-313) and Related Legislation (Public Law 106-311) and (Public Law 106-396),* HQPGM 70/6.2.8 (June 19, 2001) [hereinafter Cronin Memorandum] at 3, *available at* http://uscis.gov/graphics/lawsregs/handbook/ac21guide.pdf (last visited Oct. 26, 2005) and http://www.aila.org/infonet (document no. 01062031) (last visited Oct. 1, 2005) (provision benefits H-1B nonimmigrants "with approved I-140 petitions").

filed under INA § 203(b)(1), (2), or (3). But in § 104(c)(2), it says that to benefit the worker must be eligible for permanent resident status *"but for"* application of the per country limitations. The "but for" language can be read to mean that to benefit, the only thing standing in the way of permanent residence must be the unavailability of immigrant visa numbers, not their unavailability *plus* a petition that has yet to be approved.

Reason 2:

Let's say an argument is advanced that the word "filed" in § 104(c)(1) is clear and unambiguous. Consequently, the argument may go, a filed, not an approved petition, is all that's required to benefit under this provision. To top off the argument, the "plain meaning" rule[69] is trotted out to support the claim that, when the language in a statute is clear and not unreasonable, a court may not go outside the statute to give it a different meaning.[70] Since nothing can be clearer than the word "filed," all that's required is a *filed* immigrant visa petition. No further interpretation is needed or permitted.

"Not so fast," comes the other argument. When read together, §§ 104(c)(1) and (c)(2) *are* ambiguous, one subsection requiring a filed petition, the other offering a "but for" test. Because of the ambiguity, there is no clear expression of legislative intent, and other interpretive aides should be consulted to see if they shed any light on the meaning.[71] One such aide is the legislative history. Here's what the Senate Judiciary Committee report prepared in connection with AC21 says on this subject:

> This section [104(c)] also affords transitional protection for individuals on H-1B visas with *approved* petitions for permanent employment visas but whom the per-country limit is preventing from obtaining a permanent resident visa to stay until such a visa becomes available.[72]

So, if this part of the legislative history carries sway, it's pretty clear that Congress meant to require an approved petition to benefit under § 104(c).

Reason 3:

There's another canon of statutory construction that goes like this: Each part or section of a statute dealing with the same basic subject should be construed in connection with every other part.[73] So, look at AC21 § 104(c) and then compare it to AC21 §§ 106(a) and (b).[74] I'm afraid you may find the provisions a little hard to reconcile.

---

[69] The "plain meaning" rule has been expressed in a number of ways, but generally means that if the language of a statute is clear and unambiguous, it must be held to mean what it plainly expresses, and there is no room for alternate interpretations. *See generally* Norman J. Singer, 2A Statutes and Statutory Construction § 46.01 (6th ed. 2000).

[70] *Id.*

[71] *Id.* at § 48:01.

[72] S. Rep. No. 106-260, at 22 (2000) (emphasis added).

[73] Singer, *supra* note 69, at § 46.05 (statutory subsection may not be considered in a vacuum, but must be considered in reference to the statute as a whole and in reference to statutes dealing with the same general subject matter).

[74] When first enacted on Oct. 17, 2000, AC21 § 106 provided:

SPECIAL PROVISIONS IN CASES OF LENGTHY ADJUDICATIONS.

(a) EXEMPTION FROM LIMITATION- The limitation contained in section 214(g)(4) of the Immigration and Nationality Act (8 U.S.C. 1184(g)(4)) with respect to the duration of authorized stay shall not apply to any nonimmigrant alien previously issued a visa or otherwise provided nonimmigrant status under section 101(a)(15)(H)(i)(b) of that Act on whose behalf a petition under section 204(b) of that Act to accord the alien immigrant status under section 203(b) of that Act, or an application for adjustment of status under section 245 of that Act to accord the alien status under such section 203(b), has been filed, if 365 days or more have elapsed since--

(1) the filing of a labor certification application on the alien's behalf (if such certification is required for the alien to obtain status under such section 203(b)); or

(2) the filing of the petition under such section 204(b).

(b) EXTENSION OF H1-B WORKER STATUS- The Attorney General shall extend the stay of an alien who qualifies for an exemption under subsection (a) in one-year increments until such time as a final decision is made on the alien's lawful permanent residence.

The statute was amended on November 22, 2002 by § 11030A of the 21st Century Department of Justice Appropriations Authorization Act, Pub. L. No. 107-273, 116 Stat. 1758, which provided:

EXTENSION OF H–1B STATUS FOR ALIENS WITH LENGTHY ADJUDICATIONS.

(a) EXEMPTION FROM LIMITATION.—Section 106(a) of the American Competitiveness in the Twenty-first Century Act of 2000 (8 U.S.C. 1184 note) is amended to read as follows:

continued

Under § 106(a), an H-1B nonimmigrant is not eligible for additional time beyond the normal six-year limitation unless an immigrant visa petition or a labor certification application was filed at least 365 days before he came to the end of year six in H-1B status. Section 104(c) imposes no such requirement. An immigrant petition can be filed *during* year six, and the H-1B worker can still benefit.

Why, one might ask, would Congress give this great benefit under § 104(c) unless it contemplated that the immigrant visa petition had already been approved? How else can you explain that under AC21, one class of H-1B worker has to satisfy a 365-day rule, while another class does not? Isn't it a logical answer that one group gets to bypass the

---

"(a) EXEMPTION FROM LIMITATION.—The limitation contained in section 214(g)(4) of the Immigration and Nationality Act (8 U.S.C. 1184(g)(4)) with respect to the duration of authorized stay shall not apply to any nonimmigrant alien previously issued a visa or otherwise provided nonimmigrant status under section 101(a)(15)(H)(i)(b) of such Act (8 U.S.C.1101(a)(15)(H)(i)(b)), if 365 days or more have elapsed since the filing of any of the following:

"(1) Any application for labor certification under section 212(a)(5)(A) of such Act (8 U.S.C. 1182(a)(5)(A)), in a case in which certification is required or used by the alien to obtain status under section 203(b) of such Act (8 U.S.C. 1153(b)).

"(2) A petition described in section 204(b) of such Act (3 U. S.C. 1154(b)) to accord the alien a status under section 203(b) of such Act.".

(b) EXTENSION OF H-1B WORKER STATUS.—Section 106(b) of American Competitiveness in the Twenty-first Century Act of 2000 (8 U.S.C. 1184 note) is amended to read as follows:

"(b) EXTENSION OF H-1B WORKER STATUS.—The Attorney General shall extend the stay of an alien who qualifies for an exemption under subsection (a) in one-year increments until such time as a final decision is made—

"(1) to deny the application described in subsection (a)(1), or, in a case in which such application is granted, to deny a petition described in subsection (a)(2) filed on behalf of the alien pursuant to such grant;

"(2) to deny the petition described in subsection (a)(2); or

"(3) to grant or deny the alien's application for an immigrant visa or for adjustment of status to that of an alien lawfully admitted for permanent residence.".

365-day hurdle because the immigrant visa petition was approved?

Moreover, under AC21 § 106(b), extensions of stay may continue on a year-to-year basis until the labor certification application filed for the H-1B worker has been denied, until the preference petition has been denied, or until the adjustment of status application or immigrant visa application has been granted or denied. Under § 104(c), however, extensions may be granted until the H-1B worker's status has been adjusted to lawful permanent resident, clearly meaning that a petition had already been approved.

ANSWER B: A FILED, NOT NECESSARILY AN APPROVED, PETITION IS REQUIRED

If the USCIS finally does what it keeps saying it will do, and introduces premium processing to the I-140 immigrant visa petition, we wouldn't have to fashion arguments to support the view that an approved petition is not necessary to benefit under § 104(c). But until that fine day comes along, these are some reasons to consider:

Reason 1:

AC21 was enacted in 2000, when an approved I-140 petition was needed to move forward on all employment-based cases, so of course the legislative history cited earlier would refer to an approved petition. Later on, in July 2002, the immigration agency changed its procedures to permit the concurrent filing of an I-485 adjustment application *before* the I-140 petition was approved.[75] Because of that change in procedure, an approved petition isn't needed to file an adjustment application and to receive the ancillary benefits of travel permission and an employment document valid for open-market employment. And those benefits accrue not just to the principal alien, but to his family members as well. If you can get all of that without an approved immigrant petition, why, one might ask, should an approved petition be needed merely to get additional years of H-1B status?

Reason 2:

Rather than focusing on the words "filed" in § 104(c)(1), and "but for" in § 104(c)(2), attention

---

[75] The INS announced this change in its procedures at 67 Fed. Reg. 49,561-64 (July 31, 2002) (amending 8 CFR § 245.2).

should be paid to the words "is eligible to be granted that status" in § 104(c)(2). What does it mean to be "eligible" for permanent residence? Does it necessarily mean being the beneficiary of an approved petition at the present time? Clearly not.

Look, for example, at the supplementary information to the concurrent filing rule. When that rule was published, the INS said:

> Therefore, as a result of this interim rule, an *eligible* beneficiary of a Form I-140 visa petition for whom a visa is immediately available *will no longer need to wait for approval* of the underlying Form I-140 before *eligible* to apply for these benefits.[76]

Note that an "eligible beneficiary of a Form I-140 visa petition" is not necessarily the beneficiary of an approved I-140 petition. Note, too, that 8 C.F.R. § 245.1(c) contains a list of aliens ineligible to adjust status, and the beneficiary of a not-yet-approved immigrant visa petition is not on the list.

Reason 3:

AC21 was a remedial piece of legislation, and under the canons of statutory construction, remedial legislation is to be construed liberally.[77] Indeed, that may be why some leading scholars in the field of immigration law—including the current General Counsel of the USICS—have been of the opinion that an approved I-140 visa petition is not necessary to benefit under § 104(c).[78]

Yet another rule of construction is that ambiguous language in a remedial statute is entitled to a generous interpretation consistent with the mission of the legislation, at least if that interpretation doesn't conflict with the legislative history.[79]

While there is language in the legislative history that supports an interpretation that the I-140 immigrant petition must first be approved before one can benefit under AC21 § 104(c),[80] a broader reading of that history can also support the view that an approved petition is not required. In October 2000, when AC21 was enacted, no one anticipated the grave backlogs in immigrant visa availability that we have today.[81] At that time, other than the "other worker" category, which was backlogged across the board, there was visa unavailability only for nationals of China and India, and only in the second and third preference categories.[82] In September 1999, other than the "other worker" category, there were *no* backlogs in any of the employment-based categories at all.

The reason that Congress was so concerned with the plight of H-1B workers is set out with clarity in the legislative history. Not only fearful that U.S. companies could not "grow, innovate, and compete"[83] in global markets because of the annual 65,000 cap on H-1B approvals, Congress expressed grave reservation about the disruptions that would be caused were H-1B workers forced to depart before obtaining permanent resident status. Here's what the Judiciary Committee said about H-1B workers caught in a visa unavailability squeeze:

> These immigrants would otherwise be forced to return home at the conclusion of their allotted time in H-1B status, disrupting projects and American workers. The provision [§ 104(c)] enables these individuals to remain in H-1B status until they are able to receive an immigrant visa and adjust their status within the United States, thus limiting the disruption to American businesses.[84]

Reason 4:

I do not have the statistics to support this statement, but based on my own observations, most H-1B workers seeking an extension of stay beyond year six will qualify under AC21 § 106. For the few who do not and need relief under § 104(c), most would likely be the beneficiaries of approved labor certification

---

[76] 67 Fed. Reg. at 49,562 (emphasis added).

[77] Singer, *supra* note 69, at § 60:1.

[78] *See, e.g.,* Robert C. Divine, Immigration Practice, § 15-1(b) (2004-05 ed.) (worker for whom I-140 petition filed "*not necessarily approved,*" may obtain benefit of AC21 § 104(c)) (emphasis added).

[79] *See, e.g.,* Hogar Agua y Vida en el Desierto v. Suarez-Medina, 36 F.3d 177 (1st Cir. 1994) (presumption exists that ambiguous language in remedial statute entitled to generous construction).

[80] *See supra* note 72 and accompanying text.

[81] The Visa Bulletin of the Department of State for the month of October 2005 is available at http://travel.state.gov/visa/frvi/bulletin/bulletin_2631.html (last visited Sept. 25, 2005). In October 2005, backlogs existed worldwide for the third employment-based category, and for Chinese and Indian nationals, backlogs also existed in the first and second employment-based categories.

[82] The Visa Bulletin for the month of October 2000 is available at http://dosfan.lib.uic.edu/ERC/visa_bulletin/2000-10bulletin.html (last visited Oct. 11, 2005).

[83] S. Rep. No. 106-260, *supra* note 72, at 2.

[84] *Id.* at 22.

applications. That means that it has already been determined that these workers' skills are in short supply in the U.S. workforce. Others may qualify because of their extraordinary ability, their outstanding achievements, or because their work is in the national interest. Are these the people we should be sending home?

Reason 5:

Let's not forget that AC21 was enacted because of congressional concern about this nation's ability to attract and keep the most talented professional workers and to maintain our position as the world's leader in science, education, and business.[85] Among its provisions were four major components: an increase in the annual allotment of H-1B visas (§ 102); a remedy for agency delays in processing H-1B visa petitions (§ 105); a remedy for agency delays in processing labor certification applications and immigrant visa petitions (§ 106); and a remedy for the unavailability of immigrant visa numbers (§ 104).

Following the rule of statutory construction demanding that all sections of a statute dealing with the same general subject be construed in connection with each other[86] we find this: § 105 permits an H-1B worker to change employers and commence employment upon the *filing* of a petition by the new employer,[87] and § 106 permits extensions of H-1B status beyond the normal six-year limit if 365 days have elapsed since the *filing* of a labor certification application or immigrant visa petition.[88] It makes sense, therefore, that § 104(c)'s protection would also accrue upon the *filing* of the immigrant visa petition, which is why the statute refers to the "beneficiary of a petition *filed*" under INA § 204(a).

Reason 6:

The USCIS could broaden the scope of § 104(c) through rulemaking or policy, and there's precedent for it to do so. For example, consider the bars to admission under INA § 212(a)(9)(B),[89] which impose

stiff penalties on nonimmigrants who overstayed by 180 days or more the period granted them on their I-94s. The same law that punishes also contains a "tolling for good cause" provision. If a good faith, timely application to extend or change status had been filed, and if it remains pending for up to 120 days,[90] unlawful presence will not accrue. That statute is black and white on this: The application better not pend for more than 120 days, because if it does, unlawful presence begins to accrue.

Despite the clear language of the statute, the INS developed a policy that prolonged the tolling period for the *entire time* that a timely, good faith application remains pending, even if it takes the Service longer than 120 days to adjudicate the application.[91]

ALIENS UNLAWFULLY PRESENT.-

(i) In general.-Any alien (other than an alien lawfully admitted for permanent residence) who-

(I) was unlawfully present in the United States for a period of more than 180 days but less than 1 year, voluntarily departed the United States (whether or not pursuant to section 244(e)) prior to the commencement of proceedings under section 235(b)(1) or section 240, and again seeks admission within 3 years of the date of such alien's departure or removal, or

(II) has been unlawfully present in the United States for one year or more, and who again seeks admission within 10 years of the date of such alien's departure or removal from the United States, is inadmissible.

(ii) Construction of unlawful presence.-For purposes of this paragraph, an alien is deemed to be unlawfully present in the United States if the alien is present in the United States after the expiration of the period of stay authorized by the Attorney General or is present in the United States without being admitted or paroled.

[90] INA § 212(a)(9)(B)(iv), 8 U.S.C. 1182(a)(9)(B)(iv) provides:

Tolling for good cause.-In the case of an alien who-(I) has been lawfully admitted or paroled into the United States,

(II) has filed a nonfrivolous application for a change or extension of status before the date of expiration of the period of stay authorized by the Attorney General, and

(III) has not been employed without authorization in the United States before or during the pendency of such application, the calculation of the period of time specified in clause (i)(I) shall be tolled during the pendency of such application, **but not to exceed 120 days**. (Emphasis added.)

---

[85] *Id.* at 1-2, 10.

[86] *See supra* note 72 and accompanying text.

[87] AC21 § 105 amended INA § 214 by adding subsection (m)(1), which provides, in pertinent part: "A nonimmigrant alien...who was previously issued a visa or otherwise provided nonimmigrant status under section 101(a)(15)(H)(i)(b) is authorized to accept new employment upon the *filing* by the prospective employer of a new petition...." (Emphasis added.)

[88] See *supra* note 74.

[89] INA § 212(a)(9)(B), 8 U.S.C. § 1182(a)(9)(B) provides:

continued

[91] Memorandum from Michael A. Pearson, INS Executive Associate Commissioner, Office of Field Operations, to all INS offices, *Period of Stay Authorized by the Attorney Gen-*

continued

So, when the equities demand an expansive reading, the immigration agency will sometimes accommodate.[92] In the AC21 § 104(c) context, the same general reasoning can apply. Processing times for I-140 petitions are under the agency's control. If a petition filed in year six of H-1B status languishes for months at a service center and is not approved by the end of year six of H-1B status, why should the H-1B nonimmigrant and his employer be penalized? Doesn't it make more sense to permit extensions before the immigrant petition's approval?

Reason 7:

If the USCIS is concerned about fraudulent or frivolous filings of immigrant petitions just to allow an H-1B worker to seek extensions under § 104(c), the agency could borrow its solution to a similar problem, announced in the Yates Memorandum.[93] The problem and solution go something like this: Suppose a foreign national is eligible for a seventh year of H-1B status just as he enters year five of that status. An H-1B petition is filed requesting the rest of year five, plus years six and seven. Early in year six, there is a final denial of the I-140 immigrant petition filed on his behalf.

Even though the worker is the beneficiary of an H-1B petition approval valid through year seven, the Yates Memorandum advises that "the beneficiary will not be entitled to an extension beyond the time remaining on his or her 6-year maximum stay unless another basis for exceeding the maximum applies."[94] The same kind of remedy can be fashioned for those extending their status for three years under § 104(c).

---

eral After 120-Day Tolling Period for Purposes of Section 212(a)(9)(B) of the Immigration and Nationality Act, File No. HQADN 70/21.1.23-P, AD 00-07 (Mar. 3, 2000), *reprinted at* 5 Bender's Immigr. Bull. 286 (Mar. 15, 2000), and *available at* http://www.aila.org/infonet (document no. 00030773) (last visited Oct. 1, 2005). ("The Service has designated as a period of stay authorized by the Attorney General the entire time during which a timely filed, non-frivolous application for E/S or C/S is pending, provided the alien meets the requirements set forth below.").

[92] For an informative discussion of why the INS decided to, in effect, rewrite the law, I recommend the tape of the panel "Unlawful Presence" from the 2001 AILA Annual Conference, tape no. 54. Bo Cooper, INS General Counsel, had some very interesting things to say about INA § 212(a)(9)(B), and how and why the INS broadened the scope of the statute.

[93] Yates Memorandum, *supra* note 68.

[94] *Id.* at 8-9.

If there is a final denial of the immigrant petition during the three-year period, and no other basis for further extensions exist, the H-1B worker will have to depart.

Question 27: I've heard that an H-1B petition extension can be filed under § 104(c) when immigrant visa number unavailability precludes the filing of an adjustment of status application. But what about this? My client, the beneficiary of an approved I-140 petition, filed his adjustment application a year ago, it still hasn't been approved, and now there's been visa retrogression in his preference category. Can he benefit from § 104(c)?

Answer: I think the answer is a clear yes. After all, the facts fit squarely within the statutory provisions: he is the beneficiary of an approved petition, and he's eligible to be granted lawful permanent resident status but for application of the per country limitations. An early INS memorandum on AC21 provides some helpful authority, stating that:

> The AC21 § 104(c) enables H-1B nonimmigrants with approved I-140 petitions who are unable to adjust status because of per-country limits to be eligible to extend their H-1B nonimmigrant status until their application for adjustment of status has been adjudicated.[95]

That guidance does not state that the provision is available only to those who cannot *file* their adjustment applications; it's available to those unable to adjust status because no immigrant visas are available, which is the situation your client is in.

Despite this, the Vermont Service Center (VSC) had held a contrary view, insisting that the benefit of § 104(c) accrues only to those with approved immigrant visa petitions who are *precluded from filing* their I-485 applications because of the unavailability of immigrant visa numbers. Fortunately, the VSC has changed its opinion, agreeing that § 104(c) is also available to those with adjustment of status applications pending.[96]

Question 28: I notice that AC21 § 104(c) is titled "One-Time Protection." Does this mean that you can use this provision only one time?

---

[95] Cronin Memorandum, *supra* note 68, at 3.

[96] The author was advised of the earlier position in a telephone discussion with the VSC's Premium Processing Unit on Oct. 17, 2005. In an e-mail with the VSC on October 25, 2005, the author was advised that the Service Center has since changed its view.

Answer: The Yates Memorandum makes it clear that, despite reference to "one-time protection," a qualifying H-1B nonimmigrant may be granted more than one extension under this provision.[97] It might even be argued that in titling the provision "One-Time Protection," Congress intended that H-1B beneficiaries granted extensions under § 104(c) be provided a "duration of status" type of extension.

Question 29: I have a client who's the beneficiary of an approved I-140 immigrant visa petition, but he wanted to apply for an immigrant visa abroad, rather than adjusting status, thinking it would take less time to complete his case. His I-140 petition was completed to indicate he would consular process. Now, there's visa retrogression in his preference category, so he's unable to apply for the visa, and he's also precluded from changing courses and filing an adjustment of status application. Is he eligible for H-1B extensions in three-year increments under AC21 § 104(c)?

Answer: It is odd that the statute says that an extension of status may be granted "until the alien's application for adjustment of status has been processed and a decision made thereon," and says nothing about an application for an immigrant visa. This provision certainly is "drafting-challenged." It would make no sense whatever to restrict this benefit to those adjusting status.

Question 30: I filed an outstanding researcher petition for my client when he was already in the sixth year of H-1B status, and it's just been approved. My client is a national of China, and there are no visa numbers available in his preference category, so he couldn't file an adjustment of status application. Now, one of the principal researchers on his project has left and gone to a different laboratory. He'd like to take my client with him. I know my client's current employer can file an H-1B petition for him under AC21 § 104(c), seeking a three-year extension of stay, but can the new employer? My client isn't eligible for any further extensions of H-1B status under AC21 § 106(a), so I need to be sure that if he changes jobs, he'll be protected.

Answer: One would hope that the USCIS will follow the guidance that it issued in connection with H-1B extensions under AC21 § 106 and permit extensions by the new employer. In guidance provided recently in the Yates Memorandum, the USCIS stated: "The statute [AC21 § 106] does not require

that the labor certification or immigrant petition must be from the same employer requesting the H-1B extension."[98]

Let's look again at § 104(c) and point out the reasons why a new employer should be permitted to file a petition under this provision:

A. The statute does not require that the employer filing the H-1B petition be the same entity that filed the immigrant visa petition. All that's explicitly required is a filed immigrant visa petition and the unavailability of immigrant visa numbers.

B. Keep in mind that some immigrant visa petitions, those submitted under the extraordinary ability and national interest provisions, may be filed by the foreign national himself, who is precluded from filing a self-petition under the H-1B provisions.[99] In every such instance, therefore, the petitioner on the H-1B petition will be different from the petitioner on the immigrant visa petition. Surely, these cases must qualify under § 104(c), as must all cases in which the H-1B petitioner is different from the immigrant visa petitioner.

C. An argument may be fashioned that this provision is fundamentally "alien-based": "Any *alien*," it says, for whom an immigrant visa petition was filed, "may apply for…an extension of such status until the *alien*'s application for adjustment of status has been processed and a decision made thereon."[100] The provision, in other words, adheres to the "alien," was crafted for his benefit, and should travel with him to another employment situation.

D. As we've seen, the rules of statutory construction demand that a statutory subsection must be considered with reference to other statutes dealing with the same general subject matter.[101] Let's review, then, what the USCIS said about a sister provision, AC21 § 106(c), the adjustment portability provision.[102] In that context, the agency advised:

---

[97] Yates Memorandum, *supra* note 68, at 11.

[98] *Id.* at 9.

[99] *See, e.g.,* 8 C.F.R. § 214.2(h)(2)(i) (alien may perform services for an "employer") and 8 C.F.R. § 214.2(h)(4)(ii) (definition of U.S. employer requires existence of employer-employee relationship).

[100] AC21 § 104(c) (emphasis added). Although it is the employer who must file the extension petition, and not the "alien," in a sense, the extension does indeed run to the foreign national.

[101] *Supra* note 73 and accompanying text.

[102] Codified at INA § 204(j), that provision states:

continued

In all cases an offer of employment must have been bona fide, and the employer must have had the intent, at the time the Form I-140 was approved, to employ the beneficiary upon adjustment. It should be noted that there is no requirement in statute or regulations that the beneficiary of a Form I-140 actually be in the underlying employment until permanent residence is authorized. Therefore, it is possible for an alien to qualify for the provisions of § 106(c) of AC21 even if he or she has never been employed by the prior petitioning or the subsequent employer under section 204(j) of the Act.[103]

Of course, to benefit under AC21 § 106, an immigration visa petition must be approved and an adjustment of status application must remain pending for at least 180 days. In your case, your client was foreclosed from ever filing his adjustment application. Nevertheless, the offer of employment was bona fide, and the employer had the intent to employ your client when the petition was approved. It's even quite possible that, upon the approval of his adjustment of status application, your client may return to his original employment.

E. On a broader policy level, if relief to your client is deemed to be unavailable under § 104(c) if he changes employers, he'll be locked in his current job for years come, the very situation AC21 sought to remedy. While his co-workers who were fortunate enough to file adjustment applications before the gate fell shut can change employers after 180 days and still get permanent residence, your client will have two choices: stay put for years, or go home.

So, what advice do you give to your client? One easy answer is to have the new employer file an H-1B

Job Flexibility for Long Delayed Applicants for Adjustment of Status to Permanent Residence.—A petition under subsection (a)(1)(D) for an individual whose application for adjustment of status pursuant to section 245 has been filed and remained unadjudicated for 180 days or more shall remain valid with respect to a new job if the individual changes jobs or employers if the new job is in the same or a similar occupational classification as the job for which the petition was filed.

[103] Memorandum from William R. Yates, Acting Associate Director for Operations, BCIS, *Continuing Validity of Form I-140 Petition in accordance with Section 106(c) of the American Competitiveness in the Twenty-First Century Act of 2000 (AC21) (AD03-13)*, HQBCIS 70/6.2.8-P (Aug. 4, 2003), at 3, *reprinted at* 8 Bender's Immigr. Bull. 1462 (Sept. 1, 2003), *available at* http://www.aila.org/infonet (document no. 03081114) (last visited Oct. 22, 2005).

petition for him at the Premium Processing Unit, and see what happens. Your client should not "port" to the new employer, however, until the petition has been approved. It's to be hoped that the USCIS will soon issue guidance on this important question so we give firm answers, and peace of mind, to our clients.[104]

ONE THING MORE

Question 31: One more question. I have a client who began his sixth year of H-1B status on October 15, 2005. He's just been offered a better job elsewhere. In 2002, his current employer filed a labor certification application for him. Based on that application, the new employer would like to file an H-1B petition for him seeking the rest of year six and all of year seven. It figures that it can file a PERM application for him by February 2006. Let's plan for the worst, and assume that once my client leaves his current job, the former employer will withdraw the labor certification application.

At the end of year seven, that is, in October 2007, can the new employer file an eighth-year H-1B petition for my client seeking to benefit under AC21 § 106? Let's assume that by that time it has filed an I-140 immigrant visa petition for him that's still pending, and that, because of immigrant visa number unavailability, an adjustment application cannot be filed. Remember, even though more than 365 days will have elapsed from the filing of the PERM application when the new employer files for year eight of H-1B status for my client, its PERM application was filed while my client was already in his sixth year of H-1B status.

Answer: We tend to think of the benefits of AC21 § 106 accruing to those nonimmigrants for whom a labor certification application or immigrant visa petition was filed before they entered year six of H-1B status, but the language of the statute is broader than that. The normal limitation on H-1B status, the statute provides, shall not apply if at least 365 days have passed since the filing of an immigrant visa petition or "any" application for labor certification in a case in which the certification is required or used by the H-1B worker to obtain permanent resident status.[105]

---

[104] In early March 2006, the USCIS agreed that the employer seeking an extension of H-1B status for a foreign national under § 104(c) need not be the same employer who filed the I-140 immigrant visa petition for that worker. However, this position has yet to be issued in the form of written guidance.

[105] *Supra* note 74.

In this case, the second employer's labor certification application was filed while your client was in valid H-1B status; it was filed in February 2006, more than 365 days before his current period of H-1B status expires in October 2007; and it was even followed by an immigrant visa petition, which is still pending. The requirements of the statute have been met.

Nevertheless, this is another area calling out for agency guidance. Although I've heard of extension approvals in similar circumstances, there's no predicting how the USCIS would rule on this case.

CONCLUSION

It's been five and one-half years since the passage of AC21. For most people, a half-decade would be an inordinate amount of time to wait for an agency to issue regulations on new legislation. Not immigration lawyers. We measure time in light years. While the USCIS dawdles, many important issues are screaming out for clarification. Clients need answers, life decisions need to be made, and practitioners need to practice law with some assurance that the advice we provide today will not come back to bite us and our clients tomorrow. The practice of law really needs to be elevated above the level of a sophisticated guessing game. If this article started out with a quote from a movie, it ends with the title of a Johnny Mercer song: "Something's Gotta Give."

CURRENT STATE OF THE U.S. GUEST WORKER PROGRAM: H-2B AND H-2A STATUS FOR EMPLOYING ESSENTIAL WORKERS AND PROPOSED IMMIGRATION REFORM

*by Jay C. Ruby and Robert D. Kershaw**

HISTORICAL U.S. LABOR SHORTAGES AND EVOLUTION OF THE H-2 GUEST WORKER PROGRAM

Employers in many industries are faced with the daunting task of securing sufficient numbers of qualified skilled and unskilled laborers in an ever-shrinking U.S. labor pool. The list of industries that have recurring short-term seasonal, peak-load, or event-based demands for additional workers is a long one: agriculture, construction, fishing/crabbing, hurricane disaster relief, landscaping, manufacturing, oilfield, poultry processing, professionals sports, resorts/hospitality, shipbuilding, theme parks, and timber.

The current labor shortage is not a new problem. At the beginning of the 20th Century and again after World War II, the United States needed laborers to construct railroads, bridges, and buildings. The solution to the labor shortage in both instances was the importation of foreign laborers.

In 1943, the U.S. government created the H-2 temporary visa program to assist the U.S. Sugar Corporation to import sugar cane cutters from the Bahamas. In the 60-plus years since its inception, the H-2 guest worker program has evolved from be-

ing a useful solution to meet the demands of the U.S. economy to being, at best, a limited opportunity to meet the demands of a few employers. And, the limitations of the H-2 program have created a massive market for illegal workers. As a result, the topics of a guest worker program and comprehensive immigration reform (designed to meet U.S. labor demands in the 21st Century) have become part of the third rail of politics in Washington.

Labor shortages and related problems are persistent. Unable to locate sufficient supply of U.S workers, employers are seeking the services of skilled and unskilled foreign laborers to survive. As a result, record numbers of H-2 applications were filed in fiscal year 2005, and demographic studies confirm that U.S. employers will become increasingly dependent on foreign skilled and unskilled labor.

Within the H-2 program, there are several categories for visa qualification. Selecting the best classification for authorizing the entry and employment of foreign skilled laborers can be extremely challenging for an employer and its attorney. While the legal framework for immigration provides a veritable "alphabet soup" of temporary employment classifications for formally educated professionals, there are very few nonimmigrant visa classifications available to nondegreed skilled or unskilled laborers. While recently introduced guest-worker and immigration-reform legislation could change the landscape of U.S. immigration, at this time, the H-2A agricultural worker and H-2B nonagricultural nonimmigrant visa classifications are the only options for employing temporary essential workers.

The H-2B and H-2A temporary visa programs—the only options available to many U.S. industries—are inadequate to meet employers' needs. Only a limited number of industries can qualify, the annual application process is overly burdensome for the industries that do qualify, and the number of visas allotted annually to meet the demand of U.S. industries for nonagricultural visas is being reached so early in the year that numerous businesses that would use the H-2B visa category to meet their labor demands are being forced

---

* **Jay Ruby** is a partner with the Atlanta office of Ogletree, Deakins, Nash, Smoak & Stewart, PC, a labor & employment and immigration law firm with over 300 attorneys and 24 offices. Mr. Ruby focuses his practice on business immigration law and has been a speaker at various forums on H-2B essential workers. He received his J.D. from Louisiana State University in 1992 and his B.A. in history and political science from Indiana University in 1989, and is licensed in Georgia and Louisiana. An Indianapolis native, Mr. Ruby previously practiced in New Orleans, joining AILA in 1994 and serving on the executive committee of the AILA Mid-South Chapter from 1998–2001 and also as an H-2B mentor.

Robert Kershaw practices at Law Office of Robert Kershaw, P.C., in Austin. He received his B.A. at University of Texas at Austin, and his J.D. from Regent University School of Law. He is a member of AILA and the Alliance Defense Fund, and is president, Citizens for Common Sense Immigration Reform, Inc. Mr. Kershaw is a frequent author and speaker at immigration law conferences.

into their only alternative—using workers with questionable work documents.

The cap on H-2B visas excludes industries that want to meet their labor needs legally, and the cap should be raised significantly or eliminated. If businesses can demonstrate that they cannot find U.S. workers to meet their labor needs, they should be allowed to meet those needs with temporary, non-immigrant, H-2B workers (regardless of the number of such workers needed and regardless of whether the need is seasonal, intermittent, peak-load, or one-time need). The caps and the categories for such workers are insufficient, arbitrary, and inadequate to meet the needs of U.S. businesses. For these reasons, and for others discussed in this article, immigration reform is needed without further delay.

LEGAL OVERVIEW OF H-2A AND H-2B STATUS

The H-2A temporary agricultural program is a means for agricultural employers to bring foreign workers to the United States to perform *agricultural labor or services of a temporary seasonal nature*. "Temporary or seasonal nature" means employment performed at certain seasons of the year, usually in relation to the production and/or harvesting of a crop, and for a limited time period of less than one year.

The H-2B classification is a nonimmigrant classification available to many types of nonagricultural employers. This classification is used for a foreign laborer (or usually large groups of laborers) coming temporarily to the United States to perform *nonagricultural temporary service or labor* in the event U.S. workers cannot be found. Occupations for H-2B workers include hotel/resort staff worker, landscaper, fishing vessel worker, welder, professional athlete, electrician, construction worker, restaurant worker and cook, retail worker, poultry processor, boilermaker, and shipfitter.

STATUTORY AND REGULATORY AUTHORITIES FOR H-2A AGRICULTURAL AND H-2B NONAGRICULTURAL WORKERS

The legal framework that governs the H-2A and H-2B programs consists of federal statutes and the implementing regulations of U.S. Citizenship and Immigration Services (USCIS), Department of Labor (DOL), Department of State (DOS), and other

federal agencies. The primary statute is the Immigration and Naturalization Act of 1952 (INA).[1]

Statutes

INA §101(a)(15)(H)(ii)(a) defines an H-2A worker as someone "having a residence in a foreign country which they have no intention of abandoning and . . . are coming temporarily to the United States to perform agricultural labor or services of a temporary or seasonal nature."

INA §101(a)(15)(H)(ii)(b) defines an H-2B worker as someone "having a residence in a foreign country which he has no intention of abandoning who is coming temporarily to the United States to perform other temporary service or labor if unemployed persons capable of performing such service or labor cannot be found in this country."

INA §214(c)(5)(A) provides that employers are liable for the reasonable costs of return transportation if a worker is dismissed from employment before the end of the period of authorized admission.

INA §218 provides a broad overview of the H-2A category as well as the procedural and substantive requirements for H-2A applications for temporary labor certification and petitions for H-2A status.

Fair Labor Standards Act (FLSA) of 1938 §3(f), 29 USC §203(f), provides the definition of "agriculture."

Internal Revenue Code of 1954, §3121(g), 26 USC §3121(g), provides guidance for determining whether the services or labor is to be performed on a farm or on a ranch.

USCIS Regulations

8 CFR §214.2(h)(2)(I) sets forth the requirements for filing H-2B petitions.

8 CFR §§214.2(h)(2)(ii)–(iv) sets forth requirements for multiple and named beneficiaries. It also discusses when substitution of beneficiaries is allowed.

8 CFR §§214.2(h)(6)(i)–(iv) covers the filing of H-2B petitions and the labor certification process for all areas except Guam.

8 CFR §§214.2(h)(6)(v)(A)–(H) covers the labor certification requirements for Guam.

---

[1] Immigration and Nationality Act of 1952, Pub. L. No. 82-414, 66 Stat. 163 (*codified as amended at* 8 USC §§1101 *et seq.*) (INA).

8 CFR §214.2(h)(6)(vi) sets forth the evidence that must be submitted with H-2B petitions.

8 CFR §214.2(h)(6)(vii) covers traded professional athletes on H-2B visas.

8 CFR §214.2(h)(9)(iii)(B) sets forth validity periods of H-2B petitions and the impact on the petition when certification from DOL is not granted.

8 CFR §§214.2(h)(13)(iv)–(v) lay out the limitation on admission requirements.

8 CFR §214.2(h)(15)(ii)(C) addresses H-2B extensions of stay.

8 CFR §248.3 covers applications for change of status.

Operations Instructions, §214.2(h)

The Operations Instructions set forth the H-2B process and define "temporariness" and the conditions under which beneficiaries must be either named or unnamed, who the petitioner must be, and the role labor certification plays in the process.

DOL Regulations

20 CFR Subpart A, "Labor Certification Process for Temporary Employment Occupations Other than Agriculture, Logging or Registered Nurses."

20 CFR §§655.1–.4 contain a brief overview of the H-2B labor certification process.

Department of State Regulations

9 *Foreign Affairs Manual* (FAM) 41.53 N.4.5 defines H-2B classification.

9 FAM 41.53 N.22 covers H-2B classification for sheepherders.

9 FAM §41.53 N.23 covers H-2B classification for foreign employees of U.S. exhibitors or employers at international fairs or expositions held in the United States.

9 FAM 41.53 N.24 limits the number of H-2B visas to 66,000 during any fiscal year.

Agency Publications

DOL General Administration Letter No. I-95, "Procedures for H-2B Temporary Labor Certification in Nonagricultural Occupation" (GAL), must be read before an attorney proceeds with the application for labor certification. It sets forth the procedures for processing H-2B temporary labor certifications in nonagricultural occupations, including revised standards for determining the temporary nature of a job under the H-2B classification.

DOL Field Memorandum No. 25-98: "H-2B Temporary Non-agricultural Labor Certification Program Requirements" (Apr. 27, 1998). This memorandum provides answers to frequently asked questions about the H-2B program, especially with respect to the temporary nature of the program.

Immigration and Naturalization Service, HQ/6.2.9, "Clarification of Memo Dated July 15, 2001 Regarding Certain H-2B Adjudication Issues" (Feb. 1, 2002). This memo provides clarification on proper usage of unnamed beneficiaries in H-2B petitions.

USCIS Public Notice, "USCIS To Accept Additional H-2B Filings for FY 2005 and 2006" (May 23, 2005). This notice was issued following congressional passage of the Save Our Small and Seasonal Business Act of 2005 and covers H-2B workers who benefit from the Act and the filing requirements for "returning workers" who are exempt from the annual numerical limit.

OVERVIEW OF H-2A STATUS FOR AGRICULTURAL WORKERS

Qualifying Criteria

There are three general categories of individuals or organizations eligible to file an application:

- An agricultural employer may file an application requesting temporary foreign agricultural labor certification when it anticipates a shortage of U.S. workers to perform agricultural labor or services of a temporary or seasonal nature. "Temporary or seasonal nature" means employment performed at certain seasons of the year, usually in relation to the production and/or harvesting of a crop, or for a limited time period of less than one year when an employer can show that the need for the foreign worker(s) is truly temporary.

- The employer may be an individual proprietorship, a partnership, or a corporation. An association of agricultural producers may file as a sole employer, a joint employer with its members, or as an agent of its members.

- An authorized agent, whether an individual (*e.g.*, and attorney) or an entity (*e.g.*, an association), may file an application on behalf of an employer. Associations may file master applications on behalf of their members.

Many of the benefits that must be included in a job offer and other conditions that must be satisfied depend on the prevailing practices in the same occupation, crop, and area. Employers are advised that it is desirable to make an independent determination of factors such as prevailing wages and employer practices before filing an application.

Employer's Responsibilities Under H-2A Labor Certification

An employer who files an application for temporary foreign labor certification pursuant to H-2A regulations must meet several specific conditions.

Recruitment. The employer must agree to engage in independent, positive recruitment of U.S. workers. This means an active effort, including newspaper and radio advertising in areas of expected labor supply. The recruitment effort must be at least equivalent to that conducted by non-H-2A agricultural employers in the same or similar crops and area to hire U.S. workers. It must be an effort independent of and in addition to the efforts of the State Workforce Agency (SWA). To establish worker qualifications and/or job specifications, the employer must designate only those qualifications and specifications that are essential to carrying out the job and that are normally required by employers who do not hire foreign workers.

Wages. The wage or rate of pay must be the same for U.S. workers and H-2A workers. The hourly rate must also be at least as high as the applicable Adverse Effect Wage Rate (AEWR), federal or state minimum wage, or the applicable prevailing hourly wage rate, whichever is higher. The AEWR is established every year by DOL or every state except Alaska. Employers should consult with the SWA or DOL regional office to determine what the rate is for their state.

If a worker is paid on a piece-rate basis, the rate offered must be no less than what is prevailing in the area for the same crop and/or activity, as determined by the SWA. If the piece-rate does not result in average hourly piece-rate earnings at least equal to the amount the worker would have earned had the worker been paid at the hourly rate, the worker's pay must be supplemented to match the equivalent hourly level.

Housing. The employer must provide free housing to all workers who are not reasonably able to return to their residences the same day. Such housing must be inspected and approved according to appropriate standards.

Meals. The employer must provide either three meals a day to each worker or furnish free and convenient cooking and kitchen facilities for workers to prepare their own meals. If meals are provided, the employer may charge each worker a certain amount per day for them.

Transportation. The amount of transportation payment can be no less (but need not be more) than the most economical and reasonable common-carrier transportation charges for the distances involved. The employer is responsible for the following different types of transportation of workers:

- After a worker has completed 50 percent of the work-contract period, the employer must reimburse the worker for the cost of transportation and subsistence from the place of recruitment to the place of work if such costs were borne by the worker.

- The employer must provide free transportation between the employer's housing and the worksite for any worker who is provided housing.

- Upon completion of the work contract, the employer must pay costs of a worker's subsistence and return transportation to the place of recruitment. Special conditions apply when the worker will not be returning to the place of recruitment because of another job.

If the employer must advance transportation costs to foreign workers or provide transportation, the employer must advance such costs or provide transportation to U.S. workers as well. In addition, if it is prevailing practice in the occupation to provide transportation, the employer must provide transportation to U.S. workers as well.

Workers Compensation Insurance. The employer must provide workers compensation insurance where it is required by state law. If state law does not require it, the employer must provide equivalent insurance for all workers. Proof of insurance coverage must be provided to the regional administrator before certification is granted.

Tools and Supplies. The employer must furnish at no cost to the worker all tools and supplies necessary to carry out the work, unless it is common practice in the area and occupation for the worker to provide certain items.

Three-Fourths Guarantee. The employer must guarantee each worker employment for at least three-fourths of the workdays in the work contract period and any extensions. If the employer affords less employment, then it must pay the amount that the worker would have earned for the guaranteed number of days.

50-Percent Rule. The employer must hire any qualified and eligible U.S. worker who applies for a job until 50 percent of the period of the work contract has elapsed.

Labor Dispute. The employer must assure that the job opportunity for which H-2A certification is being requested is not vacant because the former worker is on strike or is being locked out in the course of a labor dispute.

Certification Fee. A fee will be charged to an employer granted H-2A. The fee is $100, plus $10 for each job opportunity certified, up to a maximum fee of $1,000 for each certification granted.

Other Conditions. The employer must keep accurate records of a worker's earnings, and the worker must be provided with a complete statement of hours worked and related earnings on each payday. The employer must pay the worker at least twice monthly, or more frequently if it is the prevailing practice to do so. The employer must provide a copy of a work contract or the job order to each worker.

Duration of Status

"Temporary or seasonal nature" means employment performed at certain seasons of the year, usually in relation to the production and/or harvesting of a crop, or for a limited time period of less than one year when an employer can show that the need for the foreign workers(s) is truly temporary.

Process for Filing

DOL handles the initial application process for the H-2A status. An application can be submitted by:

- filing it in person with the appropriate regional administrator and local SWA;

- mailing it to the appropriate regional administrator and local office of the SWA by certified mail, return receipt requested; or

- delivering it by guaranteed commercial delivery to the appropriate regional administrator and local office of the SWA.

Note: The appropriate DOL regional administrator is no longer the DOL regional office, but either the Chicago or Atlanta Processing Center, depending on the state of employment.

An employer should observe the following time considerations when applying for H-2A certification:

A complete labor certification application must be filed with and received by the appropriate regional administrator and local SWA at least forty-five (45) calendar days before the first date on which workers are needed. If the initial application is accepted or amended within the required time frame and complies with the regulations, the regional administrator will make a certification determination thirty (30) calendar days before the date on which the workers are needed. Delays in obtaining an acceptable application beyond the time permitted in regulations will delay the certification determination. Employers are encouraged to file before the minimum forty-five (45) calendar-day requirement. This allows more time for review, discussion, and amendment, if necessary.

Employers are encouraged to consult with the regional office of DOL's Employment and Training Administration and with SWA staff for guidance and assistance well before the 45-day filing period.

In emergency situations, the regional administrator may waive the time period specified, provided he or she has an opportunity to obtain sufficient labor-market information on an expedited basis in order to make a determination of U.S. worker availability. However, none of the minimum conditions of employment (wages, housing, and other benefits) are waived.

The regional administrator will review an employer's application promptly. Normally, within seven calendar days after receipt of an application, the regional administrator will notify the employer in writing of the decision on the application. Copies of the notification will be sent to the SWA and to the employer by means normally assuring next-day delivery.

Recruitment of U.S. Workers

Upon receipt of an employer's application for H-2A certification, the SWA must promptly prepare a local job order and begin recruiting U.S. workers in the area of intended employment. After an application is accepted for consideration, the regional administrator will direct the centralized location of the SWA to prepare an agricultural clearance order to permit the recruitment of U.S. workers by the employment service system on an intrastate and interstate basis.

When an employer's application is accepted for consideration, the regional administrator will require the employer to engage independently in specific, positive recruitment efforts within a multi-state region of traditional or expected labor supply if the regional administrator determines there is a sufficient supply of labor to be recruited.

An employer must comply with the recruitment assurances, the adverse-effect criteria, all time requirements, and other appropriate requirements established by law and regulation. If the regional administrator determines that it has, an H-2A certification will be granted for the number of jobs for which it has been determined there are not sufficient U.S. workers available. After certification has been granted, the employer must continue to recruit U.S. workers until the H-2A workers have departed for the place of work. In addition, the SWA must continue to send qualified and eligible U.S. workers to the employer if they have applied within the first 50 percent of the contract period, and the employer must hire these U.S. workers.

Upon DOL approval of the employer's application, the employer files its I-129 petition for H-2A status with the USCIS service center, which then issues the I-797 approval notice listing the beneficiaries.

OVERVIEW OF H-2B STATUS FOR NONAGRICULTURAL WORKERS

The H-2B classification is a nonimmigrant classification available to employers for hiring a foreign laborer (or usually large groups of laborers) coming temporarily to the United States to perform nonagricultural temporary service or labor, in the event capable U.S. workers cannot be found.

Qualifying Criteria: Proof of Temporary Need

While USCIS ultimately grants the H-2B status, the employer must first undergo a DOL process known as "temporary labor certification" to show that no qualified U.S. workers are available. The petitioning employer may apply for as many workers as it needs (in some instances, hundreds).

The two elements of proof that an employer must demonstrate to qualify for the H-2B status are: (1) that the position of employment in the United States is temporary in nature; and (2) the petitioning employer's "need for the duties to be performed by the alien" are temporary. This is sometimes referred to as the "double temporary" requirement.

In determining whether a position itself is temporary, USCIS and DOL regulations look to the nature of the employer's needs rather than whether the underlying job can be classified as permanent or temporary. It is the nature of the employer's need, not the nature of the duties of the job, that controls.

The petitioning employer must also show that employment of foreign workers will not adversely affect the wages and working conditions of similarly employed workers in the United States. Therefore, the employer cannot pay foreign workers lower wages than similarly situated U.S. employees. Other factors that may affect the employer's ability to obtain the temporary labor certification include the time period for which workers would be certified, the number of workers requested, and the frequency with which the employer requests H-2B status.

To show that the nature of the employment is sufficiently temporary, the employer must demonstrate to DOL that its need for the work to be performed does not exceed one year (except in extraordinary circumstances), and the need fits into one of the four following categories: (1) one-time occurrence; (2) seasonal need; (3) peak-load need; or (4) intermittent need.

One-Time Occurrence

An employer with a one-time occurrence need must prove that it has not employed workers to perform the services in the past and will not need them in the future, or that a temporary event of short duration has created the need for a temporary worker (or workers) for an otherwise permanent position.

For example, a permanent employee's illness or leave of absence may result in an employer's one-time occurrence need for a temporary worker. An employer's need for temporary workers to fulfill a specific project, such as the opening of a new manufacturing plant in an area with low population (*e.g.*, specialized foreign workers training full-time new U.S. employees or foreign workers completing a phase of a construction project) can also be examples of a one-time occurrence need.

Seasonal Need

To demonstrate a seasonal need for a temporary worker, the employer must establish that the service or labor is traditionally tied to a season of the year by an event or pattern that is of a recurring nature. The employment is not considered seasonal if the period during which the services are needed is unpredictable, subject to change, or considered a vacation period for the employer's permanent employees. The employer must specify the period(s) of time during each year ("off-season") in which it does not need the services or labor.

A classic example of recurring seasonal need is a resort hotel that has to supplement its workforce with additional housekeepers and other staff during the prime tourist season. Nonagricultural industries with recurring seasonal demands for workers include fishing, landscaping, retail, transportation (truck drivers), and professional sports.

Peak-load Need

A peak-load need can be established by showing that the employer regularly employs permanent workers to perform the same services but needs to supplement its permanent staff on a temporary basis due to short-term demand. The work must be above and beyond the employer's normal level of operation and not expected to become a part of the employer's future regular operations.

A manufacturer/contractor (shipyard, poultry processing plant, construction company) with a peak production phase often has a peak-load need to supplement its permanent work force with additional short-term laborers. An example of such a peak-load need would be a construction contractor who requires additional welders and electricians during a certain or predictable phase of particular construction projects.

Intermittent Need

An employer can demonstrate an intermittent need for a temporary employee by establishing that it has not employed permanent or full-time workers to perform the same services, but occasionally or intermittently needs temporary workers for short periods. This category could be utilized in a situation where the employer does not employ permanent employees for a certain position. For example, a convention center may have an intermittent need for a specialty chef to prepare banquets for infrequent and unusual conventions.

The temporary nature of the employer's need is a major consideration in DOL's adjudication. A continuous temporary need (year-round or more than one year) is equal to a permanent need. DOL takes into account whether the employer frequently requests H-2B visas and whether there are alternatives to hiring foreign workers. Repeated applications from the same employer become subject to increasing DOL scrutiny. In such situations, the employer

may need to assure DOL that it is not abating its responsibility to obtain an adequate domestic workforce.

Temporary Placement Companies/Job Shops

DOL generally (perhaps arbitrarily) seeks to preclude certain U.S. employers ("job shops" or temporary-help companies) from obtaining temporary labor certification, even though the applicable regulations do not provide any basis for its doing so. DOL believes such employers have a permanent need for laborers and thus, do not qualify for temporary labor certification.

In the landmark case *Matter of Artee Corp.*,[2] the Board of Immigration Appeals (Board) held that a job shop supplying machinists to General Motors had a year-round need for the services of the machinists. However, the Board interestingly raised the question of whether a job shop could ever qualify for H-2B status on the basis of a temporary need. The Board concluded that it would be possible for a temporary services contractor, or job shop, to qualify for H-2B labor certification.

Duration of H-2B Status

The H-2B classification may only be obtained in increments of one year or less (usually 10 months or less), with each new increment requiring a new labor certification and petition. Successive labor certifications can be increasingly difficult to obtain, because the positions appear less temporary to DOL with each application. With respect to employers that have recurring seasonal or peak-load need, the applicable case law acknowledges that an employer may be able to obtain temporary labor certification for the season each year if the season is less than 10 months of the year.

The maximum H-2B stay is three years, although it is unlikely that the employer will be able to extend the worker's H-2B status beyond an initial period of one year or less. For employers with a recurring seasonal or peak-load need, however, it is possible for to petition for the same worker or group of workers for each recurring season. Employers with multiple locations that have sequential or opposite seasonal/peak-load needs may obtain temporary labor certification for each location and file H-2B extensions of stay to transfer H-2B workers from one operation to another. An example might be a housekeeping cleaner working in Vail, Colorado, in the

---

[2] 18 I&N Dec. 366 (Comm. 1982).

winter and in Cape Cod, Massachusetts, in the summer and fall.

Annual Cap: 66,000 Visas

The total number of H-2B visas available each fiscal year (October 1–September 30) is 66,000. Until FY 2004, USCIS had never officially reached the annual limit. In FY 2004 and FY 2005, USCIS reached the 66,000 cap on March 9, 2005, and January 3, 2006, respectively.

In May 2005, Congress passed the Save Our Small and Seasonal Business Act (SOSSBA),[3] splitting the H-2B cap for fiscal years 2005 and 2006 into two seasons, providing for 33,000 new H-2B approvals for the first half of the fiscal year (October 1–March 30) and 33,000 new H-2B approvals for the second half of the fiscal year (April 1–September 30). In addition, SOSSBA exempted from the annual cap two types of returning H-2B workers (called H-2Rs): (1) For FY 2005, approximately 35,000 workers who were new H-2B workers seeking work dates before October 1, 2005; and (2) For FY 2005 and 2006, all "returning workers" who counted against the H-2B cap during any one of the three fiscal years preceding the fiscal year of the requested start date. In a petition for a start-date on or after October 1, 2005, the worker must have been previously approved for an H-2B work start date between October 1, 2002, and September 30, 2005. In addition, if a petition was approved only for an "extension of stay" in H-2B status, the worker was not counted against the annual cap at that time and thus the approval for the extension of stay could not be considered a "returning worker" in a new petition.

The provisions of SOSSBA are set to expire on November 30, 2006, unless extended by Congress. If SOSSBA is extended by Congress, some seasonal and peak-load employers can limit the effect of the annual H-2B cap by recruiting "returning workers" who are not subject to the cap. If SOSSBA is not extended, employers with spring and summer seasonal or peak-load need for workers will effectively be shut out from the H-2B process, as employers with fall and winter seasonal or peak-load need for workers will deplete the annually available 66,000 new H-2B visas each year. (Before the spring- and summer-need, employers can obtain DOL and USCIS approval.) In the event SOSSBA is not extended by Congress, employers with spring and summer seasonal or peak-load need for workers will be left with relatively few options. It is important to lobby Congress now to extend SOSSBA for at least one more year. Otherwise, the impact on many industries that rely heavily on the H-2B visa program, such as construction and landscape companies, will be devastating.

Filing Procedure: A Three-Step Process

Overall, the H-2B application process may take 90–120 days to complete. However, some states have quicker processing times than others, and certain occupations such as boilermakers have special procedures for obtaining expedited approval. There are three steps in the process of filing for H-2B certification.

Step 1: Determination of Prevailing Wage, Filing with State Workforce Agency, Recruitment of Qualified U.S. Workers, DOL Review, and Certification

Prior to completing Form ETA 750, "Application for Alien Labor Certification," the applicant must first determine the prevailing wage. This can be done by submitting the Prevailing Wage Request Form to the SWA prior to completing the application.

All applications for temporary labor certification are initially filed with State Workforce Agency (SWA) of the state where the foreign worker(s) will perform the services. The temporary labor certification package filed with the SWA consists of Form ETA 750 Part A, "Application for Temporary Alien Labor Certification," in duplicate original plus one copy and originals of the following documentation:

- a letter from the employer describing the temporary nature of its need for the workers (either a one-time occurrence, seasonal, peak-load or intermittent need) and the duration (less than one year) it will need the workers;

- documentation supporting the employer's temporary need (*e.g.*, a contract for a particular phase of a construction project or historical payroll records showing a pattern of hiring additional workers during a particular season of the year); and

- proof of prior unsuccessful recruitment of qualified U.S. workers (optional).

---

[3] Emergency Supplemental Appropriations Act for Defense, the Global War on Terror, and Tsunami Relief, 2005, Division B, Title IV, Pub. L. No. 109-13, 119 Stat. 231 (May 11, 2005).

If an attorney is filing on behalf of the employer, the blue G-28 form must also be included, signed by both the attorney and the employer.

An employer may file a single Form ETA 750 application for multiple unnamed workers for each occupation. A separate ETA 750 Part A application and the aforementioned supporting documentation must be submitted for each occupation. For example, a resort hotel seeking temporary labor certification for 20 housekeeping cleaners, 10 janitors, and 5 bellmen would be required to file three separate applications (one for each occupation).

Upon receiving the application, the SWA will review the job offer for completeness. A job offer containing a wage below the prevailing wage for such employment in the local area will cause the application to be returned as unacceptable; the employer then has the option of raising the offered wage. An employer filing an application for temporary labor certification must offer at least 100 percent of the prevailing wage.

DOL General Administration Letter 2-98 (GAL 2-98) lays out a three-tiered wage system. If the occupation and its prevailing wage are covered by the Davis-Bacon Act,[4] the McNamara-O'Hara Service Contract Act,[5] or a collective bargaining agreement in the Metropolitan Statistical Area (MSA) where the workers will be working, the employer must offer 100 percent of the wage. If the occupation is not covered by either of those statutes or a collective bargaining agreement, the SWA will look to the Occupational Employment Statistics (OES) Wage Survey for the source of the prevailing wage.

Once the application for temporary labor certification is filed, the SWA will create a job order and request the employer to advertise the position in a local newspaper. If the SWA refers any qualified U.S. applicants to the employer, the employer must make every effort to interview and hire the applicant. The number of foreign workers for which an employer may obtain labor certification is reduced by the number of U.S. workers it hires. Documentation must be provided to demonstrate a good faith effort to hire each applicant, list job offer letters to applicants who were hired, and explain job-related reasons for not hiring any applicants who rejected.

Because the certification process may take more than 60 days to complete, employers should start the process 120 days before the foreign workers' services are needed. An employer may not file an application for temporary labor certification less than 60 days nor more than 120 days before the foreign workers' services are needed.

Step 2: USCIS Processing of H-2B Petitions

Upon receipt of a final determination (certification or denial) from DOL, the employer is then eligible to file the H-2B petition with the USCIS service center. The H-2B petition consists of Form I-129, H Supplement and the Supplement-1 Form (for multiple workers), the original final DOL determination, a supporting letter, and documentation of the credentials of the beneficiaries (if required).

If DOL has denied the employer's application, the employer must include with the petition "countervailing evidence" proving the employer's temporary need for foreign workers. Also, employers are prudent to file the I-907 application under "premium processing" and pay the $1,000 fee to ensure processing in 15 days or less. The petitioner must also pay the petition fee and (presently under SOSSBA) an additional $150 fraud prevention fee.

A petitioning employer may petition for hundreds of workers on the same petition if they are going to the same consular post and have the same occupation. It is also possible (but perhaps not prudent) for an employer to file a petition for "unknown" workers (i.e., the employer does not list any names on the Supplement-1 form). However, USCIS usually requires the employer to show a compelling reason for not listing the names of the foreign nationals. From a strategic standpoint, the employer is better served by listing the names of the foreign national beneficiaries, especially in the event the beneficiaries will be applying for H-2B visas at a U.S. consulate or embassy. If the beneficiaries are named in the I-129 petition, the USCIS approval notice, Form I-797, will list the names of the beneficiaries—which will aid in the consular processing.

Step 3: Consular Processing of H-2B Visa Applications

Once the USCIS service center has approved the H-2B petitions, it will issue the original I-797 approval notices (listing the names of the beneficiaries) and cable the designated U.S. consulate or embassy for further processing. The exception is when the foreign worker or group of foreign workers selected is

---

[4] 40 USC §§276a et seq.; 29 CFR Part 1.

[5] 41 USC §§351 et seq.

already in the United States seeking a change of status.

Upon receipt of the I-797, each individual applicant applies for his or her H-2B visa at the U.S. consulate or embassy in his or her home country. If the visa application (Form DS-156) is approved, a visa will be placed in the passport. The length of the visa's validity is the amount of time stated in the USCIS approval notice.

In instances where groups of beneficiaries will be applying at different consular posts, the employer will require multiple original I-797 approval notices. To secure multiple I-797 approval notices, I-824 petitions for duplicate originals should be filed concurrently with the I-129 petition with USCIS.

Often, the consular processing of H-2B visa applications can be a major hurdle. Pursuant to 8 CFR §214(b), consular officers have the discretion to deny H-2B visas to applicants who lack strong ties to the home country (that is, they are unlikely to return to the home country). Other grounds for H-2B visa denial include incomplete applications, prior U.S. immigration violations, felony convictions, and failure to serve in the home country's military. U.S. consular officers presume that any applicant/beneficiary intends to immigrate to the United States. The burden of proof rests with the applicant/beneficiary to overcome this presumption and to prove nonimmigrant intent. Any documents that help to establish nonimmigrant intent (such as marriage and birth certificates of family staying in the foreign country, title to land, or a lease for a home) will demonstrate that the applicant/beneficiary has a residence that they do not intend to abandon. This will improve the likelihood that their visa will be approved.

Consular posts allow employers to substitute beneficiaries in the event a worker or group is ineligible for admission. The procedure for substituting beneficiaries is to contact the consular post and send an e-mail or fax with a list of the beneficiaries to be substituted and their names and passport information.

Pitfalls, Strategies, and Recommendations

Prevailing Wage Issues

In general, an employer filing an application for temporary labor certification must offer 100 percent of the prevailing wage, which is determined by the State Workforce Agency (SWA) for the state in which the H-2B workers will be employed.

Wage Hierarchy

DOL has a three-tiered wage system, as set forth in 20 CFR §655 and DOL's GAL 2-98.

1. Wages Subject to the Davis-Bacon Act or the McNamara-O'Hare Service Contract Act

If the occupation is covered by a government contract with a local business, the SWA will look to the Davis-Bacon Act or the McNamara-O'Hare Service Contract Act for the source of the prevailing wage. This is true even if the petitioning employer does not have a contract with the U.S. government. The mere fact that such a contract exists between the government and any employer in the area subjects the occupation and the employer to the applicable statute.

The Davis-Bacon Act generally covers occupations in the construction industry, including shipbuilding.

The Service Contract Act encompasses the virtually undefined area of "service occupations." When the government receives a "service" from an outside contractor, the occupations that provide the service would be covered by the Service Contract Act. For the most part, professional occupations (degreed occupations) do not fall within the scope of the statute. However, most skilled labor positions would fall within the Service Contract Act if such a contract exists in the MSA.

If the occupation is covered by either the Davis-Bacon Act or the Service Contract Act, the SWA's wage determination based on either act takes precedence over any other source. In other words, the petitioning employer may neither challenge the SWA determination nor substitute such a determination with an independent survey. And the employer must offer 100 percent of the wage required by the Davis-Bacon Act or Service Contract Act.

2. Wages Subject to Collective Bargaining Agreements (Union Wages)

Occupations not falling under either the Davis-Bacon Act or Service Contact Act may nevertheless be covered by a collective bargaining agreement. If the occupation is covered by a collective bargaining agreement in the Metropolitan Statistical Area (MSA), the SWA will determine that the prevailing wage for the occupation is the same as the union wage. In such an event, the petitioning employer must offer 100 percent of the union wage.

3. Wages Subject to OES Survey

The SWA looks to the Occupational Employment Statistics (OES) survey if the occupation is not covered by the Davis-Bacon Act, the Service Contract Act, or a collective bargaining agreement.

If the SWA cannot find a match in the OES survey, it may match it to a similar, yet higher-level, occupation, which may result in an inaccurate, inflated prevailing wage determination.

4. Wages from Independent Surveys

In the event the OES wage seems inflated, the petitioning employer may submit a published survey or its own survey if it meets strict criteria. Independent surveys can be obtained from a private survey company. The cost of the survey varies among the different companies. However, not all survey companies satisfy the seven criteria set forth by DOL. Also, some SWAs favor surveys from certain companies.

Proving Temporary Need to DOL and/or USCIS

This is the major substantive hurdle for most employers seeking H-2B classification. An employer must prove to DOL that it has a temporary (less than one year) need for the services of the foreign workers. DOL takes the general position that employers usually have a "year-round" need for workers—leaving employers with the burden of proving that the need for the workers (whether one-time occurrence, peak-load, seasonal, or intermittent) is temporary. Unless the employer can show that it has a temporary need for the services of the worker(s) under one of the four prongs of temporary need, DOL will deny the application. While employers in some industries such as hospitality, fishing, and landscaping have traditional seasonal needs for additional foreign laborers, employers in industries such as manufacturing and construction may have more difficulty establishing the need for workers for only a specific time within a given year.

In order to comply with DOL regulations and GAL 1-95, the petitioning employer must establish that it regularly employs permanent workers to perform the services or labor at the place of employment, and that it needs to supplement its permanent staff on a temporary basis due to a seasonal or short-term demand with temporary employees who will not become part of the regular operation. For example, the success of a resort hotel's application for certification based upon a seasonal peak-load need will generally hinge upon whether it can prove that it has a temporary need to supplement its permanent workforce on a temporary basis, due to a short-term demand, with workers who will not become part of the hotel's regular operation. Such proof might include: (1) historical occupancy rates; (2) historical payroll records showing increased numbers of employees for the occupation in question during certain months of the year; and/or (3) county lodging tax records to show that the area in general has a seasonal peak-load need.

In the event DOL does not approve the employer's application for temporary labor certification, the employer does not have a formal appeal process. Rather, the employer's remedy would be to file the I-129 H-2B petition with USCIS together with "countervailing evidence" of its temporary need for the workers. Although USCIS gives great deference to DOL decisions, it is not bound by the decision and may approve the I-129 petition if the employer can provide proof that it has a temporary need for the workers. Before USCIS approves a petition that is filed with "countervailing evidence," it must first certify the case to the Administrative Appeals Office (AAO) before the I-797 can be issued. In the event USCIS does not approve the H-2B petition, the employer may file a motion to reopen and an appeal with the AAO. If the AAO overturns the USCIS decision, the employer (if it has a seasonal or peak-load need) may use the AAO decision as part of its "countervailing evidence" for its H-2B petition for the following season, assuming the AAO makes a timely final decision.

Processing Delays and the 120-Day Constraint

The greatest pitfalls of the H-2B process are processing delays and the 120-day limitation. Pursuant to USCIS and DOL regulations, employers may not file applications for temporary labor certification with the SWA more than 120 days before the workers are needed. While it is conceivable that the SWA, DOL, and USCIS can process the application for temporary labor certification and I-129 petition in 120 days (if premium processing is selected), practitioners should advise employers of the possibility that final approval from USCIS may not come until well after the start of the temporary need. Coupled with the annual H-2B cap, the 120-day constraint can create a logistical impasse (although the split seasons created by the passage of the Save Our Small and Seasonal Business Act mitigated the effects of the 120-day constraint for some employers).

To avoid processing delays, it is important to be prepared for each step. For example, while the application for certification is pending with the SWA and DOL, the Form I-129 petition and Supplement-1 form should be completed and ready for filing with

USCIS immediately upon receipt of the approved temporary certification. Preparation of the Supplement-1 form (a manifest listing the name, date of birth, and passport number of each worker) can take some time. Furthermore, while the I-129 USCIS petition is pending, the consular Form DS-156 applications for the H-2B passport visa can be completed for each worker for filing with the U.S. consulate or embassy upon approval of the I-129 petition.

Named versus Unnamed Beneficiaries

Employers can request temporary labor certification for a specific number of "unnamed beneficiaries" on Form ETA 750 filed with the SWA. However, such requests are generally not preferred by USCIS at the H-2B petition (Form I-129) stage of the process. While USCIS will allow an employer to file an I-129 petition for unnamed workers (in "emergent" situations), USCIS usually returns such applications and requests a statement supporting the employer's reasons for not listing the beneficiary by name. In February 2002, USCIS issued a memo stating that an employer can file for unnamed beneficiaries if it has a "valid business reason" for not naming the workers in the I-129 petition.

Consular Processing Pitfalls and Substitution of Beneficiaries

Consular officers have wide discretion pursuant to 8 CFR §214(b) to deny H-2B visa applications if the foreign worker cannot produce evidence that he or she will return to the home country when the visa expires. In fact, some consular posts deny the majority of H-2B visa applications submitted after truncated interviews of the applicants. Persons with low levels of "flight risk" are those leaving behind immediate family members (spouse and children) or have permanent obligations in the home country such as a permanent job or a mortgage for a home. Each applicant must show strong ties to the home country or otherwise face the possibility of being denied. Even if DOL approves the application for temporary labor certification and USCIS approves the I-129 H-2B petition, the consular officer has the discretion to deny some or all of the consular visa applications. The employer should therefore carefully review the candidates during the recruitment process and select those who can demonstrate strong ties to the home country.

Other notable grounds for visa refusal are "insufficient documentation" and "inadmissibility." A denial based on insufficient documentation occurs when a necessary document (*e.g.*, a foreign worker's work experience letter) is missing from the application. Another common inadmissibility ground is the applicant's prior unlawful presence in the United States.

H-2B visa processing can vary from post to post. Some consulates (*e.g.*, China and the Philippines) generally deny a majority of H-2B visa applications. Others (*e.g.*, Jamaica and Mexico) tend to approve a large percentage of H-2B visa applications in instances where the applicant can prove "strong ties" to the home country. It is therefore prudent at the outset, before the employer invests time and funds in the recruitment of foreign nationals and files the applications with DOL and USCIS, to determine whether a particular post has a tendency to approve or deny H-2B visa applications.

Most consular posts permit employers to substitute beneficiaries, often by informal notification (*e.g.*, fax or e-mail list of the substituted beneficiaries and passport information). Therefore, employers are prudent to recruit additional qualified candidates to serve as alternates in the event any initial beneficiaries are denied.

It is also advisable for each beneficiary to have a letter offering employment when he or she appears at the consulate. The letter should state the job duties, rate of pay, location of the work, deductions from pay, and job benefits. The beneficiary should understand the contents of the letter. If a beneficiary does not know who he or she is working for, what he or she is doing, and how much he or she is being paid, the consular officer may not consider that the beneficiary has a legitimate job offer.

Applications for 10 or More Construction Workers

There are special procedures for obtaining H-2B certifications for construction workers. The term "construction" encompasses all types of general construction, including shipbuilding and marine fabrication.

While all employers must undergo the temporary labor certification process, U. S. employers engaged in construction and seeking the temporary services of *10 or more* workers in the same occupation within a six-month period must contact local unions representing construction workers in the same or substantially equivalent job classification. While union notification (via certified letter) does not always pose an impossible hurdle for completing the recruitment of U.S. workers for the certification process, a practitioner must determine at the outset whether union notification for the particular job site or project is a potential deal-breaker.

Applications for Canadian Boilermakers

The National Association of Construction Boilermaker Employers and the International Brotherhood of Boilermakers have arranged with DOL and USCIS to obtain expedited determinations on H-2B applications and petitions for boilermakers from the Canadian Boilermakers Union when there are insufficient U.S. boilermakers to meet contract needs. The Manpower Optimization Stabilization and Training Fund (MOST) in Kansas City, a clearinghouse for employers and workers, handles the initial processing of the application. USCIS petitions for Canadian boilermakers may be filed with USCIS without the specific names and/or evidence of the qualifications of the beneficiaries. USCIS has been instructed to expedite the adjudication of such petitions under emergent procedures.

Applications for Aerospace Engineers

If the employer is seeking certification for one or more aerospace engineers, the SWA and DOL will require the employer to first offer laid-off engineers re-employment before applying. In addition, the SWA requires contract engineering firms to identify the user aerospace companies and specify where the foreign workers will work. In addition, the contract engineering firm must supply a copy of the aerospace engineering contract with the application for certification.

U.S. Virgin Islands Employers and Special Limitation on H-2B Applications

Temporary labor certification applications filed for H-2B employment in the U.S. Virgin Islands may be approved only for entertainers and athletes and only for periods not to exceed 45 days.

Appeal to USCIS vs. Re-application

Although DOL's final determination is not binding, USCIS usually tends to agree with DOL concerning labor certification or denial, even in instances where the petitioning employer submits substantial "countervailing evidence" of its temporary need for workers. Hence, many practitioners consider an appeal to USCIS to be futile. A DOL determination denying an application for certification will contain the reason(s) for the denial. If the problem is correctable through documentation and advocacy, the practitioner can re-apply with DOL and

gain approval long before the USCIS Administrative Appeals Office (AAO) even reviews the appeal.

DEALING WITH THE H-2B QUOTA

The H-2B visa cap of 66,000 per year for nonagricultural businesses is inadequate for the needs of U.S. businesses. If SOSSBA is not extended (and expanded), U.S. businesses will continue to experience severe labor shortages, have no legal immigration program to meet their labor needs, and will continue to create an economic magnet attracting undocumented aliens to fill job positions that U.S. workers do not want. Without SOSSBA, the cap was reached on March 9 in FY2004 and on January 3 in FY2005. With more businesses applying for H-2B visa workers each year, the cap would probably be reached within the first two months of the fiscal year if SOSSBA is not extended. This would exclude major industries from the H-2B program, especially those with early spring start dates, such as landscaping and construction. In such cases, many industries will have no way to deal with the quota and will be put out of business.

If SOSSBA is extended (and for businesses with fall start dates if it is not) there are some important strategies for dealing with the H-2B cap, including the following:

- File the ETA 750A, with supporting documents, exactly 120 days from the date of need—the soonest that you can file the application.

- Start dates can be moved up a little to allow for "orientation" of workers. Orientation can involve getting established in the area, learning company policies and procedures, getting Social Security numbers, and learning about H-2B program. Orientation cannot include training unless the training requirement is listed on the ETA 750A and explained in the supporting letter.

- Expedited procedures can help assure that the employer's petition gets to USCIS before the cap is enforced. As discussed earlier, the next step in the process can be prepared ahead of time (for instance, the I-129 package can be prepared while waiting for certification, and information on beneficiaries can be obtained in advance as well).

If SOSSBA is extended, there will be additional strategies for dealing with the cap (which allows for 33,000 visas for new workers to be available on October 1, and 33,000 additional visas for *new* workers to be available on April 1). Returning workers (those who have been on an H-2B visa anytime during the prior three visa years) are exempt from the cap of 66,000. Thus, if SOSSBA is extended, utilize the following additional strategies:

- Recruit returning workers. Since they do not have to be returning to work for the same company, returning workers are preferable because they are pre-exempt from the cap. The best place to recruit returning workers is from your client's existing workforce (most will have friends who are on an H-2B visa with another company). Offer an H-2B worker a bonus if he or she can recruit a friend who is also a returning worker.

- Apply at the earliest date possible for all workers, both new and returning as "unnamed" workers. Once labor certification is received, split the certification into two petitions with different start dates if the cap for new workers has been reached. For instance, if your client needs 100 entry-level landscape laborers with February 1 start dates, apply in early October (precisely 120 days prior to February 1) for 100 "unnamed" workers. If the cap has not been reached when your certification is approved, send in your I-129 petition for all workers—new and returning—with February 1 start dates. If the October 1 cap has already been reached, split the certification into two petitions. If your client needs 50 new workers, make their start dates April 1. At least you should be able to get them in before the second cap of 33,000 is reached for new workers, and your client gets his or her returning workers when they are needed.

The most important strategy for dealing with the H-2B cap is to lobby Congress to raise the cap, or at least to extend SOSSBA. Even better, lobby for elimination of the cap (such as H-2A) and for allowing the number of H-2B visas to be determined by the proven needs of U.S. businesses.

ALTERNATIVES TO H-2 CLASSIFICATION

The H-2A and H-2B are the only nonimmigrant visa classifications that authorize the temporary employment of most skilled and unskilled agricultural and nonagricultural workers. Nevertheless, in light of the problematic annual limitations of the H-2B classification, practitioners should be aware of two alternative nonimmigrant visa classifications for certain employers: (1) The J-1 summer work/travel status; and (2) the Q-1 cultural exchange visitor status.

J-1 Summer Work/Travel Visa

Students at foreign colleges and universities are eligible for a short (generally three-month) J-1 summer work/travel visa through qualified J-1 exchange visitor programs approved by the U.S. Department of State. There are numerous DOS-approved J-1 exchange visitor programs that offer summer opportunities for foreign students to work for U.S. employers in many industries, including hospitality and parks and recreation. To qualify, the student must be enrolled in a foreign college or university (not having graduated) and be able to communicate effectively about the attributes of the culture of his or her home country.

Qualified U.S. employers seeking the services of J-1 summer work/travel students can contact the J-1 cultural exchange program sponsor to register as a sponsoring employer. The J-1 exchange visitor programs generally require the U.S employer-sponsor to provide the summer work/travel students affordable and adequate housing and positions that offer opportunities for the students to share their culture with the American public. While the J-1 option may not be viable for many U.S. employers with summer season demands for landscapers and construction workers, employers in such industries as hospitality (e.g., front-desk positions) and recreation (e.g., life guards at an amusement park) with summer peak-load need can often supplement their workforces with J-1 students.

To obtain a J-1 visa through an umbrella sponsor with DOS authority to issue DS-2019 forms (J-1 approval), a student completes a J-1 application (a set for the beneficiary and a set for the U.S. employer) and pays the applicable processing fees (which varies among sponsors). Upon issuance of the DS-2019, the beneficiary then applies for the J-1 passport visa at the U.S. consular post in his or her home country.

Q-1 Cultural Exchange Visitor Visa

Employers that offer opportunities for cultural exchanges that are open to the American public (e.g., amusement theme parks, ethnic restaurants, museums) may qualify as Q-1 cultural exchange program employers. INA §101(a)(15)(Q) allows foreign nationals to obtain Q-1 classification (valid for up to 15 months) under the following conditions:

- They must be a participant in an international cultural exchange program approved by the Attorney General.

- The purpose of the cultural exchange program must be to provide practical training, employment, and the sharing of the history, culture, and traditions of the foreign national's home country with the American public.

- Wages and working conditions must be similar to those of domestic workers.

The foreign national must be at least 18 years of age and have the ability to communicate the history, traditions, and customs of his or her home country. The Q-1 visa is valid for up to 15 months and cannot be extended. However, if the foreign national then resides outside the United States for one continuous year or more, he or she would be eligible for a new 15-month period of Q-1 status.

Productive employment in Q-1 classification is permitted insofar as the employment relates to the goals of the cultural exchange program. The work components of the foreign national's employment must be tied to the cultural components of the employer's cultural exchange program (*i.e.*, the work must serve to advance the goals of the cultural exchange). The program's itinerary must have regular events and work components to foster the cultural exchange. Furthermore the international cultural exchange program must take place in the "public eye" and not an isolated business setting.

To obtain Q-1 status, the employer files the I-129 petition and Q supplement form with the USCIS service center, along with the Supplement-1 form (listing the multiple beneficiaries); a supporting letter detailing the structure, goals, work components, and cultural components of the cultural exchange program; and documentation of the Q-1 beneficiaries' credentials, the employer's attributes for hosting the cultural exchange, the wages and working conditions of similarly situated U.S. employees, the employer's financial ability to pay the offered wages, and a memo signed by the company's employee responsible for administering the exchange program. Upon USCIS approval of the employer's petition, the Form I-797 listing the beneficiaries is then forwarded to the beneficiaries for consular processing of the visa applications. Q-1 applicants are required to present proof of "strong ties" to the home country and their credentials establishing eligibility to participate in the cultural exchange program.

The Q-1 classification (often dubbed as the "Disney" visa) may not be appropriate for employers in isolated settings, but employers offering a forum where a cultural exchange with patrons and guests can be accomplished in a public setting may qualify. Employers seeking to establish a cultural exchange program need to show that they have structured cultural events and work components designed to serve the exchange program, and document the program's itinerary.

H-2 CLASSIFICATION VERSUS EB-3 IMMIGRANT VISA

H-2 classification is appropriate for temporary positions where the employer's need for workers is for less than one year. Employers seeking year-round or permanent employment of skilled and unskilled workers must either select an appropriate nonimmigrant visa classification that has a duration of one-year intervals or longer (*e.g.*, TN, H-1B, L-1) or pursue a permanent visa application in the employment-based third preference (EB-3) immigrant visa category.

The regulations at 20 CFR §656 govern the labor certification process for permanent employment of foreign workers, whereas 20 CFR §655 sets forth the labor certification process for temporary employment of foreign nationals in occupations other than agriculture, logging, or registered nursing. Although teaching positions are often for a duration of less than 12 months, INA §212(a)(5)(A)(ii)(I) expressly recognizes "a member of a teaching profession" as an occupation within the ambit of permanent labor certification, as do the regulations (with respect to college professors) at 20 CFR §§656.21 and 656.24.

In the leading case distinguishing temporary need from permanent need, *Matter of Vito Volpe Landscaping, et al.*,[6] the Board of Alien Labor Certification Appeals held that the six applications for permanent labor certification by three employers engaged in the landscaping business for the positions of "landscape gardener" and "lawn service worker" for employment of less than 10-month duration was not permanent employment. The Board found that the positions fit the definition of "seasonal employment" because the work to be performed was to be "exclusively performed at certain seasons or periods of the year." Accordingly, despite the fact that the positions were full-time and recurring, they were not permanent.

An employer may sponsor an H-2 employee for permanent resident status as long as the job offered

---

[6] 1991-INA-300, *et seq.* (Sept. 29, 1994) (*en banc*).

is in fact a full-time, year-round position. For example, a resort hotel employing a housekeeping cleaner in peak-load H-2B status may offer the person a permanent housekeeping supervisory position if the position is a full-time, year-round job and he or she meets the minimum experience and/or training requirements of the position. However, from a logistics standpoint, the current priority date retrogression for the EB-3 immigrant visa category (priority date cut-offs as of this writing for the EB-3 skilled/professional and other worker categories are May 1, 2001, and October 1, 2001 respectively), limit the viability of sponsoring H-2 employees for permanent resident status. The current priority date retrogression is so severe that it would be difficult for an H-2 employee to maintain status long enough to be eligible to adjust status when the priority date established in the application for permanent labor certification finally becomes current.

ESSENTIAL WORKERS AND COMPREHENSIVE IMMIGRATION REFORM

Comprehensive immigration reform is badly needed. All immigration attorneys and their clients who will benefit from common sense immigration reform should lobby for reform that meets U.S. business needs, grows our economy, protects U.S. workers, provides legal status for immigrant workers, protects our borders, improves national security, and enables the United States to be globally competitive. Doing nothing about comprehensive immigration reform is really no longer an option.

At the time of this writing, Congress was debating the need for comprehensive immigration reform. There were a number of proposals, each with strong points and each lacking in some areas: (1) President Bush's general proposal; (2) the McCain-Kennedy proposal (S.1033); (3) the Cornyn-Kyl proposal (S.1438); (4) the Hagel proposals (S.1916, 1917, 1918, and 1919); and (5) legislation being crafted by Judiciary Committee Chairman Arlen Specter (known as the "Chairman's Mark"), which will likely serve as the basic bill for consideration and which contains many elements of the other proposals. Since, by the time this article is published, the debate will be far beyond any of the above proposals, it is more helpful here to focus on the issues that are tied to comprehensive immigration reform than to compare the various proposals. This section focuses on some of the problems that must be addressed, the necessary components of a viable immigration reform bill, and other areas that must be considered in any serious immigration reform.

Problems to be Addressed

National Security

National security cannot be achieved with roughly 11 million undocumented aliens within U.S. borders. U.S. immigration policies should be retooled to provide incentives for hard-working immigrants (who have no terrorism-affiliated or criminal histories) to become legitimate nonimmigrants through registration. Perhaps the only real enticement for registration will be the promise of some form of legal status that will authorize U.S. employment and eligibility for other benefits (e.g., Social Security numbers and driver's licenses). A common provision of most of the reform proposals is a three-year, renewable nonimmigrant visa, as long as the alien is filling a job position that U.S. workers do not desire or a U.S. employer cannot fill.

The reality is that finding, arresting, detaining, adjudicating, and deporting 11 million people is not only impracticable, it is inadvisable. Such action, even if achievable, could bankrupt the U.S. government and destroy the U.S. economy, particularly industries that now depend on the services and labor of undocumented workers. Because U.S. businesses rely so heavily on these workers, a discussion of enhancing national security with respect to undocumented aliens is futile without a concurrent discussion for legalizing their presence and employment. The existing H-2B program, with its annual limits and procedural constraints, does not provide a way to replenish a significant workforce in the event it were to vanish.

Protection of U.S. Workers

U.S. workers cannot be competing for jobs that registered immigrants will take for much less pay. Such a result could cause massive unemployment of U.S. workers and cripple the U.S. economy. A possible solution would be to allow employers to apply for registered workers to fill jobs that U.S. workers do not desire. The labor certification process (now used successfully in the H-2B temporary worker program) would require employers to offer the job first to U.S. workers at the "prevailing wage" for that position in that geographic area. Only after the employer proves that it could not locate qualified U.S. workers to fill the necessary positions would it then be allowed to hire registered workers. The current safeguards of the H-2B program—paying the prevailing wage and requiring U.S. recruitment—can be implemented for the protection of U.S. workers in a retooled guest-worker program. If all employers seeking to hire registered workers must meet those requirements, it can be argued that the wages and working conditions of U.S. workers will be elevated, but failure to pass a new guest worker program (with the same safeguards, no annual numerical limits, and less procedural burden) in favor of the status quo will only ensure that wages and working conditions of U.S. workers will further erode.

Border Protection

The United States, which is in need of low-wage labor, is separated by only a shallow river from a country that cannot provide jobs for its workers to feed their families. Border protection can only be achieved if there are legal channels to meet this supply-and-demand dynamic. Once legal channels are created to meet U.S. needs for low-wage labor, penalties can be aggressively enforced on employers that use undocumented labor. And fewer people will swim the river and enter the country illegally, because the market for their illegal labor will have diminished.

Global Competitiveness

At present, hundreds of thousands of U.S. jobs are being lost to entities/countries that have a low-wage labor force and can produce almost any service or product at a low cost. If this trend continues, the status of the United States as the economic leader of the world will decline. Access to skilled and unskilled labor from abroad through a viable guest worker program can only enhance U.S. employers' abilities to compete in the global economy. One could further surmise that as U.S. companies successfully compete in the global economy, their resulting growths would also add higher paying managerial, clerical, and administrative jobs for the U.S. workforce.

The Need for Economic Growth

Guest workers would not only supply the U.S. needs for unskilled/skilled labor but also fuel the economy while they are here. They will be new consumers, spending much of their earnings in the United States.

Exploitation of the Undocumented Aliens

The U.S. economy has historically benefited from the labor of undocumented aliens. Undocumented workers build homes, cut lawns, clean facilities, and own businesses employing foreign and U.S. workers alike. However, the rights afforded undocumented workers are grossly disproportionate to their contributions to the U.S. economy. Undocumented workers are often knowingly exploited by U.S. employers (paid less than prevailing wages and not afforded health care or worker's compensation) that have little fear of legal action or repercussions.

An Illegal Underground

Eleven million undocumented aliens create a huge underground economy that encourages exploitation and fosters crime like drug trafficking, prostitution, robbery, tax evasion, and human trafficking. Intelligent immigration reform that includes remedies for undocumented aliens and strict enforcement of immigration laws is needed to eliminate the illegal underground.

H-2A Temporary Agricultural Visa Program Must Be Reformed If It Is to Meet the Needs of the Agricultural Industry

The Senate proposal entitled Ag JOBS (S.359) would streamline the H-2A process and put less cost on the employer. Ag JOBS would also bring wages more in line with the marketplace and make U.S. agriculture more globally competitive. Another solution could be to include H-2A classification reform in a more comprehensive guest worker program.

Necessary Components of a Common Sense Immigration Reform Program

- **Establish a Legal Nonimmigrant Status for Guest Workers** for three years after the worker: (1) pays a fine for undocumented status in the United States; (2) registers for the guest worker program within six months of the date that the program is passed into law; (3) undergoes a thorough background check; and (4) is sponsored by a U.S. company that cannot obtain U.S. workers to fill the position.

- **The Labor Certification Process for U.S. Businesses to Qualify to Hire Guest Workers** must be required of all employers prior to hiring guest workers. The labor certification process protects U.S. workers by requiring employers: (1) to offer the job to U.S. workers first; (2) demonstrate that they cannot hire sufficient U.S. workers to fill the positions needed; (3) pay wages comparable to those paid to U.S. workers for the job duties, and (4) demonstrate that hiring the guest worker will not adversely affect the wages or working conditions of U.S. workers.

- *Background Checks* must be performed on all persons registering for the guest worker program to ensure that they have no criminal history or terrorist affiliations.

- *Renewability of Three-Year Guest Worker Visas* for another three years should be available if the worker can again pass the background check and the employer can again qualify for labor certification and demonstrate that U.S. workers are still unavailable to fill the position.

- *Combining Many Visa Categories into one Streamlined Guest Worker Program* will eliminate many confusing and overlapping visa categories. A single program will be easier to regulate and administer. However, the elimination of the H-2A and H-2B programs in favor of one comprehensive guest worker program could prove to be problematic in the future if the new guest worker program has a limited duration or is limited to current undocumented workers.

- *Earned Adjustment of Status to Permanent Resident Status (not Amnesty)* should be available for guest workers who have worked on the guest worker program for nine years, paid their taxes, obeyed the laws, and passed all background checks. These workers will have "paid their dues" by taking jobs that U.S. workers cannot or will not fill. By doing so, they will have earned permanent residency, not given amnesty.

- *Harsher Penalties for Employers and Immigrants Who Violate Immigration Laws* should be enforced. If legal paths are made available to meet U.S. labor needs, hiring of illegal aliens must be strictly prohibited by harsh penalties that no longer allow hiring of illegal aliens to be a viable option for employers or workers.

- *Mandatory Registration of All Illegal Aliens* within our borders must be required within six months from the date the guest worker program is passed into law. Failure to register within the six-month window of opportunity would disqualify anyone who has been illegally in the United States from qualifying for a guest worker program.

- *Portability of Guest Worker Visas* to other employers who have not obtained labor certification should not be allowed. However, workers should be allowed to change jobs among employers who have obtained certification (if the change is reported by the employers and the worker to USCIS).

- *Guest Workers Should be Taxed* at an established "guest worker tax rate" (possibly 10 to 15 percent) to be withheld by the employer. Guest workers should not pay for, nor qualify for, Medicare or Social Security. In all other respects, guest workers should be treated the same as U.S. workers.

- *Strict Supervision of Individuals and Organizations Allowed to Process Guest Worker Visas* is important to avoid fraud and illegalities in the guest worker program. Processing of guest worker visas should be restricted to certified and trained attorneys or other trained and certified organizations.

- *Immigration Laws Must be Strictly Enforced* (with random job site enforcement) after a guest worker program is in effect. Using illegal workers should no longer be an option. If legal programs are developed to meet U.S. businesses labor needs, the use of illegal labor should not be tolerated.

- *A Guest Worker Program Must be Economically Viable and Self-Sustaining* through guest worker taxes, fines, and penalties.

- *A Guest Worker Program Must be Politically Viable* and meet some (if not most) of the needs of groups that have an interest in immigration reform. This can be done by a common-sense, middle-of-the-road approach that considers the needs and desires of these groups.

CONCLUSION

Employers in the United States face shortages of low-wage labor—shortages so severe that they threaten the viability of many industries and the future growth of the U.S. economy. The current visa programs that allow employers to hire foreign low-wage workers, primarily the H-2A and H-2B classifications, are woefully inadequate for meeting employers' needs.

Reform of the U.S. immigration system is necessary. Appendix A is a proposal for a comprehensive, common-sense guest worker system to solve one of the most pressing problems facing the United States. But achieving such reform will require that all involved—immigration attorneys, employers, and other interested groups—press for those changes. Appendix B outlines an action plan to advocate for comprehensive reform.

APPENDIX A

GUEST WORKER PROGRAM: A REFORM PROPOSAL

Common-sense immigration reform can be the solution for many of America's needs. Following is a proposal for immigration reform—a well-planned guest worker program—that can help solve some of our greatest problems.

The Economy

Capitalism depends on a growing economy. The U.S. economy is struggling to recover from various economic setbacks (9/11 terror attacks, the dot-com implosion, Enron-type scandals, stock market losses, and losses of U.S. jobs to overseas competition). Immigration reform can be the key to growing our economy and making us globally competitive.

Guest workers spend money while they are in the United States. They also supply the vital workforce needed to make U.S. companies globally competitive. If done properly, we can actually grow our economy through immigration reform.

Presently, U.S. jobs are going overseas to countries with a low-wage workforce. We can be globally competitive. We do not have to be losing jobs to overseas competition. We have a low-wage workforce in our backyard that will make us globally competitive, if we will only utilize it properly.

First, we can grow our economy by growing our population. Population growth among U.S. citizens is near zero; we are dying at a faster rate than we are creating new Americans. This problem will only increase as baby-boomers retire and grow older, unless there is a change. Somehow we must grow our population, and there is no better way than through controlled immigration reform that adds new Americans who are hard-working, law-abiding, and tax-paying individuals.

In addition to enlarging our tax base, these individuals are spending money while they are here—buying cars, stereos, clothes, and food. They are renting apartments, buying mobile homes, and even new houses. As they become permanent residents and citizens, they become an even more established part of our growing economy. Every one of them is a new American consumer adding to our economic growth.

If there are 11 million illegal immigrants presently in the United States filling jobs that U.S. workers do not want, what would happen if they became legal U.S. consumers? A portion of their money would no longer go back to Mexico (or any other country). Many will be more inclined to spend it here in the United States. Once they become permanent residents, they will be more inclined to spend it here. If only half of the guest workers become permanent residents in nine years, there will be 10 million more permanent U.S. residents who will be likely to apply for dependent visas for their families as they improve their economic situations. If each new permanent resident has an average family of four, that is 40 million new U.S. consumers—just among permanent resident aliens. Then, another 10 million guest workers will come to take the entry-level guest-worker jobs vacated by the new permanent residents. We would have 50 million new U.S. consumers in nine years. This new influx of legal American workers will grow our economy by growing our population. Within 14 years, we will also see a dramatic increase in the population of U.S. citizens.

This population growth will exponentially grow our economy. Not only will it add new U.S. consumers, it will add new U.S. jobs. As U.S. businesses grow and are more globally competitive because their need for entry-level workers is met, they will begin adding other higher paying (management, administrative and clerical) jobs as well. The result: more jobs, more spending; more spending, more economic growth; more economic growth, more prosperity in general (and a growing tax base for government social programs and government spending in general).

As U.S. companies become more globally competitive, they will grow at home and have less incentive to go overseas. Jobs can remain with U.S. companies at home, as we not only grow our economic base at home but also grow through becoming more competitive in the emerging global economy.

National Security

A large undocumented underground population poses a threat to our national security. The problem of a vast illegal underground population can be largely eliminated through intelligent immigration reform that rewards legal immigration and punishes illegal immigration. Common-sense immigration reform can provide incentives to both U.S. companies and immigrants for legal immigration and controlled growth, as well as disincentives for illegal immigration. The tax revenues of $29 billion per year that would result from immigration reform would be more than enough to administer a guest worker program, enable more rigorous job site enforcement, and provide enhanced border security to *secure our borders—an increasingly popular goal!*

Global Competition

We are feeling the effects of global competition. The United States must become more globally competitive if we are to remain the world's economic leader into the future. But the dilemma is how to compete with overseas low-wage labor without bringing down the wages of U.S. workers. The answer is a guest worker program. Through it, we can have low wage labor. We can grow U.S. businesses by becoming globally competitive, and U.S. workers can keep the higher paying jobs, which will only grow in number as companies become more globally competitive.

In addition, a guest worker program will attract the brightest and the best from all industries from all over the world. Through a comprehensive, well-designed program, we can see America become the undisputed leader in the global economy.

Deficit Spending

Deficit spending is the result of the increasing costs of government and a decreasing tax base. Immigration reform can help solve the problem of deficit spending by increasing our taxable incomes, producing economic growth that increases tax revenues, and by providing more tax-paying workers than retirees. This proposal would supply an immediate $40 billion upfront through fines that illegal immigrants and employers registering for the program would be required to pay, and at least $29 billion per year in additional tax revenue.

Rising Taxes

Taxes are rising on both businesses and individuals because there is an increase in the costs associated with government and fewer taxpaying persons to pay those costs. Illegal immigrants often pay no taxes while utilizing government services, which only aggravates the problem. If all new immigrants are also taxpayers, there will be more tax revenues and less need for the government to tax a decreasing number of taxpayers. By increasing our tax base, we can prevent rising taxes in the future.

Slow Population Growth

Slow population growth impedes economic growth. A growing population through controlled and intelligent immigration reform can lead to growth in our economy.

Bankruptcy of Social Security

Recently we have been made more aware of the ultimate insolvency of Social Security system if something is not done soon. The numbers are alarming, especially as baby-boomers start to retire. Today there are three workers for each retiree. Soon it will be two to one, and ultimately one to one—unless something is done.

Some talk of cutting benefits. Others talk of privatizing Social Security, hoping to grow returns on investment through private investment accounts. Why not just grow the number of taxpayers by growing our working and taxpaying population through intelligent immigration reform that increases our tax base? The additional tax revenues of $29 billion a year will solve the problem of a decreasing tax base for an increasing number of retiring Americans. Also, since guest workers are not U.S. citizens or permanent resident aliens, their flat tax would not include Social Security payments nor would it allow them to qualify for Social Security benefits.

Lack of a Low-Wage Workforce

The lack of a low-wage workforce is crippling many U.S. businesses. U.S. workers do not want, and will not take, most of these jobs. If these low-wage jobs were filled with legal foreign workers, many U.S. businesses would grow and add other, higher paying jobs. The need for low-wage workers encourages illegal, non–taxpaying workers to come into the country to fill these jobs if there is not a legal means to meet employers' needs. Jobs that are essential to U.S. companies include entry-level construction jobs, janitorial, housekeeping, crop picking, and ditch digging. If U.S. employers have access to a legal low-wage workforce for jobs that U.S. workers do not want, then it will enable many of them to grow and add other higher paying jobs. *Latin America has the low-wage workforce that U.S. companies need to grow and become globally competitive.* Remember, the guest worker program will only be for jobs that U.S. employers can demonstrate that they *cannot* hire U.S. workers to fill, and the employers will be required to offer the jobs to U.S. workers every three years in order to qualify again for the foreign guest worker program.

Illegal Immigration

Illegal immigration, and the resulting illegal underground economy it spawns, fosters crime, corruption, and exploitation. It creates more economic problems than it solves. Without immigration programs in place to control the market forces of supply and demand, illegal immigration cannot be stopped when there is a magnet economy, such as we have in the United States, close to very poor economies, such as those in Latin America. Intelligent immigration reform could effectively stop most illegal immigration while at the same time, providing programs to meet the demand of U.S. businesses and protect U.S. workers. If the immigrants are going to come anyway, we should provide programs that ensure that immigration is meeting the needs of U.S. businesses, not adversely affecting U.S. workers, encouraging legal immigration for qualified persons, and strongly discouraging those businesses and individuals who would violate our immigration laws. The best program is the one that benefits everyone involved.

Decline of the American Work Ethic

In recent years, we have seen a decline in the American work ethic, partly related to our outdated and ineffective immigration programs. The American work ethic was created by the types of people historically drawn to the United States. Look at the people who want to work, even two jobs if necessary—often, they are immigrants. They are willing to work, and work hard. They are happy to have an opportunity such as they never had in their home country.

If they are willing to come here legally and work hard; if they are willing to pay taxes and obey our laws; if they are willing to take jobs that U.S. workers do not want; if they are willing to pay their dues and earn a place in our country like all other immigrants of every other generation—why don't we have the good sense to provide legal channels to let them come and do just that?

APPENDIX B

ADVOCACY FOR LEGISLATIVE ACTION

Advocacy Begins with Us!

Don't think someone else will do it. If we are going to be successful, then we are all going to have to start now to advocate for immigration reform.

Advocate (Webster's)—1. to plead in favor of; support or urge by argument; recommend publicly; 2. one who defends, vindicates, or espouses a cause by argument; upholder; 3. one who pleads for or in behalf of another; intercessor.

Each of us must begin to advocate to our elected representatives, to the media, to our clients, to our colleagues, and to our communities. We must press upon them the urgent need for immigration reform. One of the author's law firm has mailed a 35-page article advocating common sense immigration reform to every member of Congress, the President, hundreds of immigration lobbying groups and special interest groups, and to all of our clients at a cost of over $5,000, and we are just getting started. Each of us can at least write our elected representatives.

Network with Other Groups that Have an Interest in Immigration Reform

Many groups that differ on some issues can be united on others. We will have to work together if immigration reform is to be politically viable. Any immigration reform must be politically viable. To be politically viable, an immigration reform proposal must be good for America and give the major interest groups involved in immigration reform some of the things that they want and need. Some of these interest groups (and what they want):

Conservatives want our borders secured, illegal immigration stopped, and immigration laws enforced. They do not want to reward people who have broken our laws by granting them amnesty (the automatic granting of permanent resident status). They are not (for the most part) opposed to qualified individuals being able to *earn* legal status as nonimmigrant workers.

Hispanic groups want some form of legal recognition for workers who are here obeying the laws (other than their unlawful presence) and providing essential services by taking jobs that most U.S. workers do not want. Legal recognition will give workers rights that will stop much of the exploitation of Hispanic workers. Hispanic groups would also like to see some opportunity for workers to earn permanent resident status.

Big businesses need to be able to compete globally. For this to happen, they need access to low-wage labor for unskilled job positions. Companies cannot afford to pay $15 per hour for jobs that pay $3 per hour overseas; they cannot compete globally with such a disparity of labor costs. If this situation is allowed to continue, more and more companies will move overseas, resulting in the loss of more (higher paying) U.S. jobs. U.S. companies do not need to match wages overseas since there are many other advantages to doing business in the United States—they simply need access to a dependable low-wage (as well as a high-wage/skilled) labor force.

Small businesses employ most U.S. workers and must be able to make a profit to stay in business. Employees (salaries and benefits) are the largest expense for most small businesses, and most depend on both skilled and unskilled workers. They cannot stay in business if they must pay an unskilled worker $15 per hour. If a small business must go out of business, its higher paid/skilled workers are out of work also. Then, the only businesses left operating are those hiring the illegal immigrants.

Agriculture. U.S. workers cannot, and will not, meet the needs of U.S. farmers for seasonal, low-paying jobs such as crop picking. If the United States wants to be the bread basket of the world, it needs a dependable migrant workforce.

Construction companies need skilled and unskilled workers. U.S. workers, for the most part, will not take hard-labor, low-paying jobs that are necessary to support the higher paid/skilled construction workers.

Liberal groups are concerned for the most part with workers' rights, working conditions, and fair and equal treatment, all of which can be addressed through a government-controlled and supervised guest worker program. In the absence of such a program, low-wage/undocumented workers who are providing essential services have almost no rights and are vulnerable to the worst types of abuse and exploitation.

The Green Industry—landscapers, nurseries, and tree farms—find it almost impossible to hire U.S. workers, since most positions require no skills, are low-paying, and are seasonal in nature. Without a guest worker program, many such businesses are forced to rely on workers with questionable work documents. The worker may provide a Social Security card, but it was likely made in a flea market the weekend before.

Unions need members as they lose jobs to overseas competition. Unions should support a guest worker program and attempt to rebuild their numbers with these new workers. Otherwise, they will continue to lose significance and influence in American business and politics.

Many other industries—fishing, shrimping, logging, forestry, hospitality, janitorial services, quarries, manufacturing, health care, lawn maintenance—depend on some forms of unskilled/low-wage positions that U.S. workers are not willing to take. They need a legal guest worker program.

Motivate Your Clients Who Have an Interest in the H-2 Programs to Lobby their Elected Representatives

These are businesses that elected representatives will take seriously. Some of your clients may even know their congressional representatives personally or even play golf with them. If all of us get our clients to lobby their representatives, we will see legislation passed quickly. Our voices must be heard before Congress will act.

When the H-2B cap was hit in March 2004, nobody did much about it. But when it was hit on January 3, 2005, every H-2B industry began to intensely lobby their representative. The result was the Save Our Small and Seasonal Businesses Act of 2005. But SOSSBA sunsets this year. Now it is time to act again, but a lot of people are assuming somebody else will do something about it.

There is an old story about a problem that needed fixing, and four peoples' responses to the problem. Their names were Everybody, Somebody, Anybody, and Nobody. Everybody knew the problem existed. Everybody thought Somebody would take care of it. Anybody could have done something. But, you probably guessed who ended up doing something about it—that's right, Nobody. We cannot let that be the case with such an important issue as advocacy for legislative action for comprehensive immigration reform and revision of the H-2 programs to meet the present and future needs of U.S. businesses.

STRATEGIES FOR L-1AS

by Kelly M. McCown, Gerard M. Chapman, and Joycelyn L. Fleming[*]

EXECUTIVE VS. MANAGERIAL CAPACITY

Companies that have traversed international boundaries make for challenging clients. The L-1A visa category, which allows for intracompany transfer of foreign employees into executive and managerial positions in the United States, often meets their business needs. However, a successful L-1A petition requires a fact-intensive inquiry into corporate organization, personnel relationships, and the industry. In other words, the devil is in the details.

The following discussion of L-1A strategies for business immigration practitioners highlights both the substantive and the procedural law on which an L-1A case can turn. It also gives practice pointers and tips to avoid undue U.S. Citizenship and Immigration Services (USCIS) scrutiny.

The authors will discuss the executive-managerial distinction; the manager-functional manager distinction; issues for small businesses and new offices; the advantages and disadvantages of using the Blanket L visa category; the effects of corporate changes on visa eligibility; special border processing for Canadians under NAFTA; and dealing with the five- and seven-year visa limitations. Finally, we raise ethical dilemmas that may arise for practitioners handling L-1A cases, along with tips to satisfy clients without compromising professional responsibilities.

Although the distinction between executive or managerial capacity is sometimes blurred because the duties often overlap, there are separate statutory definitions for executive and managerial capacity.[1] An individual employed in an executive capacity does not need supervisory responsibilities. Thus, if the L beneficiary is more involved in directing the organization than in supervising employees, it may be a strong argument that he or she is employed in an executive rather than a managerial capacity.

Notwithstanding the statutory distinction between executive and manager, in either case it is important to outline a U.S. company's hierarchy clearly using organizational charts, detailing any direct or indirect oversight of employees or independent contractors by the L beneficiary. It may be helpful to include outside vendors or service providers managed by the L-1 beneficiary, such as corporate lawyers, accountants, suppliers, or other consultants. Another strategy in a close case may be to obtain an evaluation from an industry expert, verifying that the position requires an executive or manager and that the L employee will indeed be working in such a capacity.

Although the duties have to be "primarily" executive or managerial,[2] the L-1A employee is permitted

[*] **Kelly McCown** is a partner in the law firm of McCown & Evans LLP in San Francisco and a Certified Specialist in Immigration & Nationality Law with the State Bar of California, Board of Legal Specialization. Her areas of practice include nonimmigrant and immigrant visas for professionals and investors, consular practice, family immigration, and naturalization. She is currently the AILA Northern California Chapter chair and co-chair of Bay Area Lawyers for Individual Freedom (BALiF), the San Francisco area gay and lesbian bar association.

Gerard Chapman of Greensboro, N.C., is a board certified immigration specialist. He graduated from UNC-CH in 1973 with a B.A. in International Studies, and in 1978, he received his J.D., *cum laude*, from the University of Georgia School of Law. He is a trustee of AILF and served as chair of the AILA Carolinas Chapter and as a member of AILA's board of governors from 1998–2000. He is a founding member and board member of the North Carolina Legal Immigration Coalition (NCLIC), a group that gives educational presentations on immigration developments to businesses and other groups.

Mr. Chapman would like to thank Helen Jugovic for her extensive help with his sections of this paper. She will join his firm as an associate in August 2006.

Joycelyn Fleming is a partner at Ford & Harrison, a national labor and employment law firm, and manages the Business Immigration Law Group from the firm's Atlanta office. She is a member of AILA's Health Care Professionals Committee. She is listed in *Best Lawyers in America* for immigration in Georgia, and was named one of Georgia's "2006 Super Lawyers" by *Atlanta Magazine*.

---

[1] *See* INA §§101(a)(44)(A) (managerial) and 101(a)(44)(B) (executive); and 8 CFR §§214.2(l)(1)(ii)(B) (managerial) and 214.2(l)(1)(ii)(C) (executive).

[2] *Ikea U.S., Inc. v. U.S. Dep't of Justice*, 48 F. Supp. 2d 22 (D.D.C. 1999) (petitioner failed to establish that beneficiary's primary duties would be as a functional manager), *aff'd*, No. 99-5159, 1999 U.S. App. LEXIS 25164 (D.C. Cir., Sept. 27, 1999) (granting motion for summary affirmance). For further discussion, see the section below on "Small Business Issues."

to engage in duties that are not strictly managerial but are common to the position.[3] However, be wary of submitting evidence that may suggest that the L-1 beneficiary is engaged in clerical work or administrative duties that may not be consistent with executive or managerial capacity.[4]

USCIS takes the view that "managerial capacity" excludes a "first-line supervisor" unless the employees supervised are professionals.[5] It is therefore helpful to provide proof of the educational credentials or equivalency of the employees supervised, to show that they possess at least a baccalaureate-level education.

L-1A FUNCTIONAL MANAGERS

An individual who "manages an essential function within the organization, or a department or subdivision of the organization" can qualify for L-1A status as a functional manager.[6] The functional manager must also function at a senior level within the hierarchy or as to the function managed, and exercise discretion over its day-to-day operations.

Proving that an employee is a functional manager may require some creativity because there is little guidance defining these positions. The functional manager should not directly supervise employees.[7] To prove that a person is a functional manager, describe instead the person's authority over the function; budgetary responsibility; authority to bind the company in contract; activities at a senior level within the organization and interfacing with other senior-level employees elsewhere in the business); strategic decision-making responsibility; influence on profitability, products, or operations; management of direct or indirect reports; education and work experience; and exercise of discretion in managing day-to-day operations.

SMALL BUSINESS ISSUES AND THE L-1A

While the general L-1 rules and guidelines often apply neatly to large, multi-national corporations, small businesses also may use the category both for executives and managers and for individuals with specialized knowledge. However, special care must be taken to give the adjudicating officer enough information to make the sophisticated analysis necessary to determine that every requirement for L-1 status has been met.

In the small company scenario, it is even more important to cross-examine your client to confirm the accuracy and persuasiveness of the facts of the case. Whether it is fair or not, the USCIS adjudicator or consular officer will look more closely at this kind of case than at one filed by a large multinational, so you might as well put the client to the test right from the start.

In the end, the reviewing officer will look at the whole picture to determine whether the small business is a qualifying organization with employees eligible for L-1A status. The job of the immigration lawyer is to paint the small business picture fully and accurately, while emphasizing the regulations in favor of small businesses to center the reviewing officer on the bottom line.

How to Wear All the Hats and Still Qualify for L-1A Status

Small businesses often have the same immigration problems that new businesses face, such as proving that the company needs a manager or executive who also will have to conduct duties that cross over from executive to managerial, and activities associated with, for example, a sales position. The USCIS Operating Instructions provide help with this kind of situation:

(2) Eligibility requires that the duties of a position be primarily of an executive or managerial nature. The test is basic to ensure that a person not only has requisite authority, but that a majority of his or her duties relate to operational or policy management, not to the supervision of lower-level employees, performance of the duties of another type

---

[3] *See Republic of Transkei, et al. v. INS*, 923 F.2d 175 (D.C. 1991) (noting the INS position in commentary to the regulations at 51 Fed. Reg. 5739 (1986) that persons whose duties include executive-level public relations and lobbying will not be disqualified from obtaining L-1 status simply because of those activities).

[4] *See Calexico Warehouse, Inc. v. Neufeld*, 259 F. Supp. 2d 1067 (S.D. Cal. 2002) (upholding revocation of L-1A petition where evidence included sales invoices and shipping documents signed by beneficiary, indicating that beneficiary was performing the basic operations of the company, including nonmanagerial clerical functions).

[5] 8 CFR §214.2(l)(1)(ii)(B)(4).

[6] 8 CFR §214.2(l)(1)(ii)(B). *See Matter of Harrison Pacific Inc.*, WAC-92-192-51184 (AAO Feb. 16, 1994); "AAU Re-examines Harrison Pacific Case," May 3, 1994, *published on* AILA InfoNet at Doc. No. 94050390 (*posted* May 3, 1994).

[7] 9 FAM §41.54 N.8.2-1a ("individuals who control and directly perform a function within an organization, but do not have subordinate staff [except perhaps a personal staff], are more appropriately considered specialized knowledge employees").

of position, or other involvement in the operational activities of the company, such as doing sales work or operating machines or supervising those that do. This does not mean that the executive or manager cannot regularly apply his or her technical or professional expertise to a particular problem. The definitions are not intended to exclude from the duties of a manager or executive activities that are not strictly managerial [or executive], but are common to those positions, such as customer and public relations and lobbying and contracting.[8]

The trick, then, is to acknowledge in the statement of job duties that the executive or manager has primary responsibility for duties that fit within the scope of the USCIS or *Foreign Affairs Manual* (FAM) definitions for the position, but also point out that the other necessary duties (*e.g.*, customer relations or contracting) that are secondary to the larger set of job duties.

It is both logical and commonplace for an executive (and to a lesser extent a manager) to have personal interaction with customers and to know as much as possible about their businesses. One common way to gain that knowledge is to have the personal contact that we call public relations or marketing. Some PR and marketing can be conducted impersonally, but a chief executive or high-level manager almost always needs to have a personal relationship with the customer and will often be involved with the details of contract negotiations. This is true whether a business is large or small. Fortunately, the Operating Instructions acknowledge this reality; it is totally appropriate to remind USCIS or the consulate of this fact.

Department of State regulations even allow a case to be approved where the L-1A applicant will be the *only* employee, if his or her primary functions are executive or managerial:

> The sole employee of a company may qualify as an executive or manager, for L visa purposes, provided his or her primary function is to plan, organize, direct and control an organization's major functions through other people.[9]

Where the company will be thinly staffed, be proactive in helping your client organize the way all major functions of the company will be performed by people other than the client and if possible identify individuals and entities who will be under his or her command. In our knowledge-based economy, filled with supply chains and other cutting-edge technologies, this may be easier to prove than it was when companies only manufactured onsite and supplied hard goods directly to a small set of customers. In the "old days," it would not be uncommon for the manager or executive to be supervising production workers, which does not meet L-1A standards.[10] In today's world, managers and executives fill the role of supply chain managers as well as negotiators, PR contacts, etc. The more you can show that your executive or manager is directing traffic between independent companies or other entities, with the goal of ultimately supplying goods or services to the L-1 company's customers, the closer your case will come to satisfying the regulations.[11]

Despite your best efforts, the FAM in effect contains a presumption against granting L-1A status to applicants who have little or no staff, and this presumption probably will be harder to overcome for a small company than a larger one.[12]

Large Roles in Small Companies

Because every case will be controlled by its facts, just how much of a dual role a manager/executive can play is unclear. According to the FAM, the business cannot be so small that in reality, the individual is in

---

[8] OI 214.2(l)(5)(i)(A)(2). The *Foreign Affairs Manual* (FAM) contains virtually identical language. *See* 9 FAM 41.54 N.8.2-1(a).

[9] 9 FAM 41.54 N.8.2-1(c).

[10] OI 214.2(l)(5)(i)(A)(1).

[11] A good example of a functional manager in the traditional kind of business is a manufacturing manager who performs a liaison and quality control function between the design engineers and the production engineers in a vehicle manu-facturing company. The design engineers send drawings to the manufacturing engineer, who decides if they are in proper form to submit to the Production Department. Only when he says they are ready do they go to Production. Once the production engineers get the drawings, if they have a problem with them, they send them back to the manufacturing manager to resolve the problem, either on his own or by sending the drawings back to the Design Department for further work. The manufacturing manager does not perform the design or work, and both technically and in reality he has no direct reports. However, the function he performs is to control two of the most critical functions in the company. In the knowledge-based context with a small company, the sole executive can be approved for L-1A status if you can show that he or she is performing the same kind of "clearinghouse" function between similar service providers who are external to the company.

[12] *See* 9 FAM 41.54 N.8.2-1(b).

the United States purely to be self-employed.[13] On the other hand, it also states that the size of the petitioning company does not limit its use of the regular (non-blanket) L category as long as it has demonstrated its international nature by continuing to do business in the United States and abroad.[14] Therefore you must convey to clients that each case is fact-based, and that the petition or Blanket case must be supported by detailed descriptions of job duties and company relationships.[15]

With this in mind, the focus of the analysis for the dual-role manager or executive should be on which role is primary (specialized knowledge versus management and oversight). To qualify for L-1A status, the petition should make it clear that the transferee is not in the United States merely to be self-employed or simply practice his professional skills but to both manage and oversee the U.S. operation, though some secondary, day-to-day duties are necessary to produce the product or services. Any small business petition should go beyond mere recitals to draw the true picture of the business and its need for the intracompany manager or executive.

Echoing the FAM language, the OIs give an example of a small business where the duties are *not primarily* executive or managerial:

[N]either the title of a position nor ownership of the business are [*sic*], by themselves, indicators of managerial or executive capacity. For example, a physician may incorporate his or her practice for business purposes and may hire a receptionist, bookkeeper, and a nurse to assist in that medical practice. For L purposes, the physician is not a manager, but a person who primarily practices his or her professional skills as a physician.[16]

The goal, then, is to distinguish the example from the case of the petitioning small business. The physician example does not contemplate the typical small business that produces and sells products, negotiates and concludes contracts for services, etc. Yet, it may be helpful to use the physician's example as a starting point, remembering that the ultimate test is whether the person has requisite authority and whether a majority of his or her duties relate to operational or policy management.[17] Anticipating the small business case, *the statute itself* cautions USCIS and the State Department to be reasonable in using staffing levels to determine if the applicant will work as an executive or a manager. In using staffing levels, USCIS or the consular official is required to consider the reasonable needs of the organization, component, or function "in light of the overall purpose and stage of development of the organization, component or function."[18]

Practice Pointer: Companies with only a few employees in the U.S. operation can find it difficult to justify an executive or managerial position. Do not be deterred if you and your client believe the case warrants L-1A status. Remind USCIS and the consulate of the wording in the statute and explain in detail why, at your client's stage of development, an executive or manager is not just appropriate but absolutely necessary.

Where cases have been denied, the Administrative Appeals Office (AAO) has pointed to an apparent lack of information about who or what duties are under the individual's discretion: failure to provide a "comprehensive" business plan for a start-up; failure to provide complete job descriptions for all employees; mere "recitals" of the USCIS regulations in lieu of statements of specific job duties; and failure to indicate whether salesmen would be compensated for their efforts as agents of the company.[19] In dismissing one appeal, the AAO pointed out that both the text description and the organizational chart overview of the beneficiary's position were confusing.[20]

To help avoid such an outcome, organizational charts can be very powerful evidence, and you do not have to be limited by the traditional kind of organizational chart. For instance, if your client is a

---

[13] *See, e.g.,* 9 FAM 41.54 N.10.4: "The L classification was not created for self-employed persons to enter the United States to continue self-employment (unless they are otherwise qualified for L status) . . . "

[14] 9 FAM 41.54 N.7.5.

[15] 9 FAM 41.54 N.8.2-1(c) ("If a small or medium-sized business supports a position wherein the duties are *primarily* executive or managerial, it can qualify under the L category. *However, neither the title of a position nor ownership of the business, are, by themselves, indicators or managerial or executive capacity.*") (emphasis added).

[16] OI 214.2(l)(5)(i)(A)(4).

[17] *See* OI 214.2(l)(5)(i)(A)(2).

[18] INA §101(a)(44)(C).

[19] *See, e.g., In re [name not provided]*, EAC 99 101 53073, 2002 WL 32077614 (INS) (AAO, Jan. 22, 2002), and *In re [name not provided]*, EAC 97 051 53808, 1998 WL 34057252 (INS) (AAO, June 26, 1998).

[20] *In re [name not provided]*, EAC 99 101 53073, 2002 WL 32077614 (INS) (AAO, Jan. 22, 2002)

functional manager in a very small company, the standard organizational chart probably will present a weak picture if it only shows pure employees of the U.S. operation. In place of or in addition to the standard chart, consider creating a new one that places the beneficiary at the top or in the middle of the page, with all the outside entities and independent contractors surrounding or below him. Instead of a single chart with the beneficiary at the bottom and no direct reports, you now have a clear and accurate picture of entities and individuals who in fact report to or are supervised or monitored by the beneficiary.

In cases that are denied, many of the failures are fact-based. As an immigration lawyer, approach the L-1A case (especially for small businesses) with the same focus that a trial lawyer approaches a case: know your facts, and make your client answer questions that can make factual presentations stronger. Clients have to run their businesses, but they hire you to help them do that successfully. By pushing (but not trampling on) the client for all relevant facts, you will be serving the client well.

Part-Time or Intermittent Need for the Transferee

What about the case where a foreign entity and the receiving U.S. entity are established but will remain small? Here, the small business may not need or want the intracompany transferee to be in the United States continuously or to work full-time. USCIS has dealt with this situation in a manner that generally benefits small and large businesses alike. Although the regulations anticipate full-time employment, as long as the transferee dedicates a significant portion of his or her time to the U.S. company on a "regular and systematic basis" in managerial or executive duties that are part of or that directly affect its day-to-day operations, he or she need not work full-time in the United States.[21] In preparing such a case, consider the possibility of including a general itinerary of expected travel during a given year, lists of customers and their locations that will require the beneficiary to be both inside and outside the United States, and the type of discussions and negotiations the beneficiary will conduct at these locations. In doing so, connect this evidence with the rule that requires the beneficiary's activities to be "part of or directly affect" the U.S. operations' daily affairs.

As a further benefit, the seven-year maximum limitation on L-1A stay does not apply to individuals whose employment in the United States is seasonal, intermittent, or is for an aggregate of six months or less per year.[22] Nor does it apply to L-1 employees residing abroad and regularly commuting to the United States to engage in part-time employment.[23]

On the other hand, some activities by themselves, such as "conferring with officials, attending meetings and conferences, and participating in training are not considered productive employment and are appropriate for B-1 classification."[24] Therefore, if the transferee is going to work only part-time in the United States, it is important to provide enough information about job duties and travel plans in the L-1A petition to distinguish the proposed activities from a B-1 visa case.

Owners as L-1A Transferees

It may be less common than other fact situations, but the case law supports the transfer of a majority or substantial shareholder under the L-1A classification.[25] However, such a petition must be supported by evidence that the beneficiary's services will be temporary, and that the beneficiary will be transferred to an assignment abroad once he or she completes the assignment in the United States.[26]

Organization and Type of Business

What types of small businesses qualify as receiving and sending companies for L-1A purposes? The form of the business entity is not relevant.[27] It can be for-profit, nonprofit, religious, or charitable.[28] Even so, small businesses typically need to provide more information than larger ones to establish that the petitioner and the foreign entity are bona fide operations.

---

[21] OI 214.2(l)(5)(ii)(B); see 9 FAM 41.54 N.8.5.

[22] See 8 CFR §214.2(l)(12)(ii).

[23] Id. The regulation states very clearly, however, that this exception is to be granted only upon "clear and convincing proof that the alien qualifies for an exception. Clear and convincing proof shall consist of evidence such as arrival and departure records, copies of tax returns, and records of employment abroad."

[24] OI 214.2(l)(5)(ii)(B).

[25] Matter of Aphrodite Investments, Ltd., 17 I&N Dec. 530 (Comm. 1980).

[26] 8 CFR §214.2(l)(3)(vii).

[27] Matter of Church of Scientology International, 19 I&N Dec. 593 (Comm. 1988).

[28] Id.

For example, in addition to a statement of an authorized official regarding the ownership and control of the sending and receiving companies that even large, established organizations must submit, the OIs state that small businesses and marginal operations should submit other evidence of ownership and control. The OIs cite as evidence of ownership and control records of stock ownership, profit and loss statements or other accountants' reports, tax returns, or articles of incorporation, by-laws, and minutes of board meetings.[29]

For partnerships, a copy of the partnership agreement must be provided and even then "other evidence may be necessary."[30] The small business also may be an individual proprietorship, which in effect would be a branch office of the foreign sending company. "In cases where the business is not a separate legal entity from the owner(s), the petitioner's statement of ownership and control must be accompanied by evidence, such as a license to do business, record of registration as an employer with the [IRS], business tax returns, or other evidence which identifies the owner(s) of the businesses."[31]

Practice Pointer: Proving the corporate existence and relationships can be challenging with small businesses. To keep it from being too challenging and disruptive to the client, before you ask the client to provide multiple documents, try to obtain them from other sources. For instance, articles of incorporation are available online in many states; tax returns can be obtained from the company's outside accountant; annual reports may be downloadable from the company website, etc. In other words, use all the tools at your disposal before you ask the client for documents.

Job Titles in the Small Business

Common sense can be a big help in preparing cases and, more important, in your discussions with the client before you begin preparing an L-1A case. USCIS, like all government agencies, does not mind if you are aggressive as long as the case is supported by the facts. However, it will be skeptical of a petition if the U.S. office is staffed mostly by individuals with executive titles, and only a few people are below the beneficiary on the organizational chart. On the other hand, do not overlook the wording in

the statute that cautions USCIS and the consulate about using staffing levels in rendering a decision.[32]

A related issue may be salary. It is typical to expect an executive to earn a sizeable salary, but established case law confirms that a nonsalaried company chairman can qualify for L-1A status.[33]

Summary

Every year, small businesses create most of the new jobs in the United States. Their creativity and flexibility are the hallmarks of our vibrant economy. Foreign companies with small U.S. operations should be welcomed to the United States and generally are. However, tension arises between our desire to encourage foreign investment in the United States and the overly aggressive transfer of foreign managers and executives through the L-1A visa classification. These cases can be approved but they must be supported by clear, well-organized, and substantial proof of all substantive elements of the case.

As counsel for small L-1A companies, keep your "trial lawyer" hat on in the initial discussions of the case and all the time you are preparing it for filing. If you make proper use of charts, detailed job descriptions, and company documents, USCIS will be much more likely to approve the case. The result will be a client who succeeds in bringing one of its key people to the United States, which in turn may result in a larger and more vibrant U.S. presence, for the benefit of all.

NEW OFFICE L-1AS

L-1A petitions for executives or managers who are coming to the United States to open or be employed in a new offices can be challenging. USCIS regulations require documentation for L-1 petitions for a new office that is not otherwise required, including a showing that the physical premises secured will be adequate. Additionally, the petitioner must show that the beneficiary's foreign employment was as an executive or manager and that the proposed U.S. position involves executive or managerial authority over the new operation.[34]

---

[29] OI 214.2(l)(6)(ii)(A)(2).

[30] OI 214.2(l)(6)(ii)(A)(4).

[31] OI 214.2(l)(6)(ii)(A)(5).

[32] *See* INA §101(a)(44)(C).

[33] *See Matter of Tessel, Inc.*, 17 I&N Dec. 631 (AAC 1981), and the discussion, *supra*, of special rules for transfers of majority or sole owners of the petitioner.

[34] 8 CFR §214.2(l)(3)(v). While the regulations require the foreign employment of an L-1 executive or manager coming to work in a new office to have been in an executive or

continued

New office L-1s are approved only for one year, and the regulations require a showing that the new office will, within a year of approval, support an executive or managerial position.[35] Arguably, the position does not even have to be "primarily" executive or managerial within the first year. Proof of this element usually involves submission of a business plan that will project increased staffing levels by the end of the first year, information about the size of the U.S. investment and the financial ability of the foreign company to remunerate the beneficiary and commence doing business in the United States, and the organizational structure of the foreign entity.[36] Organizational charts to show the projected hierarchy of the U.S. entity at the one-year mark may be helpful. It is understood that an executive or manager in a new office will be more involved in day-to-day operations during the initial phases of the business, but he or she must also have authority to hire staff and make decisions about the goals and management of the organization.[37]

When it is time to file for the L-1A extension toward the end of the first year, the petitioner must show that the U.S. entity is doing business and that the new office can now support an executive or managerial position. USCIS also typically requires evidence of the number of employees and their positions, the wages they are paid, significant growth in cash flow or assets, presence of significant customers and clientele, and similar details.[38]

One problem that arises with new office L-1 petitions filed for an executive or manager comes up when the business does not grow as quickly as projected within the first year. For instance, rather than hiring five professional software engineers, what if the company hires only one computer programmer and one administrative support person, and the L-1A manager still handles mid-level technical sales and marketing tasks in addition to managerial duties? Because of the rule that USCIS does not consider first-line supervisors to be managers unless the employees they supervise are professionals,[39] and be-

cause USCIS considers managers in small companies with few employees to not be "primarily" engaged as managers,[40] it may be difficult to extend this manager's L-1A status. As a result, the company may potentially lose U.S. L-1 work authorization for the manager it relocated to establish the U.S. office.[41] It is therefore extremely critical to advise the client well in advance what proofs will be required to successfully extend the beneficiary's L-1 status beyond the year.

Where the company truly remains in "start-up mode" after a year, a better strategy may be to argue that the L-1A employee is a functional manager or even attempt to change his or her status to L-1B specialized knowledge if he or she otherwise qualifies.

BLANKET L-1 FILINGS

Many if not most L-1A applications filed are individual cases, meaning they are filed for one person with a service center. However, some companies can take advantage of the Blanket L filing procedure.[42]

---

managerial capacity, the statute contains no such restriction. For commentary on this, see C. Gordon, S. Mailman, and S. Yale-Loehr, 2 *Immigration Law and Procedure*, §24.05[4] n.37, and accompanying text.

[35] *Id.*

[36] *Id.*

[37] 9 FAM 41.54 N.12.3.

[38] *See* 8 CFR §214.2(l)(14)(ii).

[39] 8 CFR §214.2(l)(1)(ii)(B)(4).

[40] *IKEA U.S. Inc. v. U.S. Dep't of Justice*, 48 F. Supp. 2d 22 (D.D.C. 1999) (holding in multinational manager I-140 case that restaurant manager for one store was not serving an "essential function within the organization, or a department or subdivision of the organization," and noting that the duties and percentage of time to be spent on them were not adequately documented), *aff'd*, No. 99-5159, 1999 U.S. App. LEXIS 25164 (D.C. Cir. Sept. 27, 1999); *Boyang, Ltd. and Hee-Sung Jang v. INS*, No. 94-35535, 1995 U.S. App. LEXIS 28314 (9th Cir. Sept. 29, 1995) (concluding that beneficiary was conducting "first-line" duties and noting that "[w]hen a company has a very limited number of employees, it becomes questionable as to whether the operator of the business is engaged primarily in managerial or executive duties. The [INS] may reasonably conclude in such a case that a wide range of daily functions associated with running a business will be performed and that these duties are unrelated to the definitions of manager or executive.")

[41] Note, however, that courts have stated that the statute was not meant to limit managers or executives to those who supervise a large number of persons or a large enterprise. See *e.g.*, dicta in *National Hand Tool Corp. v. Pasquarell*, 889 F.2d 1472 n.5 (5th Cir. 1989); *Mars Jewelers, Inc. and J.J. Naran v. INS and the United States of America*, 702 F. Supp. 1570 (N.D. Ga. 1988) (denial of L-1 to a manager an abuse of discretion where emphasis on size of organization and number of employees supervised was excessive, *citing Johnson-Laird, Inc. v. INS*, 537 F. Supp. 52 (D.C. Ore. 1981) (L visa available to sole proprietor as well as to corporation with only two employees)).

[42] *See generally* 8 CFR §214.2(l)(4) for Blanket L procedures. *See* Memorandum of Thomas Cook, Acting Asst. Commr. for Adjudications, HQ 70/6.2.8 (Feb. 13, 2001), *continued*

A company approved for a Blanket L may *choose* to file an individual case for a given employee,[43] and in some instances *must* file an individual case, even if the Blanket L process is more desirable.

The following discussion addresses advantages and disadvantages of the Blanket L process, substantive differences between "regular" and "blanket" cases, matters of procedural significance, practice tips, and ethical considerations. The process has both advantages and disadvantages, and a number of special rules must be followed.

Cost-Benefit Analysis

In discussing the Blanket L system with clients, it is important to help them understand that the rules here are strictly interpreted. They must also weigh the potential benefits of becoming an approved Blanket L company against the costs of obtaining approval. Companies seeking Blanket L status must have enough related entities to satisfy the regulations (see below).[44] When applying for Blanket L status, the petitioner also must clearly document the nature of its relationship with all the entities it wants to have listed on the Blanket L Approval Notice.[45]

Simply put, the time and documentation required to prove those relationships may translate into excessive costs compared to the benefits of the Blanket L status. Unlike your discussion with the human resources representative about an individual L petition, preparing the documentation for a Blanket L petition may require several corporate officers and their staff to spend many hours and experience much distraction to prove to USCIS that all the intracompany relationships are satisfactory.

Background Checks

One point that deserves special emphasis in reviewing the Blanket L procedure with the client is this: the Blanket process does not relieve the beneficiaries of background checks, which can delay visa issuance significantly. In your comments about how much quicker the Blanket process can make intracompany transfers, do not omit this point about the continuing potential delays of background checks. If you stress that point, it may make the client reluctant to spend the time and money needed to get approval as a Blanket L company. But that is a much easier discussion than the one where the employer is angry because the human resources manager thought (reasonably or unreasonably) that the Blanket L process allowed employees to skip background checks.

Reading the Regulations

The USCIS regulations on Blanket L cases are found at 8 CFR §214.2(l)(4)(i) *et seq*. The rules are fairly straightforward, but they add a layer of complexity to an area that is complex enough. Even if you have prepared Blanket L petitions (both the initial one to obtain Blanket L status for the petitioner and related companies, and individual Blanket cases at the consulate), do not move blindly into the next Blanket case without reviewing the regulations and all USCIS policy memos, DOS cables, etc.

One rule change that practitioners often seem to overlook is the rule that Blanket applicants and individual applicants now must have a full year of qualifying employment with the "sending" company. The rule previously allowed Blanket applicants to show only six months of qualifying employment with a related entity.[46] Now, all individual applicants and most Blanket applicants are subject to the same one-year requirement.[47] Informing your clients of this

---

published on AILA InfoNet Doc. No. 01022003 (*posted* Feb. 20, 2001) (Blanket petition does not deal with individual aliens but rather relationships between the entities in the corporate structure; approval of Blanket petition means USCIS has determined the listed companies are qualifying organizations).

[43] 8 CFR §214.2(l)(4)(iii).

[44] Among other requirements, the petitioner must have three or more domestic and foreign branches, subsidiaries, or affiliates. 8 CFR §214.2(l)(4)(i)(C).

[45] 8 CFR §§214.2(l)(4)(iii), 214.2(l)(4)(iv).

[46] INA §214(c)(2)(A) (*repealed*).

[47] On December 8, 2004, President Bush signed the Omnibus Appropriations Act (OAA) for Fiscal Year 2005, Pub. L. No. 108-447, 118 Stat. 2809. Among its provisions is the L-1 Visa Reform Act of 2004 (L-1 Reform Act). Previously, INA §214(c)(2)(A) stated the Blanket L employee must work in qualifying employment for a minimum of six months. The Reform Act deleted the six-month reference in §214(c)(2)(A). USCIS initially advised that employees seeking admission under a Blanket L petition need to have been continuously employed by the petitioning employer for a year, 8 CFR §§214.2(l)(5)(D); 214.2(l)(1)(A); *see* Memorandum of Wm. R. Yates, Assoc. Dir. Operations, HQ 70/8, "Changes to the L Nonimmigrant Classification made by the L-1 Reform Act of 2004" (July 28, 2005), *published on* AILA InfoNet at Doc. No. 05080566 (*posted* Aug. 5, 2005). More recently, however, the DOS Visa Office clarified its policy on Blanket L classifications in response to an inquiry from AILA's DOS Liaison Committee. The Visa Office confirmed that an employer who filed a petition for initial Blanket L classification prior to June 6, 2005, may continue to bring in Blanket-qualified workers with only six months of

continued

change in the rules will serve you and your clients well if the employer (either from reading on the Internet or having used the Blanket procedure in the past) thinks it can transfer an employee after only six months with the related company outside the United States. Educating your client on this one point can save the client tremendous costs associated with the transfer itself and finding and training a replacement for the transferee.

Advantages and Disadvantages of the Blanket L

If the client after a thorough cost-benefit analysis concludes that filing the Blanket L petition is a good choice, it then becomes important to review with the client the relative advantages and disadvantages of the Blanket L status. The points that follow are not meant to be exhaustive, but they do cover most of the pros and cons that clients will want to consider. Each client's situation is different, so do not limit your discussions to the human resources manager. Even if you do not have access to higher-level executives to review these costs and benefits, strongly encourage your human resources contact to do so before giving you the green light to file the case.

Advantages of Obtaining a Blanket L

Speed of processing—The primary benefit of the Blanket process is speed of processing. A qualifying individual applicant can be presented to the U.S. consulate without a USCIS Approval Notice (I-797C).[48] (To that extent, the Blanket L process is just like an E visa application: no individual USCIS filing is required.) For this reason, the Blanket L process can save everyone involved a lot of time and money.

Advance approval of a substantive element—Approval of a Blanket L petition constitutes official USCIS recognition that the listed foreign and U.S. companies are "qualifying organizations" for the purposes of an L-1 individual visa application.[49] This means that one critical, substantive requirement has been pre-approved by USCIS, so the consulate will not need the kind of proof of corporate relationships that USCIS requires in an individual case.

Name recognition—On a practical level, a corporate family of companies that have Blanket L status can earn "name recognition" at a consulate, which may result in a quicker and more favorable review for the foreign national. Do not be lulled into a false sense of security, however. Under the regulations, the consular office cannot approve a Blanket L case unless it meets the "clearly approvable" test.[50]

Momentum—Once having obtained an L visa through the Blanket process, as long as the employee continues in the position for which the consulate issued the L visa, and as long as all necessary qualifying corporate relationships remain in place, it is reasonable to assume that the consulate will approve a renewal L visa application. In other words, the "clearly approvable" standard creates some momentum.

Quicker access to foreign nationals—This advantage is not as great as it was previously. From 2001 to early 2005, a Blanket case could be filed by a person who had held a qualifying position with a related employer outside the United States for only six months,[51] but effective June 6, 2005, all L-1A applicants (Blanket or individual) must show a full year of qualifying employment.[52]

Facilitating reassignments—An alien admitted under a Blanket L can be reassigned during an authorized stay to any organization listed on the I-797C Approval Notice without filing a change of employer petition, as long as he or she will be performing "virtually the same job duties."[53] If the job duties are not sufficiently similar, the original Blanket L petitioner must file a new I-129S (which otherwise is filed with the consulate) for approval from the service center that approved the original Blanket petition before to the proposed change.[54]

Partial revocation—Even if USCIS issues a Notice of Intent to Revoke a Blanket petition, it might revoke only part of the petition.[55] For example, if domestic or foreign affiliates or subsidiaries of the petitioner are acquired by another entity, they no longer have the right to use the Blanket process, at least based on the prior relationship with the original

---

qualifying employment. The Visa Office indicated that USCIS concurs with this policy, which is subject to continuing examination by the agencies; *published on* AILA InfoNet at Doc. No. 06040763 (*posted* Apr. 7, 2006).

[48] 8 CFR §§214.2(l)(5)(ii)(B) and (C).

[49] *See* Memorandum of Thomas Cook, *supra* note 42.

[50] *See* 8 CFR §214.2(l)(5)(ii)(E).

[51] *See* 8 CFR §§214.2(l)(5)(ii)(D); 214.2(l)(1)(A); Memorandum of Wm. R. Yates, *supra* note 47.

[52] *See* 8 CFR §214.2(l)(5)(ii)(D).

[53] *See* 8 CFR §214.2(l)(5)(ii)(G).

[54] *Id.*

[55] 8 CFR §214.2(l)(9)(iii)(A).

petitioner.[56] The remaining, properly related companies can continue using the Blanket procedure.[57]

Disadvantages of Obtaining a Blanket L

Managing client expectations (#1)—Since Blanket Ls operate through individual employees, companies may acquire unreasonable expectations about how the consulate will treat individual cases. It is prudent to occasionally remind your human resources contact (and your staff) that Blanket L cases must meet a higher evidentiary standard ("clearly approvable") than individual cases.[58] It also is helpful to remind them that other than managers and executives, only positions requiring specialized professional knowledge (with both the sending company and the proposed U.S. employer) can use the Blanket L procedure.[59]

Picking a racehorse—An applicant cannot file a Blanket and an individual case at the same time, hoping to get one approved before the other.[60] If an approved Blanket L company decides to file an individual case with USCIS, it must confirm to USCIS that it has Blanket status and must further certify that the beneficiary has not applied and will not apply for a Blanket L visa.[61] However, if the consular officer denies a Blanket L visa, the beneficiary still may apply through USCIS.[62] Obviously, this will cause a delay the client did not anticipate. On the other hand, though a last resort, this second bite at the apple may accomplish the client's ultimate objective: bringing the foreign national to the United States.

Stricter scrutiny—If the individual is denied at the consulate abroad, the consular officer is required to record reasons for the denial on the I-129S and send it to the USCIS service center that approved the Blanket L Petition.[63] Where a new petition is filed with USCIS, the petitioner must also name the consular office that denied the Blanket L visa and must

inform the service center of the reasons for the denial.[64] Under such circumstances, the individual petition almost certainly will receive greater scrutiny than if the Blanket had never been attempted. For this reason, it is critical to analyze each potential Blanket L case to determine whether it meets the "clearly approvable" standard. Obviously, if the client wants an employee to transfer quickly to the United States using the Blanket procedure, that can create significant tension when you believe the case may not be clearly approvable. If the client insists on going ahead, make your best effort to prepare a successful case without neglecting your ethical obligations to the client and the consulate.

The need to "use it or lose it"—If business patterns change temporarily and none of the qualifying organizations uses the Blanket petition procedure for three consecutive years, USCIS will send a Notice of Intent to Revoke the Blanket Petition,[65] giving the petitioner 30 days to respond.[66]

Managing client expectations (#2)—The Blanket process may create unreasonable expectations in the U.S. company, the foreign affiliate, and the transferee about the speed with which a case will be processed. If delays arise at the consulate, some or all of them may be extremely upset at the amount of time it takes to get a visa appointment at the consulate or a security clearance. Keep them informed of the possible delays.

Case presentation—It is sometimes hard to get executives and managers to realize they are not just applying for a visa stamp but rather presenting their entire case at the interview with a consular officer.

Practice Pointer: In your standard client "instructional letter" for a client filing a Blanket L-1A visa application, remind the client to read the entire package, especially the company support letter, because that document really contains all the substantive elements of the case. Without that preparation, a difficult consular officer could suspect that the beneficiary has presented a case that is not "clearly approvable," and deny it. Clients may assume too much, especially in the Blanket L context, so make sure to protect your clients from themselves.

---

[56] *Id.*

[57] 8 CFR §214.2(l)(9)(iii)(B).

[58] See 8 CFR §214.2(l)(5)(ii)(E) for reference to the "clearly approvable" standard for Blanket L alien beneficiaries.

[59] 8 CFR §§214.2(l)(4)(ii) and 214.2(l)(5)(ii)(D) both indicate that only (a) managers, (b) executives, and (c) specialized knowledge *professionals* may qualify under the Blanket L procedures.

[60] 8 CFR §214.2(l)(4)(iii).

[61] *Id.*

[62] 8 CFR §214.2(l)(5)(ii)(F).

[63] *Id.*

---

[64] *Id.*

[65] 8 CFR §214.2(l)(9)(iii)(A)(6).

[66] 8 CFR §214.2(l)(9)(iii)(B).

Regular Ls and Blanket Ls Compared

The benefits of the Blanket L approval come with a price. The company, for instance, will incur significant legal fees to prepare the package. Some of its employees will incur substantial time commitments to help document the proof USCIS requires for approval of the Blanket petition. The following summarizes the main points that need to be proved at the USCIS stage and at the consulate:

Basic Differences

For the Blanket petition filed with USCIS, the regulations[67] require proof that:

- The petitioner and all of the affiliated entities are engaged in commercial trade or services; *and*

- The petitioner has an office in the United States that has been conducting business for at least one year before the petition was filed; *and*

- The petitioner has at least three or more domestic and foreign branches, subsidiaries, or affiliates; *and*

- The petitioner (with all subsidiaries, branches and affiliates combined) must have obtained approvals for 10 or more L-1A or L-1B employees in the past year (note that any L-1Bs must have been specialized knowledge *professionals*); *or*

- The petitioner and all U.S. affiliates must have had annual sales of at least $25 million; *or*

- The petitioner and all U.S. affiliates must have at least 1,000 employees in the United States.

The L-1B "specialized knowledge" employee category is treated in depth elsewhere in this book. However, it is important to note that the Blanket L procedure is restricted to "professionals" for Blanket L-1B applicants and the requirement applies to both the position from which the individual applicant is coming and the one he or she is coming to fill.[68] This contrasts starkly with regular L-1B petitions, where the individual must possess specialized knowledge, but need not be a professional.[69]

USCIS can approve a Blanket Petition initially for three years, and indefinitely thereafter.[70] It can also revoke a Blanket petition on notice for one of

several reasons,[71] for instance, if one or more entities are no longer qualifying organizations.[72] If a Blanket L petition is revoked and there are already beneficiaries working in the United States who are otherwise eligible for L classification, USCIS must extend the Blanket petition for the time needed to support their stay.[73] USCIS also must issue a new Approval Notice stating the names of the remaining qualifying organizations and covered beneficiaries.[74] No new beneficiaries can be classified or admitted under this limited extension.[75] Therefore, after a revocation, to transfer additional employees under the Blanket procedures, the client will have to file a new Blanket L petition with USCIS.

To avoid revocation, keep the Blanket flexibility in place, and maintain the highest level of credibility with USCIS and the consulates at which the client's foreign nationals file their cases. It is advisable to file an amended Blanket L petition with USCIS to reflect changes in company relationships and add new qualifying organizations promptly.[76]

What Stays the Same?

Although much is gained by obtaining an approved Blanket L petition from USCIS, much stays the same:

- The basic substantive requirements of managerial and executive positions

- Specialized knowledge requirements for professionals

- General L concepts: five and seven-year limits, etc.

- The need for the individual applicant to have a full command of all the facts and circumstances on which the visa application is based (job duties outside and inside the United States, organizational charts and the positions and direct reports they reflect, discretionary duties the employee has conducted or will conduct, professional status of employees the applicant has supervised or will supervise, etc.).

---

[67] 8 CFR §§214.2(l)(4)(i)(A), (B), (C), and (D).

[68] 8 CFR §214.2(l)(4)(ii).

[69] *See* 8 CFR §§214.2(l)(1)(ii)(A), (D), and (E), as well as 214.2(l)(3)(ii).

[70] 8 CFR §214.2(l)(7)(i)(B)(2).

[71] *See* 8 CFR §214.2(l)(9)(iii).

[72] 8 CFR §214.2(l)(9)(iii)(1).

[73] 8 CFR §214.2(l)(9)(iv).

[74] *Id.* The new approval notice will be Form I-171C (not I-797A).

[75] *Id.*

[76] *See* 8 CFR §214.2(l)(7)(i)(C).

Procedures Compared

Many of the procedural differences between standard or regular L-1s and Blanket L-1s center on the content and presentation of the documentation presented at the consulate or the border.

Forms. DS-129S (Certificate of Eligibility) (three originals to consulate; one to corporation), copy of the I-797A Blanket Approval Notice and attachment (list of all affiliated entities); Form DS-156 and, if male, DS-157; plus employer support letter, organizational charts, etc. By comparison, with a standard L-1 visa application, the applicant presents the DS-156 and DS-157 plus all supporting materials, and the materials must include documentary proof of the qualifying relationship between the sending and receiving companies.

Practice Pointer: Consulates want to see the text of the support letter within the four corners of the I-129S (and the full text of any necessary attachments). In a regular L-1 case, USCIS will allow you to insert a phrase such as "See attached support letter" in the space on the L-1 Supplement that asks for the employee's prior and proposed job duties in the qualifying positions. For Blanket cases, the text for all the standard proof required for the requested classification normally must appear on the I-129S.

Documentation the individual must carry. The foreign national must carry a current copy of the I-797 Blanket Petition Approval Notice and Form I-129S when either (a) leaving or re-entering the United States to resume employment with the company, (b) applying for a new or revalidated visa, or (c) applying for readmission at the port of entry.[77]

No new documentation needed for some job changes. The foreign national may be readmitted to the United States to resume employment *even if* he or she is reassigned to a different organization than he or she previously worked for pursuant to the I-129S as long as the new employer is listed on the Blanket L I-797 Approval Notice and the new job duties will be "virtually the same."[78] This is a very favorable procedural rule that applies only to Blanket L foreign national beneficiaries.

A regular L still may be filed. If an employer has an approved Blanket L petition, it nevertheless may opt for the prospective employee to begin the L process with an individual petition.[79] This may be useful in uncertain cases where an individual applicant qualifies for L-1 status but you have concluded that the case will not meet the Blanket "clearly approvable" proof standard.

- Keep in mind that, if the Blanket L employer opts to file an L-1A petition as its first choice, it must certify to USCIS in its filing that the foreign national employee has not and will not apply at a U.S. consulate under the Blanket L petition.[80]

- Also keep in mind that should a U.S. consulate deny a Blanket petition for not being "clearly approvable," a second route is procedurally available.[81] A new individual petition may be filed with USCIS as long as the consular denial is disclosed.[82] Second-bite petitions are likely to receive more scrutiny than those without the history of a consular denial.

Interview of the foreign national. Because the Blanket L case must meet the higher standard by being "clearly approvable," pay extra attention to:

- The communication skills and preparation of the foreign national. For example, does he or she interview well? Will the employee have read the supporting documentation and be prepared to field questions from the consular officer? Where the case involves a functional manager position either in the United States or abroad, the alien needs to be prepared to highlight the managerial nature of his or her employment. In such a case, you should have a direct discussion with the employee to help him or her prepare for the interview. Even if you defer that discussion, you should encourage the employee to review the full application package before the interview.

- Consular processing. If you have not dealt with the consulate where the foreign national will interview recently, or at all, make reasonable efforts to learn its quirks and share that information with the employee.

- Follow up. It is important to follow up with the foreign national after the consulate approves an L-1 visa application. This is the best time to obtain the most current information about processing information at that consulate, which can be

---

[77] 8 CFR §§214.2(l)(13)(i) and (ii).

[78] 8 CFR §214.2(l)(5)(ii)(G).

[79] 8 CFR §214.2(l)(4)(iii).

[80] *Id.*

[81] 8 CFR §214.2(l)(5)(ii)(F).

[82] *Id.*

shared with future company employees applying there.

Favorable admissions rules. The regulations (much like the E visa regulations) provide that the beneficiary of a Blanket petition *may* be admitted for three years, even if the Blanket petition approved by USCIS will expire during that period.[83] Where the Blanket petition will expire while the employee is in the United States, the petitioner must file either a petition seeking indefinite validity of the Blanket petition or an individual extension application for the employee.[84]

Indefinite extensions. Once the Blanket petition has been in place for three years, it may be re-approved for an "indefinite time."[85] In a cost-benefit analysis, the front-end costs of obtaining an initial Blanket L and extending it for the indefinite period should be considered in light of the potential long-term validity of the Blanket L approval. The extension application must include Form I-129 with a report of admissions during the previous three years.[86] That report must include a list of aliens admitted under the Blanket during the past three years, and for each person listed, it must give:

- Each position held during each admission;

- The entity that employed the aliens during each such admission; and

- The dates of initial admission and final departure.[87]

Procedural penalty for failure to obtain indefinite validity. If the petitioner fails to file for indefinite validity or USCIS denies the filing, the petitioner must wait another three years to file a new Blanket petition.[88] During that time, the company's only option is to use regular USCIS L-1 filings.[89]

CORPORATE CHANGES AND L-1 VALIDITY

USCIS regulations require amended L-1 petitions when there are changes that would affect the beneficiary's eligibility for L-1 status. The regulations specify amendments when there are changes in approved relationships, additional qualifying organizations under a blanket, or a change in capacity of employment (for example, from a specialized knowledge position to a management position).[90]

Although the most conservative approach is to amend whenever there could be an adverse effect on an L-1 worker's continuing eligibility as a result of a corporate change, not all circumstances require it. A change from one managerial position to another does not require an amendment, although the petitioner should inform USCIS when it files an extension of stay for the beneficiary.[91] Nor is an amendment needed for a change in geographic location or job title, as long as the new location continues to be with the same L-1 employer and the beneficiary is still in the same type of managerial, executive, or specialized knowledge position.

For those who obtained L-1 status through a Blanket petition, a new or amended I-129 petition is not required where the beneficiary changes job duties or transfers to any organization listed on a Blanket petition if the duties are virtually the same.[92] Where the L-1 worker filed an individual petition, a transfer to a corporate entity within the same L-1 organization does not require an amendment if the employee is transferred to it but does not become its employee; but an amendment is required if he or she will become an employee of the related company.[93]

Carefully analyze the effect that corporate mergers, acquisitions, and divestitures may have on the ability of an L-1 worker to maintain valid immigration status. The challenge, especially in fast-track, complicated corporate mergers and acquisitions, is to determine whether a relationship still qualifies after an ownership change, and if so, to explain and document it in an L-1 amendment. There is little guidance for acquisitions of assets only or part of an entity, such as a division, but it can be more difficult generally for those situations to qualify.

Often, immigration is the last consideration in a corporate transaction and rarely is it given due diligence before a corporate change. Since an amendment can be filed only after a U.S. firm actually becomes

---

[83] 8 CFR §214.2(l)(11).

[84] *Id.*

[85] 8 CFR §214.2(l)(7)(i)(B)(2).

[86] 8 CFR §214.2(l)(14)(iii)(A).

[87] *Id.*

[88] 8 CFR §214.2(l)(14)(iii)(B).

[89] *Id.*

[90] 8 CFR §214.2(l)(7)(i)(C).

[91] Memorandum of James J. Hogan, Exec. Assoc. Commr., Operations, "Guidelines for the Filing of Amended H and L Petitions" (Oct. 22, 1992).

[92] 8 CFR §214.2(l)(5)(ii).

[93] *See* Hogan Memorandum, *supra* note 91.

related to the foreign firm in a qualifying capacity,[94] an L-1 worker can easily become out of status due to no fault of his or her own. Unauthorized employment causes ineligibility for a stateside extension under an amendment or a change of status. If so, consular processing of a visa and a new entry would be necessary.

A worker can remain eligible for L-1 status even if the acquiring entity closes the L-1 foreign entity at which the worker obtained the qualifying year of employment, as long as the petitioner still has at least *one* foreign entity in active business that meets the qualifying relationship to the U.S. petitioner.[95] A qualifying relationship can still exist after a corporate change if the U.S. petitioner is or will be actively engaged in business in at least one other foreign country directly or through a parent, subsidiary, or affiliate for the duration of the beneficiary's stay in the United States as an L-1 employee.

If the relationship between the foreign and U.S. entities no longer qualifies, there is a duty to notify USCIS of the change, since it affects the alien's eligibility for L-1 status. The petition may then be revoked if the change destroys L-1 eligibility. If the beneficiary no longer is eligible for L-1 status, resorting to other visa categories is necessary as soon as possible, such as E-1 Treaty Trader or E-2 Treaty Investor, if the acquiring entity and the employee meet nationality and other criteria; or the TN category for Mexican and Canadian citizens, if the position is listed in NAFTA.[96] Often, however, the only alternative is the H-1B Specialty Worker visa, which may not be immediately available if the current year's visa allocation has been exhausted.

L-1 PETITIONS FOR CANADIANS UNDER NAFTA AT U.S.-CANADA PORTS OF ENTRY

Canadian citizens may present individual or Blanket L-1 petitions for nonimmigrant worker (Form I-129) for same-day processing at U.S. Customs and Border Protection (CBP) inspection facilities for initial L-1 issuance and extensions.[97] The

petition should include all of the same components as a petition filed with a service center. Dependents may apply for L-2 status at the same time, or later with a copy of the principal beneficiary's Form I-94 and Notice of Action (Form I-797), if the employer receives one.[98] A Notice of Action (Form I-797) is issued later by mail only if the CBP facility chooses to forward the approved petition to a service center.

Mexican citizens do not have this border-processing option under NAFTA. Their U.S. employers must still submit individual L-1 petitions to a service center.

FIVE- AND SEVEN-YEAR LIMITS

It is possible to extend the five- and seven-year limits of the L-1B and L-1A categories by recapturing time the foreign worker spent outside the United States, but the burden is on the worker to document that he or she was in fact physically outside the United States for the days sought to be recaptured.[99] There is also an exception for those who work seasonally or intermittently in the United States or whose employment is for six months or less per year.[100] In either case, the beneficiary must provide documentary proof of time spent out of the United States beyond a list of dates he or she was absent.

SPECIALIZED KNOWLEDGE TO EXECUTIVE/MANAGER POSITION

An L-1B specialized knowledge worker who is promoted to a managerial position may be able to change status to L-1A, thereby becoming eligible for a maximum stay of seven years rather than five. The petitioner must have an L-1A petition approved at least six months before the end of the alien's five-year L-1B period to receive this benefit.[101]

---

[94] Letter from Jacquelyn A. Bednarz, Nonimmigrant Branch Chief, INS Office of Adjudications (Nov. 17, 1992).

[95] 8 CFR §214.2(l)(1)(ii)(G)(2).

[96] Appendix 1603.D.1 to Annex 1603, 8 CFR §214.6(c). *See also Immigration Practice Under NAFTA and Other Free Trade Agreements*, Third Ed. (AILA 2006). For more information or a table of contents, see *www.ailapubs.org*.

[97] 8 CFR §214.2(l)(17)(i).

[98] 8 CFR §214.2(l)(17)(v); Memorandum of Wm. R. Yates, INS Acting Exec. Assoc. Commr., to the field (no file number given) (Mar. 16, 1999), *published on* AILA Doc. No. 99031690 (*posted* Mar. 16, 1999).

[99] Memorandum of Michael Aytes, Acting Assoc. Dir. for Domestic Operations, "Procedures for Calculating Maximum Period of Stay Regarding the Limitations on Admission for H-1B and L-1 Nonimmigrants (AFM Update AD 05-21) (Oct. 21, 2005), *published on* AILA Doc. No. 05110363 (*posted* Nov. 3, 2005).

[100] 8 CFR §214.2(l)(12)(ii).

[101] 8 CFR §214.2(l)(15)(ii); *see* Memorandum of Wm. R. Yates, *supra* note 47 (citing *Adjudicators Field Manual* at §32.2(g)(2)).

An L-1B employee who qualifies for a change to L-1A and worked in a managerial position overseas for the requisite one year of the prior three years may also become eligible for an I-140 Petition for Immigrant Worker as an EB-1 Priority Worker.

ETHICAL CONSIDERATIONS

As restrictions and the pressures exerted by the agencies, the INA, and the regulations increase, clients and their lawyers will be tempted to push the limits of all visa categories, including the L classification. We already have mentioned the client's desire for speed and its possible expectation for positive outcomes at U.S. consulates because its Blanket petition was approved.

Unless Congress approves additional H-1B numbers (which currently seems unlikely), foreign nationals who normally would seek H-1B status may seek L-1 status. Clients whose employees were accustomed to filing Blanket L cases after only six months of qualifying employment with an overseas affiliate of the U.S. company may chafe under the new restriction that requires a full year.

Regardless of those pressures and expectations, you must not allow the client to misrepresent anything to USCIS or to the consulate. In today's world of instant electronic communication, few if any companies will suffer irreparable damage if they follow all L-1 rules.

As an officer of the court and as a licensed attorney, you are bound by your state rules of professional conduct and you should read them carefully, even though your practice is "federal." They usually include rules like Rule 3.3 of the ABA's Model Rules of Professional Conduct (governing candor to a tribunal), Rule 4.1 (regarding duties to third parties), and Rule 8.4 (regarding dishonesty).

For example, assume you have prepared and are ready to file a Blanket L petition for Company A. Just before filing, Company A sells one of the companies listed as an affiliate outside the United States. Or assume the same facts, except that the sale occurs after you have filed the Blanket petition. In both cases, Company A needs to transfer an important manager to the United State as soon as possible. In the first situation, clearly you need to revise the package that you were going to submit. In the second, if the case has been pending for several weeks with USCIS and you are expecting a decision shortly, it may be appropriate to wait for the decision, process the visa application for that one employee, and then file an amended petition with USCIS.

In cases involving functional managers, especially in small companies, it is very easy to exaggerate the nature of the duties of the employee in the United States. There is nothing wrong with being a zealous advocate, but it is inexcusable not to know the facts. Questionnaires (and the client's detailed answers to them) are invaluable tools. Read the regulations and use them to be sure that the case is factually supported and that you present all your client's facts. In responding to your questionnaire, sometimes the client will surprise you by providing new information that did not apply or was not available in an earlier case for a different employee. All you have to do is ask the questions, and all the client has to do is provide factual responses.

As all good trial lawyers know, good facts make good cases. Approach these cases (and all immigration cases) like a trial lawyer who is presenting the best case possible for the client. After you have discussed actual job duties with the human resources manager, departmental supervisor, and the employee, you can help edit a job description that accurately reflects the activities the employee will conduct. If you have a long-standing relationship with the client and you know what a standard engineer job description will encompass, it is permissible for you to use the job description from another case based on the same job title, subject to a brief e-mail to the human resources manager or department manager to be sure it is the same job.

What you must *not* do is draft a job description from scratch, with no input from the client, and with no confirmation of its accuracy, and then assume that it is accurate and complete. Nor should you file anything without the client's direct and careful review of the package and its confirmation to you that it is correct and complete.

Finally, if facts change that are material to the case, make whatever changes and file whatever amendments are appropriate without harming your client. Your vigilance and exercise of ethical responsibility will keep your client in good standing with USCIS and U.S. consulates, they will keep you out of trouble with the state bar disciplinary council (and the U.S. Attorney), and they will let both you and the client sleep easier at night.

OVERCOMING HURDLES WITH L-1B INTRACOMPANY TRANSFEREES

by Sherry L. Neal[*]

For decades, the L-1 nonimmigrant classification for intracompany transferees has been a useful method for multinational companies to transfer employees to the United States, particularly since the standards were liberalized through the Immigration Act of 1990 (IMMACT90).[1] Indeed, the L-1 classification has many advantages over other types of nonimmigrant classifications, including no annual limits on the number of foreign nationals who can qualify for the category, no prevailing wage standards, dual intent whereby a foreign national can apply for permanent residence without impact on the nonimmigrant status, and employment authorization for spouses.

Despite the many advantages, the L-1 nonimmigrant classification has its share of hurdles—especially the L-1B specialized knowledge classification that has a shorter duration of authorized stay than other nonimmigrant classifications, imprecise meaning of the term "specialized knowledge," and restrictions on working at offsite locations. Moreover, in the last few years, there has been a perception in government and the media that the L-1 category is "vulnerable and susceptible to fraud." This article will highlight the most common hurdles of the L-1B category.

INSPECTOR GENERAL'S REPORT ON L-1 VISAS

The Consolidated Appropriations Act of 2005[2] required the Inspector General of the Department of Homeland Security to examine the L-1 visa program and submit a report with recommendations to Congress.[3] Recently, the Inspector General released its report, which concluded there were "vulnerabilities and abuses" of the L-1 visa program. The report also noted the following characteristics of the L-1 category.[4]

Number of Approvals: The number of L-1 approvals began to increase in the late 1990s and hit its peak in 2001, when the government approved almost 60,000 L-1 petitions. In the years since 2001, the number of L-1 approvals has decreased to between 40,000 and 50,000 each year.

Industry: The highest percentage of L-1 visas has been in the information technology industry. In fact, from 1999 to 2004, nine of the 10 companies that had the largest number of L-1 approvals were in the information technology industry.

Nationality: The majority of L-1 approvals are for beneficiaries of India, Canada, the United Kingdom, Japan, and Germany. While there has been relatively little change in the country-percentages for L-1A managers and executives during the last four years, the percentage of L-1B specialized knowledge individuals per country has changed significantly during the last four years. For example, the percentage of L-1B beneficiaries from India increased from 10 percent in 2002 to 48 percent in 2005, while the other top four country-consumers of L-1Bs either decreased or remained constant. Canada's consumption of L-1Bs decreased from 25 percent in 2002 to 15 percent in 2005; Japan's consumption of L-1s decreased from 12 percent in 2002 to 4 percent in 2005; and the UK remained constant with 5 percent of the L-1B approvals in both 2002 and 2005.

Destination in the United States: During four of the last five years, the majority of L visas have been for work in California.

U.S. Consulate: The U.S. consulate in Chennai, India, processed 13,222 L-1 visa applications in

---

[*] **Sherry Neal** is a partner with Hammond Law Group, LLC in Cincinnati. She serves as the chair of the Ohio chapter of AILA and is a member of the National Health Care Committee (nonphysician) of AILA. Ms. Neal earned her law degree from the University of Dayton School of Law and her B.A. from Cedarville University.

[1] Immigration Act of 1990, Pub. L. No. 101-649, 104 Stat. 4978 (IMMACT90).

[2] Pub. L. No. 108-447 (H.R. 4818), *published on* AILA InfoNet at Doc. No. 04121811 (*posted* Dec 8, 2004).

[3] Division J, Title IV, Subtitle A of the Act (§§ 411–417) is also cited as "The L-1 Visa (Intracompany Transferee) Re-

---

form Act of 2004." (*Note*: The same legislation also imposed a $500 fraud filing fee on each new L-1 petition and H-1B petition to help fund government efforts to investigate fraud.)

[4] Department of Homeland Security, Office of Inspector General, "Review of Vulnerabilities and Potential Abuses of the L-1 Visa Program" (Jan. 2006), *published on* AILA InfoNet at Doc. No. 06021310 (*posted* Feb. 13, 2006) (hereinafter the Inspector General report).

continued

2005, almost three times as many L-1Bs as any other U.S. consulate. The other highest posts included London, which processed 5,903 L-1B visas, New Delhi, India, which processed 5,664 L-1B visas, Mumbai, India, which processed 4,602 L-1B visas, and Calcutta, India, which processed 3,146 L-1B visas.

These statistics are noteworthy in that they were mentioned within the same report in which the Inspector General concluded that there were "vulnerabilities and abuses" of the program. While it is too soon to gauge the impact the Inspector General's report will have on the L-1 visa program, Senator Chuck Grassley (R-IA) immediately issued a press release calling for action to close the "loopholes" in the L-1 program.[5] It is likely—at least in the short term—that consular officers and U.S. Citizenship and Immigration Services (USCIS) adjudicators will begin to closely scrutinize L-1 petitions. In fact, the officers may try to make a link between the statistics mentioned within the report and the conclusion of abuses within the report, thereby resulting in closer scrutiny of L-1 petitions from foreign nationals from India working in the information technology industry.

PROVING SPECIALIZED KNOWLEDGE

The L-1B intracompany transferee classification is for employees with specialized knowledge. 8 CFR §214.2(*l*)(1)(ii)(D) defines "specialized knowledge" as:

> special knowledge possessed by an individual of the petitioning organization's product, service, research, equipment, techniques, management, or other interests and its application in international markets, or an advanced level of knowledge or expertise in the organization's processes and procedures.[6]

Due to the imprecise definition of specialized knowledge, proving the specialized knowledge is often the most difficult hurdle in L-1B petitions. Petitioners of L-1Bs should consider the following issues in trying to prove specialized knowledge.

Be specific about the nature of the specialized knowledge: The DHS Inspector General found that L-1B petitions often "contain highly technical lan-

guage that is not readily comprehensible to an adjudicator."[7] While the report opined that the vague definition of "specialized knowledge" leads USCIS adjudicators to "believe they have little choice but to approve almost all petitions," the reverse may often be the case. If adjudicators cannot understand the specialized knowledge, they are more likely to issue requests for evidence (RFEs) and/or denials of L-1B petitions. Thus, it is imperative to be clear, concise, and specific about the type of specialized knowledge.

Recognize that the definition of specialized knowledge has two alternatives: *Either* special knowledge possessed by an individual of the petitioning organization's product, service, research, equipment, techniques, management, or other interests, and its application in international markets, *or* an advanced level of knowledge or expertise in the organization's processes and procedures. Explain how the beneficiary acquired the special knowledge or advanced level of knowledge and document it with proof, such as training certificates, performance evaluations, etc.

Distinguish the beneficiary's specialized knowledge from the knowledge in the general labor market: In a 1994, USCIS memorandum, the Acting Executive Associate Commissioner for Operations instructed officers to make a comparative assessment between the beneficiary's specialized knowledge and the knowledge in the general labor market. The memorandum states:

> The determination of whether an alien possesses specialized knowledge does not involve a test of the United States labor market. Whether or not there are United States workers available to perform the duties in the United States is not a relevant factor since the test of specialized knowledge involves only an examination of the knowledge possessed by the alien, not whether there are similarly employed United States workers. However, officers adjudicating petitions involving specialized knowledge must ensure that the knowledge possessed by the beneficiary is not general knowledge held commonly throughout the industry but that it is truly specialized.[8]

---

[5] See Press Release, Senator Chuck Grassley (R-IA) (Feb. 9, 2006), at *http://grassley.senate.gov*.

[6] 8 CFR §214.2(l)(1)(ii)(D).

[7] Inspector General report, *supra* note 4.

[8] INS Memorandum, James A. Puleo, Acting Executive Associate Commissioner, "Interpretation of Specialized Knowledge" (Mar. 9, 1994), *published on* AILA InfoNet at Doc. No. 01052171 (*posted* Mar. 21, 2001).

USCIS still follows this memorandum and has stated in recent requests for evidence that "this Service is required to make a comparative assessment ... between the claimed specialized knowledge employee and the general labor market." Therefore, petitioners must be prepared to explain how the beneficiary's knowledge is more unique or advanced than general knowledge in the industry. It is also helpful for the petitioner to describe how difficult it would be to impart the knowledge to another individual without significant economic inconvenience or business interruption.

Distinguish the beneficiary's specialized knowledge from other employees in the petitioner's workforce: When the L-1 visa program was created in 1970, the Congressional Record stated that the L-1 category was intended for "key personnel."[9] Twenty years later, Congress broadened the scope of the L-1 category through IMMACT90 and made the L-1B category more flexible for case-by-case basis. However, USCIS often cites the Congressional Record from the 1970, legislation and imposes a standard of "key personnel" that involves a comparison of the beneficiary's specialized knowledge with the knowledge of other employees in the petitioner's workforce. A recent L-1B denial states:

> The term "key personnel" denotes a position within the petitioning company that is "of crucial importance." Yet, in general, all employees can reasonably be considered "important" to a petitioner's enterprise (i.e., if an employee did not contribute to the overall economic success of an enterprise, there would be no rational economic reason to employ that person). Thus an employee of "crucial importance" or "key personnel" must rise above the level of petitioner's average employee. Accordingly, ... this Service is required to make a comparative assessment ... between the employee and the remainder of the petitioner's workforce.

In some cases, USCIS has issued RFEs asking for the names, positions, and case numbers for all other L-1B beneficiaries that the company has transferred to the United States. While there is nothing in the statute or regulations that state specialized knowledge can only be held by a relatively small number of people in the company, petitioners should be prepared to explain how the beneficiary's knowledge is unique or more advanced than the knowledge of the "average" employee.

Sometimes specialized knowledge is easier to prove to a U.S. consular officer through the blanket L procedures than to a USCIS adjudicator through the individual L procedures because the Department of State (DOS) is arguably more expansive in its interpretation of specialized knowledge.[10] However, it is important to note that for L-1B intracompany transferees to qualify under the blanket L procedures, the person must be a specialized knowledge "professional."[11] Therefore, an L-1B person applying through the blanket procedures needs proof of a college or university degree or the equivalent professional qualifications.

PLACING AN EMPLOYEE OFFSITE AT A CLIENT LOCATION

Section 412 of the Consolidated Appropriations Act of 2005 imposed restrictions on placing an L-1 nonimmigrant at a worksite other than the petitioner's or an affiliated company worksite. The statute provides:

> (F) An alien who will serve in capacity involving specialized knowledge with respect to an employer for purposes of section 101(a)(15)(L) and will be stationed primarily at the worksite of an employer other than the petitioning employer or its affiliate, subsidiary or parent shall not be eligible for classification under section 101(a)(15)(L) if—
>
> (i) the alien will be controlled and supervised principally by such unaffiliated employer; or
>
> (ii) the placement of the alien at the worksite of the unaffiliated employer is essentially an arrangement to provide labor for hire for the unaffiliated employer, rather than a placement in connection with the provision of product or service for which specialized knowledge specific to the petitioning employer is necessary.[12]

If the employee will be working at an offsite location, the petitioner must explain how the L-1B worker will be supervised and controlled. USCIS

---

[9] *See generally* H.R. Rep. No. 91-851, 1970 U.S.C.C.A.N. 2750.

[10] See 8 CFR §214.2(l)(4) for the criteria a company has to meet for blanket L approval.

[11] 8 CFR §214.2(l)(1)(ii)(E).

[12] Pub. L. No. 108-447 (H.R. 4818), *published on* AILA InfoNet at Doc. No. 04121811 (*posted* Dec 8, 2004).

and the U.S. consulates have recently asked for specific details such as the name, job title, credentials, and even the immigration status of the person "supervising" the L-1B worker at an offsite location.

PROVING EMPLOYMENT ABROAD

In addition to the requirement of specialized knowledge with a foreign-related business, the L-1B beneficiary must prove he or she was "employed for at least one continuous year within the three years preceding the admission to the United States." While this phrase seems simplistic, it actually denotes several requirements, including: (1) employment; (2) one continuous year; and (3) preceding admission to the United States.

The beneficiary can meet the criteria of "employment" regardless of whether or not the beneficiary received a salary from the foreign company. It is the power of control of the employee's activity, rather than the payment of a salary, that establishes an employer-employee relationship.[13] However, if the beneficiary was "outsourced" by another agency, then the requisite employer-employee relationship may not exist.[14] Also, the employment had to be full-time, rather than part-time.[15]

The beneficiary's employment abroad had to be "continuous." Brief trips to the United States do not break the continuity of the employment, but they do not count toward the one year of employment either.[16] For example, if the beneficiary spent one month in the United States, he or she would need to show 12 other months of continuous employment abroad since the one month in the United States does not count toward accrual of the requisite 12 months of foreign continuous employment.

The beneficiary's employment with the foreign-related business must have "preceded the time of his or her application for admission into the U.S."[17] Effectively, USCIS and its predecessor (legacy Immigration and Naturalization Services (INS)) have interpreted this to mean that the employment had to be

"abroad." However, in a February 2003, INS letter, Fujie O. Ohata clarified that U.S. territories such as American Samoa and Swains Islands are considered "abroad" and a beneficiary who worked for a foreign-related business in those areas would meet the requisite employment standard.[18]

OVERCOMING PROCESSING DELAYS AND THE FIVE-YEAR LIMIT

The L-1B category can pose challenges in timing at both ends of the spectrum: in applying for an L-1B initially and in reaching the five-year limit on L-1B status. The timing issues in applying for an individual L-1B petition can be reduced through premium processing of the petition.[19] While the regulations require USCIS to process L-1 petitions within 30 days of filing, there is no way to enforce the 30-day processing time.[20] Instead, the only method to ensure that USCIS processes the petition in an expedited manner would be to file a petition and to request that it be premium processed. In June 2001, legacy INS implemented a premium processing program that guarantees processing within 15 calendar days of filing for a premium fee of $1,000 per petition.[21]

Still, after USCIS approves the L-1B petition under the individual procedures, the beneficiary must appear at the consulate for a visa, except for Canadian citizens, who are exempt from visa requirements and can apply directly at a port of entry pursuant to the North American Free Trade Agreement. The wait time for an appointment at the consulate varies among the consulates but can take anywhere from a few weeks to a few months.[22] To reduce the waiting time for an interview, most consulates allow a beneficiary to schedule an appointment at the consulate while waiting for USCIS to approve the petition although the beneficiary needs to plan accordingly since he or

---

[13] *See Matter of Pozzoli*, 14 I&N Dec. 569 (R.C. 1974); *Matter of Tessel, Inc.*, 17 I&N Dec. 631(AAC 1981).

[14] Letter, Hernandez, Acting Branch Chief, Business and Trade Services (Feb 14, 2000), *reproduced in* 77 *Interpreter Releases* 272 (Mar. 6, 2000).

[15] 9 FAM 41.54 N11.1.

[16] 8 CFR §214.2(l)(1)(ii)(A).

[17] *Id.*

---

[18] INS Memorandum, Fujie O. Ohata, Associate Commissioner, Service Center Operations, "Interpretation of Specialized Knowledge" (Dec 20, 2002), *published on* AILA InfoNet at Doc. No. 03020548 (*posted* Feb 5, 2003).

[19] *Note*: L-1 petitions under the blanket process bypass USCIS and are processed directly at a U.S. consulate.

[20] *See* 8 CFR §214.2(l)(7)(i).

[21] "INS Regulation on Premium Processing Program," 66 Fed. Reg. 29682 (June 1, 2001), *published on* AILA InfoNet at Doc. No. 01060102 (*posted* June 1, 2001).

[22] The Department of State posts the waiting times for an interview at each U.S. consulate on its website at *www.travel.state.gov/visa/temp/wait/tempvisitors_wait.php*.

she will need the approval notice from USCIS before he or she appears at the consulate.

The five-year limit on L-1B status creates a hurdle. An L-1B specialized knowledge employee is limited to five years in the United States in L-1B status. Due to the long processing times for permanent residence petitions—particularly due to visa retrogression—an L-1B employee who wants to remain in the United States should start the permanent residence process within the first few years of entering the United States. If the employee is approaching the five-year limit and will not be able to file the I-485 application and obtain an employment authorization document before the expiration of the L-1B durational limit, the person might have to rely on the possibility of other strategies. The most common strategies include the following: (1) filing for a change of status to H-1B status, which provides the benefit of an additional year of employment authorization and also the possibility of extending beyond the six-year H-1B limit, based on the provisions of the American Competitiveness in the 21st Century Act;[23] (2) filing for change of status to L-1A status if the person has been working in a management position at least six months before reaching the five-year limit;[24] or (3) recapturing time in L-1 status for previous stays that were seasonal, intermittent, less than six months per year, or part-time when commuting from abroad.[25]

CONCLUSION

Since its inception in 1970, the L-1 visa program has been a useful method for multinational businesses to transfer employees to the United States, yet the overall number of L-1 visas is relatively low and has declined in recent years. The L-1B category has always had its share of hurdles that will only increase if the government imposes additional restrictions.

[23] American Competitiveness in the 21st Century Act, Pub. L. No. 106-313, 114 Stat. 1251 (AC21).

[24] 8 CFR §214.2(l)(15)(ii).

[25] 8 CFR §214.2(l)(12)(ii).

PRACTICE POINTERS FOR O AND P VISAS

by Kathleen L. Grzegorek, Laya R. Kushner, and Jenifer M. Brown[*]

O & P, SCENE 1, ACT 2—CUT!

This article contains a selection of practice pointers for O and P petitions and visa applications. Although not a comprehensive overview of the practice, common issues are discussed.

BUT, I DON'T THINK I'M EXTRAORDINARY . . .

Many practitioners often forget there are three distinct categories under the O-1 regulations at 8 CFR §214.2(o)(1)(i). The highest standard of "extraordinary ability" is for aliens in the sciences, education, athletics, and business; it is defined as "a level of expertise indicating that the person is one of the small percentage who has arisen to the very top of the field of endeavor."[1]

There are, however, two significantly lower standards for O-1 aliens in the arts and in motion pictures and television. For aliens in the arts, extraordinary ability means distinction, defined as "a high level of achievement in the arts evidenced by a degree of skill and recognition *substantially above that ordinarily encountered* to the extent that a person

described as *prominent is renowned, leading or well-known* in the field of arts."[2] Extraordinary ability with respect to aliens in motion pictures and television is defined as "a very high level of accomplishment in the motion picture or television industry evidenced by a degree of skill and recognition *significantly above that ordinarily encountered* to the extent that the person is recognized as *outstanding, notable or leading* in the motion picture or television field."[3]

An O-1 alien in the arts or motion pictures/television is, thus, not required to show that he or she is among the small percentage of individuals who have risen to the very top of their field. As a practical matter, showing extraordinary ability in the arts and motion pictures and television is not as daunting as it may seem. For example, a graphic designer or architect or VFX artist or producer may not have any individual press coverage or may not have won any awards, but may have had a critical role on high-profile projects that received significant media coverage or won awards. Even if not specifically mentioned in any of the press or winner of an award individually, if you can show the client had an important role and show the media coverage or awards the project received, you will likely be able to show "extraordinary ability" under the lower standards for individuals in the arts or motion pictures and television. In these cases, reference letters or testimonials from experts in the industry are extremely useful to confirm the alien's critical role and original contributions to the field.

BUT, SERIOUSLY, I TRULY AM EXTRAORDINARY!

On the other hand, many practitioners may have encountered aliens who insist they meet the criteria for an O-1. O-1 regulations require individuals to show that they have *sustained national* or *international* acclaim. Often, an alien has numerous student awards or press from student publications or press from local community newspapers, or numerous credits as an actor, but all as an extra or in un-

[*] **Kathleen Grzegorek** is a partner in the Los Angeles office of Stone & Grzegorek LLP. She is a certified specialist in immigration and nationality law by the State Bar of California Board of Legal Specialization. She has over 20 years of immigration experience serving a diverse client base with an emphasis on business immigration in the professional, high technology, academic, fine arts, scientific, and entertainment fields.

Laya Kushner is a third-generation attorney practicing immigration law, and a member of the bars of the State of North Carolina and New York, and the U.S. Supreme Court. Ms. Kushner has lectured to the immigration bar and various law schools. She received a B.A. from State University of New York at Binghamton (1991), and a J.D. from the University of Baltimore (1994).

Jenifer Brown practices immigration law with Ice Miller LLP in Indianapolis. She represents corporate clients in the hiring and retention of key professional and managerial employees, and in obtaining permanent residence based on extraordinary ability, outstanding research, and labor certification. Ms. Brown also advises on employment verification compliance and tax consequences of employing foreign nationals in the United States. She is a past chapter chair and frequent speaker on a variety of immigration topics.

[1] 8 CFR §214.2(o)(3)(ii).

[2] *Id.* (emphasis added).

[3] *Id.* (emphasis added).

credited roles. Be wary of these kinds of cases—does your documentation evidence *national* or *international* acclaim? If not, you may be the recipient of a lengthy request for evidence (RFE) or, even worse, a denial.

Similarly, someone who has been recognized for many years but has not worked for several years may not meet the standard for *sustained* national or international acclaim. The California Service Center is particularly stringent in its treatment of "has-been" actors or child actors who have not worked for a long time and whose press is dated.[4]

ONE-YEAR VS. THREE-YEAR EXTENSIONS FOR O-1 BENEFICIARIES

An initial O-1 petition (and O-2 petition on behalf of any essential beneficiaries) may be approved for a period of time to accomplish the activity, not to exceed three years.[5] Moreover, the extension period for an O-1 beneficiary (and any essential O-2 beneficiaries) are authorized in increments of up to one year to *continue or complete the same event or activity* for which he or she was admitted.[6] Therefore, it is possible to request a new period of three years on an I-129 petition requesting an Extension of Stay in two situations: (1) The I-129 O-1 Extension Petition is being filed by a new petitioner; *or* (2) the I-129 O-1 Extension Petition is being filed by the same petitioner for a *new event or activity*.[7] The first situation is self-explanatory, but it is recommended that your cover letter highlight that this is a new petitioner, and include a copy of the ISD Teleconference of October 3, 2002, Minutes from AILA.[8] The second situation happens more often. An "event" is defined as an activity such as, but not limited to, a scientific project, conference, convention, lecture series, tour, exhibit, business project, academic year or engagement, including short vacations, promotional appearances, and stopovers that are incidental or related to the event. A group of related activities or the alien's contract may also be considered to be an event.[9] The nature of arts and entertainment is such that itineraries tend to be fluid, which is supported by U.S. Citizenship and Immigration Services (USCIS) regulations that permit petitioners of O (and P) petitions to add performances or engagements during the validity period of the petition without filing an amended petition, provided the additional performances or engagements require an alien of O-1 caliber.[10] Therefore, when submitting an I-129 O-1 petition (and any accompanying O-2 petitions) that requests either an extension of stay or consular notification, it is important to note in both the attorney cover letter and supporting itinerary that the activities listed are new and separate events from those contemplated in the original I-129 O-1 petition and are *not* to continue or complete what was specified in the initial petition. To further support the request for a three-year extension, you may submit the alien's new contract, or a new list of dates for the tour, exhibit, or business project. Again, it is helpful to include a copy of ISD Teleconference of October 3, 2002, Minutes.[11]

SO, WHEN DO I FILE?

Like nearly all nonimmigrant petitions, O and P filings can be made no earlier than six months before the requested start date.[12] For many in the sports and entertainment industries particularly, the applicant is not identified until a few months or even weeks before the season or event. That is why O and P filings are routinely filed via premium processing to secure adjudication of the petition within two weeks; normal processing times fluctuate between one to four months.

In response to delays in processing times for O and P petitions, USCIS did publish a proposed rule in April 2005 that would have enabled petitioners to file up to one year before the anticipated start date. However, the proposed rule also would have required filings to be made no earlier than six months before the event. An exception was provided for an emergency need. Perhaps because of this expansive exception and the option of premium processing for any I-129 petition, the proposed rule change appears to have been abandoned.

---

[4] *See also* "Critical Analysis of the Elements that Make Up E11 Stature," 78 *Interpreter Releases* 895 (May 25, 2001).

[5] 8 CFR §214.2(o)(6)(iii).

[6] 8 CFR §214.2(o)(12)(ii).

[7] "ISD Teleconference of 10/3/02," *published on* AILA InfoNet at Doc. No. 02110470 (*posted* Nov. 4, 2002) (hereinafter ISD Teleconference).

[8] *Id.*

---

[9] 8 CFR §214.2(o)(3)(ii).

[10] 8 CFR §214.2(o)(2)(iv)(D).

[11] ISD Teleconference, *supra* note 7.

[12] 8 CFR §214.2(o)(2)(i), §214.2(p)(2)(i).

DEFINING THE FIELD: EXTRAORDINARY COMPARED TO WHOM?

One additional factor to consider in preparing an O petition is the scope of the field and how the applicant fits within it. Can the applicant better establish extraordinary ability if compared against a large pool of other professionals within the industry or against a smaller, more defined group? Where the applicant is part of a small, distinguished group of professionals within a larger field, it may be easier to establish that he or she is extraordinary within a broader class of professionals as opposed to the smaller handful of the elite who have also risen to the top. By virtue of having reached the top of the field, he or she may easily qualify as having extraordinary ability, but USCIS could ask whether the applicant is extraordinary compared to the narrower class of elite professionals. If that can be established, there should be no issue, but if the applicant does not stand out within the smaller class, you might consider broadening the field of comparison.

By way of example, if the applicant plays in the position of center in the National Basketball Association (NBA), it may be easier to document that he is extraordinary among all professional athletes as opposed to a smaller group of NBA centers. Certainly, if his statistics show that he is the best center in the NBA, it is certainly worthwhile to establish this fact. However, if he is at best average among NBA centers but still has the distinction of making it to the NBA and is thereby extraordinary among players and athletes generally, it would be worthwhile to establish his place within the broader field. One way to accomplish this is by limiting references to a specific position and instead refer to him as a player generally. Innocent but frequent references to him as a center could result in USCIS determining that he is not extraordinary among centers even if you have sufficiently established his distinction among basketball players or athletes generally worldwide.[13]

ESSENTIAL SUPPORT PERSONNEL: CAN I BRING MY PERSONAL ASSISTANT OR BUSINESS MANAGER?

O-2 regulations were specifically designed to accommodate essential support personnel in the arts, athletics, and entertainment industries, but there are two distinct categories for O-2 aliens at 8 CFR §§214.2(o)(4)(ii)(A) and (B). First, aliens accompanying an O-1 artist or athlete of extraordinary ability must be coming to the United States to "assist in the performance of an O-1 alien" and must be "*an integral part of the actual performance* and have critical skills and experience with the O-1 alien which are not of a general nature and which are not possessed by a U.S. worker."[14] Therefore, stylists, nutritionists, choreographers, dancers, roadies and crew members, producers, back-up singers, managers, and chefs can all apply for O-2s if they can show they are an integral part of the O-1 alien's performance.

O-1 aliens in the motion pictures and television must demonstrate

skills and experience with the O-1 alien which are not of a general nature and which are critical based on a *pre-existing longstanding working relationship or, with respect to the specific production*, because significant production (including pre-production and post-production work) will take place both inside and outside the United States and the continuing participation of the alien is essential to the successful completion of the production.[15]

Therefore, an O-1 director can bring in any of his or her crew, including his or her first or second unit assistant director or production manager or production assistant; or an O-1 author or producer can bring in his or her long-time personal assistant; or a technical director can bring in a crew of digital artists. With motion pictures and television, even though a director may not have a long-standing relationship with the O-2 alien, because production or post-production on a feature film or television series is scheduled both within and outside the United States, the O-2 is considered essential for stylistic and technical continuity of the production.

Petitions for O-2 aliens must be filed separately (with their own I-129 petitions and government filing fees) and advisory opinions are separate. With H-1B visas unavailable due to the H-1B cap, practitioners may want to consider O-2 petitions for certain professions, such as digital artists, graphic designers, and architects, where "teams" of talent can be brought in under the O-2 classification. While O-

---

[13] R. Deasy & P. Yanni, "Arrows in Your Quiver: Arm Yourself to Win Approvals," *Immigration Options for Academics and Researchers* 281 (AILA 2005).

[14] 8 CFR §214.2(o)(4)(ii)(A).

[15] 8 CFR §214.2(o)(4)(ii)(B).

2 aliens do not have to show individual extraordinary ability, they must be "attached" to an O-1 alien of extraordinary ability and authorized only to work with the O-1 alien. There is no provision for essential support personnel to accompany O-1 aliens in the sciences, business, or education.

Similarly, P-1 essential support personnel can be brought into the United States based on a support relationship with an individual P-1 athlete, athletic team, or entertainment group.[16] Common examples of P-1 essential support personnel are roadies, crewmembers, business managers, athletic trainers, coaches, producers, dancers, back-up singers, stylists, nutritionists, chiropractors, and musicians. Petitions for P-1 essential support personnel must also be filed with their own separate petitions and the advisory opinions will be separate.

CONSULAR PROCESSING OF GROUPS

If there are multiple beneficiaries listed on an O-2 or any P petition, it may be necessary to notify more than one American consul or port of entry. Although you may concurrently file I-824 Applications with the I-129 O-2 or P petition to request multiple consular notification, you may request that notification on the I-129 petition itself. On Page 2, Part 4, Section 1, you may insert "MULTIPLE CONSULAR OFFICE NOTIFICATION REQUESTED," and then list those consulates you wish to have notified. It is suggested that you highlight this on the I-129 petition. In the attorney cover letter, you also must list which beneficiaries will be applying at which American consulates. The authors recommend that you staple a separate list of the American consulates, stating which beneficiaries will be applying at which consulate, to page 2 of the I-129. Upon approval, USCIS should issue multiple I-797 Approval Notices, equal to the number of American consulates you request to be notified, so that the beneficiaries may each present an original I-797 Approval Notice to their consulate.

DUAL INTENT AND FOREIGN RESIDENCE

The issue of dual intent and O and P applications is de facto, not actual. Although not explicitly exempt from the concept of dual intent, as in the H and L categories, an alien applying for O-1 nonimmigrant classification, such as those in the H and L categories,

is not required to maintain a foreign residence.[17] Most other nonimmigrant visa classifications in the O and P category, such as O-2 and P, specifically state that the alien "must have a residence in a foreign country which he has no intention of abandoning." There is a requirement that the alien intend to remain in the United States only temporarily.[18]

Additionally, an O-1 visa cannot be denied solely on the basis of evidence of immigrant intent. The approval of a labor certification or the filing of a preference petition for an alien may not be a basis for denying an O-1 petition, extension, or admission. An alien may legitimately come to the United States temporarily as an O-1 nonimmigrant and depart voluntarily at the end of his or her authorized stay and, at the same time, lawfully seek to become a permanent resident of the United States.[19] However, this exemption does not apply to O-2 and O-3 applicants.

As with the O-1, a P visa cannot be denied solely because a labor certification or a preference petition has been filed, although again this provision does not apply to essential support personnel.[20]

Since O-1 and P aliens may have a dual intent and an O-1 is not required to maintain a foreign residence, what about the O-2 and O-3 applicant? An O-2 alien must have a residence in a foreign country that he or she has no intention of abandoning.[21] The criteria for residence abroad and temporariness of stay that pertain to O-1 and O-2 nonimmigrants also apply to their O-3 dependents.[22] Thus, an O-3 attached to an O-1 need not maintain a residence abroad while the O-3 dependent of an O-2 must do so.

PACKAGING EXHIBITS

Among best practices in this area are organizing exhibits by the 8 CFR §214.2(o)(3) evidentiary criteria for the individual's field, and making a list or table of the exhibits. Some practitioners write detailed explanations of each exhibit on the list; others simply provide a brief description.

---

[16] 8 CFR §214.2(p)(4)(iv).

[17] INA §101(a)(15)(O).

[18] *Kurzban's Immigration Law Sourcebook* 587 (10th ed. 2006), www.ailapubs.org, for more information and table of contents.

[19] 8 CFR §214.2(o)(13); 9 *Foreign Affairs Manual* (FAM) 41.55 N.8.2.

[20] 8 CFR §214.2(p)(15); 9 FAM 41.56 N.9.2.

[21] INA §101(a)(15)(O)(ii)(IV).

[22] 9 FAM 41.55 N.5.

The exhibits should have tabbed markers so the adjudicator can easily flip to the specific exhibit while reading the cover letter or the list of exhibits. Use bottom tabs; side tabs are usually discarded in the mailroom. Adjudicators also report that highlighting salient points in the exhibit is helpful.

Copies may be submitted: "A legible photocopy of a document in support of the petition may be submitted in lieu of the original."[23] USCIS may request originals at a later date.[24] Most practitioners prefer to keep the originals in case an extension or I-140 petition is later filed, to avoid having to copy a copy.

Exhibits can be submitted as black and white copies or color copies. If your beneficiary practices in a field that has visual impact, color copies can make a stronger case. With any copies, make sure they are easy to read and are not blurry.

Having a copy of the actual exhibit is preferable than just mentioning its existence. For example, a copy of the actual magazine cover on which the alien appeared is much more persuasive than simply stating that the beneficiary appeared on the cover.

The authors recommend editing exhibits for visual presentation and content. If you feel that an exhibit would not get a G or PG rating and might offend or titillate, seriously consider omitting it or edit it so that it is less likely to offend an adjudicator, who cannot help but bring his or her own biases as he or she assess the applications.

AGENTS AS PETITIONERS

Unlike H-1B and L-1 petitions, O-1 and O-2 petitions and all P petitions (including accompanying P-1S, P-2S, or P-3S for essential support personnel) do *not* require that the petitioner be the actual employer of the alien. Instead, a U.S. agent is permitted to file a petition for workers who are traditionally self-employed, such as artists and entertainers.[25] The regulation provides that the agent/petitioner may be: (1) the actual employer of the beneficiary; (2) the representative of both employer and beneficiary; or (3) a person or entity authorized by the employer to act for the employer as its agent.[26] Therefore, in the context of I-129 O and P petitions, the petitioner is *not* required to be the actual employer.

Since 1997, foreign employers may *not* be the petitioner for immigration purposes; a U.S. entity with a U.S. Tax Identification Number must act as petitioner for all I-129 petitions filed. The purpose of this is to prevent abuses of INA §274A.[27] The legislative history of the "Agents as Petitioners" section states that an "agent can be someone authorized to represent and act for another, to transact business for another, or manage another's affairs."[28] Therefore, almost any U.S. entity with a U.S. Tax Identification Number (Federal Employer Identification Number or Social Security number) may act as an agent for an O or P petition, provided the conditions listed in 8 CFR §§214.2(o)(2)(iv)(E) and 214.2(p)(2)(iv)(E) are met. The best way to satisfy the adjudicating immigration officer is to include an agency agreement between the petitioner and the beneficiary or beneficiaries outlining the conditions and any other terms the parties may desire.

---

[23] 8 CFR §214.2(o)(2)(iii)(C).

[24] *Id.*

[25] 8 CFR §214.2(o)(2)(iv)(E), §214.2(p)(2)(iv)(E).

[26] *Id.*

[27] 62 Fed. Reg. 18508 (Apr. 16, 1997).

[28] *Id.*

Consultation Organizations for Arts-Related Petitions

General Notes:

- Contact unions in advance to confirm whether new fees imposed/old ones changed.

- All consultation organizations have 15 days in which to respond. Thereafter, USCIS "must" adjudicate petition based on existing record, so make record of consult requests and, if not received in time, submit to USCIS with proof of efforts.

- Contact unions that charge fees for possible fee waivers if Petitioner is a collective bargaining signatory or Beneficiary is a member of target union.

- Issue for all consultation sources is whether Beneficiary meets applicable O/P standard, *not* whether U.S. worker available, prevailing wage considerations, or other policy/political matters. Consultation not providing facts supporting conclusion that Beneficiary fails to meet applicable standard is a "no objection" letter by definition.

- Union "jurisdictions" can overlap for consultation purposes. If uncertain, contact union directly. There may be activities over which no union asserts "jurisdiction," *e.g.*, fight masters, choreologists, and dramaturges. If so, Petitioner should exhaust possibilities, explain effort to USCIS, and request a consultation waiver.

- Consultation requirement waived for "management" positions over which unions by definition cannot assert "jurisdiction."

- 8 CFR §214.2(o)(5)(i)(F) requires USCIS to obtain union consultation in O-1 cases *if* petition includes non-labor consultation. As service centers inconsistent/slow to do so, avoid doing this *unless* Petitioner insists USCIS obtain the labor consult. Opera petitioners for historical reasons rely on this process more frequently.

****

For concert and solo singers, dancers, choreographers, stage and assistant stage managers, stage and assistant stage directors, and narrators in concert, recital, oratorio, opera, and dance:

The American Guild of Musical Artists (AGMA)
1430 Broadway, 14th Floor
New York, NY 10018
Tel: (212) 265-3687
Fax: (212) 262-9088
Contact: Thomas Jamerson, x.3014, or Gretchen Lees
Alan Gordon, Executive Director/General Counsel (*agmany@aol.com*)
$250 *per petition*
In general, look first to AGMA for consults involving combination of dance, music, and/or song. AGMA will consult on any matter on which AGVA will consult. AGMA unpredictable on secondary and support roles as it takes position these should be reserved for U.S. workers.

For all instrumental musicians, conductors, and music librarians:

The American Federation of Musicians (AFM)
1501 Broadway, #600
New York, NY 10036
Tel: (212) 869-1330
Fax: (212) 764-6134
Contacts: Os: Thomas F. Lee, x.218 or Theresa Naglieri, x.212
Ps: Michael Manley, x.231; Elizabeth Blake, x.259; Stanton Davis, x.230
$200.00 *per petition (payable to "AFM immigration processing") and* **$250.00** *for* <u>**expedites**</u>
P-1/P-3 questionnaire required (contact AFM)

For other performers and stage managers in live format presentations:

Actors Equity Association (AE)
165 West 46th Street
New York, NY 10036
Tel: (212) 869-8530
Fax: (212) 719-9815
Contact: Marc Kochanski, x.347
$250 *per petition*
For P-3 petitions, two most important items are cover letter and I-129 form. Most petitions addressed with these alone. AE almost always objects to English- and French-language productions outside P-2 context, and any production not under an AE contract.

For other stage directors and choreographers in live format presentations:

Society of Stage Directors and Choreographers (SSDC)
1501 Broadway, Suite 1701
New York, NY 10036
Tel: (212) 391-1070
Fax: (212) 302-6195
Contact: Will Parker, x.236
$250 *per petition*
Typical turnaround—three weeks

For performers in nightclubs, burlesque, and circuses:

American Guild of Variety Artists (AGVA),
Attn: Legal Dept.
363 Seventh Avenue, 17th Floor
New York, NY 10001
Tel: (212) 675-1003
Contact: Wade Alexander (*agvany@aol.com*)
$250 *per petition*
AGVA eccentric on consultation matters, and refuses all phone calls and faxes. It also refuses to use FedEx because it is "anti-union."

For press agents/publicists and managers (general, company, tour):

Association of Theatrical Press Agents and Managers (ATPAM)
1560 Broadway, Suite 700
New York, NY 10036
Tel: (212) 719-3666
Fax: (212) 302-1585
Contact: Tito Sanchez (*tsanchez@atpam.com*)
$250 *per petition*
ATPAM covers tour *managers, not managers otherwise exempt from consultation requirements because they are management, not labor. Same-day service promised.*

For performers in the film and electronic media (audio and visual) (one of the following):

For Film/Movies:

Screen Actors Guild (SAG)
360 Madison Avenue, 12th Floor
New York, NY 10017
Tel: (212) 827-1598 or (212) 944-1030 (main)
Fax: (212) 827-1580

Contact: Noris Boccanfuso
$250 *per petition*

Screen Actors Guild (SAG)
5757 Wilshire Blvd.
Los Angeles, CA 90036
Tel: (323) 549-6019 or (323) 954-1600 (main)
Fax: (323) 549-6520
Contact: Sally Tich
$250 *per petition*
SAG prefers that petitions to be filed with Vermont go to its NY office, petitions to be filed with California to its CA office. Petitions to be filed with Texas or Nebraska may go to either office.

For Tape/Video/TV:

American Federation of Television and Radio Artists (AFTRA)
260 Madison Avenue
New York, NY 10016
Tel: (212) 532-0800
Fax: (212) 532-2242
Contact: Donna Mirande
O-1/P-1 questionnaire required (contact AFTRA)

American Federation of Television and Radio Artists (AFTRA)
5757 Wilshire Blvd., Suite 900
Los Angeles, CA 90036
Tel: (323) 634-8100 x.116
Fax: (323) 634-8246
Contact: David Besbris
No questionnaire required

For all directors of photography (cinematographers), technical and craft personnel:

Int'l Alliance of Theatrical Stage Employees & Moving Picture Machine Operators (IATSE)
1430 Broadway, 20th Floor
New York, NY 10018
Tel: (212) 730-1770
Fax: (212) 730-7809 (dir.) or (212) 921-7699 (main)
Contact: Colleen Paul / Matthew Loeb
$250.00 per petition or $350 per petition for <u>expedites</u> (24–48 hrs) **(payable to IATSE)**

International Brotherhood of Electrical Workers (IBEW) (non-film only)
1125 15th Street, NW, Room 1113
Washington, D.C. 20005
Tel: (202) 728-6026
Fax: (202) 728-6295
Contact: Peter Potenza / Wanda Prue
Edwin Hill, International President
No longer participating due to national security concerns!

United Scenic Artists
29 W. 38th Street, 15th Floor
New York, NY 10018
Tel: (212) 581-0300
Fax: (212) 977-2011
Contact: Michael McBride
Members: free; Theater, a collective bargaining signatory: $100; Person/theater is neither: $200.

For motion picture and television producers:

Producers Guild of America
8530 Wilshire Boulevard, #450
Beverly Hills, CA 90211
Tel: (310) 358-9020 x.102
Fax: (310) 358-9520
Contact: Grant Stoner/Vance Van Petten, Executive Director
If production company is a member: free; non-members (5–7 days): $150; non-member expedites (2–3 days): $300

Association of Independent Commercial Producers
3 West 18th Street, 5th Floor
New York, NY 10010
Tel: (212) 929-3000
Fax: (212) 929-3359
Contact: Matt Miller, President
If production company is a member: free; non-members: no consultation service

For motion picture and television directors:

Directors Guild of America (West) (DGA)
7920 Sunset Blvd.
Los Angeles, CA 90046
Tel: (310) 289-2000
Fax: (310) 289-2024
Contact: Louis Zogaib

Directors Guild of America (East) (DGA)
110 West 57th Street, 2nd Floor
New York, NY 10019
Tel: (212) 581-0370
Fax: (212) 581-1441
Contact: Fred Kastner

For writers in film, television, and news (audio and visual):

Productions East of the Mississippi:

Writers Guild of America-East
555 West 57th Street, Suite 1230
New York, NY 10019
Tel: (212) 767-7800
Fax: (212) 582-1909
Contact: James H. Kaye, Assistant Executive Director

Productions West of the Mississippi:

Writers Guild of America-West
7000 West 3rd Street
Los Angeles, CA 90048
Tel: (800) 548-4532
Fax: (323) 782-4800
Contact: Jane Nefeldt

For management consultations for aliens of extraordinary achievement/support personnel:

Alliance of Motion Picture and TV Producers (AMPTP)
15503 Ventura Blvd.
Encino, CA 91436
Tel: (818) 995-3600
Fax: (818) 382-1793
Contact: Sue McDermott Mercer, Counsel
(Vanessa Pelech, Executive Asst. to Sue McDermott Mercer)
Note: All I-129 petitions and supporting letters must be current, dated, and signed and MUST BE ON COMPANY LETTERHEAD; prefers an O-1 of only 20 pages.

For management consultations for opera-related petitions:

Opera America
330 7th Avenue
16th Floor
New York, NY 10001
Tel: (212) 796-8620
Fax: (212) 796-8631
Contact: Trish Ferrell Wileman
Consultations free to members; non-members: $250

For management consultations for symphony orchestras and classical musicians:

American Symphony Orchestra League
910 17th Street, NW
Suite 800
Washington, D.C. 20006
Tel: (202) 776-0215
Fax: (202) 776-0224

For management consultations for equestrian sports, including horse trainers and riders:

United States Equestrian Federation
4047 Iron Works Parkway
Lexington, Kentucky 40511
Tel: (859) 225-6930 or (859) 258-2472 (main)
Fax: (859) 231-6662
Contact: Julie Goodman, General Counsel

WORKSTUDY: EMPLOYMENT OPTIONS FOR STUDENTS WITH F, J, OR M VISAS

*by Elizabeth S. Goss, Craig Peterson, and Scott D. Pollock**

Immigration practitioners frequently encounter foreign students who have completed a program of study in the United States but desire to remain in the country to work, and they are typically well acquainted with employment options for such students. They are often less familiar, however, with work opportunities available to students during their programs of study.

---

* **Elizabeth Goss** specializes in the representation of physicians, researchers, trainees, and students in higher education and health care, securing their temporary and permanent visas. In addition, she has extensive experience representing multinational corporations and entrepreneurial ventures in a wide array of immigration matters. Ms. Goss was the legal consultant to Tufts University and also served as the university's Foreign Student and Scholar Advisor and director of the International Office for the Health Sciences Campus and Affiliated Hospitals. Ms. Goss is actively involved in the field of human rights, having worked with the prosecutor's office of the International Criminal Tribunal in Rwanda. She is also an active author and presenter for the Association of International Educators (NAFSA). Ms. Goss is a graduate of the New England School of Law and Wheaton College. She is admitted to practice in the state bars of Massachusetts and New York and the Court of International Trade.

Craig Peterson, a senior attorney at Dorsey & Whitney LLP in Minneapolis focuses on business-related immigration matters, including both immigrant and nonimmigrant filings. While his work encompasses all types of organizations, he has particularly deep experience in immigration matters connected with academic research institutions, colleges, and universities. Mr. Peterson worked for a major academic research institution for 10 years, handling a full range of student, exchange visitor, and employment-based immigration matters. He is an active member of the Association of International Educators, working with immigration policy and practice matters on behalf of the association and its member institutions.

Scott Pollock is the founder of Scott D. Pollock & Associates, P.C., in Chicago. He received his J.D. *cum laude* in 1985 from Brooklyn Law School. He is a frequent lecturer and author on U.S. immigration law. His previous contributions to the AILA *Immigration & Nationality Handbook* include updates on F-1 students and H-1B temporary workers, and "Getting the Facts on Your Client: Freedom of Information Act and Criminal Records Searches." He has served as a past chair of AILA's Chicago Chapter, on numerous local committees, as past chair of AILA's Consumer Protection/Authorized Representation Task Force, and on the Nebraska Service Center Liaison Committee. His clients include several colleges and universities.

Becoming familiar with these job opportunities is beneficial to practitioners in several situations, such as determining whether a student has engaged in unauthorized employment or in advising a student or employer about the full range of options available and how to facilitate employment. And practitioners who advise officials at educational institutions must be fully versed on student employment programs.

This article focuses on employment options connected with the F, J, and M visas, which are the visas available to foreign students studying in the United States. It also addresses important related concerns that international students and Designated School Officials (DSOs) of U.S. Citizenship and Immigration Services (USCIS) have with applications for Social Security numbers.

F-1 STUDENT VISAS

F-1 Student Visa Eligibility for Admission

The F-1 student visa is issued to those in a full-time course of study at a college, university, seminary, conservatory, academic high school, or elementary school language-training program.[1] Canadian and Mexican citizens also may be admitted as F-3 "border commuter students."[2] All F-status students must maintain a residence in a foreign country that they have no intention of abandoning, and present documentary evidence of financial support for the duration of the academic program. F-2 visas are available to the spouse and minor children of an F-1 visa holder.[3] Like other international student nonimmigrant categories, F-1 and F-2 visa holders are subject to the reporting and documentation requirements of the Student and Exchange Visitor Information System (SEVIS).[4]

---

[1] Immigration and Nationality Act of 1952, Pub. L. No. 82-414, §101(a)(15)(F), 66 Stat. 163 (codified as amended at 8 USC §§1101 *et seq.*) (INA); *see also* 8 CFR §§214.2(f)(1)(i), 214.2(f)(6).

[2] 8 CFR §§214.2(f)(18)(iv), 214.2(f)(3); INA §101(a)(15)(F)(ii).

[3] INA §101(a)(15)(F); 8 CFR §214.2(f)(3).

[4] 8 CFR §§214.2(f)(1)(i)(A)(i)–(iii); 214.2(f)(3).

The Student and Exchange Visitor Information System

SEVIS is the USCIS web-based system for maintaining information on all students and exchange visitors in the United States. If approved by USCIS for an F-1 program designation, an academic institution will be provided through the DSO a program number and access to the SEVIS system. Once a student is accepted and meets the requirements for admission, the DSO will create a SEVIS record and issue SEVIS Form I-20.[5] Use of the SEVIS system has been mandatory for document issuance and record maintenance since 2003.[6]

Types of Employment on the F-1 Visa

Like all other nonimmigrant visa categories, the F-1 category has limitations on employment. Failure to abide by these limitations constitutes failure to maintain status.[7] Students seeking temporary employment must be specifically authorized under one of the five categories of employment available to them: on-campus employment; severe economic hardship; special student relief programs; certain employment by international organizations; and practical training (curricular and optional).[8] All of the categories require that the student be currently maintaining valid F-1 status, and each category of work authorization has specific eligibility requirements, as detailed below.[9] (F-2 spouses and children may not accept employment under any circumstances.[10]) Border commuter students are limited to employment only in the practical training category (curricular or optional), and students attending English-language programs are ineligible for any type of work authorization.[11]

On-Campus Employment

Upon obtaining F-1 status, a student is immediately eligible to work on-campus for a maximum of 20 hours per week during his or her pursuit of a full course of study up to the date of graduation, including a 30-day period prior to beginning a new program and vacation periods.[12] On-campus employment may be full-time during vacation periods, between academic semesters, and during the period of transition to the next academic level at the same institution. Students may engage in on-campus employment only at the school having jurisdiction over their SEVIS records. A transferring student may not engage in on-campus employment for his or her new institution until the transfer has been completed.[13]

A student may seek employment at the school, including teaching and research assistant positions and jobs in the school library or administrative offices. A student may also seek employment with on-location commercial firms that provide services for students on campus, including the bookstore and food services companies. A student may not seek employment with, for example, a construction company that is building a new health center on campus. The principle here is that the work is not directly related to servicing students.[14] F-1 post-graduate students may be eligible to work at off-campus sites affiliated with the school's established curriculum as defined by each institution, or with contractually funded research projects that are an integral part of the student's education program.[15] This provision was specifically enacted to allow payment to graduate students conducting research under professors who have contract-based research grants not payable through the education institutions.[16]

An F-1 student is not required to obtain formal authorization from a DSO or USCIS for on-campus employment; such authorization is considered "incident to status," and these students need only present a valid Form I-20 to a prospective employer.[17] Note that most institutions require that a student be cleared by a DSO prior to commencing employment.

---

[5] INA §101(a)(15)(F)(ii); 8 CFR §214.2(f)(3).

[6] 8 CFR §214.2(f)(1)(iii).

[7] 8 CFR §214.1(e).

[8] 8 CFR §§214.2(f)(9)(i)–(iii), 214.2(f)(10).

[9] 8 CFR §214.2(m)(14)(i).

[10] 8 CFR §214.2(f)(15)(i).

[11] 8 CFR §§214.2(f)(18)(iv), 214.2(f)(10).

[12] 8 CFR §214.2(f)(9)(i).

[13] 8 CFR §214.2(f)(9)(i).

[14] 8 CFR §214.2(f)(9)(i) and *NAFSA Advisor's Manual* (2005 release) §3.18.3.1.2. There is considerable disagreement as to whether on-campus businesses leasing space and providing services to students, such as restaurant chains or office-supply chains, are to be considered on-location commercial firms permitting F-1 students to work for those entities via on-campus employment authorization. DSOs, in general, refer to the school's legal counsel for a determination on a case-by-case basis.

[15] 8 CFR §214.2(f)(9)(i).

[16] 8 CFR §214.2(f)(9)(i) and 56 Fed Reg. 55608–10 (Oct. 29, 1991) "Supplementary Information."

[17] 8 CFR §214.2(f)(9)(i).

Off-Campus Employment

During the course of his or her studies, a student may seek authorization for off-campus employment under three circumstances: severe and unforeseen economic necessity, internship with an international organization, or employment-based on the Special Student Relief program. These forms of employment must be recommended by the DSO in SEVIS and adjudicated and approved by USCIS issuance of an employment authorization document (EAD).[18] A student may not begin employment until the card is issued and received by the student.[19]

Severe Economic Hardship

To qualify under this circumstance for off-campus employment, a student must have been in F-1 status for at least one full academic year and show that the employment is necessary due to severe economic hardship that arose after obtaining F-1 status and was caused by circumstances beyond his or her control.[20] Examples of hardship include "loss of financial aid, substantial fluctuation in the valuation of currency or exchange rate, inordinate increases in tuition and/or living costs, unexpected changes in the financial condition of the student's source of support, medical bills or other substantial and unexpected expenses."[21]

An F-1 student qualifying for such employment is allowed to work up to 20 hours per week while school is in session and full-time during vacation periods. The student may work in any type of job, related or unrelated to their field of study, and an offer of employment is not necessary for eligibility. Finally, qualification under this category does not interfere with or limit any other type of employment such as on-campus employment or practical training that the student may qualify for.[22] Termination of the work authorization occurs when the student transfers from one institution to another or when the need for employment ceases. However, employment authorization is allowed to continue when transition from one educational level to another occurs at the same institution.[23] Employment can be granted in one-year intervals when a student applies directly to USCIS

for an EAD, and employment may not commence until that EAD has been received.[24]

A student must apply for the EAD via Form I-765 with the proper filing fee and two passport-style photos, and submit accompanying documentation showing the circumstances causing the economic need, including a written statement and proof of change in circumstances such as proof of currency devaluation in the student's home country. The statement also must explain why other employment options (on-campus work authorization) are not sufficient. Generally, a simple statement is enough to satisfy this requirement. The DSO must update the student's record in SEVIS to verify eligibility for the benefit, recommend that USCIS approve the student for employment based on severe economic hardship, and print SEVIS Form I-20 with the recommendations for the student to submit with the I-765.[25]

Once the EAD is issued, a student may work up to 20 hours per week while school is in session and full-time during vacations.

Employment with an International Organization

An F-1 student may work for a recognized international organization, as defined by the International Organization Immunities Act.[26] A student is eligible for this type of employment as soon as he or she obtains F-1 student status. Work authorization is available only to the student maintaining a full course of study up to the time of graduation. Full-time employment may be authorized, and the job does not need to be related to the student's particular field of study.[27] However, a written offer of employment from a qualifying institution is required. Use of this type of employment authorization does not interfere with or limit any other type of employment, such as on-campus employment or practical training that the student may qualify for.[28] Employment can be granted in one-year intervals when a student applies directly to USCIS for an EAD, and employment may not commence until that EAD has been received.[29]

---

[18] 8 CFR §214.2(f)(9)(ii)(F)(2).

[19] 8 CFR §214.2(f)(9)(ii).

[20] 8 CFR §214.2(f)(9)(ii)(A), (C).

[21] 8 CFR §214.2(f)(9)(ii)(C).

[22] 8 CFR §214.2(f)(9)(ii)(A).

[23] Operating Instructions (OI) 214.2(f)(14)(v).

[24] 8 CFR §214.2(f)(9)(ii)(F)(2).

[25] 8 CFR §214.2(f)(9)(ii)(D).

[26] 79 Pub. L. No. 291, 59 Stat. 669, Dec. 29, 1945).

[27] 8 CFR §214.2(f)(9)(iii).

[28] 8 CFR §214.2(f)(9)(ii)(A).

[29] 8 CFR §214.2(f)(9)(ii)(F)(2).

The DSO must update the student's record in SEVIS to verify eligibility for the benefit, recommend that USCIS approve the student for employment, and print SEVIS Form I-20 with the recommendations for the student to submit with the I-765.[30] A student must apply for the EAD via Form I-765 with the proper filing fee and two passport-style photos, photocopies of Form I-94 and Form I-20 with required recommendations, and a written offer of employment from an international organization.

Special Student Relief Program

Under this program, USCIS designates certain countries experiencing crises in order to allow assistance to those students whose means of financial support came from where the crisis caused a reduction in student support and led to severe economic hardship. (Note: there is no requirement that a student be a citizen of the designated country.) Currently, USCIS has designated five countries for this benefit: Indonesia, South Korea, Thailand, Malaysia, and the Philippines.[31] If he or she comes from one of the listed countries, the student must have obtained and maintained F-1 status since June 10, 1998, and show that the crisis has led to the loss of financial support and caused severe economic hardship.

Full-time employment both on and off campus may be authorized, and the job need not be related to the student's particular field of study.[32] However, a written offer of employment from a qualifying institution is required. Use of this type of employment authorization does not interfere with or limit any other type of employment, such as on-campus employment or practical training that the student may qualify for.[33] On-campus employment authorization must be obtained from the DSO, and off-campus employment can be granted in one-year intervals when a student applies directly to USCIS for an EAD. Employment may not commence until the EAD has been received.[34] Students granted employment authorization under this provision may be allowed to register for less than a full course of study during the period of employment (undergraduates must register for at least six credit hours, and graduate students are required to register for at least three credit hours).[35]

For on-campus Special Student Relief employment, the DSO must verify the student's eligibility and update the student's record in SEVIS. Once the record is updated, the DSO authorizes the employment by annotating the student's I-20 in the employment section.[36] The I-20 is printed and given to the student. The DSO in the case is responsible for verifying all financial documentation.

If a student is applying for off-campus employment, the DSO must update the student's record in SEVIS to verify eligibility for the benefit, recommend that USCIS approve the student for employment, and print SEVIS Form I-20 with the recommendations for the student to submit with the I-765.[37] A student must apply for the EAD via Form I-765 with the proper filing fee and two passport style photos, photocopies of Form I-94 and Form I-20 with required recommendations, and documentation regarding the financial distress caused by the crises in the designated country.

Curricular and Optional Practical Training

One of two types of training can be granted for part-time (20 hours per week or less) or full-time employment to a student wishing to gain practical experience: curricular optional training (CPT) or optional practical training (OPT).[38] Curricular and optional practical training are limited to students enrolled in a SEVIS approved college, university, conservatory, or seminary who have been enrolled for at least one full academic year.[39] Exceptions to

---

[30] 8 CFR §214.2(f)(9)(ii)(D).

[31] The Special Student Relief program was created by two separate documents, published together in the *Federal Register* on June 10, 1998. The first document was the interim rule that amended the federal regulation governing F-1 duration of status at 8 CFR §214.2(f)(5), full course of study at 8 CFR §§214.2(f)(9)(i) and (ii). 63 Fed. Reg. 31872 and 63 Fed. Reg. 31874 (June 10, 1998).

[32] 8 CFR §§214.2(f)(9)(i)–(ii).

[33] 8 CFR §214.2(f)(9)(ii)(A).

[34] 8 CFR §214.2(f)(9)(ii)(F)(2).

[35] 8 CFR §§214.2(f)(6)(i)(A), (B), (F). In a Dec. 3, 2003, liaison call with DHS, NAFSA asked ICE whether a reduced enrollment authorized under the SSR notice had to be processed as a formal RCL in SEVIS. *NAFSA Advisor's Manual*, Sec 3.18, "Employment in F-1 Status."

[36] 63 Fed. Reg. 31874, 31875 (June 10, 1998).

[37] 63 Fed. Reg. 31874, 31875 (June 10, 1998) AMDOC #200302011.

[38] 8 CFR §214.2(f)(10).

[39] 8 CFR §214.2(f)(10)(i). Prior to Jan. 1, 2003, the regulations had required lawful full-time enrollment for "nine consecutive months." The current interpretations allow for those students authorized for a reduced course load or enrolled in a

continued

this rule include graduate students enrolled in programs where early participation in curricular practical training is a requirement of the program.[40] A student who had previously been enrolled for one academic year in status, falls out of status, and subsequently is granted reinstatement of status is able to use the previous time period to qualify for OPT or CPT.[41]

Curricular Practical Training

Curricular practical training is available to students whose academic program requires the work as "an integral part of an established curriculum" prior to completion of their studies.[42] A job offer is required, and the employment must qualify under the specific program at the discretion of the school and the DSO. Depending on the program at the school, CPT can be authorized for specific hours and periods of time up to one year at a time. However, the use of full-time CPT for one year or more during the same academic program renders the student ineligible for OPT.[43]

CPT authorization requires that the DSO check the student's eligibility and update the student's record in SEVIS to verify eligibility for the benefit. Once the record is updated, the DSO authorizes the employment by annotating the student's I-20 in the employment section. For on-campus Special Student Relief employment, the DSO must verify the student's eligibility and update the student's record in SEVIS to verify eligibility for the benefit. Once the record is updated, the DSO authorizes the employment by annotating the student's I-20 in the employment section.[44] The I-20 is printed and given to the student for employment. The DSO in the case is responsible for ensuring that the employment meets the regulatory requirements, and will generally require written documentation from the program advisor.

Optional Practical Training

If otherwise qualified as described above, a student may be granted a cumulative period of 12 months of practical training to use in his or her related field of study.[45] A new 12-month period is available at each degree level.[46] No offer of employment is required, but the student is expected to work or be actively seeking employment after the OPT EAD is issued. A student may use all or part of an OPT prior to the end of his or her studies, and part-time employment up to 20 hours per week can be deducted from the cumulative period at a reduced rate.[47] A student who chooses to use part or all of the OPT during studies is limited to 20 hours per week while school is in session but may work full-time during official school breaks.[48] An OPT issued for a post-completion studies period can be issued only for full-time use and must be completed within 14 months of the student's graduation date.[49]

When a student applies for optional practical training, the DSO must update the student's record in SEVIS, recommend that USCIS approve the student for employment, and print SEVIS form I-20 with the recommendations for the student to submit to USCIS with the I-765.[50] A student must apply for the EAD via Form I-765, with the proper filing fee and two passport-style photos and photocopies of Form I-20 and I-94. The application for post-completion practical training must be submitted to USCIS prior to the date of the student's program completion.[51]

---

study abroad program to qualify their time to meet the current regulations. OI 214.2(f)(10)(i).

[40] 8 CFR §214.2(f)(10)(i).

[41] Letter from Jacquelyn Bednarz, INS, to Lisa Enfield, Esq. HQ214f-C (updated 1993), *reproduced in* 70 *Interpreter Releases* 1120–21 (Aug. 23, 1998).

[42] 8 CFR §214.2(f)(10)(i).

[43] *Id.*

[44] *Id.*

[45] *Id.*

[46] 8 CFR §214.2(f)(10).

[47] 8 CFR §214.2(f)(10)(ii)(D)(i). OPT must be "directly related to the student's major area of study and commensurate with the student's educational level."

[48] 8 CFR §§214.2(f)(10)(ii)(A)(1), (2).

[49] Letter form Jacquelyn Bednarz to David Swaim (Apr. 5, 1993). 8 CFR §214.2(f)(10)(ii)(A)(3).

[50] 63 Fed. Reg. 31874, 31875 (June 10, 1998) AMDOC #200302011.

[51] 8 CFR §214.2(f)(10)(ii)(A)(3). With the advent of SEVIS and the update of the F-1 regulations, the student's post-completion optional practical training must now be issued and submitted prior to the program end-date. Previously, students were able to file for OPT during the 60-day grace period following the completion of their course of study.

SPECIAL ISSUES FOR POST-COMPLETION OPTIONAL PRACTICAL TRAINING

Early Termination

In the case of post-completion OPT, there are several triggering events that terminate the validity of a student's EAD issued for optional practical training. Once a student record is transferred to another school via SEVIS, and that student registers for classes, OPT is automatically terminated.[52]

Travel and Re-entry During OPT

F-1 students engaging in OPT prior to completion of studies follow the same procedures as other F-1 students. The OPT does not affect their ability to re-enter the United States. Post-completion OPT students who choose to travel outside the United States can be readmitted to resume employment for the remainder of the period of authorized OPT on their EAD.[53] The student must present a Form I-20 endorsed by the DSO for travel within the previous six months along with their unexpired EAD and proof that they are returning to the United States to resume employment. Students should be advised that, although the regulations allow for their re-entry to resume employment, an admitting officer still has the discretion to bar re-entry. For example, if a student does not have proof of a job offer and has only a month of OPT left, the officer may deny entry because the student has not shown evidence of resuming employment. The USCIS interpretation of travel when the OPT EAD has yet to be issued is even more nebulous. USCIS's December 15, 2004, Operations Instructions for SEVP has interpreted travel and re-entry to be allowed before the EAD is issued only if a student is re-entering to resume looking for a job or after the EAD is issued only to resume employment.[54]

J-1 COLLEGE AND UNIVERSITY STUDENT EMPLOYMENT[55]

Introduction

The J-1 visa is a feature of the Exchange Visitor Program and was created to implement the Mutual Educational and Cultural Exchange Act of 1961[56] (also called Fulbright-Hayes Act). The Exchange Visitor Program is administered by the Department of State's Bureau of Educational and Cultural Affairs (ECA).[57] The purpose of the act, and the mission of ECA, is to increase mutual understanding between the people of the United States and other countries through educational and cultural exchanges.[58] The Department of State appoints sponsors, which may be public or private entities, to facilitate activities consistent with the purposes of the act.[59] There are 13 distinct categories of exchange visitors, and ECA separately authorizes use of each category by sponsors.[60] Employment possibilities vary greatly among categories. This part of the article focuses on the employment features for college and university students.

Many colleges and universities have received designation by the ECA to operate J-1 student programs on their campuses, and are able to issue DS-2019 certificates of eligibility for J-1 students and their J-2 dependents.[61] In addition, other organizations administering international exchange programs can serve as sponsors and issue DS-2019 documents.[62] The students sponsored by other organizations are typically hosted by colleges or universities

---

[52] 8 CFR §214.2(f)(10)(ii)(B).

[53] 8 CFR §214.2(f)(13)(ii).

[54] 8 CFR §214.2(f)(13)(ii); OI found at *www.ice.gov/graphics/sevis/pdf/faq_f_reentry.pdf.*

[55] In addition to primary sources of authority, the author relied significantly on the *NAFSA Adviser's Manual* (2005 release), a publication of NAFSA: Association of International Educators.

[56] Pub. L. No. 87-256, 22 USC §2451 *et seq.,* as amended (1988).

[57] *http://exchanges.state.gov/.*

[58] 22 CFR §62.1(a). The Exchange Visitor Program assists the Department of State in furthering the foreign policy objectives of the United States. This foreign policy role of the EVP distinguishes it from the F-visa program and often explains differences between the two programs in employment and other contexts.

[59] 22 CFR§62.1(b).

[60] 22 CFR §62.5 *et. seq.*

[61] The DS-2019 form was redesignated from IAP-66 when the Department of State took control of the EVP from the United States Information Agency on October 1, 1999. At the same time, program regulations moved from 22 CFR Part 514 to 22 CFR Parts 61 and 62.

[62] *See, e.g.* Institute for International Education, *www.iie.org.*

by agreement between sponsor and host. The sponsor issuing the DS-2019 to the student controls the employment activities of its sponsored students, rather than the host campus in these cases.

Each J-1 sponsoring organization must appoint a Responsible Officer (RO), who may in turn appoint one or more Alternate Responsible Officers (AROs) to administer the program at the sponsor level.[63] The RO/ARO plays a role in any employment authorization process for students participating in its program.

Source and Types of Employment Authorization

J-1 students may be employed by the program sponsor or sponsor's designee within the guidelines of the Exchange Visitor Program and as described on the DS-2019 issued by the program sponsor.[64] J-1 students are not required to apply to USCIS for EADs; rather, they are authorized for employment with specific employers, incidental to their J-1 status.

Student employment options consist of academic training (addressed later) and the following:[65]

- employment pursuant to a scholarship, fellowship, or assistantship (usually on-campus, but not necessarily so);

- general on-campus employment (on the premises of the institution the student is authorized to attend); and

- off-campus employment necessitated by serious, urgent, and unforeseen economic circumstances arising after commencement of the J-1 program (as determined by the RO).

These three types of employment may not exceed 20 hours per week, except during official school breaks and during the student's summer vacation. During school breaks, employment may be full-time, with no limit on hours worked each week. Further, the student must be in good academic standing and engaging in a full course of study, except while on official break or during summer vacation. Finally, the employment must be authorized, in writing and in advance, by the RO.[66]

The regulation at 8 CFR §§274a.12(b)(11), 1274a.12(b)(11) implies that all employment authorizations should be recorded on the student's DS-2019. At this time, however, SEVIS, through which the RO would generate the DS-2019, does not permit entry of specific student employment authorizations on the DS-2019 for J-1 students. Scholarships, assistantships, and fellowships typically appear in the DS-2019 as funding sources, and this arguably satisfies the writing requirement. ROs record other student employment authorizations on separate documents, and procedures vary among programs.

Academic Training[67]

Academic training is intended to complement the classroom component of the J-1 student's program, and is considered part of his or her overall academic program. A student may engage in academic training before or after completion of academic study, or in combination with academic study, and may receive remuneration for it.[68] Academic training is available for degree-granting programs and nondegree programs.

Academic training must:[69]

- be recommended to the RO by the student's academic dean or advisor;

- have specified goals and objectives;

- identify the location, training supervisor, hours per week, and the start and end dates of the training program; and

- be an integral or critical part of the academic program.

Additionally, academic training must meet these general criteria:[70]

---

[63] 22 CFR §62.9(g).

[64] 8 CFR §§274a.12(b)(11), 1274a.12(b)(11).

[65] 22 CFR §62.23(g)(1)(i)–(iii). *See also* 63 Fed. Reg. 34276 (June 24, 1998), which relaxed employment restrictions and full course of study requirements for students from certain Asian countries experiencing economic difficulties. The program still exists and requires that students had begun their J-1 programs on or before June 24, 1998, to qualify. Its applicability is, therefore, increasingly rare.

[66] 22 CFR §§62.23(g)(2)(i)–(iv).

[67] 22 CFR §62.23(f).

[68] 22 CFR §62.23(f)(2). Note that the regulation indicates post-completion academic training must be paid, but USIA indicated unpaid, post-completion academic training could indeed be authorized provided the student had sufficient funds from other sources for support during the academic training period. *See NAFSA Adviser's Manual*, p. 4-90 (2005 release).

[69] 22 CFR §62.23(f)(5)(i).

[70] 22 CFR §62.23(f)(3).

- The student's purpose for participating in the Exchange Visitor Program must be primarily study, not academic training.

- The academic training must relate directly to the student's field of study.

- The student must be in good academic standing.

- The RO must provide written authorization, in advance, for the duration and type of academic training.

The RO must determine whether the academic training is warranted and the above criteria are satisfied.[71]

Time Limits

Post-completion academic training must commence no later than 30 days after completion of studies.[72] The upper limit on academic training for nondegree students, undergraduates, and predoctoral graduate students is 18 months, with the caveat that the duration of academic training must not exceed the duration of academic study.[73] The 18-month and "duration of academic study" limitations do not apply where the student is engaged in a degree program that mandates longer training, such as those requiring internships.[74] Students completing doctoral degrees may engage in academic training for up to 36 months or for a period equal to the duration of their academic study, whichever is less.[75]

The availability of the 36-month period for post-doctoral academic training varies with how the regulation is interpreted. Some ROs' interpretations limit academic training beyond 18 months to the traditional academic postdoctoral associate position consisting entirely of supervised research, and will not authorize it for other activities, such as teaching. This interpretation stems from the preamble to the

regulation published in 1993, which discusses the additional 18 months as a way to facilitate completion of research projects in this traditional setting.[76] Other ROs take a more generic view of "post-doctoral" activity and treat the 1993 preamble as an example, rather than an outright limitation.[77]

I-9 Considerations

Unlike optional practical training for F-1 students, there is no EAD from USCIS to evidence employability. Further, SEVIS does not enable the RO to place an academic training authorization or off-campus economic hardship work authorization on the student's DS-2019. As a result, procedures and documentation will vary from one RO to another, and employers often need assurance during the I-9 process that, indeed, the student is authorized to engage in employment. The student's I-94 and valid DS-2019, plus the written authorization from the RO, establish employment authorization, but attorneys and ROs must be prepared to trace these documents to specific regulations for the benefit of employers.

J-2 Dependents

J-2 dependents are permitted to apply to USCIS on Form I-765 for an EAD.[78] The regulations limit the use of J-2 dependent income to the "support of the family's customary recreational and cultural activities, and related travel, among other things." Further, "[e]mployment will not be authorized if this income is needed to support the J-1 principal alien."[79] The J-1 student, in other words, must have an independent source of funding to pursue study. This can place an RO in a dilemma when a J-1 student has lost a source of funding such as an assistantship but the employed J-2 spouse has sufficient income to support an extension of the DS-2019 document.

The J-2 status and associated EAD are valid only as long as the J-1 student is maintaining status and the student's DS-2019 is valid.[80] J-2 employment authorizations are granted in one-year increments, despite the fact that the regulation at 8 CFR

---

[71] 22 CFR §62.23(f)(5)(ii). The RO typically creates a separate document to serve as evidence that the academic training has been authorized.

[72] 22 CFR §62.23(f)(2)(ii). Note that many ROs interpret "commence" to include receiving an offer during the 30 days following completion of studies, even where actual employment activity begins later. *NAFSA Adviser's Manual*, p. 4-90 (2005 release).

[73] 22 CFR §62.23(f)(4)(ii).

[74] *Id.*

[75] 22 CFR §62.23(f)(4)(iii). Note that a single academic training authorization may not exceed 18 months. Multiple authorizations may be required for post-doctoral academic training.

---

[76] 58 Fed. Reg. 15180 (March 19, 1993).

[77] *See NAFSA Adviser's Manual*, p. 4-86 (2005 release) for detailed history on this topic.

[78] 8 CFR §§274a.12(c)(5), 1274a.12(c)(5); 8 CFR §214.2(j)(1)(v).

[79] 8 CFR §214.2(j)(1)(v).

[80] *Id.*

§214.2(j)(1)(v) appears to authorize up to four years of employment authorization.

M-1 VOCATIONAL OR OTHER NONACADEMIC STUDENTS

Purpose of the M-1 Visa

The M-1 visa is available to a student with a residence in a foreign country that he or she has no intention of abandoning, and who seeks to pursue a full course of study at an established and approved vocational or other recognized nonacademic institution (other than in a language training program).[81] M-2 visas are available to the spouse and minor children of an M-1 visa holder.[82] M-1 visas also are available to nationals of Canada and Mexico who will commute to a U.S. institution or place of study for a full- or part-time course of study.[83] Like other international student nonimmigrant categories, M-1 and M-2 visa holders are subject to the reporting and documentation requirements of SEVIS.[84]

Types of Employment on the M-1 Visa

Employment is limited to six months of post-completion practical training. Employment during an M-1 course of study is prohibited.[85] Temporary employment for practical training may be authorized only after completion of the student's course of study.[86]

An M-1 student must apply for permission to accept employment for practical training on Form I-765 with the proper filing fee, accompanied by a Form I-20 that has been endorsed for practical training by the DSO.[87] The DSO must also certify on Form I-538 that (1) the proposed employment is recommended for the purpose of practical training; (2) the proposed employment is related to the student's course of study; and (3) upon the DSO's information and belief, comparable employment is not available to the student in the country of the student's foreign residence.[88] The DSO must update the student's record in SEVIS to recommend that the USCIS approve the student for practical training and print SEVIS form I-20 with the recommendation for the student to submit with the I-765.[89]

The request for employment authorization must be submitted before the end-date listed on the M-1 student's I-20 but not more 90 days before the program end-date.[90] The I-765, I-538, I-20, and filing fee should be filed with the USCIS service center having jurisdiction over the student's location. The student may not begin employment until he or she has received an employment authorization document issued by USCIS.[91]

One month of employment authorization will be granted for each four months of full-time study that the M-1 student has completed, but the student may not engage in more than six months of employment. The student will not be granted employment authorization if he or she cannot complete the requested practical training within six months.[92] During an authorized period of practical training, the M-1 student who departs the United States may be readmitted for the remainder of the authorized period indicated on the I-20. If the practical training was not authorized prior to the student's departure from the United States, he or she will not be readmitted.[93] Authorization for all employment for practical training is automatically suspended upon certification by the Secretary of Labor that a strike or other labor dispute involving a work stoppage is in progress in the occupation at the place of employment.[94] There is no appeal from a decision denying permission to accept employment for practical training.[95]

Employment Authorization for M-2 Dependents of M-1 Students

The M-2 spouse and children may not accept employment.[96]

---

[81] INA §101(a)(15)(M)(i); 8 CFR §214.2(m).

[82] INA §101(a)(15)(M)(ii); 8 CFR §214.2(m)(3).

[83] INA §101(a)(15)(M)(iii); 8 CFR §214.2(m)(19).

[84] 8 CFR §§214.2(m)(1)(i)(A)(i)–(iii); 214.2(m)(3).

[85] 8 CFR §214.2(m)(13).

[86] 8 CFR §214.2(m)(14)(i).

[87] 8 CFR §214.2(m)(14)(ii).

[88] 8 CFR §§214.2(m)(14)(ii)(A)–(C).

[89] 8 CFR §214.2(m)(14)(vi).

[90] 8 CFR §214.2(m)(14)(ii).

[91] 8 CFR §214.2(m)(14)(iii).

[92] *Id.*

[93] 8 CFR §214.2(m)(14)(iv).

[94] 8 CFR §214.2(m)(14)(v).

[95] 8 CFR §214.2(m)(15).

[96] 8 CFR §214.2(m)(17)(i).

SOCIAL SECURITY NUMBERS

Social Security Numbers for F, J, and M International Students

A Social Security number (SSN) is not legally required to begin authorized employment in the United States. Employers may defer reporting income for a short period, or they may accept an Individual Taxpayer Identification Number (ITIN) in lieu of an SSN for reporting purposes. In practice, however, most employers expect to see an SSN and may not accept that a prospective employee is authorized without it. This is an area of concern to international students, DSOs, and other campus officials, because obtaining a Social Security card has become increasingly difficult in recent years. There are often delays and uncertainty while the Social Security Administration (SSA) verifies that the international student is authorized to accept employment.

The SSA will only issue an SSN to non–U.S. citizens who have permission to accept employment from DHS.[97] The SSA will not issue an SSN simply to enroll in a college or school.[98] DHS and the Department of State have coordinated with the SSA to facilitate issuance of SSNs to international students. Updates to SEVIS by a DSO should be accessible to the SSA within 48 hours.[99]

The SSA has issued a final rule, "Evidence Requirements for Assignment of Social Security Numbers (SSNs); Assignment of SSNs to Foreign Academic Students in F-1 Status."[100] Citing concerns about national security and identity theft, the rule requires additional evidence for F-1 students who apply for SSNs to show specific work authorization from DHS and the school and that, in the case of on-campus employment, a specific job has been offered.

---

[97] "Social Security Numbers for Noncitizens," SSA Publication No. 05-10096 (Dec. 2005), available at *www.ssa.gov/pubs/10096.html*.

[98] "International Students and Social Security Numbers," SSA Publication No. 05-10181 (Dec. 2005), available at *www.ssa.gov/pubs/10181*.

[99] "Information for Students and Exchange Visitors (F-1, M-1 & J-1 Visa Categories) Pursuing Employment in the United States," U.S. Immigration and Customs Enforcement Fact Sheet, June 14, 2004.

[100] 69 Fed. Reg. 55065–76, (Sept. 13, 2004), *published on* AILA InfoNet at Doc. No. 04091415 (*posted* Sept. 14, 2004). The revisions to the SSA regulations dealing with nonimmigrant aliens are found at 20 CFR §422.105 (presumption of authority of nonimmigrant alien to accept employment) and 20 CFR §422.107 (evidence requirements).

Social Security Numbers for On-Campus Employment

Students who have been authorized to work on campus may apply for an SSN by completing a Form SS-5, "Application for a Social Security Card," and presenting proof of immigration status, work eligibility, age, and identity. Immigration status is shown by a current I-94 arrival/departure record and an I-20 for F or M students or DS-2019 for J students. Work eligibility must be shown by a letter from the DSO that identifies the employer and the type of work, as well as a letter from the employer that describes the job, the employment start date, the number of hours that the student will work, and the supervisor's name and telephone number.

Social Security for Curricular Practical Training

An F-1 student authorized for curricular practical training must also present the Form I-20 with the employment page completed and signed by the DSO.

Social Security for Other Off-Campus Employment

An F-1 or M-1 student authorized to work off-campus must present an EAD. This applies to optional practical training, internship with a recognized international organization, or cases of extreme economic hardship.

Social Security for J-1 Students

A J-1 student must provide a letter from the program sponsor or RO, on the sponsor's letterhead with an original signature that authorizes the student's employment.

CONCLUSION

Immigration practitioners often may not be involved in the mechanics of applying for employment authorization or SSNs for international students. The statute grants authority to DSOs and requires DSOs to make recommendations and take actions to assist the student in this area. Still, all immigration lawyers must understand the eligibility categories in order to advise students properly, to provide accurate information on SEVIS forms and types of employment that are authorized for international students, and to make legal determinations regarding the implications of a student's employment during a course of study on an F, J, or M visa.

TRAINING AMERICAN STYLE

by Cora D. Tekach, Lori T. Chesser, Scott F. Cooper, and M. Mercedes Badia-Tavas[*]

INTRODUCTION

U.S. employers often seek to train or be trained by foreign nationals who need to temporarily enter the United States for this bona fide business purpose. There is a variety of situations that can present themselves. This includes scenarios where a U.S. company must train personnel from abroad on the methods, procedures, and processes of the U.S. operations to implement the same practices at overseas operations of a related entity; a U.S. company may purchase equipment or specialized goods from abroad requiring training by an expert of the foreign vendor; or a U.S. company may simply want to provide an opportunity to a foreign national to gain professional experience in the United States in his or her field of specialization as part of an exchange program. Counsel must examine the visa options available, given the statutory and regulatory parameters, policy statements, and practical requirements of the particular training program. This article will examine three visa options—the B-1, H-3, and J-1 visas—their different elements yet overlapping requirements, advantages and disadvantages, practical uses, and processing issues.

B-1 VISA STATUS FOR TRAINING PURPOSES

Potential Training Uses

U.S. Citizenship and Immigration Services (USCIS) and the Department of State (DOS) recognize that some B-1 business visitors may engage in activities that are appropriate for other visa categories.[1] The B-1 visitor for business category may be used for certain types of business-related training, largely for circumstances in lieu of the H-3[2] or J-1 status,[3] but also for the purpose of commercial or industrial training.[4] Additionally, certain educational purposes, such as providing or receiving academic training and attending conferences, are also permissible.[5] Although rarely used for this purpose, B-1 status is also appropriate for individuals who are invited to participate in the training of Peace Corps volunteers or who are coming to the United States under contract pursuant to certain provisions of the Peace Corps Act,[6] and for participants in the United Nations Institute for Training and Research (UNITAR) program or internship.[7]

[*] **Cora Tekach** is a shareholder with Maggio & Kattar, P.C., and has practiced immigration law exclusively since 1991. She is accomplished in all aspects of business immigration, and also has extensive experience representing individuals in removal proceedings. Ms. Tekach served as associate director, Information and Liaison, at AILA, and is a past president of the AILA D.C. Chapter. She also served with the Peace Corps in rural Paraguay and is fluent in Spanish.

Lori Chesser is a shareholder and vice president of the Davis Law Firm (*www.lawiowa.com*) in Des Moines, and heads its immigration practice group. She currently serves as chair of the AILA Immigration Reform Committee, and is active in organizing for immigration reform locally through Catholic Charities and other advocacy partners. Ms. Chesser practices in all aspects of business and family immigration. She co-founded the Iowa-Nebraska AILA chapter and served as its first chair. She also is a member of the boards of the Iowa Council for International Understanding and Hispanic Educational Resources, an accredited bilingual daycare provider.

Scott Cooper, a partner with Fragomen, Del Rey, Bernsen & Loewy LLP, has been an officer with the Michigan and Chicago Chapters of AILA and on national committees. He practices employment, education/research, and compliance-related immigration law. Mr. Cooper has been an active member at the state, regional, and national levels of NAFSA: Association of International Educators. He was lead author of an *Immigration Briefings* on exchange visitors. See *www.fragomen.com*, for further biographical information.

Mercedes Badia-Tavas is principal of Badia-Tavas Law Group, Ltd., in Chicago, *www.btlawgroup.net*. She has 12 years of immigration practice. She authored an update article on employer sanctions in the *Immigration & Nationality Law Handbook* (AILA 2003–04). Presently, Ms. Badia-Tavas serves as a member of the AILA National Committees on Health Care Professionals (nonphysician), National Conference Committee, AILA Chicago Chapter's DOL Liaison Committee and Advocacy Committee, and DHS/CBP Committee. She is a graduate of Tulane Law School.

---

[1] 22 CFR §41.31; INS Operations Instructions (OI) 214.2(b).

[2] 8 CFR §214.2(h)(7).

[3] 8 CFR §214.2(j).

[4] 9 FAM 41.31 N.10.1(a); OI 214.2(b)(3); OI 214.2(b)(5).

[5] 9 FAM 41.31 N.8.

[6] 9 FAM 41.31 N.10.6.

[7] 9 FAM 41.31 N.10.7.

When pursuing a B-1 in lieu of the H-3, the foreign national must be employed abroad and be classifiable as H-3. This requires that the proposed training not be available in the foreign national's own country, the individual not be placed in a position that is in the normal operation of the business, the individual not engage in productive employment (unless incidental and necessary to the training), and the training benefit the foreign national in pursuing a career outside the United States.[8] Additionally, the foreign national must continue to receive a salary from the foreign employer, with no salary or other remuneration from a U.S. source, other than an expense allowance or other reimbursement for expenses (including room and board) incidental to the temporary stay.[9]

The B-1 may be used in lieu of J-1 in circumstances in which a foreign national's travel is funded by the U.S. government for the purpose of engaging in any of a wide variety of programs.[10] For example, a Foreign Service National employee of an Embassy or Consulate abroad may travel to the United States at U.S. government expense for specific training. It will be necessary to show that the J-1 is unavailable for the purpose of the stay in the United States. In order to make this showing, the sponsoring U.S. government agency may certify that such an exchange program does not exist or that the foreign national's activities are unrelated to any existing program.[11]

B-1 visitors may be permitted to enter the United States to train U.S. workers in the installation, servicing, or repairing of commercial or industrial equipment or machinery purchased from a company outside the United States, as long as there is no "hands on" work.[12] The B-1 status also may be used for those coming to the United States for building or construction work, but only if those individuals will be engaged strictly in supervising or providing training to construction workers.[13]

B-1 visitors coming to the United States for the purpose of "usual academic activity" may accept honoraria under the American Competitiveness and Workforce Improvement Act of 1998 (ACWIA).[14] In order to qualify, the individual may not engage in activity lasting longer than nine days at any one institution and may not accept payment from more than five institutions within the previous six-month period.[15]

Typically, the B-1 may not be used in cases where the primary purpose of the stay in the United States would be for study. An exception to this rule is a student at a foreign medical school who seeks to enter the United States for the purpose of an "elective clerkship" at a U.S. medical school's hospital.[16] This exception is permitted with specific requirements having been met, such as that the individual is attending a foreign medical school and will receive no remuneration from the U.S. medical school's hospital. Further, this exception does not apply to graduate medical training.[17]

Requirements

In *Matter of Hira*, the Board of Immigration Appeals, with Attorney General affirmation, established the requirements for the business visitor B-1 visa classification. These requirements are the following:

- The foreign national must be engaged in commercial activity;

- He or she must have a clear intent to maintain a foreign residence;

- The individual's principal place of business and the actual place of eventual accrual of profits, at least predominantly, remains in the foreign country;

- The foreign national's stay in the United States must be temporary in nature (notwithstanding the fact that the business activity may be ongoing); and

- The foreign national's salary must come from abroad.[18]

Thus, it is clear that the B-1 visa applicant must show intent to return to his or her foreign residence upon completion of the training. Additionally, the

---

[8] 9 FAM 41.31 N.11.9.

[9] *Id.*

[10] DOS Cable, 04-State-13720, "B-1 In Lieu of J-1 Visas for USG-Funded Travel" (Jan. 21, 2004), *published on* AILA InfoNet at Doc. No. 04022564 (*posted* Feb. 25, 2004).

[11] *Id.*

[12] 8 CFR §214.2(b)(5).

[13] 9 FAM 41.31 N.8.

[14] INA §212(q). American Competitiveness and Workforce Improvement Act of 1998, Title IV of Pub. L. No. 105-277 (Oct. 21, 1998), 112 Stat, 2381, §431.

[15] *Id.*

[16] 9 FAM 41.31 N.10.4-1; OI 214.2.

[17] OI 214.2(b)(4), 9 FAM 41.31 N.10.4-1.

[18] *Matter of Hira*, 11 I&N Dec. 824 (BIA 1965, 1966).

applicant must show that the purpose of the intended stay is temporary with a definite time limitation. There can be no *hands on* or *productive work* (unless it is incidental and necessary to the training).[19] For B-1 issuance, there may be no salary or other remuneration from a U.S. source. Note, however, that salary paid by the U.S. entity's separate business enterprise abroad shall not be considered as coming from a "U.S. source."[20] The U.S. company may pay all domestic and foreign employees through a centralized payroll system in the United States, as long as the B-1 continues to be employed by the foreign branch and the training in the United States qualifies as a B-1 activity. In order for an employer to be considered a "foreign firm" for this purpose, the entity must have an office overseas.

If the applicant is applying for B-1 in lieu of H-3, the fact that the training may last one year or more is not in itself controlling, and it should not result in a denial of the visa. Further, the applicant must show that the proposed training is not available in the applicant's own country, and the training will benefit the applicant in pursuing a career outside the United States.[21]

If the B-1 visa applicant's travel purpose is for commercial or industrial training, there must be a contract of sale, specifically requiring the seller to perform such services or training.[22] Additionally, the foreign national must possess specialized knowledge essential to the seller's contractual obligation to provide services or training; the foreign national will receive no remuneration from a U.S. source; and the trip is to take place within the first year following the purchase.[23]

Limitations on B-1 for Training

The B-1 visa category may not be used for a foreign national seeking entry into the United States where the individual would qualify for A, G, or H-2 status (the individual must seek H-2, notwithstanding the fact that the salary or other remuneration is being paid by a source outside the United States, and the petitioner must file a labor certification).[24] If there is any uncertainty regarding whether a case may be classifiable as B-1, an advisory opinion must be requested from DOS at *legalnet@state.gov*.

H-3 TRAINING PROGRAMS

General Considerations

H-3 training programs are developed and administered by the U.S. entity offering the training to the foreign national.[25] Unlike J programs, there is no pre-approved intermediary. The training entity applies directly to USCIS on Form I-129 with a detailed statement of the proposed program with extensive documentation to support its validity.[26]

The H-3 category requires that the foreign national not have immigrant intent—meaning that he or she intends to leave the United States at the end of the training period.[27] It also requires that the training not be available in the foreign national's home country.[28] The beneficiary may not be placed in a position where U.S. workers are regularly employed,[29] and no "productive employment" is allowed unless it is incidental to training and necessary for preparing the beneficiary to perform a function outside the United States.[30] The training must prepare the beneficiary to pursue a career outside the United States[31]

The regulations provide that training may *not* be granted in certain situations, which include the following:

- Training that is too general or has no objective means of evaluation;

- Training that is not compatible with the nature of sponsor's business;

- The beneficiary already possesses substantial expertise in the training area or subject matter;

- It is unlikely the training will be used outside the United States;

- The training will result in productive employment, meaning the training involves functions, responsibilities, duties, and schedules that are the

---

[19] 9 FAM 41.31 N.11.9.

[20] 9 FAM 41.31 N.3.4.

[21] 9 FAM 41.31 N.11.9.

[22] 9 FAM 41.31 N.10.1; OI 214.2(b)(5).

[23] *Id.*

[24] 22 CFR §41.22(b); 22 CFR §41.24(b)(4); 9 FAM 41.31 N.11(3).

[25] 8 CFR §214.2(h)(1)(i), 8 CFR §214.2(h)(7)(i).

[26] 8 CFR §214.2(h)(7)(ii).

[27] INA §101(a)(15)(H)(iii); 8 CFR §214.2(h)(1)(ii)(E).

[28] 8 CFR §214.2(h)(7)(ii)(A)(1).

[29] 8 CFR §214.2(h)(7)(ii)(A)(2).

[30] 8 CFR §214.2(h)(7)(ii)(A)(3).

[31] 8 CFR §214.2(h)(7)(ii)(A)(4).

same as a U.S. worker regularly employed at the training site;

- The sponsor does not have sufficient physical plant and personnel to conduct the training;

- The training is designed to extend time granted for training of a foreign student.[32]

The period of admission on an H-3 may not exceed two years.[33] No extension, change of status, or re-admission to H or L status will be granted if the full two years has been used, unless the beneficiary has resided outside the United States for six months.[34] Additionally, an extension may be denied if labor certification has been granted or an I-140 Petition for Immigrant Worker filed for the beneficiary.[35]

The I-129 form for the H-3 petition may be filed up to six months before training is scheduled to begin.[36] The petition may be filed for one employee training at one location, two or more locations with an itinerary, or for multiple employees training at the same location. However, all aspects of the itinerary, training, and location should be the same, or separate petitions will be required.[37] Multiple beneficiaries processing at different consulates may use one petition.[38]

An H-3 petition may be denied, or an approved petition revoked and entry into the United States by the beneficiary may be denied by Customs and Border Patrol (CBP) and USCIS in case of a strike. This would occur if the Secretary of Labor certifies that a strike or other labor dispute involving a work stoppage is in progress in the occupation at the place where the beneficiary is to be trained, and that the training of foreign workers would adversely affect the wages and working conditions of U.S. citizen and lawful permanent resident (LPR) workers.[39] If the beneficiary has already entered in H-3 status at the time a strike or work stoppage commences, the beneficiary will not be considered to be out of status solely because of his or her participation in the strike or other labor dispute. However, he or she will still have

to abide by the terms of authorized stay and depart the United States at the end of the H-3 status.[40]

The spouse and minor children of an H-3 beneficiary may accompany or follow to join the trainee into the United States in H-4 status, which is not a work-authorized status. The dependent would have to qualify independently under a visa classification authorized for employment incident to status.[41]

Special H-3 Programs

The regulations specifically provide for three special programs: medical student externs;[42] nurses;[43] and special education programs.[44]

Externs may qualify for H-3 status if they attend a residency or internship program at an American Medical Association or American Osteopath Association hospital and will engage in the externship during school vacation.[45]

Nurses may use the H-3 program if they have an unrestricted license in the country where they received medical education or if the education was in Canada or the United States and the petition states that the nurse is qualified under state law to receive training.[46] Note that the foreign health care worker certifications required under Immigration and Nationality Act (INA)[47] §212(a)(5)(C) are not necessary for trainees.[48]

The special education program addressed in the regulations is for practical training and experience in the education of children with physical, mental, or emotional disabilities.[49] It is limited to 18 months' duration (as opposed to the usual two years), and the petitioner must be a facility with professional,

---

[32] 8 CFR §214.2(h)(7)(iii)(A–H).

[33] 8 CFR §214.2(h)(9)(iii)(C)(1).

[34] 8 CFR §214.2(h)(12)(iv).

[35] 8 CFR §214.2(h)(16)(ii).

[36] 8 CFR §214.2(h)(9)(i)(B).

[37] 8 CFR §§214.2(h)(2)(i)(B), 214.2(h)(2)(i)(C).

[38] 8 CFR §214.2(h)(2)(ii).

[39] 8 CFR §214.2(h)(17).

---

[40] 8 CFR §214.2(h)(17)(iii).

[41] 8 CFR §214.2(h)(9)(iv).

[42] 8 CFR §214.2(h)(7)(i)(A).

[43] 8 CFR §214.2(h)(7)(i)(B).

[44] 8 CFR §214.2(h)(7)(iv).

[45] 8 CFR §214.2(h)(7)(i)(A). *See also* 9 FAM 41.53 N.20.

[46] 8 CFR §214.2(h)(7)(i)(B).

[47] Immigration and Nationality Act of 1952, Pub. L. No. 82-414, 66 Stat. 163 (*codified as amended at* 8 USC §§1101 *et seq.*) (INA).

[48] USCIS Memorandum, William R. Yates, "Final Regulation on Certification of Foreign Health Care Workers: Adjudicator's Field Manual Update AD 03-31" (Sept. 22, 2003), *published on* AILA InfoNet at Doc. No. 03092641 (*posted* Sept. 26, 2003).

[49] 8 CFR §214.2(h)(7)(iv)(A)(1).

trained staff and a structured program.[50] The beneficiary must be "nearing" a B.A. or higher degree or have "extensive" prior training or experience.[51]

Practical Considerations

A detailed, specific outline of the training must be submitted to include the following information:

- Who will be performing the training (names of staff members and job titles);

- Where the training will be performed (including photographs of physical location);

- What course materials will be used (including table of contents for instruction manuals, for example);

- How many hours will be devoted to each aspect of training, including breakdown of classroom, hands-on, on-the-job, or other type of training; and

- The statement also should include how the trainee is to be evaluated.

The petition must be very clear regarding the proportion of time devoted to productive employment versus classroom training. The statement describing the training, submitted with the petition, should fully describe the amount of time the beneficiary will devote to classroom training, on-the-job training, and productive employment. Productive employment and on-the-job training must be minimal and justified as necessary for the training and not to displace a U.S. worker.[52] The training program must also be compatible with the nature of the employer's business or enterprise.[53] The employer must have a physical plant and sufficiently trained personnel to provide the training.[54]

Training primarily by or at academic institutions is prohibited,[55] but the petitioner may integrate outside classroom studies into a training program.[56] If classroom instruction is too theoretical, hands-on experience could supplement the program, although care should be taken in justifying the necessity of such practical experience.

Specific proof should be submitted regarding how the beneficiary will use the training outside the United States, including proof of the existence of an office abroad or other place where the person will be returning to for work after the training. The ideal situation is if the petitioner operates a foreign office that employed or will employ the beneficiary following training. In this case, a letter or other proof from the foreign office stating the training is not available at the foreign location and committing to employing the beneficiary following the period of U.S. training is advisable.

A more difficult situation arises when the U.S. company plans to open a new foreign office and will employ the U.S.-trained beneficiary there. In this case, specific plans regarding when and how the office will be opened, proof of contracts in the foreign country, letters from suppliers or customers confirming the foreign office is being opened, and similar evidence would all go to substantiate the claim that the beneficiary will have a career to pursue outside the United States at the end of the training period.

If the petitioner is training the beneficiary for a position at an unrelated third-party company abroad, the existence of a job offer with the third party also should be well documented.

If the beneficiary will work somewhere besides his or her home country at the end of the training period, proof should be provided that he or she will be authorized to work in the target location.

Legitimate reasons for H-3 training may include a corporate rotation to enable overseas employment, a desire to educate an overseas client about the employer's business as a marketing strategy, or a need to train a co-venturer in the employer's methodology to facilitate the development of a joint project.[57] However, if the employee has significant prior experience with a related entity abroad, it may appear that the H-3 training is unnecessary. This may be addressed by including the beneficiary's curriculum vitae or résumé and pointing out gaps in experience or prior training that are intended to be filled by the H-3 training program.[58]

If the training will utilize prepared course material from an outside source, evidence should be provided that such training is not available in the home country, such as the proprietary aspects of the training in

---

[50] 8 CFR §214.2(h)(13)(iv).

[51] 8 CFR §214.2(h)(7)(iv)(B)(2).

[52] 8 CFR §214.2(h)(7)(ii)(2).

[53] 8 CFR §214.2(h)(7)(iii)(B).

[54] 8 CFR §214.2(h)(7)(iii)(G).

[55] 8 CFR §214.2(h)(1)(ii)(E)(1).

[56] "Training Visa Categories In The United States," 93-05 *Immigration Briefings* 2–8, (May 1993).

[57] *Id.*

[58] *Id.*

addition to prepared course material, or the need to interact with persons in the U.S. office to fully learn applications of the course material. A copy of the contents page, or the entire course material if not too bulky, should be submitted with the petition.

The source and amount of remuneration also must be documented,[59] and care should be taken regarding this aspect lest USCIS may use it as a basis for concluding the H-3 beneficiary is being used as a ruse for productive employment. The beneficiary will not be able to seek supplemental employment while in the United States in H-3 status, so the documented amount should be sufficient for the beneficiary to live on while in the United States, and could include room and board, for instance, as another portion of remuneration.

THE J-1 TRAINEE

The J-1 visa is appropriate for industrial and other types of training where exchange activities are contemplated pursuant to the United States Information and Educational Exchange Act of 1948 (Smith-Mundt Act),[60] as well as the Fulbright-Hays Act,[61] the statutes which originally authorized the J-1 visa category.

General J-1 Training Categories

The J-1 category includes three general categories of training—graduate medical training, flight training, and industrial training. The latter accommodates almost every other type of training in specialty and non–specialty occupations, other than that in clinical health professions. Medical trainees must be sponsored by the Educational Commission for Foreign Medical Graduates, the only organization designated to sponsor physicians for post-graduate clinical training.[62] Since the attacks of 2001 and the revelation that several of the terrorists were trained by U.S.-based flight training programs, flight training sponsorship has been closely monitored. A moratorium on approval of new flight training programs and agricultural training programs was recently announced by DOS, citing a lack of resources to properly monitor

such programs.[63] The training program under the J-1 has survived years of criticism by Congress, labor and professional organizations, and several studies that have found abuse and lack of proper controls on the program by the U.S. government.[64]

Industrial Training

The use of the J-1 for industrial training has grown significantly within the past decade. DOS (and former United States Information Agency and International Communication Agency) has designated both individual sponsor organizations, as well as "umbrella" sponsors to serve as sponsors for training programs.

Sponsor organizations use various sponsorship criteria for the individual whom they will sponsor. Some, such as the American Council for International Personnel (ACIP), limit sponsorship to trainees who will train with member employers. Several U.S. foreign chambers of commerce, such as the British-American Chamber, German-American Chamber or French-American Chamber, tend to favor sponsoring individuals of the chamber's national group or for member organizations, but not exclusively. Trainees need not be nationals of the particular foreign chamber partner country. American Immigration Law Foundation (AILF) and the Association for International Practical Training (AIPT) are examples of organizations that will serve as a sponsor for any third-party employers and prospective trainees without any need for membership and irrespective of nationality or industry. The sponsoring entities can be found on DOS's website at *http://exchanges.state.gov/education/jexchanges/*. Specific employers are authorized to sponsor trainees for internal training purposes. These employers tend to be international companies in manufacturing, service, financial, educational, research, and other industries.

Advantages of Using the J-1 Category

The principal advantages of the J-1 over the B-1 for training is that on-the-job training can be an element of the program,[65] the alien need not be an employee of a foreign employer, and financial support

---

[59] 8 CFR §214.2(h)(7)(ii)(B)(6).

[60] United States Information and Educational Exchange Act of 1948, Pub. L. No. 402, 66 Stat. 6. (Smith-Mundt Act).

[61] Mutual Educational and Cultural Act of 1961, Pub. L. No. 87-256, 75 Stat. 527 (Fulbright-Hays Act).

[62] The scope of this article is limited to industrial training.

[63] 71 Fed. Reg. 3913 and 71 Fed. Reg. 3914 (Jan. 24, 2006).

[64] General Accounting Office (GAO) report, Inappropriate Uses of Education and Cultural Exchange Visas (Feb. 5, 1990) (hereinafter GAO report), *reported in* 67 *Interpreter Releases* 315 (Mar. 19, 1990). *See also* 58 Fed. Reg. 15180 (Mar. 19, 1993) (supplementary information) and 70 *Interpreter Releases* 337 (Mar. 22, 1993).

[65] 22 CFR §62.22(b) (Apr. 11, 2002).

of the trainee can come from both U.S. or foreign sources.

Contrasted with the H-3, productive employment can be the principal training setting for a J-1, and there is no requirement to show that the training is unavailable in the home country. There is also no need to file and obtain approval of a petition with USCIS before the alien applies for a visa. The J-1 applies directly for the J-1 visa with the sponsor-provided certificate of visa eligibility known as Form DS-2019.

Although a B-1 or H-3 holder may be required to be taxed as a resident for federal and state income tax purposes and must pay social security taxes, a J-1 exchange visitor enjoys an initial nonresident tax status, is exempt from FICA contributions, and may benefit from tax treaty provisions exempting J-1s from U.S. taxation altogether for defined periods. The category may help an employer avoid paying into both the U.S. and foreign social tax systems for a trainee where there is no totalization agreement in place between the United States and the trainee's home country.

Much of the criticism of the J-1 trainee program has been targeting employers using it as an employment visa and avoiding the wage and other requirements under the H-1B category. For this reason, it is imperative that counsel assures that training programs meet regulatory requirements. DOS's auditing of training programs over the last several years has prompted many trainee sponsors to more carefully review applications for sponsorship, and they are now more likely to refuse sponsorship if a training program appears incomplete or the training is in an unskilled occupation.

Another distinction between the J and other trainee categories is that J dependents (both spouse and children), who are granted J-2 visas, may apply for employment authorization once they have entered the United States in J-2 status. The dependents of H-3 foreign nationals as well as H-1B dependents in H-4 status do not qualify for work authorization. The H-4 dependents have to qualify independently for a visa that grants them work authorization, if they wish to work.

Requirements for J-1 Training Programs

DOS regulations require that a training program be designed to enhance the exchange visitor's skills in his or her specialty or non–specialty occupation through participation in structured training and that the program improve the participant's knowledge of U.S. techniques, methodologies, or expertise within the trainee's field of endeavor.[66] Such programs are also supposed to incorporate elements that will convey to the trainee knowledge of U.S. culture and society as well as expose U.S. residents to foreign cultures and skills.[67]

On-the-job training is allowed as a component of a bona fide training program and is defined as an individual's observation of and participation in given tasks demonstrated by experienced workers for the purpose of acquiring competency.[68] These bona fides distinguish a program from one involving unauthorized gainful employment.

The field in which training can be provided must be either a "specialty" or "non-specialty" occupation, as opposed to unskilled work. A "specialty occupation" is defined as "an occupation that requires theoretical and practical application of a body of highly specialized knowledge to perform fully in the stated field of endeavor,"[69] not dissimilar from the USCIS definition of an occupation appropriate for the H-1B classification. "Non-specialty" occupations are generally those that are more than skilled occupations, but not specialty occupations and generally require at least two years of training or experience.[70] Specialty programs are allowed in:

- Arts and Culture;
- Information Media and Communications;
- Education, Social Science, Library Science, Counseling, and Social Services;
- Management, Business, Commerce, and Finance;
- Health-Related Occupations (non-clinical);
- Aviation (other than flight training);
- Sciences, Engineering, Architecture, Mathematics, and Industrial Occupations;
- Construction and Building Trades;
- Agriculture, Forestry, and Fishing;
- Public Administration and Law, and other training.[71]

A particular J-1 sponsor may be restricted as to the occupational areas in which it is authorized by

---

[66] 22 CFR §62.22(d) (Apr. 11, 2002).

[67] 22 CFR §62.22(b) (Apr. 11, 2002).

[68] 22 CFR §62.22 (Apr. 11, 2002).

[69] Id.

[70] Id.

[71] 22 CFR §62.22(c)(2) (Apr. 11, 2002).

DOS to sponsor participants. Therefore, it is necessary to ensure that the sponsor's program designation allows for training in the desired field.

DOS generally relies upon the Department of Labor's former Schedule B as a reference point for unskilled occupations.[72]

The length of a J-1 training program may range from a minimum of three weeks to no longer than 18 months in duration. In October 2003, DOS notified J-1 sponsors that an alien may be sponsored under the J-1 trainee category only one time, with few exceptions. Exceptions to this limit must be obtained by contacting the Assistant General Counsel to the DOS Exchange Visitor Program Designation Branch. The agency also has said that a departure of 30 days or more serves to terminate an alien's J-1 program. This would appear to preclude a trainee from engaging in a program that contemplates return to the home country of a month or more within the authorized period of stay, even if the purpose is to allow the alien to transfer the skills gained back to the home country for a short period and then to return to the United States to continue the program.

J-1 trainees and any accompanying dependents in J-2 status must be covered by health insurance that meets DOS regulatory requirements. Willful failure to maintain such insurance is a ground for termination of the exchange visitor's program, and the sponsor is required to report such termination to DOS.

Note: Where the participant is coming to the United States to *provide* as opposed to *receive* training, the "specialist" J-1 category may be used for this purpose since it allows sponsorship of an expert in a field of specialized knowledge or skill to come to the United States for "observing, consulting, or demonstrating special skills."[73]

Training vs. Employment

Before contacting a prospective training sponsor, counsel needs to evaluate whether the proposed activities constitute a "bona fide" training program and not gainful employment.[74] It is best to request from the client a training program, broken down into training segments, which delineates for each segment:

- The period of time required;
- The type of training activity, *e.g.*, classroom training, seminars, rotation through several departments, on-the-job training, attendance at conferences, and site visits;[75]
- The skills to be acquired, *e.g.*, knowledge of company procedures and process, product marketing, or a manufacturing process;
- Who will provide continuous supervision of and conduct the periodic evaluations of the trainee.[76]

The training plan also must contemplate evaluations of the trainee's progress in the program at least at the mid-point and end of the program.[77] There also must be a determination that the trainee will not assume a position that is filled or would be filled by regular full-time or part-time employees.[78]

This exercise helps an employer construct an organized training experience to comply with federal regulations and, more importantly, to better assure a successful training experience for both the trainer and trainee. Most umbrella J-1 sponsors offer advice and assistance to the client in putting together an appropriate training program plan. Putting the program sponsor directly in touch with the employer can be good practice. If the facts do not show that a training opportunity is legitimate, other visa options should be considered.

It is important to note that the alien need not be an employee of the entity providing the training. The J-1 program is flexible in terms of the relationship between the trainee and the entity providing the training. An example is a situation where a representative of an overseas customer needs to come to a U.S. company to receive on-the-job training in a process or product. It is quite difficult, in this situation, to obtain an employment visa, such as an E, H, L, or TN, if there has not been and/or will not be an employment relationship between the U.S. company and the representative. The J program is flexible enough to allow for sponsorship of the representative in such a circumstance. The financial support for the trainee also can come from any source—the training entity, a foreign employer, or other third party, or the trainee's personal funds would all be allowable.

---

[72] 22 CFR §62.22(c)(1) and Appendix E to Part 62 (Apr. 11, 2002).

[73] 58 Fed. Reg. 15181 (Mar. 19, 1993) (supplementary information); 22 CFR §62.4(g) (Apr. 11, 2002).

[74] 58 Fed. Reg. 15187 (Mar. 19, 1993) (supplementary information); 22 CFR §62.22(b) (Apr. 11, 2002).

[75] 22 CFR §62.22(d)(1) (Apr. 11, 2002).

[76] 22 CFR §62.22(g) (Apr. 11, 2002).

[77] *Id.*

[78] 22 CFR §62.22(d)(2)(ii) (Apr. 11, 2002).

Process of Obtaining J Sponsorship

Assuming the employer provided a training schedule and otherwise arranged for a legitimate training experience and does not have its own program designation from DOS, the next step is to contact one of the umbrella J program sponsors. The sponsor will usually have a website where program information, documentary requirements, and applications can be found. It is crucial to review the sponsor's site and the application forms carefully for any restrictions specific to that sponsor's program, which may go beyond those in the regulations. For example, umbrella sponsors may require that the prospective trainee have been outside of the United States for 60 to 90 days prior to the beginning date of the proposed training program. This requirement helps the J programs avoid applications from employers seeking to use the trainee program as a continuation of earlier training or employment or to bridge gaps between one status and another, such as a student whose Optional Practical Training will expire before an H-1B is available.

Counsel also should be sure to check that the J-1 sponsor's program designation provides for the particular field of training and, for that field, allows for sponsorship for the required period of training contemplated. Sponsors do vary on these issues.

Completed applications are submitted to the prospective umbrella sponsor, which conducts a review and may request additional documentation. The umbrella programs also offer relatively low-cost health insurance to meet the regulatory requirements for such coverage for the exchange visitor and any dependents. Note that, although many employers' health plans may meet the minimum health insurance requirements, they usually do not contain provisions to cover the costs of evacuation of the trainee back to the home country in case of an illness or for repatriation of remains in case of death. Also, such insurance is available whether or not the exchange visitor will be an employee of the entity providing the training, on-the-job training is involved and regardless of the source of funding for the exchange visitor's stay. If the employer does not wish to purchase insurance through the program sponsor, it will be required to demonstrate that other insurance meeting regulatory requirements will be in place during the program.

Once satisfied that the training program is appropriate for sponsorship, the program sponsor will issue Form DS-2019, which is generated through the Student and Exchange Visitor Information System (SEVIS), the government system designed to track F, M, and J status aliens. The form may be provided by the program sponsor's Responsible Officer (RO) or Alternate Responsible Officer (ARO) to the attorney, the company, or be sent to the alien directly in the home country or through a collaborating organization in the home country. It is important for counsel to review the DS-2019 carefully to assure that the information is accurate. Biographic data (name, date of and country of birth, country of nationality, and country of residence) should be consistent with that contained in the applicant's passport. The occupational field in which the training is being provided, countries of citizenship and of permanent residence, and sources of funding are important in determining whether the two-year foreign residence requirement of INA §212(e) applies. Incorrect information should be brought to the attention of the RO or ARO to obtain a corrected DS-2019 prior to the visa application or entry to the United States. The consular officer also will have made an initial determination noted on the DS-2019 and on the J-1 visa stamp as to whether the two-year foreign residence requirement applies. However, these determinations are not always accurate and should be reviewed carefully.

Most J-1 trainee sponsors now offer expedited service that reduces what might be normally a two-month process to review the application and issue the DS-2019, to a matter of a few days. This processing time, as well as that for the J visa application, should be considered in setting the beginning date of the training program so that the program start and end dates on the DS-2019 are realistic. If the alien arrives late or the program sponsor is not prepared to commence the training when the alien arrives, it may prove necessary to seek an extension of the program to which the program sponsor must consent. DOS may need to be consulted concerning an extension of stay.

Applying for the J Visa and Entry

Before the alien may apply for the J-1 visa for admission, Form I-907 must be filed online or through the mail along with payment of the $100 SEVIS fee. A J-1 visa applicant must submit:

- Completed Forms DS-156, DS-157, and DS-158;
- A passport *valid for at least six months beyond the end date* of the DS-2019;
- Form DS-2019;
- The $100 application fee and, where applicable, reciprocity fee;

- A copy of the receipt for payment of the $100 SEVIS fee;

- A passport type photo;

- Evidence of financial support not designated on Form DS-2019 or in the case where support is from personal funds; and,

- Documentation/information establishing that the applicant intends to return to an unabandoned permanent residence in the home country upon completion of the exchange program.

The applicant should sign and date the DS-2019 as indicated prior to submission of the form with the application. Because a J-1 visa applicant must satisfy the consul of the likelihood of return to the home country, applications for J-1 visas are best filed with the U.S. consul in the applicant's home country. This is particularly true for applicants from countries where economic or political conditions are difficult. J-1 visa applicants from such countries find, at best, mixed results in third countries, such as stateside U.S. consuls in Canada or Mexico. The refusal rates for J-1 exchange visitor visa applications have dropped somewhat as a result of a DOS Visa Office cable sent to U.S. consuls last year urging them to take into account that student and exchange visitor applicants may not have the ties to the home country that apply to applicants.[79] This has had a positive impact on student visa applicants, including those under the F-1 and J-1 student categories. Trainees, other than perhaps those who are still at earlier stages in their careers, may not benefit from this less restrictive viewpoint. For example, an individual who is making a career change later in life or who is self-employed or does not have a firm position in the home country could face a refusal if other factors indicating significant ties to the home country are not evidenced. In this regard, treatment may be similar to that accorded a B-1 trainee visa applicant, although consuls treat J-1 visa applicants more favorably as a general rule. A Canadian citizen would apply directly at a port of entry for admission in J-1 status, since Canadians are visa exempt.

When the J-1 is admitted to the United States, the period of authorized stay indicated on Form I-94 is "duration of status" or "D/S." This is defined as the period from the beginning to the end of the validity dates of Form DS-2019 plus a 30-day grace period if the alien completes the exchange program. The alien may apply to change status to another category within this period unless barred by a failure to maintain status or by the two-year foreign residence requirement (see below). Note that, because the exchange program is limited to the period on Form DS-2019, any employment that is a part of the training program must end by the end date stated on the DS-2019 and may not continue during the grace period.

A change of status to J-1 visa status within the United States is possible so long as the program sponsor does not require the trainee to apply for a visa and/or enter as a J-1. Counsel needs to caution the training entity that a change is not an application that can be treated to premium processing by USCIS and that the variance in processing times can make it difficult to assure that the alien will be able to begin the training program in a timely manner. If the application to change status is filed too early such that USCIS adjudicates the case more than 30 days before the start date on the DS-2019, a service center may deny the application.[80]

Changes of J-1 category from the trainee category to another category within the J-1 visa, such as the student category, are rarely authorized by DOS, as there must be a finding of unusual or exceptional circumstances.[81] It may be possible for a trainee to depart, obtain a new J-1 visa in a new J-1 category, and re-enter the United States. Sponsorship as a J-1 professor or research scholar is prohibited until the trainee has been out of J-1 status for at least one year.

The J-1 should be provided an initial orientation soon after arrival on the local community and given information including the address and phone number of the RO, program rules, and medical insurance.

Any employment that is incidental to the training program is authorized without the need to apply to USCIS for an employment authorization document. The J-1 program sponsor must verify the trainee's

---

[79] The cable is available at *http://travel.state.gov/visa/laws /telegrams/telegrams_2843.html*. Its official citation is State Department Cable R 092051Z FEB 06. The Rice-Chertoff Joint Vision Statement is at *www.state.gov/r/pa/prs/ps/2006 /59242.htm*.

[80] The USCIS Nebraska Service Center (NSC) has taken the position on changes of status that if the start date on the DS-2019 is more than 30 days beyond the date of adjudication and the alien's status has expired during the pendency of the application, the application will be denied. NSC bases this policy on the regulatory prohibition on entry of an exchange visitor to the United States more than 30 days in advance of the start date of the DS-2019.

[81] 22 CFR §62.41 (Apr. 11, 2002).

entry to the United States within 30 days of the program start date or report to DOS the failure of the trainee to report, and the trainee's SEVIS record is terminated. The trainee is also required to report any change of residential address in the United States to the program sponsor within 10 days of such a change. Reporting this change alleviates the need to file Form AR-11 with the Department of Homeland Security. Termination of program for failure to maintain required health insurance is also reported to DOS. The trainee may not realize this until he or she travels abroad temporarily and is either refused a new J-1 visa, if such is required to re-enter, or may encounter difficulty at a port of entry if the CBP port official checks SEVIS and sees that the trainee's record has been rendered inactive.

Verification of employment eligibility where on-the-job training is included in the program may be completed in Section 2 of the I-9 form through review of the trainee's original valid foreign passport, Form I-94, and DS-2019, which are "column A" documents.

J-2 Dependents

The trainee's spouse and unmarried children under 21 years of age may apply concurrently for J-2 visas. The program sponsor provides separate Forms DS-2019 to each dependent for this purpose.

J-2s apply for work authorization with the USCIS regional service center with jurisdiction over the applicant's place of residence. This authorization may be obtained in one-year increments up to the end date on the J-1's DS-2019. The J-2 must apply with Form I-765, filing fee, documentation of valid J-2 entry and status and the J-1's valid status, and a statement from the J-2 indicating that the funds that will be earned through any employment will not go toward the support of the J-1.[82] Since it may take two to four months for such authorization to be granted, it may not prove very useful for trainees who are entering for six months or less. If the application remains pending for more than 90 days, the J-2 may apply to the district office for an interim employment authorization card. Also, trainees who enter for a program of less than a year are generally not accompanied by dependents.

Seeking J-1 Program Designation

Those employers who have ongoing training programs and foresee the need to train many foreign nationals going forward may envision cost savings due to social security and other tax exemptions for exchange visitor trainees. They also may wish to avoid trainee sponsorship fees paid to third-party umbrella program sponsors. The convenience of being able to issue its own DS-2019s to prospective trainees is also attractive.

The costs of applying for J-1 program designation, compliance with SEVIS requirements, and program administration are not insignificant, so that there needs to be the prospect of considerable volume to justify the cost and effort in seeking J-1 program designation. At a minimum, the employer must sponsor five trainees per year to maintain the program designation.

Regulations published in March 1993 by the former USIA detailed the requirements for training program sponsors.[83] These delineate both general requirements applicable to all J-1 program sponsors as well as ones specific to training sponsors.[84]

The program application is made through the SEVIS system by completing Form 3036 online at *https://egov.immigration.gov/sevis/* and paying the application fee. Additional documentation is submitted in support of the application, and a site visit is normally conducted before an approval can be issued by DOS.

The prospective program sponsor may apply for designation in any combination of specialty and/or non–specialty occupations, and may provide training within any occupation within any of the occupational fields for which a designation is received.[85] The applicant also must provide evidence of its ability to provide the training. This includes a certification that:

- There is sufficient space, equipment, and trained personnel;[86]
- The training program is not designed to recruit and train foreign nationals for employment in the United States; and,
- Trainees will not be placed in positions that displace full-time or part-time employees.[87]

---

[82] 8 CFR §214.2(j)(1)(v).

[83] 58 Fed. Reg. 15186 (Mar. 19, 1993).

[84] 22 CFR §§62.3, 62.5, 62.9, 62.22(d) (Apr. 11, 2002).

[85] 22 CFR §62.22(c)(3) (Apr. 11, 2002).

[86] 22 CFR §62.22(d)(1) (Apr. 11, 2002).

Sample training plans for each field in which training is envisioned, as well as for each expected training plan duration (*e.g.*, 3, 6, 12 and/or 18-month training plans), are also required.[88] These can be based on either planned training or examples of training plans already in existence or used, perhaps through umbrella J-1 sponsors.

Documentation to be separately submitted to DOS includes:

- Verification of the existence of the corporation and its good standing;

- Certification of U.S. citizenship of the company and that the prospective RO and AROs are either U.S. citizens or LPRs;

- Evidence of the financial ability of the sponsor to run the program; and,

- Evidence of prior experience in administering international exchange programs. Documenting experience with expatriate or other corporate international program administration is useful in this regard.

If the application languishes at the DOS Exchange Visitor Designation Branch for a number of months before it is finally reviewed, updated financial and good standing documentation will likely be required. A program sponsor is required to provide a prospective exchange visitor with information about the training program, which should include:

- A written statement concerning any stipend to be paid;

- Costs and fees that the trainee must pay;

- Housing arrangements;

- The insurance requirement;

- The applicability of INA §212(e);

- Estimated living expenses for the geographic area where the alien will be residing in the United States during the program; and,

- A summary of the training program.[89]

The RO and ARO(s) are responsible to DOS for the conduct of the exchange program. Regulations require them to be thoroughly familiar with the exchange visitor program rules and the Codebook and Instructions booklet provided by DOS.[90] The RO and AROs must provide advice and assistance to exchange visitors, conduct official communications regarding the program, and maintain custody and control of exchange program documentation, and comply with the reporting and other requirements under the Student and Exchange Visitor Program and SEVIS computer system.

The software for the SEVIS computer system is provided by DOS to the sponsor who installs it and trains its RO and AROs in its use. Although DOS has grudgingly allowed a sponsor's outside counsel to serve as an ARO, the RO or another ARO who is an employee of the sponsor and who is familiar with the program must sign the DS-2019. The RO must submit an annual report regarding program activities to DOS.

As can be seen from the above, obtaining a designation and administering an exchange visitor program for the purpose of sponsoring trainees is likely to prove undesirable except for those prospective sponsors who have an ongoing need to train many foreign nationals. The costs can easily exceed the perceived FICA savings that employers enjoy due to the exemption of J-1s from U.S. Social Security. In determining whether to seek a J-1 designation, consideration also should be given to applying concurrently for "specialist" designation, which may be advantageous as a way to bring over individuals to *provide* training or to demonstrate and convey to U.S. individuals a sponsored foreign national's expert skills in a field.

The Two-Year Foreign Residence Requirement

The applicability and potential impact of INA §212(e) must be considered in whether to have a trainee sponsored as a J-1. The two-year foreign residence requirement requires a J-1 visitor to return to his or her home country or country of last permanent residence for two years before being eligible to change status in the United States to most other nonimmigrant visa categories[91] from J-1 status or to obtain permanent residence. It also precludes issuance of an H or L visa to a former exchange visitor who has not fulfilled the requirement. This requirement applies if:

- The exchange visitor's program is wholly or partially financed, directly or indirectly, by a U.S.

---

[87] *See* 9 FAM 41.31 N.11.9.

[88] 22 CFR §62.22(f) (Apr. 11, 2002).

[89] 22 CFR §62.22(l) (Apr. 11, 2002).

[90] 22 CFR §62.11 (Apr. 11, 2002).

[91] INA §212(e); *see also* INA §248 and 8 CFR §§248.2(c) and (d).

government agency or by the government of the country of his or her nationality or last place of residence;

- The skills to be acquired by the exchange visitor have been designated by DOS as required by the exchange visitor's country of nationality or last place of residence;[92] or

- The exchange visitor participates in a program of graduate medical education or training.[93]

Although the consular officer may render an initial determination on the alien's Form DS-2019 and/or visa whether or not he or she is subject to the requirement, this is not a final determination and may be incorrect. Counsel needs to determine in advance whether the requirement will apply. The DOS Waiver Review Branch can render a determination as to the applicability of the requirement by providing an advisory opinion. Although industrial trainees are usually not government-funded for their programs, the skills list frequently applies. For example, the government of China has indicated to the U.S. Department of State that all skill areas on the Exchange Visitors Skills list are in need in China so that every J-1 who is a citizen or resident of China at the time of obtaining J-1 status is subject to the requirement.

This requirement would present a significant problem if the employer who provided the training later decides that it needs to keep the exchange visitor in the United States or bring him or her back to the United States to be employed. The alien must reside and accumulate two years of physical presence in the home country in order to fulfill the requirement. Except in rare instances, the requirement cannot be fulfilled in a third country. DOS recently underscored this policy in recently determining that a citizen of a member country of the European Union (EU) cannot fulfill the requirement through residence and physical presence in another country in the EU.

The requirement can be waived for industrial trainees in the following circumstances:

- Where the home country does not object to the alien not fulfilling the requirement;

- If the alien would be persecuted by the home country government;

- If a U.S. citizen or permanent resident alien spouse or child of the exchange visitor would suffer an exceptional or unusual hardship if the exchange visitor were required to fulfill the requirement; or,

- Where an interested U.S. government agency recommends to DOS that a waiver be granted.[94]

The J-1 exchange visitor visa can be a very useful training visa; however, the sponsor and the foreign national must be fully advised of all the advantages and disadvantages. Counsel also must investigate whether the two-year foreign residency will apply to any individual case and advise both the sponsor and affected foreign national accordingly.

CONCLUSION

Visa options for foreign nationals entering into the United States either to receive or provide training in a specialized or non–specialized field can be challenging for the U.S. company wishing to train or be trained by a foreign national in the United States; however, the economic engine of globalization has made these visa options a necessity for U.S. companies competing or expanding globally. Consequently, counsel must understand the intricate requirements of each appropriate visa classification, the nature of the client's training program, and the future goals of its clients. The selection of the appropriate visa classification for the training depends on the prospective trainee's or trainees' background and the sponsor's goals. The petition process for a particular visa classification, such as an H-3 or a J-1 visa, may be time-consuming, demand substantial documentation, and subject prospective trainees and U.S. companies to high levels of scrutiny by USCIS, DOS, and CBP. The trainee visa options are not intended to bypass restrictions in other temporary employment authorized visa categories and should be used with this purpose in mind. The authors hope this article provides practitioners with guidance regarding the types of visas appropriate for foreign nationals entering the United States for bona fide training purposes.

---

[92] 22 CFR §41.63(a)(1)(ii); 9 FAM 41.63 N.2; 22 CFR §41.62; OI 214.2(j)(1) and (7). The Exchange Visitor Skills List appears as an Appendix to OI 212.8(e) and as Exhibit II to 9 FAM 41.62 Notes.

[93] INA §212(e).

[94] 22 CFR §41.63.

U.S. GOVERNMENT FUNDING IN J-1 WAIVER CASES—
THE WORST FORM OF THE DISEASE

by Bruce A. Hake[*]

INTRODUCTION

Section 212(e) of the Immigration and Nationality Act (INA), 8 USC §1182(e), subjects certain J-1 exchange visitors to the J-1 foreign residence requirement. A person subject to this requirement must return to his or her home country (or country of last residence) for two years before he or she can apply for permanent resident status or certain other benefits.

Per INA §212(e), a person can become subject to the foreign residence requirement in three ways: (1) if his or her area of training is on the Skills List for his or her home country; (2) if he or she came to the United States for graduate medical education; or (3) if his or her J-1 program was funded by his or her home country's government or by the U.S Government. Per INA §212(e), persons subject to the J-1 foreign residence requirement can seek a waiver in four ways: (1) on the basis of hardship to qualifying relatives; (2) on the basis of a personal risk of persecution; (3) on the basis of a recommendation from an interested government agency; and (4) on the basis of a no objection statement from the home country.[1] The last option is not available to J-1s who came to the United States for graduate medical education.

Thus, one can view the J-1 foreign residence requirement as a disease: there are three ways to catch it and four ways to cure it. By far the worst form of the disease is a J-1 foreign residence requirement caused by U.S. Government funding.

My most recent article on the Hake Hardship Scale ended with this addendum:[2]

Which issue is still most uncertain? The approach here has been refined for years, and by now I feel confident about predicting the result in most cases. But there is one issue that is still shrouded in mystery: the precise role of U.S. Government funding. As discussed above, by estimating the negative effect of U.S. Government funding at "5 points" on the Hake Hardship Scale, one can come close to predicting the influence of this factor on adjudications by the USCIS [U.S. Citizenship and Immigration Services], based on available AAO [USCIS Administrative Appeals Office] decisions. But it has never been the role of the Immigration Service to discount the approvability of J-1 waiver cases based on the existence of U.S. Government funding or other "program and policy" factors. Instead, in J-1 hardship cases, it has traditionally been the Immigration Service's role to assess legal eligibility (for instance, whether or not there exists a qualifying relative) and to weigh the gravity of hardship, issues that are well within the agency's institutional experience and competence, while "program and policy" considerations have typically been reserved to the USIA [U.S. Information Agency, which was abolished in 1999] or State Department. Thus, it is arguably improper for this factor to have had any negative influence on Immigration Service adjudications, while at the same time it seems clear from experience that the factor has historically had a very strong negative influence on State Department adjudications.

The Immigration Service does not keep statistics on how many Form I-612 cases are filed or

---

[*] Copyright © 2006 by Bruce A. Hake. All Rights Reserved. Reprinted with Permission.

Bruce Hake is a lawyer in Damascus, Md. Formerly an editor of *Interpreter Releases* and *Immigration Briefings*, he has been in private practice since 1993. His practice concentrates on J-1 hardship waiver cases. *See www.hake.com/pc*. Thanks to all lawyers who helped with this paper, especially Alan Musgrave, Robert Aronson, Greg Siskind, and William Stock.

[1] For more information on J-1 waivers, see Hake, "Hardship Waivers For J-1 Physicians," 94-2 *Immigration Briefings* (Feb. 1994); Hake, "Hardship is Hardship: The Equivalency of Hardship Standards in U.S. Immigration Law," 2 *Immigration & Nationality Law Handbook* 384–93 (AILA 2001–02 ed.); Hake, "Hardship Standards," 7 *Bender's Immigration Bull.* 59–80 (Jan. 15, 2002); Hake, "The Hake Hardship Scale (Beta Version)," 1 *Immigration & Nationality Law Handbook* 237–51 (AILA 2002–03 ed.); and Hake & Banks, "The Hake Hardship Scale: A Quantitative System for Assessment of Hardship in Immigration Cases Based on a Statistical Analysis of AAO Decisions," 10 *Bender's Immigration Bull.* 403–20 (Mar. 1, 2005). Earlier versions of the last article were also published at: 1 *Immigration & Nationality Law Handbook* 490–507 (AILA 2004–05 ed.); *Immigration Options for Physicians* 49–66 (AILA 2d. ed. 2004); and 2 *J Visa Guidebook*, App. I-13 (LexisNexis: Siskind, Stock & Yale-Loehr, eds. 2005 ed.).

[2] 10 *Bender's Immigr. Bull.* at 420 (Mar. 1, 2005).

approved, much less on the underlying facts. As I have confirmed from discussions with officials of the Waiver Review Division, the State Department does not keep statistics on how many Form I-612 cases involve specific factors, including the existence of U.S. Government funding. Therefore, nobody knows exactly how important the issue is, nor exactly how it is addressed within the deliberations at the State Department.

All that is known for certain is that U.S. Government funding is a serious disability that will usually lead to defeat unless there is some special positive factor. Such factors may include spectacular levels of hardship, a spectacular risk of persecution (for a persecution waiver case), spectacularly high-level political influence, or strong national security factors. However, it may also be true that some U.S. Government funding cases can be won, in the absence of spectacular facts, if the applicant can do a persuasive job of demonstrating that approval of the waiver would fulfill the statutory purposes, as set forth at 22 CFR §62.1(a). It does seem that the Waiver Review Division is giving more thoughtful attention to the balancing of program and policy factors in U.S. Government funding cases than may have been true for the USIA. Readers are encouraged to send the author any anecdotes or insight you may have on this issue.

This short article is an attempt to go beyond that addendum. Its main contribution to the literature is an analysis and description of information gathered in response to the above concerns through a poll of lawyers with experience with J-1 waiver cases.

BACKGROUND

The exchange visitor program was created in 1948 to promote better international relationships through the exchange of cultural information.[3] That predates the first version of the INA, which was enacted in 1952. A key underpinning of the exchange visitor program was the notion that the individual would take the knowledge and skills acquired in the

United States back to his or her own country in order to promote world peace and also to aid international development.

Over time, Congress became concerned that some exchange visitors were not returning to their home countries. Therefore, in 1956, Congress created the first version of the J-1 foreign residence requirement.[4] Amendments followed in 1961, 1970, 1976, 1988, 1994, 1996, and 2002.[5]

As amended, INA §212(e) now provides (emphasis added):

No person admitted under section 101(a)(15)(J) or acquiring such status after admission (i) whose participation in the program for which he came to the United States was financed in whole or in part, directly or indirectly, by an agency of the Government of the United States or by the government of the country of his nationality or his last residence, (ii) who at the time of the admission or acquisition of status under section 101(a)(15)(J) was a national or resident of a country which the Director of the United States Information Agency, pursuant to regulations prescribed by him, had designated as clearly requiring the services of persons engaged in the field of specialized knowledge or skill in which the alien was engaged, or (iii) who came to the United States or acquired such status in order to receive graduate medical education or training, shall be eligible to apply for an immigrant visa, or for permanent residence, or for a nonimmigrant visa under section 101(a)(15)(H) or section 101(a)(15)(L) until it is established that such person has resided and been physically present in the country of his nationality or his last residence for an aggregate of at least two years following departure from the United States: *Provided,* That upon the favorable recommendation

---

[3] Information and Educational Exchange Act of 1948 (Smith-Mundt Act), Pub. L. No. 80-402, §201, 62 Stat. 6. For an overview of the history of the J program, see Schorr & Yale-Loehr, "The Odyssey of the J-2: Forty-Two Years of Trying Not to Go Home Again," 8 *Bender's Immigr. Bull.* 1810, 1812–22 (Dec. 1, 2003). The information in this background section is partially adapted from Gordon, Mailman, & Yale-Loehr, *Immigration Law and Procedure* §§22.06[1] & [2] (LexisNexis 2006 ed.).

[4] Exchange Visitors-Immigration Status, Pub. L. No. 84-555, 69 Stat. 494 (1956).

[5] Mutual Educational and Cultural Exchange Act of 1961 (Fulbright-Hays Act), Pub. L. No. 87-256, §109, 75 Stat. 527, 535; Act of Apr. 7, 1970, Pub. L. No. 91-225, 84 Stat.116; Health Professions Educational Association Act of 1976, Pub. L. No. 94-484, §601(d), 90 Stat. 2243, 2301; Act of Oct. 24, 1988, Pub. L. No. 100-525, 102 Stat. 2609; Act of Oct. 25, 1994, Pub. L. No. 103-116, §220(a), 108 Stat. 4305; and Illegal Immigration Reform and Immigration Responsibility Act of 1996, Division C of the Omnibus Appropriations Act of 1996 (H.R. 3610), Pub. L. No. 104-208, §622(b), 110 Stat. 3009, Sept. 30, 1996. In addition, the reference to INA §214(l) was corrected by the DOJ Appropriations Authorization Act, Pub. L. No. 107-273, §11018(c)), 116 Stat. 1758, Nov. 2, 2002.

of the Director, pursuant to the request of an interested United States Government agency (or, in the case of an alien described in clause (iii), pursuant to the request of a State Department of Public Health, or its equivalent) or of the Commissioner of Immigration and Naturalization after he has determined that departure from the United States would impose exceptional hardship upon the alien's spouse or child (if such spouse or child is a citizen of the United States or a lawfully resident alien), or that the alien cannot return to the country of his nationality or last residence because he would be subject to persecution on account of race, religion, or political opinion, the Attorney General may waive the requirement of such two-year foreign residence abroad in the case of any alien whose admission to the United States is found by the Attorney General to be in the public interest except that in the case of a waiver requested by a State Department of Public Health, or its equivalent, or in the case of a waiver requested by an interested United States government agency on behalf of an alien described in clause (iii), the waiver shall be subject to the requirements of section 214(*l*): And provided further, that, except in the case of an alien described in clause (iii) the Attorney General may, upon the favorable recommendation of the Director, waive such two-year foreign residence requirement in any case in which the foreign country of the alien's nationality or last residence has furnished the Director a statement in writing that it has no objection to such waiver in the case of such alien.

THE U.S. GOVERNMENT FUNDING GROUND

A J-1 exchange visitor "whose participation in the program for which he came to the United States was financed in whole or in part, directly or indirectly, by an agency of the Government of the United States" is subject to the foreign residence requirement. This provision includes exchange visitors who acquired that status before the 1970 amendment.[6]

Direct financing is defined as funds contributed to the exchange visitor or for the exchange visitor's use; indirect financing means financing by an international organization or by a private organization or institution, with funds contributed by either the United States or the exchange visitor's government.[7]

Government financing will impose the foreign residence requirement only if it is specifically provided for the purpose of supporting the exchange visitor's participation in the program.[8] Moreover, financing by an agency of the U.S. Government will impose the foreign residence requirement only if the agency financed the program specifically for the purpose of promoting international exchange.[9] In other words, the U.S. Government funding imposes the foreign residence requirement only if the funds are "earmarked" for exchange purposes.

The fact that a J-1 exchange visitor is employed by the U.S. Government (for instance, as a research scientist at the National Institutes of Health (NIH)) does not by itself mean that the person is subject to the foreign residence requirement. NIH has many classifications for J-1 exchange visitors employed by NIH, and only some of them are subject to the foreign residence requirement. Similarly, the fact that a person's J-1 employment is funded by a research grant provided by the NIH or another U.S. Government agency does not subject the person to the foreign residence requirement. As noted, the U.S. Government funding must be earmarked for exchange purposes in order for the foreign residence requirement to attach. This is usually clear from the text of the exchange visitor's DS-2019 (formerly IAP-66) form(s).

Further, note that actual U.S. Government funds do not need to be disbursed, either to the exchange visitor or to the exchange visitor's institution in the United States, for it to be considered that there is U.S. Government funding that imposes the foreign residence requirement. For example, U.S. Government funding may be deemed to exist for a Fulbright scholar whose travel and other expenses are paid entirely from foreign sources. In such cases, the State Department's Bureau of Educational and Cultural Affairs (ECA) is deemed to have inherently

---

[6] Act of Apr. 7, 1970, Pub. L. No. 91-225, §2, 84 Stat. 116. The information in the first part of this section is partially adapted from Gordon, Mailman, & Yale-Loehr, *supra* note 3, §22.06[3].

[7] 22 CFR §62.2.

[8] *Id*. Financing includes monetary payments and other forms of support, such as costs of transportation, equipment, tuition, books, supplies, and insurance coverage. *See* Cooper *et al.*, "Exchange Visitors," 93-10 *Immigration Briefings* 34 (Oct. 1993).

[9] *See* 22 CFR §62.2 (definitions of "financed directly" and "financed indirectly"). *See also* Klasko, "Demythicizing the Exchange Visitor Two-Year Return Requirement," 8 *Bender's Immigration Bull.* (Apr. 1, 2003) (myth 7).

expended U.S. Government funds for management and oversight of the program.[10]

A complete description of the Fulbright system is outside the scope of this article, but a few points may avoid some confusion. The Fulbright exchange program is the grandfather of all the J-1 programs. There are now almost 4,000 J-1 program sponsors, but Fulbright has always been the most prominent. The main program number for Fulbright exchanges is "G-1-1," or more recently "G-1-001." If you see that program number, you know the person has a serious legal disability.

Be aware that the documents from a person with Fulbright funding may not bear the name "Fulbright." For example, in one of my cases, the person came on a Fulbright fellowship in 1998 to study at the University of California. The IAP-66 does not say "Fulbright" anywhere. Instead, it says that the person came on Program Number G-1-1, sponsored by the USIA.

There is no single institution or office that governs Fulbright exchanges. Instead, the Fulbright system involves complicated arrangements between both governmental and private or quasi-public organizations both in the United States and in other countries with whom the United States engages in binational exchanges. The main input in a J-1 waiver case for a Fulbrighter comes from the State Department's ECA, the governmental agency that oversees the American side of Fulbright exchanges. However, other actors include the U.S. quasi-public Fulbright Commission, which is rooted in academia, along with the Fulbright Commission for the foreign sending country plus the education ministry for that country, among others.

An exchange visitor who has received a Fulbright or Humphrey grant is regarded as having been financed by an agency of the U.S. Government.[11] In some years past, the USIA generally agreed to waive the foreign residence requirement where the amount of a Fulbright grant was $2,000 or less. This so-called "de minimis" rule, however, has not been in effect for more than 10 years.[12]

There is no mechanism for repaying U.S. Government funding of a J program, an issue that is often raised by clients. Occasionally one hears rumors that a person was able to repay funds, but I have tried to track this down for more than 10 years and have been unable to document a single case. In contrast, it often is possible to repay funding provided by a foreign government or international organization, and some countries have a policy of requiring this before a no objection statement will be issued.

There are two kinds of J programs: "G" (for government) programs, and "P" (for private) programs. All J programs are one or the other. For example, foreign physicians in graduate medical training in the United States typically are in program P-3-4510 sponsored by the Educational Commission for Foreign Medical Graduates (ECFMG). In general, "G" programs tend to involve U.S. Government funding, while "P" programs do not, but there are exceptions in both directions.[13]

A person dissatisfied with a determination that his or her participation in an exchange program was financed by the U.S. Government may question it by submitting an appropriate statement to USCIS, if the person is in the United States, or to a U.S. consul, if the person is abroad. The State Department's determination that a program is government-financed is not binding upon USCIS, and an applicant for adjustment of status or other immigration benefits may offer evidence to rebut the presumptive effect of such a determination.[14]

In the great majority of times when I am approached by prospective clients with U.S. Government funding, I tell them that their best strategy is probably to arrange their affairs to include two years in their home country. I typically advise them to be careful not to hire another lawyer unless the lawyer has experience with U.S. Government funding cases, not just J-1 matters generally. I usually explain further that they should realize that they are up against extremely serious and weighty foreign policy goals of the U.S. Government. The core purpose of the J-1 exchanges is to reduce the

---

[10] AILA/USIA Draft Liaison Minutes, Item 7 (May 26, 1998) (on file with author).

[11] Cf. Matter of Oum, 14 I&N Dec. 340 (BIA 1973) (foreign residence requirement inapplicable where Fulbright Travel Grant preceded acquisition of exchange visitor status; the alien got the travel grant, entered as an F-1 student, and later changed status to J-1).

[12] See Klasko, supra note 9 (myth 10).

[13] See id. (myth 11). See also J Visa Guidebook, supra note 1, at App. A7-1 (State Department list of "G" programs that are not considered to involve U.S. Government funding, and list of "P" programs that are).

[14] See Matter of Ajaelo, 15 I&N Dec. 85 (BIA 1974) (immigration judge improperly rejected such evidence).

risk of war by fostering good relations among peoples of the world. When it comes to countries such as Russia and the former Soviet states, that means reducing the risk of nuclear war! Whereas the impact that any one individual might have on such a weighty concern always seems ridiculously attenuated, it cannot be denied that in the aggregate, it is a policy concern of the utmost importance. In general, the State Department really does believe that strict enforcement of the J-1 foreign residence requirement reduces the risk of war. Such a belief can (and should) only be outweighed by very serious concerns.

WHAT LAWYERS REPORT
ABOUT THE ISSUE

I sent the following 10 questions by e-mail to lawyers who are experienced with J-1 waiver cases. The respondents include very prominent and competent lawyers. In their totality, these responses represent the best data available on the impact of U.S. Government funding in J-1 waiver cases. They also confirm that my own understanding of the issue has been generally accurate.

Below are the questions, including some explanatory materials, responses from 14 lawyer respondents (R-1, etc.), and then a concluding comment by me. The responses were received by me in e-mail. I have edited the responses lightly and removed certain specific details. If a lawyer had no response to a question, nothing is listed here.

1. Approximately what percentage of J-1 waiver cases with U.S. Government funding ("USG cases") do you accept?

R-1: Less than 5 percent. In the past few years, only one case.

R-2: I guess probably a reasonably high number, but that's partially misleading because I'm pretty discouraging and a lot of people choose not to pursue after that or they look for a lawyer that tells them what they want to hear. But I probably take most of the cases as long as I've been careful to explain the chances and also go over the options. In some cases, I tell them to check with the funding agency's office in their home country first and many choose not to pursue once they realize what they're up against.

R-3: Only two or three cases.

R-4: 5 percent.

R-5: I have handled 5 to 7 such cases.

R-6: 2 in many years.

R-7: 2 in 11 years.

R-8: About 5 percent.

R-9: I probably do 2 to 3 per year. Most of my waiver cases are ECFMG-sponsored physicians and these do not involve USG funding.

R-10: Very few.

R-11: I've had fewer than a dozen inquiries for waivers involving USG funding, most were NIH. I have accepted only three. I referred the rest out and a few were consultations where NIH was doing the waiver internally to keep the J-1 researcher and the J-1 just wanted to consult with an attorney about the process, etc.

R-12: Since I don't keep electronic records summarizing this information, I'd have to make a guess that maybe 30 to 40 percent of my potential J waiver consults involve USG funding, and maybe 40 percent of them turn into representations.

R-14: Very low, total only four.

R-15: Around 15 percent.

Hake: These responses basically match my experience. So far I've had decisions in 17 USG cases, but I've also turned down hundreds of them. They tend to come in swarms in the first quarter of every year. I never accept such a case unless it involves spectacular hardship or some other very special factor.

2. Approximately what percentage of the ones you have accepted were: (a) no objection cases; (b) hardship or persecution cases; (c) IGA [interested government agency] cases (and please subdivide the IGA cases if you can)?

R-1: The case was a hardship waiver.

R-2: Probably two-third are hardships. I've done the no objection + cases with a little success. No IGAs yet. I actually don't do all that many of these cases because most people don't bother pursuing the case after the consultation. *[Hake: "No objection +" cases is a term I've used to describe no objection waiver applications that are supplemented by extensive evidence of humanitarian or other special concerns. Like this lawyer, I've had success with this approach several times, but the Waiver Review Division (WRD) currently strongly discourages this approach, preferring that hardship cases be initially filed on Form I-612 with USCIS.]*

R-3: I don't take it if it is just a no objection. Must have an IGA component.

R-4:   a. 0 percent; b. 50 percent; c. 50 percent.

R-5:   I've had at least two no-objection; two hardship; and a few IGA (all HHS [U.S. Department of Health and Human Services]) cases.

R-6:   Both were hardships.

R-7:   One hardship, one HHS researcher.

R-8:   100 percent hardship or persecution.

R-9:   Most cases are no objection or hardship/persecution (probably 80 percent). We have also applied to HHS and USDA as IGAs.

R-10: I've been doing J waivers since 1988, so it's a blur. I have pretty much quit doing hardship cases. I know I've won a couple IGA cases—State 20 back then, and HHS waiver where there was government funding. (I have always viewed HHS as the 800 pound gorilla of IGAs; USIA would nearly always agree with them.) I did have one no objection letter—got the funding agency to say OK because the individual was serving the purposes of the exchange program here in the U.S. The government funding cases I have taken were mostly hardship.

R-11: 100 percent were IGA cases—all three to DOE.

R-12: Very few are no objection—maybe 10 percent. Probably 30 percent of the remainder are hardship, the other 60 percent are IGAs.

R-14: All four no objections, and did a hardship too for one of them.

R-15: None that I recall were simple no objection cases. USG funding creates a strong program-and-policy presumption that the exchange visitor should return to the home country. For USG funding, having a foreign government raise no objection is beside the point. (So India doesn't mind that U.S. taxpayers spent a bundle to educate this person? So what? It's not India's money.) One needs to say more to inspire the waiver folks to release the exchange visitor with USG money.

Perhaps 35 percent were hardship or persecution cases. That requires much laboring over the writing.

For the rest, I do IGA waivers. Most often the client is a scientist and I am making a national interest argument against sending the exchange visitor home. Not infrequently the argument involves the claim that returning the scientist is too dangerous, sort of a Soviet Scientist argument. I'd guess 35 percent National Science Foundation [NSF], 10 percent HHS, 20 percent DOD, 20 percent Conrad cases, and 15 percent miscellaneous other agencies.

Hake: The range of experience here is broad. Of the 17 such cases I have so far had decisions in, 15 were hardship cases, 1 was a no objection, and the other was an unsuccessful IGA case (NSF) that was successful only after a high-level political intervention.

3. Approximately what percentage of such cases have you won?

R-1:   We won the case, but it took nearly a year to get a response.

R-2:   Probably two-third.

R-3:   Both, although for different reasons. One was an IGA and the other got approved for asylum, so we argued that in parallel to IGA.

R-4:   100 percent.

R-5:   All of them, except for one no-objection case. The original plan was to file this case with the NSF. However, NSF has a policy of not accepting cases for processing, unless the no-objection request was denied. We filed the no-objection request and got a denial, as expected. By then, the client got disappointed with the process and decided to go to another attorney.

R-6:   0.

R-7:   Hardship submitted at TSC 17 months ago, still pending at WRD after 14 months (USAID) funding; HHS researcher case about to be submitted

R-8:   95 percent.

R-9:   About 60 to 70 percent.

R-10: I think I won them all—some with several go-arounds. The only waiver I can remember losing was a recent hardship where both a husband and wife were subject to the foreign residence requirement in two separate countries. They approved the wife and denied the husband—absolutely absurd. He had already left the U.S., and they ultimately decided not to fight it, which made me sad.

R-11: 0 percent. They were denied by DOE.

R-12: Knock on wood, all of them (though one hardship denial from CSC is on appeal to the AAO).

R-13: 98 percent approval rate.

R-14: All four approved.

R-15: I have never lost a waiver case, but I choose carefully and I have not had a high volume.

Hake: I've won 16 of 17 so far, but I've also turned down hundreds of them. These responses confirm my impression that these cases are ex-

tremely hard to win, but that they are not hopeless if there are very strong equities.

4. What have you heard from others about the impact of USG funding on J waiver cases?

R-1: That USG funding makes it nearly impossible to win a J waiver case. My understanding has always been that DOS checks with the funding agency for their views, and those views are given an incredible amount of weight, nearly impossible to overcome.

R-2: Extremely bad, but possibly getting a little better, particularly when you have really good facts and you're from a country that is not a developing nation.

R-3: I have heard/experienced that it was impossible under USIA, even with de minimis funding from Fulbright (had an old case denied with just a $700 travel grant), but since the WRD took over from USIA in 1999, it is not as strict a rule. Still tough, but not impossible. My view has been that if you can argue, through IGA, that the work you do here will still support the underlying mission of the J-1 program, then you can get waiver approved. For example, person would work in U.S., but for a non-profit whose goal was to educate third world countries (including his home country) on economic and agricultural issues.

R-4: It is the kiss of death as far as waivers are concerned.

R-5: That, for Fulbright scholars, if the Fulbright foundation issues official support, the case would be approved. In all other cases, it is my understanding that the initial agency (USCIS or IGA) processes the case as it normally does, and the DOS does a balancing test weighing the reasons for a waiver against the interest of the program.

R-6: Almost impossible.

R-8: I think if it's hardship, DOS treats them without so much difficulty.

R-9: The general belief is that USG funding is the death knell for waiver requests.

R-10: Everyone says it is the kiss of death, but it ain't necessarily so.

R-11: Impossible to get a no objection waiver if USG funding, and depending on type of funding difficulty varies. Fulbright makes funding impossible to get a waiver.

R-12: For no objections, the WRD says it depends strongly on the attitude of the funder. They have gotten heat from the funding agencies for approving too many no objections for funded scholars. Some agencies (NIH springs to mind as one with a policy on point) usually do not care, others vary on a case-by-case basis (I just had a no objection waiver granted for somebody funded by the Smithsonian Institution, for example).

R-15: For USAID, Fulbright, and Freedom and Democracy funding, generally waivers are very hard—impossible without good grounds (and sometimes impossible even with good grounds).

Hake: These responses match what I have heard.

5. Have you noticed any changes in success rates or adjudication practices over time? Please describe.

R-2: Possibly getting a bit better for Fulbright. Can't really speak to other agencies.

R-4: Not really. My recollection over the years (20+) is that it was always hard, though more than 10 years ago, it may have been *easier*.

R-5: I understand that it may have become a bit easier to win these cases in the past several years, provided that there are compelling reasons for a waiver that outweigh competing program and policy concerns.

R-6: No.

R-8: Lately, a little bit easier.

R-9: I think that DOS is becoming a bit more lenient. I screen my USG funded cases based on amount of funding; contributions of alien; family hardship situation; possibility of release statement from USG; etc. I think that DOS will consider these factors as a supplement to the no objection.

R-10: I started when you could get waivers even with government funding—late 80s. Then went through the "just say 'no'" phase at USIA, then saw a real balancing at the DOS waiver office, and think that still holds. Rumors abound that you can now get waivers in USG cases with a no objection letter if there is a good public policy reason for a grant.

R-12: DOS is definitely looking at no objection cases more carefully than in previous years. Jinny Chun [the WRD's Chief] said so at the 2005 AILA Annual Conference. IGA waivers are harder to do at the various agencies, but I haven't yet had a waiver approved by the IGA that was rejected by DOS. However, hardship cases seem to be getting a little tougher to win, particularly in California.

R-13: It has become more difficult to get hardship cases approved, especially at CSC.

R-15: Doctor cases may be a bit easier these days. Other cases seem much the same.

Hake: I have not noticed any changes in approval rates on USG cases over the last 13 years, except only that I have the impression that about five years ago, the WRD seems to have started to give more thoughtful attention to competing factors in no objection cases. My impression is that the USIA and later the WRD always gave thoughtful attention to competing factors in hardship, persecution, and IGA cases.

6. Please describe in as much detail as possible what facts have been important in your decision to accept a USG case and in the chance of success?

R-1: The level of hardship to the USC family members. The only case we filed involved a J-1 female married to a USC male expecting a USC baby. The J-1's sister in the home country suffered from a few miscarriages. We had medical opinions confirming that those miscarriages would have been preventable in the United States. The USC husband had a computer job that he could not do at all in the home country. We focused quite a bit on the country conditions as well. If we were going to pursue an IGA waiver, I would imagine that it would have to be a compelling project that the person was going to work on.

R-2: Nationality of applicant (wealthier countries seem to be more relaxed), basis for hardship.

R-4: I need to know the agency funding, amount of funding, and the level and type of hardship or the IGA and its level of interest/need for the foreign national.

R-5: I've had clients who have received assurances from the Fulbright commission that it would support the waiver. Those cases got approved via the no objection route. Otherwise, making compelling IGA arguments or hardship arguments have worked well for me.

R-6: I tried two cases with really great hardships and both were unsuccessful despite tremendous efforts.

R-8: Depends on family members, medical issues.

R-9: Suggested above. I particularly like to explore whether the USG source might release the alien. Also, family hardship seems to be consideration.

R-10: Pretty dramatic hardship is necessary! I'm considering some "public policy" no objection cases right now.

R-11: If USAID or Fulbright funding, I do not accept the case. In the three DOE cases I took on, the

universities requesting the waiver were very supportive and understood the chance of success was less than 50 percent. I also consider the public policy argument as an important factor in my decision.

R-12: I don't care about the kind of USG funding, only the strength of the underlying IGA/Hardship/"no objection plus" case. Obviously, the higher the funding, the more we advise that the underlying case has to be strong.

R-13: Depends on the case.

R-15: The client must be able to afford my help. I don't take USG cases unless I see a reasonably promising route to success, however unusual it may be. Unless the case involves great hardship that is readily shown (*e.g.*, a woman with breast cancer and bad medicine in the home country), I will likely invest a lot of time and expense before the case is ready to file. I won't do half the job for half the fee.

Hake: I will consider accepting a case if it involves really exceptionally serious hardship, persecution, and/or public interest factors. For non-USG cases, the Hake Hardship Scale indicates that one needs "11 points plus a good story" in order to have a strong confidence of success. I estimate that more is required for a USG case. In particular, for such cases, the Hake Hardship Scale indicates that one needs at least "16 points plus a very good story." That seems to be accurate, and it is consistent with the opinions of these other lawyers.

7. Have you observed any difference in success rates or adjudication practices depending on whether the USG funding was Fulbright, USAID [U.S. Agency for International Development], or other categories?

R-1: In this instance, the funding was Fulbright.

R-2: Main experience is with Fulbright.

R-3: Perception certainly is that Fulbright is hardest, but I have always thought that it is still a presentation issue. If you just argue IGA and DOS has to choose between IGA and Fulbright, they call it "conflicting policy interests" or something like that and refuse to grant the waiver. It seems to me that even a Fulbright *could* be approved, but only if the facts circle back to outline described above—work in U.S. must still support the underlying mission of cultural exchange and not just merely be in the U.S.'s national interest.

R-4: I have never accepted a Fulbright or USAID case. I have heard from reliable sources that they are very tough to get and the cases that have presented were not sufficiently strong to try.

R-5:   No.

R-6:   No.

R-8:   All the same, difficult.

R-9:   Not really. I have had better success with Fulbright than with USAID.

R-10: Fulbright, USAID are always the heavies and used to (probably still do) object to every waiver. Can't think of any others right now.

R-11: Yes. Waiver involving other category funding seems much easier, but this is anecdotal only.

R-12: No, except as noted above on no objection cases Fulbright and USAID rarely consent (thought I have seen it happen).

R-13: I have done two Fulbright cases recently. One was for someone who only received travel funding and on the other we got an IGA to issue a support letter. Both were approved.

R-15: My sense is that USAID money makes for the hardest cases, with Freedom and Democracy money a close second. I find all USG cases hard, however. I take some but I expect to work at them.

Hake: I have not observed any difference. I think that Fulbright, USAID, and all other USG funding agencies tend to be very restrictive about acquiescing in waiver applications, but I also think that they will give thoughtful attention to cases that involve strong competing factors.

8. In a USG no objection case, how do you advise people to prepare the Statement of Reasons? [All no objection waiver applications require a statement from the applicant concerning his or her reasons for wanting to waive the foreign residence requirement and stay in the United States.]

R-1:   I would never file just a no objection case. I would always try to find hardship or an IGA in support.

R-2:   We usually prepare the cases along the lines of a hardship case and the Statement of Reasons is consistent. Given what I've been hearing from others, I'm not sure this is such a hot idea.

R-4:   I advise them to truthfully explain why they want a waiver to remain in the USA. I advise them that they should take into consideration their

audience (the Waiver Review Division) in the method that they frame their interest in a waiver.

R-5:   Personally, I think it's all about the support of the sponsoring agency. The Statement of Reasons is just a formality.

R-9:   Hard to give a unitary reply. It depends on the facts. But this really is the crux of the case. Again, we tend to provide our reasons directly to WRD rather than filtering them through the alien's home government.

R-10: Emphasize service to home country and furtherance of exchange goals by working in the U.S., or for an international organization.

R-12: Consistent with whatever else we are doing in the case. A vanilla no objection case where we are expecting to convince the funding agency not to object to the waiver, or where they have a policy of not objecting, I just say "I want to stay to work in my field" or "marry my spouse" or whatever. Otherwise, I am consistent with the underlying waiver application—"It would cause a hardship to my spouse," etc.

R-15: Make all hardship and possible persecution arguments that one has, if one has such arguments. If the home country is not a NATO country, and if the exchange visitor has expertise of military application, discuss the likelihood that one will be put to military use. If one's work in the United States is arguably of national importance, make the national interest argument.

Hake: In non-USG cases, I advise people simply to be short and honest about why they want to stay in the United States. Only one paragraph is necessary, and there are no magic words. In USG cases, on the other hand, the Statement of Reasons, in my opinion, is of tremendous importance. It should be carefully written to explain why the person's planned course of action in the United States would better fulfill the statutory purposes of the J exchange programs than would requiring the person to return to the home country.[15] Where possible, I emphasize the continuing contacts that the person will maintain with the home country and with home county institutions. In such cases, sometimes it may be wise to supplement the Statement of Reasons with a few support documents, such as letters from persons both in the home country and in the United States who will be connected to the

---

[15] See 22 CFR §62.1(a) (statutory purpose of J exchange programs).

person's planned activities in the United States. Recently the State Department advised that in no objection cases: "The attorney of record should submit materials that assist waiver officers in balancing the policy, program and foreign policy considerations."[16]

9. How do you think the Waiver Review Division [WRD] internally processes USG cases differently from non-USG cases?

R-1: I think that the WRD checks with the USG agency for their input.

R-2: I know that they'll keep a case pending forever waiting on a response from the funding agency. I wish they had a policy of granting the recommendation when the funding agency fails to respond. If they can't be bothered responding, how worried are they really that the person is not going to go back.

R-3: I view it as a burden of proof difference. If foreign funds or Skills List, USG has no stake and will defer to foreign government with no additional review. If USG invested dollars in the exchange, then you have to convince them that they didn't waste the money and that the mission of program is supported. Maybe the difference could be described as between "preponderance of the evidence" (for non-USG cases) and "clear and convincing evidence" (for USG cases)?

R-4: WRD gets a position from the USG funding agency and, I think, they also get an idea of how important it is to the agency that a waiver *not* be granted. My understanding is that this position of the USG funding agency is given great weight by the WRD.

R-8: I think if it's not hardship waiver, forget it.

R-9: Am not sure other than they consult with the funding source.

R-10: I think they weigh the program sponsor's views more heavily. And I think there are internal politics.

R-11: I suspect much more weight is placed on policy considerations and program sponsor's view on waiver.

R-12: They hold up the case and ask for a response from the funder. The funder's opinion is weighed heavily in their decision process.

R-15: They consult with the funding agencies.

---

[16] Draft Notes of AILA-DOS Liaison Meeting (Mar. 23, 2006), Response 7 (AILA Doc. No. 06040571).

Hake: Unfortunately, it appears that nobody really knows. Some cases certainly involve considerable discussion. It is unknown what process is followed in the majority of USG cases. There seems to be a consensus that the amount and source of funding is important.

10. Do you think it is advisable to seek to influence the program sponsor directly in a USG case, such as asking for help from the foreign Fulbright Commission, or do you have any other observations about the politics of USG cases?

R-1: I think it is a good idea to get input from the home country.

R-2: Absolutely. I think this makes a big difference.

R-3: I do think that is important, but I actually don't think that it is *as* important as connecting the reason for stay to purpose of program. Even if the sponsor disagrees (as they usually do), you can still override and get approval if presented properly.

R-4: If there is a good political connection to the USG funding agency, then I advise using it. If it is not very strong, then I advise against using it, though, if it looks like a negative recommendation may be coming, I advise the client to try whatever they can to influence the decision.

R-5: Absolutely. In my experience, those cases where Fulbright issued a statement of support sailed through.

R-8: No.

R-9: Absolutely yes. We always work with the foreign Fulbright office and have had success in getting their endorsement of waivers. Without this endorsement, I think the chances of success are greatly diminished.

R-10: Yes, get help from overseas folks if possible.

R-11: I know that the NIH waivers I've consulted on that were done internally at NIH and were all approved, so it does seem to help to have the program sponsor involved.

R-12: Absolutely. I've seen Fulbrighters granted no objection waivers where the Fulbright organization has been convinced not to object.

R-13: Fulbright and USAID are not very receptive to these calls. Other institutions usually do consent to the waiver being granted.

R-15: Only once, in my experience, has the foreign Fulbright agency made substantial contribution to the waiver argument, explaining changes in country conditions that I did not understand. Generally I think it's worth hearing whatever the sponsor may say. Where appropriate, sometimes I may also seek political help of various sorts.

Hake: It depends on the case. Where a person has had a cordial personal relationship with someone at the foreign Fulbright Commission, my impression is that a strong endorsement from that person can be extremely helpful.

CONCLUSION

On balance, it appears that the impact of U.S. Government funding in J-1 waiver cases has not significantly changed over the years. Such funding is a major obstacle to the success of a waiver application and the great majority of such cases have no realistic hope. But the State Department will give thoughtful attention to competing factors. Cases that have very strong equities may have a reasonable chance of success.

PROTECTING VICTIMS OF CRIME[*]

by Aimee Clark Todd, Sally Kinoshita, Sheila Neville, and Gail Pendleton[**]

INTRODUCTION

In 2000, Congress created two nonimmigrant visa categories for noncitizen survivors of human trafficking and other serious crimes—the T and U visas. Another visa had been created in 1994 for witnesses and informants in certain criminal cases—the S visa. To best serve clients who fall into these

[*] Portions of this article are excerpted and adapted from "The Law of Human Trafficking: What Legal Aid Providers Should Know," *Clearinghouse Review*, March-April 2004, by S. Neville and S. Martinez, and "A Guide for Legal Advocates Providing Services to Victims of Human trafficking," United States Conference of Catholic Bishops/Migration and Refugee Services, Catholic Legal Immigration Network (CLINIC), and the Legal Aid Foundation of Los Angeles (edited and compiled by E. Abriel) (Nov. 2004), at *www.cliniclegal.org* under "Publications."

[**] **Aimee Clark Todd** is an associate with Powell Goldstein LLP in Atlanta. Her practice concentrates on business immigration, including temporary working status and permanent residence for professionals, international transfers, investors, researchers, artists, and athletes. Ms. Todd is currently treasurer of the Atlanta Chapter of AILA, vice chair of AILA's Young Lawyers Division Steering Committee, board member of the International Family Center, and Development Committee member for Refugee Resettlement and Immigration Services of Atlanta.

Sally Kinoshita is a staff attorney at the Immigrant Legal Resource Center (ILRC), a national nonprofit technical backup center on immigration law in San Francisco. She is co-author of a number of ILRC publications including *Special Immigrant Juvenile Status for Children Under Juvenile Court Jurisdiction, Immigration Benchbook for Juvenile and Family Court Judges,* and *The VAWA Manual: Immigration Relief for Abused Immigrants.*

Sheila Neville is a staff attorney with the Immigration Unit at the Legal Aid Foundation of Los Angeles (LAFLA), where she oversees the S.T.O.P. the Traffic: Slavery Training and Outreach Project. Ms. Neville provides training and technical assistance on human trafficking and slavery issues to legal aid programs and other community-based agencies throughout the United States. Ms. Neville received her law degree from George Washington University Law School.

Gail Pendleton is an independent consultant and co-chair of the National Network to End Violence Against Immigrant Women. For 20 years, she was with the National Immigration Project, where she received AILA's Human Rights Award. She now directs the federally-funded ASISTA Project, providing technical assistance and DHS intervention on VAWA and U status.

categories, it is important for immigration attorneys to understand not only the legal requirements for T, U, and S status but also the critical need to collaborate with professionals from other disciplines who assist victims and witnesses.

It is also important for immigration attorneys to build collaborative relationships with law enforcement agencies, domestic violence and sexual assault agencies, programs that serve trafficked persons, medical providers, community-based organizations, and other agencies and individuals who are encounter immigrant victims of crime and human trafficking.

It is particularly important to work with law enforcement agencies. You should not expect automatic assistance from them if they have not been educated about these visa categories or do not yet have reason to trust you.

OBTAINING "U" STATUS FOR VICTIMS OF CRIME

Legislative Background of U Status

The Victims of Trafficking and Violence Prevention Act (VTVPA)[1] was enacted in October 2000 to strengthen law enforcement's ability to detect, investigate, and prosecute violent crimes while protecting the victims of these crimes.[2] This purpose is accomplished by giving legal status, employment authorization, and access to public benefits to victims who have gathered the courage to come forward, report the crime, and assist in its investigation and/or prosecution.

The VTPA created the U nonimmigrant category to permit noncitizen victims of crime and their families to stay in the United States and obtain employment authorization. The U status is available to noncitizens who suffer substantial physical or mental

---

[1] Pub. L. No. 106-386, 114 Stat. 1464 (Oct. 28, 2000) (hereinafter VTVPA); INA §§101(a)(15)(U), 214(o), 245(l).

[2] Cronin, Office of Programs, Victims of Trafficking and "Violence Protection Act of 2000 (VTVPA) Policy Memorandum #22—'T' and 'U' Nonimmigrant Visas," Memorandum for Michael Pearson, Office of Field Operations (Aug. 30, 2001), *reprinted in* 78(44) *Interpreter Releases* 1758 (Nov. 12, 2001) (hereinafter Interim Relief Memo 1).

abuse resulting from a wide range of criminal activity, including domestic abuse. After three years in U status, the noncitizens may be able to adjust status to lawful permanent residence. The U status is available to up to 10,000 people per year.[3]

Although U status was created several years ago, as of this writing the Department of Homeland Security (DHS) has not yet issued regulations to implement the statute. Because U.S. Citizenship and Immigration Services (USCIS) cannot grant U status at this time, it has made available through policy memoranda a form of interim relief for noncitizens who might otherwise be eligible for U status.[4] In the Violence Against Women and Department of Justice Reauthorization Act,[5] enacted in January 2006, Congress mandated that DHS issue implementing regulations for U status (as well as other provisions) within 180 days of passage of the law, *i.e.*, by July 5, 2006.

Due to the lack of a regulatory framework, the complexity of this area of law, and the vulnerable status of noncitizen victims of crime, it is important that practitioners utilize the vast resources and guidance available from the National Immigration Project (*www.nationalimmigrationproject.org*), the Immigrant Legal Resource Center (ILRC), (*www.ilrc.org*), and the ASISTA Immigration Technical Assistance Project (*www.asistaonline.org*), when representing noncitizen victims of crime. These organizations have not only gathered and created resource materials for filing for U interim relief, they also engage in regular contact with USCIS, provide training to practitioners and to law enforcement officials, and advise on changes needed in the law.

Qualifying for U Status

To qualify for U status, a noncitizen must establish that the following four criteria are met:

- He or she has suffered substantial physical or mental abuse as a result of having been a victim

of one of the following forms of criminal (or "similar") activity: rape; torture; trafficking; incest; domestic violence; sexual assault; abusive sexual contact; prostitution; sexual exploitation; female genital mutilation; being held hostage; peonage; involuntary servitude; slave trade; kidnapping; abduction; unlawful criminal restraint; false imprisonment; blackmail; extortion; manslaughter; murder; felonious assault; witness tampering; obstruction of justice; perjury; or attempt, conspiracy, or solicitation to commit any of the above mentioned crimes.

- He or she possesses information concerning the criminal activity (or in the case of a child under the age of 16, the parent, guardian or next friend of the noncitizen possesses such information).

- He or she has obtained certification from a federal, state, or local law enforcement officer, prosecutor, judge or other authority (or DHS) that states she or he has been helpful, is being helpful, or is likely to be helpful in investigating or prosecuting the criminal activity (or in the case of a child under the age of 16, the parent, guardian or next friend of the noncitizen has provided such help).

- The criminal activity violated the laws of the United States or occurred in the United States or its territories or possessions.[6]

To illustrate the potential reach of U status, consider some examples of individuals who might qualify.

- An H-4 spouse who is the victim of domestic abuse by the H-1B principal could qualify for U status if she reported the abuse to the police.[7]

- In addition, the spouse of a U.S. citizen or permanent resident abuser who does not qualify for VAWA (*e.g.*, due to a divorce more than two years ago) could qualify for U status if she reported the abuse.

- Abused individuals in same-sex relationships covered by their state domestic violence laws may also gain status through the U process.

- Even individuals who were victims of criminal activity outside of the United States can receive

---

[3] VTVPA; INA §§101(a)(15)(U), 214(o), 245(l).

[4] *See id.* Yates, Associate Director of Operations, "Centralization of Interim Relief for U Nonimmigrant Status Applicants," Memorandum for Director, Vermont Service Center (Oct. 8, 2003), *published on* AILA InfoNet at Doc. No. 03101420 (*posted* Oct. 14, 2003) (hereinafter Interim Relief Memo 2).

[5] Title VIII, Protection of Battered and Trafficked Immigrants of the Violence Against Women and Department of Justice Reauthorization Act of 2005, Pub. L. No. 109-162, 119 Stat. 2960 (Jan. 5, 2006) (hereinafter VAWA 2005).

[6] INA §§101(a)(15)(U)(i) and (iii); 214(o)(1).

[7] Note that this person also could apply for work authorization under new provisions created by Congress in VAWA 2005, but is not otherwise independently eligible for status, except for the U option.

U status if the criminal activity violated the laws of the United States and a U.S. law enforcement agency is willing to investigate and/or prosecute the crime.

An individual might qualify for more than one type of status—U, T, or permanent residence through VAWA—as a spouse who has suffered domestic violence. It is important to review the criteria and procedures for each of these categories to determine the best option for your client.

AMBIGUITY IN THE ABSENCE OF REGULATIONS

In the absence of regulations, a great deal of ambiguity arises from the statutory language. A key unanswered question is whether DHS will limit the Type of law enforcement officers from whom it will accept certifications. The statute's language is purposefully broad in this respect, but advocates fear that DHS may limit certifications from local law enforcement to chiefs of police or individuals specifically designated by chiefs of police. The National Network to End Violence Against Immigrant Women has put the agency on notice that it will challenge the regulations if DHS places limits on certifications by local law enforcement.[8] Currently, the VAWA unit grants interim relief to applicants with certifications from the frontline officers working the case.

Determination of who qualifies as a "victim" is also expected to be resolved by regulations. What is known, however, is that being a witness to a crime is not sufficient to qualify for U status or interim relief. Advocates are currently pushing for an adoption of the federal Victims of Crime Act (VOCA) definition of "victim" in the visa regulations.[9] In most cases, it will be clear who the victim is because most of the statutorily listed crimes for the U status involve a person as the victim. Less clear are situations in which the victim was not the direct target of the crime but suffered nonetheless. If an individual has

received victim compensation or victim assistance, the argument for qualification will be stronger.

Another concern stemming from the lack of regulations is the definition of "substantial harm." It is important to note that, as with the "battery or extreme cruelty" requirement for VAWA applicants, the abuse is not confined to physical abuse but also includes mental abuse. The term "substantial" indicates that the abuse must rise to a certain level of severity, but at this time there is no standard to determine whether the abuse suffered was substantial. Until regulations are published, U interim-relief requests are being accepted with evidence of abuse that would satisfy a VAWA claim.

As nonimmigrant visa applicants, U applicants must overcome the grounds of inadmissibility. Congress created a discretionary waiver for all grounds of inadmissibility except those applicable to Nazis and perpetrators of genocide, torture, and extrajudicial killings. The standard for a waiver is the "public or national interest." Although applicants for interim relief need not concern themselves with this issue, they should begin amassing evidence of positive equities that will meet the waiver's standards.

Applicants who have been convicted of an aggravated felony face a special problem. Congress did not preclude eligibility for applicants with aggravated felonies, but Interim Relief Memo 2 said that such applicants are per se ineligible for interim relief. Finally, without regulations, it is unclear exactly how "helpful" the victim must be to law enforcement. The statute does not require any specific acts, such as serving as a witness at trial or providing testimony. However, both the statutory language and experience with interim-relief applications shows that the case must have led to an investigation or prosecution in which the victim was helpful.[10]

To receive the latest information on U interim relief issues, you can join the free VAWA Updates list serve.[11] To obtain background documents, a U certification form for use by law enforcement, and other materials on U interim relief, go to the ASISTA website: *www.asistaonline.org.*

---

[8] For arguments on this issue and others identified by the National Network, see its Comments on the Proposed U Form (*www.asistaonline.org*) (hereinafter Comments).

[9] VOCA defines victim as "a person who has suffered physical, sexual, financial, or emotional harm as a result of the commission of a crime," Appendix A to VOCA. *See www.ojp.usdoj.gov/ovc/publications/infores/fraud/psvf/appenda.htm* (last visited May 20, 2006).

[10] For suggestions on kinds of helpfulness that qualify and who should make that determination, see Comments.

[11] Send your request to Christine Kellogg at *Christine@asistaonline.org.*

Length of Status and Adjustment of Status

The U status can be granted for up to four years, or longer if a law enforcement official certifies that the U principal's assistance is required in an investigation or prosecution.[12]

Individuals who receive U status, and have maintained continuous residence in the United States for at least three years since receiving the status, may apply for adjustment to permanent resident status if they show that "continued presence in the United States is justified on humanitarian grounds, to ensure family unity, or otherwise in the public interest."[13] Absences from the United States greater than 90 days or an aggregate of 180 days will not terminate continuous presence if the absence was to assist in the investigation or prosecution or if an official involved in the investigation or prosecution certifies that it is "otherwise justified."[14] A recent USCIS memo has clarified that individuals who are granted interim relief and whose U-status application is ultimately approved "will have their U nonimmigrant status recorded as of the date the request for U interim relief was approved."[15] This will help to alleviate some of the harm caused by the nearly six-year delay in issuance of U regulations.

Nonimmigrants in U status who have "unreasonably refused to provide assistance" to a criminal investigation or prosecution will be denied adjustment.[16] In addition, U nonimmigrants, who participated in Nazi persecution or engaged in genocide, are ineligible for adjustment.[17] All other grounds of inadmissibility may be waived in the public or national interest.[18]

Family Members Eligible for Derivative Status

Spouses and children of principal applicants may petition for U derivative status.[19] If the principal U applicant is under the age of 21, certain members of his or her family—specifically, parents and unmarried siblings under age 18 on the date the principal U applicant files for status—may also petition for U derivative status.[20] Amendments contained in VAWA 2005 have eliminated the need to certify that the investigation would be harmed without the assistance of the relative, as well as the requirement that the relative prove that he or she would suffer extreme hardship if U derivative status is not granted.[21] These are important changes, to ensure that victims of these serious crimes will have the support of their family members.

Application Procedures for U Status (Interim Relief)

In the absence of regulations implementing U status, USCIS issued guidance in August 2001 providing interim relief for noncitizens who appear to be eligible for U status.[22] This guidance was later supplemented by an additional USCIS memorandum in October 2003, centralizing all interim-relief filings with the VAWA unit of the Vermont Service Center (VSC).[23] This very important development has resulted in a more consistent application of U policy. A later memo addressed application procedures for eligible applicants in proceedings.[24] The VSC now issues grants of deferred action and employment authorization to qualified applicants for U interim relief.

Applicants for, and recipients of, U interim relief should be warned not to travel outside the United States. There is no procedure in place at this time for U interim-relief applicants or recipients to receive advance parole or any other re-entry document. Those who do leave and manage to return to the United States may trigger serious bars to their ability to obtain permanent residence.

Eligibility for U Interim Relief

An application for U interim relief must provide prima facie evidence that the noncitizen meets the U-status criteria described above.[25] Significantly, the USCIS memoranda promote a favorable reading of

---

[12] INA §214(p), *amended by* VAWA 2005 §821(b).

[13] INA §245(m).

[14] INA §245(m)(2). Note that for those who are granted U interim relief, there is no procedure permitting travel at this time.

[15] Aytes, Acting Assoc. Dir., Domestic Operations, "Applications for U Nonimmigrant Status," Memorandum to Director, Vermont Service Center (Jan. 6, 2006), *published on* AILA InfoNet at Doc. No. 06011763 (*posted* Jan. 17, 2006).

[16] INA §245(m)(1).

[17] *Id.*

[18] INA §212(d)(14)

[19] INA §101(a)(15)(U)(ii).

[20] *Id.*, as amended by VAWA 2005 §801(b).

[21] *Id.*

[22] Interim Relief Memo 1 at 4.

[23] Interim Relief Memo 2.

[24] Interim Relief Memo 4.

[25] Interim Relief Memo 2 at 2.

the U criteria for interim relief, stating that "it is better to err on the side of caution than to remove a possible victim" and that "[s]ervice personnel should ensure broad interpretation of the guidance to ensure an alien is not removed."[26] Practitioners should keep in mind, however, that approval of interim relief does not guarantee ultimate approval of U status, as a grant of interim relief is not an adjudication of the claim for U status itself.[27]

If the applicant is in removal proceedings, the VSC first must contact U.S. Immigration and Customs Enforcement (ICE) to determine if there is adverse information in his or her file.[28] The VSC must exercise discretion in approving the application. If approved, ICE must terminate the proceedings.

In the absence of regulations, current USCIS guidance indicates that the agency will not grant interim relief to individuals convicted of an aggravated felony.[29] However, there is nothing in the statute that restricts USCIS from granting U interim relief (or U status in the future) to these individuals. It is important to note that noncitizens in a valid status must relinquish their existing status to be eligible for deferred action (only available to those with no other status), which is the essence of interim relief. It may be that some individuals will choose to pursue U interim relief rather than remain in another nonimmigrant status in order to obtain work authorization or a route to permanent residence. VAWA 2005 clarified that there should be no restrictions on changing nonimmigrant status for those seeking U visas.[30]

Filing an Application for U Interim Relief

Applications for U interim relief should be mailed to the VAWA Unit of the VSC.[31]

No official USCIS form exists for an interim-relief application and there is no filing fee for in-

terim relief. The application materials will vary depending on the relief being requested. However, all applications should contain the following:

- A one-page cover letter serving as a roadmap to the application, highlighting how the applicant meets the eligibility criteria and listing the documentation submitted. If the applicant's qualifying spouse, child, parent, or sibling will also be seeking interim relief, the cover letter should state this.

- The applicant's declaration describing what occurred in his or her own words. Practitioners should ensure that the declaration is detailed and addresses each of the eligibility criteria noted above. However, to ensure credibility of the application, it is of the utmost importance that the declaration be in the applicant's own words.

- A copy of the applicant's photographic identification or birth certificate.

- A law-enforcement certificate dated within six months of the application that (1) identifies the certifier by name, employer, position, job title, employer's address, and phone number; (2) states that the applicant was a victim of one or more of the listed crimes (including a "similar" crime); (3) identifies the crime(s) (including, where possible, the dates and locations of criminal activity and the statute or code that has been violated); (4) verifies that the applicant is being, has been, or is likely to be helpful to the prosecution or investigation of the criminal activity (or in the case of a child under the age of 16, that the parent, guardian, or next friend of the noncitizen has provided such help); and (5) affirms that the criminal activity occurred in the United States or its territories or possessions or is in violation of U.S. law.[32] You should obtain this certificate as early as possible in the process, while the activity is fresh on the officer's mind. Until a more formal application process is created by USCIS, practitioners are encouraged to use the U visa certification form created by Gail Pendleton and Annie Benson. An updated version reflecting the 2005 changes can be downloaded from the U section of the ASISTA website at *www.asistaonline.org*.

---

[26] Interim Relief Memo 1 at 3; Interim Relief Memo 2 at 5.

[27] Interim Relief Memo 2 at 3.

[28] Yates, Associate Director of Operations, Assessment of "Deferred Action in Requests for Interim Relief from U Nonimmigrant Status Eligible Aliens in Removal Proceedings," Memorandum to Director, Vermont Service Center (May 6, 2004).

[29] Interim Relief Memo 2 at 5.

[30] INA §248, *as amended* by VAWA 2005 §821(c).

[31] The address of the VSC: USCIS Vermont Service Center, Attn: VAWA Unit, Box 1000, 75 Lower Welden Street, St. Albans, VT 05479-0001.

[32] Interim Relief Memo 2 at 4.

Optional Documentation

The information listed below goes beyond the prima facie standard required under USCIS interim relief guidance.[33] If the information is available now, it is a good idea to document it while the case is relatively "hot." Collecting it later may be more difficult.

- Documentation of the criminal activity, such as the police report, other police or court documents, and a copy of the code section describing the criminal activity.

- Documentation of the abuse suffered. In addition to the applicant's declaration, this could include witness declarations, police reports, medical reports, a counselor's report, and photographs. The counselor's report should be similar to a report for a VAWA spouse case, detailing the facts as they were told to the counselor and stating that the applicant's account of the emotional or physical abuse suffered is credible to the counselor based on his or her extensive experience counseling such victims.

Authorization to Work

To obtain work authorization, the applicant must submit Form I-765 with the required fees and photographs, which can be filed concurrently with the application for interim relief. An affidavit establishing the applicant's economic need for work authorization should be included. If the applicant cannot afford to pay the I-765 filing fee, an affidavit in support of a fee-waiver request must be included. It is a good idea to obtain deferred action and employment authorization for eligible children as well as adults—even if the eligible child is not old enough to work, the employment authorization will provide the child with a government-issued photo identification. You must specifically ask that derivatives be granted deferred action and work authorization. To facilitate the renewal process, described below, it is prudent to do this for the principal and the derivatives at the same time.

Both deferred action and the employment authorization document (EAD) are valid for a period of one year. When USCIS grants deferred action, it will send a notice to the applicant indicating the period of validity. A request for an extension of deferred action must be timely submitted annually, including copies of the documentation submitted with the original request. An I-765 application for renewed employment authorization also must be filed each year between 90 and 120 days prior to expiration of the current EAD. Applicants should apply for extensions of deferred action and the attendant EAD at the same time.

The VSC maintains a hotline for inquiries about U interim-relief cases at (802) 527-4888. (This is the same hotline that the VSC uses for VAWA self-petitions.) This line is for use by advocates and attorneys only, not applicants. Leave a message, and a USCIS adjudicator will generally call back within several days. The unit will not respond unless you have submitted a G-28 or the application's cover letter is on your letterhead (for those who are not attorneys).

It is important to note that §384 of the Illegal Immigration and Immigrant Responsibility Act (IIRAIRA)[34] prohibits immigration authorities and immigration courts from making an adverse determination of admissibility or deportability using information furnished solely by the perpetrator of criminal activity or the substantial physical or mental abuse, unless the U visa applicant has been convicted of certain crimes.[35] The immigration authorities and immigration courts are also prohibited from disclosing any information concerning individual U-visa applications for relief.[36] The penalties for willfully using, publishing, or permitting information to be disclosed in violation of IIRAIRA §384 include disciplinary action and a civil money penalty up to $5,000 for each violation.[37] Congressional intent in adding these provisions was to prevent government officials from initiating contact with abusers or relying on information from abusers to apprehend, detain, and attempt to remove victims of domestic violence, sexual assault, trafficking, or other crimes.

Strategies for Risky Cases

Individuals who submit an application or request to the USCIS run the risk of being placed in removal proceedings if they are not eligible for any form of immigration relief. Practitioners must inform clients

---

[33] See Interim Relief Memo 2.

[34] Ilegal Immigration Reform and Immigrant Responsibility Act of 1996, Division C of the Omnibus Appropriations Act of 1996 (H.R. 3610), Pub. L. No. 104-208, 110 Stat. 3009 (IIRAIRA).

[35] IIRAIRA §384(a)(1).

[36] IIRAIRA §384(a)(2).

[37] IIRAIRA §384(c).

that an application for interim relief necessarily announces to the immigration authorities that the applicant is in the United States. If the request for interim relief is not granted, an applicant who is not in valid status risks being placed in removal proceedings. Those at greatest risk are individuals requesting U interim relief who are clearly ineligible for a U-visa and individuals with aggravated felonies. Those cases could be referred to ICE for issuance of a Notice to Appear. In reality, however, the risk of exposure to removal proceedings is low. As of this writing, the USCIS policy is not to forward denied U interim relief cases to ICE. However, that policy is not statutory or regulatory and could change at any time. Clients should be informed that, in the future, weak cases that are denied may expose the applicant to removal.

While nothing is certain, some cases seem to fall squarely under the statutory requirements for U status. Others, however, may be subject to unpredictable statutory interpretations. "Slam dunk" cases might include those in which:

- An applicant is a direct victim of a crime listed in the statute, the state law is clear that this is the crime, and the crime was committed in the United States fairly recently or the investigation/prosecution is ongoing;

- An applicant contacted law enforcement and has a certificate or similar document;

- An applicant can show "substantial" physical or mental abuse flowing from the criminal activity. (The "any credible evidence" standard from VAWA applies, but "substantial" is an unknown quantity. Start marshalling corroborative evidence as noted above and as described in VAWA training materials.); and

- There are no admissibility issues. (Remember that the U visa is a nonimmigrant visa, and applicants must be admissible. There is a "public or national interest" waiver for all grounds except Nazi persecution and genocide, but practitioners should monitor how VSC adjudicates similar waivers for T-visa applicants before subjecting U visa applicants with admissibility problems to USCIS scrutiny.)

Noncitizens who do not fit neatly into these categories may still qualify for U status. If the regulations fail to fully implement the statute and the will of Congress, however, there may be a period of uncertainty for those who have received interim relief but do not appear to qualify under the final regula-

tions. Prepare a plan for challenging the regulations in that situation. Send those factual scenarios to the National Network to End Violence Against Immigrant Women for use in advocacy. The Network will organize comments on the regulation and file court challenges where necessary. As always, we will continue to work with DHS to insure that the agency implements the law as Congress intended.

Individuals who are not eligible for interim relief, or are fearful that they will not be granted interim relief, can proactively gather documentation, including the law enforcement certificate, to support the application once the regulations are issued. Be aware, however, that old law-enforcement certifications may not qualify unless they were used to request interim relief. The regulations are expected to apply the same six-month rule for certifications as applied to interim-relief applicants. Certifications obtained more than six months in the past probably will not qualify new U-status applicants.

OBTAINING "T" STATUS AND OTHER RELIEF FOR HUMAN TRAFFICKING SURVIVORS

When interviewing victims of human trafficking, you might hear comments such as:

"My boss has my passport and won't give it back to me."

"I had to work for my smugglers to pay off what I owed them for bringing me here."

"I mortgaged my family's home to pay a labor recruiter for the chance to work in the U.S. on an H-visa. I never got the job he promised. I had to work for him in his restaurant to pay off my recruiting debt back home."

"I came to the U.S. to live with my aunt and uncle when I was 13 years old. They said they were going to send me to school, but they never did. I stayed at home and babysat their children."

"When I first came to the U.S. I worked in a massage parlor. I left about a month after my contract was paid off. I'm HIV positive."

If a client made any of the above statements to you, would you consider that he or she might be a survivor of human trafficking? Trafficking cases can be difficult to identify, and your only clues may be facts that are not relevant to any other immigration remedy. In some cases, facts that at first appear to work against a client—such as illegal entry, an HIV-positive status, and work in the sex trade—could be elements of a trafficking case. Victims often are very fearful, not only for themselves but for family members in their home countries. Some do not see themselves as victims but consider their experience to be the price they had to pay for coming to the United States. They often have only their own statements as proof of what happened to them. It is critical for immigration attorneys to be able to recognize human-trafficking indicators to determine if individuals are eligible for T nonimmigrant status and other benefits designed for trafficking survivors.

The Trafficking Victims Protection Act of 2000 (TVPA)[38] is the most comprehensive anti-trafficking legislation in the world. It increases criminal penalties for traffickers, dedicates resources to the prevention of trafficking, and, perhaps most important, offers benefits and protection based on the recognition of trafficking as a human rights abuse. Subsequent amendments made by the Trafficking Victims Protection Reauthorization Acts of 2003 [39] and VAWA 2005 removed some barriers to T-status eligibility and added additional protections for victims.

Unfortunately, more than five years after TVPA's passage, only a fraction of the victims estimated to qualify for its benefits and protection have been identified. Although the TVPA provides that up to 5,000 trafficking victims a year may be issued T nonimmigrant status,[40] as of early 2006, the VSC had issued T status to fewer than 700 principal applicants since it began processing applications in 2002.[41]

If you believe you have identified a human trafficking case or would like technical assistance in representing a trafficked survivor, you can contact a member organization of the Freedom Network USA at *www.freedomnetworkusa.org*.

Legislative Background of T Status

Passage of the TVPA was preceded by the highly publicized discovery of modern-day slave operations in California and New York. In the predawn hours of August 2, 1995, state and federal law enforcement authorities in El Monte, Calif., raided an apartment building that served as a slave-labor compound. Some of the 72 Thai workers found in the building had been held captive for up to seven years. Enclosed by a razor-wire fence and unable to communicate with their families, the workers were forced to sew garments for U.S. manufacturers and retailers six days a week for up to 20 hours a day.[42]

In 1997 the claims of four deaf Mexican men led New York City police to the discovery of dozens of deaf Mexicans who were enslaved and forced to peddle trinkets in subway stations for 18 hours a day and almost no pay. Their traffickers had beaten, physically restrained, and tortured them.[43]

Motivated by the discovery of these modern-day slave operations, Congress passed the TVPA in 2000. Amendments made by the Trafficking Victims Protection Reauthorization Act of 2003 and VAWA 2005 have enhanced the TVPA's provisions for trafficking survivors and their family members.[44]

Identification of Trafficking Victims

Traffickers use a variety of methods to find victims. Employment, travel, model, or matchmaking agencies are used to lure victims. Friends and acquaintances recruit victims through word of mouth.[45] Once traffickers have victims in their hands, they use force, fraud, or coercion to make their victims work.

They confiscate and retain victims' passports and travel documents, restrict the victims' freedom, withhold wages until victims pay off their debts, keep victims under surveillance by security guards, and use threats of violence or actual violence against the victims and their families.[46] Traffickers also use the victims' fears of arrest and deportation against

---

[38] The TVPA is one of three divisions of the VTVPA.

[39] Trafficking Victims Protection Reauthorization Act of 2003, Pub. L. No. 108-1, 93, 117 Stat. 2875 (2003) (TVPRA 2003).

[40] INA §214(o)(2) (2006). There is no annual limit to the number of derivative family members who can be issued T status. *Id*. at §214(o)(3).

[41] Homer Wetherby, CAO, USCIS, Vermont Service Center, March 2006.

[42] J. Su, "Sweatshop Watch, El Monte Thai Garment Workers: Slave Sweatshops" (2001), *available at www.sweat shopwatch.org/swatch/campaigns/elmonte.html*.

[43] Deat Mexicans Held in Serfdom by Traffickers in New York, Trafficking in Migrants (Int'l Org. for Migration, Geneva, Switzerland), Sept. 1997, at 3, available at *www.iom. int/documents/publications/en/tm16.pdf*.

[44] A separate bill, the Trafficking Victims Protection Reauthorization Act of 2005, Pub. L. No. 109-164, 119 Stat. 3558) (2005), provides, among other things, additional funding to implement the TVPA and to assist U.S. citizen and lawful permanent resident victims of trafficking.

[45] *Supra* note 43, at 5.

[46] *Id*.

them. They instill a fear of law enforcement by telling victims that, because they are in the country illegally, they have no rights and will be arrested or deported by the authorities. The fear of deportation is very powerful because returning to their home country may be extremely shameful for victims. It also may be dangerous, because traffickers might seek out the victims who return home and retaliate against them.[47]

Isolation is another technique that traffickers use to control their victims. In many cases, victims must live and work at one location. This is usually the case for persons made to work as maids, nannies, and domestic workers. Making the victim live and work at one location ensures that she does not have the opportunity to interact with others and seek help.[48] Other coercive techniques include denying victims medical treatment when needed and, in particularly egregious situations, subjecting victims to extreme mental and physical abuse, including rape, forced abortions, and beatings.[49]

Qualifying for T Status

To qualify for T status, applicants must establish that they:

- are or have been a victim of a severe form of trafficking in persons;

- are physically present in the United States, American Samoa, or the Commonwealth of the Northern Mariana Islands on account of such trafficking;

- either have complied with any reasonable request for assistance in the investigation or prosecution of the trafficking acts or are less than 18 years of age; and

- would suffer extreme hardship involving unusual or severe harm upon removal.[50]

The T status applicant may submit "any credible evidence" to establish their eligibility for T status.[51]

Victim of a Severe Form of Trafficking in Persons

The TVPA states that "severe forms of trafficking in persons" include:

- sex trafficking in which a commercial sex act is induced by force, fraud, or coercion, or in which the person induced to perform such act has not attained 18 years of age; or

- the recruitment, harboring, transportation, provision, or obtaining of a person for labor or services, through the use of force, fraud, or coercion for the purpose of subjection to involuntary servitude, peonage, debt, bondage, or slavery.[52]

It is important to distinguish this definition from smuggling, in which the smuggler arranges for the illegal entry of a noncitizen into the United States for any reason.[53] By contrast, human trafficking, as defined by the TVPA's interim regulations, involves a "particular means" (force, fraud, or coercion, with the exception of minors induced to engage in commercial sex) and a "particular end" (forced labor or forced prostitution).[54]

Unlike immigrant smuggling, human trafficking does not necessarily involve crossing an international border, since a migrant may become a trafficking victim after arrival in the United States. Individuals who are voluntarily smuggled into the United States may become victims of a severe form of trafficking in persons if, for example, the smuggler uses threats of serious harm or physical restraint to force the individual into involuntary servitude, peonage, debt bondage, or slavery after arrival. Federal law prohibits forced labor regardless of the victim's initial consent to work.[55]

One of the most crucial elements of the TVPA's trafficking definition is coercion. To fill a gap left by the Supreme Court's narrow interpretation of the federal involuntary servitude statute, the TVPA defines coercion to encompass more than physical force or the threatened use of such force.[56] Under the TVPA, "coercion" includes (1) threats of serious harm to or physical restraint against any person; (2) any scheme, plan, or pattern intended to cause a person to believe that failure to perform an act would result in serious harm to or physical restraint against

---

[47] *Id.*

[48] *Id.*

[49] *Id.*

[50] *Id.* 8 CFR §214.11(g).

[51] 8 CFR §214.11(d) (2006).

[52] TVPA §103(8), 22 USC §7102(8).

[53] New Classification for Victims of Severe Forms of Trafficking in Persons; Eligibility for "T" Nonimmigrant Status, 67 Fed. Reg. 4784, 4787 (Jan. 31, 2002) (codified at 8 CFR §§103, 212, 50 214, 274a, 299).

[54] *Id.* at 4786–87.

[55] *Id.* at 4787.

[56] *See* TVPA §102(b)(13), 22 USC §7101(b)(13) (2000) (discussing *United States v. Kozminksi*, 487 U.S. 931 (1988)).

any person; or (3) the abuse or threatened abuse of the legal process.[57]

Physical Presence

Persons victimized in the past—as opposed to someone still in the trafficker's control or recently freed—must establish that their "continuing presence in the United States is directly related to the original trafficking in persons."[58] The only T status filing deadlines are for cases of victimization that occurred before October 28, 2000.[59] However, these deadlines may be waived if "exceptional circumstances," including severe physical or psychological trauma, prevented the victim from timely filing.[60]

Victims who escape their traffickers before law enforcement becomes involved in the case must show that they did not have a "clear chance" to depart the United States after the escape.[61] This determination must be made in light of the applicants' circumstances, including trauma, injury, lack of resources, or, because the traffickers seized their travel documents, lack of such documents.[62] Victims who depart and re-enter the United States are considered not physically present on account of trafficking unless their re-entry results from "the continued victimization of the alien or a new incident of a severe form of trafficking in persons."[63]

Compliance with Reasonable Requests for Assistance from Law Enforcement

Applicants for T status must comply with any reasonable request for assistance in the investigation or prosecution of acts of trafficking, unless he or she has not attained 18 years of age. The interim regulations issued by the Department of Justice in 2002 interpreted this provision narrowly by defining the request for assistance as one coming from a federal law enforcement agency (LEA).[64] VAWA 2005, however, explicitly recognizes that trafficking victims can comply with requests for LEA assistance by cooperating with state or local authorities in "the investigation of crime where acts of trafficking are at least one central reason for the commission of that crime."[65]

The "reasonableness" of a request for assistance depends on the totality of the circumstances, taking into account general law-enforcement and prosecutorial practices, the nature of the victimization, and the specific circumstances of the victim, including fear, severe traumatization (both mental and physical), and the age and maturity of young victims.[66] The determination of whether a request for assistance is reasonable is made by USCIS, not the LEA. Under VAWA 2005, DHS in consultation with the Attorney General may deem an LEA request to be unreasonable if it determines that the victim, due to psychological or physical trauma, is unable to comply with the request.[67]

Because of the requirement to comply with any reasonable request for assistance in the investigation or prosecution of the crime, the applicant must have had some contact with an LEA prior to applying for a T visa.[68] The applicant may have had this contact either by reporting the crime or by responding to inquiries from the LEA. If the applicant has not had contact with an LEA regarding the trafficking, he or she may contact the nearest DHS office, FBI field office, or U.S. Attorney's office to file a complaint, assist in the investigation or prosecution, and request an LEA endorsement. Alternatively, the applicant may contact the Department of Justice, Civil Rights Division, Trafficking in Persons and Worker Exploitation Task Force complaint hotline, at (888) 428-7581, to file a complaint and be referred to an LEA.[69] If the applicant has never reported a trafficking case to law enforcement, he or she should consult with a practitioner experienced in handling trafficking cases before reporting. It is particularly important that T applicants fully understand what may be expected of him or her in a criminal investigation and/or prosecution.

---

[57] *Id.* TVPA §103(2), 22 USC §7102(2).

[58] 8 CFR §214.11(g).

[59] The application must have been filed within one year of Jan. 31, 2002, except that a child under the age of 21 must file within one year of the child's 21st birthday or within one year of Jan. 31, 2002, whichever is later. *Id.*

[60] 8 CFR §214.11(b).

[61] *Id.* 8 CFR §214.11(g)(2).

[62] *Id.*

[63] *Id.* 8 CFR §214.11(g)(3).

[64] *Id.* 8 CFR §§214.11(a), (h).

[65] INA §101(a)(15)(T)(i)(III)(aa), *amended* by VAWA 2005 §801(a).

[66] 8 CFR §214.11(a).

[67] INA §101 (a)(15)(T)(iii), *amended* by VAWA 2005 §801(a)(3).

[68] 8 CFR §214.11(h)(2).

[69] *Id.* 8 CFR §214.11(f)(4).

Extreme Hardship Involving Unusual and Severe Harm

In assessing whether the T status applicant would face "extreme hardship involving unusual and severe harm" if the visa were denied, USCIS must consider the hardship conditions associated with trafficking in addition to those traditionally recognized under the INA. These conditions include the age and personal circumstances of the applicant, the need for medical or psychological treatment in the United States, and the likelihood of re-victimization in the home country.[70]

Waivers of Inadmissibility Grounds

The TVPRA of 2003 exempted applicants for T status from the public-charge ground of inadmissibility,[71] and VAWA 2005 exempts trafficking victims— not just applicants for T status—from the unlawful-presence ground if the trafficking "was at least one central reason for the alien's unlawful presence in the United States."[72] There are also special trafficking waivers for most grounds of inadmissibility. If the activities that make the applicant inadmissible "were caused by, or were incident to, the victimization," USCIS will give special consideration to the waiver. Applicants inadmissible on a criminal ground are required to show the connection between the disqualifying activities and the victimization.[73]

The T nonimmigrant is also eligible for any other waiver that might apply to him or her.[74] However, the interim regulations provide, that if the ground of inadmissibility would prevent or limit the applicant from adjusting to permanent residence, the USCIS will grant a nonimmigrant waiver only in exceptional circumstances.[75] A T-status applicant who is inadmissible must apply for a waiver of inadmissibility on Form I-192.

Length of Status and Adjustment of Status

The TVPA originally provided that the T status would expire three years from the date of approval,[76]

but VAWA 2005 extends its validity to four years.[77] VAWA 2005 also provides that the validity of the T status can be extended beyond four years if a law enforcement official certifies that the presence of the T nonimmigrant in the United States is necessary to assist in the investigation or prosecution of activity relating to human trafficking.[78]

Nonimmigrants in T status who want to file for adjustment of status to lawful permanent residence must have been present in the United States for a continuous period of at least three years since the date of admission as a T nonimmigrant.[79] VAWA 2005 may shorten this period for some T nonimmigrants if they have been physically present in the United States for a continuous period during the investigation or prosecution of acts of trafficking and, in the opinion of the Attorney General, the investigation or prosecution is complete, whichever period of time is less.[80]

To date, DHS has not issued regulations pertaining to the process for adjusting the status of T nonimmigrants. Currently, practitioners are filing adjustment applications for T nonimmigrants at the VSC, but the applications are not being adjudicated.

Family Members Eligible for Derivative Status

To promote family reunification, various family members of victims may apply for T status, including the spouses and children of adult victims; and the spouse, parents, children, and unmarried siblings under the age of age of 18 of child victims.[81] Child victims and child derivatives are protected from "aging out" of T status eligibility.[82] VAWA 2005 eliminated the requirement that derivative family members establish extreme hardship to qualify for T status.[83]

---

[70] *Id.* 8 CFR §214.11(i)(1).

[71] INA §212(d)(13)(A).

[72] INA §212(a)(9)(B)(iii)(V), *amended by* VAWA 2005 §802(a). This exception applies only to the unlawful-presence ground of inadmissibility at §212(a)(9)(B), and *not* to the ground relating to previous removal at §212(a)(9)(A).

[73] 8 CFR §212.16(b)(2006).

[74] INA §212(d)(13)(B).

[75] 8 CFR §212.16(b)(3)(2006).

[76] *Id.* 8 CFR §214.11(p).

[77] INA §214(o)(7)(A), *amended by* VAWA 2005 §821(a).

[78] INA §214(o)(7)(B), *added by* VAWA 2005 §821(a).

[79] The interim regulations currently provide that the T nonimmigrant must apply for adjustment within the 90 days immediately preceding the third anniversary of the grant of T nonimmigrant status. 8 CFR §214.11(p)(2). Presumably the extension of T status to at least four years will result in a change in this rule.

[80] INA §245(l), *amended by* VAWA 2005 §803.

[81] INA §101(a)(15)(T).

[82] INA §214(o).

[83] INA §101(a)(15)(T), *amended by* VAWA 2005 §801.

Application Procedures for T Status

The applicant can show that he or she is a victim of a severe form of trafficking in persons by submitting one of the following types of documentation to the VSC:

- an endorsement from an LEA on Form I-914, Supplement B, Declaration of Law Enforcement Officer for Victims of Trafficking in Persons (discussed below);

- evidence that the former INS or the DHS or one of its immigration agencies has arranged for the alien's continued presence (see discussion below) in the United States as a victim of trafficking; or

- sufficient credible secondary evidence, describing the nature and scope of any force, fraud, or coercion used against the victim (not necessary if the applicant was induced to perform a commercial sex act while under age 18).[84]

Under these provisions, T applicants are not required to submit an endorsement from an LEA. While the prologue to the interim regulations "strongly encourages" applicants to provide such an endorsement,[85] in practice it is often not possible to obtain one.

If the applicant submits secondary evidence, defined as anything other than an LEA endorsement or government evidence of status as a trafficking victim, that evidence must include the applicant's statement indicating that he or she is a victim of a severe form of trafficking in persons, credible evidence of victimization and cooperation, a description of what the person has done to report the crime to an LEA, a statement indicating whether similar records for the time and place of the crime are available, and evidence that the applicant made good- faith attempts to obtain the LEA endorsement with a description of those efforts.[86]

T-Status Denials

An applicant may appeal the denial of T status to the USCIS Administrative Appeals Office.[87] The experience of legal advocates is that the VSC will not refer denied T-status cases to ICE for removal proceedings. In cases that have been denied, advocates may also consider refiling with the VSC.

Continued-Presence Status

If a federal LEA determines that a noncitizen is a trafficking victim and a potential witness to such trafficking, the agency may apply to the USCIS Office of International Affairs/Parole/Humanitarian Affairs Branch (OIA/PHAB) in Washington, D.C., to request the victim's continued presence in the United States. "Continued presence" is an interim form of relief that allows the victim to live and work in the United States lawfully during the course of the trafficking investigation and prosecution. To ensure a victim's continued presence, USCIS grants such status as deferred action, humanitarian parole, or a stay of removal.[88] A grant of continued-presence status is not a prerequisite to an application for T status.

Eligibility for Government Benefits and Services

The TVPA provides that trafficking victims certified by the U.S. Department of Health and Human Services (HHS) are eligible for federal welfare benefits "to the same extent as an alien who is admitted to the United States as a refugee" under INA §207.[89] HHS certifies adults as victims of a severe form of trafficking if they are "willing to assist in every reasonable way in the investigation and prosecution" of the trafficking crime and have either been granted continued presence status or have made a "bona fide" application for a T status.[90] VAWA 2005 specifies that the definition of "investigation and prosecution" includes "responding to and cooperating with requests for evidence and information."[91]

Although the TVPA does not require children under the age of 18 to comply with LEA requests for assistance, HHS first consults with a federal LEA before issuing eligibility letters to child victims.

OBTAINING "S" STATUS FOR CRIME WITNESSES

In 1993 Congress amended the INA to establish the S visa for noncitizen witnesses and informants as part of

---

[84] 8 CFR §214.11(f) (2006).

[85] 67 Fed. Reg. 4784, 4788 (Jan. 31, 2002).

[86] 8 CFR §214.11(f)(3).

[87] 8 CFR §214.11(r).

[88] 28 CFR §1100.35.

[89] TVPA §107(b)(1)(A) (2000) (citing INA §207).

[90] 22 USC §7105(b)(1)(E). In cases in which the VSC has not made a bone fide determination while the T status application was pending, HHS will certify the victim when VSC grants the T status application.

[91] 22 USC §7105(b)(1)(E)(iii)(IV), *amended by* VAWA 2005 §804(b).

the Violent Crime Control Act of 1994.[92] The authority for granting S visas was originally set to expire in late 2001, but after the terrorist attacks of September 11, 2001, Congress voted to make the availability of the visa permanent.[93] From 1995 to 2004, over 500 witnesses and informants have been granted S visas, and over 300 family members have been granted derivative visas.[94]

Qualifying for S Status

For an applicant to qualify for S status, the Attorney General must determine that a witness or informant in a criminal matter:

- is in possession of critical reliable information concerning a criminal organization or enterprise;

- is willing to supply or has supplied such information to a federal or state court; and

- is essential to the success of an authorized criminal investigation or the successful prosecution of an individual involved in the criminal organization or enterprise.

For a witness or provider of information in a counterterrorism matter, the Secretary of State and Attorney General can jointly determine that the applicant:

- is in possession of critical reliable information concerning a terrorist organization, enterprise, or operation;

- is willing to supply or has supplied such information to federal law-enforcement authorities or a federal court;

- will be or has been placed in danger as a result of providing such information; and

- is eligible to receive a reward under section 36(a) the State Department Basic Authorities Act of 1956.[95]

The S status can be granted to no more than 200 criminal informants a year, and to no more than 50 terrorist informants a year.[96] LEAs may seek to parole into the United States witnesses or informants who will apply for S status.[97] All the grounds of inadmissibility can be waived in the national interest, except for INA §212(a)(3)(E) relating to participation in Nazi persecution or genocide. Nonimmigrants in S status waive the right to contest removal proceedings, except for those based on an application for withholding of deportation.

Application Procedures for the S Status

The application for S status may only be filed by the federal or state LEA directly in need of the information to be provided by the witness or informant.[98] The application is made on Form I-854, and the LEA must agree that no promises have been made or will be made to the witness or informant that he or she can remain in the United States in S or any other nonimmigrant status or parole; can adjust status to lawful permanent residence; or can otherwise attempt to remain in the United States beyond the three-year duration of the status, other than by means authorized by INA §101(a)(15)(S).[99]

Reporting Provisions

Nonimmigrants in S status must adhere to quarterly reporting requirements regarding their whereabouts and activities during the period of validity of their visas.[100] As a result, any practitioner who represents an S nonimmigrant will likely have a long and close relationship with the federal LEA to which the nonimmigrant reports. The LEA will track information about where the client lives and works, where his or her children attend school, and whether he or she has had any problems with criminal laws while in S status. As a condition of their status, S nonimmigrants may not be convicted of a criminal offense with a term of imprisonment of one year or more.[101]

Length of Status and Adjustment of Status

The S status is valid for three years and cannot be extended.[102] Before an S nonimmigrant can apply for adjustment of status, the federal LEA that originally requested the S status must file Form I-854 with the Attorney General, who forwards it for approval to DHS. Once the I-854 is approved, the S nonimmigrant may seek adjustment of status.[103]

---

[92] INA §101(a)(15)(S); "Immigration: S Visas for Criminal and Terrorist Informants," Karma Ester, Congressional Research Service, The Library of Congress (updated Jan. 19, 2005) at 1.

[93] *Id.*

[94] *Id.* at 3.

[95] 22 USC §2708(a).

[96] INA §214(k)(1).

[97] 8 CFR §212.14(a), §1212.14(a).

[98] 8 CFR §214.2(t).

[99] *Id.*

[100] INA §214(k)(3)(A).

[101] INA §214(k)(3)(B).

[102] INA §214(k)(2).

[103] 8 CFR §245.11(a), §1245.11(a).

VWP & CBP: PERFECT TOGETHER?

by Susan Borowski Storch[*]

The American Competitiveness in the 21st Century Act (AC21)[1] was enacted on October 17, 2000, along with the Visa Waiver Permanent Program Act.[2] The Visa Waiver Program (VWP), made permanent by this act, permits the entry to the United States of a foreign national without the need of a visa, if the individual is a national of one of 27 participating countries in the Program. The participating countries are Andorra, Australia, Austria, Belgium, Brunei, Denmark, Finland, France, Germany, Iceland, Ireland, Italy, Japan, Liechtenstein, Luxembourg, Monaco, New Zealand, The Netherlands, Norway, Portugal, San Marino, Singapore, Slovenia, Spain, Sweden, Switzerland, and the United Kingdom.

The major advantage of the VWP is that there is no burden on a foreign visitor to obtain a visa prior to embarking on a short-term visit of up to 90 days to the United States for business or pleasure. While the Program makes travel to the United States easier for nationals of participating countries, it has been noted that sometimes entering on the visa waiver presents unanticipated problems to the traveler.[3]

This article will consider the ramifications of the authority of U.S. Customs and Border Protection (CBP) officers in inspecting visitors upon entry to the United States under the VWP, the admission process, random exams, and failure to meet documentary requirements.

Prior to admission to the United States, VWP travelers are screened and enrolled in the Department of Homeland Security's (DHS) U.S. Visitor Immigrant Status Indication Technology (US-VISIT) program.[4] On October 4, 2005, CBP implemented a plan of "informed and enforced compliance" designed to aid carriers that demonstrate a good faith effort to comply with the Advance Passenger Information System (APIS).[5] CBP is required to collect address information as mandated by the Enhanced Border Security Entry Reform Act of 2002.[6] Specifically, this act requires that a biometric identifier feature be implemented as part of the admissions and inspections process. As a result, DHS concluded that digital photographs provided greater security against counterfeiting over traditional photographs.[7]

Under APIS, transportation carriers are required to collect address information of all passengers and make every effort to ensure that the address submitted in the APIS manifest appears to be a valid address.[8] Essentially, carriers are obligated to check that the passenger's address collected by the airline or cruise ship is identical to the address declared to CBP by the passenger on the application for entry, Form I-94W. CBP retains the authority to employ enforced compliances (penalties) to ensure that APIS requirements are handled properly by carriers. As of October 26, 2005, transportation carriers may be fined up to $3,300 per violation for transporting any visitor traveling under the VWP to the United States who does not meet the requirements of a valid passport with a machine-readable zone (for a passport issued before October 26, 2005) or a digital photograph (for a passport issued on or after October 26, 2005). "E-Passports," which include an integrated computer chip capable of storing biographic information from the data page, a digitized photograph, and other biometric information, will be required by October 26, 2006, and all VWP participating countries will need to issue secure passports that contain integrated circuit chips.

A VWP traveler holding a passport issued on or after October 26, 2005, who fails to meet these requirements, will be required to obtain a tourist visa from a U.S. consulate abroad.[9] Otherwise, upon inspection by

[*] **Susan Storch**, Of Counsel–New Business Initiatives, serves in the Iselin, N.J., office of Fragomen, Del Rey, Bernsen & Loewy, LLP, and is responsible for new business development/corporate partnerships. Ms. Storch would like to express gratitude to Nancy H. Morowitz of Fragomen, Del Rey, Bernsen & Loewy, LLP, for her legal and editorial assistance.

[1] Pub. L. No. 106-313, 114 Stat. 1251 (AC21).

[2] Pub. L. No. 106-311. 70 Fed. Reg. 64648 (Oct. 31, 2005).

[3] *See* "The Visa Waiver Program," *Immigration & Nationality Law Handbook* 597 (AILA 2005–06 ed.), which includes an historical overview of the VWP and a thorough legal analysis of the documentary requirements, individual requirements, waiver of rights, and available immigration benefits.

[4] *See www.travel.state.gov/visa/temp/without/without_1990.html.*

[5] *www.cbp.gov/xp/cgov/travel/id_visa/apis_final_rule_reqs.xml.*

[6] Pub. L. No. 107-173, 116 Stat. 543.

[7] *www.cbp.gov/xp/cgov/travel/id_visa/vwp/vwp_digital_photos.xml.*

[8] *www.cbp.gov/xp/cgov/travel/id_visa/apis_final_rule_reqs.xml.*

[9] *www.cbp.gov/xp/cgov/travel/id_visa/vwp/vwp_digital_photos.xml.*

a CBP officer, the VWP traveler may either be denied admission or detained pending removal.[10]

On October 26, 2005, DHS announced that of the 27 countries participating in VWP, only Italy and France would have limited digital photo production capabilities and that DHS would continue to work closely with these countries to certify their full compliance as soon as possible.[11] The VWP traveler is obligated to ensure that he or she meets the documentary requirements for admission to the United States.

Prior to entry, the VWP applicant is required to complete Form I-94W (green form), which includes specific questions related to inadmissibility issues. The applicant also must sign and date the Form I-94W indicating agreement to waive his or her right to a hearing before an immigration judge, if found inadmissible.[12] Further, the applicant is required to return the Form I-94W upon departing the United States. CBP advises that failure to return the I-94W creates a problem with the traveler's record in that the individual is considered an "overstay" and will be denied entry to the United States upon a subsequent entry.[13] In the event an individual returns abroad without returning the Form I-94W, CBP advises that the VWP traveler should send it in, along with documentation that demonstrates he or she departed the United States, such as a boarding pass.[14] The address designated for returning the Form I-94W with supporting documentation is ACS Inc., 1084 South Laurel Road, London, Kentucky, 40744.

Upon inspection at a U.S. airport or seaport, a VWP traveler will be subject to US-VISIT, a "check-in/check-out" system that collects biometric identifiers, verifies identity and immigration status, and tracks the entry and exit of the foreign traveler. US-VISIT is applicable to all VWP travelers between the ages of 14 and 79 and who are traveling through a U.S. port where US-VISIT is in operation.

Certain individuals are exempt from the US-VISIT requirements. In particular, registrants in the INSPASS program, an advance registration system for frequent business visitors to the United States, are exempt from US-VISIT, as well as those registered in the National Security Entry-Exit Registration System

(NSEERS). If an individual possesses an NSEERS waiver, he or she is subject to US-VISIT.

Moreover, visitors may be subject to fingerprinting and photographing upon entry to the United States. As part of the inspection process, a CBP officer has the authority to conduct extensive questioning about the VWP visitor's travel history, purpose of visit, background, employment, and other issues.[15] Further, CBP officers have the authority to conduct enforcement examinations without a warrant, ranging from a single luggage examination up to a personal search.[16] All persons, baggage, and merchandise arriving in the Customs territory of the United States from abroad are liable to inspection by a CBP officer.[17] As a reminder, travelers requesting admission under VWP are generally waiving their right to review or appeal a CBP officer's decision as to their application for admission at the port entry. In the event an individual is found to have violated the terms of his or her admission under the VWP, he or she does not retain the right to contest a removal order.[18] Upon inspection, the CBP officer determines the length of stay in the United States. VWP travelers are not permitted to extend their stay beyond this initial period of stay.

In the event Form I-94W is endorsed incorrectly by the CBP officer, CBP offices at international airports and deferred inspections locations are authorized to correct errors that occurred at the time of arrival.[19] As part of the inspections process, CBP conducts random compliance examinations (COMPEX). These exams involve random selection of air passengers or vehicles that ordinarily would not be selected for an intensive examination. CBP believes it is able to estimate the total number of violations being committed by the international public.[20]

While VWP is designed to speed foreign travelers' access to the United States for short trips of less than 90 days, applicants seeking admission to the United States must be cognizant of the documentary requirements necessary for such entrance. Above all, VWP travelers must be mindful of the wide breadth of authority of the CBP officer to render a final decision on the foreigner's travel plan to the United States.

---

[10] *Id.*

[11] *www.cbp.gov/xp/cgov/travel/id_visa/vwp/vwp_digital_photos.xml.*

[12] *Id.*

[13] *http://help.customs.gov/cgi-bin/customs/cfg/php/enduser.*

[14] *Id.*

[15] 8 CFR §§235, 1235; INA §235.

[16] INA §212(a).

[17] 19 CFR §162.6.

[18] *www.travel.state.gov/visa/temp/without/without_1990.html.*

[19] *Id.*

[20] *www.cbp.gov/xp/cgov/travel/admissibility/random_exams.xml.*

THE NEW ADMISSION CONUNDRUM

by David L.P. Garson and Gregg Rodgers[*]

There is an ancient curse that says, "May you live in interesting times." Traveling in and out of countries in the Western Hemisphere may indeed become very interesting in the near future.

Suppose your client has the ticket and itinerary for an important business trip to the United States. She has planned her meetings down to the last detail. What would happen if she cannot get a visa or is denied admission after arrival at a U.S. airport?

Three factors are changing cross-border travel and could affect on your client's business trip. First, we are entering an age where technology will become much more prevalent in our travel life. Second, international initiatives have established new requirements for passports and proof of identity. And third, the U.S. government has revised its immigration processes.

Here are some tips and information that can help you make sure your client's trip to the United States is the least of your worries.

CROSSING BORDERS IN THE AGE OF TECHNOLOGY: E-PASSPORTS

In October 2006, the U.S. Department of State (DOS) will begin to issue E-passports in conjunction with the policy of requiring all U.S. citizens to be in possession of a passport when re-entering the United States from any other country. (Passports of U.S. citizens that are not E-passports will remain valid until they expire.)

The E-passport includes a computer chip, known as radio frequency identification (RFID), embedded in the back cover. The chip stores the holder's biographical data and a digital photo that will serve as a person's biometric identifier. Facial recognition technology will be used at the port of entry to assist in reading these passports.

The E-passport initiative also impacts citizens of countries that are part of the Visa Waiver Program (VWP). Congress has required that all countries that are part of the VWP issue passports containing the RFID computer chip. All citizens of VWP countries will be required to possess an appropriate E-passport as of October 2006 to continue to enter the United States under the program. A citizen of a VWP country who does not hold a technologically appropriate passport will need to apply for a U.S. visa after that date.

The requirement that U.S. citizens hold E-passports will impact travel patterns to Canada, and Canadians will need a secure a document establishing identity and nationality by December 31, 2007.

Currently, 16 million Canadians visit the United States each year, and 14.2 million U.S. citizens visit Canada. In border areas, such as Windsor/Detroit and Niagara Falls/Buffalo, hundreds of thousands of business people, tourists, and commuters cross everyday. But only 34 percent of U.S. citizens, and only 41 percent of Canadian citizens, have a passport.

Aside from U.S. citizens carrying E-passports, crew members from Singapore Airlines and certain Australian and New Zealand citizens are carrying passports that meet the requirements.

U.S. consulates will no doubt become extremely busy when surprised individuals cannot enter the United States as they once could. Because little information has been made available to the traveling public, it is likely that individuals will be caught unaware and need a visa on an urgent basis. As governments employ the E-passport, there will be legitimate concerns about personal civil liberties, the right to privacy, trade, and tourism. The E-passport

[*] **David Garson** is a senior partner with Guberman, Garson, Bush, a Toronto-based law firm that practices solely in the field of immigration law. According to "International Who's Who of Corporate Immigration Lawyers," Mr. Garson is rated as one of the five "most highly regarded individuals" in immigration law in Canada. He is the immediate past-chair of the immigration section of the Ontario Bar Association, and is also a past-chair of the Canada Chapter of AILA and a past-chair of the Canadian Bar Association Sub-Committee, Port of Entry. The Law Society of Upper Canada certified Mr. Garson as a specialist in immigration law.

Gregg Rodgers is an owner in the Seattle office of Garvey Schubert Barer, a law firm of over 100 attorneys with offices in Seattle; New York; Portland, Ore.; Washington, D.C.; and Beijing. He concentrates his practice on the areas of business-related immigration and employment law. He is the general counsel of the Washington State China Relations Council. He is a member of the AILA General Counsel Liaison Committee–(DHS, ICE, CBP). He previously served as co-chair and chair of AILA USCBP Liaison Committee. Mr. Rodgers was also chair of the AILA Washington State Chapter for two terms. He is a graduate of Seattle University School of Law.

will generate further concern regarding domestic spying and privacy. It is unclear what additional information the E-passport can contain. A person who holds a passport may be subjecting him- or herself to types of scrutiny that is not known to the holder.

WESTERN HEMISPHERE TRAVEL INITIATIVE

The Western Hemisphere Travel Initiative (WHTI) will require all travelers to and from the Americas (Canada, the United States, Mexico, and Panama), the Caribbean, and Bermuda to have a passport or other secure, accepted document establishing the bearers' nationality and identity in order to enter or re-enter the United States. This requirement includes citizens of the Americas, the Caribbean, and Bermuda.

WHTI is a component of the Summit of the Americas process that is intended to foster cooperation among Ministries Responsible for Transportation of the Summit of the Americas countries.[1] One of the main objectives of the group of ministries is to improve port security throughout the hemisphere by developing an international standard of security. The WHTI will require a secure passport denoting identity and citizenship for all travel into the United States by January 1, 2008.

On October 31, 2005, the government of Canada submitted its official comment to the U.S. government on the Western Hemisphere Travel Initiative. Canada indicated that "the flow of Canadians and Americans across the border is a vital and historic part of the Canada-U.S. relationship, and the effective management of that flow is an important responsibility . . . . [T]he proposed changes to document requirements at the U.S. border are of concern to us and it is extremely important that we take the time required to get this right."

Canada proposed several initiatives, including strengthening the foundation for establishing identity and citizenship; working jointly to identify and assess the best options for alternative documents to

be required on the land border; conducting tests of the preferred options at high-volume land-border crossings; and making bi-national recommendations on documentary requirements.

It does not appear that the United States will be excepting Canadians from the secure document requirements. Canada is the United States' largest trading partner with over $1.6 billion in goods crossing the border each day. Currently, citizens of the United States and Canada regularly cross the border into each other's countries without a passport, doing so with other types of documentation, such as birth certificates and photo identification.

As noted above, the upcoming requirement for a passport and/or secure document is not widely understood. This situation is comparable to landed immigrants entering Canada from Commonwealth countries, who at one time did not require visas to enter the United States. When this requirement changed, there was a fair amount of consternation, and consulates in Canada were extremely busy issuing visas to individuals who were not formerly required to have them.

While perhaps not requiring Canadian citizens to have passports, it does not appear that the United States will be exempting them from presenting secure documents. The Federal Minister of Public Safety, Stockwell Day, indicated that Canadians will have to carry some form of national identification card, other than a passport, to travel outside of the country. As the possibility of a Canadian national identification card becomes more likely, the United States is relaxing its demand that Canadians obtain passports. Despite some differences with the U.S. government, it is clear that Canada wishes to work with the United States, not only for its own interest but for the interest of North American security. Still, crossing the border seems destined to be more challenging and infinitely more interesting for both Canadian and U.S. nationals.

THE PASSPORT SHOULD BE VALID FOR THE ENTIRE PERIOD OF THE TRIP, AND SIX MONTHS BEYOND

A person about to travel to the United States should check the expiration date of his or her passport at least a few weeks before departure to ensure that it will be valid for the needed period. U.S. immigration law requires that a passport be valid for at

---

[1] The members of the organization include Antigua & Barbuda, Argentina, Bahamas, Barbados, Belize, Bolivia, Brazil, Chile, Colombia, Costa Rica, Dominica, Ecuador, El Salvador, Grenada, Guatemala, Guyana, Haiti, Honduras, Jamaica, Mexico, Nicaragua, Panama, Paraguay, Peru, Dominican Republic, Saint Lucia, St. Kitts & Nevis, St. Vincent & the Grenadines, Suriname, Trinidad & Tobago, Uruguay, Venezuela, Canada, and the United States.

least six months *beyond* the final date of the visit,[2] to assure the government that the person will be able to leave the United States, either to the country of citizenship or elsewhere, at the end of the intended trip. (Canadian citizens do not need a passport for entry into the United States at this time, unless arriving from outside the Western Hemisphere.)

U.S. Customs and Border Protection (CBP) officers can deny entry to a person whose passport will expire within a specific time frame even if it is valid on the date presented. A passport valid for less than the required time may result in a shortened visit or, worse yet, a denied entry. In actual practice, however, CBP officers are usually willing to disregard this issue in cases of lengthy employment-related entries in which the passport is valid for a year or more beyond the date of entry.

The United States will consider the passports of some countries to be valid for six months *beyond* the actual expiration date, if valid on the date of presentation.[3] While this helps many people, those from other countries may be denied admission if the passport expires less than six months from the date of

presentation, or they may be admitted for a shorter period than sought.

It also is possible to get a "quick fix" at the time of arrival in the United States. A person who is told that the passport expiration date requires either denial of entry or a shortened period of authorized stay may complete a Form I-193, "Application for Waiver of Passport and/or Visa," and pay a $265 filing fee.

MAKE SURE THE INTENDED ACTIVITIES COMPLY WITH THE STANDARDS FOR THAT VISIT

Business trips are classified as "B-1" entries, and pleasure trips as "B-2." Your client might think that he will work hard on the trip, but his activities must be considered "doing business," as opposed to "working," to fit within the acceptable standards for a B-1 admission.

Acceptable activities for B-1 classification include engaging in commercial activities that do not involve gainful employment for a U.S. entity.[4] Such activities include negotiating contracts, consulting with business associates, and attending conventions, conferences, or seminars. Construction workers are not generally admissible in B-1 status, but certain people may enter to supervise or train others who are engaged in building or construction work.[5] More information about B-1 status and procedures may be found at *http://travel.state.gov/visa/tempvisitors _types_visitor2.html*.

There are several other duty-specific B-1 activities that may apply to personnel of a non-U.S. entity who are Canadian or Mexican citizens. The North American Free Trade Agreement (NAFTA)[6] has created additional occupations and professions for which a B-1 classification is authorized. Information about the specific requirements for these NAFTA-specific occupations and professions, such as research and design, marketing, sales, after-sales service, and general service is found at 8 CFR §214.2(b)(4).

---

[2] INA §212(a)(7)(B). That section states that an individual is inadmissible for nonimmigrant admission if "not in possession of a passport valid for a minimum of six months from the date of the expiration of the initial period of the alien's admission or contemplated initial period of stay. . . ." The passport also must authorize "the alien to return to the country from which the alien came or to proceed to and enter some other country during such period. . . ."

[3] From time to time, the Department of State publishes the "Table of Foreign Passports Recognized for Extended Validity." As of press time, the countries whose passports can be considered as valid for six months beyond the date of expiration include Algeria, Antigua & Barbuda, Argentina, Australia, Austria, the Bahamas, Bangladesh, Barbados, Belgium, Bolivia, Bosnia-Herzegovina, Brazil, Canada, Chile, Colombia, Costa Rica, Cote D'Ivoire, Croatia, Cuba, Cyprus, Czech Republic, Denmark, Dominica, Dominican Republic, Ecuador, Egypt, El Salvador, Ethiopia, Finland, France, Germany, Greece, Grenada, Guatemala, Guinea, Guyana, Hong Kong (certificates of identity & passports), Hungary, Iceland, India, Ireland, Israel, Italy, Jamaica, Japan, Jordan, Korea, Kuwait, Laos, Latvia, Lebanon, Liechtenstein, Luxembourg, Macau, Madagascar, Malaysia, Malta, Mauritius, Mexico, Monaco, Netherlands, New Zealand, Nicaragua, Nigeria, Norway, Oman, Pakistan, Panama, Paraguay, Peru, Philippines, Poland, Portugal, Qatar, Romania, Russia, Senegal, Singapore, Slovak Republic, Slovenia, South Africa, Spain, Sri Lanka, St. Kitts & Nevis, St. Lucia, St. Vincent & the Grenadines, Sudan, Suriname, Tunisia, Turkey, United Arab Emirates, United Kingdom, Uruguay, Venezuela, and Zimbabwe.

[4] INA §101(a)(15)(B); 8 CFR §214.2(b); 9 FAM 41.31, N.7 to N.13.7.

[5] 8 CFR §214.2(b)(5).

[6] North American Free Trade Agreement, U.S.-Can.-Mex., Dec. 17, 1992, 32 I.L.M. 296, 612 (entered into force Jan. 1, 1994). For more information on using the procedures under NAFTA, see *Immigration Practice Under NAFTA and Other Free Trade Agreements*, Third Ed. (AILA 2006), visit *www.ailapubs.org* for a table of contents or to order.

IS A VISA REQUIRED OR IS YOUR CLIENT ELIGIBLE FOR THE VISA WAIVER PROGRAM?

Visas

Obtaining a visa has become complicated and time consuming. Interviews and fingerprinting are now required in almost all cases, and it can take several weeks to schedule an interview. A visa can be issued on the day the application is considered or it may take 10 days or longer. Your client should allow for enough time to complete the required forms, to have the interview, and to receive the visa.

The first step after determining that a visa is required is to schedule a nonimmigrant visa application appointment. Most U.S. consulates provide visa application instructions that you can review before your client begins the process. You can access links to U.S. embassies and consulates worldwide at *http://travel.state.gov/visa/questions_embassy.html*.[7]

From the website, you can learn more about the procedures and forms required by the post your client plans to utilize. You also can find out about waiting times for visa appointments at *http:// travel.state.gov/visa/tempvisitors_wait.php*.

Practice Pointer: Some business people may consider the forms and questions to be a nuisance, and pay little attention to the information they submit. (Some people, for example, answer "no" to questions about prior arrests, assuming that a youthful indiscretion is not relevant.) It is imperative that all visa applicants understand that DOS has access to a wide variety of information, including arrests. An incorrect, incomplete, or false answer may, at some point, create insurmountable complications.

While many visas are valid for several years, it is important to remember that a visa is only a ticket—it does not determine the period of admission that is granted upon presentation at a U.S. port of entry. Many B-1 applicants for admission are granted six months, (the 12-month maximum is rarely granted), and extensions can be sought. This is a particular advantage over the VWP, which authorizes a 90-day period of entry, with no extensions allowed.

Visa Waiver Program (VWP)

Citizens from 27 countries[8] in the VWP[9] may be eligible to enter without a B-1/B-2 visa for up to 90 days. If your client is entering under the VWP, do not let him or her get on the plane without a visa unless (1) you know that your client is from a country in the VWP, (2) the trip fits the B-1/B-2 standards, (3) your client has a round-trip ticket, and (4) you know that the purpose of the trip can be accomplished within 90 days.

Travelers who enter the United States under the VWP must have a machine-readable passport. Most countries have begun issuing machine-readable passports, but some have not, and some people have not yet obtained a machine-readable passport. To determine whether the passport is machine-readable, look at the page that contains biographical information about the person. This page is near the front of the passport and usually includes the person's picture and date of birth. If the passport contains two lines of type similar to bar codes on consumer products (including some alphabetical characters), the passport is probably machine-readable. Those lines allow an immigration officer's computer to electronically gather some of the information contained on the upper part of the biographical page. An example of a machine-readable passport can be viewed at *www.travel. state.gov/visa/temp/without/without_1990.html#4*.

A traveler who does not have a machine-readable passport may not enter the United States under the VWP, and must obtain a visa before applying for entry to the United States. This applies to regular, official, or diplomatic passports. Families must have individual machine-readable passports for each member, including children.

Any violation of the VWP rules, including overstaying by just one day, may terminate the ability to use the VWP ever again,[10] although port officers have the discretionary authority to grant a one-time

---

[7] For extensive information on consular processing, see *The Visa Processing Guide and Consular Posts Handbook, Process and Procedure at U.S. Consulates and Embassies*, 2006–07 Ed. (AILA). Visit *www.ailapubs.org* for a table of contents or to order.

[8] Citizens of Andorra, Australia, Austria, Belgium, Brunei, Denmark, Finland, France, Germany, Iceland, Ireland, Italy, Japan, Liechtenstein, Luxembourg, Monaco, New Zealand, the Netherlands, Norway, Portugal, San Marino, Singapore, Slovenia, Spain, Sweden, Switzerland, and the United Kingdom are eligible to be considered for Visa Waiver admission.

[9] INA §217(a); 8 CFR §217.2.

[10] INA §217(a)(7); 8 CFR §217.2–.3.

admission in certain cases.[11] Because no official notice of a violation is given, your client may not know that he or she has violated the rules and faces the risk of being turned away at a U.S. port of entry in the future.

BE READY TO PROVIDE EVEN *MORE* INFORMATION TO THE GOVERNMENT UPON ARRIVAL

U.S. Visitor and Immigrant Status Indicator Technology (US-VISIT)

The US-VISIT program began on January 5, 2004, at many U.S. airports and seaports.[12] Under the program, people entering the United States using a visa must be fingerprinted and photographed. All VWP visitors traveling through U.S. ports of entry that have US-VISIT capabilities must also comply with its requirements.[13] US-VISIT is now in place at 115 airports, 15 seaports, and in the secondary inspection areas of 154 land ports. Go to *www.dhs.gov/dhspublic/interapp/editorial/editorial_0685.xml* for a list of ports at which US-VISIT technology has been implemented.

The visitor will be fingerprinted by an electronic fingerscan and photographed by the CBP officer at the time of entry. This process takes just a few seconds. The information is compared to the data collected at the consulate during the visa application process and from previous visits.

US-VISIT has a three-stage redress policy to enable individuals to inquire about the data US-VISIT has collected on them, as well as to facilitate the amendment or correction of data that is not accurate, relevant, timely, or complete. Information about the US-VISIT redress policy can be found at *www.dhs.gov/dhspublic/interapp/editorial/editorial_0436.xml*.

For more information about US-VISIT, go to the official government website at *www.dhs.gov/dhspulic/interapp/content_multi_image/content_multi_image_0006.xml*.

DHS currently is conducting evaluations of radio frequency identification (RFID) technology in three states at five land ports—two in Arizona, two in Washington, and one in New York. These "proof of concept" tests are intended to consider passive, or near-passive systems, requiring little or no action by the visitor and imposing no need to stop, interact with an official, leave a vehicle, or use a special lane. Current concepts include the use of a sticker affixed to the I-94, insertion of the RFID directly in the paper stock of I-94s, or a plastic I-94.

NATIONAL SECURITY ENTRY-EXIT REGISTRATION SYSTEM (NSEERS) (SPECIAL REGISTRATION)

Under the National Security Entry-Exit Registration System (NSEERS), some people are required to provide a great deal more information than others as they seek entry to the country. NSEERS requires detailed information about an individual and his or her plans while in the United States.

NSEERS requirements may be imposed on anyone, but are always required of citizens or nationals of Iran, Iraq, Libya, Sudan, or Syria. Male citizens or nationals of Pakistan, Saudi Arabia, or Yemen ages 16 through 45, and people with unexplained travel to Iran, Iraq, Libya, Sudan, Syria, North Korea, Cuba, Saudi Arabia, Afghanistan, Yemen, Egypt, Somalia, Pakistan, Indonesia, or Malaysia also are likely to be required to comply.

Your client may want to be prepared to provide the following information, just in case he or she is required to register under the government's NSEERS program:

- name;
- passport country of issuance and number;
- identification and description of a second form of positive identification (*e.g.*, driver's license and number);
- date of birth;
- country of birth,
- nationality and citizenship;
- height; weight; color of hair; color of eyes;
- address of residence in the United States and in country of origin;
- telephone number(s) in the United States and in country of origin;
- names, addresses, and dates of birth for both parents;

---

[11] *See, e.g.*, documents *published on* AILA InfoNet at Doc. Nos. 05033174 and 05033175 (*posted* Mar. 31, 2005).

[12] Illegal Immigration Reform and Immigrant Responsibility Act of 1996, Pub. L. No. 104-208, §110 (IIRAIRA); INS Data Management Improvement Act, P.L. 106-215 (DMIA).

[13] Visa Waiver Permanent Program Act, Pub. L. No. 106-396, 114 Stat. 1647 (VWPPA).

- points of contact in the alien's country of origin;

- name and address of school or employer in the United States (if applicable);

- name and address of former school or employer in country of origin;

- intended activities in the United States; and any e-mail addresses.

Registration under the NSEERS program involves finger scanning and photographing, just as in the US-VISIT program. In fact, a person who complies with NSEERS will not be required to take any additional steps to comply with US-VISIT. That is, compliance with NSEERS complies with US-VISIT. But compliance with US-VISIT does not fulfill compliance with NSEERS. The person registering under NSEERS will be provided with an I-94 Departure Record that includes an annotation of the Fingerprint Identification Number and "SR" for Special Registrant.

For more information about NSEERS, see *www.ice.gov/graphics/specialregistration/index.htm*.

THE GOVERNMENT MUST BE ADVISED OF ANY CHANGE OF ADDRESS

Your client will be required to complete either the white (regular) or green (visa waiver) I-94 Departure Record at the time of entry.[14] The full I-94 form, completed at the time of initial admission, includes a line for an address while in the United States, but it allows for only one address. All temporary visitors and even lawful permanent residents must notify the government of any change of address within 10 days of that change by filing a Form AR-11. See *http://uscis.gov/graphics/formsfee/forms/ar-11.htm* or, for people registered under NSEERS, *http://uscis.gov/graphics/formsfee/forms/ar11sr.htm*.

Failure to comply with this requirement may result in a denial of entry in the future.

AIR TRAVEL WHILE IN THE UNITED STATES

The U.S. government has developed "watch lists" for people it has concerns about traveling to, and within, the United States. The proliferation of these lists has made it more likely that your business client may find her name on a list, if only because

---

[14] Most Canadians admitted in B-1 or B-2 status are not given an I-94.

her name is similar to someone the government is concerned about. Inclusion on some watch lists may prevent boarding an air carrier, while inclusion on others may result in diversion of the aircraft to an alternate airport to prevent passage over critical airspace. The ability to get one's name removed from a watch list has been difficult, but widespread publicity (from embarrassment, to missed flights and meetings) has resulted in some improvement.

Some passengers have found that they are unable to obtain a boarding pass online, at curbside check-in, or from an air carrier's electronic kiosk. When this occurs, they are referred to the airline ticket counter, where they may experience a delay while the agent verifies their identity. If this happens to your clients, or if they are required to undergo additional checkpoint screening each time they fly, they may contact the Transportation Security Administration (TSA) toll-free at 1-866-289-9673, by e-mail at *TSA-ContactCenter@dhs.gov*, or by clicking on the "Contact Us" button at *www.tsa.gov*. The TSA Contact Center (TCC) has developed a procedure to expedite the check-in and screening process for individuals who repeatedly experience delays. This process may take up to 45 days to complete.

The following information should be provided to the TSA representative:

- full name

- date of birth

- telephone number

- mailing address and e-mail address

Your client might be on other watch lists that are not controlled by TSA. If so, this may necessitate more complicated FOIA action.

ACTIONS AT THE TIME OF DEPARTURE MAY AFFECT THE ABILITY TO RETURN

US-VISIT

US-VISIT exit procedures are now in operation at 12 airports and 2 seaports.[15] Anyone who was re-

---

[15] Atlanta (William B. Hartsfield International Airport); Baltimore (Baltimore-Washington International Airport); Chicago (Chicago O'Hare International Airport); Dallas/Fort Worth (Dallas/Fort Worth International Airport); Denver (Denver International Airport); Detroit (Detroit Metropolitan Wayne County Airport); Ft. Lauderdale (Ft. Lauderdale-Hollywood International Airport); Miami (Miami International Cruise Line Terminal); Newark, New Jersey (Newark International Airport); Philadelphia (Philadelphia International Airport);
continued

quired to comply with US-VISIT at the time of entry must also register their departure from the United States, but only if they do so from an airport or seaport that requires US-VISIT exit registration.[16]

Over time, mandatory "departure confirmation" will be required at more and more air and sea ports. Travelers who have been registered with US-VISIT upon entry should always check to see if departure confirmation is required at the air or seaport as they leave the United States. If this is the case, the person who was registered in the US-VISIT program at the time of entry must also locate and use the US-VISIT kiosk before leaving the terminal. This is done by following the exit registration requirements, which vary by location. Almost all departure confirmation includes "swiping" the passport data page through the scanning slot and providing fingerprints of both index fingers electronically. Some locations require that additional photographs be taken at the airport, and others may issue paper receipts. Failure to confirm departure at a port with such capabilities subjects the individual to a variety of determinations in the future, including being found in violation of the terms of admission or parole and being ineligible to receive a visa.[17]

The website *www.dhs.gov/dhspublic/interapp/ editorial/editorial_0685.xm* provides a list of ports at which US-VISIT technology has been implemented.

NSEERS

A person should exit-register if required to complete NSEERS registration upon entry. This may only be done at specific ports of departure and may take 30 minutes or longer.

NSEERS obligations may involve on-going registration with the U.S. government while in the United States, and they also may limit locations from which the person can leave the United States. A list of the ports of departure will be provided to anyone who is registered in NSEERS and is available at *www.ice.gov/graphics/specialregistration/ WalkawayMaterial.pdf*.

Anyone who was registered in the NSEERS program at the time of entry or while in the country *must* complete an NSEERS exit registration. The exit registration process can be completed only at specifically designated ports of departure; the process can take at least 20 minutes to complete, so an appropriate amount of time must be allowed. Anyone who is required to comply with exit registration for NSEERS is not required to comply with US-VISIT exit-registration procedures.

Failure to exit-register can be addressed at a consulate or port of entry.[18]

Surrender of the I-94 Upon Departure

Surrender of the I-94 Departure Record upon departure, and the consequences if it is not surrendered, can be of great importance.

An I-94 issued at a land port of entry is considered a multiple-entry document unless specifically annotated for a limited number of entries.[19] An I-94 issued at an air or sea port is considered a single-entry document unless designated otherwise.[20]

Departure by Land

An I-94 issued at an air or sea port is to be surrendered upon departure unless it was issued for multiple entries.[21] The I-94W is issued for admissions under the VWP, and it must be surrendered upon departure (to Canadian officials if by land to Canada, to U.S. officials if by land to Mexico).

However, surrender is not common for departures by land or to contiguous foreign territories or adjacent islands. Those leaving the United States through a land-border port of entry normally face difficulties in finding a place to turn in the I-94. Land ports do not apply a uniform procedure to turn in the I-94s for database entry to record departure.

Departure by Air or Sea

An I-94 issued at air or sea ports of entry is to be surrendered upon departure unless the card was issued

---

San Francisco (San Francisco International Airport); San Juan, Puerto Rico (Luis Muñoz Marin International Airport); Seattle (Seattle/Tacoma International Airport); and Los Angeles (San Pedro and Long Beach Seaports).

[16] 8 CFR §235.1(d)(1)(iii).

[17] 8 CFR §215.8(b).

---

[18] Please refer to U.S. Citizenship and Immigration Services (USCIS) Counsel Divine's memorandum on the topic *published on* AILA InfoNet at Doc. No. 04111566 (*posted* Nov. 15, 2004) and DHS Fact Sheet at Doc. No. 03120141 (*posted* Dec. 1, 2003).

[19] 8 CFR §235.1(f)(1).

[20] *Id.*

[21] *Id.*

for multiple entries.[22] The I-94W, issued for admissions under the VWP, notes that surrender of the I-94W (to the transportation line if by air or sea) is required upon departure: "A nonimmigrant alien departing on an aircraft proceeding directly to Canada on a flight terminating in that country *must* surrender any Form I-94 in his or her possession to the airline agent at the port of departure."[23] (Emphasis added.)

This directive appears to conflict with 8 CFR §235.1(f) for multiple-entry I-94s issued at air or sea ports and for almost all land port-issued I-94s, which are by regulation considered multiple-entry documents.

It is rare for an airline agent to distinguish between I-94s issued at different kinds of ports. Unless the traveler points out that land port-issued I-94s are, by regulation, multiple-entry, or points out the multiple-entry designation on an I-94 issued at an air or sea port, it will likely be collected and turned into a single-entry I-94 for departures by air. But this common practice is not mandated by law.

US-VISIT regulatory provisions have attempted to clarify that no multiple-entry I-94s need be surrendered: "This amendment clarifies that air and sea carrier passengers will continue to be issued I-94s which must be surrendered upon departure, *unless the I-94 was issued for multiple entries by the alien.*"[24]

I-94s and Automatic Visa Revalidation

Sometimes it is extremely important to retain the I-94 when traveling to Canada or Mexico. Under certain circumstances, 22 CFR §41.112(d) provides for automatic extension of validity of a visa.[25] The

law specifically allows those returning to the United States from Mexico or Canada after a trip of 30 days or less to be readmitted under an extended or changed nonimmigrant classification by presentation of a valid passport, I-94, and an expired visa. This procedure cannot work if the I-94 (either a CBP-issued card or an I-94 at the bottom of an I-797 approval notice for an extension or change of status) is surrendered or taken upon departure from the United States.

The failure of 8 CFR §235.1(f) to address whether an I-94 at the bottom of an I-797 approval notice for an extension or change of status is a multiple-entry document is a problem. The I-797 itself instructs the applicant to turn in the I-94 upon departure, but applicants for extension or change of status already have I-94s and must prove that they are legally in the United States at the time they apply for a change or extension. But how can an applicant use automatic visa revalidation if the I-94 was taken or surrendered at the time of departure?

In general, the benefit of automatic visa revalidation is not available if the individual applied for a visa while in Canada or Mexico.[26] As noted in the March 14, 2002, cable sent by Secretary of State Colin Powell,[27] a refused visa is indicated by stamping the passport on the back page in indelible ink to reflect that the applicant has been refused a visa. The term "application received," which is the language used by DOS to indicate that a visa has been applied for but not immediately issued for some reason, may be used.[28] And, as noted in the telegram, "A passport bearing the above stamp and a subsequently issued visa indicates that the refusal was overcome or a waiver of the ineligibility was granted."

Further instructions were published in a DOS cable (Ref. STATE 50158) issued in June 2002.[29] There, DOS noted:

> To help ensure INS inspectors at POEs do not overlook the "Application Received" stamp and inadvertently apply the revalidation regulation in

---

[22] *Id.*

[23] 8 CFR §231.2.

[24] Emphasis added. Implementation of the U.S. Visitor and Immigrant Status Indicator Technology Program; Biometric Requirements," 69 Fed. Reg. 467 (Jan. 1, 2004), Interim Final Rule (DHS).

[25] Citizens of countries other than Iran, Syria, Libya, Sudan, North Korea, or Cuba may travel to "contiguous territory" such as Canada or Mexico (and, for people in F, J, or M status, "contiguous territory or adjacent islands other than Cuba") for 30 days or less and return to the United States without a valid visa if they can present a current, valid passport and a current, valid Departure Record, Form I-94, issued by USCIS, CBP, or their predecessor, INS. (Those in F, J, or M status also should have a current Form I-20, Form IAP-66, or the latter's replacement, the DS-2019.) Canadian landed immigrants must present an expired visa. Travel to any other country is not permitted. Denial of a visa application submit-
continued

ted to a U.S. consulate in Canada or Mexico while there terminates the ability to seek re-entry without a valid visa under this process.

[26] 22 CFR §41.112(d)(2).

[27] *Published on* AILA InfoNet at Doc. No. 02040432 (*posted* Apr. 4, 2002).

[28] 9 FAM §41.21.

[29] *Published on* AILA InfoNet at Doc. No. 02061947 (*posted* June 19, 2002).

41.112(d)(i) to aliens who are in fact not qualified for such treatment, INS has requested, and CA has agreed to, the following two additional steps:

1. Consular officers should collect any valid I-94 in such cases, mark the back of the I-94 with the date and post name (the "Application Received" stamp can be used for this), and return the form to INS. If there is an INS office at post, the I-94 should be turned over to that office. In other cases the form should be sent as expeditiously as possible to ACS-INS, P.O. Box 7125, London, KY 40743 when using the U.S. mail or pouch or to ACS-INS, 1084 South Laurel Road, London, KY 40744 when using another delivery method.

2. If the consular officer is unable to collect the I-94 because the applicant claims it was lost, stolen, or turned in to INS, the "Application Received" stamp should be placed next to the expired visa or, in the case of a prior change of status, next to the most recent unexpired visa in the different category that might otherwise be erroneously converted and revalidated if the INS inspector were unaware of the alien's intervening visa application. This stamp is in addition to the stamp that must be placed in the back of the passport, as required for all visa refusals.

That same DOS cable clarifies DOS's position on the propriety of return to the United States with a current, valid visa after having applied for a new one and being denied. In the cable, DOS stated:

In cases where the applicant possesses a valid visa, the visa should not be revoked unless the consular officer determines either that the alien is no longer entitled to the visa classification indicated on the visa (this would include aliens in possession of valid B visas who are no longer qualified under 214(b)), or that the alien is ineligible under 212(a) or some other legal ground of visa ineligibility.

If that is the case, then the consular officer must follow the procedures outlined in 9 FAM 41.122 for revoking visas.

Admission in the Same Status Using a Visa Issued for Employment with a Different Employer

A July 8, 1997, Memorandum[30] issued by Michael L. Aytes, Assistant Commissioner of the INS confirms that:

in the case of an H, L, O or P nonimmigrant visa, the visa remains valid during its validity period regardless of a change in the beneficiaries employer. As long as the alien remains in the same nonimmigrant classification, the visa is considered valid up until the date of its expiration. An H, L, O or P nonimmigrant alien who changes employers in the United States, but remains in the same nonimmigrant classification, may use the previously issued visa to apply for admission to the United States if it is still valid.

What if Your Client Is Outside the United States and Still Has an I-94 After It Has Expired?

I-94s are not consistently surrendered or collected for U.S.-Canada flights, or from those who enter Canada by land. And some I-94s just are not collected for unknown reasons. As a result, people who do not return to the United States while the I-94 is valid will appear to have overstayed. Little, if any, information is provided to those affected by these practices. These actions can have a tremendous impact on individuals. They may be improperly denied entry and future benefits of the VWP, as well as under visa categories. Trying to rectify these situations take countless hours in needless referrals to secondary inspection.

If your client arrives in his or her home country with an I-94, he or she must take the time to return the card *and* provide documentation to the government to establish timely departure. The original card, along with original documentary evidence that the individual left the United States by the expiration date of that card (such as boarding pass, credit card purchases signed outside the United States, etc.) should be sent to:

ACS Inc.
1084 South Laurel Rd.
London, Kentucky 40744

Failure to do so will likely result in, at the least: (1) the government assuming that the person stayed beyond the time allowed and violated the terms of admission, (2) being sent to "secondary inspection" for closer questioning upon next arrival, or (3) prohibition of use of the VWP if the I-94 card was green. Any of these could result in a refused admission and immediate return to the country of origin on a future trip.

---

[30] *Published on* AILA InfoNet at Doc. No. 97071690 (*posted* July 16, 1997).

Correcting Erroneous Information

To correct outdated or false CBP-related database information, an inquiry, along with all supporting documentation, should be sent to:

Director, TECS/FOIA
U.S. Customs and Border Protection
Office of Field Operations
1300 Pennsylvania Ave. NW
Washington, D.C. 20229

If CBP determines that the information is under the jurisdiction of another entity, such as ICE, it will forward the inquiry.

CONCLUSION

If all of these procedures and requirements seem complicated, they are. Travel to the United States is not as easy as it used to be, and the penalties for violation of the standards have become more severe. Do not let your client's next trip end before the meetings start—plan for immigration as you plan for business, and you will have less to worry about.

ALL IN THE FAMILY:
HOW MESSY DIVORCES CAN MAKE A MESS OF NATURALIZATION

by Jonathan S. Greene[*]

INTRODUCTION

Divorce rates in the United States have reached all-time highs over the last 30 years; recent Census Bureau estimates suggest that about 50 percent of all U.S. marriages will end in divorce.[1] When marriages break apart, some of the worst human behavior materializes, including adultery, bigamy, and failure to support children and spouses. A fair number of naturalization issues turn on the behavior of immigrants in such circumstances. As a result, immigration practitioners handling naturalization cases must understand the problems a messy divorce case can create.

The behavior in divorce cases often ties in to the need to show good moral character in order to naturalize. Although there is no statutory or regulatory definition for good moral character, it has been interpreted as meaning character that measures up to standards of average citizens of the community in which the applicant resides.[2] The standard does not necessarily require the highest moral excellence.[3]

THAT CHEATIN' HEART

Adultery is one aspect of some divorces that can lead to a disaster when a party is trying to naturalize. Part 8 of Form N-400 requires detailed information about the applicant's marital history.[4] A naturalization applicant will be subject to a finding of lack of good moral character, absent extenuating circumstances, if he or she had an extramarital affair that tended to destroy a marriage during the statutory period.[5] Although the regulation is fairly limited in scope, before 1981, adultery was a mandatory bar to good moral character under former Immigration and Nationality Act (INA) §101(f)(2). The INA of 1952 never defined the term "adultery" or specified how to determine if sexual conduct constituted adultery.[6] As a result, court interpretations of adultery were wildly divergent depending on state law, both civil and criminal. INA §101(f)(2) was repealed by the INA amendments known as the Act of December 20, 1981.[7]

Despite the general nature of the regulation and the repeal of the prior bar, USCIS continues to interpret broadly the impact of adultery on good moral character determinations. An applicant will be found to lack good moral character when adultery is present in the following circumstances:[8]

- It destroys a viable marriage.

- It is grossly incestuous, as between parent and child, or brother and sister.

- It is commercialized, as where the petitioner prostitutes herself.

- It is flaunted openly with a willful disregard for the proprieties, causing publicized notoriety and public scandal.

- It is committed in the home under circumstances contributing to the delinquency of minor children.

---

[*] **Jonathan Greene** is a founding member of Howanski & Greene, LLC, in Towson, Md. He was chair of the AILA Washington, D.C. Chapter from 2005–06. He graduated from the University of Maryland Law School in 1996 and has practiced immigration law since then. He has written numerous articles on immigration and family law, and has been a speaker at national seminars and conferences, including those of AILA and ALI-ABA. He is also a former contributing editor to the American Bar Association *Student Lawyer* magazine.

[1] There is some debate about the U.S. rate of divorce. Simply comparing marriage to divorce in any given year yields results that differ from trying to ascertain whether any particular cohort of marriages ends up in divorce. The National Center for Health Statistics showed 7.5 marriages per 1,000 people and 3.8 divorces per 1,000 people in 2003, but there are no reliable predictions for how many divorces will result from 2003 marriages.

[2] *Matter of Mogus*, 73 F. Supp. 150 (1947); *see* USCIS Interpration 316.1(e)(1) (*available at* www.uscis.gov; follow link to "Immigration Laws, Regulations and Guides").

[3] *In re Hopp*, 179 F. 561 (1910); *see* Operations Instructions (OI) 316.1(e)(1).

[4] Form N-400, Oct. 26, 2005 version.

[5] 8 CFR §316.10(b)(3)(ii).

[6] USCIS Interpretation 316.1(g)(2)(i).

[7] Pub. L. No. 97–116, 95 Stat. 1611.

[8] USCIS Interpretation 316.1(g)(2)(viii).

- It results in illegitimate children who become public charges supported by public funds.

- The frequency of adulterous acts, the number of different persons involved, the number of illegitimate children born, and any other circumstances collectively indicate the petitioner's disregard for any standard of sexual morality.

These interpretations are much broader than the regulatory requirement of "tending to destroy an existing marriage." Be mindful of the difference between the regulations and the interpretations and be prepared to argue a case accordingly. The interpretations also apply the same approach to an unmarried applicant who engaged in sexual intercourse with a married person under criteria like those listed.[9]

Many married couples split because one spouse is committing adultery or has done so over time. Attorneys representing potential naturalization applicants who are being or have been divorced should interview clients in-depth about how the marriage ended. Clients should furnish a copy of the divorce decree and attorneys should review the document to see if it mentions adultery as a ground for divorce. If naturalization applicants mention adultery, ask to see the divorce pleadings to see if adultery was alleged as a ground for divorce and if there was any admission about adultery. Ask clients if questions about adultery were asked of them in deposition or whether they made any admissions in any other documents. If necessary, review deposition transcripts or written statements to ascertain the impact of the adultery on the marriage or whether the adultery implicated any other factors.

Even if potential naturalization applicants never have been married, attorneys should ask if they have ever been sexually involved with married persons. The same analysis of adultery could apply in such cases, especially where the applicants are deposed in a married person's divorce case.

The spouse who commits adultery often feels that the marriage is not really viable any longer. If a potential naturalization applicant has committed adultery that appears to have destroyed the viable marriage, ask the client who he or she talked to about the situation at the time. Sometimes therapists, clergy, and other confidants will sign affidavits describing the poor state of the marriage at the time the adultery occurred. If the other spouse already had

---

[9] USCIS Interpretation 316.1(f)(6).

committed adultery, the client has a better chance to argue that the marriage was no longer viable when he or she committed adultery.

OOPS! DID I FORGET SOMETHING?

Naturalization applicants who have been through divorces can face another high hurdle over support issues. Question 22g of Part 10 of Form N-400 asks if the applicant has ever failed to support dependents or pay alimony.[10] An applicant who has willfully failed or refused to support dependents will be found to lack good moral character, unless there are extenuating circumstances.[11] This failure is limited to the statutory period, but evidence of prior nonsupport may be relevant to a determination of present good moral character or a finding that there is lack of reform of character during the statutory period.[12]

Many of those who have gone through divorce have emerged with support obligations for children, former spouses, or both. If you are representing a potential naturalization applicant, thoroughly review this issue if clients are divorced or divorcing. Child support and spousal support usually will be reflected in a court order, such as a divorce decree, a contract between the spouses, or both.[13] Ask clients for a copy of

---

[10] Form N-400, Oct. 26, 2005 version.

[11] 8 CFR §316.10(b)(3)(i).

[12] INA §316(a) provides the following:

> No person, except as otherwise provided in this title, shall be naturalized, unless such applicant, (1) immediately preceding the date of filing his application for naturalization has resided continuously, after being lawfully admitted for permanent residence, within the United States for at least five years and during the five years immediately preceding the date of filing his application has been physically present therein for periods totaling at least half of that time, and who has resided within the State or within the district of the Service in the United States in which the applicant filed the application for at least three months, (2) has resided continuously within the United States from the date of the application up to the time of admission to citizenship, (3) during all the periods referred to in this subsection has been and still is a person of good moral character, attached to the principles of the Constitution of the United States, and well disposed to the good order and happiness of the United States.

INA §319(a) provides that persons married to U.S. citizens must reside in the United States for a period of three years instead of five.

[13] Spouses can be contractually bound to pay alimony or child support. During a period of separation before the entry of a divorce decree, spouses can enter into a marital settle-

continued

all court orders and agreements requiring payment of support to ascertain what was supposed to be paid and any modifications to the original obligation.[14]

Once you know about a support obligation, ask clients for proof that support has been paid. Many clients retain canceled checks or cash receipts for payment. Alimony is also often tax deductible for the payor, so client tax returns can provide information about payments.

Carefully question clients about whether they ever fell behind in their support obligations or whether any enforcement actions were ever taken against them. Clients should provide a copy of any contempt or other enforcement order, garnishment order, or wage liens. Sometimes support arrears are taken from retirement accounts via special orders, and these domestic relations orders also should be provided.

Clients who fail to pay also can be ordered to be incarcerated as part of a court's contempt power in some cases, so ask the clients if they were ever in jail because of support owed. Obtain any incarceration documents the clients might possess.

If there are orders or agreements requiring that payment be made to a support agency, your client is in for a special treat. The support agency may have had the authority to suspend your client's driver's license or professional license and intercept tax returns if payments fell behind. The support agency may have records of such actions, as well as the other government agencies involved, including the Internal Revenue Service, the state taxing authority, and the state motor vehicle administration. Ask clients if they were ever subject to any punitive action from the support agency or had their tax refunds taken or licenses suspended. Also ask them to furnish any documents they received from support agencies or that were related to support agencies. If the clients do not have such documents, you may

need to track down copies of the documents from the agencies to understand what occurred.

Willful Failure

After collecting all the client's information and documentation, it will be necessary to ascertain whether a failure to pay support was willful. Although the question on Form N-400 asks about any failure to pay support, the regulations indicate that USCIS is only interested in willful failures to pay.[15]

To evaluate the client's intent, it will not be sufficient to simply ask whether the client intentionally did not pay support. Review the documents obtained and the client's explanations to ascertain whether any nonpayment constituted a refusal to pay. Scrutinize any contempt orders or other enforcement documents for language indicating that the client refused to pay or engaged in a willful failure to provide support. Do not assume that contempt orders equal refusal; some courts will enter nonsupport contempt orders whenever payments are due, no matter what the reason for the arrearage.

USCIS has recognized circumstances where willful failure or refusal to pay support translated into a finding of lack of good moral character:[16]

- A person failed to pay support for a period of years without satisfactory explanation.[17]

- A person had the financial means to pay substantial support but instead provides inadequate support.[18]

- A person refuses to pay support because the other spouse decides to live elsewhere with the children.[19]

Extenuating Circumstances

Even if there is evidence of willful failure, a good moral character finding will not be withheld if there are acceptable extenuating circumstances. USCIS has recognized several examples of extenuating circumstances where nonsupport did not result in a finding of lack of good moral character:[20]

---

ment or other agreement that binds one to pay support to the other. Such agreements can be enforced as contracts; a non-paying spouse can be found to be in breach of contract and ordered to pay damages or be required to specifically perform the obligations of the contract. These agreements often are incorporated into divorce decrees, which make the terms of the agreement enforceable as part of a court order.

[14] Child support and some alimony obligations are subject to court modification upon material change of circumstances, for example, a significant change in the payor's income. It is critical to obtain all court orders referring to support or alimony, because the terms of original orders may have changed over the years.

[15] 8 CFR §316.10(b)(3)(i).

[16] USCIS Interpretation 316.1(f)(5).

[17] *Matter of Mogus*, 73 F. Supp. 150 (1947), *cited in* USCIS Interpretation 316.1(f) (5) n. 69c.

[18] *Matter of Halas*, 274 F. Supp. 604 (1967), *cited in* USCIS Interpretation 316.1(f)(5) n. 69e.

[19] *See Petition of Dobric*, 189 F. Supp. 638 (1960), *cited in* USCIS Interpretation 316.1(f)(5) n. 69f.

[20] USCIS Interpretation 316.1(f)(5).

- A person did not comply with a court order due to lack of employment and financial ability.[21]

- A parent met the burden of support to a reasonable extent.[22]

- The other spouse was self-supporting and did not request support.[23]

- The children were no longer minors during the statutory period and the other spouse received support from a daughter and from income-generating property.[24]

- The other spouse had successfully prevented the applicant from ascertaining the other spouse's address but the applicant had nevertheless made partial support payments through the applicant's mother.[25]

- The failure to volunteer support was motivated by concern for the child and an attempt to gain custody according to the court decree, and the applicant contributed after the court reminded applicant of the duty to pay support.[26]

The duty to pay support can be excused for numerous reasons beyond those USCIS has noted. Where the naturalization applicant withheld support after the other parent strongly interfered with the applicant's ability to have visitation with their children, one court found that to be an extenuating circumstance.[27]

Sometimes naturalization applicants have been engaged in post-divorce litigation over the amount of child support that should be paid. Imagine a client who believed he was entitled to a reduction in the

amount of child support and filed the proper court pleadings to pursue the reduction. If the state law governing the child support case does not provide for recoupment of child support that is overpaid, the client may have engaged in self-help and lowered the amount of support paid during the litigation. The strategy eventually might have resulted in the desired reduction in support without any problem from the court, even though the client had paid less than the previous court order had required in anticipation of the desired reduction. Although the client had engaged in a willful failure to pay support from the perspective of naturalization law, the actions were deemed to be justified by the state court and thus there would seem to be extenuating circumstances.

Improving the Odds

Naturalization applicants who refused to pay support without extenuating circumstances still might have an opportunity to establish good moral character. If the willful nonpayment of support occurred before the statutory period, applicants can show reform of character by presenting a strong support payment record during the statutory period. They also can pay off arrearages ahead of any schedule set by court orders, or show they are paying other forms of support that might not be required by court orders, such as college expenses for their children. Affidavits from former spouses may be useful toward establishing good moral character.

THE SMALL PROBLEM OF BIGAMY

Bigamy is not specifically mentioned as a ground for finding lack of good moral character, but it can have a negative effect in a naturalization case nonetheless. Question 22d of Part 10 of Form N-400 asks if the applicant has ever been married to more than one person at the same time.[28] If a person seeks to naturalize based on marriage to a U.S. citizen and was not actually divorced from a prior spouse, the second marriage is not lawful due to bigamy. Without a lawful second marriage, not only will naturalization be denied but permanent residence could be revoked as well. Bigamy is also a crime.

I Thought I Was Divorced

While bigamy cases often occur by design, they also can arise seemingly by accident.[29] Divorces of-

---

[21] *Petition of Schindler*, U.S.D.C. Nev., A-8476356 (1958), *unreported, cited in* USCIS Interpretation 316.1(f)(5) n. 69j.

[22] *Petition of Perdiak*, 162 F. Supp. 176 (1958); *Petition of Teofilo Manloto Nayan*, U.S.D.C. N.D. Ill, A-10130890 (1967), *unreported, cited in* USCIS Interpretation 316.1(f)(5) n. 69k.

[23] *Petition of Breitsammeter*, U.S.D.C. N.D. Ill., A-5962234 (1965), *unreported, cited in* USCIS Interpretation 316.1(f)(5) n. 69m.

[24] *Petition of Tabone*, U.S.D.C. N.D. Cal., A-4526467 (1950), *unreported, cited in* USCIS Interpretation 316.1(f)(5) n. 69n.

[25] *Petition of LeBrasseur*, U.S.D.C. E.D. Pa., A-8534353 (1962), *unreported, cited in* USCIS Interpretation 316(f)(5) n. 69o.

[26] *Petition of Sadkowy*, U.S.D.C. N.D. Ill., A-10866315 (1964), *unreported, cited in* USCIS Interpretation 316(f)(5) n. 69p.

[27] *Matter of Valad*, 465 F. Supp. 120 (E.D. Va. 1979).

[28] Form N-400, Oct. 26, 2005 version.

[29] States are split on whether the crime of bigamy has a *mens rea* component or is a strict liability offense. Washington

continued

ten can be obtained by one spouse with little involvement by the other beyond receipt of divorce pleadings. Naturalization clients may not have been the moving parties in their divorce actions and may not have received copies of their supposed divorce decrees. Those clients may have assumed they were divorced because their spouses told them so. More than a few people have discovered that leaving the responsibility to the other spouse was not a good idea because the other spouse did not follow through to secure the divorce.[30] Ask naturalization clients to produce their divorce decrees for review before naturalization applications are filed.

Not All Divorces Are Equal

Sometimes naturalization applicants have engaged in bigamy without intending to do so because they did not obtain final divorces before remarrying. A number of states, including Maryland and Virginia, have multiple categories of divorce. Some of these do not permit remarriage. For example, Maryland features two categories of divorce: limited and absolute.[31] A limited divorce resolves issues of child custody, child support, alimony, and personal property but does not address division of marital property, including real property.[32] The limited divorce also does not permit remarriage. A person who obtains a limited divorce is permitted to file a supplemental complaint for absolute divorce within 18 months and proceed to obtain the absolute divorce.[33] Only an absolute divorce permits remarriage.

An attorney who has a naturalization client with a Maryland divorce needs to ascertain which type was obtained. Maryland divorce decrees are typically titled "Judgment of Limited Divorce" or "Judgment of Absolute Divorce." Ask clients with Maryland divorces to provide a copy of the divorce decree to verify they have obtained an absolute divorce. Occasionally, a decree is inadvertently issued under the title "Judgment of Divorce." In that case, obtain a copy of the court docket to review what

type of divorce was sought. If the docket is unclear, the pleadings might need to be reviewed. If a client only provides proof of a limited divorce, investigate whether an absolute divorce was later obtained in Maryland or in another state or country.

Virginia also features two types of divorce, the divorce from bed and board, and the divorce from the bond of matrimony.[34] A divorce from bed and board, like Maryland's limited divorce, does not permit remarriage:

In granting a divorce from bed and board, the court may decree that the parties be perpetually separated and protected in their persons and property. Such decree shall operate upon property thereafter acquired, and upon the personal rights and legal capacities of the parties, as a decree for a divorce from the bond of matrimony, except that neither party shall marry again during the life of the other.[35]

A person who has obtained a Virginia divorce from bed and board can later obtain a final divorce from the bonds of matrimony, which permits remarriage.[36] But people with divorces from bed and board alone are not free to remarry.

I Went on Vacation and All I Got Was This Lousy Divorce

Sometimes clients present divorce decrees that appear to be valid but turn out to be worth less than the paper on which they are printed. For example, parties who seek to obtain customary, nonjudicial divorces in their home countries have to observe the legal requirements particular to that type of divorce.[37] Other times, divorcing spouses attempt to obtain a consular divorce, only to discover that they did not obtain what they were seeking.[38] In representing potential naturalization applicants, review the divorce documents and check with local law if there is any question about the validity of the divorce. The burden of proof rests with the naturalization applicant to provide sufficient evidence of valid termination of prior marriages.[39]

---

takes the view that a person is only guilty of bigamy if he or she intends to commit the offense. *Washington v. Seek*, 109 Wash. App. 876 (2002). In contrast, Maryland continues to find that lack of intent is not a defense. *Braun v. Maryland*, 230 Md. 82, 185 A.2d 905 (1962).

[30] *See Matter of Dabaase*, 16 I&N 39 (BIA 1976).

[31] Md. Code Ann., Family Law §7-102 provides grounds for limited divorce and §7-103 for absolute divorce.

[32] Md. Code Ann., Family Law §7-102.

[33] Md. Rule 9-202 (d).

---

[34] Va. Code Ann. §20-95 provides grounds for a divorce from bed and board and §20-91 for a divorce from the bonds of matrimony.

[35] Va. Code Ann. §20-116.

[36] Va. Code Ann. §§20-117, 20-121.

[37] *See Matter of Nwangnu*, 16 I&N Dec. 61 (BIA 1976).

[38] *See Matter of Hassan*, 16 I&N Dec. 16 (BIA 1976).

[39] *Matter of Brantigan*, 11 I&N Dec. 493 (BIA 1966).

BIG LOVE IS BAD NEWS

Polygamy and bigamy are not the same thing in immigration law.[40] What is the practical difference? Polygamy is the intentional practice of creating a single family unit that features multiple spouses, typically one husband with several wives. Bigamy results in multiple family units, sometimes unintentionally. A husband could have two families in two different cities by design or might just have failed to get a proper divorce before remarrying.

Practicing polygamy during the statutory period is a clear bar to a finding of good moral character.[41] Although the bar to naturalize is limited to the practice of polygamy during the statutory period, USCIS could consider polygamy occurring before the statutory period if the applicant's conduct during the statutory period does not reflect reform of character from the earlier period, or if the polygamy appears relevant to present moral character.[42] While USCIS is supposed to evaluate good moral character based on the standards of the average citizen in the community of residence, it is unlikely that any large U.S. community would condone polygamy as morally acceptable behavior for its average citizens.[43] There are reported to be small local U.S. communities in Utah, Arizona, and other Western states where polygamy occurs, but the practice is criminalized throughout the country and anathema to most religious communities in the United States, including the present Mormon Church.

At least one person has attempted to get around the ban on polygamy through a serial monogamy scheme in which the husband entered a series of marriages and divorces, but all the prior wives still lived with the husband.[44] Naturalization applicants inclined toward polygamy should be cautioned against the creative use of marriage and divorce; the results are likely to have a detrimental effect on a typical analysis of good moral character.

CONCLUSION

Careful practitioners who investigate a client's criminal background and health history also should thoroughly review a prospective naturalization applicant's marital history to determine whether adultery, breach of support obligations, polygamy, or bigamy could become an issue. The applicant may not be aware that personal circumstances from years ago could give rise to these issues. Where they are present, clients should be counseled about the risks of proceeding with a naturalization application, which could include denial of the application, revocation of permanent residence, removal proceedings, and even criminal prosecution once the circumstances come to the attention of the U.S. government.

---

[40] *Matter of G–*, 6 I&N Dec. 9 (BIA 1953).

[41] 8 CFR §316.10(b)(2)(ix).

[42] 8 CFR §316.10(a).

[43] *Id.*

[44] *See Utah v. Green*, 2004 Utah 76, 99 P.3d 820 (2004).

Apa, Jill A.—Nonimmigrant Waivers for Canadian Citizens and Instability in the Processing System 108

Auerbach, Randy P.—Technology for the Immigration Practitioner 11

Badia-Tavas, M. Mercedes—Training American Style 668

Badrinath, Vikram K.—Relief from Removal: Does It Currently Exist? 73

Bae, Davis C.—Best Practices for Immigration Law Office Management 1

Bacon, Roxana C.—The Importance of Advance Business Planning in the Initial Representation Decision 23

Barker, Rodney M.—Summary of AAO Decisions on "Religious Visas" 501

Berg, Royal F.—Stopping Time and Ignoring the Reality of Aging: The Simple Beauty of the Child Status Protection Act 323

Brodyaga, Lisa S.—Habeas Corpus and the REAL ID Act: Some Constitutional Concerns 204

Brown, Jan H.—Family Immigration Issues: Love Conquers All? 312

Brown, Jenifer M.—Practice Pointers for O and P Visas 648

Butte, Dagmar—Appealing Words for the BIA and AAO 184

Campbell, Boyd F.—International Adoption—A Basic Guide to the Three Visa Categories 364

Chandler, Anne—The ABCs of Working with Immigrant Children to Obtain Special Immigrant Juvenile Status for Those Abused, Neglected, or Abandoned 300

Chang, Henry J.—E-1 Nonimmigrant Status 544

Chapman, Gerald M.—Strategies for L-1As 628

Chea, Socheat.—The Immigration Judge War 160

Chehrazi, Jasmine—Why "Walk the Line"? Effective, Efficient, and Ethical Practices for Immigration Paralegals 67

Chesser, Lori T.—Training American Style 668

Chu, Newton J.—Employment Verification Systems—Where Are We and Where Are We Going? 508

Colon, Salvador—Asylum Grab Bag: Sexual Orientation, Gangs, Children, and Presentation of Background Country Condition Evidence 239

Cooper, Holly S.—Getting Out: Strategies for Challenging Unlawful Detention in Federal Court 213

Cooper, Scott F.—Training American Style 668

DelVecchio, Dyann—"Should I Stay or Should I Go?" 387

Devore, Jeffrey A.—Priority Dates: More Important Than Ever 399

Dinnerstein, Julie E.—Violence Against Women Act (VAWA) Self-Petitions 331

Dornbaum, Neil S.—A Proactive Approach to DOL Audits—BINGO Revisited 521

Eiss, James D.—How Much Is Enough? Documenting the Ability to Pay in Religious Worker
    Cases (Updated) 497

Falstrom, Carl—Managing Client Expectations 27

Ferrell, Paul W.—Making Sense of the FAM Notes on Treaty Investor Visas 562

Flanagan, Judy—The ABCs of Working with Immigrant Children to Obtain Special Immigrant
    Juvenile Status for Those Abused, Neglected, or Abandoned 300

Fleming, Joycelyn L.—Strategies for L-1As 628

Fragomen, Jr., Austin T.—Employment Verification Systems—Where Are We and Where Are
    We Going? 508

Frank, Robert—Preventative Medicine: Avoiding Removal for Noncitizen Criminal Defendants
    Using Pre- and Post-Conviction Relief 124

Gallagher, Anna Marie—Remedies of Last Resort: Private Bills and Pardons 144

Ganchan, Leigh N.—Employment Verification Systems—Where Are We and Where Are We
    Going? 508

Garson, David L.P.—The New Admission Conundrum 707

Ginsburg, Richard M.—Fraud and Misrepresentation Waivers—Planning for Success 96

Gladstone, Michael H —Security Clearances and Technology Licenses 530

Goldman, Jeffrey W.—Best Practices for Immigration Law Office Management 1

Goodwin, Jodi—What You Still Need to Know about §212(c) 84

Goss, Elizabeth S.—Workstudy: Employment Options for Students with F, J, or M Visas 658

Greene, Jonathan S.—All in the Family: How Messy Divorces Can Make a Mess of
    Naturalization 717

Greenstein, Ilana, E.—Into the Rabbit's Hole: When a Misdemeanor Is a Felony
    The *Davis/Barrett* Hypothetical Federal Felony Analysis of Drug Crimes 137

Greenstein, Ilana, E.—What You Still Need to Know about §212(c) 84

Grzegorek, Kathleen L.—Practice Pointers for O and P Visas 648

Guevara, Rómulo E.—Labor Certifications and the Law of Recruitment 424

Hake, Bruce A.—U.S. Government Funding in J-1 Waiver Cases—The Worst Form of the
    Disease 681

Han, Hilary A.—Asylum Grab Bag: Sexual Orientation, Gangs, Children, and Presentation of
    Background Country Condition Evidence 239

Hasche, Tilman—Reopening the Executed Removal Order (Appendix) 181

Hernández, Xiomara M.—Priority Dates: More Important Than Ever 399

Henner, Janet L.—Challenges in Representing Nonimmigrant Professionals: A Roundtable Q&A
    with Practitioners 571

Hirsch, Matthew I.—Why "Walk the Line"? Effective, Efficient, and Ethical Practices for Immigration Paralegals 67

Hines, Barbara—Relief From Removal: Does It Currently Exist? 73

Hornik, Philip—Waivers of the §212(a)(9)(c) Permanent Bar How to Get Them If You Need Them—And What Is a 'Removal Order' Anyway? 104

Joaquin, Linton—NACARA for Guatemalans, Salvadorans, and Former Soviet Bloc Nationals 280

Jones, David S.—Technology for the Immigration Practitioner 11

Joseph, Jeff—Getting Out: Strategies for Challenging Unlawful Detention in Federal Court 213

Kenepaske, Linda—Preventative Medicine: Avoiding Removal for Noncitizen Criminal Defendants Using Pre- and Post-Conviction Relief 124

Kershaw, Robert—Current State of the U.S. Guest Worker Program: H-2B and H-2A Status for Employing Essential Workers and Proposed Immigration Reform 605

Kinoshita, Sally—Protecting Victims of Crime 692

Kramer, Mary E.—Asylum Grab Bag: Sexual Orientation, Gangs, Children, and Presentation of Background Country Condition Evidence 239

Kushner, Laya R.—Practice Pointers for O and P Visas 648

Lawler, Martin J.—Appealing Words for the BIA and AAO 184

Leiden, Warren R.—B-1 Business Visitors (Updated) 536

Leopold, David W.—Getting Out: Strategies for Challenging Unlawful Detention in Federal Court 213

LGBT/HIV Based Asylum Handbook: Winning Asylum, Withholding and CAT Cases Based on Sexual Orientation, Transgender Identity and/or HIV-Positive Status (Excerpt)—Brief History of Lesbian, Gay, Bisexual, Transgender, and HIV (LGBT/H Asylum) Law 248

Mailman, Stanley—Appealing Words for the BIA and AAO 184

Malhotra, Anil—Intercountry Adoptions from India 375

Malhotra, Ranjit—Intercountry Adoptions from India 375

Mancini, Mark A.—Ethical Considerations for Immigration Attorneys Regarding Employment of Paralegals 44

Marcus, Daniel E.—International Adoption—A Basic Guide to the Three Visa Categories 364

Marks, Jay S.—Preventative Medicine: Avoiding Removal for Noncitizen Criminal Defendants Using Pre- and Post-Conviction Relief 124

Masliah, Noemi E.—Yes, Same-Sex Couples Can Get Married in Four Countries and Massachusetts—No, They *Still* Are Not I-130 Eligible 317

Mautino, Kathrin S.—Pulling the Rabbit Out of the Hat: Using Western Hemisphere Priority Dates to Move Business and Family-Based Immigration 409

McCown, Kelly M.—Strategies for L-1As 628

McKee, Estelle M.—Appealing Words for the BIA and AAO 184

Mehta, Cyrus D.—"Should I Stay or Should I Go?"...387

Moccio, Kathleen A.—The ABCs of Working with Immigrant Children to Obtain Special
Immigrant Juvenile Status for Those Abused, Neglected, or Abandoned 300

Montag, Jonathan D.—The Immigration Judge War 160

Neal, Sherry L.—Overcoming Hurdles with L-1B Intracompany Transferees..........................643

Newman, Mark J.—Security Clearances and Technology Licenses 530

Neville, Sheila—Protecting Victims of Crime 692

Ng, Ronald H.—Stopping Time and Ignoring the Reality of Aging: The Simple Beauty of the
Child Status Protection Act 323

Nightingale, Zachary—Here We Go Again: Motions to Reopen, Reconsider, and Rescind Before
the Board of Immigration Appeals 169

Olivas, Michael A.—*Plyler v. Doe*, the Education of Undocumented Children, and the Polity.....224

Ovink, B. John—The Hardship of Proving Hardship..114

Pelta, Eleanor—Challenges in Representing Nonimmigrant Professionals: A Roundtable Q&A
with Practitioners 571

Peterson, Craig—Workstudy: Employment Options for Students with F, J, or M Visas.............658

Pendleton, Gail—Protecting Victims of Crime 692

Pollock, Scott D.—Workstudy: Employment Options for Students with F, J, or M Visas...........658

Reich, William Z.—Nonimmigrant Waivers for Canadian Citizens and Instability in the
Processing System..108

Rizzo, Danielle—How Much Is Enough? Documenting the Ability to Pay in Religious Worker
Cases (Updated) 497

Rodgers, Gregg—The New Admission Conundrum 707

Rosenberg, Lory D.—Appealing Words for the BIA and AAO 184

Rost, Kristina K.—Managing Ethical Conflicts in a Business Practice 38

Rubin, Edwin R.—Managing Client Expectations 27

Ruby, Jay C.—Current State of the U.S. Guest Worker Program: H-2B and H-2A Status for
Employing Essential Workers and Proposed Immigration Reform 605

Schorr, Naomi—Making Do: AC21 in a Regulatory Vacuum..583

Scofield, Eileen M.G.—Employment Verification Systems—Where Are We and Where Are We
Going?..508

Shannon, Careen B.—DOL Proposes Drastic Changes to the Labor Certification Program 417

Sharma, Dhara—Summary of AAO Decisions on "Religious Visas" 501

Shastri, Avantika—Here We Go Again: Motions to Reopen, Reconsider, and Rescind Before the
Board of Immigration Appeals..169

Shenoy, Dinesh P.—Best Practices for Immigration Law Office Management.................................1

Shiron, Jr., Peter T.—A Proactive Approach to DOL Audits—BINGO Revisited 521

Silverman, Mark—NACARA for Guatemalans, Salvadorans, and Former Soviet Bloc Nationals 280

Simmons, Teri A.—B-1 Business Visitors (Updated) 536

Smith, Philip—What You Still Need to Know about §212(c) 84

Soloway, Lavi S.—Yes, Same-Sex Couples Can Get Married in Four Countries and
    Massachusetts—No, They *Still* Are Not I-130 Eligible 317

Sostrin, Rita Kushner—The Revival of Schedule A, Group II: Is "Exceptional" in Vogue? 443

Steffas, Irene A.—International Adoption—A Basic Guide to the Three Visa Categories 364

Stone, Lincoln—B-1 Business Visitors (Updated) 536

Storch, Susan Borowski—VWP & CBP: Perfect Together? 705

Sultan, Tarik H.—Challenges in Representing Nonimmigrant Professionals: A Roundtable Q&A
    with Practitioners 571

Tafapolsky, Alan—A Proactive Approach to DOL Audits—BINGO Revisited 521

Tekach, Cora D.—Training American Style 668

Todd, Aimee Clark—Protecting Victims of Crime 692

Underwood, Shannon M.—"Should I Stay or Should I Go?" 387

Virtue, Paul W.—"Should I Stay or Should I Go?" 387

Wada, Ronald Y.—PERM Strategies and *Ad Hoc* Rules for Beneficiaries with Three-Year
    Bachelor's Degrees 432

Walters, Alison—Why "Walk the Line"? Effective, Efficient, and Ethical Practices for
    Immigration Paralegals 67

Waxman, Nathan A.—National Interest Waiver: Case Study 454

Weber, Cletus M.—Technology for the Immigration Practitioner 11

Wexler, Mitchell L.—DOL Proposes Drastic Changes to the Labor Certification Program 417

Wiebe, Virgil—"Maybe You Should," "Yes, You Must," "No, You Can't": Shifting Standards
    and Practices for Ensuring Document Reliability in Asylum Cases 263

Wizner, Andrew L.—A Proactive Approach to DOL Audits—BINGO Revisited 521

Yale-Loehr, Stephen—EB-5 Immigrant Investors 480

Yale-Loehr, Stephen—Initial Interviews 32

SUBJECT MATTER INDEX

Alphabetization is word-by-word (e.g., "H nonimmigrant" precedes "Habeas").

A

A.A.-M. v. Alberto Gonzales, 306

AAO, *See* Administrative Appeals Office

ABC-registered class members asylum applications, 286–92

AC21, *See* American Competitiveness in the Twenty-First Century Act of 2000

Acosta v. Gonzales, 107

Adams v. Howerton, 318–19, 320

Adjustment of status applications
battered spouses and children and, 394
benefits of, 388–89
compared with Consular Processing, 387–90
immediate relatives and, 394
INA §245(i) and, 395–96
INA §245(k) and, 396–97
remedies upon denial of, 397–98
S visas and, 704
T visas and, 702
technical exceptions, 394–95
travel and, 392–93
U visas and, 695
unlawful status and, 393–97
work authorization and, 391–92

Administrative Appeals Office
ability to pay the proffered wage to religious workers, 504–05
adjudicators, 196
appeals before, 196–200
burden and standard of proof, 197
cumulative weight of the evidence, 199
description, 196
EB-2 degree equivalency decisions, 434–36
establishing the two-year period of experience requirement for religious workers, 501–04
expert testimony, 197–99
high-tech occupations and, 196–97
job offers for religious workers, 506–07
qualifying religious job/traditional religious function, 505–06
religious worker decisions, 499–507
style for briefs, 196
submission of new evidence, 199–200
tax-exempt, bona fide religious organization workers, 507

Adoption, *See* Intercountry adoptions from India; International adoption

Adry-Mart, Inc., 428

Adultery, 717–18

Advance parole
marriage cases and, 315
Nicaraguan Adjustment and Central American Relief Act and, 283

Advocacy
appeals before the AAO, 196–200
appeals to the BIA, 186–96
legal writing style and, 201–03
principles of, 184–85
style issues, 185–86

Agricultural workers, *See* H-2B and H-2A visas

Aggravated felony
See also Criminal issues, Removal and relief, Waivers
BIA and the *Davis/Barrett* hypothetical federal felony doctrine, 138–43
definition, 137
generally, 74–83, 129–30, 131–34, 135–36
historical background, 138
Section 212(c), 84–95

AILA*Link* software, 11, 15

Ali v. Ashcroft, 219

Altamirano-Lopez v. Gonzales, 210

Amanfi v. Ashcroft, 241, 251

American Bar Association
Model Rules of Professional Conduct, 39–40, 43, 44–45

American Competitiveness in the Twenty-First Century Act of 2000
H-1B visas and, 581–82, 583–604
I-140 portability and, 406–07
Section 104(C) and immigrant visa retrogression, 596–603

Antitrust crimes
case study, 126–30

AOS, *See* Adjustment of status applications

Apostille method of authentication, *See* Hague Convention

Armentero v. INS, 215

Arts-related petitions, *See* O and P visas

Asere v. Gonzales, 209–10

Ashbrook-Simon-Hartley v. McLaughlin, 430

Asylum and other forms of protection
authentication of documents, 264–69
bases for asylum, 248–49
children, 239–47
circuit courts of appeal and, 275–78
corroboration standards, 263–64
Department of State and, 274–75
derivative children of, 328–29
detention of, 222
document reliability, 263–79
evidence of country conditions, 244
expert witness testimony, 246–47
gangs, 239–47
immigration courts and the BIA, 274
lesbian, gay, bisexual, transgender, and HIV (LGBT/H asylum) law, 248–62
motions to reopen and, 172
NACARA, 280–99
persecution based on social group and, 239
practical tips, 245
presentation of evidence, 245–46
sexual orientation, 239–47
U.N. Convention Relating to the Status of Refugees, 248
U.N. Protocol Relating to the Status of Refugees, 248
USCIS Asylum Office guidance, 272–74

Asylum Office Procedures Manual
document authentication and, 272

Attorney-client relationships
confidentiality, 33
dual representation and, 40–42
starting and ending in writing, 5

Audits
DOL audits, 521–29
Form I-9 and, 517–18
Wage and Hour Administrator, 521–29

Authentication of documents
chain authentication, 265
China example, 266–67
consulates and, 266
field investigation, 269–72
forensic examination, 269
Hague Convention Abolishing Requirement for Legalization of Foreign Documents and, 268–69

Azerbijan
  international adoption and, 374

B

B-1 visas
  Applicant's prior immigration history and, 537
  description, 536
  eligibility for, 538–39
  entry for a temporary period requirement, 538
  H-1B or H-3 status and, 540–41
  importance to U.S. participation in the global economy, 543
  limitations on, 670
  NAFTA and, 541
  permitted business activities, 538, 539–40
  potential training uses, 668–69
  regulatory authority, agency guidelines, and policy considerations, 536–37
  requirements, 669–70
  statutory authority, 536
  unabandoned foreign residence requirement, 538
  visa application, admission, extension, and change of status, 542
  for workers in the United States, 539
BALCA, *See* Board of labor Certification Appeals
Basic Pilot Program
  employment verification and, 509
Belarus
  international adoption and, 374
Belgium
  same-sex marriages, 317
Benslimane v. Gonzales, 161, 162
Best practices
  business plans, 2, 23–26
  creating a culture and core values, 2–3
  creating good will, 3
  dealing with details, 6–7
  efficiency, 3–4
  file review, 4–5
  information and document management, 5–6
  managing a law practice, 4
  starting and ending attorney-client relationships in writing, 5
  understanding the business, 1
BIA, *See* Board of Immigration Appeals

BIA Practice Manual, 191
Bigamy
  naturalization and, 720–22
  Violence Against Women Act self-petitions and, 339
Blanket L-1 filings
  advantages of, 636–37
  background checks, 635
  companies and, 634–35
  compared with regular Ls, 638–40
  cost-benefit analysis, 635
  disadvantages of, 637
  regulations for, 635–36
Board of Immigration Appeals
  appeal advocacy, 186–96
  Child Status Protection Act decision, 327
  conclusion of the brief, 195–96
  Davis/Barrett hypothetical federal felony analysis, 138–43
  decision holding that homosexuals constitute a particular social group, 239–40
  document authentication and, 274
  draft language and checklist, 190–91
  employment of paralegals, 45, 48–56
  evidence and findings of fact, 187
  exhaustion of remedies, 187–88
  hardship case studies, 116–20
  motions to reopen, reconsider, and rescind and, 169–83
  Notice of Appeal, 189
  organization of the argument, 194
  practical considerations, 189
  statements of facts, 191–93
  substance of the argument, 194–95
  summary affirmance factors, 190
  summary dismissal factors, 189–90
  summary of the argument, 193
  supplementary parts of submission, 193
  theory of the appeal, 188–89
  theory of the case, 186–87
Board of Labor Certification Appeals
  case law, 426–28
Boer-Sedano v. Gonzales, 240, 251
Borovikova v. U.S. Dep't of Justice, 277
Bowers v. Hardwick, 319
Braden v. 30th Judicial Circuit Court of Kentucky, 215
Brown v. INS, 120
Business plans
  client selection, 23–24

developing, 2
  initial representation decision and, 23–26
  taking a client outside your plan, 24–26
Business visitors, *See* B-1 visas

C

California
  state pardon procedures, 153–54
Cambodia
  international adoption and, 374
Canada
  E-1 nonimmigrant status and, 553
  L-1 petitions for Canadians under NAFTA at U.S.-Canada ports of entry, 641
  nonimmigrant waivers for citizens of, 108–13
Cancellation of removal, 76–80
  See also Crime involving moral turpitude, Removal and relief, Waivers
CARA, *See* Central Adoption Resource Agency
Case management
  software for, 12–15
Case studies
  antitrust crimes, 126–30
  concealed dangerous weapons, 135–36
  crimes of violence, 125–28, 134
  domestic violence, 125–28, 133
  false statements to a police officer, 135–36
  hardship, 116–20
  identity theft, 131–34
  moral turpitude crimes, 125–30
  noncitizen criminal defendants, 125–36
  Sherman Act, 126–30
  wire fraud, 131–34
CAT claims
  lesbian, gay, bisexual, transgender, and HIV asylum law and, 261–62
CBP, *See* U.S. Customs and Border Protection
Central Adoption Resource Agency
  home study reports and, 377
  procedure for intercountry adoptions, 376–77
Chamberlain Group, Inc. v. Interlogix, 199
Child Status Protection Act
  age calculation, 390–91

AOS compared with CP and, 391
children of U.S. citizens and, 324–25
derivative children of an asylee or refugee, 328–29
effective date, 330
naturalization of the petitioning parent and, 329–30
priority dates and, 407–08
provisions, 323–30, 390
unmarried sons or daughters of LPRs and, 325–28
V visas and, 330
Child Welfare v. Society of Sisters of Charity St. Gerosa Convent, 377–78
Children
See also Family immigration and adoption
abused, neglected, or abandoned children, 300–311
asylum claims based on persecution by gangs, 241–43
asylum eligibility, 311
Child Status Protection Act and, 323–30, 390–91, 407–08
deportation of children left behind by immigrant parents, 243–44
Development, Relief, and Education for Alien Minors (DREAM) Act and, 233
initial interviews and, 35–36
Nicaraguan Adjustment and Central American Relief Act and, 294–95
Plyler v. Doe and the education of undocumented children, 224–38
Special Immigrant Juvenile Status, 300–311, 364–74
Western Hemisphere Priority Date program and, 410, 413–14
Chile
E-1 nonimmigrant status and, 553
China
example of authentication methods and pitfalls for asylum-seekers, 266–67
Chintakuntla v. INS, 432–33
Circuit courts of appeal
See also specific cases
document authentication and, 275–78
Clark v. Martinez, 219
Clients
effective hand-holding techniques, 29–31
fees and retainers, 37

high-maintenance, 30–31
initial interviews with, 32–37
managing client expectations, 27–31
selecting, 23–24
starting and ending relationships with, in writing, 5
taking a client outside your business plan, 24–26
Codes of conduct, 39
Colombia
example of the Apostille method of certifying documents, 268–69
Communication barriers
children, elderly persons, and the mentally ill, 35–36
cultural, 34–35
language, 34
trauma, 35
Complaints
immigration judges and, 165–68
Computer-telephony integration, 16
Conference calls, 16–17
Confidentiality issues
attorney-client relationship and, 33
8 CFR Sections 208.6 and 1208.6 and, 264–65
field investigation of documents and, 270
Consolidated Appropriations Act of 2005
L-1 visa program and, 643–44
Consular processing
benefits of, 389–90
compared with adjustment of status applications, 387–90
E-1 nonimmigrant status and, 554
O and P visas and, 651
three- or ten-year bars and, 397
travel and, 392–93
unsuccessful adjustment of status applications and, 398
work authorization and, 391–92
Cook, Thomas E.
memo on Special Immigrant Juvenile Status, 303
CP, *See* Consular Processing
Creative Cabinet & Store Fixture Co., 427
Crime involving moral turpitude, 74, 80, 97, 109, 125–28.
See also Cancellation of removal, Criminal issues, Removal and relief, Unlawful detention, Waivers

Criminal issues
See also Aggravated felony, Cancellation of removal, Crimes involving moral turpitude, Removal and relief, Unlawful detention, Waivers
avoiding removal for noncitizen criminal defendants using pre- and post-conviction relief, 124–36
case studies of crimes of violence, 125–28, 134
checklist for initial evaluation, 124–25
deportation of Salvadorans because of violent crimes, 241
domestic violence/crimes of violence/crimes involving moral turpitude, 125–28, 133
lesbian, gay, bisexual, transgender, and HIV asylum law and, 255–56
mandatory detention challenges, 215–18
visa for victims of crime, 692-704
Cross-border travel
actions at the time of departure affecting the ability to return, 712–13
air travel while in the United States, 712
complying with standards for the visit, 709
correcting erroneous information, 716
E-passports, 707–08
I-94s and automatic visa revalidation, 714–16
informing the government of changes of address, 712
National Security Entry-Exit Registration System, 711–12
passport validity period, 708–09
surrender of the I-94 upon departure, 713–14
U.S. Visitor and Immigrant Status Indicator Technology program, 711
visa requirements, 710
Visa Waiver Program, 710–11
Western Hemisphere Travel Initiative, 708
CSPA, *See* Child Status Protection Act
Cultural barriers
communication issues, 34–35

lesbian, gay, bisexual, transgender, and HIV asylum law and, 258–59

D

Davis/Barrett hypothetical federal felony analysis, 138–43
DEA, *See* Drug Enforcement Administration
Dearborn Public Schools, 430
DeCanos v. Bica, 231
Defense of Marriage Act
  same-sex marriages and, 320–21
Demore v. Kim, 216, 217, 222
Development, Relief, and Education for Alien Minors (DREAM) Act, 233
DHS, *See* U.S. Department of Homeland Security
Diomande v. Wrona, 218
Divorce
  adultery and, 717–18
  bigamy and, 720–22
  naturalization and, 717–22
  polygamy and, 722
  support issues, 718–20
  Violence Against Women Act self-petitions and, 339
DOE, *See* U.S. Department of Energy
DOI, *See* U.S. Department of the Interior
DOL, *See* U.S. Department of Labor
DOMA, *See* Defense of Marriage Act
Domestic violence
  See also Violence Against Women Act
  case studies, 125–28, 133
  motions to reopen and, 172, 179
  working with domestic violence victims, 335–36
Driver's licenses
  Form I-9 and, 516–17
Drug crimes
  Davis/Barrett hypothetical federal felony analysis, 138–43
Drug Enforcement Administration
  security clearances and technology licenses and, 531
Dual intent
  nonimmigrant professionals and, 580–81
  O and P visas and, 651
Dual representation in business immigration matters
  ABA Model rules, 39–40

analysis of, 40–43
attorney-client relationship, 40–42
terminating the relationship, 42–43

E

E-1 nonimmigrant status
  authorities for, 544
  Consular processing versus change of status, 554
  dependents of E-1 treaty traders, 556
  E-1 employees, 550–53
  exchange of items of trade and, 547
  existence of Treaty of Friendship, Commerce, and Navigation and, 545
  historical background, 544
  how, where, and what to file, 554–55
  incidental activities while in E-1 status, 555
  intention of the applicant to depart the United States when E-1 status terminates, 553–54
  international trade and, 548
  key considerations, 544–54
  labor disputes (citizens of Canada, Mexico, Chile, and Singapore), 553
  list of treaty countries, 558–61
  nationality of the treaty country and, 545–46
  overview, 544
  period of visa validity, admission period, and extensions of stay, 555–56
  procedural considerations, 554–56
  qualifying items of trade and, 547
  special provisions for employees of the Taipei Economic and Cultural Representative Office, 556–57
  substantial trade requirement, 548–49
  third country national cases, 554–55
  "trade" definition and, 546
  trade principally between the United States and the treaty country requirement, 549–50
E-2 visas
  FAM guidance, 562–70
E-3 visas
  compensation issues, 574–75, 577–78
  educational background and, 574

full-time versus part-time and multiple employers, 578
  intent requirements, 581
EAR, *See* Export Administration Regulations
EB-2 visas
  ad hoc rules for, 440–41
  compared with EB-3 category, 436–38
  recent AAO decisions regarding, 434–36
  three-year bachelor's degrees in, 432–34
  USCIS opinion letters from Hernandez and, 439–40
EB-3 visas
  ad hoc rules for, 441–42
  compared with EB-2 category, 436–38
  H-2 visas and, 619–20
EB-5 visas
  adjudication of Form I-829, 489–90
  benefit to the U.S. economy and, 484
  creating or saving jobs and, 484–85
  designated regional centers, 495–96
  deterring fraudulent investments, 491
  failure to file Form I-829, 489
  initial evidence and, 485–88
  "investing" or "actively in the process of investing" "capital" and, 483–84
  new commercial enterprise requirements, 481–83
  overview, 480–81
  pilot program, 481, 488–89
  procedures for, 485–90
  qualifying for, 481
  statutory requirements, 481–85
  termination of EB-5 status, 490–91
  theory vs. reality, 491–92
  2002 amendments, 492–94
Economic hardship
  case examples, 121
Education
  See also F-1, J-1, and M-1 visas
  E-3 visas and, 574
  institution of higher education definition, 583–88
  Plyler v. Doe and the education of undocumented children, 224–38
  three-year bachelor's degrees from non–American universities, 432–42, 573–74
EEVS, *See* Electronic employment verification system

EILA software, 13
EIMMIGRATION software, 13
El Salvador
asylum claims based on persecution
by gangs, 241–43
gang recruitment program, 241–42
hardship presumption and, 281
Mano Dura program, 242
NACARA and, 280–99
Elderly persons
initial interviews and, 35–36
Electronic employment verification
system
description, 509–10
Emotional hardship
case examples, 121
Empire Marble Corp., 431
Employment and security compliance
DOL audits, 521–29
employment verification systems,
508–20
security clearances and technology
licenses, 530–35
Employment verification systems
See also Form I-9
defending against federal investigations, 519–20
Department of Justice guidelines on
application questions, 518–19
Driver's licenses and, 516–17
Form I-9 and, 510–18
Form I-9 audits, 517–18
historical background, 508–10
nationality issues for Form I-9 purposes, 511–14
notices of unauthorized employment, 514–15
Social Security issues, 515–16
Employment-based immigrant visas
EB-5 immigrant visa category investors, 480–96
establishing priority dates, 405–06
I-140 portability under the American Competitiveness in the
Twenty-First Century Act of
2000, 406–07
labor certification system and the
law of recruitment, 424–31
national interest waiver case study,
454–79
PERM strategies and ad hoc rules
for beneficiaries with three-year
bachelor's degrees from non–
American universities, 432–42

proposed Department of Labor
changes to the labor certification
program, 417–23
religious worker cases, 497–500
retention of priority dates, 405–07
Schedule A, Group II, 443–53
Employment-based nonimmigrant
visas
AC21, 583–604
B-1 business visitors, 536–43
challenges in representing nonim-
migrant professionals, 571–82
E-1 nonimmigrant status, 544–61
E-2 nonimmigrant visa, 562–70
H-2B and H-2A status for employ-
ing essential workers and proposed immigration reform, 605–
27
L-1A visas, 628–42
L-1B intracompany transferees,
643–47
O and P visas, 648–57
EmpPet Professional/EmpPet Enterprise software, 13
Entry and exit issues
tips for cross-border travel, 707–16
Visa Waiver Program and the authority of CBP officers, 705–06
E-passports, 707–08
Escobar v. Alberto Gonzales, 242
Esq. software, 13
Ethics
ABA Model Rules, 39–40, 43
codes of conduct, 39
dual representation in business immigration matters, 39–43
effective, efficient, and ethical practice for immigration paralegals,
67–72
employment of paralegals, 44–66
ethical considerations of filing an I-
130 petition for same-sex marriage partners, 321
ethical considerations of filing for
L-1A status, 642
legal guidance, 38–39
managing ethical conflicts, 38–43
Executives, *See* L-1A visas
Exhaustion requirement
unlawful detentions and, 213–14
Exit issues, *See* Entry and exit issues;
specific visas
Expert testimony
appeals before the AAO and, 197–
99

asylum and other forms of protection and, 246–47
content of, 198
documentation on background conditions and, 247
Federal Rules of Evidence and, 246
qualifications of the expert, 246–47
sources of information relied on by
the expert, 247
USCIS and, 197–99
Export Administration Regulations
classification of articles/technology
under, 532
permission for foreign nationals to
receive controlled technology or
articles, 532–33
scope of, 531–34
technology or software subject to,
530
Ezeagwuna v. INS, 270–71, 277

F

F-1 student visas
curricular and optional practical
training, 661–62
eligibility for admission, 658
off-campus employment and, 660–
61
on-campus employment and, 659
Social Security issues, 667
special issues for post-completion
optional practical training, 663
special student relief program, 661
Student and Exchange Visitor Program, 659, 664
types of employment and, 659
Fair Labor Standards Act of 1938
H-2B and H-2A status definitions,
606
False statements to a police officer
case study, 135–36
FAM, *See Foreign Affairs Manual*
Families, *See* Children; Family immigration and adoption
Family immigration and adoption
See also Children
bureaucratic delays, 313–14
Child Status Protection Act and,
323–30
family-related and domestic violence-related immigration options (table), 351–60
intercountry adoptions from India,
375–86
international adoption visa guide,
364–74

marriage issues, 314–22
processing delays and, 312–14
quotas and, 312–13
recapturing old priority dates in
family-based cases, 401–02
review of immigration and the family, 332–33
same-sex couples and, 317–22
Violence Against Women Act self-
petitions, 331–63
Fatin v. INS, 242
FBI, *See* Federal Bureau of Investigation
FDA, *See* Food and Drug Administration
Federal Bureau of Investigation
DOL audits and, 521
Federal pardons, 151–52
Federal Rules of Civil Procedure
document authentication and, 276–
77
Federal Rules of Evidence
document authentication and, 276–
77
expert testimony and, 198, 246
Fernandez-Vargas v. Ashcroft, 106,
107
Field investigation of documents
Advocates' submission of their own
"field investigations," 271–72
competent investigatory practices in
conducting overseas investigations and, 270–71
confidentiality issues, 270
description, 269–70
File review
systems for, 4–5
Florida
state pardon procedures, 154
FNELs, *See* Foreign National Employment Licenses
Fongo v. Gonzales, 277
Food and Drug Administration
security clearances and technology
licenses and, 531
Foreign Affairs Manual
authentication definition, 265
B-1 business visitors and, 536, 537
E-1 nonimmigrant status authority,
544
fraud and misrepresentation waivers
and, 97–99
international adoption and, 364
treaty investor visas, 562–70

Foreign National Employment Licenses
International Traffic in Arms Regulations and, 531–35
Form ETA-9089
drafting PERM job specifications
on, 442
filing, 449–50
Form I-9
audits and, 517–18
common mistakes in preparing,
517–18
driver's licenses and, 516–17
nationality issues, 511–14
proof of nationality and, 512
quasi-nationals, 512–14
USCIS revisions, 510–11
Former Soviet Union
hardship presumption and, 282
NACARA and, 280–99
Forms
See also specific forms
software for, 12–16
Francis v. INS, 90–91
Fraud
EB-5 immigrant visas and, 491
initial interviews with clients and,
33
wire fraud case study, 131–34
Fraud and misrepresentation waivers
challenging the grounds for, 96–99
eligibility for waivers, 99–100
preparing applications for, 100–103
FRCP, *See* Federal Rules of Civil
Procedure
FRE, *See* Federal Rules of Evidence
Full and unconditional pardons, 150–
51
Furstenberg v. U.S., 199

G

Galicia v. Ashcroft, 251
Gallo-Alvarez v. Ashcroft, 105
Gangs
asylum claims based on persecution
by, 241–43
Garcia v. Boldin, 208
Georgia
state pardon example, 152–53, 155–
56
Georgis v. Ashcroft, 275–76
Gonzales, Alberto
See also specific court cases
memoranda to immigration judges
and the BIA, 165

Good moral character
NACARA and, 285–86
Naturalization and, 717–22
Violence Against Women Act self-
petitions and, 341–43
Goonsuwan v. Ashcroft, 207
Gorchev & Gorchev standard, 429–30
Grace Korean United Methodist Church
v. Chertoff, 438–39
Graham v. Richardson, 230
Guardian and Wards Act, 382
Guatemala
hardship presumption and, 281
NACARA and, 280–99
Guest worker program
advocacy for legislative action,
626–27
H-2B and H-2A status for employ-
ing essential workers, 605–22
reform proposal, 623–25

H

H-1B visas
AC21 §104(C) and immigrant visa
retrogression, 596–603
advanced degree relationship to applicant's job, 588–89
American Competitiveness in the
Twenty-First Century Act of
2000 and, 581–82, 583–604
B-1 business visitors and, 540–41
cap on petition approvals for fiscal
year 2006, 583
compensation issues, 575, 577–78
concurrent H-1B employment, 592
employment "at" versus employment "by" and institution of
higher education and, 590–92
extensions, 581–82
full-time versus part-time and multiple employers, 578
institution of higher education definition and, 583–88
intent requirements, 581
juris doctor (J.D.) degrees and, 589
labor certification after the end of
seven years, 603–04
nonprofit entities affiliated with or
related to institutions of higher
education, 589–90
physicians and, 594–96
preparing petitions for, 571–73
specialty occupations and, 578–79
three-year bachelor's degree issues,
573–74

"would be eligible" language of
INA §214(g)(7), 592–94
H-2 visas
alternatives to H-2 classification,
618–19
annual cap on H-2B visas, 612
border protection and, 621
components of a common sense
immigration reform program,
621–22
dealing with the H-2B quota, 617–
18
duration of H-2B status, 611–12
duration of status, 609
EB-3 immigrant visas and, 619–20
Employer's responsibilities under
H-2A labor certification, 608–09
essential workers and comprehensive immigration reform, 620–22
exploitation of undocumented aliens
and, 621
filing process, 609, 612–14
global competitiveness and, 621,
624
historical background, 605–06
legal overview, 606
national security issues, 620, 623–
24
overview of H-2A status for agricultural workers, 607–10
overview of H-2B status for nonagricultural workers, 610–17
pitfalls, strategies, and recommendations, 614–17
problems to be addressed, 620–21
proof of temporary need and, 610–
11
protection of U.S. workers and,
620–21
recruitment of U.S. workers and,
609–10
statutory and regulatory authorities,
606–07
H-3 visas
B-1 business visitors and, 540–41
general considerations, 670–71
practical considerations, 672–73
special programs, 671–72
training programs, 670–73
Habeas corpus
availability of habeas review, 204–
06
detention decisions and, 213
exhaustion of remedies and, 207
interaction of direct and habeas review from 1952 until passage of
the REAL ID Act, 206

prior to the REAL ID Act, 204–08
REAL ID Act and, 208–12
Hague Adoption Convention
accrediting entities, 373
application of, 371–72
approval/accreditation, 372–73
Central Authority and, 372
children emigrating from the United
States, 373
India, and, 382
legislative history, 371
Hague Convention
Abolishing Requirement for Legali-
zation of Foreign Documents,
268–69
contracting states list, 279
Hardship
BIA case studies, 116–20
court decisions, 115–16
economic, 121
emotional, 121
exceptional and extremely unusual,
120
Hake Hardship Scale, 681–82
INA definition, 114
medical, 121
NACARA and, 281–82. 290–92
T visas and, 702
Haynes v. DHS, 218
HEA, *See* Higher Education Act of
1965
Heikkila v. Barber, 204–05
Henry Quentzel Plumbing Supply
Co., Inc. v. Quentzel, 199
Hernandez, Efren
opinion letters, 439–40
Hernandez v. Houston Independent
School District, 225, 227, 228,
229
Hernandez-Montiel v. INS, 240, 251
Hernandez-Patino v. INS, 115
Higher Education Act of 1965
institution of higher education defi-
nition, 584–88
Hindu Adoptions and Maintenance
Act of 1956, 375, 380–82
HIV/AIDS status
making judgmental assumptions
about, 258
U.S. immigration policies and, 249–
50, 254–55
Homosexuals, *See* Sexual orientation
Honduras
asylum claims based on persecution
by gangs, 242

House Subcommittee on Immigration,
Border Security and Claims
private bill procedures, 146–47

I

ICE, *See* U.S. Immigration and Cus-
toms Enforcement
Identity theft
case study, 131–34
IEEPA, *See* International Emergency
Economic Powers Act
IIRAIRA, *See* Illegal Immigration
Reform and Immigrant Responsi-
bility Act of 1996
IJs, *See* Immigration judges
Illegal Immigration Reform and Im-
migrant Responsibility Act of
1996
asylum on the basis of sexual orien-
tation and, 250
Form I-9 and, 510–11
habeas corpus review and, 207–08
Illinois
state pardon procedures, 154–55
IMMACT90, *See* Immigration Act of
1990
Immediate custodian rule
unlawful detentions and, 214–15
ImmForms Plus software, 15
Immigrant Legal Resource Center
Winning NACARA Suspension
Cases, 280–99
Immigrant Pro software, 13
Immigration Act of 1990
Schedule A, Group II and, 443–53
Immigration and Nationality Act
See also specific sections, i.e., Sec-
tion 212(c) of the INA
adopted child definition, 364–65,
366–67
E-1 nonimmigrant status and, 544
H-2B and H-2A status definitions,
606
J-1 foreign residence requirement,
681–91
orphan petitions, 367–71
"would be eligible" language of
INA §214(g)(7), 592–94
yearly maximum of visas for appli-
cants to invest in a new com-
mercial enterprise, 481
Immigration Forms Gold software, 13
Immigration Judge Benchbook
asylum documentation and, 274

Immigration judges
  complaint standards, 166–67
  complaint structure and, 165–66
  Gonzales's memo to, 165
  immigration adjudication structure and, 165
  New York Times survey of cases, 161–63
  practical representation considerations, 163–65
  preserving the issues and, 163–64
  reasons why immigration court complaints go unnoticed, 160–61
  renewal of adjustment of status applications and, 398
  stating at trial what needs to be stated, 164–65
  unlawful detentions and, 213–14
  when and how to complain, 167–68
Immigration Law Interactive Drafting System, 13
Immigration Law Systems software, 15
Immigration Reform and Control Act of 1986
  Increased Worksite Enforcement and Penalties, 509
Immigration Works software, 14
ImmigrationTracker software, 14
Impell Corporation, 431
In absentia orders
  motions to rescind and, 176–77, 179
In re: Jose Maurico Lovo-Lara, 320–21
In re Alien Children, 229–30
INA, *See* Immigration and Nationality Act
Independent school districts
  charging of tuition to undocumented children, 224–25
India
  intercountry adoptions from, 375–86
Indonesia
  special student relief program, 661
Infanzon v. Ashcroft, 210
Initial interviews with clients
  clarifying the attorney-client relationship, 33
  communication barriers, 34–36
  establishing rapport, 32–33
  evaluating the case, 36–37
  fees and retainer agreements, 37
  gathering facts, 33–34
  purpose of, 32
INS, *See specific legal cases*

INS v. Abudu, 210
INS v. Hector, 116, 121
INS v. Jong Ha Wang, 115–16, 121
INS v. Rios-Pineda, 115
INS v. St. Cyr
  habeas corpus review of deportation orders and, 204
  Section 212(c) and, 86–89
INS v. Ventura, 161–62
INSZoom software, 14
Intercountry adoptions from India
  See also International adoption
  adoption applications, 379–80
  conflict of laws, 384–86
  documents required, 379–80
  domestic law, 380–82
  guardianship orders, 378
  handicapped children and children requiring medical attention, 379
  historical background, 375–76
  home study reports, 377–78
  problems faced, 382–86
  procedure to be followed, 376–77
  requirement before the court, 378–80
  surrogacy, 382–84
Internal Revenue Code of 1954
  H-2B and H-2A status definitions, 606
International adoption
  See also Intercountry adoptions from India
  age requirement, 365
  child's home country's law and, 370
  facts impacting procedure and outcome, 365–66
  Hague Adoption Convention, 371–73
  INA definition of an adopted child, 364–65, 366–67
  legal custody and residency requirements, 365
  orphan petitions, 367–71
  practice pointers, 366–67
  problem countries, 374
  relatives adopted as orphans, 370–71
International Emergency Economic Powers Act
  security clearances and technology licenses and, 531
International Traffic in Arms Regulations
  classification of articles/technology under, 531–32
  export by foreign persons, 530–31

permission for foreign nationals to receive controlled technology or articles, 532–33
  scope of, 531–34
Interviews, *See* Initial interviews with clients
ITAR, *See* International Traffic in Arms Regulations

J

J-1 visas
  academic training, 664–65
  advantages of, 673–74
  applying for and entry under, 676–78
  description of the J-1 visa program, 663–64
  general J-1 training categories, 673
  historical background, 682–83
  I-9 considerations, 665
  industrial training, 673
  J-2 dependents, 665–66, 678
  process of obtaining J sponsorship, 676
  requirements for training programs, 674–75
  seeking J-1 program designation, 678–79
  Social Security issues, 667
  source and types of employment, 664
  summer work/travel visas, 618
  time limits, 665
  for trainees, 673–80
  training versus employment, 675
  two-year foreign residence requirement, 679–80
  U.S. government funding in J-1 waiver cases, 681–91
Jagdish Chander Gupta v. Dr. Ku Vimla Gupta, 378
Jahed v. INS, 161
Jama v. Immigration and Customs Enforcement, 219
Jayantilal v. Asha, 378
Joaquin-Porras v. Gonzales, 241
John Clements v. All Concerned, 386

K

K Super KQ-1540 A.M., 431
K-1 visas
  for Canadian citizens, 113

Karouni v. Gonzales, 240, 251, 255
Kim v. Ziglar, 215–16
Kimumwe v. Gonzales, 241, 251
Koval v. Gonzales, 198
*Kurzban's Immigration Law Source-
    book* (Kurzban), 443

L

L-1A visas
  background checks and, 635
  Blanket L filings, 634–40
  corporate changes of validity of,
      640–41
  ethical considerations, 642
  executive versus managerial capac-
      ity, 628–29
  five- and seven-year limits, 641
  functional managers, 629
  new offices and, 633–34
  organization and type of business
      and, 632–33
  owners as transferees, 632
  petitions for Canadians under
      NAFTA at U.S.-Canada ports of
      entry, 641
  small business issues, 629–33
  specialized knowledge workers
      changing to executive/manager
      positions, 641–42
L-1B intracompany transferees
  Department of Homeland Security
      Inspector General's report on L-
      1 visas, 643–44
  overcoming processing delays and
      the five-year limit, 646–47
  placing an employee offsite at a cli-
      ent location, 645–46
  proving employment abroad, 646
  proving specialized knowledge,
      644–45
Labor certification system
  alternative publication requirement,
      428
  applicable case law, 426–28
  backlog of cases, 424
  candidate's travel expenses and,
      427–28
  certification after the end of seven
      years, 603–04
  elimination of substitution, 417–20
  employer's duty to further investi-
      gate, 429–30
  enforcement provisions, 423
  foreign national's involvement and,
      427
  "fortuitous cure," 430

good faith recruitment efforts, 425–
    26
HEA definition of an institution of
    higher education and, 587
historical background, 424
lack of experience in a particular job
    duty and, 430
obligations of the certifying officer,
    429
Permanent Electronic Review Man-
    agement system, 424
prohibition on sale, barter, purchase,
    and related payments, 422–23
qualification standards, 428–29
reduction in recruitment waivers,
    425
rejection of U.S. workers and, 428–
    30
statutory and regulatory scheme,
    424–25
subjective grounds for rejection, 431
sufficiency of documentation and,
    426, 428
tests, salary, and the overqualified,
    431
timely contact of U.S. worker and,
    427
traditional filings, 425
unchallenged job requirements, 429
validity and filing period, 420–22
verification of employment and, 431
Labor disputes
  E-1 nonimmigrant status and, 553
LaGuerre v. Reno, 205–06
Lawful permanent residents
  adjustment of status applications,
      387–98
  affirmative applications for LPRs
      who need to travel and, 95
  Consular processing and, 387–98
  marriage issues, 314–15
  priority dates and, 399–416
  relief from removal, 73–83
  Violence Against Women Act self-
      petitioners, 343–44

LawLogix software, 14–15
Lawrence v. Texas, 319
Lawson v. Gerlinski, 217
Laxmi Kant Pandey v. Union of India,
    375, 376
Legal Immigration Family Equity
    Act, 106
Legal writing style principles, 201–03
LEI Immigration Software, 15
Lesbian, gay, bisexual, transgender,
    and HIV asylum law
  application process, 257–59
  bisexual claims issue, 253
  criminal issues, 255–56
  cultural barriers and, 258–59
  dual nationality and, 256
  explanations of asylum law to cli-
      ents, 258
  initial consultations, 258
  intent of the person or persons who
      commit persecution and, 249
  marriage issue, 252–53
  Matter of Toboso-Alfonso and,
      239–41, 248–49
  multiple return trips to country of
      origin and, 254–55
  persons with HIV/AIDS and, 249
  precedential cases, 250–52
  prior government employment and,
      256
  procedure for raising CAT claims,
      261–62
  recognizing and respecting client
      individuality, 257–58
  stereotypes, 253–54
  straightforward asylum applications,
      252–53
  thorny issues, 252–56
  Visa Waiver Program and, 256
  working with HIV-positive clients,
      261
  working with lesbian, gay and bi-
      sexual clients, 259–60
  working with transgender clients,
      260–61
Lesbians, *See* Sexual orientation
LexisNexis, 11
LGBT/H asylum law, *See* Lesbian,
    gay, bisexual, transgender, and
    HIV asylum law
LIFE Act, *See* Legal Immigration
    Family Equity Act

Lin v. Gonzales, 277

Liu v. Ashcroft, 276

Lopez-Soto v. Ashcroft, 242–43

LPRs, *See* Lawful permanent residents

Ly v. Hansen, 217

M

M-1 vocational or other nonacademic
students
  employment authorization for M-2
    dependents of M-1 students, 666
  purpose of the M-1 visa, 666
  Social Security issues, 667
  types of employment, 666
Malaysia
  special student relief program, 661
MALDEF, *See* Mexican American
  Legal Defense and Educational
  Fund
Managers, *See* L-1A visas
Mandatory detention
  Section 236(c) challenges, 215–18
Mara 18 gang, 241–43
Marriage
  battered spouses and, 315
  conditional residence and its re-
    moval, 315–16
  lesbian, gay, bisexual, transgender,
    and HIV asylum law and, 252–
    53
  motions to reopen and, 175
  permanent residence and, 314–15
  same-sex couples and I-130 eligibil-
    ity, 317–22
Martinez v. Bynum, 232
Massachusetts
  same-sex marriages, 317–18
Maternity for Hire, 382
Matter of Andazola-Rivas, 116–17,
  118, 121
Matter of Blake, 92–93
Matter of Brieva-Perez, 93
Matter of Cerna, 170
Matter of Chawathe, 197
Matter of Concurrent Computer
  Corp., 428–29
Matter of Deandra-Ramos, 189
Matter of Esposito, 92–93
Matter of Frentescu, 255–56
Matter of Fritz George, 429
Matter of Garcia, 162
Matter of Hernandez-Casillas, 91, 93

Matter of Hong Kong Royale Restau-
  rant, 428–29
Matter of Jimenez, 92–93
Matter of Joseph, 214, 217
Matter of Kim, 327–28
Matter of Lopez, 170
Matter of Meza, 91–92, 93
Matter of Mogharrabi, 242
Matter of Montenegro, 92–93
Matter of Montreal, 116, 117–18
Matter of M/V Seru, 327–28
Matter of Nicole V., 199
Matter of Recinas, 117–18, 121
Matter of Shaar, 179–80
Matter of Shah, 434–35
Matter of Shaw, 563
Matter of Silva, 91
Matter of S-M-J, 244–47, 264
Matter of Toboso-Alfonso, 239–41,
  248–50
Matter of Valencia, 190
Matter of Vanguard Jewelry Corp.,
  429
Matter of Velarde-Pacheco, 162
M.B. v. Quarantillo, 306
McCarthy v. Madison, 213
Medellin-Reyes v. Gonzales, 209
Medical hardship
  case examples, 121
Mentally ill persons
  asylum issues, 259
  initial interviews and, 35–36
Mexican American Legal Defense and
  Educational Fund
  case management, 228–29
  Plyler v. Doe role, 225–30, 232–33
Mexico
  E-1 nonimmigrant status and, 553
  three-year visas for citizens of, 582
M.N. Auto Electric Corp., 426
Model Rules of Professional Conduct
  dual representation, 39–40, 43
  employment of paralegals, 44–45
Molathwa v. Ashcroft, 251
Moral turpitude crimes
  case studies, 125–30
Mortera-Cruz v. Gonzales, 106–07
Motions to reconsider
  compared with motions to reopen,
    170–71
  description, 170
  documentation for, 170
  equity-based exceptions, 177
  filing, 170

preliminary questions, 169
Motions to reopen
  adjustment of status applications
    and, 398
  bases established by case law, 173–
    75
  burden of making a *prima facie* case
    and, 171–72
  compared with motions to recon-
    sider, 170–71
  description, 171
  equity-based exceptions, 177
  government use of, 180
  ineffective assistance of counsel
    and, 173–74
  jurisdictional requirements, 171
  marriage during proceedings and,
    175
  new criminal issues, 180
  NACARA and, 289
  numerical limit to, 177
  preliminary questions, 169
  reopening the executed removal or-
    der, 181–83
  requesting *sua sponte* powers, 178
  review after the client has been re-
    moved, 178–79
  statutory and regulatory bases for,
    172–73
  stay of removal and, 179
  vacating convictions and, 174–75
  voluntary departure period, 179–80
Motions to rescind
  in absentia orders and, 176–77, 179
  description, 175–76
  equity-based exceptions, 177
  exceptional circumstances and, 176
  preliminary questions, 169
  stay of removal and, 179
  strategic choices and, 176–77

N

NACARA, *See* Nicaraguan Adjust-
  ment and Central American Re-
  lief Act
Nadarajah v. Gonzales, 221
NAFTA, *See* North American Free
  Trade Agreement
Nahatchevska v. Ashcroft, 209
National interest waiver case study
  Attorney's cover letter to USCIS,
    460–65
  Attorney's cover letter to USCIS re-
    sponding to RFE, 470–74

Attorney's guideline memo for NIW client to give to support-letter writers, 455–59
overview, 454
representative letters of support for client's NIW petition, 466–69
representative letters responding to RFE, 475–79
National Security Entry-Exit Registration System, *See* NSEERS
Naturalization
divorce and, 717–22
Netherlands
same-sex marriages, 317
New York
state pardon procedures, 155
Nicaragua
NACARA and, 280–99
Nicaraguan Adjustment and Central American Relief Act
advance parole rule, 283
analysis of cases, 280–93
application for asylum as well as suspension and, 295–96
application procedures, 286–92
approval rate for applications, 289
bars to NACARA seven-year special cancellation of removal, 297–98
case evaluation, 292–93
children turning 21 and, 294–95
continuous physical presence and absences from the United States and, 284–85
dependents and, 282, 296
exclusion proceedings and, 284
fees for applications, 289
good moral character requirement and, 285–86
hardship presumption, 281–82
hardship requirements, 290–92
motions to reopen and, 289
provisions, 280
summary of statistics, 299
suspension or special rule cancellation of removal and, 282–86
Violence Against Women Act and, 282
work authorizations and, 289
NOAs, *See* Notices of Appeal
Nonimmigrant visas
See also specific visas
challenging occupations, 578–80
compensation issues, 574–75
dual intent, 580–81
educational issues, 571–74

employment options for students with F, J, or M visas, 658–67
full-time versus part-time and multiple employers, 578
H-1B, H-1B1, and E-3 visas, 577–78
protecting victims of crime, 692–704
maximum stay, 581–82
trade NAFTA and, 575–77
U.S. employers seeking to train or be trained by foreign nationals, 668–80
U.S. government funding in J-1 waiver cases, 681–91
Nonimmigrant waivers for Canadian citizens
laws and processes, 110–13
triage of a case, 108–10
Noriega-Lopez v. Ashcroft, 210–11
North American Free Trade Agreement
See also Trade NAFTA
B-1 business visitors and, 541
L-1 petitions for Canadians under NAFTA at U.S.-Canada ports of entry, 641
Notices of Appeal
BIA advocacy and, 189
NRC, *See* U.S. Nuclear Regulatory Commission
NSEERS
cross-border travel and, 711–13

O

O and P visas
agents as petitioners, 652
Consular processing, 651
consultation organizations for arts-related petitions, 653–57
defining the scope of the field, 650
dual intent and foreign residence and, 651
essential support personnel and, 650–51
filing for, 649
O visa categories, 648–49
one-year versus three-year extensions for O-1 beneficiaries, 649
packaging exhibits and, 651–52
Oregon
Development, Relief, and Education for Alien Minors (DREAM) Act, 233

Orphan petitions
common orphan adoption situations, 369–70
INA and, 367–71
Oyedeji v. Ashcroft, 218

P

P visas, *See* O and P visas
Padash v. INS, 328
Padilla-Calderas v. Gonzales, 106–07
Paralegals
compensation issues, 72
effective, efficient, and ethical practice for, 67–72
ethical considerations for the employment of, 44–66
hiring criteria, 69–71
retaining, 71–72
training, 71
Pardons
federal, 151–52
"full and unconditional," 150–51
historical background, 144
legal authority and applicability of, 149–50
recommendations, 155–56
state, 152–53
Parlak v. Baker, 218
Perez-Gonzalez v. Ashcroft, 106
PERM
beneficiaries holding three-year bachelor's degrees from non–American universities and, 432–42
description, 425
drafting PERM job specifications on Form ETA-9089, 442
historical background, 424
Permanent Partners Immigration Act, *See* Uniting American Families Act
Pervaiz v. Gonzales, 210
Philippines
special student relief program, 661
Physicians
H-1B visas and, 594–96
Pitcherskaia v. INS, 250
Polygamy, 722
Posner, Richard
New York Times survey of cases, 161–63
Practice management and ethics
best practices, 1–10
business plan importance, 23–26
client expectations, 27–31

initial interviews with clients, 32–37

managing ethical conflicts in a business practice, 38–43

technology considerations, 11–22

Priority dates

annual allocations of immigrant visas, 400

chargeability, 401

Child Status Protection Act and, 407–08

INA §245(i) and, 407

recapturing old priority dates in family-based cases, 401–02

retention in employment-based cases, 405–07

review of terms, 399

V visa eligibility, 402–04

Western Hemisphere Priority Date program, 409–16

Private bills

contact with DHS and the effect of enactment of, 149

effect of introduction of private bills on nonimmigrant status, 148

historical background, 144

procedures in the House Subcommittee on Immigration, Border Security and Claims, 146–47

procedures in the Senate Subcommittee on Immigration, Border Security and Citizenship, 147–48

purpose and legal authority of, 145–46

recommendations, 155–56

stays of removal during consideration of, 148–49

Plyler v. Doe

education of the polity, 232–33

historical background, 225

MALDEF role, 225–30

reactions to, 231–32

Supreme Court's ruling, 230–31

Texas Independent School Districts' charging of tuition to undocumented children, 224–25

Q

Q-1 cultural exchange visitor visas description, 618–19

Quasi-nationals

Form I-9 and, 512–14

R

Racketeer Influenced and Corrupt Organizations

Department of Labor audits and, 521, 527–28

REAL ID Act of 2005

asylum on the basis of sexual orientation and, 250

cases where additional evidence may be required, 211–12

cases where no petition for review was timely filed, 209–11

corroboration standards and, 264

driver's licenses and, 516

evidence of country conditions and, 244

habeas corpus after, 208–09

habeas corpus prior to, 204–08

Recinos de Leon v. Gonzales, 163

Reduction in recruitment waivers description, 425

Refugee Act of 1980

refugee definition, 248

Refugees

See also asylum

Relief from Removal, *See* Removal and relief

Religious workers

AAO decisions, 499–507

ability to pay checklist, 500

ability to pay the proffered wage to, 504–05

documenting the ability to pay, 497–500

establishing the two-year period of experience requirement, 501–04

job offers for, 506–07

qualifying religious job/traditional religious functions, 505–06

tax-exempt, bona fide religious organizations, 507

Yates memo and, 498–99

Removal and relief

See also Cancellation of removal, Unlawful detention, Waivers

avoiding removal for noncitizen criminal defendants using pre- and post-conviction relief, 124–36

background, 73

cancellation of removal, 76–80

Davis/Barrett hypothetical federal felony analysis of drug crimes, 137–43

fraud and misrepresentation waivers, 96–103

nonimmigrant waivers for Canadian citizens, 108–13

pardons, 144, 149–56

private bills, 144–49, 155–56

proving hardship, 114–23

relief from removal, 73–83

Section 212(c), 73–76, 83, 84–95

waivers of the §212(a)(9)(C) permanent bar, 104–07

Reno, Janet

designation as precedent a BIA decision on homosexuals as a social group, 239, 248–49

Reyes-Reyes v. Ashcroft, 251, 262

RICO, *See* Racketeer Influenced and Corrupt Organizations

RIR waivers, *See* Reduction in recruitment waivers

Romania

international adoption and, 374

Romer v. Evans, 319

Rose Technology

computer-telephony integration software, 16

Rumsfeld v. Padilla, 215

S

S visas

application procedures, 704

crime witnesses and, 703–04

length of status and adjustment of status, 704

qualifying for, 704

reporting provisions, 704

Salkeld v. Gonzales, 251

Same-sex marriages

Defense of Marriage Act and, 320

ethical considerations of filing an I-130 petition, 321

historical background, 317–18

relevant jurisprudence, 318–19

Uniting American Families Act and, 321–22

Schedule A, Group II

DOL legal standards, 444–50

historical background, 443–44, 452

USCIS requirements, 450–52

Seasonal workers, *See* H-2B and H-2A visas

Section 212(h)/212(i) of the INA

advanced waiver provisions, 80–83

Section 212(a)(5)(A) of the INA

labor certification and, 424–25

Section 212(a)(9)(C) of the INA

historical background, 104

persons subject to, 106–07
"removal order" definition, 104–06
Section 245(i) and, 106–07
waivers of the permanent bar, 104–07
Section 212(c) of the INA
adjustment of status and, 94
affirmative applications for LPRs who need to travel and, 95
combining with other forms of relief, 94
continued availability of, 83, 86–88
conviction after trial versus a plea and, 87–88
"doctrine of the comparable ground" and, 90–94
historical background, 73–76, 84–85
INS v. St. Cyr, 86–89
reclassification of the underlying offense, 88–89
simultaneous application for cancellation of removal and, 94
Section 236(c) of the INA
challenging in federal court, 215–18
Section 240A(a) of the INA
cancellation of removal provisions, 76–80, 94
Section 245(i) of the INA
adjustment of status and, 395–96
priority dates and, 407
Section 245(k) of the INA
adjustment of status and, 396–97
Security clearances and technology licenses
Export Administration Regulations and International Traffic in Arms Regulations, 530–33
legal sources of technology protection and security in the United States, 530–35
practice pointers, 534–35
technology protection and immigration, 533–34
Self-petitions, See Violence Against Women Act self-petitions
Senate Subcommittee on Immigration, Border Security and Citizenship
private bill procedures, 147–48
SEVIS, See Student and Exchange Visitor Information System
Sexual orientation
history of lesbian, gay, bisexual, transgender, and HIV (LGBT/H) asylum law, 248–62
persecution based on, 239–41

same-sex couples and I-130 eligibility, 317–22
Shahwan v. Chertoff, 221
Sherman Act
case study, 126–30
SIJS, See Special Immigrant Juvenile Status
Singapore
E-1 nonimmigrant status and, 553
Small businesses
L-1A visas and, 629–33
Social Security issues
employment verification systems and, 515–16
F, J, and M international students, 667
Social Security Number Verification System
employment verification and, 508
Software options
case management and forms, 12–15
forms only, 15
research, 11–12
scanning, 15–16
Soto-Vega v. Ashcroft, 253–54
South Korea
special student relief program, 661
Spain
same-sex marriages, 317
Special Immigrant Juvenile Status
alternative forms of relief, 309–11
application for permanent residence, 309
asylum eligibility, 311
background on demographics, 300–301
DHS consent and, 304–05
eligibility for lawful permanent residence, 309
forcing the decision, 305–07
Form I-360 and, 307–08
international adoption and, 364–74
state courts and, 302–04, 307–09
T visas, 310
Violence Against Women Act and, 310–11
working with abused, neglected, or abandoned children, 301–02
Specialized knowledge
L-1A visas and, 641–42
L-1B intracompany transferees and, 644–45
Specter, Sen. Arlen
electronic employment verification system and, 509

SSNVS, See Social Security Number Verification System
St. Theresa's Tender Loving Care Home and others vs. States of Andhra Pradesh, 376
State courts
dependency proceedings, 307–09
international adoption and, 365
Special Immigrant Juvenile Status and, 302–04
State Department Country Reports, 245
State pardons
historical background, 152
mass clemency and, 152–53
procedures in states with high immigrant populations, 153–55
Strategies before the courts
advocacy principles when representing clients before the BIA, the AAO, and USCIS, 184–203
unlawful detention in federal court, 213–23
habeas corpus and the REAL ID Act, 204–12
immigration judges, 160–68
motions to reopen, reconsider, and rescind before the BIA, 169–83
unlawful detention in federal court, 213–23
Student and Exchange Visitor Information System, 659
See also F-1 and M-1 visas
Students, See F-1 and M-1 visas
Sua sponte powers
motions to reopen and, 178
Subhan v. Ashcroft, 162
Surrogate parenting, 382–84
Swain v. Pressley, 208

T

T visas
application for, 703
compliance with reasonable requests for assistance from law enforcement, 701–02
continued-process status, 703
denials of, 703
eligibility for government benefits and services and, 703
family members eligible for derivative status, 702
identification of trafficking victims, 699–700
legislative background of, 699

length of status and adjustment of status, 702
qualifying for, 700–701
Special Immigrant Juvenile Status and, 310
Taipei Economic and Cultural Representative Office
E-1 nonimmigrant status and, 556–57
TAL, *See* Technology Alert List
Technology Alert List, 534
Technology Assistance Agreements
International Traffic in Arms Regulations and, 531–33
Technology considerations
computer-telephony integration, 16
forms, 15
online resources, 17–22
scanning hardware and software, 15–16
security clearances and technology licenses, 530–35
software options, 11–15
voice recognition, 16
websites, 16
working from home, 17
TECRO, *See* Taipei Economic and Cultural Representative Office
Telephone technology
computer-telephony integration, 16
conference calling, 16–17
Texas
Department of Public Safety list of acceptable documents for issuance of a driver's license, 517
Independent School Districts' charging of tuition to undocumented children, 224–25
Thai v. Ashcroft, 219
Thailand
special student relief program, 661
Three-year bachelor's degrees from non–American universities
EB-2 category and, 432–36
EB-3 category and, 436–39
Grace Korean United Methodist Church v. Chertoff case, 438–39
H-1B visas and, 573–74
non-Indian degrees, 439
summary of "ad hoc rules" for drafting PERM applications, 440–42
USCIS opinion letters from Efren Hernandez, 439–40
Tijani v. Willis, 217
TN, *See* Trade NAFTA

Torres, Isaias
Plyler v. Doe and, 229
Trade NAFTA
See also North American Free Trade Agreement
amount of compensation and, 574–75
bachelor's degree and, 573–74
full-time versus part-time and multiple employers, 578
initiating permanent residence and, 580–81
for management consultants and scientific technicians, 579–80
Trading with the Enemy Act
security clearances and technology licenses and, 531
Trafficking Victims Protection Act
provisions, 699
Training
B-1 visas and, 668–70
H-3 visas and, 670–73
J-1 visas and, 673–80
Transgender persons, *See* Sexual orientation
Trauma
asylum-seekers and, 259
communication with persons suffering from, 35
Treaty of Friendship, Commerce, and Navigation
E-1 nonimmigrant status and, 545
TVPA, *See* Trafficking Victims Protection Act

U

U visas
absence of regulations for, 694
application procedures, 695
eligibility for, 695–96
filing applications for, 696–99
length of status and adjustment of status, 695
obtaining U status for victims of crime, 692–94
qualifying for, 693–94
Special Immigrant Juvenile Status and, 310
UAFA, *See* Uniting American Families Act
Ukraine
international adoption and, 374
Unauthorized employment notices, 514–15
United Kingdom
international adoption and, 374

United Nations
Convention Relating to the Status of Refugees, 248
Protocol Relating to the Status of Refugees, 248
Uniting American Families Act
same-sex marriages and, 321–22
Unlawful detention challenges in federal court
arriving aliens, 221
automatic stay provisions of 8 CFR §1003.19, 222–23
exhaustion requirement, 213–14
"immediate custodian" rule and, 214–15
mandatory detention challenges, 215–18
post-removal detention under *Zadvydas v. Davis*, 218–21
refugees, 222
removal period, 218–21
Uritsky v. Ridge, 218
U.S. Citizenship and Immigration Services
adjustment of status applications, 387–90
Asylum Office guidance on document authentication, 272–74
expert testimony and, 197–98
family immigration and adoption and, 313–14
Form I-9 revisions, 510–11
H-2B and H-2A status regulations, 606–07
InfoPass Internet appointment system, 313
opinion letters from Efren Hernandez, 439–40
Schedule A, Group II requirements, 450–52
special student relief program, 661
U visas and, 693
U.S. Customs and Border Protection
B-1 business visitors and, 536–37
Visa Waiver Program and, 705–06
U.S. Department of Commerce
security clearances and technology licenses and, 530–35
U.S. Department of Energy
security clearances and technology licenses and, 531
U.S. Department of Homeland Security
asylum for homosexuals and, 240
DOL audits and, 521
electronic employment verification system and, 509–10

forensic examination of documents, 269

Form I-9 revisions and, 510–11

habeas corpus review and, 208

Inspector General's report on L-1 visas, 643–44

joining motions with, 178

private bills and, 149

Special Immigrant Juvenile Status and, 303–07

U visas and, 693

unlawful detentions and, 213–15

Visa Waiver Program and, 705

U.S. Department of Justice
guidelines on employment application questions, 518–19

U.S. Department of Labor
arts and sciences field Schedule A, Group II legal standard, 444–48

audits, 521–29

Form ETA-9089 filing and, 449–50

H-2B and H-2A status regulations, 607

institution of higher education definition, 586–88

international legal standard for Schedule A, Group II, 449

labor certification system and the law of recruitment, 424–31

performing arts field Schedule A, Group II legal standard, 448–49

posting notice requirement, 450

prevailing wage determination, 450

proposed changes to the labor certification program, 417–23

Wage and Hour Administrator audits, 521–29

U.S. Department of State
B-1 business visitor regulations, 536, 537

document authentication and, 274–75

E-passports, 707–08

H-2B and H-2A status regulations, 607

Hague Convention website, 268

security clearances and technology licenses and, 530–35

Technology Alert List, 534

U.S. nationals definition, 511

U.S. Department of the Interior
security clearances and technology licenses and, 531

U.S. ex rel Accardi v. Shaughnessy, 206, 212

U.S. ex rel Marcello v. INS, 205

U.S. Immigration and Customs Enforcement
asylum for homosexuals and, 240

automatic stay provisions of 8 CFR §1003.19, 222–23

defending against investigations by, 519–20

deportation of children left behind by immigrant parents, 243–44

DOL audits and, 521

field investigation of documents and, 269–70

Forensic Document Laboratory, 269–70

Special Immigrant Juvenile Status and, 302–05

unlawful detention and, 218, 219

U.S. Nuclear Regulatory Commission
security clearances and technology licenses and, 531

U.S. Supreme Court
See also specific cases

exhaustion requirement and, 213

habeas corpus prior to the REAL ID Act and, 204–06

INS v. St. Cyr, 86–89

Plyler v. Doe decision, 230–31

U.S. Treasury Department
security clearances and technology licenses and, 531

U.S. v. Calderon-Pena, 206–07

U.S. Visitor and Immigrant Status Indicator Technology program
cross-border travel and, 711, 712–13

USCIS, *See* U.S. Citizenship and Immigration Services

US-VISIT program, *See* U.S. Visitor and Immigrant Status Indicator Technology program

V

V visas
alien beneficiaries in the United States, 403–04

alien beneficiaries outside of the United States, 404

application procedure, 403–04

Child Status Protection Act and, 330

eligibility for, 402–03

termination of V status, 404

VAWA, *See* Violence Against Women Act

Veterans Administration Medical Center, 429

Victims of crime
background of visas for, 692

obtaining U status, 692–94

Victims of Trafficking and Violence Prevention Act
provisions, 692–93

Vietnam
international adoption and, 374

Violence Against Women Act
abuse (physical battery or extreme cruelty) and, 340–41

adjustment interviews, 346–47

criteria for, 338–43

description, 336–37

divorce and, 339

documents that may be helpful in preparing, 361–63

family-related and domestic violence-related immigration options (table), 351–60

filing, 344–45

forms flow chart, 350

good moral character and, 341–43

historical background, 331

immigrant status of the abusive spouse, parent, son, or daughter and, 339–40

joint residence and, 341

lawful permanent residence eligibility, 343–44

motions to reopen and, 172–73

NACARA and, 282

overview, 334

petitioner's statement, 337–38

post-approval, 346

post-filing, 346

privacy protection, 343

resources, 347–48

Special Immigrant Juvenile Status and, 310–11

terminology, 334

victims of bigamy, 339

working with domestic violence victims, 335–36

Visa Waiver Permanent Program Act
provisions, 705

Visa Waiver Program
advantages of, 705

cross-border travel and, 710–11

lesbian, gay, bisexual, transgender, and HIV asylum law and, 256

participating countries, 705

U.S. Customs and Border Protection officers and, 705–06

VisaManager software, 15
Visas
  See also Employment-based immi-
    grant visas; Employment-based
    nonimmigrant visas; *specific vi-
    sas*
  annual allocations of, 400
  burden of proof and, 197
  E-visa applications for Canadian
    citizens, 112–13
  international adoption and, 364–74
  K-1 applications for Canadian citi-
    zens, 113
  unmarried sons or daughters of
    LPRs and, 325–26
  Western Hemisphere Priority Date
    program and, 414–15
Voice Over Internet Protocol, 16
Voice recognition software, 16
VOIP, *See* Voice Over Internet Proto-
  col
Voluntary departure period
  motions to reopen and, 179–80
VTVPA, *See* Victims of Trafficking
  and Violence Prevention Act
VWP, *See* Visa Waiver Program

W

Wage and Hour Administrator audits
  Corporate Bingo, 529
  creating a team for, 523
  final meeting, 526–27
  gap analysis, 523–24
  government enforcement of I-9
    regulations and independent
    contractors, 527
  initial meeting, 525–26
  investigation, 526
  lacking resources for, 524–25
  process of, 525–27

public access files and self-audits,
  522–23
reasons to be proactive, 522
remediation, 525
RICO claims, 527–28
vulnerability to, 522
working proactively with the investigator, 527
Waivers
  See also Aggravated felony, Cancel-
    lation of removal, Crimes in-
    volving moral turpitude, Crimi-
    nal issues, Removal and relief
  fraud and misrepresentation, 96–103
  national interest waiver case study,
    454–79
  nonimmigrant waivers for Canadian
    citizens, 108–13
  reduction in recruitment, 425
  Section 212(a)(9)(C) permanent bar,
    104–07
  Section 212(c), 73–76, 84–95
  Section 212(h), 80–82, 120, 134
  Section 212(i), 82–83, 99–100
  U.S. government funding in J-1
    waiver cases, 681–91
Wang v. Attorney General, 162, 177
Weapons
  concealed dangerous weapons case
    study, 135–36
Websites
  client input and, 16
  client reporting and, 16
Western Hemisphere Priority Date
    program
  after-acquired spouses of permanent
    residents, 411
  children and, 410, 413–14
  common examples, 411–12
  derivative family members and, 410
  examples of WHPDs today, 412–15

historical background, 409
immediate relatives and, 410
invalid visa petitions and, 414–15
labor certifications and persons who
  would not be employed and, 410
multiple registrations and, 414
1976 savings clause, 409–10
practical problems and solutions,
  415
questions to discover a potential
  WHPD, 415–16
relatives of lawful permanent residents and, 410
Western Hemisphere Travel Initiative
  description, 708
Westlaw software, 12
WHTI, *See* Western Hemisphere
  Travel Initiative
Winning NACARA Suspension Cases
  (Immigrant Legal Resource Center), 280–99
Wire fraud
  case study, 131–34

Y

Yates, William
  memo on H-1B visa extensions, 582
  memo on religious workers' ability
    to pay, 498–99
  memo on Special Immigrant Juve-
    nile Status, 303, 304
  memo on spousal immigrant visa
    petitions, 320–21
Yeboah v. U.S. Department of Justice,
  306

Z

Zadvydas v. Davis, 218–21
Zhao v. Gonzales, 278